9 ^{99}

ELEANOR
AND
FRANKLIN

JOSEPH P. LASH

Foreword by Arthur M. Schlesinger, Jr.

Introduction by Franklin D. Roosevelt, Jr.

ELEANOR
AND
FRANKLIN

*The story of their relationship, based on
Eleanor Roosevelt's private papers*

KONECKY&KONECKY

Konecky & Konecky
156 Fifth Avenue
New York, N.Y. 10010

This edition published by special arrangement
with W.W. Norton & Company, Inc.

Grateful acknowledgment is made for permission to quote from the
following: to Harper & Row, *This is My Story* and *This I Remember*,
by Eleanor Roosevelt; to *McCall's,,* "I Remember Hyde Park," by
Eleanor Roosevelt; to Pauli Murray, "Mr. Roosevelt's Regrets"; to the
Society of Authors on behalf of the George Bernard Shaw Estate,
Candida ; to Little, Brown and Co., *Behold This Dreamer*, by Fulton Oursler,
copyright © 1964 by Fulton Oursler, Jr.; to Simon & Schuster, *The Secret
Diary of Harold Ickes*, copyright © 1953.

ISBN: 1-56852-075-1

Printed in the United States of America

To my wife Trude

Contents

Foreword by Arthur M. Schlesinger, Jr.   *ix*
Introduction by Franklin D. Roosevelt, Jr.   *xiii*
Author's Note   *xv*
Preface   *xvii*

I CHILDHOOD AND YOUTH

1. Eleanor's Father   *3*
2. Her Mother   *14*
3. The World into Which Eleanor Was Born   *21*
4. The Crack-Up   *34*
5. Her Mother's Death   *39*
6. "He Lived in My Dreams"   *46*
7. The Outsider   *59*
8. The Spark Is Struck   *74*
9. Young in a Young Country in a Young Time   *88*
10. "For Life, for Death"   *101*
11. Mother and Son   *111*
12. Journey's End   *121*
13. Epithalamion   *132*

II WIFE AND MOTHER

14. Honeymoon   *145*
15. Settling Down   *152*
16. The Wife of a Public Official   *167*
17. The Roosevelts Go to Washington   *183*
18. Bringing Up Her Children   *193*
19. The Approach of War   *200*
20. Private into Public Person   *208*
21. Trial by Fire   *220*
22. Reconciliation and a Trip Abroad   *228*
23. The Rebellion Begins   *237*

III   THE EMERGENCE OF ELEANOR ROOSEVELT

24. A Campaign and Friendship with Louis Howe   249
25. Baptism in Politics   259
26. The Tempering—Polio   265
27. Her Husband's Stand-In   277
28. The 1924 Campaign   287
29. Life without Father   293
30. A Life of Her Own   304
31. Smith's Defeat, Roosevelt's Victory   309
32. Return to Albany   321
33. Roosevelt Bids for the Presidency   337
34. "I Never Wanted to Be a President's Wife"   350
35. Mrs. Roosevelt Conquers Washington   359

IV   THE WHITE HOUSE YEARS

36. The Politics of Conscience   381
37. Mrs. Roosevelt's "Baby"—Arthurdale   393
38. Publicist for the New Deal—Columnist and Lecturer 418
39. Without Louis Howe—The 1936 Campaign   434
40. Wise As a Serpent, Guileless As a Dove   452
41. Changes at Hyde Park   473
42. Life with Mother and Father   485
43. The Divided White House   498
44. A Gathering Storm   512
45. The Youth Movement   536
46. From Pacifist to Antifascist   555
47. A Spiritual Shock   571
48. Mrs. Roosevelt and the Communists   585
49. FDR Administers a Spanking   597
50. The Third Term   612
51. A Job to Do   634
52. GI's Friend, I: Journey to Britain   654
53. A Consciousness of Color   669
54. GI's Friend, II: The First Lady and the Admiral   682
55. The 1944 Campaign   692
56. Death of the Commander-in-Chief   713

Bibliographical Note   727
References   728
Index   751

Foreword by Arthur M. Schlesinger, Jr.

I BEGAN TO READ THE MANUSCRIPT OF this work with a certain apprehension. I knew that no one was better qualified by close and sympathetic acquaintance to write the biography of Eleanor Roosevelt than Joseph P. Lash. But one also knew of Joe Lash's profound, almost filial, devotion to Mrs. Roosevelt and feared that affection might conflict with the austere obligations of the biographer. Moreover, his friendship with Mrs. Roosevelt covered only the last twenty-two years of a long and varied life, and one wondered how someone coming along at the verge, so to speak, of the last act could do justice to the earlier years—above all, to an intense and crucial girlhood lived so many years before in what was not only another century but another world. Nor could one be certain that Mr. Lash, for all his experience as a newspaperman, would not be lost in the staggering mass of Mrs. Roosevelt's personal papers; even a professional historian might well have been daunted by this form of total immersion.

My apprehension was unjustified. Mr. Lash has written, I believe, a beautiful book—beautiful in its scholarship, insight, objectivity, and candor. He portrays Eleanor Roosevelt's anguished childhood with marvelous delicacy and understanding, and he skillfully evokes the social milieu in which she grew up—the old New York of Edith Wharton, where rigid etiquette concealed private hells and neurosis lurked under the crinoline. He perceives and reconstructs the complex reciprocity of the partnership between Eleanor and Franklin Roosevelt with immense subtlety, sensitivity, and honesty. He faithfully records the moving, often painful, process by which a tense and humorless girl overcame personal insecurity and private adversity and emerged as a powerful woman in her own right, spreading her influence not only across her own country but around much of the planet. As he does all this, he gives a story long familiar in its broad outline a fresh and compelling quality.

A word about the author. Mr. Lash, born in New York City in 1909, graduated from the City College of the City University of New York in 1931 in the depth of the Depression. In the next year he became an officer of the Student League for Industrial Democracy, a Socialist youth organization; and in 1935, when the Comintern Congress in Moscow gave the international Communist movement a more moderate party line, he overcame his earlier distrust of the American Communists and led the SLID into one of the first American experiments in a "united front" against fascism—the American Student Union. American students were politically concerned as they would not be for another thirty years, and Joe Lash was one of their more conspicuous leaders. In the

Popular Front enthusiasm after 1935, he moved closer to the Communists and was discussing a job with the *Daily Worker* in August, 1939, when the news came through of the Nazi-Soviet Pact.

For the idealistic fellow-travelers of the period, the pact was a stunning blow. It separated the democrats from the Stalinists; and Lash found himself in growing conflict with his Communist associates in the ASU. Then in November, 1939, three months after the pact, Lash, with other youth leaders, received a summons from the House Committee on Un-American Activities, already well embarked on its long career of saving the republic by hit-and-run investigations of the radical left. It was in this connection that he had his first serious encounter with Mrs. Roosevelt.

The president's wife had a conviction, hard to oppose but not widely shared, that the youth constituted the future of a nation; and, in this time before the young had quite become a distinct and impassioned constituency, she sought to find out on behalf of her husband what they believed and needed. She not only advised the student leaders of 1939 how they should conduct themselves before Congressman Dies's committee but attended the hearings herself and took half a dozen of the young firebrands back to the White House for dinner. Joe Lash, after Stalin's deal with Hitler, was both in inner turmoil and somewhat isolated within the ASU; his personal dilemma appealed to Mrs. Roosevelt. Moreover, she soon found she could rely a good deal more on his word and judgment than on that of his pro-Soviet colleagues.

Soon she invited him to Hyde Park. In spite of considerable disparities in age and background, a warm friendship developed. This continued when as a soldier he went to the South Pacific and in the years after the war when he wrote for the *New York Post*. Clearly he filled some need in her own life—in particular, perhaps the compelling emotional need, so perceptively analyzed in the pages that follow, to offer help, attention, tenderness, and to receive unquestioning love in return. Mrs. Roosevelt may have made occasional mistakes in her desire to provide succor, but her trust in Joe Lash was not misplaced. He has now repaid this trust by writing a book which, because it sees Eleanor Roosevelt with love but without illusion or sentimentalism, makes her, in her fortitude and in her triumph, an even more remarkable figure than we had supposed before.

Americans over thirty, whether they admired or detested her, will not forget Mrs. Roosevelt. But for those under thirty—and this was the group she cared about most—she can only in the 1970s, I imagine, strike faint chords of third-hand recollection, probably arousing faint memories of maternal benevolence. As the young read this book, they will discover that while the do-good thing was there all right, while an indestructible faith in human decency and possibility was the center of her life, all this was accompanied by an impressive capacity for salty realism and, on occasion, even for a kind of quasi-gentle mercilessness. She was, in fact, a tough old bird who saw earth as well as stars. People mixed with her at their peril, as even such tough citizens as Harry S. Truman, Cardinal Spellman, Carmine de Sapio, and Andre Vishinsky learned. Her air of artlessness was one of her most deadly weapons; no one could slice off a head with more benign innocence. But her toughness was tempered by tolerance and tied to a belief in humanity.

The young will discover, too, how contemporary the past may, after all, be. They will find students in revolt, marching, picketing, fighting cops, heckling presidents. They will see the first American war against poverty and the greatest American effort to humanize industrial society. And they will see in Eleanor Roosevelt herself, though she would doubtless have smiled over the overwrought ideology and dramatics of Women's Lib, the most liberated American woman of this century.

But what Mr. Lash understands so well and sets forth so lucidly is that her liberation was not an uncovenanted gift. She attained it only through a terrifying exertion of self-discipline. It was terrifying because the conviction of her own inadequacy was so effectively instilled in Eleanor Roosevelt as a child, and because her adult life had so much disappointment and shock, that it required incomparable and incessant self-control to win maturity and serenity. If her mastery of herself was never complete, if to the end of her life she could still succumb to private melancholy while calmly meeting public obligation, this makes her achievement and character all the more formidable. Her life was both ordeal and fulfillment. It combined vulnerability and stoicism, pathos and pride, frustration and accomplishment, sadness and happiness. Mr. Lash catches all this and, in a remarkable American biography, recreates for a new generation a great and gallant—and, above all, a profoundly good—lady.

Introduction by Franklin D. Roosevelt, Jr.

MY MOTHER'S WILL named me her literary executor, responsible for her private papers which she deposited with the Franklin D. Roosevelt Library at Hyde Park, New York. After consulting with my sister Anna and my brothers, I asked Joseph P. Lash to undertake the very extensive research and the writing of this biography based on these papers. Joe Lash has been a close friend of mine and of my entire family for over thirty years, and during this period I have developed great respect for his integrity and objectivity. In inviting Joe to go through my mother's papers, I was also mindful of the fact that in 1947 she had selected him to assist my brother, Elliott, in editing volumes III and IV of my father's letters. She further attested to her confidence in Joe in the authorization she gave him to go through her papers while she was still alive in connection with the book he was writing on the youth movement of the thirties.

The library at Hyde Park houses the papers of both my father and my mother and of many who were associated with them during their public careers. Those careers cover the period in American history during which time the United States grew from a nation isolated not only by geography but often by national policy into the most powerful country in the world, the most advanced industrial society, as well as a nation of great social conscience. That transformation is reflected in the papers in the Roosevelt Library, which make it a fascinating and unique collection of source materials.

Each of us sees a person differently. My brothers and sister in our family conclaves have often argued vehemently, though lovingly, about our parents. It was natural that Joe Lash would see some matters differently from us. I read this book carefully while it was in preparation. I had many sessions with the author, and we discussed his assessments and reconstructions and occasionally disagreed. But I felt from the beginning that this had to be the writer's book.

My parents are figures in history. They were also human beings with foibles and frailties as well as great strength and vitality. Their marriage lasted forty-five years. To us, as children, they were wonderful parents. Inevitably, there were times of tension and unhappiness as well as years of joy and companionship. For this book to be of value to the present generation the whole picture, insofar as it could be ascertained, had to be drawn.

Many people have written about my mother's contribution to my father's work. This book documents her part in that work. They were a team, and the

Roosevelt years, I believe, were more fruitful and creative as a consequence of that partnership.

It was my hope that Joe Lash would present a portrait of my mother that would be objective yet sympathetic and recapture something of her reality as she moved through eight of the most significant decades in our country's history. This book fulfills my hope.

Author's Note

WHEN I FINISHED my little book, *Eleanor Roosevelt: A Friend's Memoir,*
I did not think that I would again be involved in writing about Eleanor Roosevelt, but then Franklin Roosevelt, Jr., invited me to do a biography based on his
mother's papers and I accepted happily. Not the least part of my pleasure was
the prospect of again working closely with my old friend Franklin.

Many people have aided in the writing of this book, but I particularly want
to acknowledge my indebtedness to Eleanor Roosevelt's children for talking
with me freely and at length. Anna Roosevelt Halsted's vivid recollections were
invaluable, and our many three-hour luncheons were among the most pleasant
parts of my research. The footnotes list the names of the many relatives,
friends, and co-workers of Mrs. Roosevelt who were kind enough to share their
memories with me. My sessions with Eleanor Roosevelt's two remarkable cousins, Alice Longworth and Corinne Cole, and with Mrs. Roosevelt's ninety-
six-year-old uncle by marriage, the late David Gray, were especially memorable, as were my many talks with such long-time friends and collaborators of
Mrs. Roosevelt's as Esther Everett Lape, Marion Dickerman, Earl R. Miller,
Dr. David Gurewitsch, and Maureen Corr.

Dr. Viola W. Bernard read the first half of the manuscript and devoted
several evenings to giving me a psychiatrist's view of Eleanor Roosevelt's psy-
chosocial development. She was very helpful; however, she is not responsible
for the way I have made use of her observations, nor, for that matter, are the
others who talked with me.

The distinguished New Dealer and wise counselor, Benjamin V. Cohen,
read the entire manuscript and made helpful comments, as did Nancy and
James A. Wechsler, who provided a constant support through their friendship.
Mrs. Suzanne P. Roosevelt, who was trained by her father to look at a writer's
copy with a grammarian's eye, reviewed part of the manuscript. A promising
young writer, Noemi Emery, helped me with some of the research and made
many useful observations.

Living in a lovely old house, Wildercliffe, overlooking the Hudson, I spent
three winters going through Mrs. Roosevelt's papers at the Franklin D. Roosevelt Library at Hyde Park, and immersing myself in the Dutchess County countryside and traditions. Research is a lonely task, but the loneliness in this case
was offset by the companionship of the Richard Roveres and of the staff of the
Roosevelt Library: Dr. Elizabeth B. Drewry, its former director; her successor,
Dr. James O'Neill; William J. Stewart, the assistant director; James White-

head, the curator; Jerry Deyo, the archivist; and Joseph Marshall, in charge of the Search Room.

The typing was done by my sister, A. Elsie Lash, a formidable task to which she gave all of her free time because of her devotion to the memory of Mrs. Roosevelt.

It was my good fortune when I turned the manuscript in to W. W. Norton & Company to have it reviewed by Evan W. Thomas, an exacting but sensitive critic.

The spare words with which I have dedicated this book to my wife do not convey the help she has given me in its writing. There is scarcely a page which does not bear her imprint.

JOSEPH P. LASH

Preface

THE FIRST ROOSEVELT, Claes Martenszen van Rosenvelt, arrived from Holland in the 1640s when New Amsterdam was a tiny settlement of 800 huddled in some eighty houses at the foot of Manhattan. Who Claes Martenszen was, whether solid Dutch burgher in search of larger opportunities or solemn rogue "two leaps ahead of the bailiff," as his witty descendant Alice Roosevelt Longworth has suggested, is not known. In either case, by the eve of the American Revolution when New York had become a bustling port of 25,000, there were fifty Roosevelt families, and Claes's descendants were already showing an "uncanny knack" of associating themselves with the forces of boom and expansion in American economic life.

In the Roosevelt third generation two of the brothers, Johannes and Jacobus, took the family into real estate with the purchase of the Beekman Swamp, a venture that was to have "a lasting effect on the city and their own family fortunes." It was these two brothers, also, who started the branches that led ultimately to Oyster Bay (Johannes) and to Hyde Park (Jacobus). The pre-Revolutionary Roosevelts were prosperous burghers but not of the highest gentry, and in civic affairs they were aligned with the popular faction against the aristocrats.

The first Roosevelt to achieve gentility and distinction was Isaac, the great-great-great-grandfather of Franklin, who for his services to the American cause was called "Isaac the Patriot." Isaac was a trader in sugar and rum but ended his business career as president of New York's first bank. At his death Philip Hone, the diarist, spoke of him as "proud and aristocratical," part of the "only nobility" the country had ever had.

It took the Johannes-Oyster Bay branch of the Roosevelts a little longer to advance from trader to merchant prince. Isaac's cousin James, after service with the Revolutionary army, founded Roosevelt & Son, a hardware business on Maiden Lane that swiftly expanded into building supplies. When James's grandson, Cornelius Van Schaack Roosevelt, was head of the firm, it imported most of the plate glass that was used in the new homes being built in the prospering nation. Cornelius' chief distinction was his wealth; he was listed among the five richest men in New York. His son, on the other hand, the first Theodore, retired from business early in order to devote himself to civic activity and was one of the most esteemed men in the city.

By the beginning of the twentieth century the Roosevelt family was one of the oldest and most distinguished in the United States. Its men had married well—a Philadelphia Barnhill, one of whose ancestors arrived with William Penn; a Yankee Howland, whose family had arrived on the *Mayflower*; a Hoffman of Swedish-Finnish descent, one of the richest heiresses in Dutchess County; and one of the Bullochs of Georgia. The Hudson River Roosevelts led the leisurely life of country squires and Johannes' clan was building its country houses, stables, and tennis courts along the north shore of Long Island.

Conscious of having played their part in the transformation of New York from a frail Dutch outpost into a cosmopolitan city and of the country from a handful of seaboard colonies into a continent-spanning imperial republic, the Roosevelts had a firm sense of their roots. While most of them had changed their church affiliation from Dutch Reform to Protestant Episcopal, they remained faithful churchgoers and believers in the Protestant ethic, which sanctified a ruthless competitive individualism on the one hand and, on the other, the love and charity that were the basis of the family's strong sense of social obligation. Standards of honor, conduct, and manners—the caste marks of the old-stock upper class—were further bred into the Roosevelt sons at Groton and Harvard. They went on to become bankers, sportsmen, financiers, and, in two cases, president of the United States. The Roosevelt women, however, were essentially private individuals concerned with supervising large households and launching their daughters into fashionable society. With a few notable exceptions, they led lives of genteel conformity and escaped public notice—until the advent of a girl who was to become known as First Lady of the World.

I

CHILDHOOD AND YOUTH

1. Eleanor's Father

ELEANOR ROOSEVELT was born on October 11, 1884. Anna Hall Roosevelt, her mother, died when she was eight and her father, Elliott Roosevelt, when she was ten.

"He was the one great love of my life as a child," Eleanor wrote about her father almost forty years after his death, "and in fact like many children I have lived a dream life with him; so his memory is still a vivid, living thing to me."

Seeking to give some shape and meaning to his brief existence, she called him a "sportsman." He was that, but as one contemplates the promise of his early years, it is the pathos of wasted talents, the stark tragedy of an enormously attractive man bent on self-destruction that reaches across the decades to hold us in its grip.

Elliott's brother Theodore became president of the United States, one of its outstandingly "strong" chief executives. What made Theodore resolute and Elliott weak? It was a question the many who loved Elliott sought to answer all their lives, for the pain of Elliott's death remained in their hearts to the end of their days, such was the spell this man cast over those around him.

It was her father who acquainted Eleanor Roosevelt, his gravely gay Little Nell, with grief. But he also gave her the ideals that she tried to live up to all her life by presenting her with the picture of what he wanted her to be—noble, brave, studious, religious, loving, and good.

The story of Eleanor Roosevelt should begin with him.

Elliott Roosevelt was the third of four children born to Theodore Roosevelt, Sr., and Martha Bulloch. They were a remarkable group. Of Anna, the oldest, born in 1855, whom the family called "Bye" or "Bamie," her niece Alice was to say, "If Aunty Bye had been a man, she would have been President." Theodore Jr., born in 1858, was followed two years later by Elliott, who was called "the most lovable of the Roosevelts." Corinne, the youngest, born 1861, called "Conie" or "Pussie" by her brothers, was described by Clarence Day, whose family's Madison Avenue brownstone adjoined Corinne's in the 1880s, as "a dignified but lively young lady who . . . knew how to write poetry, turn cartwheels and stand on her head."

A childhood friend, recalling the family, spoke of their "gusto," "explosions of fun," "great kindliness and generosity of nature," their "eager friendliness." They were all unabashedly demonstrative in their affections. "Oh! my darling Sweetest of Fathers I wish I could kiss you," a thirteen-year-old Elliott wrote. His southern grandmother's outbursts of affection were so embarrassingly effusive, they were called her "melts."

Their mother, Martha "Mittie" Roosevelt, was a flirtatious southern belle whose dark hair glowed and whose complexion seemed to young Corinne like "moonlight." A vivacious hostess, a spirited and daring horsewoman, she made as lively an impression on New York society as she had on the ante-bellum Savannah society of the early fifties. In the years after the Civil War, Martha Roosevelt was among the five or six gentlewomen of such birth, breeding, and tact that people were "always satisfied to be led by them," acknowledged Mrs. Burton Harrison, one of New York's smartest hostesses.

The children adored her. To Elliott she was "his sweet little China Dresden" mother, and Bamie spoke glowingly of "darling little mother's exquisite beauty." She told stories better than anybody, said Corinne, and her way of describing things was inimitable. Many of these stories were about her "little black shadow," a slave she had been given at birth. She was, however, completely helpless when faced with the smallest everyday task. She was habitually, almost compulsively tardy, and household accounts were a mystery to her. Even when they were very young, her children felt protective toward her, and Theodore Sr. insisted that Bamie, when she was fourteen, take over the reins of the household.

Mittie's Savannah friends later said that the younger Theodore "got his splendid dash and energy" from his southern mother, but the children themselves never doubted that it was from their father that they inherited their zest for life and love of people. The male Roosevelts were solid, industrious, worthy Dutch burghers, and—also in the Dutch tradition—they were a humorless, sobersided lot. But Theodore Sr., who belonged to the seventh generation of American Roosevelts, was also blessed with vivacity and tenderness, and in him there began to emerge that special blend of grace, vitality, courage, and responsibility that is called charisma and that his contemporaries found irresistible.

A big, powerful, bearded man, he moved easily and comfortably in the worlds of Knickerbocker society, business, philanthropy, and civic enterprise. Her father, Corinne said, was "unswerving in duty . . . yet responsive to the joy of life to such an extent that he would dance all night, and drive his 'four-in-hand' coach so fast . . . that his grooms frequently fell out at the corners!" When Bamie came out in the winter of 1873–74, she had a hard time getting her father—he was then forty-two—to go home from a dance, and he was so popular that she felt like a wallflower.

Theodore Sr. was only twenty-nine when the Civil War broke out, but in deference to the feelings of his wife, whose grandfather had been the first post-Revolutionary governor of Georgia and whose brothers served with the Confederacy, he bought a substitute and limited himself to noncombatant work with the Union armies. Even though this was of sufficient importance to earn him the friendship of Lincoln and a lifelong intimacy with John Hay, the fact that his father did not enlist in the Union fighting forces remained a sore point with young Theodore.

The Confederacy was a living presence in the Roosevelt household. Mittie's sister Anna—later Mrs. James King Gracie—the children's beloved Aunt Gracie—lived with them in New York during the war, as did Grandma Bulloch, and the three women did not hide their passionate southern loyalties, on the occasion of one southern victory, a family legend has it, even breaking out the Confederate flag. The two Bulloch brothers were not included in the post-Civil War amnesty and settled in Liverpool as exiles. From then on, the family never went abroad without visiting Uncle Jimmie and Uncle Irvine in Liverpool.

Theodore Sr. was the son of Cornelius Van Schaack Roosevelt, in whose stately house on Union Square Dutch was still spoken on Sundays. It was he who shifted the family firm into banking and investment. When Cornelius died in 1871, he left ten million dollars to his four sons.

Theodore headed the plate glass division of Roosevelt & Son, but after the Civil War he devoted more and more time to philanthropy and civic enterprise and finally withdrew from business altogether. He was one of the founders of the Metropolitan Museum of Art and the Museum of Natural History, helped start the Orthopedic Hospital, contributed substantial amounts to charities, took a continuing interest in the Newsboys' Lodging House, and led a Mission Class for poor young men.

Public concern for poverty, social welfare, and reform were something new in the elder Theodore's days, as indeed unemployment, slums, and the exploitation of children were new. Fashionable New York, then centered on lower Fifth and Madison Avenues, was only a stone's throw from the tenements on the East Side and the squatters' shanties on the West Side, but most of the wealthy were content to keep them out of sight and out of mind. "At a time when most citizens of equal fortune and education" were not willing to accept any responsibility for reforming and philanthropic enterprises, Theodore "was always engaged in them," commented a colleague in many of those undertakings.

He was not content to serve on boards; he needed to be actively involved with those he sought to help. In the Newsboys' Lodging House he knew the boys by name and was familiar with their histories, and whenever he came they would gather round and he would question each one as to what he was doing and would "give him advice and sympathy and direction." He often brought his children with him, and they remained interested even after his death; one of Eleanor Roosevelt's earliest memories was being taken by her father to the Newsboys' Thanksgiving dinner. Theodore Sr. had a special feeling for children, was full of tenderness when speaking to them, and could not bear the thought of their being shut up in institutions. He had what he called a "troublesome conscience," a burden or a blessing of which his granddaughter Eleanor also would complain.

First and foremost, however, Theodore Sr. was a family man fully involved in the upbringing and education of his children. It was a matter of deep concern to him that Theodore Jr., Bamie, and, later, Elliott suffered from ill health and handicaps which, if not corrected, might seriously limit their activities. The most acutely afflicted was Bamie, who suffered from a curvature of the spine, while Theodore Jr. was sickly and asthmatic. It was largely for Theodore

Jr. that the upstairs back of the house was transformed into a large play and exercise "piazza" so that he could build himself up on the exercising devices. The equipment was also a source of joy for the other children, especially Elliott, who quickly became the leader in their youthful sports and won all competitions.

The children's education was centered in the home. Aunt Gracie taught them their letters and there was an occasional tutor, but it was their father who really opened up new worlds of learning for them. On picnics and rides, or before the fire in winter, he discussed authors with them and had them recite their favorite poems. He was a firm believer in the educational effect of travel, and when Elliott was nine took his whole brood on a twelve-month Grand Tour of Europe, and three years later on an even more extended and strenuous pilgrimage to Egypt, the Holy Land, southeastern and central Europe. The children were left in Dresden, where they stayed with German families for "purposes of board and instruction," and where they remained for five months while their family's new house on Fifty-seventh Street was being built. They were getting on in German grammar, Elliott wrote his father, adding "We have learned three pieces of German poetry." But on July 4, he rebelled against the glories of German culture being preached day after day by Fräulein. "Don't you think America is the best country in the world?" he asked his father. "Please, when you write tell me if we have not got as good Musick and Arts as the Germans have at the *present* time." When in September, 1873, the Fifty-seventh Street house was nearing completion—though a hand-carved circular staircase had missed its connection on the second floor by three feet—the children set out for home.

Upon their return Theodore Jr. was given a tutor to prepare him for Harvard. Elliott wanted very much to enter St. Paul's, but he now suddenly began to suffer from severe headaches and dizzy spells. His father, feeling that health was more important than formal education, sent him abroad in 1874 and in 1875 South with a friend of the family who was a doctor in the hopes that two months of outdoor life and hunting would build up his constitution. He loved the shooting, but, he confessed to his "dear funny little Bamie," he was also homesick. "Sometimes I long for Home—what a sweet word it is. I wonder what you all are doing this beautiful moonlit night. I can see you now. Conie and Thee home from dancing class and full of it have finished their storeys and are gone upstairs to study. Papa's pet or the belle of New York is entertaining some friends in the parlor and Father is in his study. And Mother?"

He was lonely, as his loving letter to his father written on his fifteenth birthday showed.

Mar 6th 1875
Saturday.

My own dear Father.*

I got your kinde "Father" like letter with Muzes to day oh! it was so nice to feel you had thought of me on my birthday. . . .

---

* Holograph letter in Halsted File at Franklin D. Roosevelt Library with spelling and punctuation as in the original.

Dear old Govenor—for I *will* call you that not in publick but in private for it does seem to suit you, you splendid Man just my ideal, made to govern & doing it so lightly & affectionately that I can call you by the name as a pet one.—its not such a long time since you were fifteen & any way as I was saying to Mrs Metcalfe today you are one of the few men who seem to remember they were boy's once them selves & therefore can excuse peices of boyish folly committed by their boy's.

Do you think it would be a good plan to send *me* to school again perhaps as I am not going to college I could make more friends there. I will do just as you think best, mon père.

I gave you my plan of study in my last letter but I would just as leif study at school as at home for Thee is way behind or rather before me & perhaps although I don't now I may in future years see it was best for me.

I feel rich too in the prospect of my allowance, next first of January, it seemes a long way off.

Are we going to Oyster bay next summer dont you think Thee & I could spunge on all of our uncles & you & have a sail boat. I *know* we could manage her & would not I think be likly to drown. My darling Father you have made me a companion & a very happy one I don't believe there is any boy that has had as happy & free of care life as I have had.

Oh. Father will you ever think *me* a "noble boy", you are right about Tede he is one & no mistake a boy I would give a good deal to be like in many respects. If you ever see me not stand by Thee you may know I am entirely changed, no Father I am not likly to desert a fellow I love as I do my Brother even you dont know what a good noble boy he is & what a splendid man he is going to be as I do No, I love him. love him very *very* dearly & will never desert him & if I know him he will *never* desert me.

Father my own dear Father God bless you & help me to be a good boy & worthy of you, good by.

Your Son.

[P.S.] This sounds foolish on looking over it but you touched me when you said always to stand by Thee in your letter.   E.R.

When Theodore Sr. finally gave in to Elliott's pleadings and allowed him to enter St. Paul's in September, 1875, the boy's happiness was brief. "I am studying as hard as I can," he wrote his father on October 1, "and I think all my teachers are satisfied with me." But after a letter full of casual gossip, he added an ominous postscript:

Private

Yesterday during my Latin lesson without the slightest warning I had a bad rush of blood to my head, it hurt me so that I can't remember what happened. I believe I screamed out, anyway the Doctor brought me over to his house and I lay down for a couple of hours; it had by that time recovered and after laying down all the afternoon I was able to go on with my afternoon studies. I lost nothing but one Greek lesson by it. It had left me rather nervous and therefore homesick and unhappy. But I am all well now so don't worry about me. I took some of my anti-nervous medicine, and I would like the receipt of more. You told me to write you everything or I would not bother you with this, but you want to know all about me don't you?

P.S. II   Don't forget *me* please and write *often*.   Love from Ellie

"Poor Ellie Roosevelt," Archibald Gracie wrote his mother, "has had to leave on account of his health. He has 'ever been subject to rush of blood to his head' and while up here he exerted himself too much both physically and mentally. He studied hard and late. One day he fainted just after leaving the table and fell down. . . . His brother came up to take him home. . . ."

The various doctors who were consulted did not agree on the nature of his malady. According to some reports he had a form of epilepsy, but there is no other record of epilepsy in the family and the seizures of which we have accounts were too infrequent to fit such a diagnosis. Some doctors who have read this account have noted that Elliott's seizures occurred when he was confronted with demands that evidently were too much for him and have suggested that they may have been, without Elliott's realizing it, a form of escape.

It was the elder Roosevelt's view that bodily infirmities were to be conquered by a strenuous outdoor life and Spartan discipline. He had told the frail and asthmatic Theodore in 1870: "You have the mind but not the body. . . . You must make your body." And that was exactly what Theodore proceeded to do. Outdoor life was now to cure Elliott; he was sent to Fort McKavett, a frontier post in the hill country of Texas, where the Roosevelts knew many of the officers, including the commander, General Clitz. This may seem to have been an inappropriate treatment for a medical ailment, but in wealthy families of that era travel was the standard prescription for illnesses, nervous disorders, and unhappy love affairs, and Elliott did seem to function more effectively away from his family and school. With an unusual ability to fit into any situation and a zest for adventure, the sixteen-year-old quickly and without complaint made the transition from the comfortable, closed, and protected life of New York society to the rough equalitarianism of the frontier.

Graham, Young Co., Texas

Dear Father: Jan. 12th, 1876
I have gone through some regular roughing since I last wrote you at Weatherford. After we left there we came on slowly camping at night and shooting all that we wanted to eat for we have never been on short rations yet thank goodness. The weather up to last night was very warm and pleasant but suddenly one of those frightfully cold north winds sprang up and from being too warm with our coats off, the addition of blankets, ulsters and muflers of all kinds did not keep us even tolerably warm. Ed and I left them: that is the two wagons; at about half past five and went on for three or four miles and made a camp fire and prepared everything for them, but we waited and watched and no wagons so at last we concluded that they had gone on to Graham not having seen the fork we turned up it being so dark. We were camped by a house so as we had no blankets and it was most fearfully cold we tied our horses to the gate post and left the saddles on to keep them warm and as Ed said I had a "persuasive air with me" I went up to the little log hut and knocked. The door was opened and the master appeared and I talked with him for a while and then a friend of his appearing on the scene he offered to take Ed with him and the first fellow took me in. The hut was crowded and a single fire burning so although there were chinks on all sides and a cold wind blowing still we kept fairly warm. There were three girls two quite good looking so I made the rest of the evening pass

quite pleasantly only I was a little worried about the other chaps not having turned up. At about ten o'clock the landlord or rather ranch man came in with "Gentlemen your beds are ready" where at, as I had been riding since seven o'clock and not had a mouthful to eat either I got up and making my good night to the ladies, the elder of which being the mistress sat pipe in mouth in the chimney corner; I rose followed by some six others all pretty rough looking chaps and followed mine host into an adjoining room no roof but logs and the merest frame work of walls. Three rolls of blankets on the floor, three men took one, two another and a cow boy from way out west and I took the third. I used Tar who had stuck to my heels all the evening in mortal terror of two other dogs belonging to the house, for a pillow partly for warmth and partly to drown the smell of my bed fellow. In this manner I shivered through the night up to five when "breakfast gentlemen" brought us all to our feet and without more ado we ran for the fire in the next room and were served by the old lady still pipe in mouth with bacon and bread a frugal meal but if you laugh at it think I had not a mouthful since six a.m. the day before, roughing it! eh? . . .

Your affectionate
Son.

In two visits Elliott spent over a year with the 500 men, women, and children who lived in Fort McKavett. Officers and enlisted men delighted in regaling the attractive young easterner with tales of Mexican War days and Indian fights. There were elaborately organized wild-turkey shoots in which Elliott did his "fair share of the shooting, also of the eating." He became "chums" with the post commander, boxed, sat on the piazza listening to the post band, read every paper he could lay his hands on, and argued politics. "So Hayes is really counted in," Elliott wrote his father, March 4, 1877. "I wish you could hear the dismal forebodings that the Democratic members of our party (I was the only Republican) have for the 'Old Union' we have had some glorious pitched battles, 'you bet'!" There were also whist parties until three in the morning, and although he assured his family that he neither smoked nor drank, "for wine we drink catawba and the General knows what a good bottle of that is like I can tell you."

The old trouble with his head seemed to be gone but all his attempts to follow an organized course of reading and study came to naught. "It strikes me it's just a sell my being down here . . . altogether I feel like a general fraud, who ought to be studying," he confessed to his father. He was troubled, but not enough to resist the temptations of the "glorious" life at the fort.

Soon after Elliott returned to New York in 1877, his father became ill with what was later diagnosed as intestinal cancer. For weeks Elliott scarcely left his father's room. That winter, wrote Corinne, "Elliott gave unstintingly a devotion which was so tender that it was more like that of a woman and his young strength was poured out to help his father's condition." Elliott wrote in his diary of his father's "cries for ether," the mercy of "a chloroform sleep," and new agonies on awakening until the final release of death on February 10, 1878, at the age of forty-six.

The family was devastated, and the children vowed to lead lives that would reflect credit on their father's name. "We have been very fortunate,"

Theodore Jr. wrote Bamie after he returned to Harvard, "in having a father whom we can love and respect more than any other man in the world."

Eighty-nine years later, Theodore Sr's granddaughter, Alice Roosevelt Longworth, contrasting her own style and outlook with that of her cousin Eleanor, said that Eleanor "was a do-gooder. She got that from my grandfather. It took with Eleanor, but not with me. I never did those things. They bored me."

Legacies of approximately $125,000 came to each of the children at the death of their father, which gave them an annual income of about $8,000. Of the $125,000, half was given outright, half a trust for life. Each of the children would receive another $62,500 at the death of their mother. And thus their annual income would be about $14,000 if they held onto their capital.

For Elliott, the most sensitive of the children, the death of his father was not only a terrible sorrow but a disaster. Without his father's stern, demanding, but loving guidance he was lost. Although intelligent and eager to learn, he was discouraged by the realization that he was hopelessly outdistanced by his contemporaries. Restless, spoiled by admiration and success out West, he was not prepared to start at the bottom of some business and patiently work his way up. And then there was the strong pull of the exciting world of society and sport, where he was a leader by the sheer force of his personality. His inheritance made it possible for him to live in this world.

Theodore, whom Elliott visited frequently at Harvard, admired his younger brother's social skills and his great popularity with the girls. Although his every instinct was combative and competitive, Theodore was so fond of his brother, he wrote an aunt, that he could "never hold in his heart a jealous feeling toward Elliott" and "gloried" in his accomplishments. This did not stop him from keeping a sharp eye on who was the better man. "Nellie stayed up from town," he wrote in his diary in 1879, "and so I spent the day with him: we rowed around Lloyd's—15 miles, and virtually racing the whole way. As athletes we are about equal; he rows best; I run best, he can beat me sailing or swimming; I can beat him wrestling and boxing. I am best with the rifle, he with the shotgun, etc., etc. . . . ." Elliott, although he wrote in 1880 that every day he was "more happy in the dear old brother's good company," must have been somewhat overwhelmed by a brother who, a friend noted, "always thought he could do things a little better than anyone else," and, if he couldn't, set out to overcome the infirmity with awesome resolution. The time was past when Elliott had to shield his older brother from bullies.

The year Theodore graduated from Harvard, Elliott decided to undertake an expedition to India to hunt tiger and elephant, and to the Himalayas for the elusive ibex and markhor. He was pulled by the lure of adventure but was also pushed by the realization that Theodore, who had been his father's favorite son, was returning to New York and would become the head of the family. Another consideration contributed to his decision to abandon New York: he had begun to drink heavily, so much so, one family report has it, that a girl whom he wished to marry refused him unless he changed his ways—which he apparently was unable to do.

Elliott and Theodore spent two months hunting out West before Elliott left for the Orient. It was a happy trip, and they enjoyed "the return to the old delight of dog and gun," Elliott wrote his mother, but it was also the occasion for an uneasy report by Theodore on what he called Elliott's "epicurean" appetites. Only half in jest he reported after a week's hunting in Iowa:

As soon as we got here he took some ale to get the dust out of his throat; then a milk punch because he was thirsty; a mint julep because it was hot; a brandy mash 'to keep the cold out of his stomach'; and then sherry and bitters to give him an appetite. He took a very simple dinner—soup, fish, salmi de grouse, sweetbread, mutton, venison, corn, macaroni, various vegetables and some puddings and pies, together with beer, later claret and in the evening, shandigaff.

When Elliott set out on his big expedition to India, aware that his glorious adventure was also a flight, he assured Bamie that the duties of paterfamilias would be attended to,

and by a far better man. Thee is well able and no mistake—shrewd and clever, by no means behind the age. What I have often smiled at in the old Boy are I am now sure some of his best points—a practical carrying out in action of what I, for example, am convinced of in theory but fail to put into practice.

Even as Elliott was journeying through India his brother won election as assemblyman from the "brownstone district" of New York and completed his first literary venture, *The Naval War of 1812.*

"Has not our dear Thee done well at home this winter," Elliott wrote Bamie from Kashmir, "and his plans for occupying the position he should as Father's son and namesake seem [to be] going so splendidly smoothly—all success to him." Elliott diagnosed correctly that he lacked "that foolish grit of Theodore's." And while he, too, was interested in politics and had helped his brother found the City Reform Club to interest "respectable, well-educated men—young men especially" in the political questions of the day, and he, too, loved being with the Newsboys, and he, too, had a literary flair, as was evident in his letters, he was incapable of sustained effort except in sports, and followed the easier and ever more tempting path of achieving success and approval through his charm and his accomplishments as sportsman and man-about-town.

He would make frequent "new starts" in his short life, but the question of "paterfamilias" was settled for good.

His trip to India was a series of glittering triumphs. On shipboard to England the James Roosevelts of Hyde Park, just married, asked him to make their rooms in London his headquarters. He had "long talks and walks" with Thomas Hughes, the author of *Tom Brown's School Days*, and agreed to dine with him in London. His partners at whist were "kind enough to wish me to go to Cannes to play whist with them all winter!" And most important to Elliott, Sir John Rae Reid, "the mighty hunter and second Gordon Cummings has taken me under his especial wing—given me a dozen letters to India and I breakfast with him next Sunday at twelve and on Monday we buy my guns, etc."

From the moment of his arrival in Bombay he was treated like a "grand prince." He could hardly account for it, he wrote his mother, "for if ever there was a man of few resources and moderate talents I am he, yet all events and people seem to give me the best of times on my holiday visit. . . . I am 'up' at the club and have 'dined,' 'Tiffined' and breakfasted 'out' every meal."

The officers of His Majesty's Forces in India, the princes of India, and the Society of the Bombay Club were charmed by this young man from New York and pressed invitations upon him. Nevertheless, he retained a certain critical detachment. He exulted over an intoxicating feast at Sir Sala Jung's, regent of the Nizam of Hyderabad, to which they were driven in a cortege that was itself a princely pageant and were escorted into dinner "through long lines of motionless blacks holding flaming torches." But he also commented, "This is a picture of a native state—under, unwillingly, British protection. England in power—natives high and low discontented."

"Oh! these people," he wrote en route to Kashmir and the Himalayas,

what a puzzle to me this world becomes when we find out how many of us are in it. And how easy for the smallest portion to sit down in quiet luxury of mind and body—to say to the other far larger part—lo, the poor savages. Is what *we* call right, right all the world over and for all time?

He was appalled by the "ocean of misery and degradation" that he found on the subcontinent, such total degradation that it

might teach our "lovers of men" to know new horrors and sadness that the mortal frames and still more the Immortal Souls of Beings in God's image made, should be brought so low. The number and existence of these some millions of poor wretches has upset many preconceived notions of mine.

The journey to Tibet along the Astor Road was shadowed by mishap. In Srinagar he was held over for a week by fever. Impatiently, he pushed on and reached Thuldii in the highest Himalayas, but "that beastly fever" clung to him and he was forced to abandon the expedition and return home without having hunted the ibex and markhor that he had sought.

India had made him deeply conscious of his lack of education. "How I do crave after knowledge, book learning . . . education and a well-balanced mind," he exclaimed in the Himalayas as he tried to catch hold of "finer subtleties" of description, history, and analysis. Few Americans had had his opportunity, and he wanted to write about his experiences, which would have made as colorful a book as Theodore's about the West. He drafted an account of a tiger shoot in Hyderabad and an elephant hunt in Ceylon. The drafts were good, but he did not persist. The manuscripts did not see the light of day until 1933 when they were edited, along with his letters, and published by Eleanor under the title *Hunting Big Game in the Eighties*.

While the youthful Elliott was disturbed by the way the British held India "in a grip of iron," the way of life of the British rulers—hunts, polo, racing—suited him quite well. "I am very fond of this life, Bammie," he wrote at the end of his trip.

No doubt about it. I thought to rather put a slight stop to my inclinations by a large dose of it, but—for the great drawback that none of you are with me to enjoy it, it would be very nearly perfect in its way. Not, I think, "our way" for that means life for an *end*. But this for the mere pleasure of living is the only life.

He found it necessary to justify his trip—"There seemed little for me to do in New York that any of you my own people could be proud of me for, and naturally I am an awfully lazy fellow"—and he faced his return to New York with some anxiety.

I know Sister Anna will keep her eyes open and about her for chances for the boy. If some of the wise and strong among you don't make a *good* chance for me on my coming home I'll make but a poor one for myself I fear. . . .

But fate now intervened in the form of a sparkling debutante, Anna Rebecca Hall.

2. *Her Mother*

———

ELLIOTT WENT INTO real estate on his return from India, and even though he dutifully reported to his office on lower Broadway his 1 al life was as man-about-town. Because of his Himalayan exploits he seemed more glamorous than ever and had a kind of Guardsman masculinity that captivated young and old alike. He had the ability when talking with you, said Fanny Parsons, a friend of Corinne's, of shutting out the rest of the world and making you feel as if you were the most important thing to him.

If he noticed me at all I had received an accolade, and if on occasion he turned on all his charm, he seemed to me quite irresistible. But all the time I knew that his real worship was at the shrine of some mature and recognized belle of the day.

The leading debutante the winter Elliott returned was Anna Hall. He described her excitedly as "a tall slender fair-haired little beauty—just out and a great belle."

Anna, then almost nineteen, was the eldest of four Hall sisters. All four—Anna, Elizabeth (Tissie), Edith (Pussie), and Maude—were society belles, and all were considered slightly but attractively mad. Anna was the most competent, and she was also a little cold. Elliott was all spontaneity and tenderness, while beneath her youth and beauty Anna was a creature of rules and form. She belonged to Edith Wharton's "old New York," an ordered and hierarchical society "which could enjoy with discrimination but had lost the power to create."

The Halls were descendants of the landed Livingstons and Ludlows, and their Tivoli home on the Hudson was on property originally deeded to the lords of Livingston Manor through letters patent of Charles II, James II, and George I. The marriage of Anna's father, Valentine G. Hall, Jr., and her mother, Mary Livingston Ludlow, represented a merger of a wealthy mercantile family of New York City with the landed gentry of the Hudson. The first Ludlow had settled in New York in 1640, and as early as 1699 a Ludlow was one of provincial notables, meaning men of property, and had sat as a member of the Assembly of the Province of New York. The Ludlow social standing, patriot or Tory, was of the highest, but along the upper reaches of the Hudson, from Tivoli to Germantown, they were overshadowed by the Livingstons.

Anna Hall's grandmother, Elizabeth Livingston, the granddaughter of Chancellor Livingston, eloped with Edward H. Ludlow, a doctor. Imperious and strong-willed, she made her young husband give up his profession because she did not like a doctor's hours. He went into real estate where values were booming and in the period after the Civil War became the city's most respected realtor. That did not soften his wife's disdain for those who carried on the world's business. Once when some business associates came to see him at their house on fashionable Fourth Avenue, she stormed into the parlor, turned off the gas, and announced, "Gentlemen, my husband's office is on lower Broadway." They retired in confusion.

Eleanor remembered her great-grandmother as a very old lady whom she, her Aunt Maude, and Grandma visited regularly on Sundays. One Sunday Grandma Hall was ill and Eleanor and Maude went alone. The old lady refused to accept their explanation for Mrs. Hall's absence and told them to go right back and summon "Molly," which they did. Mrs. Hall dutifully got out of bed. When one of Eleanor's cousins, who was also the old lady's granddaughter, inherited some blue Canton china, she asked her father why so many pieces were missing. "Well, my mother used to throw the plates at my father and myself and so a good many of them were broken," he explained. When Mrs. Ludlow wanted something or felt irate, she banged the floor with her cane, which Eleanor remembered as a very long one. "I was terrified of her," Eleanor later said, adding half in amusement, half in admiration, "she was *character*."

A picture of this iron-willed lady shows a plain but strong mouth, and if the upper half of her face is covered, the mouth and chin are those of Eleanor Roosevelt.

She and Edward Ludlow had two children—Edward, "the gentlest of men," and Mary, who was mild, submissive, and beautiful. Both married children of Valentine G. Hall.

The senior Valentine Hall was an Irish immigrant. He settled in Brooklyn and by the time he was twenty-one had become a partner in one of the largest commercial houses in the city and had married his partner's daughter. The firm—Tonnele and Hall—enjoyed "unlimited credit" throughout the world. "He had remarkable business ability," his contemporaries said, and before he was fifty retired from business "with a large fortune" that included considerable real estate from Fourteenth to Eighteenth Streets along Sixth Avenue. He lived another thirty-five years but contributed little to civic welfare except for his support of religious enterprises.

His son, Valentine G. Hall, Jr., was a gentleman of solemn dignity who, after some sowing of wild oats and a period of penitence that included attending a theological school, assumed his place in society and executed its obligations and those of his church with punctilious regard. He did not go into business but lived the life of a leisured gentleman. He fathered six children—four daughters and two sons, Valentine and Edward; the Ludlows said he was good for little else. That was not his opinion of himself. In 1872 instead of building a larger town house, he built Oak Terrace at Tivoli, next to the house of his brother-in-law.*

* A family story which Eleanor told with amusement had it that when her Grandfather Hall needed more money to complete his Tivoli house he went to his mother who

Its finest room was the library, presided over by a bust of Homer. There, together with a resident clergyman whom he supported, he pursued his interests in the classics and in theological doctrine.

Valentine Jr.'s preoccupation with theology gave a puritanical tone to Tivoli life that was unusual for the Hudson River gentry. He was troubled by man's innate depravity. "I awoke this morning about half-past seven," he wrote in his journal when he was twenty-seven. "Instead of getting up immediately as I should have done, I gave way to one of my many weaknesses and lay instead until the clock struck eight building castles in the air. Oh! how much time, precious time, we waste in worldly thoughts." His austere ways reminded a neighbor of "one of the olden Christians," and the family clergyman later wrote that "no one could ever forget the morning and evening devotions, the Sunday afternoon recitation of favorite hymns."

In the Roosevelt household religion was seen as the affirmation of love, charity, and compassion; in the Hall household at Tivoli it was felt that only a ramrodlike self-denial was acceptable to God. Religion was also used to justify domestic tyranny. Valentine Hall, Jr., was a despot who had little intellectual respect for his wife. He had married her when she was quite young and had always treated her like a child. He alone decided the education, discipline, and religious training of his children. He did not even permit his womenfolk to go into the shops to choose their own clothes. He ordered dresses to be sent home where they were strewn around the parlor, and the women were allowed to make their choices. At Tivoli youthful spirits constantly rubbed against externally imposed standards. While the Roosevelts welcomed "joy of life" as the greatest of heaven's gifts, the Halls considered pleasure of the senses to be sinful and playfulness an affront to God. As the Hall children grew up, their instincts were often at war with their moral precepts, and they had an especially strong sense of duty and responsibility.

Anna Hall's education, except for religion and manners, was sketchy. A great deal of attention was given to correct posture, dancing, and the social graces; one's debut was more important than the cultivation of one's mind except for a smattering of language, literature, and music. A scrapbook that Anna kept on a trip to England and Ireland the summer before she made her debut contained photographs of the accepted shrines of the culturally refined—Sir Walter Scott's study, Abbotsford Abbey, Holyrood Palace, Windsor Castle. The poems that she transcribed into her exercise book were by the approved poets of the period—Longfellow, Browning, Owen Meredith—and she preferred those that pointed to a moral and suggested a rule of conduct.

"would go to the wardrobe and rummage around" and emerge "with a few thousand dollars." Eleanor thought that this harked back to her great-grandmother's immigrant origins "because in Ireland it would be perfectly normal to keep your belongings in whatever was the most secret place in your little house. You would not deposit them in a bank, and this was what . . . my great-grandmother evidently had carried into the new world and proceeded to do." Eleanor added that "as neither of her sons ever added to the fortune but both of them seemed well provided for, I think, it is safe to say that the original immigrant great grandfather must have made a considerable fortune."

The same exercise book contained the beginning of a story she had written. Its language was conventional and its emotions stereotyped, its setting in a British castle suggesting the fascination that British titles had for girls in the 1880s—a form of escape both romantic and decorous. Its theme was the redemption of a dissolute London aristocrat by an equally aristocratic girl of nineteen. High-minded and self-controlled, Anna turned naturally to a man of ardor and bravura, even if he was weak.

When Anna was seventeen her father died without leaving a will, which meant that the properties had to be administered by the court. Valentine Hall had never taught his wife how to budget and to keep accounts. Mary Hall, who knew nothing about disciplining her children since that had been her husband's prerogative, was left with four daughters and two sons between the ages of three and seventeen. Anna, the oldest, was "the strongest character in the family, very religious"; she "took hold and tried to control the family." But since she was also the most beautiful, she was married within three years of her father's death.

In the brief but strenuous New York season of 1881–82 Anna was acclaimed as one of society's most glamorous women. "She was made for an atmosphere of approval," a friend said, "for she was worthy of it. . . . Her sweet soul needed approbation." Elliott's courtship provided just that, for where she was reserved and circumspect, Elliott was demonstrative and ardent.

It was the springtime of the year, the springtide of their love; their hope was high and their dreams radiant. Elliott introduced her to his Newsboys and she began to do volunteer work at the Orthopedic Hospital. Gallant messages arrived accompanied by flowers and proposals that they ride or dance or boat or dine together. On Sundays there were the church parades along tree-shaded Fifth Avenue past the fashionable residences, the young men top-hatted, the girls elegant, stopping to chat, while horses and carriages jogged northward toward Central Park.

For the wealthy, the New York of the eighties was gracious and society a self-contained little island of brownstones that stretched from Washington Square to Central Park along Fifth and Madison Avenues, with a few Knickerbocker hold-outs at Gramercy Park and Stuyvesant Square—the "Second Avenue set," Elliott called them. Almost everyone to whom Elliott doffed his hat was connected in some way to either the Roosevelts or the Halls.

Anna and Elliott's courtship was ritually decorous.

"My dear Mr. Roosevelt," wrote Anna in her strong, precise handwriting,

Thank you many times for your very pretty philopena present. I think it was wicked of you to send me anything, yet I must tell you how much pleasure it gave me. I would try and thank you for your note, but feel it would be useless. Let me only say that I fully appreciate your kindness.

Hoping soon to see you, Believe me   Yours very sincerely,
                                         ANNA R. HALL

Monday, March 12th.   11 West 37th St.

And a note from Elliott, impatient to shorten the hours away from her, greeted his "dear Miss Hall" at breakfast.

It will be, I hope, so delightful an afternoon that I will be at the hospital at half after four instead of five, it being so much more pleasant an hour for driving than the later.

I trust that you can get through your work there by that time. Accept these few flowers and wear them for the little children to see. They say that the "lovely lady" always has some with her. Even the flowers are happier at being your servants I am sure.

With regard I am   Faithfully Yours
6 West 57 St.   ELLIOTT ROOSEVELT
Friday

According to Fanny Parsons, Anna and Elliott decided to become engaged at a Memorial Day house party given in the hope of encouraging just this event by lovely Laura Delano, the youngest sister of Mrs. James (Sallie) Roosevelt. The party was at Algonac, the stately Delano mansion overlooking the Hudson at Newburgh. The Roosevelt clan immediately welcomed the nineteen-year-old Anna with an outpouring of affection mingled with relief that as a family man with "something to work for in life," Elliott might perhaps settle down.

"He is such a tender, sympathetic, manly man," Bamie wrote to Anna, that she, though older, had "ever turned toward him in many sad moments for help and strength." Corinne, suffering from a "quincy sore throat," scratched out a note in pencil to express her delight that Anna had made Elliott "so grateful and happy a man. He loves you with so tender and respectful a devotion, that I who love my darling brother so dearly, cannot but feel that you as well as he, have much to be thankful for." Theodore wrote his "dearest Old Brother" that "it is no light thing to take the irrevocable step you have just taken, but I feel sure that you have done wisely and well, and we are all more than thankful to have so lovely a member added to our household circle."

Felicitations poured in, as did invitations to call. From Hyde Park, Elliott's cousin James Roosevelt sent his "warmest congratulations," adding, "Your Godson [F.D.R.] thrives and grows. I have just been teaching him now to climb a ladder in a cherry tree. Your Aunt [Sara] says—'she will send you a line to express her congratulations.'"

Elliott spent most of the summer in town, but on week ends he was at Tivoli and the whole "Tivoli crowd" along the Woods Road came to congratulate the couple. There were tennis and "jolly drives," reading out loud and an evening of fireworks at the R. E. Livingstons'. Moving serenely through it all, reported Elliott to his mother, was his willowy Anna, wearing the magnificent "tiger claw necklace" that Elliott had had made after his return from India.

Weekdays in town were not all work. There were "all night talks" with Theodore and frequent dashes out to Hempstead to ride, hunt, and play polo. "The 'Meet' at Jamaica yesterday afternoon was a very pretty one and we had a glorious run," Elliott wrote Anna. "Mohawk [his hunter] did grandly and gave me a good place in the first flight from start to kill." Afterward they "dined quietly at the kennels," and then Elliott sat "cosily over the big wood fire gazing into the flames and wishing for and thinking of my Sweet Heart."

"A jolly afternoon's polo yesterday," he reported a few days later. He was one of the best polo men at Meadow Brook, and his brilliance in this "emperor" of sports thrilled Anna, although she must have worried about the game's hazards. "You will have to hurry up and marry me," he warned her,

if you expect to have anything left to marry. It seems to me that I get from one bad scrape into another. That beastly leg gave me so much pain that I went to the Doctor and I'm in for it this time, I'm afraid, not to get on a horse for a week and not to walk about more than is absolutely necessary. Oh! my! *Poultices*! *Ointment*! and three evenings alone by myself at 57th St. with my leg on a chair.

Was he really in such a hurry to marry Anna? He was often melancholy that summer and had some sort of seizure at Tivoli. "My old Indian trouble has left me subject to turns like I had Monday from change of weather or some such cause," he wrote Anna reassuringly. The trip down on the train had been "pretty bad," he confessed, but "Herm Livingston and Frank Appleton were on board and very kind so I pulled along very well."

Anna was troubled by his sudden depressions. "Please never keep anything from me," she pleaded with him, "for fear of giving me pain or say to yourself 'There can be no possible use of my telling her.' Believe me, I am quite strong enough to face with you the storms of this life and I shall always be so happy when I know that you have told and will tell me every thought, and I can perhaps sometimes be of some use to you."

She should not worry, he replied. "I know I am blue and disagreeable often, but please darling, bear with me and I will come out all right in the end, and it really is an honest effort to do the right that makes me so often quiet and thoughtful about it all." And in Anna's moments of doubt and despondency, Elliott comforted and cheered her: "Darling if you care to, we will read some of my favorite chapters and verses in the little Testament together." He had carried that little book all around the world and it had been a "comforting and joyous though silent companion."

Mrs. Hall agreed to a December 1 wedding date. Would Anna really like diamonds for a wedding present, Elliott asked her as summer drew to a close, or would she prefer "a little coupe or Victoria?" He thought he could afford to buy one for her if she would find it useful and enjoy the driving.

As the wedding day neared, Mrs. Hall, although happy for her "darling child," could not help but feel anxious about entrusting her to this dashing young man, so different from her sternly pious husband. "I pray you and Elliott to enter your new life with your hearts turned to God," she wrote her daughter on the eve of the wedding. "Go to him tonight before retiring and in His presence read your Bible and kneel together and ask Him to guide you both through this world which has been so bright to you both, but which must have some clouds, and dearest Anna and Elliott for my sake, and for both of your dear fathers' sakes never fail to have daily prayers."

The wedding ceremony was at Calvary Church, two blocks from Elliott's

Twentieth Street birthplace. It was described by the *Herald* as "one of the most brilliant social events of the season. . . . The bride was every bit a queen and her bridesmaids were worthy of her." The *Herald*'s account of the wedding ended, "It is the desire of the bride to be back by the 11th inst. in order to be present at the time of the Vanderbilt ball."

On their way south they stopped in Philadelphia, and Elliott promptly penned a reassuring note to Mrs. Hall.

Your kind letter we received today and both your children, for I feel for Anna's sake you will consider me one now too, are deeply and truly with you in the spirit of what you say. We both knelt before the Giver of every good and perfect gift and thanked him the source of perfect happiness for His tender loving kindness to us. Dear Lady do not fear about trusting your daughter to me. It shall be my great object all my life to comfort and care for her.

An invitation to Eleanor's parents to attend the Patriarchs Ball. Only those who "belonged" were invited.

3. *The World into Which Eleanor Was Born*

AFTER HIS MARRIAGE Elliott went to work for the Ludlow firm, the city's leading real-estate establishment. His earnings there supplemented the better than $15,000 annual income that he and Anna had between them. Their income did not permit a gold service or servants in livery drawn up in line in the English fashion as were to be seen at the more formal entertainments of such friends as Mrs. Astor and the Cornelius Vanderbilts. But, in an era when there were no taxes and wages were low, the young couple were able to maintain a well-staffed brownstone house in New York's fashionable Thirties. Anna had her coupe in town and ordered her dresses from Palmers in London and Worth in Paris while Elliott stabled four hunters at Meadow Brook.

The Elliott Roosevelts were among the gayest and most lively members of the younger set—the newspapers called them "the swells"—who pursued their pleasure in the great Fifth Avenue houses, at Meadow Brook, Tuxedo, Newport, Lenox, and the fashionable watering places of Europe. They were prominent members of New York society at a time when the merger between the old Knickerbocker families and the post-bellum barons of oil, steel, and railroads had already been accomplished, and, in emulation of Europe's aristocracies, especially England's, New York society had become a well-defined, self-conscious, codified hierarchy. It was, said Mrs. Winthrop Chanler, "a closed circle to which one either did or did not belong."

Anna and Elliott belonged. They and their friends set the fashion in dress and manners, and the anxious ones knocked at their doors. Anna's graceful beauty and charming manners were everywhere acclaimed. "Fair, frail and fragile, and therefore a good illustration of beauty in American women," a society columnist rhapsodized. Her father's discipline had not been in vain. He had insisted that she and her sisters walk regularly in the country with a stick across their backs held in the crook of their elbows, which had produced an unmistakable bearing. "The proud set of the head on the shoulders was the distinctive look of the Halls," recalled Mrs. Lucius Wilmerding, whose mother was a close friend of Anna. When *Town Topics* took the young ladies of society to task for their stoop and slouch compared to the "superb" carriage of English girls, it excluded Mrs. Elliott Roosevelt from its strictures and recommended her as a model.

Mr. Peter Marié, writer of *vers de société* and a great beau, was noted for the beautiful women at his entertainments. No greater compliment could be bestowed upon a lady than to have Mr. Marié request a photograph from which he would have some well-known artist paint a miniature for his famous collection. Anna's beauty was accorded this gallant tribute: she was one of his "brilliant creatures." Robert Browning was so taken with her beauty that he came to read to her while she was having her portrait painted during a summer she and Elliott spent in the Engadine.[1]

When Anna and her friends launched the Knickerbocker Bowling Club it became the fashionable thing to do. While the well-turned-out coaches of other women promenaded in Central Park, she and her friends jogged an extra three miles up semirustic Riverside Drive to the Claremont Restaurant for afternoon tea. She was among the women who inaugurated the series of dances at Sherry's, when the "swells" decided that the Assemblies and Patriarchs' Balls had ceased to be select. She was, to use the phrase of one of her contemporaries, "tuned to a ballroom pitch."

She loved the cotillions at eleven and supper at midnight, the Tuesday Evening Dancing Class, the evening at the opera, the annual kennel and horse shows, the amateur theatricals, the polo and tennis matches, the meetings of philanthropic boards, and all the other occasions that constituted a New York season. While a few emancipated spirits considered conformity to society's pleasures and disciplines bondage to a "chain of tyrannical trifles," for Anna Hall Roosevelt they were the very substance of a happy, contented life.

Anna was proud of her handsome husband who was one of society's great gallants. His haunts were the Knickerbocker Club and Meadow Brook, his pleasure a fast game of polo, the cross-country steeplechase, the hunt ball, and the horse show. A young lady's cup flowed over, said Daisy Harriman, when she was asked down to Meadow Brook. "All New York aped the English," Mrs. Harriman said of society in the eighties, especially so in the annual Coach Parade, when the swells in green coats and gray top hats, with lovely ladies gracing the boxes of their four-in-hands, would make the circuit of Central Park. Elliott was a mainstay of this ritual, which ended with dinner at the Brunswick, its dining room festooned with whips, whiffletrees, and coach horns. John Sargeant Wise, son of a well-known Whig politician from Virginia, said that Elliott was "the most lovable Roosevelt I ever knew," adding that "perhaps he . . . was nothing like so aggressive or so forceful a man as Theodore, but if personal popularity could have bestowed public honours on any man there was nothing beyond the reach of Elliott Roosevelt."[2]

In New York, Meadow Brook, Bar Harbor, and Newport, Anna and Elliott gave themselves to a strenuous, fun-loving life. "We play our polo matches on Monday, and Saturday next we go out on Mr. E. T. Gerry's yacht the 'Electra' to see the race tomorrow for the Goelet Cups. We dine, dance, play tennis, polo, sail, swim and live in the open air all the time. It will do you lots of good," Nell assured his "dearest Bye," urging her to join them.

And this letter from Anna to Bamie described their summer:

34 Catherine Street

Newport

Dearest Bamie,

I want to write you just a few lines in answer to your letter. We arrived here on Saturday & spent until Monday with the Wilsons. Of course I was in bed all day Sunday with one of my headaches. Elliott went everywhere though, & they were awfully kind and made things as pleasant as possible for us.

Elliott's match will come off tomorrow. The Harvards beat the Westchesters on Wednesday. Every one seems to think that Meadow Brook will beat them though. Elliott is very much excited over it, & is playing very well. We have been to the Casino every morning watching the tennis matches. . . . I suppose this is the gayest week here, but I do not care much for it. I liked Bar Harbor much better. The air there is bracing & then you always got to bed early. The life here is too much like New York. This afternoon I am going with Mrs. Vanderbilt to some teas. This evening we dine with the Whitneys.& then Elliott is coming home.

I may go to the Kernochan ball for half-an-hour, but doubt it. I am not feeling my best and am on my back—which accounts for this being in pencil.

Last night we had a very jolly spree. First we dined on the Morgan's yacht after a delightful sail to Bristol & then drove home by moonlight on the coaches. There were three coach leads. . . .

On Monday they play in pairs at polo & if Elliott loses on Monday or Wednesday we will go up the Hudson on Thursday, but if not we will stay for the final game on Saturday.

I shall be delighted to reach Tivoli and see them all. I really feel quite homesick here . . . [rest of letter missing].

There were times when Elliott was full of large plans—to get wealth "for his little wife's sake," to become active in Republican politics, to pull together and publish his notes on India. But his will was as weak as his hopes were high, and the attractions of society and sports quickly reasserted themselves.

In the summer of 1884 Anna was pregnant, and, always of frail health, she often felt unwell and had to rest a great deal. The family was anxious, all the more so because in February of that year Theodore's wife, his adored Alice Lee, had died two days after giving birth to baby Alice. It had been a time of double tragedy in the Roosevelt household, for their beloved mother, Mittie, had died only a few hours earlier. "There is a curse on this house," Elliott cried as he opened the door to Theodore, who had rushed down from Albany; "Mother is dying and Alice is dying too."

Anxiety grew as Anna's confinement approached, and there was general relief when, on October 11, a baby girl was delivered—without complications. Though Elliott and Anna had wished ardently for a "precious boy" and the little girl was "a more wrinkled and less attractive baby than the average," to her father she was "a miracle from heaven." Anna and Elliott named their first-born Anna after her mother and Bamie, their favorite sister and sister-in-law, and Eleanor after her father who had been called "Ellie" and "Nell." Between her parents' disappointment that she was not a boy and the death threat that her advent into the world had represented to her mother, Eleanor, in a sense, came into the world guilty and had to reinstate herself.

As usual, Bamie was on the scene being helpful. From the time of the older Theodore's death, the family had turned to her at moments of crisis. Elliott in particular relied on "the busy Bye" to set his "little world to rights." It was Bamie who notified members of the family, including Aunt Gracie, who immediately replied:

Bamie's telegram at 11.30 this morning brought us the joyful news. I am over-joyed to hear of itty girl's (not itty "precious boy jr") safe arrival and just long to have her in my arms. How well I remember when I held you darling Ellie for the first time. My heart beat so I could hardly hold you! And you were so rosy and so beautiful! Kiss Anna for me.

Eleanor—she never called herself Anna Eleanor except in official documents and in signing checks—was born into a secure golden world in which significant or even ominous events around the globe were hardly noticed—or, if they were, they seemed remote and without relevance to the lives of her parents and their friends.

The foreign cables in the newspapers of October 11, 1884, reported the growth of the empires whose dissolution would occupy so much of the agenda of Eleanor's final years at the U.N. Egypt, which had been part of the Ottoman Empire when her father had sailed up the Nile in a dehabeah in 1873, was coming under the rule of Great Britain, and, at the request of the khedive, it was reported, British troops were in the field seeking to suppress the "wild and fanatical" forces of El Mahdi. The same column of foreign notices reported that Paris had heard that "Chinese bands" had been driven off from "Western and Southern Tonquin." "My fleet is closely watching the coast," General Brière de l'Isle reported to Paris. "I assume immediate command of the troops and am about to leave Hanoi." In India Elliott had questioned the universality of the western concepts of right and civilization in defense of which the white man was allegedly assuming his burdens. But gradually he had lost interest in the rights and wrongs of imperialism, and his social ties were now aligned with the propertied classes of western Europe, especially of England.[3]

The foreign cables also noted briefly that "the outrages against the Jews in Morocco have been stopped." New York society had little sympathy for an anti-Semitism that expressed itself in physical brutalities and political repression, but it was nevertheless openly anti-Semitic. Attendance at the Patriarchs' balls at Delmonico's was falling off, *Town Topics*, the self-styled "Journal of Society" noted, adding that the chief beneficiaries of these entertainments now were "the Hebrews," who arranged their own festivities for the days following a Patriarchs' ball so that they could take advantage of the lavish decorations the Patriarchs left behind. Even so enlightened a woman as Mrs. Winthrop Chanler could write of a Jewish friend that "she seemed to descend from prophets rather than from money lenders." Elliott and Anna shared New York society's bias against immigrant foreigners generally, and against the eastern European Jews particularly.

Politics, except on the highest levels of government and statesmanship, was not an occupation for gentlemen in 1884. Theodore's willingness to run for assemblyman in the "brownstone" district—in Eleanor's day it would be known as the "Silk Stocking" district—distressed some members of the family. "We felt that his own father would not have liked it, and would have been fearful of the outcome," Cousin Emlen said. "Uncle Jim, Em and Al bitterly opposed to my candidacy of course," Theodore had noted in his diary in 1881, but Elliott stood by him like a "trump." Elliott even joined his brother in going into the Twenty-first A.D. Republican Club.

The chief item in the newspapers that October, and Theodore's major preoccupation, was the close of the Cleveland-Blaine campaign. Theodore was not happy with a presidential candidate whom he regarded as a special-interests jobber. He had opposed Blaine at the Chicago convention and until a few weeks before Election Day had managed to avoid campaigning for him. But in the end, to the distress of the Reformers, he chose regularity and stumped for Blaine. Presumably Elliott, who, like his sisters, followed his brother in political matters, voted for him, but Anna's side of the family found Grover Cleveland's honesty as well as conservatism more than satisfactory. And, indeed, a substantial part of high society voted for Cleveland. A few days before Eleanor was born Grandfather Ludlow was quoted as saying: "I have been a Democrat for years and will probably vote for Cleveland, but I am not a politician. . . ."

The Roosevelts had all been Democrats before the Civil War but became firm Lincoln Republicans during the war. So did Valentine Hall, although a little less staunchly, motivated by economic self-interest as well as patriotism. A friend who came in after dinner just before the 1864 Lincoln-McClellan race ended announced that he had sold all his stocks. Valentine Hall considered that stupid. "He should have held on until after Lincoln's election," he thought. Everything would go up. He scared another friend with the warning that if McClellan were elected, the Democrats would surely repudiate the debt. But Valentine Hall did not wholly approve of Lincoln, either. When the president sent in a general to take charge of riot-ridden New York, he thought the action "despotic." As for Lincoln's political associates, their pockets were "filled too." He prayed, worried about his health, and though in his twenties, bought a substitute in order to escape military service, as many gentlemen did.

The Oyster Bay Roosevelts stayed Republican, but the Dutchess County branch reverted to the Democratic party. One Roosevelt who voted for Cleveland was the gracious squire of Hyde Park.

Cleveland was the first Democrat to occupy the White House since 1860, but his policies differed little from those of his Republican predecessors. Not until Theodore became president did either Republican or Democrat assert the national interest in any way that angered the rich and privileged.

The Cleveland victory saw the final suppression of the Negro vote in the southern states. "Let the South alone," William E. Dodge, New York capitalist, Grant Republican, and close friend of the elder Theodore, had urged in 1875, and that is what Republican administrations did, beginning with President Hayes, for whom the elder Theodore had worked hard. By 1884 the South had nullified the Fourteenth and Fifteenth Amendments insofar as they applied to Negroes, and white supremacy was effectively re-established.

Because of the Bulloch connection in Georgia, the Roosevelts always had a large circle of southern friends. And because of these southern ties, Elliott and Theodore were undoubtedly sympathetic with the restoration of white rule in the South, although as president, Theodore would shatter precedent and rouse the South to a fury by having Booker T. Washington as a White House luncheon guest.

He was to shatter precedent as well by his enlightened approach to the rights of the workingman, and it was in the year of Eleanor's birth that he began to question the interpretation of the laissez-faire doctrine to which he and most of the members of his class had always subscribed. In 1884 Samuel Gompers of the Cigarmakers Union took Theodore on a tour of the slum sweatshops, and the young assemblyman agreed to sponsor a bill to prohibit the manufacture of cigars in tenements even though it violated his laissez-faire principles. And when the courts, quoting Adam Smith, invalidated his bill saying that they could not see "how the cigar-maker is to be improved in his health or his morals by forcing him from his home and its hallowed associations," Theodore began to be aware, as he wrote later, that complete freedom for the individual could turn out in practice "to mean perfect freedom for the strong to wrong the weak." He would be the first president since Jackson to use the power of government against Big Business—in the 1902 coal strike.

The trade-union movement in the eighties was in its infancy. Labor was cheap. The propertied wanted to keep it that way and rationalized their privileged position by arguing that any man worth his salt could improve his status. The day Eleanor was born, an Episcopal congress met in Detroit to answer the question *Is Our Civilization Just to Workingmen?*. "Labor's complaint is poverty," said the keynote speaker, the Reverend Dr. R. H. Newton. "Poverty is the fault neither of the laborer nor of nature. The state crosses the path of the workingman and prevents him from making a fair fight. Labor fails to get favorable legislation; capital secures all it asks."

To the respectable and the upstanding, whether wealthy or not, this was "rot" and heresy. Their laissez-faire individualism was not troubled by the fact that at a time when half-a-million-dollar yachts and million-dollar mansions were being built, thousands of unemployed were looking for work, bread, and shelter, that the average income of eleven million out of the twelve million American families was $380 a year. They approved of industrialists like Pullman, who proclaimed that "the workers have nothing to do with the amount of wages they shall receive." In 1893 they were relieved when the Supreme Court declared unconstitutional a 2-per-cent tax on income of $4,000 and over; a good friend and Roosevelt family advisor, Joseph Choate, had argued the case, denouncing the tax as a "a communist march on private property."

"Unfair" taxes and the threat of the nascent labor movement may have invaded the after-dinner conversations of the men, but matters involving politics were of no concern to gentlewomen. *Godey's Lady's Book*, the widely read arbiter of feminine taste and interest in the 1880s, made it a matter of policy to avoid references to public controversy and agitating influence. In 1884 the closest it came to discussing a woman in public life was "Queen Victoria as a Writer." Women's suffrage had become an important issue, but it had no supporters in the Roosevelt family among either the men or the women.

Family letters and recollections provide few glimpses of Eleanor's childhood, yet they were obviously critical years. In Eleanor's later portrayal of these years she emerges as a child who was full of fears—of the dark, of dogs, horses, snakes, of other children. She was "afraid of being scolded, afraid that other people would not like me." She spoke of a sense of inferiority that was almost overpowering coupled with an unquenchable craving for praise and affection. She described her mother as the most beautiful woman she ever knew but also as representing cold virtue, severity, and disapproval, while her father embodied everything that was warm and joyous in her childhood.

Her contrasting memories of her mother and father emerged in a brief account of her first visit to Hyde Park that she included among the explanatory footnotes to her father's letters, in *Hunting Big Game in the Eighties*. On January 30, 1882, "a splendid large baby boy" (Sara Roosevelt's description) had been born to the James Roosevelts. They asked Elliott to be one of the godparents of Franklin Delano, as they decided to name him.

To see this godchild, Eleanor wrote, was the reason

for that visit which I paid at the age of two with my parents to Hyde Park and I am told that Franklin, probably under protest, crawled around the nursery (which has since been our children's), bearing me on his back. Also, I am told, that I was sent down at tea time to the library in a starched white frock and stood bashfully at the door till my Mother saw me and called "Come in, Granny." She often called me that, for I was a solemn child, without beauty and painfully shy and I seemed like a little old woman entirely lacking in the spontaneous joy and mirth of youth.[4]

From her mother Eleanor received the indelible impression that she was plain to the point of ugliness. As a young woman Anna had been captivatingly beautiful, her face and head so classic in outline that artists had begged to paint her. Anna had been, a friend of the family said, "a little gentlewoman." Eleanor, in her anxiety for people to do right, was more the little schoolmistress, saved from primness only by her grave blue eyes and the sweetness with which she admonished the grownups. To paraphrase Carlyle, who was speaking of the founder of one of the world's great religions, she was one of those who "cannot but be in earnest; whom Nature herself has appointed to be sincere." She is so "old-fashioned," her mother said apologetically. Eleanor, who sensed her mother's disappointment in her, considered this a reproach, but behind the reproach was a mother's bafflement over her little girl's precocious sense of right and wrong and the sadness in her appraising eyes. But these same traits amused and charmed her father, who called her his "little golden hair."

My father was always devoted to me, however, and as soon as I could talk, I went into his dressing room every morning and chattered to him often shaking my finger at him as you can see in the portrait of me at the age of five which we still have. I even danced for him, intoxicated by the pure joy of motion, twisting round and round until he would pick me up and throw me into the air and tell me I made him dizzy.[5]

Eleanor's first nurse was French. "My mother had a conviction that it was essential to study languages, so when I was a baby, she had a French nurse for me, and I spoke French before I spoke English." What this nurse was like, Eleanor nowhere said, but in later life she spoke French as fluently as English, which suggests that this first nurse had the baby's confidence.

While Eleanor's own warmest memories of her early childhood years were all associated with her father, that attractive man was, in fact, putting his little family through a grim ordeal. Nervous and moody, he spent much of his time with the Meadow Brook men, often in reckless escapades and drinking sprees that worried his family and mortified Anna. In the spring of 1887, dissatisfied with himself and his business prospects, he gave up his partnership in the Ludlow firm. Anna prevailed upon him not to risk another Long Island summer. An extended stay in Europe, away from his cronies, she hoped, would enable him to get hold of himself and regain his health. So, on May 19, the Elliott Roosevelt family, a nurse for two-and-a-half-year-old Eleanor, and Anna's sister Tissie sailed for Europe on the *Britannic*.

One day out, the *Britannic* was rammed by the incoming *Celtic* in a fog. "The strain for a few minutes," Anna wrote Bamie, "when we all thought we were sinking was fearful though there were no screams and no milling about. Everyone was perfectly quiet. We were among those taken on life boats to the *Celtic*." Eleanor's recollection of "wild confusion" was significantly different, and closer to reality.

As passengers described the collision to newspapermen, the prow of the *Celtic* struck the *Britannic* a slanting blow, glanced off and then struck again, her nose entering the *Britannic*'s side fully ten feet. Several passengers were killed, a child beheaded, and many injured. The sea foamed, iron bars and belts snapped, and above the din could be heard the moans of the dying and injured. Grownups panicked. Stokers and boiler men emerging from the depths of the *Britannic* made a wild rush for the lifeboats until the captain forced them back at the point of his revolver. The air was filled with "cries of terror," Eleanor's among them. She clung frantically to the men who were trying to drop her over the steep side of the ship into the outstretched arms of her father, who stood in a lifeboat below. Although the sea was calm, the life-boats were pitching, and the distance seemed vast to Eleanor. The transfer was finally completed despite Eleanor's struggles and they were rowed to the *Celtic*, which took them back to New York.[6]

Anna and Elliott decided to go through with their plans, because Elliott's health depended on it. But Eleanor, in terror, refused to go and remained unmoved even by her father's endearments and pleas. The puzzled young parents turned to the Gracies, and Eleanor was left to spend the summer with them. "We took a cab," Aunt Gracie wrote to Corinne,

and called for our sweet little Eleanor and brought her out here with us. She was so little and gentle & had made such a narrow escape out of the great ocean that it made her seem doubly helpless & pathetic to us. . . . She asked two or three times in the train coming out here, where her "dear Mamma was, & where her Papa was, & where is Aunt Tissie?" I told her "They have gone to Europe." She said "where is baby's home now?" I said "baby's home is Gracewood with Uncle Bunkle & Aunt Gracie," which seemed to entirely satisfy the sweet little darling. But as we came near the Bay driving by Mrs. Swan's she said to her uncle in an anxious alarmed way "Baby does not want to go into the water. Not in a boat." It is really touching. . . .

Aunt Gracie's hopeful interpretation of Eleanor's acquiescence may have calmed her own anxiety but showed little real understanding of the ordeal the two-and-a-half-year-old child was going through in numb silence. She had not been able to overcome her terror of the sea. She had disgraced her parents, and as a punishment they had deserted her and she had lost her home.

This violent experience made an indelible impression on Eleanor. She never lost her fear of the sea. Throughout her life she felt the need to prove that she could overcome her physical timidity by feats of special courage. Desertion of the young and defenseless remained an ever present theme—in her reading and her compositions for school; the mere suspicion that someone she loved might have turned away from her always caused the same taut, hopeless bewilderment.

Anna remained uneasy about the separation, "I do so long for her," she wrote from Paris, "but know it was wiser to leave her." And even if Anna had understood how seriously the child was being hurt, she could not have acted differently, because her troubled husband needed his wife's reassuring presence and love if he was to get well.

By August he was "a thousand times better," but he did not wish to risk exposure to his family until he was "really strong and fit to work hard." They returned to New York after six months and Elliott, full of good intentions, joined his Uncle Gracie's banking and brokerage firm. But he also rejoined the hard-drinking, hard-riding Meadow Brook crowd. In spite of his family's misgivings he began to build a large, handsome house in Hempstead, L. I. Polo and hunting became more the center of his life than ever, and he became an ever more reckless rider. One day the hunt started from the Mineola Fair Grounds, the hounds streaking across the Jackson and Titus farms. Forty started out but by the time they were taking the fences of the Titus place only Elliott was following the huntsman. He could hear his companions shouting "don't follow that Irishman, you will be killed" when he was thrown at the third fence and broke his collar bone. On another occasion he arranged a hair-raising midnight steeplechase. "Your father was one of the greatest sports I ever knew," Joe Murphy, the Meadow Brook huntsman, later wrote.[7]

Anna and Eleanor shared Elliot's excitement about the new house in Hempstead—Anna because she hoped it might steady him, Eleanor because it meant she would spend more time with her father. The family rented a cottage nearby to be able to supervise the construction. "Anna is wonderfully well, enjoys everything . . . even the moving and looks the beautiful girl she is. Little Eleanor is as happy as the day is long, plays with her kitten, the puppy & the chickens all the time & is very dirty as a general rule. . . . Baby Eleanor goes up to look after it [the house] every day and calls it hers," a delighted Elliott informed Bamie.

The idyll was brief. In June, 1888, Elliott, exhausted by his hectic life, became seriously ill, and though he rallied miraculously, his family was far from reassured. "Elliott is very much better," Theodore wrote. "I lunched with him Wednesday, and he is now able to go out driving. I wonder if it would do any good to talk to him about his imprudence! I suppose not. I wish he would come to me for a little while; but I guess Oyster Bay would prove insufferably dull, not only for Elliott but for Anna." Soon Elliott was back on his feet, playing polo with Theodore in Oyster Bay. "I know we shall be beaten," Anna confided to her sister-in-law, "since Elliott can barely stay on his pony." Elliott's team lost. "We have great fun here at polo," Theodore wrote Cabot Lodge. Theodore worked and played strenuously, but he found the pace set by Anna and Elliott too frantic and ultimately meaningless. "I do hate his Hempstead life," he confided to Bye. "I don't know whether he [Elliott] could get along without the excitement now, but it is certainly very unhealthy, and it leads to nothing."

For Eleanor, Hempstead was a happy place. She was not too far away from her cousin Alice, with whom she loved to play. "She and Eleanor are too funny together," Anna reported. They both went to Aunt Gracie's for lessons every morning. "Alice is looking so splendidly and plays so beautifully with Eleanor," was the report. But when Elliott left to go cruising on the *Mayflower*, the 100-foot sloop that had won the America's Cup several years before, Anna made a point of letting him know that "Baby is well but very fiendish." Eleanor's anger did not last, however. Soon she was caught up again in the excitement of her full summer life. "Eleanor is on the piazza building a house with blocks and seems very well and happy," Anna wrote in her next report. "She won't hear of going home as she says, she would not have Alice any more. Aunty and Uncle Bunkle took Alice and Eleanor sailing yesterday. They did enjoy it so much. They are coming over from Sagamore Hill to lunch, and tonight we tea there."

The relationship between Alice and Eleanor, both born in 1884, may not have been as serene as their elders assumed. The two cousins were very different. Though a frail child, "Baby Lee" was as proud, self-assured, and competitive as her father. Golden-curled and saucy, her blue eyes flashed an endless challenge, while Eleanor was gentle, docile, shy, and already painfully aware of her ungainliness. For two years Eleanor wore a steel back brace to correct a curvature of the spine, "a very uncomfortable brace." Alice, like Eleanor, idolized her father, and also felt rebuffed and neglected by her mother—in her case, her stepmother. Her response was to rebel, to turn tomboy, which she knew annoyed her stepmother, while Eleanor, much as she would have liked to imitate Alice, withdrew into injured melancholy. Alice seemed "older and cleverer," she said much later, "and while I always admired her I was always afraid of her."

The summer of 1888 had been a time of closeness to her parents and happiness for Eleanor, who was going on four. "The funny little tot had a happy little birthday," her father wrote to Bamie, thanking her for Eleanor's birthday present, "and ended by telling me, when saying good night (after Anna had heard her say her prayers) that she 'loved everybody and everybody loved her.' Was it not cunning?"

That fall and winter were to be the last time Anna, Elliott, and Eleanor enjoyed life as a family. By late spring, 1889, they were finally and fully settled in their "country seat," which they called "½-way Nirvana." Anna was pregnant again and expecting to spend a quiet summer.

It was only a few weeks later that Elliott, rehearsing with friends for an amateur circus to be staged at the Waterbury place in Pelham, fractured his ankle in turning a double somersault. The break was incorrectly diagnosed as a sprain, and he was in agony for two weeks after the plaster had been broken off. There were days of such pain "that he could eat nothing and at night he would sob for hours." His leg had to be rebroken and reset. He told Eleanor what the doctors were going to do. She gave him courage and comfort, but it was a thoughtless act, considering that she was not quite five. He did not complain, but Eleanor, being a child of amazing sensitivity, did not have to be told; as leaves moved to the wind, she stirred to the thought of others in pain. If a playmate was injured she wept, and her father was the person she most loved in the world. Her eyes brimmed with tears as he pulled himself on crutches out to the waiting doctors. Eleanor never forgot this experience.

Elliott Jr. was born October 1, 1889, and this event evoked the first letter, dictated to Pussie, from Eleanor, who had been sent to Tivoli to stay with her grandmother.

Dear Father:

I hope you are very well and Mother too. I hope little brother doesn't cry and if he does tell the nurse to give him a tap tap. How does he look? Some people tell me he looks like an elephant and some say he is like a bunny. I told Aunt Pussie today she would be very unhappy if she were a man because his wife would send her down downtown every day she could only come home on Sunday and then she would have to go to church. Goodby now dear Father, write me soon another letter. I love you very much and Mother and Brother too, if he has blue eyes.

Your precious little
Eleanor.

"And," added Pussie, "Totty [the name by which her Hall aunts called her] is flourishing. She has quite a color and tell Anna the French lessons are progressing, although I am afraid the pupil knows more than the teacher."

"Eleanor is so proud of her baby brother and talks of nothing else," was the next report from Tivoli.

Elliott and Anna were equally pleased. The birth of their first son was the fulfillment of "their hearts' desire." Elliott, in spite of his continuing pain, doted on "Baby Joss," as the new arrival was called. But even though Elliott was with his new son, Eleanor sensed no change in her father's attitude toward her. She never doubted that she was first in his heart.

With her mother, however, the birth of little Ellie and a year later of Hall did make a difference. Forty years later, in 1929, Eleanor wrote a story for a magazine whose fictional heroine, Sally, was obviously herself.

Her forty-fifth birthday. . . . As she looked [into the fire] pictures formed in the dancing flames, first, there was a blue-eyed rather ugly little girl standing in the door of a cozy library looking in at a very beautiful woman holding, oh so lovingly, in her lap a little fair-haired boy. Through Sally's heart passed the old sensation, the curious dread of the cold glance which would precede the kindly and indifferent 'Come in Sally, and bring your book.'

In her autobiography, published in 1937, she was more explicit about her feelings of being left out when her mother was with the two little boys, Ellie and Hall. Her mother did not consciously exclude her; she read to Eleanor and had Eleanor read to her and recite her poems, and Eleanor was allowed to stay after the boys had been sent off to bed. But what Eleanor emphasized was standing in the door, "very often with my finger in my mouth," and her mother bidding her "Come in Granny," with that voice and look of kind indifference. Child psychologists had not yet discovered the connection between the "finger in the mouth" and the hunger for affection. To visitors her mother would explain that she called Eleanor "Granny" because she was "so old-fashioned."

"I wanted to sink through the floor in shame, and I felt I was apart from the boys."[8]

To Eleanor her mother's sigh and exasperated voice were further proof that only her father understood and loved her. And her father was leaving her again. His foot had to be stretched every day to prevent its shortening. He had begun to take laudanum and morphine and to drink ever more heavily to kill the excruciating pain in his foot. When his behavior became hostile even to those he loved most and he threatened suicide, the doctors prescribed a complete rest, and at the end of December, 1889, he embarked on a trip to the South—without saying good-by to his wife and children. His wife desperately tried to reach him through his love for the children. "Eleanor came rushing down when she heard the postman to know if there was a letter from you and what you said. I told her you would not be here for two weeks and she seemed awfully disappointed, but was quite satisfied when I told her you were getting well."

Eleanor's whole life was spent waiting for her father. "Eleanor lunched with us yesterday," wrote Tissie; "she rushed to the stairs every time the bell rang to see if it was her Papa. I shall be so glad to see my *dear* Father, she kept saying. She certainly adores you."

4. The Crack-Up

THE SOUTHERN CURE did not work. Elliott's drunken sprees became more violent and dissipated. In 1890, in a final desperate effort to hold the family together, they decided to lease their houses in town and Hempstead, sell their horses, and go abroad for a tour of mountain resorts and watering places. Anna declined the Gracies' offer to leave the children with them, and Eleanor, almost six, and baby Elliott accompanied their parents on a restless, troubled journey that ended in disaster.

They went directly to Berlin, and Anna's first extended report to Bamie was bright and hopeful. Count Bismarck got them "splendid places" for the parade of the garrison. Count Sierstorff took them to see the cavalry drill. And the only moment of danger came when Buffalo Bill, who was also in Berlin, offered Elliott whiskey to drink to his health. Sierstorff was wonderful, Anna reported, took the glass out of Elliott's hand, and told Buffalo Bill it was against doctor's orders.

From Berlin they proceeded to Reichenhall, in Bavaria, where the Germans were "all of a class that no one would think of meeting," Anna wrote. But Elliott took the baths and drank the waters and except for "awful attacks of depression" was sleeping well and his foot had stopped hurting.

"Elliott is really studying German now," she added, "and I hope he will take some interest in it. Eleanor is beginning to speak a little but teaching her to read is hopeless. She is as good as gold."

After a month in Reichenhall they went on to Munich and then to Oberammergau for the Passion play before heading for Vienna and Italy. Their expenses, lamented Anna, seemed enormous. "I don't know how it is, but we don't seem to be able to travel under $1,500 a month," even though they were not buying things. On the way to Vienna they stopped to visit the estate of Count Arco, and that was a disaster. "Elliott was an angel up to Wednesday night. Then I *think* he drank champagne for dinner, though he denies it." Anna was ill and had to stay in bed, but she tried to accompany Elliott everywhere, "excepting when they were shooting." Elliott, however, finally eluded her, and she found him drinking brandy and water. "I was furious and said so. It affected him at once. . . . I am sure it is the first alcohol he has touched in two months."

That fall they moved south to Italy. From Venice, at the end of October, Elliott wrote "Dear Anna's Mother" that though they had "done so much and worked so hard over our amusements . . . the children and Anna are both very well." Lots of sightseeing and visiting but her great delight of course; as mine; is in Baby "Joss." He gets stronger and fatter and rosier every day. I am afraid he is a son of his father, though, for he is not at all a "good boy." Eleanor is so sweet and good with him and really is learning to read and write for love of it making it possible to tell him stories which he cannot understand.

He told her of

the little things such as Ellie's feeding the pigeons on the Piazza at St. Marks, the lovely music on the Canal in decorative Gondolas by the band of the "32" Regiment, the delight that Eleanor and I have taken in the Lido Shore, wandering up and down looking over the blue Adriatic watching the gray surf and catching funny little crabs!

For Eleanor, the high point in Venice was her father acting as gondolier and singing along with the other boatmen.

They moved on to Florence and then Naples, because, said Anna, "it is warmer." From Sorrento in November, Anna wrote to Bamie that Elliott

goes sailing every day & takes the children in the morning. I went one afternoon but cannot stand it. Elliott generally takes a nap in the boat in the afternoon. Last night I only got four hours sleep owing to a dear sweet letter from Aunt Annie which completely upset Elliott. Don't repeat this, but beg them to write brightly. Elliott is so nervous everything upsets him. First he sobbed, then got furious and went out, said he would never go home, etc. and worked himself into a perfect fever of excitement.

To her mother she wrote more reassuringly.

This is the most beautiful place, right on the bay with Naples, Vesuvius and Capri opposite and only a little way off Pompeii. Elliott takes both children sailing every morning, while I have an Italian lesson from the Priest here, and later in the afternoon we drive and then go on the water for the sunset.

Pregnant again and unwell, Anna was in bed much of the time, and when Elliott proposed a trip to Vesuvius she begged off. He took Eleanor and her nurse, Albertina. The three were late getting back and Anna had worried herself into a state close to hysterics. For little Eleanor it was an exciting but exhausting trip. Years later she recalled the endless journey down the slope and how it took all her self-control to stand it "without tears so that my father would not be displeased." Fear of her father's displeasure also seared Eleanor's memory of the donkey that she was given in Sorrento.

"You are not afraid are you?" The tone was incredulous, astonished, and the man looked down from his horse to the child on her small donkey. The eyes were kind, but she sat shivering and hung back, looking at the steep descent. A steely look came into the man's eyes and in a cold voice he said: "You may go back if you wish, but I did not know you were a coward." She went back and the man went on sliding down the hill after the grown-ups—the nurse and the little donkey boy escorted the five year old girl along the dusty highway back to Sorrento, Italy.[1]

In her autobiography Eleanor recalled another episode with the donkey and the little donkey boy, whose feet were cut and bleeding. "On one occasion we returned with the boy on the donkey and I was running along beside him, my explanation being that his feet bled too much!"

Grasping at externals, Anna thought Elliott was getting better in Sorrento. Not that she supposed he could as yet stand temptation, but she hoped for great things from the next two months; perhaps by the beginning of March they might be able to return home. But she did not feel she could manage the homeward trip alone. She was expecting a baby in June and pleaded with Bye to come over. As the winter rains started and the children took sick "in the nasty wet cold," the doctors prescribed a cold, dry climate, and the family settled down for the winter in the old university city of Graz in Austria, in "the beautiful mountains of southern Styria." At first they all felt "the benefit" of the "hardy, honest and healthy climate," and Elliott even managed to get off a cheerful report to Theodore, chiefly about his children.

Tell Alice that Eleanor takes French lessons every day and tries hard to learn how to write so she won't be far behind when we return. Eleanor is learning to skate too, quite well. She has some little German friends with whom she coasts and plays snow balling all day. She really talks German *very* well. Little Boy understands both German and English but can only say "Nein" "Mama" and "da-da" as yet. He is so fat and well. Eats all the time. He looks just like little Ted used to those days at Sagamore when I used to laugh so at his back view digging holes in the walk. And playing he was as big as the other children. Do you remember?

Ever lovingly yours,
Nell.

But the Graz interlude was brief, and on the advice of Vienna specialists Elliott entered the Mariengrund sanitarium for treatment. Bamie was sent for, and persuaded the Vienna doctors to allow her to stay at Mariengrund with him.[2]

April brought a precipitate dash to Paris. It is not clear why, but the departure was so hurried that the children were left behind and traveled to Paris with their nurse Albertina and her husband—Elliott's man Stephen. At one stop the train went off before Eleanor and Albertina managed to get back on, causing much fright and telegraphing back and forth. At the suggestion of the doctor whom they engaged to take care of the pregnant Anna, the family rented a house in Neuilly.

Since it was a small house, it was decided that Eleanor would be better off in a convent, where she would be out of the way when the baby arrived and able to improve her French. The six-year-old child saw this as a banishment. She was miserable, made to feel like an outsider by the other little girls, whose religion she did not share and whose language she spoke awkwardly.

Loneliness, the sense of exclusion, the hunger for praise and admiration led to the episode of the penny. When one of the other little girls became the center of excitement and attention because she had swallowed a coin, Eleanor went to the sisters and announced that she, too, had swallowed a penny. It was a pathetic but revealing bid for the limelight. The sisters did not believe her but could not budge her from her story, so they sent for her mother, who took her away in disgrace. Her father "was the only person who did not treat me as a criminal."

In Paris Elliott's behavior became more frightening and erratic. He disappeared for days on end and then turned up depressed, penitent, full of promises to reform; he made violent scenes and then tried to reassure his family. Anna and he were "quietly happy," he wrote his mother-in-law. "Anna and I walk together in the morning . . . we often sit and read for two hours at a time while the children play; that is Joss does, for Eleanor is at school except in the afternoon when she comes, too, and feeds the fishes and the ducks." But to his Meadow Brook cronies he wrote boastfully about his good times with the Jockey Club set hunting boar with the Duc de Grammot's hounds.

. . . the horns played a little and then we galloped in single file up and down miles of beaten forest roads (without a chance of danger or excitement unless one should be to sleep in the saddle and fall out) guided by clever Piquers until we killed. It was fun and interesting but how I did long for a gentle school (over Hempstead Plains even) with you or one of your kind.

The family's breakup came soon after the birth of Hall in June, 1891. Elliott seemed to lose control of his actions completely. He feared that he was losing his mind, and the terrified family became afraid to have him with them.

The more frenzied Elliott's excesses, the more his unhappy, sorely tried wife, backed by Bamie, took refuge in strength and rectitude. In desperation, during one of his wilder, more prolonged bouts of drunkenness, they finally had him placed in an asylum for medical treatment. He said they "kidnapped" him. Anna, Bamie, and the children sailed for home, Anna agreeing not to get a divorce if Elliott consented to stay under the care of physicians for six months at the Château Suresnes outside of Paris.

Fearful, however, that he would dissipate the remainder of his estate, the family applied to the U.S. courts to have him adjudged insane and incapable of taking care of himself, and to have his property, which Theodore valued at $175,000, placed in trust for his wife and children. In their affidavits, Theodore and Bamie said that as long ago as 1889 they had noticed the deterioration in Elliott's physical and mental condition, his inability to concentrate, loss of memory, irrational behavior. Three times he had threatened to commit suicide.[3]

The months during which the proceedings dragged on were anguished ones for the family, none of it made easier by the sensation the court move had created in the press. A reporter for the *World* tracked Anna down at her mother's house in Tivoli where she was staying with her children. She was afraid that she would be "nasty" but could not risk having her mother talk to him. Was Elliott really insane, the reporter wanted to know. "I said no doctor had ever thought him so excepting from alcohol," she replied, "and that I considered any man irresponsible when under the influence of alcohol."

Elliott alternately cooperated and resisted. In one letter to Anna, he first accused her of the most "abominable" things and sounded like a "madman," she wrote Bamie, and then after picturing himself as the injured party, abruptly changed his tone and said that she was a "noble woman" and that he trusted her entirely. "His letter is so hopelessly sad and I so long to help him, not to make him suffer more."

The family was divided over the recourse to the courts. The doctors disagreed over the cure. Elliott himself wrote to the court, objecting to the proceedings. Finally, Theodore, who was then a member of the Civil Service Commission and living in Washington, made a hurried trip to Paris. He persuaded Elliott to come home and make a new start, promising that the legal proceedings would be discontinued if Elliott would place most of his money in trust for his family. Elliott agreed to take a course of treatment for alcoholism in the United States, resume a business connection, and prove himself worthy of being reunited with his family.

A woman to whom Elliott had turned in Paris, who met him with welcoming love rather than lectures, passed harsh judgment on Anna and Theodore. While she was clearly a biased witness, Eleanor was not wholly unsympathetic when in later years she came into possession of the journal entries in which this woman's feelings were recorded.

"This morning," this woman wrote,

with his silk hat, his overcoat, gloves and cigar, E. came to my room to say goodbye. It is all over, only my little black dog, who cries at the door of the empty room and howls in the park, he is all that is left to me. So ends the final and great emotion of my life. "The memory of what has been, and never shall be" is all the future holds. Even my loss was swallowed up in pity—for he looks so bruised so beaten down by the past week with his brother. How could they treat so generous and noble a man as they have. He is more noble a figure in my eyes with all his confessed faults, than either his wife or brother. She is more to be despised, in her virtuous pride, her absolutely selfish position than the most miserable woman I know, but she is the result of our unintelligent, petty, conventional social life. And why is it that the gentle, strong men always marry women who are so weak & selfish. Perhaps the feeling of protection & care given to a feebler nature is part of the charm. If she were only large-souled enough to appreciate him. . . .

In later years Eleanor said that it might have been more helpful to her father if her mother had responded to his drinking with love instead of highminded strength. Her mother was a good woman, she said, and very strong, but if something was right there was no excuse for not doing it. Her father might not have been able to conquer his drinking, she later concluded, but would have been happier if he had felt loved.

How much six-year-old Eleanor knew of her father's crack-up is unclear. She said that it was only after her mother died that she began to have any awareness that there was something seriously wrong with her father. But she was so bound up with his moods and actions that she could not have been wholly shielded from the sad events that were taking place in the tiny household. But, whatever she heard or saw, her sympathies were with her father.

5. Her Mother's Death

ELLIOTT RETURNED to the States anxious to redeem himself in the eyes of his family, especially his wife. She had stipulated a year of separation during which he would have to regain command of himself, stop drinking, choose an occupation, and stick to it.

He went, in February, 1892, to Dwight, Illinois, the headquarters of Dr. Keeley and the "Keeley cure" for alcoholism, but undertook this new course of treatment and probation rebelliously. He considered it "wicked and foolish" and only agreed to it because "it *is* Anna's wish." After drying out in Dwight, he felt that he should return to New York and undergo his final probation "*in my family* with the aid and strengthening influence of Home." To start anew in some western or southern city, as his family was insisting, would only separate him further from his wife and children. He had wanted to see Anna before he went to Dwight so that she should "see me as I *am*. Not as she last saw me, flushed with wine, reckless and unworthy but an earnest, repentant self-respecting gentle-man." But Anna had refused to receive him.

As the five-week treatment drew to a close, Elliott was less rebellious and was prepared to "do *anything* required of me by my loved ones to prove the completeness of my cure and the earnestness of my desire to atone." His brother-in-law, Douglas Robinson, proposed that he go to southwest Virginia to take charge of the large Robinson holdings there. Bamie and Theodore sided with Anna but the Robinsons, especially Corinne, joined the Gracies and the Liverpool Bullochs in taking Elliott's part. The Robinson properties covered a vast, almost primeval wilderness of virgin forest, laurel thicket, and high peaks, which the Douglas Land Company had decided to begin to tap. This meant bringing in railroads, improving mountain trails, settling boundary disputes, selling land to homesteaders.

The work was difficult and hazardous but "by meeting the mountaineers upon their own grounds" Elliott was soon considered a "friend," the Washington County paper wrote. "Children loved him; negroes sang for him; the poor, the needy and the unfortunate had reason to bless him; the young girls and the old ladies 'fell for him;' and men became his intimate friends."[1]

He quickly assembled "a stable of choice mounts," gathered "a rare assortment of dogs, including terriers, setters, pointers, 'coon' dogs, hounds," and hunted everything from snakes to bears. . . . He dropped into homes and fitted into every family circle, eating apples by the open fire, reading poetry,

talking of local things or about his own wife and children." He always functioned best away from his strong-minded wife and very successful brother but
does not seem to have recognized this. And although he carved out a place for
himself in Abingdon, he felt exiled, and his letters home were full of remorse
and pleas that the "homeless and heartsick and lonely" sinner be forgiven and
allowed to return to his family. "You who know no sin which compares with
mine," he wrote his wife, "can hardly know the *agony* of shame and repentance
I endure and the *self* condemnation I have to face. I need indeed be brave to
make my fight. . . ."

Anna had an equally anguished time, torn between wanting to try again
yet not daring to hope that Elliott would change. She made few moves without
consulting Bamie. "This letter from Elliott worries me so that I send it to you,"
she wrote from Tivoli. "I am so awfully sorry for him. My heart simply aches
and I would do anything I could that could really help him. . . . It seems to be
dawning on him for the first time that he is not coming home this Autumn."

It was the summer of 1892, when Anna was nearly thirty. She suffered
from backaches and headaches, complained that her eyes were giving out, and
was to have an operation in the fall. Eleanor was then sleeping in her mother's
room and spent hours rubbing her mother's head with her strong, competent
fingers, happy, she said, to be of some use to her suffering parent. Only seven,
she was already taking care of her mother.

The life of a beautiful young woman separated from her husband was not
an easy one in New York society of the 1890s. Anna was aware of how easily a
woman alone might be considered to have overstepped the line of correctness
and propriety. When she and Eleanor went to Bar Harbor she was continually
preoccupied with how much fun and gaiety she could allow herself. A string of
queries went off to Bamie. Should she "matronize" dinners? Could she go
rowing or driving in the afternoon with a man, although, of course, she would
not go more than once or twice with the same man? It was

an awful temptation when one feels desperately lonely and wildly furious with the
world at large, not to make up one's mind to pay no attention to criticism as long as
one does no wrong and to try to get some fun out of the few years of our youth. I
hate everything and everyone so and am most of the time so miserable that I feel
anything one could do would be a comfort to forget for one moment.

Many members of her family were at Bar Harbor—her sister, Pussie; her
brothers, Vallie and Eddie; Cousin Susie and her husband Henry Parish. There
were endless discussions about Elliott. "Something was wrong with my father
and from my point of view nothing could be wrong with him," Eleanor wrote
much later. But no one told her anything, and the anxious talks, which she now
strained to catch, left her confused, torn between her adoration for her father
and the distress of her mother.

Anna returned to New York in the autumn, determined to start a new life
for her children and herself, a life that would be more than a waiting for a transformation in her husband that deep down she knew would never happen and

that would provide a buttress against the now pleading, now threatening letters with which Elliott bombarded her. She moved to a new house at Sixty-first Street and Madison Avenue, two blocks away from Bamie. Her gracious hospitality and charm quickly attracted a widening circle of admiring friends who gathered round her while she presided over the silver tea urn. But no matter how busy her day, she explained to friends, the evening hours from six to seven o'clock were resolutely and dutifully devoted to her children. "If anyone comes to see me during that hour, they must understand they are welcome, but the children are of the first importance then, and my attention must be given to them. I play with them any way they may want. I get down on the floor and we play horse or we play tag, or I read for them—anything, that they may remember the hour happily as 'mother's hour,' and feel assured that nothing whatever is to interfere with it."[2]

A friend was present one day when the children were brought in at six o'clock sharp. "She took the baby in her lap, kissed 'Josh' and moved the footstool for Eleanor to sit upon. A bit of biscuit was given to each, and then they were kissed goodnight 'as tonight Mamma is very tired' and waved to bed, only little Eleanor remaining at her mother's feet."

Anna began to plan her children's education. Little Ellie would go to kindergarten next year, so that was easy; but Eleanor presented a problem. Anna was sure that Eleanor should have a good basic education. She felt keenly her own lack of systematic study, and lamented that her knowledge of history and science was so scanty that she was not able to answer Eleanor's questions. She no longer accepted the premise that beauty and breeding were all that a girl of wealth needed—and, besides, Eleanor would not have beauty to help her succeed as a woman.

At seven Eleanor had had a smattering of reading and writing which had been taught to her by various relatives. Great-Aunt Gracie had tried to teach Eleanor and Alice to read, as she had their fathers. Eleanor adored her, was fascinated by her expressive hands as she told them B'rer Rabbit tales and stories of the vanished ante-bellum life on the Roswell plantation in Georgia, but she did not learn to read. Another great-aunt, Mrs. Edward Ludlow, whose Hudson River estate bordered her grandmother's, was dismayed to find, when Anna and the children returned from Paris, that seven-year-old Eleanor could not read and hadn't the slightest knowledge of the elementary household tasks that little girls usually learn by playing house in the nursery. Great-Aunt Maggie scolded the embarrassed Anna and sent her companion over every day to make sure that the child got her lessons. And to Eleanor's great sorrow, the nurse, an Alsatian woman whom Eleanor feared, was directed to teach Eleanor to cook and sew, which quite possibly is the reason that Eleanor never was interested in cooking or learned much about it. She did not like Madeleine.

Mrs. Ludlow's reprimand confirmed Anna in her decision to begin Eleanor's formal schooling immediately. In the fall of 1892 she turned part of the upper floor in her house into a schoolroom for Eleanor and a few other girls her age, and invited Frederic Roser, whose classes for the daughters of the highest society were then very fashionable, to teach the little group. Mr. Roser did not like to teach the youngest girls and assigned his assistant, Miss Tomes, to the class.

Eleanor remembered her first days in school as a time of agony and mortification. She was asked to spell simple words such as "horse" that her mother knew she knew, but frozen by shyness and the presence of her mother, who sat in on the class, she misspelled every one. Her mother reproached her—she did not know how Eleanor would end up, she said. Forty years later Eleanor still remembered vividly her feeling of utter misery because of her mother's disgust with her. "I was always disgracing my mother." Perhaps her behavior in the classroom was also a rejection and punishment of her mother, whom she blamed for exiling her beloved father.

Anna realized that her already shy and awkward daughter suffered deeply under the discord in the family and tried to comfort her, making a special effort for her. Anna read to her daily, and Eleanor listened silently and politely but without the rapt attention she had always given to her father. Years later Eleanor's strongest childhood reading memories were associated with her father. "I had a special interest in *The Old Curiosity Shop*, because my father used to call me 'Little Nell' after the child in that story, and I first really learned to care for Longfellow's poems because my father was devoted to Hiawatha." At the age of eight she learned almost the entire poem because she was eager to surprise her absent father when she saw him again.[3]

Her sons were a comfort to Anna. "Ellie is a saintlike child, simply perfect, never grumbles or complains of anything and is so loving and attractive," while Baby Hall was a "lovely boy with a strong will" who "rules Ellie even now." Only Eleanor was a problem. She was now so afraid of "strange children" that when her mother took her to children's parties on Saturday afternoons she would break into tears and have to be brought home. Anna arranged to have some boys and girls come in on Friday afternoons to play and stay for tea so that Eleanor could begin to make some friends, but the plan was never carried out. Anna had her operation and Eleanor spent her eighth birthday with the Gracies. "Mother wishes she could be with you," Anna wrote her. "I enclose a letter from Father to you."

Abingdon, Va.
Oct. 9/92

My darling little Daughter,

Many happy returns of this birthday little Nell. I am thinking of you always and I wish for my Baby Girl the greatest of Joy and the most perfect happiness in her sweet young life.

Because Father is not with you is not because he doesn't love you. For I love you tenderly and dearly. And maybe soon I'll come back all well and strong and we will have such good times together, like we used to have. I have to tell all the little children here often about you and all that I remember of you when you were a little bit of a girl and you used to call yourself Father's little "Golden Hair"—and how you used to come into my dressing room and dress me in the morning and frighten me by saying I'd be late for breakfast.

I gave a doll to the little girl you sent the Doll's jewelry to, small Lillian Lloyd and she has called it Eleanor and another little friend of mine the daughter of my good and dear friend Mr. Blair of Chicago has named her most precious doll Eleanor too; after you they are both named. Some day you must meet little Lillian and little Emily and they will be glad to know you in person; they say they know your photograph so well.

Now I must stop writing dearest little Nell, do take care of yourself and little Brothers, Ellie and Brudie, and kiss them for me. Love dear Mother for me and be very gentle and good to her 'specially now while she is not well. Goodbye my own little Daughter. God bless you.

Give my best love to Aunt Gracie and Uncle.   Your devoted Father
                                                  Elliott Roosevelt.

From Aunt Gracie's, Eleanor went to Tivoli and from there wrote her father.

                                                  Oak Terrace
My dear Father:—   Tivoli-on-Hudson
    Your present which you and Mamma sent me was lovely. It is just what I want for washing the doly's clothes which Aunt Pussie and Auntie Maud gave me. I got a ball, walking doll, violin, music boxes, and a bell to draw around the piaza. The candy Auntie Tissie brought up looks lovely, but I have not tasted it as I do not eat between meals, but will have some after dinner. Elsie, Susie and Kittie Hall are coming to dinner and Auntie Maud is going to have Punch and Judy after dinner which I think will be great fun don't you. I was very glad to get your letter and please thank the clerk for the picture. I thank you again for the present you sent me. I hope you are all well and now I must close dear Father from your little daughter

                                                  Baby

Eleanor received two other birthday letters from friends in Abingdon. One was from Lillian Lloyd, daughter of the Episcopalian rector.

Dear Eleanor:
    I want to write so badly that Mother is holding my hand. Your nice letter came today. I wish I could play with you. Wont you come down and play with my pretty doll and my brother Hubard and spend a week? I named my pretty doll ELEANOR ROOSEVELT LLOYD. . . . I love your papa dearly, better than any man but Father. He has my picture with my Maltese cats in it. They are dead.
    Send me your picture, Eleanor, if you can't come soon. . . .

The other was from the daughter of Daniel Trigg, whose farm was just outside Abingdon. She also mentioned how often Eleanor's father spoke of his daughter, how fond she was of Eleanor's father, and how she hoped Eleanor would soon come down to Abingdon. The letters from the Abingdon children were loving and innocent, but for Eleanor they made the pain of separation from her father almost unbearable.

Elliott had wanted to come north for Anna's operation but was asked to stay away. To explain why Anna did not want him to come even though she was seriously ill, Corinne relayed to Elliott what she had heard from Anna's mother. Elliott responded by writing directly to Mrs. Hall.

Did she say she wanted to die, that I had made her so utterly miserable that she did not care to live any more. And did you say that was what your poor child had been suffering in silence all these past killing months?

He was relieved when he heard that Anna was better but insisted that "in danger my place and my right is to be near her." But Anna did not want him. A new illness at the end of November was diagnosed as diphtheria. "I ought to be with her unless my presence is *actually distasteful* to her," Elliott wrote imploringly, but Mrs. Hall telegraphed "Do not come," which Elliott understood to be Anna's command.

Letters crossed in the mail. Mrs. Hall again wrote sharply that he should not come. Her letters hurt him, he wrote on December 6. They had no right to doubt his word, "and I have pledged it to my wife never to force myself upon her. . . . You need not fear that even if called to my wife's deathbed that if not at her request I would present myself there." The next day he wrote again.

I am only terribly sad that I should be so repugnant to her. . . . It is most horrible and full of *awe* to me that my *wife* not only does not want me near her in sickness or trouble but *fears* me. And, before God I say it, I am honestly worthy of her trust and Love—for even in my drinking I never did a *dishonorable* thing, nor *one cruel act* towards my wife or children.

Resigned to staying away from New York, he begged Mrs. Hall to telegraph C.O.D. about his wife's condition. She died that day, and the message reached him while he was at Daniel Trigg's, several miles out in the country. Hurriedly driving over the muddy road to town, he packed a bag hastily and flagged the night train to New York.

Eleanor's account of her mother's death, written almost forty-five years later, did not dwell on the loss of her mother but on the return of her father. "Death meant nothing to me, and one fact wiped out everything else—my father was back and I would see him very soon." Her mother died on December 7, 1892. Her father did not come to see her immediately. Later she realized, she wrote, "what a tragedy of utter defeat" her mother's death meant for her father. "No hope now of ever wiping out the sorrowful years he had brought upon my mother—and she had left her mother as guardian for her children. My grandmother did not feel she could trust my father to take care of us. He had no wife, no children, no hope!"[4]

She wept for her father, not for her mother. Yet that engaging man's capacity for love and devotion was fatally flawed: it was totally self-centered, without steadiness or altruism. He made large promises, was full of warmth, charm, and affection, but there was no follow-through, no constancy, little on which his family could build.

Eleanor refused to recognize this, but the rest of the family, especially Bye and Theodore, saw him clearly and approved Anna's decision, stated in her will, to make her mother the children's guardian. "Good as I firmly believe your advice to have been," Elliott informed Mrs. Lloyd, the wife of the Episcopalian rector in Abingdon, and sorely as I think myself I need my little ones with me, I will return without them. I have not found one person in either my wife's or my connection who encourages me in the slightest degree when I propose that the children join their Father. If I have a comfortable home they might come down and visit me for a while during the summer. But all seem to think that the proper place for them now is with their Grandmother and surrounded by everything in the way of luxury and all the advantages, both educational and otherwise to which they have been accustomed.

Elliott sought to comfort his daughter as well as himself with a gleaming vision of their making a home together again.

After we were installed (at Grandma Hall's house) my father came to see me, and I remember going down into the high ceilinged dim library on the first floor of the house on West 37th Street. He sat in a big chair. He was dressed all in black, looking very sad. He held out his arms and gathered me to him. In a little while he began to talk, to explain to me that my mother was gone, that she had been all the world to him, and now he had only my brothers and myself, that my brothers were very young, and that he and I must keep close together. Some day I would make a home for him again; we would travel together and do many things which he painted as interesting and pleasant, to be looked forward to in the future together.

Somehow it was always he and I. I did not understand whether my brothers were to be our children or whether he felt that they would be at school and college and later independent.

There started that day a feeling which never left me—that he and I were very close together, and some day, would have a life of our own together. He told me to write to him often, to be a good girl, not to give any trouble, to study hard, to grow up into a woman he could be proud of, and he would come to see me whenever it was possible.

When he left, I was all alone to keep our secret of mutual understanding and to adjust myself to my new existence.[5]

6. "He Lived in My Dreams"

ELLIOTT'S LETTERS to his daughter were tender, chivalrous, playful, and, above all, full of protestations of love. After his death she would carry them around with her for the remainder of her life. People who lived on in the memories of those alive, she said, were not dead. She read and reread her father's letters, and each time it was a fresh invocation of the magic of his presence.

"I knew a child once who adored her father," she wrote in 1927.

She was an ugly little thing, keenly conscious of her deficiencies, and her father, the only person who really cared for her, was away much of the time; but he never criticized her or blamed her, instead he wrote her letters and stories, telling her how he dreamed of her growing up and what they would do together in the future, but she must be truthful, loyal, brave, well-educated, or the woman he dreamed of would not be there when the wonderful day came for them to fare forth together. The child was full of fears and because of them lying was easy; she had no intellectual stimulus at that time *and yet she made herself as the years went on into a fairly good copy of the picture he had painted.*[1]

In his letters her father addressed Eleanor as "Father's Own Little Nell," and that was the way she signed herself in the letters to him. His first letter after his return to Abingdon reported on his new puppies. "They are both in the armchair beside me and the old Dog is curled up at my feet in the rug dreaming, I suppose of all the rabbits he *did not* catch today!"

What shall he write about, his next letter asked.

Shall I tell you of the wonderful long rides, of days through the grand snowclad forests, over the white hills, under the blue skies as blue as those in Italy which you and I and little Ellie, though he was so little he cannot remember it, used to sail over Naples Bay to beautiful Capri. I am afraid in those young "Nell days" you were a little seasick and did not enjoy it as much as you will in the day that is coming when you have worked hard at your lessons and gotten that curious thing they call "education."

After Anna's death "Professor Roser," as Elliott dubbed him, had inquired of Grandma Hall about her plans for Eleanor's education, expressing hope that he would not lose such a promising student. Mrs. Hall consulted Elliott. There was no question "as to the wisdom of Eleanor's undoubtedly remaining in his class. Will you write therefore and have the matter attended to? The tone of his note is very nice, did you not think so? Our little girl is a good little girl and conscientious, I believe, as he says."

His January 20 letter sought to impress on Eleanor the importance of education.

The next time you go walking get your maid to take you where they are building a house and watch the workmen bring one stone after another and place it on top of the one gone before or along side, and then think that there are a lot of funny little workmen running about in your small Head called "Ideas" which are carrying a lot of stones like small bodies called "Facts," and these little "Ideas" are being directed by your teachers in various ways, by "Persuasion," "Instruction," "Love," and "Truth" to place all these "Fact Stones" on top of and alongside of each other in your dear Golden Head until they build a beautiful house called "Education"—*Then!* Oh, my pretty companionable Little Daughter, you will come to Father and what jolly games we will have together to be sure—And in your beautiful house "Education," Father wishes you such a happy life—But those little fact stones are a queer lot, and you have to ask your teachers to look well after the Idea workmen that they don't put some in crooked in the walls of your pretty House. Sometimes you'll find a rough hard fact that you must ask your teacher to smooth down and polish and set straight by persuasion, love and truth. Then you'll find a rebellious little factstone that won't fit where it ought to, though it is intended to go just there like the little factstone "music"—may be you will have to get your teachers to use Instruction, maybe a great deal of it to get that small stone to fit, but it must go there and it *will*, if the little Idea workmen stick at it long enough. Then there are what seem to be stupid, wearisome, trying factstones that you can't see the use of in your dear house, that the Ideas are building! Like—"Going to bed regularly and early fact stones," "*Not eating candy* fact stones," Not telling *always* exactly the Truth fact stones," "Not being a teasing little girl fact stones" instead of a precious gentle *Self* amusing and satisfied one.

There are lots of others like those I have mentioned and to have them put in order you must *beg* your teachers to use all four powers of Persuasion, Instruction, Love, Truth and another force too, *Discipline!* Of all the forces your Teachers use, Father and you too, Little Witch, probably like Love best, but we must remember the little fact stones as I said at first are such a queer lot, that we have to trust to your Teachers, who know by Experience in building other Education houses in little brains, how much the Idea workmen can do and how also the character of the fact stones, what forces to apply. Think of your brain as an Education House; you surely always wish to live in a beautiful house not an ugly one, and get Auntie Maude darling to explain what Father means by this letter tale. Little Terrier says I must go to bed. Goodnight *my* darling little Daughter, my "*Little Nell.*"

Miss Tomes was a good teacher who knew how to hold the children's interest, and Eleanor was a diligent pupil. Despite her initial humiliation, she gradually gained self-confidence—only long division eluded her. Usually Mr. Roser urged his girls to skip it on the assumption that well-bred women did not go on to college and would not need mathematics, but her father, while sympathetic, urged her not to give up.

I know division, especially long division, seemed to me at your age a very tiresome and uninteresting study. I too longed to be in fractions—or *infractious* but I found afterwards that it had been better,—as it turns out nine times out of ten, that I stood out against my own impatience and lack of desire to become informed, and devoted myself—howbeit against the grain—to the study of the life and the interests of those of God's creation, whom He calls not his own.

Arithmetic aside, she did well. "Your letter was undoubtedly without mistake, so far as the spelling is to be considered, and I congratulate and praise you upon the same. You should be proud of, my daughter, Mr. Rosa's [sic] unlooked for compliment as to your book, and commendation of the good behavior of so young a child." She was also doing well in French, not surprisingly since she had spoken French before English and there had always been someone who spoke French in the house as long as her mother had been alive.[2] She liked her French teacher Mlle. LeClerq, and even though she thought memorizing passages of the New Testament in French a waste of time, she dutifully did so. "I have received your beautifully written French note of the 26th," her father wrote her. "I see well que vos leçons de français vous fait beaucoup de bien, même en style et en facilité il faut me corriger toujours quand je fait des fautes en vous écrivant."

Eleanor's school work was soon so good that she was singled out for advanced work. Bursting with importance, she reported to her Uncle Eddie.

Dear Uncle Edie   March 2d, (1894)
I hope you are well and Mr. Wright also. Are you having a lovely time in Morroco with hunts and pig sticks and oh so many horses, I should think you were having a beautiful time with so many things to do. Are the people out there very bad ones?
Now I want to tell you about what I am going to have next May in schooll, a written examination in History and Geraphay and I am the youngest one who is to have it.
With a great deal of love from all and a great deal from me I am your little niece.

                                                   Eleanor.

At Easter time she sent her father books and he sent her white violets, "which you can put in your Prayer book at the XXIII Psalm and you must know they were Grandmother Roosevelt's favorite flower." Eleanor did not have to be told what the XXIII Psalm was; her mother had encouraged her to learn by heart many verses from the Bible. "Is there anything else in life that can so anchor them to the right?" had been Anna's view. Elliott was no less religious. He sang in the choir of the little Episcopal church in Abingdon and was a favorite of the local clergy. She wore his flowers to church, Eleanor wrote her father, who replied, "I thought of *You all day long* and blessed you and prayed for your happiness and that of your precious small brothers." There were always special "love messages" for the little boys, Ellie and Brudie, in his letters to her.

Tragedy struck the little household again in May, when both boys came down with scarlet fever. Elliott hastened to New York and sadly telegraphed the Ludlows, to whom Eleanor had been sent, to prepare the little girl for the worst. In addition, he wrote his daughter "to let you know that dear little Ellie is very, very ill and may go to join dear Mother in Heaven. There is just a little chance that he may not die but the doctors all fear that he will."

"Dear father," Eleanor replied,

I write to thank you for your kind note and to tell you how sorry I am to hear Ellie is so sick, but we must remember Ellie is going to be safe in heaven and to be with Mother who is waiting there and our Lord wants Ellie boy with him now, we must be happy and do God's will and we must cheer others who feel it to. You are alright I hope. I play with the [name indistinct] every day.

It is so cold here that Uncle Ned wears a fur overcoat. I met a lady that used to live down at hemmestid and she new me right away.

Goodbye give my love to all and Ellie and Brudie to and for you O so much love.

Nell.

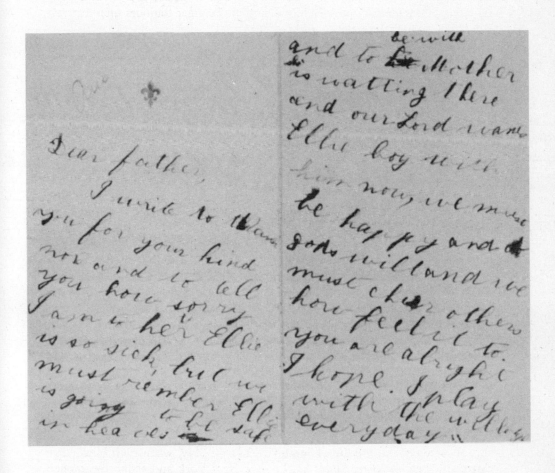

(Letter continued on next page)

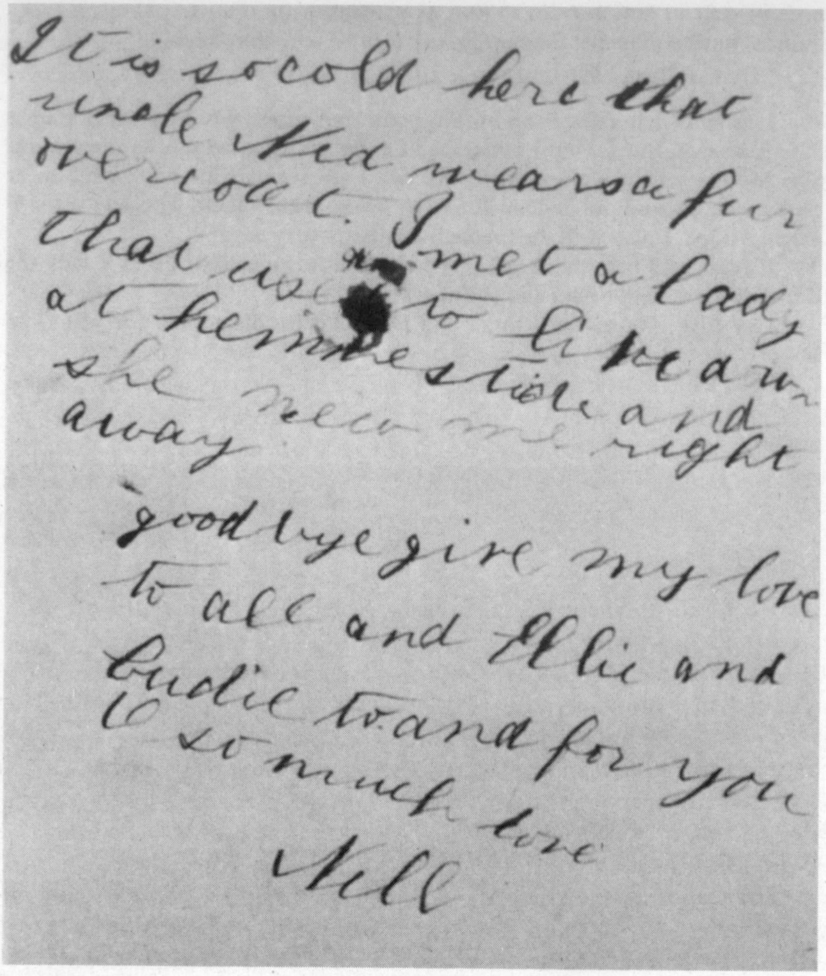

It is so cold here that
uncle Ned wears a fur
overcoat. I met a lady
that used to live an
at her — stile and
she — right
away

goodbye give my love
to all and Ellie and
Budie to and for you
so much love
Nell

My darling little Nell,   Monday [May 29, 1893]
    I am so glad you wrote Father such a sweet note on Saturday. I received it today and it has comforted me a great deal to know my little daughter was well and happy.
    Ask Aunt Maggie to tell you what a sad day today was for all of us. I do not want to write it to you though I would tell you if your dear golden head was on my breast; my dear, *loved* little Nell. But do not be sad my Pretty, remember Mother is with Ellie and Aunt Gracie now.
    I sent Morris, my groom, on with your pony and cart tomorrow afternoon's boat so that he will deliver him to you on Wednesday morning with Father's tender love to his sweet Daughter. You must get Aunt Maggie's coachman to teach you how to drive him. He is *perfectly gentle* and only needs reasonable handling for you to drive him *alone*. Tell Aunt Maggie this. In fact let Aunt Maggie or Uncle Ned

read this letter. I wish I could be with you to teach you how to drive myself but that can not be. Thank Aunt Maggie for asking me to come on after the 22nd and say that I am writing her.   With a heart full of love,
                                                    Ever fondly, your Father.

Sympathetic and considerate as Grandma Hall and Great-Aunt Maggie were, Eleanor had only one thought, one purpose—to rejoin her father. That alone would be home. But the family dared not entrust the children to him. "I cannot tell you dear little girl," he wrote her two weeks after Ellie's death, "when you are coming home until I have seen Grandma and consulted her." Mrs. Hall informed Elliott that she did not want him to come to Tivoli during the summer, and that in August Eleanor would be going to Newport. Elliott pleaded with her to bring his children to the city or the seashore "where I can see them and enjoy a little love which my heart craves and for lack of which it has broken. Oh, Mrs. Hall, I have tried so hard and it has been so lonely & weary and the break down seems to me natural in my strained condition. Above all believe me it was not drunkenness. Let me see you soon please Mother. . . ."

It was difficult not to yield to these entreaties, and Mrs. Hall turned to Bamie for advice. She would do anything she could, Bamie told her, but Elliott had turned against her, and if she appeared to be intervening he would take the opposite position. She could no longer influence him. She was heartbroken, but he had put it out of her power to do anything for him unless he specifically asked for something. His greatest chance of stability of purpose in regard to his children "lay in the management being purely between you and himself." There was only one exception to her hands-off attitude: if Elliott tried to take the children from Mrs. Hall, she and Theodore felt that "for Anna's sake" they would have a right to stop him.

Her father's visits brought Eleanor rushing down the stairs to fling herself into his arms, but their reunions were not wholly without anxiety for her. In later years she recalled how one time he called to take her driving in what appeared to be a very high dog cart. On the way to Central Park, along Madison Avenue, a streetcar frightened Mohawk, her father's high-spirited hunter. When the horse shied, her father's hat flew off, and when it was retrieved, Elliott looked at his daughter and asked, "You weren't afraid, were you, little Nell?" She was but she did not want to disappoint him by admitting it. When they reached the park and joined the procession of carriages and horses, her father said teasingly, "If I were to say 'hoop-la' to Mohawk he would try to jump them all." Eleanor prayed he would not. Yet despite her "abject terror," she later wrote, "those drives were the high point of my existence."

Worse trials beset the eight-year-old as, for instance, on one occasion when her father came to take her for a walk. "My father had several fox terriers that he seemed to carry everywhere with him," Eleanor recalled. "One day he took me and three of his fox terriers and left us with the doorman at the Knickerbocker Club. When he failed to return after six hours, the doorman took me home." It was a shattering experience for a child who was already obsessed with a fear of being deserted by those whom she loved, and when she spoke of it in later years, she sometimes added the terrible detail that she saw her father carried out. It was no wonder that Grandma Hall disapproved of his visits so strongly.

While the adults in the Roosevelt and Hall families feared that the hapless Elliott might commit some irredeemable folly in a moment of lonely despair, his letters to his daughter continued to be full of tenderness. He wanted her to learn to ride, "for it will please me so and we can have such fun riding together after you come to the city next fall." She was swimming a little in the Hudson, she told him. That was splendid, he commented, and was Brudie "learning new things, too?" She had a bad habit of biting her fingernails. He wanted her to stop: "I am glad you are taking such good care of those cunning wee hands that Father loves so to be petted by, all those *little* things that will make my dear Girl so much more attractive if she attends to them, not forgetting the big ones. Unselfishness, generosity, loving tenderness and cheerfulness."

But his letters were also full of excuses—why he had not written in "so long," why he had not been able to see her, why he would not be able to visit her. Nor did his vivid accounts of what he did with the children at Abingdon give Eleanor unmixed pleasure. "Little Miriam welcomed me with the fox terriers at the station though I came by an entirely unexpected train," Elliott wrote. "The little girl had been down to *every* train for two days." Realizing perhaps that Eleanor might be jealous of the girls who could be with him, he added, "No other little girl can ever take your place in my heart." Another letter must have caused even sharper pangs of envy.

Miriam, Lillian and the four Trigg children all on their ponies and horses and the fox terriers Mr. Belmont gave me (to comfort me in my loneliness) go out about sunrise and gallop over these broad fields for one or two hours; we rarely fail to secure some kind of game, and never return without roses in the cheeks of those I call now, my children.

In the fall of 1893, he moved in and out of New York, and had become evasive with everyone in his family concerning his whereabouts and intentions. He told the faithful Corinne that he was going to Abingdon, but ten days later she discovered he was still in town. Corinne and Douglas went to his hotel almost daily, but could never find him in. He would promise to come to stay with them or Theodore or Uncle Gracie and then would telephone to break the engagement.

He disappeared from his usual haunts, and they learned only later that, although he received mail at the Knickerbocker Club, he was living under an assumed name on West 102nd Street with a woman whose name was unknown to the family. Theodore and Bamie sadly and reluctantly gave up.

To Bye, Theodore wrote in July, 1894,

I do wish Corinne could get a little of my hard heart about Elliott. She can do, and ought to do nothing for him. He can't be helped, and he simply must be let go his own gait.

He is now laid up from a serious fall; while drunk he drove into a lamp post and went out on his head. Poor fellow! if only he could have died instead of Anna!

Eleanor had known for many months, from the talks and whisperings of the grownups, that something was desperately wrong with her father. She also knew it from her own experience. Her father would send her a message that he was coming to take her for a drive and then not appear. Unthinkingly, he would arouse her hopes that she would be coming "home" to him. He disappointed her in almost everything, yet her love never faltered, her trust never weakened.

With the arrival of summer, 1894, Grandma Hall again closed her Thirty-seventh Street house and Eleanor moved to Tivoli and later to Bar Harbor. A handful of Eleanor's letters to her father that final summer have survived.

Dear Father: June 14th, 1894

I hope you are well. I am very well and so is every one else. We moved to the country and that is why I have not written before we were in such a hurry to get off for it was so hot in New York. We have two people staying with us—cousin Susie Hall and Mable Drake—do you know her? tell me in your next letter. I rode my pony to-day for the first time this summer. I did not go very far but tomorrow I am going for a long ride with Uncle Valley won't it be fun. I wish you were up here to ride with me. Give my love to the pupies and every one else that you know. Madlein Brudie and I often drive with my pony.

With a great deal of love I am your little daughter

                                                        Nell

Dear Father   July 5th, 1894

I would have written before but I went to Cousin Susie. We are starting to-day for Bar Harbor we are in a great flurry and hurry I am in Uncle Eddie's room. The men are just going to take the trunks away. We are to have lunch at 15 minutes before twelve. We are going to Boston in the one o'clock train. Brudie wears pants now.

Good-bye I hope you are well *dear Father*.

With a great deal of love to everybody and you especially I am your little daughter

P.S. Write to me at W. 37th St.   Nell

Dear Father: July 10th, 1894

I hope you are well. I am now in Bar Harbor and am having a lovely time yesterday I went to the Indian encampment to see some pretty things I have to find the paths all alone I walked up to the top of Kebo mountain this morning and I walk three hours every afternoon. Brudie walks from 4 to 5 miles every day. Please write to me soon. We eat our meals at the hotel and the names of the things we get to eat are to funny Washington pie and blanket of Veal are mild to some other things we get. I have lessons every day with Grandma.

With a great deal of love, I am your little daughter

                                                        Nell

One of Eleanor's last letters to her father. He died a few weeks later.

Dear Father: July 30, 1894.

I hope you are well. I enjoyed your last letter very much. I went fishing the other day I had great fun I caught six fish don't you think I did well for the first time. I am having lessons with Grandma every day and go to a french class from half past eleven till half past twelve. Alice Fix died three days ago and was buried yesterday was it not very sad.

Goodby dear dear Father I send you a great deal of love I am your little daughter

Nell

With a Knickerbocker Club return address, Elliott wrote his "little Nell" that her letters from Bar Harbor had been his "great delight."

When you go to the Indian encampment you must say "How" to them for your old father's sake, who used to fight them in the old claims in the West, many years before you opened those little blue eyes and looked at them making birch bark canoes for Brudie and Madeleine to go paddling in and upset in the shallow water, where both might be drowned if they had not laughed so much.

Give my love to all the dear home people and all of my good friends who have not forgotten me.

Would you like a little cat, very much like the one you used to have at Hempstead and called an "Angostora" kitten instead of what was his correct name, "Angora?" If so, I have a dear friend who wants to make you a present of one. Let me know after you have asked grandma.

Please do not eat all the things with the funny names you tell me you have,—that is, if they taste like their names—for a Washington pie with a blanket of veal, and Lafayette left out, would be enough to spoil your French-American history of the latter part of the last century, for some time to come, possibly for so long that I might not be able to correct your superstition. The blanket was what Washington needed and the pie should have been laid out of veal and the neglected Lafayette should have eaten it.

Again with dear love, I am   Your affectionate father
                                              Elliott Roosevelt.

On August 12 Theodore wrote Bamie from Washington: "Elliott is up and about again: and I hear is drinking heavily; if so he must break down soon. It has been as hideous a tragedy all through as one often sees."

On August 13 Elliott wrote his last letter to his daughter.

Darling Little Nell—

What must you think of your Father who has not written in so long, but we seem to be quits about that. I have after all been very busy, quite ill, at intervals not able to move from my bed for days. You knew that Uncle Gracie was back. He is so happy at "Gracewood." You know he was going to ask you there. Are you going?

Give my love to Grandma and Brudie and all—I was very much amused by hearing my Darkey coachman in his report of Stable News say that he had trained all the Dogs to drive together, four and six in hand, and built a wee cart with wooden wheels. It was really funny to see this great big fat "Irish" colored man in this little cart! and six small Fox Terriers driving for all they were worth. I saw

Auntie Corinne and the others the other day. They were so funny—They are very well and sent love to you all. How is your pony and the dogs at Tivoli, too? Tell Madeleine and Brudie that Father often thinks of them—With tender affection ever devotedly

Your Father
Elliott Roosevelt

The next day Elliott had a fall, was knocked unconscious, and died with none of his family about him, moaning in his delirium for his sister Corinne.

From the *World*, August 16, 1894:

The curtains of No. 313 West 102nd Street are drawn. There is a piece of black crepe on the door-knob. Few are seen to pass in and out of the house, except the undertaker and his assistants. The little boys and girls who romp up and down the sidewalk will tell you in a whisper; "Mr. Elliott is dead," and if you ask, "Who is Mr. Elliott?" "We don't know, nobody knows," they will answer.

At the door a sad-faced man will meet you. "Mr. Roosevelt died at 10 o'clock Tuesday evening." he will say. In a darkened parlor all day yesterday lay a plain black casket. Few mourners sat about it. Beneath its lid lay the body of Elliott Roosevelt. Few words will tell of his last days. . . .

The physician and a valet were the only watchers at the end. The first of the family notified was James K. Gracie of Oyster Bay, an uncle of Elliott Roosevelt. To him was left the duty of breaking the news to the others. Many of them did not know that Elliott Roosevelt was in New York. Few of them had seen him for a year. At the clubs no one knew his address. Even the landlord from whom he rented his house knew him only as Mr. Elliott. Under that name he has lived there with his valet for over ten months. He sought absolute seclusion.

Many people will be pained by this news. There was a time when there were not many more popular young persons in society than Mr. and Mrs. Elliott Roosevelt. . . .

Elliott was buried at Greenwood, the Roosevelt burial place. Grandma Hall did not take Eleanor to her father's funeral, and even the flowers she sent from herself and the children arrived too late. Grandma Hall was deeply sorry about that: "Elliott loved flowers and always brought them to us, and to think not one from us or his dear ones went to the grave with him grieves us deeply."

There was one comfort in his death—the harsh and bitter memories were washed away, Theodore wrote Corinne.

I only need to have pleasant thoughts of Elliott now. He is just the gallant, generous, manly loyal young man whom everyone loved. I can think of him when you and I and he used to go round "exploring" the hotels, the time we were first in Europe; do you remember how we used to do it? And then in the days of the dancing class, when he was distinctly the polished man-of-the-world from outside, and all the girls from Helen White and Fanny Dana to May Wigham used to be so flattered by any attention from him. Or when we were off on his little sailing boat for a two or three days' trip on the Sound, or when we first hunted; and when he visited me at Harvard. . . .

Elliott had spent a few weeks of that final tormented summer with the woman who had been his mistress in Paris, who had summoned the doctor to her house on the New England shore and tried to make Elliott rest. He had often spoken to her of his sister, Corinne Robinson, and she now wrote Mrs. Robinson,

will you not tell me how he died? He seemed so much stronger when he left, that even the physician was astonished at his vitality, and I hoped for his children, he would try to take care of himself. He was so strong, and had such a gay, sweet nature, that I could not realize seeing him with my children, so interested in their work and play, that he was mentally and physically so worn out.

I do beg of you to have his children's memory of him—a beautiful one; his tender courtesy, his big—generous heart and his wonderfully charming sweet nature, ought to be kept before them. If in saying this, I am overstepping the line of discretion or courtesy, I beg you to forgive me.

Believe me, dear Mrs. Robinson, your brother suffered greatly, only as a big tender man like him could suffer—and while he was here, and I watched him sick and half wandering in his mind while he slept, he spoke constantly of you, how you had held to him and alone had given him the love he needed. Of course you do not need for a stranger to tell you this, but I know what a grief your brother's death must be to you, and it may be a little consolation to you to hear this.

I cannot forgive myself for not keeping him here, where he was loved and guarded, and where he might have regained some strength so as to have gone back a little more able to meet his lonely fight there—but it is too late to even regret. One thing you can do for him—see to it that he does not lose the place he deserves in his children's lives. He loved them, and ought to have been with them.

Two years later, when Mrs. Hall asked that his body be moved to the family vault at Tivoli, Corinne was grateful. "I want to write you a few lines to thank you for having let me know that all was safely accomplished and that Elliott now lies by Anna and his boy. I cannot help but feel glad that it is so, and I must tell you once more how deeply I appreciate the feeling which led you to wish him brought to Tivoli, a feeling which I dared not think could be there, or I should never have laid him at Greenwood."

With her father's death, wrote Eleanor Roosevelt in 1933, "went for me all the realities of companionship which he had suggested for the future, but as I said in the beginning he lived in my dreams and does to this day."[3]

Perhaps it was fortunate for Eleanor that her father died when he did. As Theodore Roosevelt said, now he could again think of Elliott as "the gallant, generous, manly, loyal young man whom everyone loved." By his death Elliott made it possible for his daughter to maintain her dream-picture of him. But somewhere, rarely admitted to conscious awareness, Eleanor carried another picture of her father—the father who sent her messages that he was coming and did not appear, who left her in the cloakroom of his club, who aroused her hopes that she would be coming home to him, hopes that were always disappointed, the father who lacked self-control, who could not face responsibility, who expected to be indulged. Repressing this picture exacted a price: her own sense of reality was impaired. She tended to overestimate and misjudge people, especially those who seemed to need her and who satisfied her need for self-sacrifice and affection and gave her the admiration and loyalty she craved. Just as her response to being disappointed by her father had been silence and depression because she did not dare see him as he really was, so in later life she would become closed, withdrawn, and moody when people she cared about disappointed her.

Although idolization of her father exacted a price, it was also a source of remarkable strength. Because of her overwhelming attachment to him, she would strive to be the noble, studious, brave, loyal girl he had wanted her to be. He had chosen her in a secret compact, and this sense of being chosen never left her. When he died she took upon herself the burden of his vindication. By her life she would justify her father's faith in her, and by demonstrating strength of will and steadiness of purpose confute her mother's charges of unworthiness against both of them.

7. The Outsider

"POOR CHILD," Mrs. Hall wrote Corinne after Elliott's death; she "has had so much sorrow crowded into her short life she now takes everything very quietly. The only remark she made was 'I did want to see father once more.'"

Her father's death deepened Eleanor's feeling that she was an outsider. She was a shy, solemn, insecure child, tall for her age, badly dressed, with blonde hair falling about her shoulders, and did not make friends easily. She would have to regain her trust in the world before she could act upon the lesson her Grandfather Theodore had impressed upon his children—receive people's love and people will love you.

To some extent her separateness was self-imposed. She wanted to be left alone "to live in a dream world in which I was the heroine and my father the hero." At school her first compositions reflect this fantasy life.[1]

The Tempest

We were all crowded in the cabin, no one had dared to go to bed for it was midnight on the sea, and there was a dreadful storm raging. It is a terrible thing in winter to be tossed about by the wind, and to hear captain calling through the trumpet "Cut away the mast." So we all sat there trembling, and none of us dared to speak, for even the bravest among us held our breath while the sea was foaming and tossing, and the sailors were talking death. And while we sat there in the dark, all of us saying our prayers, suddenly the captain rushed down the stairs. "We are lost!" he shouted. But his little girl took his cold hand and said. "Is not God on the ocean just as well as on the land?" Then we all kissed the little girl, and we spoke more cheerfully, and the next day we anchored safely in the harbor when the sun was shining brightly.

This little sketch reversed what had actually happened at sea in 1887 during the collision of the *Britannic* and the *Celtic*, when Eleanor had been terrified and her father had acted as the strong and confident captain. In making the girl the heroine, she betrayed what she wished had happened—that she had been calm and brave and had won the approval of her father and all the passengers so that all would have "kissed the little girl." The poignant tale underscored again how greatly she craved admiration and affection, and yet the reversal of roles also reflected what had happened between the time of the collision and her father's death. In those years her father had been the one who needed help and in reality as well as in fantasy, she had been the one to sustain and comfort him.

Eleanor lived with her grandmother in the brownstone on Thirty-seventh Street, a fashionable part of New York. In addition to the Roser class and French lessons with Mlle. LeClerq, she now attended a music class taught by Frank Damrosch and was brought by her governess to the exclusive Dodworth's, where girls in velvet curtsied to boys in blue and learned the waltz, the two-step, and the polka. But despite her busy life, she was a child as bereaved and lonely as Antoine Lemaire, the hero of another of her early compositions who is cast out of his home by his parents and is befriended by a musician who teaches him to play the violin. Antoine is a "born genius" and plays superbly, but, wrote Eleanor, "the thing which the boy yearned for most was love."

Grandma Hall was well disposed and kindly, but her hands were full with her own rather unruly children, Eleanor's aunts and uncles—Pussie, twenty-one; Maude, sixteen; Vallie, twenty-five; and Eddie, twenty-two. Grandma was only fifty-one, but her temperamental family exhausted her and she withdrew—or, as Eleanor later put it, she was "relegated"—to her own bedroom where her children expected her to sit by the window and mend their clothes. She did everything within her comprehension for Eleanor and Hall, yet they were neglected youngsters, starved for the thousand little parental attentions that build up the security and self-esteem of children.

That is the way some of Eleanor's schoolmates in the Roser classes remembered her.[2] She attended them until she was fifteen. Her classmates were Helen Cutting, Margaret Dix, Jessie Sloane, Gwendolyn Burden, Ruth Twombly, Valerie Hadden, and Sophie Langdon.

"It must have been in our early teens," Helen Cutting (Mrs. Lucius Wilmerding) recalled. "She was visiting me in Tuxedo."

" 'Let's go out and do something,' I urged."

Eleanor put her off. "I'll finish the letter I'm writing to Hall. Then we can go out."

"But you wrote him yesterday."

"I write him every day. I want him to feel he belongs to somebody."

Her stay with Helen was one of the rare occasions she was allowed to be away from home. The less her grandmother was able to control her own children, the more rigidly she sought to rein in Eleanor and Hall, and guidance usually meant saying "no." When the father of another of Eleanor's Roser classmates, Jessie Sloane, invited Eleanor to spend a summer out West with his daughter, Eleanor begged to be allowed to go. She had never wanted to do anything as much. Jessie was the prettiest girl in class, and Eleanor, who was gawky, her prominent teeth in braces, admired her for her loveliness. Her grandmother said no.

The girls were reaching the age when they were sensitive about their clothes. Margaret Dix (Mrs. Charles Lawrance), the daughter of the rector of Trinity, "the oldest, wealthiest and most fashionable" parish in the country, first made her appearance in the classroom in a DePinna sailor dress. "A titter in the class—my skirt's too short!" she later wrote.

Eleanor's skirts were always too short. She had few dresses and those she did have were shapeless and fell straight from the shoulders. She wore black stockings and high button shoes, and her grandmother insisted on long flannel underwear from November to April.

"A group of us little girls would go to Central Park to skate and play," Helen Cutting has said. "In the spring we went without our coats. Eleanor played very hard and like all of us would fall into puddles and get covered with mud and grime.

" 'Couldn't you put on a clean dress?' we asked her the next day.

" 'My other dress is in the wash,' she answered."

One day she spilled ink on her dress. When she took it off and tried to wash it in a basin, the ink spot spread all over the dress. "But she had to wear it," said Helen. This was not because of a lack of money but because of a lack of attention and care. Although Grandfather Hall had died intestate and thereby created financial problems for his wife, she received more than $7,500 a year for the care of Eleanor and Hall from various trusts left in their name.

The Thirty-seventh Street house was a dark, gloomy place, "grim and ill-kept," as Helen Cutting remembered it. "Nobody cared how it looked. Eleanor did not have her little friends there often. I don't remember having a meal there."

Eleanor's cousin Corinne, the daughter of her Auntie Corinne (Mrs. Douglas Robinson), lived in a brownstone at Forty-ninth Street and Madison Avenue. "My mother would ask me to go to have supper with Eleanor," recalled Corinne, who was two years younger than her cousin. "I never wanted to go. The grim atmosphere of that house. There was no place to play games, unbroken gloom everywhere. We ate our suppers in silence." It was not a house for children, Corinne added. "The general attitude was 'don't do this.' "[3]

It was also a frightening house. Eleanor's uncles had begun to drink heavily and she was afraid of them. She slept in a hall bedroom on the top floor next door to the room that Madeleine, the governess, occupied with Hall. Madeleine was sweet with Brudie, as Hall was called, but tyrannized Eleanor, pulled her hair "unmercifully," and berated her so violently that if Eleanor did something wrong, she preferred punishment at the hands of her grandmother. It was not until she was fourteen that she dared to tell her grandmother how often Madeleine made her shed bitter tears and was at last taken out of her care.

"I remember Madeleine," said Corinne. "She was a terrifying character. It was the grimmest childhood I have ever known. Who did she have? Nobody."

Eleanor's unhappiness made her even more determined to succeed. Some of her classmates considered her a "grind." They thought she worked harder than the other girls because things did not come easily for her, yet she had a very good memory, turned in compositions that were well written and imaginative, and recited poetry quite well. If she was a grind, it was because she set herself high standards. She wanted to learn, to excel, and thereby gain approval and praise.

Margaret Dix, the clergyman's daughter and, therefore, in the eyes of the other girls—except Eleanor—"a thing apart," had to win acceptance. But she was quick, gay, and mischievous. She inked in faces on her fingernails and held them up behind the teacher's back for the other girls to see. "They would giggle," Margaret recalled. "Eleanor would turn away. That would shock her. She only wanted to be a student."[4]

The Twombly mansion, where the Roser class met when the Cutting house was not available, was next door to St. Thomas' Church at Fifth Avenue and Fifty-third Street. The day the duke of Marlborough married Consuelo Vanderbilt in one of the most fashionable weddings in society's annals, Margaret found the occasion irresistible and slipped out during the recess to watch the wedding. "Eleanor would never have stepped out of a class to watch a wedding," she said.

Margaret recalled her schooling in the Roser class approvingly: "Mr. Roser gave me an excellent education." A more general verdict was that voiced by Eleanor's cousin Corinne, who was enrolled in a younger class:

I cannot understand why on earth our mothers fell for the Roser classes. They were held at all the big houses. I wish you could have seen Mr. Roser. A Prince Albert coat. Side whiskers, Not one grain of humor. Nobody in the world as pompous as he. And the things he decided to have us learn!

In the single paragraph that Eleanor Roosevelt devoted to the Roser classes in her autobiography she wrote admiringly of his assistant, Miss Tomes, but with reserve about Mr. Roser himself. He envisaged himself as a headmaster in the British public-school tradition, was learned in a literary kind of way, and expressed himself forcefully. The girls were obliged to stand when he came into the classroom, whereupon he would bow formally and indicate to the "young ladies" that they could be seated, addressing them as "Miss Roosevelt," "Miss Cutting," "Miss Sloane." He had a quotation from some great man or writer, most often from Dr. Johnson, for every occasion. The textbooks—the Nelson School Series, most of them written by William Francis Collier, LL.D., D.D.—were imported from England. History was taught from Dr. Collier's *The Great Events from the Beginning of the Christian Era Till the Present Time*, the present time being 1860, when Dr. Collier had produced this particular text, whose aim was "To give in a series of pictures such a connected view of the Christian Era as may be pleasantly readable and easily remembered." Implausible as the Nelson textbooks appear today, they were, nevertheless, not inferior to the McGuffey reader and Webster Speller that were in use in common schools all over the United States at the time. And if the Reverend Dr. Collier presented Victorian England rather than the American Republic as history's crowning triumph, the aberration would be corrected at home, since most of the Roser pupils came from families whose genealogy was in itself American history.

Mr. Roser was a pedant and rhetorician who expressed himself in a manner that he considered aphoristic.

Self control is necessary at all ages. We cannot begin too soon to acquire this virtue.

Without order in the classroom there can be no lesson given.

Whatever breaches the order of the class constitutes an act of disorder.

There is a distinction between reasonable and unreasonable merriment.

Occasionally Mr. Roser was driven to less pompous utterances. "Some girls talk too much," he once exploded.

He courted the rich and taught precepts that the wealthy found agreeable. "What is more natural to a good person than to help the poor?" one of his homilies began, and proceeded, "and if we yield to our emotions at the sight of a poor man we shall be surprised to hear that we are not diminishing wretchedness but increasing the number of street beggars." The notion that the poor were victims of their own failings, that no man who was sober, industrious, and prudent went hungry, was part of the Protestant ethic of individualism.

What did young, compassionate Eleanor make of such preachments? Charity, not prudence, even when it was disguised as benevolence, ruled her heart. She felt sympathy and solicitude even for what was alien and hostile. In Italy when she saw her donkey boy's bruised feet, she made him mount the animal while she trotted alongside. While she was in a stagecoach on Fifth Avenue, Eleanor saw an impoverished man try to snatch a purse from a woman sitting nearby, terrifying Eleanor so much that she jumped from the moving vehicle. But afterward she remembered, even more vividly than her fright, the face of the "poor, haunted man."

Eleanor found two Roser subjects difficult—grammar and arithmetic—and her mastery of them was due more to her excellent memory than to her ability to reason. The hours devoted to literature, especially poetry, were more satisfactory. The girls had to recite, and medals were given for the best performance. Gwendolyn Burden did Caroline Norton's "Bingen on the Rhine," which began "A soldier of the Legion lay dying in Algiers," and had them all in tears. Helen Cutting recited "The Old Clock on the Stairs" with a perceptible French accent since she had spent so much time abroad. Eleanor declaimed "The Last Leaf on the Tree," and was awarded a medal for her performance. She loved poetry, and memorized Tennyson's "The Revenge" in one day. Impressed, Mr. Roser had her recite the whole poem. They had no work that day, Helen recalled with delight, for Eleanor took up all the time with the ballad of brave Sir Richard Grenville, "who fought such a fight for a day and a night as may never be fought again."

It was the era of the "Delsarte System" of elocution, which assigned an appropriate flourish or pose to every mood and emotion—remorse, the hand to the head; rejection, the right hand flung out and down as if casting off a scrap of paper. Margaret Dix was a mimic and entertained her classmates with take-offs of their poetry recitations. She often portrayed Eleanor, standing stiffly erect, her face turning from left to right in approved elocutionary style, the hand outflung, the tip of her tongue in a circular movement moistening her lips. Eleanor and Margaret were not congenial.

Some of Eleanor's compositions have survived. Mr. Roser's comment was often a prim "your handwriting is not satisfactory." Even then Eleanor's penmanship was strong, angular, and highly individual. Sometimes Mr. Roser was impressed by Eleanor's vivid imagination, and he would append a "recommended for printing" comment to the end of the exercise, meaning that in his view it was worthy of publication, although apparently there was no school magazine or paper.

One of the first of her compositions, "Gilded Butterflies," showed her to be, as always, the moralist, but she also displayed a growing power of observation. The "butterflies" were characters suspiciously like the people around her, especially her young aunts.

Gilded Butterflies

Lying one hot July day on my back in the long grass lazily watching the daisies nod their heads as the scarcely felt breeze passed over them I was disturbed by a sound of voices and looking around I could see nothing but a few harmless butterflies fluttering here and there. Listening again I discovered that the voices came from the butterflies. Curiosity sharpening my ears I began to understand what they were saying. Listening to the one which was now speaking I heard him say "Pooh! I'm not going to sit on a daisy always. I have higher aspirations in life. I am going to know a great deal and to see everything. I won't stay here to waste my life. I mean to know something before I've finished."

Then he flew away and I saw a big fat portly old butterfly. He looked after him and said "Dear, dear, dear how dreadful it is to be discontented. For my part I'd rather stay where I am. I've seen life. I've met great men and been to large dinners in the crowded cities and now that it is ended it's a rest to be in the country and to see the flowers from which I can sip as much honey as I want, and besides, here I can be comfortable."

Just then a beautiful young butterfly arrived. "Dear me I am so tired. I've been to at least six dinners and about as many dances in the last week but then it is such fun. What would life be worth if there weren't any dinners, teas or dances but there aren't enough. There ought to be more. O my! there's an old gentleman, I must go. I never can stand these old people."

And she lifted her lovely gilded wings and fluttered by making a great noise and almost blowing the old gentleman off his comfortable seat. His old wings flapped as he muttered, "Poor little gilded butterfly what a lot you've got to learn."

Then came one who settled down next to the old man and said, "O dear, dear what a nuisance it is always racing and tearing for your food and then you don't get anything. Every one gets there before you. What bother life is. I wish I was dead. There are nothing but daisies and buttercups never any change. Now if I were only a genius, or rich then I could buy genius! Then he stopped and the old man gave a low chuckle. Then I heard a soft, lovely voice near my ear so low it was like a whisper. The voice said "Child, learn a lesson from the gilded butterflies and be contented in this world and you will find happiness."

An even more charming fable, written when Eleanor was thirteen or fourteen, was "The Flowers Discussion." Its references to a "conservatory" in which orchids, camellias, and even "a huge palm tree" were growing suggest the kind of great houses where young Eleanor was welcome. This composition was rewarded with the Roser imprimatur "recommended for printing."

The Flowers Discussion

"I am by far the most beautiful." These were the words I heard as I awoke from a nap I had been taking in a conservatory.

I was rather surprised to see that the speaker was a tall red rose which grew not far from me. There was evidently a hot discussion going on among the plants as to which excelled the others. I knew that if they saw I was awake the discussion would cease & as I wished to hear how it ended I feigned sleep.

After the red rose had spoken the beautiful lily raised its head. "You, the most beautiful?" I heard it say. "Look how straight you hold your head. You have no grace. Now mine bends over gracefully & then I am white which is by far a prettier color than red. I rest every eye which looks at me while you tire it. Besides you hurt people with your thorns. I never do. I smell far sweeter than you. Most people think so. Now you see that I excell you all" & she looked around with a proud glance.

There had been several interruptions during her long speech from the smaller flowers but now for a moment there was silence. Then the orchid spoke. "Indeed, you the most beautiful of all the flowers. What an idea. Why if any one is beautiful I am. Look at my varied coloring & how gracefully I hang, far more gracefully than you. Besides everyone likes me. No conservatory is complete without me while any can go without you."

Then a little white camelia spoke. "I hear someone coming. Whichever flower they choose as the prettiest shall excell." The flowers hardly had time to murmur "yes" when in came a little boy of not quite two. He gave a cry of delight as [he] entered. He looked around & then made straight for the orchid & stood by it drawing his finger lightly over the flower murmuring as he did so "Pitty flower pitty flower." His nurse picked it for him & he passed out.

As soon as he had disappeared the discussion began again, the rose & the lily averring that it was not right to stand by his decision. He was too small. This time the modest little violet who had not as yet spoken said "someone is coming. Stand by their decision" & the flowers said yes again. This time a young girl & her lover entered. They seated themselves under a huge palm tree & the young man said "which of all these flowers do you love the best?" "I love the white rose best, she is so sweet and pure," the young girl said. Her lover picked one for her and they went out.

They had hardly gone when the discussion began again. This time it was the orchid who said "The white rose is too small a flower to excell us all & besides the one which excells is king & imagine the white rose ruling us." All the plants laughed at the idea of their obeying the white rose & even I had to smile at the thought of the little flower ruling the haughty red rose, lily & orchid.

The discussion continued for several minutes when the pansy said, "Be quiet. Someone is coming." An old man & his wife now appeared. The flowers whispered as they entered "We will abide by their decision." The old couple seated themselves & the old man said "Is it not beautiful here Jennie. Which of all these flowers do you love the best?" The old wife looked around. "I love them all." she said & then as though she were thinking not talking "As a baby I loved the orchid, then the lily & the rose. As a young girl I loved the violet for it is the flower you picked for me when you told me of your love. Yes I loved it best then. I love it best now.

I thought so, the old man said. Then they went out. I wondered what the flowers would say to this, but I was soon to find out for the old couple had hardly gone when the rose broke out with "The violet excell all of us? The violet rule us? Why the white rose could do it better."

"Yes, indeed," cried all the plants. I could plainly see that all the flowers were bent upon excelling & I do not know how long the discussion would have lasted had not the violet said "Why none of us excell. We are all beautiful in our own way. Some are beautifully colored. Others smell sweetly & again others are graceful. We were all made well. From this day we are all equal."

The other flowers listened & to some it seemed strange that the flower which had been chosen to excel should say this but they all agreed and from that day they were equal.

But I always have and always will love the violet best.

As she passed from childhood to adolescence, the beauty of nature spoke to her awakening senses. The changes of the seasons, the play of light on the river, the color and coolness of the woods began to have the profound meaning to her that they would retain throughout her life. When she was a young girl, she wrote a half century later, "there was nothing that gave me greater joy than to get one of my young aunts to agree that she would get up before dawn, that we would walk down through the woods to the river, row ourselves the five miles to the village in Tivoli to get the mail, and row back before the family was at the breakfast table."

The summer months in her grandmother's house on the Hudson were among her happiest, even though none of her friends lived close by except Carola dePeyster, whose parents' house was five miles away and with whom she exchanged visits twice each summer. All the great houses along the Woods Road were on land rising in terraces.[5] Below, the Hudson was wide, slow, and majestic, while westward the Catskills rose in hushed silence.

A stone gatehouse led into the Hall estate, and the road went by large stables and came out onto a lawn that was shaded by towering oaks. The driveway went past a lawn tennis court said to have been one of the first built in the United States. Vallie and Eddie were both outstanding tennis players, each in turn winning the National Championship for singles and together for doubles. There was an old orchard behind the water tank and a sluggish little stream in which Eleanor and Hall caught tadpoles.

The children loved Oak Terrace, as the high-ceilinged drafty house with fourteen bedrooms was called. On the first floor there were reception, dining, and music rooms and the massive library wing. The large crystal chandeliers were not used, and the rooms were lit by kerosene lamps. Two bathrooms served the square bedrooms upstairs. On the third floor there were the servants' quarters, and the kitchen and storerooms were in a deep cellar, with a dumbwaiter to transport meals to the dining room. Staples were stored in barrels, and every morning Eleanor accompanied her grandmother to the storeroom and watched her measure out exactly what the cook would need. There was also a big, old-fashioned laundry in the cellar, presided over by Mrs. Overhalse, a neighboring farm woman. Eleanor was told that she could help the kindly lady, and she turned the wringer and learned to iron. There were enormous washes "because for every dress" her aunts wore "there were at least three petticoats." Eleanor often watched as her aunts dressed for the evening. "The top dress was pinned to the petticoat all the way round the edge so that the flounces would come straight and they would fall correctly." She watched with envy, wondering when her turn would come.

There were always errands to be run for her aunts and uncles, but in return they played games with the children. They had campfires and evening picnics in the hemlock grove. Uncle Vallie taught her to jump her pony, Captain. Aunt Pussie read her poetry, and Pussie and Maude occasionally permitted Eleanor to accompany them on a drive through the countryside, and she would sit with her legs dangling from the rear of the Hall buggy.

Sunday was a special day in the household. The family drove to church in the victoria, with Eleanor sitting in a little seat that faced backward. Sometimes the victoria swayed so much that she would begin to feel seasick. St. Paul's Church, on the Woods Road, had been built by the Livingstons, Ludlows, dePeysters, Halls, and Clarksons, and its tree-shaded churchyard was little more than a family burial place with a row of vaults built into the side of a hill. The front pews in the little church were reserved for the Livingstons, with Eleanor's branch on the right side. There was a special door for John Watts dePeyster by which that eccentric man came into a transept that was reserved for him. Before church Eleanor gave a Sunday school lesson to the coachman's little daughter. She also recited a hymn and collect to her grandmother.

There was a minimum of cooking, most of the Sunday dinner having been prepared the day before. In the afternoon no games, not even croquet, were allowed, only walks. The religious pattern that had been set by Grandfather Hall was even followed on weekdays. "My grandmother always had family prayers in the morning to which everybody including every servant in the house and even the coachman was expected to come and there were always evening prayers though all the outside people were not expected to come." After her aunts and uncles were grown up, Eleanor noted, "they weren't so good about observing all these rules."

She was a scrupulously well-behaved girl in class, but at Tivoli she sometimes broke her grandmother's rules, playing games along the high gutters of the house with Hall or sliding down the roof of the ice house and getting her clothes dirty, for which she would be sternly scolded. She even practiced high-kicking, although she had to do it secretly because when she expressed admiration for ballet dancing, her grandmother told her that no lady did anything like that.[6]

Most of all, Tivoli was a place for reading. There were long summer days when she would lie on the grass or climb a cherry tree with a book, sometimes forgetting to appear at meals. On rainy days the attic was her favorite spot. She often awakened at dawn and just as often violated her grandmother's injunction that she was not to read in bed before breakfast. The library was full of her grandfather's heavy theological works, but there were also Dickens, Scott, and Thackeray, and "sometimes a forbidden modern novel which I would steal from my young aunts, purely because I heard it whispered that the contents were not for young eyes."

Eleanor read everything, disappearing into the fields or woods, often to "cry and cry" over such books as Florence Montgomery's *Misunderstood* and Hector Mallet's *Sans Famille*. The heroes of both these books were orphaned outcasts with whom she obviously identified. *Sans Famille*, which became *No Relations* in English, began with the declaration "I was a foundling," and the adventures of this waif were reminiscent of those of Antoine Lemaire in Eleanor's composition for Mr. Roser. *Misunderstood* was a great favorite of the Victorians; as a young girl Sara Delano also sobbed over its pages. In that book the lad Humphrey welcomed death because it would reunite him with his mother and end an existence that had been rendered "miserable" by his father's partiality for Humphrey's little brother. She still enjoyed them, Eleanor Roosevelt wrote in 1950, but she thought them "very sentimental, foolish books to allow a rather lonely child to read."* Sometimes she made a play out of the book she was reading, in which she was the principal character and her brother, six years younger, the supporting cast. *Robinson Crusoe* especially lent itself to such dramatization. The desert island was a secret place in the woods a quarter of a mile away from the main house. Hall was "poor Friday," and in that role was "forced to do many strange things."[7]

Another fictional waif who engaged her sympathy was Peter Ibbetson, the main character in the du Maurier novel by that title which swept romantic young America at the end of the century (probably one of the books she purloined from her aunts). Peter Ibbetson, orphaned at twelve like Eleanor, retreated to an "inner world" where he achieved happiness by learning to "dream true"—that is, to evoke at will the people he loved and to carry on a fantasy life with them in his "private oasis." Generally her reading was not censored, but if she asked inconvenient questions the books prompting them disappeared. On Sunday mornings the book she was reading was taken away "no matter where I was in it," and she was given what were called "Sunday books," works of religious edification.†

At fourteen Eleanor had definite opinions, was reflective, and was capable of a crisp expression of her views. An essay on "Ambition" exists only as a draft, and toward the end the corrections she made in it become somewhat illegible, but the main ideas are clear. She was ambitious. She wanted to succeed.

* She was often asked in later years to list her favorite girlhood books. "I loved Dickens' *Old Curiosity Shop* and *Tale of Two Cities*; Longfellow's Poems; Kipling's *Light That Failed*; Walter Scott's *The Talisman*; *Sarah Carew*; *The Prince and the Pauper*; *The Little Lame Prince*; Ouida's *Dog of Flanders* and *Nuremberg Stove*." On another occasion she added *Oliver Twist* and *Dombey and Son* as among the books she remembered from girlhood and "with great enthusiasm a long book called *Thaddeus of Warsaw*, which was a historical novel, touching on one phase of Poland's efforts to remain a free nation." In an article for *Girl Scout Magazine*, August, 1933, she said that she had read George Eliot's *The Mill on the Floss*, *Romola*, and *Silas Marner* as she "grew a little older." Also, "a book which could not be found today in any library—*The Gad Fly*—gave me hours of pleasure."

† *The Sunday at Home: Family Magazine for Sabbath Reading* (Religious Tract Society, London).

Ambition

Some people consider ambition a sin but it seems to me to be a great good for it leads one to do & to be things which without it one could never have been. Look at Caesar. It was because he was ambitious that they killed him but would he ever have been as great a man had he not had ambition? Would his name ever have come down to us if he had not had enough ambition to conquer the world? Would painters ever paint wonderful portraits or writers ever write books if they did not have ambition?

Of course it is easier to have no ambition & just keep on the same way every day & never try to do grand or great things, for it is only those who have ambition & who try & who meet with difficulties, they alone feel the disappointments that come when one does not succeed in what one has meant to do for the others say "It was meant that we should not succeed. Fate has so decreed it" and do not think of it again. But those who have ambition try again, & try till they at last succeed. It is only those who ever succeed in doing anything great.

Ambition makes us selfish and careless of pushing others back & treading on them to gain our wish it is true, but we will only be able to push back the smaller souls for the great ones we cannot tread on. Those who are ambitious & make a place & a name in the great world for themselves are nearly always despised & laughed at by lesser souls who could not do as well & all they do for the good of men is construed into wrong & yet they do the good & they leave their mark upon the ages & if they had had no ambition would they ever have made a mark?

Is it best never to be known & to leave the world a blank as if one had never come? It must have been meant it seems to me that we should leave some mark upon the world & not just live [&] pass away. For what good can that do to ourselves or others? It is better to be ambitious & do something than to be unambitious & do nothing.

Ambition is essential for any kind of success. Even those best men who condemn ambition, must have it or they would never do anything good. For it is their ambition that makes them wish to do better things than other people.

Therefore it seems to me that after all people have said against it ambition is still a good thing.

While she considered ambition a virtue, wanted to achieve great things and even echoed Roser's social Darwinism with the suggestion that only the fittest survive—and deserve to survive—these were not really the beliefs by which she lived. Highest in her scale of values were loyalty, friendship, service to others. And women, she lamented in another composition, lacked these qualities, which were so much more desirable than mere beauty. Thus did she seek to come to terms with her own lack of good looks. Her distaste for women who kissed one moment and the next tore each other's characters to shreds was also the response of a judgmental young girl to the mercurial crushes of her schoolmates and aunts—some of whom, at least, thought her too high-minded, too serious, too good.

Loyalty and Friendship

Loyalty is one of the few virtues which most women lack. That is why there are so few real friendships among women for no friendship can exist without loyalty. With a man it is a point of honor to be loyal to his friend but a woman will kiss her best friend one moment & when she is gone will sit down with another best friend & pick the other's character to pieces.

It may seem strange but no matter how plain a woman may be if truth & loyalty are stamped upon her face all will be attracted to her & she will do good to all who come near her & those who know her will always love her for they will feel her loyal spirit & have confidence in her while another woman far more beautiful & attractive will never gain anybody's confidence simply because those around her feel her lack of loyalty & by not having this great virtue she will lose one of the greatest gifts that God has given man, the power of friendship. . . .

She was, of course, talking about herself. She was the "plain" one, who by her truth and constancy would gain the love and confidence of those around her. She would succeed by the strength of her character since she did not have beauty to fall back upon. The first entry in a briefly kept journal is a careful copying out of a long poem, "My Kate," by Mrs. Browning:

> She was not as pretty as women I know, yet one
> . . . turned from the fairest to gaze in her face
> And when you had once seen her forehead and mouth
> You saw as distinctly her soul and her truth. . . .
>
> She never found fault with you, never implied
> Your wrong by her right, and yet men at her side,
> Grew nobler, girls purer as through the whole town
> The children were gladder that pulled at her gown.

"So like Aunt Pussie," Eleanor wrote at the bottom of the poem. "How I wish I was like her. I don't suppose I ever will be though."

Actually, Pussie, who was the most volatile of the Hall sisters, was not very much like Mrs. Browning's Kate. Pussie was constantly involved in tempestuous love affairs whose ups and downs she shared with Maude and Eleanor, much to their delight. She was also frequently depressed, and when she was she locked her door and talked to no one for days. She was an accomplished pianist, briefly tried her hand at painting, shared her literary enthusiasms with Eleanor, and even took her to meet the great Italian actress Eleanora Duse. Eleanor devotedly served her lovely aunt, rubbed her temples when she complained of headaches, and once even groped tremblingly down three flights of stairs in the dark of night to get her some ice from the backyard icebox at Thirty-seventh Street. Because Eleanor adored Pussie, she invested her with Kate's nobility, but because Pussie was irresponsible as well as irrepressible, she was scarcely a woman, as Eleanor herself later realized, at whose side men grew nobler and girls purer.

"I have a headache journal tonight," Eleanor wrote on November 18, 1898.

I am feeling cross. Poor Auntie Pussie she is so worried. I am going to try and see if I can't do something for her tonight. I have studied hard two lessons but I can't think of a composition. I suppose I can think tomorrow. Am not going to tell you—unless something happens. I've tried to be good and sweet and quiet but have not succeeded. Oh my.

A page from a journal that Eleanor kept when she was 15.

She was setting herself very high ideals, an entry for November 13 indicated.

> To be the thing we seem
> To do the thing we deem enjoined by duty
> To walk in faith nor dream
> Of questioning God's scheme of truth and beauty.

"It is very hard to do what this verse says," Eleanor commented, "so hard I never succeed & I am always questioning, questioning because I cannot understand & never succeed in doing what I mean to do, never, never. I suppose I don't really try. I can feel it in me sometimes that I can do much more [than] I am doing & I mean to try till I do succeed."

The final entry in the journal, dated November 18, also reported that

Alice did not come. I never will see her I am afraid. I wish I could but I don't dare ask if she is coming to lunch. I *do hope* I will see her. Goodnight journal.

In 1898 Alice was in open rebellion against her stepmother and had been sent to New York to stay with Auntie Bye, now married to Commander William Sheffield Cowles. Alice had grown into a defiant, hoydenish girl who coasted down steep hills with her feet on the handlebars of her bike, rode her pony hard and recklessly, and once, to get an evening out with her teen-age gang (of which she was the leader although its only girl member), had one of the boys call for her dressed in his sister's clothes, a ruse that was discovered.[8]

Not surprisingly, she considered Eleanor too mild. "She was full of duty, never very gay, a frightful bore for the more frivolous people like ourselves." Although Eleanor looked forward to Alice's visits, they never turned out to be as happy as she had anticipated. Alice was a tease, and when she and the other girls excitedly discussed the "facts of life," Eleanor was embarrassed. Once they were all chattering away in Alice's room at Auntie Bye's—Eleanor, Alice, Gwen Burden, Jessie Sloane, Margaret Dix, and Helen Cutting. "No one should talk about things like that," Eleanor indignantly protested. When they told her that everything they were saying could be found in the Bible, she lapsed into injured silence. "What is the meaning of whore?" she asked her grandmother when she returned home, adding, "It is in the Bible." "It is not a word that little girls should use," Mrs. Hall said severely.

Later on, her schoolfriends enlightened her.[9]

After her parents' death Eleanor saw little of her Oyster Bay relatives. Grandmother Hall had said that she wanted the children to be "influenced by their father's family as well as by their dear Mother's" but frightened by the gay and strenuous life led by the Teddy Roosevelt clan, she kept Eleanor away, and Theodore's wife did not press Eleanor to visit Oyster Bay. Aunt Edith was standoffish and reserved toward all but her immediate family, but when Eleanor did go to Sagamore Edith saw the child's future with remarkable prescience. "Poor little soul, she is very plain," she wrote Bamie. "Her mouth and teeth seem to have no future. But the ugly duckling may turn out to be a swan." Whatever Aunt Edith's attitude toward her, Uncle Ted's affection was huge and vehement. He loved all his nieces, having what Alice called a "tribal affection," but Eleanor was his favorite because she was Elliott's daughter and "he was very devoted to Uncle Ellie."

"Eleanor, my darling Eleanor," he greeted her as he helped her out of the carriage at Sagamore and crushed her to his chest. "He was a bear," Edith reported, and "pounced upon her with such vigor that he tore all the gathers out of Eleanor's frock and both buttonholes out of her petticoat." Eleanor loved the day and a half she was allowed to stay at Sagamore, but keeping up with her uncle and her cousins turned into another series of mortifying proofs that she was inadequate. Alice was much better at sports. Eleanor did not even know how to swim, she had to confess the first time she went to Oyster Bay, whereupon Uncle Ted told her to jump off the dock, which she obediently did, only to come up panicky and spluttering.[10]

Then he organized a race down Cooper's Bluff, a steep sandy cliff, with each cousin holding onto the hand of another, and Uncle Ted in the lead. Rolling, tumbling, sliding down, she was "desperately afraid" the first time, but then realizing that there was little to fear, entered into the fun. Her Uncle Ted did everything with a boyish zest, chasing the children through the haystacks, into which they burrowed like rabbits, and through the barn in the game of hide and go seek. In the evening around a campfire he would pull out whatever book he had in his pocket and read to them; on rainy days he took them to the gun room and read to them there. A week end in Sagamore was a test of self-control and perseverance, of hiding fears and doing things to the best of her ability, but when Eleanor returned to her lonely existence at Tivoli or Thirty-seventh Street she was again the outsider.

The only other occasion on which she saw her father's family was at the Christmas party that Auntie Corinne gave at Orange. That was the only time she was with boys her own age, and the experience gave her "more pain than pleasure." The other young people knew each other so much better, she was poor at winter sports, and she thought that she danced awkwardly and was not dressed properly.

"Mother would have Eleanor stay with us," her cousin Corinne recalled.

We were a gay ebullient family. Eleanor was just sad. For the big party she was dressed by her grandmother in a short, white nainsook with little blue bows on either shoulder, the hem above her knees all hanging like a child's party dress but she was 14. She was in Alice's age group and Alice had on a sophisticated long dress. We begged her to borrow a dress, but she was noble, martyred and refused.

"We all felt the same way about her—Mother, Auntie Bye and I," Corinne added. "We loved her. We admired her and we were sad about her."[11]

But finally, when Eleanor was just turning fifteen, Grandmother Hall decided it was not good for her to remain at home. Her son Vallie was becoming increasingly difficult to handle, and Pussie had turned out to be a sophisticated but wildly romantic woman who had young men to tea and smoked cigarettes.

"Your mother wanted you to go to boarding school in Europe," Mrs. Hall told Eleanor. "And I have decided to send you, child."

Finishing school in Europe meant Allenswood and Mlle. Souvestre, who had done such wonders in 1869 for Auntie Bye and whom Eleanor's parents had met and liked in 1891 when they were living in the suburbs of Paris.

Another stage of her life was beginning. The years of being an outsider were over.

8. The Spark Is Struck

A YEAR AFTER Eleanor arrived at Allenswood, on the outskirts of London near Wimbledon Common, its remarkable headmistress, Mlle. Souvestre, wrote Mrs. Hall:

All what you said when she came here of the purity of her heart, the nobleness of her thought has been verified by her conduct among people who were at first perfect strangers to her. I have not found her easily influenced in anything that was not perfectly straightforward and honest but I often found she influenced others in the right direction. She is full of sympathy for all those who live with her and shows an intelligent interest in everything she comes in contact with.[1]

Eleanor blossomed in the warm, friendly environment of Allenswood—it was as if she had started life anew. Behind her were the people who pitied her because she was an orphan or who taunted her for her virtues, and for the first time in her life all fear left her and her personality began to shine forth. "As a pupil she is very satisfactory," Mlle. Souvestre's evaluation continued, "but even that is of small account when you compare it with the perfect quality of her soul."

Bamie had been sent to Mlle. Souvestre in 1869 when the latter was headmistress of Les Ruches in Fontainebleau, outside of Paris. Because of an internal crisis precipitated by her co-principal, Marie Souvestre had given up Les Ruches, and years of "cruel sadness" had followed. In the mid-eighties she founded her new school in England.*

"The elite of many countries" sent their daughters to Allenswood—the Chamberlains, the Roosevelts, the Siemenses, the Stracheys. Henry James thought well enough of the school to suggest that his brother William send his daughter there in 1899, and described the sixty-five-year-old Mlle. Souvestre as "a most distinguished and admirable woman" who

has had for many years a very highly esteemed school for girls at high, breezy Wimbledon, near London (an admirable situation)—where she has formed the daughters of many of the very good English *advanced* Liberal political and professional connection during these latter times. She is a very fine, interesting person, her school holds a very particular place (all Joe Chamberlain's daughters were there and they adore her,) and I must tell you more of her.

* A fictional account of the crisis at Les Ruches and a vivid portrait of Mlle. Souvestre are to be found in *Olivia* by "Olivia" (1949). *Olivia* was the pseudonym of Dorothy Strachey-Bussy, the sister of Lytton Strachey who was a pupil at Les Ruches and a teacher at Allenswood when Eleanor was there.

"The one shade of objection," he wrote Mrs. William James a few days later, "is that it is definitely 'middle-class'. But *all* schools here are that." By "middle-class" James meant to differentiate between the upper bourgeoisie and the intellectual elite to which he, as a man of genius, belonged.[2]

While the majority of the 35 to 40 girls enrolled in the school when Eleanor arrived were English-speaking, French was obligatory inside the classroom and out. This was no hardship for Eleanor, and, indeed, in the first few bewildering days she was reassured to see the other new girls having difficulty with the language. At her "first meal," a classmate recalled, "when we hardly dared open our mouths, she sat opposite Mlle. Souvestre chatting away in French . . . we admired her courage."[3]

The American newcomer was turned over to Marjorie Bennett, an English girl who was to be Eleanor's roommate. "Bennett" showed her around the school and explained its rules. Allenswood had some of the austerity and strictness of a British public school. "Its strict discipline suited the temperament of the youthful 'Totty.' "[4] The girls wore long skirts, usually black, white ruffled blouses, and boaters out-of-doors. Their day was fully programmed, and punctuality was mandatory. They made their own beds. Bureau drawers and closets had to be arranged as laid down in the rules and ready for inspection at any moment. At meals everything taken onto a plate had to be eaten. After breakfast there was a brisk walk in the commons in good weather and foul, and in London's damp chill Eleanor gladly began wearing her flannels again.

Classes went on throughout the day with special periods set aside for the preparation of lessons. To encourage concentration, the pupils were obliged to lie down on the floor after their midday meal and fix their minds for an hour on a single thought, which they later discussed at tea in French. Although athletics were not worshiped here as in the British public schools, two hours of exercise in the afternoon were obligatory. Eleanor went out for field hockey. She was not good at sports, but, as one of her classmates put it, "full of duty again,"[5] she persevered and made the first team, one of "the proudest moments" in her life, she said. There was an afternoon snack, more classes and study, and then the bell that alerted them to dress for dinner. Leadership in the school was marked in many ways, and the most ceremonial was to be chosen to sit opposite Mlle. Souvestre at dinner. To occupy this place, Dorothy Strachey wrote, "was an education in itself." It was this girl's duty to rise at a nod from Mlle. Souvestre as a signal that dinner was ended. In time, Eleanor was awarded this coveted honor. "Sou," as the girls called their headmistress, had her favorites. As the students filed by to say good night, she embraced some girls, kissed some, and extended a gracious hand to the rest.

Eleanor, who was drawn to girls who had difficulties, soon developed her own circle of friends. Carola von Passavant, the daughter of a wealthy Frankfort family, arrived in Allenswood shortly after Eleanor. It was her first time away from her parents and her first time out of Germany. The English girls were "very cool and stiff," the other German girls not sympathetic. Mlle. Souvestre saw that Carola was having an unhappy time and asked "Totty," as Eleanor was called at the school, to watch out for her. "That she did and I was thankful for it."[6] Eleanor, Carola, and Marjorie Bennett formed a trio. Eleanor also made friends with Hilda Burkenshaw ("Burky"), whose father was an officer with the British forces in India, and with Avice Horn, who had been sent from Australia to get her education "at home." Two rather schoolmistressy girls, the Gifford sisters, Helen and Leonie, who later started the successor school to Allenswood, were also among Eleanor's intimates.

Eleanor took French with Mlles. Souvestre and Maître, German with Fräulein Prebitsch, and Italian with Signorina Samaia, a mouselike woman with skirts that swept the floor who had come with Mlle. Souvestre from Fontainebleau and was now the school's energetic administrator. She studied English literature with Dorothy Strachey, who remembered her as "a tall, slim, elegant young girl who was so much more intelligent than all the others!"[7] and English history, Latin, and algebra with a variety of instructors. She had three years of drawing and design, and her schoolgirl notebooks were adorned with baroque lettering. She toiled away at music—three years of piano lessons and one of violin—but with indifferent results. "I struggled over the piano and was always poor," she wrote many years later. "I could not draw much less paint. I envied every good actress but could not act!" She wanted "desperately to have some form of artistic expression," but soon realized that she had no particular gifts.[8] Classes in the dance and three years of "needlework" rounded out her course of study. Allenswood placed little emphasis on science, and there was little concern with American history and government. Beatrice Webb, who was otherwise a good friend and admirer of Marie Souvestre, criticized the school's "purely literary" training.[9]

In contrast to Mr. Roser's decorous homilies, which had almost turned learning into a chore, Eleanor found the teaching at Allenswood lively and stimulating. According to her teachers, she was eager to learn and keenly interested in all her class work. Her workbooks showed a steady development in standards of taste and judgment, and—after the months when Mlle. Souvestre felt she was "a little bit likely to be influenced in her studies"—a sturdy insistence on thinking for herself.

The girls were encouraged to go to the theater in London and Paris during the holidays. Eleanor sat in the topmost gallery at the Comédie Française and stood and shouted, as did everyone around her, for Sully, then going blind, in *Oedipus Rex*.[10] She and her friends saw *L'Aiglon* with Sarah Bernhardt and *Cyrano de Bergerac* with Coquelin in the leading role. Was it because she remembered these occasions through "the rosy glasses of youth" that she felt in later years they represented the greatest days of the theater?[11] "Cyrano," Eleanor, the Allenswood student, wrote,

seems to me to be a very able piece of work in which the workman has made good use of everything which could make his readers laugh or cry. It is not a burlesque but it is very amusing and the duel scene in which Cyrano fights and rhymes at the same time is very clever. I do not wonder that Coquelin has made such a success of the part, for on the whole Cyrano is a very sympathetic character and Coquelin is a wonderful actor. I notice his voice which M. told me was so disagreeable but I think it serves admirably in this part and helps to enhance the comic effect . . . it is a play essentially written for the stage and though interesting to read many of the fine points can only be brought out by perfect acting. . . .

But she was not sure, she added, that *Cyrano* merited more than one or two readings: Shakespeare, on the other hand, was "a continent."

What distinguishes men of great genius? It is the power of creation and generalization. They gather into one character scattered personalities and they bring to the knowledge of the world new creations. Do we not believe in Don Quixote's existence as in that of Caesar? Shakespeare is something terrible [she first used word "gigantic" but crossed it out] in this respect. He was not one man but a continent. He had in him great men, entire crowds, and landscapes.

Men of genius, she went on,

do not need to pay attention to style, they are good in spite of their faults and because of them, but we, the lesser ones, only prevail by perfect style. Hugo will surpass everyone in this century because of his inspiration, what inspiration! I hazard here an opinion which I would not dare speak anywhere. It is that the greatest men often write very badly and all the better for them. It is not in them that we must look for perfect style but in the secondary writers (Horace, Labruyere)—One must know the masters by heart, adore them, try to think as they do and then leave them forever. For technical instruction there is little of profit to draw from the learned and polished men of genius.

The nature of the poetic mission and understanding intrigued her, and she returned to the subject.

To a poet nothing can be useless. He must be conversant with all that is terribly awful and wonderfully beautiful. He must be able to admire alike what is splendidly great or elegantly small. The plants of the garden, the insects and birds of the air are all important, for he knows most who is best able to vary his scenes and to furnish his readers with moral and useful instruction.

But the knowledge of nature "is only half the task of a poet," she wrote in the same essay.

He must be acquainted with all the different modes of life. He is required to estimate the happiness and misery of every condition, to trace the power of the passions, and to observe all the changes through which the mind passes owing to the different customs and climates from infancy to old age. He must free himself from the ideas of his time and regard right and wrong apart from the customs of his age. He must [word indecipherable] nature and consider himself above the criticism of his time trusting to posterity to acknowledge his merit. He must consider himself the arbiter of the thoughts of future generations as a being superior [?] to time and place.

Her notebook on English literature began with *Beowulf,* devoted a considerable amount of space to the Age of Chaucer and ended with the Age of Johnson. A separate notebook was filled with the passages from Shakespeare's plays that she considered worth transcribing. Her readings in French literature were equally extensive, and in Italian she read *The Divine Comedy* and *Orlando Furioso.*

Age of Dr Johnson.

The importance of prose.
The age of philosophy
The influence of France
The Rise of philosophical History
The rise of the modern novel. Sentimental & realistic.
The decadence of poetry.

Samuel Johnson 1709-1784.

London. 1738
Vanity of Human Wishes 1749.
Irene. 1749
The Rambler & The Idler. 2 periodicals.
Dictionary 1755. (letter to Chesterfield.)
Rasselas, prince of Abyssinia 1759.

The Rise of the Modern Novel

The novelists. decline of the theatre & increase of reading public.

Richardson. The first novelist. The true stories of ordinary people
Pamela 1740. or Virtue Rewarded
The novel of Sentiment & Sensibility. Tragedy of the
human heart.

A page from Eleanor's English literature notebook.

Her report cards showed a steady progression and mastery:

FRENCH LANGUAGE

SEPTEMBER TO DECEMBER, 1899 — "has begun too recently to be able to judge but interests herself very much in her lessons"

JANUARY TO APRIL, 1900 — "she works admirably in French and history and is the first out of a class of nine."

MAY TO JULY, 1900 — "works at French with much intelligence and taste, has made progress but cannot yet work on her own well enough"

SEPTEMBER TO DECEMBER, 1901 — "works with application"

MAY TO JULY, 1902 — "very advanced"

GERMAN

SEPTEMBER TO DECEMBER, 1899 — "works very well, spelling needs improving"

JANUARY TO APRIL, 1900 — "very good pupil, is always interested in her work"

MAY TO JULY, 1900 — "excellent"

SEPTEMBER TO DECEMBER, 1901 — "worked well"

MAY TO JULY, 1902 — "very industrious—has made remarkable progress."

LATIN

SEPTEMBER TO DECEMBER, 1899 — "is going over the elements with good results"

JANUARY TO APRIL, 1900 — "has worked splendidly. Excellent"

ITALIAN

SEPTEMBER TO DECEMBER, 1901 — "very good student, she works with zeal and much intelligence"

MAY TO JULY, 1902 — "excellent student, she speaks and writes Italian easily."

ENGLISH LITERATURE

SEPTEMBER TO DECEMBER, 1899 — "Intelligent, as far as can be seen in the few lessons she has had"

JANUARY TO APRIL, 1900 — "Intelligent, but she is not quite up to the level of the class she is in."

MAY TO JULY, 1900 — "Good"

SEPTEMBER TO DECEMBER, 1901 — "Works very well. Very satisfactory."

MAY TO JULY, 1902 — "Very good. Her progress was very marked this term."

The Allenswood years shaped Eleanor's tastes in literature, music, theater, and the arts generally, but what made those years among the most important in her life was its headmistress, the seventy-year-old Mlle. Marie Souvestre. The daughter of Emile Souvestre, a well-known philosopher and novelist and an innovator in the field of adult education, she inherited his interest in ideas and the arts as well as his moral zeal in politics. Strongly anti-Royalist, almost radical in his sympathies, he had been obliged on occasion to take refuge in Geneva.

His daughter was just as staunchly outspoken and nonconformist in her views. She was at home in the world of high politics and high culture and was welcome in all the great Liberal houses in England. Although her body had thickened with age, she was a woman of striking presence. Her forehead was strong and unlined, her face finely featured, her hair silvery white, and her eyes penetrating. She communicated a sense of force and authority and gave a Gallic flavor to any company she was in. Her lectures in history and literature were wide-ranging discourses on social movements. Beatrice Webb spoke of her "brilliancy of speech," which Dorothy Strachey said "darted here and there with the agility and grace of a hummingbird" and which influenced the literary style and taste of Lytton Strachey. "Cette grande femme," he called her.[12] No one read Racine like Marie Souvestre. She gave the French classics, one of her pupils said, "a new vividness and reality and a wider meaning." Her special gift was "the intense enthusiasm she could inspire in the young for things of the mind, for courageous judgment, and for a deep sense of public duty."

Mlle. Souvestre's classes were conducted in her library, a spacious book-lined room that was always full of flowers. The sculpture and paintings seemed quite daring to the girls—the work of such artist-friends as Rodin, Puvis de Chavannes, Barbedienne. The occasions Eleanor treasured most were the evenings when she and a few other girls were invited to Mlle. Souvestre's study, where for a few hours after dinner Mademoiselle read aloud, encouraged them to recite poems, and talked with them.

A passionate advocate, Mlle. Souvestre "often fought seemingly lost causes," but causes, Eleanor noted, that "were often won in the long run." She was a Dreyfusard, and for years before Captain Dreyfus was vindicated, the spellbound girls heard every move in the case over and over again. From that time on, Eleanor later said, she became conscious of the feeling in herself that "the underdog" was always to be championed.

When the Boer War came along, Mlle. Souvestre was Pro-Boer. She had a great many friends in government circles; in fact, one of her old pupils was a daughter of an Englishman high in the government at that time. But that did not deter her from being a pro-Boer running a girls' school in England or from her outspoken criticism of British policies. On the other hand, she was scrupulously fair and allowed the British girls to celebrate their victories in South Africa, although she would take the rest of us into her library and talk to us at length on the rights of small nations while the British celebration was going on.[13]

Despite the vigor of her convictions, or perhaps because of them, she insisted that her students think for themselves. Intellectual independence and a lively sense of curiosity, she felt, were the most important traits she could develop in her girls. She wanted them to become personalities without losing the grace, the sweetness, the elegance which she felt were "the charm and smile of life." She herself had broken free from the constraining circle of inherited ideas, and she wanted the girls she cared about to do the same, to be open-minded, curious, and to reach out. Eleanor, who had been taught by her mother and grandmother that conformity was the way to win society's approval, was a little upset with the demand that she be herself and self-reliantly say what she, not her teacher, thought.

Mlle. Souvestre's class sat on little chairs in her library, the headmistress in "a tall, straight armchair," with Signorina Samaia "on a little stool close and behind." Mlle. Souvestre talked, gave them a reading list, and asked them to do an essay based on their reading. Later, when the girls read their essays, she devastated those who parroted what she had said. A half-century later Eleanor could still see the indignant headmistress, as one of the girls read her paper aloud, take it away and tear it up. "You are giving me back what I gave you and it does not interest me." She insisted that her girls sift things through their own intelligence. "Why was your mind given you but to think things out for yourself?"

Challenged, Eleanor began to seek points Mlle. Souvestre had not made, and felt that it was even more satisfactory to come up with an idea that she had not found in the assigned reading. She glowed when Mlle. Souvestre returned a paper with the comment "well thought out," even if she added, "but you have forgotten this or that point."

Beatrice Webb was less impressed by Mlle. Souvestre as a thinker. She lamented Mademoiselle's reliance on the sparks of intuition rather than the rigors of scientific method in arriving at social judgments. Like her father, Mlle. Souvestre was primarily a moralist in politics, and she was concerned more with social justice than with social analysis. In this regard she strengthened Eleanor's disposition toward a social idealism based on intuitive reason and the promptings of the heart rather than intellectual analysis.

In what did Mlle. Souvestre succeed, a pupil later asked, and answered her own question —"in exciting, in amusing, in passionately interesting the intellect, in putting such a salt and savour into life, that it seemed as if we could never think anything dull again."

Mlle. Souvestre's fervent concern with public affairs and politics was another novelty for Eleanor; at Grandma Hall's there had been fashionable indifference. Uncle Ted's exploits in Cuba, his progress to the governorship, the vice presidency, and presidency were, of course, discussed at Tivoli, but as part of the family chronicle, not because they were national events. Politics, so far as the women were concerned, was still strictly the business of the men, as it had been in Grandfather Hall's day. Mlle. Souvestre, on the other hand, was "a radical free thinker," an intimate of the group that surrounded Frederic Harrison, leader of the English Positivists, who was a staunch supporter of trade unionism and an advocate of the "religion of humanity."

The headmistress was sensationally different from the devout Christians who directed the English public schools in her attitude toward religion: she called herself an atheist. That shocked Eleanor. If Grandma Hall had had the slightest inkling of this, she would surely have summoned Eleanor home immediately, regardless of Auntie Bye's devotion to the Frenchwoman.

As Mlle. Souvestre explained it, she could not comprehend a God who occupied Himself with the insignificant doings of individual men, and she considered pathetic the belief that He passed out rewards for good behavior and punishment for bad. Right should be done for its own sake; only the weak needed religion. These views were held by a large body of anticlerical opinion on the continent, but they were new and startling to Eleanor.

Did Christians do right only because of the rewards that were promised in heaven? Eleanor puzzled over this for many years, and in the end concluded that the charge was meaningless so far as her own feeling about God was concerned. "I was too young then to come back with the obvious retort that making those around you happy makes you happy yourself and, therefore, you are seeking a reward just as much as if you were asking for your reward in your future life."[14]

But she also maintained that listening to Mlle. Souvestre's anticlericalism did her no harm in that it prompted her to re-examine her own beliefs. She could not accept Mlle. Souvestre's concept of a God indifferent to man and his activities on earth. Eleanor felt that God commanded what her own heart bid her do. Eleanor has "the warmest heart that I have ever encountered," Mlle. Souvestre noted on Eleanor's first report. Religion and prayer touched mystic chords in Eleanor that bound her to her dead father and to all humanity. Mlle. Souvestre's indifference to religion did not interfere with Eleanor's enjoyment of the Passion play which Aunt Tissie took her to see or of the Christmas midnight mass that she and Burky attended with Mlle. Souvestre in Rome. She concluded, with pathetic eagerness, that the headmistress could not be an atheist "at heart for she was as much moved as we were by the music and the lights!" Beatrice Webb questioned Marie Souvestre's ability to appreciate religious feeling. Yet one of Mademoiselle's dearest friends, the French evangelist the Reverend Charles Wagner, did not consider it a violation of his friend's basic convictions to confide her soul to the hands of the Lord at her funeral in the Church "de L'Oritoire Saint-Honoré." So Eleanor may have been more discerning than Mrs. Webb in ascribing some religious sentiment to Mlle. Souvestre.

While Marie Souvestre's agnosticism produced no answering echo in Eleanor, the elder woman's "uncompromising sense of truth"—Beatrice Webb called it her "veracity"—and her "intolerance of pettiness and sham" did. In later years Eleanor did not hesitate to disagree with church or bishop when their actions or words seemed to conflict with Christian spirit or when religious institutions lent support to cruelty, prejudice, and human degradation.

Although Allenswood was notably emancipated if measured against other finishing schools, it was totally innocent in regard to preparing young ladies to deal with the world of men. Except for a few elderly gentlemen teachers, the girls were as cloistered as in a nunnery. On one occasion when Eleanor and Audrey Hartcup, then two of the oldest girls at the school, went into the library to say good night to Mlle. Souvestre, they found her in conversation with Mlle. Samaia and the older brother of one of their classmates. "Mlle. Samaia threw up her hands in horror and shooed us out!" The next day Eleanor and Audrey cornered her and tried to make her understand the absurdity of such squeamishness in view of "how freely we mixed with members of the opposite sex—when at home." If Eleanor, one of the most proper of young ladies, felt that Mlle. Samaia was being overly protective, it must have indeed been a cloistered existence.

Mlle. Souvestre was the most influential figure in Eleanor's early years, second only to her father. Headmistress and pupil were strongly drawn to each other. Marie Souvestre, like Eleanor, had been very attached to her father, who had died when she was quite young, and there were other bonds between the two. Mlle. Souvestre admitted to having a special feeling for Americans, and then there was the family tie. "Believe me," Mlle. Souvestre wrote Mrs. Hall, "as long as Eleanor will stay with me I shall bear her an almost maternal feeling, first because I am devoted to her aunt, Mrs. Cowles, and also because I have known both the parents she was unfortunate enough to lose." But according to Corinne, Eleanor's younger cousin whose first year at Allenswood overlapped Eleanor's last and who also gained a preferred place in the affections of the school's headmistress, the crux of the relationship was Mademoiselle's realization that "she could give a great deal to that really remarkable, sad young girl."

The headmistress' motherly solicitude for Eleanor extended to her clothes, her health, her grooming. She was outraged by Eleanor's made-over dresses but hesitated to say so at first because she was afraid of hurting the sensitive girl. During Eleanor's second year at Allenswood, however, when she and Burky were spending the between-year holiday with a French family in order to improve their French, Mlle. Souvestre, who was also in Paris, finally expressed herself on the subject of Eleanor's clothes. Mlle. Samaia was directed to take Eleanor to a dressmaker, and the dark red gown that was made for her gave Eleanor as much pleasure as if it had come from the most fashionable house in Paris. "I can well remember this red dress," a schoolmate recalled more than sixty-five years later.

Mlle. Samaia also undertook to break Eleanor of the habit of biting her fingernails. She had little success until one day when Eleanor was rereading her father's letters and came to the passage that admonished her to take care of her personal appearance. It hit home, and from that day forward, she said, she let her nails grow.

Her grandmother had alerted the school to her delicate health. "You would enjoy seeing her so well, so rested, so ready for all out-of-door exercises," Mlle. Souvestre wrote Mrs. Hall. "She does not any more suffer of the complaints you told me about. She has a good sleep, a good appetite, is very rarely troubled with headaches and is always ready to enjoy her life." A year later Mlle. Souvestre again reported on Eleanor's physical condition.

She looks always very thin, delicate and often white and just the same I have rarely seen such a power of endurance. She is never unwell even when she seems so. Her appetite and sleep are excellent and she is never tired of walking and taking exercise.

Photographs of Eleanor at this period show a tall, slim, narrow-waisted girl with soft, wavy hair arranged in a pompadour and braided in the back. Her most distinctive feature was her eyes; blue, serene, and soft, in their gaze one forgot the overly prominent teeth and the slightly receding chin. Her soul, said Mlle. Souvestre, was a radiant thing, and it could be glimpsed in her eyes. Like her father, she had the faculty of concentrating all her attention and sympathy on the person she was with. "She is conscientious and affectionate," the headmistress wrote Mrs. Hall in one of many such reports, "full of regard for others, and of a fineness of feeling truly exquisite. She desires only the good."

Eleanor's schoolmates agreed. Burky, who felt "tired" by comparison with Eleanor, later expressed her gratitude to her for her companionship during holidays, even though "my mind and my body could not keep up with all the things you absorbed so readily and so intelligently." Eleanor was so consistently helpful that even the girls her age looked upon her "as one of the older ones." Avice Horn's sister Dorothy characterized Eleanor "as being entirely sophisticated, and full of self-confidence and *savoir faire*," and Eleanor's cousin Corinne gave this picture of the position that Eleanor held at the school:

When I arrived she was "everything" at the school. She was beloved by everybody. Saturdays we were allowed a sortie into Putney which had stores where you could buy books, flowers. Young girls have crushes and you bought violets or a book and left them in the room of the girl you were idolizing. Eleanor's room every Saturday would be full of flowers because she was so admired.

Mlle. Souvestre's aim was to make her girls "cultivated women of the world," and because she knew so many men of arts and letters in all countries she was able to give a few fortunate older pupils special advantages when she took them abroad on vacation. Eleanor was one of those chosen for this privilege.

"If you have no objection to this plan," she wrote Mrs. Hall in February, 1901, "I am thinking of taking her with me to Florence during the Easter holiday. It will be short but I think she may nevertheless derive some benefit of a fortnight in Italy and she is very eager to come with me."

All the practical details of the journey were turned over to the sixteen-year-old girl. Eleanor packed for both of them, looked up train schedules, secured the tickets, arranged for the hansoms and porters. She loved every part of her assignment, and traveling with Mlle. Souvestre was a "revelation" to her: eating native dishes, drinking the *vin du pays* (diluted, of course, with water), being with the people of the country, not one's countrymen. She learned the pleasures of a meal of wine, cheese, bread, and coffee, and the virtue of flexibility in travel; of revising plans in order to see a friend or a church or a painting.

In France they were entertained by M. Ribot, a former prime minister. In Alassio they called on Mrs. Humphrey Ward, the novelist. In Florence they stayed with a painter who was doing a gigantic church mural of the Last Supper. While in Florence Mlle. Souvestre told Eleanor to take her Baedeker and go through the sublime city street by street, church by church; "Florence is worth it," said Mlle. Souvestre. And "so, 16 years old, keener than I have probably ever been since and more alive to beauty, I sallied forth to see Florence alone."[15] In addition to the excitement and joy of discovery, there was the pleasure of discussing everything she had seen with Mlle. Souvestre afterward. "It is impossible to wish for one self a more delightful companion in traveling," Mlle. Souvestre wrote Mrs. Hall. "She is never tired, never out of sorts, never without a keen interest in all that she sees."[16]

On her way back to England Eleanor stopped in Paris, where she wanted to get gifts. Like her father, she took pleasure in giving, and also like him she tried to find "just the thing" which would make the recipient feel loved and valued. A list of those to receive presents started with her family:

> *Maude's baby* [Maude was Mrs. Larry Waterbury]
> *Joe's baby* [her Uncle Eddie Hall had married the beautiful Josie Zabriskie]
> *Pussie*
> *Cherub* [Hall]
> *Grandma*
> *Vallie*
> *Tissie* [Mrs. Stanley Mortimer]
> *Cousin Susie* [Mrs. Henry Parish]

It also included teachers and her closest school friends, and ended with the redoubtable Madeleine, who had caused her so much grief.

In Paris she ran into the Newbold family, whose Hyde Park estate bordered on that of the Roosevelts'. Mlle. Souvestre did not think Eleanor needed to be chaperoned, and the Newbolds promptly reported to Grandma Hall that they had seen Eleanor in Paris alone. Eleanor worried about her grandmother's reaction to this news; she was to go back to the United States in July and she wanted desperately to return to Allenswood in September. "I sincerely hope she may be able to do that," Mlle. Souvestre wrote to Mrs. Hall. "I am sure another year of a regular and studious life will be in every respect mentally and physically beneficial. Her health though excellent is perhaps not yet settled enough to make it desirable for her to face all the irregularities of a society life. . . . She is very desirous of seeing you and is often anxious for you, now that so many of your daughters are married and away." (Tissie spent a good part of the year abroad; Maude had married Larry Waterbury, the famous polo player; and Pussie, although still unmarried, was totally preoccupied with herself.)

It was Pussie who came to London to accompany Eleanor on her return to America. The voyage was emotionally exhausting. Pussie, in the throes of a romantic crisis about a man she had met in London, was full of tears and of avowals that she was going to jump overboard. It was a bad beginning of an unhappy summer, whose only bright note was a visit to Farmington, Connecticut, where Auntie Bye had recently moved. Eleanor helped her aunt get settled, and in the guest book next to her name she wrote "the laborer is worthy of his hire." She was thrown together with Pussie again in Northeast Harbor, Maine, where Pussie was staying with Mrs. Ludlow and Eleanor with Mrs. Ludlow's daughter, her cousin Susie.

Something Eleanor said nettled Pussie. Because she had taken Pussie's threats to jump overboard seriously, Eleanor may have expressed surprise at the speed with which Pussie became involved in a new romantic interest in Maine. Whatever the provocation, Pussie retaliated with gibes intended to hurt Eleanor where she was most vulnerable. She ridiculed Eleanor's appearance, reviving her mother's lament that she was the ugly duckling among all the beautiful Hall women; no men would ever be interested in her, Pussie taunted. But Eleanor, long reconciled to her plain looks, could not be provoked, so Pussie thrust more savagely. Who was she to talk selfrighteously in view of her father's behavior? She hysterically told Eleanor about her father's last years and of the grief and shame his behavior had caused her mother and all the family. Distraught and shattered, Eleanor ran to her grandmother for consolation and denial, whereupon she was told that Elliott *had* ruined her mother's life.

Eleanor was thrown into despair, and wanted only to get back to Allenswood and Mlle. Souvestre. Her grandmother hesitated, but Eleanor's determination and entreaties finally prevailed and Mrs. Hall agreed to let her return for a third year if she could find a chaperone for the voyage. Eleanor went to New York and on her own engaged a "deaconess" through an employment agency to accompany her. With the help of her aunts, she bought her first tailor-made suit with an oxford-gray skirt that fashionably trailed the ground. Accompanied by the respectable-looking deaconess and dressed modishly, she turned away from that unhappy summer and returned to the peace of Allenswood.

It is a measure of how much she had grown in self-assurance that her encounter with Pussie did not cause her to withdraw into feeling unloved except by a father who was dead. Instead, her last year at Allenswood strengthened her leadership qualities.

She was happy and contented, yet she also "knew the sadness of things," a sadness that shadowed even her moments of greatest joy and achievement. She could not abandon herself to frivolity and merriment like other young people. Mlle. Souvestre later talked with Corinne about "Totty," and after enumerating her virtues "would throw up her hands and add 'mais elle n'est pas gaie.' " "She took a serious view of life," Helen Gifford recalled, "and once confided to me that all she wished for was to do something useful: that was her main object."[17]

Because her mother had bred in her an ineradicable sense of inferiority and plainness, Eleanor felt that she could never count on beauty in gaining people's affection—only helpfulness. "The feeling that I was useful was perhaps the greatest joy I experienced," she later wrote. Happiness, she reasoned in an essay she wrote for Mlle. Souvestre, lay in what one did for others rather than in what one sought for oneself.

There is no more fleeting notion than that of happiness. Certain people seem to find happiness in a thoroughly egoistic life. Can we believe however that those socialites who look as if they were enjoying happiness in the bustle of worldly pleasures are actually happy? We don't believe so, for the pleasures of the world are precarious, and there must be moments, even in the gayest and most brilliant life, when one feels sad and lonely in the midst of a frivolous crowd where one cannot find a single friend.

On the other hand, it often happens that those whose existence seems saddest and dullest are in fact the happiest. For instance you sometimes meet a woman who sacrifices her own life for the sake of other people's happiness and is happy nevertheless because she finds in her devotion the best remedy against sadness and boredom. . . .

If no life is without sadness, none is without happiness either, for in the saddest life there are moments of happiness, sometimes produced by comparing the present peace of mind with past sufferings.

Most of all, those who are not looking for happiness are the most likely to find it for those who are busy searching forget that the surest way to be happy is to seek happiness for others.

Eleanor wanted to return for a fourth year, but her grandmother insisted that she come home and be introduced into society since she would be eighteen in October.

"The more I know her the more I see what a helpful and devoted grandchild she will be to you," Mlle. Souvestre wrote to Mrs. Hall at the beginning of 1902, adding, "Ah! to me! What a blank her going away must leave in my life!" And in her final report in July she said, "Elinor [*sic*] has had the most admirable influence on the school and gained the affection of many, the respect of all. To me personally I feel I lose a dear friend indeed."

As for Eleanor, she wrote in an exercise that described Allenswood to an interested parent, "I have spent three years here which have certainly been the happiest years of my life."

9. *Young in a Young Country in a Young Time*

———

ELEANOR WAS almost eighteen when she returned to the United States in the early summer of 1902. There was a lively perception in her eyes, her face was sensitive and intelligent, and although she was tall, her movements were quick and graceful—like those of a colt, someone said. Full of dreams and hopes, her sky-reaching mood matched that of the country. Reform was in the air. The century was young, and the United States, raucous and self-confident, was responsive to the prophecies of Eleanor's uncle, its most youthful president, that this was destined to be an American and, therefore, a better century. The nation was ready to embark on "a new quest for social justice," historian Harold U. Faulkner wrote, and Roosevelt "instinctively . . . responded to the widespread desires for a better civilization and, rushing to the head of the movement, he rose to unprecedented heights of popularity as the reform wave surged onward."[1]

Radiant, full of optimism, Theodore Roosevelt delighted in the presidency, and the nation was infected with his enjoyment of the office. For the first time not only was a president's policy always on stage, but so was his personality—the warming smile, the outsize teeth, the striking phrase sometimes uttered with a screech, the explosive laugh. Never before had the private lives of the president and his family been so fully and continuously reported. The country adored reading about his dash with children and friends down Cooper's Bluff, his wandering off into the meadows to read an afternoon away, or such greetings to Alice's friends as "Children, come with me—I'll teach you how to walk on stilts."[2] Alice, now dubbed "Princess," was on the front page almost as often as her father, and he, even in his Harvard days, had been, one professor complained, "a great lime-lighter." He now used his showman instincts to promote his public purposes. "On the whole," William James wrote in 1902, "I have rejoiced in Roosevelt so far."[3] His use of the word "rejoiced" caught precisely the national mood of sheer pleasure in its young president. The nation was enchanted, and so was Eleanor, who, soon after her return, made the rounds of her Oyster Bay kin—Auntie Bye and Auntie Corinne, Uncle Gracie and Uncle Ted.

The advance of technology and the resultant new domestic comforts bolstered the sense that the new century would be a better one. "How wonderful the telephone is and how I should miss it at Hyde Park," Mrs. James Roosevelt noted in her journal. Eleanor's family was replacing coal stoves with gas, and kerosene lamps and gas jets with electricity. They were using automobiles as a means of transportation, not only as playthings. When Alice and another girl motored alone "all the way from Newport to Boston" that summer, the newspapers hailed the journey as representing progress in travel by motor, while their families lamented the shift in moral standards among the young implied by the absence of a chaperone.

New York, too, was changing from the quiet city Eleanor had known as a child. It was now Greater New York, a teeming metropolis of 3.5 million people, and the population was still surging upward as immigration, almost wholly from eastern and southeastern Europe, approached a million a year. "More money," the city departments cried. The budget would soon pass the hundred million mark, the editorials warned, while Fusion Mayor Seth Low bewailed the unreasonable limitations that Albany placed upon the city's borrowing powers.

It was a divided city. Jacob Riis had called his book on the subject, published in 1890, *How the Other Half Lives*. A decade later the split was deeper. There was the New York of Eleanor's family and friends, whose resplendent homes along Fifth Avenue now stretched from Washington Square to the upper eighties. Concentration of wealth was "the outstanding feature of American economic life" in the new century, and on Fifth Avenue it was reflected in the French châteaux, Rhine castles, and Italian Renaissance mansions that replaced the old brownstones.

The other face of New York was the huddle of East Side slums, where two thirds of the city lived in 90,000 tenements, most of them of the gloomy "dumbbell" type in which ten out of the fourteen rooms on a floor were windowless. The male head of the household earned $600 a year, for which he worked a ten-hour day, six days a week. Children and women were "sweated."

These were the ugly realities raising portentous thunderheads over the glitter and elegance of Fifth Avenue when Eleanor returned. But the omens, if more menacing, were not new; what was new were the reforming impulses that could be felt everywhere, especially among women, whose position was changing. The women's rights movement had made enormous strides since 1848, when Elizabeth Cady Stanton had launched it. When she died, just as Eleanor returned, she was no longer a figure of mockery, and some even called her "the greatest woman the world has ever produced." Even Theodore Roosevelt, who was not yet a convert to women's suffrage, called her death a loss to the nation.

By the opening of the new century, American women had broken out of their traditional sphere.

When I read in the papers and heard in the Club that a dozen women of great wealth were standing along Broadway handing bills and encouragement to the girl shirtwaist strikers of last winter, I was not a bit surprised. Nowadays I can hardly go to a reception or a ball without being buttonholed by somebody and led into a corner to be told about some new reform. It is perfectly amazing, this plague of reform, in its variety, in its volume and in the intensity of earnestness with which it is being pushed.[4]

Some well-born women went further. Charlotte Perkins Gilman challenged members of her sex to seek "economic independence" and to use their economic power for social reform, not simply to salve their consciences by charitable donations. When Professor Vida Scudder of Wellesley advocated "a new Franciscanism" and appealed to students to go into the slums and staff the growing settlement-house movement, a few New York debutantes responded. Mary Harriman and Nathalie Henderson enrolled in Barnard to study economics and sociology and then launched the Junior League, one of whose purposes was to assist the settlements.[5]

Eleanor returned to the United States feeling that she was on the threshold of life, ready to be swept up by such an undertaking. After three years under Mlle. Souvestre's influence, she was open to the reforming currents that were in the air, and she wanted to go on with her education.

But society decreed that at eighteen, young girls who "belonged" came out. The debut was a tribal ritual, "the great test," the society columns cruelly proclaimed, of a young girl's social talents.[6] The approaching rites filled Eleanor with dread, but it never occurred to her not to comply—a resolve that worried Mlle. Souvestre. Her letters cautioned Eleanor against permitting society to "take you and drag you into its turmoil. Protect yourself," she urged.

Give some of your energy, but not all, to worldly pleasures which are going to beckon to you. And even when success comes, as I am sure it will, bear in mind that there are more quiet and enviable joys than to be among the most sought-after-women at a ball or the woman best liked by your neighbor at the table, at luncheons and the various fashionable affairs.[7]

But society, echoed by her Hall relatives, decreed that her first obligation was to be introduced. So Eleanor prepared for the ordeal.

The social season did not begin until November, and Eleanor spent the intervening months at Oak Terrace in Tivoli. It was a sobering experience. After the protected surroundings of Allenswood, she was suddenly brought face to face with "the serious side of life." It was lonely at Tivoli. Aunt Maude, closest to her in age, was now settled in her own house and was leading a very gay life that was the talk of the society columns. Aunt Pussie, Eleanor reported to Mlle. Souvestre, was involved in "worldly excitements." She was as temperamental as an artist, and when she was at Tivoli she was likely as not to be depressed and would refuse to speak to anyone. And then "she would emerge perfectly delightful and bright and happy as a May morning." The whole family, added Eleanor, who had become quite impatient with her aunt, "had been through a wringer wondering what was the matter and then nothing."

Pussie was quite attached to Hall, Eleanor's eleven-year-old brother, and considered him her child. Eleanor wanted Hall with her although she felt bad about it, she wrote Mlle. Souvestre, because it made her aunt so sad. Mlle. Souvestre consoled her. It was hard for Eleanor to be faced with such problems so soon, but Mademoiselle was pleased that Hall had elected to go with Eleanor. Since Pussie was so busy with society and her gentlemen, the headmistress thought she would easily forget these "regrets of a sentimental character."

The loneliness of Tivoli could have been borne, even when Hall was staying with his Oyster Bay cousins, if it had not been for Uncle Vallie, whose alcoholism was a never-ending nightmare to Eleanor. He would stand at a window with a gun and shoot at members of the family as they crossed the lawn so that they had to take shelter behind the trees. Vallie was often joined in his escapades by his younger brother even though Eddie was now married to the beautiful Josie Zabriskie. Her Allenswood classmate, Leonie Gifford, came to stay with Eleanor, but throughout her visit Eleanor was on tenterhooks. The strain was too much, and she decided that she could no longer invite friends to Tivoli. Two young men, Duncan Harris and Charley Draper, dropped in unannounced and were baffled by her desperate maneuvers to keep them from having a drink with Vallie, who they knew was entertaining the current amateur doubles champions that day.[8] Only once did she depart from her "no guests" rule, and that was when she invited young Franklin Roosevelt, who knew the situation at Tivoli well enough not to be frightened off by Vallie's sudden eruption. Of the visit, Franklin noted in his Line-A-Day diary, "Vallie has been exemplary—I seem to have a good effect on him."

The spectacle of her two uncles losing control of themselves instilled in Eleanor, she said, "an almost exaggerated idea of the necessity of keeping all of one's desires under complete subjugation." She warmed to vitality but disliked abandon, especially the maudlin behavior induced by alcohol. When people let themselves go in that way, she turned rigid and cold. The intensity of her reaction to her uncles was undoubtedly fed by the repressed knowledge of her father's behavior, something that she could not acknowledge but which, after Pussie's outburst the summer before, must have been close to the surface of consciousness.

Between Vallie and Pussie, she had a "liberal education" that summer in how people who were emotionally unstable "can make life miserable for the people around them." She began to have an understanding of what her mother had suffered, although it did not alter her feelings toward her father.

After the new school term began at Allenswood, Mlle. Souvestre wrote Eleanor that she was sorely missed at the school. "There are many new girls with us," Mlle. Souvestre wrote. "As is their custom, the English girls pay no attention to them and leave them alone. You would have known how to act so that they would have felt at ease and happy in conditions so different from their usual life." What a "great void" your departure has created, Mlle. Samaia wrote her. "Tell me when the big season starts in New York," Mlle. Souvestre demanded.

For Eleanor, the coming of autumn only increased her dread of her debut and her first winter in society. Would her Roser-class schoolmates still see her as a girl apart? Would there be the whispered "she has no father or mother, she is so pathetic," or would she be able to repeat her Allenswood triumph and establish a place for herself in New York?

For some, the New York season began with the autumn ball at Tuxedo, but it was the sound of the bugle opening the horse show at Madison Square Garden that announced to the city that society was once more "at home." Splendid animals pranced on the tanbark, and elegant folk thronged the boxes. One of the stalls belonged to Franklin D. Roosevelt's older half brother, James "Rosy" Roosevelt, who had married an Astor, looked Edwardian, worldly, and attractive, and was "a real honest snob." The night the horse show opened James's daughter Helen, who was engaged to Theodore Douglas Robinson, was there with him, as was Eleanor. "Two handsome members of the Roosevelt family," reported the *Herald*, which omitted to note that young Franklin Roosevelt, down from Harvard, was also in the box that evening; he was an unimportant Roosevelt. The center of attention was Alice, who made several circuits of the Garden in a lovely white gown and the strikingly large hat that had already become her trademark, this one of white plumes.

Although the newspapers noted Eleanor's presence at the show and Franklin wrote in his diary, "Dinner with James Roosevelt Roosevelt, Helen Roosevelt Roosevelt, Mary Newbold and Eleanor Roosevelt at Sherry's and horse show," in her own account of her coming out Eleanor failed to mention the occasion. For her the pinnacle was still to be scaled.

The big Assembly Ball at the Waldorf Astoria took place on December 11. To New York society, said the *New York Times*, it is what "the Drawing Room in Buckingham Palace is to the fashionable world in London." A debutante did not feel she had come out until she had curtsied to the patronesses who received the guests in the smilax-decorated foyer, had entered the great ballroom in her white gown and long white gloves, and had danced in the cotillion with a handsome young man.

Almost all the debutantes considered the ball an ordeal—"ninety-nine per cent of us," said Helen Cutting; "no, I would make that ninety-nine point nine per cent."[9] They all worried over what their peers would say about their gowns, their looks—above all, whether they would be asked by young men to dance. For Eleanor the evening was even more trying because of the inevitable comparisons with her mother's splendid debut. The week before the Assembly, *Town Topics* had commented that Eleanor's coming out recalled the brilliant days of New York society in the late eighties when Mrs. Elliott Roosevelt was one of its "leaders." Society would be thinking of her mother and, she was sure, how far the daughter fell short of being a belle.

She stayed in town that autumn with Pussie, who never let her forget that it was unheard of for a Hall girl not to be a belle at every party. Fourteen years after her debut Pussie was still much admired and much wooed, still had more partners than she could possibly accept for both the cotillion and supper. Both Pussie and Maude caused "raised eyebrows" in New York society; they "broke practically every rule that could be broken" but were always forgiven because of their great beauty and charm. Living with Pussie only added to Eleanor's feelings of gloom and foreboding.

There were five Misses Roosevelt making their appearance in society in 1902. Alice, who had come out the previous January with "the most gala White

House ball since the days of Dolly Madison," was coming to the Assembly, as were Christine, Elfrida, Dorothy, and Eleanor—all eighteen years of age. The town was talking about "the Magic Five" and twittering away over who was the prettiest, the most attractive, the most sought after. That Alice was the wittiest—not only among the debutantes but in society generally—was already agreed.

The Assembly, according to Eleanor, was "utter agony." She was adequately gowned in a Callot from Paris, but she knew no one and would have been totally ignored by the men, she claimed, were it not for Forbes Morgan, a suitor of Pussie's, and Bob Ferguson, who was fifteen years older and had been devoted to her mother. They danced with her and introduced her to others at the ball, but she was not a popular debutante, she felt, and left as soon as she could, ashamed that she should be the first girl on her mother's side of the family not to be a belle.

Her agony, though real, was self-inflicted, and revealed more about the immense importance she attached to being a success than it did about how others regarded her. So far as looks were concerned, *Town Topics* commented rather cruelly, the Roosevelt girls were "interesting-looking, but they are not pretty."[10] And what constituted a "popular debutante"? Before going to the Assembly Ball, Eleanor had attended the largest of the dinners that preceded it, an elaborate affair thronged by young men and women given by the Reverend Dr. and Mrs. Morgan Dix for their daughter Margaret. Two days before the Assembly she was at Sherry's for the dinner-dance given by the Emlen Roosevelts for their daughter Christine, and the day after the Assembly she attended the reception and small cotillion given by Mrs. Hilborne L. Roosevelt for Dorothy. The following week she went to a dinner and dance at Sherry's for Gertrude Pell and assisted at Elsie Waterbury's afternoon reception and supper. Before departing for Washington for New Year's at the White House, Aunt Tissie took sixty of Eleanor's friends to see Julia Marlowe in *The Cavalier*. After the play the elegantly begowned ladies and top-hatted young men went by omnibus to Sherry's for supper and informal dancing. In Washington Eleanor was invited to all the big parties and went to most of them. In all, it was hardly the life of a "Miss Lonelyheart."

After the exhausting New Year's gaieties, Eleanor returned to New York for more dinners and private dances in the splendid mansions along Fifth Avenue. "Now comes the critical test of the winter as to who shall be left and who shall be chosen," wrote the *Herald*, adding that a few debutantes—but by no means all—would be invited to the Astor ball, "the most important event of the winter season." To be included on Mrs. Astor's list meant distinction for the girl who had just made her debut. Eleanor was included, and she was also invited to all the so-called "small" dances—those presented by Mrs. Ogden Mills, Mrs. John Jacob Astor, the Elbridge T. Gerrys, the Whitelaw Reids. These entertainments usually began at eleven after the opera, and consisted of dancing until midnight, supper, a cotillion, and further dancing until early morning. Eleanor did not enjoy these parties and left as early as possible. That first winter, she said, society was the all-important thing in her life, but it nearly brought her to "a state of nervous collapse."

"She wasn't a belle by any means," recalled Duncan Harris. "She was too tall for most of the young men. But she was an interesting talker. And she was always gracious and pleasant." Her contemporaries remarked upon her exquisite manners, and older men found her sympathetic and were impressed with her grave thoughtfulness. To her surprise, several times she found herself seated next to the host—but what did such victories matter? At eighteen she would have preferred younger, if less exalted, dinner companions. With men her own age, however, she was insecure and quick to consider them "fresh," and she was overly "proper." During her last month at Allenswood, Leonie Gifford's brother had come to visit his sister, and the two Giffords, Eleanor, and Marjorie Bennett went for a walk in the common. She and Marjorie tossed a coin to decide who should walk with whom. "You walked with me," Walter Gifford reminded her two decades later, "and when I congratulated you on winning the toss you very coldly told me you had lost it, which was rather galling for a 17-year-old male in a very high collar."

The winter over, she was glad to get back to Tivoli. "I only arrived at six last night and I've just finished my third book. I never quite realize when I'm away how much time there is for reading here." She laughed over Charles Flandrau's *Harvard Episodes* and *The Diary of a Freshman* but the third book, *La Gioconda*, "is just tremendous. . . . I suppose D'Annunzio meant to show that fate is inexorable and that one may sacrifice all and get nothing for it if such is our destiny. Certainly he did not show men in a very favorable light." She made these comments in a diary she began to keep at the end of May, 1902, because, she wrote, she hoped to do "something which I will want to remember later on." But she also had literary aspirations, and in the briefly kept journal she dramatized an encounter between her grandmother and the cook.

"Do you know Totty I simply cannot get rid of the cook!" was the way Eleanor began the episode; "she simply won't go." Then Eleanor recreated the scene between her grandmother and the cook, Mary Ann—"the scene which had led up to this startling announcement."

G'ma. "Mary Ann, Mrs. K wants you to go back to her on Monday."

Mary Ann. "Sure Mam and I couldn't think of such a thing (feeble attempt at protest from my G'ma) why should I be after leaving you when the young ladies are so nice and I'm quite completely settled for the summer. (Another attempt at speech on my G'ma's part—unsuccessful of course.) Why now Ma'am I've been with Mrs. K's sister, Mrs. B., and with her brother's sister-in-law and with her cousin so it's natural you know she should want me back but I told her when I was going I wouldn't come back and you don't think I'd be after laving you now?"

Here there was a pause for breath and her grandmother managed to say something.

G'ma. "But Mary Ann if we have a great deal of company can you make ice cream and do all the other work?"

Mary Ann. "Why to be sure, Ma'am an' I can do anything, anything you want, of course ye'll give me some help and don't you worry about me I kin do things just perfect. You just send word to Mrs. K. I can't come back. I'd do it meself but I can't write you know."

"So G'ma retired," Eleanor finished, "to do as she was bid and Mary Ann is still our cook."

The entry (and the diary) ended with a pathetic declaration: "I won't write again until I've been to the Poor's. Wish me good luck please. I'm usually so hopeless on a house party!"

Despite this self-depreciation, she had begun to develop a circle of friends. Her eyes, Laura Delano later asserted, softened the hearts of all the men, young as well as old, and her face did things that were suddenly lovely.[11] Her male friends came from the group that worked for the Astor Trust—Duncan Harris, Nicholas Biddle, and especially Robert Munro Ferguson, who was the center of a "Ferguson cult" among New York society women. He was a member of an ancient Scotch Highland clan, and his brothers were pillars of the British Liberal establishment and members, along with Asquith, Haldane, and Grey, of the closely knit group called the "Limps." Bob Ferguson had come to the United States in the late 1880's and had been a Rough Rider in the Spanish-American War; Teddy Roosevelt considered him one of the bravest men he had ever known. He had been a frequent visitor at Eleanor's house while her mother was alive and was a favorite of Auntie Bye's. A tall man, rather sad looking except when his face broke up in twinkles, he invited confidences. He was not all surface and Eleanor was strongly drawn to the silent, sensitive, attractive Bob.

Bob Ferguson introduced Eleanor to Bay Emmett, the painter, and escorted her to parties at Miss Emmett's studio in Washington Square. "Not a Four Hundred thing, although it was the Four Hundred,"[12] the Emmett parties were extremely informal and supposedly very Bohemian, although some young men did not stay long because no hard liquor was served. That made the parties even nicer, as far as Eleanor was concerned, and thus she was not, as was customary for her, among the first to leave.

By the autumn of 1903 her Tivoli family was beginning to depend on her a great deal, looking upon her as the strong one. She could cope with Pussie's emotional crises, and when a drunken Vallie, eluding Mrs. Hall in Tivoli, would turn up in New York, it was Eleanor who took command. She gladly assumed responsibility for Hall. Anna Roosevelt had entered Hall's name on the Groton list for his year, and after her death, the headmaster, Reverend Endicott Peabody, wrote Eleanor's father that although Hall was twenty-third on the list, he was sure that Groton would be able to take him. It was Eleanor who accompanied Hall to the school, saw him installed, and chatted with Dr. Peabody and the masters, especially William Amory Gardner (WAG), on whose yacht the *America* her father had sailed. It was the first of what would be many trips, for she thought of Hall as being as much her son as her brother.

She went through her second winter in New York calmly. Just as at Allenswood she had taken the younger girls under her wing, she now eased the ordeal for those in the new crop of debutantes who were close friends. Though society had lost its terrors for her, she did not look forward to another round of parties, she was ready for something more. She joined a German and a Bible class.

Mlle. Souvestre had cautioned her against a preoccupation with social success, and the good example that Auntie Bye set proved Mlle. Souvestre's point to Eleanor. At home in the world of society, Mrs. Cowles did not let herself be limited by its conventions. People said of her, as they did of Eleanor, that she was no beauty but that her quick intelligence and cordiality made them forget that fact. In New York she had turned her drawing room "into a rendezvous for civic reformers, artists, writers, journalists, politicians"[13] at a time when society "fled in a body from a poet, a painter, a musician, or a clever Frenchman."[14] Her at-homes in Washington, Eleanor observed, brought "every kind of person into that house." She enjoyed people, drew them out, and made them feel at their best; later she would discuss them with Eleanor, commenting with sympathy, sometimes with spice. When Eleanor stayed with her, Bye was delighted to take her "soft-eyed" niece—so alert, so shyly curious—everywhere and to encourage her interest in public affairs.

The most important visitor to Bye's little house on N Street was Theodore

*An invitation to the White House during a visit with
Auntie Bye, Mrs. William Sheffield Cowles.*

Roosevelt, who came so frequently to talk with his sister that her home was called "the little White House." Eleanor would talk to her about them afterward, enough so that she could say later,

There was never a serious subject that came up while he was President that he didn't go to her at her home on N. Street and discuss with her, that was well known by all the family. He may have made his own decisions, but talking with her seemed to clarify things for him.[15]

Uncle Ted's disdain for society no doubt fed Eleanor's maturing determination to free herself from its demands. "It was one of Roosevelt's definite contributions to his time," wrote Mark Sullivan, "that he, being a Harvard man, and of inherited wealth, showed to others of his class ways to spend their lives with satisfaction to themselves and advantage to their country."[16] It was a doctrine that he particularly preached to the young.

He did not have much success with Alice, who, he wrote his sister Corinne in 1903, was "spending most of her time in Newport and elsewhere, associating with the Four Hundred—individuals with whom other members of her family have exceedingly few affiliations." Eleanor, however, found his attitude congenial.

One day Eleanor was on the Hudson River train with an elderly relative who never hesitated to state his views. Referring to the newspaper he was reading, he demanded, "What is this Junior League?" Not waiting for her answer, he rasped out his disapproval of girls who gave plays and made themselves conspicuous. He did not like it even if it was in the name of charity. "Young girls are getting altogether too bold nowadays!" Eleanor kept quiet. That was a time, she said, when young people did not disagree with their elders.[17] But her interest had been stirred, and later when she was asked why she didn't join the Junior League, she was the readier to do so because it had been criticized. She was acquainted with Mary Harriman and Nathalie Henderson, who were rallying the debutantes to give entertainments to help finance the "college settlements." While all debutantes were automatically inscribed as associate members on the lists of the Junior League, only a few were volunteering for active work in the settlement houses.

Eleanor soon joined this group. Along with Jean Reid, the daughter of Whitelaw Reid, she was assigned to work with the settlement house on Rivington Street. After a brief introductory lecture in "practical sociology," they plunged into teaching calisthenics and dancing to a group of young East Side girls, although they had had no previous training in how to manage children in groups. Jean played the piano, Eleanor was the teacher. "I had been in calisthenics classes and in dancing classes," wrote Eleanor, "and all I could do was put to use methods I had seen used and which I thought were good." The results were sometimes ludicrous. "The contribution of the college settlements to the education of the middle class," observed the historians Mary and Charles Beard, "was perhaps greater than its services to the poor."[18]

Until then Eleanor's contact with poor children had been slight: she had helped her father serve Thanksgiving dinner to the newsboys; she had assisted Uncle Vallie in decorating the Christmas tree for children in Hell's Kitchen; and she had trailed along with her aunts to sing at the Bowery Mission. But these activities had been charity, a continuation of the kind of work that had been started by her grandfather. Now she saw misery and exploitation on a scale she had not dreamed possible, and the pleas for legislative reform were more compelling to her because she saw the conditions to which they were addressed.

The Rivington Street Settlement, two blocks south of Houston Street in one of the most densely populated parts of the city, was a harsh introduction to social realities. When the settlement was founded in 1889 the neighborhood had been German. Then it had become predominantly Jewish; and now it was changing again as Italian emigrants flooded into the country. Settlement workers urged the residents to welcome the Italians and not to use the derogatory term "dago." The settlement activities were practical—kindergartens for the young children, a gymnasium, classes in cooking, carpentry, art, and dancing, picnics in the woods and at the beach, and a summer camp in the country—and the settlement was also the center of neighborhood effort for civic improvement. The headworker, in her report for the year Eleanor was there, hailed the advances that had been made—cleaner streets, tenements with more light and air, new schools—and then she added: "That further improvements will follow is assured by the fact that the neighborhood is beginning to demand them and to speak for itself, a most encouraging sign."[19]

The settlement's policy of encouraging slum dwellers to stand together and claim their rights was one phase of Eleanor's education in the realities of social change. Another was in the relationship of law and politics to social conditions. The girls and young women in the clubs and classes often failed to appear, and when the settlement workers investigated they found the explanation in the excessively long hours the poor were obliged to work. The College Settlement Association enlisted the help of Miss Mary Van Kleeck of Smith College to make a study of working hours of women in factories. Such a report, it was hoped, would prod state authorities into enforcing the law that limited the hours that women and children could work to sixty per week.

The Van Kleeck report startled the city. Ten hours, it noted quietly, "make a long day spent watching and feeding a needle which sets 4,000 stitches a minute; or treading in standing position the pedals of an ironing machine." Yet Miss Van Kleeck found that it was "not uncommon" for young girls in factories to work twelve, thirteen, and even fourteen hours a day, six days a week, at a weekly wage of $6.

Eleanor took her duties at Rivington Street very seriously—too much so, in the view of her cousin Susie, in whose home on East Seventy-Sixth Street Eleanor was staying. When her afternoon at Rivington Street conflicted with a party, Cousin Susie insisted that Eleanor give up the class; Eleanor gave up the party. "She says I am the most obstinate person she knows as she would have preferred my giving out this afternoon and going to-night!" Cousin Susie pitied the man Eleanor might marry. For her part, Eleanor pitied Cousin Susie's husband, Henry Parish, whom the family described as "a dear sweet man" except that he never dared stand up to his wife and at Newport kept his bottle of Scotch hidden in his hatbox. Cousin Susie was a very tall, very proper woman, who in motion reminded the younger people of "a full-rigged ship."[20] She was strait-laced and opinionated and refused to have anything to do with people who were outside Society. Nevertheless, she was very kind to Eleanor, and although Eleanor refused to be frightened by Susie's apprehensions about her safety on Rivington Street, she was devoted to her and her husband.

Eleanor liked the settlement-house children and they liked her.

Poor Jean [Reid] has grippe and couldn't go to Rivington Street with me today, so I took my first class alone and I've not had such real fun for weeks. The children were dears, a little obstreperous at times but I hope they enjoyed it in the end as much as I did. Two of them walked back to the cars [?] with me and we had such a nice talk, I cannot see how Caroline and Gwendolyn after going once could miss as they do. I don't believe either of them really cares for children or they would love going down there and not treat it as a burden. I stayed very late and only got home at a quarter to six and it was such a relief to know that I didn't have to start out for the Barker's at once.[21]

Jean recovered and returned to the class, and Eleanor was relieved that she too enjoyed the assignment: "I thought she might hate it and refuse to go again!"[22]

When Gwendolyn Burden needed help in Ludlow Street in her sewing class, Eleanor volunteered, "but the children were not as nice as mine and I am glad I do not have to go regularly." Occasionally she had disciplinary problems at Rivington Street and had to send children home, which she "hated" doing, but on the whole the experience, after the agonies of trying to shine in society, was a reassuring one. Her class at Rivington Street, she summed up, was "the nicest part of the day."[23]

She quickly emerged as one of the leaders of the Junior League. Of a meeting at Nathalie Henderson's, she reported that it had been "a little trying . . . I made myself disagreeable to Mary Harriman by telling her I could not call meetings at a moment's notice and by opposing several of her suggestions successfully!"

The settlement house was part of a network of reform organizations that included the Public Education Association, the Women's Trade Union League, and the Consumers League. Eleanor became a member of the Consumers League, a militant group devoted to combating the abuses disclosed in the Van Kleeck report. The league was headed by the redoubtable Maud Nathan; Eleanor's aunt, Mrs. Douglas Robinson, was a vice president, as was Mrs. Fulton Cutting, Helen's mother. It operated by means of a "white list" that named the retail establishments which dealt "justly" with their employees and which the league's members and friends were urged to patronize. To get on the "white list" a retail firm, among other requirements, had to give equal pay for equal work, observe a ten-hour working day, and pay a minimum wage of $6 per week. Another of the League's major goals was to obtain legislation that would prohibit child labor, and, in particular, the cruel "sweating system" where children of kindergarten age toiled away in their slum homes at such jobs as making artificial flowers.

The league's key committee was the one that determined whether a merchant had complied with the league's standards. The Rivington Street headworker was on that committee, and Eleanor became involved in its activities.

Her first trip to check on conditions in department stores proved to be valueless. Did the women have stools to sit on behind the counters when they were not waiting on customers, she was asked afterward. She had not looked, she confessed; it had not occurred to her that perhaps they could never sit down and rest. "And if I had looked I would not have understood what it meant until someone else pointed out its meaning." But she was a willing pupil, and the league asked her to investigate the sweatshops in which artificial feathers and flowers were being made.

I was appalled. In those days, these people often worked at home, and I felt I had no right to invade their private dwellings, to ask questions, to investigate conditions. I was frightened to death.

But this was what had been required of me and I wanted to be useful. I entered my first sweatshop and walked up the steps of my first tenement. . . . I saw little children of four or five sitting at tables until they dropped with fatigue. . . .[24]

She was finding a vocation and a role, and she applied herself with scrupulous diligence to the settlement tasks. Already her debutante friends were classing her with Mary Harriman and Nathalie Henderson, whom they regarded as "superior beings," and even among her more frivolous debutante associates she was not an object of fun. Would-be scoffers were deterred by Eleanor's dignity and universal helpfulness. She did not have "social lightheartedness," but girls liked to tell her their most intimate secrets because she gave everyone the feeling that she was interested in them, as indeed she was.

Among the young men, too, she had many admirers, including some whose interest was serious. But they had missed their chance. A young man who knew his mind had asked her for her hand, and she had become secretly engaged.

10. *"For Life, for Death"*

FRANKLIN ROOSEVELT's most fateful action as a gay, charming, princely young man of twenty-one was to pick shy, somewhat plain Eleanor Roosevelt to be his wife. It showed remarkable perspicacity. We can only guess at his reasons; his courtship letters were burned—by Eleanor Roosevelt, probably in 1937 when she was writing the first volume of her autobiography and his youthful avowals of constancy unto death were perhaps too painful to reread. She said she burned them because they were too private. He preserved hers.

Franklin was a junior at Harvard when he encountered Eleanor after her return from Allenswood and began to see in her an appealing woman rather than interesting cousin. They had run into each other occasionally before she went abroad. At a Christmas party in 1898 at the West Orange country house of Eleanor's aunt, Corinne Robinson, a sixteen-year old Franklin, then a Groton student, had asked an unhappy, pathetically dressed fourteen-year-old Eleanor to dance, for which she had been deeply grateful. But it had not been just cousinly chivalry. A few weeks before the Robinson party Franklin had written his parents to ask, "How about Teddy Robinson and Eleanor Roosevelt? They would go well and help to fill out the chinks at a Hyde Park Christmas party." It was about this time, too, that he was said to have remarked to his mother, "Cousin Eleanor has a very good mind."[1]

Still, his interest in Eleanor was scarcely distinguishable from his lively awareness of a number of other teen-age girls, including Alice Roosevelt, with whom he exchanged a few teasing letters. And they did not correspond while Eleanor was at Allenswood, although both were already conscientious letter writers. But one day during the summer of Eleanor's return from finishing school, Franklin saw her on the train to Tivoli, hastened over, and took her to the car in which his mother was sitting. Eleanor remembered the occasion all her life. Sara, although her husband had died two years before, was still entirely in black, with a heavy veil that fell from her hat to the ground, as was the custom for widows. Eleanor was held spellbound by her beauty, and the son was as handsome as the mother—tall, slender, with sloping shoulders. His nose, pinched at the bridge, gave him a patrician aspect; his eyes were a cool grayish-blue, arch and gay and jauntily self-confident. And Eleanor, however insecure she may have felt, was outwardly self-assured, clothed with the authority of three years abroad. Eleanor at seventeen, said Caroline Drayton, one of her contemporaries, was "dear [and] affectionate . . . simple [and] spontaneous."

She had a Gibson-girl figure, a pensive dignity, the charm of tenderness, and the sweetness of youth.

Franklin's interest was revived, and later that autumn when the social season was under way he came down from Harvard for some of the debutante parties. Although Eleanor nowhere mentioned his presence at the social affairs that were such "agony" to her, her name began to appear in his diary with increasing frequency. He noted that she was at the horse show, and two weeks later, when he was again in New York for Christine Roosevelt's dance, his diary read "Lunched with Eleanor." And before he went to Hyde Park for Christmas he shopped with his mother until 3:30 but then slipped away for "tea with Eleanor."

After Christmas week in Hyde Park and New York he, too, was invited to Washington for the New Year's festivities, and stayed with Mrs. Cowles. She was "Cousin Bamie" to him, and he was one of her favorites in the younger generation. He went to afternoon tea with Alice at the White House and noted in his diary that Eleanor was staying with Alice. At the New Year's Day reception, he and Eleanor stood in the "inner circle" and watched with fascination the thousands filing through the White House to shake hands with the president, who afterward went out for his customary canter "as fresh as a daisy," according to the papers. They all dined with the president, and then "to theatre and sit near Eleanor." "Very interesting day," the young man commented in his diary.[2]

A month later, Eleanor was among those his half brother Rosy invited to celebrate Franklin's twenty-first birthday, an affair that Franklin described as "very jolly!" At the end of the school year in June there was a house party at Hyde Park, and Eleanor's name began to appear in Sara Roosevelt's journal as well as in her son's diary. "Muriel [Robbins, Franklin's cousin, also called Moo], Eleanor and her maid, Franklin, Lathrop Brown and Jack Minturn came yesterday. Mary Edmund and young Hollister came to dine. Had singing after dinner."[3] They all walked to the river "in the rain," Franklin recorded, dined with the Rogers, who were next-door neighbors, played tennis and blind man's bluff. It was a long week end. Eleanor arrived on Saturday, and Franklin took her to the train on Tuesday.

He then dashed back to Cambridge to pick up his diploma. He had obtained it in three years but planned to return to Harvard to do graduate work and, what was more important to him, to run the *Crimson*, of which he had been elected president. His degree in his pocket, he boarded the *Half Moon*, the family's sixty-foot schooner, in New Bedford, raced her off Newport and then sailed her back to Hyde Park. Again there was a house party which Eleanor, accompanied by the inevitable maid, attended, along with those whom Sara described as "my six young people." They sailed, dined on board the *Half Moon*, went on a hay ride, took the cliff walk along the river. A week later Sara noted in her journal that everyone had had tea with Eleanor at Tivoli, but if she suspected that Franklin's interest in Eleanor was becoming serious, she said nothing, not even when, before going abroad July 24, he invited Eleanor to come to Campobello after he returned. She arrived on August 28, and on September 3 Sara noted, "Eleanor left at six with her maid. We took her to Eastport, on the *Half Moon*." A more perceptive observation was made by Mrs. Hartman Kuhn of Boston, whose red-shingled, green-shuttered summer home was next to the Roosevelts' at Campobello. When Franklin and Eleanor announced their engagement fifteen months later, Mrs. Kuhn wrote Eleanor that she could not pretend to be surprised: "The first summer at Campo I saw most clearly how Franklin admired you. . . ."

Few saw that that admiration was turning into love. Already Franklin was a man who masked his deepest feelings in debonair banter, preferring to gain his way by diplomacy and charm rather than by frontal assault. Indeed, many of his contemporaries belittled him as being all shining surface and artifice. Young Corinne Robinson taxed him with lacking conviction and laughingly called him "hypocrite" and "feather-duster."[4] His Oyster Bay female cousins did not consider him a great prize in the matrimonial sweepstakes. "He was the kind of boy whom you invited to the dance, but not the dinner," said Alice; "a good little mother's boy whose friends were dull, who belonged to the minor clubs and who never was at the really gay parties."[5] But this was said years later when envy and politics had sharply divided the Oyster Bay and Hyde Park clans.

Some of the Delanos had their own theory to explain Alice's spitefulness. "Alice was angry about Franklin's choosing Eleanor," Franklin's cousin Laura Delano maintained. "That's always in the picture. She was angry because she didn't catch him."[6] In the course of researching this book, when the author asked Mrs. Longworth about this, her expressive face registered incredulity, alarm, and horror, not wholly unmixed with interest, as if her very active mind were examining the story for all its possibilities. "I liked him, of course," she finally said, but he was too "prissy," too much of "a good little mother's boy" for her. And since she was not entirely persuaded that the interviewer believed these protestations, Mrs. Longworth told the *Washington Post* that she had "tape recorded her denial, so that future generations can hear in her own voice and words just how absurd she considers such a suggestion to be."[7]

No other contemporary of Eleanor, Alice, or Franklin confirmed Laura Delano's intriguing theory; on the contrary, everyone was skeptical of it, but they also disagreed with the Oyster Bay portrait of Franklin as a mollycoddled lightweight. "They exaggerate" was the dry comment of a contemporary who went to the same balls, attended the same football games, moved in the same social circles, and was Republican in her sympathies.[8] As an undergraduate, Franklin led a strenuous social life in Boston and New York and suffered from no lack of invitations to dinners as well as dances. His diary was sprinkled with the names of young ladies with whom he teased and flirted, and when the news of his engagement to Eleanor was disclosed more than one young female heart must have fluttered with regret. No, he could pick and choose, and his choice of Eleanor showed that beneath his surface gaiety there was seriousness and a life plan. "We used to say 'poor Franklin,' " Alice Longworth acknowledged. "The joke was on us."

While neither his mother nor his friends seemed to perceive the strength of his feeling for Eleanor, she, persuaded of her plainness, refused to believe it. He had stayed on at Campobello after she left, a good part of the time in the company of Evelyn Carter, daughter of the governor of Barbados, who made no secret of her interest in him. From Campo he went to Oyster Bay to stay with the Emlen Roosevelts; Alice Parker, an attractive debutante whom he had seen in London, was also a guest. And Miss Carter turned up again at Lenox while Franklin was visiting Mrs. Kuhn before returning to Hyde Park. But if these dalliances caused Eleanor to wonder about the young man's intentions, she should have been reassured by her overnight stay at Hyde Park on her way back to Tivoli from Groton, where she had left Hall. Franklin took her on a long ride through the woods in the morning and in the afternoon on a drive in the dog cart. Their talk was intimate and relaxed. She told him of her worries about "the Kid," as she called Hall, and he spoke of his plans for the *Crimson* and his indecision about whether to enroll in the law school or the graduate faculty. She must have sensed that he was eager to please her, for he left for Cambridge the next day, ushered at the football game, and then went immediately to Groton so that he could report to her that "the Kid" was getting on "finely" and was "much liked." No matter how devoted he was to Groton, he hardly would have left Cambridge the week end that he was preparing, almost singlehandedly (since most of the staff was not yet back), to get out the first issue of the *Crimson* if he had not wished to impress the young lady in Tivoli with his thoughtfulness.

She, too, was interested, even to the point of being a little jealous, as her first letter to him after his return to Cambridge reveals, but she was also on guard for a rebuff.

[Oct. 3, 1903]
Tivoli
Dear Franklin   Friday
Many thanks for your note & the "token from the sea," which I think you should have sent to someone else however, don't you?
Hall wrote me that he had seen you at Groton last Sunday. It was kind of you to look him up when you must have had so much to do. I hope he is all right. I can't tell much from his letters.
Did you have to work very hard on the "Crimson"? I hoped someone would turn up to help in the end.
I am so anxious to hear what you have decided to do this year & also whether you can come here on the 16th. I am hoping that you will be able to get down & of course I would like you to come back here after the game on the 17th if Cousin Sally does not mind & you are willing to stay in this quiet spot.
Please don't do anything you don't want to do however as I shall quite understand if you decide to go to Hyde Park instead of coming here.
Yours in haste,
Is the address on this right?   Eleanor Roosevelt.

"It is not so much brilliance as effort that is appreciated here," wrote Franklin in his first editorial, addressed to the freshman class—the "determination to accomplish something." He felt that with Eleanor at his side his own great dreams would stand a better chance of realization. "It was nice of you to write me," Eleanor said in her next letter, "and you know quite well you need not apologize for writing about yourself. I should think history and political economy would be most interesting and much the most useful for you in the future and *of course* you are going to get an A.M."

An indignant reproach in the same letter made it clear that this was more than cousinly advice. "What were you thinking of when you wrote not to tell me whether you could get down on the 16th and come to me or not?" she asked. She cared a great deal, even if convention prescribed that she betray no interest in him and even if her grandmother looked askance when she received a letter from a man. Franklin had not replied to Eleanor because he had wanted to find out first what his mother was planning for the week end of the Harvard-West Point game. Who was coming on the sixteenth, he had written her. "Are H. [Helen] Cutting, Eleanor and Moo [Muriel Robbins] coming to us?" Everything was arranged satisfactorily, and although it poured on the day of the game it was a joyful week end for Franklin and Eleanor. "Harvard wins 5 to 0," he recorded in his Line-A-Day. "Eleanor and I catch train, others miss it, drive up from Poughkeepsie." An unexpected participant in some of their gaieties was Alice Roosevelt, who that week end was a guest of the Ogden Millses at their estate a few miles up the Hudson at Staatsburgh; she came down, escorted by a young man, for tea.

"Cousin Sally [Sara Roosevelt] was very sad after you left on Sunday," Eleanor reported to Cambridge, "and the only thing which cheered her at all was the thought of having you on the 3d all to herself." The romance was flourishing. She now signed herself "Your affectionate cousin" and made her plans with his in mind. She had been invited to a party at the Levi Mortons' and was unable to decide whether or not to go; however, "I think I'll chance there being someone there I like and accept."

She worried about his health. "I suppose you are hard at work now, but please be a little careful of your eyes, for it is really foolish to fool with them you know, and besides it worries Cousin Sally so when you are not all right. She spoke of it several times after you had gone." But then, a little conscience-stricken that she might sound too schoolma'amish, she apologized. "I am afraid this letter has a good deal of horrid advice in it. Please remember, however, that you have told me I was 'grandmotherly' and don't blame me too much!"

Grandmotherly! Do Prince Charmings fall in love with "grandmotherly" young ladies? Yes, if under his gay surface the prince harbors large ambitions that require a helpmate rather than a playfellow to bring them to fruition. "Even at that age," recalled Isabella Greenway, who, as a debutante, took New York society by storm in 1904, "life had, through her orphanage, touched her and made its mark in a certain aloofness from the careless ways of youth. The world had come to her as a field of responsibility rather than as a playground."[9]

Neither young Roosevelt was leading a monastic life. Franklin's letters to his mother spoke of a "small dance" at the golf club, a visit to Beverly, a swimming party at the home of Alice Sohier, a Boston belle, week ends at New Bedford. Eleanor moved from one country house to another: one week end she was at Llewellyn Park, Cousin Susie's estate in the fashionable Oranges; she spent another at Ophir Hall, the Westchester establishment of Whitelaw Reid, owner of the *New York Tribune* and the father of Jean Reid, Eleanor's associate at Rivington Street; and she accepted the invitation of Franklin's cousin Muriel Robbins to attend the Tuxedo Ball. The Boston Brahmins had created Brook Farm; New York society had Tuxedo Park, a 600,000 acre country club community thirty miles from New York City whose "cottages" were casemented in the English style, whose clubhouse was staffed with English servants, and whose grounds were enclosed by a high fence to guard against intruders from the lower orders.

"I am glad you think I am going to enjoy the Tuxedo Ball," she wrote Franklin. "I do not feel quite so confident as I haven't seen any of my last winter's friends in so long that I fully expect to be forgotten." Did she go to the ball in order to prove to him that she was not too "grandmotherly"? "Tuxedo was great fun," her next letter insisted, "and I only wish you had been there, though I don't doubt you had a more restful time wherever you were, as we were up till all hours of the night, which nearly finished me." She would be going up to the Mortons' on the 3:30 train and if he did not have to go up earlier "it would be splendid to go up together." There was a mild rebuke in this letter, one that would be repeated often in the future. "By the way do you know you were an 'unconscionable' time answering my last letter and you would not be hearing from me so promptly if I did not want you surely to lunch with me on the 14th." Sara Roosevelt's entry in her journal for November 14 indicated that the Morton week end had worked out as Eleanor had planned.

Got up at 7 and at 7:30 Franklin and Lyman came from Boston. After they had their baths, we all had breakfast and we all lunched with Eleanor at Sherry's, also her cousin Mrs. Parish. We came up at 3:30 and Eleanor, Franklin and Lyman went up to Ellerslie to the Mortons to spend Sunday.

Ellerslie was another palatial country house, high above the Hudson at Rhinecliff, owned by Levi P. Morton, who had been governor of New York and vice president under Benjamin Harrison. The Morton girls were sophisticated and fun-loving, temperamentally closer to Alice than to Eleanor. "I am glad you enjoyed the Morton's," Eleanor wrote Franklin, "as I thought it very pleasant." Her praise of the party was tepid, but her comments on a poem that Franklin had sent her on his return to Cambridge were much livelier. She thought it was "splendid" poetry, "but what ideals you have to live up to! I like 'Fear nothing and be faithful unto death,' but I must say I wonder how many of 'we poor mortals' could act up to that!"*

In mid-October Franklin invited her to Cambridge for the Harvard-Yale game, after which he hoped to join her at Groton during her visit to Hall. She would accept, she replied, if Muriel Robbins and her mother also were going.

---

* Efforts by the Library of Congress and others to trace the poem from the line quoted by Eleanor were unsuccessful. Perhaps it was written by young Franklin Roosevelt, in which case the loss to history caused by Mrs. Roosevelt's destruction of his courtship letters is even more regrettable, even though the last part of the line, indeed the whole sentence, echoes the Bible, Revelations 2:10.[10]

Muriel's brother Warren was at Harvard and they could chaperone her. On Saturday, November 21, Franklin wrote in his diary:

In town at 10:30 and Eleanor and I walk to the Library, see the pictures, and then walk up Beacon Hill. I out to lunch in Cambridge and lead the cheering at the Harvard-Yale game, 16–0, but our team does well. Show Eleanor my room and see them off to Groton.

The next day he followed Eleanor to Groton and spent the day with her, beginning with church in the morning and ending with chapel in the evening. During this visit to Groton he proposed to her. How he put it we do not know. Some biographers have written that he said, "I have only a few bright prospects now," to which the nineteen-year-old Eleanor is said to have replied, "I have faith in you. I'm sure you'll really amount to something someday."[11] This account leaves one dissatisfied. Another version seems more in character. According to this account, Franklin said that he was sure he would amount to something some day, "with your help," and the surprised girl replied, "Why me? I am plain. I have little to bring you."[12]

Eleanor returned to New York trembling with excitement even though she was beset by questions. She found Franklin irresistible, but was he sure? Was she? What would happen to her brother Hall? What was her duty to her grandmother? And, as so often in her life, her joy was shadowed by tragedy. Her Great-Uncle James King Gracie had died, and her first letter to Franklin after the Groton week end first dwelt on that. "I am more sorry than I can say for he has always been very kind and dear to us and he and Aunt Gracie both loved my Father very dearly and so it is just another link gone." She was worried, too, about her Aunt Corinne, for whom the death was a terrible blow and who was "almost crazy" with grief.

In spite of it all I am very happy. I have been thinking of many things which you and I must talk over on Sunday. Only one thing I want to tell you now. Please don't tell your Mother you have to come down to see Mr. Marvin on Sunday, because I never want her to feel that she has been deceived & if you have to tell her I would rather you said you were coming to see me for she need not know why. Don't be angry with me Franklin for saying this, & of course you must do as you think best. Ellen told me they were all coming down Saturday night by boat so you will have plenty of company. Please don't get tired out this week & try to rest a little bit at Fairhaven. I am afraid this letter sounds very doleful, for I really am sorry about dear Uncle Gracie & the whole day has been a bit trying so please forgive me & the next will be cheerier & more coherent I hope! Goodnight,

Always affectionately
Eleanor Roosevelt.

Her next letter reveals something of what she and Franklin had said to each other that Sunday in Groton. It represents the first time she felt free to give voice to the strength of her feeling for Franklin.

[Nov. 24, 1903]
Tuesday night

Franklin dear,
   I promised that this letter should be cheerier so I don't suppose I ought to

write to-night for the day has been very trying. I wanted to tell you though that I *did* understand & that I don't know what I should have done all day if your letter had not come. Uncle Gracie's funeral is to be on Friday at ten. I have been twice to-day to Auntie Corinne's & I have promised to spend to-morrow morning there also. She looks so worn & I wish I could do something more to help her. She seems to have every thing to arrange & settle. Teddy came this afternoon I am thankful to say so he will be some help to her & a great comfort. I am dreading Friday. I know I ought not to feel as I do or even to think of myself but I have not been to a funeral in ten years & it makes me shudder to think of it. The others have all gone to the play so I am all alone to-night as I would of course go nowhere this week, & I have been thinking & wishing that you were here. However, I know it is best for you not [to] come until Sunday & for me also as I should be a very dreary not to say a very weary companion just at present & there are so many things I know I ought to think of before I see you again. I am afraid so far I've only thought of myself & I don't seem to be able to do anything else just now.

Do you remember the verse I tried to recite to you last Sunday? I found it to-day & I am going to write it out for you, because it is in part what it all means to me:

> Unless you can think when the song is done,
> No other is left in the rhythm;
> Unless you can feel, when left by one,
> That all men else go with him;
> Unless you can know, when upraised by his breath,
> That your beauty itself wants proving;
> Unless you can swear, *"For life, for death!"*
> Oh, fear to call it loving!
>
> Unless you can muse in a crowd all day
> On the absent face that has fixed you;
> Unless you can love, as the angels may,
> With the breath of heaven betwixt you;
> Unless you can dream that his faith is fast,
> Through behooving & unbehooving;
> Unless you can die when the dream is past—
> Oh, never call it loving![13]

I wondered if it meant "for life, for death" to you at first but I know it does now. I do not know what to write. I cannot write what I want. I can only wait & long for Sunday when I shall tell you all I feel I cannot write.

Goodnight. I hope you will all have a very happy Thanksgiving at Fairhaven & please don't get tired out by working at night.

Always devotedly
Eleanor.

She had wondered whether she, too, cared enough to be able to say that it was "for life, for death," and she discussed her feelings with Cousin Susie on her return to New York. Whatever her cousin's response, Eleanor's "great curiosity" about life and her "desire to participate in every experience that might be the lot of woman" pulled her toward marriage. She was swept up by "the urge to be a part of the stream of life," and it seemed entirely natural and right to her to say yes to Franklin.[14]

Franklin, meanwhile, had gone to Fairhaven, the Delano clan's gathering place, where he told his mother that he had proposed to Eleanor. "Franklin gave me quite a startling announcement," she wrote in her journal. Then he went to New York, where there was a note from Eleanor: "Mrs. Parish wants you to lunch with us tomorrow if you can and also to take tea with us. I do hope that you will come to both if you can for I want you every minute of your stay."

"It is impossible to tell you what these last two days have been to me," she wrote him afterward, thinking he was on his way to Cambridge, "but I know they have meant the same to you so that you will understand that I love you dearest and I hope that I shall always prove worthy of the love which you have given me. I have never known before what it was to be absolutely happy."

But Franklin had not left New York. His mother had returned, and it is not difficult to sense the surprise and disapproval in the terse entry, "I find Franklin still in New York." The next day he went to Seventy-sixth Street and accompanied Eleanor to see Sara. "I had a long talk with the dear child."[15]

To Sara, Franklin's announcement meant surrendering her exclusive relationship with her son and her plans for their life together after he left Harvard. She did not surrender easily. Could they *really* be sure they cared enough, she asked them. They were young—shouldn't both of them think it over and see what the lapse of time and being away from each other would do to their feelings? Her father, Warren Delano, had married at thirty-three, after he had made a name for himself and had something to offer a woman. Franklin was only twenty-one and Eleanor was just nineteen; they had plenty of time.

These were the reservations that Sara expressed, but Eleanor thought an additional reason was her desire that he should make "a more worldly and social match."[16] There was probably another constraint that was never voiced but that was always in the background—Eleanor's father's alcoholism, not to mention her uncles'. Girls were carefully chaperoned, and Eleanor radiated purity and innocence, but the maid who invariably accompanied her reflected her own or her family's awareness that she was more vulnerable than other girls her age to rumor and gossip if she overstepped the strict line of decorum that society drew for young ladies. As uneasy as Sara may have been about Eleanor's flawed heritage, she kept it to herself. She only pleaded with them to keep their engagement secret for a year, during which time she would take Franklin on a cruise as a test of how they really felt. They agreed to her conditions.

After Franklin returned to Harvard, he wrote his mother a comforting letter.

I know what pain I must have caused you and you know I wouldn't do it if I really could have helped it—mais tu sais, me voila! That's all that could be said—I know my mind, have known it for a long time, and know that I could never think otherwise: Result: I am the happiest man just now in the world; likewise the luckiest—And for you, dear Mummy, you know that nothing can ever change what we have always been & always will be to each other—only now you have two children to love & to love you—and Eleanor as you know will always be a daughter to you in every true way—

Eleanor sent a sympathetic and understanding letter to Sara, tenderly buttressing Franklin's point that Sara was gaining a daughter, not losing a son.

> 8 East 76th Street
> Dec. 2d, 1903,
> Wednesday.

Dearest Cousin Sally,

I must write you & thank you for being so good to me yesterday. I know just how you feel & how hard it must be, but I do so want you to learn to love me a little. You must know that I will always try to do what you wish for I have grown to love you very dearly during the past summer.

It is impossible for me to tell you how I feel toward Franklin. I can only say that my one great wish is always to prove worthy of him.

I am counting the days to the 12th when I hope Franklin & you will both be here again & if there is anything which I can do for you you will write me, won't you?

With much love dear Cousin Sally,
Always devotedly

> Eleanor.

Eleanor's days were full of activity but they were dominated by thoughts of her beloved, to whom she wrote now with ever deepening commitment.

Dearest Franklin,

Though I only wrote last night I must write you just a line this morning to tell you that I miss you every moment & that you are never out of my thoughts dear for one moment. I was thinking last night of the difference which one short week can make in one's life. Everything is changed for me now. I am so happy. Oh! so happy & I love you *so* dearly. I cannot begin to write you all I should like to say, but you know it all I am sure & I hope that you too dearest are very, very happy. I am counting the days to the 12th & the days in between seem so *very* long.

She was generous to Sara in spite of the onerous conditions the older woman had exacted from them.

I found the sweetest, dearest letter here from your Mother last night. Boy dear,* I realize more and more how hard it is for her & we must both try always to make her happy & I do hope some day she will learn to love me. She is coming to town to-day for a few days & says she will telephone me & try to see me.

She had told Cousin Susie of Sara's reaction to the engagement. Cousin Susie felt, Eleanor wrote Franklin, "as I do that your Mother's feelings ought to be considered first of all." Cousin Susie also thought it would be all right to tell Eleanor's grandmother what they had decided, and Eleanor went to Tivoli to see Mrs. Hall. "I have told her that I shall not be definitely engaged until next year and she has *promised* me to tell no one that I am even thinking of such a thing, so I hope all will go well."[17]

Was she sure that she was really in love, her grandmother asked. "I solemnly answered 'yes,' " she wrote in her autobiography, "and yet I know now that it was years later before I understood what being in love was or what loving really meant."[18]

*Eleanor's father had been addressed as "Boy dear" and "Boy darling" by his Aunt Ella.

11. *Mother and Son*

———

AT THE OLDER WOMAN'S REQUEST, Eleanor met Sara Roosevelt two days after Franklin's return to Cambridge. The session turned out to be quite painful, the first of many duels that in time would cause all of them great agony. The gracious lady, despite her protestations of regard for "the delightful child of nineteen whom I had known and loved since babyhood," was determined to create difficulties for the two young people. And in the contest of wills that Sara foresaw with her equally stubborn son she did not scruple to take advantage of Eleanor's touching eagerness to "always try to do" what the older woman wished. But if Sara had seen the letter that Eleanor wrote at her request to Franklin, she would not have drawn much comfort from it. Although Eleanor had transmitted Sara's views to Franklin, as Sara had asked, in doing so she made it perfectly clear what she herself wanted.

[Dec. 4, 1903]

Boy darling,   Friday evening

I have rather a hard letter to write you tonight & I don't quite know how to say what I must say & I am afraid I am going to give you some trouble, however I don't see how I can help it.

I went to the apartment this morning & saw your Mother there for a few minutes & then we went out together & had a long talk. She is coming down next Friday to meet you & she wants us to lunch & dine with her & then she wants you to go to Hyde Park with her Sunday morning. Helen and Cousin Rosie have been asking when you were coming home. She thinks they are sure to hear you are in New York & say that you are loafing & never coming home & she also says that if we go to church together we are sure to be seen. She also thinks that you ought to go home on account of the place, & your interest in it. She asked me to write you & I tell you all this dear because I think it only fair. Of course it will be a terrible disappointment to me not to have you on Sunday as I have been looking forward to it & every moment with you is very precious as we have so little of each other but I don't want you to stay if you feel it is your duty to go up & I shall understand of course. I realize that we may be seen if we go to church together, but we will have to choose some small church. However, I suppose your Mother feels more strongly on the subject than I do & I am afraid I must leave the whole thing to you to decide. Whatever you do I shall know to be right but I don't think your Mother quite realizes what a very hard thing she was asking me to do for I am hungry for every moment of your time, but you mustn't let what I want interfere with what you feel to be right dearest.

Now for the second thing. Cousin Sally said she did not think you would want to go on a trip now & she said she thought of taking a house in Boston for three months. She said she hoped I would come & stay once or twice during that time but if she took the house she did not want you to be coming to New York. I can understand how she feels but I'm afraid I can't promise not to want you more than twice in all that time. However I think you & she will have to talk it over next Saturday & decide that also. We also spoke about the holidays but I think that will wait until I see you as these were the only two things she asked me to write about.

I haven't had a letter from you this evening & I am wondering what has happened. I did so want it, but I hope it will come in the morning. I am going to Tivoli by the early train & coming down by the 7.19 on Sunday.

Oh! boy dear, I want you so much. I'm worried & tired & cross & I don't know what I ought to do. Please be very careful of yourself dearest & don't work yourself to death & when you can write me what you decide about Sunday.

Always your loving
Eleanor.

The decision was now up to Franklin, who was already aware of his mother's feeling; she had taken the precaution of writing him herself. As she had anticipated, he was not impressed by her arguments, although as a devoted son he was prepared to abide by her wishes if she insisted on them.

Alpha Delta Phi Club
Dec. 6, 1903,
Sunday.

Dearest Mama—

Yours of Friday came yesterday & I have been thinking over what you say about next Sunday—I am so glad, dear Mummy, that you are getting over the strangeness of it all—I knew you would and that you couldn't help feeling that not only I but you also are the luckiest & will always be the happiest people in the world in gaining anyone like E. to love & be loved by.

I confess that I think it would be poor policy for me to go to H.P. next Sunday—although, as you know and don't have to be told, I always love & try to be there all I can—I have been home twice already this term & I feel certain that J.R.R. & Helen w'd be sure to smell a rat if I went back for *part of a day* just a week before the holidays, for they would know I had been in N.Y. a whole day. *Also* if I am in N.Y. on Sunday *not a soul* need know I have been there at all as if we go to Church at all we can go to any old one at about 100th St. & the rest of the day w'd be in the house where none c'd see us. Of course I suppose you have told no one you w'd see me Saturday. Now if you really can't see the way clear to my staying in N.Y. of course I will go to H.P. with you—but you know how I feel—and also I think that E. will be terribly disappointed, as I will, if we can't have one of our first Sundays together—It seems a little hard & unnecessary on us both & I shall see you all day Saturday which I shouldn't have done had the great event not "happened." . . .

I am going to accept all invites for Xmas but don't you think we might have a house party for one or two days—Go ahead & ask whoever you want, we might have two girls & E. and if you name date & telegraph I will try to get two or three fellows—Indeed I don't intend to give up things—it w'd not be right to you or E—& she also will keep on going to things—You can imagine how completely happy I am—it gives a stimulus to everything I do. . . .

Ever your loving son   F.D.R.

All week the battle of wills raged, although it was couched in terms of endearment and respect; and all week Eleanor was on tenterhooks awaiting the outcome. He should not work too hard, she cautioned Franklin, "for I don't want to receive a wreck next Saturday. I am growing more and more impatient as the time draws near and I can hardly bear to think that you may not be able to stay here on Sunday." That was Tuesday. On Wednesday she still was hopeful that Sara would not insist on Franklin's going to Hyde Park, "for then I shall have you all to myself on Sunday," but she was afraid that his mother was going to want him on Sunday. "You see it is hard for her to realize that any one can want or need you more than she does, so I suppose I ought not to mind, only I do mind terribly, as you only can understand dear, however I mustn't complain, must I?" Sara evidently tried to force their hand by telling Rosy and his daughter Helen that Franklin was coming to Hyde Park. "I cannot tell you how sorry I am about Sunday," Eleanor wrote resignedly the next day, "but I am not in the least surprised as I knew your Mother would insist on your going to Hyde Park and since she has told Cousin Rosie and Helen it is certainly impossible for you to stay here without running the risk of their knowing it."

But young love prevailed over filial affection. However Franklin managed it, he and Eleanor spent Sunday as well as Saturday with each other. "We have had two happy days together," she wrote him after he had returned to Cambridge, "and you do not know how grateful I am for every moment which I have with you."

"She had already lived through so much unhappiness," a cousin commented, "and then to have married a man with a mother like Cousin Sally."[1] James Roosevelt had died in 1900 when Franklin was in his freshman year at college, and from that time on the forty-six-year-old Sara had focused all her thoughts, love, and energy on Franklin. For two winters she had rented a house in Boston to be close to him; they had traveled abroad together; when they were apart he wrote to her with a remarkable faithfulness. There was almost nothing she would not grant him except what was perhaps beyond the power of a lonely woman to grant an only child—independence.

"She was an indulgent mother but would not let her son call his soul his own" was the way a loyal friend of Eleanor's, quoting P. G. Wodehouse, sought to describe the strong-willed dowager's relationship with her son.[2] Except for Eleanor, no one ever exercised so strong a sway over his development, and Eleanor would always insist that not even she had so great an influence. Sara claimed Franklin as her own, even against her husband: "My son Franklin is a Delano, not a Roosevelt at all," she would assert with a proprietary air after he became president, and, strangely, in his final years his face came more and more to resemble his mother's. But the kinship was more than physical. In his will James Roosevelt had written: "I wish him [Franklin] to be under the influence of his mother." It was an unnecessary stipulation. He already was.

Handsome Sara (Sally) Delano was twenty-six, half as old as James Roosevelt, a widower of quiet dignity, when they were married in 1880. The marriage united two of the great Hudson River families, but the disparity in their ages had caused some astonishment in society, an amused surprise that had been reflected in a letter that Eleanor's father wrote home from London in 1880.

The sly old chap took great pleasure as indeed "Aunt Sara" (they passed for my Aunt and Uncle) did also, in relating to me the incidents and course of The Love Affair. When he slipped off before breakfast while he used to visit us in the country and say it was for his a.m. walk, the gay young dog went to post billets to his fair mistress. But truly they are a devoted couple and very kind to me.

The Delano family lived at Algonac, a stately brown and buff Victorian mansion with wide lawns overlooking the Hudson at Newburgh. Sara was born in 1854, the seventh child in a brood of eleven—six boys and five girls. Three years later her father, having lost his first China-trade fortune in the panic of 1857, returned to China to make "another million." This time it took him six years, and in 1862 he sent for his family, and Mrs. Delano and her children, including eight-year-old Sara, embarked on the square-rigger *Surprise* for the 128-day voyage. After their return to the United States at the end of the Civil War, Warren Delano invested his new wealth judiciously in coal and other securities; Sara's share of the legacy at his death was over a million dollars.[3]

Warren Delano was a patriarch, and everyone in his large Algonac household gave him unquestioning obedience. That was the custom of the times, said Sara later. But the Delano children went beyond custom: they were sure their father was infallible and knew best about everything. If her father frowned upon a young man, said Sara, that was the end of him, and she even permitted her father to help her with the letter so telling the gentleman. Perhaps James Roosevelt, twice her age, reminded her of her father, and perhaps that was a strong part of his attraction for her.[4]

James was a seventh-generation Roosevelt. His grandfather, born in 1760, also named James, had been the first of the Jacobus line to settle on the Hudson, after an attempt at gentleman-farming in Harlem had to be abandoned because of its rocky soil. The elder James died in 1847—"a highly respectable gentleman of the old school," wrote Philip Hone—and his son Isaac (1790–1863) completed his family's withdrawal from New York—and from public activity. Isaac was an eccentric. He attended Princeton and obtained a medical degree at Columbia, but never practiced because he was unable to stand the sight of blood or human pain. He turned instead to botanical research and led a secluded country existence in Dutchess County.

His son James (1828–1900), Franklin's father, was more enterprising. He went to Union College and then for two years did the Grand Tour, at one point in the turbulent year of 1848 even enlisting in Garibaldi's Red Shirts, who were then besieging Naples. But a siege can be a tedious affair, and James soon returned to the States. After attending Harvard Law School, he devoted himself to his investments and to cultivating a life of dignified rural amenity on the Hudson in the manor style of the British nobility, whom he much admired. He made several bids for great financial power by putting together mergers in coal and railroads, and even though the mergers failed his fortune was large enough to enable him to sustain the leisured life of a Hudson River gentleman at Springwood, his 1,000-acre Hyde Park estate. "English life to perfection," said Ward McAllister, who passed through Hyde Park and was enchanted with the avenue of old trees, the little village church, the gracious estates, and well-appointed houses.

Not the least of Hyde Park's English flavor came from James Roosevelt himself, a tall man with mutton chop whiskers who was rarely without his riding crop. He bred trotters and built a famous herd of Alderneys that he crossed with Jerseys and Guernseys.[5] He took the cure annually at a German spa, hunted in Pau, shot grouse in Scotland, and as a patriarch was among those who decided who belonged in New York society. While declining to take part in politics as not quite gentlemanly, he fulfilled a squire's obligation to the village, where he was a member of the Democratic caucus, belonged to the Volunteer Fire Company, was warden and vestryman of the church, and served as town supervisor. And as president of a small railroad he was entitled to take his private railroad car, the "Monon," to any part of the country. Such was the man and style of life to which Sara Delano happily accommodated herself.

James' first wife, Rebecca Howland, had died in 1876, and their son, James Roosevelt Roosevelt ("Rosy"), was a river grandee much in the mold of his father. Rosy and Sara were the same age but it was the widower who courted her, and in her eyes James Roosevelt was a delightful gentleman—high-minded, courteously persistent, and well descended. They worshiped the same household gods, had the same convictions about education and manners, *noblesse oblige*, and honor. They shared a love for the tranquil, secluded life of Hudson Valley and agreed that its old families, to most of whom they were related, embodied and defended the precious old standards in which they had been bred.

Warren Delano was not at all pleased with his daughter's choice. Although he was fond of the Hudson River squire—"the first person who has made me realize that a Democrat can be a gentleman"—he felt that James was too old for Sara. But this time she would not be swayed by his wishes, and on October 7, 1880, they were married at Algonac in a ceremony that, according to a New York paper, was witnessed "by a small number of the best representatives of New York Society." That afternoon they drove the twenty miles to Hyde Park, and by evening Sara, installed as mistress of Springwood, contentedly set about giving her husband the worshipful devotion and care she had bestowed upon her father—and removing all traces of her dead predecessor, Rebecca Howland.

Her diaries reflected the sedate, patterned existence into which she slipped without, if one is to judge by what she wrote there, pang or travail.

We drove to church in our new Victoria. In the afternoon James rowed me down to Rosedale. We hung our new water colors. The neighbors all have been to see us ... so we are busy returning a visit or two each day which gives an object for our drives. James keeps busy. He goes to town at least once a week and has school meetings, etc. I always go to the train with him and go for him again so he is not so long away from me. James is too devoted to me.

If their life together was not as bland as these entries suggest, if the realities were different, the code under which she had been reared would have obliged her to pretend otherwise. It would have been an affront against form and manners to have acknowledged the truth if the truth were unpleasant. This same attitude would be bred into her son Franklin. "If something was unpleasant and he didn't want to know about it, he just ignored it and never talked about it. . . . I think he always thought that if you ignored a thing long enough it would settle itself."[6] James adored her and she leaned on him, endowing his every action with an almost cloying significance. Yet she was no Grandma Hall, satisfied to be cherished, protected, and helpless; she was a woman of dominating will and active mind. When James died she assumed management of Hyde Park and, over her son's protests, kept it as a gentleman's estate rather than farming it as a business. She astutely used the money she had inherited to bolster her position as matriarch. It was perhaps an ideal marriage: she was wholly reverential, always deferred to her husband's wishes, and had everything her own way.

In 1882 the circle of her contentment was complete. A son, Franklin, was born. From then on her diaries reported equally on the doings of "dear James" and "darling Franklin." Franklin's was a happy boyhood. His parents doted on him, and as the first grandchild in the vast Delano clan (a cousin having died) he was petted and made much of by aunts and uncles. His father loved "riding and driving, sailing and ice-boating, skating and tennis" and could not wait to have his son join him as a companion in these interests. Whatever the boy wanted, he was given. A pony? As soon as his legs were long enough to straddle its back. A boat? He had the use of his father's yacht the *Half Moon*, a Campobello sea captain to teach him how to handle it, and a twenty-one footer of his own. A gun? His father handed him one at eleven. There were the neighboring Rogers boys and Mary Newbold for him to play with, trees, cliff, and a river in which to test his mettle, and a succession of nurses, governesses, and tutors to serve and instruct him and for whom he could do no wrong. He did not require strict handling, his mother said, because "instinctively" he was "a good little boy."[7] When he developed an interest in birds, he was encouraged to begin a collection, as he was with stamps. And the wishes and interests that his parents did not anticipate or were reluctant to grant, he learned to obtain by charm and persuasion. What is impressive is the steadiness and professionalism that he brought to these occupations. His interest in birds resulted in the most complete collection of Dutchess County birds in existence; his philatelic interest so impressed his Uncle Fred Delano that Fred turned over his albums to his young nephew, and their combined collection became one of the world's most famous.

In later years Franklin said, "All that is in me goes back to the Hudson." His boyhood world was ordered and harmonious, his childhood secure, happy, and protected—so different from Eleanor's storm-tossed early years. "He never saw ugly moods or emotions," Sara's biographer wrote on the basis of what Sara told her. "He was never the inwardly shrinking victim of conflicting interests, envenomed jealousies or ill-tempered words."[8] If anything, he was over-protected. "Much of his time, until he went to Groton, was spent with his father and me," Sara wrote, and though she disagreed with the assessment, there were "many people who pitied him for a lonely little boy, and thought he was missing a great deal of fun."[9] Geraldine Morgan, a Livingston from Staatsburgh who called herself a tomboy, said that Franklin was unable to make the Hyde Park baseball team recruited from the great houses; that, because he spent so much time with his mother and father, he found it difficult to play with the other children; and that the children who knew him felt sorry for him.[10] In the little memoir *My Boy Franklin,* Sara insisted that she had never tried to influence young Franklin against his own tastes and inclinations, and yet she also disclosed that it was only "eventually" that she had allowed his golden curls to be shorn, and that when, at the age of five, he had become melancholy he had "clasped his hands in front of him and said 'Oh, for freedom' " when she asked him why. She had been genuinely shocked.

That night I talked it over with his father who, I confess, often told me I nagged the boy. We agreed that unconsciously we had probably regulated the child's life too closely, even though we knew he had ample time for exercise and play.

The training and discipline of young Franklin were left to Sara, who had forceful opinions on the kind of man she wanted him to become. "Never, oh never," she confessed later, had it been her ambition for him that he should become president. "That was the last thing I should ever have imagined for him, or that he should be in public life of any sort." She had only one goal in mind for him:

that he grow to be a fine, upright man like his father and like her own father, a beloved member of his family and a useful and respected citizen of his community just as they were, living quietly and happily along the Hudson as they had.[11]

If the role of a country squire ever appealed to young Franklin, he was opened to larger ideals, different styles of life, and new heroes when he entered Groton in 1896. His cubicle at Groton was austere and cramped compared to his quarters at home, but it was his own and he loved it. The school's headmaster, the Reverend Endicott Peabody, was a stern and exacting disciplinarian, but his influence upon young Franklin was, next to his parents', greater than anyone's. Dr. Peabody's repeated theme, inside chapel and out, was service, particularly public service. "If some Groton boys do not enter political life and do something for our land it won't be because they have not been urged," he would say.

Groton helped shape Franklin's outlook, but it was not as liberating an influence on him as Allenswood was upon Eleanor. Because Franklin's regard for Endicott Peabody equaled Eleanor's for Marie Souvestre, the differences between headmaster and headmistress—not wholly to be explained by Groton's being a school for boys and Allenswood for girls—are not without interest.

Mlle. Souvestre was an agnostic—indeed, she called herself an atheist—who insisted that no area of human belief should be immune from critical inquiry and objective study. The Reverend Peabody "was by nature a believer rather than an inquirer. Theological perplexities and subtleties simply did not affect him."[12] In politics, Souvestre frequented the great Liberal houses, was a friend of Beatrice Potter Webb and a follower of Harrison's religion of humanity. Peabody was a conservative with an abiding faith in the status quo who shaped Groton into a splendid mechanism for instilling into the sons of the old-stock, white Anglo-Saxon Protestant upper class the elements of a "manly Christian character" that would make them worthy and capable of ruling America. Souvestre sided with the oppressed minorities everywhere. Peabody believed in the superiority of the Anglo-Saxon peoples, especially the English, and considered the Spanish-American War "the most righteous war that has been undertaken in this country." Souvestre's closest friends were in the artistic community and her library was adorned with avant-garde works. Peabody distrusted art and artists, and Groton boys with serious artistic interests had to hide them if they did not wish to be labeled outsiders. Souvestre was impatient with pupils who studied by rote and mechanically repeated what they had heard from her or had read in a book. Interest should motivate study, the rector agreed, but if interest was not aroused "the work should be done as a matter of duty." Souvestre, a Dreyfusard, was prepared to uphold the truth even if it meant undermining authority. At Groton "obedience came before all else"; rules and good form were upheld at the price of curiosity, sometimes of truth. In short, Peabody's values were those of order, hierarchy, discipline, and power; Souvestre's were those of heart, vision, and spirit.[13]

When Franklin left Groton he was attuned to the rector's admonitions that Groton boys should go into politics and public service. But service to whom, politics for what ends? To uphold the established order, as the rector preached, or to change it in favor of the victim, as Mlle. Souvestre believed? Roosevelt's answer in the great crisis of the thirties would be to conserve the system through the institution of change, a course that reflected the teachings of the rector tempered by those of Mlle. Souvestre as transmitted through Eleanor Roosevelt.

Sara's hopes that her son would lead the quiet life of a country gentleman were undermined from another quarter—Theodore Roosevelt. Franklin's enthusiasm as a boy at Groton and a young man at Harvard for "Cousin Theodore" was undisguised. Indeed, it was in connection with the Theodore Roosevelts that young Franklin showed that, devoted as he genuinely was to his mother, he could be as stubborn and determined as she. At the end of his first year at Groton (1897), while his parents were taking the annual cure at Bad Nauheim, Bamie wrote and asked whether Franklin could spend the Fourth of July week end with her at Oyster Bay. When his mother refused the invitation for him, he wrote back, "Please don't make any more arrangements for my future happiness." A few days later Theodore came to Groton to talk about his adventures as New York police commissioner—a talk that Franklin called "splendid"—and while there he also invited Franklin to Oyster Bay. The young man promptly accepted and wrote his parents: "I hope you will not refuse that too."

Theodore Roosevelt's compelling personality made a large impact upon the younger generation, and his influence was particularly felt at Harvard, which Franklin entered in 1900, where Theodore's example counteracted the Gold Coast cult of "Harvard indifference." He was a "great inspirer," said Eleanor, and Franklin was one of those whose inclination to enter politics definitely matured under his influence. At Harvard, Franklin was a clubman, went out for the crew, and took a heavy schedule of courses, but he spent most of his time on the *Crimson*, which he later said was probably "the most useful preparation I had in college for public service."

An undergraduate paper that he wrote on the Roosevelts in New Amsterdam should also have warned his mother that he would go with her as far as he could but that he was independent, self-reliant, and thought for himself. To Sara, the Roosevelt and Delano family trees—which she knew in every detail and which she would frequently expound (in later years, much to the irritation and impatience of her daughter-in-law)—were the basis for her feeling of caste and exclusiveness. Franklin's genealogical researches, however, had a democratic emphasis. In a sophomore essay, "The Roosevelt Family in New York before the Revolution," he wrote:

Some of the famous Dutch families in New York have today nothing left but their name—they are few in numbers, they lack progressiveness and a true democratic spirit One reason,—perhaps the chief—of the virility of the Roosevelts is this very democratic spirit. They have never felt that because they were born in a good position they could put their hands in their pockets and succeed. They have felt, rather, that being born in a good position, there was no excuse for them if they did not do their duty by the community, and it is because this idea was instilled into them from their birth that they have in nearly every case proved good citizens.[14]

It is true that Franklin was as strong a traditionalist as his mother, and later became a founder and pillar of the Dutchess County Historical Society, but he recognized what his mother did not, and the recognition was implicit in his Harvard essay, that in order to survive America's aristocracy had to justify itself by its works and a willingness to accommodate to change. This was Eleanor's feeling, too, although genealogy never had the fascination for her that it did for Franklin.

Franklin knew his own mind, and was determined to shape his own destiny. Although he was a devoted and loving son, if his views differed from his mother's in matters that he considered important to himself, he held his own course. He preferred to achieve his objectives by diplomacy, patience, and charm, but if it came to a direct collision, he, too, could be stubborn. That was the case with his decision to marry Eleanor.

Eleanor signed the letter she wrote Franklin after their week end together in New York "Little Nell," her father's favorite name for her. It was a sign of how completely she had surrendered her heart to her young lover by admitting him into her most precious secrets and endowing him with all the virtues she had ascribed to her father. "For many years," she later wrote, her father "embodied all the qualities I looked for in a man." But although he was her father's godson, Franklin was not like her father, nor was her father the "par-fit, gentil knight" that in her dream world Eleanor imagined him to be. In this inability to see the man she loved as he really was, she set the stage for much disappointment for herself.

Franklin, like Eleanor, was caught up in the tide of young love. He copied and sent to her his favorite poem from the *Sonnets from the Portuguese*. We can only guess which one it was. It "is an old friend of mine," Eleanor wrote back, "and queerly enough I read it over the other evening also and thought how beautiful and expressive it was." Why did he reread her old letters? she went on. "They really are not worth it. However, I don't suppose I ought to talk as I have kept all yours and probably read them far oftener than you read mine, but you write nice letters and I love them and mine are very often dull I fear."

She was wrapping Christmas presents and he was in the midst of class elections. He had been nominated for class marshal, but, as he had warned his family, he was not elected. The biggest prizes seemed to elude him, at Harvard as well as at Groton. He had entered Groton two years after the other boys in his form, was not a success at athletics, was not elected prefect, and was not one of the really popular boys. "He knew things they didn't; they knew things he didn't," Eleanor later said, commenting on the consequences of his entering his form two years late. "He felt left out. It gave him sympathy for people who are left out." At Harvard he not only missed election as class marshal but was not taken into Porcellian, Harvard's most exclusive club, which was by far "the greatest disappointment" in his life, he later confided to Bye's son, Sheffield Cowles.[15] After he became president, his Republican relatives ascribed his attacks on Wall Street and his hostility to bankers like Morgan and Whitney to his resentment about not making Porcellian. "He was getting back at them," they maintained. He had been disappointed, Eleanor agreed, and even developed something of an inferiority complex as a result; but the blow to his self-esteem at Harvard, like his loneliness at Groton, had widened his sympathies. His childhood had been secure and happy, and his cheerfulness contrasted with Eleanor's gravity. But there was a sense in which he, like Eleanor, was an outsider, and this, too, drew them together, especially since she supported and encouraged him in his large dreams.

She was overjoyed, she wrote him when he was chosen permanent chairman of the Class Committee, "for I know how much it meant to you and I always want you to succeed. Dearest, if you only knew how happy it makes me to think that your love for me is making you try all the harder to do well and oh! I hope so much that some day I will be more of a help to you."

12. *Journey's End*

FOR FRANKLIN AND ELEANOR January, 1904, was shadowed by Franklin's impending departure for the Caribbean. If Sara had hoped that a five-week winter cruise would dampen the romance, the urgency of their meetings in January should have told her otherwise.

"I am sorry to part with the old year," Eleanor wrote Franklin on New Year's Eve; "it has been so good to me but the new is going to bring us both I hope still more perfect joy and love, if that is possible. Twelve is striking so goodnight darling 'a Happy New Year to you—.' "

They spent the next two days together in New York, and while Franklin jovially reported to his mother, who had returned to Hyde Park, how they had gone to a play and to church and been to Aunt Corinne's for an "uproarious lunch" and all had tea later at Cousin Susie's, there were things he did not tell her, such as how they had slipped away from Aunt Corinne's early and that he was planning on returning to New York the following week end.

Even with the prospect of seeing him again on Saturday, for Eleanor the hours seemed to drag. "What will you do when you have to stand five weeks?" Cousin Susie admonished her. Eleanor was mortified that anyone else should see how out of humor she was; it spoke badly for her self-control, she felt. She told Franklin that he should not laugh at her work in the Rivington Street Settlement. If he were in New York to take up all her time "I would not be going I'm afraid, but one must do something or not having the person who is all the world to me would be unbearable."

Despite all their stratagems for concealing their relationship, some began to suspect. When challenged or teased, Eleanor found the slightest deviation from a truthful, candid reply excruciatingly difficult. Was she ever going to marry Franklin, her Aunt Pussie asked her flatly one day. She had no right to ask that, replied Eleanor, who was easily exasperated with Pussie; when she intended to marry, she would let Pussie know. But since she was secretly engaged, this was an evasion and it embarrassed her. "I suppose I could have got out of it without telling such a story if I had thought and I am really quite remorseful."

At a luncheon one day Eleanor's friends began to discuss the approaching marriage of one of their friends, Edith Poor, to a British officer. "Can you imagine loving a man well enough to go to South Africa with him?" the girl next to Eleanor asked her. "Luckily," said Eleanor, someone else chimed in and answered for her. To dissemble made her dreadfully uncomfortable.

For the sake of appearances, Eleanor agreed to accept Lyman Delano, Franklin's cousin and also a student at Harvard, as a supper partner at a theater party and dance to be given by his Aunt Kassie. Lyman was interested enough in Eleanor to get angry when she seemed to elude him. He wrote her from Harvard that he was expecting to come to New York for Aunt Kassie's party—would Eleanor go to supper with him? To avoid difficult explanations, Eleanor accepted. But, she consoled Franklin, "I'll dance with you," and besides, they would be together at Groton before the party and would come to New York on the train together. At the party Lyman wanted to know how she had come down from Boston and by what train, "and when I said the twelve," Eleanor reported to Franklin later, "he said 'why had I not let him know, as he would have met me and been delighted to come down with me!' I did not say that I was escorted by someone else."

In Franklin a relaxed attitude toward the truth produced neither guilt nor embarrassment. Although his trip to New York the second week end in January had been planned the week before, after he was back in Cambridge he wrote to his mother:

Now I must confess—on Saturday I found I had no engagement and went to N.Y. on the 10 o'clock—E. and I had a quiet evening and went to Church together on Sunday—I lunched at the Parishes' & came on here again on the 3 o'clock getting here at 10, just in time to write my editorial. You know I positively couldn't help it—There was nothing to keep me here and I knew I should be in a much better humor for a short trip to N.Y.!

Countless young men in love have resorted to similar omissions and excuses in communications with their parents, and Franklin's dissemblings were not unusual. Eleanor's scrupulousness was. She had, she said, "painfully high ideals and a tremendous sense of duty at that time, entirely unrelieved by any sense of humor or any appreciation of the weaknesses of human nature."[1]

There was a deep strain of puritanism in her. Grandfather Hall had preached a stern gospel of duty and self-control, and both Grandfather Roosevelt and Uncle Theodore, for all their joy of life, had been accused of priggishness in their youth. Grandma Hall and Cousin Susie both dinned it into her that passions should be mastered, not yielded to. "I don't think I seem a great success at conquering 'my natural inclinations' which seems to be our aim in life," she confessed to Franklin in the course of bewailing her inability to get along with Pussie. Her conscience spoke to her with a strong voice, and it was powerfully reinforced by the repressed knowledge of what self-indulgence had done to her father. Paradoxically, her earnest correctness and the tight control she kept over herself were not, on the conscious level at least, her defense against being like her father but were her way of complying with her father's wishes. He had wanted her to be good, loyal, well educated, truthful; he had wanted her to be the virtuous person he wished he could be and which perhaps she could help him to be; he had wanted her to work against the pleasure-seeking side in him. He, too, had lovingly called her "Granny." Perhaps she appealed to Franklin because he needed someone to temper his fun-loving, easy-going, frivolous side.

She could be quite censorious and prim. Alice was in New York, she informed Franklin, "looking well but crazier than ever. I saw her this morning in Bobbie Goelet's auto quite alone with three other men! I wonder how you would like my tearing around like that. I'm seriously thinking of taking it up, it seems to be the fashion nowadays." Bobbie Goelet was one of the gayest and wealthiest young men about town—"None of us had very much money compared to Bertie and Bobby Goelet," said Duncan Harris, who then worked at the Astor Trust; "they were the big party boys." Bobbie Goelet was also one of the reasons Eleanor disapproved of Pussie, who was to marry Forbes Morgan on February 14. Eleanor was to be her maid of honor and the day before the wedding was busy arranging the house for the ceremony. Pussie, on the other hand, spent a good part of the day with Bobbie Goelet, and Eleanor could not understand "spending the last afternoon like that." But then there was little that Pussie did of which Eleanor approved. She could not forget what Pussie had said about her father. After one of Eleanor's flare-ups with Pussie, Cousin Susie told Eleanor that her face looked as if it were made of stone. Eleanor should read the thirteenth chapter of Corinthians, Cousin Susie had suggested, "and though she said it laughingly I am quite discouraged with myself for I don't think I shall ever learn how to take Pussie charitably." A few days later Cousin Susie lectured her again, this time on the subject of forgiveness. "She says I do not know the higher meaning of the word because I never forget. Of course it's true and that makes it all the more disagreeable I suppose. . . ." Eleanor vowed to try to be a better person, "and according to Cousin Susie the first step is peace with Pussie so peace it is to be until we fight again!"

Eleanor's mood softened the day of the wedding: "Pussie was married this afternoon at half past four and really looked so lovely." The ceremony affected Eleanor strongly. "It is a pretty solemn thing when it comes to the point of this getting married and I do not see how anyone who has not a great love in their heart can go through with it. Have you ever read the service through Honey? I wish you would sometime for each time I hear it, I think it more beautiful and it means so much, one's whole life in fact."

She was very firm about not yielding to what she considered her baser instincts. She came very near "gambling" at bridge, she confessed to Franklin, at a dinner party at General and Mrs. Bryce's on Washington Square. Afterward their daughter Leila organized the young people for bridge and suggested that Eleanor and Beatrice Mills play at the same table, which terrified Eleanor, who seldom played bridge. It was a favorite diversion at the Mills' house parties,* and Beatrice was a skilled player. "You can imagine my feelings when I had to say that I never played for money and objected distinctly to having my partner carry me!"

Harnessed to a narrow moralism, Eleanor's ability to say "no" might have landed her in the ranks of the battle-ax feminist crusaders had she not married Franklin, Alice Longworth asserted.[2] She was, moreover, by temperament a "yea-sayer." Overflowing with vital energy, she was eager to experience the

---

* The palatial Mills' house at Staatsburgh, a few miles north of Hyde Park, is described by Edith Wharton in *The House of Mirth*, where it is called Bellomont.

world in all its aspects and, like her preceptor Mlle. Souvestre, believed it to be woman's particular function to add a grace note to life. However, she was not as forbidding as she depicted herself in the episode at the Bryces'. Although she was not good at games, she was an easy conversationalist, quick to appreciate merit in others; she took pains to draw shy people out and would not spoil other people's pleasure if she could help it. Outwardly, little ruffled her. One time a group of young men—Bob Ferguson, Nick Biddle, and Otway Bird of Westover, Virginia—descended upon one of her tea parties and in high spirits proceeded to telephone her friends, talk Indian language to them, and beat on tom toms. "Finally they left to my great relief," Eleanor recalled, "and I'm glad to say Cousin Susie was out during the whole performance or I'm afraid she wouldn't have approved!" At a dinner party given by Charles Barney, she was seated between Mr. Barney and Bronson Winthrop, the bachelor descendant of Governor Winthrop. "Luckily, I can, with some effort, succeed in making Mr. Winthrop talk but I cannot imagine why I was put next to the host when there were a good many older girls there! I suppose I must resign myself to being considered twenty-five however!" It was part of her code that one tried to put other people at ease, and she was critical of Laura and Ellen Delano, Franklin's cousins, because they would not make the effort to talk with people who were newly introduced to them.

At the Whitelaw Reids' annual ball Edmund Rogers took her into supper, and she had such "nice partners" that she stayed until 4:00 A.M. "for the first and last time this winter." She was "burning the candle at both ends," she confessed to Franklin, and she could never do that for very long.

It was an equally strenuous month for Franklin. He would arrive back in Cambridge from a week end in New York and then doze through his morning classes. "It is dreadfully hard," he wrote his mother, "to be a student, a society whirler, a 'prominent and democratic fellow' and a fiance all at the same time—but it [is] worth while, especially the last and next year, tho' hard will be easier."

Two plays greatly impressed Eleanor that winter, one negatively, the other positively. She went with Maude Waterbury to R. C. Carton's *Lord and Lady Algy*, a popular stock comedy that everyone enjoyed—except Eleanor. The intoxication scene in the second act was the most vivid in the play, and it spoiled the entire work for her. But she saw *Candida* by George Bernard Shaw several times, and was fascinated by Candida, whose love for and care of her husband, James Morell, a popular clergyman and Christian Socialist, made him strong and master of the house. The play's most eloquent speech is made by Candida to the wastrel poet Marchbanks, and its account of what she does for Morell foreshadows the role that for many years Eleanor would have in Franklin's life.

Now I want you to look at this other boy here—my boy—spoiled from his cradle. We go once a fortnight to see his parents. You should come with us, Eugene, and see the pictures of the hero of that household. James as a baby! the most wonderful of all babies. James holding his first school prize, won at the ripe age of eight! James as the captain of his eleven! James in his first frock coat! James under all sorts of glorious circumstances! You know how strong he is . . .—how clever he is—how happy! [*With deepening gravity*] Ask James' mother and his three sisters what it cost to save James the trouble of doing anything but be strong and clever and happy. Ask me what it costs to be James' mother and three sisters and wife and mother to his children all in one. . . . Ask the tradesmen who want to worry James and spoil his beautiful sermons who it is that puts them off. When there is money to give, he gives it; when there is money to refuse, I refuse it. I build a castle of comfort and indulgence and love for him, and stand sentinel always to keep vulgar little cares out. I make him master here, though he does not know it. . . .

This outpouring is a revelation to Marchbanks, who gives up his suit; he says despairingly of Candida, upon whose hurt feelings he had hopefully played, "it is she who wants somebody to protect, to help, to work for. . . . Some grown-up man who has become as a little child again." Eleanor must have identified with the character of Candida, since she, also, wanted somebody to protect and to work for. She had already begun to take care of Franklin. She worried about keeping his relationship with his mother on an even keel: "Boy dear, do you realize you've not written your Mother for over a week," she admonished him. Just as Candida had the will and self-discipline to make a happy marriage, so did she.

January sped past, and the week of Franklin's departure for the Caribbean arrived. Then—dreadful disappointment—Henry Parish had to go to Lakewood for his health, and "of course Cousin Susie goes too so I shall be here alone and no one not even you dear can come to the house till they get back." She hated to upset their plans for being together before Franklin left, "but I cannot help it as long as it is not proper for me to have you come to see me when I'm not chaperoned. . . . I don't know what to do but perhaps you can think of something and you know that I will do anything which I possibly can rather than miss seeing you for a whole day before you leave."

Franklin was equal to the emergency. He wrote his mother:

I have just heard from E. that Mr. and Mrs. Parish have gone away and I couldn't see her [*i.e.*, no chaperone] if I went to N.Y. on Wednesday. I find I can get off from here Tuesday night and I feel that I must see all I can of E. these last few days—so I am telegraphing you tonight to see if you won't have her up at Hyde Park—coming Wednesday a.m. and staying till Thursday. Nobody need know a thing about it and she wouldn't be any trouble as far as getting off is concerned—for I can pack all my things in half an hour. If you decide not to telegraph her I think I must go down Thursday so as to have all day Friday with her. . . .

On February 6 Franklin, Sara, and Franklin's Harvard roommate, Lathrop Brown, sailed on the *Prinzessen Victoria Luisa*. "F. is tired and blue," his mother noted. And Eleanor, who fled the city to spend the week end with Muriel Robbins at Tuxedo, confessed when she began her first letter: "I could not write last night. I felt as though you had gone so far away and altogether the world was such a dreary place that I was afraid to trust myself on paper. . . . I wonder if you know how I hated to let you go on Friday night, five weeks seems a long time and judging by the past two days they will be interminable."

The only consolation was that on his return Franklin would join her in Washington, where she would be visiting Auntie Bye. He gave her three mailing addresses in the Caribbean, and she wrote something each day, sending him three fat letters in which she told him about the people she had seen, the things she had done in society, the books she had read, the plays she had attended, what she had been doing at the settlement house, and occasionally even breaking away from the purely personal to comment on the news.

"The papers are nothing but war and fires," Eleanor's first letter reported. The war referred to was the one between Russia and Japan, the fire the one which had gutted Baltimore. The latter affected the Delano family, for Mrs. Warren Delano III of Barrytown was Jennie Walters, the daughter of one of the richest men in Baltimore, whose inheritance had included many properties in Baltimore.

She had see Nick Biddle, Eleanor wrote in relation to the larger conflagration in the Far East. "He wants to go to the war but I think it would be foolish when he is getting on so well at the office to throw it all up and I do hope he won't go." "Everyone is talking war madly at present," Eleanor added a few days later, "and the Japanese certainly seem to have made a good beginning. I do hope that they will win for I suppose that their defeat might bring about an international war. Besides they are, from a distance at least, such a plucky and attractive little people, don't you think so?"

Did Franklin, like Nick Biddle, itch to get to the battlefront? He had talked excitedly about enlisting in the Navy in the Spanish-American War, but scarlet fever ended that dream; and he wanted to go to Annapolis, "only my parents objected."[3] "Thank heavens," she wrote, "you are not out there dear, even as a correspondent." Both were sufficiently interested in the Far East to read *Chinese Characteristics*, a book by a Christian missionary, A. H. Smith, which combined penetrating observations of Chinese traits with the argument that China's needs will be met "permanently, completely, only by Christian civilization." The book had impressed Eleanor, and she lent it to Franklin.

She liked to share her literary enthusiasms with him, and one of the books she wanted him to read was Balzac's *La Peau de chagrin*. There was a stoic strain in her, and perhaps the appeal of the book was its thesis that every aspiration of the heart, brain, or will that is fulfilled must in the end be paid for. "There are so many things I want to cover and read with you some day when we have time," she wrote Franklin. Another book that she wanted him to read with her was Ruskin's *Sesame and Lilies*. What in this work particularly attracted her? Was it the metaphor of the library as a silent storehouse where the reader is privileged to hold communion with the kings and prophets of all ages? Or was it Ruskin's passionate outcry against the exploitation and injustice rampant in England and his denomination of idleness and cruelty as the two most heinous sins? Or did she want to see what Franklin's reaction would be to Ruskin's appeal to women to exercise their power against injustice and war? How different in this respect was Ruskin's outlook from that of the Reverend

Dr. Morgan Dix, Margaret Dix's father, who weekly inveighed not only against women's suffrage but even against college education for girls. But Eleanor was far from a feminist. She did not go to Barnard as some of her friends did, and she was vigorously opposed to women's suffrage. She even declined an invitation to become a founding member of the Colony Club, the most exclusive of women's clubs, as did Franklin's mother, who said, "She could not see any reason for a women's club and would never have any reason to go inside one."[4]

Eleanor attended church faithfully and was very interested in Janet McCook, one of the girls in society who went to Barnard and also taught Bible classes; she later received an M.A. and became something of a Biblical scholar. Eleanor, who attended Janet's classes and often discussed religion with her, went with her to hear a popular preacher, Dr. G. Campbell Morgan, a leader of the Northfield Extension Movement. "It was really very interesting and impressive but quite at the end he called upon all those who felt themselves to be *really* Christians to get up and that flavored too much of a revival meeting to me but it was interesting to see." She went to hear him a second time, but she felt that his sermon was addressed "to the crowd whose emotions must be touched and that kind of thing does not appeal much to me."

So with attendance at church and the opera and a few parties and Bible classes and lessons in German, the weeks passed, and at last she could write Franklin that she was leaving for Washington. "My class in Rivington Street bade me a sad farewell today for two weeks and they all promised to be good with Helen and I feel sure they will be as bad as they can be." She was reluctant to leave, for there were many things in New York she hated to miss, "but I love being with Auntie Bye and I hope it won't be too gay, for a perpetual society would kill me."

She arrived in Washington and was "Immediately taken out calling!" Friends came to tea, and then "A. Bye and I went to dine with Uncle Theodore. I am sorry to say A. Edith is away but we had a very pleasant dinner during which I just sat still and listened while the men discussed the appointments for the Panama Commission," she wrote in her last letter to Franklin, whose cruise ended in Nassau. There they were the guests of the C. T. Carters, whose daughter, Evelyn, flirtatiously entertained Franklin and Lathrop. On their way back to Washington, Franklin and his mother stopped briefly in Palm Beach, where they found, according to Sara, "much dressing and display, crowds of overdressed, vulgar people."

A note was waiting for Franklin at the Shoreham in Washington. "Just a line to tell you how *more* than glad I am to have you here at last. I will be home as near twelve as possible Honey, and I hope you will be able to get here. Auntie Bye will I think, be in about then also." Shortly after their arrival Mrs. Cowles called. "Went to Bammie's to tea. Eleanor at Bammie's," Sara noted.

Sara was not ready yet to concede defeat, and tried once more to separate the young couple. She forgot the episode, she said, but years later Mabel Choate reminded her of it.[5] Sara took Franklin to see Joseph Choate, whom Theodore had summoned home from his ambassadorial post in London in connection with the Russo-Japanese War, and asked the ambassador to take Franklin with him to London as his secretary. But Mr. Choate had already engaged a secretary, and, in any event, he felt that Franklin was too young for the job.

Sara had lost.

"Darling Franklin," his mother wrote him when she returned to Hyde Park from Washington,

I am feeling pretty blue. You are gone. The journey is over & I feel as if the time were not likely to come again when I shall take a trip with my dear boy, as we are not going abroad, but I must try to be unselfish & of course dear child I *do* rejoice in your happiness, & shall not put any stones or straws even in the way of it. I shall go to town a week from Friday just to be with you when I can. I have put away

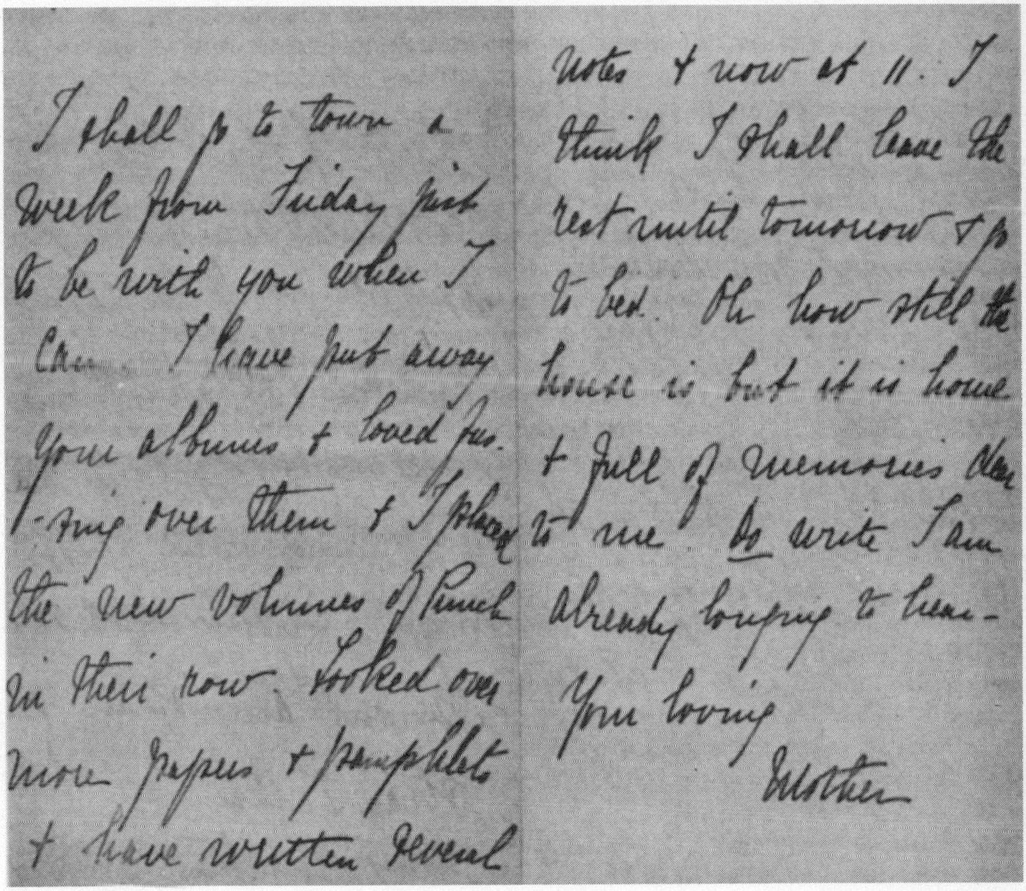

I shall go to town a week from Friday just to be with you when I can. I have put away your albums & loved fuss-ing over them & I placed the new volumes of Punch in their row. Looked over more papers & pamphlets & have written several notes & now at 11. I think I shall leave the rest until tomorrow & go to bed. Oh how still the house is but it is home & full of memories dear to me. Do write I am already longing to hear—

Your loving

Mother

your albums & loved fussing over them & I placed the new volumes of Punch in their row. Looked over more papers & pamphlets & have written several notes & now at 11 I think I shall leave the rest until tomorrow & go to bed. Oh how still the house is but it is home and full of memories dear to me. *Do* write. I am already longing to hear.

Back in Tivoli, Eleanor was full of compassion for Sara. "I knew your Mother would hate to have you leave her dear," she wrote Franklin in Cambridge, "but don't let her feel that the last trip with you is over. We three must take them together in the future that is all and though I know three will never be the same to her still someday I hope that she really will love me and I would be very glad if I thought she was even the least bit reconciled to me now. I will try to see her whenever she comes in town if she lets me know."

". . . don't let her feel that the last trip with you
is over," Eleanor wrote Franklin at about the same time.

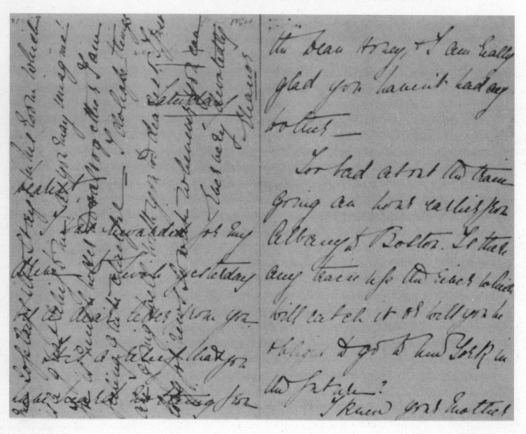

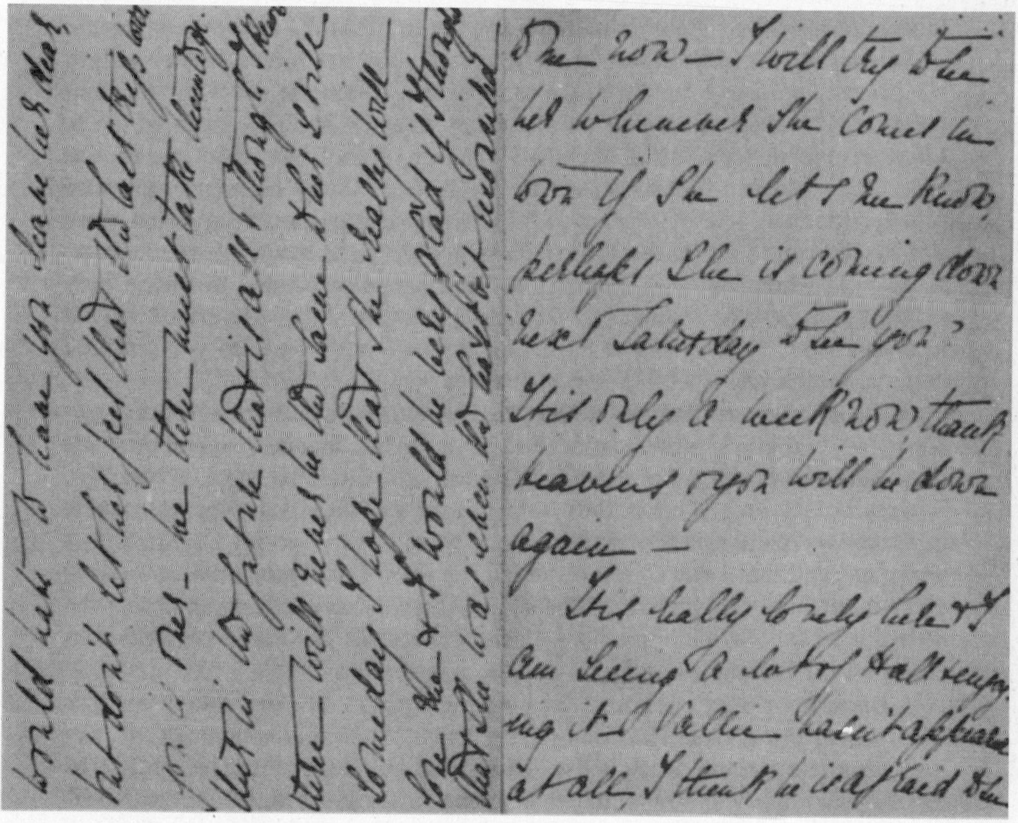

Dec 20th — I will try to see
her whenever she comes to
town. If she lets me know,
perhaps she is coming down
next Saturday to see you?
It is only a week now, thank
heavens, & you will be down
again —

It is really lovely here & I
am seeing a lot of Halbwachs,
my it I'd like have laughed
at all, I think he is afraid she

13. Epithalamion

SARA STILL RESENTED THE MATCH, but prudence as well as breeding now required that she yield gracefully. She realized, moreover, that her best hope for preserving a close relationship with her son lay in Eleanor's extraordinary sense of duty and in the girl's eagerness to be accepted by her future mother-in-law.

Sara's letters to Franklin began to report the things she did with "the dear child": they had spent the afternoon together; Eleanor had accompanied her to the dressmaker's for a fitting; they had had tea; Eleanor has been "as sweet as ever." Sara invoked Eleanor to get Franklin to do things he might otherwise refuse. "Much as I want to see you," she wrote him in early May, even more she wanted him to attend the Thayer-Russell wedding; it would please the Russells—with whom the Delanos had been intimately associated in their China ventures—to have one member of the family there. And then she added, almost in desperation, "I am going to have Eleanor here next week, so you will find her, and I think you will be willing to do what I ask."

Eleanor, whose resentment had given way to magnanimity and duty, was sorry for Franklin's mother and tried to ease her anguish. Sometimes she arranged to be elsewhere so that Sara and Franklin could be alone. When Mrs. Warren Delano invited her to Barrytown for the Fourth of July, she was unable to accept and confessed to Franklin that it was "just as well for Cousin Sally's peace of mind that I can't." She assumed the role of mediator between mother and son, urging Franklin to be forbearing; "We will have to learn to accept the little things," she wrote him after a clash between the two, "and not show our annoyance. I know it is harder for you."

Because of Sara's jealousy, Eleanor rejoiced at all signs that Franklin's family liked and accepted her. She spent a day at Algonac, the home of Mr. and Mrs. Frederic Delano Hitch (Mrs. Hitch was Franklin's Aunt Annie). The place was as lovely as Franklin had said, she wrote him. Mr. Hitch "petrified" her, but Mrs. Hitch took her around the house and grounds and for a long afternoon drive and could not have been sweeter. From Tuxedo she reported with delight that another of Cousin Sally's sisters, Mrs. Price Collier, had asked her to call her "Aunt Kassie." And Franklin was meeting with equal acceptance from her own Hall family, she wrote him happily. They liked him so much, she said in mock despair, that she feared they would not think her half good enough when they learned of the engagement. His mother and Mrs. Parish had had a long talk, and Sara had been "sweet" to Cousin Susie. "I don't think Honey, your Mother could be anything else. Everyone has to fall in love with her."

Helen Roosevelt and Eleanor's cousin Theodore Douglas Robinson were to be married in June at Hyde Park. Eleanor and Helen, who was Franklin's niece, were the best of friends and Eleanor carefully followed the preparations and decisions that Helen made since she soon would confront many of them herself. Uncle Ted was coming for the wedding and Eleanor, Alice, and Corinne were to be among the bridesmaids.

Never had spring been so wonderful as that year—to Eleanor's wide-awake senses it seemed that she heard "all the lovely summer noises beginning" as she walked through the woods. She would awaken early and lie in her bed dreamily, wishing she had Peter Ibbetson's capacity to imagine what her lover was doing. She wondered "how life could have seemed worth living before I knew what 'love' and 'happiness' really meant." She could not see enough of Franklin. When they were together, the world and its cares were banished, but at the moment of separation an uncontrollable sadness would well up in her. She hated partings, and sometimes was overwhelmed by melancholy, almost depression. "A woman's moods are sent her," she wrote Franklin apologetically, "just as a man's temptations."

Eleanor spent the Fourth of July week end in Oyster Bay at Sagamore. Young Corinne and Isabella Selmes were staying nearby with Lorraine Roosevelt at Waldeck, the home of the West Roosevelts. There was dancing, "a nice hen party for lunch," and a great deal of tennis, which Eleanor played poorly; Corinne won the tournament despite an injured leg. Eleanor accompanied her cousin to the doctor in New York, and afterward the two girls lunched with Bob Ferguson and Nick Biddle. The latter, a young man of great gaiety, was taken with Eleanor, but Corinne, who was not aware of her cousin's feeling for Franklin, thought that perhaps Eleanor was interested in Bob.[1]

Eleanor was better than Franklin at playing the Victorian charade that she and Franklin were friendly cousins, not plighted lovers. Her lapses of candor caused twinges of conscience, but to have violated the pledge to Sara to keep their engagement secret would have caused her greater inward stress. Franklin was the opposite: he found it difficult to hide his feeling for Eleanor—or probably he did not wish to and took the pledge to his mother less seriously than Eleanor did. The result was a Shakespearian comedy of errors at Islesboro in Dark Harbor, Maine, where Eleanor went to visit her Aunt Corinne and young Corinne. Caroline Drayton was there, too, and the three girls were reading Browning together when Franklin and some Harvard classmates appeared on the *Half Moon*. The two Corinnes were soon persuaded that Franklin was quite in love with Eleanor but that she did not seem interested in him, which, they thought, was a pity. They noted that Franklin took Eleanor canoeing but that Eleanor seemed indifferent.[2] After the *Half Moon* had departed Eleanor wrote Franklin at Campobello saying that aunt and cousin "both undertook to talk to me seriously yesterday about you, because they thought I did not realize how serious you might be, etc. and I led them on very wickedly and made believe I was much worried at the thought that you might really care for me in more than a friendly way! May I be forgiven for all my white lies, but it seems like I can't help doing it!"

She did not lack attentions from other men, and her Dark Harbor letters were filled with chitchat about Boston boys who had gone to Groton and Harvard and who were "attractive" and "interesting." There was Howard Cary, who was much in evidence at Dark Harbor. His intense, searching eyes seemed to be asking for answers she could not give him, and he invited her to go climbing with him, to explore the other side of the island, to come to dinner, to tea. And when she lunched with Caroline Drayton "it brought me a rather terrifying proposal which I was obliged to accept and in consequence Mr. Drayton and I are going walking together tomorrow morning! I haven't yet recovered from the shock and my terror is great!" Was she wholly teasing? She evidently enjoyed the attentions of other men, and with feminine instinct realized that such interest on their part enhanced her appeal to Franklin and also served to bridle any inclination he might have to philander. The name that cropped up most often was Nick Biddle's. She had seen him frequently in town and invited him to Tivoli in June. He amused her: "Never have I known anyone able to talk the steady stream that Mr. Biddle does," she reported to Franklin. One of her friends thought they were secretly engaged, and even the astute Mrs. Cowles was puzzled. Auntie Bye had written her, Eleanor informed Franklin, that she wanted a long visit to Oldgate in the autumn "and wanted to have you and Nick Biddle while I was there but thought she had better have you at different times! I really think the family must think me either a dreadful flirt or an awfully poor one, I don't quite know which." Franklin was not leading a cloistered life, either. Evelyn Carter was back on Campobello, staying with Mrs. Kuhn, and one of Eleanor's comments in a letter from Dark Harbor was almost too nonchalant: "I did not know you had Edith Weekes with you."

But this was all froth on the waves of their love. Franklin impatiently urged her to abbreviate her stay at Dark Harbor, and she did her best to accommodate him without wounding Aunt Corinne's feelings. The quickest route to Campobello was by way of Millbridge, and Franklin begged her to take it so that he could meet her there. That would not do, she wrote primly; if the train missed connections, they would be stranded, and even with her maid to chaperone them, that would not be proper. "That is one of the drawbacks dear, to not announcing our engagement, and though we did not think of it at the time, it is one of the things we gave up until January 1st." But she, too, was longing to get to Campobello. Although she had greatly enjoyed Islesboro, "I want a quiet life for a while now and above all I want you."

Franklin's fondness for Campobello was second only to his feeling for Hyde Park, and Eleanor soon came under the enchantment of the "beloved isle," as the James Roosevelts had named it when they first discovered its beauty and peace in 1883. It was pine-smelling and spruce-laden, nine miles long and from one and a half to three miles wide. Franklin took Eleanor for walks over mossy paths and showed her his favorite picnic spots. In the morning the fog rolled in and shut out the world, but in the evening spectacular sunsets were arrayed in the western sky. At Franklin's urging Eleanor ventured onto the tennis court, but even though she loved him dearly she did not see why she had to prove her inability over and over again—play with Evelyn, she entreated him. She went sailing on the *Half Moon* and portrayed a willow tree in the end-of-the-season *tableaux* at the club for the benefit of the island library; Franklin impersonated "a very funny 'Douglas' in kilts." They made eighty dollars, Sara recorded, plus twenty-five cents that Eleanor later sent from Tivoli—"I came away and entirely forgot that I owed it . . . for a ticket the night of the *tableaux* as I took a small boy in."

The happy time they had together in Campobello was over "oh! so quickly," Eleanor lamented, and Franklin's feelings mirrored her own. "I wish you could have seen Franklin's face the night you left Campo," Mrs. Kuhn wrote. "He looked so tired and I felt everybody bored him. He could not stand Evelyn's chatter."

And increasingly Eleanor could not stand the chatter and triviality of the social game. She spent a week end on Long Island with Aunt Tissie, and wrote Franklin that a number of ladies were coming to tea and bridge. "If you ever find me leading this type of life, stop me, for it's not the way to happiness." Her high-mindedness vexed some of her relatives. She had "the queerest time," she reported of her visit to her Aunt Joe (Eddie Hall's wife): "I don't go there very often and in between times I forgot the impression it always makes on me to see Joe and all the other women there smoking and I find myself constantly the only one who does not do one thing or another, which makes me uncomfortable as they always say 'Oh! well, Totty hasn't been here enough to fall into our ways' and I dare not say that I hope I never shall! Somehow I can't bear to see women act as men do!"

In the autumn of 1904 Franklin entered Columbia Law School. He had planned to go to Harvard Law School, but Columbia meant he could be near Eleanor, and that consideration was more compelling than his fondness for the Yard and Gold Coast society. "I am anxious to hear about the first day [at Columbia Law]," Eleanor wrote from Tivoli, "and whether you found any old acquaintances or had only Jew Gentlemen to work with!"* Most of the young-sters in her Rivington Street class were Jewish and although that did not inhibit her solicitude for them, she did share society's prejudice against Jews.

Occasionally Franklin met her at the settlement, and once, when a child in her class became ill, he accompanied Eleanor to the tenement in which the child lived. After they came out he drew a long breath of air. "My God," he said, aghast. "I didn't know people lived like that!"

Sara was as pleased as Eleanor that her son was in New York. He should move his chair closer to the light "so as to see the print of those charming and comprehensible law books!" she gaily advised him, adding, "I am so sorry I cannot be there to explain any difficulties you meet with." But law school com-manded little of Franklin's attention that first year, and even the presidential

* An inspection of the 1907 class roster showed 21 Jewish names in a graduating class of 74.

election does not seem to have been much on his mind, or on Eleanor's, although the campaign was reaching its climax and there must have been a great deal of discussion of Uncle Theodore's prospects the first week in October when they were visiting Auntie Bye at Oldgate in Connecticut. But they were absorbed in each other and in the approaching announcement of their engagement. When? Who would write letters to whom? How soon after should their wedding follow? On October 7 Franklin selected a ring at Tiffany's, "after much inspection and deliberation," and gave it to Eleanor on October 11, her twentieth birthday. "I am longing to have my birthday present from you for good," she wrote him from Tivoli that evening, "and yet I love it so I know I shall find it hard to keep from wearing it! You could not have found a ring I would have liked better, even if you were not you! This sounds odd but is quite sensible."

They disclosed their engagement at the beginning of December. Franklin had planned to be at Fairhaven, where the Delano clan would be assembled at Thanksgiving, to announce the news himself, but he came down with jaundice and had to remain in New York. Excited letters were promptly sent to Franklin and Eleanor from Fairhaven telling them what the family's response had been. "All those who know you think it is the luckiest thing that ever happened to Franklin," Muriel Robbins reported. Lyman Delano wrote to both of them: "I have more respect and admiration for Eleanor than any girl I have ever met, and have always thought that the man who would have her for a wife would be very lucky." And to Eleanor he wrote that he would have given anything if she could have been in Fairhaven on Thursday morning "when Franklin's letters came. I never saw the family so enthusiastic in my life and I am sure your ears would have burned if you could have heard some of the compliments paid you."* Lyman's father, Warren Delano, the senior member of the clan, wrote Franklin that "Eleanor must have no doubt about being taken in by all her fiance's family—certainly by those who have learned to know and appreciate her." Another note was struck by Mrs. Hitch, who, aware of the wrench in the relationship between her sister and Franklin that the announcement foretold, wrote Eleanor that she was thankful you "already love my dear Sister" and expressed her pleasure to Franklin "that your devoted Mother will have a devoted daughter in Eleanor."

Eleanor's Hall relatives rejoiced that she would at last have a home of her own, but their hearts ached somewhat at the thought of her leaving Tivoli and Cousin Susie's. She would miss "dear Eleanor very much," Grandma Hall wrote Franklin, but was thankful that Eleanor was "going to marry such a fine man as I believe you to be." Maude, a believer in spiritualism, horoscopes, and

---

* Grace Tully, Franklin Roosevelt's secretary during the White House years, once asked him why he departed from custom and congratulated the prospective bride as well as groom. "With the mock sense of injury he sometimes affected, he said that when his engagement was announced, all the congratulations were showered on him for securing Eleanor as a wife. He felt, he said, that some people at least should have congratulated her for securing him as a husband." Grace Tully, *F.D.R. My Boss* (New York, 1949), p. 120.

fortune tellers, drew a circle in wishing "Totty" happiness, "a perfect circle no break anywhere," and then added, "Do be good to Grandma I think she will miss you frightfully." Cousin Henry, who usually was not given to speaking in a personal vein, wrote Eleanor that she filled a place in Susie's life: "Much as I am to Susie, you are more and I pray that you always will be." Pussie was in ecstasy. "I've always loved Franklin & must write him a tiny line tonight just to ask him if he knows and appreciates what he has won," she wrote, but asked how Hall felt. "I know that he had a secret longing that Mr. Biddle would be the one."

He had to throw away three unsatisfactory starts, Mr. Biddle confessed to Franklin in his congratulatory note. Another disappointed suitor, Howard Cary, wrote him from Cambridge, "You are mighty lucky. Your future wife is such as it is the privilege of few men to have." He was mortified that at Islesboro he had "thoughtlessly put her in a position which must at times have been embarrassing." And Howard's mother, only half in jest, lamented to Eleanor, "and so you are not going to be my daughter-in-law after all."

Letters of congratulations also poured in upon them from friends and former classmates at Allenswood, Groton, and Harvard. "I am afraid I shall bear [Franklin] a grudge though," one of Eleanor's co-workers in the Junior League wrote, "if in consequence we are to lose the most efficient member of the League." Many of the letters to Franklin told him how lucky he was, that he could not have made a better match. "It has been a dream of mine for some years that you would be a man widely useful to your country," Groton's second in command, the Reverend Sherrard Billings, wrote him, "and a sympathetic wife will be a great help to you on the road to realizing my dream and I am thankful and glad." The previous spring when Dr. Peabody had officiated at Flossie Twombly's wedding to William A. M. Burden, Eleanor had said to Franklin, "It seems quite necessary for a Groton boy to have him," and the rector now shifted an engagement to preach in a Cambridge church in order to be able to officiate at their marriage.

The Oyster Bay side of the family was delighted with the news. "Oh, *dearest* Eleanor—it is simply too nice to be true," wrote Alice from the White House; "you old fox not to tell me before." Young Corinne Robinson bubbled over—"Hurrah, hurrah, hurrah," she wrote, and recalled that when Franklin and Eleanor had come to Orange in the fall she had suggested to Franklin that he was in love with Eleanor and had called him a hypocrite and gay deceiver when he had denied it.

"My own darling soft-eyed child," Auntie Bye wrote Eleanor, "your letter has given me great joy. I love Franklin as you know on his own personal account because he is so attractive & also because I believe his character is like his Father's whom Uncle Will & I always feel was the most *absolutely* honorable upright gentleman (the last in its highest sense) that we ever knew." She was thankful, Auntie Bye went on, "to feel you care for someone in a way that gives you the right to make him first over everyone & be everything to him." Aunt Corinne was equally moved by the news. "I can only hope that when the time comes for [young] Corinne to tell me such a piece of news, that I shall feel as completely satisfied."

Uncle Theodore, always in the pulpit, sermonized a little in his letter to Eleanor: "Married life has many cares and trials; but it is only in married life that the highest and finest happiness is to be found; and I know that you and Franklin will face all that comes bravely and lovingly." A happy married life, he advised Franklin, was more important than political success.

White House
Washington

Dear Franklin,   Nov. 29th 1904

We are greatly rejoiced over the good news. I am as fond of Eleanor as if she were my daughter; and I like you, and trust you, and believe in you. No other success in life—not the Presidency, or anything else—begins to compare with the joy and happiness that come in and from the love of the true man and the true woman, the love which never sinks lover and sweetheart in man and wife. You and Eleanor are true and brave, and I believe you love each other unselfishly; and golden years open before you. May all good fortune attend you both, ever.

Give my love to your dear mother.

Your aff. cousin
Theodore Roosevelt

A few days after the announcement of their engagement Eleanor and Franklin saw Auntie Bye and asked her to find out if Uncle Ted would be able to attend the wedding, which, like Pussie's, would take place in the adjoining Seventy-sixth Street houses of Cousin Susie and her mother, Mrs. Ludlow. A few days later Auntie Bye forwarded Theodore's note: "Tell dear Eleanor that I can attend the wedding if it takes place before March 17." Eleanor promptly wrote the president that the ceremony was scheduled for March 17 and expressed her pleasure that he could come. "I want you & Aunt Edith so much & as I am to be married in the house do you think you could give me away?" Not only would he do so but, wrote Aunt Edith, she and Uncle Theodore had been talking about the wedding and "he feels that on that day he stands in your father's place and would like to have your marriage under his roof and make all the arrangements for it." They would understand if she wished to adhere to her original plans, "but we wish you to know how very glad we should be to do for you as we should do for Alice." Despite the warmheartedness of this offer, Eleanor and Franklin decided to keep the wedding at Cousin Susie's and have the invitations sent by Grandma Hall. Eleanor would have "a bevy of pretty bridesmaids," she wrote to Helen Robinson, including Alice Roosevelt, Ellen Delano, Muriel Robbins, Isabella Selmes, Corinne Robinson, and Helen Cutting. "You angel," Alice replied to her invitation,

to ask me to be your bridesmaid. I should love to above anything. It will be too much fun. Let me know where I am to hat (&) clothe myself so I can arrange about fittings. . . . Really you are a saint to ask me. . . .

Before the wedding the engaged couple took time off to attend Uncle Theodore's inauguration. He had defeated conservative Democrat Judge Alton

B. Parker by 2.5 million votes, a landslide, and one of the votes came from Franklin. "My father and grandfather were Democrats and I was born and brought up as a Democrat," he later explained (1938), "but in 1904 when I cast my first vote for a President, I voted for the Republican candidate, Theodore Roosevelt, because I felt he was a better Democrat than the Democratic candidates."[3]

They traveled to Washington in Emlen Roosevelt's private car and stayed with Auntie Bye. During the ceremonies on March 4 they sat on the Capitol steps just behind the president and his family and heard his ringing appeal: "All I ask is a square deal for every man." They went to the White House to lunch with the president and again joined him and his immediate family on the reviewing stand for the parade and at the inaugural ball that evening. Then they hurried back to New York, Eleanor, at least, thinking that was the last inauguration of a member of her family that she would attend.[4]

With the wedding less than two weeks off, many parties were given for them, and wedding presents began arriving. There were in all 340 gifts— flatware and china, glass candlesticks, silver candlesticks, several silver tea sets, cut glass and vases of many descriptions, four inkstands, thirteen silver trays, and thirteen clocks. For Franklin there were golden cigarette cases and a dozen bottles of Madeira, and for Eleanor there was a great deal of jewelry, including a handsome pearl dog collar with diamond bars, a gift from Sara. There were water colors from Uncle Ted and Aunt Edith and a sketch of Auntie Bye from Ellen Emmet. They were given enough sets of books to fill a library—two of Jane Austen, three of Robert Browning, two *Golden Treasuries*, and one set each of Campbell, Motley, Emerson, Mrs. Browning, Symonds, Stevenson, Rossetti, Charlotte Brontë, Whittier, Cowper, and Longfellow's *Dante*. Bridesmaids helped Eleanor acknowledge her presents, and Isabella Selmes was so carried away she began to sign her own name instead of Eleanor's.[5]

Cousin Susie helped Eleanor buy her trousseau and linen, and Sara went with her to Pach's for her wedding photo. On March 6 Sara noted in her journal "Tried on my lace dress for my dear Franklin's wedding. Mama's black lace over white."

On March 16 Sara wrote:

Mr. and Mrs. Peabody came at 3.15. I took them up to see Eleanor's presents. Back to tea. Had Bammie, Corinne & Douglas, Mr. & Mrs. Jack Morgan to dine. This is Franklin's last night at home as a boy.

Franklin, meanwhile, was busy with his ushers. Since Rosy, his half brother, was ill, Lathrop Brown was to be his best man, and the ushers were Nicholas Biddle, Owen Winston, Lyman Delano, Warren Robbins, Charles B. Bradley, and Thomas Beal, who had sailed on the *Half Moon* with him the previous summer. He had designed a diamond tie pin for his ushers based on the three feathers in the Roosevelt crest, and he gave Eleanor a watch with her initials in diamonds and a pin with the three feathers to hold it.

On Friday, March 17, Pussie sent Eleanor some last-minute advice:

Try & forget the crowd & only think of Franklin—& if you are wise you will drink a cup of strong tea half an hour before you go down stairs. It will give you color & make you feel well. *No* sugar or cream in it.

She sent three kisses, "one for Father & Mother & Ellie."

From Maude came a note with the hope "that she will always try & think of me as her sister, one who loves her very much." A cable signed "Souvestre" was handed her: "Bonheur," it said.

Downstairs all was in readiness. The two large drawing rooms that opened into each other glowed in candlelight and the reflected tints of the heavy furniture. The yellow brocade with which the walls were hung picked up the glow as did the portraits of the Livingstons and Ludlows. White lilacs, lilies, and pink rosebuds relieved the stately dignity of the two rooms, and clematis and palms shaped the brocaded walls into a tabernacle of blossoms. An altar had been set up at the back of Mrs. Ludlow's drawing room, where an enormous shower bouquet of pink roses combined with palms to form a bower in which the ceremony would be performed.

Outside, traces of winter were still on the street, but the day was balmy, and windows everywhere were open, crowded with spectators. Many little boys had come from the St. Patrick's Day parade and were holding American and Irish flags as they awaited the arrival of the president. The carriages and cars of the guests continuously pulled up to the canopy, and finally everyone had arrived and was seated. Grandma Hall in black velvet and Franklin's mother in white silk trimmed with black lace were ushered to the front. Off in a little room on the side Franklin, Lathrop, and the rector were reminiscing, a little distractedly, about Groton; upstairs the bride and her bridesmaids were waiting for the president. A few moments before 3:30 the squeals of the children, a clatter of hooves, and the shouting of commands signaled his arrival, and— top-hatted and buoyant, a shamrock in his buttonhole—he bounded out of the open landau and hastened upstairs.

The Landers Orchestra, discreetly screened, began to play the wedding march. The bridesmaids, in taffeta, with demiveils and three silver-tipped feathers in their hair, moved with measured step down the circular stairway and up the aisle formed by satin ribbons held by the ushers. Behind them came the gravely beautiful bride on the arm of her uncle. A few, remembering her mother, gasped—today she looked like the beautiful Anna, they thought. Past and present were everywhere. Her satin wedding gown was covered with Grandmother Hall's rose-point Brussels lace, which Eleanor's mother had also worn at her marriage. The veil that covered her hair and flowed over her long court train was secured with a diamond crescent that had belonged to her mother. March 17 was her mother's birthday.

At the altar she was met by Franklin. Alice took her bouquet of lilies of the valley and the rector began the Episcopal wedding service. Once he faltered—the light was dim and he could not lay hold of the words, he explained later. Eleanor knew the service so well she could have helped him out, but he recovered quickly. The vows were exchanged. Hand touched hand. It was done.

"Well, Franklin," the president's high-pitched voice could be heard saying, "there's nothing like keeping the name in the family." He kissed the bride and marched off to the double dining room where refreshments were being served. Others pressed forward to congratulate them, but as the dining room began to crackle with the president's sallies and the guests' appreciative laughter, the bridal couple soon found themselves abandoned. Dr. Dix and his daughter Margaret, arriving a little late for the reception, found Franklin and Eleanor standing quite alone. Eleanor was taking it calmly, Margaret observed, but Franklin was a little put out.[6] The Dixes traipsed off after the others, and soon the newlyweds, too, decided they might as well follow. Ushers and bridesmaids gathered round while Franklin guided Eleanor's hand as she cut the cake. Even the president was made to attend and take his piece. At five the president left, to shouts of "Hooray for Teddy" from the little boys still waiting outside; the president beamed and shook his fist smilingly. Eleanor and Franklin went upstairs to dress, and soon they, too, departed in the traditional shower of rice. With Isabella, they stopped to see Bob Ferguson, who was ill in bed, and then left for Hyde Park, which Sara turned over to them for an interim honeymoon.

Sara, at Tuxedo Park, where she had gone with her sister Kassie, finished the day's chronicle:

March 17th. Took Mrs. Peabody out in the electric to do some errands. Had all the ushers to lunch. Left at 2.30 for 76th Street. Franklin is calm & happy. Eleanor the same. All the family at the wedding. Dora, Annie & Fred, Fred & Tilly, Kassie & all & Mlle. Mathieu. About 200 at the ceremony, a large reception afterward. Theodore Roosevelt, President, gave Eleanor away.

Then she wrote her "precious Franklin and Eleanor" that it was "a delight to write you together & to think of you happy at dear Hyde Park just where my first happiness began."

And the president, addressing the Friendly Sons of St. Patrick at Delmonico's after the wedding, spoke in words intended as much for the Vanderbilts, Sloans, Burdens, Chanlers, Winthrops, Belmonts, and van Rensselaers who had applauded his quips in the Ludlow-Parish dining room as for his immediate audience:

American is not a matter of creed, or birthplace, or descent. That man is the best American who looks beyond the accidents of occupation or social condition, and hails each of his fellow citizens as his brother, asking nothing save that each shall treat the other on his worth as a man, and that they shall join together to do all that in them lies for the uplifting of this mighty and vigorous people.[7]

It began with Theodore Roosevelt as the American century but would progress toward a more ecumenical outlook; and in the broadening of loyalties that the United Nations would represent, the marriage that had been celebrated that day was destined to figure significantly.

II

WIFE AND MOTHER

14. Honeymoon

SOME SITUATIONS brought out Eleanor's competence, and others touched the secret springs of her insecurity; her marriage did both. The pathos of orphanage was ended, but the poignancy of wishing to please and be fully accepted by her young husband and his mother began.

For five years before her marriage, beginning with the beneficent influence of Mlle. Souvestre, she had begun to assert her individuality, sense her potentialities, and emerge as a tower of strength to those around her. Suddenly the pattern was reversed, and in return for the privilege of loving and being loved she stifled any impulse to assert herself. "I want him to feel he belongs to somebody," she had said of Hall in the 1890s to explain why she wrote him so often, and it reflected her own yearning to belong, to be part of a family whose members came first with her as she came first with them. She had had the self-discipline to do what she thought needed to be done to bring that about, and now that she wanted to be fully accepted by her mother-in-law she was prepared to dismiss her own wishes and values to gain Sara's love.

There was, moreover, that conscience of hers; if there was any conflict between what she might enjoy doing and what she ought to do, the voice of duty prevailed. The result was that she totally subordinated herself to her husband and her mother-in-law. Their wills became hers; not what she wanted, but what they wanted, mattered.

Since Franklin had to finish his year at Columbia Law School and they could not yet leave on an extended honeymoon, they were to have a week to themselves in Hyde Park and then stay at the Hotel Webster in New York. When Franklin finished his exams they would depart for a three-and-a-half-month honeymoon in Europe. Fifty years later, Eleanor's recollections of the week at Springwood focused on "Elespie"—Elspeth McEachern, the highly competent Scotswoman who, under Sara's direction, ran the efficient and spotless household at Hyde Park. She had been at the door to welcome Sara as James' bride in 1881. "She was in the house when we went to Hyde Park the day of our wedding," said Eleanor, "and she looked me over critically and appraisingly, wondering if I could come up to her expectations as the wife of 'her boy.' "[1]

When they returned to New York on March 25, Sara was there to greet them. "Went to F. & E.'s apartment at Hotel Webster," she noted in her diary;

"arranged flowers and went to my French lecture. Returned to find my children and brought them home to lunch with me."

Now that Eleanor was faced with the fulfillment of her dream—an intimate normal life of her own with the man she loved—she was frightened. In her grandmother's house she had never had a chance to learn what went into a serene, well-run household. The hotel apartment was a godsend, because Franklin would not discover how little she knew about managing a household right away. All she had to do was "a little mending."

Despite her inner anxieties, on the surface she was busy cheerfulness and left Franklin free to prepare for his examinations. She arranged for Hall to stay with them at the hotel when he came down from Groton; she went with Franklin and Sara to the wedding of Lucius Wilmerding and Helen Cutting; and there was much family visiting—the large Delano clan, the Oyster Bay and Hudson River Roosevelts. Helen and Teddy Robinson returned from their honeymoon trip around the world, and Sara had everyone to dinner—"Rosy, Corinne and Douglas, Bammie, F. & E." Eleanor had many things to take care of for her own forthcoming honeymoon—purchases to be made, trunks to be packed, letters of credit arranged, tickets to be picked up. She organized it all competently—and quickly. On June 6 Sara wrote, "Franklin got all their luggage put on board the *Oceanic* & lots of friends came to say goodbye. We had Rosy, Helen & Teddy to dine." Then, overcome with a sense of her good fortune, she added, "My dear Franklin & Eleanor."

For Eleanor her honeymoon was a bittersweet affair. Its sweetness was recorded in the long, detailed letters she wrote to her mother-in-law at the time; its harsher side emerged only in her reminiscences three or four decades later when she had become a freer, more independent woman.

"There were certain subjects never discussed by ladies of different ages," she wrote thirty-five years later, "and the result was frequently very bewildered young people when they found themselves faced with some of life's normal situations!" She was commenting on the scene in *Life with Father* where Father announces that he will tell his son "all about women" and then informs him promptly that there are certain subjects never discussed between gentlemen.[2]

And to the extent that there was any discussion between generations of what a woman faced, it was in terms of marital duty. That was Grandma Hall's view. It was also Sara's, so one of her grandchildren, Franklin Jr., learned one day when he sat on the edge of "Granny's" bed and she pressed him to tell her about his girls. The young man parried the question. "What was life like with Grandfather?" he wanted to know. "Did you have any fun?" She was not at all unwilling to answer the charming young man. "Well, you know, we were Victorians. I knew my obligations as a wife and did my duty."[3]

That was the case with Eleanor. Sex was an ordeal to be borne, she would later confide to her daughter Anna.[4]

She began her honeymoon trip fearful that she would be seasick and become a burden to her nautical husband, who was never more at home with himself than when on the water. But after four days out Franklin reported to his mother, "Eleanor has been a *wonderful* sailor and hasn't missed a single meal or *lost* any either." And she exulted, "Franklin has been a wonderful maid & I've never been so well looked after." With Eleanor there to prod Franklin, for once Sara would not feel she was being neglected. Almost daily they sent her long letters full of information and affection. Eleanor's effusive avowals of love were pathetic evidence of her eagerness to be fully accepted by the older woman. "Thank you so much dear for everything you did for us," she wrote from the *Oceanic*. "You are always just the sweetest, dearest Mama to your children and I shall look forward to our next long evening together, when I shall want to be kissed all the time!"[5]

She shared amused observations about Franklin with the adoring Sara. "The stewardess informed me the other morning that my husband must be English, he was so handsome and had the real English profile!" she wrote archly. "Of course it was a great compliment but you can imagine how Franklin looked when I told him." Eleanor was always observant, always learning, her heart easily stirred. They toured the ship with the captain, and "it was very interesting, but I am more sorry than ever for the Steerage passengers." Some Japanese were on board on their way to supervise two Japanese battleships being built in England; Franklin spent most of his time "*trying* to talk to the Japs," Eleanor reported, "and they have proved interesting companions."

After a stop in Liverpool to visit Eleanor's Confederate relatives, the Bullochs, and to weep a little with Aunt Ella, whose heart still ached over her "Ellie boy," they went on to London. Wherever they went in Europe there were family connections or friends of the family to introduce them into the highest circles of society, politics, and art. Their greatest joy, however, was to poke around London, Paris, or Venice—just the two of them. For Eleanor it was a new experience to be able to do the things she had always wished to do without worrying about the cost or what "G'ma" or Cousin Susie would think. Some places had special meaning for her because she had first seen them with her father or Mlle. Souvestre, and she delighted in exploring them anew with Franklin; for his part, he could not wait to take his bride to his favorite bookseller, mountainside spot, or café.

They walked themselves weary in London while Franklin searched for rare books and prints, and ordered, he teasingly wrote his mother, "thousands of dollars worth of clothes." They lunched at the Embassy with the Reids, Eleanor reported, and "I sat next to Mr. Reid!" They had supper at the Carlton and, she said, "were much entertained by some of the English women. It is quite out of date here to appear with your own face or hair. In fact it really looks immodest!" She visited Allenswood, "but it was dreadful without Mlle. Souvestre." She had died a few weeks earlier.

Doing Paris with Franklin was an even greater joy. She went shopping for clothes and ordered "thousands of dollars worth of linen," according to Franklin, while he spent "all I owned" in the first bookshop he entered. He accompanied her to the dressmaker's but insisted that he had dozed off while she ordered "a dozen or so new dresses and two more cloaks." Eleanor scribbled a P.S.: "Don't believe *all* this letter please. I may be extravagant but——!!!" Franklin enjoyed introducing his new wife to the world of high fashion. "This

A.M. we went out and Franklin got me such lovely furs," Eleanor wrote; "I don't think he ought to give them to me but they are wonderful and of course I am delighted with them." They dined in out-of-the-way places, ordered *spécialités de la maison*, and, since Franklin thought he spoke French well, they had a gay time talking with the *patrons*. Although Franklin's French was hardly as good as Eleanor's, it was good enough for some hard bargaining with booksellers. He would not let Eleanor come along on these bargaining sprees, because her sense of fairness interfered with hard trading. Her Italian, however, was fair, while his was only poor, so in Italy he had to rely on Eleanor for such transactions. In Paris they also visited "Cousin Hortense" Howland, the French woman who had married a brother of James Roosevelt's first wife and whose salon was described in Proust as a meeting place of the Jockey Club. "You would have laughed if you could have heard Mrs. Howland flatter Franklin yesterday," Eleanor wrote. "This isn't true," Franklin commented in the margin; "Eleanor got buttered on both sides!"

For Eleanor, Venice was full of memories of her father and Mlle. Souvestre. Of course they hired a gondola and gondolier. Charles Stuart Forbes, an artist and kinsman, lived in Venice and was their guide. They visited the Palace of the Doges and the artistically interesting churches with him, and at the end of tiring days they all went to little Italian restaurants where they learned the pleasures of superbly cooked but simple Italian food.

They had tea at the Lido, and again Eleanor's strait-laced attitudes asserted themselves. "It is a lovely island with a splendid beach but I never saw anything like the bathing clothes the ladies wear. . . . But Franklin says I must grow accustomed to it as France is worse!" For Eleanor a decorous bathing costume consisted of a skirt, a long-sleeved, high-necked blouse, stockings, slippers, a sun-bonnet, and gloves. They left Venice reluctantly. Franklin, who had expected to be disappointed with Venice, found the reality "far more wonderful than he had imagined." Eleanor felt that "nothing could be quite so lovely," but then the stern voice of conscience welled up "as long as you wished to be idle!"

From Venice they proceeded to the Dolomites and to Cortina. "An old lady's Paradise," Franklin complained, "and I feel like Satan all right." But among the not-so-old female guests was Kitty Gandy, the attractive owner of a fashionable New York hat shop. She joined them at bridge and, according to Franklin, was "quite nice (smoked all my good cigarettes) and promised *me* a new ostrich feather hat for next winter." When Eleanor, a poor mountain climber, declined to accompany him up the 4,000-foot Faloria, Miss Gandy gaily volunteered. To his letter describing the jaunt, a piqued Eleanor appended: "E.R. spent the morning with the Miss VanBibbers climbing up the landslide, to meet a husband who never turned up till after they got home!" Much later, in her autobiography, she confessed that she had been unspeakably jealous of Kitty Gandy and hadn't breathed easily until they left Cortina to drive through the Alps to St. Moritz. The drive over the Stelvio was "wonderful," and Franklin, in an exuberance of good spirits, leaped out of the coach to pick wild flowers for Eleanor—"the wild jasmine smells sweeter than anything I ever had," she wrote. Aunt Tissie, who often stayed at St. Moritz with her family, had reserved rooms for them, and Eleanor had been a little anxious as to what they might find awaiting them, since Tissie's "ideas of the necessities of life and ours differ"; but, she reported, "we are surviving her extravagance." She went to have her hair washed while "Franklin found a paper and devoured it." They had tea and then went down to dinner, "since when I have been writing this and he has been mending his Kodak and occasionally telling me that I have a wonderful husband, so I suppose he is being successful!"

Fashionable St. Moritz did not respond to their young romantic mood. Eleanor always remembered—and recounted with a smile—that they were underdressed for the Palace Hotel and the management relegated them to a table—with a view of the lake, to be sure—well out of sight of the other guests. Fifty years later, when she was world-famous, she returned to St. Moritz but stayed at a rival hostelry and explained to her companions why she was amused by the aggrieved message from the management of the Palace Hotel: "But why didn't Madame Roosevelt stay with us!"[6]

Their next destination was Franklin's boyhood haunts in southern Germany, where they journeyed through the Black Forest. From St. Blasien Franklin reported: "We are full of health and bursting with food (at least I am) and the only unkind word Eleanor has ever said to me is that she would like to see me bust!" Her letter, Eleanor insisted at the beginning of a twelve-page report, was bound to be "unbearably dull"; all her letters were dull, she said deprecatingly, compared to Franklin's "amusing ones." "We are having such a nice lazy time," she reported from St. Blasien. She was reading Anatole France in French, but "he occasionally disgusts me so that I have to stop." Sara had sent them a check, and she had decided to spend her share in Paris. "How I would like to kiss you and *tell* you instead of writing my thanks."

On their return to Paris her clothes and furs were awaiting her for fittings. And awaiting Franklin were his law-school grades, which—not surprisingly for the year in which he was married—included two F's. They immediately cabled for his law books so that Franklin could study on board ship on the way home. He wanted to take make-up examinations in the autumn, Eleanor wrote. "I'm not very confident about his passing but it won't hurt him to try and the work will be that much gained next winter."

In Paris Franklin ran into some college friends who took Eleanor and Aunt Dora to a very "French" play, hoping to shock the ladies, Eleanor reported, a little irritated with their sense of humor. The only one shocked was Eleanor; Mrs. Forbes did not lift an eyebrow. Eleanor's primness came out again at Voisin's, where she saw, she wrote, *Mrs.* Jay Burden and *Mrs.* Harry Whitney with Mr. Bertie Goelet and Mr. Meredith Hare, "so you see it is not fashionable to go out with your husband!"

The honeymoon drew to an end with a visit to Novar, the home of the Ferguson clan, and to Mr. and Mrs. Foljambe, friends of Sara's who lived in a part of England that included Sherwood Forest and was known as the "Dukeries." The opulent estates there eclipsed the great houses on the Hudson, and for Eleanor the visit to Osberton-in-Workshop, as the Foljambe estate was called, was "terrifying." There was a punctilious emphasis on correct behavior, and dinner was austerely formal. Guests of such a great house, it was assumed, would all know each other and thus there were no introductions. After dinner, bridge was played for money, which was against Eleanor's principles, and so arrangements were made for her to be carried by her partner. She was the more embarrassed by this to-do because she was convinced she played badly. She described her feelings at Osberton-in-Worksop with a metaphor whose grisliness underscored her insecurity: she felt like "an animal in a trap" who did not know how to get out or how to act where it was.

Franklin took the Foljambes in his stride. They were flattered by his interest and eagerness to learn all about Osberton. After touring the farms and talking with Mr. Foljambe, he breezily informed his mother that his plans for Hyde Park "now include not only a new house, but new farm, cattle, trees, etc."

The visit with the Fergusons, old friends of Eleanor's father and mother, was more relaxed. Bob's older brother Hector remembered her as a golden-haired three-year-old. Bob Ferguson and Isabella Selmes, who had been married in July, were visiting the family. Eleanor drove over in a two-wheeled cart to see them and wrote Sara delightedly: "It is impossible to imagine how sweet [Isabella] and Bob are together for I would not know him for the same man. He has become demonstrative if you can believe it and they play together like two children."

While they were with the Fergusons, they received news that Theodore Roosevelt had scored a considerable diplomatic triumph when the Japanese and Russian peace plenipotentiaries, meeting at Portsmouth, New Hampshire, reached agreement on terms of a settlement of the Russo-Japanese War. The Fergusons were part of the Foreign Office establishment, and Sir Ronald Ferguson had played a role in bringing the meeting about. "It is nice news, isn't it?" Eleanor wrote. "We had really begun to think it would not be and I think Uncle Ted must be gratified to have done so much towards it." Franklin jauntily waved the flag. "Everyone is talking about Cousin Theodore saying that he is the most prominent figure of present-day history, and adopting towards our country in general a most respectful and almost loving tone. What a change has come over English opinion in the last five years!" Also while Franklin and Eleanor were at the Fergusons', Sidney and Beatrice Webb came to lunch. "They write books on sociology," was Eleanor's meager description of the couple, "and Franklin discussed the methods of learning at Harvard while I discussed the servant problem with the wife!" Did her exclamation point mean that she sensed that talking with Beatrice Webb about servant problems had been an opportunity wasted? The door was open, as at Uncle Ted's, to talk of high politics, culture, and science. Therefore, when Lady Ferguson asked Eleanor to explain the difference between federal and state governments and Eleanor could not get beyond the fact that there *was* a difference, since Uncle Ted had been governor of New York and now was president of the United States, her mortification was extreme. Fortunately, Franklin came to her rescue—as he did again when she was asked to open the flower show. "She opened it very well," Franklin insisted, "and wasn't a bit rattled and spoke very clearly and well—but I had an awful time of it and wasn't even introduced." Eleanor's account was different. "We opened the flower show at Novar last Saturday and Franklin made a very good speech." In this case, Eleanor was the more accurate reporter; Franklin's talk was graceful and humorous—it was, as his wife said, "a very good speech."

He was fortunate "in having a Highland nurse," he said, "so that I passed my early years with kilts on the outside and oatmeal and scones on the interior." If he began on a note of intentional humor, he ended on one that was unintentional. American women instead of cooking vegetables in water "nearly always cooked them in milk, and this of course makes them more nutritious, besides bringing out the flavor."[7] Little as Eleanor knew about cooking, she knew her husband was drawing on his imagination when he spoke of cooking vegetables in milk and it was a relief when he ended. But his audience loved it and she loved him for coming to her rescue.

As they left for home they received a letter from Sara expressing her delight and gratification over the way they had made her feel she was never far from their thoughts. "I never knew such angels about writing and I *am* so glad Eleanor says that although you have had such a perfect time you are now anxious to see 'home and mother' again!"

15. *Settling Down*

AT THE NEWLYWED'S REQUEST, Sara had rented for them the Draper house at 125 East Thirty-sixth Street, just three blocks from her own, and furnished it and staffed it with three servants. If she had looked forward to finding and furnishing her own first house, Eleanor gave Sara no hint of this. "You are an angel to take so much trouble with the house," she wrote from St. Moritz, and thanked Sara for having done "wonders" for them in the way of "a bargain," for now they could get settled "so much sooner than if we waited to choose a house on our return. Altogether we feel jubilant over it and I am looking forward so much to getting it in order with you to help us." Eleanor's requests were minimal: she wanted their bedroom painted white, the kitchen and basement whitewashed, the telephone, if there was one, to remain—and was there a house safe?

Only when Sara offered to spend a considerable amount of money to wire the house for electricity did they demur. "You are a dear, sweet Mama, to want to put it in for us," Eleanor wrote from Paris a month before their return, "but we are pulled two ways for we will only have the house two years."

They moved into their "14 foot mansion," as Franklin called it, as soon as they returned, and two days later he took his make-up exams at Columbia Law School. Sara had sent his law books to London with the advice, "You can do a good deal even crossing an ocean, if you set apart two or three hours a day for work." He had a retentive memory and a good mind, and with Eleanor to see that he stuck to his studies, he passed.

Through the remaining two years at law school Eleanor's quiet confidence in Franklin's abilities fortified him against indolence and irresolution. He passed his bar exam in the early spring of 1907, was sworn in in May, and in September wrote from Campobello to his mother in Europe that by the time she returned he would be "a full-fledged office boy" with Carter, Ledyard and Milburn. "I shall think of you on the 23rd beginning work," his mother wrote back. "I know you will in many ways be glad to start. Try to arrange for systematic air and exercise and keep away from brokers' offices, this advice free gratis for nothing."

While Franklin was busy learning his way around the municipal courts, Eleanor devoted herself to her mother-in-law. Every day she drove with Sara in her brougham up Fifth Avenue and through Central Park, and they had at least one meal a day together. Eleanor consulted Sara on servants and menus and on where to shop and what to buy, and she listened dutifully to Sara's daily briefings about Franklin's health. Often she had to beg off when Helen Robinson or Nathalie Swan or Corinne Robinson wanted to "have a little gossip." She had to lunch with Mama, she excused herself. No, she could not go to the lecture or to the theater with them—she was driving or dining with Mama.

Under the firm guidance of her mother-in-law she was becoming a conventional young society matron.[1] Franklin did not mix socially with his fellow students or professors. The young couple's social life was to be restricted to the group in which they had been raised. New York was throbbing with vital movements in art, politics, and welfare, but for Franklin and Eleanor, New York was limited to the interests of a small group of families of impeccable social standing and long-established wealth. Before her marriage, Eleanor had begun to break loose from this narrow framework through her work at the Rivington Street Settlement and with the Consumers League. But now she was told by Sara and Cousin Susie that if she continued with this work she risked bringing the diseases of the slums into her household. Eleanor's impulse to do things for the less fortunate was to be restricted to serving on proper charitable boards and to making modest donations, the appropriate activity for a young matron, just as the older members of Franklin's family approved of his election as a vestryman of St. James' Episcopal Church and his membership, like his father before him, in the Eagle Engine Company of Hyde Park and the Rescue Hook and Ladder Company of Dutchess County.

The Franklin Roosevelts, while not really wealthy, were well off. Franklin had a $5,000 income from a $100,000 trust fund, and Eleanor had an annual income of $7,500. Also, Sara could always be counted on for generous checks on special occasions. So their life was comfortable and without financial worry.

They were not members of the fastest, gayest crowd, although they saw a good deal of the Teddy Robinsons, who were. Franklin rode and hunted, but hunt-breakfasts, polo, and steeplechasing were never as important to him as they were to Teddy. The Robinsons engaged in such madcap pranks as turning up at dinner dressed in baby clothes. Eleanor was totally incapable of "letting go" in that way, but if Franklin had been married to someone else he might have joined the fun. He enjoyed gay escapades that Eleanor had little use for and that often left her feeling inadequate.

If he wanted to go on a "bat" with his male contemporaries, she encouraged him. She packed him off to Cambridge for a "real spree" with his Fly Club brethren, which gave her a chance to fix up the house, she said, "so it will look a little better for you." In June she bundled him off to Cambridge again, for she realized that the true son of Harvard needed the stimulus of a return to the Yard and participation in commencement festivities.

Eleanor got on easily with older people, and joined her mother-in-law and her friends in their discussions of art, literature, and music. Almost everybody in society was organizing classes. Sara Roosevelt had one in history at her home. "Such a funny combination of people," remarked Helen Robinson, since it consisted mostly of Sara's contemporaries, with only Helen and Mary Newbold and Eleanor representing the younger generation. Around the corner, Eleanor attended the class Aunt Jennie (Mrs. Warren Delano) had in her home in "modern" literature—George Eliot, D. G. Rossetti, Browning, Swinburne, Meredith, Matthew Arnold. She still turned up regularly at the Bible class conducted by Janet McCook.

The pattern of Franklin and Eleanor's life during the the first year of marriage was set by Sara, at least to the extent that Eleanor's deliberate self-effacement kept her from expressing her own preferences. No wonder Sara was thankful—she understood what she had gained. In 1905, on Eleanor's twenty-first birthday Sara wrote that she prayed that her "precious Franklin may make you very happy, and thank him for giving me such a dear loving daughter. I thank *you* darling for being what you are to me already."

But Eleanor had Franklin's love and a home, and that was what counted for her. In September Franklin went to New York and she stayed in Hyde Park alone, their first day apart. "I feel quite lost and sad without you," she wrote him, "and it was horrid coming home last night so I don't think we will try this experiment again, do you think? Incidentally I hope you miss me dreadfully too!"

Insecure, unsure of her adequacy as a woman, another of her anxieties when she married Franklin was that she might prove barren.[2] But not long after they returned from their honeymoon she knew she was pregnant. The pregnancy was a difficult one, and for the last three months she was quite ill, but with those around her she remained calm and cheerful. "Eleanor and I walk every morning at ten. She is wonderful, always bright and well," Sara noted. Eleanor had little patience with her own physical ailments and did not allow them to keep her from doing what had to be done. This had always been one of her nobler attributes, but it had sometimes made her insufferably righteous toward others who were less self-disciplined. Her pain and nausea while carrying Anna, however, humbled and softened her, and although she still refused to yield to her own infirmities, she became more tolerant of those who did.

In December, 1905, Alice Roosevelt announced her engagement to Nicholas Longworth. Since the wedding on February 17, 1906, took place only a few weeks before Eleanor's confinement she was unable to attend, but Franklin went with his mother. "Alice looked remarkably pretty and her manner was very charming," Sara reported to Eleanor. Cousin Theodore was, "as always, cordial and interesting." "So Alice is really married," the family noted with considerable surprise and even more relief.

On May 2, Sara wrote, "Eleanor and I had our usual walk and in the afternoon she and I drove from 2:30 till four, and Eleanor and Franklin lunched here. I went there to dine. We played cards. Eleanor had some discomfort." The next day, Miss Spring, a trained nurse, called Sara at nine. "I went over and Dr. Ely soon came. At 1:15 a beautiful little girl was born, 10 pounds and one ounce."

Eleanor always remembered the first time she held Anna in her arms, "just a helpless bundle but by its mere helplessness winding itself inextricably around my heart." The mother's pleasure in the birth of her first child was only slightly marred by her knowledge that her mother-in-law had yearned for a boy.

Eleanor had scarcely recovered from childbirth when she began to worry about what would happen once the trained nurse left. Stubby Blanche Spring was so competent and sensible that Eleanor became quite attached to her, and felt rather lost when the nurse was no longer with them. "Miss Spring left," Sara noted in her diary. "Poor little Eleanor is upset by it though she is brave."

Miss Spring urged Eleanor to care for the baby herself, but Sara argued that a nurse must be employed. So Eleanor added a nurse that Sara engaged to the household staff of cook, housemaid, and butler. Later she bitterly regretted yielding on this point; if she had insisted on caring for her own children, she felt, instead of turning them over to nurses and governesses, as was customary in her group, she as well as the children would have been happier. In retrospect, she also regretted having been insulated from the household's vital activities; she and Franklin, she said later, would have been better off during the first years of their marriage if they had not had a staff of servants. But Sara shaped their style of life, and when Eleanor had misgivings and consulted her Cousin Susie, she found that Susie was as much a traditionalist as Sara.[3]

The baby was christened "Anna Eleanor" at St. James Church on July 1, 1906. The child's godmothers were Isabella Ferguson and Muriel Robbins, and the godfather was Edmund Rogers. A lunch party for thirty-four at Springwood followed the ceremony.

For Sara, the presence of a grandchild was a fascinating experience, and she found it more difficult than ever not to spend all her waking hours with her son and his family. There were times, nevertheless, when Eleanor escaped her mother-in-law, and managed to join her friends at lunch, to call on them at their homes, and sometimes even to entertain them at dinner. Those were the years when most of her bridesmaids and Franklin's ushers were themselves getting married, settling down, and excitedly reporting to each other on their babies. Helen Robinson's son Douglas Jr. was born on November 8, 1905; Helen Wilmerding (née Cutting) gave birth to a son in January, 1906; and Isabella Ferguson had a daughter in September, 1906. "Will you marry me 21 years from today?" the Robinsons telegraphed the Fergusons on behalf of Douglas Jr. "Sorry," the answer came back, "just eloped with Peter Biddle" (Peter was Nick and Elizabeth Biddle's one-month-old son). The Robinsons took Douglas to call on little Anna Eleanor. "Douglas rather terrifying Anna by his amorous advances," Helen recorded, "as they sat on the floor together. He wanted to hold her hand but she was quite rebellious."

Soon after Anna's christening the Franklin Roosevelt household left for the first of many summers on Campobello Island. Resolutely Eleanor set about mastering her fear of water, because life on Campobello would be tedious for her if she didn't sail. If she wanted to keep her children company—not to mention her husband—she had to learn about boats. They went up to St. Andrews in the launch, Franklin informed his mother, "and though slightly rough in Passamaquoddy Bay for a few minutes E. did not show the least paleness of cheek or tendency to edge towards the rail!" Eleanor even learned to fish: "F. and I fished yesterday afternoon and caught twelve flounders," she announced laconically.

She wanted to participate in other sports with her husband, but her feelings of awkwardness and shyness as well as her husband's self-centeredness deterred her. Franklin loved golf, and Eleanor practiced secretly, but when she went golfing with him she played so badly and Franklin was so impatient with her that she gave it up then and there. During their courtship he had tried to coax her onto the tennis court, but he now accepted her protestations that she would only spoil the game for others—so she was relegated to entertaining the guests on the sidelines. At Hyde Park, too, her efforts to join in outdoor activities were unsuccessful. Her ankles were too weak for ice-skating. She enjoyed riding and tried Franklin's horse Bobby, but he was used to Franklin's handling and she could not control him. When Sara, who could handle Bobby (the horse at one time had been hers), took the view that there were not enough people at Hyde Park to justify two saddle horses, Eleanor meekly said that she preferred not to ride.[4] As a result, the only outdoor pleasures she shared with her husband were long walks and picnics.

It was not customary for wives to go on long cruises with their husbands, but Eleanor was left out of the carefree active summer life on Campobello more than most young women of her time. She did not complain, however, and at the end of each summer she would busy herself provisioning the *Half Moon* for Franklin and Hall for a run to Nova Scotia or westward to Bar Harbor.*

The first few summers at Campobello the Franklin Roosevelts lived with Sara, who managed not only the household but everything else with great firmness. Franklin was an expert sailor and he loved the *Half Moon*, but for many years Sara, not Franklin, gave the captain his orders, and only when her son had guests at Campobello was the boat turned completely over to him. Sara also kept the management of Hyde Park firmly in her own hands. She allowed her son to take some responsibility for the woods and the roads but meticulously kept his operations and hers separate.

Back in New York during the winter of 1906–7, Eleanor led an even quieter life than before, because she still had not completely recovered from her difficult pregnancy and tired easily. Occasionally, however, she and Franklin accepted an invitation to one of the big balls. The night of the Sloane dance, they had the Teddy Robinsons and the Biddles to dinner, went to a play, and then stopped at Mama's to "prink a little" before proceeding to the Sloanes', where they stayed through the cotillion and supper. Sometimes Eleanor encouraged Franklin to go alone or to stay on after she left. At Hyde Park it was cus-

---

* But secretly she resented her exclusion from the active handling of the boats on which her menfolk sailed. In 1935 Emma Bugbee of the *New York Herald Tribune* was with her in Campobello, and they went sailing. "I shall never forget the satisfaction with which she took the helm from Captain Calder, who had handled Roosevelt family boats for years," Emma later wrote. " 'I never get a chance to sail the boat myself,' she beamed. 'There are always so many men around. . . . One always has to let the men do the sailing' " (*New York Herald Tribune*, July 7, 1963).

tomary to dine, dance, and see the New Year in at the Rogers "with a great deal of noise and a punch bowl." There was ice-skating on the Hudson and tobogganing and skating on the Rogers pond. There were even baseball games on the spacious front lawn when the weather permitted. "We all went to a dinner of 50 at the Rogers," Sara noted New Year's Eve. "A dance after it. . . . E. does not seem at all well." Helen and Teddy were also at the party. "We dined at the Rogers tonight," Helen wrote, "a great big dinner as Edmund has a lot of men with him, & F.D.R. & Eleanor, Sylvia & Corinne are all staying at Cousin Sallie's & were all at dinner. It was great fun. . . . Teddy stayed till quite late . . . & I was tired, so we slept till 10.30 this morning."

Corinne also remembered the party. Eleanor had left with Sara after dinner; Franklin had stayed on, at Eleanor's urging, and had had "a lovely time," Corinne recalled. "It was an all-night affair and he could not have left before three or four in the morning." The next day when Corinne finally arose, she went in to see Eleanor and afterward ran into Franklin in the foyer. "He was pale as a sheet and furious. His mother had upbraided him for staying out so late, especially with his wife unwell, and had forced him to come down for breakfast at 8 A.M." Corinne and Franklin went for a walk and stopped in a greenhouse. "Suddenly there was a clatter of pipes and Franklin literally jumped. 'Are you afraid Mama is after you again?' I teased."[5]

If Eleanor was hurt by Franklin's easy acquiescence in her pulling back from most of the gay life of the young-married set she never said so, but much later she confessed that she had sometimes been jealous. She well remembered a young bride, Eleanor wrote in 1931 in a draft of an article, "The Tests of a Successful Wife" (and the reference, although in the third person, appears to be autobiographical), "who wept many tears because after an absence of some weeks, her husband on his return talked to her more about his business than about his love for her with the result that she thought the romance and glamor of marriage were gone forever."

Franklin, self-centered and flirtatious, would gladly have joined in every game or mischievous escapade of the moment. Banter came easily to him, and he was an incorrigible tease. Although Eleanor could laugh robustly, she was usually overserious, sensitive, and felt insecure in casual relationships. Thus, not wishing to spoil her husband's fun, nor expose herself to embarrassment and humiliation, she increasingly withdrew.

Their different temperaments, values, and upbringing created problems of adjustment for both. She had high and precise standards of how her young husband should behave. If he disappointed her—if he, like her father, was as invariably late as she was prompt; if he forgot an anniversary by which she set much store; if he was sometimes less than frank; if, without suspecting the inner distress it caused her, he agreed to domestic arrangements she did not like—she did not speak to him about it. Instead, she withdrew into heavy silence. The depressions were a form of passive reproach: she did not dare to be defiant, for that meant risking the approval of those whom she wanted to love her. She called them her "Griselda moods," and she was, like Patient Griselda in Chaucer's "The Clerk's Tale," the medieval archetype of "wifely obedience . . . all meekness, all yielding, all resignation." Eleanor not only nursed her hurts and disappointments in silence, but performed her wifely duties so excellently, was so helpful, self-effacing, competent, and understanding that, also like Griselda, "Ech her lovede that looked in her face."* Franklin loved and admired his wife but was often puzzled by her "Griselda moods" and wished she would speak up. He wanted to live up to her expectations and was aware of his shortcomings, even if he ·.as not unduly weighed down by them. It made him unhappy to see his wife sad or depressed, and at those times he left her alone, hoping it would blow over.

There were other differences between the two. Franklin executed his vestryman's duties at St. James Church faithfully, but often skipped Sunday services to play golf. Eleanor went to church regularly; it took time for her to become reconciled to his casual churchgoing habits. Franklin was dilatory about writing, while she was the most dependable of correspondents. "I was horribly disappointed with your hasty little scrap of a note yesterday after not getting anything for two days," she wrote from Campobello. It was a recurrent reproach.

In the excitement of the moment he often neglected his duties and forgot his promises, assuming that eventually, if others were involved, Sara or Eleanor would square things for him. And they did.

Eleanor took care of the amenities. When babies were born she sent notes of congratulations and ordered the gifts. When someone was ill, she called; when friends or relatives died, it was she who wrote. When Sara was not with them, it was Eleanor who said to Franklin, "I think Mama would love a letter from you" or "Don't forget Mama's birthday is the 21st." When Sara returned from Europe it was Eleanor who advised Franklin to have a man at customs "to see Mama through quickly . . . she expects us to 'smooth' things." She had an obsession about paying bills promptly; Franklin could be quite casual about this and tended to overlook them. She did not want to bother him in the midst of his Cambridge festivities, Eleanor wrote him in June, 1907, but "this has just come and I thought you said you wrote the man a note. . . ."

Whether gladly or not, she accepted the role of prodder and manager in family affairs in her marriage, just as she had for her brother. On the whole, life seemed good. When two of her bridesmaids, Ellen Delano and Muriel Robbins, wrote her in the spring of 1907 about their young men, she commented to Franklin, "God bless them both and may their husbands be as good to them as you have been to me."

Her preparations at the end of 1907 for the birth of her second child were

---

* The parallels between Chaucer's Griselda and Eleanor go much beyond this point. The prince's subjects at first could not understand why, with all the beautiful girls in the realm to choose from, he settled on Griselda. But then as she took charge of his household, they recognized her "rype and sad corage," and before long all were her liege supporters, for

> So wyse and wordes hadde she
> And jugements of so greet equitee,
> That she from heaven sent was, as men wende,
> Peple to save and every wrong t'amende.

a model of serene efficiency. "It is a very active infant or infants (!)," she wrote her mother-in-law, "and I have never felt so well but it will stick out in front and I have great difficulty keeping my clothes from rising up to my chin! Miss Spring says if it is twins she will run away!!" On December 16, Miss Spring again came to stay.

Eleanor wrote out a list of things for Franklin to do.

F.D.R. List

Tell Sara she can have Mrs. Keenan for the afternoon & evening on her Sunday out & on Thursday evenings. Speak to Mrs. K. yourself. Tell Nurse to put Anna to sleep in her *crib* until I am well enough for her to go in her cage & to bring her down to you in the mornings as soon as you call & then you get the nursemaid when you leave to bring her sewing & stay with her till Nurse can come for her. Telephone G'ma—47 Germantown, Cousin Susie, Isabella 331 Plaza. A. Corinne 6605 - 38th St. Helen 1008 79th St. Telegraph A. Bye 1733 N. St.

Milk tags for cans to be given Sara about Jan. 3d are in left hand drawer of my desk. Address envelopes for bills next to tags.

She bought and wrapped the Christmas gifts and filled the stockings, "even [for] Baby Anna and Miss Spring," Sara reported in some astonishment. On December 22, 1907, Eleanor, Franklin, and Hall dined with Sara and at 10:30 walked home. An hour later Hall was sent back to Sara's to spend the night there, as Eleanor's pains had begun. Franklin called his mother at 2:45 in the morning.

"I flew over and found Franklin to greet me with 'a son all right Mummy.'" Sara wrote in her diary. "I hope it will be *James*."

Franklin, elated, could not wait to inform the world. He called Helen and Teddy before breakfast, and Helen arrived almost immediately. Franklin showed her the "cunning baby," she reported. "He is lovely & looked like a 3-weeks-old child instead of only 7 hours! Weighs 10 lbs. 5 oz."

On the day that James was christened, Sara noted in royal phrases, "I gave presents on the place and house in honor of the named." As for Eleanor, her "heart sang," and she greeted the birth of a son with "relief and joy."

Despite James' size he was a sickly baby. He came down with pneumonia, and even after he recovered he was not completely well. The winter was difficult, for both baby and mother—"one of the times" in her life, Eleanor wrote, which she "would rather not live over again." To be near their doctor, the Roosevelts rented a cottage at Seabright, New Jersey, for the summer of 1908. Sara preferred not to be in Campobello without her children, and commuted between Hyde Park and Seabright during the hot summer months as did Franklin.

That summer Franklin had one of the first Fords around—it had no windshield, was cranked by hand, and was prone to frequent blowouts. "Has Franklin done anything rash yet—such as driving across the lawn and through the hedge?" Hall inquired. But it was Eleanor, not Franklin, who banged into the gate post when she was learning to drive. She gave up the attempt after the mishap, appalled at having damaged something that was Franklin's. She preferred the victoria, in which she and the children took drives along the beach.

Franklin and Eleanor enjoyed their children, whose first lispings were chronicled in detail. "She kept her eyes fixed on the door and said 'pa pa pa' all the time," Eleanor reported of Anna, aged eight months. There wasn't a funnier sight, she told her mother-in-law, than Franklin coming up the hill with Anna on his back, her "two short legs sticking straight out of either side of his head." Anna's first steps were duly noted. "She began on Sunday going from him [Franklin] to Cousin Susie and does better all the time but she loves it so that she really runs instead of walking which is the cause of many tumbles and subsequent tears."

In later years Eleanor described herself as having been a model of innocence and ignorance in her methods of child training. A believer in fresh air, she cradled Anna in a wire contraption rigged up outside a window until outraged neighbors, who allegedly threatened to report Eleanor to the Society for the Prevention of Cruelty to Children, compelled her to give up the experiment. But the other young wives thought her a pioneer, "How well I remember the Tuckermans, etc. on 37th Street agitating over the baby outside the window," Lily Polk later recalled, "and how wise the younger ones thought it and when we copied you how daring we felt!"

Though Eleanor knew what habits she wanted to encourage in her children, she was not sufficiently sure of herself to overrule the formidable array of mother-in-law, nurses, and English governess. In these early years she yielded to their authority against her own better judgment. "Anna is upset today so I am told though I haven't seen her long enough to judge for myself. Mama and Nelly think so, however, so she has gone to bed and had a dose of castor oil." On another occasion she thought that Anna wasn't well, but Sara disagreed. The doctor came and said Anna "should have calomel and I expect all would have been well before had I given it but Mama is so against it I didn't dare!" But if Sara and a nurse disagreed, the headstrong Sara laid down the law: "I told Nurse Watson she *must* get up and turn her [Anna] over and soothe her," Sara once noted in her diary.

When Anna was sixteen months old, Nurse Nelly had to be away. "I am to take charge of her and put her to bed tonight," Eleanor wrote, and noted the next day, "I never knew before how easy it was to take care of Anna." When Nurse Nelly returned, the baby was pleased, but, wrote Eleanor, "I am glad to say I think she missed me a little last night!"

In the autumn of 1908 Franklin and Eleanor moved into a house Sara had had built for them at 49 East Sixty-fifth Street. She had announced her intentions at Christmas in 1905, and the following year had acquired the land and hired Charles A. Platt, the designer of the Freer Gallery of Art in Washington, D. C., to draw up plans for adjoining houses—one for herself and one for the young couple—like the Ludlow-Parish houses on Seventy-sixth Street. The two houses' drawing and dining rooms opened onto each other, there was a connecting door on the fourth floor, and they had a common vestibule.

When Franklin came home on their first evening in the new house, he

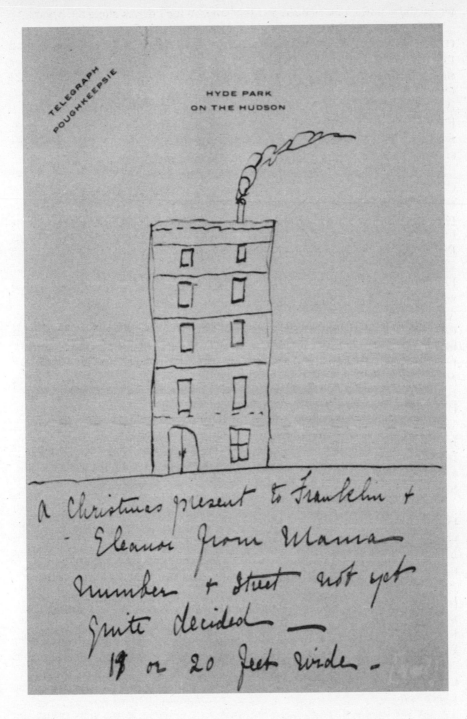

found his wife in tears. This was not her house, she sobbed. She had not helped plan it, and this wasn't the way she wanted to live. Why hadn't she told him this before, her bewildered husband asked. They had gone over the plans together—why hadn't she spoken up? He told her gently that she was not seeing things as they really were, and quickly left the room.[6]

If Sara knew of Eleanor's unhappiness, she did not admit it, even to herself. "Some of [my] friends were surprised," she told her biographer twenty-five years later, that Franklin and Eleanor had not lived with her after their marriage. That had never occurred to her, she blandly averred; she valued her independence too highly.[7] "You were never quite sure when she would appear, day or night," Eleanor later said of the connecting doors.[8]

With all her benevolence and breeding, Sara was an autocrat and rather enjoyed being regarded as the "redoubted madam" by her staff. She would have been surprised and hurt, however, if she had been told she was trying to rule her children's lives. She was a matriarch who belonged completely to a past generation; she sought to dominate her children's lives as she had dominated her husband's—from behind a façade of total generosity, submission, and love.

"Last night we had such a funny time," Eleanor wrote from Seabright to Nova Scotia, where Franklin was on a hunting expedition with Hall.

You would have enjoyed it for Anna gave Mama a little exhibition of her will power! She wished to sit on a certain chair and Grandma thought by talking to her and diverting her mind she could be made to sit on another and the result was shrieks and G'ma rapidly took to the desired chair.

When she ceased to weep I said "Oh! Anna where did you get all your determination from?" and she looked up at Mama and said "Gaga!"

Of course I almost expired for it did hit the nail so beautifully on the head.

Sara's husband had advised her never to be materially dependent upon her children, but it was all right, she told Eleanor, to have her children be dependent on her. "I think she always regretted that my husband had money of his own from his father and that I had a small income of my own," Eleanor said many years later. Their son James stated it more bluntly: "Granny's ace in the hole . . . was the fact that she held the purse strings in the family. For years she squeezed all of us—Father included—in this golden loop."

Few in the family were aware that Eleanor found total subordination to her mother-in-law increasingly oppressive. She did confide, often tearfully, Laura Delano said, in Laura's mother, Mrs. Warren Delano, who lived around the corner. But if she could tell Aunt Jennie, Laura wondered, why couldn't she have had it out with her husband and her mother-in-law?[9]

A few of her closest friends eventually became aware of the situation and concluded that she kept silent because she did not wish to do anything that might disturb the relationship between mother and son. Moreover, she could not bear being scolded or rebuked herself. She had developed a sixth sense for Sara's velvety "yes" that really meant "no," and was so sensitive even to these indirect reproaches that she preferred to swallow her discontent. That was the period, a friend recalled, when she was saying "Yes, Mama" or "No, Mama" three or four times in a row.[10] She was "very dependent" on her mother-in-law, Eleanor said forty years later; she had needed Sara's help "on almost every subject and never thought of asking for anything which I felt would not meet with her approval."[11] But this self-subordination exacted its toll in self-doubt, bottled-up anger, and withdrawal into those "Griselda moods" that her husband found so puzzling.

Whatever Eleanor's private frustrations, Sara was oblivious of them in her diaries, which were a serene chronicle of the things she did with Franklin and Eleanor and their children: "A little dinner for F. & E." "To town early. Arranged flowers for F. & E.'s lunch of 22 for the T.R. family." "Today E. & I walked to church." In 1908 Eleanor was pregnant for the third time, and a diary she kept briefly before the baby was born revealed only that, like other young wives, she moved in a world that was still limited to family and old friends, to familiar surroundings and activities. She was very precise in noting the time Franklin came in and when he went out alone. She dined alone with Sara, she recorded in January, 1909, while Franklin went to a dinner party with Teddy Robinson, played poker at the Knickerbocker Club, and "returned home 4 A.M." Two weeks later there was a similar entry: "F. went to Harvard Club dinner & got home 3:30 A.M. Dined with Mama."

On Wednesday, March 17, she wrote, "St. Patrick's Day. Mother's birthday. Our fourth wedding anniversary!" The next day Franklin Jr. was born.

Again Sara recorded the event.

March 18th Eleanor had her beautiful hair washed, etc. and nails done. At 2 she went to drive with me. We got home at 4. At 5.30 Dr. Ely came. At 8.10 her second son was born. Franklin got home at 4.45 so he was there very soon after Eleanor got home from her drive. The baby is really lovely and very big, 11 lbs.

Franklin Jr. was indeed the biggest and most beautiful of all Eleanor and Franklin's babies. Eleanor had regretted letting Miss Spring go too quickly after the birth of James, and this time she insisted on keeping Miss Spring for several months.

In the summer of 1909 they returned to Campobello but stayed in a house of their own. Mrs. Hartman Kuhn, who had owned the cottage next door to Sara's, had become as fond of Eleanor, who frequently read to her, as she had always been of Franklin. She had died in 1908, and her will stipulated that Sara could have her house for $5,000, if she purchased it for Franklin and Eleanor. Sara did so.

This was the first house that Eleanor felt was her own. "I have moved every room in the house around," she gaily reported to her husband, "and I hope you will like the change," and he should bring up his caribou and wolf skins to spread in front of the fireplace. Now Franklin and Eleanor could have whomever they wished as guests. Although Sara had encouraged them to invite friends when they stayed with her, her opinions of suitable guests had not always coincided with Eleanor's. Furthermore, Sara did not want her children to form close attachments outside the family circle. Eleanor liked Miss Spring, from whom she had learned a great deal, but when she lunched with Miss

Spring she did not dare mention it to Sara and cautioned Franklin not to do so, "for Mama always seems to dislike my doing things with her!" Even after her first summer in her own house in Campobello Eleanor was fearful of Sara's reaction to the announcement that she was inviting Miss Spring to come up for part of the next summer.

"I broke it to Mama Miss Spring was coming up and put it all on you," she advised her husband. Unable to stand up for herself and say "this is what I want," she made use of others. It was a conscious tactic that she would employ in the White House years with great subtlety and sophistication in order to get Franklin to do the things which he might otherwise refuse to do if the suggestions came directly from her.

Eleanor was content at Campobello. The pace there was more sedate than at Bar Harbor or Newport. The summer families had a club of sorts and were satisfied with an occasional dance for which a Victor talking machine provided the music. Eleanor even liked the Bay of Fundy's fogs and its prolonged periods of foul weather, for she was an avid reader and enjoyed reading aloud to family and guests in front of the fireplace in the large living room.

She always arrived at Campobello determined on self-improvement. One summer she and Sara read all of Ferrero's volumes on Rome. She began to study Spanish with the help of recordings. "All my Spanish things are here," she wrote Franklin, "but I am waiting for you to put my phonograph together!" Franklin did, but at the end of the summer she confessed she might never learn the language because she still had not mastered the art of making the phonograph work.

Until his marriage, Hall spent part of his summers at Campobello. Franklin enjoyed and admired his brilliant young brother-in-law, who had been chosen senior prefect at Groton. Whenever Hall arrived, a covey of girls would immediately gather around him, and Franklin and Eleanor spoke teasingly about "Hall and his harem." Hall looked up to his sister, whose selflessness and devotion he appreciated. "I despair of hearing from Eleanor about herself," he wrote Franklin from Groton. "I hope you will drop me a postal some time just to let me know how she is getting on."

When Franklin had to be in New York, Eleanor tried to pinch-hit for him with the children in outdoor activities, and during the summer of 1909, when James was a year and a half and Anna a little over three, she took them sailing on the *Half Moon.* "I think they will sail rather seldom together as James goes round and round the cockpit and won't sit still and Anna kicks him whenever she can." James had his defenses against Anna, however: "He is very naughty and poor Anna's arm is all blue where he bit her yesterday."

There were fond letters from Eleanor and the children.

Dearest Honey—
The enclosure was dictated jointly by Anna & James on the *Half Moon* this afternoon. We got off at three but the wind was light & we didn't get up to G. South Bay but the chicks had supper on board & loved it.
This morning I took Anna & James to the beach & as there was no wind & the

sun was hot I put on Anna's bathing suit & she waded until just before we came up when she sat down & kicked & splashed & then ran home & slept 2 hours! She is mad about it & James weeps because he can't sit down & when I say he must stop wading he kicks & howls with rage! . . .

Ever so much love. E.R.

(Enclosure)

Dear Fadder,

I had my bathing suit on & go in the water & walked & sat down & splashed. (James) took off his shoes & stockings & was angry as he couldn't walk to the boat. In the morning I say "Good morning Half Moon, Captain, Mother, Old Mother Hubbard.

(Anna) I wouldn't like to go away from Campobello.

(James) Poor Fadder go to New York.

(A. & J.) Like Fadder to come back soon.

Anna's kiss . . . made by herself.

James' kiss

Your loving
Anne & James

And there were the detailed orders from an efficient wife in cool Campobello to a husband in the sweltering city. "I enclose my list of things to be done," she wrote Franklin, "and I am sorry for you."

Ask Mary if she knows of two good, *honest* cleaners to come on Monday, Sept 13th & start at the roof & clean down & be through on Sept. 21st. To take great care with the white paint & get it clean also sun the children's mattresses on the roof & beat them well the last day. I think it would be well for you to ask Harriet to do the library & tell her to take all the books out, wipe them & put them back. She ought to do it in three days & as she can't work steadily I would tell her that we will only pay her $1. a day. The other cleaners get $1.50.

Telephone R. H. Morisson 73rd St. & 3d Avenue to clean all the chimneys between the 9th & 11th as it must be over before the cleaning begins. Also find out from Max if the [word indistinct] cap is on the chimney as we don't want more work than necessary done after the house is clean.

Bring me Aug. & Sept. Harper's when you come. Go to Putnam's & order some nice book not more than $5. sent to Miss Ellen Shipman, Windsor, Vermont, with enclosed card.

If Mary knows no cleaners ask Harriet.

I am anxiously waiting for the wash trunk. Was Mary at the house when you got home? Will you ask her when the trunk left? Don't forget to look in both houses for [words indistinct]. Tell me what Dr. Dailey's bill was. Send Hall his check book.

Subsequent letters supplemented these instructions.

Their return to New York that autumn was shadowed by the illness of Franklin Jr. Although he weighed eleven pounds at birth, he seemed delicate, like James, and Miss Spring was with the family at Campobello most of the summer to care for him. They were worried about his rapid breathing, but they were not prepared for the worsening in his condition that set in late in October. Sara reported the course of the crisis in her journal and the reaction of the three of them to the tragedy.

Oct. 29. Baby cried often in the morning, but was sleeping sweetly in the pram at 12.30 when I went in a motor to the Olins for lunch. Mrs. Howard with me. At 2, Annie the housemaid telephoned me to come as Baby was ill. I *flew* home. . . . Dr. Gribbon was here, holding precious Baby. He just got there in time as the little heart had almost stopped. . . . I telephoned E. She and F. came at 8.30 bringing Miss Spring. Dr. Gribbon stayed till 11.

Oct. 30th. . . . they all leave on the 9.30 train. . . . Dr. Winters in N.Y. confirms Dr. Gribbon that it is serious heart trouble. Some hope is held out. Darling Eleanor is brave and Franklin helps and supports her hopeful spirit.

Oct. 31st. Eleanor says Baby had a fair night and is quiet. They are hopeful. At 2.30 Franklin telephoned me not so well. I went to town, though just as I left, F. said "don't come down." I simply had to go. When I got there, E. said, "Oh, I am so glad you came." . . .

Nov. 1st. At a little before 5 I went in. Dr. Carr said "He is holding his own." At a little before 7 A.M. F. telephoned me to my room. "Better come, Mama, Baby is sinking." I went in. The little angel ceased breathing at 7:45. Miss Spring was asleep in her room but Dr. Carr and Miss Battin did what they could. F. and E. are most wonderful, but poor E.'s mother heart is well nigh broken. She so hoped and cannot believe her baby is gone from her. He was 7 months and 9 days old, a beautiful flower he always seemed and yet the delicacy certainly was there and he could not overcome it.

Nov. 2nd. I sat often besides my little grandson. It is hard to give him up and my heart aches for Eleanor.

Nov. 5. F. and E. came home (i.e., H.P.) and it is such a sad homecoming. E. is perfectly marvelous the way she bears it.

Nov. 7th. All to church. E. brave and lovely.

For many months Eleanor's life was darkened by the baby's death. She felt she was in some way to blame and reproached herself for not caring for him enough. The baby's death reinforced her sense of inadequacy as a woman and as a mother. When Elliott, born ten months later, turned out to be a more agitated and excitable baby than Anna and James had been, she blamed that, too, on her moodiness while carrying him. Only gradually did she conquer her grief for her dead baby, and she often laid flowers on the quiet little grave in the St. James churchyard and recalled the sad burial scene.

Such tragedies, as she well knew from childhood, were part of the human condition. Religion comforted her, as did her love for Franklin. "I miss you dreadfully and feel very lonely," she wrote him from Campobello the next summer, "but please don't think it is because I am alone, having other people wouldn't do any good for I just want you!"

"Success in marriage," she told an interviewer many years later, "depends on being able when you get over being in love, to really love . . . you never know anyone until you marry them."[12] Five years after her marriage, just before Franklin entered politics, their friends considered them an exemplary couple and thought Eleanor remarkable for the way she fulfilled her role as wife, mother, mistress of her household, and daughter-in-law.

16. The Wife of a Public Official

AFTER TAFT'S ELECTION in 1908 Theodore Roosevelt invited various younger members of the family to the White House for a final visit before inauguration day. Eleanor and Franklin went down early in January, and a week later it was the Teddy Robinsons' turn. "It is rather horrid to feel that is the last time that we will be at the White House in that way," Helen wrote.[1] Franklin had other thoughts. Imbued with Theodore's ideals of public service, he already contemplated a career modeled on Uncle Ted's that would bring him to the White House on his own. To his fellow law clerks he outlined a political timetable like his uncle's—the state legislature, assistant secretary of the Navy, the governorship, and then, with "any luck," the presidency. The law office was only a way station on the road to the livelier world of politics, and "he intended to run for office at the first opportunity."[2]

Franklin's mother did not welcome the idea that her son might become involved in the "messy business" of politics, as she later told her biographer. She did not see why she should receive all these people whom she had never called on and whose families she did not know. Eleanor, however, was neither surprised nor upset by his plans.[3] While Franklin was still in law school she had written Auntie Bye, "he will not find himself altogether happy with the law he is studying at Columbia unless he is able to get a broad human contact through it."[4] A career in politics would assure him of a life full of excitement and variety in which his ability to get along with people would be important.

Franklin had always voted from Hyde Park. Like his father, he was active in village and county affairs, but with Eleanor at his side to encourage him he brushed aside his mother's pleas that he follow his father and lead a "peaceful life among the family, the friends and neighbors at Hyde Park." When John Mack, Democratic district attorney in Dutchess County, dropped into the Carter, Ledyard and Milburn offices early in 1910 to talk Dutchess politics and discuss the possibility of Franklin running for the state legislature, he found an attentive listener.

Eleanor had known enough men in public life to realize that if her husband embarked on a political career it would mean that the family would have to move about a lot, be very adaptable, and make many sacrifices. But she wanted her husband to have large plans, and if realizing those dreams meant she would have to make adjustments, she was prepared to do so—to live in Albany if that was required and to see that his household ran smoothly. Politics was neither new nor threatening to her. She followed public affairs, read the *New York Times* regularly, and, like her husband, had been stirred by Uncle Ted's appeals to the younger generation to devote themselves to the public good. And deep within she must have realized that Franklin's entry into politics would mean an expansion of her horizons as well as his.

In June she and Franklin lunched with Uncle Ted on his return from Europe and Africa, and no doubt they discussed Franklin's decision to go into politics. Theodore was planning to return to the political wars himself, to fight the conservative drift in the Republican party under Taft. Would Uncle Ted be campaigning in Dutchess County, Franklin asked Auntie Bye a few weeks later. "Franklin ought to go into politics without the least regard as to where I speak or don't speak," Theodore advised Bye. Franklin was "a fine fellow," he went on, but he wished he had Joe Alsop's views. Joe Alsop, whom Auntie Corinne described as "a very strong man," had married young Corinne and was involved in Republican politics in Connecticut. And in Herkimer, New York, Teddy Robinson was preparing to run for the state assembly as a Republican.

She had heard an amusing account, Aunt Ella wrote Eleanor from Liverpool, of how Franklin, Teddy, and Joe Alsop were "all in the limelight and Uncle Ted in the extraordinary position of being the arbiter of the Republican destinies. He has certainly infected you all with large ambitions as citizens and I am sure will be proud of you all."[5]

It was a measure of Franklin's independence that, admiring Theodore as greatly as he did, he stuck with the Democrats. Eleanor, although she worshiped her uncle and had been raised in a household and milieu where "Republicanism and respectability went hand in hand,"[6] followed her husband's political allegiance. Any suggestion that she should not would have shocked her, and she certainly did not envisage a political role for herself. She was an antisuffragette, and vigorously so. Pussie was the only advocate of the women's vote in the family. "The most surprising part to me," Hall commented to Eleanor in 1908, "is that she is trying to convert you of all people." Two years later Eleanor was still disagreeing with Pussie over the suffragette issue, and evidently with some violence, to judge by Hall's reproving remark: "I thought you had more self control."

While Eleanor insisted that politics was a man's domain, she wanted to share her husband's interests and accomplishments, a somewhat contradictory position that was also held by other strong-minded women of that transitional era. Beatrice Webb did not recant her public opposition to women's suffrage until 1909, even though she had renounced her romance with Joe Chamberlain rather than yield to his insistence that he should have the final word in their marriage.[7] Eleanor made no such demand, but she did want to be part of her husband's life away from home as well as in it.

She was at Campobello most of the summer of 1910 when Franklin was meeting with the Dutchess County leaders and party workers. Her letters begged him to keep her informed about his political prospects; it was difficult enough being at Campobello without him, she wrote, but if he did not write she would feel quite lost. And if he was unable to come up as he had planned, "I shall weep." Franklin hoped to run for the assembly, but the incumbent, Lewis Stuyvesant Chanler, finally told him he had no intention of bowing out. This left the state senate seat, which had only once been won from the Republicans, in the 1880s by Roosevelt's neighbor, Thomas Jefferson Newbold. Franklin's chances of winning, Mack cautioned him, were one in five. Undaunted, Franklin decided to make the bid.

On September 23, 1910, Eleanor gave birth to Elliott, an eleven-pound fourteen-ounce baby. Two weeks later, on October 6, the Democratic leaders meeting in convention in Poughkeepsie formally nominated Franklin Roosevelt for state senator. Sara now discovered that pride in her son was stronger than anxiety over the hordes of strangers she might have to receive. She sat proudly through the meeting as he made his acceptance speech, she recalled two decades later, her head held high, sure as she heard his statement of principles that *noblesse oblige* would shape his career in politics as it had that of her old friend Theodore and the sons of her highborn friends in England.[8] In her diary at the time, however, she limited herself to the more pragmatic comment, "Franklin will be here now a great deal."

Eleanor did not hear the speech. Immobilized in New York City with her newly born baby, she had to be satisfied with the lilies, at that time her favorite flower, that Franklin had sent her. "Much love and good luck to you in your campaigning," she wrote him as he set out to reverse the 5 to 1 odds by the unorthodoxy of his campaign tactics. "In the coming campaign," he had pledged in his acceptance speech, "I need not tell you that I do not intend to sit still. We are going to have a very strenuous month." He hired a red Maxwell touring car and decked it out with flags, and "at the dangerous pace of about 22 miles an hour" he and the congressional candidate, Richard Connell, a spread-eagle orator, toured the district, stopping at every country store, talking to every farmer, speaking in every village.* Not even a fall from a moving street car slowed him down. Eleanor spent twenty-four hours soaking his elbows and knees in disinfectant and he was off again. The Saturday before the election Eleanor heard him make his final speech outside the Nelson House in Poughkeepsie, later known as his "lucky corner"—the first time she had heard him make a political speech. She agonized over his slow delivery and frequent pauses,[9] but he managed, nonetheless, to convey warmth, friendliness, and self-confidence. The voters responded. On Election Day, Sara recorded, in the proper order of their importance to her, "Anna weighs 42.8; James 35.13. Franklin elected State Senator with about 1,500 majority."

---

* In later years he often regaled his wife and children with the song that he and Connell sang as they neared some port of call:

> Are we almost there?—Are we almost there?
> Said the dying girl as she neared her home.
> Be them the tall poplar trees what rears
> Their lofty heights against Heaven's big dome——
> Are we——al——most there——
> (agonized diminuendo)

It was a Democratic sweep in which the governorship as well as both houses of the legislature were captured by the party, but Franklin ran far ahead of the state ticket. His unparalleled 1,140 majority in a rock-ribbed Republican district was noted by politicians throughout the state. "Telegrams coming all day for Franklin," Sara recorded. Eleanor returned to New York to be with her baby, but a new period was beginning in her life, for Franklin had said that if elected he wanted his family with him in Albany. "We're thinking of your move to Albany," Isabella Ferguson wrote Eleanor from Cat Cañon in New Mexico. The Fergusons and their two children had cut loose from fashionable New York and were literally tenting down in the southwest desert because the dry air and hot sun had been recommended for Bob's lungs. Eleanor's impending move represented almost as drastic a break with her previous style of life as the Fergusons' had.

The change began in November when she and Franklin, without Sara, went to Albany to look for a house. They picked a large brownstone with an enormous library and a small garden. Although it seemed quite palatial compared to their narrow New York house, "it is a comfort to have only three stories instead of six," Franklin commented. Three weeks later they returned with Sara, who approved. "A fine house can be made comfortable."

Albany in 1911 was a cluster of low roofs dominated by a few church spires and the architectural pile on a hill that constituted the center of the state government. For most of the legislators the city was little more than a dormitory and their brief stays were confined to the stretch of pavement between the Hotel Ten Eyck, the capitol, and the railroad station. It was also a pleasant city for those who wanted to live there, with broad avenues, narrow tree-shaded streets, and a spacious park full of lovely walks and drives where Eleanor and the nurses could take the children. Among the brownstones and red brick homes were a few gabled roofs to remind newcomers of the city's Dutch antecedents. The small, compact Albany society was dominated by a few old families of Dutch lineage, and it bid the Roosevelts welcome.

Eleanor was the wife of Albany's most talked-about young politician, and her initiation into official life was swift, sudden, and thorough. On the Sunday before Governor Dix's inauguration, with the children, their three nurses, and a household staff barely settled, she and Sara were arranging furniture and hanging photographs when politicians who had come to Albany for the inauguration began to drop by to take a look at Franklin.

The next day, wife, mother, and brother-in-law accompanied the new senator to the assembly chamber, where they listened to the governor's speech and then hurried home because Franklin had announced "open house" for his constituents. A block away, they saw a dense, cheering crowd in the front of their house—the delegation from Franklin's senatorial district, "four hundred strong!" as Franklin told the story. There was a band and the Hyde Park Fife and Drum Corps, both "working overtime," and "all finally managed to get into the house, shaking hands as they passed into the Dining Room." To Eleanor the catered luncheon seemed endless, but Sara thought she "managed splendidly," and Franklin recorded proudly that both "E.R. and S.D.R. . . . made a hit with the whole delegation."

Eleanor's initiation was not yet over. She and Franklin drove to the executive mansion to pay their formal respects to Governor and Mrs. Dix, and when they returned half the Dutchess County delegation was back at the house to await the departure of their train. It was late afternoon before Franklin coaxed them out and led them down to the station. Scarcely had Eleanor and Sara gone back to moving furniture when the governor called and invited Franklin and Eleanor to come up to the mansion for a "family party" and a little informal dancing; so they quickly dressed and hurried over.[10] The next night they were again with the governor, this time as guests of Colonel and Mrs. William Gorham Rice, old friends of the James Roosevelts. Colonel Rice had been President Cleveland's secretary, and he and Governor Dix were Cleveland Democrats, as Franklin's father had been and as his half brother Rosy still was. Mrs. Rice welcomed Eleanor to Albany with a list of places to shop and a ceremonial offering of "ole Keuken," a cake that was still eaten by the families descended from the original Dutch colonists. Another guest at the Rices' was Thomas Mott Osborne, the former mayor of Auburn. A man of wealth, he was the leader of the anti Tammany liberal wing of the Democratic party, which he had nurtured along with the help of an upstate newspaperman named Louis Howe.

On Wednesday Sara returned to Hyde Park. "It seems like a very strange dream," she wrote Franklin and Eleanor, "to be here and to think of you dear things all settled in that big Albany house and my boy sitting in the State Senate, a really fine and dignified position, if only lived up to as it should be and I know it *will* be by my dear one. . . . I was *so* interested today and were I to be with you I should be very often in that gallery."

For the first time since her marriage, Eleanor was out of immediate reach of Sara and Cousin Susie and had to depend upon herself. Although she was shy and uncertain, necessity was a good teacher. In the few days she had been in Albany, she had met hundreds of new people, had had to cope with all kinds of new situations, and had discovered not only that she could manage, but that she liked it.

She had a lively intellectual curiosity, was as interested in people as her husband was, and found the political atmosphere invigorating. When Franklin turned their State Street house into the headquarters of the insurgents a few days after the session began, Eleanor took it in her stride. At that time U. S. senators were still chosen by the state legislature, and Tammany leader Charles F. Murphy wanted Chauncey M. Depew's successor to be "Blue-eyed Billy" Sheehan. Edmund R. Terry, an independent assemblyman from Brooklyn who had been a classmate of President Taft's at Yale, began the rebellion against Boss Murphy's designation of Sheehan. Franklin was the first senator to join the assembly insurgents and was made the spokesman for the group. He quickly became "the shepherd of the flock," Terry wrote, "and his house was during the early days of the insurgency a harbor of refuge nearly every evening."

Eleanor spent many of these evenings with the men, and later estimated that she got to know at least thirty of them "very well." For her it was a seminar in the more practical side of politics. She made the men feel at home in the library; sometimes she sat with them, but more often they slipped into the living room to talk with her. Terry was one of the most faithful. A prolific writer of verse, he read it to her by the hour while she knitted. At the end of the evening, with Terry's help she brought in crackers, cheese, and beer, which became the signal that it was time, gentlemen, to adjourn.

The press came to the house, another new experience for Eleanor. Louis Howe, a poky little man in disheveled clothes, was often there as reporter and adviser, and Eleanor invited his wife and daughter to lunch. Another day Mr. and Mrs. Sheehan were her luncheon guests. The former Buffalo boss hoped he could soften Franklin's opposition in a direct confrontation, and the men withdrew, leaving the ladies to make polite, uncomfortable small talk. It was sticky going. Finally the parley ended and the Sheehans left. "Did you come to any agreement?" Eleanor anxiously asked. "Certainly not," her husband replied. The struggle went on.

Sara came to Albany. "He is working bravely," she wrote. Uncle Ted also approved: "Just a line to say that we are all really proud of the way you have handled yourself." Franklin felt the same way about his distinguished relative. "Are you an admirer of your uncle-in-law?" a reporter asked him. "Why, who can help but admire him? ... My uncle-in-law will come back all right, no matter what some people believe." Sheehan spread the word that Franklin was really Theodore's agent and was trying to split the Democratic party. "Why I haven't seen my distinguished cousin since the first of the year," Franklin said laughingly, and then added, a little inaccurately, "We've had absolutely no communication on this subject." As Franklin's fight made him known throughout the state, the mail began to pour in, and Eleanor received her first fan letter: "I know very well he never could do so well, and be so brave, if he were not upheld and strengthened in every way by his wife." It was one of the few nonfamily letters she saved from that period.

The meetings continued night after night, and when the children, whose nursery was directly above the library, began to complain about the cigar smoke, Eleanor moved the nursery to the third floor. She presided over frequent dinners and larger entertainments that mixed politicians and local society. She met thirty-three-year-old Robert Wagner, whose nomination as president pro tem of the state senate Franklin had seconded on behalf of the upstate senators. Alfred E. Smith, assembly majority leader and another of Murphy's protégés, came to dinner. When British Ambassador James Bryce addressed a joint session of the legislature, Franklin and Eleanor gave a party for about one hundred people at which Ruth Draper did her monologues and Tammanyites, insurgents, and Albany cliff dwellers rubbed shoulders. "Mr.

Grady gratefully acknowledges the honor and accepts the gracious compliment of the invitation of Mrs. Roosevelt to her at home," one reply read, from Senator Tom Grady, the courtly, eloquent, but somewhat bibulous Tammanyite. Although Franklin had helped to depose Grady as senate leader, he liked the young man's wife. "Be with the insurgents," he wrote Eleanor on St. Patrick's Day, "and if needs be with your husband every day in the year but this—to-day be 'wid us.' "

When Sheehan finally withdrew from the race, Murphy put forward the candidacy of Justice O'Gorman, a man of integrity though a former Tammany sachem. The insurgents went along, and newspapermen wrote that Roosevelt had been scalped by Tammany. They failed to note that Franklin Roosevelt's name had become nationally known in connection with the movement for direct, popular election of senators and that he had become identified as part of the progressive wing of the Democratic party. As for Eleanor, she asserted that the rights and wrongs of the Sheehan fight meant very little to her, although she was appalled at the reprisals against some of the more vulnerable insurgents. Franklin, however, later said that the struggle was the beginning of his wife's "political sagacity."

When, at a banquet given by the Columbia County Society, a reporter asked Franklin how country women compared with those in the cities, he replied, "I'm afraid I'm a little prejudiced in that direction," and flashed his broad smile. "I haven't been married long enough to compare any woman favorably with my wife—and she came from the country, from Columbia County which is one of the reasons I am at this banquet. If all country girls are like her, then there can be no comparison—and you must pardon me if I make none."

Their close friends knew how helpful she was to him. "She did everything quietly but calmly and most efficiently," Langdon P. Marvin, one of Franklin's law partners, later recalled. "She was a great manager in the family and in the household and everybody loved her." She was also, he added, "the ardent backer" of her husband, even though he was not able to budge her when he began to shift his position on women's suffrage.[11] His conversion was less than wholehearted at first. With an eye on his rural constituents—and perhaps also on his mother and his wife—he hedged his stand, saying that the voters should express their views through a referendum before the legislature acted. That, said the beautiful and relentless suffragette, Inez Mulholland, who lobbied Senator Roosevelt on the issue, was "a very stupid and expensive way" of going about it.

Miss Mulholland had come to Poughkeepsie in May, 1911, to fire up the feminist troops, of which the Vassar faculty was a powerful contingent. She marshaled the members of the Dutchess County chapter of the Equal Suffrage League in a series of street-corner meetings and house-to-house canvasses.[12] Senator Roosevelt finally took the correct stand, but without help from his wife, who still considered men superior beings. Nor is there any evidence that Eleanor intervened on behalf of another crusader for women's rights, Frances

Perkins, just out of college, who had joined the staff of the Consumers League and, as a lobbyist in Albany for the fifty-four-hour bill for working women, was having difficulty with Franklin.

Eleanor was not yet "the evident force" that she subsequently became, observed Marvin. Within the privacy of the family, however, she was a sympathetic and interested listener who through her questions and comments helped Franklin clarify his opinions by talking them out, as she had seen her Auntie Bye do with Uncle Ted.

She went to the senate gallery regularly to listen to the debates and occasionally visited the assembly side to follow the progress of a bill. She read political materials, including such recondite documents as the proceedings of the 1884 Democratic national convention, which Colonel Rice had sent to her. By the beginning of July, when she transported her large household to Campobello, she had the knowledge of a political insider to whom Franklin could write in the crisp shorthand that political professionals use about such varied items as the race-track-gambling bill, the ups and downs of his fight for a direct primary, or his intricate political maneuvers to defeat a Republican reapportionment bill.

It was a disturbed summer. No sooner had Eleanor arrived in Campobello than Franklin reported he was having trouble with his sinuses and that he felt "like a rag and have lost nearly ten pounds. . . . I can't tell you how I miss you and Mama does not in the least make up." Eleanor promptly returned to Albany to nurse him. "Eleanor came in all the heat," Sara noted, adding five days later, "Poor Eleanor returns alone to Campobello." Franklin stayed to push his direct-primary bill. When the legislature recessed without action, he hastened to Campobello, but he had to leave again early in September. "I feel lonely and depressed and wish you were here," she wrote him. "Take care of yourself and write often and tell me everything."

She realized that she would often have to manage without him in the summer. She was a conscientious manager. Henry Parish, the banker who was married to Cousin Susie, taught her to keep her household accounts, and his lessons were supplemented by those Franklin gave her. She budgeted carefully. "I enclose Edgar's bill which is a dreadful surprise to me," she wrote her husband from Campobello. "I had no idea that you had told him to spend so much on the pool or that he had to work so many days in the winter. This year we must make it plain that we want no work done!" Sometimes her efforts at frugality and careful planning ran athwart Sara. Eleanor and Franklin had decided that instead of opening their townhouse in New York for the few autumn months before they were back in Albany, they would stay with Sara and board out the servants they wanted to keep. Sara was upset over the proposed arrangements, Franklin warned; she wanted the servants to stay. "Do just as you think best dearest," he wrote Eleanor, "and you know I'll back you up!" his letter ended.

"Really, Honey, it becomes ludicrous!" Eleanor protested in a spurt of independence:

She made an offer then withdrew it and now wants to renew it! I think she had better decide another time before speaking and as I wrote you it would be foolish to get new servants and put them in her house as Lydia is going. I expect to let Emily go also as I overheard a conversation which made me decide that she talked too much even though she might seem nice to me! ... After Cousin Susie is in town I'm sure she will love having us stay there if we want to anytime and I would rather do it than go to Mama's now! I simply wrote Mama all my plans were already made and no one would be in her house and I did not expect to go there!

Eleanor's view prevailed. It usually did when she considered it worthwhile to make a stand.

When they returned to Albany for the winter of 1911–12 they moved into a new house. Their friends were glad to see them both. They were "exceedingly popular ... their home ... the scene of good fellowship and real family life."[13] People were as interested in Eleanor as they were in Franklin, and she was now an old Albany hand. She called on the wives of the new legislators and helped make them feel at home, and she dropped in on the wives of newspapermen. Her thoughtfulness and kindness made friends for Franklin everywhere. Teddy Robinson had been elected to the assembly from Herkimer in November's Republican comeback, and the two families saw each other often. For Franklin's birthday Eleanor had the Robinsons, Hall and his fiancée, Margaret Richardson, William Church Osborn, the Rices, and some senatorial colleagues with whom Franklin worked closely. Sara was not there. "I planned to go up and surprise you today," she wrote, "and spend one night but as Hall and Margaret get there today I think it would be foolish and also I should have to sleep with you and Eleanor!" As a birthday gift, she "enclose[d] a little motor car for the winter."

Eleanor found marriage to a man at the center of public activity stimulating. Everyone had something interesting to contribute to her education and, in turn, she gave everyone the feeling that she was interested in them. Eleanor's "dinner record" was crowded with the names of Cleveland Democrats, progressives, and regulars. She and Franklin went to play bridge with Mr. and Mrs. Louis Howe, although Eleanor felt that neither bridge nor Mr. Howe contributed to an attractive evening. Franklin wanted her to go, so she went.

Franklin was a key man in the 1912 legislature. "We are safely organized," he informed Eleanor, who was in New York City, at the beginning of the year. "The Committee appointments were handed down. I drew Chairman of Agriculture, ranking member of Conservation (the old Forest, Fish and Game) and also member of Codes, Railroads and *Military Affairs*! This isn't bad and I am particularly glad that the other members of Agriculture give me control of the Committee as against our New York City friends." Franklin was even being talked about as a possible candidate for governor. On their wedding anniversary Eleanor gave a political luncheon attended by the governor, the lieutenant governor, Senator O'Gorman, and a gentleman whom she described in her dinner book as the "Secretary of Tammany Hall."

By April, however, his political prospects had darkened. The Republican resurgence dimmed his chance of re-election in 1912, and the Tammany bosses detested him. The Democratic boss of Albany, "Packy" McCabe, upbraided Roosevelt as a "political prig" and said it was time the party leaders stopped coddling these "fops and cads . . . these political prudes," phrases that echoed those used against Theodore when he was an assemblyman. One hope that Franklin and his fellow progressives had of breaking Murphy's stranglehold on the state Democratic organization was to align themselves with the burgeoning Wilson movement. Although initial efforts to drum up Wilson support at the state convention were a fiasco, Franklin and William Church Osborne decided to convene a Wilson Conference. But before the preparations were complete Franklin and Hall embarked on a winter cruise to Panama, leaving Eleanor to cope not only with the move back to town but with the Wilson movement as well.

Osborne wrote Eleanor to ask whether there was any objection to signing Franklin's name to the call for the conference, saying he was quite sure it was all right "under the approval he [Franklin] gave; but I should prefer to have your advice on the matter." Eleanor's reply was deliberately noncommittal, which did not help him much, Osborne commented dryly, and left him "in something of a quandary." Osborne's letter, she wrote Franklin, "has given me an uncomfortable day but I can only hope I've done as you would wish." More of a pragmatist in politics than the uncompromising Osborne, he wanted to move slowly. Moreover, he had many irons in the fire, as Eleanor's next letter indicated. "Louis Howe told me to tell you," she wrote, "that Evans etc., were grooming you to run for Governor against Mr. Wadsworth! Also he had a long talk with Mr. C. Osborne and felt that you could count on help from him next autumn."

She had arranged to meet Franklin in New Orleans on his way back, since they did not like to be separated any longer than necessary. "I simply hated to have you go on Saturday," she wrote him after he sailed, and he was also upset. "It is hard enough to be away from the chicks, but with you away from me too I feel very much alone and lost. I hereby solemnly declare that I REFUSE to go away the next time without you. . . ."

Her husband's involvement in the Wilson campaign created a dilemma for Eleanor, since she was devoted to her Uncle Ted. Late in March she had lunched with Auntie Bye and Uncle Ted who, with characteristic energy, was preparing his assault on Taft's renomination. When she joined Franklin in New Orleans in April they went to Cat Cañon for a three-day visit with the Fergusons and found Bob and Isabella passionately absorbed in Theodore's forthcoming campaign. The younger "progressive" elements were hitching themselves to Theodore's star, they told the Roosevelts. Franklin's law partners, Langdon Marvin and Harry Hooker, were for Teddy. Even Sara was in conflict.

Whatever Eleanor's private sentiments, her duty was to be at the side of her husband, who had accepted the chairmanship of the New York State Wilson Conference, and she accompanied him to Baltimore for her first national convention. Many people she knew were there, including Alice and Kermit. Theodore was preparing to run as a third-party candidate. "Pop's been praying for Clark," Kermit told Franklin. Alice looked bad, Eleanor thought; in fact, all of Theodore's supporters who came to Baltimore seemed to her "restless and unhappy."

She found the convention sessions tedious. A moralist in politics, she felt that the ritual of noisy demonstrations, parades, and seconding speeches, while colorful, did not contribute to the thoughtful consideration of the party's purposes and policies. After the first roll call Champ Clark, the candidate of the conservatives, was in the lead; but he could not muster the two-thirds majority for the nomination. As the balloting dragged on, Eleanor saw less and less of her husband, and decided to take the children to Campobello and await the results there. But the significance of the battle between Wilson and Clark had not escaped her; what struck her most was "the contempt in which the New York delegation was held and the animosity shown toward the big financiers. If we are not going to find remedies in Progressivism then I feel sure the next step will be Socialism."[14] This was a remarkably sage and sophisticated perception by someone who only a few years earlier had been the shyest of apprentices in politics.

"Wilson nominated this afternoon," Franklin wired her in Campobello, "all my plans vague splendid triumph." Eleanor rejoiced not only for her husband's sake but because she felt that Wilson offered the best chance for the alleviation of social injustice. However, she felt bad for Uncle Ted, who, she suspected, would not have committed himself so irrevocably to running as a third-party candidate, had he foreseen Wilson would be the Democratic nominee. Wilson's nomination and Theodore's third party transformed the political scene. With the prospect of a Bull Moose candidate in his district who would divide the Republican vote, Franklin's doubts about running for re-election evaporated. He began to press hard for renomination, touring his district tirelessly, rousing his workers, flashing the smile that overcame all resistance. "It appears that Tammany and the 'Interests' are really making an effort to prevent my renomination," he wrote Eleanor, but he thought Tammany's ally in Dutchess County was spineless and would yield in the end.

As Franklin predicted, his Tammany opposition did collapse, and on August 24 he wired Eleanor, "Received designation by unanimous vote. Will wire Sunday if I can leave." He also notified his mother, who was in Paris. She replied, "In one way I wanted you all in New York, but to be sensible and unselfish, I am glad . . . I hope the 'bull moose' party will endorse you." But the Bull Moosers entered a candidate against him. The Democrats on their side closed ranks around Wilson, and Osborne and Roosevelt quietly shelved their independent Wilson organization. This brought Franklin an anguished plea from Louis Howe, who had been on Osborne's payroll: "If you can connect me with a job during this campaign, for heaven's sake help me out." A few weeks later Franklin was flat on his back with typhoid and asked Eleanor to see if Howe would run his campaign. That eccentric-looking little man had early sensed Franklin's possibilities and had cultivated his friendship. Franklin had reciprocated these overtures, somewhat to the dismay of Eleanor and Sara, who were put off by Howe's untidiness, his tobacco-specked vest, and a face that he himself cheerfully called "one of the four ugliest" in the state. Nevertheless, Howe had a sixth sense for the movement of public opinion and was something of a genius at political analysis. He loved power, Eleanor later wrote, but recognized his own limitations. In 1911 he spotted Franklin as the instrument through which he could realize his own ambitions. For his part, Franklin sensed that here was the perfect aide, brilliant politically but no potential rival. But many years were to pass before Eleanor appreciated Howe's remarkable qualities.[15] A man of great sensitivity, he could not have failed to notice how uncooperative Eleanor was after he hurriedly came down from Horseneck Beach in Massachusetts to take over Franklin's campaign. She fussed over his chain smoking, seemed impatient with the length of his visits, and generally made herself a nuisance, she confessed later, to the man who was to carry the district for her husband.

The fact that she herself was feeling ill no doubt accentuated her irritability. It was Sara who discovered that something was radically wrong when she arrived one day to find her daughter-in-law "so hot I was frightened." Characteristically, Eleanor shrugged off her symptoms; she would get to bed early and be well in the morning. But Sara was not to be put off so easily, and insisted on taking Eleanor's temperature, which was over 103. She summoned the doctor at once and his tests showed that Eleanor, too, had typhoid. A trained nurse was brought in and Eleanor went "into the fever." It was a week before her temperature began to come down. "She sees no one but Franklin, not even me!" Sara reported to Eleanor's Aunt Maude.

Thus the crucial election drew to a close with both Franklin and Eleanor flat on their backs. "Poor Franklin," Eleanor wrote Maude, "has had a horrid time just up and down. . . . He hasn't been able to campaign at all so he feels a little uncertain of election." But Howe was doing a first-rate job, and with the Bull Moose candidate expected to draw off Republican votes, Franklin's chances were good.

Theodore's campaign was roaring to a finish. Isabella wrote Eleanor that she had spent the day with Uncle Ted in Albuquerque: "He was more loveable than ever and of you he said so much that warmed my heart." Eleanor's Uncle Eddie Hall came to tell her that he had registered so he could vote for Theodore. Sara went to Theodore's windup rally with the Parishes one night and the next she was at Madison Square Garden to hear Woodrow Wilson. On election night, however, when Eleanor and Franklin were so weak they could barely sit up, Sara chose to go with Harry Hooker to Bull Moose, not Democratic, headquarters. But there was little cheer there. "Governor Wilson has a landslide," Sara noted in her diary. "Franklin is elected with about 1,500 majority."

"Howe did gallant work under very adverse circumstances," Osborne wrote Franklin. "He was about as loyal and wholehearted as a man could be." And Sara noted critically, "Mr. Howe here a good deal." By December,

Eleanor could begin to jest about the fact that both she and Franklin had been ill. Her Christmas presents would be small, she informed Maude, "as the campaign was more expensive than it would have been had Franklin been well and of course the doctors' bills are a bit high for our joint autumn entertainment! However, we ought to be thankful as we got off cheaper than if we had had it separately!" They were not taking a house in Albany this time, only a small apartment, and they planned to be there only from Tuesday to Thursday because, wrote Eleanor, Franklin "thinks he won't have much work this year."

Eleanor was twenty-eight as Franklin's term in Albany ended. She presided over a large household that had to be moved several times a year—from Sixty-fifth Street in New York, to Hyde Park, to Albany, and in June to Campobello. And on each occasion it was like a small army on the march: a nurse for each of the three children, three to five other domestics, and a vast number of trunks, valises, hat boxes, and pets. The trip to Campobello meant an early train to Boston with a stopover during the day at the Hotel Touraine, then a sleeper to Eastport, Maine, and finally the *Half Moon* or the motor launch to Campobello—in all, a considerable exercise in logistics. When Franklin could not be with them, Eleanor handled it alone with a minimum of fuss. She had already developed a reputation within the family for crowding an incredibly large number of activities into a morning. "She got hats, ordered dresses, etc.—all very quickly and I dropped her off at Susie Parish's before one," Sara noted in admiration. When she moved her family down from Albany, Eleanor "had to work awfully hard," Sara recorded, "and think very hard before she got away and she seemed to remember everything, even tho' at one day's notice she moved a whole day earlier than planned."

Eleanor dressed smartly—even the style-conscious Pussie was delighted to get her hand-me-downs. She was slim and tall and the sheath gowns of the era did justice to her Gibson Girl figure. She had tapering, expressive fingers and masses of soft brown hair full of golden tints. Her profile, with its overly prominent teeth and receding chin, was not attractive, but, like Auntie Bye, she had an inner radiance that prevailed over physical looks. Her eyes, as Beatrice Webb had said of her own mother, caressed one with sympathy and studied one with intelligence. Even the self-deprecating Eleanor admitted that her eyes were her best feature. She was glad that her children had inherited their father's looks—his fair skin, his smile, his jutting jaw—but their eyes, she thought, came from her side of the family, and they were good eyes, she said.

The Halls still turned to her in every crisis, and the crises were frequent. "Eleanor has been here every day," Grandma Hall wrote. "She is so good." Tivoli was decaying. Presided over by the violent-tempered Vallie who brandished a gun at visitors, and Grandma Hall, now a roly-poly lady in a black dress and bonnet, Oak Terrace was no longer a proud Hudson house but the setting for a Gothic tragedy. "I am so sorry about Grandma," Eleanor wrote Maude,

and one's hands are tied unless Vallie can be removed from Tivoli, which of course she won't agree to now. . . . I wish you and I could talk it over as I would do anything to make these next years easier and happier for her. Can't I let you have some money?

An equally urgent problem was what should be done with Eddie's three children, whose beautiful mother had died. "I feel after this," Eleanor wrote when Eddie had disappeared on another prolonged bat, "he should not dream of taking the children to his own house this spring and hope no one will make it possible so long as the Zabriskies are willing to keep them." Her stern advice echoed Auntie Bye's admonition fifteen years earlier to her own family that under no circumstances should Eleanor's father be permitted to have his children. But Eleanor had never acknowledged the wisdom of keeping herself and her father apart; the world of reality and the dream life she lived with her father were still separate.

Eleanor was Maude's confidante in matters of the heart as well as her mainstay in disentangling her private affairs, including some large debts. Maude, with her masses of red hair, great warmth, and puckish sense of humor, charmed men and women alike. She had turned down a Whitney to marry Larry Waterbury, and at one time the society pages were full of her doings. "Seated in a big automobile at the Jockey Club races at Newport last summer, Mrs. Waterbury performed the feat of eating half of a large watermelon without removing her white gloves—and without soiling them." Although Larry Waterbury was attractive and an outstanding polo player, he had no money. The two lived beyond their means, and contracted heavy gambling debts, and finally the marriage broke up. When Maude decided to sell her pearl collar, "Totty" was her agent in the negotiations with Tiffany's and Black, Starr and Frost. To free herself of debts, Maude, like Lily Bart in *The House of Mirth*, tried running a dress shop and even considered, until Eleanor discouraged her, serving as a hostess in a new restaurant whose owner was eager to have society patronage. Eleanor loved having her aunt at Campobello. Would Eleanor mind, Maude inquired, if a Mr. David Gray joined her on the island?

Eleanor could not quite make up her mind about the romance but she welcomed Mr. Gray to Campobello and undertook to chaperone them. "If you think best casually mention to Mama that Mr. Gray is boarding in the village," she wrote Franklin, "but if you think the surprise is better for her, just let it go." The son of a Buffalo editor, David Gray was witty and charming, wrote fashionable stories about the hunting life, and was much in demand in society.

Eleanor kept Franklin informed of her reactions to Mr. Gray. He had "the best anthology I've ever seen called *The Home Book of Verse*, compiled by a man called Stevenson. You can give it to me for my birthday as he has mended the turntable so I don't need a new one!" Mr. Gray read poetry well, and they were having "a grand poetry orgy," her next letter said. He was a delightful companion "but something is lacking and it worried me. I wish you were here and could form an opinion." He read them a story he had just written. "He certainly has the gift of the short story. Whether he has it for the big things is not yet proved and I wonder if it ever will be." How did Eleanor like him, Maude asked after they had been at Campobello several weeks. "I told her I did not feel I knew him yet. . . . I somehow shall never feel quite straight about it all till I've told him all my fears for them and seen how he takes it."

Meanwhile there was Sara to be dealt with. Appearances meant a great deal to her. Once Harry Hooker, one of Franklin's law partners, had come to Campobello while Franklin was away, and "Mama has chaperoned us pretty carefully," Eleanor noted with amusement. When Eleanor first mentioned David's name to Sara she "fairly snorted," and Eleanor foresaw trouble. Publicly Sara was kind, gracious, and devoted to Maude, but she "confided in Laura (who promptly told me)," wrote Eleanor, "all her outraged feelings in regards to Maude, David and me. . . . I know I'm in for a grand scene with Mama and tears one of these days."

David finally allayed Eleanor's misgivings: "I think you will like David Gray," she advised Franklin. If Maude ever made up her mind to marry him, "he will take good care of her. He strikes me as a man who has enjoyed life, had some big disappointments but kept his ideals, though up to now he has wanted a big incentive for work."

Her doubts about her brother Hall's marriage were of a different kind. A handsome young man, Hall had graduated from Harvard Phi Beta Kappa in 1912 and was about to enter engineering school. Eleanor had great faith in his abilities and wanted to be sure the girl he married would bring out the best in him; she thought of Hall as her oldest child, and if he was ever in trouble she was at his side. "Eleanor is a wonder," a friend remarked who saw them together; "it was delightful to see the sweet feeling between that sister and brother." When Hall first brought Margaret Richardson, a lovely Boston debutante, to meet Eleanor, Eleanor had some reservations. Margaret was a sportswoman who rode, played tennis, and enjoyed camping trips and dancing. "Hall is holding you up as an example to me," Eleanor teasingly reported to her. They were different types, and Eleanor could not get on "an intimate footing" with Margaret, she confessed to Franklin, and Margaret had the same problem with her. Eleanor "was perfectly lovely to me," Margaret recalled, "but I never felt at home with her."[16] Eleanor thought a woman should stir a man to large undertakings and be able to keep up with him intellectually, not just be someone to have fun with, and she was not sure Margaret was the right person for her brother. After Hall and Margaret were married, however, she counseled him not to make too many demands on his young wife. Hall had just awakened to poetry and philosophy, which were like wine in their effect on him, Eleanor observed in a letter to Franklin, adding, "He expects Margaret to feel as he does and to grasp things just as quickly and it is very hard on her for she has been accustomed to a sleepy atmosphere. He is impatient of her family and wants her to keep out of the atmosphere of Boston which she has always been in! Oh! these periods of readjustment, they are hard all round, aren't they?"

Painful as the process had been, she had made the adjustment from innocent bride to manager of a large household, from sheltered wife of a fun-loving young lawyer-about-town to competent helpmate of a promising public official.

Politics was already for her as well as for her husband a way to self-fulfillment. It was an activity she could share with him, a domain where she could be helpful, unlike sports and frivolities where she so often felt inadequate and excluded. Politics pivoted around Franklin and the family pivoted around her, but she was more than the mother of his children, the custodian of the hearth. He respected her judgment and valued her opinions—how much so he attested in a letter he wrote Maude. He wanted Maude to come back to Campobello next year, "as I know what a delight it is to Eleanor to have you and I am afraid I am sometimes a little selfish and have had her too much with me in past years and made life a trifle dull for her really brilliant mind and spirit."

17. The Roosevelts Go to Washington

IN MID-JANUARY, 1913, Franklin had been summoned to Trenton for a talk with President-elect Wilson about New York patronage. Franklin wanted to serve in the new administration himself, but when he, Eleanor, and Sara went to Wilson's inauguration, he still did not know whether he would be able to get the post he most coveted, the assistant secretary of the Navy, the position that Theodore Roosevelt had held before moving on to the governorship of New York and the presidency.

The morning of the inauguration he ran into Wilson's new secretary of the Navy, Josephus Daniels, homespun editor of the *Raleigh News and Observer*, prohibitionist, pacifist, and progressive. They had met at the Baltimore convention, where Josephus had instantly taken to Franklin, "as handsome a figure of an attractive young man as I had ever seen . . . a case of love at first sight."[1]

"How would you like to come to Washington as Assistant Secretary of the Navy?" Daniels queried.

"How would I like it? I'd like it bully well," Franklin replied. "All my life I have loved ships and have been a student of the Navy, and the assistant secretaryship is the one place, above all others, I would love to hold." He is "our kind of liberal," Daniels told the president two days later when he brought up Roosevelt's name.

After his confirmation on March 17, Franklin elatedly pulled out an assistant-secretary-of-the-Navy letterhead, impressively embossed in the corner with the office's insignia of four stars around an anchor, and wrote his "own dear Babbie," as he called her. She had remained in New York to hear what was to be "our fate."[2]

I didn't know till I sat down at this desk that this is the 17th of happy memory. In fact with all the subdued excitement of getting confirmed & taking the oath of office, the delightful significance of it all is only just beginning to dawn on me. My only regret is that you could not have been here with me, but I am thinking of you a great deal & sending "wireless" messages!

He was already at work, he went on gaily, "signing vast quantities of 'stuff' about which I know nothing," and would she have calling cards made for him, "by next Monday if possible"?

Eleanor meanwhile had written Franklin:

A telegram came to you from Mr. Daniels so we know you are confirmed & finally launched in your work!

P.S.
March 17th.
Many happy returns of to-day dear. I ordered your 17th of March present as we couldn't do anything else together!

Franklin also had written his mother, "I am baptized, confirmed, sworn in, vaccinated—and somewhat at sea!" She was grateful that her son had thought of her in the moment of his success: "You can't imagine the happiness you gave me by writing to me yesterday. I just *knew* it was a *very* big job, and everything so new that it will take time to fit *into* it." Big jobs, in Sara's mind, required appropriate signatures: "Try not to write your signature too small," she added, "as it gets a cramped look and is not distinct. So many public men have such awful signatures, and so unreadable!"

Shortly after Franklin began his new job he was invited to Raleigh, North Carolina, Josephus Daniels' home town, to address the Agricultural and Mechanical College. Daniels was one of its trustees and was proud of this college of farm boys, as he was of his young aide.

Eleanor, wearing a big hat and a dress with a high choke collar, according to the local paper, accompanied Franklin who sported a derby. "I am a hayseed myself," the pince-nez'd patrician northerner said at one point in his speech, "and proud of it."[3]

Eleanor, more fastidious in her choice of words, would never have called herself "a hayseed," and she was suddenly conscious of a kind of upper-class insularity. "There seems to be so much to see and know and to learn to understand in this big country of ours," she wrote Maude afterward, "and so few of us ever try to even realize that we ought to try when we've lived in the environment that you and I grew up in."[4]

The Wilson years in Washington thrust them on—Franklin toward national leadership, Eleanor toward wider sympathies and a radical independence.

Franklin had to learn the ropes of his new position, and so did Eleanor, whose job was to make things easier and pleasanter for him. But what were the duties of the wife of the assistant secretary? "When I see Eleanor," Theodore wrote Franklin in congratulating him, "I shall say to her that I do hope she will be particularly nice to the naval officers' wives. They have a pretty hard time, with very little money to get along on, and yet a position to keep up, and everything that can properly be done to make things pleasant for them should be done." Auntie Bye, the wife of an admiral and as knowledgeable in the ways of the Navy and the Capital as anyone, gave Eleanor similar advice. Mrs. Cowles also briefed her in the Washington ritual of calls.

As long ago as 1823 General Jackson had protested the practice—"There is nothing done here but vissitting [sic] and carding each other—you know how much I was disgusted with those scenes when you and I were here, it has been increased instead of diminishing"[5]—but in 1913 it was still a "sacred rite." Ladies in white gloves, carrying cardcases, went forth daily on their appointed rounds, and none was more determined or conscientious than Eleanor: Mondays the wives of the justices of the Supreme Court, Tuesdays Congress, Thursdays Cabinet, Fridays diplomats. Wednesday would be the day she received, but she was sure no one would call on her.

A letter to Maude described her first weeks in Washington that spring.

I've paid 60 calls in Washington this week and been to a luncheon at the Marine barracks, the kind, where the curtains are drawn & candles lit & course after course reduces you to a state of coma which makes it almost impossible to struggle to your feet & leave at 4 P.M. I've received one long afternoon next to Mrs. Daniels until my feet ached and my voice was gone & since then I've done nothing but meet people I saw that day & try to make them think I remember them quite well! We've been out to dinner every night, last night a big Navy League affair for Mr. Daniels where there was some really good speaking. Mrs. Daniels is a dear & I'm looking forward to knowing her better. Mrs. Bryan is nice too though not so attractive, but some of the others are not so exciting.

Ten days later she was still at her calls. "I got here yesterday about 2 and started out at 3 to call on the Navy Yard people & the Justices' wives, about 20 calls in all and the same number almost everyday this week!"

As the wife of the assistant secretary she considered it her duty to master Navy protocol and ceremony, to keep her poise when the guns thundered out a seventeen-gun salute when her husband boarded a flag ship, and to shake hands only with the officers, not the enlisted men, as the Marine guard on the quarter deck presented arms. There were sterner tests of her self-command. The secretary invited members of the cabinet and their wives to join him and the assistant secretary in watching the Navy at target practice at Hampton Roads, "the most spectacular sight on sea or land," he called it. The men went to the firing division and the women were brought aboard the *Rhode Island*, the battleship that was towing the target. The executive officer of the *Rhode Island*, Commander Yates Stirling, detailed an officer to each lady to explain anything she might wish to know. Lieutenant Emory Land was assigned to Eleanor.

As Eleanor recalled the day, the sea had been quite rough and she had begun to feel queasy. When the young officer asked her if she would like to climb the skeleton mast, she quickly agreed—anything to distract her from the way she was feeling would be a relief—and up the mast she went. It was a dizzying climb, but she got over her seasickness. The impression she made on the *Rhode Island*'s officers was totally different.

She wanted to see all there was, and when I went to the wardroom, where all were assembled, she had donned a suit of dungarees, trousers and all, and Land was taking her up the mast to the top, an excellent place from which to witness the firing. None of the other women seemed willing to risk climbing the mast.[6]

Even in New York and Hyde Park there was no escape from her duties as the wife of the Navy Department's second-in-command. When the secretary did not require them, a 124-foot converted yacht, the *Sylph*, and an older but larger dispatch boat, the *Dolphin*, were at Franklin's disposal, and he made frequent use of them for trips down the Potomac and occasionally up the Hudson. He could also thumb rides on other ships. One time Eleanor asked Maude if she were going to Tivoli, because "if so we want you to go up the River 8 A.M. Saturday with us on a destroyer." When they moored off Hyde Park, Sara went on board with Anna and James, and fifty sailors came up to the house for ice cream.

Life at Campobello was also considerably changed as a result of Franklin's new position. Not only did Eleanor see even less of him, but he was as likely as not to bring a large naval vessel along when he was able to get away from Washington. The first time this happened was when Franklin ordered one of the fleet's most powerful ships, the *North Dakota*, to anchor off Eastport on the Fourth of July week end of 1913. The job of entertaining the ship's senior officers fell on Eleanor, who arranged teas, bridge, games, dinners, and other festivities. After the week end, Franklin left but the *North Dakota* lingered on, delayed by a dense fog. Eleanor played bridge with the captain, the commander, and the paymaster until she was sure they must be quite sick of her; but the children loved it. Eleanor dressed three-year-old Elliott in a blue sailor suit, and when he boarded the ship he faced the stern and saluted the flag as his father had instructed him. He even displayed "a real swaggering walk." Finally the fog cleared and the *North Dakota* departed, "thank heavens." But a few days later Eleanor heard alarming rumors that a flotilla would be turning up in August. "Is it so?" she wrote pleadingly to Franklin. "I could hardly bear such excitement again."

"No, no more battleships coming," he reassured her. "I may come up in a destroyer later, but that means only 3 officers!"

"I shall welcome you on a destroyer or with whole fleet," she wrote back, "if you will just come a little sooner on their account but of course the destroyer will be easier to entertain!"

The Navy yards were under Franklin's jurisdiction, and in the autumn Eleanor accompanied him on a tour of Gulf installations. It was her introduction to the exertions, excitements, and crises of an official inspection. Diminutive, handsome, sharp-tongued Laura Delano also went along. She was having a stormy love affair, and the Roosevelts thought the trip would be good for her.

From the moment they arrived in New Orleans, they were "busy every minute." After breakfast they left with a delegation of "prominent political (not social) citizens," Eleanor said, drawing a distinction that still seemed immensely important to her. At the Navy yard Franklin "counted every rivet," she noted impatiently; a time would come when such inspections would not seem tedious, when she would painstakingly do the same. They were due to dine with a "real old bird," a retired admiral, in one of New Orleans' most elegant cafés, but "of course Franklin had to be late so we started off alone." Not usually given to gourmandizing, Eleanor nevertheless noted that their dinner was exceptional, ending, as it did, "with coffee poured into burning brandy, the prettiest thing and also the best thing I ever tasted," one of the few occasions on which she had anything good to say about liquor. She was less keen on the champagne that was served the next morning before breakfast en route to Biloxi on a yacht. While Franklin inspected the harbor, she and Laura were motored around Biloxi, and in the evening they all attended a banquet "where husbands and wives sat side by side and salad came after the soup!" Afterward she and Laura "just sat down and laughed for 15 minutes." At Pensacola, where they arrived at six the next morning, and at Brunswick they followed the same hectic schedule of tours, picnics, and receptions, their tour ending with a twenty-four-hour train trip back to Washington. It was an exhausting, demanding journey with little sleep and less privacy, but one kept silent about headaches and weariness and extended never-failing courtesy to everyone because, Eleanor said, the point of her presence was "to make life pleasanter" for her husband, not to add to his burdens.[7] The trip, moreover, had been stimulating. It confirmed her view that "it is always good to break away from accustomed surroundings."

In Washington they lived in Auntie Bye's house at 1733 N Street, which they had sublet from her. The red brick residence on a narrow tree-shaded street had a "postage stamp of a lawn" and a little garden in back with a rose arbor where Eleanor liked to breakfast when the weather permitted. Sara, after her first visit, noted: "Dined at 1733 N. Street. Moved chairs and tables and began to feel at home."

Washington is never as vibrantly alive as in the first months of a new administration. New policies, new men—all things seem possible. The 1912 election had boiled down to a race between Theodore Roosevelt and Woodrow Wilson, but whatever the differences between Wilson's New Freedom and Roosevelt's New Nationalism, both philosophies recognized the need for social change and both were energized by the nation's reforming and humanitarian impulses. Bull Moosers and Wilsonian liberals alike felt a quickening of spirits with the end of Wilson's inaugural address: "Here muster, not the forces of party, but the forces of humanity. I summon all honest men, all patriotic, forward-looking men, to my side."

Since they were related to Theodore and were members of Wilson's official family, Eleanor and Franklin Roosevelt seemed to represent what was best and most promising in both camps. The belief that Franklin was a coming man in politics and would some day be the heir of both progressive traditions enhanced Washington's fascination with him. "It is interesting to see that you are in another place which I myself once held," Uncle Ted had written him, and Josephus Daniels had the same thought. "His distinguished cousin T.R. went from that place to the Presidency," he wrote in his diary. "May history repeat itself."[8] Franklin himself was not averse to pointing up the Theodore Roosevelt analogy. Two days after becoming assistant secretary of the Navy, he assured newsmen that there need be no fear of a repetition of what happened "the last time a Roosevelt was on the job"—a reference to Theodore's reversal of department policies in accordance with his own ideas while his chief was away.[9] Eleanor thought it was "a horrid little remark." Now many men in addition to Louis Howe were busy planning Franklin's future. "My head whirls when I think of all the things you might do this coming year," Eleanor teased him, "run for Governor, U. S. Senator, go to California! I wonder what you really will do!"

They were invited to nearly all the big parties, including occasional dinners, musicales, and receptions at the White House, and Eleanor did her own share of entertaining. Her first big dinner was in honor of Mr. and Mrs. Daniels. "Our dinner went off quite well," she reported to Sara, "and I think the cook is good." The only untoward event was that "the Sec. and Mrs. Daniels came early but luckily I was ready." They gave a dinner for Secretary of State and Mrs. William Jennings Bryan, the most pacifistic member of the cabinet, at which the other guests were chiefly admirals and generals. They dined with Justice and Mrs. Charles Evans Hughes. It was very pleasant, noted Eleanor, and after dinner the attorney general and the justice talked to her and she was fascinated by what they had to say but was unhappy when one of the guests began to play the piano, for that made conversation "rather scrappy." Franklin, she said with mock disdain, "indulged entirely in children. Nona McAdoo and Miss Hughes at dinner and Miss Wolcott afterwards." A few days later they were guests of General John Biddle, who lived next door. "I had Justice Holmes [on] one side (you may remember the speech of his which we read last winter). He is brilliant and full of theories and epigrams and Franklin thinks Mrs. Holmes wonderfully clever and quick so we both enjoyed ourselves." On her other side was Vice President Marshall, who had recently warned the Wall Street plutocracy that "if the tendency of certain men to accumulate vast fortunes is not curbed America may face socialism or paternalism." Eleanor questioned him about the speech; he had not been correctly quoted, he told her, but "nevertheless," she wrote Maude, "he is a good deal of a socialist with a desire for the millennium and it seems to me no very well worked out ideas so far of how we are to get there."[10]

While she did not advocate socialism, she did not approve of Henry Adams' pessimism, either. A frail one-man Greek chorus, the aristocratic, cynical Adams was at that period commenting sourly on the passing Washington scene from his study overlooking Lafayette Square. He had ceased going out socially in Theodore Roosevelt's day, but he would stop his victoria in front of the Roosevelt house on N Street and ask to see the children, whereupon all of them, including the dog, would climb into his carriage. Justice Holmes said that Adams turned everything "to dust and ashes" but Adams was nevertheless attracted by this golden couple and invited them to lunch. Sometimes Eleanor stopped in alone for a cup of tea, "rather exhausted after an afternoon of calls," recalled Aileen Tone, "Uncle Henry's" secretary-companion, who had taken charge of him after his stroke. "She had the routine of calls so well organized that she kept to a schedule of six minutes a call. Uncle Henry liked her—it was difficult not to," Aileen continued; Eleanor had "a kind of universal friendliness and kindness that enveloped you."[11]

All the Roosevelts stopped by to see Uncle Henry whenever they were in Washington, and Eleanor had a quiet, old-fashioned kind of charm of which Adams approved, even though her desire to reform the world, rudimentary as it was at the time, "was not much in Uncle Henry's line." Once, when Franklin was impatiently holding forth about the Wilson administration, Adams stopped him and, according to Eleanor, said, "Young man, I have lived in this house many years and seen the occupant of that White House across the square come and go, and nothing that you minor officials or the occupants of that house can do will affect the history of the world for long!" Eleanor did not consider this good doctrine to preach to the young. Adams' pessimism, she concluded later, was "an old man's defense against his own urge to be an active factor in the work of the world, a role which Henry Adams rejected in his youth."[12]

Washington during the Wilson administration was no longer the slow-moving, parochial Capital it had been when Theodore Roosevelt first arrived there in the 1890s, "where an old resident knew by sight everyone who kept a carriage" and its social life had consisted of walking, driving, bicycling, and paying calls.[13]

Society consisted of three groups—old Washington families called "The Aborigines," top-ranking officials who were also social register, and diplomats. Franklin and Eleanor were immediately placed on the lists of all three. There were the "cave dwellers" like the Misses Patten who knew everyone and at whose Sunday afternoons the latest gossip could be heard (official Washington was said to have three means of communication—telephone, telegraph, and tell-a-Patten). "I called on the Misses Patten this p.m.," Eleanor reported in 1916 when the social tide was running strong against Germany, "and heard the latest German tale."

Another early dinner guest at the Franklin Roosevelts was Belle Hagner, who had been a highly popular Washington debutante and had served as Edith Roosevelt's social secretary and had stayed on in that position with Mrs. Taft and the first Mrs. Wilson. The William Corcoran Eustises were also guests of the Roosevelts. They lived in the Corcoran House, a landmark on Lafayette Square. Mrs. Eustis was the former Edith Morton, daughter of Levi P. Morton, a Dutchess County neighbor of the Roosevelts and vice president under Benjamin Harrison; Willie Eustis was a member of one of the First Families of Virginia. Edith Eustis said the Franklin Roosevelts were "the most attractive and nicest young couple I know." Other families (mostly Republican) of distinguished lineage and public eminence who were kind to them were the Longworths, the Lodges, the Henry Whites, and the William Phillipses.

The Metropolitan and Chevy Chase country clubs were the gathering places of the socially acceptable and politically powerful; businessmen were not admitted—neither were Jews nor, of course, Negroes. (One reason Washington high society suspected Woodrow Wilson of social radicalism was his refusal to accept honorary membership in the Chevy Chase Club.)[14] Franklin spent a great deal of time at both. Their acceptance mattered to him. They were the people who counted, and their recognition eased the pain of his exclusion from

Porcellian.[15] Eleanor later said that it was Louis Howe, who had come to Washington as Franklin's aide, who saved Franklin from the snobbishness and total dedication to pleasure-seeking represented by the Metropolitan Club. The Howes lived near the Roosevelts, and every day Louis and Franklin walked to the Navy Department together. Eleanor and Grace Howe shopped together and occasionally the Howes were guests at 1733 N Street, but although Eleanor was unfailingly courteous, she still discouraged intimacy.

In the diplomatic circle the young Roosevelts inherited most of Uncle Ted's and Auntie Bye's friends and made many of their own, especially among the younger embassy people. The British ambassador, Sir Cecil Spring-Rice, had known Eleanor's parents, and he and his wife became good friends of the young Roosevelts. The French ambassador, Jean Jusserand, who had been a member of Theodore's "walking cabinet," also befriended them.

Within this larger Washington society, the Roosevelts had their own circle of friends, sufficiently intimate, said Eleanor, that protocol could be ignored when they dined together, as they often did. This group included the Charles Hamlins, the William Phillipses, the Franklin K. Lanes, and the Adolph Millers.

Charles Hamlin was assistant secretary of the treasury, a post he had also held under Cleveland. His wife "Bertie" was from Albany and had met Franklin when as a young boy he had come to Albany for his Uncle Ted's inauguration as governor. They lived near the Roosevelts, and although Franklin did not find them exciting, he felt they would make real friends, he told Eleanor.

William Phillips was assistant secretary of state. He was a protégé of Colonel House, who had brought him into the Wilson administration and who often used the Phillips home as his base when he was in Washington. Caroline Phillips, a granddaughter of *the* Mrs. Astor and a voluminous diarist, was an old friend of Eleanor's.

Franklin Lane was secretary of the interior, appointed sight unseen by Wilson on Colonel House's strong recommendation. Mrs. Lane, it was said, had set up "a code of calling which exceeded in exclusiveness anything attempted by the White House," but nevertheless the Lanes were not primarily occupied with social affairs. Lane was known for his buoyant temperament and good advice; although he was a Democrat, he had been appointed to the Interstate Commerce Commission by Theodore, who valued his counsel. A western progressive, he argued the need for government to experiment with a distribution of wealth that would be more equitable than the existing economic order while not destroying individual initiative. A young couple could not have had a wiser mentor or a better friend.

Adolph Miller, an economist brought to Washington by Lane as one of his top aides, was subsequently appointed to the newly established Federal Reserve Board. Although Miller was a strict Dutch Calvinist and not an ebullient conversationalist, his wife Mary was pleasant and gay. Eleanor found both the Millers and the Lanes to be a "joy," and noted that "talk with them is real talk."

These were the friends Franklin and Eleanor saw informally, often on

Sunday evenings when Eleanor scrambled eggs in a chafing dish and served cold cuts, a cold dessert, and cocoa. They called themselves "the Club." "Franklin Roosevelt was always gay and amusing. The Lanes and Millers were brilliant conversationalists. Those evenings were among the best of that Washington sojourn," Phillips later wrote.

How little did any of us imagine the great role that Franklin was to play in the future! I knew him then as a brilliant, lovable, and somewhat happy-go-lucky friend, an able Assistant Secretary of the Navy, but I doubt if it ever occurred to any of us that he had the making of a great President. . . . His wife, Eleanor, whom we all admired, was a quiet member of the little group. She seemed to be a little remote, or it may have been that Franklin claimed the attention, leaving her somewhat in the background.[16]

Eleanor was essentially domestic, said Phillips, "and her interest in public affairs was centered in her husband's career rather than in any thought of a career of her own." Franklin overshadowed her. Although she was still basically shy, occasionally there were thunderclaps that heralded the political activist and militant equalitarian she was to become in later years. For example, she had a violent political argument with Fred Adams, who had married Ellen Delano. "He is most pessimistic about the 'common people,' considers us the worst governed people in the world and would prefer a monarchy! He has about the grasp and vision in big things of a child and it is discouraging to think that he is only one of many who think and feel like that about their country!" She could not see how Laura, Ellen's sister, could admire Adams: "It would be deadening to see much of him, much less live in the house with him."[17]

Cousin Susie's preoccupation with herself also irked Eleanor. Now living alone with Henry Parish in big houses in New York and Orange, she complained constantly of her ailments. "She thinks she is dying," Eleanor scoffed, "someone else to think about would be her best cure."

Harry Hooker was in love. Eleanor lunched with the young lady and her mother "and came away with the feeling that Hooligan (Hooker) would never win out unless he could make his own life a big thing and not hang around Tuxedo." She told him so that evening. He should really go to *work* for the progressives, she advised him and not always keep the young lady first in his mind. "Harry came up to dine," she reported to Franklin, "and went home about 9.45 after my having all your theories passed on to him as mine and if they have the desired effect he'll go to supper after his progressive meeting tomorrow night with all 'the boys.' "

Another example of Eleanor's independent thinking was displayed in 1914 during the family contretemps resulting from Rosy Roosevelt's announcement that he had finally persuaded Betty Riley, the gentle Englishwoman who had been his companion for many years, to marry him. Betty had tried to discourage him, because she felt that her lower-middle-class origins were not worthy of his social standing. Sara would have agreed. She was shocked by Rosy's decision and deplored his behavior as a threat to "standards," feeling that it showed he lacked principle. She wanted Eleanor's moral support, but did not get it. "She told me yesterday," Eleanor wrote Franklin, "she could talk it all over with Helen [Robinson] and Helen understood her point of view but I made her feel like a stranger by my curious attitude and I assured her I had no attitude and no opinion and she became enraged and said, *that* she couldn't understand!" The marriage took place before Sara was able to get down to Hyde Park, but Rosy later accepted her invitation to come to Campobello. "Somehow it fills me with amusement for Mama is so happy to be 'the one' and yet feels she must not let me think she approves!"

But such stirrings of nonconformism went unnoticed in Washington society, which saw her as an official's wife who was doing her job, "the embodiment of 20th century activity," one friend marveled. Eleanor was doing her job "a little better than anyone else" was the surprising verdict of Alice Longworth, who herself refused to play the game of calling and being called upon.[18] Alice did only what amused her, but such was her wit and temperament that she could establish her own rules. Eleanor envied Alice's ability to disregard convention,[19] little aware that one day she too would go her own way—but in the interest of those who needed help, not for the sake of her own amusement.

18. Bringing Up Her Children

IN 1927, ELEANOR ROOSEVELT, by then much freer and more self-reliant than she had been in the years when she was giving birth to one child after another, wrote an article entitled "Ethics of Parents" in which she briskly and self-confidently summed up her views in a seven-point code.

1. Furnish an example in living.
2. Stop preaching ethics and morals.
3. Have a knowledge of life's problems and an imagination.
4. Stop shielding your children and clipping their wings.
5. Allow your children to develop along their own lines.
6. Don't prevent self-reliance and initiative.
7. Have vision yourself and bigness of soul

The next generation will take care of itself.[1]

It was observed of Pestalozzi, the great educator, that he could not bring up his own children, and it must be noted that this admirable statement of Eleanor Roosevelt's was written after her youngest child had been delivered to boarding school and she could be more objective about parenthood.

While the Roosevelt children were at home and in their most impressionable stage, Eleanor was ambivalent—on the one hand, she was too deferential to the child-rearing views of her mother-in-law and the nurses and governesses who were usually selected by Sara, and on the other, she was too much of a disciplinarian, reflecting her own austere upbringing.

Two children were born during the years that Franklin was assistant secretary of the Navy. In August, 1914, the second Franklin Jr. was born. Again, as with Elliott, her confinement and recovery took place while Franklin was involved in a political campaign, this time an unsuccessful bid for the Democratic senatorial nomination in New York. August was also the month when war broke out. Eleanor followed these events as best she could from Campobello. She was leading a very quiet life, she assured her husband, and saw no reason for the baby to arrive "before the date, the 26th." She had arranged with Dr. Ely, one of the country's leading gynecologists, to come up for the delivery, but Miss Spring was to arrive on August 12.

It was fortunate that Miss Spring came early and also that Franklin dashed up for a visit, for on the sixteenth Eleanor felt the baby was about to appear. She awakened Franklin, and he sailed over on the *Half Moon* to get old

Dr. Bennett from Lubec. The doctor arrived, but the baby did not. For almost a day everyone sat around while Eleanor felt guilty over the trouble she was causing and sought to persuade Dr. Bennett to leave and take care of his other patients. Finally, late on the seventeenth the second Franklin Jr. made his appearance—another better-than-ten-pound baby. Afterward Dr. Bennett expressed surprise to Miss Spring that when it came to having babies summer people were no different from Down-Easters: "She is just like one of us."

As soon as Franklin was sure Eleanor and the baby were all right he hurried back to his primary fight. Her letters mixed reports about bowel movements with political encouragement. They had put up the poster Franklin had sent them; James wanted more campaign buttons; "I have a little more milk." The baby thrived but Franklin's six-week bid for the Democratic nomination did not—Tammany's candidate, James W. Gerard, defeated him. "I wonder if you are disappointed," his mother wrote consolingly. "I hope not. You made a brave fight and now you can return to the good and necessary work of the Navy Department which must have missed you all these last weeks." Eleanor was so involved with the new baby that the campaign made little impression upon her, but like Sara she thought that Franklin was quite content to get back to his desk at the Navy Department.

Eleanor's last baby, John Aspinwall, was born March 13, 1916. In February she was still dining out almost every night and being hostess at large Navy receptions—"as 225 came last time I don't think there is anyone left to come!" Caroline Phillips, who was also pregnant, dined with her the evening of March 13. After dinner Franklin went out, and at ten Caroline left. Shortly afterward Eleanor called Miss Spring, who summoned the doctor, and by the time Franklin returned the baby had almost arrived—"born at 11 p.m. in Washington," Sara recorded in her diary. John's was the only birth Sara was not on hand for. Later, John, like the other boys, was brought to St. James Episcopal Church in Hyde Park and christened in his father's christening dress. Henceforth Washington matrons who complained that they could not run their households were told it could be done: "Eleanor Roosevelt . . . has five children and moves them all six times a year—and does everything else besides!"

In later years Eleanor blamed herself for the way she brought up her children: she had been too stern with them; she had not done enough things that they wanted to do and too many that she had thought it was good for them to do; she had deferred too much to nurses and to Sara.[2] The results of this training were described by Mrs. Frances Theodora Parsons, a friend of Eleanor's parents and a well-known writer of books on nature. She was at Susie Parish's when Eleanor was there with Anna and James. Eleanor admired Mrs. Parsons' creativity and sweetness with the children, but Mrs. Parsons was less complimentary about Eleanor. She met James and Anna "primly parading on the asphalt drive with their nursery-governess one June morning," she recalled in *Perchance Some Day*. "I invited them to join me in a hunt for wild flowers up the mountain path. But they were too much appalled by steep curves and outcropping rocks to derive any pleasure" from the expedition.[3] That was before

Eleanor had become an independent woman, Mrs. Parsons explained. "I can remember at twenty-two expecting my year old baby to sit on the sofa beside me while I poured tea with all kinds of good things on the tray. Her manners had to be so perfect that she would never even reach or ask for these forbidden goodies!" Eleanor later wrote.[4]

Eleanor's nurses and governesses were supplied by agencies that tradition-ally served New York's upper-class families, and the schools to which she sent Anna, James, and Elliott were the accepted ones in her milieu. Before she moved the children to Washington in 1913, Anna, then seven, briefly attended classes in New York. Maude had suggested the progressive Ethical Culture school, but Anna was sent to Miss Davidge's. In Washington Anna went to the Misses Eastman, and James and Elliott to the Potomac School. These schools were well-staffed and highly exclusive.

Like other young Washington matrons, Eleanor gave much thought to education, a subject that she discussed endlessly with Caroline Phillips and Lily Polk, who had children the same age as her own. She was principally concerned with what she and Franklin could do to reinforce the classroom. She believed that the early years were decisive and that the home was more important than school; if a child was not taught habits of self-control at home and if parents did not encourage curiosity by the way they responded to a child's queries, formal education was likely to be unproductive.

Eleanor tried a number of ways to teach her children to concentrate. She spent time with them on their lessons and reading to them. She also had a French governess to help them learn French. Elliott "goes to Mlle. now for French every morning & I think has learnt a good deal though if you ask him to say anything he promptly refuses." She had borrowed one of her methods of teaching concentration from Mlle. Souvestre. After lunch she had the children lie flat on the floor.[5] "Relax your muscles completely," she softly commanded. When they were physically relaxed and, she hoped, mentally focused, she read to them. It is difficult to say whether these efforts were effective. The Roosevelt children did show an unusual ability, when interested, to concentrate on what was being said and to pick up ideas and information aurally, but their father and mother had the same faculty and it may have been an inherited rather than a learned trait.

The children did not suffer from lack of motherly care and attention. John was "three months old [and] weighs 14 lbs 13 oz.," Eleanor noted, "which is 15 oz. more than F. jr. weighed." She worried if she had to be away from the children. Before Eleanor left with Franklin on his inspection tour of southern naval facilities, Anna had asked anxiously what would happen if they had to buy anything "or got lost or put into prison." Eleanor was also apprehensive about how the household would manage if a crisis developed while she was away, and the longer she was gone, the stronger her fears became. But after she returned she was able to report to Sara, "All was well here."

Sometimes there *were* mishaps while Eleanor was away. One summer when they were at Campobello she went to St. Andrews to do some shopping, and when she returned she discovered Elliott had fallen into the smoldering ashes of a fire the children had made on the beach while the nurse had wandered off and burned his arms and legs. In the four-page letter that went to Franklin describing what had happened, Eleanor was careful not to alarm him unduly—"he only cried a little & Nurse says they are only skin burns" and they applied Unguentine.

She was as composed and cool-headed in dealing with Elliott as she was in writing Franklin, and later concluded that the spirit with which one faced life's little calamities was the important thing, since children cannot be totally shielded from misadventures. But then when Franklin, perhaps because her letter was so reassuring, made only passing reference to Elliott's injuries, she was indignant. "You are casual about Elliott's burns . . . he is a very brave young man!"

Because she had been full of fears when she was a child, Eleanor wanted her children to be venturesome and to meet adversity with fortitude. She was pleased when Anna and James entered the swimming pool. "One thing their lessons did for them is that they'll put their heads under & go in to their necks & James seems less timid than Anna," she reported. Since Anna was ten and James nine, it might not appear to be much of an achievement, but the point is that she was determined to have them face up to their fears. She admired spunk-iness and detested sniveling. Once when Elliott bit James hard she spanked him with a slipper and explained that no matter whose fault it was, boys didn't bite. Elliott's feelings were hurt and "he made such a long upper lip he looked like a rabbit," but she was pleased with his insistence that "it didn't hurt so very much, Mother!" Another show of defiance was also reported half approvingly: "Elliott went for me with both fists." There were times, however, when she was not so enamored of Elliott's temper. She took him to the Spring-Rice dancing class to look on, "but he is so shy with people and you never are sure that he'll do as you tell him without a scene so it isn't an unmixed joy." Then she added firmly, "The new baby is not going to be allowed to grow up like this!"

Sara often deplored and frequently hindered Eleanor's efforts at shaping the children's character. "Anna and James thrive and have a good time," Eleanor wrote Franklin, "though Mama thinks them much abused." When they all went sailing, she reported on another occasion, "the chicks became obstreperous and I most severe and Mama unhappy!" When James fell off his pony while they were visiting Hyde Park he was scratched but Eleanor did not think he was really hurt; "but of course he cried hard and Mama brought him in and had him lying down before I knew anything was wrong or I would have made him get on again if only for a minute."

Sara should not have interfered with her daughter-in-law's decisions, but Eleanor, as she later realized, was too stern a disciplinarian. She had disliked her mother, but it was her mother's and grandmother's tendency to say "no" rather than her father's life-affirming "yes" that took charge when she was confronted by unruliness in her children. She thought the discipline she had undergone as a child had been beneficial, "and so when I found myself responsible for the bringing up of children, I enforced a discipline which in many ways was unwise."[6] Having seen what self-indulgence had done to her father and uncles, she was puritanical and repressive toward herself and overly severe in curbing what she considered the "wildness" of her children. "They have been the wildest things you ever saw," she complained to Franklin, "and about ready to jump out of their skins." "Let the chicks run wild at Hyde Park," he advised her. "It won't hurt them." His reaction was the same when she appealed to him to end some roughhousing between James and Elliott: "Oh, let them scrap. It's good exercise for them."

Franklin did not like to administer discipline. As public responsibilities more and more cut down the time he was able to spend with his "chicks," he wanted the hours he was with them to be full of fun, excitement, and affection. His mother had always tried to run him, and he shied away from doing the same to his children. He was loath to hurt anyone's feelings, and preferred to be the agent of good tidings. When one of the children had to be punished, the task usually fell to Eleanor, and if she insisted that it was Franklin's responsibility, wrote James Roosevelt in his engaging memoir, *Affectionately, F.D.R.*, "the punishment simply was not administered."[7]

Sara, however, was the real culprit in undermining the children's discipline. Even the Hyde Park servants thought so. Sara overheard talk in the servants' part of the house that she spoiled the children, that she was "chicken-hearted," and the criticism made her cross, she wrote to Eleanor. Then she added:

But one sh[d] keep as clear of the opinion of that class as possible I am sure, for they blow hot & cold, the best of them, & if any of them speak to me of how *nice* the children are, I shall not even answer. One thing that makes for good behaviour at table is that we all know everything goes upstairs & outside.

"We 'chicks' quickly learned," wrote James, "that the best way to circumvent 'Pa and Mummy' when we wanted something they wouldn't give us was to appeal to Granny."[8] But Franklin was away so often that it was Eleanor who bore the brunt of Sara's interference. The older woman was motivated by darker, more complicated forces than an overindulgent love of her grandchildren: she was Eleanor's rival for the affections both of the children and of Franklin. James wrote that his grandmother was "in constant competition with Mother" over how the children should be raised. In the article that *McCall's* published posthumously, "I Remember Hyde Park," Eleanor at the end of her life spoke more plainly than ever about this arrangement *à trois*.[9] The Big House at Hyde Park was her mother-in-law's and Franklin's home, but not hers: "For over forty years, I was only a visitor there." In the dining room Franklin sat at one end of the table, Sara at the other, and Eleanor on the side. It was the same in the large library-living room, in the new wing that Sara added to the house in 1915 after consulting Franklin but not her—the two large armchairs on either side of the fireplace were occupied by Franklin and his mother, while Eleanor "sat anywhere."

When Sara had realized that the marriage between Franklin and herself could not be prevented, Eleanor went on, explaining why the Big House had been such an unhappy place for her, "she determined to bend the marriage to the way she wanted it to be. What she wanted was to hold onto Franklin and his children; she wanted them to grow up as she wished. As it turned out, Franklin's children were more my mother-in-law's children than they were mine." This was partly her own fault, she admitted, for having permitted Sara to keep her "under her thumb."

Hall understood his sister's problems with "Cousin Sally," as he called Sara, and with the nurses and governesses that Sara selected for Eleanor. "Are the legions of law and order too strong for you or have you managed this summer without too assiduous attentions?" he sympathetically inquired.

Eleanor tried to lead the children in games and sports. She went fishing with them—"James and Anna and I fished off the float yesterday morning and got about 11 flounders in about an hour and a half." She taught them croquet and found it "a good exercise for her temper" to take their disregard of the rules calmly. She accompanied Anna and James to their dancing class at Lady Spring-Rice's. She took James on a tour of Annapolis and could "hardly drag him past the football practice field." All the children had an assortment of dogs and rabbits—"We had a great tragedy yesterday, one of the bunnies died. . . . The chicks were very sad but they buried it with great ceremony and are going to put a mound of stones above him today and that seems to be a great consolation." When she played with her children she tried to forget herself, to enter into the spirit of the occasion and to be like a child herself, but she was not easygoing in such matters. The moralist in her was always in command, standing between herself and her children, whose irrepressible spirits cried out for acceptance, not judgment. "She felt a tremendous sense of duty to us," Anna later said. "It was part of that duty to read to us and to hear our prayers before we went to bed, but she did not understand or satisfy the need of a child for primary closeness to a parent." "I was certainly not an ideal mother," Eleanor wrote later. "It did not come naturally to me to understand little children or to enjoy them. Playing with children was difficult for me because play had not been an important part of my own childhood."[10]

Even without Sara, Eleanor's overly active conscience would have been both a burden and a blessing to her children, but Sara made escape from the demands of that conscience more difficult. Sara spoiled the children, but she was also very conventional and she imposed her essentially Victorian standards of good behavior on the children by "a procession of 'proper' English 'nannies,'" wrote James, that she "foisted on our household."[11] Their really intimate lives, said Anna, "were run by nurses and governesses."[12] One of these nurses, whom James called "Old Battleaxe," tyrannized the children, cuffing them about, locking them in closets, subjecting them to humiliations, all in the name of discipline. Eleanor discovered that she was also "a secret drinker," and that was her end. "From the time I got rid of that person," she said many years later, reminiscing with her children, "and took over the selection of the type of nurses I wanted, I began to have more confidence in my ability to handle the children."

There was a severe polio epidemic in 1916, which frightened Franklin and Eleanor, and Franklin was glad his family was at Campobello. "The infantile paralysis in N.Y. and vicinity is appalling," he wrote back after leaving them on the island. "*Please* kill all the flies I left. I think it really important." Eleanor tried to do as he wished: "The flies are fairly well exterminated," she reported.

Franklin spent little time at Campobello that summer, and Eleanor was restless and when Franklin intimated he might have to cut short his holiday at Campobello, she proposed to bring the family down earlier: she and the children could "easily go down from here by train alone." But Franklin did not like that idea. "No one is thinking of moving children by rail," he told her. And he wanted his family to stay there until he could get the *Dolphin* to bring them back directly to Washington rather than have them go to Hyde Park as they usually did in September, but that would not be until mid-September. Eleanor did not share Franklin's anxieties about having the children stay at Hyde Park.

I think the chicks will be safest at Hyde Park and even Mama does not seem to worry. They are exposed *possibly* anywhere and all we can do is to keep them as well as we can and I think the long season in Washington would be worse for them than the risks at Hyde Park.

But having made clear how she felt, she would not press the point. "of course if you decide it best to go to Washington or to stay later here I will do as you think best."

She yielded to him even though she found it "annoying to have to stay here just the one year I really want to get back!" The *Dolphin* finally picked them up at Eastport at the beginning of October. It was commanded by William D. Leahy, who recalled later that the forty-two-hour journey to New York City was considerably enlivened by the children, who took over the ship. They went to Hyde Park after all, Franklin finally agreeing with Eleanor "that H.P. is really no more risk than a long autumn in Washington."

It was Eleanor's "complete unselfishness," William Phillips wrote, that kept the household on an even keel, although Sara's "jealousy made life difficult in many ways" for her.

Caroline was always impressed by Eleanor's willingness to efface herself so that there would be no trouble between mother and son. It was her thoughtfulness of other people rather than of herself which made it possible to preserve a calm and tranquil attitude in such domestic difficulties.

No wonder we all admired her.[13]

But was her attitude so admirable? She did not think so in later years. Neither did her children.

19. The Approach of War

ACCORDING TO BILL PHILLIPS, who knew him as well as anyone in World War I Washington, Franklin did not seem fully mature. "He was likable and attractive, but not a heavyweight, brilliant but not particularly steady in his views," Phillips later wrote. "He could charm anybody but lacked greatness."[1] What was more, he was inclined to cockiness in his relation with his superiors, especially Daniels; if audacity did not more often lapse into presumption, he probably had Eleanor to thank for it.

She tried to discipline his brashness, because although she appreciated her husband's abilities and loyally supported his ambitions, she also knew that he could be egocentric and impulsive and give the impression that no one could refuse him anything. She took pleasure in passing on any praise of him that came her way, but usually coupled it with a chastening qualification. Harry Hooker "talked of you last night in a wonderful way and so did Maude and David the other day"—that was the garland; then came the bramble: "It is a great responsibility to feel such trust in one's character and brains and I'm glad it doesn't lie on my shoulders. I'd be bowed down!" Adulation bothered Eleanor. It intoxicated her husband.

His exuberant self-esteem usually amused her, but occasionally she dressed him down sharply. She read in the papers that Franklin had launched his campaign for senator with a statement "congratulating" his old political ally William Church Osborne on his resignation as New York Democratic state chairman by using such snide phrases as "had Mr. Osborne been in the thick of every political contest" and "had Mr. Osborne's political experience been deeper. . . ." "Isn't it just a bit patronizing?" Eleanor rebuked her husband. "If I were 'he' I would rise up and smite you for an impertinent youth."

Bill Phillips recorded an exchange between Franklin and Eleanor that he thought characterized Eleanor's steadying influence on her husband in those years. It took place in a hotel suite in San Francisco which the Phillipses shared with the Roosevelts in March, 1915, when they accompanied Vice President Marshall to the opening of the Panama Pacific Exposition. One morning while the four of them were breakfasting together, Eleanor asked Franklin whether he had received a letter from a certain person. " 'Yes,' said F.D.R. and drank his coffee. 'Have you answered it, Dear?' she asked. 'No,' said he and swallowed some more coffee. 'Don't you think you should answer it?' 'Yes,' was the reply. 'Don't you think you should answer it now?' 'Yes.' " Phillips added, "He answered it then and there. I gathered that the letter might never have received a reply without the watchful eye of his wife."[2]

When Josephus Daniels had cleared Roosevelt's appointment as assistant secretary with Elihu Root, then senator from New York, Root had cautioned him that "whenever a Roosevelt rides, he wishes to ride in front," and it was not long after his confirmation that Franklin was confiding to Eleanor how much better he could run the department than his chief. He and the secretary had slaved all day

on all the things he *should* have decided before and as I expected *most* of them were turned over to me! The trouble is that the Secretary has expressed half-baked opinions on these matters and I don't agree. I know that he would decide right if he'd only give the time to learn. However, he has given me *carte blanche* and says he will abide by my decision.

Eleanor thought this showed Mr. Daniels to be a man of magnanimity and strength. "I think it is quite big of him to be willing to let you decide," she cautioned Franklin. "Most people want to put their opinions through at all costs whether they are half-baked or not! It shows great confidence in you."[3]

At an early meeting of his cabinet President Wilson had referred to the Diary of Gideon Welles, Lincoln's secretary of the Navy, which had prompted Eleanor to read it and to point up its moral to her husband. She was struck by the "pettiness" of the men around Lincoln. "It was very wonderful we ever came through the Civil War. There seems to have been poor management at the War Department and so much jealousy and littleness among Cabinet members."

It was easy to underestimate Daniels, and Franklin did. The secretary's porkpie hat, string tie, and country-editor pleasantries gave him a look of rustic innocence, but underneath there was stubborn character and coherent conviction, and his feeling for power and how to hold onto it was just as strong as his ambitious young aide's. If Franklin raged impatiently against Josephus in the privacy of the N Street dining room, Bill Phillips felt equally strongly about his chief, William Jennings Bryan, who was Daniels' closest political associate. Both secretaries were pacifists, and neither was willing to look at his department through the eyes of its career men—the professional diplomats at State, the admirals at Navy.

To Daniels, navalist meant imperialist, while Franklin was an early disciple of Alfred Thayer Mahan, the great theoretician of sea power in relation to world politics. The admirals considered Franklin a sympathetic soul and cultivated him enthusiastically. The outbreak of war seventeen months after he joined the Navy Department brought Franklin's impatience with the secretary to a boiling point. If Eleanor had misgivings about her husband's hawkish views, she suppressed them and sided with him in the controversies he had with Daniels over the size and pace at which the Navy should be built and the aggressiveness with which the United States should assert its maritime rights against Germany.

The coming of the war shook the foundations of the world in which Franklin and Eleanor had grown up. To Caroline Phillips it seemed "like the end of the world."[4] Like Caroline, Eleanor watched gloomily as diplomatic efforts to damp down the blaze that had been kindled at Sarajevo yielded to inflammatory ultimatums and intimidating mobilizations. "It does seem unthinkable that such a struggle should take place," she wrote her husband from Campobello, where she was awaiting the birth of the second Franklin Jr., and comforting her French and English household help, whose relatives were being called to the colors. "I wonder if war can be averted," she wrote on August 2. War in fact had already begun, and a long letter Franklin wrote her that same day described the situation at the department. He had

found everything asleep and apparently utterly oblivious to the fact that the most terrible drama in history was about to be enacted. . . . These dear good people like W.J.B. and J.D. have as much conception of what a general European war means as Elliott has of higher mathematics. They really believe that because we are neutral we can go about our business as usual. . . .

"I am not surprised at what you say about J.D. or W.J.B. for one could expect little else," she wrote back. "To understand the present gigantic conflict one must have at least a glimmering of understanding of foreign nations and their histories. I hope you will succeed in getting the Navy together and up to the mark for I think we're going to need its moral support."

Franklin thought a long drawn-out struggle could be averted: "I hope England will join in and with France and Russia force peace *at Berlin*!" Eleanor concurred, and wrote, "The only possible *quick* solution to me seems the banding together of France, Russia and England and then only if England can gain the decisive victory at sea." Three days later a harried Franklin wrote again: "I am running the real work, although Josephus is here! He is bewildered by it all, very sweet but very sad!" Eleanor's reply was sympathetic: "I can see you managing everything while J.D. wrings his hands in horror. There must be so much detail to attend to all the time and so many problems which must, of course, be yours and not J.D.'s."[5]

Over at State the Phillipses were equally discontented with Bryan. William was working sixteen hours a day while "Mr. Bryan spends his time talking local politics with Senators and Congressmen," Caroline recorded, "and has not the slightest realization of the importance of this momentous struggle in Europe, consequently the whole initiative falls on William's and Mr. Robert Lansing's, the Counselor, shoulders. Without the latter, William would really be quite alone."[6]

The illusion persisted that the war might be ended quickly. The captain of the *Half Moon* told Eleanor of a rumor about a big naval battle in which thirty-seven German and six English ships had been sunk. "What a horrible loss of life, if true. One can only hope such a disaster will end the war," Eleanor wrote Franklin, who replied that he was disappointed "that England had been unable to force a naval action—of course it is the obvious course for Germany to hold her main fleet back and try to wear out the blockading enemy with torpedo and submarine attacks in foggy and night conditions."

As the hopes of a quick Allied victory faded, the dreadful consequences of a prolonged struggle loomed larger in Eleanor's mind. "I fear whichever side wins it will be a fearful slaughter," she wrote her husband, adding, "the Belgians have certainly done wonders." She was pro-Ally.

Germany's militarism and its intrigues in the Caribbean, especially in Mexico, the refusal of the Central Powers to submit the Serbian question to arbitration, the invasion of Belgium, despite treaty pledges, and Belgium's "glorious and unexpected resistance," as Franklin put it, all served to turn most Americans into Allied sympathizers, even though the country generally supported Wilson in his proclamation of complete neutrality. In the fervidly pro-Ally circles in which the Roosevelts moved, however, there was less sympathy for the president's subsequent plea that Americans should be neutral in thought as well as in action.

When Franklin lunched with Sir Cecil Spring-Rice at the Metropolitan Club, he informed Eleanor, the German ambassador, Count Johann Heinrich von Bernstorff, was at the next table "trying to hear what we were talking about. . . . I just *know* I shall do some unneutral thing before I get through." Eleanor also disdained Wilson's plea for impartiality of thought. Sara was always passing on the latest anti-German tidbit; she had heard, for example, that "the big gray building of the German Brothers across the river from Hyde Park (North of it) is full of ammunition."

Eleanor was still in touch with a German schoolmate, Carola von Passavant, whose brother had stayed with her and Franklin during a visit to the States just before the war broke out. In January, 1915, Carola wrote Eleanor:

Although this war is most terrible, it also makes us feel proud and happy, as it shows clearly all the good qualities, mental and physical strength of our nation. I do not know whether the feelings in America are with us, or against us now. I wonder what sort of an opinion you have formed about the Germans in this war?

Usually the promptest of correspondents, Eleanor delayed her reply until May 14, when she wrote:

. . . you asked questions which I did not just know how to answer. . . . This whole war seems to me too terrible. Of course it brings out in every nation wonderful, fine qualities for it calls for self-sacrifice and unselfishness, two qualities which are not apt to shine in uneventful and prosperous times but every people believes that it is right! War also brings out in all nations certain qualities which are not beautiful and I wish it could be wiped from the face of the earth though I recognize that in our present state of civilization there comes a time when every people must fight or lose its self-respect. I feel that it is almost too much to expect that we shall be spared when there is so much sorrow and suffering in so many countries abroad.

As to the opinions we have formed of the Germans in the war, I can only speak for myself, for my husband as you know is a member of the government and not allowed to express any opinions, but I think among the people here there is great respect for the people of Germany and also for the wonderful efficiency and preparedness of her army. Sympathy is pretty well divided I think on both sides but I think Count Bernstorff has been unfortunate in talking too much at first and though Dr. Dernburg has made very able speeches he has alienated many who felt he was trying to appeal to the popular sympathy over the heads of the Government. Just now you know the feeling is very tense but I cannot help hoping some understanding may be reached. . . .

The tense feeling to which Eleanor referred was over Germany's U-boat campaign. A week earlier, a German submarine had sunk the *Lusitania* on the high seas, with a loss of twelve hundred noncombatants, including 120 Americans. The United States was shocked and angered. Theodore Roosevelt wanted to go to war, and when Wilson said, "There is such a thing as a man being too proud to fight," Roosevelt accused him of cowardice and weakness. The Wilson cabinet was divided between Bryan, who favored compromise and arbitration, and those who favored strong action to compel Germany to end submarine warfare against unarmed merchantmen. On June 8, Bryan resigned to head a countrywide peace campaign.

"What d'y' think of W. Jay B?" Franklin wrote his wife. "It's all too long to write about, but I can only say I'm disgusted clear through. J.D. will *not* resign!" Their letters crossed. "I'm so glad Bryan is out," Eleanor commented, "but I can't help admiring his sticking to his principles. How about J.D. I wonder, and how would his resignation affect you! It is all most exciting but above all how will this affect the German question?"[7] In her autobiography two decades later Eleanor wrote that Bryan's pacifism had appealed to her and that she was one of the few people in official Washington who had not laughed at the miniature plowshares made out of old melted down swords that he sent around: "Anti-war germs must have been in me even then."[8] That is clear, too, from her letter to Carola. There were women who went considerably further, who not only actively preserved their detachment but, impressed with war's futility, sought a peace without victory. In 1915 an international women's congress met at The Hague, under the presidency of Jane Addams, and outlined a peace platform that was the forerunner of Wilson's Fourteen Points. There were forty-seven women in the U. S. delegation, including Dr. Alice Hamilton and Professor Emily Balch, but such movements and actions were still outside Eleanor's ken. Her husband was a leader of the preparedness faction within the government, and she was vigorously pro-Ally, as were her friends. Sir Cecil Spring-Rice was contemptuous of Bryan, whom he portrayed as sighing for the Nobel Prize. German policy, moreover, affronted American feelings.

Anger over the *Lusitania* had scarcely begun to subside when the White Star Liner *Arabic* was torpedoed without warning. "An outrage," commented Eleanor, adding the next day, "We are all wondering whether there are to be more words or action of some sort over the *Arabic*. The Germans are certainly not treating us with great consideration!"[9] Franklin thought the president would act, he replied, "as soon as we can get the facts. But it seems very hard to wait until Germany tells us her version and I personally doubt if I should be quite so polite."

"I think we have a little too much patience with Germany, don't you," Eleanor wrote back. Sara, as usual, was more emphatic. "I feel a little as T.R. feels, in fact a good deal," she wrote her son, adding shortly afterward, "there is one thing that he [Wilson] must remember—the time for dealings with the German criminals is over. Diplomatic relations with Germany are henceforth impossible." But the German government retreated. It disavowed the *Arabic* sinking and revealed that its submarine commanders had been ordered not to sink passenger liners without warning or making sure of the safety of noncombatants.

The U-boat crisis converted Wilson into an advocate of preparedness, vindicating a position that Franklin had long held, particularly with regard to the fleet. His strong feelings on the issue had in fact brought him close to insubordination. "He was young then and made some mistakes," Daniels wrote in 1944. "Upon reflection, although I was older, I made mistakes too."[10]

While Eleanor and Franklin had sympathized with Theodore's demands in 1915 for a tough line against Germany, they had serious reservations about Uncle Ted's politics in 1916. At the Republican convention that year, Theodore made his peace with the party. Although the nomination of Charles Evans Hughes on a platform of "straight and honest" neutrality represented a rejection of both his leadership and his policy of interventionism, Theodore supported the Republican ticket. When a relative said that Uncle Ted in 1916 had shown himself to be a bigger and a finer man than ever before, Eleanor could only express her astonishment. At the time Theodore was abandoning the progressives, Wilson was pushing through Congress most of the planks that Roosevelt had advocated in 1912. The mood of the country was fiercely noninterventionist. The Democrats answered Hughes' slogan of neutrality with the cry "He kept us out of war," and ardent progressives as well as Socialists swung over to Wilson. The election was one of the closest in U. S. history, but Eleanor thought Wilson was certain to lose.

Eleanor was at Hyde Park with the children as the election drew to a close. The Lanes and Millers were there, too, at Sara's invitation. (Lane called Sara "the ducal lady" and Franklin "the lord lover.") Sara was at her most gracious, and Lane reported that they all had "an exquisite time" before they left Eleanor and her children to go to New York City to hear the returns at headquarters.

It was a gloomy night for Democrats; Hughes appeared to be elected when Lane and Roosevelt left the dispirited gathering to return to Washington. But the next day it turned out that the western states were ranged in the Wilson column, and the outlook had altered drastically. "What a close and exciting election," Eleanor wrote her husband, "and all weighing now apparently on California. I can't help feeling Hughes will win in the end but it won't be such a walkover as it appeared to be." To Franklin this was "the most extraordinary day" in his life. "After last night, Wilson may be elected after all," and if he was, Franklin intended to wire his conservative Uncle Warren Delano, who was violently "agin the government" that "the Republican Party has proved to its own satisfaction I hope that the American people cannot always be bought." Then in a postscript addressed as much to himself as to Eleanor, he added, "I hope to God I don't grow reactionary with advancing years."

Despite Wilson's victory, 1916 ended, Eleanor said, with a sense everywhere of impending catastrophe.[11] Franklin was more and more outspokenly interventionist. "We've got to get into the war," he would say to Daniels, who invariably answered, "I hope not."[12] When, on January 22, 1917, Wilson called for a negotiated settlement, a "peace without victory," and an organized postwar order based on self-determination, disarmament, and freedom of the seas, Eleanor, in a departure from Franklin's interventionism, was enthusiastic. "I think the Allies are wild but it may be successful," she wrote Sara.[13] Spring-Rice was cynical about Wilson's motives: "Peace under the President's auspices must mean the permanent glory of the Democratic party in the person of its head."[14]

Germany spared the Allies the necessity of formally rejecting Wilson's bid by resuming unrestricted submarine warfare. On February 3, the president, while not completely abandoning his hopes of a peace without victory, announced a break in relations with Germany. Ambassador Bernstorff was handed his passports.

Franklin, meanwhile, had been sent to the Caribbean to inspect the Marine operations in Haiti and Santo Domingo and to determine whether the approaches to the Panama Canal were wholly secure. Haiti was not entirely pacified and evidently there was some danger in going there—or so Eleanor thought. Franklin was tired and needed the change, she wrote Sara; "also it is good for all men, young men especially, I imagine, to occasionally do something with the spice of risk in it otherwise they lose the love of it and Franklin hadn't had a chance for a long time now!"

This was another side of Eleanor. She was the daughter of her father, with a taste for adventure and a desire to feel not only the balm but the tang of life. Soon there would be hardship and danger enough for everyone.

When Wilson broke relations with Germany, Daniels ordered Roosevelt to return to Washington "at once." But throughout February and March Wilson continued to debate whether or not to declare war. He felt that war was inevitable, but the cost would be so great and the responsibility so heavy that he wanted it to be clear to the world that Germany left no other course open to him.

Daniels shared the president's feelings. "If any man in official life ever faced the agony of Gethsemane, I was the man in the first four months of 1917," he later wrote. "From the very beginning of the war in Europe I had resisted every influence that was at work to carry the United States into the war." Roosevelt felt that Wilson had the power to arm merchant vessels without congressional authorization, as did Lane. "We wait and wait," Lane wrote his brother on February 16. "Daniels said we must not convoy—that would be dangerous. (Think of a Secretary of the Navy talking of danger!)"[15] In his diary Roosevelt noted on March 9, "White House statement that Wilson has power to arm and *inference* that he will use it. J.D. says he will by Monday. Why doesn't President say so without equivocation?"

Again, Germany took the decision out of the president's hands with the Zimmerman telegram, which instructed the German representative in Mexico

City to propose an alliance with Mexico in the event the United States entered the war, in return for which Mexico would receive "the lost territory in Texas, New Mexico, and Arizona." Fury swept both the country and the administration. On March 18 German submarines torpedoed three American vessels. Two days later the cabinet, including Daniels, advised Wilson to ask Congress for a declaration of war. "The Cabinet is at last a unit," Lane wrote. But the president, he added, "goes unwillingly." So did Daniels.

Congress was summoned to meet on April 2 "to receive a communication concerning grave matters." It rained on April 2, "a soft, fragrant rain of early spring," Wilson's son-in-law, William E. McAdoo, noted. The president's address was equal to the solemnity of the moment. There was no alternative to war, he explained. Autocracy was the foe of liberty, and "the world must be made safe for democracy."

... It is a fearful thing to lead this great peaceful people, into the most terrible and disastrous of all wars, civilization itself seeming to be in the balance. But the right is more precious than peace, and we shall fight for the things which we have always carried nearest our hearts. ...

"I went," Eleanor wrote, "and listened breathlessly and returned home still half-dazed by the sense of impending change."[16]

The period of privacy, of exclusive devotion to her family and preoccupation with purely social duties, was at an end.

20. *Private into Public Person*

———

A YEAR AFTER AMERICA'S ENTRY into the war Eleanor wrote her mother-in-law that she was taking on still another assignment: "I'm going to have charge of the knitting at the Navy Department work rooms," in addition to the hours spent at the Red Cross canteen. "It is going to mean part of every day now except Sundays taken up at one place or another but that doesn't seem much to do, considering what the soldiers must do."[1] Eleanor had never shunned work, but the war harnessed her considerable executive abilities to her always active sense of responsibility. The war gave her a reason acceptable to her conscience to free herself of the social duties that she hated, to concentrate less on her household, and plunge into work that fitted her aptitudes. Duty now commanded what she could take pleasure in doing.

During the first few weeks Eleanor was so busy helping entertain the high-ranking allied missions that came hurrying to Washington that she didn't have time to think about what the war demanded of her as a person. The young couple's friendship with British Ambassador Spring-Rice and French Ambassador Jusserand, Franklin's duties with the Navy Department, and the social circles in which they moved meant a great deal of partying with members of the British Mission, headed by Arthur Balfour, whom Eleanor found "charming in the way that a good many Englishmen are and very few of our own men," and with the French Mission, with "Papa" Joffre as the center of attraction.

Marshal Joffre brought sobering news that dispelled the lingering illusion in New York and Washington that all that would be required of the United States would be money, foodstuffs, war materials, and the fleet to see to it that they got safely to Europe. At a luncheon at the Phillipses that included the Lanes, the Eustises, the Roosevelts, the Longworths, and Mrs. Borden Harriman, the Marshal made it clear that France wanted American troops, and as quickly as possible: "You should send 25,000 troops at once, and then again 25,000 and again and again, just as fast as possible."[2] Eleanor later accompanied Franklin to a Navy League reception for the head of the British Naval Mission. Franklin in his remarks sought to awaken the public to the true state of affairs. The British and the French Missions had been given "fair words, and again fair words," he said, but they had a right to ask about "the number of men that have left America for the other side. . . . It is time that they [Congress and the people] insist on action *at once*. Action that will give something definite—definite ships, definite men—on a definite day."

Eleanor applauded; "Franklin listened to all the polite platitudes and false hopes and was called on to speak last," she wrote Sara, at which time he "said all he has pent up for weeks. It was solemn and splendid and I was glad he did it and I think a good many people were but I shouldn't wonder if the Secretary was annoyed. Mr. Belmont was furious and said he took much too dark a view!"[3]

Franklin espoused a plan to lay a mine barrage across the North Sea to bottle up the submarines in their nests as part of an aggressive antisubmarine strategy. And it *was* originally Franklin's idea, Eleanor claimed. There has been dispute about that claim, but none that he became its chief advocate at a time when Daniels questioned its practicality and the British admiralty dragged its heels. "Franklin has asked to see the President to present his plan for closing the North Sea," Eleanor wrote Sara on May 10, 1917, "but 3 days have passed and he hasn't been granted an interview." She thought Franklin "very brave," Sara wrote back, "and long to hear that he could show his plan to the President." Franklin did not get to see Wilson until June 4, when he obtained the president's support for the establishment of an interdepartmental commission to inquire into the project's advisability. "If it hadn't been for him, there would have been no Scotch mine barrage," Admiral Harris later said,[4] and if the barrage came too late to be a decisive factor in winning the war, the delay was not Franklin's fault.

Theodore Roosevelt visited Washington during the hectic first weeks of the war. Blind in one eye, bothered by the fever he had picked up in the Brazilian jungles, the former president nevertheless came charging into the Capital with characteristic bravura to press his proposal that he be sent to France at the head of a division that he personally would raise. He stayed with Alice, and Franklin and Eleanor saw a good deal of him. When Uncle Ted visited them, the two youngest children, Franklin and John, were soon made aware of his presence. Full of electric vitality, Theodore burst into their room at the top of the house. "Oh, ho, ho," the old lion roared; "these two little piggies are going to market," and he hooked a happily protesting child under each arm and charged down the stairs.[5]

But apart from such family interludes there was little to cheer Theodore. "Though he was kind to us, as he always was," Eleanor said, "he was completely preoccupied with the war."

Franklin thought it was good policy to permit Uncle Ted to go to Europe and arranged for him to see the secretary of war. Sara also approved. "I hope he will be allowed to go," she wrote. More substantial support came from France. "Our *poilus* ask, 'Where is Roosevelt?'" Clemenceau wrote Wilson. "Send them Roosevelt—it will gladden their hearts." But the War Department was afraid a Teddy Roosevelt division would drain off the best officer talent. The war would be won by professionalism, discipline, and organization, it felt, not by gallant charges up the French equivalent of San Juan Hill. "The business now in hand," Wilson coldly announced on May 18, "is undramatic, practical, and of scientific definiteness and precision."

"I hated to have him disappointed," Eleanor wrote, "and yet I was loyal to President Wilson."[6]

All four of Theodore's sons went into the service, and he repeatedly urged Franklin to resign and put on a uniform. But General Leonard Wood, the most prestigious soldier in the Army and a Republican, said in July, 1917, that it would be "a public calamity if Franklin, an advocate of fighting the war aggressively, left at this time." Daniels was equally firm. A year later Eleanor became quite angry with her distinguished uncle when he brought up the subject again at Douglas Robinson's funeral, urging her to use her influence to get him to don a uniform. It was her husband's own business, she felt, and she knew, moreover, how anxious he was to get into the Navy. She was quite prepared to have him serve, but there were decisions a man had to make alone.

When her brother Hall, who was just getting established professionally, teamed up with Theodore's youngest son, Quentin, to go into the fledgling air force, she backed him up, even though he had to cheat a little on the eye test to qualify. But Grandma Hall asked why he didn't buy a substitute, as gentlemen had done in the Civil War, which outraged Eleanor. "Gentlemen" owed the same duty to their country as other citizens, and it would be unthinkable, she flung out at her grandmother, to pay someone to risk his life for you.[7]

The episode stood out in Eleanor's mind as another step on her road to independence. Under the impact of the war, her viewpoint was changing. A letter from Cousin Susie full of complaints about minor inconveniences caused by the war evoked an impatient exclamation: "How can one be like that in these days?"[8]

On all sides noncombatants were being urged to do their bit. "It is not an army we must shape and train for war," said Wilson, "it is the nation." Women, on the point of achieving suffrage—to which Eleanor was now a convert— broke loose from the Good Samaritan services to which tradition had assigned them and rallied to the war effort in every capacity except actual fighting in the field. "Is there any law that says a yeoman must be a man?" asked Daniels when the Navy faced a shortage of office workers. "Then enroll women!" Eleanor yearned to serve, but how? Her first ventures were awkward. Food administrator Herbert Hoover appealed to the country to conserve food; society responded by reducing the eight-course dinner to three, decreeing one meatless day a week, and pledging "simplicity in dress and entertainments." There was an end to calls.

Eleanor introduced her own austerity rules in her household, and her food-saving program was selected by the Food Administration "as a model for other large households," the *New York Times* reported. "Mrs. Roosevelt does the shopping, the cooks see that there is no food wasted, the laundress is sparing in her use of soap, each servant has a watchful eye for evidence of shortcomings on the part of others; and all are encouraged to make helpful suggestions in the use of 'left overs.' " And Mrs. Roosevelt added, according to the reporter, "Making ten servants help me do my saving has not only been possible but highly profitable."[9]

The story produced guffaws all over Washington. Franklin wrote:

All I can say is that your latest newspaper campaign is a corker and I am proud to be the husband of the Originator, Discoverer and Inventor of the New Household Economy for Millionaires! Please have a photo taken showing the family, the ten cooperating servants, the scraps saved from the table and the hand book. I will have it published in the Sunday Times. . . . Uncle Fred says "It's fine, but Gee how mad Eleanor will be!"

Uncle Fred was right about Eleanor's reaction. "I do think it was horrid of that woman to use my name in that way and I feel dreadfully about it because so much is not true and yet some of it I did say. I never will be caught again that's sure and I'd like to crawl away for shame."[10]

Although chagrined, she did not give up. She went to a meeting called by Daisy Harriman to muster support for the Red Cross. Mrs. Harriman proposed the formation of a motor corps auxiliary, but since Eleanor did not drive, she joined the Red Cross canteen, helped Mrs. Daniels to organize the Navy Red Cross, and joined the Comforts Committee of the Navy League, which distributed free wool to volunteer knitters and on Saturdays collected the finished articles.

The war kept Franklin in Washington, and Eleanor had to move the household to Campobello alone. She managed very well, as usual, and as soon as the family was settled went to Eastport to talk about the Red Cross. She wrote that she also brought "6 pyjamas to make and am going to learn to use the machine to make them myself!" She had begun on the machine, she reported the next day, "and hope to work more rapidly as I go on!" A week later she rejoiced that the last pyjama top would be finished that night, "and then I take 6 pair back tomorrow!"

During the summer Franklin was hospitalized with a throat infection, and Eleanor hurried to Washington to be with him. She returned the middle of August, bringing word to Sara that Franklin had petitioned the secretary to be allowed to go overseas in order to urge the British admiralty to use more aggressive antisubmarine tactics.

At the end of the summer, for the first time, Eleanor varied the routine of moving her family off Campobello. She shepherded her whole flock as far as Boston, saw the four younger ones, their nurses, and maids settled on the train to New York, and then Huckins, the Roosevelt chauffeur, drove her and eleven-year-old Anna west along the Mohawk Trail to visit Hall and Margaret and their children in Schenectady. "The views are wonderful and Anna is a most enthusiastic companion," she wrote her husband in Washington. She preferred to do such things with Franklin, but if he wasn't available she would do them nonetheless, and she was determined also to learn to drive. It was another small declaration of independence.

There was also the remarkable letter dated October 14, 1917, that Sara sent Franklin and Eleanor. In 1959 Eleanor told her son James that it had followed an argument about the future of Hyde Park, with Sara on one side and herself and Franklin on the other. Sara wanted the estate to stay in the family, the way Algonac and Fairhaven were kept by the Delanos and her English friends held on to their ancestral acres. Franklin dissented vigorously, Eleanor mildly, but dissent she did. He refused to make any such promise, Franklin declared and then, according to Eleanor's later recollection, forcefully voiced his own social and political credo, an exposition that caused Sara to write the following letter a few hours after her children had left for Washington.

Dearest Franklin
& Dearest Eleanor,
. . . I think of you almost in New York and I am sorry to feel that Franklin *is* tired and that my views are not his, but perhaps dear Franklin you may on second thoughts or *third* thoughts see that I am not so far wrong. The foolish old saying "noblesse oblige" is good and "honneur oblige" possibly expresses it better for most of us. One can be democratic as one likes, but if we love our own, and if we love our neighbor we owe a great example, and my constant feeling is that through neglect and laziness I am not doing my part toward those around me. After I got home, I sat in the library for nearly an hour reading and as I put down my book and left the delightful room and the two fine portraits, I thought: after all, would it not be better just to spend all one has at once in this time of suffering and need, and not to think of the future; for with the *trend* to "shirtsleeves," and the ideas of what men should do in always being all things to all men and striving to give up the old-fashioned traditions of family life, simple home pleasures and refinements, and the traditions some of us love best, of what use is it to *keep up* things, to hold on to dignity and all I stood up for this evening. Do not say that I *misunderstood,* I understand perfectly, but I cannot believe that my precious Franklin really feels as he expressed himself. Well, I hope that while I live I may keep my "old fashioned" theories and that *at least* in my own family I may continue to feel that *home* is the best and happiest place and that *my* son and daughter and their children will live in peace and happiness and keep from the tarnish which seems to affect so many. Mrs. Newbold's theory that children are "always just like their parents," is pretty true, as *example* is what really counts.
When I *talk* I find I usually arouse opposition, which seems odd, but is perhaps my own fault, and tends to lower my opinion of myself, which is doubtless salutary. I doubt if you will have time dear Franklin to read this, and if you do, it may not please you. My love to our fine little James, and to you two dear ones.
Devotedly
Mama

At the time this was written Eleanor was deeply involved in war work, an experience that was propelling her toward a more radical assertion of independence. "Today I go canteening " had become Eleanor's password. Washington was a major railroad junction, with as many as ten troop trains a day sitting on the sidings in the Washington yards. The Red Cross set up canteens manned by volunteers to provide the waiting soldiers with soup, coffee, and sandwiches. When a train came in the Red Cross ladies were there, lugging baskets of sandwiches and buckets of steaming coffee that had been prepared in the tin shacks where the volunteers worked. His mother was "up at five this morning to go to the canteen," James complained to his grandmother; "do not you think that Mother should not go so early?"

Edith Benham Helm described Eleanor at the canteen:

We also had a small room where we sold, at cost, cigars, cigarettes, chewing tobacco, picture postcards and candy bars. Here Mrs. Roosevelt shone. We had to make change at quick order when the men were lined up buying the supplies and we were supposed to turn over our finances in perfect order to the incoming shift. In all my experience there were only two women whose financial affairs were in perfect condition. One was Miss Mary Patten and the other, Mrs. Roosevelt.[11]

Eleanor, who once had not known how to keep her own household books, worked out the canteen's accounting system, and Mrs. Helm considered her "the dynamo" behind the canteen service.

Before the troop trains pulled out, the canteen workers picked up the postcards they had furnished for the men, censored them, and saw that they were posted. But handling the mail on top of her other canteen duties was too much even for her, as it ran to about five hundred pieces of mail a day. "This post office game isn't going to work," she informed her husband. "It needs two or three people a day." She persuaded the Red Cross to set up a special unit under Mrs. Vanderbilt.

When she was not at the canteen she gave out wool to knitters and collected the finished products. Then she was placed in charge of the knitting at the Navy Department, which meant supervising more than forty units whose captains reported to her. At the same time she learned that if Mrs. Daniels, who was ill, was not well enough to preside at a Navy Department rally the next day to organize for war work, she would have to preside. She did it—"I hated it but it was not as terrifying as I expected." Then she was asked to report to an assemblage of Red Cross workers on how the Red Cross knitting operation was organized. She was "petrified" when it was her turn to speak in the huge DAR auditorium, but she managed to get through her report, she wrote Sara, "and I hope I was heard."

She did everything that was asked of her. "I pour tea this p.m. at the Navy Yard for a Navy Relief party"; "I am collecting for the Red Cross at the Shoreham Hotel Lobby from 9–12 tomorrow a.m. and then canteen from 1–6." "Sometimes," she wrote Franklin, "I'd rather like to have a little while with you when neither of us had anything we ought to do, but I suppose that isn't to be hoped for till after the war!" Once when Franklin came to pick her up at the canteen they "were so busy he just turned in and worked too for an hour and enjoyed it! We had about 3,700 men during the day." The only concession to family life she made was always to be at home at tea time with the children and to keep them with her until they went to bed.

The winter and spring of 1918 were an anxious time. "I don't think there is any doubt that the Germans will put everything they can muster into a spring offensive," Eleanor wrote Sara.[12]

Sir Cecil Spring-Rice, the British ambassador, was acutely conscious of the dangers of the interval before the weight of the fresh American divisions began to be felt on the western front. Wilson did not like the ambassador, whom he called "that highly excitable invalid," and in January, 1918, Spring-Rice was recalled. "I feel very badly about the Spring-Rices," Eleanor wrote. "I shall be very sorry to have them go, it will really make a big difference here." The Spring-Rice children, Betty and Anthony, brought Anna pictures of themselves as parting gifts, and the ambassador gave Franklin and Eleanor a pen-and-ink drawing of the Washington monument which he had done himself; there was a poem on the back addressed to "sons of honour, richly fathered, scions of a sturdy brood. . . . Tell again your father's story" and ending with a warning: "Woe to them who lounge and linger when the foe is at the gate." Within a month Sir Cecil was dead. Eleanor framed the poem and drawing and hung them on the wall.

The sorrow and tragedy of the war was always with her. Franklin reported that a transport had been sunk and they feared a thousand men were lost. "All through dinner I felt like Nero." When the word came that Theodore's youngest son, an aviator, had been killed, "Think if it were our John," Eleanor wrote Franklin; "he would still seem a baby to us." She grieved for Aunt Edith and Uncle Ted, "but I suppose we must all expect to bear what France and England have borne so long."

Sir Cecil was not the only friend who passed from the world's stage that spring. At the end of February they dined with Henry Adams for the last time; on March 27 his "nieces" found him dead.

Franklin and I went to Mr. Adams funeral at two and I felt very sad for he was a very interesting man and the house had so many associations and now all is ended. There are not too many houses or [interiors] of that kind in this country and the end of things is sad. Alice invited us to lunch next Sunday almost before the Service was over and it offended me and made me angry, it seemed to be lacking in feeling, but Franklin said we'd go.

It was not always easy for Eleanor to follow Franklin into new experiences and to entertain new people whom he considered important to his career. When he brought Felix Frankfurter home, she sensed his brilliance but was bothered by what she considered his Jewish mannerisms—"an interesting little man but very jew," she commented.[13] In her anti-Semitism she belonged to the world of Henry Adams and Spring-Rice, whose hostility to materialism and the new power of money was mingled with dislike of Jews. She had to go to a party given by Admiral Harris for Bernard M. Baruch, "which I'd rather be hung than seen at," she complained to her mother-in-law; "mostly Jews."[14] Two days later she wrote, "The Jew party [was] appalling. I never wish to hear money, jewels and . . . sables mentioned again." Brandeis was exempted from this dislike, as were the young Henry Morgenthaus who had recently settled at Fishkill in lower Dutchess County. Even Sara approved of the Morgenthaus. "Young Morgenthau and his wife called this p.m.," she wrote Eleanor from Hyde Park, "and while they were here Mrs. F.W.V. [Vanderbilt] came bringing 5 people, and we had a pleasant tea. Young Morgenthau was easy and yet modest and serious and intelligent. The wife is very Jewish but appeared very well."

In May, 1918, the Red Cross proposed that Eleanor go to England to organize a Red Cross canteen there. "I really won't go abroad," she assured Sara, "but it is a fearful temptation because I feel I have the strength and probably the capacity for some kind of work and one can't help wanting to do the real thing instead of playing at it over here."[15] Why did she refuse? She was not sufficiently independent to manage such an undertaking, she later wrote, adding that in her heart of hearts she felt her primary obligation was to stay with her children. She did not want to admit this, even to herself, but that is what she felt.[16] And she knew the family—Grandma, Cousin Susie, Sara— would not approve.

Some were even critical when Franklin went abroad on naval business in July. "I think the family are funny not to be interested in F's trip," she wrote Sara,

for if it served no other purpose, it is really the only way of knowing the "real thing," the problems over there and the men whom this war is daily changing. It is too silly to think you can sit here at a desk and realize them and adequately deal with them, even men of the highest imagination can't and they say so. I hear it all the time.

The next day Franklin was received at Buckingham Palace. To bolster Sara, Eleanor sent her newspaper clippings about the event. Franklin "is surely making a hit," she observed. "The enclosed is from the *Washington Post*. I often think that you must wish his father could be here to be proud with you of Franklin."

She was working hard and tirelessly. Sara wanted her to come up to Hyde Park in May, but when Eleanor told the Navy Department workers that she was thinking of leaving, "they groaned. I really have no right to go unless it is a necessity." One day when there was a rush at the canteen she cut her finger to the bone while using the bread-slicing machine. She applied a bandage and kept on working, and although she saw a doctor later, she carried a scar for the remainder of her life.

She saw Alice at a party. Alice, who amused guests by turning back somersaults, expressed an interest in working at the canteen. "I'm taking Alice down to the canteen but I doubt if she does much and they told me they were almost afraid to take her on!" There were no trains the afternoon Alice came down and she decided, said Eleanor, that "she did not like scrubbing and ironing."

Sara's sister, who lived in Washington, reported that "Eleanor is the 'willing horse' and they call upon her at all hours, all the time." Washington was sticky and torrid that July, especially in the tin shacks in which they worked, but Eleanor made light of the discomfort: "I've come to the conclusion that you only feel heat when idle."

They had eight trains on July 17, a "very hectic day" made more so because the president's daughter Margaret came in to work with Eleanor's shift. Eleanor had

to introduce her to officers, etc. Mrs. Wilson now has a uniform and comes and works fairly regularly and yesterday late the President came down and walked down the tracks and all around and they tell me seemed much interested. I rather wish I'd been on duty there instead of the station.

A week later she had second thoughts about the president's wife.

We've become the fashionable sight and yesterday Mrs. Woodrow Wilson came to look on and brought Lady Reading [the wife of the British Ambassador] and Mrs. [Newton D.] Baker and Miss Margaret Wilson worked with us! It rather tries my soul but it is good for my bump of deference.

While Franklin was in Europe she finally had the family chauffeur, Huckins, teach her to drive. She was able to drive their Stutz to the canteen with Huckins on the running board, but just when she learned to handle it, the axle broke. She then used their older Buick, but its brakes "don't hold very well so I've just escaped street cars occasionally. However, Huckins says I'm doing finely." When General Headlam, head of a British military mission, came up from Washington to visit West Point and stayed at Hyde Park, Eleanor drove him about in the Ford, "once nearly dumping him but otherwise all serene." By the end of August she was driving her children and assorted relatives up to Tivoli and back. She was also making a new effort to learn to swim, and thought she might at last succeed.

Sara was happy to have her daughter-in-law at Hyde Park, if only because it meant that Franklin's letters to Eleanor from Europe would be promptly read to her. Please, Eleanor implored her husband, "when you don't write Mama, send messages to her otherwise I have to invent and that is painful! . . . I hate not being with you and seeing it all. Isn't that horrid of me!" She envied him his opportunities and she was lonely, but she hoped he could accomplish "a good deal . . . for I know that is what you really want."

Franklin delayed his departure from Europe because he wanted to avoid the Democratic primary at the beginning of September. The previous summer he had made his peace with Tammany, to the distress of Eleanor and Sara. Just before he had left for Europe he had had to squelch a plan to nominate him for governor that Tammany was prepared to sponsor, and in the process had come out for upstater William Church Osborne, an old comrade in the political wars against Tammany. A letter from Eleanor reported that Louis Howe was in an agitated state because Franklin's support of Osborne was interfering with his appeasement policy toward Tammany. Howe told her, Eleanor reported, that

he alone kept you from being nominated for governor and now he doesn't know what to do as you came out for Osborne and he is staying in the race and Al Smith wants your endorsement and he, Mr. H. could get no answer as to what the White House wanted you to do, etc! My guess is he's making himself one little nuisance.

However, I soothed him by suggesting that as you were out for Osborne you'd have to stick till he withdrew which would doubtless be soon.

As Howe had foreseen, however, Osborne declined to withdraw from the primary and came to Howe to solicit Franklin's help. Howe told him that Franklin would be out of the country, and therefore out of politics, for a long time, and asked Eleanor to pass the word to Franklin confidentially that "the President and Mr. Daniels think that the political situation will be considerably eased if he does not reach this country until at least a week after the primaries, which are sometime in the first week of September."

In a speech in Paris Franklin said that he intended to volunteer for the Navy, and a letter to Eleanor from Brest explained that his place was "not at a Washington desk, even a Navy desk." He added that he expected to be back in the States about September 15.

She next heard that he was ill in Paris, "so I expect it has been a little too strenuous but the trip back if devoid of incidents will be restful!" His illness was more serious than she knew. On September 19, the *Leviathan* docked and Eleanor received a call to come to the pier with a doctor. She summoned Dr. Draper, and two hours later an ambulance drew up at Sara's Sixty-fifth Street house and four Navy orderlies carried Franklin inside. His illness was diagnosed as double pneumonia.

As a consequence, she and Franklin did not get back to Washington until October 18, and a few weeks later the war was over. "This has been an exciting day," Eleanor wrote on November 11, 1918.

The Secretary got me a ticket for the gallery so I heard the President make his speech to Congress and F. went on the floor with Mr. Daniels. The galleries were packed and it was most inspiring. At the mention of Alsace-Lorraine's evacuation the whole place rose and cheered and the French wept. There was not as much enthusiasm for feeding the Central Powers![17]

"The feeling of relief and thankfulness was beyond description," she later wrote.[18]

At the war's end her attention shifted from the canteen to the wounded, who were being returned to military hospitals. There were men who would never be well enough to go home again, and Christmas no longer was exclusively a family party. Her children, Sara noted, "had a Christmas tree and supper with 12 soldiers from Mrs. Lane's Convalescent Home and 12 sailors from the Naval Hospital." Each man was given a cornucopia of candy, a box of cigarettes, and a tie. "Sec. and Mrs. Lane there and Mrs. (Gladys) Saltonstall played violin and everyone sang."

Except for Eleanor, everyone in the household—all the children, Franklin, and most of the servants—was felled by the influenza epidemic that swept through Washington that winter. Eleanor worked round the clock, putting to good use all the lessons she had learned from Miss Spring. When the children were asleep, she hurried off to assist the Red Cross unit set up to provide help for government offices whose employees were absent with the flu.

After everyone recovered, Eleanor and Franklin went to Europe (more will be said about this journey later) and when they returned on February 24, Eleanor thought her work was "practically over." But soon afterward she agreed to take charge of the Red Cross recreation room at the Naval Hospital. She visited the hospital wards daily, handing out cigarettes, bringing flowers, saying a word of cheer. Her new duties also included reviewing appeals from families of sailors and marines who were in need of help.

"I am taking two ladies of Navy Department Red Cross Auxiliary to St. Elizabeth's this p.m.," she wrote Sara at the end of March. "We have 400 men in the insane asylum there and the Chaplain asked that we go to see the Doctor in charge and find out what could be done for them as very few organizations take any interest in them and many of the men are not insane but shell shock patients."[19] The chief doctor took them through the two naval wards, and pity filled Eleanor's heart. St. Elizabeth's, a federal hospital, was starved for funds, short of attendants, lacking equipment. The men were locked in and moved restlessly around their cagelike porches; they were not permitted to go outside for exercise or sports. Eleanor told the doctor that the Navy Red Cross would supply newspapers, games, a phonograph, and records for a Navy recreation room that the Red Cross would build.

St. Elizabeth's was under the jurisdiction of the Interior Department, headed by Eleanor and Franklin's friend, Franklin Lane, who feared that the program Eleanor and her friends had devised for the Navy boys in the hospital would be considered discriminatory. "It is more and more clear to me," he wrote her, "that we could not have the Navy men treated better than the Army men or the civilians without causing a great deal of trouble." There was a time when Eleanor would have let the matter rest there, but now she asked why the government should not improve the whole hospital, military and nonmilitary. She wanted Lane to visit St. Elizabeth's to see conditions for himself, and although he declined, he appointed a departmental investigatory commission, whose report to the House Committee on Appropriations confirmed the inadequacy of the care provided at St. Elizabeth's. A larger appropriation was voted and the doctors were able to transform the hospital into a model institution.

Far from decreasing, her public activity was so great that, Eleanor lamented late in 1919, she hardly had time to breathe. She had a hand in obtaining rest rooms for the girls who worked in the Navy Department; she was responsible for a ball for the benefit of Trinity Parish; she even agreed to sit in a booth at the New Willard Hotel to help the membership drive of the American Women's Legion. Theodore Roosevelt had died in January, 1919, and a Women's Memorial Committee was being organized. She agreed to work hard for it if someone else took the chairmanship, stating, "This is positively the last thing I'm going to do!"

But there were compensations. On New Year's Eve a Staten Island mother wrote her:

I want to thank you as the mother of one of the boys who was in the Naval Hospital at Washington from the first of April until July 8th for the kind words—the little favors—the interest you took in my son, which was so much appreciated by him and also his mother.

Perhaps you can't recall the boy. He lay in the T.B. ward. . . . He always loved to see you come in. You always brought a ray of sunshine with you, always had something to say to him. . . .

Eleanor acknowledged that being able to help gave her a deep sense of satisfaction. "One of the boys in the Naval Hospital died today," she wrote Sara, "and the little wife who is to have a baby in October and the mother had to borrow money to come to him so the Navy Department Auxiliary is going to refund it and I must go to see them this p.m. It is nice to be able to do such things isn't it?"[20]

In 1920, when Franklin accepted the Democratic nomination for vice president and Eleanor resigned from the Navy Relief Society, the board of managers adopted a resolution praising her for her "valuable services, . . . unfailing interest in the work of the society, . . . patience, good judgment, tact, and amiability."

Once during the war when Sara had been deploring the fact that the war caused a decline in moral standards, Eleanor had remarked that she might be right, "yet I think it is waking people to a sense of responsibility and of obligation to work who perhaps never had it before." She was one of the awakened.

She said, when she was asked to go to work for the Theodore Roosevelt Memorial, and she repeated it in one form or another throughout her life. "I begin to feel that only a hermit's life will ever give me joy again." But her commitment to public activity had been made. The sleeping princess, as Archibald MacLeish later wrote, had been awakened.[21] She would never again be content with purely private satisfactions, and for the rest of her life she would look at the injustice of the world, feel pity for the human condition, and ask what she could do about it.

21. *Trial by Fire*

THERE WAS ANOTHER REASON why there was no turning back to a wholly private life for Eleanor: her discovery of the romance between her husband and her social secretary, Lucy Page Mercer. In the shaping of Eleanor Roosevelt the Lucy Mercer affair, while neither hammer nor anvil, was the flame whose heat hastened and fixed the change from private into public person. Franklin's love of another woman brought her to almost total despair, and she emerged from the ordeal a different woman. Ended was the subordination to her mother-in-law and to the values and the world Sara represented; emergent was the realization that to build a life and interests of her own was not only what she wanted to do but what she had to do. "The bottom dropped out of my own particular world," she wrote. twenty-five years later, "and I faced myself, my surroundings, my world, honestly for the first time. I really grew up that year."[1]

She forgave her husband and they continued to live together, but their relationship was different. She no longer allowed herself to be taken for granted, either as a woman or an instrument of his purposes. And because—to paraphrase Santayana—she felt great things greatly and had the power to relate them to the little things she felt keenly and sincerely, her life became an inspiration to women everywhere. Her relationship with her husband not only stands as one of the most remarkable in American history but had considerable effect upon its course.

The depth of Eleanor's feeling about the Lucy Mercer episode can be gauged by the fact that it is one of the few events that she did not mention in her books and about which she found it difficult to speak. Occasionally in later life Eleanor discussed it with a few of her closest friends, including the writer of this book, when she saw they were puzzled by some of her domestic arrangements or when she thought her own experience might help them disentangle their own problems of love and marriage, but even then she was very reluctant to speak of it. If it were not central to an understanding of husband and wife it might be passed over with the same reticence, but it must be dealt with, even though the story is known only in outline.[2]

Eleanor employed Lucy Page Mercer, then twenty-two, in the winter season of 1913–14 to help with social correspondence three mornings a week. Lucy, an efficient social secretary and a charming person, soon became a household familiar. By late spring 1914 Franklin was writing Eleanor in Hyde Park that he had arrived safely in Washington, gone to the house, "and Albert telephoned Miss Mercer who later came and cleaned up." (Albert was the Roosevelt chauffeur and general handyman.)

Sara approved of Lucy. In the spring of 1915 when she came down to stay with the children during Franklin and Eleanor's trip to the San Francisco Exposition, a letter that reported such news as "Babs [Franklin Jr.] is splendid, had his one big movement," also included an enthusiastic reference to Eleanor's social secretary: "Miss Mercer is here, she is *so* sweet and attractive and adores you Eleanor."[3]

Sara's approval was in character—Lucy, descended as she was from the Carrolls of Maryland, had an irreproachably patrician background. Her mother had been a famous Washington beauty and her father was Major Carroll Mercer, one of the founders of the Chevy Chase Club, where Franklin played golf, and a pillar of the Metropolitan Club, another favorite haunt of Franklin's. But the family had fallen on hard times and the marriage had broken up, so Lucy's mother had brought her up to be able to earn a living as a social secretary—a job, Jonathan Daniels has written, for young ladies of "impeccable social standing and slim purses." Lucy did her job well, said Aileen Tone, who performed similar functions for Henry Adams. Lucy would sit down on the floor of the living room, Aileen recalled, strew bills, letters, and invitations about, and in the twinkling of an eye have everything in order. "She was a charmer," Aileen added. Lucy Mercer's loveliness, good taste, and exquisite manners enabled her to maintain her footing socially. When Eleanor was short a woman for a dinner party or luncheon, she invited Lucy. Men fell in love with Lucy—"every man who ever knew her," some said; she was good-looking enough "to be generally admired," one of the young men at the British Embassy said, and her voice had the quality of dark velvet. She knew how to please a man, to make his life easy and agreeable, to bolster instead of challenge him.

She had qualities of femininity that Eleanor lacked, and Eleanor was aware of her own shortcomings. Because she could not relax, others found it difficult to be wholly relaxed with her. Duty came first, not fun or pleasure. She still felt awkward at parties, and at dances she put in an appearance and then vanished. While Arthur Schlesinger, Jr., may have exaggerated when he described the Eleanor Roosevelt of that era as "a woman sternly devoted to plain living, invincibly 'sensible' in her taste and dress,"[4] she herself often spoke of the "Puritan" in her that held her back from high living, frivolity and indolence.

Franklin, on the other hand, was, as Lane dubbed him, the "gay cavalier," the "lord lover"—debonair, fun-loving, and able to enjoy making a night of it with the British Embassy "boys" or his intimates at the Metropolitan Club. Franklin was one of the handsomest men in Washington, admired by men and women alike. Walter Camp, the famous Yale coach who came to wartime Washington to keep its executives in trim, described Roosevelt as "a beautifully built man, with the long muscles of an athlete."[5] The assistant military attaché at the British Embassy, Arthur Murray, spoke of Roosevelt as "breathing health and virility."[6] Bill Phillips remembered him as "always amusing, always the life of the party."[7] After Auntie Bye had seen Franklin in Washington, Admiral Cowles (her husband) reported to Franklin that Bye had thought him brave and charming, "but," Cowles added, "the girls will spoil you soon enough Franklin, and I leave you to them."[8]

Eleanor also teased him about his popularity with the ladies. He was going back to the department at five o'clock, she reported to Sara, to review "the yeomen F" (female).[9] She thought that was entertaining, but she might have been happier had the secretary assumed that duty. When Franklin went to Europe in 1918 she was amused at all the lovely creatures in the Navy Department and the Red Cross who took an interest in his safe arrival abroad. The wife of a Marine captain, she wrote Franklin, "told me she knew you were on the way and had been so worried! She's one of my best cooks on the canteen, so it hasn't interfered with her work!"[10] Everyone was so nice about Franklin's safe arrival in Europe, she reported to Sara: "I wish I could tell you how many people speak as though they were lying awake nights over him!"[11]

She knew that she did not satisfy the frivolous, flirtatious side of Franklin's nature. She liked the company of older people while he complained that they were always invited to the stodgy parties where he was usually given the "honor" of taking the oldest dowager present in to dinner. Her letters from Campobello and Hyde Park were filled with expressions of pleasure that he was having a gay time,[12] which reflected an awareness that companionship and love that were not freely offered were not worth having. But she was also jealous, and undoubtedly the more firmly she urged him to go to a party alone, the more she wanted him to say no. She disciplined herself to treat his flirtations as summer shadows. She had long ago learned to repress her jealousy, to think tolerantly, even fondly, of possible rivals when her adored father had filled his letters from West Virginia with accounts of all the things he did with the little girls in Abingdon. She could treat Franklin's dalliances lightly so long as she was sure of his love, sure that she came first with him.

She began to feel uneasy about her husband being alone in Washington during the summer of 1916, the year of the polio epidemic when Franklin insisted that she remain at Campobello until the end of September and she did not want to stay. That was the summer he portrayed himself a veritable wallflower in his letters to Eleanor. "Yesterday I had a very busy time as the Secretary went to Annapolis and left me a thousand loose ends to tie up. I stayed here until just in time to dress for dinner and went out to Chevy Chase with the Blues—a nice dinner. Everybody danced afterwards, except self who lost his nerve, and Mrs. Blue and the Miss Somebody [he couldn't catch her name] who had a sore on her leg—so I had a peaceful evening—and really enjoyed watching the antics of the three or four hundred other bipeds on the floor."[13] That was the summer, too, when their chauffeur, Golden, went joy riding through Washington in the Roosevelt car and cracked up both the car and himself. "Isn't it horrid to be disappointed in someone," she wrote to Franklin commiseratingly, "it makes one so suspicious!"[14] Suspicious only of servants, or was the comment meant to have a broader application?

In 1917 she delayed her departure to Campobello for reasons that may be surmised from a letter Franklin sent her the day after she left.

I really can't stand that house all alone without you, and you were a goosy girl to think or even pretend to think that I don't want you here *all* summer, because you know I do! But honestly *you* ought to have six weeks straight at Campo, just as *I* ought to, only you can and I can't! I *know* what a whole summer here does to people's nerves and at the end of the summer I will be like a bear with a sore head until I get a change or some cold weather—in fact as you know I am unreasonable and touchy now—but I shall try to improve.[15]

Eleanor was nervous about Lucy Mercer that summer; when she reluctantly left Washington she put Lucy and Mary Munn in charge of the Saturdays when she gave out yarn and collected the sweaters, scarves, and socks that had been finished. Eleanor had insisted that Lucy, who had begun to work in the Navy Department as a yeoman (F), third class, in June, be paid and that the relationship be strictly a business one. She had given Franklin notes on how she wanted her "wool Saturdays" to be handled while she was away. "Your letter of Thursday is here and one from Miss Mercer," she wrote him on July 23. "Why did you make her waste all that time answering those fool notes? I tore them and the answers up and please tear any other results of my idiocy up at once. She tells me you are going off for Sunday and I hope you all had a pleasant trip but I'm so glad I'm here and not on the Potomac!"

The trip to which Miss Mercer referred combined duty with pleasure. "The trip on the Sylph was a joy and a real rest, though I got in a most satisfactory visit to the fleet," Franklin wrote her.

Such a funny party, but it worked out *wonderfully*! The Charlie Munns, the Cary Graysons, Lucy Mercer and Nigel Law, and they all got on splendidly. We swam about four times and Sunday afternoon went up the James to Richmond. We stopped at Lower and Upper Brandon, Westover and Shirley and went all over them, getting drenched to the skin by several severe thunderstorms. Those old houses are really wonderful but *not* comfy![16]

Nigel Law, the third secretary of the British Embassy, was a bachelor and a companion of Franklin's in relaxation at the Chevy Chase Club and at the Lock Tavern Club on the Potomac. Before Eleanor left Washington, she had spent a week end on the *Sylph* at which Lucy Mercer and Nigel Law were present. Did the presence of Nigel Law allay her worry about Lucy?

She was glad he had enjoyed his trip, Eleanor commented, "but sorry you found things not quite right in the fleet. The party sounds delightful to me except the Graysons' but I think you were clever to take them."[17] Eleanor's letter went on to talk of household matters such as reminding him to deposit three hundred dollars into the household account on August 1 as she intended to draw on it that day to pay bills, but she did not manage to conceal her disquiet completely. She was writing for train accommodations early, she announced, but he would see very little of her in Washington in the early autumn because she would have lots of things to do in New York. "I think in spite of all their troubles Mrs. Munn and Miss M. like to run my Sats. so I shall have no scruples there and I don't think I shall have to take over the packing room." Then, in a reference to his protestations of how lonely it was in Washington in the summertime, she remarked "I'm glad you are so gay but you know I predicted it! I hope you'll have this Sunday at H.P."

Then Franklin informed her, "I do miss you so very much, but I am getting busier and busier and fear my hoped-for dash to Campo next week for two days will not materialize. Nor can I get to H.P. for Sunday, as I found my absence last Sunday has put me too far back."[18] "I am sorry," she wrote back, "you can't get to H.P. this Sunday before Mama leaves. I know she will feel badly about it. I hope you won't try to come here. It is too far away and you ought not to do it. It will be better to take 2 weeks at H.P. in September and October."[19] But it was a reproach, because only four days earlier she had written, "I am praying no one will come to stay this summer, I am having such a delightful, unbothered time. . . . I wish you could come but I want no one else!" And there was another reproach: "I don't think you read my letters for you never answer a question and nothing I ask for appears!"

Although she was having a "delightful, unbothered time" at Campobello, when Franklin came down with his old throat infection at the end of July Eleanor rushed to Washington and did not return to Campobello until the middle of August. En route back she wrote, "I hated to leave yesterday. Please go to the doctor twice a week, eat well and sleep well and remember I *count* on seeing you the 26th. My threat was no idle one."[20]

She did not say what her threat had been, but whatever her suspicion of an attachment between her husband and Lucy, it is obvious that she hadn't mentioned it while in Washington, for on August 20 Franklin wrote her, "I had a very occupied Sunday, starting off for golf at 9 with McIlhenny, Legare, and McCawley, quick lunch at Chevy Chase, then in to town and off in car at 2:30 to the Horsey's place near Harper's Ferry. Lucy Mercer went and the Graysons and we got there at 5:30, walked over the farm—a very rich one and run by the two sisters—had supper with them and several neighbors, left at nine and got home at midnight! The day was magnificent, but the road more dusty and even more crowded than when we went to Gettysburg."

This time Franklin did get to Campobello as he had promised. "It is horrid to be without you," Eleanor wrote him on September 2, the day after he left, "and the chicks and I bemoaned our sad fate all through breakfast." But she continued to be reserved and wary toward Lucy, as indicated by a genteel dispute between the two over Eleanor's insistence on paying Lucy for handling her "wool Saturdays." Eleanor sent a check, which Lucy declined to accept. Eleanor was immovable and Lucy finally said she would abide by her wishes since Eleanor was mistress of the situation. She apologized for having been unbusinesslike, but then she returned the check as the last two collections were not made, on the assistant secretary's instruction; furthermore, on Saturday, July 21, she had not been present, and she had participated the previous Saturday only to the extent of answering questions and listing what came in. Eleanor sent this letter on to Franklin with the comment, "I've written Miss Mercer and returned the check saying I knew she had done far more work than I could pay for. She is evidently quite cross with me!"[21]

"*You* are entirely disconnected and Lucy Mercer and Mrs. Munn are closing up the loose ends," Franklin replied.[22]

That autumn the Roosevelts moved into a larger house at 2131 R Street, and wool distribution and collection were shifted to rooms at the Navy Department. Lucy Mercer, who had been promoted to yeoman, second class, was released from her Navy duty on October 5, 1917, "by special order of Secretary of the Navy"—perhaps for hardship, since her father had died a few days earlier—but she still helped Eleanor as social secretary and Eleanor still asked her to fill in when she needed an extra woman for a lunch or dinner party.

On the surface all went on as usual, but Eleanor must have had a sense of impending catastrophe. That winter she wrote almost daily to her mother-in-law, whose standards in regard to the obligations that a husband owed his wife and family were precise and unbudgable. Her letters to Sara at this time were as warmly affectionate as they had been the year of her honeymoon. It was as if she were seeking to protect herself against the disaster she saw coming by shielding herself in the older woman's lee.

"Much love always dearest Mummy," Eleanor wrote on January 22, 1918. "I miss you and so do the children, as the years go on I realize how lucky we are to have you and I wish we could always be together. Very few mothers I know mean as much to their daughters as you do to me." "I wish you were always here!" she wrote a month later, "There are always so many things I want to talk over and ask you about and letters are not very satisfactory are they?" She rejoiced when the time came for Sara's spring visit. "We are all thrilled at the thought of having you, I am particularly hungry for a sight of you, only a stern sense of duty has kept me from running away to see you a number of times."

Sara sent Franklin and Eleanor a letter and telegram on their wedding anniversary and Eleanor replied,

Thirteen years seems to sound a long time and yet it does not seem long. I often think of what an interesting, happy life Franklin has given me and how much you have done to make our life what it is. As I have grown older I have realized better all you do for us and all you mean to me and the children especially and you will never know how grateful I am nor how much I love you dear.[23]

Sara reciprocated Eleanor's regard.

When Aunt Kassie's daughter, "Little Kassie," married George B. St. George, the latter's mother was delighted with her daughter-in-law. "Well, Kassie, you are running a close second to my Eleanor as a daughter-in-law," Sara commented. Kassie demurred: "Oh, Aunt Sallie, I never could be as good and lovely as Eleanor is."

For some her very goodness was a goad. The romance between Franklin and Lucy did not escape Alice's keen eyes. She saw Franklin out motoring with Lucy, and called him afterward. "I saw you 20 miles out in the country," she teased. "You didn't see me. Your hands were on the wheel but your eyes were on that perfectly lovely lady."[24]

"Isn't she perfectly lovely?" he replied.

Alice encouraged the romance. Franklin dined at Alice's when Eleanor was out of town, and she also invited Lucy. It was good for Franklin, Alice maintained. "He deserved a good time. He was married to Eleanor."[25] Moreover, since she considered Eleanor "overly noble," Alice was not beyond enjoying a little one-upmanship at Eleanor's expense. Alice and Eleanor had run into each other at the Capitol, but Eleanor had left Alice at the door, she reported to Franklin, "not having allowed her to tell me any secrets. She inquired if you had told me and I said no and that I did not believe in knowing things which your husband did not wish you to know so I think I will be spared any further mysterious secrets!"

When Franklin returned from his 1918 trip to Europe in September stricken with double pneumonia, Eleanor took care of his mail, and in the course of doing so she came upon Lucy's letters.[26] Her worst fears were confirmed. Her world seemed to break into pieces. After her wedding there had been a period of total dependency and insecurity from which she had slowly begun to emancipate herself. But Franklin's love was the anchor to which her self-confidence and self-respect were secured, and now the anchor was cut. The thought tortured Eleanor that, having borne him six children, she was now being discarded for a younger, prettier, gayer woman—that her husband's love belonged to someone else. The bottom, she wrote, dropped out of her world. She confronted her husband with Lucy's letters. She was prepared to give her husband his freedom, she told him, if after thinking over what the consequences might be for the children he still wanted to end their marriage.

He soon discovered that divorce might have disagreeable consequences in addition to the effect upon the children. Sara was said to have applied pressure with the threat to cut him off if he did not give up Lucy. If Franklin was in any doubt about what a divorce might do to his political career, Howe was there to enlighten him. Lucy, a devout Catholic, drew back at the prospect of marriage to a divorced man with five children. Eleanor gave him a choice—if he did not break off with Lucy, she would insist on a divorce. Franklin and Lucy agreed never to see each other again.

"I know that marriage would have taken place," Mrs. Lyman Cotten, a North Carolina cousin of Lucy, told Jonathan Daniels, "but as Lucy said to us, 'Eleanor was not willing to step aside.' "[27] Mrs. Cotten is incorrect, not in her impression of what Lucy may have told her, but as to the facts. Franklin may have told Lucy that Eleanor would not give him a divorce, but this was not the story as Eleanor's friends heard it or as Auntie Corinne heard it from Cousin Susie or as Alice Longworth heard it from Auntie Corinne.[28] "I remember one day I was having fun with Auntie Corinne," Alice said; "I was doing imitations of Eleanor, and Auntie Corinne looked at me and said, 'Never forget, Alice, Eleanor offered Franklin his freedom.' And I said, 'But, darling, that's what I've wanted to know about all these years. Tell.' And so she said, 'Yes, there was a family conference and they talked it over and finally decided it affected the children and there was Lucy Mercer, a Catholic, and so it was called off.' "

With Eleanor the paramount, perhaps the only consideration in preserving the marriage was the children, and no doubt Franklin's affection for his children was the major reason for his hesitation. Lucy's guilt feelings as a Catholic and Sara's threat were undoubtedly also influential, but for years Eleanor believed that the decisive factor with Franklin had been his realization that a divorce would end his political career.

A long letter dated February 14, 1920, from Eleanor to Sara full of chit-chat about the children and political news ended with the sentence, "Did you know Lucy Mercer married Mr. Wintie Rutherfurd two days ago?"

In later years Eleanor confided to her most intimate friends, "I have the memory of an elephant. I can forgive, but I cannot forget."

22. *Reconciliation and a Trip Abroad*

"No woman marries the man she really marries," Josephus Daniels declared[1] at a party the Roosevelts gave in December, 1918, to celebrate the approaching marriage of Sallie Collier, Aunt Kassie's gayest daughter. The secretary addressed himself to Sallie but it was Eleanor who paid attention. She and Franklin were now each trying to be the partner the other had hoped for when they married. He knew how deeply he had wounded her and sought to do the things that pleased her; she was making an effort to be gay, even frivolous. There was a kind of wistful camaraderie to their relationship. "Last night's party was really wonderful and I enjoyed it," she informed Sara, and Franklin reported the same reaction. Eleanor talked to "heaps and heaps of people" he wrote, "and I actually danced once."[2]

Sunday was still sacred to Chevy Chase and golf, but in the afternoon instead of the morning. Franklin "went to church last Sunday and goes again today, which I know is a great sacrifice to please me," Eleanor noted. Once his casual habits of attendance at church had upset Eleanor, but now she could jest about it. When Franklin was informed that he had been made a vestryman at St. Thomas where they worshiped in Washington, Eleanor described the news as a "fearful shock" to him and expressed the hope that he would decline.[3]

He spent more time with the children. He took James with him to Chevy Chase and let the youngster caddy, and helped Anna with her algebra until Miss Eastman suggested it might be better to drop algebra altogether and concentrate on arithmetic. He read Eleanor his official report to the secretary on his European trip. She thought it very good and undertook to edit the diary he had kept during the trip with a view to publication. "We had a good deal of dictating in the evening for the first time," she wrote Sara.[4] She merged into a single account diary notes, letters, and new material dictated by him, and then dictated the combined account to a stenographer in Franklin's office. A month later they were still working on it—"luckily I'm not as sleepy as last night so I hope we can have some dictating"[5]—but in the end the account was only half completed and was not published until Elliott edited his father's *Personal Letters*.

With the war over, Washington was no longer the focus of excitement and action, and Franklin was restless. *Town Topics*, the society gossip sheet, even said he had resigned and might be slated for a diplomatic post. "Mrs. Franklin Roosevelt," the item added, "has always been retiring and not overwhelmingly in love with Washington." Eleanor thought that was "a funny notice, however, I'm glad I'm retiring enough not to merit any further comments." Yet Franklin was "very discontented with his work. . . . Don't be surprised if we are back with you next winter, if we are not in France," she wrote Sara.[6] It was to Europe that they went.

Franklin proposed to the secretary that a civilian should go to Europe to direct the liquidation of the naval establishments there, and if he were sent, Eleanor should accompany him. "Today the Secretary told Franklin he could sail about the 19th but I still feel it is uncertain," wrote Eleanor, but she nevertheless quietly finished her Christmas shopping "as I felt if we were going I wanted to have everything ready."[7] Daniels, who was not enthusiastic about the idea, signed his orders reluctantly, perhaps as much in the interests of the marital truce as in those of the Navy. "Franklin says we may sail on the 28th and I can probably go."[8] She thought the children, who were recovering from the flu, would be well enough by then. "I never hated to do anything so much and yet I think I'd worry more about Franklin if he went alone. It is rather a horrid world I think."[9]

One of the few things they did in New York before they boarded the U.S.S. *George Washington* was to review the triumphant U. S. fleet in a blinding blizzard. A photograph of Eleanor on the bridge of the reviewing ship, one of the most extraordinary of the thousands taken of her, showed a face ravaged and severe, purged of all softness as if she, not Franklin, was the one who had survived a wasting illness. The night before they sailed Franklin, Eleanor, and Sara dined at the Colony Club with Captain Edward McCauley, the *George Washington*'s skipper. Franklin was "full of enthusiastic anticipation of the adventure before us," he recalled, and in spite of her qualms Eleanor also looked forward to the journey. On New Year's Day they embarked. "Very comfy and well settled in our suite," she noted in the diary that she began to keep.

It was an eventful moment to be going to Europe. Four years of slaughter had ended, leaving 9 million soldiers dead, 22 million wounded, and immeasurable civilian devastation. Mankind's eyes were now on the Paris Peace Conference, where almost all the great and mighty on the Allied side were in attendance. Wilson, the most powerful of them all, had become the inspired spokesman for a new order of things. Eleanor had seen the president a week before he sailed, at "a really historic party at the French Embassy. The President and Mrs. Wilson came and the Ambassador spoke and then the President and everyone drank to Strassbourg and the President. The National Anthems were played and with all the uniforms and pretty dresses it was a brilliant scene and as Caroline said it will be nice to tell our grandchildren about."[10]

Both Eleanor and Caroline had been critical of Wilson, but both were becoming true believers. Caroline left an account of her change of heart, which became complete when she heard Wilson's address to a joint session of Congress just before he sailed for the Peace Conference:

It began the night that I heard him speak at the French Embassy. . . . On Monday last, this experience was more than ever vivid. I was poignantly moved by the ordeal he was facing. I prayed with all my strength for his support, and I felt as though some spiritual aid was really reaching him through my prayers. My conclusion is that in the ordinary things of life he makes continual blunders, has poor judgment of men and affairs, is self-conscious, shy, uncertain, but in the really big things he has a real vision and inspiration which make him a great leader, in fact the *only* man who can lead the way in the upbuilding of a new and better world out of the chaos of the old one. . . .[11]

Eleanor thought Wilson had a remarkable understanding of man in the mass but little of men as individuals. She considered him an inept politician and had criticized his appeal to the country in the November elections to return a Democratic Congress, an appeal which had boomeranged. She thought self-righteousness made him too partisan.[12] But like Caroline she was unhappy over Wilson's blunders because she cared deeply for his ideals.

Eleanor was thirty-five when she sailed for Europe, her first trip abroad since her honeymoon fourteen years earlier.[13] The ocean, like much else, had lost most of its terrors: "Quite a blow and some roll," she noted in her diary; "I feel proud to be so good a sailor so far." It was indeed a "blow"; Livingston Davis, Franklin's partner in Chevy Chase convivialities as well as his assistant for operations and personnel, also kept a diary on that trip. "A heavy sea," he noted that same day; "whole dining room wrecked by heavy roll, also my breakfast landing on top of waiter's head."

Eleanor's sure-footedness compared with 1905 was more than nautical. She entered into all shipboard activities, went to the movies, joined in the singing led by a YMCA man, turned out daily for the "abandon ship drill," and was present for every meal. If a man interested her, she sought him out. She talked with Walter Camp, who exercised the men daily. "I like him," she wrote, and it was for her benefit as well as Franklin's that he came to their suite to show them his back exercises. Charles M. Schwab, the steelman, was another passenger. When Wilson had named him head of the Emergency Fleet Corporation in the spring of 1918 Eleanor considered the appointment "the first sign that the President [was] waking up" to the need for stronger leadership in war production. He and Franklin spoke to the crew, and Eleanor noted that she had "a little walk and talk with him." Bernard Baruch, who had once been a Roosevelt dinner guest, was another illustrious shipmate. Since he was seasick most of the voyage he stayed below, and Eleanor's diary did not refer to him until they reached Paris, when he sent her "a lot of roses." There were Chinese and Mexican delegations aboard on their way to the Peace Conference. "At four Eleanor gave a tea to the Chinese mission," Livy (Davis) noted. "Most of the conversation was in French."

Theodore Roosevelt had died while they were en route. "I feel it must have been sudden and I am so sorry for Aunt Edith and the boys in Europe," Eleanor wrote. She was sorry, too, that the last few years had been so full of disappointments for Uncle Ted. In Europe, when Wilson was informed of the passing of his old antagonist he dictated a cool message of condolence to Mrs. Theodore Roosevelt and remarked to his intimates that Roosevelt had no constructive policy to his record. Eleanor's evaluation of her uncle's role was more just: "Another great figure off the stage," she wrote sadly in her diary.

The news about Uncle Ted's death came while she was reading *The Education of Henry Adams*, which she had given Franklin for Christmas. Theodore was for her a symbol of "active participation in the life of his people," while Adams symbolized withdrawal from life. "Very interesting," she commented on the Adams book, "but sad to have had so much and yet find it so little."

"A wonderfully comfortable and entertaining trip," Eleanor summed up the voyage as the *George Washington* approached the port of Brest. After the landing ceremonies, demobilization business claimed the men of the party, while Admiral Henry B. Wilson took Eleanor and Mrs. Thomas C. Spellacy, the wife of the U.S. attorney from Connecticut who was Franklin's legal advisor on the mission, on a drive through the town and its environs. "Every other woman wears a crepe veil to her knees," Eleanor noted. An exhausted Mrs. Spellacy begged to be allowed to sit in the car during the last part of their tour of the city and naval base and stayed behind when Eleanor walked with the admiral to a shop that sold the work of war widows.

The next day they were in Paris. Eleanor had never seen anything like it, she reported. "It is full beyond belief and one sees many celebrities and all one's friends." In one respect her outlook had changed little since her honeymoon visit; the women still scandalized her. "The women here all look exaggerated, you wonder if any are ladies though all look smart and some pretty." Now, however, puritan ethic was fortified by social outrage. "In contrast to this element are the women in plain black and deep mourning that one sees in all the streets."

She and Franklin went to tea with Mrs. Wilson at the Palais Murat, and it seemed to Eleanor that all of Washington was congregated there. She attended a luncheon given by Admiral Benson's wife, at which Mrs. House and Mrs. Lansing were also present, and noted, "Much talk of the President's not having been to the front yet and Mrs. Wilson only having seen two hospitals." Eleanor helped remedy the latter complaint, according to Miss Benham, Mrs. Wilson's social secretary, who wrote that Eleanor "swept Mrs. Wilson up into her project of visiting the war wounded in the hospitals."[14] Although the president had not yet visited the front, Eleanor did so on the way to Boulogne with Franklin. It was a journey through recently fought-over battlefields that, said Franklin, "we shall never forget." Eleanor, he added, had a "very achy side and shoulder" but insisted "on doing everything and getting out of the car at all points of interest." The land was gashed by trench systems and scarred by barbed-wire entanglements. "Ghastly," Franklin exclaimed at the Somme battlefield. "In the bigger places the Cathedral is *always* destroyed, and the town more or less, mostly more," Eleanor noted. "The streets are all clear, all is neat and clean but you feel as though ghosts were beside you." Their army guides, who had been through the fighting at St. Quentin, described the attack the previous September in the face of massed machine guns and the breakthrough in the Hindenburg line at the St. Quentin Canal. "An almost incredible feat," said Franklin. "How men ever did it I cannot imagine," wrote Eleanor. When they finally arrived at

Amiens for the night, they were informed that express orders forbid ladies to go to the front, "but as I'd been," wrote Eleanor, "there was nothing to do about it!"

"Eleanor laid out with pleurisy," Livy recorded when they reached London. Admiral William S. Sims met them at the station and took them to the Ritz, and when Muriel Martineau, one of Eleanor's bridesmaids and Franklin's cousin, came to see them, she immediately called a doctor, who ordered a protesting Eleanor to bed. Franklin and his staff had a great deal to do in London, but he came back to the hotel for lunch and later for tea, and at the end of the day dined at the hotel, "bringing me my dinner. He has been too sweet in looking after me," Eleanor recorded. In the next few days she ran a temperature, admitted to feeling tired and even conceded she might have a touch of influenza, but when Franklin insisted on taking her temperature and, finding that it was over 100, would not let her go out, she was furious. "He made me back out to my rage."

After she recovered she had reunions with those of her Allenswood schoolmates who were in London. They recalled the years that were among the happiest in her life, and although she was deeply fond of them she had progressed beyond them in the breadth of her interests and sympathies. Lady Gertrude of Osberton came to call. Eleanor's honeymoon stay at Osberton had been a nightmare; now she was at ease and self-assured. Lady Gertrude was "a dear old Lady" but Eleanor had scant sympathy for her lament that Osberton was ruined because the woods had to be cut down to pay the death duties. And she was amused by Lady Gertrude's distress that her grandson, who had been a prisoner of war, had married his nurse, a Polish woman; "of course one would prefer an Englishwoman even though she was nice and had twice saved his life," Lady Osberton said.

Yet interlaced with judgments and reactions that showed how much Eleanor had grown since her honeymoon days were avowals of allegiance to Sara that were as affectionate as those of 1905. "I do hope we never have to separate again. As I grow older I miss you and the children more and more. I think instead of becoming more independent I am growing into a really clinging vine!" Her old puritan conscience was as outraged in London as it had been in Paris. She and Franklin dined with a British admiral, and she was shocked: "Just wait till I get home and tell you what these respectable people now let their daughters do, your hair will curl as mine did!" Franklin, however, was intrigued. One lady so fascinated him, Eleanor wrote, that it was with difficulty she "dragged" him home at eleven o'clock. "We have nothing like some of their women or some of their men!"

She learned anew how cold London could be in the winter. "I don't wonder they consume much wine here, they have to in order to rise above the cold houses or the cheer would indeed be cold cheer!" She wore spats, a flannel petticoat, and her heavy purple dress "all the time" and never felt even "mildly warm." She was disappointed in herself for minding: "Decidedly we are growing effete at home from too much comfort and I always thought myself something of a Spartan!"

Franklin left on the thirty-first of January for Brussels and the Rhineland without Eleanor; it would be easier for everyone, he told her, not to have women along in the occupied areas. "I hate to miss the trip to Brussels and Coblentz," she wrote in her diary, "and to have him going off without me."

She stayed on in London with Muriel Martineau and then returned to Paris, but it was depressing without Franklin. "I hope he arrives. Somehow I feel lost and lonely in a strange town alone and I do get so blue. I suppose it must be the result of pleurisy!" She decided that activity was the best cure for melancholy.

She and Aunt Dora, who all through the war had refused to abandon her beloved Paris, visited the Val de Grâce Hospital. "It is here that Morestin operates and he has been so successful with the horrible face wounds," she wrote. The sight of shattered faces devastated her, and much as she tried she could not help but feel revolted "even though one does not show it." Aunt Dora seemed to love hearing about the various operations, but it made Eleanor feel ill. She even found the plaster casts oppressive, and "could hardly bear to look at the men with the horrible face wounds." But she did.

The next day was waiting-for-Franklin day, and from 6:00 P.M. on she began her waiting in earnest. Lieutenant Commander John M. Hancock, one of Franklin's aides, came to dine at 8:00; they waited until 8:15 but "still no sign, so we dined." Livy joined them after dinner and stayed until 10:30, when he pleaded sleepiness and went to bed. At 11:30 Hancock felt "it wouldn't do for him to wait longer so he left." Finally, at about 12:30 Franklin and his party turned up. Eleanor had a cold supper waiting for them and Admiral Long, who met them in the hall, "came up with some liquid refreshment." They were laden with "loot" from the battlefields and were "full of a delightful and interesting trip," she reported. The party broke up at 1:30, probably due to her.

A few days later they prepared to sail for home, again on the *George Washington*. Eleanor was relieved that young Sheffield Cowles and David Gray were going back with them; Paris was "no place for the boys, especially the younger ones, and the scandals going on would make many a woman at home unhappy." Sara sounded a similar theme. "One hears a great deal here from returning officers and privates," she wrote. "One tale is that the common soldier behaves better than the officers, asking 'where is Napoleon's Tomb' 'where is the Louvre gallery' etc. The officers say: 'Where is Maxim's?' "

The president and Mrs. Wilson were also to be on board the *George Washington*. The Covenant of the new League of Nations had been finished on February 12, and Wilson was returning, House said, "to confront his enemies in the Senate." Sara had kept her children apprised of the way sentiment had turned against Wilson, at least in the circles in which she moved. She had stayed away from Mrs. Whitelaw Reid's, she informed them, because everyone had told her that Mrs. Reid did nothing but criticize the president and the administration "and I am rather tired of it." At a luncheon, another report went, she had sat next to Mrs. Berwind, who said that her husband looked upon Wilson as the "head of the Bolsheviki in this country." People generally were "so nasty about the Peace Conference and League of Nations that when anyone is full of admiration of our President and his ideals it is a pleasant surprise."

The boat train on which the Roosevelts were passengers preceded the president's by twenty minutes, and as they flashed by between lines of troops and roofs crowded with Bretons their train was mistaken for the president's. "The troops present arms and gaze in the hope of seeing the President," Eleanor noted in her diary. "It rains gently as usual." A newspaperman gave them a copy of the Covenant. "The High Contracting Parties," they read, "in order to promote international cooperation and to achieve international peace and security. . . ." They read the twenty-six Articles eagerly and had high hopes that the new machinery could effectively safeguard the peace. In Brest they joined the French dignitaries who were there to bid the president good-by. "Great consternation and great upsetting of plans" when Mrs. Wilson and Miss Benham—on the president's insistence, but contrary to Navy custom—went on board ahead of the president. Eleanor and Franklin went in to talk with the president and Mrs. Wilson. "The President is not very flattering about the French government and people," she recorded. Franklin left to go to the bridge as the vessel got under way, and stayed for nearly an hour's chat with the president, who was also there.

Auntie Bye's son Sheffield, a tall, lantern-jawed, kindly young man, saw a great deal of Eleanor on that trip. "She used always to be telling Franklin, 'I met so-and-so. He's an interesting fellow. You should talk with him. He's interested in more than sailing,' " he recalled.[15] Eleanor did the same kind of reading as his mother, he noted; "I was surprised how much she referred to Mother and was influenced by Mother."

On the fourth day out the president and Franklin made an official inspection of the ship, but "I can't say the President looked as though he saw much!" Eleanor noted. She herself visited the sick bay, and her inspection was thorough. "The arrangements for sick and wounded are ideal in every way. Splendid operating room, cleanliness, good food and good nurses." It was a far cry from the young woman who had complained that Franklin had inspected "every rivet."

One evening the crew put on an entertainment in which a boy dressed up as a chorus girl chucked the president under the chin. "Consternation and later reprimand but the President took it calmly," noted Eleanor. On Washington's Birthday they were invited to lunch with the president and Mrs. Wilson along with Dr. Grayson, Captain McCauley, Miss Benham, and the U. S. ambassador to Russia. The talk, Eleanor said, was, as usual in such cases, "chiefly stories," but two things the president said made a deep impression on her. He had read no papers since the beginning of the war, Wilson told them; Joseph P. Tumulty, his secretary, "read all and cut out important news or editorials," for him. "This is too much to leave to any man," she exclaimed in her diary. She also noted that the president spoke of the League, saying, "The United States must go in or it will break the heart of the world for she is the only nation that all feel is disinterested and all trust."

Eleanor accepted that. Her visits to the hospitals and battlefields of

Europe had imbued her with an implacable hatred of war, a sentiment that would be a ruling passion with her for the remainder of her life. Two days later when they landed in Boston and rode in the fifth carriage in the president's procession, she noted approvingly that the streets "were all packed with people wildly shrieking. I never saw a better crowd or more enthusiasm." At the luncheon following the parade she was seated next to Governor Calvin Coolidge. It was, despite her best efforts, a wordless encounter. She thought Mayor Peters of Boston made "a courageous speech," coming out for the League despite the hostility of his Irish constituents. Governor Coolidge meant to speak guardedly but committed himself to "feeling sure the people would back the President." It was the president's speech, however, that set his listeners on fire, a "fighting" pronouncement, the *New York Times* reporter said, in which the president threw down "the glove of defiance to all Senators and others who oppose the League of Nations." "A very wonderful speech," was Eleanor's comment.

On the train to Washington, Miss Benham had tea in their compartment, and when they went to say good-by to the president and Mrs. Wilson, Eleanor had "a nice talk with him" and Mrs Wilson gave her and Mrs. Spellacy a "bunch of flowers." They were home the next morning: "Greeted by chicks and Mama. All very well and very happy to be together again."

Back in Washington they soon discovered that the opposition was not at all daunted by Wilson's thunderbolts. When they dined with Alice Longworth, Eleanor found the atmosphere "very partisan"—so much so that it was too much for Franklin's customary good nature and he became "rather annoyed."[16] Nevertheless, Alice and her husband were invited to dinner at the Roosevelts', along with the leader of the Senate Democrats, to meet Sir Edward Grey, who had come to Washington as special ambassador to try to persuade Wilson to compromise with Senator Lodge and accept his reservations to the Covenant. "All seemed to enjoy it," Eleanor wrote of her dinner. "Lord G. said to Alice 'I would like to have a list of the books which you have read and I've never even heard of'! She really is extraordinary and kept us all entertained."[17]

Grey's mission was a failure, both with Alice and with Wilson. In a cold rebuff, Wilson, immured behind White House walls after his stroke, declined to receive Grey, and Alice remained a principal crusader against the League. When the Senate rejected the Covenant, the leading irreconcilables adjourned to the Longworth house for a celebratory snack, where, Alice wrote, "Mrs. Harding cooked the eggs."[18]

Eleanor took no part in the League fight, as political activity was still Franklin's domain. Nor did she take part in the final battle for women's suffrage. Although she declined Alice Wadsworth's invitation to join the National Association of Anti-Suffragists and counseled Sara to do likewise, when Franklin went to Hyde Park to vote in November, 1918, he went alone, even though New York women had acquired the vote by state referendum in 1917.

But she was venturing into new fields and was privately expressing views on politics and public affairs that were crisply unequivocal and quite sophisticated. When Wilson dismissed Secretary of State Lansing because he had convened cabinet meetings during the president's disablement without authorization, she was indignant: "I think it will be awkward for whoever is next Secretary of State for he will be branded as a rubber stamp. The President's letter can only be considered that of a sick, peevish man and I think everyone is more seriously worried than at any time."[19] And when New York lawyer Bainbridge Colby was named to succeed Lansing, she was harsh: "Mr. B. Colby is a good speaker and an agreeable person to meet. His 'mind will go along' excellently. He's a nonentity and has never shown in any job much capacity and of course he has no qualifications for this one, except that I feel sure he will never hold an opinion at variance with the President as long as it pays him not to!"[20] Official Washington's unhappy experience with an incapacitated president who was protectively isolated from his cabinet and political associates by his wife and physician made an indelible impression on Eleanor and would influence her own conduct in the final months of Franklin's administration when his strength began to fail.

In the fall of 1919 when Franklin went to New Brunswick for some hunting, Eleanor undertook to keep track of the Industrial Conference for him. Organized under the chairmanship of Secretary Lane, the conference was trying, amid the wave of postwar strikes, to formulate a modus vivendi between employer groups and unions. This activity brought Eleanor in touch with a new range of problems and people. "Heard Mr. Fish of the Employer group speak against a compromise resolution which was brought in on the collective bargaining issue, responded to with much heat by Mr. Wheeler of the public group. Nothing done so far!" The next day she reported, "The industrial conference came to a smash and the labor delegates walked out. Now the public groups are trying to pick up the pieces having asked the employers to withdraw. The President's letter was fine but did no good, even the *Tribune* gave it high praise this morning. The coal situation looks a little better today but the A.F. of L. has called a general conference for November and is preparing for a big struggle."[21]

The labor movement was beginning to engage Eleanor's sympathies. An International Congress of Working Women took place in Washington at the end of October, 1919, and she went to a tea for the delegates. It was "of course a very advanced and radical gathering presided over by Mrs. Raymond Robins," but evidently its radicalism did not frighten her for she found it "interesting and amusing."[22]

She then invited some of the women to lunch with her. The U. S. delegation, in addition to Mrs. Robins, included Rose Schneiderman of the Cap Makers, Maud Swartz of the Printers, Leonora O'Reilly of the New York Women's Trade Union League, Mary Anderson of the Boot and Shoe Workers Union, Fannia Cohn of the Ladies Garment Workers, Julia O'Connor of the Telephone Operators, and Lois Rantoul of the Federal Employees Union. The time was coming when she would call many of these women her friends.

23. *The Rebellion Begins*

THE YEARS IN WASHINGTON were drawing to a close. Outwardly they were a time of triumph; they were also a time of deep inner travail.

"I do not think I have ever felt so strangely as in the past year," Eleanor wrote in her diary at the end of 1919, "perhaps it is that I have never noticed little things before but all my self-confidence is gone and I am on edge though I never was better physically I feel sure."[1]

At Christmas time she sent close friends photographs of her family. The handsome group included the five children, Franklin, and, on Eleanor's insistence, Sara. "It looks alarmingly like the ones of families that end up in the White House," a close friend wrote. What "a grand success you've made."

Success! When the rock upon which she had built her life and sought to lay to rest the sense of failure and inferiority had been shattered? Tightly, desperately, Eleanor clung to the old familiar ties and attachments—family, friends, and duties—yet she could not shut off the moods of black despair that seized her when she felt that no one belonged to her and she was of no use to anyone. There were moments when her belief that life had meaning slipped away from her. "There are times," she later said, "in everyone's life when the wish to be done with the burdens and even the decisions of this life seems overwhelming."[2] This was such a time for her. She often took refuge in Rock Creek Cemetery, sitting in front of the haunting memorial that Henry Adams had commissioned Augustus Saint-Gaudens to erect to his wife. The cowled bronze figure had inspired Spring-Rice to write a sonnet, a copy of which was found among Eleanor's bedside papers at her death:

> O steadfast, deep, inexorable eyes
> Set look inscrutable, nor smile nor frown!
> O tranquil eyes that look so calmly down
> Upon a world of passion and of lies! . . .

Mrs. Adams, a victim of prolonged depressions, had committed suicide, but the seated figure did not evoke thoughts of despair in Eleanor. The lips were full. The hand was strong. The beautiful face was that of a woman who had achieved absolute self-mastery. Henry Adams had sometimes called the figure the "Peace of God," a peace, Saint-Gaudens said, that was "beyond pain and beyond joy," and for Eleanor these were the years when sometimes she envied the peace that Mrs. Adams had achieved, and sometimes wondered whether such peace could be achieved in life through self-mastery.[3] "There was a time."

she would write a friend in 1941, "when I thought happiness didn't matter but I think differently today."[4]

As civilized as she and Franklin were, they had some very bad times, although inner strain flared only rarely into open conflict. "Found F.D. and E. very cool as he had been to the Fly Club dinner night before," Livy Davis had noted in Paris.[5] "Dined alone," Eleanor recorded on April 10, 1919. "Franklin nervous and overwrought and I very stupid and trying, result a dreadful fracas."

It was a time for her of harsh self-reproach and depreciation, of desolating conviction that she had failed as a woman and was in some way responsible for Franklin's involvement with Lucy. But bitter as the experience was, it also matured her. Slowly she won through to the realization that she could not achieve fulfillment through someone else. "Somewhere along the line of development we discover what we really are," she wrote in 1941, "and then we make our real decision for which we are responsible. Make that decision primarily for yourself because you can never really live anyone else's life not even your child's. The influence you exert is through your own life and what you become yourself."[6]

She buried herself in work, especially in her work for St. Elizabeth's where she could find her way back to a firm feeling that she was of some use, where she could feel herself needed. "My experience has been," she wrote in later years, "that work is almost the best way to pull oneself out of the depths."[7] To wean her from self-pity and private woe there were, in addition to her duties with the Red Cross, her children, her household, as well as her obligations as the wife of one of the most promising public men in Washington.

In her final months in Washington she made considerable changes in her household. Servants had ceased to intimidate her. When Blanche, her personal maid, did not do her job, she cheerfully informed Sara, "I blew her up the other day,"[8] and while she did not think it had "much effect" the expression bespoke her growth in self-assurance.

In the choice of governesses she also struck a new note. "I feel when we do *burden* ourselves with one," she told Sara, "it should be to acquire a language not just to be kept up in English to which they devote most of their winter."[9] Their last year in Washington she gave Anna and James the choice of having a governess who would supervise them or making a pledge to perform their chores and duties without supervision. Both chose freedom.

In 1913 Daniels had reproached her for having white household help. Housework should be done by Negro servants, he had said, and the statement had shocked her. But now in 1919 difficulties with her white help persuaded her to restaff her household, except for an English nurse, with Negro servants— cook, kitchen maid, butler, and housemaid. Paradoxically, this was not a compromise with the southern view that such jobs were menial and for Negroes alone but a rejection of New York society's conviction that only whites were qualified and trustworthy enough to serve inside the house. It was Eleanor's first intimate contact with Negroes. "Well, all my servants are gone and all the darkies are here and heaven knows how it will all turn out!" she informed Sara.[10]

Her first big dinner under the new arrangements was to take place on March 13, and she was curious to see how "my darkies manage," but she had already found them "pleasanter to deal with and there is never any question about it not being their work to do this or that."[11] The dinner went off without mishap but sometimes there were problems. On the eve of a buffet luncheon for Marine officers the butler developed pleurisy, which she thought an odd disease for midsummer. "With darkies," she generalized, "one is always suspicious even of a death in the family."[12] But her new cook, Nora, more than made up for the butler's absence and proved to be "a host in herself. . . . She cooked the hams (4) made a wonderful grapefruit punch and vegetable salad in enormous quantities and black coffee in the same quantities." Eleanor never regretted having made the change, although there was a long journey ahead before she freed herself of racial stereotypes and bias.

When in the summer of 1919 racial violence swept Washington, triggered by returned servicemen, her thoughts were of Franklin's safety, not of the causes of the racial outbreak. She and the children were in Fairhaven rather than Campobello, because, she had explained to Sara, it was "a long and expensive commuting trip" to Campobello and that is what it would be for Franklin "and for me."[13] Her anxiety when she did not hear from Franklin seemed excessive, its intensity a reflection of her own edginess. "You seem to have had pretty bad race riots in Washington," she wrote him on arrival at Fairhaven. "Have you seen anything of them?"[14] She was more agitated the next day. "No word from you and I am getting very anxious on account of the riots. Do be careful not to be hit by stray bullets." The riots had not spread to R Street, he assured her, and he had taken pains "to keep out of harm's way."[15] But the mail was slow in reaching Fairhaven. "Still no letter or telegram from you and I am worried to death," she wrote him. "Even if something is wrong why don't you let me know. I'd always rather know than worry. I couldn't sleep at all last night thinking of all the things which might be the matter."[16] She seemed unduly disquieted. Evidently Franklin thought so too. "Your telegram came last night at ten," he informed her; "as I was in my pyjamas and couldn't get Western Union I did not answer it till this a.m. as soon as I got to the office."[17]

If she was strained and jittery in matters involving Franklin, when it came to a crisis involving the children Eleanor was remarkably poised, as she had demonstrated a few weeks earlier at the time of the A. Mitchell Palmer assassination attempt. "Mother's" self-control on that occasion became a legend in the family. Shortly before midnight on June 2, 1919, a bomb went off in front of the house of Attorney General Palmer, shattering its front, killing a man, and blowing out the front windows of the Roosevelt house across the street. Franklin and Eleanor, who arrived shortly after the blast, raced into their house to see what had happened to James, who was the only child at home.

"James did not hear the explosion but heard the ensuing confusion," she wrote Sara.

However, I stated nothing was the matter 'just an explosion' in the most matter-of-fact tone as though it was a daily occurrence and he returned to bed and sleep at once. We went over at once and offered to take the Palmers in but they preferred to get out of the street.

Now we are roped off and the police haven't yet allowed the gore to be wiped up on our steps and James glories in every new bone found! I only hope the victim was not a poor passer by instead of the anarchist![18]

She was now asserting a more direct supervision over her children's upbringing. She was discontented with Anna's school—she thought it "stuffy," an expression that indicated her changing standards. Frequent conferences with the Misses Eastman on ways to improve Anna's grades produced middling results. She took Anna to the theater to encourage an interest in the drama, and sent her to music and dancing classes, and when the young men from the British Embassy came to luncheon Anna was sometimes invited to join them in the hope that the combination of handsome young men and good conversation would widen her interests. She was tall, with yellow hair that tumbled over her shoulders, and looked older than her thirteen years. Her parents took her with them to Annapolis, and she was invited to next year's plebe hop. "I declined," her mother wrote Sara.[19]

James also failed to make good grades at the Cathedral School, which he and Elliott now attended. That distressed Eleanor because he needed good grades to qualify for Groton, and it was taken for granted that when they reached their twelfth birthdays all the boys would be handed over to Dr. Peabody. Eleanor tried a winter of getting up early to hear James' lessons before he went off to school, and there were tutors and stern lectures, but all with indifferent results. James continued to do better as left end on the football team than on his exam papers. Elliott's marks were "very good," she informed Sara, but "James is worse than last month, 12th in a class of 26, average way below the class, the only decent mark is 93 in History. I just told him I did not care to discuss it as unfortunately no one else could study for him and he evidently did not care to make use of any of his advantages. He wept as usual and it will have as much effect as usual. I think this summer I shall have him work an hour longer than Anna daily."[20]

Of all her children the two youngest, Franklin Jr. and John, were the ones Eleanor seemed to enjoy most. She was overprotective of Elliott, perhaps because he carried her beloved father's name and seemed to have his proneness for physical mishaps, but with "the babies" she was more relaxed than she had been with the older children, could take their outbursts of wildness more calmly, and on the whole seemed to have more fun with them. Franklin Jr. was the "sunshine" boy, as James later dubbed him. "I went out for a walk with little Franklin this morning," he wrote his grandmother, "and everytime he saw a child he would say hallow as if he knew them." Franklin at five was a flatterer. "I love you very much. I want to kiss you," he wrote his grandmother, adding, "Please give me a light like Anna's and a firecracker." He amused his mother. "I asked Franklin Jr. last night what I was to ask Santa Claus to bring him and without prompting he reeled off more things than you ever heard of. I gasped and he added, 'and John just the same!' "[21] John was already showing the instincts of a businessman; "I feel sure he owns everything by now," Eleanor wrote Sara after the children had been with their grandmother for a week in 1918.[22] She read them a children's life of their Uncle Ted. "Granny, I intend to run for the Presidency, and am beginning my campaign at your tea," Franklin Jr. announced to Sara while he was still in short pants. John had no such interest. Aunt Tissie at Fairhaven was so taken with John's pleasing ways that she told him he would be president some day. "I am *not* going to be President," he replied firmly.[23]

Franklin Jr. and John made a team. Together they went to a party at the Bill Phillipses and had a "fine time," according to their mother, "except for the fact that they did not get enough cereal to eat." On John's fourth birthday she arranged a "Mother Goose" party for "the babies." This was Franklin Jr.'s time to be little Jack Horner as the others had been before him, and she had a large pie filled with little toys which he handed out after supper with much excitement. As the youngest were a pair, so were Anna and James. Elliott was left out, the others sometimes allying themselves against him, spurred on by the feeling that their mother spoiled him. "The other boys ate up his dessert at dinner, because he ate so slowly he wasn't ready for it, and they wouldn't tell him where the w.c. was so just before leaving he had an accident in his pants which upset him a good deal but I think all will go well from now on!"[24]

Gladys Saltonstall, who spent a Sunday evening with the Roosevelts in 1919, found Eleanor's warm, maternal relationship to her children especially attractive."I secretly envied her."[25] But others who knew the household better doubted that Eleanor gave her children what they needed. Margaret Cutter, who then was her sister-in-law, felt that while Eleanor loved the children she "did not make them her friends."[26] "She did her duty," cousin Corinne remarked. "Nobody in the world did her duty more than Eleanor Roosevelt. But with the children I don't think you can have an understanding of them unless you enjoy them."[27] It was their father who taught them to ride, to love sailing, who during the winter was "the moving spirit in coasting and tobogganing," and who filled their Washington week ends with joy. He was "my childhood hero," said Anna, while "it was Mother's duty to counteract my tomboy tendencies and to teach me to sew and knit."[28] "I don't think Mother shared in the day-to-day fun in life at all," James agreed, "in things like skating, sledding, etc. She was very good about making arrangements, but she did not participate. We had more real fun with Mother when we were all much older when we went to the play with her, met people at her house, a few Sunday evenings."[29]

The burdens and perplexities of bringing up her own children made Eleanor appreciate more fully. the heavy charge that had been placed on Grandma Hall when in 1892 she had taken in Eleanor and her two brothers. "My grandmother died," she wrote in her diary on August 14, 1919. "A gentle good woman with a great and simple faith. It is only of late years that I have realized what it meant for her to take Hall, Ellie and me into her home as she did. Pussie and Maúde were wonderful about it too."

Not since the early days of their marriage when Franklin was a law clerk had Eleanor spent so much time with him, but time spent together can be abrasive as well as healing. He now often came home for lunch and tea, but good as his intentions were, he was still his old unpunctual self. He dallied at the office until an outraged telephone call from the "Missus" caused him to stuff papers in his briefcase, grab his hat and cane, and bolt for home. Even when she called for him at the office, she could not get him to leave on time. "Waited 35 minutes and returned to find Paul Hammond playing with the children waiting for us," she noted on one such occasion. Outwardly she smiled, inwardly she seethed.

They picnicked together in the country. They walked in the woods. Together with the Phillipses and the Millers they canoed up the old B & O Canal, lunched, and came back by way of the Potomac. The river ran fairly fast in spots. Pleasant but "not real excitement," Eleanor commented afterward.[30] Danger and roughness gave spice to life, and she did not like a slack and tepid existence. She tried to show Franklin that, but for him there were sanctuaries that belonged to men alone, into which he would not admit her.

If she did not hear from him she worried and when he was away she missed him, but when they were together he easily upset her, as was the case at the end of that 1919 summer. "I'm glad you enjoyed your holiday dear, & I wish we did not lead such a hectic life, a little prolonged quiet might bring us altogether & yet it might do just the opposite! I really don't know what I want or think about anything anymore!"[31] Yet when in October he went off to the Canadian woods with Livy and Lieutenant Commander Richard E. Byrd to hunt moose, she wrote him like a newlywed. "I hated to have you go off alone and shan't feel quite happy till you are safely home again," she wrote within hours after he left. When the postman brought his first letter she wrote in her diary, "No moose yet but sounds well, thank goodness. It was a joy to hear."[32]

She tried to be the kind of person he wished her to be. When he went off to a poker game, she used the time to make up the household-accounts book as he liked to have it done. "Now that I've done it, it doesn't take so long," she wrote Sara. "I hope Franklin will be pleased."[33] She took more time selecting her clothes. While they were in Paris she had ordered two dresses at Worth, and Franklin and Sara approved. The cape that Sara did not like she gave away to the "darling housemaid." She bought three hats ("$91—isn't it too awful . . . but I really took a long time to choose") from Miss Gandy, the mountain-climbing lady of whom she had been so jealous on her honeymoon.[34] In February, 1920, she splurged again, buying an evening dress and a gray satin afternoon dress at Miss Converse's. Franklin liked her in the evening dress, she noted a few weeks later with relief and pleasure.

The winter of 1920, a tonsillectomy was added to Franklin's usual ailments of sinuses and colds. "He looks rather poorly for him," Bertie Hamlin noted in her journal. Franklin asked Eleanor not to cancel their social engagements; Eleanor was getting out 2,000 invitations for Navy teas, he told Bertie. She got through the luncheons and the one big dinner they had scheduled, although it was "horrid" to do so without Franklin. Even with Franklin, dinner parties had again become ordeals. During one dinner that winter she went upstairs to tuck the children in and hear their prayers, and stayed away so long that Franklin became anxious. "I just can't stand to greet all those people," she said in tears. "I know they all think I am dull and unattractive. I just want to hide up here."[35]

Franklin was thirty-eight on January 30, and she had a party to celebrate the occasion: "all are coming as a character in a book, so it ought to be amusing."[36] The Lanes, Millers, Polks, Hallowells, McCauleys, Rodgers, and Alice and Nick Longworth were the guests. Their costumes were nowhere recorded, nor whether Eleanor found the evening bearable. On her own birthday the previous October she had noted, "I am 36. Margaret and Hall sent me a book, Mama and Tissie and Franklin wired" (Franklin was away making a speech in Rochester). It gave her pleasure to plan and organize gay birthday parties for others, but she always found reasons why hers should not be celebrated, especially when her feelings had been deeply hurt. Why should anyone wish to celebrate her birthday? She was not averse to making Franklin feel a little guilty.

Some of the gayest parties the winter of 1919–20 were given by Mrs. Marshall Field, whose liveliness, despite her age, evoked Washington's admiration. "We stayed at Mrs. Field's last night till 12:30 p.m. ending with a Virginia reel! On Sunday night too!" Eleanor reported.[37]

But other evenings turned out less happily. There was one disastrous revel at the Chevy Chase Club, of which there are two accounts. One is Eleanor's told years later when she could bear to speak of it; the other told by Alice Longworth with her usual "detached malevolence."[38] The women had, as usual, swarmed about Franklin, and he had been very gay while Eleanor felt more and more miserable. Finally she decided she would not be missed if she departed. He should stay and enjoy himself, she whispered to Franklin, but she was going home. She didn't, "as a rule," let him stay behind at a dance, said Mrs. Longworth. "She was rather firm about that; but this time she let him stay at the country club, and he came in with the Warren Robbinses. And it was they, of course, who hastened to tell me the next morning all about what had happened."

Eleanor had forgotten her latchkey and, unable to get in, had settled down on the doormat, propping herself against the wall, feeling sorry for herself and cross with Franklin. When he finally did turn up, close to dawn, Eleanor rose in the vestibule "like a wraith," said Alice, to confront him. The rest of the story we have from Alice.

"But darling, what's happened? What are you doing here?"

"Oh, I forgot my key."

"But couldn't you have gone to the Adolph Millers'? You could have spent the night there, or you could have gone to Mitchell Palmer's house, where there's a guard."

"Oh, no, I've always been told never to bother people if you can possibly avoid it." Here, Alice, in telling the story, interpolated, "So noble, so noble."

"You must have been hideously uncomfortable," Franklin went on.

"Well, it wasn't *very* uncomfortable."

She was quite sure, Eleanor commented later, that she had made Franklin "feel guilty by the mere fact of having waited" in the vestibule. They were not, she said in a massive understatement, the best years of her life.

Her immense physical vitality seemed to drain away, one of the few times in all her years that she registered such a complaint. "I was dead," she wrote on April 19, attributing her exhaustion to dinner guests who stayed "till 11.30."[39] The next day she noted again "I was a dead dog," having dined with Aunt Kassie at eight. And the evening after that she went to the Army and Navy League Ball. "I stood and received till 11 p.m. and went home 11:30 dead again." This would have been a normal reaction for most women, but Eleanor was always able to tap hidden springs of energy and her exhaustion was not normal. In May when she was at Hyde Park, she and Sara had a quiet dinner "but I might as well not have eaten it for I promptly parted with it all!"[40] She insisted it was "just weariness," but the weariness was only another manifestation of the conflict within her between a nature seeking to find its true vocation and the life of conformity that the effort to please her husband and mother-in-law had shaped.

While she sought to rebuild her relationship with Franklin, she began to turn against Sara. In July, 1919, when she had left Hyde Park and taken her younger children to Fairhaven, she confessed to her husband, "I feel as though someone had taken a ton of bricks off me and I suppose she feels just the same."[41] But Sara evidently was not aware of Eleanor's inner stress. "A letter from Mama this morning," Franklin wrote her. "It will amuse you as she says everything is going very smoothly."[42] At the end of September they all returned to Hyde Park. "Mama and I have had a bad time," she noted on October 3, "I should be ashamed of myself and I'm not. She is too good and generous and her judgment is better than mine but I can *learn* more easily."[43] (The italicized word is almost undecipherable, but "learn" seems to fit the context best.)

On a Sunday two days after this rebellious entry, Eleanor wrote, "Went to Church but could not go to Communion."[44] The words were austere and their implication stark, for she was the most faithful of churchgoers, the most sincere of communicants, for whom prayer was not a matter of rote but a daily influence in her life. Religion was of the utmost seriousness to her and prayer a kind of continuing exchange with God, a way of cleansing the heart and steadying the will. To say that she could not take Communion meant that she could not say that she "truly and earnestly" repented of her sins and that she was in a state of "love and charity" with those around her, as the Episcopalian Communion service required. She was temporarily cut off from divine grace, a condition that she must have found insupportable.

That week end she lost her temper with her mother-in-law, one of the rare times in her life she did so. Her letter of October 6 begging Sara's forgiveness disclosed how deeply alienation and despair had taken command of her feelings. "I know, Mummy dear, I made you feel most unhappy the other day and I am so sorry I lost my temper and said such fool things for of course as you know I love Franklin and the children very dearly and I am deeply devoted to you. I have, however, allowed myself to be annoyed by little things which of course one should never do and I had no right to hurt you as I know I did and am truly sorry and hope you will forgive me."

Although she was remorseful, her rebellion against Sara and the way of life Sara represented was only beginning, and it spread to Cousin Susie. When Eleanor went to New York to have dinner with the Parishes, "we had in some ways a very stormy evening."[45] She was finding Cousin Susie's self-indulgence and her unfriendly attitude toward people outside of her little circle difficult to bear. Eleanor "fairly jumped with joy," she wrote, when she and Franklin did not have to spend a summer week end with Cousin Susie, "though I'm sorry of course she isn't well."[46]

By the time she and Franklin left Washington her estrangement from Sara's and Cousin Susie's outlook was very deep. In early December, 1920, she spent an evening in New York talking with Sara and her two sisters, Dora and Kassie, and wrote Franklin afterward: "They all in their serene assurance and absolute judgments on people and affairs going on in the world, make me want to squirm and turn bolshevik." She was beginning to follow the "remorseless logic" of her love for others. Her desire to serve, which deference to her mother-in-law and Franklin had confined to the family circle, was breaking free. Humiliation and despair did not quench her ardent nature. Tenderness flowed into new channels. She clipped a poem, "Psyche," by Virginia Moore, out of the newspaper and wrote on it "1918," meaning that it conveyed her own slow climb out of the depths. It, too, like the Spring-Rice sonnet about the Saint-Gaudens statue, was filed among her bedside papers.

> The soul that has believed
> And is deceived
> Thinks nothing for a while.
> All thoughts are vile.
>
> And then because the sun
> Is mute persuasion,
> And hope in Spring and Fall
> Most natural,
>
> The soul grows calm and mild,
> A little child,
> Finding the pull of breath
> Better than death, . . .
>
> The soul that had believed
> And was deceived
> Ends by believing more
> Than ever before.

But her soul, which ended by "believing more," was moving toward wider, more general sympathies. Speaking of her wartime experience, Eleanor later wrote that from then on she saw herself and others more realistically. "No one is entirely bad or entirely good," and she no longer was sure of what was right and what was wrong; out of it all she emerged "a more tolerant person, far less sure of my own beliefs and methods of action, but I think more determined to try for certain ultimate objectives."[47]

III

THE EMERGENCE OF
ELEANOR ROOSEVELT

24. A Campaign and Friendship with
Louis Howe

"SHALL WE HAVE TO FIGHT EACH OTHER THIS FALL?" Alice Wadsworth, the wife of the incumbent Republican senator asked Eleanor. "I'd hate to have either of our good men beaten—so let's go after different jobs!"[1]

It was 1920, a presidential election year and the end of the Wilson years. The "club" dispersed. Lane resigned to take a job with Edward L. Doheny's oil company at $50,000 a year; it was strange employment for a man who had been one of the most progressive members of Wilson's cabinet, but he was already suffering with the illness that in a few months would kill him. Phillips was posted as U. S. minister to The Hague. Franklin spent much of his time out of Washington touring New York State to prepare the way to run either for governor or senator in the 1920 elections.

When Franklin left for San Francisco to attend the Democratic national convention, Eleanor did not know which office he would finally seek, but in either case he would need, if not the sponsorship, at least the neutrality of Tammany at the state convention. She was, therefore, surprised to read in the papers that he had helped wrest the state standard from a Tammany stalwart when the New York delegation refused to join in the demonstration in Wilson's honor. "You and Tammany don't seem to agree very well. Mama is very proud of your removing the State standard from them! I have a feeling you enjoyed it but won't they be very much against you in the State Convention?"[2]

Her letters to him sounded as if she, too, wanted to be in San Francisco. Two of his old Poughkeepsie supporters, John Mack and Thomas Lynch, were with him. "I can't help thinking what fun you will all have together." Politics interested her more than she sometimes acknowledged. She would like to have heard William Jennings Bryan's speech about the Democratic platform, she said, and then added a terse comment on the platform itself that might well apply to most such documents—"too much self praise and recrimination, too long but better than the Republican on the whole."[3]

She wished she could meet Franklin in Washington after the convention was over and hear all about it, she wrote, but on July 4 she transported her brood to Campobello. She did not dream that her husband might end up being the vice-presidential candidate, and since McAdoo, Cox, Palmer, and Smith seemed to be in a stalemate over who the candidate would be, Eleanor's major anxiety was that Franklin's arrival at Campobello would be delayed. "Please, please don't let your staying an extra day make any difference in coming up to us!"[4] She still did not know what had happened when she wrote him, "I suppose you started tonight for the East. I heard tonight in Eastport Cox was nominated but am in the dark as to the rest. I wonder if you are really satisfied."[5] Then the telegrams began to arrive. "It would have done your heart good to have seen the spontaneous and enthusiastic tribute paid when Franklin was nominated for Vice President today," Daniels wired her; "Franklin was nominated by acclamation," Lynch informed her. "This certainly is a world of surprises," she wrote Sara that evening. "I really think F. had a better chance of winning for the Senatorship but the Democrats may win, one cannot tell and at least it should be a good fight."[6]

So little was known about Eleanor that a long profile of Franklin Roosevelt in the Democratic *New York World* stated in the last sentence of the last paragraph, "Mrs. Roosevelt 'goes in' but little for society, finding her occupation in the management of her home and the welfare of her one daughter and her three sons." A Washington society reporter gave a somewhat different picture in the *New York Times*: "Mrs. Roosevelt is one of those women who, while she is absolutely at ease in the frilliest of social frills—she was born to them—yet finds them unimportant in her scheme of life."[7] After describing the Roosevelt family, the reporter continued, "She has her own circle of warm friends. She is—well, as one of her friends put it, she is too much of a Roosevelt to be anybody's prize beauty, but she's pure gold. . . . Few women are so generally esteemed by their acquaintance as Mrs. Roosevelt. . . . She was up to her eyes in war work . . . [but] she is essentially a home woman. She seems to particularly dislike the official limelight. . . . Just how she would endure the Vice-Presidential status . . . remains to be seen." "Papers are demanding your picture," Howe wired her from Washington. "Is there one at the house here that I can have copied?" "Are no pictures of me," she replied. As a result, the *Daily News* that Sunday published a picture of some other woman that it had cropped from a photograph of the Roosevelts at a baseball game, thinking it was the candidate's wife.

The *World* sent a correspondent from Eastport to Campobello to interview Eleanor. He came away with a brief, rather stilted statement that could hardly have satisfied his editor. "I am very much pleased and happy to know of Mr. Roosevelt's nomination," she said, "But I realize that it will take up much of his time during the coming campaign, and he may not have much time to enjoy a rest here. While he may not have looked for the honor, I am proud of his nomination and hope he will be elected."[8] An *Evening Post* reporter who went to Hyde Park, on the other hand, found a great dowager, quite at ease, overawed neither by press nor by the honors accorded to her son. "There is a stark and undeniable atmosphere of noncompromise about this house and its lady," the reporter commented, and found everywhere and in everything about Springwood—in the commodious and sturdily built mansion, the stone walls, the spreading trees—"a stamp of ancient solid things, of good beginnings which have persisted well."[9] Sara declined to talk about Franklin except for his connection with Hyde Park, the one place on earth, she said, that he loved best. In such surroundings, the perceptive reporter remarked, "there is no necessity ever to speak of what is one's belief; it is so certain and so sure."

Hyde Park did not want to be left out of the homecoming ceremonies that were being planned in Poughkeepsie, Sara advised her son. A rousing village welcome was being prepared, with their neighbor, Mr. Newbold, as chairman. "If and when you are elected, you will belong to the nation, now you are 'our boy' of Hyde Park and Dutchess." Motherly hopes were soaring: "My regards and best wishes to our future President."[10]

But Democratic national prospects were not good, as Eleanor had indicated in her letter to Sara. The country sensed that since Wilson's illness the government had been rudderless, and this was held against the Democrats. The people were tired of the heroic mode. There was a revolt against high taxes. The country was ready, as the Republican nominee Senator Harding phrased it, for a "return to normalcy." But for Roosevelt no political campaign was a lost cause. When Cox's representative in San Francisco had awakened Charles Murphy to tell him that Roosevelt was Cox's choice for vice president, the Tammany leader said, "He is not well known in the country." To campaign was an opportunity for Franklin to project himself onto the national stage and to conduct himself in such a way that no matter what happened in 1920, the party would turn to him in 1924.

Eleanor's hopes for Franklin's early arrival at Campobello dimmed as he conferred with local leaders on his way East and stopped off at Columbus to meet with Cox, a meeting at which the two men announced they wanted the election to be a plebiscite on the League of Nations. Eleanor finally went to Hyde Park instead. "In order to share the day with her husband, Mrs. Roosevelt traveled all night and all day from Eastport, Maine," the *New York Times* reported. She arrived too late for the "homecoming" at Springwood, where village neighbors with a band at their head met Franklin at the gate and escorted him to the house, but she did catch up with him for the ceremonies in Poughkeepsie.[11]

Sara wrote her son after the homecoming ceremony, "I will say nothing of my feelings on Tuesday last and in fact always for you know. I know you and I will never forget Tuesday the 13th of July, 1920! I kept wishing for your Father but I believe he knew and was with us. . . ." Happy mother, unhappy wife. Eleanor could not identify with Franklin's triumphs in that instinctive and impulsive way. "Whatever Franklin achieves must be largely due to you," she had written Sara.[12] That was conviction, not courtesy.

Their closest friends saw it differently. Eleanor is "your real 'running mate,'" Aunt Kassie wrote. Isabella was thrilled because if Franklin was elected, Eleanor would also be in a position to do much to benefit the country, and she marveled at the steady progress Eleanor had made. The thought of Eleanor as the wife of the vice president caused Pauline Emmet to glow: "How splendid you will be dearest Eleanor (we must win!) graceful and gracious and charming!"

Eleanor was happy for Franklin, happy that he had attained something he wanted, but her feeling was also one of detachment and objectivity, as if she were looking at someone else's life from the outside. There were married couples who could say, as Beatrice Webb did of her marriage, "apart we each of us live only half a life, together we each of us have a double life." Eleanor had wanted that sort of relationship with Franklin, but the Lucy Mercer affair had killed her feeling that she really shared in his life or that she had abilities of her own. This was his career, not hers, his potentialities that were being realized, while hers continued to be circumscribed by family and friends.

She was ready for something more—how much so is suggested in an interview she gave at Hyde Park during the homecoming ceremonies. Mrs. Roosevelt, the reporter wrote, "is first of all a domestic woman, but she has one outside interest, she admitted on Wednesday to a reporter of the (Poughkeepsie) *Eagle News*, in the only interview she granted. That is politics."

"Yes, I am interested in politics, intensely so, but in that I think I am no different from the majority of women, only that, of course, I have followed my husband's career with an interest that is intense because it is personal. But I have never," and she emphasized her words, "campaigned for him. I haven't been active in politics in any way, and so you see there isn't much of a story to be found in me.

"My politics? Oh yes, I am a Democrat, but," and here she paused, "I was brought up a staunch Republican,—and turned Democrat. I believe that the best interests of the country are in the hands of the Democratic Party, for I believe they are the most progressive. The Republicans are,—well, they are more conservative, you know, and we can't be too conservative and accomplish things.

"I am particularly interested in the League of Nations issue and I am firmly in favor of it, though I think we should adopt it with the reservation that Congress shall vote on whether or not we shall enter a war. But the League of Nations is, I believe, the only way that we can prevent war. We fought for it, and we should adopt it. If we don't adopt it, it will be useless. The U.S. must be part of the alliance."[13]

These were the careful comments of a woman who was thinking for herself. The reporter was charmed by this "womanly" woman, as he described her. "Her hair is blond and fluffy, and her eyes of a deep shade of blue, make her look far younger than one would have imagined the mother of half-grown children to be. She is constantly smiling,—not the set, vapid smile of one who assents pleasantly rather than discuss a problem, but rather the smile that portrays a personality intensely interested in the questions under discussion and with a personal viewpoint on each of them." The reporter was interested that "as Mrs. Roosevelt sat and chatted . . . the Democratic nominee for Vice President frequently entered the library to ask her advice on questions that had come up. . . ."

Back in Campobello Eleanor followed Franklin's progress through the papers. He and Cox were going to see the president, he wrote her, but he still planned to get to Campobello: "I can hardly wait. I miss you so much. It is very strange not to have you with me in all these doings."[14] "I like all your interviews," she replied, "and am dying to hear about your talk with the President. Oh! how I wish I could be in two places at once!"[15]

Franklin made the journey to Campobello on the destroyer *Hatfield*, piloting the vessel through the treacherous Lubec Narrows himself. While he was on the Island, he told the press, he intended to do some shooting, take cliff walks, begin work on another toy sailboat for the children, and teach James how to handle the *Vireo*, the boat that he had brought up, lashed to the deck of the *Hatfield*, to replace the *Half Moon*.[16] At the end of the week he, Eleanor, and Anna left for Washington, after which they would go to Dayton to attend the ceremony at which Governor Cox would be officially notified of his nomination. In Washington Eleanor arranged to give up their house—another indication of how little they expected to win—and Franklin said his good-by to the Navy by means of a formal letter of resignation to the president and an affectionate longhand note to Daniels. "You have taught me so wisely and kept my feet on the ground when I was about to skyrocket—and in all there has never been a real dispute or antagonism or distrust." In his diary, Daniels wrote, "He left in afternoon, but before leaving wrote me a letter most friendly and almost loving which makes me glad I had never acted upon my impulse when he seemed to take sides with my critics."[17]

While Eleanor and Anna went to Dayton with Franklin, Sara returned to Hyde Park with James and Elliott to prepare for Franklin's notification. Young Henry Morgenthau, Jr., managed the ceremonies at Springwood. Sara later grumbled to her children about what the crowds of politicians had done to her immaculate lawns,[18] but in her diary she wrote, "Very fine and impressive. About 500 came in the house. About 8,000 in all outside." Party notables, including Daniels, McAdoo, and Goveror Smith were on Sara's porch, which one reporter called a "wonderful front porch—a long, broad stone veranda" that, he implied, put into the shadow the front porch from which Harding had said arrogantly he would conduct his campaign. The reporters wrote approvingly of the vine-covered stucco house and the old, wide-spreading trees, and described James and Elliott and their cousin Cyril Martineau as youngsters whose yellow hair stood on end like bristles, while Anna's tow hair fell down her back nearly to her waist. Eleanor Roosevelt wore a plain blue and white dress without ornaments, the press reported, and listened to her husband intently, perched on the balustrade that ran around the veranda with her feet resting on the edge of a camp stool.

When Franklin went West for his first campaign trip, Sara, Eleanor, and the three children returned to Campobello. "Keep some kind of diary *please*," he wrote her from St. Paul, "as I know I will miss some of the things that happen!"[19] That was his last letter. From then on if the family heard from him at all it was by telegram. "Splendid receptions Minnesota, South and North Dakota," he telegraphed on August 16. "So sorry miss Franklin's birthday give him my special love. All well. Telegraph Wednesday noon care Station Master Northern Pacific Railroad, Spokane, Washington."

Franklin's campaign office was still after her for photographs. "Bachrach in Washington has a good one with F. Jr. when a baby," she replied to Charles McCarthy on August 25, but those taken of her alone were rather poor. "I take such bad photographs." She went on to talk about the campaign:

I am glad you feel Franklin's chances are good for I would be sorry to have him beaten after so much work & I really think & hope "Cox & Roosevelt" can do better for the country the next four, very hard years than "Harding & Coolidge." Personally, I had wanted Franklin out of government service for a few years at least, so in spite of the honor I really feel rather unselfish when I wish for his success!

Would it be possible for you to send me some copies of Franklin's speech of acceptance & some campaign buttons both Cox & Roosevelt? Several people are asking & writing for them & I would be most grateful if you can let me have them.

"Dearest, dear Honey," she wrote him on August 27, "I am positively hungry for news of you and it seems a long time since your last telegram and they are meagre enough." Her letter was full of family and political news. "So far the Republican papers having nothing very bad against you have simply been trying to treat you like an amiable, young boy, belittlement is the worst they can do." The Republican side of the family was lining up for Harding, a later letter reported. "Did you see that Alice is to go on the stump for Harding and that Auntie Corinne is to speak for him in Portland, Maine, on September 8th, starting his campaign there. Ted also speaks in Maine." Mrs. Selmes, Isabella's mother, had been at Henderson House when Franklin was nominated and reported that everyone there was "so nice" about Franklin. But Franklin's success in the West worried the Republican high command. "Do you know," said the engineer on the Roosevelt train, "that lad's got a 'million vote smile'—and mine's going to be one of them." Theodore Roosevelt, Jr., was dispatched by the Republicans to trail Franklin. "He is a maverick," young Theodore said in Sheridan, Wyoming. "He does not have the brand of our family." This personal attack galled Franklin, and it was the beginning of bad feeling between the Oyster Bay and Hyde Park clans. Franklin thrust back shrewdly, although not personally, by recalling that "in 1912 Senator Harding called Theodore Roosevelt, first a Benedict Arnold and then an Aaron Burr. This is one thing, at least some members of the Roosevelt family will not forget."

Eleanor was restless at Campobello. When Franklin agreed to go to Brooklyn on Labor Day, she wrote to Sara a little irascibly, "Of course it is hard to refuse but I do think he should have cut Monday out and come here directly, however, there is no use in saying anything."[20] A reminder to Franklin to write to Aunt Dora revealed her own feelings: "I hate to add these personal things when you are under such a strain and wish I could do them but I can't and they are the kind of things which do mean so much to other people who don't happen to have all the interesting things you have to fill their minds."[21] He was in the privileged position; he had interesting things to do, and she was no longer content to sit on an island off the northeast coast of Maine while he had all the fun.

On September 20 Louis Howe wrote her that the staff was struggling with the Roosevelt pictures and packing as well as they could, and then he added, "I do not think Franklin has told you, but I am resigning for a month in order to avoid the civil service rules and going off with Franklin on the next western trip." And Franklin had not told Louis that he had also asked Eleanor to join the campaign train.

How this came about is not clear. She had written her husband at the beginning of September, "I would love to go down but as I know you must go on campaigning I would just be in the way." If she thought of herself as a burden, her friends saw her as a political asset. When Grace C. Root sent congratulations on Franklin's nomination, she added, "and not at all the least to you whose comprehension of things political might well be envied by the suffrage sisters!" Alice Wadsworth, relieved that "so far as *our* men are concerned the victory of one does not necessitate the defeat of the other," took it for granted that "both of us will probably be busy with *politics*—thanks to this dratted Suffrage!"

The 1920 election was the first national election in which women voted. "The woman's hour was striking," Mrs. Catt proclaimed at the victory convention of the National American Woman Suffrage Association. A candidate's wife could have an important effect upon his fortunes, and Franklin wanted Eleanor at his side. Before joining him, however, she took James to Groton, the first of four trips to deliver a son to the rector's Spartan disciplines. James was only twelve and it was difficult to leave him at boarding school, but it was family tradition, so she unpacked his trunk, arranged his cubicle, and finally said good-by to the Peabodys and to James. She would go through the same melancholy experience with each of the boys, increasingly dubious that separating youngsters from parents at so early an age was good for either; but it was Franklin's wish and she yielded, just as she did a few days later when James came down with a digestive upset and Franklin, on the basis of a reassuring message from the rector, urged her to stay with the train and let Sara go to Groton instead. It was the first time she had not been with an ill child and it was hard not to hasten back to her son's bedside, but as she wrote Sara, "I am going gaily on."

"This is the most killing thing for the candidate I ever knew," was her first report to Sara from the *Westboro*, as their campaign car was called.[22] There were good crowds, she wrote from Charleston, and she was particularly pleased to find that "Franklin has certainly made strides in public speaking and gets enough praise everywhere to turn anyone's head."[23] Days aboard a campaign train were more hectic than any she had ever experienced. "F. made 2 speeches & drove 26 miles over awful roads before we ever got any breakfast!" she reported from Kentucky. "There have been two town speeches since then and at least one platform speech every 15 minutes all day! We had coffee & sandwiches for lunch & a very hurried supper & now he still has to get off at Bowling Green at 10:10 for a speech in a hall! I never will be able to do without at least four large cups of black coffee again *every* day!"[24] She was relieved to learn from Sara that James' ailment had been diagnosed as colitis. "I don't know when I'll be back though I really don't see that I'm of the least use on this trip."

This was not Franklin's view, according to a few lines he added to the same letter. "I am still alive, tho' it has been about the most strenuous week of the campaign. It has been a great comfort to have Eleanor. Some day when this is all over I will regain my normal mode of life—& then I won't be horrid to you as I was last Sunday—& I will really try to do the many little things that do count! It is too bad about James."

Eleanor was able to leave the train in Terre Haute, Indiana, have a bath at the hotel, and write Sara.

We had a splendid meeting at Bowling Green last night, in the open at 10:30 p.m. must have been over a 1,000 people there. Franklin's voice is all right again & I should say he came through yesterday finely & it certainly was a big day, he must have talked to and tried to shake hands with at least 30,000 people, the newspapermen think. We arrived in this town about 12, a big crowd waiting came to shake hands & when Governor Cox's train came in we all went to speak to him & he had to say a few words & shake all the hands he could. He looks well but his voice is much worse than F.'s. F. went with him to Indianapolis, also Mr. Howe, Mr. McIntyre (whom I like very much) & Mr. Prenosil (the A.P. man). They return at 8:48 & we get on the train & go on to St. Louis.

Of course Franklin's looks bring all sorts of admiring comments & then we get asked if he's "Teddy" frequently. I almost hope he does not get elected for so many people are coming to see us in Washington & I shan't remember their names or faces.[25]

In St. Louis the station crowds appeared to her to be "rather apathetic," but she thought that was due to the "German descent" of so many of the city's inhabitants. In any case, Franklin had an "appreciative audience" in the armory, and afterward he had his hair cut "at 11 p.m. the only chance he had & then it was done on the car surrounded by an admiring audience of newspapermen!" She wanted Sara to send her "1 clean nightgown & shirt & 3 chemises & 3 drawers & any black stockings & handkerchiefs I may have. F. says he has enough." In a postscript about Franklin's impact on the crowds, she said his "head should be turned if it is ever going to be for there is much praise and enthusiasm for him personally almost everywhere."[26]

They went westward as far as Colorado and then returned East by another route. In Cincinnati mail and laundry caught up with them. Eleanor was still amazed at the pace and unhappy over her own uselessness. "I tell Franklin he will never settle down & give up the inevitable large cup of black coffee & cream with every meal again but I really think he will be so glad to rest he won't want to move for days. We enter N.Y. State the a.m. of the 21st & I shall go on to N.Y. as my only use has been so far that people are curious to see his wife but that won't be so in the East. . . ."[27] That Sunday in Cincinnati she was taken to church, "as they thought it wise to announce in the paper where *we* would go but only *I* went." Franklin's voice was again showing strain, she reported, and little wonder: "It is becoming almost impossible to stop F. now when he begins to speak, 10 minutes is always 20, 30 is always 45 & the evening speeches are now about 2 hours! The men all get out & wave at him in front & when nothing succeeds I yank his coat tails! Everyone is getting tired but on the whole the car is still pretty good natured! They tell us Gov. Cox's is all on edge."[28]

When the train reached Buffalo, Franklin went to speak in Jamestown, while Eleanor, with Louis Howe, decided to visit Niagara Falls, which she had never seen. This was a sign of their budding friendship. It had taken Eleanor a long time to appreciate Louis. At times she had resented his influence with her husband and had been swift to find fault with him. When Franklin went to

Europe in 1918, she had complained that "the only item *every* paper gives is that Mr. Howe is running your office during your absence so he saw that was widespread news and how the naval officers must hate it!" But Howe was a sensitive, perceptive man who refused to be deterred by her coolness; he knew the blow she had been dealt by the Lucy Mercer business. She was the only woman on the *Westboro*, and he saw that many things bewildered or irritated her. At the end of the day Franklin would be tense and high-strung, and the men would gather at the end of the car to review the day's events, play a little poker, and hoist a few bourbons. Roosevelt "did not take life seriously enough," Steve Early, who was Roosevelt's advance man, later recalled. "He was just a playboy preferring poker to speech conferences."[29] Eleanor disliked the playboy in her husband; she felt he should save his strength and go to bed, and that a candidate for vice president should set an example.

She expressed her discontent obliquely; for example, she worried because she thought the car's porter was not able to get enough sleep because his berth was close to where the men played cards. She was timid with the newspapermen and wanted to be of more use than simply sitting with a rapt look listening to her husband make the same speech over and over again.

Louis sensed all this: her loneliness, her great sadness, her lack of self-confidence, her need of appreciation. He was aware also of her abilities—her good judgment, remarkable vitality, and organizational gifts. He saw the way people responded to her warmth and courtesy. He began to tell her, and she desperately needed to hear such words, that she had a real contribution to make to her husband's campaign. He brought drafts of speeches to discuss with her. He explained the ways of newspapermen and encouraged her to meet them as friends. By the end of the trip she was on good enough terms with the press to be amused rather than upset when, from the rear of a hall, some of the reporters made funny faces at her to try to break the look of total absorption she adopted for her husband's speeches. They teased her when the ladies crowded around the candidate, and she took it good-naturedly. She was grateful to Louis for that. Together they discussed the issues of the campaign and the politics of the towns through which they traveled. Eleanor discovered that Louis had a wide range of knowledge, a nice sense of humor, a feeling for poetry and the countryside. Louis knew when to be silent and when to speak up. By the end of the trip they had become fast friends. His daughter Mary was at Vassar. "Will you ask Mary Howe to come up on Sunday?" Eleanor wrote ahead to Sara.

On the Monday before the election Franklin wound up his campaign with the traditional appearance in Poughkeepsie. The central issue, he said at the end of the campaign as he had at the beginning, is "whether the U.S. is to finish the war or to quit cold, whether we are to join the other forty odd nations in the great working League of Nations that will serve to end war for all time or whether we will turn our back on them. . . ." But he was a realist. Harding was a 10 to 1 favorite in the Wall Street betting. At 10:45 on Election Day morning, he and Eleanor and Sara arrived at the polling place in Hyde Park. It was raining but the village people were there and gave him a cheer. He was vote number 207 and Eleanor's was number 208, her first vote. Sara also voted, as did Rosy's wife Betty. But the hope that the millions of newly enfranchised women voters would cast a peace vote by voting for Cox, as Mrs. Catt had appealed to them to do, was quickly dashed. The special wire that brought the results into Springwood, where Franklin held open house for friends and neighbors, showed early in the evening that a Republican avalanche was in the making. "We all feel very badly over the result of the elections," Eleanor wrote Franklin a few days later.

Franklin took it philosophically, as did the inner group around him. They all were sure another chance would come. He hoped, wrote Renah Camalier, his secretary on the *Westboro*, "that when the clan meets again four years hence, it will have sense enough to see that there is but one man to put at the head of the ticket, that man, of course, being none other than my 'old boss.' " The Roosevelt organization dispersed except for Miss Marguerite LeHand. Young, pretty, highly competent, with a dry sense of humor, she had worked for Charles McCarthy in the Roosevelt offices at Democratic headquarters, and Franklin asked her to work for him permanently. She told him she would let him know "as soon as I have talked with my people. You were very nice to ask me." A month later she wrote him, "If you would still like to have me, I will be in New York on January third."

Louis was uncertain what he should do when a Republican secretary of the Navy took over—whether to go on Franklin's payroll or accept an outside business connection. Eleanor now became his staunch advocate, as he was hers. All the Howes spent Thanksgiving at Hyde Park with the Roosevelts, and afterward, Franklin left with Louis for Washington to join Hall for a hunting trip in Louisiana. "I have enjoyed Mrs. Howe," Eleanor wrote him. "I don't think she would bore you and she's a plucky little thing. They left at 9.03 cat and all, to take the midnight [train] and Mary went back to Vassar." The next day she added to the same letter, "I had a line from Louis also this morning telling me of your trip and safe departure from Washington."[30]

On Christmas Franklin sent the men who had been with him on the *Westboro* cuff links engraved with his initials and theirs, the beginning of the famous Cuff Links Club. The men in turn remembered Mrs. Roosevelt. "I wish you would send me a dollar and your visiting card," Louis Howe wrote Tom Lynch. "The boys have decided to send Mrs. Roosevelt a little pin for Christmas as a souvenir of the campaign and this is your assessment." "The very pretty pin you sent Mrs. Roosevelt," Lynch wrote Howe after the holidays, "was shown to me last week and will say you have very good taste, the gift was appreciated very much."

Eleanor had frequently suffered from her husband's uncommunicativeness, and she now had an ally in Louis, who gave her the feeling she craved of a closer identification with her husband's work. And Louis, who was never sure he knew all that was going on with the boss and even less sure of his influence, now had reinforcement in "holding Franklin down."

Long ago he had set his hand to making a king; now he began to make a queen.[31]

25. *Baptism in Politics*

BY THE TIME the family moved back to New York Eleanor had a plan: she intended to help Franklin in whatever way he asked and permitted, but she would also have work of her own to do.

"All men who make successes of their work," she counseled a lonely woman years later,

go through exactly the same kind of thing which you describe and their wives, in one way or another have to adjust themselves. If it is possible to enter into his work in some way, that is the ideal solution. If not, they must develop something of their own and if possible make it such a success, that they will have something to interest their husbands.[1]

Franklin charted a strenuous schedule for himself. He joined a law firm which became Emmett, Marvin and Roosevelt. He became vice president at $25,000 a year in charge of the New York offices of Van Lear Black's Fidelity and Deposit Company of Maryland, the third largest surety bonding house in the country. He was a Harvard overseer. He agreed to head the Navy Club and the Greater New York Boy Scout Council. He also had ideas for some books he wanted to write. It was too much of a program, Eleanor protested. "Of course I know your remarkable faculty for getting through work when you get right down to it," but if he was to carry through on his commitments, he would have to cut out most formal parties, she said hopefully.[2]

Her own program was more modest. She enrolled in a business school to learn typing and shorthand. She found a housewife to teach her to cook. She began active work in the League of Women Voters. Unable to move back into 49 East Sixty-fifth Street because the Lamont lease still had six months to run, she and her family camped in Sara's house, but Eleanor quickly made it clear she did not intend to return to the old pattern of always being available for a meal, a drive, or pouring tea for Sara's friends and charities—in short, of subordinating her own interests to Sara's. She no longer felt the old obligation to write Sara about everything, nor did she share confidences with her or come to her with problems. She brushed aside Sara's view that a woman in her social position should confine her activity to serving on philanthropic boards. She did not want to be a name on a letterhead, an ornamental woman, without a job of her own to do. She wanted to be fully involved—with work, with people.[3]

A comment on Franklin K. Lane's death illuminated her frame of mind as well as the respect in which her wartime friends held her. Lane had checked into the Mayo Hospital in Rochester, Minnesota, and one of his last letters before undergoing the operation from which he did not recover was to Eleanor.

Just because I like you very much, and being a very old man dare to say so, I am sending this line—which has no excuse in its news, philosophy or advice;—has no excuse in fact except what might be called affection, but of course this being way past the Victorian era no one admits to affections. I will not belittle my own feeling by saying that I have a wife who thinks you the best Eastern product—and probably she'd move to strike out the word Eastern. At any rate I think I should tell you that I am to be operated on tomorrow by Dr. Will Mayo and am glad of it. We shall see what we shall see. . . . I'd love to see you and the gay cavalier—but let us hope it won't be long till we meet! Au revoir.

"It is a loss to the country," Eleanor wrote in her diary when she learned of Lane's death, "and I do not feel that we who are privileged to be his friends can gauge our loss but we must try in his memory to make the world a little better place to live in for the mankind which he loved so well."[4]

Among the organizations she turned to in the hope of being able to help improve the world was the League of Women Voters, the successor to the National Woman Suffrage Association. Its leaders had emerged from the long suffrage struggle as militant advocates of better working conditions for women, children's rights, reform of the political process, and peace. Mrs. Frank Vanderlip, the chairman of the New York State league, invited Eleanor to join the board and keep track of the league's legislative program. Eleanor hesitated, doubtful that she was equipped to handle such an assignment. She could have the help of a lawyer, Elizabeth F. Read, Mrs. Vanderlip said, to go through the Albany calendar and *Congressional Record* with her and indicate the bills of interest to the league.

Eleanor decided to accept, and one morning each week she went to Elizabeth Read's law office to review the documents and to select the bills she wanted to brief herself on more fully. She became acquainted with Esther Everett Lape, who had been active with Elizabeth Read in the suffrage movement, and shared a small apartment with her on East Eleventh Street. Esther, an energetic member of the league's state board who has taught at Swarthmore and Barnard and was an effective publicist, combined a driving political activism with tact and sensitivity; Elizabeth—calmer, more scholarly, more practical—stayed in the background. Both were highly qualified professional women. They were co-editors of the *City-State-Nation,* a weekly legislative review issued by the league, and although they were volunteers, they did an expert job. Franklin had stolen his wife's copy of the review, he wrote Esther Lape, and "I wish that the subscription list . . . might contain as many names of men as of women."[5]

Esther and Elizabeth's careful, documented workmanship shaped Eleanor's standards in her approach to public issues and helped her to do serious, sustained work. They were liberal in outlook but it was a pragmatic liberalism with which Eleanor sympathized. At meetings of the state board Esther was impressed with the way Eleanor "wanted always to know exactly what she could do before the next monthly meeting."[6] Her serenity had a stabilizing effect upon the board; she had a way of calmly rising above intramural disputes over personalities and jurisdictions to keep the board's attention focused on the league's larger purposes. "The rest of us," recalled Esther, "were inclined to do a good deal of theorizing. She would look puzzled and ask why we didn't do whatever we had in mind and get it out of the way. As you may imagine, she was given many jobs to do." Within a year the most tangled problems of reorganization were turned over to her to unsnarl.[7] Esther and Elizabeth were impressed with their new friend's attitude and performance, with her insistence upon doing her own work, with the strength and clarity that lay beneath the shyness. The esteem was mutual. Eleanor came to depend greatly upon their counsel and soon she was often spending evenings with them. They were cultivated, sensitive women with a strong sense of privacy, enormously useful citizens who had found in domestic arrangements that did not include men a happy adjustment. Their tender relationship was not unique in the suffrage movement, especially among women of great professional competence. They and several of their counterparts would in the next few years play a big part in what Eleanor herself called "the intensive education of Eleanor Roosevelt."

At the end of January, 1921, Eleanor attended the state convention of the League of Women Voters in Albany as a delegate from Dutchess County. It was a lively introduction to the league's activities. The Republican machine still smarted from the league's campaign against Senator Wadsworth, who had opposed the suffrage amendment even after New York voters had passed it. Regulars in both parties thought it was time that the women, heady with success, were tamed. The newly installed Republican governor, Nathan L. Miller, enraged the convention with a denunciation of the league as a menace to American institutions because of its social-welfare program and lobbying activities.

"I want to tell you why Governor Miller has suspicion of you," cried Mrs. Carrie Chapman Catt, the white-haired leader of the suffrage struggle and its most eloquent spokesman. "The League of Women Voters constitutes the remains of that army which for 50 years in the State of New York fought the battle for the enfranchisement of the sex." The women now intended to bring to the new struggle for welfare legislation the hard-hitting tactics they had learned in the suffrage battles.

The male politicians were very critical, but Miller's frontal attack soon proved to have been a blunder. Although Republican women outnumbered the Democrats by 5 to 1 at the convention, the league, led by Mrs. Vanderlip, a Republican, protested the governor's speech and reaffirmed the right of women "to work as a group outside the political party for political measures." The governor beat a quick retreat: he had been misunderstood, he said. The politicians realized that more subtle methods would have to be used to keep women in their place.[8]

Eleanor had long followed politics as an observer, but this was her apprenticeship in political activity on her own. Her role at the convention was limited to explaining to the delegates the work of her legislative committee: all bills introduced into the legislature would be reviewed, and the good and bad features of the key measures circulated to the league's membership. The next few months showed that there was more to the committee's activities than that.

The league decided to sponsor a bill requiring the political parties to give equal representation to men and women at all levels, and it was Eleanor's job to get the bill drafted and to obtain bipartisan sponsorship for it.[9] When the politicians in the legislature moved to weaken the direct primary law by excluding the governorship and other state-wide offices from its stipulations, the board asked Eleanor and Esther to formulate the league's opposition to the measure.[10] Eleanor led a state-board discussion of proposals to reorganize the state government which ended with the board's reaffirmation of its support of a longer term for governor, an executive budget, a shorter ballot, and departmental consolidation, reforms that in time would all be adopted. She had interested FDR in the work, enough so that the league minutes of March 1 read "on motion duly made and seconded, it was voted that a vote of thanks be sent Mr. Roosevelt for his help in the Legislative work." He was not making Governor Miller's mistake.

Franklin enjoyed coaching his wife in political tactics. The re-election of Narcissa Vanderlip as state chairman of the league was contested on the grounds that there had been electioneering in the vicinity of the polls. A committee was set up to investigate. Esther and Eleanor were both supporters of Mrs. Vanderlip and quite enraged over the investigation. At dinner at Sixty-fifth Street they told Franklin about the situation. "Eleanor, you be there early and sit up front," he advised. "Just as soon as the report is read, you get up and move that it be tabled. That motion is not debatable."

"It worked," recalled Esther gleefully. "You should have seen their jaws drop." Eleanor made a striking figure, thin and very tall. She had on a rose colored suit, and a long fur, that went around her neck and down. It gave her a special pleasure to do what Franklin had told her to do.

In April, 1921, Eleanor was in Cleveland as a Dutchess County delegate to the league's second national convention. "I've had a very interesting day and heard some really good women speakers," she wrote her husband.

Mrs. Catt is clear, cold reason, Mrs. Larue Brown is amusing, apt, graceful, a Mrs. Cunningham from Texas is emotional and idealistic, but she made nearly everyone cry! I listened to Child Welfare all the morning and Direct Primaries all the afternoon, lunched with Margaret Norrie, drove out at five with Mrs. Wyllis Mitchell and called on Mrs. (Newton) Baker, dined and heard some speeches on Child Welfare and attended a N.Y. delegates' meeting and am about to go to bed, quite weary! Meetings begin tomorrow at ten.[11]

Twenty years later Eleanor still recalled the speech of Minnie Fisher Cunningham, veteran of a hundred reform battles in Texas, who made her feel "that you had no right to be a slacker as a citizen, you had no right not to take an active part in what was happening to your country as a whole."[12] She was moved particularly by Mrs. Cunningham's plea "that she hoped the day would not come when her children would look at her and say: 'You knew certain conditions existed and you did nothing about those conditions.'"

Mrs. Catt may have been "clear, cold reason" on the subject of direct primaries and other measures to weaken boss control of political parties, but she was all flame and passion when she ripped into President Harding, who in his first address to Congress a day earlier had declared "this Republic will have no part" in the League of Nations. Mrs. Catt threw aside a prepared speech.

You have heard politics all day. I can't help saying something I feel I must. The people in this room tonight could put an end to war. Everybody wants it and every one does nothing. . . . I am for a League of Nations, a Republican league or any kind the Republicans are in.

She summoned the women, most of whom were by now on their feet, to "consecrate" themselves

to put war out of the world. . . . Men were born by instinct to slay. It seems to me God is giving a call to the women of the world to come forward, to stay the hand of men, to say: "No, you shall no longer kill your fellow men."[13]

There was dead silence, followed by wave after wave of applause. Not until Eleanor Roosevelt achieved her full powers would another woman have a comparable authority over female audiences; but Eleanor had many years of training, discipline, and speechmaking ahead before she achieved such mastery. Back from Cleveland, a diary entry for April 23 noted that "worked in a.m. at typewriting review of legislative work for winter." The next day, Sunday, she went back to her typewriter after church, finished her notes on legislation, "and wrote out speech for Tuesday" for the Dutchess County chapter of the League of Women Voters. Margaret Norrie, her Staatsburgh neighbor, made the main report on the Cleveland convention. "I added a few words," Eleanor noted. The next day she went to New York to have her hair done and again say "a few words on legislation" to a league luncheon at the Colony Club. Speaking in public was a torment; her cultivated voice—which in conversation was relaxed and warm—rose several octaves and became high-pitched, and frequent distracting giggles reflected her self-consciousness. She was, however, determined to do better.

Regardless of the difficulties she had making speeches she was doing her job, and at the May meeting of the Dutchess County league was nominated for chairman but withdrew in favor of Margaret Norrie.[14] Also at that meeting she became involved in public controversy for the first time—in defense of civil liberties. In an article in the *Delineator* Vice President Coolidge had alleged that women's colleges were filled with radicals, Vassar being one of his targets, and in particular Professor Winifred Smith, who worried the vice president because she had contrasted the "moderation and intelligence" of the Soviet representative in Washington with the "narrowness" of the congressmen who were demanding his deportation. Coolidge thought Professor Smith's reactions were dangerous. Eleanor introduced the club's resolution on the subject. The club knew Miss Smith as "a public-spirited and devoted citizen," her resolution read, and in times of "public excitement" the national interest was best served by "calm and critical judgment." The resolution ended with a protest against "all thoughtless aspersion on such public-spirited citizens."

The *Poughkeepsie Eagle News* headlined the censure of the vice president: "Mrs. F. D. Roosevelt Offers Resolution Taking to Task Husband's Victorious Rival." The local press was "indignant" over the resolution, Eleanor noted in her diary, and added, "Foolish of me ever to do anything of the kind."[15] The criticism bothered her less than the fact that she had involved her husband. It was a problem she would face often in later years—did she have a right to engage in controversy if her husband might be adversely affected?

The circles in which Eleanor moved were greatly concerned with equal rights for women, and so was Eleanor. But the harsh stridency of some feminists irritated her; she was not what Franklin and Louis sarcastically called a "she-male." She attended a Westchester County Democratic dinner where Franklin spoke, as did Harriet May Mills, who had been president of the New York Women's Suffrage party and was now a leading Democrat. Eleanor admired Miss Mills but thought she overdid the women question.[16] Eleanor enjoyed masculine society and working with the men. From Cleveland she had written Franklin, "Much, much love dear and I prefer doing my politics with you."[17]

Even though she was developing her own interests, her first choice still was to enter into her husband's work. Now the summer began that was to leave him crippled, with his survival as a public man dependent on her resolution, her encouragement, her readiness to serve as his proxy in politics. He had always needed her, more than she was ever able to recognize or than he usually could bring himself to say. After the summer, there no longer was need for words.

26. The Tempering—Polio

FRANKLIN WAS IMPATIENT to get back to Campobello in 1921. For the first time since he began to campaign for public office, he planned to spend most of the summer on his beloved island. He needed its peace and he looked forward to being with his family. Public office had a disciplining effect on him, and when he was out of office he was restless, reckless, irrepressible. "Found Franklin in bed after a wild 1904 dinner and party," Eleanor noted May 24. Harriet, the maid, "frightened" her with the announcement that Mr. Roosevelt was in bed, but then when she learned why, she was "very indignant with him!"[1] Just before they went to Campobello, young Sheffield Cowles was married to Margaret "Bobbie" Krech, and Franklin's "uproarious" behavior at the wedding festivities surprised the Oyster Bay contingent, who had always thought of him as a little lacking in earthiness. "It was the Roosevelt spirits," they said, a claim that irritated Sara, who was sure her son was a Delano.

Orders went to Captain Calder at Campobello to get the *Vireo* and the motor launch in readiness, also the tennis court. Louis Howe, who had left the Navy Department, was planning to come to Campobello with his wife and his son, Hartley, which would give Franklin and Louis plenty of time to blueprint Franklin's bid for the governorship in 1922.

Sara was not in her house. Although sixty-seven, she returned to her pre-war practice of a yearly voyage to Europe to see her sister Dora and other Delano relatives. In London the spirit of adventure overcame caution, and she and Muriel Martineau took a twin engine aeroplane from London to Paris.

It was five hours from London to Paris. I had been told four hours, but I would not have missed it and if I do it again I shall take an open plane as one sees more and it is more like flying. Poor Muriel soon began to feel ill and had to lie on the floor all the way and had a horrid time.

"Don't do it again," her son hastily cabled her, and she agreed. "In thinking it over I believe you really mean it, so I shall try not to fly back." After settling his family at Campobello, Franklin had to rush to Washington to deal with a Republican effort to "smear" his and Daniels' record. The specific charge was that they had sanctioned the use of entrapment procedures at Newport Training Station in a drive against homosexuality there. Louis brought Eleanor a copy of the report signed by two Republican senators. She was anxious to hear what Franklin intended to do. "Of course," he wrote back, "as I expected I found all the cards stacked, only even worse than I thought."[2] The Republican majority reneged on a promise to give him an opportunity to be heard. A Roosevelt press release denounced the committee's methods, denied any knowledge of the entrapment procedures and certainly of any supervision of them, and protested Republican use of the Navy as a political football.

"It must be dreadfully disagreeable for you and I know it worries you though you wouldn't own it," she wrote back, "but it has always seemed to me that the chance of just such attacks as this was a risk one had to take with our form of government and if one felt clear oneself, the rest did not really matter."[3] When she saw the newspapers the next day she was indignant, "but one should not be ruffled by such things. Bless you dear and love always." She added a postscript: "I liked your answer. You will be starting a week from today."

The presence of the Howes and other guests, including the Bibescos, enlivened the summer for her while Franklin was away. It was a sign of her growing fondness for Louis that she relaxed her puritan scruples about liquor. "Mlle.," the governess, had fallen into the water while cleaning the *Vireo,* "and I've just had to give her a little gin in hot lemonade," Eleanor informed her husband, "as she has never warmed up since!"[4] This was quite a concession from Eleanor, who was a strict teetotaler and a supporter of the newly ratified Prohibition amendment. Sara's attitude was more relaxed. She wrote from Paris,

I rather enjoy being where one had red and white wine on the table, very little said on the subject and no drinking of spirits, and I feel, as I always have, that we should have made our fight against the *spirits* and the saloon, and encouraged the French habit of wine and water, but Americans really like their whiskey best now, just as the English do.[5]

For the visit of Elizabeth Bibesco, the daughter of Herbert Asquith, leader of the British Liberal party for over a quarter of a century, Eleanor even permitted a cocktail to be made. "I had to break the lock of your drawer to get at the whiskey!" she informed Franklin, who no doubt was slightly startled and amused. It turned out to be a "very bad cocktail" made by Jefferson Newbold, but Elizabeth "was sweet and I like her better than ever."[6]

Louis was an ideal guest. A do-it-yourself carpenter, he had acquired Roosevelt's passion for model boats and had begun working with Captain Calder to build a workbench for Franklin in the boathouse. He was also an irrepressible writer of doggerel and a water colorist, and his place cards were a continuous delight. He had been a mainstay in the Drama League Players in Washington both as director and actor and was always ready at Campobello to entertain the children and play with them. He was a "godsend" when it came to keeping track of the island workmen who came to repair the pump. "Mr. Howe has endless patience in batting the ball to Elliott and Hartley," Eleanor wrote Sara, "and he thinks Elliott will be good though I can see no signs as yet."[7] But sometimes Eleanor's energy and enterprise were too much even for the willing Louis. She read aloud to them in the evenings, "but Grace and sometimes Louis snore before I get far and Russell [James' tutor] goes to bed before I begin and Mlle. won't go to bed but props her eyelids up with her fingers!"[8]

On July 30 Eleanor wrote Sara that she had expected Franklin that day but instead he was coming on Van Lear Black's yacht, the *Sabalo*. She was glad, she said, because the heat was awful and a trip by train would further tax his vitality. "I thought he looked tired when he left," Miss LeHand advised her. Thus began the harsh events that Eleanor later called "trial by fire," that left her husband unable to walk.

The cruise of the *Sabalo* proved strenuous. The weather in the Bay of Fundy was foul and the visibility low; Franklin was obliged to take the wheel for hours. Dropping anchor in Welchpool Harbor, he plunged into entertaining his guests. They went fishing for cod and he baited the hooks; at one point he slipped overboard and "never felt anything so cold as that water." His pace was too much for his New York visitors, who discovered that imperative business required their presence in New York.[9]

The tempo of the household slackened only slightly. Roosevelt took his babies sailing on the *Vireo*; he and Louis worked on model boats; he played tennis with the older children; after supper they all turned out for baseball. Some friends sailed in on a yawl "and they spent a late evening with us ending up with a midnight supper!"[10] Though Franklin complained of feeling dull and tired, the vigorous life continued. On August 10, when the family was out on the *Vireo*, they spotted a forest fire and went ashore to flail at the flames with pine boughs. After the fire was under control, they dog-trotted, eyes smarting and smoke besmudged, for a dip in the relatively warm waters of Lake Glen Severn, then jogged back. Perhaps because he could not shake his loginess, Franklin took a quick dip in the Bay's icy waters but did not get "the glow I expected." When they returned to the house he sat around in his wet bathing suit looking through the mail, too tired to dress, and at supper complained of chills and aches and soon went to bed.

The next morning he felt worse. As he got out of bed his left leg dragged; soon it refused to move at all, and by afternoon his right leg was also powerless. His temperature was 102. Though he managed a smile and a joke for Anna when she brought him his tray, Eleanor was worried and sent for the family physician, old Dr. Bennett in Lubec, who thought it was a cold. But by Friday, August 12, paralysis had set in from the chest down. Eleanor, apprehensive, had sent the rest of the household on a previously planned three-day camping trip. A letter to Franklin's half brother, James Roosevelt Roosevelt, described the inception of the crisis. Harried and apprehensive as she was, the letter was composed, clear, and poignant.

Campobello
August 14, 1921

Dear Rosy,   Sunday

We have had a very anxious few days as on Wed. evening Franklin was taken ill. It seemed a chill but Thursday he had so much pain in his back and legs that I sent for the doctor, by Friday evening he lost his ability to walk or move his legs but though they felt numb he can still feel in them. Yesterday a.m. Dr. Bennett and I decided we wanted the best opinion we could get quickly so Louis Howe (who, thank heavens, is here, for he has been the greatest help) went with Dr. Bennett to Lubec and they canvassed the nearby resorts and decided that the best available diagnostician was the famous old Dr. W. W. Keen of Philadelphia and he agreed to motor up and spend the night. He arrived about 7:30 and made a most careful, thorough examination and the same this morning and he thinks a clot of blood from a sudden congestion has settled in the lower spinal cord temporarily removing the power to move though not to feel. I have wired to New York for a masseuse as he said that was vital and the nursing I could do, and in the meantime Louis and I are rubbing him as well as we can. The doctor feels sure he will get well but it may take some months. I have only told Franklin he said he could surely go down the 15th of Sept. He did say to leave then but not before on account of heat and to go to New York but it may have to be done on a wheel chair. The doctor thinks absorption has already begun as he can move his toes on one foot a little more which is encouraging. He has told the Dr. here just what medicines to give and what treatment to follow and we should know in the next ten days or two weeks how things are going.

Do you think you can meet Mama when she lands? She has asked us to cable just before she sails and I have decided to say nothing. No letter can reach her now and it would simply mean worry all the way home and she will have enough once here but at least then she can do things. I will write her a letter to quarantine saying he is ill but leave explaining to you or if you can't meet her to Uncle Fred or whoever does meet her. I hope you will think I am doing right and have done all I could. Of course write me if you think of anything else. I do not want particulars to get into the papers so I am writing the family that he is ill from the effects of a chill and I hope will soon be better, but I shall write Uncle Fred what I have told you and Langdon Marvin as Franklin cannot be at the office to relieve him.

> Affly always,
> Eleanor

For two weeks, until a trained nurse could come up from New York, Eleanor slept on a couch in Franklin's room and took care of her husband day and night. All the tenderness, solicitude, and devotion that so often were dammed up by his jaunty flirtatiousness now poured forth as she bathed him, rubbed him, attended to his every need. Looking at his collapsed legs brought to mind Michelangelo's *Pietà*, that universal symbol of woman, the mother, grieving over the broken body of man, the son, the piece of sculpture that in her girlhood, reminding her of the wasted body of her father, had moved her to tears. She took her cue from Franklin's courage. Her vitality was equal to his darkest moments. Sometimes with Louis, often unaided, she raised and moved her husband's large, heavy frame. Dr. William W. Keen, who was witness to her twenty-four-hour ministrations, was worried.[11]

You have been a rare wife and have borne your heavy burden most bravely. You will surely break down if you too do not have immediate relief. Even then when the catheter has to be used your sleep must be broken at least once in the night.

In later years the old doctor never ceased to praise Eleanor's tireless consecra-

tion. "She is one of my heroines," he wrote Roosevelt in 1926; "don't fail
to tell her so." He was equally impressed with Franklin's courage and cheerfulness; indeed, he confided to Eleanor, he had "rarely met two such brave,
cheerful and delightful patients. You see I count you as one although you are
not going to take my medicine!"[12]

Franklin's cheerfulness at the time was a fugitive affair, as Eleanor's next
letter to Rosy hinted. His temperature had returned to normal, she wrote on the
eighteenth, "and I think he's getting back his grip and a better mental attitude
though he has of course times of great discouragement." She had not yet told
Franklin that Dr. Keen had warned that his recuperation would take a long
time. "I dread the time when I have to tell Franklin and it wrings my heart for it
is all so much worse to a man than to a woman but the 3 doctors agree he will
be eventually well if nothing unfavorable happens in the next ten days or so and
at present all signs are favorable, so we should be very thankful."

Dr. Keen had brought another doctor into the consultations, but in the
meantime Uncle Fred, on the basis of Louis Howe's description of the illness,
had consulted doctors in New York who leaned toward a diagnosis of infantile
paralysis. "On Uncle Fred's urgent advice," Eleanor wrote Rosy,

which I feel I must follow on Mama's account, I have asked Dr. Keen to try to get
Dr. Lovett here for a consultation to determine if it is I.P. or not. Dr. Keen thinks
not but the treatment at this stage differs in one particular and no matter what it
costs I feel and I am sure Mama would feel we must leave no stone unturned to
accomplish the best results.[13]

Dr. Keen tracked down Dr. Robert W. Lovett, a specialist in orthopedics, at
Newport, and he went to Campobello immediately. Dr. Lovett promptly diagnosed infantile paralysis, but would not commit himself as to the future course
of the illness. Eleanor, determined to know the worst, begged Louis to ask
Lovett what the chances were of Franklin's recovering the use of his lower
limbs, because she felt that the doctor would be more frank with someone who
was not a member of the immediate family.

It was impossible to tell, Lovett replied, but whatever chance there was
depended on the patient's attitude. "If his interest in resuming active life is
great enough, if his will to recover is strong enough, there is undoubtedly a
chance." Eleanor should be prepared "for mental depression and sometimes
irritability."

When she heard the diagnosis of polio she felt a momentary sense of panic
because of the children, in addition to her anxiety over Franklin.[14] She had
thought of polio as a possibility, she wrote Dr. Peabody at Groton, and while
"it seemed incredible" she had kept the children out of Franklin's room, but
that did not mean they were safe.[15] Lovett assured her, however, that since the
children were not already stricken they had probably not been infected. When
the trained nurse at last arrived from New York, Lovett and Keen, impressed
with Eleanor's skillful care of her husband, felt that she should continue to
share the nursing responsibility.

She also acted as Franklin's secretary and scribe. She wrote Langdon Marvin not to come up because "you wouldn't be allowed to see me if you came." Franklin could not get to the Sulphur Spring meeting, she advised the Fidelity and Deposit home office, but in her letter to Dr. Peabody asking whether James should return to Groton in September in light of his father's illness, she added, "Franklin says to tell you he can still do lots of work on the committee he hopes!" Miss LeHand, meanwhile, not knowing that Franklin was ill, had asked for a raise in salary. Mr. Roosevelt could not jump her to forty dollars but might manage to get her thirty-five, Eleanor wrote.

The most difficult letter was to Sara, who was due to arrive August 31.

> Campobello
> August 27, 1921
> Dearest Mama,   Saturday
> Franklin has been quite ill and so can't go down to meet you on Tuesday to his great regret, but Uncle Fred and Aunt Kassie both write they will be there so it will not be a lonely homecoming. We are all so happy to have you home again dear, you don't know what it means to feel you near again.
> The children are all very well and I wish you could have seen John's face shine when he heard us say you would be home again soon.
> Aunt Jennie is here with Ellen and we are having such lovely weather, the island is really at its loveliest.
> Franklin sends all his love and we are both so sorry he cannot meet you.
> Ever devotedly
> Eleanor

Louis went to New York. "Everything in connection with your affairs is in the best possible shape," he reported. "I took breakfast with 'Uncle Fred' before your mama arrived, and filled him full of cheery thoughts and fried eggs. That night, being so exhausted with his day's labors, he decided to take dinner with me and we went together to the movies."[16]

As soon as she arrived Sara went to Campobello. The façade of cheer she found there did not fool her, but if Eleanor and Franklin were able to put up a brave front so would she. She was heartsick, but noted that Eleanor was doing "a *great* deal" for Franklin and commented, "This again illustrates my point that the lightning usually strikes where you least expect it." She wrote her sister, Doe (Mrs. Paul R. Forbes):

> It was a shock to hear bad news on my arrival at the dock, but I am thankful I did not hear before I sailed, as I came directly here, and being very well and strong I could copy the happy cheerful attitude of Eleanor and even of poor Franklin, who lies there unable to move his legs, which are often painful and have to be moved for him, as they have *no* power. He looks well and eats well and is very keen and full of interest in everything. He made me tell him all about our four days in the devastated region, and told me what he saw when there. Dr. Lovett, the greatest authority we have on infantile paralysis, pronounced it that and says he *will* get well. At best it will be slow.[17]

"He and Eleanor decided at once to be cheerful," she reported to her brother Fred, and the atmosphere of the house is all happiness, so I have fallen in and follow their glorious example. . . . Dr. Bennett just came and said "This boy is going to get well all right." They went into his room and I hear them all laughing. Eleanor in the lead.

Franklin persuaded his mother to go to Louise Delano's wedding as there was little for her to do at Campobello. "I am glad you sent her off to the wedding. It will do her good," Rosy wrote from Hyde Park. "Poor Tom Lynch I told him today about you, and he burst out crying." Lynch was not the only one. "I simply cannot bear to have beautiful, active Franklin laid low even for a time," Mary Miller wrote when the news caught up with her. Everyone found it difficult to think of "such a vigorous, healthy person ill," but they admired the "magnificent spirit," as Adolph Miller put it, which Franklin and Eleanor were showing. Husband and wife did not yield to self-pity, and they discouraged weeping and wailing by those around them. In the letters that Eleanor wrote for him, Franklin set a tone of optimistic banter that he expected those close to him to follow. "After many consultations among the medical fraternity," his letter to Langdon Marvin said,

my case has been diagnosed by Dr. Lovett as one of poliomyelitis, otherwise infantile paralysis. Cheerful thing for one with my gray hairs to get. I am almost wholly out of commission as to my legs but the doctors say that there is no question that I will get their use back again though this means several months of treatment in New York. . . . The doctors say of course that I can keep up with everything and I expect to do this through Mr. Howe, my former assistant in Washington who will act as my go-between from 65th Street to 52 Wall and the F & D Company.[18]

Howe and Miss LeHand went along with his tone of cheerful badinage. "By the way, Mr. Howe took me up with him in a *taxi*," Miss LeHand wrote Roosevelt; "isn't that scandalous? I love scandal! . . . I have moved my desk and typewriter into your office right beside the telephone. Do you object?" Eleanor was grateful. "Your letters have amused him and helped to keep him cheerful." "Dear Boss," Louis wrote,

I loved the way Eleanor telegraphed to go into Tiffany's to buy a watch for Calder without mentioning whether it was to be a $1200 Jorgerson or a Waterbury Radiolite; also to have it inscribed without mentioning what to inscribe on it! Lord knows I have acted as your alter-ego in many weird commissions, but I must positively refuse to risk my judgment on neckties, watches or pajamas.[19]

The watch was purchased and given to Captain Calder by Eleanor when the private railroad car that Uncle Fred had obtained pulled out of Eastport with Franklin aboard. It was the captain who, with the aid of some island men, had carried Franklin down the hill to the Roosevelt wharf on a stretcher that he had improvised and placed him on a motorboat for the two-mile crossing to Eastport. There, Louis, who stage-managed the whole move, skillfully diverted the waiting crowd while the stretcher was placed on a luggage cart and pulled up to the train. Each jolt was agony for Franklin, but Calder and his men could not have been gentler as they passed him through a window into the waiting car. Eleanor was deeply grateful to the captain and promised to let him know how Franklin stood the trip as soon as they arrived in New York. Her thoughtfulness as well as Roosevelt's evoked the sea captain's admiration.

I went over to see Dr. Bennett yesterday afternoon and learned from him just how Mr. Roosevelt is taking everything. Isn't it wonderful to think how bravely and hopefully he is facing it all? . . . Say to Mr. Roosevelt that I carried his message to the engine driver who was so careful on the way to Ayer's Junction and he was more than proud.[20]

Calder also thanked her for the watch,

which I can accept from you and Mr. Roosevelt, as the spirit in which it is given is so different, also for the real good friendly note which accompanied the same. Who could dare be disloyal to a friend like you? I only hope that Anna can be just like you as she grows older.

In New York Franklin entered Presbyterian Hospital and his case was taken over by Dr. George Draper, Harvard friend and orthopedic specialist. Whether Franklin could recover the use of his leg muscles was wholly uncertain. "I told them very frankly that no one could tell them where they stood," Lovett advised Draper. The case was a mild one and Lovett thought that "complete recovery or partial recovery to any point was possible, that disability was not to be feared." But then he hedged; it could go either way, he admitted. It looked to him "as if some of the important muscles might be on the edge where they could be influenced either way—toward recovery, or turn into completely paralyzed muscles." The doctor's ambiguity heightened the strain on Eleanor. A little later Draper wrote Lovett that he was concerned about his patient's "very slow recovery both as regards the disappearance of *pain*, which is very generally present, and as to the recovery of even slight power to twitch the muscles." Draper shrank from the moment when they would have Franklin sit up and he would "be faced with the frightfully depressing knowledge that he cannot hold himself erect." He felt strongly that

the psychological factor in his management is paramount. He has such courage, such ambition, and yet at the same time such an extraordinarily sensitive emotional mechanism that it will take all the skill which we can muster to lead him successfully to a recognition of what he really faces without crushing him.[21]

Eleanor understood the psychological factor better than anyone. Franklin came back to New York believing he would soon be well enough to leave the hospital on crutches and resume work. At Campobello, all of them—Franklin, Louis, herself—had taken it for granted that he would soon be able to work again. They were returning to New York rather than Hyde Park, she had written Rosy, not only because that was where he could best be treated, but so that he could carry on his "various business activities." His determination to remain active was supported by his wife and by Louis, who underwrote his loyalty and faith in his friend's recovery by giving up his personal and family life and moving into the Roosevelt home in order to handle Franklin's affairs.

But the charade of a busy man of affairs which all three played at Campobello was based on the assumption of a relatively speedy and complete recovery. What would happen when Franklin realized that it might take years to regain the use of his legs or the even more somber possibility of permanent disablement? Any suggestion of retirement would diminish his recuperative powers, Dr. Draper felt. Eleanor was sure that if her husband was to hold onto the will to recover, he had to cling to his faith that he would return to politics and business.

Franklin was discharged from Presbyterian Hospital on October 28, but his record read "not improving" and some of the most painful days were ahead. At home he set about his exercises, but he was still running a temperature and his muscles were still tender.

Now the most excruciating pain began. The tendons behind his right knee began to jackknife and lock, and his legs had to be placed in plaster casts into which *wedges* were driven deeper and deeper, to stretch the muscles. It was as if his legs were on the rack. Not since Eleanor had seen her father go to have his leg rebroken had she witnessed such pain. But Franklin had a toughness and resilience her father had lacked, and he bore is stoically. He and Eleanor had taught the children to face illness and injury without tears or complaint; pain was to be borne silently. He followed his own Spartan precepts. Those who called him "feather duster," the political opponents who derided him as "Mama's boy," simply failed to see the iron fortitude behind the smiles and cheer. And if there were moments, as there must have been, when he was tempted to cry out against his fate, to surrender to his infirmities, Eleanor was there to brace him against them.

Their biggest problem was Sara. In her view, public service was an affair of *noblesse oblige*, not civic duty, and the life of a public man, especially of a politician, was less attractive than the quiet, secluded existence of a country gentleman. She now adamantly preached its virtues to Franklin and Eleanor. She was, moreover, genuinely afraid for her son. She was fearful that the callers whom Eleanor encouraged to come to the house sapped his vitality, that keeping up with his interests tired him. And she was sure that her mother's heart knew better than Franklin or Eleanor or Louis or the doctors what would speed his recovery. (She was not the only Hudson River matriarch with such views. Her good friend Mrs. Robert Livingston had prevailed upon her son to abandon the law and withdraw to the vacuous life of a country squire when his eyesight began to bother him. In later years his contemporaries, viewing his squandered talents, would say that Franklin had had Eleanor and Louis to save him from his mother while Robert Livingston had been unprotected.)[22] All through the winter a struggle between the two women went on, usually with politeness and courtesy but sometimes with acrimony.

As Franklin and Eleanor stood firm in the contest of wills, Louis became the target of Sara's resentment, but it was Eleanor who bore the brunt of the struggle. Sara could be ruthless. With her, family was all that counted, and she resented outsiders with whom her children had close relationships. When Louis moved into the house, rather than being grateful to him for thus "marrying himself irrevocably to his crippled friend's future," Sara doggedly fought the influence with Franklin and Eleanor of "that ugly, dirty little man," as she called him.[23] She found it difficult to be civil to him and, in disapproval, withdrew to Hyde Park.

Sara was not content simply to argue with Eleanor over Franklin's care; she also used the children, too young to understand what was going on, shaken by the sight of their splendid, spirited father prostrate, their house astir with strangers. Since they were also resentful of Louis, Sara played on their resentment, especially Anna's. She was fifteen years old and having a difficult time fitting in at Miss Chapin's, where she felt she was treated by students and teachers as an "outsider." "I hated it but Mother decided I had to like it because she hoped I would develop the same feeling for Miss Chapin that she had for Mlle. Souvestre. So it was a year of complete withdrawal on my part from Mother, and Granny was feeling very excluded too."[24]

Anna was supposed to have the large room with bath on the third floor, but Eleanor had turned it over to Louis, relegating Anna to a cubicle on the fourth floor. Eleanor was sharing a room with the youngest boys, sleeping on a cot, but Anna did not think of that: "I agreed completely with Granny that I was being discriminated against." Moreover, Anna was confused by her mother's switch in attitude toward Louis; Eleanor and Sara had always agreed about that "dirty little man," and now only Sara was being consistent.

Granny, with a good insight into my adolescent nature, started telling me that it was inexcusable that I, the only daughter of the family, should have a tiny bedroom in the back of the house, while Louis enjoyed a large, sunny front bedroom with his own private bath.

Granny's needling finally took root; at her instigation, I went to Mother one evening and demanded a switch in rooms. A sorely tried and harassed mother was naturally anything but sympathetic; in fact, she was very stern with her recalcitrant daughter.[25]

Eleanor carried a tremendous load. Since she was relieving the trained nurse, household arrangements could be complex. If she wanted to go out, as she did to take Anna to *Tosca* (she could not "resist seeing Anna at her first opera"), she had to make special arrangements with the nurse. Franklin wanted visitors and she saw to it that they came, but she also had to make sure they did not stay too long and would see them herself if necessary. Franklin had his ups and downs, and the one person with whom he did not have to dissemble was his wife.

"I am sorrier for you than Franklin," Caroline Phillips wrote from The Hague, "and I know what an ideal wife you are." It was, Eleanor said, the "most trying winter" in her life. Once Anna came upon her mother unexpectedly and found her slumped down in a chair, the picture of total dejection. Only Louis knew how to cope with Eleanor's moods. She must not give up in despair, he counseled; she had a great future, and so did Franklin. He could usually make her come out of her shell, but Anna only came to appreciate this later. At the time she was angry and resentful and it upset her to see Louis sitting in a comfortable armchair with her mother at his feet: "I would be violently jealous."[26]

Sara encouraged Anna to believe that her mother cared more for Louis than for her and this brought Eleanor close to the breaking point. Once that winter her self-discipline failed and the outward serenity and composure with which she usually guided the household shattered. She was reading to Franklin Jr. and John when she was suddenly swept by uncontrollable sobbing. The boys quickly left the room and so did Elliott, who happened to come in, saw his mother in tears, and fled. Louis tried to calm her but could do nothing. Finally she locked herself in a bathroom in her mother-in-law's house, until she was able to regain control. It was the only time that she went to pieces in that way, she said.

Sara's interference, on top of the burdens, was almost too much for Eleanor. "That old lady [Sara] with all her charm and distinction and kindliness hides a primitive jealousy of her daughter-in-law which is sometimes startling in its crudity," Caroline Phillips wrote in 1936 after a long talk with Helen Robinson in which she learned of the way Sara had used Anna against Eleanor.[27]

In the late spring of 1922 Anna came down with the measles and on top of that the mumps.[28] She was sent to Hyde Park, and when Franklin went to Boston to be fitted for braces, Eleanor went to Hyde Park too. One day Anna was writing a letter to her cousin, Helen Robinson, and "had just finished a few lines to the effect 'that the thing I like most about being up here is that Louis Howe is not up here,' when Mother walked in." Anna tried to hide the letter, but Eleanor sternly insisted that she wanted to read it. "I burst into tears," said Anna, "and gave it to her. She read it sitting at the end of the sofa and then said very coldly to me she would have to see to it I had no further contact with Louis the next winter when school started."

Sara was to take Anna and Jimmy to Europe later that month and the conversation turned to that.

Suddenly to my horror Mother burst into tears and out poured her unhappiness. She had always looked forward herself to taking Jimmy and me to Europe, but she did not have the money to do so. So Granny was.

Eleanor softened when she saw how upset Anna was and said "she would really try to make things easier for me with regard to Louis," Anna noted.

After this incident, mother and daughter began to open up to each other. Their rapprochement was strengthened as a result of a run-in between Anna and her father. One day Anna was on a ladder shifting some books in the library at Hyde Park while Franklin directed her from his wheelchair when an armful of books slipped and crashed to the floor. "I saw Father start, and an expression of pain passed swiftly over his face. My apologies were interrupted by his voice very sternly accusing me of being too careless for words and no help at all." Anna fled in tears and ran into Mother. To her I sobbed out my story and my grief. . . . Mother told me of the battle Father was waging against great odds; of the naturalness of his nervous reaction; how lucky we were to have him alive and to be able to help him get well; how much more patience and grit he had to have than we; until I felt very sheepish and even more ashamed—but in a different way, a more adult, understanding way. Back I went to the library where, of course, I not only found forgiveness but also a sincere and smilingly given invitation to resume my place on the library ladder.[29]

Whatever the strain, Eleanor did not yield to Sara. After it was all over, Dr. Draper told his sister, Alice Carter, that if it had not been for Eleanor and Mr. Howe, Franklin would have really become an invalid.[30] Eleanor refused to treat Franklin as an invalid and did not allow others to do so. The struggle with her mother-in-law was finally over. "She dominated me for years," Eleanor later said. Franklin's illness completed her emancipation "and made me stand on my own two feet in regard to my husband's life, my own life, and my children's training."[31] She and Franklin both emerged from the ordeal tempered, tested, and strengthened. If she had yielded to Sara, Eleanor later said, she would have become "a completely colorless echo of my husband and mother-in-law and torn between them. I might have stayed a weak character forever if I had not found that out."

27. *Her Husband's Stand-In*

ELEANOR ROOSEVELT now began a period of intensive public activity. Chroniclers of the Roosevelt era have studied her emergence in the years after her husband was stricken from the point of view primarily of the help it was to him. She became his stand-in with the Democrats. She kept his name before the public. She brought people to see him—key party officials and public personalities and the less well known whose points of view she felt should interest him.

All this was true. Equally true, although rarely noted either by herself because of modesty or by others because they were more concerned with Franklin Roosevelt, was her effectiveness in the organizations in which she worked. Interested in neither titles nor honors, she moved swiftly into positions of leadership. She became known for the honesty and vigor of her opinions. She accepted responsibility because there was a job to be done, and with the same ardent good will took on both "donkey work" and assignments that produced headlines. Her lack of pride and vanity and her sincere dedication to the public good inspired confidence in her fairness and judgment. By the time Franklin returned to political office some of the foremost women of the time, who had long been leaders in the struggle for women's rights, saw in Eleanor a new leader to whom they could pass on the torch.

Even before polio disabled Franklin, Louis had been encouraging her to take up interests of her own and to go into politics. As it became clear that Franklin would not return to public activity for a long time, Louis added an irresistible argument: Eleanor had to become actively involved in Democratic politics in order to keep alive Franklin's interest in the party and the party's interest in him. Doubtful as she was of her ability, once Louis put it to her as a matter of duty, his suggestions became easier for her to accept. And beneath the implacable promptings of conscience, there now were also the stirrings of ambition—the desire to show that she could succeed in this man's world of politics—and, even deeper, a repressed but sweetly satisfactory awareness that the fate of the man who had hurt her so deeply now depended upon the success she made of her work for him.

So when Nancy Cook, assistant to Harriet May Mills, chairman of the women's division of the Democratic State Committee, called to ask her to preside at a money-raising luncheon, she suppressed an impulse to say "no." Sara was among the hundred women gathered at the luncheon tables, and although she had undoubtedly come to give her daughter-in-law moral support, the presence of this increasingly critical lady could only have added to Eleanor's terror of the occasion. "I trembled so," she later wrote, "that I did not know whether I could stand up, and I am quite sure my voice could not be heard."[1] Since a few thousand dollars were raised as a result of her plea for funds, somebody must have heard her, and her performance was strong enough that she was subsequently asked to serve as chairman of the Finance Committee for the women's division. She invited Miss Cook, whose brisk enterprise she liked, to spend a week end at Hyde Park. Nancy was a striking, crisp-haired, crisp-voiced young woman with eager eyes, whose resourcefulness as an organizer and talents as a designer and craftsman (she was skilled at jewelry, pottery, copper, and brass work as well as cabinet making) made it easy for the members of the women's division to accept her managerial propensities. Through Nancy, Eleanor soon met Marion Dickerman, a soft-spoken, tall ("as a Gothic church window," someone said) woman of high principles and mournful countenance. They hailed from upstate New York, where they had been active in the suffrage movement, and had gone overseas to serve as volunteers in a British hospital. They returned home as the New York suffrage leaders were casting about for someone to run against Thad Sweet, the upstate Republican Speaker of the Assembly, who had blocked the progressive measures sponsored by the women. Finding that Marion lived in his district and was a Republican, they persuaded her to run against him. Nancy became her campaign manager. Backed by the Democrats, Socialists, Prohibitionists, and the women's groups, Marion's candidacy frightened Sweet sufficiently, though the district was traditionally Republican, that his backers slashed the tires of the women's cars, denied them halls to meet in, pressured the local printers to refuse their work. Marion lost but doubled the vote against Sweet. Harriet Mills was impressed with Nancy's work and asked her to come to New York City to work with her. Marion came down too, to teach and to work for the Foreign Policy Association. They found an apartment in Greenwich Village. Marion came with Nancy to Hyde Park.[2] That was the way the friendship began. During the next few years Nancy, Marion, and Eleanor were almost inseparable.

On Franklin's urging, Eleanor put in as much time in Dutchess County politics as she did at the offices of the State Committee. An upstate Democrat had to have a firm local footing, Franklin felt, if he was not to be at the mercy of the New York bosses. He also believed that Democratic weakness upstate was a result of the neglect and apathy of those same bosses toward upstate issues and that systematic hard work could diminish, if not overcome, Republican upstate majorities. Franklin was the strategist and Eleanor the chief of the troops at his command. She and John Mack's daughter set out to organize the women in the county. That meant more speaking, and Louis took her in hand and coached her. He came to her meetings, sat at the back of the hall, and afterward gave her his critique. He was hard on her nervous giggle: "Have something to say, say it, and then sit down," was his terse advice.

The 1922 State Democratic convention was to take place at the end of September. William Randolph Hearst had gubernatorial aspirations. Franklin backed Al Smith and undertook to mobilize upstate support for him and especially to ensure a Dutchess County delegation committed to the former governor. Henry Morgenthau, Jr., helped, as did Mack, Tom Lynch, and Eleanor, who was his most tireless worker. She presided over a Dutchess County luncheon at which Elinor Morgenthau offered an anti-Hearst resolution that was unanimously adopted. She met the press and fired away at the Republicans: "It is impossible to be both a Republican and a progressive under the leadership of Governor Miller in this State."[3] She gave a picnic at Hyde Park for the wives of forty upstate mayors. She and Franklin received the Odd Fellows and Rebeccas at Hyde Park. One evening that summer as dessert was being served, Eleanor rose and said she had to go to speak in the Village. "It's only beginning," Rosy laughingly warned his younger half brother. "Once they mount the soapbox, mark my words, they never get off."[4]

Sara, who was in Europe with Anna and James, seemed to be feeling more benevolent about Eleanor's activities. "Eleanor's work among the women, will, I trust, bear fruit," she wrote Franklin.[5] Despite her political chores Eleanor took a refresher course in driving, and three times a week chauffeured Franklin and the two youngest children to Vincent Astor's place in Rhinebeck to use his "swimming tank." There were mishaps. "Your running into our gate post was all right," Sara comforted her, "so long as you were not hurt."[6]

On August 13 Franklin addressed an open letter to Smith calling on him to run again, as the choice of "the average citizen," Smith said he was available. A telegram from Louis in Syracuse to Franklin in Hyde Park described the outcome: "AL NOMINATED WITH GREAT ENTHUSIASM. MORGENTHAU AND YOUR MISSUS LED THE DUTCHESS COUNTY DELEGATION WITH THE BANNER THREE TIMES AROUND THE HALL . . ." "Everything went along first rate," Smith wrote Roosevelt after the convention. "I had quite a session with our lady politicians as Mrs. Roosevelt no doubt told you. I was delighted to see her taking an active part and I am really sorry that you could not be there but take care of yourself —there is another day coming."[7]

The "lady politicians" had demanded two places on the ticket, but when Smith pledged to appoint women to high places in his administration, they gave way.

During the campaign Eleanor worked mainly in Dutchess County and learned how party politics worked on the village level. What she saw was not pleasant, especially the purchase of votes, but rather than withdraw in well-bred disgust, she was spurred on to work harder. On Election Day she chauffeured voters to the polls in the family Buick. The Republican margin in the county for Miller, which had been 6,200 in 1920, was reduced to little over 1,000. "I think what has been done in the county is amazing," Mrs. Norrie wrote approvingly to Franklin, "and I believe, now the start is made, a great deal more can be done."[8] So did Franklin and Eleanor. He was having a "strenuous time" over Hudson River politics, Franklin wrote a few months later. "We are doing some fine organizing work—especially with the aid of the ladies."[9]

"What job is Smith going to give you?" Hall wrote her from the West

Coast after Smith's landslide election,[10] but a job on the public payroll was not what Eleanor had in mind. She was in politics primarily to serve her husband's purposes and beyond that to advance a point of view that began to take shape in her mind as she took on increasing responsibilities in the party. It was crystallized in an article entitled "Why I Am a Democrat," which the Junior League *Bulletin* asked her to write and which was to be run with one by Mrs. John Pratt on "Why I Am a Republican."[11]

She first discussed political parties and why principles, not personalities, should govern one's party allegiance. She felt that the Democratic party gave higher priority to human needs than did the Republican party. "On the whole the Democratic Party seems to have been more concerned with the welfare and interests of the people at large, and less with the growth of big business interests." Her next point showed how far she had moved from the viewpoint of the group with whom she had been raised.

If you believe that a nation is really better off which achieves for a comparative few, those who are capable of attaining it, high culture, ease, opportunity, and that these few from their enlightenment should give what they consider best to those less favored, then you naturally belong to the Republican Party. But if you believe that people must struggle slowly to the light for themselves, then it seems to me that you are logically a Democrat.

This Jeffersonian trust in the people was even more strongly reflected in Eleanor's growing involvement with the Women's Trade Union League. Founded in 1903 by Jane Addams and others "to aid women workers in their efforts to organize . . . and to secure better conditions," the Women's Trade Union League was the most militant women's group, and many of its leaders were aligned with the socialist movement. Eleanor joined the league in 1922 after attending a luncheon at the invitation of Mrs. James Lees Laidlaw. Rose Schneiderman, a redheaded packet of social dynamite who directed the New York League, said she first met Eleanor at a tea given by Mrs. Willard Straight to interest her friends in purchasing a home for the league. Rose was captivated by Eleanor's "simplicity" and "her lovely eyes." Eleanor was interested in Rose, too, and invited her to Sunday night supper at Sixty-fifth Street. While Eleanor scrambled eggs in a chafing dish and the silver coffee urn burbled, Rose recalled, "We talked about the work I was doing. Mrs. Roosevelt asked many questions but she was particularly interested in why I thought women should join unions."[12]

Rose and her associate, Maud Swartz, who had received her trade-union training in the British labor movement and was full of amusing stories about the trials and tribulations of a labor organizer, represented a new kind of friendship for Eleanor. Esther and Elizabeth, Nan and Marion, came of old American stock and were cultivated, well-bred women. But Rose, who had emigrated from Russian Poland and whose accent was still marked by the Lower East Side, was a fiery soapboxer. Her speech after the Triangle fire in 1911, the *New York Times* reporter said, brought emotion "to a snapping point." It took some time before Eleanor ventured to ask Sara to invite Rose and Maud to Hyde Park, as Sara was almost feudal in outlook. "She judged people almost solely by their social position," Eleanor later wrote, but "only people who knew her well could tell when she was really being rude."[13] "Of course, I can understand the point of view to which Cousin Susie and Sally arrive (a la Ku Klux)," Hall commiserated with her,

but could never contemplate its use as they see it their duty to inflict same. If I lived in New York we should either never meet or else they would "lay off" of personalities. My feeling of the entire tribe is that they lack sympathy (original Greek meaning). I am only disturbed lest my children be brought up in the atmosphere of protection and utter uselessness to society.[14]

Eleanor went to work for the Trade Union League with the energy and thoroughness that characterized all her undertakings. While Dorothy Straight raised the $20,000 to make a down payment on a five-story brownstone at 247 Lexington Avenue, Eleanor, assisted by Mrs. Thomas W. Lamont, agreed to head up a committee to raise funds to pay off the mortgage, which in the end amounted to $35,000. Evening classes for women workers were organized at the new headquarters, and Eleanor came one night a week to read to the girls—to teach and to be taught. Marion Dickerman taught a class in literature. In 1925 Eleanor invited Rose and Maud to Campobello, and when she had to leave briefly while they were there she left the two women in charge of Franklin Jr. and Johnny and two of their friends. She had "more faith" in Maud Swartz handling the boys, she wrote Franklin, than she did in their tutor.[15]

Eleanor explained to her sons what the two women were doing and asked if they would like to give a Christmas party for the children of WTUL members. The boys agreed, but Sara was horrified. The diseases the two boys might pick up. . . . But this argument no longer carried weight with Eleanor. When she shyly approached Rose with the proposal, Rose was delighted. The invitations went out from Franklin Jr. and Johnny; Nancy Cook dressed the Christmas tree; Eleanor purchased the gifts—clothing, roller skates, dolls—and a cornucopia of candy for each child. At the last moment her boys balked; they could not understand "giving" presents: Christmas was a time for "getting" presents. They were more reconciled to their role the following year when it was explained to them that they were, in fact, deputies of Santa Claus.[16] For the Roosevelt boys this was their first contact with children of the slums and with trade unions. For their mother, it was another manifestation of a radical equalitarianism.

A Christmas party for slum children might still be considered in the Lady Bountiful tradition, even if it was under trade-union auspices, if it had not been buttressed by Eleanor's systematic work on behalf of league objectives—the forty-eight hour week, minimum wages, the abolition of child labor, the right to organize. She had become an influential figure in the League of Women Voters, the Women's City Club, and especially in the Democratic party, and wherever she carried weight, she rallied support for league programs. "Always generous and understanding, she never refused me anything I asked her," Rose wrote; for her part, Rose taught Eleanor all that she knew about trade unionism.[17]

Through Eleanor, Rose and Maud also became Franklin's teachers and spent many hours with him. Frances Perkins later said that Franklin's whole attitude toward trade unions might have been different had he not seen the theory and history of the trade-union movement through the eyes of these women. A labor leader once said to Madam Perkins that "you'd almost think he had participated in some strike or organizing campaign the way he knew and felt about it," and she credited his comprehension and grasp to the hours he had spent with Rose and her associates.[18]

In her article for the Junior League *Bulletin* on why she was a Democrat Eleanor had listed as a final reason the party's approach to the prevention of another war. The Democrats, she felt, were "more conscious of our world responsibility and more anxious to see some steps taken toward international cooperation than were the Republicans." It was a mild statement of the case. The times were not hospitable to militant advocacy of the League of Nations; the mood of the country was indifference, the policy of the Harding administration isolationist. Franklin, who had become head of the Woodrow Wilson Foundation, muted his support of the League and sought instead to keep an interest in Wilsonian principles alive. Wilson's attitude toward Franklin softened, especially after polio made Franklin a fellow in suffering. They exchanged letters, and when Eleanor went to Washington she called on Mrs. Wilson.

When Wilson died in early February, 1924, Franklin was on his houseboat in Florida waters. "I wired Mrs. Wilson today for us both," Eleanor wrote Franklin; "a people had never more surely contributed to a man's breakdown."[19] The president "must have been glad to go." She was aghast at Lodge's fulsome tribute to the dead president in the Senate: "I must say if I had been Lodge I would not have made his speech in the Senate, would you?" She took Anna to the hastily organized memorial service in New York at Madison Square Garden, which "was really almost filled even in the top gallery. Mr. John Davis and several others made good speeches but Rabbi Wise made the most stirring one."[20] That gifted orator called on his listeners to "embalm in oblivion the names and deeds of those who, to punish your and my leader—the hope-bringer of mankind—struck him down and broke the heart of the world!"

Franklin thought Wilson's death might help revive bipartisan faith in Wilson's ideals, but to Eleanor it seemed that the country was "so seething in partisan politics just now, it would seem hard to lift any subject out of them."[21] She spoke from melancholy personal experience. A promising and substantial effort to move international cooperation back into the realm of practical politics was foundering in a flare-up of faction and cowardice.

The previous May, Edward M. Bok, the former editor and publisher of the *Ladies' Home Journal* and a talented publicist, had proposed a nationwide competition for "the best practicable plan by which the U.S. may cooperate with other nations to achieve and preserve the peace of the world." To stimulate interest in the contest he offered $100,000 as the prize, half to go to the winner on the selection of the plan and the other half to be given to him when the plan received serious consideration in the Senate. It was, as the *New York Times* said, one of the most "princely" prizes ever offered for a noncommercial idea. Bok asked Esther Lape to direct the project, and she agreed to do so if she could have Eleanor Roosevelt work with her as a member of the policy committee. Bok readily agreed, and to establish the nonpartisan character of the competition they also asked Mrs. Frank Vanderlip, a Republican, to join the initial group.

The competition was announced on July 2, 1923. It was the lead story in the *New York Times* and rated headlines in all the great metropolitan dailies. "Isn't the American Peace Award going fine?" an exultant Bok wrote Franklin a month later, "and surely a great deal of the credit is due to that wonderful wife of yours. I am wondering whether she and Esther Lape ever sleep!"[22] Eleanor and Esther had assembled an impressive policy committee and had persuaded the big national organizations to set up a cooperating council. "She has been very busy with the Bok Award," Franklin wrote Hall. "I think it is a fine thing for Bok to start and will undoubtedly do much to hasten our eventual participation in world reconstruction, though I doubt if we see any immediate results. What do you think of it?"[23] Hall was more skeptical of its producing results: "The voting public of this part of the world, at least," he wrote, "has fallen into a state of lethargy as regards cooperation with the European Powers." Esther asked Franklin for a statement on the award. He was cautious. "I handed out a serious protest against the title," Roosevelt wrote Bok, "on the ground that it might make people think that we could get permanent peace by the mere establishment of a formula."[24]

With a quarter of a million inquiries and plans pouring in by the thousands, Eleanor was more sanguine than her husband and brother. The purpose of the competition, she said in her speeches, was not only to focus public thinking upon the form of association Americans felt their country ought to have with the rest of the world, but to submit the winning plan to the supreme test of practicality—passage in the Senate. "Esther wants me to do rather a job at the Bok office the next few weeks," she wrote Franklin at the end of October (the deadline for entries was November 15, 1923). "I told her after Election I'd devote my major activities to her and let up a bit on the Democrats!" On the closing day of the contest 700 plans were received, bringing the total to 22,165. "Amazing indeed, is the interest that has been called forth from every part of the country, and from every walk of life," the *Times* commented. On January 7 the winning plan was released. Again it was the lead story in the *Times*, which also published the full text. Briefly stated, it called for U. S. entry into the World Court and conditional support for the League of Nations, in effect cooperation without membership.

Promptly the Senate isolationists raised the cry that it was "a pro-League proposal pure and simple." An inquiry was launched headed by Senators Reed and Moses, two leading "irreconcilables," designed to show that the competition was a sinister propaganda exercise, that it was a rigged contest, and that the committee of jurors had been packed. Women crowded the hearing room, with Alice Longworth in a privileged seat on a huge leather sofa in back of the committee. Bok was treated with kid gloves at the hearing but Reed's examination of Esther Lape was so severe that other Senators chivalrously came to her aid. How was the policy committee chosen, Reed demanded. Mrs. Roosevelt was the first one invited to join, Esther replied, and then Mrs. Vanderlip; Mr. Bok had left the selection of the remainder to the three women. "Do you mean that you three ladies then selected the rest of the members of the Policy Committee?" Reed asked incredulously. He was not alone in his outrage at such female presumption. "THREE WOMEN ENGINEERED BOK PEACE PRIZE CONTEST," was the Republican *New York Herald*'s headline. "The great Bok peace prize contest," the head of the *Herald*'s Washington bureau wrote, "was managed by two matrons of social distinction and a highly educated and most efficient young unmarried woman." Front-page photographs of Eleanor, Esther, and Mrs. Vanderlip accompanied the story. Franklin's unofficial press representative in Washington, Marvin McIntyre, came up to Esther, Elizabeth, and Eleanor after the committee excused Esther. "I think we're a thousand percent!" he told them. Miss Lape was one of "the most marvellously acute witnesses" to appear on the Hill, the *Boston Transcript* correspondent wrote. "They never went on with the hearings," Esther said. "They used Wilson's illness as a pretext to adjourn them."[25] But the isolationist orators called the Bok Peace Award a "peace-at-any-price" enterprise and equated internationalism with treason.

When Eleanor and Esther went to Washington March 17 to try to persuade some senators merely to introduce the winning plan, they were treated with cordiality and friendliness, but they were turned down. "It is discouraging to see people on an errand like this," Eleanor wrote her husband. "They have so little courage! They agree that their private views are met but the party isn't for it!"[26]

For Eleanor it was an intense education in the substantive issues as well as the politics of internationalism. Together with Esther and Elizabeth she read all of the entries, twenty of which Esther published in a book called *Ways to Peace*. The contest also helped Franklin crystallize his thinking on international cooperation. He had little sympathy for the isolationists ("You have doubtless seen the grand hullabaloo in the Senate over the Bok Peace Award," he wrote George Marvin. "What fools Reed, Moses, etc. are. Eleanor is just back from Washington, where she went to hold Esther Lape's hand"), but he also had a healthy respect for political realities.

My objection to the accepted plan is that it is not practicable, i.e. politically practicable. The dear judges must have known that in choosing that plan they would revive the League of Nations very largely along existing lines. My plan avoided this by providing for an International Conference to establish a brand new permanent International organization.[27]

Because of his wife's membership on the policy committee, Franklin had not submitted his plan, but he did show it to Esther and it shaped his own approach to international cooperation when he was president.* The fundamental commitment to internationalism was there, but as a politician he thought it prudent to avoid open battle. Perhaps he felt he was bearing sufficient witness to the internationalist cause through the activities of his wife; since the public identified her advocacy with his convictions, that added to his reputation as a statesman without increasing the risks to him as a politician. He lapsed into relative silence but Eleanor pressed on. Public opinion admittedly was apathetic, even hostile; all the more reason to go forward with the work of education and organization. In her engagement book she transcribed the lines

> Never dreamed, though right were worsted
> Wrong would triumph,
> Held we fall to rise, are baffled to fight better.

The peace-award group evolved into the American Foundation, whose main purpose was to work with those who shaped national opinion to promote U. S. entry into the World Court. Esther was the member-in-charge, Elizabeth the foundation's legal scholar, Eleanor the activist. A succinct statement on the "next step" in international cooperation that Eleanor wrote in 1925 when the House of Representatives approved U. S. participation in the World Court's activities and for a brief moment it looked as if U. S. acceptance was certain, revealed that although she would not compromise on goals, she advocated being flexible on tactics; a strong sense of practicality tempered her utopianism. Her speech was prepared for a meeting of women's clubs, and Louis went over it and made a few changes, chiefly shortening some of her sentences. Entry into the World Court was a first step in America's acceptance of its international responsibilities, she stated. She was concerned with the "attitude of mind" with which a next step should be approached:

Many of us have fixed ideas of what we think our own country and the various other countries of the world should do, but if we rigidly adhere, each to our own point of view, we will progress not at all. We should talk together with open minds and grasp anything which is a step forward; not hold out for our particular, ultimate panacea. Keep it in our minds, of course, but remember that all big changes in human history have been arrived at slowly and through many compromises.

The speech also showed how strongly her approach to politics was grounded in religious conviction:

The basis of world peace is the teaching which runs through almost all the great religions of the world, 'Love thy neighbor as thyself.' Christ, some of the other great Jewish teachers, Buddha, all preached it. Their followers forgot it. What is the trouble between capital and labor, what is the trouble in many of our communities, but rather a universal forgetting that this teaching is one of our first obligations. When we center on our own home, our own family, our own business, we are neglecting this fundamental obligation of every human being and until it is acknowledged and fulfilled we cannot have world peace.

---

* It is Esther Lape's recollection that Franklin did submit his plan and that "his objection to the winning plan was simply that it was not his."

Peace was "the question of the hour," and for the women "this should be a crusade":

The abolition of war touches them more nearly than any other question. Now when many of the nations of the world are at peace and we still remember vividly the horrors of 1914–1918 and know fairly generally what the next war will mean, now is the time to act. Usually only the experts, technical people, busy with war plans know, but at the moment we all know that the next war will be a war in which people not armies will suffer, and our boasted, hard-earned civilization will do us no good. Cannot the women rise to this great opportunity and work now, and not have the double horror, if another war comes, of losing their loved ones, and knowing that they lifted no finger when they might have worked hard?[28]

28. The 1924 Campaign

SHORTLY AFTER the Bok Peace Award controversy quieted down and Eleanor was again concentrating on politics, Josephus Daniels wrote Franklin that he was relieved to learn that

I am not the only "squaw" man in the country. . . . I think the *World* showed good taste when it announced that you were taking the helm of the Smith campaign they published the picture of your wife. I have had that experience on similar occasions and have always wondered how the newspapermen knew so well who was at the head of the family.

Franklin replied in the same tone:

You are right about the squaws! Like you I have fought for years to keep my name on the front page and to relegate the wife's to the advertising section. My new plan, however, seems admirable—hereafter for three years my name will not appear at all, but each fourth year (Presidential ones) I am to have all the limelight. Why don't you adopt this too? It will make it much easier to put that Democratic national ticket of Daniels and Roosevelt across in 1928 or 1932.[1]

Was Franklin wholly jesting? In less than two years Eleanor had moved into a position of state leadership. Newspapers called her for statements and she was beginning to speak over the radio as well as on the stump. Her voice was still high, sometimes shrill, but her speaking style had improved and she gamely stuck by the rules Louis had laid down. The traits of helpfulness, modesty, and energy that made her universally admired within the family now inspired equal admiration in the public arena.

Franklin esteemed his wife's abilities highly, but he never happily surrendered the limelight to anyone. "Eleanor has been leading an even more hectic life than usual," he wrote Rosy. "Bok Peace Award, investigation by the Senate, Democratic females, in Philadelphia, etc. etc.—I think when I go away she will be more quiet as she will have to stay home more!"[2]

Eleanor understood how difficult it was for Franklin not to be front and center, especially in politics. "You need not be proud of me, dear," she wrote him on February 6, 1924:

I'm only being *active* till you can be again—it isn't such a great desire on my part to serve the world and I'll fall back into habits of sloth quite easily! Hurry up for as you know my ever present sense of the uselessness of all things will overwhelm me sooner or later!

She had a stoic, almost fatalist, sense of resignation, yet like Marcus Aurelius, whose *Meditations* she admired, she was strongly motivated by a sense of the efficacy of moral effort. If the two attitudes were contradictory, it is a contradiction philosophers have never been able to resolve.

Directed by Franklin, coached by Louis, with a group of highly able women as co-workers—Esther, Elizabeth, Nancy, Marion, Caroline O'Day (widow of a Standard Oil heir), Elinor Morgenthau, Rose and Maud, a group to which in 1924 was added Mary W. Dewson, the new civic secretary of the Women's City Club—she was becoming a major force in public life. Whenever Eleanor was mentioned, wrote Isabella, who was now Mrs. John Greenway, "I say 'there is probably the greatest woman of this generation!' " A great many people were beginning to feel that way about her.

She made her office in the women's division of the Democratic State Committee. Caroline O'Day, socially prominent and strongly antiwar, had succeeded Harriet May Mills as chairman and Eleanor was chairman of the Finance Committee. Their efforts to organize the women, especially in the rural counties where there was no men's organization, and to obtain recognition from the men, involved hard, often tedious work. Eleanor's journeyings with Nancy Cook or Marion Dickerman were fragmentarily recorded in her engagement book: "Left Massena in the rain. . . . The man Nan wanted to see was away." "Ran out of gas" in Ithaca and "searched for Mrs. T. unsuccessfully." "A good supper at St. James, proprietor a Democrat." "Gloversville—lovely country—meeting about 20 women and stayed till 3." Although they had requested modest lodgings, in one hotel they were ushered into a "palatial suite. . . . Think F.D.R. may have to send us money to get home on."

By the spring of 1924 all but five counties of the state were organized, and the men were impressed. "Organization is something to which they are always ready to take off their hats," Eleanor said, but she realized how much women still had to learn before they would belong to the game as completely as did the men. In an interview with Rose Feld of the *Times* she related what she told women as she went around the state. "They have the vote, they have the power, but they don't seem to know what to do with it." Their lack of progress stemmed from the hostility of the men, and Eleanor summed up the real masculine attitude toward women in politics:

You are wonderful. I love and honor you. . . . Lead your own life, attend to your charities, cultivate yourself, travel when you wish, bring up the children, run your house, I'll give you all the freedom you wish and all the money I can but—leave me my business and politics.

Her message to women was: "Get into the game and stay in it. Throwing mud from the outside won't help. Building up from the inside will."

A woman needed to learn the machinery of politics; then she would know how "to checkmate as well as her masculine opponent. Or it may be that with time she will learn to make an ally of her opponent, which is even better politics."[3]

At the Democratic state convention in April, 1924, called to launch the Smith boom for the presidential nomination, Eleanor led the women in rebellion against male monopolization of power. The issue was the selection of the delegates-at-large; the prime antagonist was Charles F. Murphy, the Tammany boss. "I have wanted you home the last few days," she wrote Franklin on the eve of the Albany meeting,

to advise me on the fight I'm putting up on two delegates and two alternates at large. Mr. Murphy and I disagree as to whether the men leaders shall name them or whether we shall, backed by the written endorsement of 49 Associate County Chairmen. I imagine it is just a question of which he dislikes most, giving me my way or having me give the papers a grand chance for a story by telling the whole story at the women's dinner Monday night and by insisting on recognition on the floor of the convention and putting the names in nomination. There's one thing I'm thankful for I haven't a thing to lose and for the moment you haven't either.[4]

Murphy held firm and Eleanor raised the flag of rebellion at the women's dinner at the Hotel Ten Eyck.

"We have now had the vote for four years and some very ardent suffragists seem to feel that instead of gaining in power the women have lost," she challenged her audience. If women wanted to achieve the objectives for which they had fought in winning the right to vote, they must not limit themselves to casting a ballot. "They must gain for themselves a place of real equality and the respect of the men,"[5] and that meant working "with" the men, not "for" them.

Then she went on with great deliberation,

It is always disagreeable to take stands. It is always easier to compromise, always easier to let things go. To many women, and I am one of them, it is extraordinarily difficult to care about anything enough to cause disagreement or unpleasant feelings, but I have come to the conclusion that this must be done for a time until we can prove our strength and demand respect for our wishes. We cannot even be of real service in the coming campaign and speak as a united body of women unless we have the respect of the men and show that when we express a wish, we are willing to stand by it.

The next day she headed a committee that called on Governor Smith, and when he supported the women's demands, Murphy capitulated. "Upstate women at the Democratic convention won the principal points in their contention that the selection of women delegates and alternates-at-large should be made by them rather than by Charles F. Murphy and other men leaders," the *New York Times* reported. "We go into the campaign feeling that our party has recognized us as an independent part of the organization and are encouraged accordingly," Eleanor told the press. "No better evidence could be shown that it is to the Democratic Party that the women voters of this State must turn if they desire to take a real part in political affairs." Governor Smith, she added, had been "a powerful factor" in bringing about this "very satisfactory conclusion."

That afternoon she presented the resolution to the convention that the

New York State delegates to the Democratic national convention should be pledged to the governor. The resolution was adopted with a shout, and the chairman appointed Eleanor and Miss Martha Byrne to go to the governor's office to escort him to the platform. "It was Mrs. Roosevelt," noted the *New York Times* editorial, "a highly intelligent and capable politician," who introduced the Smith resolution at the convention.[6] The *Times* considered that a mark in Smith's favor.

The fight at the state convention she won, but the next she lost. Cordell Hull, chairman of the Democratic National Committee, appointed her chairman of a subcommittee of Democratic women to canvass the women's organizations and formulate planks on social-welfare legislation to submit to the Platform Committee at the national convention. The subcommittee she assembled was a strong one—the veteran Texas reformer, Minnie Fisher Cunningham, Mrs. Dorothy Kirchwey Brown of Massachusetts, who headed the Child Welfare Committee of the League of Women Voters, Mrs. Norrie, Elinor Morgenthau, Maud Swartz, Gertrude Ely, liberal Democrat from Bryn Mawr, Charl Williams of Tennessee, who was credited with lobbying through that state's legislature the final vote needed for ratification of the suffrage amendment, and Mrs. Solon R. Jacobs, former Alabama member of the Democratic National Committee and influential in the League of Women Voters. The subcommittee held hearings and drafted strong pro-league and Prohibition enforcement planks, equal pay for women workers and a federal department of education, but its major objective was to commit the party to a resolution calling on the states to ratify the child-labor amendment. When the male-dominated Resolutions Committee rejected this proposal, Eleanor's committee sat outside its doors until the early hours of the morning demanding that it reconsider. The Resolutions Committee refused, by a vote of 22 to 18.

The resolute fight Eleanor and her friends made for progressive planks distinguished her group from two other claimants to leadership among women. One was Miss Elizabeth Marbury, who had been Democratic national committeewoman from New York since the passage of the suffrage amendment, for which she had fought. Though a remarkable woman, Miss Marbury gave the men no trouble; her chief interest in politics in the twenties, except for her opposition to Prohibition, was social, and her salon was famous for its mingling of high figures from the world of politics, fashion, and art. Eleanor and her colleagues were on good terms with her, but simply bypassed her. On the other side there were the embattled females of the Woman's party, who were too masculine for Eleanor's taste. Moreover, she thought the Woman's party opposition to protective legislation for women on the basis of equal rights was downright reactionary.

Although Eleanor's group was defeated in the Resolutions Committee, forces were gathering that in time would give them what they sought in the field of social-welfare legislation, including the abolition of child labor. Franklin Roosevelt returned to the political wars to nominate Alfred E. Smith with a speech that Walter Lippmann said was "perfect in temper and manner and most eloquent in its effect" and lifted the convention for a moment above "faction and hatred."

The national convention over, Roosevelt returned to his exercises, happy to have a legitimate reason to stand aside from the doomed national campaign, but Eleanor was deeply involved, more in support of the re-election of Smith as governor than in the campaign of John W. Davis. Because the national party had evaded the issue of ratification of the child-labor amendment, she was the more determined that the state convention should not. She appeared before the Platform Committee carrying a mandate from thirty women's organizations to urge a child-labor plank, and it was approved. She also represented the Women's Trade Union League in a plea for planks on the eight-hour day and minimum-wage legislation and these, too, were included in the platform.

Her speech seconding the renomination of Smith was one of the state convention's high points. A day earlier the Republicans had nominated her cousin Theodore Roosevelt, Jr., to oppose Smith, the same cousin who had called Franklin "a maverick" Roosevelt in 1920. Salt had recently been rubbed into that wound by Nicholas Longworth. "Mama is wild over Nick L. having called you in a speech a 'denatured Roosevelt,' " Eleanor wrote Franklin. Nick "was just trying to be funny," she told Sara, but she, too, was angry.[7]

"Of course he [Smith] can win," Eleanor said in her seconding speech. "How can he help it when the Republican convention yesterday did everything to help him?" The delegates did not miss the thrust, and applauded appreciatively. In the spring she had feigned concern because Louis Howe had rejoiced that some of the oil from the Teapot Dome scandal had spattered Teddy.[8] "I told him I was ashamed of such vindictiveness but he's been waiting to get even he says a long time!" In the campaign Louis' "vindictiveness" went further, and now he was actively abetted by Eleanor. Louis persuaded Eleanor and her lady Democrats to follow Teddy around the state in a motorcade that featured a huge teakettle spouting steam, and in her speeches Eleanor referred to her cousin as "a personally nice young man whose public service record shows him willing to do the bidding of his friends." Eleanor later said the teakettle affair was a "rough stunt."[9] The Oyster Bay clan sizzled, Louis beamed, and we may assume that Franklin shed few tears.

There is a glimpse of Eleanor on the stump in the upstate rural areas, in her own words.

"I guess you're campaigning," the speaker, a bedraggled woman who looked fifty but probably was thirty, stood beside our car. . . . We were on a narrow back road in a hilly country and we were campaigning so we acknowledged it and asked her politics, meanwhile taking a look at the farm and buildings. Everything bespoke a helpless struggle, the poor land, run down buildings, the general look of dirt and untidiness so we were not surprised to hear "Oh, I ain't got much time for politics but Mr. Williams the R.F.D. man says I must vote for Coolidge because he ain't had a chance yet and I've always been a Republican anyways."

"No," she went on, "he ain't done much as I can see for farmers, leastways I never had a worse time. . . ."[10]

Eleanor was one of the few New York Democrats who stumped in the rural districts, and her talks with farmer's wives shaped her approach to agricultural distress. Her theme was rural-urban interdependence, which placed her in disagreement with those who felt that a conflict between city and countryside was inevitable. "I live in both city and country and so realize that the best interests of both are to be promoted by better understanding of each other's situation and cooperation rather than conflict." Because city problems had been so obvious "all of the best brains in the land have concentrated on solving them" and things had improved, and rural backwardness could also be overcome "if city and country people will consider the rural problem as a joint problem vital to both and give their best thought to solving one of the greatest problems confronting our nation today."[11]

Coolidge swamped Davis, who drew only 24 per cent of the vote, not much better than LaFollette's 16 per cent. But in New York, despite the Republican landslide, Smith won re-election.

29. *Life without Father*

BY THE END OF the 1924 election campaign she had become one of the busiest women in New York public life, but her responsibilities as wife, mother, and daughter-in-law were in no way diminished. A crippled husband needed more attention than ever before, both during the months when he was in New York attending to business and politics and the household revolved about him, and in the long stretches when he was away from New York in search of recovery and had to be kept in touch with every household detail and especially with his growing children.

Franklin's determination to recover the use of his legs turned into a hunt for warm waters and balmy skies. He had discovered in Vincent Astor's heated swimming tank that his legs regained some of their power in warm water. In early winter 1923 he rented a houseboat, the *Weona II*, on which he drifted through the waters off Florida in search of good fishing and sandy beaches, and this was to be his pattern for four winters. In the summer he went to Marion, Massachusetts, to work with Dr. William McDonald on the exercises that this outstanding neurologist had devised for polio victims.

While Franklin was away Eleanor remained in New York on Sixty-fifth Street and had to be both father and mother to the children, who in 1924 ranged in age from eight (John) to eighteen (Anna). Alone, too, she had to bear the brunt of Sara's harassment and discontent.

She made it seem easy and effortless, but a few lines in a thinly veiled autobiographical article that she wrote for *Vogue* in 1930 suggested how difficult those years were for her and her loneliness in facing them.

Her husband was a busy man, loving her and loving his children, but as she sat there she realized clearly that for years to come other interests must come first with him and the irony of ironies she, who just now was groping for help, must be the one to make these other claims seem all important because she knew so well that without them the man would never be satisfied, and would never feel completely fulfilled.[1]

Her major comfort was Louis. Except for week ends which he spent with his family in Fall River, he lived in the house. Eleanor had moved him up to the fourth floor, but he came to breakfast, was often at dinner, and was always ready to counsel her. There was little she did not talk over with him. The children continued to be resentful of Louis. "I had the room next to his," James recalled.

We shared the bathroom. I thought him some kind of buddhist monk who burned incense. I didn't realize until later it was some kind of a health thing. I kind of resented the fact that he lived in the house and only later realized his contribution to Mother and Father.[2]

Sara remained a source of anxiety. The more confidently Eleanor formulated her views on the rearing of children, the more firmly she resisted Sara's interference, but the older woman had her own ways of bending the children to her will. "Those were the years," Franklin Jr. recalled, "when Granny referred to us as 'my children. Your mother only bore . . . you.' "[3] She countermanded Franklin and Eleanor by permitting the children to have things their parents withheld as a form of discipline. If she felt neglected, she would threaten to leave the offenders out of her will. "She would sometimes say before all the children together—'. . . is nicer to me than the rest of you. I think I will leave my money to him.' "[4]

James and Elliott were at Groton, but Anna, Franklin Jr., and Johnny were at home, the boys at the Buckley School, Anna finishing at Miss Chapin's. Eleanor arranged for each of the children in turn to spend part of their holidays with their father. She was in touch with Franklin's many friends who wanted to visit him—the Ledyards, de Rhams, Tom Lynch, Livy Davis, the Morgenthaus, Sir Oswald and Lady Cynthia Mosley. Disabled though Franklin was, he was usually gay and full of high jinks, and people were more than ever drawn to him.

Eleanor could squeeze in only brief visits, but she was not at home on a boat. Franklin loved a relaxed atmosphere with much laughter, prankishness, and hours devoted to stamp albums and book catalogues, which did not suit Eleanor, who was content only when she was doing something useful. Fortunately, Miss LeHand (now known as Missy) could go down and stay. Warm, competent, and attractive, she was totally devoted to the Roosevelts. Sara disapproved of this arrangement almost as strongly as she did of Louis living in the Sixty-fifth Street house, but Eleanor was grateful to the young woman. She knew that lack of mobility made the daily routines of life cumbersome and difficult for Franklin, and Missy's presence freed him from housekeeping anxieties and enabled him to stay in touch with the political world through a vast political correspondence, while it eased Eleanor's sense of guilt because she was unable to do more for him.

She herself went down for the first time in 1923, and the log of the *Weona II*, written by Franklin, suggested she was not unhappy to depart.

Eleanor, Louis Howe, Esther Lape went fishing along the viaduct and caught 20 "Jacks." They packed each other's belongings (sic) and none of their own. From 3 p.m. till 5 they paced the hurricane deck in store clothes waiting anxiously for the train bearing the relief crew—(all of which were 2 hours late).[5]

Although Eleanor may have had reservations about joining Franklin in the South, her arrival each year was eagerly awaited. "Could we commence the Sabbath in any better way than to proceed to the station to greet the heavenly

Mrs. Roosevelt [who] was expected on the morning train from Miami," wrote Julian Goldman, department-store magnate and legal client of Franklin's. The *Weona II* had been replaced by the *Larooco*, a ramshackle houseboat that Franklin and John S. Lawrence, Boston banker and Harvard friend, had jointly purchased. Frances de Rham recorded on the same day, "Mrs. F.D.R. unpacked—candy, mail, etc. and the serious business of cruising began. Mrs. F.D.R. entertained us at lunch with stories about the children." Her final entry that day reported "E.R. sleeps on deck peacefully!" Mrs. Roosevelt, Goldman elaborated,

vindicated my high opinion of her by seizing the Heavenly deck for her sleeping quarters. Mosquitoes, flies, etc. mean nothing to her so long as the Citronella holds out. . . . The afternoon was spent by FDR . . . in catching a Fish—with Mrs. F.D.R. . . . knitting and reading. . . . After the usual evening meal Mrs. FDR . . . joined Capt. Charley in Evening Services which were concluded by all singing 'Onward Christian Soldiers.' "

Further entries in the log noted that they played bridge "at which E.R. and J.G. are again winners!" They tied up at Key West and Eleanor and Missy went ashore for mail, tickets, and papers.

Find the Admiral occupying most of the front page of the papers again with project for rejuvenating Democratic Party. . . . J.G. and E.R. spend many hours in conversation—many subjects ranging from love and marriage to the price of clothes—Mr. Goldman perfectly happy![6]

In her diary Eleanor wrote, "Mr. G. is so good and so nice but loves to talk about himself." Goldman left and the Henry Morgenthau, Jrs., arrived "tired and hot hollering for a bath. All overboard and have delightful half hour in the water. FDR swimming *much* better."

A few days later Louis appeared "only 4 hours late . . . *much* conversation. . . . 4 beds arranged on the deck after violent discussion as to where which snore would annoy the least!" Louis and Eleanor played piquet, the rest parcheesi. The women swam in the early morning, clinging to the float because of sharks. "Much festivity in the evening," the log for March 17 reported, "due to the fact that it is the 20th wedding anniversary of the FDR's. Speech, green table-cloth, place cards and refreshments! Moving speech by H.M. Jr. and a presentation to the Hon. FDR of a pair of *linnen* panties." The next day there was "heavy gloom at the departure of E.R. and Missy."

"Missy weeps because last A.M. on boat!" Eleanor noted. The exclamation point indicated her own feeling that getting back to terra firma was scarcely a reason for tears.

Though she was not enthusiastic about life on a houseboat, Eleanor felt it was helping her husband. When in 1925, discouraged by the costliness of the *Larooco* and the vagaries of wind and tide, he wrote that he might sell it and concentrate on Warm Springs, she replied,

I am sorry you ever thought of giving up the boat. I think you must have had a touch of that sadness which in spite of all its sunshine the Florida landscape always gives me! It is a bit dreary as a country but I liked the life better this time than ever before and tho' I'd like to find an ideal spot where you could swim daily still I do feel it is the best thing now to do. I think you gain more at Warm Springs but it won't be practical in winter for a long time if it ever is and Florida does you *general* good which is important. I thought watching you swim you used your legs more than last summer. Don't worry about being selfish, it is more important that you have all you need and wish than anything else and you always give the chicks more than they need and you know I always do just what I want![7]

Eleanor accompanied Franklin when he first visited Warm Springs in 1924 at the suggestion of George Foster Peabody. The New York banker and philanthropist had acquired the ownership of this rundown resort built around "a miracle of warm water" gushing from a massive fissured rock "that never varied in temperature or quantity."[8] At the end of his first stay, Franklin wrote, "I walk around in water 4' deep without brace or crutches almost as well as if I had nothing the matter with my legs."[9] Warm Springs "does my legs more good than anything else." He saw its possibilities as a therapeutic center and began to negotiate for its purchase.

The financial end worried Eleanor. "Don't let yourself in for too much money," she begged Franklin,

and don't make Mama put in much for if she lost it she'd never get over it! I think you ought to ask her down to stay for a week, she's dying to go and hurt at not being asked. I'll bring her if you want and Missy could move out while she stayed.[10]

Roosevelt purchased Warm Springs from Peabody in 1926 for $195,000, most of it money he had inherited from his father. Basil O'Connor, who in 1925 had become Franklin's law partner, did the legal work on the transaction. "Something tells me Peabody's doing all right," he commented.[11] Dr. LeRoy W. Hubbard, a New York orthopedic surgeon with considerable experience in polio therapy, was persuaded to supervise the medical end, and brought Helena T. Mahoney, a trained physiotherapist, with him as an assistant.

"I know you love creative work," a dubious Eleanor wrote May 4, 1926,

my only feeling is that Georgia is somewhat distant for you to keep in touch with what is really a big undertaking. One cannot, it seems to me, have *vital* interests in widely divided places but that may be because I'm old and rather overwhelmed by what there is to do in one place and it wearies me to think of even undertaking to make new ties. Don't be discouraged by me; I have great confidence in your extraordinary interest and enthusiasm. It is just that I couldn't do it.

Warm Springs prospered under Franklin's leadership and was approved by the American Orthopaedic Association. "Sixty-one patients is grand but I don't see where you put them," Eleanor exclaimed a year later. In 1928 the Edsel Fords contributed $25,000 with which to enclose the pool in glass so that it could be used the year round. Franklin built a cottage which became, next to Hyde Park, the place that he loved best, and he stayed there for longer and longer periods. "I can't bear to have you away," Eleanor wrote him at Thanksgiving, 1927. "Next year if you don't come home, I shall go up to Groton!" She was "not keen to get into Warm Springs life at all," she told him when Johnny, her youngest, was about to enter boarding school, yet she would have to get involved, she felt, if she stayed "long or often." The atmosphere of the rural South, with its poverty and the degradation of Negro and poor white, depressed her.

She felt, too, that Warm Springs was Missy's domain, and there were times she resented this and was even jealous. On her way to join Franklin in Florida in 1925 she had chatted on a train with a lady who told her how she lived in New York in the winter and in Long Beach during the summer and was now on her way to Cuba to "visit some folks." No, her husband did not mind; he was busy with the Elks and Masons at night and was at his office all day. "An unconscious tragedy told," Eleanor commented in her diary. She had escaped that kind of loneliness by developing interests that were her own but that also fitted into Franklin's long-range political plans. Nevertheless, she, too, was a lonely woman. "No form of love is to be despised," she wrote in her diary on the same trip, quoting from *The Constant Nymph*, which she was reading. Franklin did not offer the love for which she yearned, and she had to build her life around the acceptance of that fact. Theirs was now a carefully arranged relationship, but while behavior and action could be managed, she had less control over her feelings. She still was attracted by this man, still hoped and grieved that he could not show her the tenderness and unselfish devotion for which her spirit thirsted. So she was grateful to Missy and treated her almost as one of her children, and kept the pangs she suffered to herself.

Real maturity, she wrote at the end of her life in the little book *You Learn by Living*, was the ability to look at oneself honestly and acknowledge the fact that there is

a limitation in me. Here is a case where, because of some lack of experience or some personal incapacity, I cannot meet a situation; I cannot meet the need of someone whom I dearly love. . . . Either you must learn to allow someone else to meet the need, without bitterness or envy, and accept it; or somehow you must make yourself learn to meet it. . . . There is another ingredient of the maturing process that is almost as painful as accepting your own limitation and the knowledge of what you are unable to give. That is learning to accept what other people are unable to give. You must learn not to demand the impossible or to be upset when you do not get it.

That was the code she had worked out for herself; but her heart sometimes mutinied against that which her mind accepted as harsh necessity.

There were other reasons why she did not wish to become involved in Warm Springs. She was reluctant to have to fit into a life and place that belonged wholly to Franklin. Hyde Park bore the imprint of Sara's personality; Warm Springs that of Franklin's. She was developing her own style of life and did not want to give it up. She was, moreover, more useful to Franklin in New York. None of this persuaded Sara, who was constantly after her to spend less time on public activity and more with her husband and children. "It is nice to have Eleanor back,"[12] she wrote her son, "but I feel badly to have you so long without her." But this rarely was an issue between husband and wife.

Since Franklin was unable to help his younger sons in outdoor activities, Eleanor set about overcoming her own disabilities. She learned to ice skate; she finally mastered swimming by taking lessons at the Y; and she even made an attempt at tennis. "I practiced serving for half an hour today and nearly had apoplexy!" In 1925 she, Nan, and Marion took Franklin Jr., Johnny, Hall's son Henry, and Dr. Draper's son George Jr. on a camping trip through the Adirondacks in the old seven-passenger Buick, then up to Quebec and to Campobello. If there were no public camping sites, Eleanor, the most persuasive member of the group, talked farmers into giving them permission to pitch tents in their fields. "Where are your husbands?" one farmer wanted to know. "Mine is not with me and the others don't have husbands," she replied. "I don't want women of that kind," the farmer said with finality.[13] Their arrival in Campobello was described in a letter Franklin, who was at Marion, sent to Rosy.

All goes well. Eleanor and the rest of the caravan reached Campobello in safety, the only accidents being first, Franklin Jr. cutting his foot with the axe, instead of the tree; second, skidding off the road into the ditch and having to be pulled out; and third, upsetting a dray just as they approached Lubec and dumping the load of lumber and the small boy who was driving it—total cost of damages, $10.[14]

James and Elliott spent the summer of 1925 on the C. M. Ranch in Wyoming. Judging by a letter sixteen-year-old James sent Eleanor, Sara evidently had tried to enlist him in her campaign to keep Eleanor at home.[15] "I did think that you were trying to do a little too much travelling and that you would get too tired out," he wrote, "but I guess you're the best judge of what you can do."

She made regular trips to Groton for the special events open to parents and to consult with the rector and the masters on less auspicious occasions. "I wonder if the Rector can't be induced to have a better science department," she wrote after one such visit.[16] There was a steady flow of letters from James and Elliott to Eleanor, which she forwarded to Franklin, and to Franklin, which he forwarded to her. She often intervened for Elliott. She had wanted to send him to public school but was too unsure of herself to insist in the face of tradition and the resistance of Franklin and Sara. Elliott was having a hard time with his older brother and needed encouragement. Eleanor thought Franklin should invite him South, and Franklin did. James entered Harvard in 1926, but although Elliott's grades improved he did not want to follow family tradition. "I wonder if his desire to go to Princeton will be a disappointment to you," she wrote her husband. "I think not being with James is a good thing and of course if he has his choice he will feel the obligation to make good."[17] In the end Elliott refused to go to college at all and wouldn't speak to Eleanor for months when she insisted that he had to pass his entrance examinations whether or not he went on to college.

Eleanor had an easier time with James. He had resented his mother's new friends, especially Louis, but by the end of 1926 he was playing bridge with Louis and being tutored by Marion Dickerman. Eleanor did not want him to go to Harvard. Franklin talked vaguely about sending him to Wisconsin University, but it was clear he hoped James would choose Harvard. James did, as did all the boys except Elliott.

James' first reports from college were full of the papers he had to write, the books he had to read, and the freshman elections, in which he was chosen class secretary-treasurer. Some of the undergraduate rites did not appeal to Eleanor; election to the Hasty Pudding and Fly Clubs involved substantial initiation fees and heavy drinking. "Too bad James needs the money," she wrote her husband. "You never can get away from your gold diggers, can you? I can't say three nights drunk fills me with anything but disgust!"[18] She and Franklin were worried that James would be too interested in social life and having a good time, and their fears were borne out when he was placed on probation. He had to give up running for the student council and his work with the Phillips Brooks House, and wrote a contrite letter to his mother: "I have learned what we talked about and it is better to learn it now when I can make the changes." The letter impressed Eleanor. "He's taking it very well and tho' I'm sorry about it still I think it was the best thing [that] could have happened."[19]

At the end of his freshman year James went abroad to bicycle around England, he told his parents. Eleanor suspected the real reason was to see Lucy Archer-Shee, whom James thought he wanted to marry, "but of course she or he may have changed a number of times before he is earning $5,000 a year which is the minimum I told him he could marry on much to his dismay!"[20] The next year James wanted to go abroad again, this time with Sara, who would finance the trip. His parents thought he should work that summer, but were not arbitrary. Eleanor had long ago concluded that discipline and scolding were ineffectual if the inner motivation to act differently was lacking. "I've had long talks with James and Elliott and the net result is that I think perhaps we've been making a mistake," she wrote Franklin.

It all comes down to the old question of necessity. If they saw the need it would be logical but as it is it is tyranny. Mr. Rawle has told James that the work of the college years is in college and the holidays should be used to see things they may not for many years have another chance to see or do, and work in a job should be left to be undertaken at the close of college and then pursued unrelentingly. His inclination, and Elliott's also, runs along with this and so it seems an unreasonable request. James looked very badly and was plainly troubled about money when he arrived and I think we can push too far and therefore hope you will let him go abroad with Mama and return in August stipulating that on his return he stay at H.P. You could tell him that he must get rooted there if he ever hopes to go into politics. Mama will pay his way over and back and the $500 you would have paid to take him to Houston will cover his time over there. Mama says she will give him a Ford in the autumn and I think now he's proved steady you'd better let him have it. She'll help on his allowance too I know. . . . I will stay with the little boys this summer and economize in every way on the house and tutor and travelling so you ought to be able to make your political contributions and still get by.[21]

Eleanor's greatest problems were with Anna, who was having a most difficult time. Eleanor was experiencing the usual anxieties mothers have about pretty daughters who have become conscious of the world of young men. "I was so guarded that even at 18 I was not allowed to go to a movie without a chaperone," Anna later said. "And on that Mother went along 100 per cent with Granny." Anna did not wish to come out. "Granny said I had to—and Mother went along." Her grandmother picked out her clothes and Cousin Susie invited her to tennis week at Newport "along with a couple of suitable young men to squire me. And Mother went along."22

When Anna finished Miss Chapin's, Sara again took her abroad in the winter and spring of 1925, and Anna gave her some hard times on the trip. To Sara's horror, a distant cousin took the girl on a tour of the Rome slums. Then an English lord became interested in her, and in desperation Sara telegraphed London to have a former governess come down and take charge. When they returned, Anna confided to her mother that she would never again travel on the continent alone with Sara. "We've had lots of talks and she's a dear and I'm glad you'll have a chance to give her some good advice."23 The advice was needed about what Anna should do now that she was finished at Miss Chapin's. Sara did not want her to go to college, and cautioned her on the dangers of becoming a grind because young men would be intimidated by her and she would end up an old maid. This fear was not high on Eleanor's list. Her letters to Franklin spoke of "the inevitable young man" that was always somewhere in the vicinity. Anna had a feeling for outdoor life and a talent with animals, and felt that the summer she had spent with the Greenways on their Arizona ranch camping out on the desert was the best of her life. Her parents talked her into taking what she called "a short-horn agricultural course" at Cornell. Eleanor consulted with Henry Morgenthau, who suggested she first attend the Geneva (New York) State Experimental Station for six weeks as "it would provide the practical background for her Cornell course." Anna did not want to go, and when Eleanor drove her to Geneva they didn't say a word to each other the entire time. "Just now I am more worried about Anna than anyone," she wrote Franklin afterward.24

Though Anna no longer sided with her grandmother against Eleanor, she did not take her mother's admonitions kindly. "She doesn't care to write me, I evidently was too severe and we have not had a line since," Eleanor noted. Anna accepted her father's good-humored advice with better grace. "I am so pleased at her letter to you," Eleanor commented. "She has evidently not resented what you wrote in the way she did my letter and I'd rather have it that way for then you can be sure she'll take your advice on anything important."25 She should not worry so much, Franklin advised her; it was just a matter of being nineteen.

Anna and James were both at the age when going out meant making a night of it, and Eleanor caught catnaps waiting for them to come in. "Wednesday night it was 4 a.m. and today 6 a.m.," she noted wearily, adding, "I will say, however, that even my suspicious nature could not imagine that he'd had too much to drink!" She napped on the sofa in Anna's room until Anna came in, and it was after one particularly trying vigil that she told Anna about the Lucy Mercer affair. It was the "first really adult conversation I had with my mother," Anna later said.[26]

Sara needn't have feared that Anna would become an old maid. The Cornell course, short as it was, was abandoned abruptly when Anna became engaged to Curtis Dall, a stockbroker about ten years her senior, and she was married at twenty. "I got married when I did because I wanted to get out," she said, to escape the tension and conflict between her mother and grandmother.[27] Typical of the friction between the two older women was the row precipitated by Sara's wedding gift to Anna and Curtis.

On Thursday Anna told me Mama had offered to give them an apartment . . . as a wedding present but she was not to tell me as she thought I would dissuade them from taking it. . . . While it is a lovely thing for her to do I am so angry at her offering anything to a child of mine without speaking to me if she thought I would object and for telling her not to tell me that it is all I can do to be decent and I've really tried to be thoughtful since Aunt Annie died. Sometimes I think constant irritation is worse for one than real tragedy now and then. I've reached a state of such constant self-control that sometimes I'm afraid of what will happen if it ever breaks![28]

It was not only Sara's deviousness that angered Eleanor. She felt that the luxurious apartment, which Anna did not want, would commit the couple to an expensive style of life that was Sara's, not theirs, and that they would be able to maintain it only by continual subventions from Sara.

Sara wrote a bland letter of explanation to her son. "I am sorry I could not consult with you and Eleanor, but as it is my wedding present, I feel I should do it alone, also two other people had options on it."[29] Eleanor had first decided not to say anything to Sara, but she finally did. "Eleanor dear," an upset Sara wrote her afterward:

I am very sorry that I hurt you *twice*, first by not letting Anna tell you before it was decided and then by saying I would not give it to them. I certainly am old enough not to make mistakes and I can only say how much I regret it. I did not think I *could* be nasty *or* mean, and I fear I had too good an opinion of myself. Also I love you dear too much to ever want to hurt you. I *was hasty*, and of course I shall give them the apartment. I only wanted them to decide for *themselves* and surprise you and Franklin. No doubt he will also be angry with me. Well, I must just bear it.

Devotedly
Mama

Eleanor sent this letter on to Franklin, saying, "I answered quite politely and apologized for answering her questions frankly and commenting on her subsequent remarks and told her you never demeaned yourself by getting angry over little things so you see I've been thoroughly nasty but I'll try to behave again now for a time."[30]

Anna and Curtis moved into the apartment in the autumn of 1926. "I want to help her," Eleanor wrote her husband,

but not be about and do the superintending for I'm too executive not to do it all and then she'd never feel it was her own. Then next week I'll go and do some arranging with her when she knows what she wants. Mama says I'm cruel to 'leave the poor child alone'![31]

Eleanor sent Franklin a column by Angelo Patri, an educator, on the relationship that should exist between parents and children. "The enclosed meets my views and I think you'll like it too," she commented. "You are entitled to one life—your own," Patri urged. "Live it, start the children on their way and then plunge back into your own again." Eleanor elaborated her own views on the subject in an article, "Ethics of Parents," that she submitted to *Colliers* in 1927.[32] "Why not try letting our children go for a change?" she asked. The fact that parents and children lived in the same house does not mean "inner understanding" of the younger by the older generation. It was important to help young people "in the way they wished to be helped and not in the way we think they should be helped." With too many parents their attitude "comes down to this very often. 'Do as I wish and I will help you in every possible way, but otherwise, oh, no!' " That statement reflected her bitter experience with Sara, but when she went on to say, "How about abstaining from criticism or advice when it is not asked?" she was voicing a lesson that she herself had had to learn. "I have yet to see the time when the unpleasant truths we 'feel it our duty' to tell our children really helped a difficult situation, but of course it relieved our own minds."

Colliers did not publish the article. "I have made three or four attempts to rewrite the story," associate editor Walter Davenport wrote her. "Each effort injured rather than helped. . . . At any rate, none seemed to arouse the enthusiasm of Mr. Chenery [the editor]." Eleanor filed the manuscript and started work on a piece for the *North American Review* on "Why Democrats Favor Smith," which was published.

Her first grandchild was born in March, 1927. "Such a 36 hours as we have had!" Eleanor reported to Franklin. Anna had her child at her mother's house.

everything was prepared but we waited all day. It wasn't hard and the new way is marvelous but it was long and tedious for the child. However, after an active second night the young lady appeared at 5 A.M. The boys will tell you about her. She weighs 7½ pounds, her eyes are blue, so far her hair is black, her mouth large, her ears very flat. Anna is tired but sleeping a lot. . . . Mama is thrilled.[33]

Sara wrote her son she was

sorry the young grandfather could not be here for the great event. Eleanor sat all last night with Anna and came to my room this morning perfectly dressed and her hair perfect as if she had just left the dinner table! I think she is a wonder!

Sara never reconciled herself to the new order of things—Eleanor's living her own life, Franklin's mixing the search for recovery with continued activity in business and politics, Franklin and Eleanor's unwillingness to interfere in the lives of the children as she had in theirs. "I wish you could read Mama's last letter to me," Eleanor wrote Franklin in exasperation.

She is afraid of everything in it! Afraid of your going over bad and unfrequented roads, afraid I'll let the children dive in shallow water and break their necks, afraid they'll get more cuts! She must suffer more than we dream is possible![34]

Franklin had less patience with his mother than Eleanor. "I have seen a strong man struggle half his life for emancipation from the gentle but narrowing control of his mother," Eleanor wrote in the "Ethics of Parents" article, "and achieve it in the end only through what seemed heartlessness and entire lack of consideration." After a surge of annoyance and anger, Franklin's good nature and jollity reasserted themselves. He had his problems with Sara, but there was not the tension between Franklin and his mother that there was between Eleanor and Sara. Perhaps he sensed that the struggle was over him, but in any case he tried to stay out of it. He would sympathize with Eleanor, and then would add, "I have always told you that if you give Mama an inch she will take an ell."[35] Eleanor's letters were full of her difficulties with Sara: "Mama has done nothing but get in little side slaps today." "Mama was awful last Sunday and made us feel each in turn that we'd like to chew her up." Sara, like her son, would be horrid one moment and surprised that all was not forgiven and forgotten the next. She considered the two houses on Sixty-fifth Street "absolutely comfortable and well planned and nice in every way" while Eleanor was looking at cooperative apartments so that they might move after John went to Groton.[36] Sara criticized Eleanor's clothes, posture, taste, and activities one day, and the next praised her extravagantly. "Eleanor is a wonder, so busy, and so sweet and so amiable all the time."

That is what she really thought—but jealousy often warped her judgment and reactions. "Your library will have no chintz covers," Eleanor indignantly wrote Franklin,

because Mama told me she could make it attractive in half an hour and everyone liked her house better than mine and we had all the things to make a nice room only it needed taste, so I told her to go ahead and do it. Later she said she never liked to interfere so she didn't think she would and I said nothing would be done so I think you'll probably return to have to do it yourself! If it weren't funny I would probably blow up but I shan't.[37]

A week later she was still stubborn. "It wouldn't cost much to put slip covers in the Library, but I'm just obstinate after Mama's remarks and it is either done by her or not at all!"[38]

Eleanor could be stubborn with Louis, too, and not only over the issue of Prohibition. "It has been so hot that the furnaces have been let out in the house and in consequence a cold wave has swept in from the West and taken unfair advantage of us," he wrote his chief in Warm Springs.

I expect to spend the balance of the springtime sitting around 49 East 65th Street in my overcoat with a quilt over my shoulders, for I rashly suggested to your Missus that one hot day did not make a summer and in consequence, as you can easily guess, 20 below zero would not let her admit that she was wrong by having the furnaces started up again.[39]

30. A Life of Her Own

ELEANOR'S BEST DEFENSE against Sara was to get away from her, and by June, 1927, when she was writing Franklin that she "simply couldn't stand" staying at Hyde Park with Sara, she had a place of escape when Franklin and the children were not there, a place that she could share with her friends without having to negotiate with Sara whether it was all right for them to come. Sara was perfectly polite, always cordial, but she resented Eleanor's new friends. Rosy, whose reactions were much like Sara's, wrote Franklin, "Hope your Parlour Socialists are not living too much on the fat of the land with you, against their principles!!"[1]

Eleanor knew how the family felt about her friends, and when Franklin began to talk about a swimming pool near the Big House at Hyde Park, she persuaded him to combine it with a cottage that she, Nan, and Marion wanted to build beside the Val-Kill brook. "My Missus and some of her female political friends want to build a shack on a stream in the back woods and want, instead of a beautiful marble bath, to have the stream dug out so as to form an old-fashioned swimming hole," Franklin wrote Elliot Brown,[2] a friend from his Navy days whom he asked to supervise the probject.

"We used to go up to Hyde Park for weekends and take the boys," Marion recalled.

We were having a picnic and Eleanor said, "This is our last weekend because Granny is closing the house for the winter." Franklin said "You girls are very foolish. Why don't you build a cottage for yourselves?" So we got to playing with the idea. Franklin then said, "if you mark out the land you want, I will give you a life interest with the understanding that it reverts to my estate with your death." So we drew up a paper that Louis, Franklin, Nan, Eleanor and I signed.[3]

Franklin, who had forceful views on the architectural style that was appropriate to the Hudson, decided the cottage should be made of fieldstone and he worked with Henry Toombs, the architect, on the plans. The bids the women received seemed exorbitant. Finally Franklin told them, "If you three women will go away, Henry and I will build the cottage." On New Year's Day, 1926, the three women had their first meal there sitting on nail kegs, a crate being used as a table. The following spring Sara was writing her son that while she, Curt, and Anna were at the Big House, Eleanor and the little boys were at the cottage, but they came over here for some hours today and tomorrow they lunch here. We three are invited for supper tomorrow at the cottage and they all lunch here on Sunday. Eleanor is so happy over there that she looks well and plump, don't tell her so, it is very becoming, and I hope she will not grow thin.[4]

"The cottage is beginning to look sweet," Eleanor wrote her husband, on "Val-Kill Cottage" stationery.[5] Nan and Marion lived there, but she used it often.

I was delighted after I took all to the train at five to go back and say goodbye (to Mama) and come over here for a quiet evening with Nan. I've written two editorials and three letters and we have had supper and the peace of it is divine, but we have to take the 10:05 down tomorrow.[6]

The children loved the Big House, as did their father, but Eleanor never felt at home there. Even when Sara was away her spirit and presence were everywhere. "This house seems too queer without you," Eleanor wrote her, "and there is no doubt in my mind but houses reflect the central spirit and are just empty shells without them!"[7]

Nan's undertaking to build the furniture for the cottage evolved into a more ambitious plan to start a furniture factory nearby to produce authentic copies of early American pieces. Both Franklin and Eleanor shared a long-time concern with a better rural-urban balance, and with his encouragement Eleanor helped establish the shop "primarily . . . to carry out a theory . . . about establishing industries in agricultural counties to give men and boys a means of earning money in winter and something interesting to do." Nan went to the Metropolitan Museum in New York, to the Chicago and Hartford museums, and later to Monticello, to copy designs. Skilled Norwegian and Italian cabinet makers were employed to train the local boys. But Nan was the moving spirit here, hanging over her bottles and jars in search of the stain she wanted with the "passion of a medieval alchemist," and every piece, after the stain was applied, was rubbed and polished until the wood had the texture of velvet. Eleanor put up most of the capital—out of her growing earnings from radio and writing, as well as some of the little money she had inherited.[8]

As a first project, the women built the furniture for Franklin's new cottage in Warm Springs. "The furniture from the Val-Kill shop is a great success," Franklin wrote. By the spring of 1927 they were ready for their first exhibition, which was held at the Roosevelt Sixty-fifth Street house. The price list ranged from $40 for "trestle-table, round" to $175 for a large maple chest of drawers. "The work is handwrought and beautifully finished in every detail and copied with exactness from genuine antiques," said the *New York Times*.[9] Eleanor and Nan persuaded Abraham & Straus to send up buyers,

and though they say they only sell cheap furniture, they've ordered $610 worth and are making an exhibit of it. . . . I'm going to try Sloane's . . . and perhaps ask Grover Whalen if the Wanamaker shop in Philadelphia might be interested.[10]

Their early brochures spoke of "Roosevelt Industries," and Eleanor tried to interest the local women in weaving and other handiwork. She recruited women for a weaving class from the Hyde Park League of Women Voters and joined the class herself, but she did not have Nan's flair for design and craftsmanship. Her contributions to Val-Kill were those of executive, merchandiser, and inspirer.

Val-Kill Industries did not fully satisfy her need to do things herself, to develop skills of her own, to be useful professionally. In touch now with many professional women, she was bitter over her own inadequacies. "If I had to go out and earn my own living, I doubt if I'd even make a very good cleaning woman," she said. "I have no talents, no experience, no training for anything."[11] So when Marion, who was teaching at and vice principal of Todhunter, a private school for girls in New York City, was offered a chance to buy the school, Eleanor said, "I have no more children at home. Why don't we buy it together?"[12] With the shining example of Marie Souvestre in the back of her mind, she had always found teaching appealing. Franklin approved of the plan to buy the school and of Eleanor's decision to teach in it.

Her first efforts as a teacher evidently were disappointing. "I can't say I am set up by the exams my children did," she wrote Franklin. "I only flunked one but the others were none too good."[13] Yet when Marion asked her to take on a heavier schedule the following year she agreed.

She taught courses in literature, drama, and American history. Her drama course began with Aeschylus and ended with Eugene O'Neill, and her class in nineteenth-century English and American literature was equally wide-ranging. Notes for this class included biographical data on the writers she dealt with as well as remarks on their style and characteristics. She found her Allenswood notebooks quite useful. She was the moralist in literature; at that time it constricted her taste. She, Esther, and Elizabeth gave one night a week to reading French literature. Esther, on a trip to Paris, sent her André Gide's *Les Faux Monnayeurs*. The homosexual theme shocked her. "I read the book as the story of a sensitive relationship sensitively told," Esther said. "She read it in terms of a forbidden subject. She couldn't bring herself even to consider homosexuality. Generally her reaction was not so final, but in this case it was."[14]

In her history class, she emphasized "the connection between things of the past and things of today." Her examinations were given in two parts, one designed to test a knowledge of dates and facts, the other to encourage the girls to think for themselves. "Give your reason for or against allowing women to actively participate in the control of government, politics and officials through the vote, as well as your reasons for or against women holding office in the government." "How are Negroes excluded from voting in the South?" "What is the object today of inheritance, income and similar taxes?" (Most of her students came from families of wealth and high social standing.)

She was educating herself as well as her pupils. There were such reminders and admonitions to herself in her classbook as "look up Vikings" or "trace the trade routes better," and the general injunction, "be more exact." She used the "project method" in her homework assignments. When the class reached the Declaration of Independence she asked the girls to read any life [of a signer] you like. Get any pictures you can. Visit the museum and see if you can find anything in the museum belonging to them. Write about any present day descendants. Look up furniture of the Colonial period in the museum. Make book with pictures.

Later she gave a class in current events, called "Happenings," for the older girls. "I would like them to see the worst type of old-time tenement," she wrote Jane Hoey of the Welfare Council.[15] She took them to courts, police line-ups, markets, and settlement houses so that they might have a first-hand picture of how the city was run.

Her courses in modern history and current events made greater use of newspapers and magazines than they did of textbooks. A teacher should start from a young person's own present interest, she felt, and lead them into a wider and deeper understanding of the world into which they were going. "It is the teacher's function," she told Eunice Fuller Barnard, the education editor of the *New York Times*, "to manage this relating process, to seize all opportunities, however unpromising, to make all history and literature and the seemingly barren study of the machinery of government somehow akin to the things pupils are doing in their daily life."[16] She modeled herself on Mlle. Souvestre. The *Times* observed that

no slipshod phrases escaped her, and again and again a girl was asked to define her terms. Nor did sonorous phrases parroted from textbook or dictionary get by. "That's what the book says," Mrs. Roosevelt would smile serenely. "Now, how would you put it?"[17]

Todhunter was progressive in its use of the project method in teaching, but it was also traditional.

We still have frequent tests and mid-term and final examinations as well as reports and marks of the traditional school. For we believe that the girls will have to take certain hurdles in life, and that hurdles in school are an important preparation.[18]

The way the school day began was also traditional. Promptly at ten minutes of nine, the hundred uniformed girls, ranging from five to eighteen, marched into the assembly room

to a stirring march on the piano. . . . And Mrs. Roosevelt and Miss Dickerman, stately figures in tailored dark red gowns and low-heeled oxfords, like those the girls are required to wear, stand behind a long table in front to receive them. There is a hymn, a prayer and announcements, and a friendly talk about school plans in which the girls take part. Then comes another song of the girls' own choosing, which may be as popular as they please. The morning I was there they sang "Polly-wolly-doodle" with great relish. And they march out again to classes.[19]

"Teaching gave her some of the happiest moments in her life," said Marion. "She loved it. The girls worshipped her. She was a very inspiring person." When Franklin was elected governor of New York in 1928, she determinedly retained her ties with Todhunter, leaving Albany on Sunday night, teaching two and a half days and returning to the capital Wednesday afternoon.

Many, perhaps a majority, of Todhunter girls were drawn from Social Register families. Eleanor tried to broaden their horizons and widen their sympathies, but the very concept of a "private" school gave her difficulty. In Europe, she noted, obligatory military service brought together men from all social backgrounds thus for a time wiping out class distinctions. Public schools should do this in the United States, "but unfortunately many of our children are so closely confined amongst the little groups of people which form their immediate circle of family and friends, that they have very little opportunity to develop any knowledge or judgment of human beings as a whole."[20] To bring up young people in the belief

that their own particular lives are typical of the whole world is to bring up extraordinarily narrow people and every parent should demand of the school in which they place their children that if possible, there be a wide range of types in order that the child may be given an opportunity to develop its knowledge of the world and its own powers of choosing desirable companions.[21]

She was critical of mothers who did not inquire how well a school stood scholastically "but only whether the children that her daughter will meet will benefit her when she is ready to enter into that strange thing called 'society,'" a word which, she indicated, had lost its magic and meaning.

There was a time in New York City when the City was comparatively small and much was heard of "the four hundred." Perhaps there were really only four hundred people who could afford the gaieties and elegant leisure of the society of the day, which was represented by an old lady in a magnificent house, who gave remarkable parties to a few people, many of whom, while they may have belonged to the society of the four hundred, scarcely can have been said to have either ornamented or elevated its standing in the greater social organization we call civilization.

But today there was no such thing

in the larger cities at least, as any one group which may be called "society." . . . there is no such thing possible in this country as an aristocracy of society based on birth. We set up a material basis as the final criterion of social eligibility, certainly in our larger cities.[22]

During her Washington days when she had come to New York she had told Sara that the people she wanted to see were Ruth Ledyard, Pauline Emmet, Nathalie Swan, Helen Wilmerding, Caroline Trevor, Mary Morgan, Helen Robinson, and Cousin Susie. She was still fond of these people, but she saw much less of them. "I've had a long sobbing letter from Cousin Susie who says I've only been there twice all winter so I must make an effort to see more of her!" She still paid her dues to the Monday Evening Sewing Class and the Colony and Cosmopolitan Clubs, but she no longer took "society" seriously. The most satisfactory friends, she had now discovered, were those with whom she worked.

31. Smith's Defeat, Roosevelt's Victory

POLITICS in one form or another took more and more of Eleanor's time as the 1928 presidential campaign neared. "Women should not be afraid to soil their hands" by getting into politics, she urged everywhere. "Those who are not make the best politicians."[1] Together with Caroline O'Day, Elinor Morgenthau, Nancy Cook, and Marion Dickerman, she infused energy and purpose into the work of the women's division of the Democratic State Committee.

There was a great deal of drudgery. She had raised $6,000 toward the women's budget, she wrote her husband. "I have $24,000 to raise, do suggest some people to do it."[2] Each year it was a new struggle. "I hate the money-raising job and I wish I could resign," she wrote Franklin.[3] But she never did, and when, that same year, they began to publish a monthly magazine, the *Democratic News*, she took on the job of advertising manager as well as editor. "I've visited 12 or 15 men, can't do more than four a day and only have four ads, so far," she lamented.[4] "I'm learning the advertising business," her next letter exulted.

I spent an hour with Mr. Franklin Simon, who gave me advice, an "ad," and several names. This p.m. I'm getting my rate card done with H. M. Jr.'s "ad" man, so you see this bulletin is going to be a real business proposition before we get thro' if hard work can do it.

She wrote the editorials, solicited contributions from prominent Democrats—including her husband—and kept in touch with a network of correspondents in every county. Behind the scenes Louis was her chief collaborator. He taught her the tricks of layout, headline writing, and composing a terse lead, occasionally doing the job himself. Louis was pleased with Eleanor's progress as a politician and advised Franklin that his "Missus" was "gaining in political wisdom every day."[5]

She often went to Albany to do battle with recalcitrant legislators on behalf of legislation for women and children. When the assembly held a hearing, the manufacturers' lobby brought shop girls to Albany who asserted they were perfectly content with a 50- and 54-hour week, that a 48-hour bill would eliminate jobs. "What we want most of all is protection from the non-working and professional uplifters," an employee of the BMT declared. Disregard the "sob stuff," Eleanor urged the assemblymen when she rose to speak. The "great majority of the working women of this State are really in favor of this bill and would like to see it become law. I can't understand how any woman would want to work 54 hours a week if she only has to work 48 and could receive the same rate of wages."[6] The battle for the 48-hour law went into the 1926 and 1927 legislatures where she again clashed with the lobbyists for industry.[7]

Throughout the twenties the drive for progressive social and labor legislation in New York was directed by the Joint Legislative Conference, which had been initiated by the Women's Trade Union League and included the Consumers League, the League of Women Voters, the Women's City Club, the industrial board of the YWCA, the American Association for Labor Legislation, the WCTU, and the New York Child Labor Committee. One of its most stalwart members was Mary W. "Molly" Dewson, civic secretary of the Women's City Club, a no-nonsense lady who combined tough-mindedness with vision. She had worked for twelve years as superintendent of parole for girls in Massachusetts, gone to France during the war with the American Red Cross, and after the war, as research secretary of the National Consumers League, had helped Felix Frankfurter prepare the economic briefs in the District of Columbia and California minimum-wage cases. She had first met Eleanor the autumn of 1924, when, according to Molly, the president of the Women's City Club had introduced her to "a tall, slender woman who was hastening out of the room. 'This is our new Vice President, Mrs. Franklin D. Roosevelt,' she said. . . . In that fleeting second, I felt her human warmth, sincerity and genuine interest in other persons."[8] Molly lived in the same cooperative house on West Twelfth Street as Nan and Marion, and she, too, became a co-worker of Eleanor's.

The program of the Joint Legislative Conference, Molly wrote in her memoirs, included such long-standing progressive objectives as unemployment compensation, minimum-wage legislation, old-age pensions.[9] The work of the conference, she thought, had had a large educational effect upon Franklin Roosevelt through Eleanor, who had served as chairman of the conference one year and who, by 1926, was militantly walking the picket line with Rose Schneiderman and using her considerable political influence within the Democratic party on behalf of the advanced goals of the conference. She had developed into a hard-hitting campaigner whom the Democrats frequently asked to present the party's viewpoint in debates, as she demonstrated in the 1926 senatorial campaign when Justice Robert F. Wagner was the Democratic candidate against incumbent James Wadsworth. Eleanor would have preferred Owen D. Young to Wagner, but Wagner was better than Wadsworth, whom she smilingly shrugged off in a debate as "a country squire of the 17th century in politics . . . in the 20th century." Warming up to this theme, she added that he had a "Marie Antoinette type of mind."

In 1926 she was elected to the holy of holies of the suffrage movement—the Leslie Commission, the group of nine women who presided over the disbursement of the fund that Mrs. Frank Leslie, widow of the publisher of *Leslie's Weekly*, had left Mrs. Catt in 1914 with which to advance the cause of women's rights. "You have qualified," Mrs. Catt wrote Eleanor on her election as a director. "I should add that you were nominated and seconded by two 'black Republicans.' "[10]

There were other signs of Eleanor's growing effectiveness. Radio was coming into its own and she was often asked to present the woman's viewpoint. She had become a practiced lecturer. Pearl Buck, a graduate student at Cornell in the mid-twenties, was on the committee to meet and escort her the day she came to Ithaca to lecture to the Home Economics Department. "It was her energy that struck me most that day." Her clothes were nondescript—an ankle-length purple satin dress, a brown tweed coat, bright tan oxfords—but her disregard of style did not matter. She had "a disarming kind of shyness. She was full of self-confidence and was anxious to please." Her speech was "good," and then there was a luncheon "invented" by the Home Economics Department. "It seemed to be mostly raw cabbage. . . . It was an uneatable meal so far as I was concerned. Mrs. Roosevelt ate it with great gusto, however, and congratulated the head of the department on having achieved this meal. . . . I remember her gay, high-pitched voice commenting on everything." Miss Buck was on the receiving line before dinner. "She shook each hand vigorously. She was the soul of good humor and not a whit tired." Then they proceeded to dinner "and when we saw her off on the train I was completely exhausted."[11]

It was Louis Howe who had almost literally pitched her into the lecture circuit. "When I expressed some idea he thought was good he would snarl, 'For goodness sake, why don't you put it on paper?' Or else in his gruff but sweet manner he would say, 'Get out and talk,' "[12] Magazines had begun to invite her to write for them, and paid her generous fees. One article—"What I Want Most Out of Life," which appeared in *Success Magazine* in May, 1927—was highly personal yet representative of the new perplexities confronting women: what should they do with their vote and their growing leisure? "I suppose if I were asked what is the best thing one can expect in life, I would say—the privilege of being useful," the article began. She was particularly concerned with the woman over forty, whose children were grown and away from home and who did not have to worry too much about contributing to the family budget. She regretted that more women were not interested in politics. "More than anything else, it [politics] may serve to guard against the emptiness and loneliness that enter some women's lives after their children are grown." Even while children are growing up mothers should become

accustomed gradually and while they are still comparatively youthful, to having lives, interests and personalities of their own apart from their households. . . . Home comes first. But—in second and third and last place there is room for countless other concerns. . . . And so if anyone were to ask me what I want out of life I would say—the opportunity for doing something useful, for in no other way, I am convinced, can true happiness be obtained.

It was not, in essentials, too different from the analysis of how to achieve happiness that she had written for Mlle. Souvestre a quarter of a century earlier.

Redbook asked her to write on women and politics, and she did a piece entitled "Women Must Learn to Play the Game As Men Do."[13] She was elated when *McCall's* offered her $500 "and only 2,500 words. . . . I suppose James will tell me he 'wouldn't write for such a magazine' as he did about the *Redbook* but I am glad of the chance!"[14]

S. J. Woolf, who interviewed her for the *New York Times Magazine*, was thoroughly taken with her:

Seated at a small desk . . . she posed for a drawing, spoke about women in politics, answered innumerable telephone calls, arranged her son's departure from the city and directed household affairs; and all before 10 o'clock in the morning for at that time she had to leave to give a talk at the girls' school at which she teaches.[15]

"She is the strongest argument," Woolf concluded, "that could be presented against those who hold that by entering politics a woman is bound to lose her womanliness and her charm." Mlle. Souvestre would have liked that.

By 1927 Democratic women were strongly organized throughout the state. Whenever Governor Smith's legislative program bogged down, he called Caroline and Eleanor to Albany to ask them to help get his bills through, and women by the hundreds came to the state capital at their call. They worked in a more disciplined way than the men, whom Eleanor ventured to criticize for their "inability to comprehend the value of sustained organization. Men think they can organize the vote six weeks before election, but women generally believe in all-year-round active political work."[16] In 1926 the women had achieved one of their goals—election to the Democratic State Committee on an equal footing with the men. To the six hundred women who gathered to celebrate the victory, Eleanor hailed it as the "breaking down of the last barrier." But once inside the fortress, they found it empty. Eleanor bridled at the "cut and dried" way in which matters were handled at State Committee meetings.[17] The power lay elsewhere, and the men still held it alone.

Alfred E. Smith, who was the governor of New York during the years of Eleanor's emergence, considered her a valuable ally—partly as the representative of her husband and partly in her own right as a leader among women. Eleanor admired the governor. Reflecting her rebellion against Sara and Sara's values, the fact that Smith had worked his way up from Oliver Street on the Lower East Side and still spoke its language of the streets added to his appeal. Franklin made the keynote speech at the 1926 convention that renominated the governor, and Eleanor was a member of the platform committee and spokesman for the women. Franklin could not campaign actively, but Eleanor could and did. "The Governor does get what he wants, doesn't he?" she wrote after election day the following year when an amendment he had opposed was defeated.[18]

What Smith most wanted was the Democratic nomination for president in 1928, and Eleanor was prepared to support him, even though she did not admire him unqualifiedly. She brought Florence Kelley, the veteran social reformer, in the hope of converting him to the child-labor amendment. He stormed at the frail, elderly woman, paced angrily up and down his office, and finally Mrs. Kelley left in despair. Eleanor knew the governor well enough to understand that his show of anger masked his defensiveness; after Mrs. Kelley left she said to him, "You know that you are opposed to this amendment because the Church is opposed," and Smith agreed.[19] Some felt Smith's

Catholicism disqualified him, but Eleanor quoted her Uncle Ted as having said he hoped to see the day when a Catholic or a Jew would become president.[20]

In the *North American Review* she argued the case for Smith, saying that unlike Wilson, who was "the Idealist, with no knowledge of practical politics, and therefore without the ability to translate his dreams into facts," Smith combined idealism with a "practical knowledge of how to achieve political results."[21] The issue in the 1928 elections, she wrote in *Current History*, was the age-old conflict between Jeffersonians and Federalists.

The Democrats today trust in the people, the plain, ordinary, every-day citizen, neither superlatively rich nor distressingly poor, not one of the "best minds" but the average mind. The Socialists believe in making the Government the people's master; the Republicans believe that the moneyed "aristocracy," the few great financial minds, should rule the Government; the Democrats believe that the whole people should govern.[22]

In promoting Smith's candidacy with the Southern Women's National Democratic Organization, she argued that Smith, "in greater degree than any other man in public life, [has] the faculty of taking a complex problem of government and simplifying it so that people can go to the polls and vote on the issue intelligently," which she considered one of the most important functions of a leader in a democracy.[23] The governor's stand on Prohibition distressed her, but compared to his other qualities "his personal attitude on Prohibition is of minor importance." Mrs. Jesse W. Nicholson of Texas, the head of the Women's Democratic Law Enforcement League, bitterly opposed Smith's candidacy because he was a wet. If the league, whose membership was largely southern, was so concerned with upholding the Constitution, Eleanor wrote Mrs. Nicholson, why was it not making as great an effort "to enforce the 14th and 15th amendments relating to the right of all citizens to vote?"[24] Bravo, wrote George Marvin, writer, diplomat, and former Groton master, who addressed Franklin as "Francisco." "Whenever she gets ready to run for anything, she can count on two humble but husky votes in this 'Section.' "[25]

She had difficulties over Prohibition in her own household. When in 1924 she accompanied Mrs. Norrie to a convention of women in Washington to press for strict enforcement of the Volstead Act, she apologized to Franklin: "I know you will probably feel with Louis it is politically wrong to come but I do believe in it." While she felt that the Eighteenth Amendment

works imperfectly I don't want it repealed or modified, for with all its faults, its virtues make it good. . . . Prohibition makes it harder to get alcohol. . . . There is less drinking now among young people than there was among our fathers. It is the example of the parents that is so dangerous.[26]

Franklin, whose approach to Prohibition was firmly political and opportunist, teased her about her support of Smith despite his wetness. "Thanks for sending me that awful picture of my Missus," he wrote Stanley W. Prenosil, the AP man who had covered his 1920 campaign. "She is apparently looking at a fly on the ceiling with the hope of finding out how to be wet and dry at the same time."27

Although Smith's "Kitchen cabinet" included neither Franklin nor Eleanor, he counted on them to play a major part in his drive for nomination and election. "Mrs. Moskowitz practically told me yesterday that you were to nominate the Governor," Eleanor informed Franklin.

You will have to work hard to keep up your standard of four years ago! Also I am to head up a Woman's Committee for pre-convention activities and we are to have an office in the Biltmore with Mrs. Moskowitz, etc. It won't mean much work once it is started but there was an implication of future work which horrified me as I ought to let them know I have to be at home this summer and yet you can't refuse what you haven't been offered, can you?28

"Elinor and Henry Morgenthau are like children in their joy that she [Elinor] should be made a delegate-at-large," Eleanor wrote wonderingly, a few weeks before the Democratic national convention in Houston. "I never realized any one could care so much and only hope nothing happens to change the minds of the mighty!"29

One of her purposes in going into politics had been to keep Franklin's name before the public, especially the politicians. She succeeded. Mrs. Roosevelt's activity with the Democratic women, the *New York Herald Tribune* wrote in 1927, "has caused a revival in Tammany circles of the talk that Governor Smith favors Franklin D. Roosevelt . . . as Democratic candidate for Senator next year." Wherever she went in Democratic circles, people asked about Franklin. "I told everyone at the State Committee meeting yesterday you were going to Houston without crutches!"30

Franklin's return to the political scene would mean her withdrawal—there never was any doubt in her mind about that. She was sure that was the way it should be and had to be. But was she wholly content with the prospect? She did not go with him to Houston, but Elliott and Louis did, and when Sara sailed for Europe with James she was left in charge of Hyde Park, a chore she hated. Her last letter to Franklin before he left Warm Springs for the convention reported that "it is horrid, rainy weather and I am quite unreasonably depressed, partly because I feel uncomfortable about servants. . . ."31 She would go to the railroad station to say good-by to Marion, Elinor, and Henry when they boarded the train for Houston, she added, and if Franklin saw Mrs. Nicholson of Texas, "give her an extra polite dig for me!" She would listen on the radio "and expire if it doesn't work!" It was not the letter of a woman who was satisfied to be removed from the scene of the action. When Smith was nominated on the first ballot she sent him her personal congratulations and to Franklin wrote that she was meeting Marion at the station and rather hoped the governor would be on the train as the papers had indicated he might be.

She had worried whether Franklin's nominating speech in Houston would meet the high standard of the "Happy Warrior" one. It did, said the *New York Times* editorially: "It is seldom that a political speech attains this kind of eloquence . . . a model of its kind." At state headquarters, Eleanor reported, "everyone was talking of your speech and feel you did untold good to the Governor's cause." But there was also dissatisfaction among the women, who were unhappy because they had not been consulted

by the men leaders as to what women from New York should be given this or that place. It would be so easy for the men to do. I can't understand why they prefer to stir up this current of discontent! However it is none of my business. I'm doing just what Mrs. Moskowitz asks me to do and asking no questions, the most perfect little machine you ever saw and after the National Committee meets and they appoint permanent people I'm going to get out and retire.[32]

She was not allowed to do so. In July the Democratic National Committee drafted her and Mrs. Nellie Tayloe Ross of Wyoming, the first woman governor, to head up the women's work in the campaign, with Mrs. Ross touring the country and Eleanor directing the work at headquarters. "She does a thorough job of it," the *New York Evening Post* reported. She was at her desk at nine, except when she had a class at Todhunter, and stayed until the work was done, which was often after midnight.

Always courteous, never showing the slightest sign of impatience, she sees nearly every person who wants to talk to her and there are hundreds of them. It is said that she also dictates a personal answer to every letter she receives –about 150 a day.[33]

Malvina Thompson, young, tart, shy, a blend of New England and the Bronx, who had worked for the Red Cross and the Democratic State Committee, became Eleanor's personal secretary, and the campaign sealed a relationship that lasted through "Tommy's" life. She was also assisted by young Grace Tully, who had received her training as Cardinal Hayes' secretary. Under Eleanor's supervision, committees were organized to appeal to independent voters, business and professional women, college women, working women, social workers, new voters. Congresswoman Mary T. Norton ran the Women's Speakers Bureau and witty Mrs. June Hamilton Rhodes, the publicity department.

"Every morning," Eleanor wrote in a post-election account of the women's organization in the campaign, she "called a meeting of the various executive secretaries and went over their work with them, each one listening to the problems and questions of the other, thus learning what was going on and thus avoiding duplication. All work done in the various bureaus was under [my] direct supervision."[34] She prodded the states in which the organization was unsatisfactory and ironed out the inevitable disputes. One trouble spot was the midwest region, whose headquarters were in St. Louis. She telephoned Molly Dewson at her summer house in Maine.

Harry Hawes says the women in the Midwestern Headquarters of the Democratic National Committee are fighting and I must come out, but I cannot possibly leave headquarters in New York. Will you go in my place? I know only two women whom it would be safe to send and you are one of them.[35]

Of this request Molly later wrote, "scattered all over this country are, I imagine, a great many persons who have never been able to say 'no' to the Roosevelts or even 'I will think it over and telephone you.' I am no exception." The choice was a wise one, for Senator Hawes begged Molly "to stay through the campaign." After that, no campaign would be run without Molly's help.

Sara, still in Europe with James, wrote Eleanor that "I long to hear that my Franklin was not used up by Houston."[36] When she and James reached Vittels in the Vosges she informed Franklin that she had been given a first-hand account of the convention by Bernard Baruch.

Mr. B. Baruch is here and he came to our table last evening when he finished dinner and said he had been at the Convention and heard your fine speech. He seems to think Smith has a good chance, chiefly because many Republicans are anxious not to have prohibition. . . . Mr. Baruch says Elliott was perfect, helping you and taking the sheets as they fell from your hand. How lovely to have had James four years ago and Elliott now.[37]

Baruch also reported to Sara that the Smith forces were trying to draft her son for governor, but Roosevelt was firmly determined to avoid a draft for the governorship. Eleanor was less certain that he should turn down the nomination if it were offered to him. Agnes (Mrs. Henry Goddard) Leach, who was New York State chairman of the League of Women Voters, recalled being at Hyde Park around the time of the Houston convention. In the middle of luncheon Franklin was informed that Belle Moskowitz wanted to talk to him on the telephone. He refused to take the call, but then he was told Smith was on the phone and so he had himself wheeled out for what proved to be a long talk. "What did Smith want?" Eleanor asked on his return. "The same old thing," he replied. "He wants me to be the candidate for Governor. It's ridiculous."

"I don't think you should say it's ridiculous so quickly," Eleanor cautioned him.[38]

When the delegates began to arrive for the state convention in Rochester at the end of September, Franklin was ensconced in Warm Springs and evidently expected to stay there, for he had instructed Eleanor to have the *Times* and the *World* sent there for three months. Always buoyant and hopeful, he thought that with a few more years of exercises at Warm Springs he would be able to walk without braces. Moreoever, he and Louis did not believe that 1928 was a good year for the Democrats, and he deliberately put himself out of immediate reach of Smith and his friends. As a result, their pressure to have him run focused on Eleanor and to a lesser degree on Louis. "My conviction that you should not run is stronger than ever and Eleanor agrees with me in this," Louis wired him on September 25. Tammany leader George Olvaney, Louis informed Franklin the next day, "has been trying to reach Eleanor who is speaking in New Hampshire apparently to persuade her to persuade you," and Franklin should let them know whether his decision "not to run is still final." If Franklin would head the ticket, Colonel Herbert Lehman told Eleanor, Lehman "would gladly run as Lt. Governor" so that Franklin could feel he "could go away each winter and leave [a] competent person in charge."

"I have to go to Rochester but I wish I didn't have to go for everyone makes me so uncomfortable," she wrote her husband. "They feel so strongly about your running and even good explanations can be made to sound foolish. The Governor called me yesterday and I told him to call you."[39] Smith had telephoned her from Milwaukee, and she arrived at the Hotel Seneca in Rochester almost at the same time he did. Roosevelt had sent a telegram to the governor reaffirming his reasons for refusing to run—that Smith did not need him in order to win and that he needed two more years to get rid of his leg braces; he owed it to his family to follow through his curative program to the end. A haggard Smith closeted himself with Mrs. Roosevelt. He wanted to know Franklin's *real* objections to accepting the nomination—health? Warm Springs finances? Would the governorship endanger his chances of walking again? At two she emerged from the governor's suite. "Will Mr. Roosevelt run?" the reporters wanted to know. "I don't think it is possible," she answered. Was she willing for him to run? She told them what she had told the county leaders who were insisting that it had to be Roosevelt: "It is entirely up to him. I am not trying to influence him either way." The reporters admired her poise.

The county leaders went into session again, but the discussion always came back to Roosevelt. Franklin was refusing to take Smith's calls and Eleanor agreed to get her husband on the phone; the rest would be up to Smith. As soon as Franklin answered, Eleanor turned the receiver over to Smith and raced for the train in order to be back in New York in time for the opening of Todhunter. "All day long," the *New York Evening Post* commented on the day's activities, "Mrs. Roosevelt had been in conference with the leaders, quiet, unruffled, probably the calmest person in all the crowded hotel."[40]

When she heard that he had yielded to the party's entreaties she wired Franklin: "Regret that you had to accept but know that you felt it obligatory." The pressure on Roosevelt was described in a Lippmann editorial in the *World*: "The demand for Mr. Roosevelt came from every part of the State. It could not be quelled. It could not be denied. The office has sought the man."

Sara was surprised but accepted the decision in good spirit, considering her earlier opposition to her son's remaining in public life. "Eleanor telephoned me before I got my papers that you have to 'run' for the governorship," she wrote Franklin.

Well, I am sorry, if you do not feel that you can do it without too much self-sacrifice, and yet if you run I do not want you to be defeated! . . . Now what follows is *really private*. In case of your election, I know your salary is smaller than the one you get now. I am prepared to make the difference up to you.

One member of the family had no doubts. Anna wired her father, "Go ahead and take it," to which he replied, "You ought to be spanked."

But what did Eleanor really think about her husband's candidacy? When the press caught up with her at Democratic headquarters, she said

I am very happy and very proud, although I did not want him to do it, he felt that he had to. In the end you have to do what your friends want you to. There comes to every man, if he is wanted, the feeling that there is almost an obligation to return the confidence shown him.

The reporters questioned her persistently about a story that had appeared in that morning's *World* under the headline "Mrs. Roosevelt's 'Yes' Final Factor." Based on what "intimate friends" of Mrs. Roosevelt told its reporter, it asserted that she had been on the phone with her husband in the late afternoon, that he had told her he might not be able to refuse in the end, unless she was not satisfied to have him run. "Mrs. Roosevelt held the receiver in silence for several minutes," the story stated. "The decision was left to her. Then she assured Mr. Roosevelt that she was of the opinion that he might enter the campaign, and, if elected, accept the office without harmful effects."[41]

She would not deny that she had talked to him, but insisted, "I was very surprised at the nomination. I never did a thing to ask him to run." Had she had a hand in changing his mind, the reporters wanted to know. "My husband always makes his own decisions. We always discuss things together, and sometimes I take the opposite side for the fun of the thing, but he always makes his own decisions."[42]

She did not think it right, as she had told Smith and John J. Raskob, then chairman of the National Democratic Committee, to ask him to do anything he felt he should not do, but did she herself want him to run? Edward J. Flynn, the Bronx Democratic leader, at Smith's request, had been sounding out Roosevelt during the summer on his real reasons for resisting the nomination. Flynn felt that among other things Roosevelt was concerned about what would happen to Warm Springs and the considerable money—all his fortune, in fact—that he had put into it if he could no longer give it his full attention. Eleanor, who was always practical and hard-headed in money matters, would no doubt have wanted to be assured on this score, as she would have had to be persuaded in her own mind that her husband had gone as far as possible to recover the use of his legs. But in the end it seemed to Flynn "that she was anxious that he should run, and that she would be happy if he would consent to it."

Thirty years later when she saw *Sunrise at Campobello*, she noted that the play depicting Franklin's victory over polio could have been a play about almost any other victim of infantile paralysis. There was another drama, she went on, "which came later in my husband's life" when "he made his decision as to whether he would devote himself to his efforts toward recovery or accept his disabilities in order to play a more active role in the life he was leading." Perhaps that was a subject for another play, she added.[43] "I think the most wonderful thing Eleanor did was to encourage him to run in 1928 when most people thought he was not up to it," said Esther Lape.[44]

If she did influence his decision, she kept it well hidden. Her account of what happened in Rochester in *This I Remember* ended with the ambiguous remark, "I sometimes wonder whether I really wanted Franklin to run."[45]

Her husband's decision to run did not alter Eleanor's primary political responsibility, which was to the Smith campaign organization. She kept an eye on the state through Elinor Morgenthau, Caroline, and Nancy and even helped them with the campaign caravans they were sending out all over the state, but she had her hands full with national problems. Her mail reflected the unprecedented bigotry and snobbery elicited by Smith's candidacy. "Can you imagine Mr. and Mrs. Smith in the White House as the leading family of the nation?" one letter from a Republican woman "who had always admired you" asked. Eleanor defended Smith in the Junior League *Bulletin*, saying that his "human" sympathies were wider than Hoover's; men worked "*under*" Hoover but "*with*" Smith; Hoover stressed "material prosperity," Smith would be concerned with "the human side of government." The many letters demanding to know how she, a supporter of the Volstead Act, could support a man who, if elected, would nullify Prohibition, were relatively easy to answer. But the southern propaganda was irrational. If Smith were elected, the pope would be coming to the United States on a battleship, "AL SMITH THE NEGRO LOVER" leaflets throughout the South proclaimed. "I want to assure you," Eleanor wrote an Alabama Democrat,

that Gov. Smith does not believe in intermarriage between white and colored people. He has a full understanding of conditions as they are in the South and would never try to do violence to the feelings of Southern people . . . the Democratic Party has always better understood and sympathized with Southern feelings and prejudices than has the Republican.

As Election Day approached, Smith's defeat seemed likely, but Eleanor was a good trooper and sought to counteract a mood of defeatism. "I bring you good tidings," she told 2,500 women Democrats. "All the women of the country have been passing before me at my desk at headquarters. . . . The tide has turned and Gov. Smith's most recent speech has made us all feel that we are going to roll up a better and better vote."[46] But the day before election the betting odds favored Hoover and also Roosevelt. She made the traditional end-of-the-campaign swing through the Hudson Valley with Franklin, who was wearing the battered felt hat in which he had campaigned in 1920. The campaign ended with "Mr. Ottinger and I coming through it with the most kindly of feelings," he said. What were her husband's chances of success, a reporter asked Eleanor. "I don't know the State situation. I haven't been active with the State. I feel sure the Governor is going to win, though."[47]

She spent Election Day working at the polls, and in the evening was hostess at a buffet supper for their friends at the Biltmore. At nine Smith came by. "Frank, let's go down and hear the verdict." For a brief moment it looked as if Smith were carrying New York and the South, but then the returns moved decisively the other way. At midnight Smith dictated a telegram of concession, buttoned up his topcoat, put on his brown derby, and walked out. With heavy heart, Eleanor went to the Biltmore. "I may be here all night," Franklin said. It was "as exciting as a horse race." By morning he appeared to have survived the Democratic debacle. Smith lost New York by 103,481 votes; Roosevelt carried it by 25,564.

Smith's defeat notwithstanding, Eleanor had made her mark. Elizabeth

Marbury, Democratic national committeewoman from New York and considered the dean of women politicians, conferred the accolade. "They won't need people like me. They've got their Mrs. Roosevelt now."[48]

But Eleanor grieved for Smith. "If the rest of the ticket didn't get in, what does it matter?" she said to a reporter who asked her how she felt about her husband's victory. "No, I am not excited about my husband's election. I don't care. What difference can it make to me?"[49]

But of course it would make a great deal of difference. Even before Election Day she had written the Democratic state chairman, resigning from the Democratic State Committee: "It seems to me now that my husband is actually back in active politics, it is wise for me not to be identified with any of the party committees."[50] She could not withdraw from a Consumers League dinner, she wrote Franklin, who had returned to Warm Springs after the election, "because I promised long ago but it is my last appearance as a speaker on any subject bordering on politics!"[51]

32. *Return to Albany*

———

A TRIUMPHANT ROOSEVELT departed from Warm Springs and left it to his wife to arrange the move into the executive mansion. She was a far different person from the anxious young woman who had accompanied the ebullient new senator to Albany eighteen years earlier. She accepted an invitation from Mrs. Smith to come to Albany, and with great dispatch decided on the changes that would have to be made to fit the comfortable, loose-jointed mansion, with its turrets, cupolas, and broad red-papered halls, to the needs of the gregarious Roosevelt family.

The first structural change she wanted represented an act of thoughtfulness: to join the ladies' cloakroom to the back hall so that it could be used as a servants' dining and sitting room because the pantry where the servants had been eating was "not really decent."[1] Governor Smith's zoo was to be dismantled, and the three monkeys, one elk, one deer, one fawn, and six dogs dispersed. Republican approval was obtained to remove the three greenhouses and install a swimming tank—a real saving, Franklin carefully pointed out to the press, since the annual upkeep of the greenhouses was $6,000 for flowers which could be obtained from commercial florists for $750.

For her husband's bedroom Eleanor chose the "grandest sunny" room in the mansion, a corner room of the second floor with two exposures and a palatial dressing room and bathroom. The library downstairs would be his study and workroom, and the room upstairs that Smith had used as his office at the mansion would, with chintz curtains and Val-Kill furniture, make a cozy family sitting room and serve as her workroom. She suggested that the only single bedroom in the mansion be given to Missy; "We can talk that over," she wrote Franklin.[2]

How did she visualize her life in Albany, she was asked at a news conference. She would make the executive mansion into a home for her husband, she said, take the social side of things off his shoulders, and see that the house was run smoothly. She would carry on with the furniture factory at Val-Kill ("sold everything," she reported to her husband after their exhibit that autumn)[3] and with the weaving enterprise that she had recently started at Hyde Park village. These activities, she felt, were helpful to her neighbors and satisfied her craftsman's instinct. She was even more determined to continue her three-day teaching schedule at Todhunter School—"I teach because I love it, I cannot give it up." And she would arrange her life so that she could be immediately available to her children.[4] John, her youngest, had just joined Franklin Jr. and Elliott at

Groton, and James was at Harvard. She must be able, at a moment's notice, to dash up to Groton or Cambridge, as she did soon after Franklin's election when "F. Jr. checked into the infirmary with a belly-ache in the right side" and Johnny, "the poor lamb," was on crutches after having banged his knee on a door "in a rush for crackers after calisthenics." She also discovered on that trip that Elliott, in his eagerness to get on the football team, had never told the school about his old rupture, which was giving him trouble. James, whom she visited in Cambridge on the way home, disclosed that he had become secretly engaged to Betsy Cushing, "a nice child . . . but I regret that he wishes to tie himself down so young . . . in any case we can do nothing about it."⁵ "A lot of things can happen to four boys away at school," she told the press with motherly understatement.

Mistress of the mansion, mother, teacher—thus she envisaged her role in the weeks after election. But the women with whom she had worked expected more of her; they rejoiced in Roosevelt's victory as much because it brought Eleanor into the executive mansion as because it put him into the governor's chair. They were sure she would transform the position of First Lady into one of unique usefulness. "What a First Lady you will make," exulted Emily Newell Blair, the one-time suffrage leader and veteran Democratic politician. "How splendid it is to have one in that place with the political acumen and feeling for women that you have."⁶

Eleanor was eager to make a place for women in government, and under her tutelage her husband had come to a more genial and enlightened view of woman's quest for equality; but she knew that basically he still considered politics a man's business. Having freed himself from his mother's domination, he would become impatient and evasive if she pressed her point of view in ways that did not fit his purposes and defer to his moods. She would need self-control as well as feminine intuition and guile not to irritate him. They dealt differently with both people and problems. Her responses were structured by the logic of love; his by the logic of power and governance. Her imagination was active on behalf of others and flowered in deeds of kindness; he was concerned with using others to further his political career and purposes. She disregarded convention and sometimes was impatient with legality when it stood in the way of benevolence; he often yielded to expediency and the more comfortable course. When she disapproved, tension would arise between them. But she had an inner conviction that he shared her concern to make life better for others; that, too, was part of his political purpose, and she believed that with tact, humility, and a service of anonymity she could be of help to him and to the causes to which she now was so actively committed.

Even before the new governor assumed office, she was influential in shaping the character of his administration. Roosevelt was uncomfortably aware that Smith meant to remain the power in the state. Smith had always patronized Roosevelt, the Hudson River patrician, and treated him, Roosevelt later wrote, as a piece of "window dressing that had to be borne with because of a certain value in non-New York City areas." Robert Moses, with his gift for wounding invective, had summed up the attitude of some of Smith's circle toward Roosevelt with the gibe "He'll make a good campaigner but a lousy Governor." The governorship need not interfere with Roosevelt's polio therapy, Smith had accommodatingly assured him in September. Once he was sworn in, he could decamp for the winter to Warm Springs, leave Lehman in charge, and return for a few days before the legislature adjourned. The suggestion that he govern by proxy had amused Franklin in September; it irked him when it was renewed with even more insistence after his victory and Smith's defeat. Smith pressed him to retain the Smith cabinet intact, and particularly to keep Robert Moses as secretary of state and Belle Moskowitz as his speech writer and strategist. The situation worried Roosevelt and he discussed his anxieties with his wife and Louis. They supported him in his determination not to be a front man for Smith.

They were particularly uneasy about keeping Mrs. Henry Moskowitz. She had been a Bull Moose progressive and was a brilliant publicist, but she was so arrogant that even Eleanor, the most tractable and cooperative of colleagues, found it difficult to work with her. She was politically astute and totally committed to Smith—as dedicated, persevering, and suspicious in his behalf as Louis was in Roosevelt's. "By all signs I think Belle and Bob Moses mean to cling to you," she warned her husband, "and you will wake up to find R.M. Secretary of State and B.M. running Democratic publicity at the old stand unless you take a firm stand."[7] Her next slightly anti-Semitic remark underscored how strongly she felt. "Gosh! the race has nerves of iron and tentacles of steel!" Roosevelt was perfectly clear in his own mind that he did not want Belle as part of his political household, but he could not bring himself to tell Smith. Eleanor was aware of how difficult it could be for him to be the messenger of bad news and how he hated situations where his charm and persuasiveness were impotent, but she kept after him. "Don't let Mrs. M. get draped around you for she means to be," she prodded in a letter to Warm Springs. "It will always be one for you and two for Al."[8]

"I hope you will consider making Frances Perkins Labor Commissioner," she wrote him, starting another campaign. "She'd do well and you could fill her place as Chairman of the Industrial Commission by one of the men now on [the] Commission and put Nell Schwartz (now Bureau of Women in Industry) on the Commission so there would be one woman on it." Then, as if she sensed male feathers being ruffled, she hastily added, "These are suggestions which I'm passing on, not my opinions for I don't mean to butt in."[9] And knowing that men will often hear with pleasure from other women what they will not accept from their wives, she had made sure that she would not be the only woman to make this suggestion. She instigated an invitation to Warm Springs for Molly Dewson, a reformer who nevertheless understood the political game; men liked Molly's down-East saltiness. She had come to Eleanor to ask how she could cash in on her services in the campaign and interest the governor-elect in the legislative program of the New York Consumers League, of which she was president.[10] "Go to Warm Springs to see Franklin before others see him," Eleanor advised, and promptly made it possible.

Molly arrived in Warm Springs well briefed. In the course of talking to

Roosevelt about minimum-wage legislation she shifted the discussion to the department responsible for the administration of labor standards. "Why don't you appoint Frances Perkins your Industrial Commissioner?" she interjected. Franklin gave Molly the impression that he was not surprised by her request and that he was thinking about it favorably.[11]

The final confrontation between Roosevelt and Smith came during a four-hour meeting soon after his return from Warm Springs. All during December the battle had been fought behind the scenes and through stories planted by both sides, mostly in the Democratic *World.* "While [Smith] will retire to private life, probably to banking," wrote Ernest K. Lindley, who had covered Smith for many years, "no one doubts that he will continue to be a very powerful, if not the dominating influence in the Democratic Party in this State." Roosevelt means "to administer the office in his own name and by his own right," wrote another correspondent for the *World* on the same day. "This means," the story continued, "there will be changes in the Smith Cabinet." Lieutenant Governor-elect Herbert Lehman—a protégé of Belle's—confirmed on his return from Warm Springs, where he had gone to discuss the legislative program, that Roosevelt intended to be much more active as governor than had generally been assumed at the time of his nomination. And Roosevelt, tanned, buoyant, and "fit as a fiddle," underscored Lehman's observation. "I am ready," he announced as he left Warm Springs, "to carry on the duties of Governor of New York and to remain constantly on the job during the entire legislative period."

Eleanor had alerted Franklin that Smith wanted to see him as soon as possible after his return, and three days after Roosevelt's arrival in New York the two men talked. Moses "rubs me the wrong way," Roosevelt told Smith flatly, and that finished the campaign to keep him on. He was less definite about Belle, and an added complication was Smith's disapproval of Roosevelt's plan to appoint Frances Perkins as labor commissioner.[12] He was proud of Miss Perkins, Smith said—it was he who had appointed her chairman of the Industrial Commission, and she had performed ably—but a cabinet post carried administrative responsibilities, and, he said, "men will take advice from a woman, but it is hard for them to take orders from a woman." Smith's attitude did not surprise Eleanor. She had caught a glimpse of it in the way he had talked about the visit paid him by Nellie Tayloe Ross when she was governor of Wyoming, when Smith had gloated over her inability to produce the kind of figures that he always had at his fingertips. He did not feel a woman should be governor of a state or head of a department.[13]

Roosevelt, nevertheless, appointed Miss Perkins and also, as Eleanor had suggested, put Nell Schwartz on the Industrial Commission.

To the end of her life Eleanor would deny that she had had any part in the naming of Miss Perkins, and yet she kept a watchful eye on developments just to make sure there would be no last-minute hitches. At Miss Perkins' request, she arranged for her to come to Hyde Park to have a relaxed talk with the governor-elect and to make sure that their ideas agreed on how far her writ would run. It was a "very satisfactory talk," Miss Perkins informed Eleanor afterward, "under conditions which couldn't possibly have occurred otherwise."[14] She wanted Eleanor to know "how much the women of the State admire your prospective relationship to Government." But that relationship, Eleanor knew, and her closest collaborators soon perceived, depended on how well she buried her tracks and how persuasively she disavowed that she had any influence. Molly sensed the hazards in Eleanor's path; if she had not emphasized how much Mrs. Roosevelt had helped her, she later wrote, it was "because I thought she was in a delicate position, and the less I said about her in connection with my work, the better."[15] Defeated on Moses and Perkins, Smith still fought on for Belle, and he appealed to Perkins, who was on good terms with both men, to intercede with Roosevelt. She did, but Roosevelt turned her down. Belle was "very, very able" and had done "a great deal for Al," as she would for any man who was governor, he conceded. But, and Miss Perkins suddenly became aware how much the man leaning back in his armchair had grown in strength and maturity, "I've *got* to be Governor of the State of New York and I have got to be it MYSELF. . . . I'm awfully sorry if it hurts anybody particularly Al."[16]

The battle to be governor in his own right was won, but Frances Perkins, who saw it from the inside, believed that Roosevelt might well have drifted into accepting Mrs. Moskowitz if it hadn't been for Eleanor.[17]

On the afternoon of January 31 the Smiths were at the executive mansion to await arrival of the Roosevelt motorcade from Hyde Park. When it came into view preceded by motorcycle outriders, Smith went down the steps. "God bless you and keep you, Frank," Smith greeted him. "A thousand welcomes. We've got the home fires burning and you'll find this a fine place to live." As Smith came toward him, Roosevelt added, "I only wish Al were going to be right here for the next two years." Mrs. Smith kissed the governor-elect and Smith embraced Mrs. Roosevelt. Both sides were cordial and considerate, a more difficult script for Smith to follow, for these final days in Albany with their outpourings of affection and "Auld Lang Synes" were something of a wake, but he carried it off in splendid style.

That evening Irving Lehman, associate justice of the court of appeals and Herbert's brother, swore in the new governor and lieutenant governor. Leaning on James's arm Roosevelt took the oath of office on the Old Dutch Bible that had been in the Roosevelt family since before Isaac the Patriot's day. Theodore Roosevelt had been sworn in as governor thirty years before in the same room.

The executive mansion quickly took on the easy informality of the Roosevelt household. It was always full, its nine guest rooms usually occupied, and large groups sat down to every luncheon and dinner. Informal meals were taken on the sun porch; the big state receptions and dinners were held in the large dining room. They came off "with full dignity," wrote one newspaperman who was often a guest at the mansion, "but with less stuffiness than such occasions acquire in the hands of less skilled hostesses."[18] House guests mingled with political leaders. Roosevelt's closest aides, and Eleanor's, became members of the household. Every afternoon when she was in Albany Eleanor served "a good substantial tea with chocolate cake" in the family sitting room, and whoever was in the house was invited: family, secretaries, newspapermen, friends, state troopers, distinguished guests. The servants were swept up in the warmth and friendliness of the governor and his lady, for their outstanding trait was that they enjoyed people.

A movie theater was set up in the hall on the third floor. Books, magazines, and papers were everywhere. Dogs raced through the halls—Chief, a large police dog, and the first Falla, a black Scottish terrier named after Murray of Fallahill, a remote Scotch ancestor. There was naturalness, noise, laughter, and continuous commotion. It was a home, not an official residence. At the center was Eleanor, managing the household, making life comfortable for its members, making guests feel at home, and making it all seem easy.

There is a picture of the Roosevelt hospitality in the diaries of Caroline Phillips. She and William arrived on a Friday afternoon to visit their old friends. "A very efficient-looking English butler" showed them upstairs "to a comfortable sitting room where we found Eleanor presiding over a tea table as quiet and peaceful as though she had nothing at all to do." Caroline noted, a little wonderingly, all the household people who drifted in for tea. John A. Warner, Al Smith's son-in-law and the head of the state police, and his wife came for dinner. And afterward they watched a movie starring the Barrymore brothers. "All the servants, black and white, seventeen in all, sat behind the house party and enjoyed the show with us." The Phillips marveled at the way Franklin and Eleanor were handling their jobs, "entering into the lives of their friends and household with greatest sympathy and courtesy. . . . Eleanor never seems to worry."

The fixed points in Eleanor's schedule during the Albany years were the Sunday evening train to New York and the noon train back on Wednesdays so that she would be in time for her Wednesday "at homes" from 4:30 to 6:00 P.M. Each Sunday before she left she obtained from Franklin a complete list of the people who would stay in the house while she was away and wrote out precise instructions for Harry Whitehead, the mansion's major-domo—menus, seating order at table, assignment of rooms, cars to meet guests, issuance of invitations. She settled servant problems, considered proposals for the purchase of labor-saving equipment, and made decisions on the one hundred and one little matters that are involved in the management of a large household. When friends expressed admiration for the ease and dispatch with which she managed the governor's house, she dismissed the praise: "Everything is done for me. I simply give the orders."[19]

Missy offered to take over some of the responsibility when Eleanor was away, but Eleanor firmly declined. She was grateful to the young woman, because if Missy were not living in the mansion it would be difficult to continue teaching. Yet it made her unhappy that Missy served as hostess at the all-male dinners Franklin gave while she was in the city and that he accommodated himself so genially to her absences; she would have liked him to protest.

Often Eleanor took early Sunday supper with Franklin and their guests, but usually the pre-supper talk flowed on until there was only time for her to gulp down milk and crackers and dash for the train. As a belated birthday present Nan and Marion had given her "a new kind of brief case bag" whose chief virtue was supposed to be an almost infinite expandability, and it soon bulged with the letters and documents that poured in upon her as the governor's wife. On the train she penciled out the replies she would dictate to Miss Thompson in New York—at the women's division office that she continued to share with Nancy. She also marked students' papers and worked on her lesson plans for the coming week. She had classes at Todhunter from nine to one on Monday, nine to five on Tuesday, and nine to eleven on Wednesday, which left time for her many other activities, and her calendar was always packed tight from morning to night. "If Mrs. Roosevelt did not hit two birds with every one stone, she never could have carried out her schedule," remarked Molly, who had been told to come and pour out her woes while Eleanor was on her way to the dressmaker.[20]

She worked with Louis Howe, whom she kept informed of Franklin's activities. Louis had remained in New York City, since the right position could not be found for him in Albany. To be the governor's secretary did not seem fitting, and he could not have headed a department. He, therefore, continued as Roosevelt's political chief-of-staff. Since he liked to work behind the scenes, the city seemed a better place from which to handle Roosevelt's political mail, so he continued to live at 49 East Sixty-fifth Street and serve as assistant to the chairman of the National Crime Commission. A guest room was set aside for him at the mansion for week ends. It was not as satisfying as being able to control access to Franklin, as he had done for so many years, but he adapted to the governor's necessities, as did every one else around Franklin. Moreover, there was always Eleanor. At times the two seemed like conspirators in their efforts to hold the governor to a course of action they favored.[21]

Eleanor's political activities underwent a period of experimental adaptation. She no longer made political speeches, resigned from the boards of civic organizations that lobbied for legislation in Albany, and for a while declined to attend any meetings that "savor[ed] of politics," as she told Henry Morgenthau, Jr., when he invited her to a conference of master farmers. She also refused invitations to local Democratic dinners in four upstate counties, "so you see I'm being most discreet," she assured her husband.[22] She would miss not having "direct political responsibility," she told a farewell luncheon of the Women's City Club, especially after having worked so long to make women feel their political obligations.[23]

But this withdrawal from political activity was more a matter of form than substance. She removed her name from the masthead of the *Democratic News*, but continued to edit it behind the scenes, wrote editorials anonymously, and assigned the articles to be written.

By May, Franklin had lifted the prohibition on attending political gatherings as long as she did not make political speeches. In fact, he wanted her to go: it took another burden off his shoulders. The meetings were often exhausting affairs. She attended a Democratic luncheon on Staten Island, which she described to Franklin: "Arrived at 12:30, stood and shook hands till 1:30, ate till 3:30; talked till 5:20; home here at 6:40 nearly dead! They nominated you for President & you are the finest Gov. ever & I have all the virtues & would gladly have dispensed with half could I have left at four!"[24] A week later she was going to a Democratic dinner in Cohoes, "so let me know if you want anything done."

Her feminine grace and sympathy did not interfere with her hard-headed astuteness as a politician. When the Women's Democratic Club of Buffalo wanted to know whether a woman could be elected to office, she answered, "I think there is more opportunity now than ever before for women in politics if they will keep their ideals high and go in with the purpose of being of service rather than with the purpose of obtaining an office." Offices would come as a matter of course when the service was rendered. "Why not try to run one Buffalo woman this coming autumn in a district which has some chance?" was her closing advice.[25]

She championed the representatives of the women's groups lobbying for protective legislation for children and women workers. All through the twenties they had arrived faithfully on the Monday Empire State Express while the legislature was in session, had spent long hours waiting in corridors and anterooms to see legislators, and then were brushed off. Now they went to the executive mansion "for tea, or dinner or even to stay overnight."[26] Sometimes she lectured the women on the realities of wheeling and dealing in the legislative halls. "My dear girls," she told a League of Women Voters' delegation brought to Albany by Mrs. Leach, "you don't know what you are talking about," and then proceeded to tell them what the men really thought. "Of course, I have Franklin so they don't dare talk that way to me."[27]

Molly, who did not require lectures on lobbying, was also helped by Eleanor on occasion. She came to Albany to lobby for a bill to reduce the working hours of women in retail stores. A compromise bill had passed and was ready for the governor's signature, but it was strongly opposed by business, and the governor had arranged a public hearing. Molly found the hearing room "packed with elegantly tailored, prosperous looking gentlemen, the merchants, and not a single backer of the bill except . . . [for the] representative of the League of Women Voters. Somehow the Women's Conference had not received their notice of the hearing."

She was pouring out her disgust later to Eleanor over a cup of tea when Franklin came rolling in in his wheel chair, looking, Molly thought, as fresh and cheerful as if he were going off for a week end. Immediately Eleanor said, "What are you going to do about the bill?" with what Molly felt was a touch of anxiety in her voice.

"Sign it, of course," he debonairly answered, and held out his hand for tea.[28]

The twenty-fifth anniversary of the Women's Trade Union League took place in 1929. The Finance Committee headed by Mrs. Roosevelt and Mrs. Lamont had raised most of the money to pay off the mortgage on the league headquarters. They were arranging to celebrate the event with a party at the clubhouse when a letter came from Mrs. James Roosevelt inviting them to have their party at Hyde Park. Eleanor urged the governor to appear. "Don't forget the Women's Trade Union League party on June 8 from 2–6 PM, you are the *pièce-de-résistance*," she reminded him.[29] A boat was chartered and shop-girls and trade-union leaders made the trip up the Hudson.

"Did your ears ring all evening on Saturday?" Rose Schneiderman wrote Roosevelt afterward. "You were the main topic of conversation all the way down the river. The girls were saying over and over again, 'was not the Governor great' 'what a kind face he has' and 'How democratic he is' etc. etc. . . . As for myself—well, I wish there were a million more like you and Eleanor."[30]

Sara issued the invitation, Mrs. Lamont turned over the check, Franklin starred. Eleanor stayed in the background, but she was the link with the Women's Trade Union League, and it was often Eleanor who was in the lead on labor issues, rather than Franklin, on occasion even joining a picket line.[31] In April she presided at a luncheon of the Women's Trade Union League where the discussion centered on the five-day week. Merwin K. Hart, the manufacturers' lobbyist, commented that Mrs. Roosevelt would not want to be told she could work only five days a week. Taken by surprise, she agreed, but then qualified her agreement. "Work is living for me. The point is whether we live in our work."[32] Repeating a single motion throughout the day in a factory was drudgery, not to be compared with doing work that one enjoyed. And when in October, 1930, the International Ladies Garment Workers Union struck against the fashionable Fifth Avenue dressmakers and David Dubinsky was arrested for disorderly conduct, Eleanor came to his aid and endorsed the ILGWU's efforts to organize the unorganized.

"The Legislature adjourned, thank the Lord," Eleanor wrote, as the first session came to an end.[33] Franklin left for Warm Springs, and she began preparations for a trip to Europe which Franklin had suggested she take with Franklin Jr., who was called "Brother," and Johnny, together with Nan and Marion. The prospect of showing her sons her favorite places in Europe was appealing, but it also worried her. She was not sure she could handle Brother, going on fifteen, and Johnny, thirteen, and their inevitable wrestling matches. "I'm getting colder and colder feet about going abroad," she confessed in May. "It seems such a fearful effort."[34] She also fretted about the costs. There were large doctors' bills that spring, between Johnny's knee and Brother's broken nose and Elliott's rupture and James's digestive troubles—"if Franklin gets thro' under $6,000 he will be doing well." There were other money worries: "James asked me to beg you to send his check as he says it is a necessity. I wonder if you have forgotten Louis too? He has said nothing but Mary, when they were leaving last night, asked him for money & he was so hesitant to give it I wondered if he was short!" Sara as usual came to the rescue. "I am glad Mama is giving you a present because now I hope we will be able to pay all our many demands!"[35]

It was also Sara who a month later almost undid the European trip during a family dinner at the Big House. Eleanor was reviewing their plans for the trip—they were taking over the Buick and Chevvy and she, Nan, and Marion would do the driving; perhaps they might even do some camping. Suddenly Sara reared up, disapprovingly—it would be undignified for the wife of the gov-

ernor and two of his sons to motor in an old touring car and even worse for the
governor's wife to drive herself. Here young Franklin, unaware of the gathering
storm clouds, chimed in, "Mom will probably land us in the first ditch," and
described how the day before she had driven them into a gatepost, ending,
cheerfully if illogically, "But we'll be all right." Eleanor then turned to the head
of the table where Sara always sat opposite Franklin, and said in a cold voice,
"Very well. I will take your grandsons in a manner consistent with what you
think their positions ought to be." With that she hurried out of the dining room
and took refuge on the screened porch. Here Franklin intervened, and in a
voice more stern than Franklin Jr. had ever heard him use before—"or
after"—told him to go after his mother, apologize, and not to return without
her. Young Franklin was appalled to find his mother in tears and horrified that
he should have hurt her so—"and there was the Old Man chained to his chair
by his legs or otherwise he would have gone himself after Mother," he commented in recalling the incident.[36]

But Franklin did not contradict Sara. She again had her way, and the incident cast a shadow over the entire trip. The Chevvy was left behind. Nan and
Marion took the Buick but Eleanor rented handsome chauffeur-driven limousines everywhere they went, beginning with a Daimler in England, and made
the boys sit in the back with her although they longed to be up front with the
driver. Not until Belgium, where they had a driver who charmed them all and
who placed a little bouquet of flowers in the car for Eleanor every morning, did
she relent. "Brother paid for that remark very dearly," commented Marion
Dickerman. "Eleanor could be very hard."[37]

Before going abroad, Eleanor and the boys accompanied Franklin on an
early-summer trip through New York State that was to become an annual
event. During his first bout with the legislature, the governor had suffered several rebuffs from the Republican-controlled body, a fate he knew would be
repeated unless he could build greater support for his objectives in the upstate
areas. The city-oriented Democrats had long given up the farm areas as irre-
trievably Republican, but Roosevelt's formula was to cultivate the rural areas,
and six years of crisscrossing the state on behalf of the women's division had
convinced Eleanor that Democratic policies and organization could find a foothold upstate if the leadership worked at it. Roosevelt planned a summer cruise
along the state's inland waterways that would enable him to inspect hospitals,
mental institutions, and prisons as well as carry his programs to the people,
especially the farmers. To Henry Morgenthau, Jr., who had sampled rural opinion on the issues of the 1929 legislature, he wrote, "What hits me most is the
very high percentage of ignorance."

Eleanor joined enthusiastically in the preparations for the trip. A farm
woman had written her a bitter letter against the Department of Education and
school consolidation, she informed Dr. Frank Graves, the commissioner of
education, and she wanted someone in his office to line up the facts for her "as
concisely as possible." She intended to talk to the woman when she was in the
western part of the state. "I think it would be a very good thing to put in the
Women's *Democratic News*," she added, "besides being a very necessary thing

for my own education."[38] The tour had another purpose. In May when Franklin had gone to Warm Springs there had been a flood of stories that he was an exceedingly tired man, which disturbed Eleanor and Louis. "It looks like a deliberate campaign to show how much will now have to be done when you are away," she wrote Franklin. "Lehman would not do it & I think others are responsible";[39] she detected "Belle's hand" in the operation. The most effective antidote to innuendos about the governor's physical capability was to go out and meet the citizenry face to face. So on July 7 Franklin, accompanied by his wife and sons, took command of the "good ship *Inspector* which has a glass roof" and headed westward along the Barge Canal to Buffalo.

There were frequent debarkations to meet local officials and inspect state institutions. The protocol of these inspections called for a tour of the grounds by automobile with the superintendent as guide and Roosevelt as commentator, pointing out for the benefit of the press what he wanted the legislature to do. Debarred by his crippled legs from going through the buildings, the governor would excuse himself and say Mrs. Roosevelt would be happy to do so. This was a new responsibility for Eleanor. She had at times looked at state hospitals for crippled children and similar institutions, but it was one thing to visit as a guest and quite another to inspect on behalf of the governor, who carried the ultimate responsibility for the management of these institutions. Franklin was not easily satisfied; the usefulness of the information—on which he had to act—depended on the ability of his deputies to spot the telling detail, fix it in their minds, and report it back coherently. He had made hundreds of inspections when he was assistant secretary of the Navy, and he knew what to look for; he now proceeded to instruct his wife.

Her first reports produced explosions of dissatisfaction. Was there overcrowding? It had not seemed so to her. How had she reached that conclusion? Had she estimated the distance between beds? Had she looked behind doors and into closets to see whether cots had been folded up and stacked away out of sight?

He was equally severe in regard to the food that was being served. The first time, she simply reported what she had read on the menus. He advised her to look into the pots in the kitchen and to make sure that what she saw there corresponded with what was listed on the menus. She began to look for the telltale signs, the grimace, the slightly cynical smile that might suggest morale problems between patients and staff or between staff and superiors. And then there was the problem of remembering it all. Franklin had a "really prodigious memory," and Eleanor had to discipline herself to hold the things she saw in her mind until she had passed them on to him.[40]

Her education in the techniques of inspection was further advanced by Corporal Earl Miller, a state trooper assigned to the governor's detail who often accompanied Eleanor when she went out alone. They became friends and he was soon giving her hints on the techniques officials used to take in unwary visitors. The surest way to get a true picture, he suggested, was to arrive unannounced, which she began to do; unhappy officials often could not conceal their consternation.[41]

It was a hard school. Once Franklin asked her to look at some upstate tree plantings that were to serve as a shelter belt, and he was clearly disappointed by her inability afterward to answer his questions. "I put my best efforts after that into missing nothing and remembering everything."[42] Before the Albany years were finished, she "had become a fairly expert reporter on state institutions."[43]

Eleanor continued to have mixed feelings about dropping everything to take the boys to Europe while her husband stayed behind to do the world's battles; it was too reminiscent of her lonely summers at Campobello. "Like most things in life," she confessed, "I want to go and yet I don't want to leave."[44] But they sailed from Montreal on July 26 after Franklin gave them a farewell dinner at the Mount Royal Hotel. "Well we are off & I am going to try to give the boys a good time and while I don't expect you to write please send me frequent cables," she wrote Franklin. "One for instance on Monday after you have been to Dannemora!"[45] Her mind was on the state's business, not Baedeker. There had been an outbreak of riots at Dannemora and Auburn prisons caused by overcrowding, poor food, and the enactment of the Baumes Laws, which made life sentence mandatory for fourth offenders. "I think the Baumes law makes reward for good behavior impossible and takes incentive away," her second shipboard letter stated. "Do write me what you find and your conclusions. The surplus will vanish in prison repairs if this goes on."[46] But he did not write, preferring to cable and telephone. "Hope you have a good trip. What shall I do with your casket?" his first communication read. "No one could imagine what it meant," Eleanor informed him, "but then I remembered the lunch basket which we discovered we left behind our first day out. . . ."

The boys disembarked at Belfast, where they joined James, who was staying with his fiancée at a country house overlooking the River Boyne that the Cushing family had taken outside Dublin. After a trip through the Lake district—in two cars—Nan and Marion went on to visit friends in Scotland, while Eleanor took the boat back to Dublin, where she found her boys very much involved with horses. James had even spent all his money on a colt that a fast-talking Irishman said could be trained to win all the races. When James later wired his father for his return passage, saying he would repay him out of his winnings, Franklin replied, "So happy about horse, suggest both of you swim home."[47] From the boys' talk Eleanor picked up the news that Elliott had gambled on the canal trip and lost twenty-five dollars to Corporal Miller and forty-five dollars to another member of the governor's staff. "I had a talk with him about gambling but I did not realize it was for sums like that he had played."[48] She was quite worried about Elliott. It was the summer he was refusing to go on to college. Franklin should talk to him about the right use of money, she advised, but without telling him they knew about his gambling losses.

In Dublin she went to the horse show and the races with her children. At a lunch at the legation, she met the "very nice Governor General" of Ireland, and the children of the founder and president of Czechoslovakia, the young Masaryks, were there—"very nice as usual"—and also "a most unpleasant

Maharaja who strangled his wife (one of them) & threw her body down a well & looks it." Gossip had it that it had been the wife's punishment "for having disagreed with her lord and master." For the rest of the tour, they kept away from the world of officials. A Labor government had just come to power in London, but Eleanor made no effort to get in touch with political people, even though Franklin had suggested she go and see Prime Minister Ramsay Mac-Donald. This was to be a sightseeing trip for her boys, she insisted, and though she saw some old school friends in London and Aunt Dora in Paris, nothing was allowed to interfere with an exhaustive inspection of historical and cultural sites. She tried to keep the boys so busy during the day that they would be too weary for roughhousing, but almost every night she had to separate "two very angry brothers." They loved shopping at Harrod's and Burberry's: "I assure you I am ruined but they are swank and happy," she wrote Franklin. But they were bored with cricket and seeing the sites, and Eleanor was weary "of my incubus of a motor car," and so all were glad to cross the Channel for a tour of the Low Countries and the Rhine down to Bingen. In Luxembourg Nan, Marion, and the two boys toasted Franklin in the local champagnes; Eleanor "joined in, in Evian water!" Outside of Reims they inspected the Poméry wine cellars, where Eleanor observed that "very young boys were working under very unhealthy conditions" and Brother happily did some tasting. "F Jr. has had a taste of everything and likes it but I won't let him have it as a rule!" she reported.

At her husband's specific request they toured the battlefields, the underground forts at Verdun, Château-Thierry, Belleau Woods, and placed flowers near Quentin Roosevelt's grave. The rows and rows of crosses made a profound impression on the boys. "The thing that surprised me most was how France or Germany could go on and continue to be a world power when it had lost so many men," John wrote to his father.

Eleanor was disappointed not to find a letter from Franklin in Paris. "I hate not knowing what you have done about Elliott, and a thousand other things," she wrote. Had young Nesbitt, the son of a Hyde Park woman with whom she had become friendly, gotten into Cornell, she wanted to know, and would Franklin advance him money if he needed it.

As they were leaving Paris for Cherbourg, Franklin's only letter finally arrived, with the information that he intended to leave for Warm Springs soon after she returned. "I am very glad to be going with you as it will give us a little while to catch up & talk things over," she replied contentedly. She was glad she had made the trip, she finally concluded, "& will enjoy it in retrospect when the anxiety & necessary difficulties with two healthy youngsters is past. They have been good but a certain amount of trouble is inevitable. I think next summer we will separate them for a while." But her trials with the boys were not over. On their way to Cherbourg they visited Chartres and spent a night at Madame Poulard's at Mont-Saint-Michel, but the boys were in such a quarrelsome mood that she left them behind when she went to climb the ramparts and look at the old abbey and church. On her return, there was a commotion in the streets, and as she approached Madame Poulard's she heard screams. Franklin

Jr. had pushed Johnny out of the window and was holding him head down dangling by the heels.[49]

They returned September 15. Todhunter classes resumed on October 1 and as vice principal she was soon involved in the preparations for the reopening of the school. Being mother, mistress of the executive mansion, and the governor's stand-in were all parts of her job, but the activities that she considered her own were teaching, writing, lecturing, helping run the Val-Kill Furniture Factory. She had agreed to serve as a member of the committee selecting books for the Junior Literary Guild. "She tells you with pride that this is a paid job; not her only one, for her school pays her a salary, too," Ida Tarbell wrote.[50] *Vogue* asked Eleanor to do an article, and she was pleased that the editor thought it "splendid," she noted in her reply to him, but he had said nothing about payment. "The only reason that I feel I must do this on a business basis is that other magazines pay me and I do not feel that unless it is for a purely educational or charitable publication, that it is quite fair not to ask the usual compensation."[51] She could use the money, but more important to her was the professional recognition that payment signified.

Though the activities that gave her the greatest satisfaction were those that she did in her own right, the public's growing interest in her was a result of the way she used the executive mansion as a springboard for good works, revealing the First Lady had a heart awake to the problems of other people. There was a person at the center of government, the individual citizen discovered, who answered any plea for help and took up every complaint against a bureaucrat. Neither by design nor appointment, and with her husband's concurrence, she began to perform an office that later generations would call "ombudsman."

She entered into the lives of her petitioners and thought of them as human beings, not cases. There were heart-rending appeals from the families of patients in the mental hospitals, which she sent on for investigation to Dr. Parsons, the commissioner of mental hygiene. "I enclose his report," she wrote to the family of a Miss P., "which indicates that the patient has a mild mental disturbance to which, generally speaking, she makes a satisfactory adjustment, but from time to time she overboils in the manner indicated in the letter." And thanking Dr. Parsons, she wrote, "I hope she eventually may be settled, . . . poor thing, she does not sound very happy." She was swamped with letters from old people begging her help with pension problems. She had every one of these "pathetic letters" reviewed in the hope that somehow they might be entitled to some kind of help. She looked into all requests for pardons, and if clemency was impossible, as was usually the case, "I can sometimes relieve their sorrow a little."

One of her most touching and insistent correspondents was a mother with a son in jail. "When she found I could not help her free him she begged that I go see him which I did. Now she begs that I go weekly and read the Bible to him!" A woman of eighty, so poor she could not pay for a dog license, had applied for an exemption. She sent Eleanor the "unfeeling letter" the state supervisor of dog licenses had written her; could Mrs. Roosevelt use her influence with the governor to have the tax remitted? It was Mrs. Roosevelt who paid the tax. She was overwhelmed by the trust people had in her. "I am the farmer's wife, that wrote you two years ago," one letter began. "You remember, I laid out my case then. Will you now see that I get my pension." "The farmer's wife," commented Eleanor wonderingly, "when there are dozens of them daily!"

But no letter went unanswered. Sometimes she sent a petitioner to his local district leader for help, but she did not leave it there. "Will you be good enough to let me know just what help your District Leader gave you," she added. If she could do nothing in Albany, she would appeal to one of the many friends she had made throughout the state to look into a case for her, to see whether help might not be available locally.

Sometimes she showed these letters to Louis and, after she got to know him, to Corporal Miller, but as often as not she disregarded their warning that she was being taken in. "You're nothing but a cop," she said to Corporal Miller.[52] The appeals for help became a flood after the stock-market crash, and the rise in joblessness taxed even her resourcefulness in finding something affirmative to say to her correspondents. She strongly advised people not to come to New York to look for work: "At the present time there are countless numbers of people out of employment here and I am not able to get positions for any one." But still she did not give up. Did he have a job for Mr. K., statistician and Yale graduate, she asked Tom Lynch, who was now president of the State Tax Commission. "He has cried in my office like a whipped child."

Often she showed letters to her husband. "How shall I answer or will you?" she would pencil on the plea.

She functioned in a highly unorthodox way that defied all proper administrative charts. If she had been less tactful, less sensitive, if she had not always been careful to stay within the limits set by Franklin and to check with him to be sure that her activities were consistent with what he wanted done, her acts of compassion and her desire to be helpful could have degenerated into a scandal of meddlesomeness.

Roosevelt encouraged his state officials in the belief that he and "the Missus" were a team. She understood, and she was loyal. When she disagreed with him she told him, but it was kept within the family. He was the captain of the ship. "I sat next to you in the Senate chamber when the twenty million dollar relief bill was passed," an irate upstate judge wrote her. "Officials in Albany told me you were the boss. . . ." She had not been in the senate chamber when the relief bill was passed, she replied, "so you were wrong in thinking you sat next to me. Also any officials who told you I was boss of anything, were equally wrong."[53] Some members of Roosevelt's administration undoubtedly grumbled to their wives when she made requests they considered inconvenient, but more often they were glad to oblige. Not only was she the governor's wife and a political power in her own right, but, most important of all, she was a useful champion when their own programs were in trouble—or when they wanted the governor's support for new ideas.

It was to Eleanor that Frances Perkins came with a plan to overhaul and modernize the moribund Public Employment Service and its neglected network of state employment offices. Eleanor immediately saw its political implications as well as economic uses. "It looks good to me for it would take in employment of middle-aged and physically handicapped, etc. and you'd get the jump on Hoover, but they won't move till you let me know what you think," Eleanor wrote Franklin; the letter reached him a few days before the collapse of the stock market.[54] Roosevelt, according to Perkins, "at once saw the point of developing a good modern well-supported State Public Employment Service."

Eleanor had gotten to know a vast number of women in the small towns and rural areas and was now systematically getting to know more of them. Together with Elinor Morgenthau and Nancy Cook she was a faithful participant in the Home Economics Weeks that were organized by Cornell's Bureau of Home Economics and which annually brought thousands of rural women to Ithaca. Eleanor admired Martha van Rensselaer, the moving spirit behind the bureau, for the way she had made the bureau into a down-to-earth, sensible service to upstate women.

The women's division was ready for the 1930 gubernatorial campaign. Eleanor brought Molly Dewson into the division, and with Nancy Cook and Caroline O'Day they mapped strategy, organized meetings, issued literature—all behind the scenes. Her editorials in the *Democratic News* rallied the workers in the precincts to speak for the whole ticket. Her final editorial criticized the one-issue campaign of Republican candidate Charles H. Tuttle, who had concentrated on Tammany and corruption: what about the other big state-wide questions—taxation, farm relief, labor legislation, control of utilities, unemployment and public works, power?

What does it mean to be a candidate's wife, an interviewer wanted to know as the campaign drew to a close. "It doesn't mean a thing!" Eleanor replied. "In this particular case, at any event, the candidate's wife will go on pursuing the even tenor of her ways. Politics does not excite me. It never did. I take things as they come. If my husband is reelected, I shall be pleased. And if he isn't—well the world is full of interesting things to do."[55] In the meantime, however, she made sure that not the smallest thing was left undone that might help get her husband elected.

Roosevelt's landslide victory exceeded all expectations. He was swept in with a margin of 725,000, and was the first Democrat ever to carry upstate New York—by 167,000, which included Hyde Park, to Eleanor a "greater satisfaction than anything else." "Mrs. Roosevelt was a very great factor in Franklin D. Roosevelt's reelection," noted Molly Dewson, who was not given to flattery.[56]

The victory celebrations at Hyde Park on election night were prolonged, and Eleanor, who had to get ready for class next day, penciled a good-night note to her husband. "Much love & a world of congratulations. It is a triumph in so many ways, dear & so well earned. Bless you & good luck these next two years.—E.R."

33. *Roosevelt Bids for the Presidency*

IN A YEAR OF DEMOCRATIC SUCCESSES, Roosevelt's was the handsomest. Overnight he became front runner among the Democratic aspirants for the presidency. It gave Eleanor pleasure to see him move toward the prize that he wanted above all others. She better than anyone appreciated how much determination and self-mastery his victory represented. She was happy, too, in the joy that the triumph brought her gnarled little friend Louis Howe, who behind the scenes had masterminded the comeback. Both men were now within sight of the goal they had been pursuing almost from the time of their first encounter. But she herself was a "fatalist," and the larger the ambition, the greater her feeling of its insubstantiality. She obtained her sense of fulfillment in service to others; to search out some hidden or defeated aspiration in the heart of a human being and then, in ways of her own, "to help this aspiration assume reality" gave her the greatest, perhaps the only, real joy in life. She had helped Franklin surmount the apparent devastation of his hopes by poliomyelitis. Now that he was the leading candidate for president, "that prospect did not interest me particularly."[1]

Her hopes were centered on a wholly different concern—making their marriage once again a covenant of spirit and feeling and not an arrangement to benefit the children and Franklin's career. A wife's job, Eleanor told an interviewer who had been advised by a group of distinguished women that she was "the ideal type of modern wife," was to be partner, mother, homemaker—and in that order, she emphasized. At one time she had placed the mother's role first, "but today we understand that everything else depends upon the success of the wife and husband in their personal relationship."[2]

She wanted to be close to her husband, to share, to be treated as equal not as instrument. But he had been brought up in a society where the ideal marriage was one that joined masculine egotism to feminine self-devotion. He was, moreover, self-centered in the way men become when they learn that few can refuse them anything. She could say "no" to him, and that was a part of her problem—how to press her point of view without making him feel guilty. For when that happened he became elusive, and as he was a consummate actor if he wished to be, he could keep even Eleanor guessing as to his true feelings and purposes. This made her feel shut out and destroyed the sense of companionship that she craved. She never gave up the hope that he would change. Perhaps now, in a common effort to make life better for other people, they could find their way to a new kind of partnership and at last efface the hurt he had done her in the Lucy Mercer affair.

The day after Roosevelt's victory, Jim Farley, the breezy politician whom Louis had groomed and nudged into the Democratic state chairmanship, told the press, "I do not see how Mr. Roosevelt can escape becoming the next presidential nominee of his party, even if no one should raise a finger to bring it about." Roosevelt had not told Farley he had made up his mind to run, but the statement had been carefully drafted with Louis, who, Jim assumed, knew the Boss's mind. A few days later Ed Flynn, whose rather nominal duties as secretary of state sheltered his role as one of Roosevelt's closest political advisers, was let in on the decision. They decided that the friendly, outgoing Farley was the man to send out to the regular organizations to round up delegates as the representative of the Friends of Roosevelt, an organization that Louis would direct. It was not Franklin who told Eleanor that he had decided to make his bid for president in 1932, although, of course, she had long known that the presidency was his goal. It was from Louis that she learned of his decision and that Louis was already at work planning the final strategy.[3]

Even though Franklin had not asked her how she felt about his running for the presidency, she was prepared to put her full strength—which was considerable—into the battle for the nomination, and he knew he could count on her. New York politicians, Farley said, recognized that she was "a strong and influential public figure in her own right."[4] Women figured importantly in the campaign plans and Farley, a new convert to women's role in politics, stood a little in awe of the work of the women under Eleanor's leadership. He was also grateful to her. "It wouldn't matter what Mrs. Roosevelt asked me to do, I would do it," he later told Emma Guffey Miller, Democratic national committeewoman from Pennsylvania. "If it hadn't been for her I would never have gotten where I am for she gave me my first big chance."[5] But it was political realism about the effectiveness of the women's organization more than gratitude to Eleanor Roosevelt which swayed the men. Farley credited the women's division with Roosevelt's margin of victory in 1928, and the 1930 campaign became known as the "waffle-iron" campaign because of the effective appeal the women had addressed to the housewives.[6] According to Farley's calculation, in counties where Eleanor's women were at work the total party vote picked up 10 to 20 per cent. "We felt the same kind of a job could be done on a national scale," he said.[7] As the recognized leader of the Democratic women of the state, Eleanor was the logical person for this job, but as the wife of the man who was both governor and candidate, she could not work openly, so Molly Dewson agreed to serve as her deputy. Molly hit it off well with Howe and Farley, and the team was complete.

By the spring of 1931 Louis had opened up the Friends of Roosevelt offices, and his "letter writing mill" was going full tilt.[8] So was Molly's, for whose signature Eleanor prepared the letters, and who, said Howe, managed a campaign correspondence "quite as large" as Farley's, though she did not use the green ink that became his trademark. In July Farley, in his role as Exalted

Ruler of the Elks, made a highly productive western tour. At Eleanor's suggestion, Molly followed in his tracks a few months later. Her voluminous reports to Eleanor were also read by the men and perhaps were written with that in mind, for they reflected her and Eleanor's concern that Franklin should discuss the issues and that the women should not be ignored. At the end of her trip Molly reported from Salt Lake City: "I certainly got into pleasant relations with the ladies. . . . They undoubtedly were glad to see me. After all they are on the political coach, only by the eyelids—yet Hoover won by the women's vote." The women she had talked with considered Roosevelt "O.K." and a "vote getter" but Newton D. Baker, Wilson's secretary of war and a leading internationalist, also was "well liked." They were eager to hear Roosevelt "discuss national and international issues."[9]

Eleanor's campaign tasks for her husband were not limited to the women's division; she also helped the writers who wanted to do biographies of Franklin. Earle Looker, who had Republican inclinations and was a friend of the Oyster Bay Roosevelts, wanted to write a book about the Democratic Roosevelt. Eleanor furnished him opportunities to observe Roosevelt at first hand, and provided him with information. Looker did a great service for Roosevelt when the inevitable whispering campaign began about the candidate's physical incapacity to handle the presidency: he proposed publicly to challenge Roosevelt to submit to an examination by a panel of eminent physicians to be selected by the head of the New York Academy of Medicine. Roosevelt agreed and had the examination. The reprints of the panel's wholly affirmative findings, published by Looker in *Liberty*, were mailed out broadcast by Louis. "If polio did not kill him, the Presidency won't" was Eleanor's unsentimental reply when she was asked whether Franklin was physically up to the presidency.[10]

She was equally helpful to Ernest K. Lindley, who had covered Roosevelt, first for the *World* and then for the *New York Herald Tribune*. An outstanding reporter, he made his *Franklin D. Roosevelt: A Career in Progressive Politics* a sympathetic but objective biography that is still a source book for Roosevelt's Albany years. Roosevelt, who feigned dismay at the "whole library" of life stories that were being written about him, was not very cooperative with Lindley, but Eleanor and Louis were.[11]

Eleanor also took on such delicate, time-consuming tasks as the cultivation of Elizabeth Marbury, the still powerful Democrat, who wrote suggesting that Roosevelt come to Maine. "The best I can do is to send Eleanor to see you about the 20th of July," he replied. An ailing Missy accompanied Eleanor on a week's trip that included a stay in Newport with Cousin Susie and a stopover in Portland with Maude and David Gray. Eleanor was more concerned with Missy's health than with Miss Marbury's loyalties; Missy "smoked less today," she reported to her husband, "and I thought seemed more ready to sleep tonight. She is eating fairly well." They arrived at Miss Marbury's in time for lunch "& Miss Marbury has talked politics ever since except for a brief time when Missy & I went in swimming! Molly Dewson is here too for the night & tomorrow there is a grand jamboree!"[12]

Although she declined either in speeches or interviews to discuss politics or her husband's chances for the nomination, she was nevertheless an effective representative of his candidacy in the course of her extensive travels. In Winston-Salem, North Carolina, she spoke to the Altrusa Club, a nationwide organization of professional women, at a time when new Tammany scandals were breaking almost daily in New York City. Roosevelt's association with Tammany was seized upon by his rivals in order to embarrass him, and the nation watched developments as an index of his political independence. Eleanor did not deal with the issue directly in Winston-Salem; her subject was general and high-minded—"The Individual's Responsibility to the Community." In the course of her speech, however, she talked naturally about Tammany and how she had been raised to think that Tammany men had "horns and a tail," but "when one's party is not what one feels it should be, it is better to get into the organization and purify it from within instead of standing without and criticizing." Critics were disarmed. The *Times* correspondent observed that "Mrs. Roosevelt made many friends for herself and Governor Roosevelt. It was remarked by many political-minded folk at the dinner that she was a splendid advance agent, if such she could be termed, for her husband."[13] In Atlanta she spoke before the League of Women Voters. She sounded the theme that it was up to the women to end war, the reporter for the *Atlanta Constitution* wrote admiringly, "alternately bringing laughter with stories of her own education in politics and holding her listeners tense with her eloquence, Mrs. Roosevelt exhibited a versatility and political background worthy of the traditions of the Roosevelt family." She herself admitted to Molly that the time spent in North Carolina had been "rather profitable," although "nine speeches in three days was a bit strenuous!"[14]

Within New York State she continued to serve as Franklin's proxy. "I do not often go to the big places," she told Ida Tarbell with her usual modesty, "but often to the little places where they have difficulty in securing speakers. I don't do it as well as I wish I did, but after all what they want is to see the Governor's wife."[15] The *New Yorker* saw it differently: "No woman has a better grasp of the intricacies of state business and she has a decided flair for putting things aptly."[16]

She did not like to travel in the big state car, preferring to use her own and drive herself. This made Franklin uneasy, and he insisted that Earl Miller, now promoted to sergeant, accompany her.[17] Miller, one of the handsomest troopers in the state, a former amateur welterweight champion, an excellent horseman who did trick riding at the state fair, and an instructor in judo and boxing at the State Police School, was something of a self-styled Lothario. He had been Al Smith's bodyguard for four years and when the Roosevelts came to Albany was kept on the mansion detail. The boys in the barracks did not envy him his assignment with "that old crab," but Eleanor, with her kindliness and insatiable curiosity about people, quickly made a conquest of him. Soon he was telling her the story of his life—his beginnings in Schenectady, his years as circus acrobat, his war years in the Navy, his unhappy first marriage. Solicitude for his troubles made it easier for her to accept his helpfulness and brusque gallantries, and his barracks-room language, his cynicism, and his roughneck qualities were a new and interesting experience. She got to know his family and invited his niece to stay at the mansion. Earl, who had had no home since he was twelve, trans-fered the affection he would have felt for his parents to "the Boss" and "the Lady." Eleanor encouraged his friendship, and he helped her overcome fears that still remained from her years of self-subordination. He urged her to take up riding again and took care of her horse. He helped her gain enough confidence in her driving that she told Louis—who often insisted on doing the driving and sometimes "scared her pink"—that she would "never take him again unless I'm doing *all* the driving."[18]

While she could deal with the press, she hated to be photographed because she was convinced she was ugly. She and Louis had a game—who could find the ugliest photograph of himself. "Please don't let them take my picture," she would plead with Miller. "Try to smile," he encouraged her; "smile for just one picture." He even stood behind the photographers and made funny faces at her.[19] Miller was not the only one who, from her photographs, had expected to encounter a woman of formidable plainness. The *New Yorker* correspondent was surprised at how "unjustly" the camera dealt with Mrs. Roosevelt because it could not capture "her immaculate freshness of appearance, her graciousness, and the charm of a highly intelligent, forceful and directed personality." In time, coached by Miller and pushed by necessity, she became as relaxed with photographers as with newspapermen.

Her friendship with Earl was cemented by the assistance he gave her with her alcoholic Uncle Vallie and with Franklin's old Groton tutor and crony of Navy days, George Marvin, who had similar problems. Marvin, full of self-pity, turned up in Albany lamenting his wasted literary talents and asking for help. Franklin had no time for him, so Eleanor undertook the task of rehabilitation, getting him a job with Henry Morgenthau's Conservation Department. But the process was painful and marked by frequent backslidings. When word reached her that George was on a tear, Earl was sent into action.

And when Vallie's drinking sprees resulted in his hiring a taxi and roaring up to the executive mansion, she and Miller took him back to Tivoli. At one point Vallie began associating with a young neighbor who had been arrested for raping a ten-year-old girl and who managed to smuggle in liquor. When the young man induced Vallie to buy a car and to permit other members of his family to stay at Tivoli, Eleanor decided the time had come to step in. She took Vallie to his room while Miller proceeded to read the riot act to the young man. He told him to leave and followed him to the county line, where he warned him that if he returned he ran the risk of arrest. Vallie was more difficult: Earl had to subdue him by force. "As I wrestled him down, the cords stood out in his head. 'Hey! you're quite a strong fellow.' " Vallie finally conceded.[20]

Earl became part of the mansion household. He had been eating out in the kitchen with the other troopers, but was asked to eat with the family. He gave Eleanor the appreciation that her husband and her four sons so often neglected to show her. He took her side rather than Franklin's. And to be squired around by this handsome state trooper who paid her small masculine attentions and treated her as a woman appealed to long dormant feminine qualities in her. She even liked his lapses into a roughness that Nancy and Marion considered rudeness.[21] She became as devoted to Earl as she was to Louis; she loved everyone who gave her strength to meet and surmount difficult trials and fears.

Those she loved she mothered, as she did almost everyone who served her and Franklin. Gus Gennerich, a New York policeman who was Roosevelt's personal bodyguard, was another member of the family entourage. He had little education and always remained the New York "cop," but he was engaging and affectionate and loyal. The Roosevelts considered him a friend, and Franklin always insisted that he be considered part of his personal party. Eleanor often visited Gus's old and ailing mother, and she stayed with Gus after his mother died until the funeral.[22]

No matter what she may have felt about Missy's closeness to Franklin, Eleanor's maternal tenderness enveloped her as well. Inevitably, a romance developed between Earl and Missy which ended when Earl and Ruth Bellinger, a second cousin of his first wife, decided to get married. "Glad Earl told Missy," Eleanor wrote Franklin. "I was sure she would rather know from him."[23] Earl and Ruth were married at Hyde Park, with Anna Dall as bridesmaid and Elliott the best man.

The marriage ended gossip, at least temporarily, concerning Eleanor's relationship to Earl. It was not surprising that the habits and friendships of both Franklin and Eleanor caused raised eyebrows and provided food for "inside stories" at many dinner tables. Eleanor's frequent trips with Earl as her only companion, Missy's presence in the mansion and her role as the governor's hostess in Eleanor's absence, the affectionate familiarity among all of them, the obvious delight they took in each other's company left even good friends puzzled and confused as to the true character of their relationships.

When Bill and Caroline Phillips visited the Roosevelts in Albany, the observant Caroline noted that Earl Miller came to tea, but she could not quite figure out what his function was; she gave him the title of "Major" and decided he was probably an aide. She also noted that there was "a secretary whom everyone called Missie [*sic*]," who was, she commented, "a very nice young woman."[24] Missy's status also intrigued the Henry Goddard Leaches, who were among the guests that week end. Franklin proposed that they all motor down to Hyde Park for luncheon, and Eleanor said to Agnes Leach, "You'll understand that Franklin will not drive with us. He has this new car and he wants to show it off to Missy." Agnes concluded that he was very fond of Missy, and mentioned it later to Elinor Morgenthau. "Oh no," Elinor protested. "He loves Missy. She's quite essential to him. He loves Missy but as to an affair—no."[25] At Hyde Park they were met by Nancy Cook, "Eleanor's great friend," Caroline wrote in her diary, "short, stocky Miss Cooke [*sic*], with her poppy-out blue eyes and short wiry grey hair . . . was as always warmly embraced by Eleanor. She is a most determined person who began by being a paid worker at some Democratic organization and then a sort of political secretary to Franklin and she now runs the Val-Kill furniture factory at Hyde Park, as well as the Roosevelt family!"

The Phillipses came away from the week end with their two old friends feeling that they were both "living on *top* of their arduous job in a magnificent way. . . . The only flaw I could find in Eleanor is her disdain for any interest in food! . . . our meals were very unattractive, I must say. She was laughing at her mother-in-law who wanted to discuss with her what dishes would be most delicious for a dinner party, 'as though,' said Eleanor, 'anyone now-a-days had time to spend twenty minutes planning what to eat!' "

Eleanor's determination not to waste time on food made her insensitive to her husband's wishes, and she insisted that he was as indifferent to food as she was. "I am sorry to tell you that my husband and I are very bad about food. I do not know of any particular dish which he likes unless it is wild duck and the only recipe for that from his point of view is that it should fly through the kitchen."[26] It was no secret to others, however, that Roosevelt did not like the "plain foods, plainly prepared" that were served at the mansion, but evidently there was little he could do about it except when Eleanor was away. "Goodness, the Governor has no preferences," she told S. J. Woolf of the *New York Times*. "If I should give him bacon and eggs three times a day he would be perfectly satisfied."[27] She could be stubborn and she was always on guard against the pleasure-loving side in her husband.

Eleanor wanted her husband to talk to her about everything—friendships, managing the children, homemaking, and of course, politics and public affairs. She wanted to be his confidante and counselor, to be privy to his hopes and to be turned to when he met disappointment. But the nearer they came to the nominating convention and the decisive battle, the more ambiguous he became about his basic convictions and the less time he had for anything except the political game. When she feared that his pursuit of the presidency was engulfing her hopes of a true partnership, when it seemed to her that politics instead of being an instrument for the ennoblement of humanity was turning into a naked pursuit of an office, which, if achieved, would transform her into a ceremonial marionette, when it became evident that the more insistently she pressed these matters with him, the less he took her into his confidence, she fell into black despair.

She was worried about her children and the fact that her husband rarely saw them. Anna was having problems with her marriage. Elliott, not yet twenty-one, was restlessly moving from one job to another and rushing into marriage; he seemed "terribly young to prefer monogamy," commented David Gray,[28] and David's reservations were mild compared to Eleanor's. The youngest boys were driving too fast and too recklessly. Her husband did not take the drastic measures she urged, either because of the pressure of public duties or disinclination to face disagreeable situations. The fact that Franklin was governor meant a sacrifice for the children, she said; they could not be "first" with their father. At times she understood and accepted this as the inevitable consequence of his career as a public man but at the other times she was resentful that they should be robbed of his time, his companionship, his guidance. The reflected limelight was particularly injurious—favors were done for them; they were offered jobs and opportunities. There were always strings attached but they were too young to see that. "It may be so small a thing as being invited to park their cars where others are not permitted to," Eleanor said, unburdening herself to a friendly reporter. "It is bad for children to be allowed to infringe the rules."[29] She found herself in the role of "perennial deflator . . . sometimes it seems to me that I am everlastingly saying 'no.' " Her sigh as she said this reflected the burden that was thrown upon her by her husband's unavailability as disciplinarian. And if she did try to get Franklin to accept the responsibility for disciplining one of the children, "the punishment simply was not administered."[30]

In December, 1931, she wrote an article entitled "Ten Rules for Success in Marriage."[3] Though most readers probably assumed it described her relationship to her husband, actually it depicted what she wished her marriage to be and what it was not. The article even discussed the circumstances under which divorce was justifiable, a hazardous topic for a public figure and a radical departure from the traditions of her grandmother and mother-in-law, who belonged to the generation described by Edith Wharton as dreading scandal more than disease. When in 1922 Hall had taken her to a little New York restaurant to tell her that he intended to divorce Margaret, she had been concerned with what it would mean "to the family, all of whom believed that when you made your bed you had to lie in it." But now she observed succinctly, "It is far better for two people who cannot get along to separate than to lead a quarrelsome life. If there are no children, I would say that divorce is justifiable when either husband or wife, or both find that life together has ceased to have any spiritual value."

Her formula for married happiness emphasized "unselfishness—thoughtfulness—consideration of others. In marriage selfishness shows itself in one way that is particularly common, through the desire of either husband or wife to be the dominating person in the household." Expect to disagree, she said, but "do not dominate. In this respect victory for one is failure for the partnership."

But Franklin always had to be in command. He was a showman, and his charm and magnetism were so overpowering that the household naturally gravitated around him; everyone's interests were subordinated to his. A woman in love with a man could accept this, but that kind of love had died with the Lucy Mercer affair, Eleanor told herself. She was not in love with him. Yet she was prepared to render him a labor of love by serving his work (a distinction that she drew in an article for King Features, the Hearst Syndicate, published in February, 1933, on the role of a public man's wife) if he would be thoughtful, considerate, and treat her as a partner and confidante. Perhaps these longings for a full partnership were inherently unfillable given her emotional needs and insecurities, and Franklin, on his side, could not be tenderly confiding and open in the way she craved. As she explained to her son James years later, "His was an innate kind of reticence that may have been developed by the fact that he had an older father and a very strong-willed mother, who constantly tried to exercise control over him in the early years. Consequently, he may have fallen into the habit of keeping his own counsel, and it became part of his nature not to talk to anyone of intimate matters."[32]

Many years later she wrote to a young friend in the service:

There is one thing I've always wanted to say to you, when you do come home and get engulfed in work, will you stop long enough now and then even if T. is working with you to make her feel she is *first* in your life even more important than saving the world? Every woman wants to be first to someone sometimes in her life and the desire is the explanation for many strange things women do, if, only men understood it!

Stubbornly she fought for a more tender, intimate relationship with her husband. Life away from him was difficult; life with him could be equally so. In the spring of 1931 Sara, who was in Paris, became ill with pneumonia. Franklin wanted Eleanor to go to France, but she felt that it would do his mother much more good if he went without her, so he took Elliott instead. A touching letter from Eleanor followed. "I think I looked so tired chiefly because I hated to see you go, though I knew it was the best thing for you to do & the sensible thing for me not to go. We are really very dependent on each other though we do see so little of each other. I feel as lost as I did when I went abroad & I will never do that again. . . . Goodnight, dear. . . . Dear love to you. . . . I miss you & hate to feel you so far away." Franklin's visit, she wrote eighteen years later in *This I Remember*, "gave his mother just what was needed to accelerate her recovery."[33]

There were acute differences over issues and the compromises he felt obliged to accept in order to win the nomination. During the twenties she had developed a set of strongly-held views and she used every channel in advancing them with her husband. "What did he think? . . . What was his reaction?" she would anxiously ask Louis, if he was in Albany, before she went in to sit on Franklin's bed and say good night. Or if she were leaving Albany, she would say to Missy, "You work on him."

As the Depression deepened and joblessness spread, she pressed more urgently for action. She was "not excited about the Communists," she told the Southern Women's Democratic Organization, but she was concerned about "the great number of people in New York who cannot get work."[34] Before the Brooklyn Emergency Unemployment Committee, she spoke of the right to work "as fundamental and inherent in our civilization. Suddenly to find that no work is to be had turns people bitter." She understood that bitterness and pleaded for the "alleviation of distress . . . now."[35] She was unhappy that Franklin was as elusive on the issue of child-labor legislation as Al Smith had been. Molly, on behalf of the advocates of unemployment compensation, asked Eleanor to urge the governor to make it a major objective. Eleanor regarded her thoughtfully as they drove through the congested garment district, Molly recalled, and then said, "I will speak to Franklin about it. I do not know whether he will consider it wise to take on another measure."[36] It was she who brought to her husband's attention a hard-driving, militant social worker named Harry L. Hopkins, whom Roosevelt selected to head up the state's program of unemployment relief.[37]

Some of Roosevelt's closest advisers—Sam Rosenman, his counsel and speech writer, and Doc O'Connor, his law partner and a political counselor, thought Eleanor was dangerously idealistic. Not long after Rexford G. Tugwell was drafted as a member of the Brains Trust in the spring of 1932, he was stunned to hear O'Connor say to him and Ray Moley, Columbia University professor and the first to be recruited into the Brains Trust, that he hoped they knew one of their first jobs was "to get the pants off Eleanor and onto Frank." Sam agreed.[38] Eleanor's "well-meant probings" annoyed them, so much so that they tended to avoid the dinners at the mansion that preceded a work-out with the Brains Trust. Conversation at dinner, Tugwell noticed, tended to be controlled by Eleanor, who always had "some good cause to further" and who "was apt to chide her husband when he claimed more than he should have for his efforts during the past four years."[39] Although Eleanor's "pronouncements infuriated Doc and Sam," Tugwell took them less seriously. He felt that even if her views were not profound, "they went cautiously in the right direction."[40]

The sharpest disagreements between Eleanor and her husband were occasioned by his shifts on Prohibition and the League of Nations. She remained a teetotaler, an ardent advocate of Prohibition, and a supporter of the Women's Christian Temperance Union. She would not have liquor or wine at her table and it offended her to learn that cocktails were served at the mansion in her absence. It had been difficult for her to go along with Franklin when at the 1930 Governors' Conference he suggested a states' rights solution of the enforcement problem. She had had great hopes for the Volstead Act, yet "when I see the terrible things that have grown out of it, such as graft and bootlegging, one begins to wonder about it," and she was realistic enough to see that enforcement was not working. But when Franklin went beyond states' rights and called for repeal of the Eighteenth Amendment, Eleanor disagreed sharply. "She was," commented Sam Rosenman, "a rather inflexible person, rather high-minded and averse to compromise. She had very set ideas."[41]

Although Louis was disdainful of Sam and Doc and was usually allied with Eleanor, on the Prohibition issue he, too, considered her unrealistic.[42] Eleanor's ally in this case was Sara, who was also a Prohibitionist by conviction. "I don't want my son to be elected if he has to be elected on a 'wet' ticket," she told a group of Roosevelt's political associates. But Roosevelt and Howe approached the issue politically, and were quite reconciled to see the "great experiment" torpedoed.

The other source of tension between Eleanor and her husband in the spring of 1932 was his retreat from supporting the League of Nations and the World Court. After he became governor, Roosevelt, one of the country's most prominent Wilsonians, fell silent on the issue of adherence to the Court on the grounds that as a governor he should stick to state affairs and not get involved in foreign-policy issues. Eleanor, on the other hand, continued to work with Esther Lape for ratification of the World Court. Pleas for action over her signature were sent to all Democratic senators, and she asked the Democratic national committeewomen from their states to get after any senators who did not respond.[43] "You do stick to the Court through thick and thin," Mrs. Catt wrote her admiringly in March, 1930.

Until 1932 Roosevelt had managed to escape attack on the issue through a policy of public silence and private assurances to World Court partisans that he was still with them. Now William Randolph Hearst, launching a boom for Speaker of the House John Nance Garner of Texas, began to fulminate against internationalism and the Wilsonians, urging instead an "America First" policy. His first blast named Roosevelt, Newton Baker, Owen D. Young, even Al Smith, but the attack was soon limited to Roosevelt. In front-page editorials with big black type the Hearst papers quoted his pro-League of Nations statements in 1920. By the end of January Howe was advising Franklin that "You may have to make a public statement before we get through, if this gets any more violent." The struggle over whether to appease Hearst raged among Roosevelt's advisers. Rosenman thought Eleanor was rigid on this issue, too, even more so than on Prohibition: "She had an awful lot of faith in the World Court as the only thing to rally around once the League of Nations was out of the question."[44] Roosevelt tried to avoid public repudiation of the League and the Court by sending Jim Farley to the editors of Hearst's *New York American* to reassure them about Roosevelt's views on internationalism. The assurances should be given "to the public, publicly, not to me privately," Hearst stated on the front page next day. Finally, Roosevelt capitulated, and in a speech to the New York State Grange said he did not favor American participation in the League of Nations. He was even ready to turn his back on the Court, but Hearst seemed satisfied and the Wilsonians were up in arms. Cordell Hull, who had been drawn to Roosevelt by his internationalism and was one of the most influential supporters of his candidacy, was deeply upset by Roosevelt's speech. Colonel House warned Howe, "What you said about the League has already strained their loyalty, and many of them have told me that if you take the same position on the World Court they cannot support you."

Agnes Leach was one of the angry Wilsonians who had occasion to see Roosevelt at the time. "I couldn't believe my eyes," she said to him. "That was a shabby statement. I just don't feel like having lunch with you today."

Franklin was taken aback. "I am sorry you are in that mood. One reason I wanted you here today is that Eleanor is very fond of you and you can make peace between us. She hasn't spoken to me for three days."[45]

When Eleanor heard about the incident she immediately phoned her friend "Agnes, you are a sweet, darling girl. I hear you upset Franklin very much. I didn't know you had it in you." He was eager for Eleanor's approval, Mrs. Leach felt, and cared "a terrific lot about her opinion" even if he disregarded it.

Roosevelt's reversal on the League, his ambiguities on Prohibition, and his efforts to avoid a showdown with Tammany produced widespread doubt about the strength of his convictions. Heywood Broun called him a "a corkscrew," Elmer Davis thought him the "weakest" of the candidates for the nomination, and Walter Lippmann described him as "an amiable man with many philanthropic impulses" who was "not the dangerous enemy of anything." (Eleanor saved that column.) Many years later, Eleanor's radio and television agent,

Thomas L. Stix, who idolized her, confessed that he had voted for Norman Thomas in 1932. "So would I," she reassured him, "if I had not been married to Franklin."[46]

Political discontent merged with personal unhappiness, as is revealed briefly in a letter she sent Molly after having lunch with her: "Of course there is no other candidate who will do more what we want. I simply had a fit of rebellion against the male attitude. I've had one before but sober sense does come to my rescue & I feel better when I realize that I've thought primarily about myself."[47]

"Can't you see that loyalty to the ideals of Woodrow Wilson is just as strong in my heart as it is in yours," one of Roosevelt's letters to an irate Wilsonian began, and went on to explain that his ideals had not changed, only his methods of achieving them—"and for heaven's sake have a little faith." He might almost have been arguing with his wife.

"It was all unnecessary," wrote Mrs. Charles Hamlin to Josephus Daniels about Roosevelt's repudiation of the League. But was it? A moment came in the Democratic convention three months later at the end of the third ballot when the stop-Roosevelt movement still kept him short of the two-thirds vote needed for nomination. Several states—Mississippi, Arkansas, and Alabama— were being held in the Roosevelt ranks with difficulty. If Roosevelt did not gain decisively on the fourth ballot, his ranks might break and disintegrate. After consulting with Howe, Farley went to work on Texas, which along with California had been voting for Garner. Hearst was one of the keys to the California-Texas alliance, and Roosevelt leaders telephoned him at San Simeon to urge him to support a switch. He agreed. Would he have done so if Roosevelt had not satisfied him on the issue of the League? There is no absolute answer to the "ifs" of history, but it seems a reasonable conjecture that if Roosevelt had not compromised on this issue he might not have won the nomination. And if he had not been president when the Hitler menace broke out, would another man have promoted the Wilsonian cause as faithfully and effectively as he did?

Franklin was the politician, she the agitator, Eleanor said in later years.[48] "Mrs. Roosevelt's hand is almost exactly complementary to the hand of her husband," an authority in palmistry wrote. "By this I mean she has just the sort of character that will supplement and aid the character of the Governor."[49] They made a splendid team, but that was not the way it seemed to her at the time. She was a deeply divided woman as the convention neared. She was happy for Franklin—and Louis—as the states fell in line ("So Tennessee is in!" she wrote him on May 21, as things went according to schedule; "Jim Farley grins more broadly with each State!"), but she saw her husband's entry into the White House as portending a kind of gilded captivity for her.

Friends were baffled by her calmness, almost detachment, as the convention began. She took several hours off on the opening day to drive through a thunderstorm to visit Margaret Doane Fayerweather, an old friend who was recuperating from a very serious operation. For an hour she sat at Margaret's bedside, her knitting needles busy. Not till she left was there a word of politics. Then Margaret, unable to contain herself asked, "What are your plans?"

"Well, we shall either be flying to Chicago—or staying quietly at home."

"We shall be praying that you will be flying to Chicago."

"The time when we shall need your prayers will be if Franklin is nominated and elected."[50]

When the long night of the nominations began she was with Franklin, who was in his shirtsleeves, silent, waiting. Sara was at the governor's mansion as were Elliott and John, Missy, Grace Tully, and Sam Rosenman. When the speechmaking ended and the balloting began it was 4:20 A.M., and Eleanor sent out pots of coffee to the newsmen, who had established a listening post in the garage. As roll call followed roll call, Franklin chain-smoked and Eleanor knitted a turtle-neck sweater for asthma-wracked Louis who was in Chicago. At 9:15 A.M., after the inconclusive third ballot, the convention recessed. Sara found the suspense too upsetting and left for Hyde Park, indignant that some of the "gentlemen" in the New York delegation had voted against her son. The others tried to get a little sleep. Eleanor was the first to come down and was preparing to have breakfast with Louis Howe's grandson when she encountered two Associated Press reporters on their way out after the all-night vigil. Would Miss Hickok and Mr. Fay join her, she asked them. The breakfast went pleasantly, but to the two reporters Eleanor seemed withdrawn, not at all involved in the drama of the tense hours between the third and the final ballots. Fay thought she was worried that her husband would not get the nomination. More perceptively, Lorena Hickok, a woman in her late thirties, observed, "That woman's unhappy about something."[51]

At dinner that night the telephone call came for which Roosevelt had been waiting. "F.D., you look just like the cat that swallowed the canary," said Missy. Later the news was on the radio: McAdoo announced that California had not come to Chicago to deadlock a convention but to elect a president and was switching to Roosevelt. "Good old McAdoo," said Roosevelt, smiling contentedly. "The rest of the study was a bedlam," Grace Tully recalled. "Mrs. Roosevelt and Missy LeHand embraced each other. Both embraced me. John and Elliott tossed scratch paper in the air and shook hands as if they hadn't seen each other in years. Mrs. Roosevelt came down out of the clouds before the rest of us. 'I'm going to make some bacon and eggs,' she announced."[52]

Albany neighbors gathered on the front lawn to cheer. Roosevelt exchanged quips with the photographers and reporters who had come crowding in from the garage. The women reporters, including the owl-eyed Miss Hickok, found Mrs. Roosevelt scrambling eggs. "Mrs. Roosevelt, aren't you *thrilled* at the idea of being in the White House?" one of them "gushed." Mrs. Roosevelt's only reply, Miss Hickok noted, was a look so unsmiling that it stopped all further questions along that line. Lorena Hickok's intuition that here was a woman strangely unhappy as her husband moved toward the presidency became a bond between the two women, and before the campaign was over she was receiving Eleanor's confidence. "I'm a middle-aged woman," she said to Miss Hickok on her forty-eighth birthday. "It's good to be middle-aged. Things don't matter so much. You don't take it so hard when things happen to you that you don't like."[53]

34. "I Never Wanted to Be a President's Wife"

THE MORNING AFTER THE NOMINATION Roosevelt flew to Chicago as a way of serving notice on the country that a new energetic leadership was prepared to take command. Eleanor accompanied him, as did Elliott and John, Sam, Missy, Grace, and two bodyguards, Gus and Earl. Eleanor was the first to emerge from the plane. "A fine job, Mr. Farley. Congratulations!" she said, extending her hand to the beaming chairman. Struck by her poise and composure, Emma Bugbee of the *New York Herald Tribune* commented that she was "one of the calm people of the world."[1] Someone asked her whether her life would not "belong to the public after this," and she quickly replied, "It never has and never could."

It was a discerning question. There was in her a craving for experience, a fear of pomp and ceremony. She did not wish to be shielded from the world but to take part in it and change it. She wanted to live a life without artifice, to do things herself, to live the truth. She had an ascetic strain—she called it the Puritan in her—and inner drives that in other times and other places had led women to renounce worldly pleasures and take vows of poverty and service. She carried about with her a prayer by Henry Van Dyke entitled "The Footpath to Peace," to which she added the words "with oneself." Among the prayer's injunctions were "to think seldom of your enemies, often of your friends and every day of Christ"; she had circled the phrase about Christ. "Christ was born in a manger," she wrote a few months later, "and worked all his life and in that way we were taught that the highest and best things in life may be linked with material hardship and the simplest of living." As completely as she could, she wanted to live according to Christ's teachings.

She feared that all these things would become impossible once she was First Lady, that she would become a prisoner of protocol and tradition. Louis, an inveterate scribbler of verse, had addressed himself to her anxieties in early 1932.

> We are the hooded brotherhood of fears.
> Barring the pleasant path that lay ahead.
> Who, grim and silent, all these futile years,
> Have filled your timid soul with numbing dread. . . .
>
> Fool! Had you dared to speed your pace
> Our masking cowls aside to tear
> And meet us bravely face to face
> We would have vanished into air.

Louis' assurances that there would be plenty for her to do in the White House did not end her worries; the closer Franklin came to the nomination, the more certain she became that she did not want to be First Lady. Nancy and Marion had accompanied Louis to Chicago, and Nancy received a letter from Eleanor saying these things. When she showed it to Louis, he ripped it to shreds and told her not to breathe a word of it to anyone.[2] From her own personal standpoint, Eleanor later wrote, she did not want her husband to be president: "It was pure selfishness on my part, and I never mentioned my feelings on the subject to him."[3]

Her dread of what she called "captivity" in the White House did not prevent her from pitching into the campaign with her usual vigor. While some of the party's conservatives were opposed to a strong women's division, especially a "militant" one, a major appeal was nevertheless going to be directed to the distaff side of the electorate. Molly moved over from Friends of Roosevelt to direct the drive, again as Eleanor's deputy. There was an easy and understanding relationship between the two. "I hate people to be grateful to me," Eleanor wrote Molly in Maine, where she had been sent to rest before the campaign, "just as much as you apparently hate them to be grateful to you so you need not worry. I love working with you for just the reasons I imagine you like working with me and you need not ever worry that I will not speak perfectly truthfully to you or that you should hesitate to say whatever you have on your mind to me."[4]

While Molly rested in Maine, Eleanor organized and staffed the women's division. She presented the Democratic National Committee, which Farley had assembled in New York for a strategy session, with the plan developed by Molly for work in the states. There was to be a vice chairwoman in every state to head up the women's work and a committeewoman in every county, especially in the rural areas, with whom Molly could correspond directly and to whom headquarters could send literature and gasoline money. The men agreed, although they were reluctant to have any money come into their states that was not channeled through them. They also agreed that the women in charge of their states would draft their work plans and send them to Eleanor. For the wife of the presidential candidate to hold such responsibility and to wield such authority was unprecedented in American politics, but in Eleanor's case it seemed the natural thing to do.

Eleanor and her colleagues had learned their lessons well in 1930 and knew exactly what they wanted. They did *not* want, a chagrined Howe discovered, the twelve-page brochures the men, including himself, had drafted. The women marched into his office, he later reported, "their noses visibly turned toward Heaven," and announced loftily, "You surely don't expect us to send that to our women do you?" "Why not?" Howe inquired. "Well, I don't know about you men, but we women have no time to waste reading through stuff like that." Women, Howe learned, had an "appalling desire for figures"; they preferred leaflets which presented a single argument. Finally they were given their own printing budget and told to produce their own literature. The ladies' "Rainbow Fliers," as they came to be called, were printed by the millions and were so successful that the men made extensive use of them. "They were written solely by women. No man had a hand in them," Molly commented rather smugly.[5]

Eleanor turned over to Molly a list of the "safe states" and the "fighting states," where Louis figured the election would be won or lost. The women precinct leaders in the latter states were notified just how their districts had voted in 1928 and how many additional votes were needed for a Democratic victory in 1932. The most intensive campaigning was done by a corps of "grass trampers," women who went from door to door and whose indefatigable work Louis later credited with bringing out the women's vote; he "would rather have a half-dozen women field workers than a hundred men any day," he concluded. Moreover, they made the same amount of money go twice as far; in fact, they were sometimes too frugal, and in a campaign it was necessary to use money speedily.[6]

Farley's and Molly's offices were at the Biltmore Hotel, while Louis and Eleanor remained across the street at the old Friends of Roosevelt office. One of Eleanor's jobs was to keep the channels of communication open between Farley and the ever-suspicious Howe, and she could occasionally be seen hurrying across Madison Avenue with Louis in tow to straighten out a misunderstanding, smooth over a hurt feeling. After the Walker hearings ended with Tammany Mayor Jimmy Walker's sudden resignation, Franklin took off on his campaign train accompanied by James and his wife Betsy and Anna Dall. Roosevelt liked to have his children with him, and he was especially fond of Betsy, who was pert, vivacious, and enjoyed coquetting with her irresistible father-in-law. From time to time Eleanor flew out to join the campaign train, and she was in Chicago when the whole family attended a World Series game between the Cubs and the Yankees. She was not a model of attentiveness, Jimmy later claimed, having slept through most of the game, one in which Babe Ruth and Lou Gehrig each hit home runs.[7] But during that same stay in Chicago when Bobby Fitzmaurice, who handled transportation schedules, fell ill, it was Eleanor who took the "Commissioner of the Ramps," as Roosevelt had fondly dubbed him, to the hospital, just as, a few weeks later, when Missy's mother died, it was Eleanor who accompanied Missy to Potsdam, New York, for the funeral.

The Depression was reaching its nadir and the grim signs were everywhere—the lengthening bread lines, the Hoovervilles, the silent, sullen countryside in which smoldered the fires of rebellion, the horrifying use of troops and tear gas to rout the veterans from Washington. Eleanor shifted her emphasis from the alleviation of distress to the need for basic change. A financial system that was "man-made" was also "man-controlled," she told the Chatauqua ladies. "We must reorganize our economic structure so it may be possible for those willing to work to receive adequate compensation." Her ideas were not more advanced than her husband's, Tugwell noted, but she was willing to talk about them "when he was not yet ready for commitment."[8] She counseled the girls of the Junior League to prepare themselves for the big changes that were coming by learning to earn their own living and to pull their weight by making a contribution to the world. When one of her Todhunter girls remarked that "you can get anything you want in the world if you have enough money," she asked the entire class to bring in "a list of things you think the Depression has taught people who have money and also a list of what you think it has done to people who are unemployed and have nothing." She urged "a spirit of mutual helpfulness" in easing the hardships of the Depression but insisted that the country's leaders probe deeply into its causes with a view to fundamental reform.

It was considered unseemly for her to campaign for her husband, but it was decided she should take the stump for Herbert Lehman, who had been nominated for governor over Tammany's objections and faced a hard fight. While Roosevelt, in Pittsburgh, to the delight of the conservatives among his advisers, condemned Hoover for his "reckless and extravagant" spending policies and promised a 25 per cent reduction in federal payrolls, Eleanor, in Syracuse a week later, was not so sure economy was such "a very wonderful thing . . . it can do a great deal of harm." The Republicans had cut $21 million out of the state budget, but "practically all of that came out of the appropriation for the Department of Public Works . . . [which] means that thousands of young engineers, draftsmen and laborers were thrown out of work." Since the Republicans subsequently were obliged to appropriate not only what they had cut out of the budget, but more for public relief, she wanted to know which would have been better—"to pay that money out in salaries for labor on public works, or to pay it in unemployment relief?"[9]

Roosevelt's goal was to get elected, and his rhetoric was shaped by that; Eleanor—as she ladled out soup on the bread lines, gave lifts to tramps, and sent hungry men to her house with instructions that they should be fed—was increasingly preoccupied with the necessity not only for fundamental changes but for preparing the country to accept those changes. Otherwise, she felt, Franklin's task might prove to be an impossible one.

She poured out her anxieties to Lorena Hickok on a midnight drive from Poughkeepsie to New York. She had attended Franklin's final rally but insisted on driving back to town afterward so that she could meet her nine o'clock class in the morning. "Of course Franklin will do his best if he is elected. He is strong and resourceful. And he really cares about people," she said, according to Hickok. "The federal government will have to take steps. But will it be enough? *Can* it be enough? The responsibility he may have to take on is something I hate to think about."[10]

The next day she was back in Hyde Park to cast her ballot and then returned to New York to prepare the buffet supper that she and Franklin gave for family, friends, and newsmen before going to the Biltmore Hotel to await the returns. Whatever her misgivings about becoming First Lady, outwardly she was as gracious and composed as ever. At the Biltmore, Franklin withdrew to a small suite upstairs to receive the returns with Flynn, Farley, and a few intimates. Eleanor stayed downstairs in the ballroom to greet the hundreds of party workers who had gathered to celebrate the victory that appeared to be in the making.

Smilingly she moved from ballroom to State Committee and National

Committee quarters, but as the returns began to come in she slipped off to give Elliott's wife a glimpse of the lights and crowds and excitement on Broadway on an election eve and to bring Sara down to headquarters. As the fateful hour arrived, Louis turned gloomy, and as if to emphasize his behind-the-scenes role, secluded himself with his wife and son in his deserted offices across the street, calling Roosevelt and Farley on the telephone but refusing to acknowledge that the early returns were as good as they seemed. When victory seemed certain, Eleanor and Farley went over to get him. The "two people in the United States," Roosevelt saluted Howe and Farley, "more than anybody else, who are responsible for this great victory."

The reporters assigned to stay with Eleanor were, as one of them wrote, "incredulous" at her composure in the midst of the klieg lights and the mounting hysteria of victory. Nothing seemed to penetrate her "profound calm." She consented to a press conference. Was she pleased at the outcome of the election?

"Of course I'm pleased—if it really is true. You're always pleased to have someone you're very devoted to have what he wants." Then she paused and went on gravely, "It's an extremely serious thing to undertake, you know, the guidance of a nation at a time like this. It's not something you just laugh off and say you're pleased about."

The reporters had been reading Hickok's stories with their hints of Mrs. Roosevelt's reluctance to become First Lady. Did she anticipate returning to Washington and its social functions? one asked. "I love people. I love having people in my house. I don't think I know what 'functions' are," was her smiling response.

Would she miss New York? would she find life in Washington too restricting? the reporters pressed on. "I'm very much a person of circumstance," she said, again avoiding a direct reply. "I've found that I never miss anything after it's gone. The present is enough to deal with. Life is always full, you know."

The next morning the invisible bands whose fetters she had feared began to tighten. The police guard outside the Sixty-fifth Street house had been doubled, there were Secret Service men about everywhere, and the crowd of reporters outside was prepared to dog her footsteps all day. She was up early, and only Louis and Anna's daughter Sisty, who attended Todhunter and whom she would take to school, joined her at breakfast. A reporter for an afternoon paper sent in a message begging her to come out so that they might have a story for the early editions, and she interrupted her breakfast to oblige. She told the press what she intended to do that day. She "refuses to allow the new honor that has come to her husband to interfere with the varied interests of her own life." the *Sun* reporter wrote.

But at Todhunter the fiction she had insisted on maintaining—that she was just like any other teacher—was ignored. The girls could no longer be restrained. They stood as she entered, and one of them presented her with an Egyptian scarab to bring her good luck. "We think it's grand to have the wife of the President for our teacher," the girl shyly said.

She was not the wife of the president yet, she laughingly insisted, "and anyway I don't want you to think of me that way." In what was meant to be a reassurance to herself and a plea to those who knew her, she added, "I'm just the same as I was yesterday."

To Lorena Hickok, whom she now called "Hick," who accompanied her to Albany the next day, she unburdened herself more fully than she ever had before. "If I wanted to be selfish, I could wish Franklin had not been elected." She gazed out of the window at the long-familiar and reassuring vistas of the Hudson and the Catskills and continued, according to Hick, "I never wanted it, even though some people have said that my ambition for myself drove him on. They've even said that I had some such idea in the back of my mind when I married him. I never wanted to be a President's wife, and I don't want it now." She looked at Hick. "You don't quite believe me, do you?" she asked.

She was glad for Franklin, she went on, "sincerely. I couldn't have wanted it to go the other way. After all, I'm a Democrat, too."

"Now I shall have to work out my own salvation." Life in Washington was going to be difficult, but there was not going to be any First Lady—"there is just going to be plain, ordinary Mrs. Roosevelt. And that's all." She would very likely be criticized, "but I can't help it."

The criticism was not long in coming. She continued to do what she had done for ten years—to live her own life as teacher, publicist, and business executive. She accepted a commercially sponsored radio contract, wrote articles for the Hearst syndicate and for the North American Newspaper Alliance, and edited a MacFadden magazine, *Babies—Just Babies.* Although most of the proceeds went to charity and good works, many people reproached her for "commercializing her position" as the wife of the president-elect. When she continued to speak her mind on controversial issues, part of the press said she was embarrassing her husband.

She had contracted with MacFadden to edit *Babies—Just Babies* with Franklin's approval and after much discussion in the family. It gave a job as her assistant to Anna who was estranged from her husband. There was widespread ridicule as well as disapproval of the venture; the *Harvard Lampoon* parodied the magazine with an issue entitled "Tutors, Just Tutors." She had absolute control over the magazine's contents, she said defensively. "The job with the magazine I shall keep," she told the press. Versatility and enterprise, the *Hartford Courant* said, were admirable in a woman generally, "but the fact remains that being the first lady of the land is a full-time job in itself and that the dignity of the President and of the country cannot but suffer when his name is used for commercial purposes." Other papers echoed the *Courant* and suggested that "as a matter of propriety and in keeping with the dignity of the exalted position her husband is about to hold she ought to abandon some of her present occupations."[12] The debate became more heated when during a nationwide broadcast sponsored by a cosmetics firm she remarked that the average girl today "faces the problem of learning, very young, how much she can drink of such things as whisky and gin and sticking to the proper quantity." She was not urging girls to learn how to drink, but she was underscoring Prohibition's failure to curb excessive drinking; the conditions brought about by Prohibition, she said, required more strength of character and discipline than had been required of girls in her own youth. But that point was ignored by the drys and the "shocked protests" poured in. She was criticized in verse as well as prose.

Dear Madam: Pray take this tae mean
A kindly counsel fra a freen.
That ye hae reached the White House door
'Is just because the folk were sore.
Noo, though ye talk an' though ye write
Fair words wi' brilliant sapience dight,
'Tis better far for ye, I ken,
To curb the tongue an' eke the pen . . . M'Tavish

She defied convention in other ways that offended society. She went to Washington to call on Mrs. Hoover and look over the White House. She had received a telegram from Mrs. Hoover's secretary asking where she would like to have the White House car pick her up and whether she would like her military aide to be in uniform or civilian attire. No car and no military aide, she had replied; she would go down on the midnight train, have breakfast at the Mayflower, and walk to the White House. But that was not the end of the affair. Soon after breakfast Franklin's cousin, Warren Delano Robbins, who was then chief of protocol in the State Department, turned up with his wife and an official limousine to take her to the White House. No, Eleanor told them; she intended to walk.

"But Eleanor, darling, you can't do that," Warren protested. "People will recognize you! You'll be mobbed!" They argued with her, but to no avail. She liked to walk, Miss Hickok would accompany her, and that was that.

Whatever Ike Hoover, the chief usher, may have thought about her disregard of protocol in arriving at the White House, he could not but admire the dispatch with which she let him know what she wanted. She "rattled it off as if she had known it her whole life. She had already decided on every last detail of the social plans for Inauguration Day; told me who the house guests would be and what rooms they would occupy, though this was five weeks in the future; gave the menus for the meals, both regular and special; told me what household effects she would bring; what servants should be provided for; what the family liked for meals and when they like to have them; in fact, everything the Chief Usher could wish to know except what the weather might be on March fourth."[13]

She had her defenders as well as critics. The *Nashville Tennessean*, recalling the way "Princess Alice" had been the joy of the newspaper world in the Theodore Roosevelt era, said approvingly, "It begins to look as if Anna Eleanor Roosevelt is going to make Alice Roosevelt Longworth look like Alice-Sit-by-the-Fire."[14] And Heywood Broun did not see why she should conform to the traditional idea of a president's wife and limit her role to saying "Yes, dear, you're entirely right" to her husband. "I would hold it against her rather than in her favor if she quit certain causes with which she has been associated simply on account of the fortuitous circumstances that he happens to have been chosen as President."[15] He was "delighted to know that we are going to have a woman in the White House who feels that like Ibsen's Nora, she is before all else a human being and that she has a right to her own individual career regardless of the prominence of her husband."

Despite such defenders, Eleanor thought it best to retreat. She intended to do no more commercial radio work, she announced; her writings would be confined to subjects that did not touch politics or her husband's interests, she would give up teaching, and she would refrain from linking her name to anything that might be used in advertising promotion.[16] The press applauded. "The President's wife, indeed, during the term of her husband is in the position of a queen, as far as the public is concerned," wrote the *Baltimore Evening Sun*.[17]

The episode confirmed her worst apprehensions that she was going to be a prisoner in the White House "with nothing to do except stand in line and receive visitors and preside over official dinners."[18]

While she was in Washington to call on Mrs. Hoover, Mrs. Garner had come to call on her. A plain woman, she had for years served as her husband's secretary and cooked his lunch on an electric grill in his office. She, too, was worried over what she could properly continue to do now that her husband was vice president-elect. Anxiously, she asked, "Mrs. Roosevelt, do you think I can go on being Jack's Secretary?"

"I most certainly do!" Eleanor replied with vehemence.

Mrs. Garner's question may have influenced her own thinking about what kind of useful role she could play in her husband's administration that would not provoke public criticism and that would enable her to be the counselor and confidante of her husband. As she listened to the men surrounding the president-elect, she began to feel that the gravest danger facing him as president was that he would never hear the truth, that everyone would say yes to him. "From my life in Washington I know how difficult it is to keep in contact with public opinion once a man gets there." She was getting an enormous amount of mail—pleas for help, cries of despair, threats of rebellion. Why couldn't she serve as her husband's "listening post" and see to it that he obtained a balanced picture of what the country was thinking and feeling?[19]

She mentioned the "listening post" theme in remarks before a farewell dinner the Women's Trade Union League gave her. Some critics, she said, had asked her what right she had to set herself up "as knowing what other people are going through, what they are suffering. I cannot understand fully, of course. Yet I think I understand more than the people who write me think I do. . . . Perhaps I have acquired more education than some of you [who] have educated me, realize. . . .

"I truly believe that I understand what faces the great masses of people in the country today. I have no illusions that any one can change the world in a short time. Things cannot be completely changed in five minutes. Yet I do believe that even a few people, who want to understand, to help and to do the right thing for the great numbers of the people instead of for the few can help."[20]

That is what she hoped her husband would be able to do. That is what she hoped she would be able to help him to do.

Finally she approached Franklin, but she did so hesitatingly, tentatively, afraid she already knew what his answer would be. Perhaps he would like her to do a real job and take over some of his mail, she suggested. He looked at her "quizzically" and softly turned her down; Missy would consider it interference, he said. "I knew he was right and that it would not work, but it was a last effort to keep in close touch and to feel that I had a real job to do."[21]

Eleanor could not have been her husband's secretary. She was not a Mrs. Garner, content to subordinate herself totally to her husband. A forceful personality in her own right, every whit as strong-willed as her husband, and with a clearer sense of direction, she would have found it difficult to handle his mail and make it exclusively a reflection of his thinking and purposes.

Though she knew this was true, her husband's rebuff hurt. The day before the inauguration she asked Lorena Hickok to pick her up at the Mayflower, where the Roosevelt and Howe families were staying until they moved into the White House. She directed the cab driver to take them out to the cemetery in Rock Creek Park, where they left the cab and walked to the cluster of pines that enclosed the Saint-Gaudens memorial to the wife of Henry Adams. They sat down on the stone bench that faced "Grief," as the statue had come to be called. After they had both gazed at the hooded figure in hushed silence, Mrs. Roosevelt spoke, quietly, almost as if she were speaking to herself, about what the statue meant to her.

"In the old days when we lived here, I was much younger and not so very wise. Sometimes I'd be very unhappy and sorry for myself. When I was feeling that way, if I could manage, I'd come here alone, and sit and look at that woman. And I'd always come away somehow feeling better. And stronger. I've been here many, many times."[22]

The wound left by the Lucy Mercer affair was still open, still painful. She was a woman of sorrow who had surmounted her unhappiness and managed to carry on, stoical toward herself, understanding and tender toward others. She had turned her sorrow into a strengthening thing before, and would do so again. As First Lady she would not be able to live her own life, but she would be able to render a service of love to her stricken country.

35. Mrs. Roosevelt Conquers Washington

INAUGURATION DAY dawned gray and chill. When Eleanor slipped out before breakfast to walk her Scottish terrier, the streets around the Mayflower were almost deserted and, in the dull, windy morning, cheerless.

They seemed to mirror the mood of the country. The greatest productive machine in the history of mankind had slowed almost to a halt. With at least thirteen million unemployed, no one felt his job was safe. Banks everywhere were closing, and almost everyone feared for his savings. Eviction and foreclosure had sent an icy finger through the middle class on the farm and in the city. For the first time there was not merely hunger but fear of starvation. "World literally rocking beneath our feet," wrote Agnes Meyer, the wife of the head of the Federal Reserve Board, in her diary.[1] In New York two young Socialists had been arrested by the police in the middle of the night for pasting on the closed banks stickers that said "Closed! Socialism Will Keep Them Open." Their evangelistic message was proclaimed to unseeing eyes. While the secretary of war of the departing administration had concentrated troops around some of the nation's cities because of what "Reds and possible Communists" might do, it was fear and apathy that endangered the republic, not revolt.

The Roosevelts recognized that the nation's crisis was primarily one of the spirit. Fear was the worst thing that had happened to the country as a result of the Depression, Eleanor had written in December, "fear of an uncertain future, fear of not being able to meet our problems. Fear of not being equipped to cope with life as we live it today." What people needed was to have something "outside of one's self and greater than one's self to depend on. . . . We need some of the old religious spirit which said 'I myself am weak but Thou art strong oh Lord!' "[2]

Franklin Roosevelt soberly expressed the same feeling on the way to Washington. Religion and a belief in God, he said to Farley, as he looked out at the stricken countryside, "will be the means of bringing us out of the depths of despair into which so many apparently have fallen."

Before going to the White House to pick up the outgoing president and his wife, the whole Roosevelt household and the new cabinet attended services at St. John's Episcopal Church. The old rector of Groton, although he had voted for Hoover, was there at Roosevelt's invitation to lead the congregation in prayer: "May Thy son Franklin, chosen to be our President, and all of his advisers, be enlightened and strengthened for Thy service and may he direct and rule according to Thy will." Eleanor's head bowed low. The stirring hymn of faith and resolve rang out: "Eternal Lord strong to save."

Two limousines, with Roosevelt in the first and Eleanor in the second, moved toward the White House. There they were joined by the Hoovers. The crowds along Pennsylvania Avenue cheered. Roosevelt waved and doffed his silk hat, but Hoover, his face set stonily forward, was unresponsive to either the crowds or Roosevelt's effort to make conversation. What would Mrs. Hoover miss most? Eleanor asked her companion as they rode in the car behind. Not being taken care of, was the reply, not having train reservations made for her, not having her wishes anticipated and attended to. Eleanor made a silent vow never to permit herself to become so dependent.[3]

The immense crowds in the Capitol plaza cheered, but the country waited. On the inaugural stand the cold wind blew, and Eleanor, in a velvet gown and coat of "Eleanor blue," which it had taken her less than thirty minutes to select, was not dressed warmly enough. But she was impervious to the cold, intent on the response of the listening throng to her husband's words. Roosevelt's buoyant voice carried a message of action. In later years when the country had recovered its faith in itself, the electric line "the only thing we have to fear is fear itself," addressed to the crisis in spirit and morale, would be the one by which the speech was recalled. But on that gray day the millions of Americans who listened on their radios were most stirred by the call to battle stations: "This Nation asks for action, and action now. Our greatest primary task is to put people to work." If necessary to meet the emergency, he was prepared to ask Congress for power "as great as the power that would be given to me if we were in fact invaded by a foreign foe."

Here the president received his greatest burst of applause. Eleanor found it "a little terrifying. You felt that they would do *anything*—if only someone would tell them *what* to do," she commented afterward at the White House. She had a feeling "of going it blindly. We are in a tremendous stream and none of us knows where we are going to land." But what was important was "our attitude toward whatever may happen. It must be willingness to accept and share with others whatever may come and to meet the future courageously, with a cheerful spirit."[4]

She and the president set an example. His "exuberant vitality . . . high spirits . . . tirelessness . . . gave a lift to the spirits of millions of average men, stimulated them to higher use of their own power, gave them a new zest for life," wrote Mark Sullivan of the opening days of the Roosevelt presidency.[5] And Bess Furman of the Associated Press, reporting on Mrs. Roosevelt's debut as mistress of the White House, ended an exultant story, "Washington had never seen the like—a social transformation had taken place with the New Deal."[6] Eleanor was spontaneous, sensible, and direct, and the result was a shattering of precedents. She would run the little wood-paneled elevator herself, she firmly told Chief Usher Ike Hoover. When, because of constant interruptions, Hick was unable to finish an interview with Eleanor in the sitting room, they retreated to the bathroom. In her eagerness to get settled, she pushed furniture around herself. The thousand guests who had been invited for tea turned into three thousand, and for the first time tea was served in the East Room as well as the State Dining Room; Mrs. Henrietta Nesbitt, the Hyde Park neighbor whom Eleanor had brought to Washington as housekeeper, sent out repeatedly for more sandwiches, more little cakes. The tea guests had scarcely departed when dinner guests began arriving—seventy-five Roosevelt relatives, including Alice Longworth, all of whom Eleanor greeted at the door instead of waiting until they were assembled to make a ceremonious descent.

The most radical break with precedent was her decision to hold press conferences, the first ever given by a First Lady, in the White House, on the record. The contrast with Mrs. Hoover could not have been more marked. That silvery-haired, kindly woman had shielded herself from public notice. The handful of women who were assigned to keep track of her, who were known as the "Green Room girls," were permitted to observe her only at a distance at official receptions, teas, tree plantings, charity bazaars, and public appearances with the president. The few occasions on which she appeared in the press in her own right were in connection with the Girl Scouts. Behind the screen of protocol, within the confines of the White House, there was a motherly human being whose warmth, had the nation been permitted to share it, would have done something to relieve the impression of severity the Hoovers created. But only in the final days of the campaign did the Hoover managers realize that it had been a mistake to keep Mrs. Hoover at arms' length from friendly reporters. On the Roosevelt campaign train, Mrs. Roosevelt was talking daily to Lorena Hickok of the Associated Press, and out of the blue Bess Furman, the redheaded AP correspondent traveling with the Hoover campaign special, was told she could interview Mrs. Hoover, the only interview she was granted in four years of covering the First Lady. The ground rules, Mrs. Hoover informed her, were that she should not be directly quoted; Miss Furman would have to write about the biographical details Mrs. Hoover would now furnish her as if she had obtained them from a library.[7]

Mrs. Hoover had conformed to a pattern of behavior established for First Ladies from the time of Martha Washington. It was not a model Eleanor Roosevelt could follow without stultifying herself, and it was not a model she thought appropriate in a democratic society where the channels of communication between the people in the White House and the people in the country should, she felt, be open, lively, and sympathetic. So when Hick suggested that she hold press conferences, Eleanor agreed, and Bess Furman, whom she consulted, approved enthusiastically—as did Franklin and Louis. On Monday, March 6, two days before her husband's first press conference, an astonished and somewhat disapproving Ike Hoover, or so Eleanor thought, accompanied her into the Red Room, where thirty-five women reporters had assembled. The conference had been restricted to women, she explained, in order to encourage the employment of newspaper women and to make it more comfortable to deal with subjects of interest primarily to women. To further emphasize that she was in no way encroaching upon Franklin's domain, she had stipulated that no political questions could be asked. She brought with her a large box of candied fruits which she passed around—to hide her nervousness, she later claimed.

The first news conference did not produce much news, but the women were elated, although some of them, especially May Craig of the *Portland* (Maine) *Press Herald*, having fought hard to break down masculine professional barriers, were uncomfortable that men were excluded. However, the attitude of the men was "Why in the world would we want to come to Mrs. Roosevelt's conferences?" Byron Price, the manager of the AP, predicted that the institution would last less than six months.[8] However, a few weeks later, when a bill to legalize 3.2 beer went up to Congress, Roosevelt was asked at his news conference whether beer would be served at the White House if the bill were passed; that would have to be answered by his wife, he replied off the record. Eleanor was on her way to New York, so Ruby Black of the United Press raced out to catch her at the airport. Would she, a teetotaler, permit beer to be served at the White House? "You'll have to ask my husband," was Eleanor's guarded reply. Told that the president had referred the press to her, she burst into laughter. She would have a statement for them at her next news conference, she promised. By Monday, when the women reporters trooped in for their meeting with Eleanor, masculine scorn had turned to anguish, and some of the men begged the women to fill them in later.

Beer would be served at the White House to those who desire it, Eleanor's mimeographed announcement read. She herself did not drink anything with an alcoholic content, but she would not dream of imposing her convictions on others. She hoped, however, that the availability of beer might lead to greater temperance, and to a reduction in the bootlegger's trade.[9]

The scoffing ceased. Eleanor proved to be such a good news source that Emma Bugbee, who had been sent by the *New York Herald Tribune* to report on the First Lady's inauguration activities, was kept in Washington by her Republican employers for four months. "Well, if it's going to be like that," Emma's office said, after their reporter had lunched with Mrs. Roosevelt and had been taken through the living quarters of the president's family, something Mrs. Hoover had not done until the final months of her husband's regime, "you had better stay down."[10] Another Monday the press conference became a classroom in diets—patriotic, wholesome, and frugal; the women learned the recipe for Martha Washington's crab soup and for dishes that Andrew Jackson ate in the days "when the onion and herb were as important as the can opener."[11] Sheila Hibben, the culinary historian whom Eleanor had invited to the news conference, even ventured a theory of history about White House menus: "The more democratic our Presidents have been, the more attention they paid to their meals." The lecture on the wholesome, inexpensive dishes that other First Ladies had served their husbands led up to an announcement that with the help of Flora Rose of Cornell, Eleanor had served "a 7-cent luncheon" at the White House—hot stuffed eggs with tomato sauce, mashed potatoes, prune pudding, bread, and coffee. In London a woman read this menu and exclaimed to a friend that "if Mrs. Roosevelt can get her kitchen staff to eat three-penny, ha-penny meals, she can do more than I can with mine!"

"Oh, I don't know what she gives the servants," the friend replied. "She gives them to the President—and he eats them like a lamb."

Malnutrition, Eleanor concluded, was not only a result of a lack of food, but often of a lack of knowledge of menus that cost little and had high nutritional value. She thought the White House should set an example in the use of simple and nourishing foods. "Perhaps because of the depression we may teach people how really to feed their children."

Bess Furman contrasted the news-conference styles of president and First Lady: "At the President's press conference, all the world's a stage; at Mrs. Roosevelt's, all the world's a school."[12]

Eleanor's ban on political subjects did not mean a ban on issues of consequence and controversy. She hit out at sweatshops. She urged women to patronize the merchants who provided decent working conditions. She called for the elimination of child labor and urged more money for teachers' salaries. When in April the foreign dignitaries came flocking to the White House to confer with the president on the forthcoming World Economic Conference, she startled her press conference with the passion of her anti-isolationist plea. "We ought to be able to realize what people are up against in Europe. We ought to be the ready-to-understand ones, and we haven't been. . . . We've got to find a basis for a more stabilized world. . . . We are in an ideal position to lead, if we will lead, because we have suffered less. Only a few years are left to work in. Everywhere over there is the dread of this war that may come." She spoke, wrote Emma Bugbee, with "an intensity her hearers had never seen in her before."[13]

With many of her press-conference regulars, what began as a professional relationship soon ripened into friendship. Before the inauguration, Ruby Black (Mrs. Herbert Little) had shown Eleanor a photograph of her fourteen-month-old daughter. Eleanor had said she would love to see the child, and Ruby had thought it was an expression of courtesy rather than of intent. A week after she was in the White House, however, Eleanor telephoned her—could she come the next day to visit Ruby? She did, driving her little blue roadster to Ruby's house and making friends with the child. Newswomen found themselves being given lifts in the White House car, receiving Easter lilies from the White House greenhouses, lunching at the White House table, being invited to Hyde Park. Eleanor's gestures of thoughtfulness were not matters of calculation, of "being nice to the press"; one natural act of friendliness led to another. But friendship did not encroach upon journalistic responsibility. The women asked the questions to which they or their editors felt the public was entitled to know the answers. When a reporter cautioned the First Lady that an answer might get her into trouble, her colleagues made their displeasure known; the First Lady could take care of herself, they felt. And she did.

"Sometimes I say things," she said to her press conference,

which I thoroughly understand are likely to cause unfavorable comment in some quarters, and perhaps you newspaper women think I should keep them off the record. What you don't understand is that perhaps I am making these statements on purpose to arouse controversy and thereby get the topics talked about and so get people to thinking about them.[14]

Most of the correspondents were friendly—too friendly, some of the men grumbled. The women alerted her as to what was on the public's mind and the questions she should be prepared to answer, and sometimes she consulted a few of them about the answers she proposed to give. Even the most "hard-boiled" were willing to help. This was, after all, a male-dominated capital and the women should stand together. Sometimes Eleanor blundered. Mrs. Mary Harriman Rumsey was running into public-relations difficulties as head of the Consumers Division of the National Recovery Administration, and Eleanor talked to Bess Furman and Martha Strayer, of the *Washington News*, about taking on second jobs, for which they would be paid, to help out Mrs. Rumsey. No, they told her regretfully; they were for the NRA and the whole New Deal, but accepting money from the government in any way could mean the loss of their jobs.[15] Publicity and newspaper work were closely allied, but the line between them was sharply drawn, particularly in Washington. They were right and she was wrong, and she did not press the offer. Lorena Hickok, who suddenly realized that her close relationship with Mrs. Roosevelt was affecting her detachment as a journalist, resigned her job with the AP to work for Harry Hopkins in the new relief administration, but her intimacy with Mrs. Roosevelt was unique. Friendship was another matter. Most of the women reporters felt they could be friends with the mistress of the White House without losing their objectivity, and marveled that she wanted to be their friend. In a city where human relations were usually governed by a careful consideration of interests and motivations were usually suspect, Eleanor's warmth and good will were refreshing. "I always thought when people were given great power it did something to them," Martha Strayer wrote to Eleanor. "They lost the human touch if they ever had it. To have been able to see you at close hand, demonstrating the exact contrary, means truly a great deal to me."[16] A few weeks after the inauguration, the Gridiron Club, a male journalistic stronghold, gave its annual dinner, which was attended by the president and his cabinet but from which women were barred. Eleanor organized a Gridiron Widows buffet supper for newswomen, cabinet wives, and women in government. "God's gift to newspaper women," the feminine press fraternity murmured.

What enchanted the press captivated the public. As First Lady, Eleanor's approach to people great and small remained as it had always been: direct and unaffected, full of curiosity and a desire to learn—and to teach.

On her return from a trip down the Potomac on the *Sequoia* with Prime Minister James Ramsay MacDonald and his daughter Ishbel as guests, she and Ishbel went on board a fishing schooner from Gloucester, Massachusetts, filled with fishing captains who had come to the Capital to ask for help for this "oldest industry." She invited the skippers to visit the White House, and twenty-seven came, escorted by their congressman. Eleanor herself took them around, and after the tour of the public rooms invited them to go through the family quarters on the second floor. Down the wide hall the weather-beaten men trailed, peering into historic rooms as Eleanor opened the doors and told some of the history that had taken place in them. The men chortled when she hastily closed a door behind which she had spotted Anna sleeping, and concluded, as one skipper put it, "There ain't too many ladies in her position who would have done what she did."[17]

A few weeks later she entertained Sara and the members of the Monday Evening Sewing Class at luncheon. Helen Wilmerding, a friend from the day of the Roser classes, was in the group. "All the old tribe we grew up with in New York have turned towards you like sun flowers," she wrote Eleanor later. "At first they were naturally more anxious than other people as to how you would stand up against the difficulties of your position. You are one of them and they cared more. Now they are sunflowers I need say no more." Eleanor appreciated Helen's note "very much," she replied, "for I felt the old crowd might disapprove of many things which I did."[18]

The "old crowd" was also somewhat astonished by the growing elegance of her clothes. In the twenties it had been fashionable to deplore Eleanor's lack of interest in what she wore. It conformed with society's stereotype of a strong-willed woman of good works to see her in bulky tweeds and a hair net, and to whisper that without a corset her stomach showed. Eleanor had dressed acceptably in the governorship years, but now the top couturiers of the country, who naturally wanted her patronage, pressed their advice and most stylish models upon her. If she did not devote more time than in the past to the selection of clothes, she was more willing to be guided by friends like June Hamilton Rhodes, who had helped in the campaign and now worked as a fashion publicist for the elegant Fifth Avenue shops. "I got a lot of clothes for myself and Anna in one afternoon last week," Eleanor wrote Franklin three weeks before the inauguration. "It is better to have plenty and not buy any new ones for quite a while!"[19] But the dress shops argued that such restraint in shopping did not help business recovery, and she evidently agreed, for in May, Lilly Daché shipped her six blue velvet hats "of the June Hamilton Rhodes material" and asked her to return those that did not please her entirely. "Mrs. Roosevelt kept all of the hats as she likes them all very much and would like to have you send a bill for them," replied Malvina "Tommy" Thompson who had come to Washington as her secretary.

"Your dress, hat and coat were lovely," Helen Wilmerding commented after the "old crowd's" visit to the White House. "I wanted to snatch them off and put them on myself. . . ." Gentle Helen had not been among those who had mocked her taste in clothes, but since so many of her contemporaries had considered Eleanor a little dowdy in her dress, Helen's letter must have given her considerable gratification.

"Everyone makes very low prices," Eleanor had remarked on the afternoon she devoted to getting her White House wardrobe. She did not spurn them. She used to comment with amusement on the Scotch streak in Franklin, but it was a characteristic she shared. However, in spite of the Fifth Avenue shops' low prices, she was quite prepared to switch to less fashionable and less obliging establishments if that was the only way to get fair conditions for labor. "I feel sure that you will understand," she wrote to Milgrim's, "that I will have to wait before coming to you again until you have some agreement with your people which is satisfactory to both sides." A distraught Mr. Milgrim telegraphed her within the week that the ILGWU's strike had been settled and that both sides were satisfied. "I was quite upset when I received your letter and am very anxious to explain the facts when you come in for your fitting which will be ready Thursday, October 12th."[20]

This pro-labor gesture was in September, but in March she had already yielded to her incorrigible reforming impulses and struck out into precisely the kind of activities she thought she would have to give up as First Lady. "Friends who have wondered how long it would be before Mrs. Roosevelt's instinct for civic and social reform would assert itself in Washington had the answer today, when the story of her inspection trip to Washington's alleys was told for the first time," wrote Emma Bugbee.[21] Mrs. Archibald Hopkins, eighty-one, a "cliff dweller" with a social conscience, asked her to tour Washington's alley slums with her. By focusing public attention on these disease- and crime-ridden back streets perhaps they might be able to persuade Congress to do something about them. Eleanor made the tour, driving in her roadster. She reported her grim findings to the press and even suggested that Congress should act. Mrs. Hopkins' committee had prepared a bill to reconstruct the alley slums, she pointed out, and while it was a rule with her that she did not comment on pending legislation, she would say, "Of course I am sympathetic with the general theory of better housing everywhere." She spoke to Franklin about what she had seen and about the bill, and he permitted her to indicate to Mrs. Hopkins that he would help at the right moment. She enlisted the aid of the president's uncle, Frederic A. Delano, head of the National Capital Park and Planning Commission. "I have talked with Franklin and Uncle Fred about the bill," she reported to Mrs. Hopkins. "Franklin thinks that at the special session it will be quite impossible to get through any local bills of any kind, but I feel quite certain that at the regular session it can and will be done. Uncle Fred talked to me the other night and he feels he has convinced Senator King [chairman of the Senate District Committee] that the bill should be pushed. If it should happen to slide through well and good, but if it does not get through do not feel discouraged, for I feel sure it will go through at the next session."[22] Discouraged? Mrs. Hopkins, who had first visited the White House in Abraham Lincoln's time, at last had an ally on the distaff side. She felt invincible.

District institutions, Eleanor believed, should serve as a model for the nation. Instead, voteless and at the mercy of an economy-minded Congress that was, in addition, singularly indifferent to the Negroes who would be the chief beneficiaries of improved services, the residents of the District had among the worst hospitals, nursing homes, and jails in the nation. Her interest in the District would be a continuing one.

The Hoover action that had most offended the country was the eviction of the "bonus army" veterans from Washington in 1932. That Mr. Hoover, a Quaker, could have authorized the use of military force to drive jobless veterans out of their squatters' shacks seemed to Eleanor a dreadful object lesson in what fear could make a well-intentioned man do. As a consequence, when the

Veterans National Liaison Committee informed the White House that the veterans were returning to Washington and expected the new administration to house and feed them, she pressed her husband to treat them with consideration and see to it that there was no repetition of the previous summer's panic. Louis—whose official title was secretary to the president and who called himself "the dirty-job man"—took on the job of handling the new bonus army.[23] The Veterans Administration directed to house the men lodged them in Fort Hunt, an old army camp across the river, provided them with food, medical care, even dental service. A military band entertained them. Louis kept in daily touch with the leaders and received reports on the mood among the men, including the activity of the Communists. The veterans having presented their case by the middle of May, Louis told them that twelve hundred of them could be enrolled in the CCC and tried to persuade them to pass a resolution to go home. The men debated and dallied, and then Louis played his trump card: he brought Eleanor to visit the encampment. The men were pleased and heartened to see the First Lady among them and quickly took her over, proposing that she tour the camp. She went with the men through tents, barracks, and hospital, ending up at the mess hall, where she mingled with the men in the mess line and was persuaded to make a little speech. She reminisced about World War days and her work in the railroad yards when the "boys," perhaps some of those who were here, had come through Washington on their way overseas. She also spoke of her post war tour of the battlefields where they had fought and concluded, "I never want to see another war. I would like to see fair consideration for everyone, and I shall always be grateful to those who served their country." She led the men in singing "There's a Long, Long Trail" and departed amid cheers. "Hoover sent the army. Roosevelt sent his wife," said one left-wing veteran, who was chagrined over the Communists' loss of influence. Soon afterward the bonus marchers passed a resolution to disperse. "It is such fine things as that which bring you the admiration of the American people," wrote Josephus Daniels from Mexico City, where he was the U.S. ambassador.[24]

Eleanor and Louis had not allowed the Secret Service to accompany them to the encampment, and there was considerable relief when they returned safely to the White House. Eleanor's insistence on not being shadowed by police and Secret Service enhanced the country's image of her as a woman unafraid, seeking to be herself, but it was a sore issue with those responsible for the safety of the president and his family. After the attempt on Roosevelt's life in Miami on February 15, 1933, he wanted to ask the Secret Service to assign a man to protect her. "Don't you dare do such a thing," she warned him. "If any Secret Service man shows up in New York and starts following me around, I'll send him right straight back where he came from." But Colonel Starling, the head of the presidential detail, brought the matter up repeatedly with the president and Louis. He was particularly worried over her insistence on driving herself around unescorted. She was unbudgeable, they explained.

Local police found her as stubborn as the Secret Service. When she came to New York to visit the headquarters of the Women's Trade Union League, she found four policemen in front of the building.

"What are you doing here?" she asked.

"We're here to guard Mrs. Roosevelt."

"I don't want to be guarded; please go away."

"We can't do that, the captain placed us here," the head of the detail explained in some embarrassment. She went inside and called Louis, who phoned police headquarters. The captain came immediately. "Please take them all away. No one's going to hurt me," Eleanor said to him.

"I hope not," the captain said doubtfully, but complied. Americans were "wonderful," she said. "I simply can't imagine being afraid of going among them as I have always done, as I always shall."[25]

She refused to succumb to fear. By self-discipline she had conquered her childhood dread of animals, of water, and of physical pain, and she kept these fears at bay by simply defying them.

She was an inveterate air traveler, sometimes pressing air personnel to fly even when they thought the weather too hazardous. The fledgling airlines found her a stalwart advocate of air travel, quite willing to lend herself to their promotional efforts; the country was benignly responsive to her sense of adventure and her delight in sponsoring the new and promising enterprise. In order to impress the public, especially women, with the ease and safety of air travel, Amelia Earhart invited Eleanor to join her on a flight to Baltimore in evening dress. Hall Roosevelt went along, as did a few newspaperwomen and Miss Earhart's husband, George Palmer Putnam. How did she feel being piloted by a woman, she was asked. Absolutely safe, was her reply; "I'd give a lot to do it myself!" She seriously discussed learning to fly with Miss Earhart and went so far as to take a physical examination, which she passed. But Franklin thought it was foolish to spend time learning to fly when she would not be able to afford a plane and she came to the same conclusion.[26]

Not long after she was settled in the White House she made her first transcontinental flight, to Los Angeles to see Elliott. Such a journey still was an event, and it was even more so when undertaken by the First Lady. From Fort Worth to the Coast, C. R. Smith, the president of American Airways, accompanied her, as did Amon G. Carter, the publisher of the *Fort Worth Star-Telegram*. Both men admired her stamina and poise; "her rapid air tour," wrote Carter, "twice spanning the continent, was a physical feat calculated to take the 'bounce' out of a transport pilot." She came through it "smiling."[27] Will Rogers found her performance sufficiently impressive to write a letter about it to the *New York Times*. Yes, it was a real boost for aviation, he said, "but here is really what she takes the medal for: out at every stop, day or night, standing for photographs by the hour, being interviewed, talking over the radio, no sleep. And yet they say she never showed one sign of weariness or annoyance of any kind. No maid, no secretary—just the First Lady of the land on a paid ticket on a regular passenger flight."[28]

Not since Theodore Roosevelt's days had the White House pulsated with such high spirits and sheer animal vitality. Colonel Starling took the Hoovers to

Union Station and on his return to the White House a few hours later found it "transformed during my absence into a gay place full of people who oozed confidence."

"You know how it was when Uncle Ted was there—how gay and home-like," Roosevelt had remarked at Cousin Susie's before the inauguration. "Well, that's how we mean to have it!"[29]

As the official residence of the president, tradition and law limited the extent to which 1600 Pennsylvania Avenue could reflect the tastes and habits of the family that occupied it, but within those limits the Roosevelt personalities soon placed their gregarious and buoyant stamp on the historic dwelling.

There were grandchildren all over the place. Anna was separated from her husband, and she and her two children, Sisty (Anna Eleanor), six, and Buzz (Curtis), three, stayed at the White House. Betsy and Jimmy and their daughter Sarah often visited, James to do chores for his father, Betsy because she was a favorite of her father-in-law. Franklin Jr. and Johnny, lively teen-agers, were in and out. There were nurseries on the third floor and a sandbox and jungle gym on the south lawn. There were also Eleanor's dogs Meggie and Major, both of whom had to be exiled to Hyde Park before the end of the year, Major for having nipped Senator Hattie Caraway and Meggie after biting reporter Bess Furman on the lip.

Some staid officials found the Roosevelt exuberance a little unsettling. The housekeeper was instructed to keep the icebox full for midnight snacks, and White House guards to let the teen-agers in even if they turned up in the early hours of the morning. What kind of place is this, an indignant Johnny wanted to know, when a fellow can't get into his own house? Eleanor had her own run-in with a too literal interpretation of regulations when Colonel Ulysses S. Grant III, in charge of public buildings and grounds, informed her that she could not attach an old-fashioned swing to the limb of a White House tree because it might injure the bark. "Well, of course, I shall do whatever he tells me, but for the life of me I cannot get this point of view." Eventually the children got their swing.[30]

But she would not do anything that detracted from the mansion's dignity, because it was a house that belonged to the nation. "I think it is a beautiful house with lovely proportions, great dignity, and I do not think any one looking at it from the outside or living in it can fail to feel the spell of the past and the responsibility of living up to the fine things which have been done and lived in that house."[31] The family quarters on the second floor were spacious but not intimidating. There were four large two-room suites, one at each corner of the floor, the larger room twenty-six by thirty feet, the smaller fourteen by seventeen feet. On the southern side the two corner suites were separated by the Monroe Room, a sitting room which Mrs. Hoover had furnished with authentic reproductions of Monroe furniture, and the Oval Room. On the opposite side of the house, looking toward Pennsylvania Avenue, there were two smaller guest rooms. The whole floor was bisected by a regal hall, eighteen feet wide, and the ceilings were seventeen feet high.

When Eleanor returned from the inaugural, she found the high-ceilinged rooms and the long hall devoid of all personal belongings a little depressing, but with the help of Nancy Cook and a White House warehouse full of old furniture, the family rooms soon bore the Roosevelt imprint.

Franklin took the Oval Room as his study, covering the walls with his naval prints and his desk with the gadgets and curios that he had collected all his life. Flanking the fireplace were the flags of the United States and of the president, and over the door he hung a pastel painting of Eleanor of which he was very fond. A door next to his desk led into a small bedroom. Eleanor felt that the bed there was too cumbersome and large, and ordered one made at Val-Kill. There were two bedside tables, one usually covered with documents and memoranda, the other with pencils, pads, and a telephone. Eleanor often left letters on this table with sections underlined and a notation in the margin, "F—read."

Her own suite was next to Franklin's in the southwest corner of the floor. The larger room had been Lincoln's bedroom, but she slept in the dressing room and used the other as her sitting room and study. She liked to be surrounded by photographs, and her walls were soon adorned with the framed portraits of family, friends, and people she had known and admired. Her Val-Kill desk was by a window overlooking a handsome magnolia that had been planted by Andrew Jackson. The view from her desk, as from the president's bed, swept across the south lawns to the Washington monument. Louis occupied the southeast suite and Missy had a small apartment on the third floor that had been used by Mrs. Hoover's housekeeper.

The western end of the second-floor hall had been used as a conservatory by Mrs. Hoover, who had fitted it out with heavy bamboo furniture, a green fiber rug, palm trees, and large cages of birds to give it an outdoor, California-like air. Eleanor turned it into a family sitting room where she presided over the breakfast table in the morning and the tea urn in the afternoon. The small silver tea service had been a wedding gift from Alice and the silver statuette of Old Mother Hubbard—a dining-table bell—had belonged to her mother. It was always at her right hand, its head, to the delight of the children, nodding solemnly back and forth when she rang.

When Eleanor saw that the breakfast tray had been brought in to Franklin, she would go in soon afterward to say good morning and exchange a few words. She did not stay long because he liked to be left alone to eat his breakfast and glance through the papers. In times of crisis there were always officials waiting in the hall to see him before he was wheeled over to the executive offices. Normally the three who went in after he had finished his breakfast to discuss the day's schedule were Louis, press secretary Steve Early, and Marvin McIntyre, who was in charge of appointments. The executive offices were practically under the same roof, but Franklin was "just as much separated as though he went to a building farther away," according to Eleanor. His day was taken up with a succession of people and crises, and he had little time for private affairs. It was sometimes hard on the children, who were having problems. Anna had decided to divorce Curtis ("So the news of our family is out," Sara lamented). Elliott was settling in Texas—"nothing could pay me to go back East again"—and was also separating from his wife. "That is terrible about Elliott and Betty," Johnny wrote from Groton, wanting to know whether there was anything he or Franklin Jr. could do. He, too, was making important decisions. He intended to work that summer at camp as a counselor, and "I'm going to Princeton College." Franklin Jr., senior prefect at Groton and bound for Harvard, alone among the children seemed to be serene. "It must be very satisfying to feel you've been married twenty-eight years,—especially in these times," he wrote his parents on their wedding anniversary, adding, "But to get to the point, first of all please don't forget to bring my full dress, all my stiff shirts. . . ."

"We laugh about it a great deal when I formally make an appointment for the children to see their father at given hours when something comes up which really must be discussed and decided but it is not as much a laughing matter as we make it out to be. . . ."[32] Usually Eleanor did not see Franklin until he returned from the executive offices to get ready for dinner. They rarely dined alone, and while conversation flowed freely at the dinner table, it was inevitably of an impersonal sort. After dinner, officials often came in to work with the president, leaving Eleanor to entertain their guests and bid them good night. Then she would go to her desk to work on her mail. Before she went to bed—"and sometimes that is very late"—she took her dogs for a walk around the White House circle and drank in the beauty and stateliness of the White House, with its portico "lighted only by the lights from the windows, and yet shining out in its whiteness against the darkness." Sometimes during the first few months officials stayed until the early morning and Eleanor did not dare to go to bed for fear of missing something that might happen while she was asleep.[33] In any event, she did not go to bed before going in to say good night to her husband, sit on his bed, and chat for a while. It was often the only chance she had to talk with him about the things she really had on her mind.

However late she stayed up, her day usually began at 7:30 A.M. with exercise or a ride in Rock Creek Park. Her horse, Dot, which she had bought from Earl, was stabled at Fort Myers and brought over to the park in an army van. Missy was occasionally her companion on these rides, but more often it was Elinor Morgenthau, with whom she was closer than any other woman in official Washington. Eleanor, in her riding habit and with a velvet ribbon around her soft, light-brown hair, became a familiar figure along Washington's bridle paths. Once her horse reared, frightened by a newspaper that blew across her path, and she was thrown. "I slid off very gracefully right into the mud," she told the reporters, who inevitably heard of the mishap.[34]

After breakfast she went to her desk and saw in turn the head usher, the social secretary, and the housekeeper. Ike Hoover, who had come to the White House during the administration of Benjamin Harrison and who died soon after the Roosevelts arrived, was succeeded as chief usher by Raymond Muir, a tall, dignified lawyer from the Veterans Bureau—always polite, always unruffled. The usher's room, which was at the right of the entrance as guests came in, was the clearing house of the establishment. Muir kept track of everyone who came into the White House living quarters—family, guests, people who had appointments with anyone in the White House. He saw that guests were met by a White House car and escorted them to their rooms if Eleanor could not do so herself. Mrs. Edith Helm was Eleanor's social secretary, as she had been Mrs. Wilson's. Mrs. Helm was tall, distinguished, erect, and correct, and bore the unmistakable stamp of someone who had grown up in one of the services. The daughter of an admiral and the widow of an admiral, she knew Washington's customs and conventions. Every morning she and Eleanor went over her lists and invitations and table orders. And finally Eleanor talked with Mrs. Henrietta Nesbitt, the housekeeper, who did the buying, prepared the menus, and supervised the household staff. Ike Hoover had been concerned because Mrs. Nesbitt was not a professional housekeeper, but Eleanor preferred Mrs. Nesbitt to a professional manager because she was conscientious and something of a business woman, and she was grandmotherly and unpretentious. She would do Eleanor's bidding, not vice versa.[35]

By the time Eleanor was finished with Mrs. Nesbitt, Tommy (now Mrs. Frank J. Scheider) had gone through the mail and taken out all the personal letters, communications from government officials, and any other letters that looked as though they might require immediate attention—some fifty letters a day, only a small proportion of the mail that Eleanor received. "Letters and letters and letters," she said of the first weeks in Washington. "Wire baskets on my desk, suit cases of mail going home even on Sundays" with Tommy, "a sense of being snowed under by mail." That first year 300,000 pieces of mail came to the White House addressed to her, and she loved it.

The letters that were not kept for Eleanor's immediate attention were sent to the Correspondence Unit, where they were opened and classified. (It was unofficially called the social bureau, indicating the nature of the bulk of the First Lady's correspondence in previous administrations.) There were two divisions: one, under Mrs. Helm, handled the social correspondence; the other, under Ralph Magee, worked with Tommy on the remainder of the mail. Magee's unit used form letters dating back to the Cleveland administration, which did not seem adequate to Eleanor, so she rewrote some; but generally she tried as far as was humanly possible to see that a letter received personal attention either from Tommy or herself. Some letters Tommy answered directly, and to others she dictated replies for Eleanor's signature, but for the fifty or so letters which were of special interest, Eleanor made a note of the kind of answer she wanted Tommy to compose or, in cases involving personal friends or controversy, she dictated a reply herself. In addition, there were letters she answered in longhand—to Hick, Earl, Nancy and Marion, her children, and old friends. So when she was not on the telephone, receiving callers, or otherwise engaged, there was always the basket of correspondence to get through, even if it meant working through the night after the last dinner guest had departed or slipping away from the movie that was being shown in the hall outside the president's study. However she managed to do it, by morning there was always a basket of outgoing mail on Tommy's desk.

When she was not writing letters, she was writing articles. With Louis Howe acting as her agent, she contracted to do a monthly 750-word piece for the North American Newspaper Alliance at $500 an article. They asked her to write "as one woman to another, of your problems as the woman of the household."[36] She signed the contract after exercising her option to cancel her arrangement with MacFadden to edit *Babies—Just Babies*. Criticism did not faze her, but ridicule did. Even her friends spoofed her about *Babies—Just Babies*. At the annual party of the Women's Press Club one of the songs began:

> We are new to the business of running the show,
> We're babies, just babies, just babies.[37]

When in addition to the ridicule there were editorial differences with publisher MacFadden, she decided to withdraw, and the magazine ceased publication. That same month, May, Louis Howe negotiated a contract for her with *Woman's Home Companion* to do a monthly column, "I Want You to Write Me," for which she received $1,000 each month. In addition, Anna was paid $325 a month for handling the correspondence that came flooding into the magazine as a result of the column. A friendly congressman alerted Marvin McIntyre that there was Republican criticism in the House Appropriations Committee of the number of letters that Eleanor referred to the Women's Bureau of the Department of Labor to be answered for her. It was assumed that this mail was the result of the *Woman's Home Companion* columns, and when it was pointed out that the mail that came in to the magazine was answered there, the criticism was dropped. [38] But there were other complaints.

He did not mean to be impertinent, a member of the staff of the *Writer's Digest* wrote, but weren't these writing offers made to her because her name would attract attention? She did not think him "the least impertinent" for asking such questions, Eleanor replied. "I do not like to think that my name is entirely responsible for my receiving these offers, although I realize it must be a part of it, as I cannot very well divorce myself from my name. I always honestly try to do every job to the best of my ability."[39]

But if there were many critics, most of the country approved. Here was the wife of the president, wrote historian Mary R. Beard, who through a massive correspondence, articles, press conferences, and speeches was giving "inspiration to the married, solace to the lovelorn, assistance to the homemaker, menus to the cook, help to the educator, direction to the employer, caution to the warrior, and deeper awareness of its primordial force to the 'weaker sex.'" The country was accustomed to "the Great White Father in the White House" instructing his people "in right conduct," commented Mrs. Beard; now the "Great White Mother emerges as a personality in her own right and starts an independent course of instruction on her own account." Mrs. Beard, a long-time feminist, clearly thought the country as well as the women had gained by this step forward in feminine evolution.[40]

Were they having guests the next week end? Franklin asked Eleanor at the beginning of April. "Probably a house full," she replied. Perhaps she had better put off some of them, he suggested. Why? Were they having some guests he had not mentioned? "I think, perhaps a few Prime Ministers." In April Eleanor discovered that "there were certain social duties which were entirely mine and which must be performed even if the skies seemed about to fall."[41]

Formal entertainments such as that occasioned by the visits of Ramsay MacDonald, Edouard Herriot, and the host of other foreign dignitaries who arrived to discuss the preparations for the London Economic Conference had an obligatory, ceremonial character. If she was sad because children and friends had to be seated at remote ends of the table, she reminded herself that it was the "people's hospitality" that she was dispensing, not her own, and that men and women had to be treated according to rank and precedence. Even with American public officials, the respect for their office and the pleasure their status conferred upon them were high among the inducements that had brought them to Washington, and this had to be recognized. "It is really the position which is invited and not the person!" And it was not Eleanor Roosevelt, the person, she realized, whom officials were anxious to meet, but the "wife of the President."

That was equally true of the thousands who came to her afternoon teas and receptions. Conventions came in great numbers to Washington in April, and they had to be received. One group would come in at four and another at five. Sometimes it was much worse, as in the case of the Daughters of the American Revolution, when Eleanor shook the hands of 3,100 women in an hour and a half: "If you don't think that rather trying, you want to try it sometimes."[42] A visit to the White House was an exalted occasion to the women she received. They wanted it to be memorable, and the smartly turned-out junior military aides who attended the First Lady and the very dignified ushers who escorted the guests to the Red Room or the Green Room helped make it so. With the help of Mrs. Helm, who admonished Eleanor gently and insistently upon the importance of protocol, she finally came to realize that the handshaking and receiving were more important than she thought. "I was a symbol which tied the people who came by me in the long ever-recurring receiving lines to their government," she noted later.[43] Once she understood the significance of the receptions and teas, she no longer rebelled. "Four hundred will be quite easy to have for tea," she assured Ruth Morgan, who was organizing the conference on the Cause and Cure of War.[44]

Nor was she unappreciative of ceremony that was evocative of American history or symbolic of the responsibility and power of the presidential office. She quickly came to know the history of the White House—its rooms, its portraits, its china—and enjoyed telling guests about it. Her pulse quickened to the ceremony of piping the president aboard the yacht *Sequoia* for the trip down the Potomac with the MacDonalds, and when they came back it was she who told the press of the little ritual at Mount Vernon that was performed by all passing naval vessels: "the bell rings, the flag dips, the sailors man the rail; if there is a bugler aboard he sounds taps; everybody stands at attention in silence."[45]

Although entertainment, especially of foreign visitors, was rigidly prescribed by protocol, even here her personality quickly made itself felt. MacDonald was accompanied by his daughter Ishbel. "What a difference," Bess Furman wrote, from their previous visit to the Hoovers in 1929, when Ishbel had been "shielded" from the press by Mrs. Hoover. Eleanor held two press conferences in the White House for the prime minister's daughter, who was a political personality in her own right, and had her sit in on her own. With the press in tow they went everywhere together, including a visit, unprecedented for a First Lady, to a congressional hearing on the thirty-hour bill while Frances Perkins was testifying. A young Republican congressman named Everett Dirksen gallantly vacated his seat for the Democratic First Lady. MacDonald wrote from London that they had felt themselves "so much at home at the White House."

Most of the formal entertaining decreed by protocol and tradition was over by inauguration day, but in the autumn Eleanor would have to confront her first social season, and a "deep gloom" settled upon her as she went over the dates and lists for the state functions. "One thing is certain," she told Mrs. Helm, "I can't even have a headache between the middle of December and the beginning of Lent!" Tuesday and Thursday nights were set aside for the large formal parties that were dictated by custom. The dinner for the vice president was usually the first, in December. She knew that the president's dinner was "a command," Mrs. Garner wrote from Uvalde, but they wanted to stay in Texas for Christmas and "you know how Mr. Garner feels about dinners—so why not forget that it is a custom to give a dinner for the Vice President?" She had talked it over with the president, Eleanor replied, "and he says there is no reason why the dinner for the Vice President could not be given just as well in January. . . . I do not think the order in which the dinners come matters at all."[46]

Her success as a hostess was due neither to stamina nor to her adherence to protocol but to her constant thoughtfulness for her guests, the little human gestures that made them feel welcome and at home amid all the trappings of power and ceremony. When the Amyas Ameses, who lived next door to the James Roosevelts in Cambridge, arrived to spend Easter at the White House Eleanor was at a meeting. After saying good evening to the president the Ameses were taken to one of the guest rooms opposite his study, and as they were unpacking there was a knock on the door, and there was Eleanor bearing a bowl of fruit. Mrs. Ames was pregnant and occasionally nauseous; James had told his mother of this, so Eleanor asked if her guest would like to have a snack between meals, and if so, what? "Cocoa and rye twist," Mrs. Ames said hesitantly. Eleanor saw to it that there was always a thermos and a plate of bread on the bedside table. On Easter Sunday when the whole household went to the cathedral for the service, Mrs. Ames went along doubtfully. "You won't want to stay through the whole thing," Eleanor told her; "I've arranged for the car to come back early and you can slip out before the sermon." She inquired whether there was anyone the Ameses wanted to see in Washington, and when they mentioned the Francis Plimptons, she invited them for Easter dinner. "The White House had an aura of power and impressiveness about it, but they were themselves," Mrs. Ames later recalled. "They acted as if they had always been there. It was like visiting friends in a very large country house. One was put instantly at one's ease. She was the fantastically most thoughtful hostess I have ever met in my life."[47]

In 1913 when Eleanor, then twenty-eight years old, had arrived in the nation's Capital as the wife of the assistant secretary of the Navy, the social lists had dictated whom she received and entertained. The day was now long past when society as such had any interest for her; social standing did not foreclose an invitation to the White House, and neither did it insure one. Miss Mary Patten came, as full of gossip as ever, and so did the shy, almost speechless parents of a young hitchhiker to whom Eleanor had given a lift in upstate New York and had undertaken to get into a CCC camp, wiring Tommy that if he should turn up at the White House he should not be sent away. She reproached her cousin Muriel Martineau for thinking "we are not going to be able to see everyone just as we have always done," and also Rose Schneiderman, who had been to Washington on union business and had not let her know: "Please always come to lunch or to see me. I always feel badly when I miss any of my friends."

To be a successful hostess she felt one really had to give oneself to one's guests. This was easier to do when the people who were closest to her, who represented the private realm in her life, were somewhere near. Their arrivals, departures, and birthdays were carefully recorded in the little diary she began to keep on March 4. "Said goodbye to Hick." "Said goodbye to Earl & Ruth." "Nan to stay." "Rock Creek Cemetery with Hick." "Marion and 10s come 7:30 Hick for night." "E.R., Marion & Nan start upstate & Campo." "Hall's birthday." "Anna & children arrive." "Sisty's Birthday Party." "L.H. birthday. . . . Supper for L.H." After the inaugural ceremonies, Elizabeth said to Esther, "Eleanor cares about having her friends go through things with her." She did and invited them to one big dinner after another. She never let go of a friend.

The two events she added to the list of formal entertainments were the White House Gridiron Widows party and a garden party for women executives in the government, many of whom had never been to the White House. The Roosevelt receptions and parties were "so carefully avoided by the 'nice people,' " a Washington cave dweller was heard to say, that Eleanor "had to invite the people who worked for the government in order to have any attendance at all." When these Washingtonians read the social news from the White House and found the names of those present unidentifiable, they sat back, disapproved, enjoyed Alice Longworth's cruel take-off of her cousin, and thought nostalgically of the days when the Washington that counted agonized over whether Alice, as the wife of the Speaker, or Dolly Gann, as sister and hostess of Vice President Curtis, should have social precedence.

These were trying days for Alice Longworth. Until the arrival of Franklin and Eleanor she had been Washington's "Roosevelt." She was still one of the most entertaining people in Washington as well as one of the most malicious. She had always been the star, Eleanor the retiring one, but now it was Eleanor of whom everyone talked. Even her burlesque of Eleanor, which everyone implored her to do, lost some of its savor when at a White House party Eleanor invited her to perform it for her. "Alice has a talent for that sort of thing," she said amiably, shrugging off questioners who hoped perhaps to stoke up a feud. It did not add to Alice's pleasure in the arrival of the Franklin Roosevelts to hear Auntie Corinne say that Eleanor was more like Theodore "than any of his children." Only a few of the Oyster Bay Roosevelts had not campaigned for Hoover; Auntie Corinne had refused to serve as a Republican elector—"You must understand my own beloved niece is the wife of the Democratic Candidate"—and Kermit Roosevelt had turned up at the Biltmore election eve to congratulate Franklin. But Alice Longworth had campaigned for the Republican ticket. Like her seventy-year-old stepmother, who had come out of retirement to introduce Hoover at a Madison Square Garden rally, she could not bear the idea that the name Roosevelt should be associated in the public mind and affection with someone other than Theodore. But after the election, Eleanor set aside political differences and wrote Alice, inviting her to feel free to come to all the parties, even though she must never feel any obligation to come.

By the end of Roosevelt's first hundred days, he had piloted the greatest budget of remedial laws in American history through Congress, and Eleanor had demonstrated to herself and to an astonished country that the White House, far from being a prison, was a springboard for greater usefulness. The opportunities that came to her were not of her own making. As First Lady she automatically commanded national attention, was showered with good will, and could get anything she wanted. As the wife of a president who was lifting the hearts of the nation with the example of his forcefulness, courage, and energy, she shared in the adulation that flowed from a reviving people toward the White House. It was not a life and existence that she had shaped or willed for herself; it was something that was happening to her by virtue of her husband's election and success. The pattern was set by him. The purposes she served were his. Her real self, she felt, was buried deep within her.[48]

Yet there was more to it than that. For by the end of the hundred days, she as much as her husband had come to personify the Roosevelt era. She as much as he had captured the imagination of the country. Far from being a prisoner of the White House and having to content herself with riding, catching up on her reading, and answering mail, as she had predicted to friends, she found herself so busy that she had no time to have her hair washed and would gladly have seen "the days so arranged that one never had to sleep."[49] Most of the women who molded public opinion shared the view expressed by Fannie Hurst in her broadcast from the Chicago World's Fair on the women who were making history for their sex: never before had the White House had "a woman so closely allied to the tremendous responsibilities of her position as wife of the

President. . . ." Her mail, which at the end of the hundred days was heavier than ever, showed that hope was returning to the country, that morale and self-confidence were bounding upward. That represented the nation's response to Roosevelt's fulfillment of his pledge of "action, and action now," and it also expressed the nation's recognition that in Eleanor as well as in Franklin it had again found leadership.

Cissy Patterson, whose fast behavior had shocked Eleanor in her debutante days, interviewed her for the *Washington Herald*, of which she was the publisher. What was Eleanor's secret, she wanted to know—the whole country was astonished by her energy and her ability to move through "these cram-crowded days of hers with a sure, serene and blithe spirit." They were old acquaintances, Cissy said, who had moved in the same social circles, and she knew what a transformation had taken place in Eleanor. She was not satisfied with Eleanor's first answer—that she was blessed with a robust constitution. Nor did her second reply ("When I have something to do—I just do it") seem very enlightening. How did she escape the "sick vanity" and "wounded ego" that drained the vitality of most people? "You are never angry, for instance?"

"Oh, no. I really don't get angry. . . . You see I try to understand people."

"But when you were young, were you free like this? So free—so free of yourself?"

"No. When I was young I was very self-conscious."

Then how had Eleanor achieved mastery over herself? Somewhere along the line there must have been a struggle.

"Little by little," Eleanor replied. "As life developed, I faced each problem as it came along. As my activities and work broadened and reached out, I never tried to shirk. I tried never to evade an issue. When I found I had something to do—I just did it. Really, I don't know—."

Cissy then ventured the opinion that Eleanor was "a complete extrovert, of course." Either Eleanor didn't care for the question or did not care "for Dr. Freud," Cissy thought, for she did not answer. "She just glanced up over her knitting needles, with those clever grey eyes of hers."

Cissy gave up her effort to get Eleanor to talk about her "night of the soul." However Eleanor had achieved her self-mastery, of one thing Cissy was certain: "Mrs. Roosevelt has solved the problem of living better than any woman I have ever known."[50]

IV

THE WHITE HOUSE YEARS

36. The Politics of Conscience

An ALERT PUBLISHER rushed into print a 40,000 word compilation of articles and speeches that Eleanor Roosevelt managed to put together in the course of getting settled in the White House. The book, entitled *It's Up to the Women*, had as its unifying theme the reforming role that women must assume if the nation was to come through the crisis of the Depression successfully. It chattily interlaced workaday advice on menus, household budgets, child rearing, and getting along with one's husband and children with apostolic appeals to women to lead in the movement for social justice, to join and support trade unions, to set up consumers' groups to police the NRA, and to enter politics.[1]

The new order of things, Eleanor exhorted, should reflect not only "the ability and brains of our men" but also "the understanding heart of women," because especially in times of crisis women had "more strength of a certain kind than men."[2] "Perhaps it is better described as a certain kind of vitality which gives them a reserve which at times of absolute necessity they can call upon."[3] Above all, she wanted women to take the leadership in the movement to abolish war, and hoped that the adventure of building a better world might take the place of the excitement and glamor of war. She did not expect much from the men when it came to manifesting a will to peace: "Only the women and youth of any country can initiate this change. They will have the men to help them later on in the fight, but they will meet some of the same unbelief and lethargy that they have come up against in the past."[4]

It's Up to the Women was a call to action. It also indicated that the First Lady had her own set of priorities—peace, the abolition of poverty, and a concern for youth, women's rights, and the rights of minorities generally. Mary Beard concluded her enthusiastic review of the First Lady's book with the surprised observation that "the implications of some of her economic statements reach to the borderlands of political, social and cultural change."[5]

Eleanor's role as mistress of the White House was thrust upon her by virtue of being the president's wife, yet she also actively sought to shape that role in accordance with the laws and purposes of her inner being. "I am not a philosopher," she said.[6] Indeed, she was acutely conscious of her lack of a college education, which left her, she felt, at a disadvantage in the analysis and judgment of competing intellectual claims. Nevertheless, she did have a philosophy of living shaped by her religious upbringing and fed by a seemingly inexhaustible spring of human sympathy that turned the Golden Rule into a vital and moving force in her approach to men and institutions. In a Washington crowded with rebels and reformers her rigorous effort to live by the Golden Rule moved her into the vanguard of those who wanted the New Deal to mean a new, better order.

Her speeches and writings called for the building of a new world, and though her language was that of the Gospel and the Declaration of Independence rather than the *Communist Manifesto*, her underlying message was revolutionary. People "must understand what it is in the past which held us back, what it is in ourselves, in human nature as a whole, which must be fought down if we are successfully to have a new deal." The nation's goal had to be the creation of "a new social order based on real religion" rooted in people leading the lives "they would live if they really wished to follow in Christ's footsteps."[7]

She had her own concept of utopia. She sketched it softly, in phrases disarmingly modest and simple, in an article she wrote shortly after becoming First Lady, "What I Hope to Leave Behind Me." She would like to live in a community where every individual had an income adequate to provide his family with the ordinary comforts and pleasures of life but no individual had an income so large that he did not have to think about his expenditures. Such a community, she felt, "would have the germs of a really new deal for the race." But it would not happen without a shift in thought and a reconstruction of values—less concern with creature comforts and more cooperation in everything that might help people "acquire a little more graciousness and freedom in life."[8] If that was the type of community the Technocrats, who were much in the headlines at that time, were aiming at, she could view it sympathetically.

Eleanor Roosevelt was fundamentally a moralist. She believed that the Depression was caused as much by defects of spirit and character as of institutions. The nation had gone through a ten-year "orgy" of speculation and quick profits, "of money bringing returns which required no real work." Selfishness and a preoccupation with material things had been the hallmarks of the decade. Selfishness, she felt, had been responsible for America's imposition of higher tariffs and had flawed Americans' relationship with each other—the financial East ignored the distress in the farmlands, and everywhere the rich paid little attention to the poor.[9]

In the frenzy to make money, Americans had lost some of the qualities that made life worthwhile, the ability to enjoy simple things—a landscape, "the breath of a crisp October day," "the play of the sun and shadow," "the view from a high hill"—and above all the joy that came from sharing: "As I grow older I realize that the only pleasure I have in anything is to share it with some one else. . . . I could not today start out with any zest to see the most marvelous sight in the world unless I were taking with me someone to whom I knew the journey would be a joy."[10]

If the Depression had taught men any one thing, Eleanor hoped it was the lesson of "interdependence"—that "one part of the country or group of countrymen cannot prosper while the others go down hill, and that one country cannot go on gaily when the rest of the world is suffering." Perhaps the Depression might reunite the country and give it the sense of community that comes from shared hardships. The Pilgrim Fathers, in the small settlements that they had wrested from an unyielding continent, knew that to survive "they must survive together. . . . In our complicated modern civilization, we are so separated from each other, that we forget our interdependence. The depression has brought it back to us. . . . If we can get back to the feeling that we are responsible for each other, these years of depression would have been worth while."[11]

She invoked the Sermon on the Mount in order to persuade people, especially "the old crowd" with which she had grown up, to accept changes that meant higher taxes and fewer luxuries. If the country did just the temporary and expedient things "we will find ourselves again just where we are today, still building a civilization on human suffering."[12] What distinguished such pleas for benevolence and altruism from sentimental exhortation was the psychological understanding behind them. The personal disasters she had surmounted had taught her that although moments of stress and danger could paralyze and destroy, they could also liberate and strengthen. She had turned her father's death into a constructive, sweetening influence in her life. And instead of crushing her, the Lucy Mercer crisis and her husband's paralysis had become occasions of personal transcendence and growth. In the face of great emotional excitement, wrote William James, "proprieties and their inhibitions snap like cobwebs" and men are given courage to say "Yes" to life's challenges.[13] That was how Eleanor had responded to personal disaster; that was how she now responded to the nation's ordeal. It was a time of hardship and distress, but it was also a time when men and women might be more disposed than usual to subordinate selfishness, faction, and private interest to the common cause. Such moments had to be seized before hardness and the old cautions returned and used in order to bring about a basic reconstruction of institutions.

The National Industrial Recovery Act represented the kind of basic reform the nation needed, and Eleanor hoped the NRA codes would be charters of "fair play" among the various elements in the industrial process. But since she was also a realist about the relationship of power to justice, she helped the unions in their drive to organize under Section 7A, and when the codes turned into agreements for administered prices and restricted production she did her utmost to get consumer representation on the code authorities and state recovery boards and to strengthen the consumers' division under Mary Harriman Rumsey. "I wish I could tell you or that *you knew* how much you have helped the whole range of consumer problems and policies," Mary Rumsey wrote her. Eleanor was equally clear-eyed about another great pillar of the New Deal reconstruction, the Agricultural Adjustment Act. It seemed senseless when people were starving and in rags to pay farmers to plow under cotton and slaughter piglets: "While it may be necessary to raise farm prices, I do think some way should be found to take things which are not needed and give them to people who, in any case, will not be able to buy them."[14]

With seeming naïveté, she asked the AAA administrator over the telephone, "Why do you dump all these little pigs into the Mississippi, when there are thousands of people in the country starving?" Before the startled official could reply, she went on, "Why not give the meat away to them?" Her strong objections to the destruction of food in the midst of hunger led to a scheme that anticipated the food-stamp plan. "Surplus farm products are being fed to the hungry instead of being destroyed because she asked a government official a question," reported Ruby Black in *Editor and Publisher* at the beginning of 1934.[15] "Of course all the male officials are convinced they would have thought of it themselves," Ruth Finney later wrote in the Scripps-Howard newspapers, "but they had not done so up to the time she insisted it was the thing to do."

Eleanor's greatest hope for bold, innovative moves to bring idle men and idle resources together lay with the Civil Works Administration set up by the president in November, 1933, and charged with the task of putting four million unemployed to work. "I hope that Mr. Hopkins, in his new corporation, will do some of the things which need to be done. He is really a remarkable person and gradually things may work out."[16]

She approved and defended her husband's program, but there was a radical charge to her advocacy of the New Deal that was absent from his. By the end of 1933 there was some improvement in the economic situation and considerable recovery of confidence. There was "more hope in the air," Eleanor wrote her friend Florence Willert in England, "in spite of the fight we have on our hands over here just now."[17] The fight was being waged by an owning class, which, its nerve restored, was beginning to resist further changes.

Eleanor devoted the opening lecture of her civics course at the New York Junior League to the need for continuing deep-rooted reform. She sought to bring home to the three hundred debutantes and society matrons who crowded the small auditorium the hunger and the cold that Lorena Hickok was reporting from the Dakotas, the desperation in Appalachia. People "simply won't live that way," she warned. She begged her listeners to make the effort to put themselves into the minds and hearts of the wretched and deprived because if they did so they would not be able to complain about higher taxes and government interference.

She told the story of a man who had gone to jail for stealing food to feed his starving family. He had been a model prisoner and was released for good behavior, yet as he left he swore to the warden he would do the same thing again if necessary. "I wouldn't blame him," Eleanor commented, and as her audience stirred uneasily she added, "You would be a poor wishy-washy sort of person if you didn't take anything you could when your family was starving."[18] The protests flooded in; editorialists and correspondents were horrified that the First Lady should seem to be encouraging lawlessness and violence. "I certainly did not tell the story of the starving man's stealing to feed his family to promote or encourage lawlessness or dishonesty," she answered one such critic. "I was merely trying to bring home to my audience, which was made up of people who know little of the suffering of poverty, that people were being driven to desperate ends." Give a job to the man whose case she cited, and to others like him, she said, and they would be the "most loyal and law abiding citizens."[19]

"Nothing I said in my talk justifies starting a revolution by violence," she replied to another critic.

I simply pointed out the historical fact . . . that revolutions do not start until great groups of people are suffering and convinced of the hopelessness of their cause getting a fair hearing. I have always made it a point that we are going through a revolution without violence and I hope it will continue to be so, but certain changes must come and we should be willing to have them come.[20]

She directed her appeal to women and young people particularly, because she thought they were less involved with the past than the men and, therefore, freer to consider new ideas and accept drastic change. At Mrs. Meloney's annual *New York Herald Tribune* Forum she called upon youth to become socially militant and to face the fact "that it has to change politics, it has to change business ethics, it has to change the theories of economics and above everything else, it has to change—well, its own weaknesses." Young people should not be afraid of new ideas and should stick with them "until they have decided whether there is anything in that new idea which is worth while or not."[21]

Her praise of a little book, *Prohibiting Poverty*, by Prestonia Mann Martin, the granddaughter of Horace Mann, showed her own readiness to examine the most visionary of blueprints in the search for solutions. The book was in its fourth printing when it came to her attention in the autumn of 1933. Many of its ideas echoed Edward Bellamy's *Looking Backward*. At the heart of Mrs. Martin's "National Livelihood Plan" was the concept— taken over from Bellamy—of a Young Workers Corps or industrial army into which all young people of both sexes would be conscripted from the ages of eighteen through twenty-five. This Young Workers Corps—or National Service Corps, as Mrs. Martin also called it—would produce the "seven cardinal necessities" for everyone—food, clothing, shelter, transportation, etc. His eight-year service to the nation finished, the young "Commoner" would become a "Capital," free "to engage in the pursuit of wealth, fame, power, leisure. . . . He may continue to work or not, as he chooses. His basic livelihood is in any case secure." The National Livelihood Plan, summarized Mrs. Martin, "is a project whereby collectivism would be applied to the production of Necessaries while individualism would be reserved for the production and sale of Luxuries and Surpluses for profit."

It was utopian and simplistic and its implementation would have involved a fantastic degree of regimentation. "Where would I be if I listened to that?" Franklin commented dryly when Eleanor gave it to him to read. Utopias taken literally are easy to caricature, but they must be seen, and that is how Mrs. Roosevelt saw *Prohibiting Poverty*, after an impetuous endorsement that was without qualification—as a stimulant to thought and debate, not as a working blueprint. *Prohibiting Poverty* was a utopia that was drafted by a woman and, therefore, more likely to interest women, Eleanor felt. It dramatically advocated a national purpose that she favored as strongly as the Socialists did, that given America's technological progress, poverty could and should be abolished. She was especially enthusiastic about Mrs. Martin's proposal that the energies of the young, rich as well as poor, girl as well as boy, should be enlisted in the war against want and in the service of the nation.

At the time Eleanor was in almost daily conference with Harry Hopkins on work projects for the unemployed, especially for women and young people. "It may be possible to try out some of these ideas under the emergency relief," she wrote an admirer of *Prohibiting Poverty*. "I wish they could lead us to the point where every one would have security, as far as the basic necessities of life are concerned."[22] Izetta Jewel Miller, a Democratic stalwart who had been commissioner of Welfare in Schenectady, asked whether she (Mrs. Miller) could do anything to promote the plan. Eleanor replied:

I am afraid that we are due for some criticism for our work there. In the first place, operation. There is a germ of something along that line in the C.C.C. and in the Federal Relief camps for unattached women and girls that are being started this summer. I always speak about the book because the more people read it the more they will try to think along the lines of development for the young people of this country.

Mrs. Martin asked if her announcement could state that "Mrs. Roosevelt says everyone should read *Prohibiting Poverty*." Yes, Eleanor replied, "if you will qualify it by saying that I am not sure at the present time that all of the plans could be put into operation immediately, but I think it has many things that we should be thinking about constantly."[23] She pushed the book's thesis as "an informing power of the mind," not as a dream to be realized in practice.[24]

Among the Bellamyites who were delighted to discover an ally in the White House was Upton Sinclair, whose own plan, End Poverty in California (EPIC), was then sweeping that state and preparing the way for his race for the governorship. At the heart of the EPIC approach was its insistence on state responsibility for bringing together idle men with idle factories and exchanging their products with those of state-encouraged agricultural colonies. Sinclair and his wife were old friends of Prestonia Mann Martin, and he wrote the First Lady to ask if she would permit them to call upon her.[25] "Our friends gather round eagerly to ask what you are like, and more especially, what you think," he wrote after he and Mrs. Sinclair had visited the White House. He sent her a copy of *End Poverty in California*. "I will probably not be governor," he added, "but at least I hope to get some new ideas at work in this state."[26]

He was soon writing Eleanor again. He had heard from a friend that she was going to announce publicly her interest in his plan to end poverty in California. She pulled back from his effort to embrace her. Her reply, which was prudently marked "Private—not for publication," stated, "Some of the things which you advocate I am heartily in favor of, others I do not think are entirely practicable, but then what is impracticable today is sometimes practicable tomorrow. I do not feel, however, that I am sufficiently in accord with your entire idea to make any public statement at present."[27]

She was the teacher, the moralist, the dreamer, but she was also highly practical. The president carried the responsibility. Her proddings and probings had to be carried on in a way that would not embarrass him politically. When Sinclair, having captured the Democratic primary, turned to Mrs. Roosevelt in his effort to obtain White House support in the election, Roosevelt instructed his wife, "(1) Say nothing and (2) Do nothing"—and she loyally complied.

There was another sign of her intense practicality—the way she backed up her exhortations to women to take leadership in the fight against war and social injustice with hard-headed political organization. Many women held important positions in the Roosevelt administration, she noted in *It's Up to the Women*, and were, therefore, in a stronger position to shape policy than ever before. The book did not say what insiders in Washington knew, that at the center of this growing New Deal political sisterhood was Eleanor Roosevelt.

"About the most important letter I ever wrote you!" Molly Dewson scribbled on the margin of a seven-page enclosure she sent Mrs. Roosevelt a few weeks after the Roosevelts arrived in Washington. The letter reported on Molly's talk with James Farley, the postmaster general, about women's patronage. He would make no appointments of women, Farley assured Molly, without consulting Eleanor, so Molly felt safe about the lists she had left with him, which described the jobs the Democratic women wanted in categories of descending urgency. "Imperative recognition" covered the four appointments to the staff of the Democratic National Committee, followed by the names of fourteen women who warranted "Very Important Recognition" and twenty-five for whom jobs were sought under the classification of "Very Desirable Recognition." Postmasterships and comparable minor appointments were listed under the heading of "Worthy of Lesser Recognition."

"I think they are '100 percent' friendly toward recognizing the work of the Women and that they will probably do it," Molly's letter continued. But she cautioned Eleanor that the men were lobbying for jobs so insistently "that continuous pressure will have to be brought on Mr. Farley on behalf of the women. I mean continuous in the sense of pressure on behalf of one woman today and another woman tomorrow."[28]

Mrs. Roosevelt and Molly Dewson were determined that women's voices should be heard at every level of the new administration, and they worked as a team to bring this about, although as far as the world knew Molly was the chief dispenser of the New Deal's feminine patronage. The relationship between Eleanor and Molly was harmonious and sympathetic. They had a common conception of the importance of building party organization and of using the influence of women to achieve the objectives of the New Deal.

Eleanor persuaded Farley to make the women's division a full-time functioning department of the Democratic National Committee, and then she and the president prevailed upon Molly Dewson to come to Washington to head the department. On January 15, 1934, despite her ban on political subjects, Eleanor presented Molly at her press conference to describe the new setup of the women's Democratic organization. When Molly said that women Democrats had long hoped for such an organization and were now about to achieve it "for many reasons," Ruby Black of the United Press, who knew Mrs. Roosevelt's decisive role behind the scenes, mischievously blurted out, "name three." Eleanor gave her a humorously reproving glance, and Molly, after a pause, said, "This Democratic party really believes in women, and the plan was presented to it properly."[29] Molly arrived in the capital with the names of sixty women qualified on the basis of their work in the campaign and their past records to hold high government positions. By April, 1935, the Associated Press reported that there were more than fifty women in such positions,[30] and many of them made public pronouncements under Eleanor's auspices. Secretary of Labor Frances W. Perkins announced the establishment of camps for unemployed women at one of Eleanor's press conferences. It was in Eleanor's sitting room that Mrs. Mary Harriman Rumsey, the chairman of the NRA Consumer's Advisory Board, described her group's efforts to combat rising prices through local consumer organization. And the plans of the Civil Works Administration to provide 100,000 jobs for women were first disclosed by the new director of the CWA's women's work, Mrs. Ellen S. Woodward, at a joint press conference with the First Lady.

"I do happen to know, from my close connections with the business and professional women, of the resentment felt against Hoover because he did not recognize women," Judge Florence E. Allen of the Ohio supreme court wrote Eleanor in expressing her pleasure in the new administration's appointment of women.[31] Such recognition did not come automatically—not even in the New Deal. Molly fought vigorously to enlarge the number of positions open to women. Sometimes she won her point on her own, but if not, she went to Eleanor, and Eleanor, if she ran into difficulty, turned to Louis or Franklin. Occasionally nothing worked. When Secretary of State Hull recommended the appointment of Lucile Foster McMillin to the place on the Civil Servic Commission that traditionally had gone to a woman, Molly complained to Eleanor, "Don't you really think that Secretary Hull has enough recognition and power in his own job not to take away from the regular organization women the few jobs that have always been marked out for them?" Why didn't he appoint Mrs. McMillin to a diplomatic post? But then, she added apologetically, "Of course, I realize I may be asking more from you than is possible at this stage of woman's development."[32] Hull had his way and Mrs. McMillin was named Civil Service commissioner, but several years later he did name two women as American ministers—"the first time in our history that women had been named to head diplomatic missions," he would proudly write, adding with male condescension, "They both proved competent, and made excellent records."[33]

Harry Hopkins was much more receptive to the wishes of the women, especially Eleanor. He was as passionate a reformer as she and just as ready for bold experimentation. He cultivated her interest in the Civil Works Administration and encouraged her to take the lead in setting up the women's end of the CWA. "You may be sure that under the new Civil Works program women will not be overlooked," Eleanor assured a woman correspondent who was upset that the president's announcement of the CWA omitted specific mention of women. A program for unemployed women was hammered out at a White House conference called and keynoted by Eleanor and attended by the leading figures in the field of social welfare. By the end of 1933, 100,000 women had CWA jobs.

The irascible and aggressive Harold L. Ickes was touchier to deal with. When Eleanor went to him with a request, she was usually careful to preface it with the statement that the president had asked her to do so. This was the case when she urged that the post of assistant commissioner of education, "which is now held by a woman [should] be retained by a woman" and that under the plan to provide work for unemployed teachers, half the positions should be allotted to women. Ickes agreed on both points.[34]

While she sought through patronage to build up the women's division of the party, Eleanor insisted that appointments had to be on the basis of merit, not just party loyalty, particularly as she felt that "during the next few years, at least, every woman in public office will be watched far more carefully than a man holding a similar position."[35] Farley, under pressure from a female party worker for one of the top jobs in the administration, turned to Eleanor, who noted that "as head of the Children's Bureau, she [the woman in question] would be appalling. . . . I imagine she is entitled to something if it can be had and I also imagine that she needs the money badly, but I would not sacrifice a good job for her."

While pressing for the appointment of Democratic women, Eleanor would not agree to the removal of outstanding women who happened to be Republicans. The head of the Children's Bureau, Grace Abbott, a Republican, had been one of the three top-ranking women in Washington under Hoover. Although she militantly championed children's rights, ambitious Democrats tried to use Miss Abbott's party affiliation as an excuse for Farley to force her out. Eleanor advised Farley to write the woman who was after Dr. Abbott's job "that no change is being made in the Children's Bureau and that Miss Abbott has the backing of most of the organized groups of women interested in child welfare."[36]

Although she wanted the Democrats to become the majority party, which it was not in 1932, Eleanor did not hesitate to urge women to be ready to reject the party and its candidates "when the need arises."

This will not be disloyalty but will show that as members of a party they are loyal first to the fine things for which the party stands and when it rejects those things or forgets the legitimate objects for which parties exist, then as a party it cannot command the honest loyalty of its members.[37]

Basically what she hoped might result from the inclusion of women was a humanization of government services and programs.

At a dinner honoring the new secretary of labor, Eleanor stressed that the post had been given to Frances Perkins "not only because there was a demand on the part of the women that a woman should be given a place in the Cabinet, but because the particular place which she occupies could be better filled by her than by anyone else, man or woman, with whom the President was acquainted."[38] But beyond that, Miss Perkins exemplified the new type of public servant who was being brought to Washington by the New Deal.[39]

When Frances Perkins says "I can't go away because under the new industrial bill [NIRA] we have a chance to achieve for the workers of this country better conditions for which I have worked all my life," she is not staying because she will gain anything materially for herself or her friends, but because she sees an opportunity for government to render a permanent service to the general happiness of the working man and woman and their families. This is what we mean as I see it by the "new deal."

If this attitude toward public service struck people as new, "the women are in part responsible for it."

Louis Howe, who shared Eleanor's view that women were in the forefront of the revolution in thinking that was back of the New Deal, believed that revolution would soon make it possible to elect a woman president. "If the women progress in their knowledge and ability to handle practical political and governmental questions with the same increasing speed as they have during the last ten years, within the next decade, not only the possibility but the advisability of electing a woman as President of the United States will become a seriously argued question," he wrote, adding that if politics continued to divide along humanitarian-conservative lines and the people decided they wanted a New Deal approach to such issues as education, recreation, and labor, "it is not without the bounds of possibility that a woman might not only be nominated but elected to that office on the grounds that they better understand such questions than the men."[40]

Louis was so persuaded that the country might in the not-too-distant future say "Let's try a woman" that one day he came into Eleanor's sitting room, propped himself cross-legged on a daybed, and said, "Eleanor, if you want to be President in 1940, tell me now so I can start getting things ready."[41]

One politician in the family was enough, was her reply to such proposals, seriously meant or not. She did not deceive herself about the real attitude of the country, and doubted that the election of a woman was as imminent as Louis thought. "I do not think it would be impossible to find a woman who could be President, but I hope that it doesn't happen in the near future. . . . I do not think we have yet reached the point where the majority of our people would feel satisfied to follow the leadership and trust the judgment of a woman as President." Some day it might come to pass "but I hope it will not be while we speak of a 'woman's vote.' I hope it only becomes a reality when she is elected as an individual, because of her capacity and the trust which a majority of the people have in her integrity and ability as a person."[42]

Women would have to learn that no amount of masculine chivalry was going to give them leadership if they could not actually "deliver the goods." They should leave their "womanly personalities" at home and "disabuse their male competitors of the old idea that women are only 'ladies in business.' " Women must stand or fall "on their own ability, on their own character as persons. Insincerity and sham, whether in men or in women, always fail in the end in public life."

It's Up to the Women, which came out in November, 1933, was her first book, and like most first authors she soon was inquiring of her publisher, Frederick A. Stokes, how well it was going. "The book is not running away but is selling very steadily," he replied. Eleanor wanted to be successful, and she cared about her influence. Women leaders were conscious that the New Deal meant that more women were involved in government, that more strongholds of masculine privilege were being infiltrated, and that Eleanor Roosevelt was at the hub of this movement. "For some time I have had a collection of statesmen hanging upon my wall," wrote Carrie Chapman Catt, "but under the new administration, I have been obliged to start a new collection and that is one of stateswomen. Now it is ready and you are the very center of it all."[43]

Fundamentally Eleanor was neither stateswoman, politician, nor feminist. She was a woman with a deep sense of spiritual mission. Like Saint Theresa, she not only "had a powerful intellect of the practical order" but was a woman of extravagant tenderness and piety. There was always some prayer in her purse to recall her to her Christian vocation. Christ's story was a drama that re-enacted itself repeatedly in her thoughts and feelings. Amid the worldliness, the pomp, and the power of Washington she managed to hold vivid and intimate communion with Christ with a child's innocence and simplicity. Christ's life in this world, she wrote in a Christmas message,

lasted only a short thirty-three years. This life began in a manger surrounded by poverty and the only thing apparently which the Christ Child was given was an abundance of love. All his life was spent in want as far as material things were concerned. And, yet from that life there has sprung the Christian religion and what we know as Christian civilization. . . .

Christ died a horrible death, probably at the time it was looked upon as a death of shame. He was buried by those who loved him in a borrowed tomb for he had never acquired any property of his own and yet from that death of shame and that borrowed tomb, has come to us all the teaching which has made progress possible in the love of human beings, one for another.

What a tolerant person Christ was! He rarely condemned any one. Only when the money changers desecrated his Temple did he allow himself to drive them out.

To those who were weak, however, and to those who had aspirations or a desire to do better, he was the understanding and forgiving master.

Her greatest admiration, she wrote in *It's Up to the Women,* went to the women in all ages "whose hearts were somehow so touched by the misery of human beings that they wanted to give their lives in some way to alleviate it." Preaching and exhortation were of little value unless followed up by living example. "The reason that Christ was such a potent preacher and teacher was because He lived what He preached," and missionaries—social as well as religious—"who want to accomplish the double task not only of alleviating human suffering but of giving faith to the people with whom they come in contact, must show by their own way of living what are the fruits of their faith."[44] She did so every hour of every day. She had disciplined herself never to evade an issue or an appeal for help, and in every situation she asked not only what was to be done but what she herself must do.

Among the many letters she received when she entered the White House was one from a young woman, Bertha Brodsky, who, in wishing her and the president well, added apologetically that she found it difficult to write because her back was crooked and she had to walk "bent sideways." Eleanor immediately replied with words of encouragement, her whole being alive with pity and sympathy. She sent the letter to the doctor in charge at the Orthopedic Hospital in New York, asking whether a free bed could not be found for Bertha. It was, and when Eleanor came to New York she visited the young woman, who was almost entirely encased in a plaster cast, although her eyes and mouth showed "a determined cheerfulness." The girl came from a very poor Jewish family, her father eking out an existence with a small paper route, and before the visit ended it was as if Bertha had become one of Eleanor's children. She visited her faithfully and sent flowers regularly. There was a package at Christmas, and flowers were sent to Bertha's mother at Passover. When Bertha was released from the hospital, Eleanor called Pauline Newman of the Women's Trade Union League, who found a job for her. She also helped Bertha's brother find a job, and when Bertha acquired a serious boyfriend she brought him to Eleanor to have her look him over. Eleanor attended Bertha's wedding, counseled her in moments of early marital strain, and was godmother to her child. "Dear Messenger of God," Bertha addressed her.

Her relationship with Bertha was not untypical. She yearned for situations that imposed duties. She responded to every appeal for help, indeed, sought to anticipate them. To friends who felt that she ought to save her energies for more important things, Eleanor replied that "whatever comes your way is yours to handle." Sometimes she was duped, but that was a risk she was prepared to take, and she even refused to condemn those who were not wholly honest with her. "I do not attempt to judge others by my standards," she said,[45] and she refused to dwell on injury.

Speaking of the Saint Theresas of this world, William James wrote at the beginning of the century:

The world is not yet with them, so they often seem in the midst of the world's affairs to be preposterous. Yet they are the impregnators of the world, vivifiers and animators of potentialities of goodness which but for them would lie forever dormant. It is not possible to be quite as mean as we naturally are, when they have passed before us. One fire kindles another; and without that overtrust in human worth which they show, the rest of us would lie in spiritual stagnancy. . . . If things are ever to move upward, some one must be ready to take the first step, and assume the risk of it.[46]

To many New Dealers Eleanor seemed innocent on the subject of economics, and to the Marxists she appeared to be a sentimentalist about the struggle for power, yet long after the ideologists of the New Freedom and the New Nationalism, the Technocrats and the Bellamyites, the Socialists and the Communists retired or were driven from the battlefield, she would still be striding toward some further frontier of the struggle to liberate mankind's potentialities.

37. Mrs. Roosevelt's "Baby"— Arthurdale

"IF YOU WANT to see just how bad things are," Clarence Pickett, the executive secretary of the Quaker social-action organization the American Friends Service Committee, advised Lorena Hickok, "go down to the southwestern part of the state [Pennsylvania] and into West Virginia." Hickok had checked in with Pickett before setting out on her travels as confidential agent for Harry Hopkins to report to him and to Eleanor on poverty in the United States.[1]

Pickett did not exaggerate the distress in Appalachia. Hickok's vivid communications from the coal towns registered incredulity that Americans could sink to such levels of degradation and hopelessness. No coal was being mined. Some of the miners had not worked for eight years. Human beings shuffled around like ghosts, and a miasmic silence hung over grimy company houses that clung to mountainsides along polluted gullies.

The only circumstance of hope that Hickok found was the work of the Quakers and the Agricultural Extension Service of the state university. They had persuaded some of the miners to launch a program of self-help: subsistence gardens had been dug into the unyielding hillsides; a furniture making cooperative was thriving; the women were sewing and making clothes out of materials sent by the Red Cross; and, added Hickok, all of it "has done marvels for their morale."[2]

Nothing galvanized Eleanor into action more quickly than afflicted human beings in whom some spark of aspiration and hope still glowed. She was coming down, she informed Hickok, to see what the Friends were doing and hear what they had to propose. Pickett sent her a map "which will help you find Crown Mine, 14 miles south of Morgantown," and on August 18 Eleanor arrived, driving alone. That day and the next the Quaker workers took a tall woman whom they did not identify, wearing a dark blue skirt, white blouse, and a white ribbon around her hair, to see the most hopeful families and the most defeated ones. She listened to the miners' wives and took their babies on her lap. She went into the hovels alongside of Scotts Run, one of the worst slums in the county, where mine tipples rusted and the gully that was used for cooking and washing water also ran with sewage. The men, black-listed because of strikes, had been so long out of work that not even the Quakers could stir them out of their "sit and spit" listlessness.

What point was there in hating "our poor Communists," the two Quaker workers in the area, Alice Davis and Nadia Danilevsky, said to Eleanor when

Hickok expressed her loathing for the Communists.[3] Their organizers were having as difficult a time as the Quakers in getting the beaten-down miners to stand up for their rights. Eleanor listened carefully and took notes. These two women had done relief work in Russia after the Revolution, an experience that had disenchanted them with Communism; they knew what revolution had done to Russia and did not want it for the United States. That gave special authority to their plea for help from Washington.

Action followed swiftly upon Eleanor's return to Washington. The little girl with the bad eyes should be sent to a hospital at her expense, she wrote Alice Davis. The CCC boy did not have t.b., as his parents had feared, but leg ulcers, and was now recovered. At a White House dinner she had told the story of the little boy who had clung to a pet white rabbit which his sister said they were going to eat, and William Bullitt had promised to send her a check for $100 in the hopes that it could keep the bunny alive.[4]

But these small acts of kindness did not touch the basic question of policy—what should be done with the thousands of miners who would never find work again in the mines, who were, in effect, stranded communities? The Quakers and the Extension Service workers in Morgantown thought they would have to be resettled in an area where they could make a living or, at the very least, grow their own food and begin to recover their self-respect. To the president, to whom Eleanor reported her findings, this seemed to be exactly the sort of situation the new Subsistence Homestead Program was designed to meet. The program had been authorized by the National Recovery Act, an omnibus bill which included a revolving fund of $25 million to set up "subsistence homesteads" with a view to achieving a better rural-urban balance.[5]

Urbanization and rural decay were old preoccupations of both the Roosevelts. "The bigger the city, the less thought of man," Eleanor had heard Franklin tell the students of North Carolina A. & M. back in 1913. A Jeffersonian faith in the virtues of a yeomanry had been a sympathetic theme in their friendship with Franklin K. Lane, who at the end of the war had urged a federal program to help returning soldiers acquire subsistence farms near their places of work—a form of soldiers' settlements. Eleanor's sponsorship of the Val-Kill industries was based on the theory she shared with her husband that men and women would stay on the farm if interesting and remunerative winter work could be found for them. Like her husband, she thought rural life superior to urban. Cities were absorbing and stimulating because of "the variety of human existence" to be found in them, she had written in 1930, "but I would rather live where trees and flowers and space and quiet give me peace."[6] As governor, her husband had advocated the development of rural-industrial communities, and the creative surge of his first hundred days as president gave him his chance to push his back-to-the-land ideas.

"I really would like to get one more bill," Roosevelt wrote Senator George Norris, "which would allow us to spend $25 million this year to put 25,000 families on farms at an average cost of $1,000 per family. It can be done. Also we would get most of the money back in due time. Will you talk this over with some of our fellow dreamers on the Hill?"[7]

He got his $25 million but there had been no discussion of the provision either in committee or on the floor of Congress. Ickes, who was given the Subsistence Homestead appropriation to administer, did not know what was intended. The housing people had their eye on the money, but Roosevelt knew what he wanted. He saw it as the beginning of a program under which in time a million families might be resettled into planned communities. The government would buy the land, build the houses, acquire the livestock and farm machinery, bring in roads, water, and utilities. The homesteaders would have thirty years in which to pay.[8] It was her husband's idea, Eleanor said of Arthurdale, as the first new community came to be called; "It's a plan he has talked about ever since I can remember." When she told him what the Friends thought needed to be done for the stranded miners, he decided this was the place to launch the homestead program.[9]

"The President thought you would be interested in knowing what is being done in the State University at Fairmont, West Virginia," Eleanor wrote Ickes after her talk with Franklin. The Extension Service people were doing "splendid work" in preparing the miners to go back to the farms:

The President thought this might be a good place to start and that perhaps it would be a good idea to send some one down to get more detailed information than I have. The conditions there are appalling, but the spirit and morale are good, and the people are doing everything they can to help themselves—whole families are weaving, making simple furniture, etc.[10]

Howe already had spoken to him, Ickes informed Eleanor; he (Ickes) had immediately dispatched two men to Morgantown, "and we are expecting an early report. It all sounds very interesting indeed and if the conditions are favorable we hope to go ahead at once with a subsistence project there."[11]

At the president's request, Ickes appointed M. L. Wilson, farmer-philosopher and former professor of agricultural economics, to head the Subsistence Homestead Division. "I'm interested in this and Mrs. Roosevelt's tremendously interested in it, and I think M. L. Wilson is the best man to take it over," the president had said.[12]

Wilson had scarcely settled his family in Washington when he and his wife were invited to the White House. What does one wear to dinner with the president? he amiably inquired at Garfinckel's, Washington's leading department store. Nor did he know what he would do with his car if he arrived at the White House in it. So he and Mrs. Wilson drove to within a few blocks of the president's house, parked and took a taxi the remaining way. Once inside such anxieties vanished before the thoughtfulness of the Roosevelts as hosts. The talk, moreover, was heady, the company congenial. The other guests were Frances Perkins, the Henry Wallaces, General Hugh Johnson, Admiral Byrd, the Leonard Elmhirsts, Louis Howe, and Nancy Cook. Most of the talk was about West Virginia and the possibility of resettling the miners. But it was more than that. New vistas of human betterment cast their spell over the evening. The real bond between the Roosevelts and Wilson was the dream they shared that the resettlement program could show the way to a new type of civilization for

America. Rural sage, president, First Lady, Louis Howe, and the Elmhirsts, who were engaged in their own experiment in rural revitalization on a 2,000-acre medieval manor in Devon, England, exchanged ideas and hopes on the reshaping of village communities in order to serve the growth of a new type of socially minded individual.[13]

Dorothy Elmhirst, like Eleanor, had belonged to New York society when it was Society. She was the youngest child of William C. Whitney, financier and secretary of the Navy in Cleveland's first cabinet. Like Eleanor she had attended a Roser class which had met in her father's Fifth Avenue mansion, and also like Eleanor she had broken free from her environment and upbringing to become a woman of broad sympathies and unorthodox ideas. She and her husband Willard Straight had founded the *New Republic*. After his death she had married Leonard Elmhirst and with him had purchased Dartington in Devonshire, where they were trying out some of his ideas on how to halt the drift away from the countryside. In order to raise the standard of living they had introduced light industries and built housing, and they had encouraged the development of arts and crafts as a part of rural life and everyday amenity. Leonard Elmhirst, a student of medieval history, embellished his description of Dartington with references to the manorial system, where there had been security, a sense of belonging and rootedness, and, to a considerable degree, self-sufficiency. Everyone was fascinated. The Dartington concept was not too far from Wilson's "community idea."

"The conversation was very jolly. You felt completely at home," said Wilson. As he bid Mrs. Roosevelt good night she said she would ask Clarence Pickett of the Quakers to come down immediately so that they could talk further. "That's when we got started with Mrs. Roosevelt," Wilson added, as if he were recalling the advent of a hurricane.[14]

A few days later Wilson was informed by E. K. Burlew, Ickes's assistant, that it was evident "the President and Mrs. Roosevelt were going to have a great deal of interest in this. I think they will want Clarence Pickett to be associated with you in charge of it." The "rip-snorting pragmatist and Iowa farm-boy," as Wilson described himself, spent an afternoon with social-gospeler Pickett, who had been raised on a farm in Kansas, and they became friends. They agreed that Pickett would handle the resettlement of stranded miners in Appalachia and Wilson would concentrate on stranded farmers.[15]

Both men would have liked time in which to think their plans through carefully but West Virginia was not far from violence and the Roosevelts felt that a speedy demonstration of the government's concern was essential. "The situation has been considerably complicated," Pickett wrote after Eleanor's visit to West Virginia, "by the excessive interest of the President and Mrs. Roosevelt and Colonel Howe. They want to establish one colony very quickly and have worked out some plans already, part of which are good and part of which are questionable."[16]

Louis Howe was as interested in resettlement as the president and Eleanor. To him its most promising feature was the chance it afforded to encourage industrial decentralization. The program, "if successful," he said on WNBC, "will revolutionize manufacturing industry" within twenty years and might be the answer to urban congestion.[17] Howe seemed to Wilson "all skin and bones," a man who sensed that he was in a race with death, and for that reason, thought Wilson, in a hurry to launch these new programs. He badgered, cajoled, and ordered Wilson and Pickett into action in West Virginia. A local committee composed largely of university agricultural experts recommended the purchase of the Arthur Farm, fifteen miles southeast of Morgantown, near Reedsville, as the site for the first project. Used as an experimental farm by the university, the 1200-acre estate could be acquired cheaply since it was about to revert to the state for unpaid taxes.

But how did one purchase a farm as the agent of the government? "There were endless rules," Pickett discovered, "about purchasing land, letting contracts, and the circumstances under which local people might or might not be employed."[18] Had the limitations been respected Pickett doubted the four settlements for the stranded miners would ever have been built. Howe set them an example in cutting through bureaucracy and red tape. The president, Mrs. Roosevelt, and he were all agreed that the Arthur estate should be purchased, Howe told Wilson. He wanted it appraised and he wanted an architect to go down and draw up plans for a community house, and he wanted this done in "two days." He also wanted a topographical map—he wasn't sure what for, but the president said they should get one made immediately

The Treasury Department, after a phone call from Howe, provided the architect. Interior sent down the appraisers, but the topographical map engendered a minor crisis. The Land Office, "full of old people," was "flabbergasted" by Wilson's request and referred him to the Army. Burlew, a long-time Interior official who knew everything about the department, finally dug up two civil engineers in the Reclamation Service. It would take them thirty days to make a map, they reported to Wilson from Reedsville. "Where did you get them?" an indignant Howe wanted to know. Wilson said Burlew had provided them. "Who the hell is this man Burlew?" Howe flung out at him. Wilson explained that he had been around Interior a long time and was very knowledgable. "Rabbit," Howe said, turning to his secretary, "get me E. K. Burlew in the Interior Department." When Burlew came to the phone, Howe introduced himself and said coldly, "I don't care how they do it or what they do to do it, I want that map in a week," and then hung up. Howe then asked Wilson if he was in a position to buy the farm after it was appraised. Did he have a disbursing officer? "No, we haven't got anything yet—just Clarence Pickett and I and about three or four stenographers."

"You'd better get somebody who can pay some money pretty quickly because we're going to buy that farm," Howe said, bringing the interview to an end.

"What kind of an unreasonable man is Howe?" Burlew complained to Wilson, careful, nonetheless, to fulfill Howe's order. With the assistance of personnel from the Coast and Geodetic Survey and an Army plane, the map was provided within two days. Howe's face lit up when Wilson brought it in. "You go back and buy that place right away."[19]

On October 13 Ickes announced the purchase of the Arthur estate and said that 200 families would be resettled on this first project. Bushrod Grimes, a native of the area and the Extension Service worker in charge of the subsistence garden program in the county, was appointed manager of Arthurdale. (The new settlement was also called Reedsville, the town to which it was closest.)

"Yesterday Mr. Grimes took a group of men out to work at Arthurdale," Alice Davis reported to Eleanor. "I can't tell you what a delight it is to us that this plan has gone through. We had been looking toward it for such a long time with no real hope of substantial support, that we can hardly believe it when it happens. . . . None of us can ever tell you how grateful we are for what you have done for this community."[20]

All Eleanor's executive ability, her doggedness, and her influence were now placed at the disposal of the fledgling project, for she firmly believed that what was done in a single community might show the way to a nation. She saw Arthurdale as a laboratory for all the new communities. She wanted it to have the most advanced educational system, a model public-health service, producer and consumer cooperatives, and a program of handicrafts and music that would preserve the folk culture of Appalachia. This was a job Franklin had given her to do. Arthurdale was her "baby" and she interested herself in every detail— the selection of the homesteaders, the choice of a principal for the school, the initiation of a children's clinic. She shopped for refrigerators and inspected plumbing fixtures. Pickett took her to see a self-help group, the Mountaineer Craftsmen's Cooperative Association, which produced attractive maple furniture, including the Godlove chair. That led to a decision to transfer the Association, which was operating out of a junk shop in Morgantown, to Arthurdale and to equip the new homesteads with its products.[21]

Eleanor hired some of the staff. "This is just a note," she informed M. L. Wilson, "to tell you that I have taken on Nancy Cook and Eric Gugler as the advisory experts on the housing end of the West Virginia project." She had promised them expenses "plus whatever they deem their duties worth not in excess of $30 a day, which I understand is the pay for experts."[22] Guests came to the White House, heard the story of Scotts Run, and departed as recruits in a New Deal crusade. "It is magnificent, the way you are directing this big undertaking," wrote Dorothy Elmhirst, whose fund had agreed to finance a small clinic and hospital. "My dear, I am going back to England so proud of my country at last."[23]

By November 7 the first contingent of 25 miners and their families had moved from the coal-camp shacks to Arthurdale, temporarily quartered in the old Arthur mansion. Nine days later another 11 families followed. They would help to put up the fifty prefabricated houses that Louis Howe had ordered. There was even talk that some homesteaders would be eating Thanksgiving dinner in their own houses.

Henry Goddard Leach wrote Eleanor asking if she would do an article for the *Forum* about the "model mining village." Arthurdale was not a mining village, she corrected Leach. "It is for miners transplanted to a farming district with an industry planted there to give them a cash crop."[24] The key to Arthurdale's economic soundness—whether the transplanted miners would be able to make a living and also pay the government back the $1.5 million it had advanced to the project—was the establishment of an industry. In October the Public Works Administration allocated $525,000 to the Post Office Department in order to erect a furniture factory in Arthurdale where items of post-office equipment would be produced. The proposal seemed to pinch a neuralgic nerve in the body politic, and by January Congress was resounding with protests from the defenders of free enterprise. The factory would "wipe out private industry," Representative Taber warned. "Just a proposition to further the socialistic programs already launched by the administration," agreed his Republican colleague, Representative Foss of Massachusetts. Republican ideological protests were given point by more down-to-earth anxieties voiced by Democrats. The proposal would work an injustice on unemployed furniture workers "in my state and in every state which has a furniture factory," objected a North Carolina congressman. Representative Ludlow of Indiana, whose district was the home of the Keyless Lock Company which manufactured locks for post-office boxes, went to see Louis Howe. The Arthurdale factory would take away business from it and throw men out of work, he complained, and he was sure that when Mrs. Roosevelt learned that the furniture-factory plan would cause distress and unemployment in Indianapolis she would gladly consider some alternative proposal to create employment in West Virginia. Howe sought to reassure Ludlow by telling him that the items to be manufactured at Arthurdale would not be competitive with those on which the Keyless Lock Company was a bidder.

Howe thought he had pacified Ludlow, but a House rider on a Treasury appropriation bill, January 26, 1934, introduced by Ludlow, prohibited the expenditure of Post Office funds for equipment manufactured at Arthurdale. "Three hundred EPIC Clubs pledged to end poverty in California by putting unemployed at productive labor are prepared to go to bat with reactionaries on this issue," Upton Sinclair wired from California. Eleanor sought to restrain Sinclair, because support from the former Socialist would only confirm congressional fears that a factory in Reedsville was a plunge into Socialism. "The chance for a government factory is still possible," she informed him. "I think a great deal has been made of this prematurely."[25]

The project would not harm industry, Ickes told a news conference. "It will be used as a yardstick to determine if the government has been paying too much for post office equipment, and thereby may hang a tale and may be the reason why some are opposing it."[26] Despite administration assurances, the House at the end of February reaffirmed its prohibition, brushing aside an impassioned plea for the project by its newest member, Eleanor's old friend Isabella Greenway, now a congresswoman from Arizona. Blocked in the House, the administration turned to the Senate, where Kenneth McKellar, the chairman of the Committee on Post Offices, was sympathetic.[27]

As administration pressure continued, so did the attacks. Dr. William A. Wirt, the Gary, Indiana, school superintendent, was enlivening the Capital with his exposé of an alleged conspiracy by "brain trusters" to foster a revolution with Roosevelt cast in the role of an American Kerensky, and he cited the Reedsville project to prove his point. It was a "communistic" plot to subvert the economy of Morgantown, West Virginia, he charged, for in resettling the miners at Reedsville they would be lost to Morgantown's rent and tax rolls. None of them had paid any rent or taxes for years, Eleanor noted, nor could she understand how it was communistic "to give people a chance to earn their own livings and buy their houses." In the Senate, Thomas D. Schall, the blind senator from Minnesota, came to Dr. Wirt's defense. Not only was Mrs. Roosevelt spending $25 million of the taxpayer's money on this "West Virginia commune," but she was profiteering on her own furniture factory in Val-Kill, charging fivefold the average price for its wares because she was the wife of the president. She intended to answer him at her news conference, Eleanor notified the senator, but before she did she wanted to tell him what she intended to say and give him a chance to retract. Would he come to the White House? He made an appointment but did not appear. The Reedsville factory would produce post-office boxes, not furniture, she subsequently told the press. It would be a yardstick operation and cost only a fraction of the $25 million. As for the Val-Kill furniture factory, it had always shown a deficit, and not one of the four investors ever received a salary or even traveling expenses.[28]

Bernard M. Baruch, whom Eleanor had begun to interest in Arthurdale, was delighted with her "beautiful handling of Senator Schall,"[29] and she invited him to see Arthurdale for himself. On June 7, 1934, when the first homesteaders were formally installed in their newly built houses, he and Mrs. Ickes went along. The hardheaded Baruch was moved. "I can never get out of my mind the faces of those people I saw the day we went to Reedsville," he wrote six months later. Baruch carried great weight on the Hill, where a considerable number of senators and representatives were beneficiaries of his largesse, but even Baruch's sympathetic interest in Arthurdale did not change House sentiment about the factory. In mid-June the proposal to have the government finance a factory was finally killed. "We are now busy figuring out, as we decided that it was better to drop the effort of putting through a post-office factory for fear of having a great deal of 'hot-air' in Congress and another attack on Reedsville written into the record, what shall be the industry down there," Eleanor wrote Baruch.[30]

The defeat of the government factory was a major setback. The efforts to get an industry for Arthurdale were further hampered by the rulings of Comptroller General McCarl, who refused to allow government funds to be used to subsidize private industry on the projects. McCarl is "not only a Republican," fumed Ickes, "but . . . a reactionary Republican."[10] At Baruch's suggestion, Eleanor spoke with Gerard Swope of General Electric, who was a supporter of the resettlement idea. For a brief period a subsidiary of General Electric operated a vacuum-cleaner assembly plant in Arthurdale but closed it down for a lack of orders. Throughout the thirties Eleanor tried to get an industry for Arthurdale. Businessmen who wanted entrée to the White House would raise her hopes with big schemes and promises, and one even established a branch of a shirt factory, but at no time during the decade was more than a third of Arthurdale's labor force employed by private industry. As the prospect of employment faded, the problem of how the homesteaders were to pay for their homes and achieve a decent standard of living became less soluble. It produced a series of clashes between Eleanor and Ickes.

The prime question was: if the government were creating a new community in which a factory it would build and the farmlands it would purchase would set the levels of livelihood, what should those levels be? Eleanor thought that Arthurdale—indeed, the $25 million set aside for the whole resettlement division—should be used as seed money to show what could be done through social and economic planning to create a better life for people. If the objective was to place "as many people as possible in as cheap houses as possible, then I think the 25 millions had much better be turned over to the relief administration," she stated. This was also Pickett's view. "It was only secondarily a relief measure," he said; "primarily it was thought of as the beginning of a decentralization program for workers in industry. It was hoped it might find wide application. The picture was of millions of workers living in small homesteads with some two or three acres of land for gardening."[32] If this was utopianism, then even the Chamber of Commerce shared it, because after a visit to the new community its president, Henry I. Harriman, endorsed Arthurdale and the program of the resettlement division as "fundamental and far-reaching" in that it would show the way "to the necessary decentralization of industry" and "the relief of mass congestion in the cities."[33]

In deciding what industry should be brought to Arthurdale, Eleanor wrote Baruch, at a time when she and Wilson thought they would have some choice in the matter, the important thing was "that a family shall have a sufficient means of livelihood and the assurance of an ability to pay their expenses covering a standard which we hope to establish as something to shoot at in all rural industrial communities."[34] That standard, she felt, should include indoor bathrooms, a new type of rural school that would be the center of community life, and an innovative rural health program. Shown four alternative budgets for the homesteads by Ickes, she chose the most costly. She and Howe fought for refrigerators. Charles F. Pynchon, a Chicago building contractor whom Ickes, distrustful of Wilson, named to manage the Homestead Division in a businesslike way, omitted refrigerators from the Arthurdale plans. Everyone owned an icebox, he assumed, and the homesteaders could bring along their old ones. But few of the miners had them, Pynchon was told, when a furious Howe upbraided him for the omission: "I know Mrs. Roosevelt will be shocked because she has been looking over and picking out refrigerators for some time." Howe was in charge of the "Electrical Committee" reviewing Arthurdale's electrical requirements, the same letter said, and did not understand why he was never consulted. "I think I will have to request the firing of the man in charge of electrical matters as the President is particularly anxious that the electrical part is done under my supervision and in close contact with me."[35]

At times Ickes seemed to agree with Mrs. Roosevelt that resettlement should be a pioneering division within the government and that Arthurdale should be *the* demonstration project. He had heralded the purchase of the Arthur estate as the beginning of an experiment that would show "the way to a new life for many others."[36] But he was a suspicious administrator who liked to keep a tight control over every reach of his domain, and Wilson's direct access to the White House vexed him. His office planted a secretary on the unsuspecting Wilson who notified Burlew whenever Wilson was called to the White House. Obsessed by the fear of graft, Ickes insisted that the homestead communities be administered by Washington. Wilson, a Jeffersonian, wanted them to be self-governing, the responsibility local. So did Eleanor. "She was a great community person," Wilson observed, "and she believed that since these units were small, since they were experimental, there must be a maximum amount of local interest and local initiative in them." In the spring of 1934 Ickes overrode Wilson and federalized the fifty projects that had been announced, whereupon Wilson resigned and returned to Agriculture as assistant secretary.[37]

The first fifty projects were of three types—experimental farm colonies, homestead-garden colonies located within commuting distance of some type of industrial employment, and four settlements for stranded miners in Appalachia. Of these Arthurdale alone escaped the secretary's executive clutch.

"I am becoming worried about the Reedsville, West Virginia project," he wrote in his diary, December 2, 1933.

I am afraid that we are due for some criticism for our work there. In the first place, we undertook it too hastily. Colonel Howe, in a rash moment, told the President that we would start work within three weeks. . . . The result has been that we have rushed ahead pell-mell. I am afraid that we are spending more money than we have a right to spend. Another thing that bothers me is that Colonel Howe, with I think the approval of Mrs. Roosevelt, wanted us to enter into a contract for some 60 or 75 knockdown houses. I understand that these houses are only about ten feet wide and I am afraid that they will look a good deal like a joke.

Howe's prefabs became an albatross around Arthurdale's neck. He had ordered the fifty Cape Cod houses at a cost of $1,000 apiece over the telephone. Eleanor had tried unsuccessfully to argue him out of doing so, and when she visited Arthurdale she went straight for the first of the prefabs which had been put up. Pickett reported to Wilson her great disappointment. "She said she should have stopped Louis Howe from ordering those houses. She was afraid they would turn out to be just exactly what they were when she saw them." Their size was less a problem than their flimsiness, designed as they were for Cape Cod summers, not Appalachia winters.[38]

"We had fifty families out there in freezing winter weather sleeping under tents," Howe later said defensively. "We had to find accommodations for them somehow."[39] The houses were a blunder whatever the excuse. The blunder was compounded when the foundations that had been prepared for them proved to be too large. As a consequence the homesteaders who had hoped to be in their houses by Thanksgiving did not move in until June 7, 1934.

At Eleanor's suggestion, Eric Gugler was asked to redesign and reconstruct the houses. The president liked Gugler, she told Wilson and Pickett. "Eric Gugler turned out to be a very excellent person," said Wilson afterward. "He did a marvellous thing, but he said from the start, 'When you change plans, it's going to cost a lot of money.' "[40]

Ickes resented Eleanor's involvement in Arthurdale and was exasperated by her refusal to subordinate human values to cost consciousness, a point on which she was stoutly supported by Wilson and Pickett.[41] The debate over the size and design of the homestead houses, and, more generally, the standard of living that should be aimed at in the new settlements was fundamental and prophetic of later controversies over what constituted poverty and the government's responsibility to end it. Eleanor's view was that everyone had a right to a decent standard of living.[42] Ickes feared that failure to keep the costs down might mean loss of "the popular support that is absolutely essential if we are to carry through the program at all."[43] On the issue of the Arthurdale houses, the president at first sided with his wife. Ickes went to the White House to look at the sketches Gugler had prepared for these houses, and recorded in his diary that they

were very attractive indeed but the cost of the thing is shocking to me. The President said we could justify the cost, which will run in excess of $10,000 per family, by the fact that it is a model for other homestead projects. My reply to that was to ask what it was a model of, since obviously it wasn't a model of low-cost housing for people on the very lowest rung of the economic order. . . . I don't see how we can possibly defend ourselves on this project. It worries me more than anything else in my whole department. The theory was that we would be able to set up families on subsistence homesteads at a family cost from $2,000 to $3,000 and here we have already run above $10,000 per family. I am afraid we are going to come in for a lot of justifiable criticism.[44]

The criticism was not long in coming. An article in the anti-administration *Saturday Evening Post*, "The New Homesteaders," focused on Louis Howe's prefabs, how "the camp houses" had been "slowly tortured" into shape and buried "in a meringue of wings, bay windows, fireplaces, porches, terraces and pergolas." Eight wells had been drilled and abandoned when the architect changed his mind about the location of the houses. Each enameled sink was equipped with a "large size patented grease trap which cost $37.50," and which the author said was unnecessary. Arthurdale, he wrote, was an example of New Deal bungling and an object lesson in what happens in a planned economy.[45]

A newspaper friend sent a batch of clippings prompted by the article to Eleanor in Hyde Park. Rumors about the houses had been around a long time, the reporter said; "should we have told you?" Eleanor should be prepared to "explain frankly" when she returned to Washington.[46] She had tried to get Howe and Ickes to make a statement that these houses "had not worked out," she replied, and "that they were being made liveable, and that they would not cost the people moving in any more, as the basis for rent was to be set on the earning power of the community and not on the cost of development. For the first homesteads many things will have to be tried out which could not be paid for by the homesteaders." The homesteads were a demonstration of community building

to show what might happen if industry could be decentralized and associated with agriculture and at the same time they are to experiment to find out how much of comfort and pleasure can be put into the lives of people living in this type of community. . . . I think all this should have been said long ago but that again is not my business. . . . I am begging them now to be entirely honest and very explicit. I am afraid I would always be more frank than is considered advisable by many.[47]

She was sure to be asked about Arthurdale at her first news conference when she came back to Washington, she advised Ickes, and she was writing out her statement "so that I will be sure to say the things which you all want me to say."[48]

Arthurdale also drew the fire of the Communists. While conservatives complained that the government was subsidizing a life of middle-class affluence, the Communists attacked the homesteads as a design "for permanent poverty." Harold Ware, the Communist party's agricultural expert, collaborated on an article for *Harper's* in which he not only made fun, in a heavy-handed way, of Howe's truckloads of ready-made summer houses, but laboriously uncovered fascist implications in the homestead movement. If the West Virginia projects were a pattern for anything, they were "a pattern for the decentralization of poverty" and the establishment of "a state of serfdom." Ware supported this last charge with a reference to the thirty years that the homesteaders had in which to pay for the houses.[49]

"Of course, the Reedsville project is just one big headache and has been from the beginning," Ickes grumbled in his diary. There was Howe's initial mistake. "And then Mrs. Roosevelt took the Reedsville project under her protecting wing with the result that we have been spending money down there like drunken sailors—money that we can never hope to get out of the project. This project has been attacked in a number of articles and magazines and newspapers, and we are distinctly on the defensive about it."[50]

Ickes thought the president was swinging around to his views on cost: "As the President remarked to me: 'My Missus, unlike most women, hasn't any sense about money at all.' He added with respect to Louis Howe that Louie didn't know anything about money, being as he is an old newspaperman, although he did pay tribute to Louis's political sagacity."[51] Two days after Ickes made this entry the voters overwhelmingly endorsed the New Deal in the 1934 congressional elections. Buoyed up by this unprecedented vote of confidence, Roosevelt was determined to push forward with his program, including a massive expansion of the subsistence homestead movement. He had also decided to take the program away from Ickes. The day after the president told Ickes he was considering turning over the Subsistence Homestead Division together with a rural-housing program to Harry Hopkins, Ickes wrote in his diary, "I won't be at all put out if I lose Subsistence Homesteads. It has been nothing but a headache from the beginning."[52] But he continued to grumble about Eleanor's role in the affair.

I am very fond of Mrs. Roosevelt. She has a fine social sense and is utterly unselfish, but as the President has said to me on one or two occasions, she wants to build these homesteads on a scale that we can't afford because the people for whom they are intended cannot afford such houses. The President's idea is to build an adequate house and not even put in plumbing fixtures, leaving that sort of thing to be done later by the homesteader as he can afford them. He remarked yesterday that he had not yet dared say this to the people (undoubtedly meaning Mrs. Roosevelt) who wanted the houses built with all modern improvements.

Roosevelt may have considered his wife extravagant, although within the family she was noted for frugality, or he may have been easing the blow to Ickes at the expense of his wife, for the president shrank from hurting people's feelings and many men have directed resentment away from themselves with the protest that they could not do anything with their wives. Whatever Ickes's impressions of the president's views on plumbing, Roosevelt told Tugwell and Dr. Will Alexander, when they took over the Resettlement Administration, the successor agency to the Subsistence Homestead Division: "These people ought to have plumbing. There's no reason why these country people shouldn't have plumbing. So put in plumbing. Put in bathrooms." But try as the Resettlement people did to get plumbing "within an economic budget," they never managed it. "It was always something that they couldn't pay for," Alexander recalled. On one occasion Tugwell went over to the White House to inform "the Boss" that "if he has his plumbing, he's got to let us subsidize it." Tugwell was gone all morning. His aides, all agog and sure that great matters of state must have been under discussion, demanded to know what had kept him when he returned. He had explained to the Boss their difficulty with fitting bathrooms into a house that the homesteaders would be able to pay for "and he [Roosevelt] got to drawing privies." The presidential anteroom was crowded with ambassadors, bankers, politicians, and the president had spent the morning drawing privies, Tugwell reported. Privies it was in the end. Resettlement became the Farm Security Administration in 1937, and the new agency eliminated indoor plumbing from the houses built in the South.[53]

Most of the Arthurdale houses, however, had already been built, and all had bathrooms. The cost issue there was how much the government should charge the homesteaders for the houses and how much should be considered government subsidy. Mrs. Roosevelt asked Baruch to examine the figures and give her a businessman's judgment. "You have told me to treat this as if it were my own matter," Baruch agreed, "and I propose to follow out your request until you tell me not to."[54]

She was grateful to Baruch for his help, and their relationship in the course of their work for Arthurdale had blossomed into friendship. There was, no doubt, an element of calculation on both sides, but also there was genuine affection. Baruch, before Chicago, had been one of the leaders of the stop-Roosevelt drive and while he had sought to make up for his mistake by the generosity of his campaign contributions, it was Roosevelt's policy to give him the feeling he was an insider while in fact keeping him at arm's length. When Baruch came to Hyde Park after the Chicago convention it had been Eleanor who drove him around, and increasingly it was Eleanor and Louis through whom he maintained access to Roosevelt. Eleanor had known Baruch in a distant way when he had served Woodrow Wilson. At that time she had been cool toward him both because he was Jewish and because he was a Wall Street speculator, but she was a different woman now and had come to appreciate his acumen in business and public affairs. He was ready to give advice, and she welcomed it. She knew she tended to be too trusting, to be carried away by her hopes, too inclined to believe that will alone could defeat economic realities. "I want you to be hardboiled, for it is a kind of 'hardboiledness' which is helpful," she had entreated him in a letter of thanks for agreeing to underwrite most of the costs of the experimental school at Arthurdale.[55] The tall, spare figure had become a familiar presence in her sitting room.

After a little trouble in getting what he called the "rock bottom figures," Baruch concluded that of the $1,597,707 that had been budgeted for Arthurdale, $1,037,000 would have to be charge-off to the government. To ask the homesteaders to pay more than $3,000, he thought, would place unbearable burdens upon them.[56] A million-dollar charge-off to the government did not seem lavish to him. The excess of actual costs over estimates was "not much larger relatively than a great many business and engineering precedents in other pioneering. . . . You are to be congratulated on your implacable insistence on accurate figures revealing the truth." And Eleanor could quote him if she wished.[57] She herself assembled statistics on the millions private industry spent on research; if such outlays were justified to develop new ways of manufacturing, the government was justified in putting "a little money into experimenting in new methods of living," she wrote. (These figures were included in a defense of Arthurdale which she did not publish because Ickes's man Pynchon thought that further publicity would only add fuel to the controversy.)

Risks had to be taken; one could not wait around for perfect solutions. "We do not think for a moment that we are doing anything more than experimenting," she wrote Florence Willert. "We know a lot of things have got to be thought through, but also think it is better to do something than to sit by with folded hands."[58]

The contrasting reports that came to her at the end of 1934 from Arthurdale and nearby Jere vindicated government action on the basis of plans and concepts that everyone realized would have to be revised not once but often.

The Communists were making considerable headway among the Jere miners, reported Alice Davis, the Quaker relief worker who had first shown her around Scotts Run and who was now county welfare commissioner, and it seemed to her "just a race against time—whether we can get them into decent living conditions and decent ways of thinking before they are led to violence." The local unemployed organized by the Communists had marched on the Welfare Board and threatened to throw Alice and her caseworker into the river. "Of course, we laughed and said we furnished everything for stringing ourselves up but the rope, and they'd have to get together and make that themselves—but their faces were all twisted with hate and if they had had a little smarter leadership and a little more practice they *would* have put us in the river." She might be working with the Communists herself, she added: "If you and Mr. Roosevelt had not come to lead the people, I think many of us might have been thinking differently."[59] Eleanor put that letter into Franklin's bedside basket.

A few weeks later a wholly different report from West Virginia went into the president's basket, and Eleanor also sent a copy of it to Justice Louis D. Brandeis, who at dinner at the White House had been fascinated by her account of the efforts of the resettled miners, so like those of the Palestine settlers, to make a new life for themselves. This report was from Elsie Clapp, the progressive educator whom Eleanor had brought in as principal of the school in Arthurdale. It was about Christmas in Reedsville.

Such joy. I wish you could have seen it. The toys you gave reached every boy, girl, child, baby. And, best of all, out of their abundance, the homesteaders on their own initiative made up several Christmas boxes for some people near us who are very poor and miserable. . . . We cut our tree, brought it in and decked it. We gathered our Christmas greens from the woods. . . . Christmas Eve at seven-thirty we gathered in the Assembly Hall. Carols which the children acted out orally, the old Bible story, presented by everyone. . . . The whole Christmas drew the community together. . . I was needed only to help. It was theirs entirely.

Eleanor set great store by the school. It would be up to the school, she had told Elsie Clapp when she interviewed her for the job of principal, not only to educate the children but to reawaken hope in the homesteaders, show them how to live more satisfying lives, indeed, to breathe life into this new community. The assignment did not faze Miss Clapp, a protégé of John Dewey who had been applying progressive education principles to rural education at the Ballard Memorial School in Kentucky. But she would need to bring in teachers with special training and get the advice of the best educators in the country, she told Eleanor, who agreed to both conditions and said she would find the money to employ qualified teachers. Eleanor also helped to establish a National Advisory Committee that included John Dewey, Lucy Sprague Mitchell, and Dean William Russell. Jessie Stanton, the director of the Bank Street Nursery School in New York, set up the nursery school in Arthurdale, the first in the entire area. "If I can teach these mothers," Miss Clapp told Eleanor, "that cold pancakes and coffee aren't good for babies, my two-year-olds will be much healthier." The curriculum was adapted to the special needs of the community, the learning experiences organized around life problems that the community faced. Under Elsie Clapp's leadership, the school became the center of almost every community activity. She fostered a regional cultural movement, and a summer music festival that she and the homesteaders inaugurated featured "Jig-Dancing," "Ballad Singing," "Mouth-Harping," a "Fiddlers' Contest," and a "Square Dancing Contest" in which Eleanor was a participant.[60]

An expensive experimental school did not seem a legitimate charge upon the government, so Eleanor raised most of the operating expenses from private sources. Baruch was the most generous, beginning his contributions with a check for $22,000, a response, he wrote, to Eleanor's "rare combination of intelligence and great heart."[61] In order to be able to contribute herself, Eleanor resumed commercially sponsored radio broadcasts, the proceeds of which went to the American Friends Service Committee to be earmarked for the purposes she indicated. In the autumn of 1934 she received $18,000 for six 15-minute broadcasts of which $6,000 went for the salary of Elsie Clapp, another $6,000 to establish the handicraft center at Arthurdale under the direction of Nancy Cook, and the remaining $6,000 for health work.[62]

At times she seemed to be almost a commuter between Washington and Reedsville. When she was asked whether it was not a burden to travel to Arthurdale so often, she cut the questioner short with the reply that she enjoyed the company of the homesteaders. She liked them. She knew the names of the children, kept track of their ailments and their achievements. She chatted with their mothers about canning recipes and joined in the Virginia reel with their fathers. She had a "folksy and homelike way with the homesteaders," Wilson recalled, "as though she had always lived in the community and had just come back from having gone for a couple of weeks."

She had tried repeatedly to get Ickes to visit the project while the homesteads were still under his jurisdiction and wrote him that Baruch had come away "tremendously impressed" after his first visit, so much so that he was going "to help us to make it into the kind of experiment which we would all like to see." She hoped that the secretary would plan to go down, "for I feel that after all the trouble and anxiety that this project has caused you, you will get a sense of satisfaction from meeting the people and seeing how well it is turning out."[63] Ickes had promised he would go with her in August, but the visit never took place.

Although Ickes professed relief over the transfer of the homesteads to Tugwell, the shift rankled him. He became harshly critical of Eleanor, whom at times he even suspected of being part of a cabal to oust him from the cabinet. At the state dinner for the cabinet given by the president and Mrs. Roosevelt at the end of 1934, little pleased him: the menu hardly constituted a "Lucullan" repast, he disliked the domestic wines Eleanor insisted upon serving, and "the champagne was undrinkable." By January, 1935, he had come to the conclusion that Mrs. Roosevelt did not do her husband any good with her active involvement in public affairs. He began to cultivate Missy.[64]

Eleanor Roosevelt did present a problem to a strong, self-centered administrator like Ickes. He was never quite certain whether she was acting on the president's behalf or on her own. Nor was the president beyond taking advantage of the ambiguity.

Rexford G. Tugwell, who inherited the Subsistence Homestead Division from Ickes when, in May, 1935, Roosevelt combined it with the rural rehabilitation program of Hopkins's FERA and the soil-reclamation activities of the AAA, was also baffled by his relationship as Resettlement administrator to the First Lady, even though they were on terms of genuine cordiality. In December, 1933, when Tugwell was assistant secretary of agriculture, she had, at his urging, visited the department's National Research Center near College Park, Maryland, where Tugwell thought the nearby submarginal land could be turned into a garden city. A man of superior intelligence, more detached about his ambitions than Ickes, Tugwell admired the First Lady's relationship to government. She had rallied to his support when the food and drug interests fell upon him because of his sponsorship of an effective food and drug bill. The conservative press dug up a poem he had written as an undergraduate and quoted the line "I shall roll up my sleeves—make America over!" to prove his subversive intent, which had only strengthened Eleanor's admiration for him. They had enjoyed each other's company when they found themselves on the same plane bound for Puerto Rico, an historic visit prolific in New Deal benefits for this hitherto neglected Island dependency.[65] They were good enough friends so that when she invited him for dinner or to Hyde Park he brought along his assistant, Miss Grace Falke, whom he later married, and when he delivered a speech at Dartmouth on the New Deal, Eleanor felt able to admonish him on the foolhardiness of his title, "Wine, Women and the New Deal." "Your sense of humor has led you into a trap, I am afraid," she wrote, envisaging a deluge of WCTU protests.[66]

She wanted to be helpful to Tugwell in his role as Resettlement administrator, but she considered Arthurdale her special responsibility. She fought stubbornly for what she considered to be the interests of the homesteaders, for she knew that Tugwell was basically wary of the back-to-the-land concept of resettling the unemployed and of industrial decentralization. In fact, he would have been happier if Roosevelt had not placed the Subsistence Homestead Division, which already was under fierce attack, in the Resettlement Administration.

Tugwell considered resettlement realistic as a way of moving farmers off exhausted soil but not as a remedy for industrial unemployment or urban congestion. People go to employment, not employment to people, he had stated, as if it were an iron law of economics; and if industries could be persuaded to decentralize, the new communities which formed around them would become company towns. Nor did he believe urban growth could be halted. But Eleanor refused to accept as inevitable what she felt ought to be resisted, even if the man she was opposing was as brilliant as Tugwell. She was, Tugwell wrote in *The Democratic Roosevelt*, "naive about many things—after all, she had a very defective education."

So although they were confederates, they had reservations about each other. He consulted her on the staff for the Resettlement Administration; she was enthusiastic about his plans for a Special Skills Division to instruct and encourage the settlers in the arts and crafts. She sent him an article on Arthurdale she had written for *Liberty*, which she wanted him to review. "This is a very moving little story," he commented. No, he had no objections to publication, but even if he had, they might have been difficult to offer since her note also said, "Franklin has seen this." She also urged him to expedite decisions on Arthurdale's requests for school-construction materials, which had been sitting "for ages on a desk in Washington." "I hope you will be patient with us for a month or two," he entreated her.[67]

Like Eleanor, Tugwell believed that these new communities should set a pattern for a new America and that the managers of the homesteads, therefore, had social and educational responsibilities, not simply economic and engineering ones. He convened a conference at Buck Hills Falls to assess these responsibilities. How could these communities be vitalized, Tugwell asked the group, which included anthropologists and psychiatrists as well as rural planners and managers. "A community does not consist of houses, and it does not consist of houses and schools and roads and water systems and sewers either. There is something else to a community besides that. We are trying to find out what it is if we can, and, if we can to bring it into being, to make it come alive."[68]

The homesteaders were long-time casualties of the Depression, said Eleanor, who followed Tugwell onto the platform. They were not going to recover all of a sudden; they had lost their initiative and had suffered certain physical changes which had affected their mental and spiritual ability to face the world: "It is not purely a housing problem. You cannot build houses and tell people to go and live in them. They must be taught how to live. Therefore this is a resettlement problem."[69]

Tugwell's emphasis on the social aspects of community building pleased Eleanor, who hoped there would soon be another conference on the same theme and that it would be held at Reedsville, which was, after all, supposed to be the demonstration center. She thought Arthurdale had come to life as a community and that it had done so because of Elsie Clapp's remarkable work with the school and the nursery. Baruch agreed with her. Whatever the cost of the school, he said, "the money has been well spent because it has demonstrated what can be done especially in the way of salvaging and redeeming old and young people. What has been done there can be duplicated in other places."[70]

Arthurdale had achieved the sense of community for which Tugwell was groping, and Eleanor hoped that that spirit would not be a casualty of the reorganization. She liked the plan which Tugwell had told her about at Buck Hills to form community corporations which would lease the land and houses from the government and in turn give long-term leases to the individual homesteaders. Outright sale of the houses, Tugwell feared, might expose the colonists to speculators and make land-use planning and corporate commercial farming more difficult. But Eleanor foresaw difficulties at Arthurdale, where the homesteaders had been led to believe that ownership of their homes would be vested with them individually, not with the community, and that the costs would be based on what they could pay. "I am afraid I am complicating your life very much," she wrote Tugwell apologetically after Buck Hills, "and I do not mean to do that but I thought I ought to tell you that I had told Franklin about it as I think he will be discussing it with you."[71]

Her readiness to go over Tugwell's head to the president did complicate the administrator's life and, carried away by the First Lady's patronage, the homesteaders also bypassed Resettlement Administration channels, and were even condescending to the administrator. "There is one thing I want to suggest to you," Eleanor cautioned Elsie Clapp,

namely, Mr. Tugwell has the complete responsibility and when we are with him, I think you should make it a point to make him feel that we recognize his responsibility and do not even suggest that I do anything except stand ready to help in an unofficial way on educational and health questions. If you can, try to make him realize that while you feel identified with the people, and that they do seem to be your own, that you also fully realize the main responsibility is his, and that they are "his people" and not "my people."[72]

It was sensible advice, but her own willingness to defer to Tugwell's "complete responsibility" was less than wholehearted. Limited funds compelled the Resettlement Administration to reduce the wages of the homesteaders who were employed on community construction projects, and the cuts were devastating the homesteaders, a frantic Elsie Clapp told Eleanor. "I quite realize that what has been done is necessary," Eleanor in turn wrote Tugwell, "but I think it ought to have been done in each of the homesteads not by a mere notice, but by some one who really understood the reason and who could put it to the people." If there was to be a wage reduction, she went on, there would have to be a corresponding reduction in the payments made by the homesteaders on their homes. "I can imagine that your problems are so many that what may happen to the people in one homestead does not loom very large, but after all this is the first and the one most criticized and under the public eye. I hope you will not think me an interfering old hen."[78] Despite the disarming final sentence, she did not relax her pressure on Tugwell. The homesteaders sent her a petition, underscoring the injustice of wage reductions without corresponding reductions in what they had to pay. She sent it straight to the president, telling him, as she informed Elsie Clapp, that "my feeling was that in the effort to be efficient from the economic standpoint, I thought perhaps the division was forgetting the important human element, and that I hoped he would keep in mind the fact that I wanted him to go down and get a picture of the human side for himself."[74]

Eleanor felt a responsibility to the homesteaders, to whom the government had made commitments, many of them through her. Sympathetic as she was with Tugwell's efforts to rethink the government's homesteading policy, she felt a new approach must take those commitments into account. "The opportunity to interpret thinking that lies behind some of the projects has not been easy with the present administration," the normally patient Pickett complained to her.[75] Yet she was alive to Tugwell's problems. When Elsie, in her zeal for the homesteaders, charged into Washington to get action on an Arthurdale payroll which had been delayed because of Treasury funding problems, Eleanor rebuked her. "The fact that you visited the Treasury caused three people to telephone Mr. Tugwell to find out if you were speaking with authority for him. As you know this would annoy a man who feels that his Administration must begin to function." It would be wiser for Elsie to keep out of the administrative side, she suggested, and if problems did arise to go through regular channels or through her.[76] She urged both Pickett and Elsie to be patient. Tugwell was "tired," as were many of the men who since March 4, 1933, had been working to the limit of their energies. She sensed, moreover, that Tugwell was "quite overcome to find that the old administration had worked out none of the fundamental problems."

When Baruch went to Reedsville to try to sort out the problems there that urgently called for decision he went alone because Eleanor thought the settlers might say things to him they would be reluctant to say in front of her. Baruch's survey had a wider application than Arthurdale. While some of its problems were unique, the more basic difficulties were characteristic of many of the new communities. A decision had to be made soon, he informed Eleanor, about how Arthurdale was to be governed. Would it be local or would it continue to be run from Washington? In any event, he wrote, "there must be some method of getting quicker decisions than there is now." Those in charge at Arthurdale, when Baruch finally got them to speak frankly, complained sharply of "their inability to get decisions or to cut the red tape, even in getting materials." The size of the community had to be settled; there would soon be 125 houses—should the government still aim for 200 as originally planned? Not if the people in them could not get work, Baruch felt, and he was highly pessimistic on that point. All the problems stemmed from that fact. The homesteads, he advised, should be sold at a price low enough to give the homesteaders the chance to own them eventually, but the carrying charges could not be twenty dollars a month; a figure of $100 a year would be more realistic, especially in Arthurdale, where the possibilities of self-support had been further diminished by the belated discovery that its soil was not suitable for commercial crops.

It would be impossible to carry out the plan for a rural-industrial community as originally envisaged, Baruch advised Eleanor, but she must not feel that the effort had been wholly a wasted one. Arthurdale had demonstrated that there could be "human rehabilitation" after long periods of unemployment. Elsie Clapp's school had been particularly helpful in that connection, but there, too, they had to ask themselves whether the heavy private subsidies should continue or whether it was not time to normalize the school's relationship to the county and state educational system. "If we will learn not to put people where they cannot earn enough to care for themselves, whatever the cost, it will be cheap," Baruch concluded.[77]

It would take the war to show that the government was able, when the will was there, to direct industry to move to where people were, but Eleanor, while she abandoned neither the effort to get an industry for Arthurdale nor a vision of rural-industrial communes that would provide an escape from both urbanism and rural decay, was intellectually too insecure to press her own philosophy in the face of the practical judgments of a Baruch or the theoretical convictions of a Tugwell: "I think it is fairly well proved," she wrote a few months before a defense manufacturer began to operate in Arthurdale, "that even if industry is going to decentralize at all, it has to locate first and then the community grows around it."

Tugwell's emphasis as resettlement administrator was on land reform. His program sought "to take poor people off poor land and resettle them where good land, good organization and good advice might rehabilitate them." In addition he promoted the brilliant concept of the "greenbelt towns," garden communities built in wooded areas adjacent to industrial centers, with low-cost housing as their cores.

Eleanor supported both programs, as did the president, but the mood of the country and especially of Congress was becoming hostile to the whole idea of planned communities. Although Tugwell contemplated sixty "greenbelt" projects, only three were built because they were attacked so savagely. And in the 1936 campaign, when the Republicans made the Resettlement Administration an issue, Tugwell noted that "we had no defenders and were told to keep quiet ourselves."

The environment had become unfriendly to social planning and experimentation, and this reinforced the individualistic and competitive attitudes of the settlers within the communities whom Eleanor, Tugwell, and Dr. Alexander had hoped to imbue with the community idea. It was difficult to build new communities with old minds. For years the miners had felt themselves to be social and economic outcasts, and now their deepest wish was not to be something special but to be like other Americans. "I realized when we began," Eleanor told the Women's National Democratic Club,

that there must be an educational program when you take people from an area where they had been living for some time under impossible conditions, but I had no conception what the problem was. I understand it a good deal better than I did three years ago. . . . When these people were moved, they had to learn to stand on their own feet and make their own decisions, and sometimes they didn't quite know what was expected of them . . . nobody understood why these people didn't take hold. There is always grave danger in anything that is experimental. One must not do too much for people, but one must help them to do for themselves.[78]

The homesteaders had been encouraged to start cooperatives at Arthurdale and other settlements, but this, too, called for education. "They wanted cows tied to their back fences," Eleanor later said. "They trusted nobody, not even themselves. They had an eye out all the time to see who was going to cheat them next."[79]

"We were doomed to failure from the start," Tugwell wrote fifteen years later. The human stock was sound, he felt, but "the environment was hostile to the development of character" and to the development of the commitment and self-discipline necessary to make the communities work.[80]

The one instrumentality that had helped to reshape attitudes was Elsie Clapp's school at Arthurdale. Yet even this heavily subsidized school, with its progressive methods, made the homesteaders uneasy; they wanted their children to be taught the three R's like the rest of the children in West Virginia. Moreover, Arthurdale's bleak economic prospects worked against the initiative and self-reliance that the progressive curriculum sought to instill. Men without jobs found it difficult to plan and to keep ambition alive. That was the point made by the educational foundations when Baruch asked them to help finance the school. Without industries, without jobs, they told him, the school could not succeed. "I want to say again that in this I heartily concur," Baruch wrote to Eleanor.[81]

She went along with Baruch's conclusion, although reluctantly. He had spoken with Elsie Clapp about taking her task force of teachers to another community where the economic prospects might be more conducive to the long-term support of a costly experiment in progressive education, and Eleanor hoped the group might return to Arthurdale if the economic situation there were to become more stable. But without Baruch's moral as well as financial support she did not feel she could insist on going on with the school. She met with Tugwell and his aides to inform them of Baruch's decision and her own concurrence, as well as Elsie Clapp's. She had expected Tugwell to welcome the news since he considered it time the homesteaders tied in with the West Virginia school system, but Tugwell was unhappy, she reported to Baruch, and "rather took my breath away" with the statement that "the morale at Arthurdale and conditions there were ninety per cent better than in any other homestead, entirely due to the school." Her five-page single-spaced report to Baruch on what she had done about the school situation asked for his approval: "I hope you will feel I have acted wisely and have done what you would have done, for I value your good opinion and cooperation more than I can tell you."[82] She let him out of his commitment, but she continued to subsidize some of the school salaries. In 1939 her contribution was $2,677.49.

Eleanor went to Arthurdale to tell the homesteaders the decision about the school and explain the importance of carrying on the work "on their own responsibility and to tie themselves in in every possible way with the State, the county and the general neighborhood." She was not withdrawing her support for Arthurdale, she sought to reassure them. "I stressed to them that I was not in any way lessening my interest and would be there as often as I had been in the past" to work with their own school people.[83]

She kept her word by continuing to go to Arthurdale at commencement time to hand out diplomas until her last year in the White House. She also continued to bring friends to Arthurdale and to enlist their help for special projects—such as a library—voted by the homesteaders. In May, 1938, the president yielded to her proddings and made his often deferred visit to Arthurdale, hailing it as an example of "the awakening of the social conscience of America." Businessmen who cultivated Eleanor in the hope of obtaining access to the president suddenly realized that she was cultivating *them* in the hopes of getting an industry for Reedsville. Arthurdale struggled along, but at the end of the thirties the weekly reports on employment showed that the majority of the homesteaders were still on the government work-relief payroll. The problem of an industry and full employment was finally solved in World War II; when the government began to offer defense manufacturers generous tax incentives and subsidies to expand their plants and facilities, Eleanor, backed by Baruch, pressed the men in charge of the defense program to keep the needs of the homestead communities in mind. Arthurdale's employment problem vanished when the Hoover Aircraft Corporation, attracted by its labor force and railroad facilities and with little risk to itself since the government was underwriting the expansion, leased several of the buildings the government had built in Arthurdale and began operations.[84]

Arthurdale was a chastening experience. It taught Eleanor that a president's wife who undertakes a specific job in the government faces double jeopardy: she is without real authority yet she is expected to perform miracles. When she does assert leadership it is resented and resisted. And if she does not, officials try to anticipate what she wants done. Tugwell was one of the most strong-minded and independent men in the Roosevelt administration, and yet he had been at a loss as to how to deal with the First Lady. "I had been told that he did not tell me his exact feelings because he felt everything I wanted must be carried out," Eleanor wrote Baruch.[85]

Eleanor's patronage of Arthurdale and the subsistence homesteads insured them plenty of publicity and attention, which had its good aspects, especially in helping the underprivileged feel that the government cared about them. Officials tried harder as a result of Eleanor's interest to make the experiment succeed. The public conscience was stirred. Eleanor's visit to the farm homestead project near Memphis was "a great encouragement to the families," Will Alexander, administrator of the Farm Security Agency, the successor to the Resettlement Administration, wrote her in late 1939, and then added: "Of course, our most discouraged and bewildered group are the families in the Migratory Labor Camps, about whom John Steinbeck wrote in *Grapes of Wrath*. It would mean a great deal to them if you could some time visit one of their Migratory Labor Camps."

But there were also adverse consequences to the publicity that attended Eleanor's sponsorship and interest. A pilot program by definition must go through a period of trial and error, of mistakes and failure. Eleanor's presence not only mobilized the administration's friends but attracted its enemies, and critics pounced upon every mistake and magnified it to the limit. In this respect, Arthurdale might have benefited from less publicity.

Then there was the effect of Eleanor's involvement on the homesteaders themselves. Her readiness to help and her belief in the experiment and in the homesteaders gave them courage and was an added incentive to succeed. "I do not believe in discouraging people when there is anything to encourage them about," she replied to a critic who taxed her with closing her eyes to the problems in one of the settlements; "I think there is a tremendous amount in the psychology of hopefulness," she wrote Major Walker, one of the top officials of the program, complaining that every time the regional staff people visited the homesteads there was a slump in morale.[86] But the homesteaders, as she herself noted on other occasions, were not angels—far from it—and her efforts to be helpful to them made them dependent and too easy on themselves, so much so that on one occasion when the school bus broke down they brought it to the White House garage for repairs. Presidential aide "Pa" Watson stopped that.[87] That was an extreme case, but too many homesteaders, Eleanor confessed in 1940, seemed to feel the salvation for all their problems was to turn to the government, and she was disappointed by their unwillingness to shoulder their share of responsibility.[88]

"How do you get these people to consent to such a program?" she asked David E. Lilienthal, head of the Tennessee Valley Authority, when he came to the White House to talk to her about the effect of the TVA on people. Lilienthal, who considered her "a beautiful spirit" but felt that she had a "social worker angle on a world that is tough and bitter and hardly amenable to such tampering with systems," had long hoped for a chance "to teach her some reality about economics." He saw his opportunity when she gave a troubled account of the efforts at Arthurdale and Crossville "and how she now saw that bringing in factories from the outside wasn't the right way, even when it could be done; that our way of making something happen out of the materials at hand, and by knowing the particular problems intimately, was much wiser." When Eleanor repeated her question about how the TVA got people to change their way of doing things, Lilienthal told her of "grass roots methods, and the technique of demonstration and learning by doing and by example. And being close to the problem because we are a regional, not a Washington outfit."

"She is a very intelligent person," Lilienthal noted in his journal, "and she got it, and I think will pass it along to a member of the household who, God save the mark, can stand some education along the same line."[89]

But neither the conceptual mistakes of Eleanor Roosevelt and of M. L. Wilson nor the political vulnerability of Tugwell explain why this bold and imaginative attack on rural poverty and urban congestion was in the end liquidated by Congress. It was the firm commitment of the Farm Security Administration to the goal of ending rural poverty that alarmed the conservatives, because it threatened the traditional power structure in agriculture in general but particularly in the South, where many of the FSA benefits flowed to the Negro. And so when the war came, giving the New Deal's enemies the chance to kill off some of its most innovative programs under the pretext of cutting non-defense expenditures, the FSA was included. There were 99 communities at the time of its final liquidation; 10,938 homesteads had been built at a total cost of $108,095,328, or at a unit cost of $9,691, which included the cost of community facilities and management. Arthurdale, with a unit cost of $16,635, had been the most expensive.[90]

"These projects represent something new," President Roosevelt said in his Arthurdale address, "and because we in America had little or no experience along these lines, there were some failures—not a complete failure in the case of any given project, but partial failures due to bad guesses on economic subjects like new industries or lack of markets." But there were lessons to be learned from this "bold government venture," lessons that would save "a hundred times their cost in dollars."[91]

But the lessons were not learned. Instead of a planned approach to the related problems of the flight from the farms, urban congestion, and industrial decentralization, the outcome was left to the unchecked operation of social and economic forces that ultimately produced the crisis of the cities.

When Eleanor Roosevelt appraised the Arthurdale experience in the second volume of her autobiography, she acknowledged that money had been spent wastefully and that the financial returns to the government had not been satisfactory, but in extenuation she pointed to the human beings saved. "Oh, yes, the human values were most rewarding," she stoutly maintained.[92]

Her defensiveness was a tribute to the hold that the free-enterprise ethic had regained in the postwar era. "Sell it off—regardless" was the attitude of the National Housing Agency, which fell heir to Arthurdale.[93] The final cost to the government of liquidating Arthurdale's 165 houses, hillside inn, forge, weaving room, furniture-display room, and 57,250 square feet of factory space in 1946 was in the neighborhood of two million dollars. To Americans of the 70s, accustomed to the expenditures of billions on space and weapons research and hundreds of millions on health research, this will scarcely seem like heedless extravagance.

If experiments like Arthurdale were not justified, Eleanor wrote to a critic in 1934, then "we must go along the beaten path and he contented [*sic*] with the same type of living which has driven people out of rural districts in the past and into the cities where they have become equally unhappy under present industrial conditions."[94]

Unhappily, what in 1934 was a defense of a New Deal program turns out three decades later to have been accurate prediction.

38. Publicist for the New Deal—
Columnist and Lecturer

HAD THE CENSUS TAKER in 1932 asked Eleanor Roosevelt her job or profession, she would have said "teacher." But when she moved to the White House she had to give up professional teaching. Was there anything, she asked herself, that she could do professionally which would reflect her own knowledge and experience and not be entirely the result "of somebody else's work and position? . . . I turned naturally to speaking and writing."[1]

In 1934 she resumed the sponsored radio talks that she had given up when her husband had become president. People, especially women, were interested in her views. Speaking to them gave Eleanor a sense of fulfillment, and the largest audiences were those to be reached over the radio networks. Moreover, she wanted the money, chiefly for Arthurdale, and she decided to risk the criticism that she knew would come and see if she could ride it out. She would not touch the money from those talks herself, she explained to the press; her fees would be paid directly to the American Friends Service Committee to be disbursed at her direction. This announcement muted most of the criticism that had caused her to give up commercial radio in 1933, but not all of it. Her first sponsor was the Simmons Mattress Company, and the other mattress manufacturers, alarmed lest the nation flock to the Simmons product, protested to President Roosevelt that it did not seem fair for the First Lady to use her prestige to assist some single manufacturer. The president sent the protest to his wife. "Ask the President if he wishes me to answer?" Eleanor queried. Howe advised against it. "I agree with Louis," wrote Steve Early, and a notification finally came back: "No ans. F.D.R."[2] A few weeks later, however, when a small manufacturer objected directly to her, she did defend herself by asking if she should not write for a single magazine because it would be unfair to its competitors, or buy from a favorite dress designer. "The principle involved in my broadcasting for a particular firm holds true in everything I do."[3] It was a debater's answer, and the criticism never wholly abated; but she was willing to accept it, and so, evidently, was Franklin. Her definitive reason was, "I could not help the various things in which I am interested if I did not earn the money which makes it possible."

Simmons paid her handsomely. "I think you are entirely right that no one is worth $500 a minute," she replied candidly to an irate citizen. "Certainly I never dreamed for a minute I was!" Her fees, it was noted, placed her in the same class as the highest-paid radio personalities of the time such as Ed Wynn.[4]

Her broadcasts were sufficiently popular to bring her another sponsor as soon as the Simmons series ended, this one the American typewriter industry, for whom she did six fifteen-minute talks on child education. These were subsequently issued as a pamphlet. Her 1935 sponsor was Selby Shoes who, for sixteen fifteen-minute talks, paid her $72,000, all of it sent directly to the AFSC. An article in *Radio Guide* praised her as a radio performer. Coached by studio technicians, who were enchanted with her because she was not a prima donna, she began to learn everything about radio delivery—timing, modulation, spacing—and by 1939 she was dubbed the "First Lady of Radio" by WNBC:

Her microphone manners are exemplary. . . . She listens to suggestions from production men and cooperates in any plan to improve the reception of a broadcast. She arrives in time for rehearsals and accepts direction with no more ado than if she were an obscure personality. . . . She is not averse to a little showmanship here and there, but eschews tricks. Her voice is well-pitched and she speaks softly. . . . It is not an accident that Mrs. Roosevelt's radio voice is studied by students of speech.[5]

In 1936 Betty Lindley, the wife of Ernest Lindley and long a personal friend, became her radio agent and negotiated a contract with Pond's for thirteen talks at $3,000 apiece. Of this amount $200 was set aside for studio expenses, $300 went to Mrs. Lindley, and the remainder to the AFSC to cover the budget of the Arthurdale school; "after that it seems to me that the school should be taken over by the state."[6] She suffered a few mishaps as a radio performer. In her final broadcast for Pond's there were a "few terrible seconds" when a page disappeared from her script. If she had been following her own train of thought instead of a script as she was required to do, she could have handled it without a break, she said. As it was it took her "a second or two" to collect her thoughts.[7] What made her an outstanding radio performer was not so much her mastery of technique as her constant awareness of her unseen audience. She tried consciously to envision the women who were listening to her under conditions of the greatest diversity—on lonely ranches, in mountain cabins, in tenements—and to remember that they were weighing her words against their own experience. She made her listeners' interests and problems her own and tried out of her own experience to say meaningful things simply and concretely.

Her ability to identify with her listeners, to illustrate her thesis with homely stories, and to advance her point of view with such kindness and courtesy that even the most violent adversaries were stilled was even more evident in her lectures and speeches, where she was not bound by a script. Her custom, when she addressed live audiences, was to speak from a single page of notes. "Have something to say, say it and sit down," she advised students of public speaking, as Louis had advised her. "At first write out the beginning and the end of a speech. Use notes and think out a speech, but never write it down."[8] She did not like to speak if she did not have something affirmative to say. Often as the chairman introduced her she prayed for Divine guidance to say something that might be helpful to the people in front of her. Like Gandhi, Schweitzer, and other semi-religious figures with whom she later would be grouped, she was always the teacher. Everything she said was infused with moral purpose and affirmed the supremacy of love and truth.

Her speeches generally contained a challenge, but it was issued with such graciousness and modesty that few took offense. "Be conciliatory, never antagonistic, toward your audience," she advised, "or it may disagree with you, no matter what you say." Before the DAR convention she championed progressive methods in education, a campaign to eradicate illiteracy, and the "grand" adult-education work of the Relief Administration, and her tradition-bound audience listened attentively. She even poked gentle fun at a superpatriot's proposal to restrict the right to change laws to people of old stock (she and the president between them had only one ancestor who arrived later than colonial days, she noted, "so if anyone would have a right on that peculiar status, we would still qualify"), and ended with a plea for patriotism that "will mean living for the interests of everyone in our country and the world at large, rather than simply preparing to die for our country."[9] Novelist Dorothy Canfield Fisher wrote that she had "fairly bounded into the air with joy" because she had never dreamed that someone in authority could say right out what Eleanor had said to the DAR.[10]

A few weeks later she spoke extemporaneously at a federal prison for delinquent girls and women in Alderson, West Virginia. Her speech was Lincolnesque in its simplicity and feeling. She had been moved by the way the girls had sung the spirituals, she began, and then quoted the 121st Psalm: "I will lift up mine eyes unto the hills from whence cometh my help." That was the keynote of Alderson, she noted, set as it was in the mountains and run by a progressive penologist, Dr. Mary Harris, to help those who were there over the rough spots. That was also what government in general was now trying to do—"help the people it governs" over the rough spots. There was a new concept of social justice and government abroad in the land. "The fundamental change is just this, that instead of each person being out for himself for what he can get for himself . . . people must think . . . of the people around them" and ask of any action not only "what will be the effect . . . on me, but what will be the effect on those around me?" She then told of a recent visit to Puerto Rico and of a little rural school there that had been started by an obscure, humble individual but which was transforming the whole approach to rural education. "So when you get a chance to push something that is new and that helps the life of the people around you to be better, just remember what I have told you about Puerto Rico and help it along." Then she went into her own philosophy of life:

It is a wonderful thing to keep your mind always full of something that is worth while doing. If you can get hold of something that you feel is going to help the people around you, you'll find that you're so busy trying to add one more thing to it that you won't have time to be sorry for yourself or to wonder what you're going to do with your spare time. . . . If I get sorry for myself, I'm no good to anybody else. It is just the best tonic I know, to get so interested in everybody that you want to see them happy always, and somehow or other you'll find that you haven't time for any of the things that filled your mind, that kept you from being a really useful person in the community that you were living in.[11]

It was a speech the girls understood, delivered with such earnestness and evident good will that even the most hardened yielded to its spell. "My prediction was correct," Dr. Harris wrote her afterward; "many of the girls have referred to it and quoted from it to me, and what I hear myself is only a small part of the comment it aroused."[12]

Her speeches held her listeners because they reflected her own efforts to think through to what was right and true. "You talk the language of the new America," wrote Frank P. Graham, the president of the University of North Carolina, after her talk at the university. A Negro woman, explaining her willingness to wait an hour and a quarter to get into one of Mrs. Roosevelt's lectures, put it more colloquially: "She's got a message. And gosh! she's given it to 'em hot!"[13]

By the end of 1935 Eleanor was in such demand as a speaker by forums and other groups accustomed to paying fees that she signed a contract with W. Colston Leigh to do two lecture tours a year under his management at a fee of $1,000 per lecture. The Leigh brochure advertised five subjects on which she was willing to speak:

RELATIONSHIP OF THE INDIVIDUAL TO THE COMMUNITY

PROBLEMS OF YOUTH

THE MAIL OF A PRESIDENT'S WIFE

PEACE

A TYPICAL DAY AT THE WHITE HOUSE

One thousand dollars was a large fee, larger than she would have commanded—at least at the outset—had she not been the president's wife, and since she did not feel obligated to turn over the whole of these fees to the American Friends Service Committee, some saw this as further proof that she commercialized and cheapened the First Ladyship. But she shrugged off such criticism, sensing perhaps that no one had done more to ennoble the First Lady's role; and if people came to her lectures because they were curious about the First Lady, they stayed and felt they had obtained their money's worth because of the personality with which they had come in contact.

Her first tour for Leigh began with an appearance at Grand Rapids, "and as usual I was very nervous until I found myself standing up and actually speaking." A confidential report to Leigh from his own correspondent in Grand Rapids was ecstatic. The audience of 1,700 to 1,800 "listened intently to every word." The observer noted that Eleanor was especially admired for the "dignified, authoritative manner" with which she handled all questions, including those meant to embarrass her. "Of course, everyone was amazed at all that she was able to do in a few hours that she was in the city. . . . I am sure that she won over all of the Republicans who heard her that evening, and there were many."[14]

Eleanor liked Leigh because he was "hard-boiled" and sought to protect his lecturers from being overwhelmed by local hospitality, but Leigh's best efforts to shield her were unavailing. "All goes well but very hectically," she wrote Franklin. "It would be easy to be a lecturer or the wife of the President but both, Oh! my." She was to speak in Omaha on a Sunday evening to the Delphians, and would like to have a "quiet day," Tommy advised the local committee. A sympathetic reporter described that "quiet day." It began with Eleanor and Tommy's arrival by train at 7:00 A.M., when they were met by a half dozen Delphians and given flowers. En route to the hotel they were trailed by two detectives who kept themselves out of sight because Eleanor's distaste for bodyguards was by now well known. At 10:30, after they had bathed and breakfasted, Tommy let in the press for a half-hour's questioning. As they filed out, a delegation of WPA supervisors came in. "This time," the reporter noted, "Mrs. Roosevelt asked the questions." They were succeeded by representatives of the National Youth Administration, who invited her to inspect an exhibit of NYA handicrafts, which she did after lunch, donning low-heeled oxfords because she insisted on walking to the exhibit. An hour later, having changed to an afternoon dress, she met some forty Delphians at tea. Then came a group of women Democrats. After dinner in her suite alone with Tommy when she wrote her column, she looked in on a private party at the hotel, toured an exhibit in the hotel of bug extermination devices on display for the convention of the National Pest Control Association, and, thus "rested," wrote the reporter, "the First Lady left at 7:45 for the city auditorium to give the speech for which she had come to Omaha."[15]

In 1937, Leigh persuaded her to do the first three-week tour. A "bit too long," she confessed to Bess Furman afterward. "Two weeks is all I can do in one-night stands and keep feeling polite towards the people who meet you at seven a.m. with bouquets and flowers and expect you to wear a smile!" Sometimes the hotels were poor, she wrote her husband, and sometimes, as was the case with the Danville, Illinois, hotel from which she was writing, they were "delightful. When they like you we get much attention. When they don't we are completely neglected!" Yet exhausting as these tours were, when local sponsors wanted to make special arrangements for her, she objected. The lecture committee in Jackson, Mississippi, distressed to learn there would be no Pullman car from Meridian to Jackson, were arranging for a special car when Eleanor wired, "I do not mind riding in day coaches. Please do not put yourself or the railroad to extra expense."[16]

She might gently complain to her husband, to Bess, or to Tommy, but to those receiving her it was their comfort, their feelings that were always paramount with her. At Oak Park Junior College in Illinois she had been told that the subject of her speech would be "Peace" and was prepared to speak on that when she suddenly heard the chairman announce, "Mrs. Roosevelt will speak on 'A Citizen's Responsibility to the Community.' " She had no notes but went right ahead, saying "a little prayer that I would get through without them!" He was grateful, the embarrassed man wrote afterward, for her "courtesy in not changing the subject matter after I had announced it and the ability with which you handled the surprise subject."[17]

Women, of course, were interested in what she wore and how she carried herself. "I have seen five queens, and this queen is regal," remarked a cultivated Frenchman who watched her model a gown at a debutante cotillion. Dress designers chose her as "the best dressed woman in the United States" in 1934. "To have that title," she commented, especially in the light of her family's feeling that she never paid sufficient attention to her clothes, had been one of the "funniest" but also one of the "grandest" things that had happened to her. "I have come to the conclusion," she advised dress designer Lilly Loscher, "that a dress for this type of trip should be low cut but should have very thin sleeves coming over the shoulder which would not interfere with having a long-sleeved jacket to go with it. It should either be of lace or some crepe material which does not require a lining and which does not crush. If it is lace and has to have lining, the lining should be put into the dress because it is very annoying to have a lot of little snaps to keep straps together across the shoulders."[18]

She had a cultivated diction and pronounced her words with a singular clarity, although a few patriots objected to her preference for "*shedule*" to "*skedule*." Her platform voice was no longer a monotone but an instrument of shading and cadence, capable of a controlled intensity or easy relaxation. But it remained high pitched until she was taken in hand by Mrs. Elizabeth von Hesse, a voice teacher: "Our Dear First Lady—may I speak frankly and to the point? I am a teacher of speech, particularly of tone production. . . Mrs. Roosevelt, if I were permitted I would give you a simple set of exercises for the development of resonance and depth of tone that would give you richness of quality. You could project your voice without losing any of its beauty." The exercises were such that she could do them while dressing, even while riding. Eleanor was about to reply that she was "too busy" but changed her mind. What would they cost and what did Mrs. von Hesse think could be accomplished in two or three days "if I gave you an hour each day?" Not everything could be done in one week end, Mrs. von Hesse replied, but a set of exercises and speech habits could be established that would give her more effective use of her resonant chambers on which depended the richness of tone and would help her achieve "better diaphragm control."[19]

Mrs. von Hesse came down, charging $50 for the week end, and within a few months Eleanor was being congratulated on the improvement. Her voice did "carry better and more easily," Eleanor agreed, but she was playing truant from her exercises when she traveled: "I could probably exercise my head and my voice, but my body is out of the question because trains and hotel rooms do not lend themselves to space enough and there is a feeling the floor may not be clean which may have something to do with it."[20]

Because of her success with Eleanor Roosevelt, Mrs. von Hesse's professional reputation boomed, but when Mrs. von Hesse discussed with Colston Leigh lecturing under his management, Eleanor hastily wrote "I would not want to be used as Exhibit A, with a comparison of my defects and improvements," adding, however, that it was "quite all right for you to state in your publicity that I have had lessons from you."[21]

A "one-season-wonder" in the lecture field, Drew Pearson and Robert S. Allen wrote disparagingly in their newspaper column, "Washington Merry-Go-Round." As reporting, this was wildly inaccurate, since in November, 1938, when the column appeared, Eleanor had been lecturing for three years; as prophecy it was even worse since until nearly the end of her life she was one of Colston Leigh's most sought-after speakers. Evidently Pearson and Allen recognized their blunder because a few months later they wrote that "a check-up of Mrs. Roosevelt's lecture audiences shows that she has definitely made friends for her husband, despite large fees charged by her agent." The columnists particularly admired the way she subjected herself to a "grueling fire of questions" after her lecture, and her effective replies. In Akron, Ohio, she was asked, "Do you think your husband's illness has affected your husband's mentality?" Except for a slight firmness about her jaw, she betrayed no emotion as she read out the question, and replied: "I am glad that question was asked. The answer is Yes. Anyone who has gone through great suffering is bound to have a greater sympathy and understanding of the problems of mankind."[22] The audience rose and gave her an ovation.

Because she spoke from notes rather than from a text she had to think about what she was saying, and this kept her speeches "a little fresher," she thought, and prevented her from becoming bored.[23]

The naturalness, good sense, and spiritual energy, which made her a durable presence on the lecture circuit, also explained her success as a newspaper columnist. Two months after her arrival in Washington the United Feature Syndicate asked her to do a daily two-hundred word article "on topics of general interest with particular emphasis on the home." Regretfully she had turned it down because of prior commitments to the North American Newspaper Alliance and to the *Woman's Home Companion*. In 1934 the latter publication, on its own initiative, increased her fee, but in 1935 it decided that "two years was about as long a time as we should continue a special feature of this type."

A few months later the United Feature Syndicate renewed its invitation to do a daily column, a diary of some four hundred to five hundred words in length. "When do I start?" was Eleanor's speedy reaction; her second question was, "What's my deadline?"[24] On December 31, 1935, she sent off her first piece of copy, carefully marking it PRESS RATES COLLECT.

No columnist had a more newsworthy setting or a more fascinating cast of characters upon whom to report. Her first column described the White House family quarters teeming with young people during the Christmas holidays. Her husband was in bed with a cold, she reported, "so I said a polite good night to everyone at seven-thirty, closed my door, lit my fire, and settled down to a nice long evening by myself." There had been sixteen that day for lunch, and one young guest had burst out, "Every meal is different in this house. Yesterday we talked about philosophies of government. Today we have talked about movies and punging." Eleanor did not explain, although a good reporter would have, that "punging" is a form of sleighing. The discussion about philosophies of government had been occasioned by Franklin Jr. and John who, in discussing a sociology course at Harvard they were taking with Professors Zimmerman and Boldyraeff, had described the professors as being highly critical of the AAA, whereupon the president had suggested inviting the professors to dinner so they could confront Henry Wallace and Chester Davis. Eleanor's concluding comment revealed that she was not going to shun controversy: "There are so many things which you do not have to consider if you are developing and studying a thing in a classroom. . . . It is quite different to be faced with actual situations that have to be met in one way or another in a given period of time."[25]

It soon became evident that her appeal as a columnist was not based only on her relationship to the president. Readers were enchanted with the personality that disclosed itself in little flashes such as "I sallied forth and in two brief hours ordered all my Winter clothes" or how she had spent "half an hour having a whole new monetary system thrust upon me" or how, when speaking about the District Training School for Delinquent Girls, she had stated, "Never have I seen an institution called a 'school' which had so little claim to that name." She discoursed on plays and books, expressing her judgments crisply and unambiguously. "Crude in a way because the thoughts hit you like hammer blows," she said of Irwin Shaw's anti-war play *Bury the Dead*, "but it was a great performance." "One line from S. A. Behrman's play *End of Summer* will stick in my head for a long time—'At the end of every road you meet yourself.'" She had just finished Santayana's *The Last Puritan*: "There is all together too much concentration on himself in Oliver's makeup. He was a fine character but missed, I think, the greatest fineness which is the ability to minimize your own importance even to yourself." John Golden was "funny" when he said there will never be any great women writers in the theater "because women do not know as much as men." The assumption of male superiority amused her "because as a rule women know not only what men know, but much that men will never know. For how many men really know the heart and soul of a woman?"[26]

She stayed away from politics but sometimes could not resist a gentle if oblique thrust. When the Supreme Court climaxed a series of rulings cutting down New Deal measures with its decision holding the AAA unconstitutional, she painted this picture of a relaxed reaction in the White House: she had gone down to the White House swimming pool for what she thought would be "a rather quiet and subdued swim at six o'clock. . . . My husband was already in the water, and before I reached the door, I dropped my wrapper, plunged into the water, and swimming about very quietly, I inquired hesitatingly how they were all feeling. To my complete surprise instead of either discouragement or even annoyance, I was told that everyone was feeling fine, and on that note we finished our swim." At dinner instead of the events of the day they discussed, violently, the Holy Roman Empire, the Dark Ages, and the Renaissance. At midnight she went in to say good night: "With the new day comes new strength and new thoughts."[27]

It was a picture of grace under pressure and at that moment of constitutional crisis her portrait of a steady-handed, nonvindictive president was worth more than a score of political pronouncements. As Anne O'Hare McCormick wrote two years later, after the tension-filled days of the Munich crisis, "No one should underestimate the reassuring effect on public opinion of the figure of the many-sided father of a family who slips in and out of the diary of the accomplished White House character who manages to sublimate the typical American woman in the person of the First Lady of the Land."[28]

Sometimes readers complained because Eleanor refused to be a pundit or to deal with serious matters all the time. "I am asked to write a diary and I cannot write on politics," she replied to one such critic; "I simply tell small human happenings which may interest or amuse the average reader. . . . Daily happenings are trivial, certainly, and not worth your time to read, but it may help some people to feel that lives they think must be important are after all filled with homely little things." To another faultfinder she wrote, "I learned a long time ago that too much crusading for any cause is almost as bad as too little. People get weary of too much preaching."[29]

She loved doing her column and longed to be accepted as part of the newspaper fraternity. She noted aprovingly that at a Hyde Park picnic "before long we had to find a quiet spot where Mr. [Heywood] Broun could write his column." She wrote and filed her column under the most adverse circumstances; neither illness, travel, nor crowded calendars were permitted to interfere. She would arrive late in the day, she informed Flora Rose, the head of Cornell's Home Economics Department, and would ask if she could have a stenographer when she arrived "as I will have to do my daily column and get it off right away." When winter storms forced her to take a train rather than fly to Washington after visiting her daughter Anna in Seattle, her biggest worry was where would she file her column: "Yesterday all wires were down along the railroad for almost five hours and I thought I would never get my column filed in time. Today I'm taking no chances and am getting it off while we wait. . . . It is good for my typing anyway, as I have to do it myself, but I am a bit sorry for those who have to read it." On another occasion she dictated the column to Tommy, who was balancing her typewriter on her lap while Elliott drove them from Denton to Fort Worth, Texas.[30]

In September, 1936, she came down with the grippe and a fever so high that Franklin canceled some campaign speeches to hurry back to the White House to be with her. Who was doing Mrs. Roosevelt's column? he asked Tommy, and said he would be very glad to do it for her. "His offer was deeply appreciated," Eleanor reported to her readers. "We want to pass it on to you so that you will realize what you missed, but we refused courteously and rapidly knowing that if it once became the President's column we would lose our readers and that would be very sad."[31]

"Mrs. Roosevelt is a magnificent trouper and a real newspaper person to carry on under such circumstances," George Carlin, the manager of the United Feature Syndicate, said to Tommy.[32]

Eleanor's fellow-columnists enjoyed giving her advice, usually in their columns. "Of course Mrs. Eleanor Roosevelt is new at the column-and-diary profession or racket and one should not be too harsh," wrote Franklin P. Adams, whose "Conning Tower" in the *Herald Tribune* was devoted to a diary in the style of Samuel Pepys once a week. "In . . . yesterday's 'My Day,' . . . she tells of having tried to get, though not where, a Chuddar shawl for Colonel Howe, probably Louis McHenry Howe. She tried in three places, unnamed, and at the fourth, also unnamed, found that an effort would be made to get the shawl. . . . We are not her editor, but if we were we would say, 'Get names.' " The manager of the syndicate sent the column to her, saying "I agree with his comment heartily." She had not wanted to advertise the shops, she replied, or to use names without asking people's permission, but she would try to do better in the future. "I fear I have been trained to be too careful."[33]

Similar advice was offered by Damon Runyon a year and a half later. He wanted to know what she had for lunch, who were the interesting people to whom she referred, and what was interesting about them. She took the criticism in good spirit and tried to bear it in mind, but when she was hurried, which was often the case, her sentences were sometimes wordy, her verbs weak, her nouns abstract—so much so that the syndicate occasionally felt obliged to delete. Of one such paragraph, William Laas, the managing editor, complained that "the guests are not named, nor are the organizations they represent, and the question under discussion is not stated in so many words. These essential details are left rather mysterious."[34]

"I realize you are right," was her contrite reply.

She was not the only Roosevelt to begin a column in 1936. Alice Longworth had been recruited by a rival syndicate and was enlivening the Republican press with her political asperities. "I think Alice is having a grand time," Eleanor wrote their mutual friend Nan Wood Honeyman. "She certainly writes well. I wish I were as free as she, though I do not wish ever to be as bitter."[35]

The difference between the two was the basis of a skit, "Alice and Eleanor, or These Little Girls Make Big Money," which was put on at the stunt party of the Women's National Press Club in March, 1936. It showed a tall lady in riding clothes with a knitting bag at her side sitting at a desk next to a tea table. She poured tea, knitted, and picked away at her typewriter. The sign at her desk read, "Roosevelt, E." At another desk, labeled "Roosevelt, A.," sat a woman with a large handbag, a lot of cigarettes, and newspapers. She smoked, glanced at a paper, wrote fitfully, strode up and down. They finished their columns simultaneously and, crying "copy," left the stage. Then two distraught editors appeared. One, tearing his hair, read a tender, domestic little piece about a lovely tea hour around a roaring fire with Harry Hopkins reading fairy tales and Rex Tugwell piling logs on the Red Flames. That, screamed the hysterical editor, appeared in hundreds of newspapers under the name of Alice

Roosevelt Longworth. The other editor, equally upset, found that under Eleanor Roosevelt's name there had appeared a column about the New Deal perishing of a potato diet and on the verge of being borsched to death.

The copy boy, the skit ended, was to blame, for "he had put Eleanor's syrup on Alice's desk and Alice's vinegar on Eleanor's desk."[36]

Whatever Eleanor's stylistic shortcomings, the column was popular. When editors left it out for a day readers protested. "I have a feeling," Bruce Bliven wrote in the *New Republic*, "that the New York sophisticates are all wrong and that the country as a whole likes the sort of person Mrs. Roosevelt has in her column demonstrated herself to be—friendly, unpretentious, possessed of inexhaustible vitality, a broad interest in all sorts of people and a human wish for their welfare." Her column was then appearing in 59 papers; a week later, right after the 1936 election, the *Pottsville* (Pennsylvania) *Republican* was added, a subscription that her syndicate considered "next only in importance to the President's carrying Pennsylvania." Though her circulation was smaller than some other columnists', it was respectable. In February, she appeared in 62 papers with a circulation of 4,034,552; Westbrook Pegler was in 110 papers with 5,907,389; Dorothy Thompson was in 140 papers with 7,500,000; Heywood Broun was in 42 papers with 2,829,487; and Raymond Clapper was in 49 papers with 3,653,000.[37]

When Eleanor first became a fellow-columnist, Westbrook Pegler approved of her; "about the only two things in the world that Pegler seems to like are 'Snow White and the Seven Dwarfs' and Eleanor Roosevelt," wrote Carlin.[38] Pegler's enthusiasm bubbled over in a column datelined San Francisco, March 17, 1938, in which he described her day there:

It had been another routine day in the life of one who is stingily described as the "most remarkable" and "most energetic" woman of her time in this country, but who deserves more than that. I think we can take the wraps off and call her the greatest American woman, because there is no other who works as hard or knows the low-down truth about the people and the troubles in their hearts as well as she does.

Pegler went on to describe Eleanor's lecture on peace, a performance that he considered the more creditable "because she works in the straitjacket of diplomatic and political restraints. . . . Mrs. Roosevelt has been before us for five years now. We know her better than any other woman, and she knows the country better than any other individual, including her husband, and the profit is all on our side."

But not long after this column appeared Pegler soured on the New Deal, the Roosevelts, and the American Newspaper Guild, and he began to challenge Eleanor's credentials as a columnist. She was no more eligible for membership in the American Newspaper Guild, which she had promptly joined, he insisted, than he for membership in the DAR; she was "gainfully employed" as a journalist, as the guild constitution required of members, only because she was the wife of the president. The first step toward rehabilitating the guild would be to get rid of those who did not belong, starting with her. The president, with whom Mrs. Roosevelt discussed the column, advised her to ignore it. "Why get into a bad-smells contest?" he said.

She was not going to get into an argument with her "kindly fellow columnist," she wrote a few days later. She acknowledged that as the wife of the president she was in a different position than other columnists: "That has not always been the case and will not always be so in the future. In the meantime, I must worry along as best I can, facing situations that I find myself in, and doing the best I can with them as they are."[39]

In a private letter George Carlin, a good friend of Pegler's whom he also syndicated, protested Pegler's challenge to Mrs. Roosevelt's eligibility: "Big names come and big names go, but a big name goes nowhere unless, through the quality of the daily delivery, the author can hold a following." Recalling that in 1936, the year "My Day" had first appeared, Alice Longworth had also begun a column along the same lines, Carlin continued:

If you will remember back, as long as I can remember, it had been the aim of newspapermen to get interviews with Princess Alice for twenty years without result. It had been thought that if she ever wrote, her stuff would make a great feature. The only trouble with the idea was that when it came to writing, she just couldn't write. Her stuff fell by its own weight and disappeared from the column field.

My Day goes on and on, not because it is written by the wife of the President of the United States, but because it is an honest projection of one of the great personalities of our own time; a woman great in her own right, and, as a newspaper columnist, possibly the best trouper of them all, never known to miss a deadline.[40]

Much as she enjoyed doing her column, Eleanor's secret aspiration was to write a novel or a play—she had always been a fervent admirer of creative writers. "I have always been sorry that I did not have the courage to go to see you when you were living in Poughkeepsie," she wrote Dorothy Canfield Fisher, who, since she considered Eleanor Roosevelt the greatest woman in the country, was somewhat overwhelmed by this unaffected, almost hero-worshipful tribute.[41]

Eleanor did not think she had the technical knowledge to write a novel but she had long toyed with the thought of doing an autobiography. The preface and footnote material that she supplied for the volume of her father's letters she had edited had brought pleas from family and friends for more stories about her early years. Her conversation was filled with anecdotal material from those years, and on the Florida Special on the way back from Puerto Rico in 1934 she had held a group of correspondents spellbound with reminiscences of her wedding day twenty-nine years earlier and how Uncle Ted had stolen the show from her and Franklin. She discussed the project of an autobiography with her literary agent, George Bye,* in the summer of 1936. He immediately saw its

---

* Her first literary agent was Nannine Joseph. But since Nannine was also Franklin's agent Louis Howe placed Eleanor with George Bye, telling Nannine it was not right for her to be the agent for both the president and First Lady. Nannine became Eleanor's agent again in the late forties.

possibilities and begged her to begin, and by autumn, as she traveled with the president on the campaign train, sections were being dictated to Tommy.

Most authors would have considered writing an autobiography a full-time assignment in itself, but Eleanor did not slacken any of her other activities. She performed the election chores her husband assigned her, filed her column, did her lecture stint, discharged her official duties as White House hostess, and, of course, dealt with her voluminous mail. Some literary advice that she offered a farm woman from the Ozarks at that time shed light upon how she approached her own autobiography. Mrs. Alma W. Johnson of Rogers, Arkansas, had not sought literary guidance; like thousands of others she just wanted to pour out her troubles to the sympathetic soul in the White House. But Eleanor found in Mrs. Johnson's chatty twenty-page account of rural vicissitudes a sweetness of spirit so moving and readable that she sent it to Henry Goddard Leach, who published the "poignant document" in the *Forum*. The publishing world became interested, and Simon & Schuster thought there might be a book in her life story. But Mrs. Johnson did not quite know how to begin, so Eleanor dispatched a long letter of encouragement and advice:

Block out your early youth, start with your very first memory, putting in as many incidents as possible which will show up your relationship to your parents, the effect of circumstances upon you, the things you learned and the way your character was formed by the circumstances of your life and the influence, conscious or unconscious, of your parents.

If you do that and will send those chapters to me, I will correct grammatical errors and spelling and send them to Simon and Schuster.[42]

Although the lady in the Ozarks, even with Mrs. Roosevelt's help, was unable to produce a satisfactory draft chapter, Eleanor, adhering to the plan of work that she had outlined, and with her incredible ability to shut off the outside world and concentrate upon the task at hand, made steady progress with her own story. By late autumn an exhilarated George Bye was showing the first part of the book to Bruce and Beatrice Gould, who had recently taken over the *Ladies' Home Journal* and were on the lookout for features with which to reverse the magazine's declining fortunes. They promptly purchased the serial rights for $75,000 and urged Eleanor to push on. "An evening buried amongst old letters," she wrote. "Why does one keep old letters?" Some, unfortunately for future biographers, went into the fireplace that winter. The people at the *Ladies' Home Journal* were "all aglow" with what they had seen, Fannie Hurst reported; they were delighted with her "fine clear prose" and the "simplicity and forthrightness of the narrative."[43]

Although she was little more than halfway through, Eleanor was sufficiently satisfied with what she had written to attend a party that the Goulds gave to celebrate the appearance of the first installment. She was so excited at the prospect of being the guest of honor at a literary party that she first went to the wrong address. She finally arrived at the right place, breathless, wearing a large black hat whose sweeping lines reflected her exultation. Radiant and happy, she took her place in the receiving line along with the Goulds and other *Journal* authors, including Dorothy Thompson. "I have written as simple and as truthful a story as I could write," she told reporters at the party. "It was quite a job, but most exciting, all of it." She had such a good time at the party that she stayed "an unconscionable time." As she said her good-bys to the Goulds, she astonished them with the remark: "I can't tell you what it means to me to have this wonderful recognition for something I have done myself not on account of Franklin's position."[44]

The Goulds were not happy with the later chapters. While the early ones had been vividly evocative of a New York society that had vanished and of a childhood that had been unexpectedly painful and insecure, and were, the couple felt, "moving and veracious" and written with "startling honesty and courage," some of the chapters she was now bringing in were "superficial and thin." Suddenly her story had stopped being "the story of a human being and become almost a mere chronicle of events," Gould wrote her. "Now I don't think your life has become suddenly less interesting. But you have ceased suddenly to write about the most interesting aspects of it." He wanted her to tell "the inner story . . . because it is all women's story made more important because you are the person you are and occupy the position you occupy."[45]

She came to his office to work on revisions. They wanted the revealing phrase and telling detail. Could she give an exact description of her mother-in-law? Could she remember her husband's first words when he realized he had polio? Bruce Gould, a brusque man, burst out at one point, "But this chapter is simply a listing of places you went and people you met. It has nothing to say—in fact—it's terrible!" Mrs. Gould cast a reproving glance at her husband, but Eleanor took his criticism quietly. Insecure as a writer, she welcomed tough editing. She was herself a disciplined worker willing to do the best she could and would not waste time bewailing her failures and frustrations, but she offered a sympathetic shoulder to other writers on which to weep. "You do get yourself into a state of jitters," she consoled novelist-friend Martha Gellhorn, who was in the throes of a new book. "It is better to write it all down and then go back. Mr. Hemingway is right. I think you lose the flow of thought by too much rewriting. It will not be a lifeless story if you feel it, although it may need polishing."[46]

The Goulds rightly perceived that the later chapters dealing with her years in Washington and her own entry into politics after her husband was stricken with polio were not as well written as the early ones. But it was not, as they thought, that the chapters were "hastily written," but because there was so much she could not say. She could not let herself go as she had in speaking of her childhood. "Freedom is necessary for the development of the creative spirit," she had once said in explaining why women were not as creative in some of the arts as men. Women were obliged to defer to conventions to a far greater extent than men, and that blunted their creativity.

Franklin went over the manuscript carefully. He was a good editor, and in the earlier chapters his comments were chiefly stylistic, such as "the contrasts must be emphasized." In the final chapters, however, he was concerned with substance. He was displeased with her account of his efforts to get into a uniform during the war, which she had written from her own point of view, to explain why she had been unwilling to try to influence his decision either way. He made a large X through this section, commenting, "This is *at least* unfair to me." He wrote out his version of what had happened and she included it as he wrote it. He did not like some of the phrases she used describing the onset of his polio, such as "one night he was out of his head," and she deleted them. When she said that Elliott had never really liked Groton as James did, his comment was "too rough," even though it was an understatement, and when in writing about her brother Hall's divorce she quoted Mrs. Selmes as having said, "If you love a person, you can forgive the big things. Infidelity under certain circumstances need not ruin a relationship," he struck out the phrase about infidelity.[47]

Anna and John were also unhappy about the last chapters when she left the manuscript with them during a visit to Seattle. There was an undercurrent of "bitterness" in the later part of the work, and although it dealt with a most difficult time in her life, it did not show how she had mastered her bitterness and developed her present philosophy of life. They felt that her quarrel with Anna over the room that she had given to Louis Howe should be left out and hoped that she would modify expressions that made it appear "that you had little part in, and little interest in, your husband's career." She softened offending passages, rewrote others.[48]

As she reworked the last chapters, the Goulds began to purr. She had picked up the "dramatic thread" again, Bruce wrote encouragingly, but he pressed her to deepen her account of her husband's illness with additional material on how she felt upon seeing that her whole life would have to be revised. "What you have given of your philosophy of learning to adjust yourself to the difficult business of life is so sound, so illuminating, that you cannot blame us for wanting more."[49]

Nothing in *This Is My Story* as it finally was published was false but much was said circumspectly. The Lucy Mercer affair went unmentioned, and her struggle with her mother-in-law was muted; her "night-of-the-soul" could be glimpsed but dimly. And yet, in retrospect, considering that she was First Lady when the book was written, it was astonishingly frank, and this was the public's appraisal of the volume when it appeared.

There had been some criticism of the Goulds within the rabidly anti-Roosevelt Curtis publishing organization because they had accepted a Roosevelt book, but their editorial judgment was swiftly vindicated when the "smash success" of *This Is My Story* became a major factor in helping the *Ladies' Home Journal* overtake *McCall's* and the *Woman's Home Companion*. "Even more pleasing than this liking expressed in numbers was the exciting discovery that Eleanor Roosevelt's biography was read, in effect, by everyone—in government, parlors and slums."[50]

Following serialization, the autobiography was to be published in book form by Harper & Brothers. In advance of the book's appearance Eleanor had several sets of the *Ladies' Home Journal* containing the complete autobiography bound in limp leather and marked in gold letters for Franklin D. Roosevelt, Anna Roosevelt Boettiger, Malvina Thompson Scheider, and Earl R. Miller.* The copy she gave Franklin was accompanied by a jingle:

> This may not look it but it is,
> A book which will some day appear
> It promises to be a whiz,
> So little less you'll get my dear!

On her way through New York City in early November she went to Harper's to receive her copy of the book. "It looks much more important than I had ever imagined it would be, but I am still inexperienced enough to feel a real thrill and to be very proud when Mr. [Cass] Canfield said that they considered it a good piece of work and were glad to be the publishers."[51]

The book was widely acclaimed because the experiences she described in it were, she discovered, widely shared. The "harmless childish weaknesses of character" that she had written about in language that was "classic" in its "plain simplicity," said Dorothy Canfield Fisher, are universal. The painfully honest account of her struggle to overcome shyness and insecurity, wrote educator Alice V. Keliher, "will help young people in their adjustments to life more than anything else written." Women embraced the story as their own. "I saw so much in the story so far that every woman experiences," wrote one.

Old Bishop Atwood touched on another aspect of the book's appeal Eleanor had been too harsh in judging her own character, the bishop thought, but had "succeeded in making a living picture of a social life now in the past." Karl Bickel, the former president of the United Press, thought it was one of "the greatest human documents he had read in modern times," and Captain Joseph Patterson, the president of the *Daily News,* in a bold black scrawl let her know that "I think your book is splendid; and that it may become a classic." There was praise, sweet to her ears, from Alice Longworth, who at a party was heard to say "Have you read it? Did you realize Eleanor could *write* like that? It's perfect; it's marvellous; she can *write* . . . all at the highest pitch."[52]

As Alice Longworth acknowledged, Eleanor could write, but the basic appeal of *This Is My Story,* like the basic appeal she had as a lecturer and columnist, flowed from her personality. "You see I think you are a kind of genius," wrote Dorothy Canfield Fisher. "Out of your personality and position you have certainly created something of first-rate and unique value—not a book or statue or painting—an example."

* Franklin, for Christmas, 1936, had distributed bound copies of the speech he had delivered at Chatauqua, New York, in August, 1936, "I Have Seen War, . . . I Hate War." Copy number 1 went to his wife; number 2 to his mother; the next five to children; number 8 to Missy; number 9 to Daisy Suckley, a Hudson River neighbor; number 10 Grace Tully; number 11 to Marvin McIntyre; number 12 to Steve Early; number 13 to Doc McIntire; number 14 to Bill Bullitt; numbers 15 to 24 to the members of the cabinet beginning with Secretary of State Hull.

39. *Without Louis Howe — The 1936 Campaign*

THE 1936 CAMPAIGN was the first without Louis Howe. For Eleanor, whose life had been molded by this misshapen eccentric genius almost as much as by Mlle. Souvestre, his death left a void as impossible to fill as it was for Franklin, with whose rise to the presidency Louis' name would be forever linked.

Louis' final decline began in the autumn of 1934 when his breathing became more labored, his eyes more sunken, his thin frame more wasted. He found it an ordeal to walk to the office and began to stay in his paper-littered bedroom off the Lincoln room. It was directly across the hall from Eleanor's sitting room, and his pajama-clad figure, wracked with coughing, was often seen shuffling from one room to the other. In January, 1935, he took a turn for the worse, and the annual Cuff Links party of those who had been associated with Roosevelt's 1920 campaign was canceled. Franklin and Eleanor had no heart for a party without Louis, who had always been the impresario on such occasions, dreaming up stunts and writing scripts with Eleanor as a willing accomplice. In March, Eleanor warned his children, Mrs. Mary Baker and Hartley, that while there was no immediate danger, their father needed cheering up and letters would help. Ten days later, after a bronchial collapse, he drifted into unconsciousness. "He seems to cling to life in the most astonishing manner," Eleanor reported to Molly Dewson, "but I am afraid it is the end."[1]

But he rallied, opening his eyes two days later to ask for one of his Sweet Caporals. For another year, much of it spent under an oxygen tent, he battled for breath and life. When Louis' wife Grace could not be at the White House, Eleanor watched over him faithfully. She kept track of what he ate, insisted that he follow the doctor's orders, kept him informed on the comings and goings in the White House, and encouraged him in his hopes that he would manage the 1936 campaign as he had the others.

When the doctors recommended that he be moved to the Naval Hospital it was Eleanor who took him there in the White House limousine and did not leave until she saw him settled. He went "peacefully," she reported to Grace, and only got into a "tizzy-whiz" because no telephone had been arranged.[2]

From his hospital bed he continued to plot strategy for the coming campaign by way of memos dictated to his secretary, Margaret Durand ("Rabbit"), and the telephone. When the inspiration seized him he insisted that "Hacky," the White House switchboard operator, put him through to

Franklin immediately whether the president was at Hyde Park, Warm Springs, or in bed. The president finally requested that Louis' direct line to the White House be available only from 10:00 A.M. to 4:30 P.M., but he also asked his chief aides to treat Louis with respect and courtesy no matter what orders he issued by phone.[3]

The president visited Louis at the hospital and those were moments of cheer, for Roosevelt was a great jollier, but there were not as many visits as Louis wished. Not only were the pressures of the presidential office remorseless, but Roosevelt had a faculty for blotting from consciousness the people who were unable to keep up with him. It was Eleanor, who had taken so long to appreciate Louis, who was steadfast to the end. She came to see him every day she was in Washington, "but yesterday he was too busy," she wrote Grace Howe, for sometimes he played the same game with her he did with Farley— that "he was still a busy man of consequence." She brought friends like Baruch, who promised to be helpful to his son Hartley and also to underwrite the Good Neighbor League, an organization that Howe felt would be needed in the campaign to appeal to Republicans and Independents.

He was saving his strength for the campaign, Louis informed Rabbit, and when the time came he would leave the hospital and move his operations to the Biltmore Hotel in New York. All of his friends joined in the sad charade that Louis would be with them in the campaign.* On the day Louis died Eleanor wrote Farley, "The President tells me that everything is to clear through both you and Louis and anything you are not entirely sure about is to come to him." That night, April 18, he slipped quietly away while asleep. Franklin was informed while he was at the Gridiron Dinner and Eleanor as she was giving her annual party for the Gridiron widows. The president ordered the White House flags to be half-masted, and the funeral services were held in the East Room. The choir of St. Thomas' Church, which Louis had joined when he first came to Washington with Franklin, sang the music he had always liked. The president and the First Lady accompanied the body to Fall River for the burial. "There is nothing to regret," Eleanor wrote in her column, "either for those who go, or for those who stay behind—only an inheritance of good accomplishment to be lived up to by those who carry a loving memory in their hearts."

There was one comforting thought, General Hugh Johnson wrote her: "In his impaired health he would have been very miserable as the campaign advances—and he not able to get into it vigorously." Eleanor agreed: "It was the happiest solution for Louis." She was grateful to Baruch: "You were wiser than the rest of us. You knew that it was medicine, food and drink to Louis to know that he was still in there fighting, doing something for Franklin."[5]

Even before Louis' death, she had felt that as a consequence of Louis' illness, Franklin was seeing a narrower range of people and his mail was being analyzed with insufficient sensitivity. "F.D.R.," she penciled on an aggrieved

---

* Although Louis played along, he had moments of doubt. "But you will be there," protested John Keller, a young man who came to the hospital to read to him. "No," Louis disagreed softly. "I will not be there. Franklin is on his own now."[4]

letter, "I think this letter answering is really vital. That was how L. H. built your popularity. I don't like R.C. but he's right about the way they feel. Couldn't one person take over this mail? E.R." He was "entirely right," she informed the writer, Russell Carney: "Louis Howe's not being on hand has meant that many people were not appreciated and had been forgotten." Molly Dewson complained that she was not able to get to see the president although the 1936 campaign was coming up and she had to get the women's division in readiness. Eleanor arranged for her and other women's division leaders to spend an evening with him. Afterward Molly commented, "I miss Louis Howe awfully."[6]

One of the jobs Louis had performed for Franklin was to keep track of the Roosevelt coalition, to evaluate by the statistical methods that were then available the inroads that were being made into the president's support from both left and right. The large followings attracted by the radical demagogues Huey Long, the Reverend Charles E. Coughlin, and Dr. Francis E. Townsend demonstrated that more rather than less action by government was necessary. Yet, on the other side, big business was outspokenly hostile to the New Deal, and men like the duPonts, Alfred Sloan, and John J. Raskob in alliance with conservative Democrats like Alfred E. Smith, Albert Ritchie, and John Davis had established the American Liberty League to oppose Roosevelt and his New Deal reforms.

The progress of the demagogues frightened the New Dealers, who raised an anguished cry for more vigorous leadership by Roosevelt. In early 1935, they were asking what had happened to FDR. What should she say in reply? Eleanor asked Franklin, sending him several letters that reflected the liberals' complaint. Perhaps she also shared their restlessness, but in selecting these letters for his attention her primary purpose was to make sure that with Louis no longer analyzing the White House mail, Franklin was aware of the questions among significant groups of his supporters. She felt, more strongly than her husband perhaps, that the New Deal could not be considered complete, but she also believed that significant changes in national direction could not simply be declared. They had to be worked at long and patiently.

A young man who described himself as still in difficult circumstances said he was prepared "to starve a little . . . if I knew that the man in Washington who captured my imagination and admiration in 1933 was unchanged." "Would you like to answer or shall I?" Eleanor queried her husband, adding, "It is rather nice." Franklin asked her to write and presumably indicated the reply she might give. "Nothing has happened to F.D.R., but reforms don't come in two years."[7] An Iowa Republican who had voted Democratic in 1932 confessed that she was beginning to lose hope because the old order seemed unchanged. "I would write her," Roosevelt suggested, "that there is one thing to learn and that is not to believe everything she reads in the newspapers. Also tell her that the position of the Administration has not varied one iota and that it still has the same objectives."[8]

Molly Dewson was another who communicated to Eleanor her alarm over the president's failure to exert more vigorous leadership. Eleanor replied to Molly along lines suggested by Franklin:

> These things go in cycles. We have been through it in Albany and we are going through it here. . . . He says to tell you that Congress is accomplishing a great deal in spite of the fact that there is very little publicity on what they have done. . . . The relief bill and the [social] security bill are bound to go slowly because they are a new type of legislation. If he tried to force them down the committee's throat and did not give them time to argue them out, he would have an even more difficult Congress to work with. . . .
>
> Please say to everyone who tells you that the President is not giving leadership that he is seeing the men constantly, and that he is working with them, but this is a democracy after all, and if he once started insisting on having his own way immediately, we should shortly find ourselves with a dictatorship and I hardly think the country would like that any better than they do the delay.
>
> The ups and downs in peoples' feelings, particularly on the liberal side, are an old, old story. The liberals always get discouraged when they do not see the measures they are interested in go through immediately. Considering the time we have had to work in the past for almost every slight improvement, I should think they might get over with it, but they never do.
>
> Franklin says for Heaven's sake, all you Democratic leaders calm down and feel sure of ultimate success. It will do a lot in satisfying other people.[9]

Sometimes even Roosevelt became impatient and was tempted to twist arms and apply the whip to Congress, and it was Eleanor who urged patience and perseverance. She lunched with some friends of World War I days—Caroline Phillips, Mary Miller, Anne Lane. "She was as dear, as affectionate, as simple and spontaneous as she was at 17 when I first knew her 35 years ago," Caroline recorded in her diary. But she also looked "very tired" and was "worried about the harm Huey Long is doing." The president was ready "to take the whip to Congress and abandon his conciliatory attitude. Eleanor tries to prevent this, but has only a limited influence," Caroline noted.[10]

In mood and objective she was allied with the New Dealers, but she felt that education, not the "whip," was the way to move ahead. Congress must have time, she counseled an Iowa progressive who wondered whether the president had deserted the progressive group in Congress for big business: "If he went on the air and forced legislation through, there would be the cry of 'Dictator,' and no willing cooperation."[11] In Warm Springs at Thanksgiving time she urged her husband to adopt "the same method he had used in Albany of holding a school of his own members in Congress so that they can get a chance to talk out their own ideas and he can get his across to them."[12] But Roosevelt felt he did not have the time, he told Sam Rosenman, who agreed with Eleanor about a school for legislators, "and besides, there are so many of them that we could never get around to all."[13]

Eleanor had strong convictions, but she respected her opponents and believed, moreover, that in a democracy reforms had to be both gradual and subject to revision. The objectives set forth by people like Huey Long, she wrote a correspondent, were fine; the problem was to obtain them "without too much dislocation and too much hardship to everyone concerned."[14]

Nor did her strong disagreement with the American Liberty League alter her warm feeling for Al Smith, one of its chief architects. Louis had been "a hater" in politics, "the most intense hater I have ever known," she said; he never forgot and rarely forgave a politician who had crossed the president. But Eleanor, as columnist Arthur Krock noted, did not seem to take "her husband's political wars personally. She has seen a lot of feuds and reconciliations in politics." Krock's comment was prompted by the one-day sensation caused when it was disclosed that Eleanor had invited Al Smith to stay at the White House when he came to Washington to address the American Liberty League on January 25, 1936. Smith declined the invitation. Had not Mrs. Roosevelt understood, Krock wondered, that the invitation to Smith, when he was coming to Washington with the avowed purpose of blasting the president, would be considered suspect? People had to understand Eleanor Roosevelt's "simple and candid" nature, he was told by White House aides. She considered the White House her home. She was an extraordinarily direct person with a feeling of warmth for Smith, and had invited him without considering the political implications. The president had had nothing to do with it.[15]

One of the most bitterly fought measures in the 1935 Congress was the social security bill. There were differences among its advocates over a national versus a state approach, over the size and method of contribution, over whether it should be a new agency or lodged within the Labor Department. And there was the more basic opposition of the Republican party to the principle of social security, which conservative businessmen felt would lead to the "ultimate socialistic control of life and industry."

Eleanor's "old crowd" reflected the virulence of the conservative opposition. She invited the ladies of the exclusive Fortnightly Club to hold their March meeting at the White House and proposed that "social welfare" be the topic of discussion. Her cousin Helen Robinson, since the Club's Board of Governors did not dare write directly, was asked to convey to Eleanor their fears that they would not feel free while receiving her hospitality to criticize the administration and to disagree with pending legislation. It had not occurred to her that the social security bill was political, but if the board could think up another subject, she would have no objection: "Of course, I would have expected them to criticize administration measures where they touch on politics. I cannot see why everyone should be expected to think the same way about anything."[16]

Faced with strong opposition to the very principle of social security, Molly Dewson, although she had strong views on the specific features of the bill that were in contest, said she would take a bill "anyhow it's drafted." Eleanor felt similarly. She did not expect to get a complete "security program" in the next two years, she told her news conference, but hoped to see the program launched. Asked about the differences among the proponents of social security, she replied: "I have always been amused to note that those who want a great deal more, and those who want a great deal less done, find themselves, unconsciously to be sure, working together and preventing the accomplishment of a moderate middle-of-the-road program."[17]

"You've done more to influence thought in the past 21 months, than anyone except your husband," one of her newspaper regulars wrote her at the beginning of 1935.[18] Educate! Educate! Educate! That was her theme. It was part of the bond between herself and Molly Dewson. Molly sent her a leaflet advertising a Democratic rally in Michigan with speakers on the "New Work Relief Program" and on the CCC. "Dear Eleanor," Molly scrawled on it, "Aren't the men fun imitating the girls and becoming 'reporters' on special subjects instead of making general gas talks."[19]

She was "much more interested in possible far-away developments and [the] steady increase of women's influence, which, I feel, tends to ameliorate bad social conditions," she told Martha at an early stage in their friendship, "than I am in any immediate political developments." In a last interview that he gave to Bess Furman of the Associated Press, Louis Howe was equally sanguine about the long-range ameliorative effects that women could have on politics:

> If politics divides, as it may, very sharply along the lines of the humanitarian and there are ten years in which to see how this experiment of females in government is working . . . and if they make good, and if the great mass of the people conclude they want New Deal ideas in recreation, labor, schools, and want to support that line—and if in time there arises some woman who gets the confidence of the people as a whole, there might be the argument advanced that the problems of the day are problems which have been neglected by man since George Washington, and men don't seem to understand what it's all about. The people may say: "Let's try a woman out." I don't think it's at all probable but there's nothing so clear now as the humanitarian issue.[20]

Eleanor had swiftly discouraged Louis when he had broached the idea that she might be the person the country might turn to—with a little prompting from him. But the idea was occuring to others. A Missouri congressman sent her a local column proposing that she be named the vice-presidential candidate in 1936 as a way of rescuing that post from oblivion; the congressman seconded the nomination. But, as Eleanor wrote Martha Gellhorn, she was interested in the mobilization of women's influence for basic reforms and sensed instinctively that she would be more effective as an educator if she were "in politics but not of it."*

Roosevelt's strategy for the 1936 election placed heavy stress on the campaign as an opportunity to educate and inform the electorate. He outlined his plans to the women at the dinner in mid-December, 1935, that Eleanor had arranged at Molly's request. It would be a New Deal, not a Democratic party, appeal, with a special effort made to reach the new groups which had a stake in the continuance of the Roosevelt policies—workers, farmers, Negroes, young people, women, independents. The opposition was formidable because of the

* A distinction drawn by the sociologist Daniel Bell, discussing Eugene Victor Debs.

wealth it commanded and because it had the support of 85 per cent of the press,
and thus there had to be a major effort to counter its propaganda and get the
truth into every home. The women's division had the most experience with a
campaign based on truth-telling and falsehood-exposing. Roosevelt counted on
the women's division, he told them, and wanted the party to make wide use of
their educational techniques. Molly sent Farley a post-dinner synopsis of the
session with the president with the admonition that "in carrying out his ideas,
we rely on you." To insure doubly that Farley did not pigeonhole the decisions,
Molly sent a copy to Eleanor.[21]

Under the plans outlined by Roosevelt the women were to be given more
space at headquarters, their budget was to be increased, and they were to have
the help of the men in obtaining government officials as speakers. His active
campaign would begin with his address at the Jackson Day dinners, he told the
women, and from that date on the ban on government officials making political
speeches was off and the whole organization should be geared to countering
Republican propaganda in the Republican-controlled press. He also said that
he wanted a "Friends of Roosevelt" type of organization set up to appeal to
those not functioning in the regular party organizations and an effort made to
vitalize the Young Democrats through a national contest for the best speech on
the New Deal.

Molly immediately drafted a letter that she asked Farley to send to the
members of the cabinet. "Dear Henry, Frank, Harry, Harold, Frances, Arthur,
etc." it read,

> The President has told the Women's Division of the National Democratic
> Committee to go ahead full steam in answering the avalanche of Republican propa-
> ganda after January 8th, when the Democratic campaign will open with the Jack-
> son Day Dinners.
>
> He also said that after January 8th there is no ban against government officials
> speaking at political meetings. No one knows the record better.
>
> Will you please have prepared for the use of the Democratic National Com-
> mittee a list of those in your department who are excellent, good and fair speakers
> upon whom we may call. . . .

During Howe's tenure the political chain of command had been clearcut:
Roosevelt, Howe, Farley. That, at least, was how Molly Dewson saw it. "Mrs.
Roosevelt told me in January that the 'high command' which I presumed meant
the President, Mr. Farley and Mr. Howe had decided that the bulk of literature
issued in the campaign should be the Rainbow Fliers. This statement was based
on the reception given the fliers in the 1932 campaign."[22] With Louis gone the
question of who was to carry out the commander-in-chief's directive became
acute. Theoretically it was Jim Farley, national chairman, postmaster-general,
and chief dispenser of patronage. He was loyal and effective, a professional
politician who, however, did not particularly appreciate the New Deal as a
movement of ideas and values or have much rapport with many New Dealers.

Farley was a technician, not a progressive crusader. During a national
reconnaissance tour in late winter, 1936, Molly picked up reports on the West

Coast that Farley was building a machine to make him president in 1940. "Just imagine JAF as President!!" she wrote incredulously to Eleanor; "for one thing he had better turn Methodist." Eleanor, who had a warm feeling about Jim, discounted the report: "Molly, I can't believe this is Jim's idea." She got along with the national chairman, but the exchange between the two women indicated their awareness of his limitations. Molly was under attack that spring by Emma Guffey Miller, the Democratic national committeewoman from Pennsylvania and sister of Senator Joseph Guffey, a highly influential Pennsylvania Democrat. Molly did not think Farley supported her in that contest with sufficient enthusiasm. "I go to your defense with loyalty and ardor practically every day," she wrote him. "The few times I have disagreed with you I have told you and no one else except Mrs. Roosevelt to whom I feel primarily responsible." Eleanor intervened on Molly's side. Farley retreated: "Regarding appointments," he wrote Eleanor, "please be assured that I will discuss them with you, and be governed by your wishes on anything I do relative to the activity of women."[23]

Like the president, Eleanor doubted that Farley and his headquarters staff, oriented as they were toward the traditional party organizations, were able to run a New Deal rather than a Democratic party campaign. Edward L. Roddan,* formerly the White House correspondent of the International News Service, was sent into headquarters to back up the redoubtable Charlie Michelson. Eleanor, like Franklin, communicated directly with Roddan although Michelson was supposed to be in charge of countering the attacks of the opposition. "Would you tell Mr. Michelson for me," Eleanor wrote Roddan, that she had heard that *Hell Bent for Election* by James P. Warburg, in which this young dissident Democrat charged that Roosevelt had carried out the Socialist rather than the Democratic party's program, was being "tremendously read and quoted, and perhaps should be answered." She had also heard that Marriner Eccles, the administration's leading defender of deficit spending, was very good at explaining "the whole monetary situation. Could he be induced to write an article . . . ?" The pamphlet the committee had prepared, "Little Red Schoolhouse," was good for speakers and reference material, but the average person would have to be given "something a little easier to read. I have just given the President some campaign leaflets [the Rainbow Fliers] and something of that kind is more useful for the average people in cities or rural districts."[24]

The communications to Roddan reflected White House dissatisfaction with the Farley-Michelson leadership. Roosevelt was almost abrupt in rebuking Farley after Farley's address to Michigan Democrats in which he predicted that "the governor of a typical prairie state" would be the Republican presidential nominee. "He, Too, Came from 'A Typical Prairie State'" the Republicans countered in a leaflet carrying a picture of Abraham Lincoln. "I thought we had decided any reference to Landon or any other Republican candidate was inadvisable," Roosevelt sternly wrote Farley. When an unrepentant Farley subse-

---

* One of "the three musketeers," as the three press-association correspondents assigned to the White House were dubbed. The other two were Frances L. Stephenson of the Associated Press and Frederick A. Storm of the United Press.

quently referred to Alfred M. Landon as the "synthetic" candidate, Roosevelt called in both Farley and Michelson and told them that no further statements should be issued without White House clearance. Roosevelt was in charge of the campaign, and to the extent that anyone was serving the role that Louis had in previous campaigns, Eleanor did in part, sitting in on budget meetings and through the women's division as well as through talks with Farley, trying to school him in her husband's concept of a New Deal campaign.

She accompanied her husband on the "nonpolitical" tour that he just happened to take at the same time the Republicans were meeting in Philadelphia. There were stops and speeches in Arkansas, Texas, Oklahoma, and Indiana. The nomination of Governor Landon was no surprise, Eleanor reported in one of her "nonpolitical" columns during the trip, but what platform would he run on? "For once the Republican Party seems to be made up of as many varying elements as the Democratic has often been!" But she was concerned about the Democratic platform: "We are on the move and things are better, but we have not yet arrived and we must not lull ourselves to sleep with a false sense of achievement."[25]

Two weeks later the Democrats convened in Philadelphia. Molly organized a breakfast for women delegates in order to deploy her forces. Eleanor thought it wiser not to come: "I would love to be at a breakfast in Philadelphia but am afraid I will only be able to come over for the day with Franklin. Otherwise, I might get myself into trouble!"[26] Although she was not at Philadelphia, her influence was felt. For the first time women were granted parity with the men on the platform committee, a measure of how far they had traveled since 1924 when Eleanor and her feminine colleagues had sat outside the locked door of the Resolutions Committee. "Women are more interested in the policies of the Democratic Party than in any question of power or patronage, and we are exceedingly grateful that the Convention has taken this tremendous step," a delighted Molly Dewson commented. Eleanor had conveyed the women's views on the Republican platform to Franklin, who was personally supervising the drafting of the Democratic document: "It might be useful in Democratic planks of interest to women." The women were jubilant over the Democratic document. "I have been telling you girls for years why I believed in the Democratic Party," Molly exulted to her cohorts, "but I could never tell you in such beautiful language." On every seat in the convention hall the women's division had placed a packet of Rainbow Fliers. There were 219 women delegates and alternates at Philadelphia compared to the 60 who had been at the Republican convention, and eight of the Roosevelt seconding speeches were made by women. Their large role at the convention symbolized the recognition they had achieved under Roosevelt. Much of the credit belonged to Molly Dewson, the best "she-politician" of his time, said Michelson, but Frances Perkins, after she had finished her formal speech at the women's breakfast, brought the audience to its feet in a spontaneous ovation when she added,

I know that many women in this country when they go to vote in November for Franklin Roosevelt will be thinking with a choke in their throats of Eleanor Roosevelt. . . .

She has gone out courageously, in the face of unfavorable criticism, not only to meet the people as a friend but to use that contact to make of herself a channel through which the needs and hopes and desires of people could be carried to places where solutions could be found to their problems.

If ever there was a gallant and courageous and intelligent and wise woman, she is one.[27]

While this eulogy was being delivered in Philadelphia, Eleanor was at the Arthurdale commencement handing out diplomas. Two days later she accompanied the president to Philadelphia for his acceptance speech before the more than 100,000 people packed into Franklin Field. The Philadelphia Symphony had played, Lily Pons had sung, and John Nance Garner had formally accepted renomination as vice president. But it was a crowd that was waiting for Roosevelt. He arrived at the podium on the arm of his son James—after a "frightful five minutes" when in the crush his steel brace had buckled and, out of sight of the crowd, he had fallen. Composed, buoyant, and smiling, he came forward.

"We have conquered fear," his speech began, and he proceeded to recall the troubles of 1932–33 and what his administration had done to overcome them. Now there were "new difficulties, new problems" which must be solved. Freedom was "no half-and-half affair. If the average citizen is guaranteed equal opportunity in the polling place, he must have equal opportunity in the market place." This nation was poor, indeed, if it could not "afford to lift from every recess of American life the dread fear of the unemployed that they are not needed in the world." When he said "this generation of Americans has a rendezvous with destiny," the huge crowd "nearly went crazy," said Agnes Leach one of the leaders of the women.

"The greatest political speech I have ever heard," commented Ickes. For ten minutes the crowd roared its approval, as Roosevelt, surrounded by his family, stood and waved. Eleanor's thoughts were less on the drama than on the expectations of the people as a consequence of her husband's speech: "A man must come to a moment like this with a tremendous sense of responsibility, but that must be very much augmented when he realizes by watching the crowd about him what his thoughts and words are going to mean to innumerable people throughout the nation."

To her schoolgirl friend Bennett (Mrs. Philip Vaughn) she wrote the same day: "For the good of the country I believe it is devoutly to be hoped that he will be reelected, but from a personal point of view I am quite overcome when I think of four years more of the life I have been leading!"[28]

Elated by the convention, several of the women—Molly, Agnes Leach, Caroline O'Day, Democratic national committeewoman Mrs. William H. Good, Frances Perkins, and Dorothy Schiff Backer, a recruit from the Republicans—turned up at Val-Kill the next day to rehash the convention and get their marching orders from Roosevelt. The president was in no hurry; he had his own clear picture of how he intended to pace his campaign: August in Washington with "nonpolitical" forays into the areas of flood and drought, no political speeches in September either, and four or five major political speeches in October. Two weeks after the convention he took off on a cruise with three of his sons; his destination was Campobello, where Eleanor would report to him on the situation at headquarters. "We are losing ground every day," Ickes fretted. "Meanwhile, the President smiles and sails and fishes and the rest of us worry and fume."[29]

While Franklin was cruising on the *Sewanna*, before going to Campobello his wife stopped in at headquarters to meet with Farley, who dealt with her as one professional to another, for she was a woman, he felt, who had a "real 'sense of politics' " and a "genuine gift for organization work."[30] She also had sessions with Molly Dewson, Stanley High, a former clergyman whose journalistic aptitude made him a fluent speech writer, and Michelson. Afterward she drafted several brisk memoranda. The basic one went to the president with copies to Farley, Michelson, High, Early, and Molly Dewson: "My feeling is that we have to get going and going quickly." She listed the questions she had brought up in her conferences at headquarters, to which she thought there ought to be answers in black and white that would reach "us" at Eastport by July 27 or 28 "when the President expects to be there." She urged that the publicity-steering committee be organized immediately, asked that minutes be kept of its meetings and that a copy be sent to the president, "and if the committee is willing, one to me as well." Some of the questions: Who was responsible for suggesting answers to charges, etc.? Who would actually do the radio work under the aegis of the publicity committee? Who was in charge of research? ("I gather if the President o.k.'s it, the aggressive campaign against Landon's record will begin before Landon's acceptance speech.") Who was collecting and organizing the Landon data? There were twelve questions in all, ending with the suggestion that Representative Sam Rayburn of Texas, who was to head the Speakers Bureau, should come in "at once to plan the policy and mechanics" and the additional suggestion that it would be well

to start some Negro speakers, like Mrs. [Mary McLeod] Bethune to speak at church meetings and that type of Negro organization. More and more my reports indicate that this is a close election and that we need very excellent organization. That is why I am trying to clarify in my own mind the functions at headquarters and have the President see a picture of the organization as clearly as possible in order that he may make any suggestions that he thinks necessary.

A supplementary letter to Farley expressed the hope "that when Ed Flynn gets back you will draw him into headquarters not only for consultation but for some definite responsibility. He is a pretty good executive organizer and Louis found him very valuable in the last campaign." Louis had trained her well.[31]

The memos she requested arrived at Campobello: two pages from Charlie Michelson; a "things are beginning to click" outline from Stanley High, who was heading up the Good Neighbor League; an explanation from Steve Early that he had been tied down at the White House and able, therefore, to spend only one day at headquarters; a letter from Rayburn's assistant saying he would reply when he arrived in New York (which turned out to be August 18); and a nine-page single-spaced letter from Farley. Yes, he would draw in

Ed Flynn "full time." They were keeping minutes at headquarters and Eleanor and the president would receive copies. Leon Henderson, formerly chief economist of the NRA, was being brought in to head up research. Eddie Roddan was compiling the material on Landon. He (Farley) would cooperate in every way with the Labor party that Sidney Hillman was organizing in New York State and thought it would bring an added 150,000 voters to the national ticket. He reviewed the situation state by state and promised to send her all reports and letters that came in from the states. So far as Negro participation in the campaign was concerned, Will Alexander, Tugwell's deputy at the Resettlement Administration, was drafting the committee's plans. Farley did not think it wise to move too actively in August, he summed up, except to tool up the headquarters operation; but the president should, as he had planned, travel widely and inspect New Deal projects.

Though Farley was optimistic he was not yet ready to predict, as he did just before election, that Roosevelt would carry forty-six out of the forty-eight states. Far from it. In early August he forwarded to Eleanor a supporter's dream that Roosevelt "would win the election by a large majority, carrying 37 states . . . [including] Mr. Landon's home state," and his accompanying comment was that "we must get a few laughs out of the campaign." Uncertain about the outcome, Farley felt that the more militant New Dealers should be sidelined during the campaign, meaning especially Rex Tugwell and Harry Hopkins. Was it accidental that when the president's schooner pulled into Welchpool, Harry Hopkins was there, he and his wife having come as guests of Eleanor Roosevelt?

She herself was a controversial figure in the 1936 campaign, and some of the president's more skittish advisers, although not Farley, "felt that she ought to stay in the background."[32] Her support of Negro rights (see Chapter 44), her insistence on pursuing her own career, her outspoken views, often slightly in advance of those of her husband, and the widespread complaint that she had commercialized the First Lady's role caused some politicians to fear that the campaign might well turn into a referendum on whether the public preferred the old or new style of presidential wife. Alice Longworth hinted at this in an article she wrote on the ideal qualifications of a president's wife. She by no means disapproved of Eleanor's conduct as First Lady; in fact, as an activist herself with an insatiable interest in politics, she rather admired her cousin, but in her article she wondered whether people might not feel that "we didn't elect her, what is she horning in for?"[33]

The American Liberty League made Eleanor a primary target in its efforts to lure the Democratic South away from Roosevelt. Early in 1936 Raskob, duPont, and Sloan helped finance a gathering of southern Democrats if Macon, Georgia. Its purpose was to assault the New Deal root, branch, and leaf, and to launch a presidential boom for Georgia Governor Eugene Talmadge, idol of the wool-hat boys who referred to Roosevelt as "that cripple in the White House." As the "grass roots" Democrats filed into the hall for the meeting every seat had on it a copy of the *Georgia Woman's World*, featuring a two-column photograph which Vance Muse, the promoter of the meeting, described as "a picture of Mrs. Roosevelt going to some Nigger meeting, with two escorts, Niggers, on each arm." Harry Hopkins accused Sam Jones, a Washington public-relations man who worked for the Republicans, of having hatched the plans "to smear Mrs. Roosevelt in Georgia."[34]

Among the hate items circulated anonymously in the campaign was a bit of rhymed scurrility directed at both the Roosevelts:

> You kiss the negroes
> I'll kiss the Jews
> We'll stay in the White House,
> As long as we choose. . . .

Steve Early and Marvin McIntyre, both southerners and both among the president's more conservative advisers, were unhappy about Eleanor's racial views. Steve was furious, she knew, although he did not say anything to her, about her garden party for the girls from the reformatory in the District of Columbia. Eleanor had visited the District's Training School for Delinquent Girls early in May, 1936, and, "horrified" by the conditions she found there, she determined to draw the attention of Congress and the District commissioners to them. Consequently, she invited the head of the school to bring her girls, three-quarters of them Negro, to the White House. "They were treated exactly as any other guests are treated and taken to see exactly what any other guests are taken to see." She made one concession to local custom: the girls, Negro and white, remained in separate groups, segregated as they were at the school, and were served refreshments in separate tents. A few Negroes were offended that Eleanor, too, had deferred to the pattern of segregation, but the bulk of the Negro press realized that the important issue was not the segregation but that the First Lady had received as White House guests a group of girls most of whom were colored. The *Afro-American* noted that she did this in the wake of criticism "for appearing at colored gatherings and posing for photographs with colored people. . . . When she's right, the President's wife knows no such word as retreat." She knew that Steve had blown up to others, including the president, about this garden party; "Franklin, however, never said anything to me about it."[35]

She so worried some of the president's aides that there were reports she was considering curtailing some of her outside activities in view of the elections. To a friend who wrote expressing the hope that one such report was in error, she replied, "The piece in the paper had no basis—in fact I have neither talked to anyone or considered doing anything different from what I have always done."[36] Carrie Chapman Catt had been apprehensive that the campaign would increase the attacks on Mrs. Roosevelt. "The wife of a President or any other high official, suffered more from attacks upon him and his policies than did the man himself," she cautioned her friend, adding that she was sure "these were not altogether comfortable times for you." She was wasting her sympathy, Eleanor gently advised her: "I think I am more hardened to criticism than the

President is, and it makes very little dent upon me, unless I think there is some real justification and something should be done."[37]

In March, the newspaper women had put on a skit at their annual party that underscored how drastically Eleanor Roosevelt had transformed the role of First Lady. A solemn-faced delegation appeared before a masked woman to inform her that her husband had been nominated for president and that she, as well as he, had to prove she was equal to the office. Then the delegation fired such questions at her as:

"How many speeches can you make in twenty-four hours?"

"Have you ever gone down in a coal mine?"

"Can you write a newspaper column with one hand and shake 500 hands with the other?"

"How's your radio voice?"

"How many places can you be at the same time?"

"Can you remodel a White House kitchen?"

"How many states of mind are bounded by Reedsville, West Va.?" At this point the prospective First Lady fainted away.[38]

Ignoring the testimony of the newspaper women that the people liked their activist First Lady, the Republican strategists decided to make a campaign issue out of the proposition that Mrs. Landon would be different. Miss Nathalie Couch, a head of the Republican women's division, flew out to Topeka, Kansas, and after conferring with the Landons said she knew of no plans for Mrs. Landon's participation in the campaign. She expressed pointed admiration for the way Mrs. Landon was conducting herself, particularly her attempts to stay in the campaign background. "Mrs. Alf M. Landon does not intend to accompany her husband on any of his campaign trips and will devote the time from now until election to the care of her family," the *New York Times* began its account of one of the rare press conferences Mrs. Landon held. As the wife of the governor she had never held a press conference, Mrs. Landon noted, and intimated she would hold few in the future. "If Governor Landon is elected, Mrs. Landon will spend her time in the White House," Republican women orators proclaimed at their rallies.[39]

The homebody image the Republicans tried to create of Mrs. Landon caused great amusement among the Democratic women working in the campaign. "She did not dare open her lips. She was kept under very close control."

It was not Republican strategists alone who completely misread how women felt about the President's wife. A Democratic decision that although Eleanor could accompany the president on his campaign train she should stay out of sight did not survive the train's first stop. "Then it was discovered that the crowds wanted Mrs. Roosevelt. If she failed to appear on the platform they shouted for her until she did appear, and they cheered her just as heartily as her husband, sometimes more heartily. She smiled and waved but made no speeches. She never does when her husband is about."[40] Scripps-Howard columnist Thomas Stokes was struck by the way the faces of women "would blossom in smiles and up went their hands in salute" when they spotted Eleanor on the train, and wondered whether in the long run "the quiet pervasive influence of Mrs. Roosevelt" through women and the home "might not outweigh that of her husband."[41]

She celebrated her fifty-second birthday on the campaign train while it was crossing Nebraska and Wyoming. The Union Pacific Railroad provided a cake "large enough not only for our own party but for everyone on the train to share it." There was a telegram from the White House staff: "This is to assure a gracious lady who fills her days with good deeds on behalf of others that the home folk appreciate all of her kindness to them. All the workers in the Executive offices join me in wishing you joy and happiness on your birthday." It was signed by Steve Early.

She continued to do her column all through the campaign but it was carefully nonpartisan. The only marked deviation from this posture was a ladylike thrust at Cousin Alice, who was campaigning for Landon.* She did not name her cousin but referred to Alice's attack on the president, headlined "His Mollycoddle Philosophy Is Called Typical of Roosevelt," in which Alice had contrasted Franklin Roosevelt's philosophy of security, dependency, and the so-called easy life with Theodore Roosevelt's credo of the strenuous life. It was Alice's view that her father had conquered his childhood disabilities and taught the nation the Spartan virtues of toughness and self-abnegation while Franklin Roosevelt, having learned to adapt to his illness, now was teaching the nation how to live with the Depression rather than to overcome it. "No man," wrote Eleanor, "who has brought himself back from what might have been an entire life of invalidism to physical, mental and spiritual strength and activity can ever be accused of preaching or exemplifying a mollycoddle philosophy. Most of my mollycoddles have had too much ease, too much dependency, too much luxury of every kind."[43]

By the time they returned from the western tour, it was becoming clear that a Roosevelt victory, perhaps even a landslide, was in the making. "The western trip was almost too successful," Roosevelt wrote Bill Bullitt. Eleanor had never seen crowds like those they were encountering in New England, she wrote as the campaign drew to an end. In Providence she was overcome by nostalgia for Louis Howe. She and Tommy went into the station restaurant for a cup of coffee and she thought of the many times she had been there with her friend and mentor: "I could see his little figure walking through that familiar station with the coat hanging from the sagging shoulders and the clothes looking much too big for him."

In the final days of the campaign the Republicans threw discretion to the winds. Landon, a man of moderate, often progressive, views and genial temperament, lost control of the campaign to the most reactionary and intransigent Republican politicians, and Molly Dewson deluged Eleanor with samples of Republican scare literature. The railroads were warning their men that if Roose-

* Mrs. Longworth had seconded Landon's nomination, and as a columnist covering the Democratic convention wrote, "The talk is quite general that Mr. Roosevelt now is laying the groundwork for a third term" and asked the president to disavow such ambitions.[42]

velt were re-elected the roads would be nationalized and thousands fired. Grocers were being advised their businesses would be destroyed by administration taxes and regulations. One national GOP bulletin directed all state headquarters in the final days of the campaign to stress that the administration was controlled by the Communists. Eleanor's old friend and ally in the labor wars, David Dubinsky of the ILGWU, had been nominated by the American Labor party as a Roosevelt elector; the Republican National chairman called Dubinsky—a Socialist and intransigent anti-Communist—a Communist, the American Labor party little better, and every day called upon Roosevelt to repudiate Dubinsky. Far from being daunted by these charges of Communism, Eleanor wrote Judge Dorothy Kenyon, who had explained that she was supporting the American Labor party as a party with "an enormous future," that "I, too, must admit that the American Labor Party tempts me!"[44]

The most reckless Republican tactic was the so-called pay-envelope campaign in which corporations inserted warnings in their employees' pay envelopes that some future Congress would divert the insurance funds of Social Security to other uses. An indignant Roosevelt ordered his speech-writing team to take the gloves off for the wind-up rally at Madison Square Garden; they gave him what he wanted and he added a few punchlines himself. It was a speech designed to stir the audience to fighting pitch. It succeeded. There was a ringing enumeration of Roosevelt's commitments to the farmer, the consumer, the unemployed, the home owner, and the slum dweller, and after each pledge, almost like an incantation, "for all these things we have only just begun to fight." But the section that brought the vast crowd to its feet, that carried overtones of hubris, and was seized upon by the Republicans as confirmation of their charges that Roosevelt aimed to make himself dictator, was his harsh, almost exultant defiance of his enemies and detractors:

Never before in all our history have these forces been so united against one candidate as they stand today. They are unanimous in their hate for me—and I welcome their hatred.

I should like to have it said of my first administration that in it the forces of selfishness and of lust for power met their match. I should like to have it said of my second administration that in it these forces met their master.[45]

If Eleanor liked the speech, she did not say so in her column, which spoke only of the emotional quality of the audience's reaction. She had her own test of what a campaign speech should be. On the campaign train she had written, "And then when you listen to all of the President's speeches, you sharpen your critical faculties by asking yourself whether it is successfully informing the people of the nation." The Garden speech was a call to battle whereas she wanted campaigns to be schools in citizenship. Moreover, having gone through many campaigns in which the voters on both sides warned that victory for the other meant the doom of the republic, she no longer took such rhetoric seriously. "I wish," she wrote in mid-October, "I could convince myself that the defeat of either candidate would be so serious that it would make the victory for the side one believed in seem even more important. But the most I can feel is that we may have more difficult times if the opposition candidate is elected." And in another column that week end she wrote that her letters showed that the people wanted her husband's re-election "for very definite reasons, that they expect the next four years to bring some very definite achievements." She thought this was a good omen, for it showed that people were "really thinking and beginning to realize that their help is needed in order to accomplish any real forward steps."

How could she be so serene, people asked on the eve of the election. There was no point in making a fuss over the inevitable, was her reply: "What happens tomorrow is entirely out of our hands, the record of the past four years, the campaign that has been waged, all are over and whatever the decision may be one accepts it and builds as useful and pleasant a life as one can under whatever circumstances one has to live."[46]

The Roosevelts listened to the returns at Hyde Park. There was a buffet supper for family, friends, and close political associates, and by 6:00 P.M. everyone settled down to the business of listening to the returns. The president was in the dining room with his sons, Missy, Sam, Tom Corcoran, leader of the new crop of bright young New Dealers, and McIntyre, with four telephones at hand. Corcoran improvised songs on his accordion; "Oh, Landon Is Dead," was one of them. Harry Hopkins moved in and out, as did Henry Morgenthau, Jr. Most of the guests were in the library being entertained by Mrs. James Roosevelt and Eleanor, who was wearing a flowing white chiffon gown with a huge red rose in her belt. She worried about the food, about the guests who had not yet arrived, about the grandchildren who were not yet asleep. She did not have the president's capacity for sitting back and savoring the moment, letting others worry about the details.

The results were not long in making themselves evident. "Very quickly the people who can compute percentages seemed to be confident that the verdict of the people was in favor of the President." Eleanor, as usual, was not so easily convinced, but when the leaders of the women's division, who had been listening to the returns at the Biltmore Hotel in New York City, telephoned that they were sure of the outcome and wanted to drive up to Hyde Park with Nancy Cook, she bade them come. "They were so much elated by the results of their labors and the success of Governor Lehman and the State ticket and of Mrs. O'Day that they did not leave until about two a.m.!" She finally induced Franklin and the children to go to bed around 3:00 A.M. after talking on the telephone with Elliott and his wife in Texas.[47] "You were right—so right," Roosevelt wrote Farley, who the day before election had predicted that he was "still definitely of the opinion that you will carry every state but two—Maine and Vermont."

Eleanor found the feeling of the country toward her husband as revealed in the election returns and the messages that flooded in upon her afterward "a little awe-inspiring. . . . You cannot help saying over and over again to yourself: 'What a responsibility for one man to carry!' Of course, no man could carry it unless the people carried it with him." Behind this last statement was a concept that later times would call "participatory democracy." That is what she had wanted the campaign to be. She thought the mandate her husband had received, overwhelming though it was, needed to be continually revitalized and renewed by an involved citizenry. The "fundamental" task, "for the leader of a democracy, is to bring to the people the realization that true democracy is the effort of the people individually to carry their share of the burden of government."[48]

To her husband she put it more concretely. He needed to build someone as his successor. The party organization had to be transformed, as the women's division had been, into an instrument of education and citizen involvement in public affairs.

"Do let me know," she wrote him just before he boarded the cruiser *Indianapolis* for a trip to Latin America, "if you've decided anything about Harry Hopkins, Ed Flynn, or Eddie Rodden. The people in certain positions seem to me very important these next few years."[49]

Then she struck a gayer note. "You should hear the messages that come to us everywhere, by letter, by wire, by telephone! You could be a king or a dictator and they'd fight for you! Lucky you have no aspirations!"

40. *Wise As a Serpent, Guileless As a Dove*

————

BY THE BEGINNING OF Roosevelt's second term, his wife had become a virtuoso in making her views known and her influence felt throughout the vast reaches of the federal government. Of her husband it would later be written that "there never was a prominent leader who was more determined about his objectives and never one who was more flexible about his means." Something similar might be said about his wife's adeptness in the uses of government, except that in her case the flexibility related to the ways by which a woman exercises influence in a milieu where power was in the hands of the men. She had learned from experience that if women wanted to be effective in politics and government they needed "the wisdom of the serpent and the guileless appearance of the dove!"[1]

Since she held no office and possessed no authority except that which derived from her husband, she left it to official Washington to guess what she did at his request and what she did on her own, what she did with his knowledge and what she did in order to place a situation before him and thus prod him and his aides into action. Officials received invitations to lunch with her at the White House, and when she steered the conversation into some field of interest to her, everyone wondered if the president had put her up to it, and usually she did not enlighten them. Sometimes she invoked the president, as in the case of a conference on leisure and recreation, when she wrote that "the President thinks it would be a very good thing if we could have a meeting on leisure time activities. He does not want to have it a White House Conference, but he felt if it could be called he could give it his blessing." What the recipients of the letter did not know was that because of her interest in the problem she had gone to the president and suggested the national conference in the first place. How could they know, when the president himself liked to keep his associates guessing as to his wife's authority since it often served his purposes to have her test a plan's acceptability before he embraced it fully.[2]

They assumed that if anyone knew where the president was heading, she did, and to a large extent they were right. How often, remarked Grace Tully, had she heard "Mrs. Roosevelt examining the Boss on what was going to be done about such and such a situation." But he did not disclose himself fully to anyone, and much that Eleanor wanted to know he did not tell her. Sometimes his reticence reflected a reluctance to discuss the seamier side of politics. (For example, Esther Lape was interested in a friend's candidacy to become ambassador to Russia, but Eleanor reported that she could not find out anything, for "these little political deals are not the things they tell the ladies readily as you know.") More often Franklin kept silent because he wanted to keep open as many options as possible. "I'm just not *ready* to talk about that yet, darling," he would say to her. On a lovely October day in 1937 in Hyde Park when the maples and oaks were in full autumnal glory the president talked with the press, and Eleanor in low-heeled shoes with a ribbon around her hair listened intently as the reporters tried to find out how he intended to "quarantine" an aggressor. She would have liked to have asked some questions, too, she wrote the next day. Of course, she could ask him in private, "but it always seems to me a little unfair to force anyone to talk shop when they might be thinking of something else."[3]

Yet when at her own press conference she was asked about the frequent coincidences between views expressed in her column and by the president, she replied with the conciseness for which the press admired her: "You don't just sit at meals and look at each other." During one insistent dinner-party cross-examination Anna cautioned her, "Mother, can't you see you are giving Father indigestion?" Some of Roosevelt's friends felt she hurried him unduly. If there were matters she could not take up with him at dinner because of the presence of guests, she could bring them up when she went in to say good night or good morning—"if there's anything we want to talk about, we do." And on occasion she even hurried through the columned portico that led to the executive offices and slipped into his office to ask or tell him something, whispering in his ear if others were present. But she did not like to do that: "I always feel I am taking too much time and there are too many people waiting."[4]

She had other ways of finding out about Franklin's policies and plans. Often she passed on letters from troubled citizens to him asking how she should answer them, and occasionally these letters reflected her own uneasiness about some development. A Philadelphia woman asked her to use her influence "to defeat the awful increase in military preparedness." "FDR what is the answer?" she wrote across the top. "The answer to this type of letter is, I think, this," he replied, and summed up the argument against unilateral disarmament. "Write a letter along these lines," she in turn instructed Tommy.[5] A student at the University of Puerto Rico sent her a chapter of a book that dealt with democracy represented by the New Deal and asked, "Did I catch the real spirit of the New Deal?"

"FDR you are a better judge than I. Did she?" Eleanor inquired.

"I think this is pretty good," the president replied.

"Tell her an authority to whom I submitted her chapter thinks it 'pretty good,' " she instructed Tommy.[6]

"I was talking with a man the other day, and he said . . . ," she began a speech to a group of women. Impressed by the shrewd analysis that followed, one of her hearers asked, "Who was that man you talked to?"

"Franklin," said Mrs. Roosevelt.[7]

The officials in her husband's administration assumed she had his backing and knew she had a large public following, but the most important source of her influence was a personality that radiated goodness. "Charismatic authority," wrote Max Weber, represents leadership to which men submit "because of their belief in the extraordinary quality of a person." When the English novelist and pacifist Vera Brittain arrived at the White House for lunch she felt herself in the presence of a natural aristocrat; photographs of Eleanor had not prepared her for "the resolute, penetrating blue-grey eyes beneath their strongly marked brows" that caused her to forget every other feature of the First Lady's face and to hang on to every word she said.[8]

Eleanor refused to admit that she had any influence because of the power of her own personality, insisting that what she was able to accomplish had little to do with her as an individual. Rather, it had "a great deal to do with the circumstances in which I found myself."[9] She continually minimized her own importance. She advised a Texas woman whom she was encouraging to write and who decided an article about Eleanor Roosevelt was the way to break into the magazine market "not to tell only good things. . . . It will be more interesting if it is not too flattering. After all, you have only had the experience of helpful things whereas there are many people whom I have not been able to help and who probably feel that I could have done so if I had had the right understanding of their problem." When you know your own weaknesses, she said to a friend whose mother she had visited in her grocery shop, you know you are no better than other people, but because of your position you have a greater chance to do good. That is all. "You don't permit yourself false airs." She carried in her purse the prayer attributed to St. Francis in which the petitioner asks the Lord to grant "that I may not so much seek to be consoled as to console, to be understood as to understand, to be loved as to love . . ." We look at life as through a glass; the poet invests it with more poetry than it has in fact; the politicians see it as the struggle for power; Eleanor Roosevelt surrounded it with love. She profoundly influenced the thinking of some of her husband's aides, partly because she was the wife of the president but mostly by example. She insisted on being her natural self, and as Washington came to know her as a person rather than as a personage and began to sense her kindness, her genuine interest in people, her lack of egotism and boastfulness, it realized that here was no designing female Rasputin but a woman of mercy right out of First Corinthians. She ruled because she had learned to serve, and service became a form of control. She wanted people to feel that their government cared about them, and because she was in the White House she felt an added obligation to make people feel they knew her, had a right to tell her about themselves and to ask her for help.[10]

She showed compassion for all living things. "Can you suggest anything?" she asked Frances Perkins about a case that had come to her attention. "His legs are useless, his father is a drunkard, the home is very poor but he has put up a grand fight for an education." To Harry Hopkins at the Works Progress Administration, she wrote: "These poor gypsies seem to be having a difficult time. Is there any chance of their being put on a homestead in Florida or Arkansas, where they could be warm and where they might carry on their cop-

persmith work as well as farming? It seems to me the only solution for them."
When Steve Vasilikos, the peanut vendor who stationed his cart near the White
House, was driven away by the police, Eleanor wrote Steve Early from a
sickbed at Hyde Park that he should take it up with the district authorities: "I
would myself miss him on that corner. We had better let him stand at the White
House gate." A protest against the manner in which Army mules were disposed
of brought a memorandum to Steve Early: "Could the War Dept. either explain
the reasons for doing so or make the whole situation clearer as I am quite sure
they do not sell them without making sure they will have good homes."[11]

She transgressed against all the rules of tidy administration, though this, of
course, was in the New Deal style. She asked help for supplicants whom
officials often thought were malingerers and charlatans, and sometimes
were. "Aside from the fact that I am disappointed in finding your story was
made up entirely out of whole cloth," she wrote a woman in California, "I feel I
must call your attention to the fact that when a letter is received which is as
untrue as yours, it takes the time and energy of people here in Washington to
follow it through which really should go toward trying to help someone who is
really in difficulty."[12] She had not expected Governor Brann of Maine to help
an applicant personally with a loan which she had referred to him, she wrote,
slightly appalled, but since the governor and his aide had done so, Tommy
informed them that "the money she [Mrs. Roosevelt] has is all pledged at the
moment, but she does not want you and the Governor to suffer and she will
take over the note and pay as she can."[13]

Officials often took her suggestions as commands when she had really
meant them to use their own judgment, she said, but it was also true that she
made her wishes known rather forcefully. Sometimes she was naïve and sometimes she asked for things that really meant a great deal of effort, yet only the
most overweaning in her husband's administration did not respond to the disinterested desire to be helpful that was back of her steady flow of communications to all the government departments. It might violate all the rules of political economy, but how was one to say no to a woman who felt the exhilaration
of battling wind and snow on a wintry day and then immediately thought of
what the foul weather meant to the poorly housed and poorly clothed?[14]

Her methods of getting the bureaucracy to respond varied with the degree
of her outrage. Usually she sent a letter with a query—how should she answer?
What was being done? Couldn't something be done? "Right in the mails she got
a great many of these appeals," Will Alexander recalled. "She looked at the
thing and decided whose business it was in the government to find out about it,
and sent that letter with her own initials on it and wrote, 'Find out about this
letter. You know what it's all about.' You'd better do it. She never forgot."[15] If
she felt very strongly she invited the appropriate official to lunch and, since her
right ear was slightly deaf, placed him on her left regardless of protocol. Or she
asked him to tea. The day she received a delegation of sharecroppers in the Red
Room she invited Henry Wallace and Dr. Alexander to be present. Sometimes
she marched over to the offices of an agency in order to insure speedier action.
On a letter she had from the National Federation of Federal Employees pro-

testing the lack of housing for middle-income workers at a naval gun factory, she wrote,

Take to Mr. Hillman and Mr. Knudsen. Make appointment for me on Tuesday at 12 with Mr. Hillman and Mr. Knudsen together if possible. Call Mr. Hillman and ask if it can be so arranged and I will go to their office. I want to talk about housing. If Tuesday not possible would Thursday at 11:30 do?[16]

If an administrator's response to a letter seemed inadequate, she took it up with the president. She sent Acting Secretary of War Louis Johnson complaints she had received from residents of Maroc, California, that the Air Force's use of Maroc Dry Lake as a bombing range was endangering life and property; she did not like the Army's reply. "Give whole thing to F.D.R. and say I think answer of Mr. Johnson a bit lame!"

Experience and intuition taught her to which officials she was obliged to use the formidable words, "The President has asked me . . . " The readiness to do her bidding did not follow ideological lines. With Wallace and Ickes she usually invoked the president's authority. Wallace steered clear of her. On the way over to the White House, Wallace warned Will Alexander, whom he had just appointed administrator of the Farm Security Administration, "Now, Will, I want to give you some advice. You want to let that woman alone. She's a very dangerous person. You don't want to get mixed up with her." Wallace did not trust her judgment, Alexander thought. "I, of course, trusted Mrs. Roosevelt almost more than anybody I ever saw."[17] Ickes was as distrustful of her judgment as Wallace. With Hopkins and Jim Farley it was quite the opposite. Hopkins' aides were under standing instructions to give her whatever help she required, and Farley did her bidding even when he did not quite understand what she was after. Although Chester C. Davis, who succeeded George Peek as administrator of the AAA, was the leader of the "agrarians" as opposed to Rex Tugwell's "liberals" in the Department of Agriculture, he was a relaxed, kindly man, and Eleanor found him open-minded. When she came back from a trip to upper New York State where farmers had complained to her about the operations of the Federal Loan Bank she got in touch with Davis about the matter. "Here is a concrete letter showing just what I mean," she followed up a few days after speaking to him about it. "Will you see that someone takes it up and looks into other conditions which I feel sure they will find throughout New York State?" No mention of the president.[18]

She lunched regularly with the wives of the cabinet and hoped her example might inspire some of them to join her in some of her undertakings. Few did. Young Jane Ickes, newly married to the secretary, wrote her in October, 1938, that because of a common devotion to progressive causes, Mrs. Roosevelt might be able to give her some advice on how to avoid Washington's pitfalls. Eleanor replied that she would be happy to do so.

I think, however, that the person who can help you more than anyone else is Mrs. Morgenthau. She has succeeded in doing work which interests her in Washington, on things which are not controversial and which, therefore, do not jeopardize her husband's position. I think the general feeling is that our husbands have to do enough jeopardizing for themselves and therefore we should do as little as we possibly can along that line!

It is a little easier for me. . . . Because of my years and old affiliations, I am apt to be blamed singly and not to put quite so much on my poor husband.[19]

She comforted herself with the thought that the country realized she had her own point of view with which Franklin might not agree. And he did have his ways of conveying to people that in her activities and opinions she was an independent personality. Once she entered his office while newsmen were jammed around his desk for a press conference. She wanted to bid her husband good-by as she prepared to leave in order to attend Cornell Week. The president looked out at the falling snow and told her to telephone if she got caught in a snowdrift.

"All right. I will telephone you from a snowdrift," Eleanor called over her shoulder as she left the room.

"And she would, too!" the president told the newsmen. This was more than husbandly admiration; it was testimony to his wife's independence.

Once she asked him whether her advocacy of the anti-lynching bill might hurt his efforts to get southern votes for his rearmament program. "You go right ahead and stand for whatever you feel is right," he said. She was not wholly persuaded that he had meant what he said and repeated her question. "Well, I have to stand on my own legs. Besides, I can always say I can't do a thing with you."[20]

Franklin never tried to discourage her, she wrote later, discussing some of the controversy she had created.[21] But it was more than that. He approved. Just because he had to ease up on his efforts to get New Deal legislation, he wanted her to press harder. It helped politically with the groups whose claims he had to postpone and, more important, it helped him resist the temptation of following the easiest course. That was her old role. One of the reasons he had married her was to keep him from sinning. "She had stronger convictions than he on the subjects of social welfare and social progress," observed Arthur Krock, who had occasionally been invited to small family dinners by Eleanor. "She was also a very determined woman—determined not only to make a career for herself so that she would not be just the President's wife, but also to make a career that would in her opinion put pressure on her husband to pursue the path of social and economic reform that he was embarked upon." She was not, she said in later years, "what you would call a 'yes-man' because that wasn't what he needed." Nor was it what the president particularly wanted, she added. "He might have been happier, if he had always been perfectly sure that I would have agreed. He wasn't. And it was probably good for him that he wasn't. But there must have been times when he would have liked it if he didn't have to argue things." She acted as a spur, she said, "because I had this horrible sense of obligation which was bred in me, I couldn't help it. It was nothing to be proud of, it was just something I couldn't help."

Rexford Tugwell recalled:

No one who ever saw Eleanor Roosevelt sit down facing her husband, and, holding his eye firmly, say to him, 'Franklin, I think you should . . .' or, 'Franklin, surely you will not . . .' will ever forget the experience. . . . And even after many years he obviously disliked to face that devastatingly simple honest look that Eleanor fixed him with when she was aware of an injustice amenable to Presidential action or a good deed that he could do. . . . It would be impossible to say how often and to what extent American governmental processes have been turned in new directions because of her determination that people should be hurt as little as possible and that as much should be done for them as could be managed; the whole, if it could be totalled, would be formidable.[22]

They were, in the White House years, consorts rather than bosom companions. Her relationship to him was less intimate than some wives had with their husbands after three decades of marriage but she was more influential. She had a point of view, a platform, a following, and he was a large and secure enough man to respect her for it.*

Cabinet officers often grumbled, some of them used her, but generally they complied with her requests. Some, like Henry Morgenthau, Jr., did so because there were times when they wanted her to find out what the president's mood was before they went in to see him, sometimes even to intercede with him.

On one occasion Morgenthau, sensing presidential displeasure with his views on tax policy, wrote in his diary that he had gone to Eleanor Roosevelt. "I told her that if she would be willing to accept the responsibility I would like to place myself in her hands as I felt that Franklin and I were drawing further and further apart. She said she was going to talk to the President." A few days later the president seemed to have softened toward Morgenthau's views and remarked at the cabinet meeting that "he and his wife had a discussion on economics in the country. . . . When he got through he gave me a searching look," Morgenthau wrote in his diary. When Morgenthau and Hopkins were trying to get the president to approve a $250,000 special outlay for milk for needy children in Chicago and were getting no response, Morgenthau went to Eleanor. "I'll ask Franklin about it tonight," she told him, "not as though you said anything, but as though I were troubled." Her intercession worked, commented Morgenthau.[23]

The bristly Ickes occasionally sought her patronage for one of his projects. When she was in Knoxville, for example, he wanted her to drive through the newly opened Great Smoky Mountains National Park. She did and expressed her pleasure in a column. He even tried to enlist her in his empire building. The wife of the naval governor of Samoa complained to her about the sanitary con-

---

* The *World-Telegram* in January, 1933, had spoken of a "connubial Presidency" after Eleanor, citing the danger of presidential isolation, said that her correspondence was an avenue

through which WE [*World-Telegram* capitals] can keep in touch with the public.

Not in the history of the American democracy and of the Presidency has a mistress of the White House spoken to the public in this extensive way, and so far as we know, not in the history of the democracies anywhere has the wife of a President, in alluding to the performance of the Presidential duties, used the first person plural "we" or "us." In the case of Mrs. Roosevelt she welcomes the public to write not in the capacity of a representative of the President but as one member of a sort of co-partnership of interest.

ditions on that island after thirty-seven years of United States' ownership. She sent the letter to Ickes because Roosevelt had placed the Division of Territories and Island Possessions in the Interior Department. But in doing so, Ickes informed Eleanor, the president had excluded Samoa and Guam. "Needless to say, I would be happy if in the process of governmental reorganization Samoa and Guam should be transferred to the Division of Territories and Island Possessions." Eleanor, however, did not take up the hint.[24]

She was glad to agree to requests to receive the staffs of federal agencies at the White House, but she deftly put such visits to her own use. The assistant to the public printer, Jo Coffin, brought the women who worked in her office to tea at the White House. "The nicest thing of all," she informed Eleanor afterward, "was the little conference when you gathered the girls around you on the lawn. You spoke of the urgent need of raising the standard of living of the colored people." The Children's Bureau brought its child-welfare field staff to Washington. "The opportunity for informal discussion of problems with Mrs. Roosevelt following the delightful tea was the highlight of the conference," Katherine Lenroot, chief of the bureau, wrote Tommy.[25]

Eleanor was careful in dealing with the members of Congress, fully aware of how jealous that body was of its status and how quick to resent what it considered pressure from the president or his wife. Occasionally a flare-up of moral indignation caused Eleanor to depart from her rule not to comment publicly on what Congress was doing, but she did so circumspectly, almost always asking Franklin's permission beforehand. If she sent a letter to a senator or representative, the note that accompanied it was studiedly neutral; it was simply for the gentleman's information to do with as he saw fit and generally elicited a courtly letter of thanks. But even in this area, when she was confronted with injustice she was not to be contained, especially if there was some bond of fellowship, either political or social, to make a direct appeal for help to a congressman appear to be the most natural course. That was the case in the matter of the sharecroppers.

Sherwood Eddy, clergyman, reformer, and publicist, came to her with an agitated account of the reign of terror in Arkansas instigated by the landlords to keep their sharecroppers out of the Southern Tenant Farmers Union. Many had been evicted, and Eddy wanted to resettle them on a cooperative farm he had purchased at Hill House, Mississippi. He asked Eleanor if these sharecroppers could be placed on relief until the first crop was brought in. "Is there any way in which you could be helpful, if you feel he should be helped?" she in turn asked Hopkins. "I want to be sure, of course, that you think something should be done, but I was horrified at the things he told me." It was Tugwell's job, Hopkins told her, and Tugwell, with whom she promptly communicated, said the Resettlement Administration would be prepared to take over the farm but they must then have the management of it. Eddy refused, and Eleanor informed Clarence Pickett, who had brought Eddy to her, that "under the circumstances I do not know what more could be expected" of the government.[26]

She did, however, write Senate Majority Leader Joseph Robinson, an old acquaintance. Eleanor had been on the delegation in 1928 that had gone to Arkansas for Robinson's notification ceremonies as vice-presidential candidate, and she wrote him without invoking the president's name. She was troubled about what the leaders of the sharecroppers and Eddy had told her, she said; "I am very anxious about it and know you must feel the same way"—would it be possible to send someone down on a mission of reconciliation? Robinson proved to be wholly on the side of the planters; there was no trouble between landlords and tenants except that which was instigated by "a group of agitators from time to time," he replied, going on to say that the landlords were willing to provide houses for the tenants who had been evicted "but they were prevented from doing so by the agitators." Eleanor pressed no further. She had made her views known and done all she could, and there was no point in alienating a mainstay of Franklin's working majority in the Senate. "The situation is a difficult and complex one," she wrote Robinson mollifyingly. "The whole system is apparently wrong and will take patience and a desire on all sides to straighten things out ultimately."

Yet her desire not to irritate Robinson did not hold her back a few months later when the Emergency Committee for Strikers' Relief telegraphed her that there was "a new reign of terror against 5,000 tenant farmers in Arkansas. Wholesale arrests of striking farm workers. Thirty-five Negro and white men held in small jail at Earle . . . workers charged with vagrancy. . . ." She requested Hopkins to have someone investigate and let her know if this was true. Their man in Arkansas had confirmed the arrests, Hopkins informed her a few days later, and the Department of Justice had a man down there to see whether there had been any infringement of federal law. Her next request was for Hopkins to arrange relief for the sharecroppers.[27]

Eleanor's efforts to improve the social-welfare institutions of the District of Columbia usually involved Congress and usually meant getting the president's explicit approval. Jail Lodge #114 of the American Federation of Government Employees called her attention to the "unsatisfactory working conditions" in the District jail. "Take up after I've been there," she noted on their letter, meaning that she should take it up in her column, and in the meantime she had Tommy send the substance of the letter to District Commissioner George Allen. Allen readily acknowledged that the complaint had merit, but it all went back to getting more money from Congress. "Would it be proper for me unofficially to draw attention of Committee to this condition?" Eleanor queried her husband. "Yes—sure—!" was the economic reply. A two-page letter detailing the conditions she had found in the District jail went to all members of the Appropriations Subcommittee concerned with the District's budget. "We did a good job for the National Training School for Girls," Senator Copeland replied; "Let's help the jail!" Senator Capper went further than his colleague: "I spent a couple of hours at the jail and became convinced that you had not overstated matters. . . . I think it is wonderful that you are interested in a matter of this kind."[28]

The head of the League of Women Voters consulted Katherine Lenroot, the chief of the Children's Bureau, on how to persuade the Appropriations

Committee to vote more money for improved children's services in the District. Miss Lenroot's advice was to ask Mrs. Roosevelt to convene a conference of citizen's groups and interested congressmen. Eleanor questioned whether such an approach might not stiffen congressional resistance, and the president, to whom she mentioned her doubts, agreed. "The President thinks the Congressional Committee might look upon it as an effort to coerce them," she wrote the league, but if they would get her a list of all the things the Social Service agencies wanted, she would ask the chairman "if he would get the Committee together and let me come up there and tell them that I realize I have more opportunity to see things first-hand than many of them," and they might like to know what she had learned. Congress did approve a budget for child welfare, but she was distressed, she wrote the chairmen of the House and Senate subcommittees a few weeks later, that no coordinator was named. "I know your deep interest in seeing that the children of the District are well cared for. This seems to me so vital that I am writing to you in the hope that you will immediately exert your influence to clear up that point." It was a moment when Roosevelt's influence with Congress was at its lowest point, and Eleanor's note ended, "I am sending this simply as a private citizen and I hope that you will not mention that I have sent it to you."[29]

Cautious as were her early approaches to Congress, by the end of the thirties they were increasingly unorthodox, occasionally even daring. In January, 1934, she told the Citizens Committee on Old Age Security, "I could not possibly appear before a Congressional hearing on anything," but later she began to accept invitations to testify before congressional committees. She appeared before the Tolan Committee, which was investigating the problems of migratory workers, and was prepared to testify before a Senate subcommittee on discrimination against Negroes in defense industry. And in December, 1939, she created a sensation when she turned up uninvited at hearings of the House Un-American Activities Committee when it had subpoenaed her friends in the American Youth Congress.*[30]

Often she used a report on what she had seen on one of her endless journeys around the country as a peg with which to begin an exchange either with her husband or with the director of a government agency. "I can't say what happens to these reports," she was quoted as saying. "Some of them may never be read at all. Some of them I know have been. But I made them because I have been trained that way." She usually made notes on the things she thought might interest the president, and local officials and the public generally took it for granted that what she saw went back to him. "No other President has had a trusted emissary going about the land talking to poor people, finding out what is good and what is bad about their condition, what is wrong and what is right in the treatment they receive," wrote Ruth Finney.[31]

Eleanor was as proficient as the president in the nonpolitical tour and inspection. Wherever she went she toured government projects, saw an endless stream of visitors, questioned reporters about local conditions—often as closely as they asked her about larger matters—and avoided public discussion of poli-

* See Chapter 49, "FDR Administers a Spanking."

tics. Irrepressibly curious and a sympathetic questioner, she arrived in a community as her husband's inspector general, or so the local people thought, and came away its confidante.

"I would never presume to make recommendations," she insisted, speaking about the reports she submitted. But she defined "recommendations" in a Pickwickian sense, meaning they were not commands. "I forgot to tell you the other day how much impressed I was by the hospital for tubercular Indians at Shawnee, Oklahoma," she wrote Ickes in one of those missives she insisted were not recommendations. "I did feel, however, that the occupational therapy work might be made of more value if they could develop some of the arts, in which some of the Indians must have skill and do a little better work than is being done at the present time." If less than a command, this was more than a suggestion. Ickes was in a benign mood; he thanked her for her letter: "It is gratifying that you found time during your busy trip to visit the Indian Sanitorium."[32]

Except for the homesteads, she was more deeply involved with the WPA than any other New Deal agency, and she did not hesitate to offer advice, often quite bluntly. She criticized the poor public-relations job the agency did, stating that some project officials seemed to avoid publicity "for fear of stirring up trouble. This is an age old attitude and never leads anywhere successfully." She admonished Aubrey Williams that the NYA representative in a discussion over which she had presided had been "rather dull. . . . Do you think a little coaching as to how to keep an audience on the *qui vive* would be advisable?" She returned from a visit to New York City and was immediately on the phone to Williams about the difficulties encountered there by the WPA-sponsored nursery school: "I think Dr. Andrus [the director of the nursery] is probably more interested in doing a good job than in government regulations. There ought to be a way by which both can be accomplished." Aubrey's follow-up report caused her to explode:

The habit of having situations which arise investigated by the people about whom the complaint is made seems to me a most pernicious one and entirely futile. Exactly the same thing happened in the Illinois gravel pit situation. I do not see how you could expect a fair report from the people who are being accused of doing things which are not justifiable.

On the back of one of the letters in the series exchanged on this matter she wrote, "Give me these. Ask if he, Mrs. [Florence] Kerr & Harry [Hopkins] if he is in town would like to come & dine & talk NYA & WPA matters over. Will gladly have Mrs. Woodward also if they like." Her test of successful management was whether the job got done rather than whether a regulation was complied with. In Chicago she met at Hull House with the supervisors of Hilda Smith's Workers and Adult Education projects: "The main difficulty seems to be that Mr. Maurer because of the set-up has to contact so many people every time he does anything that most of the time is spent running around to the people above him rather than supervising the teachers." Couldn't Aubrey "dynamite" the WPA official in charge?[33]

Often she worked through the women in her husband's administration. She and Molly Dewson kept a watchful eye over all appointments on the distaff side to make sure that women were not overlooked. The right of women to be considered on the basis of merit for all jobs was still far from established. She protested Hull's plan to send a woman to succeed Mrs. Owen in Denmark; she and Molly would "far rather" see him "send a man to Denmark and put a woman in some other place." In 1937 Molly accepted an appointment as one of the three members of the Social Security Board, and Mrs. Emma Guffey Miller, sister of Senator Guffey and Democratic national committeewoman from Pennsylvania, maneuvered to succeed her. Eleanor and Molly considered Mrs. Miller too close to the old-line organization, too traditional in her political methods. "Molly has had a conception of work for the Women's Divison which I consider very valuable," Eleanor wrote Mrs. Miller, who had mounted a considerable campaign against Molly; "she has put education first and I think the women needed that more than anything else." Molly, backed by Eleanor, succeeded in having Jim Farley name Mrs. Dorothy McAllister of Michigan as director of the women's division. There was a weekly, sometimes daily, flow of memorandums from Mrs. McAllister asking for help, reporting on developments, building up regional meetings around her. Columnists spoke of the influence that Felix Frankfurter wielded in Washington through the many young lawyers, most of them graduates of Harvard Law School, whom he had spotted strategically throughout the New Deal. "Frankfurter's hot dogs," Hugh Johnson derisively named them. The women who looked to Eleanor for their marching orders and support were as numerous and perhaps more militant than Frankfurter's disciples.[34]

When women in the administration were attacked, as happened frequently, Eleanor defended them. There were periodic campaigns against Frances Perkins. "She has been quietly shoved in the wings," columnist Ray Tucker wrote in 1935, and her job was really being handled by the department's strong man, Edward McGrady. "FDR, this is being widely said. Is it part of the attack or has she not done well?" was Eleanor's query to her husband. "This is columnist's stuff and really silly," he assured her.[35]

Frances Perkins was one of the first targets of Representative Martin Dies, who accused her of malfeasance because she had not ordered the deportation of Harry Bridges, the radical leader of the Pacific Coast's longshoremen. When Dies threatened Miss Perkins with impeachment proceedings, her friend Ann (Mrs. Arthur Osgood) Choate sent an urgent call for assistance to Eleanor. She had talked with the president, Eleanor advised Mrs. Choate, who said he would appeal to the chairman of the House Judiciary Committee, Representative Hatton W. Sumners, on the basis of masculine chivalry to bring the matter to a vote—either to go ahead with impeachment proceedings or definitely turn them down. Then Eleanor offered some advice:

I realize that Frances is under a strain and I wish she could take it more lightly because I think it is purely a political attack, and in public life women must accustom themselves to these things in the way that men have. She is alone and I wish that the women of this country, particularly in the organizations, could be induced to realize what the true story is on the whole Bridges question. Frances has it and, it seems to me, could give it to the heads of the different organizations if they would only request it. Then their backing could be made vocal. At present, many of the Federation of Women's Clubs members, who met down here, are down on Frances because they believe she is a Communist. When you get women started along those lines they are like sheep. They think Dies is doing a wonderful job and do not realize that he is doing something to make himself personally popular with the sole idea of being candidate for President, and Miss Perkins was the easiest victim.

Frances does not know how to get on with newspaper people and neither has she a secretary who can do it. I did suggest that she try to get someone who would handle the press for her, but so far as I know she has never done it.[36]

Eleanor helped Frances, although she sensed a reserve in Frances's attitude toward her—perhaps it was Frances's fear that working too closely with Eleanor might make life more difficult for her in the man's world of the labor movement. The labor leaders had originally urged Roosevelt to appoint a man, and one of the stories current in Washington which, while not wholly accurate, was said to be in character so far as Eleanor was involved, described her as commiserating with her husband for the bad hour he must have put in with the labor leaders when he told them he had already made up his mind to appoint Miss Perkins. "Oh, that's all right," Roosevelt was said to have replied. "I'd rather have trouble with them for an hour than have trouble with you for the rest of my life." But it was Molly, not Eleanor, who had organized the campaign for Frances in 1933, and when in 1939 Roosevelt asked his wife to tell Miss Perkins, if she got the chance, not to oppose a reorganization measure that took the Employment Service out of the Labor Department, Eleanor passed the job on to Molly: "I think if you speak to her, it will have more weight than if I were to do it?"[37]

As at Albany, civic organizations prospered under Eleanor's patronage. She brought the White House closer to the civic-minded through their organizations, and by getting them a hearing from the president enabled him to hear viewpoints that otherwise might not have reached him. Organizations like the League of Women Voters, the National Association for the Advancement of Colored People, the National Public Housing Conference, the National Consumers League, the National Sharecroppers Fund, and the Conference on the Cause and Cure of War as well as the more radical groups such as the Workers Alliance and the American Youth Congress suddenly felt themselves on the inside of government, holding their sessions at the White House, being briefed by the First Lady on the president's plans and difficulties, and, because of her sponsorship, getting a hearing from press and public. "What on earth would I do without you in the White House?," Lucy Randolph Mason, a key CIO official in the South, exclaimed after an expression of interest by Eleanor had finally brought intervention by the Department of Justice in the case of a union organizer who had been badly beaten in Georgia.[38]

Eleanor's assistance to the housing groups when they convened in Washington in January, 1937, to press for passage of the Wagner Housing Act made up for what they considered the president's lack of enthusiasm for the bill in the previous session of Congress. Eleanor addressed the conference, invited its leaders to the White House to fill them in on the president's thinking, and relayed messages from them to the president and from the president to them.[39]

This time, with an assist from the president, the Wagner-Steagall bill was approved, and in September the United States Housing Authority was created. Nathan Straus was appointed administrator, and he promptly wrote Eleanor, hailing her as "one of the first 'housers' in the country" and expressing the hope that he could discuss his problems with her. "We are all very much pleased that, when it is organized, you will be able to have the new housing group at the White House for one meeting at which you will preside. . . ." He regularly sent her the figures on the housing loans that he had approved and reports on the progress of the projects, and he even discussed the design of the apartments with her. To install closet doors, as she had suggested, would add approximately \$225 to the cost of a dwelling unit, he advised her; every extra feature added to the costs and if he did not keep rehousing down to minimal standards he might endanger his hope to rehouse all slum dwellers. She did not protest, as she was more realistic now than she had been in 1934 about what Congress might be expected to sanction. "Surely closet doors are not worth \$225 per house!" she agreed. "Come to lunch to talk it over."[40]

She mediated between Esther Lape's Committee of Physicians and the president in regard to improved medical services. Esther had moved the American Foundation, of which she was the member-in-charge, into the field of the organization of medical care. Organized medicine, particularly the American Medical Association, had successfully resisted the inclusion of compulsory health insurance in the social-security system when it was set up, and in order to keep the issue alive Roosevelt had appointed an Interdepartmental Committee to develop a program to strengthen the nation's health services. But this committee had gone about its studies in a leisurely manner and Roosevelt appeared to have forgotten about the group when Esther moved in. Together with a group of liberal doctors she had completed a massive survey of medical practitioners on whether and how medical care should be reorganized. The report, published in two large volumes, showed that the AMA's opposition to government involvement in the delivery of medical services and the maintenance of standards did not represent the views of the medical profession in general.

Esther wanted the president not simply to glance at the survey but really to digest it, she told Eleanor, even though she knew better than to expect the president to go through two fat volumes. Earlier Esther had mentioned some thoughts she had on government's relationship to business, and Eleanor told her to write them down and she would give them to Franklin. "Oh, he would not be interested," Esther protested. "Franklin is interested in any idea that can be written down on one page," Eleanor replied. Although the President had told Esther and Elizabeth when they had talked with him in July, 1936, that he would meet with their Physicians Committee "if they had agreed upon any clear point of view," Eleanor found him reluctant to do so when she brought up

Esther's request for a meeting in February, 1937. She pried the reason out of
him. "Somehow or other, Franklin had it in his mind that he would in some
way have to line up with someone and he was not ready to do that." When
Eleanor assured him that this would not be the case, she was able to arrange a
date. She "infinitely" preferred one, Esther hastily notified her, when Eleanor
could be present, even if it meant some delay. She sent along the names of her
Physicians Committee.[41]

Franklin did not want to have dinner. "Lunch with me first," Eleanor had
Tommy wire Esther. "Thursday April 8th. As much time as they want." In
their talk with the president the doctors urged a partnership between government, medical schools, and hospitals in order to raise the standards of all medical care and to provide medical attention for the indigent. The first practical
step was to establish a Planning Commission to formulate a national policy,
they said, which led to the rediscovery of the Interdepartmental Committee
under Josephine Roche, and the president asked Dr. McIntire to talk Esther's
proposals over with the committee "and let me have a recommendation."

When the AMA learned what was going on at the White House it lifted
the statement of principles Esther's committee had left with the president and
endorsed them. Esther was not sure whether to be elated or alarmed, she wrote
Eleanor; "Of course they tacked on some nullifying clauses designed to lodge
everything with the AMA. This will never do. But it is revolutionary to have
these principles put forth under those auspices." In any case it was more important than ever to go ahead with the Planning Commission.[42]

The president evidently thought so, too, for, Eleanor telegraphed Esther,
"Franklin thinks it important to move at once. Will see you Monday or Tuesday a.m." In the end, Roosevelt decided not to appoint a new commission but
to have Josephine Roche's committee bring in a report, which it did in February, 1938.

Guided by the Roche Report and urged on by Esther and her group,
Roosevelt suggested to his Interdepartmental Committee that they convene a
conference to secure the backing of medical science as well as public-health and
citizens' groups for a program of action. Esther had reservations about the
Roche Report, which she felt did not sufficiently reflect medical and administrative realities. But the president had one central concern: "Esther, my interest
is in getting *some* kind of medical care to the submerged third that has now
practically none."[43] The conference was held in July, 1938. Out of it emerged
the Wagner Health Act of 1939, but the AMA raised the cry of "socialized
medicine" and the bill never came out of committee.

Esther refused to give up. Her group of doctors were "the genuine representatives of a powerful group of leading medical scientists opposed to the reactionary policy of the AMA," she wrote Eleanor begging her once more to
arrange a meeting with the president. "Could you have the meeting here in September?" Eleanor queried her husband. By September war had broken out in
Europe and Roosevelt had little time to think about health legislation, and in
fact though there would have to be some health proposals ready for the 1940
session, he was hesitant about meeting with Esther's group. "Franklin says he

does not want to get into any difficulty with the AMA just now when he has so much to contend with, and asks that this just be an off-the-record meeting." He saw them at the house rather than in the executive offices, and Eleanor served tea.[44]

Franklin was in retreat on domestic legislation in general. Although he adopted the reasoning of Esther's group, the "beginning" he suggested fell far short of their hopes. He asked Congress to authorize the construction of small hospitals in the needy areas of the country, "instead of waiting for a complete and perfected plan," such as the Wagner bill, "which would cost an awful lot of money."[45] This proposal, however, never emerged from committee either.

Roosevelt wanted medical care for the needy, but it is questionable whether he would ever have become as involved as he did without Esther's committee and Eleanor's mediation. Eleanor made a career of supplying the president with ideas of what might be done, placing him in touch with people and programs that otherwise might not have gained his attention.

Ickes did not approve of circumventing channels to reach the president, and called it getting in to see the president "through Mrs. R.'s back door." But this "back door" route to the president was open with Roosevelt's acquiescence. It enabled him to talk with people without the press knowing it and without the formality of giving them appointments. He recognized his wife's right to have as guests people who interested her as well as her friends, and if as a consequence Quaker pacifists, radicals, reformers, youth leaders, and "housers," who somehow neither he nor his secretaries ever managed to find time for, had a chance to talk with him, it was no disaster. He liked people and dominated the table talk no matter who the guests were, although he might comment to his staff the next morning that "Eleanor had a lot of 'do-gooders' for dinner and you know what that means." However, it was healthy for his staff to be aware that there were routes to his presence that they did not control. Eleanor did not abuse this prerogative. When she sensed that someone bored or irritated her husband, she had them to lunch or tea, and if she felt he might not want to see someone for political reasons, she made inquiries beforehand and guided herself accordingly. In any case, the list of dinner guests was always sent up to Missy, and if the guests did not interest him, Franklin pleaded work and dined in his oval study.[46]

As the thirties drew to a close, the jobless seemed to Eleanor to be a standing indictment of the American economy and an unredeemed claim on its conscience. She had grown close to Hopkins and the WPA because he and his top people were as ready as she to try unorthodox, even radical, methods to help the jobless. Franklin sensed political danger in the work projects started by the WPA for unemployed artists, musicians, writers, actors, and women, but Eleanor was all for them. There was "not the slightest doubt" in Aubrey Williams' mind "that had it not been for Harry Hopkins and Mrs. Roosevelt, for she was a powerful influence in support of width and variety in the work projects, the work program would have been much more limited in its variety and character."[47]

Eleanor wanted the well-off to visit the WPA projects because that would help them understand that "the unemployed are not a strange race. They are like we would be if we had not had a fortunate chance at life. . . . It is very hard for people who do not come face to face with suffering to realize how hard life can be." At Hyde Park Eleanor read aloud Martha Gellhorn's first story from *The Trouble I've Seen*, a series of WPA sketches, and some of her listeners wept. Then she was invited to the Colony Club to give a reading from the book. She trembled at the prospect, she said, but steeled herself to do it because it was important for the well-to-do to understand the situation of the unemployed.[48]

Because she felt the country had not as yet faced up in a fundamental way to the problem of the machine age, she was insistent that no plan, no point of view be rejected without someone giving it careful scrutiny. "There is a Mr. Albert Lytle Deane," she wrote Harry Hopkins, "who has submitted a plan to me. I, in turn, presented it to the President and he thinks it might be worthwhile to you to see Mr. Deane, and if, after talking to him, you think the plan has merit, the President will be glad to have you talk to him about it." Hopkins was a little annoyed: "Mr. Deane has discussed his plan with every official here in Washington at some time or other," he replied, and attached an analysis of the plan by Leon Henderson, who had found "very little of value" in it. Eleanor was not deterred. She wanted to be sure new ideas were not kept from the president. "This was sent me by a little man," Eleanor advised her son James, who was then acting as one of his father's secretaries, "and I just thought there might be something in it somewhere which would help you people who are working on the Supreme Court plan."[49]

A Tennessee farmer sent her a detailed proposal for establishing a silk industry in the United States. "He wants a silk industry. It was looked into but should we look further?" The president was sufficiently intrigued to send the proposal on to Wallace, inquiring, "Is there anything in this idea?" The labor costs were prohibitive, Wallace replied. "Did anyone go over this to find out if there is anything in it?" Eleanor asked her husband in regard to still another plan. "What can we say to Mrs. Roosevelt about this?" the president asked Lauchlin Currie, one of his administrative assistants. "A crank, and not worth bothering with," was Currie's summary judgment. But as long as someone looked into these matters Eleanor was satisfied. Usually they were wild goose chases, but one of the plans she passed on to Franklin was sent by Alexander Sachs, an economist with Lehman Brothers. In 1936 he had submitted a plan for agriculture, but in 1939 he came to the White House as the intermediary for Albert Einstein and other scientists who wanted to apprise the president about nuclear fission.[50]

In her search for a solution to the unemployment problem, Eleanor was as open to suggestions from the business community as from the labor movement and the left. It was through her* that John Maynard Keynes' letter on the 1937 recession dealing with the impasse between the business world and the New Deal reached the president. Keynes wrote:

I think the President is playing with fire if he does not now do something to encourage the business world, or at any rate refrain from frightening them further. If one

* Leonard Elmhirst sent it to her, requesting that she pass it on to the president.

is purporting to run a capitalist system, and not something quite different, there are concessions that have to be made. The worst of all conceivable systems is a capitalist one kept on purpose by authority in a state of panic and lack of confidence.[51]

Baruch—also through Eleanor—was another who advised the president to ease up on the business community. He sent her the statement he had made before the Special Senate Committee on Unemployment in which he had warned that it was wrong to rush from a "regulate nothing" position to a "regulate everything" position. She was not persuaded, Eleanor wrote Baruch later, but she was ready "to see us let business have some of the reforms which they think will solve their difficulties, not because I agree but because I think there is much in the psychological effect."[52] Her old friend Harry Hooker, now a Wall Street lawyer and counsel to Myron Taylor of U. S. Steel, was distressed to hear her say there was no solution known to her or to anyone else for full employment, and sent her a nine-page plan which called for repeal of the capital-gains tax, reduction in income taxes, and a ban on New Deal speeches attacking business. "Whether we like it or not, Capitalism is timid," Hooker summed up his recommendations.[53] Eleanor reported them to her husband, adding that she had also heard from a reputable economist that the way to bring about full employment was a large-scale housing program. She was for trying both. Fine, the president commented, but where was he going to get the money?

The First Lady was in advance of almost everyone in the administration in her emphasis on how much remained to be done despite New Deal achievements. At a Youth Congress dinner in February, 1939, a Republican speaker dismissed agencies such as the NYA and the CCC as ineffective and wasteful. "American youth does not want to be mollycoddled," the Republican official asserted; what it wanted was jobs. Eleanor was moved to make an impromptu answer. She agreed that WPA and NYA might not represent "fundamental" solutions; they were, she said quietly, stop-gap measures. But the NYA "gave people hope at a time when young people were desperate," and with the NYA and WPA we had "bought ourselves time to think." Although she believed in the measures enacted by the New Deal, she also noted that "they helped but they did not solve the fundamental problems. There is no use kidding ourselves. We have got to face this economic problem. And we have got to face it together. We have got to cooperate if we are going to solve it." Heywood Broun, who was in the audience, was so moved by her speech that he consulted his journalistic colleagues: "Am I just going into an impulsive handspring or is this one of the finest short speeches ever made in our times?"[54]

Because Eleanor was in advance not only of her husband but of almost all of his cabinet in urging that the "fundamentals" of the unemployment problem be confronted, she had to be careful not to give the opposition a chance to raise the cry of "petticoat government." Although the charge was completely inconsistent with the efforts to portray Roosevelt as a "dictator," that did not deter the administration's critics. When she was in Dallas in March, 1939, to lecture, Eleanor was presented by Governor W. Lee O'Daniel, a conservative Democrat. In his introductory remarks he said, "You've possibly heard of her husband. Any good things he may have done during his political career are due to her and any mistakes he may have made are due to his not taking up the matter with his wife." Was this southern courtliness or subtle Democratic aspersion? Eleanor promptly entered a gentle disclaimer: "A President's wife does not see her husband often enough to tell him what to do." Simeon Strunsky, who wrote the "Topics of the Times" column, enjoyed that. "Many a man who has had the privilege of talking with the President for five minutes in the course of a year or a whole administration has been known to go on ever after mysteriously assuming responsibility for most of the President's acts"; the First Lady was "too modest."[55]

But she knew the pitfalls of appearing to have any influence with Franklin. He had spent half a lifetime escaping the domination of his mother, and he resisted any kind of domination, especially a woman's. And Eleanor was a very strong-minded woman. "If the term 'weaker sex' is to be transferred from the female to the male of our society," commented Grace Tully, Missy's assistant, "much of the psychological groundwork must be credited to Mrs. Eleanor Roosevelt."[56] "Men have to be humored," Eleanor wrote in answer to Raymond Clapper's assertion that women were too emotional to be entrusted with large matters of policy. "I know that men have to believe that they are superior to women, and women from the time they are little girls have to learn self-discipline because they have to please the gentlemen. They have to manage some man all their lives." She loved the passage in Stephen Vincent Benét's "John Brown's Body" which described the lady of the plantation:

> She was often mistaken, not often blind,
> And she knew the whole duty of womankind,
> To take the burden and have the power
> And seem like the well-protected flower . . .[57]

Once, a student leader suggested the text of a message the president might send to a youth meeting; he noticed Tommy getting restive and finally she said tartly, "The President will write his own message." Later Tommy came to the young man and said apologetically she had not meant to hurt his feelings but if Mrs. Roosevelt were to go to the president and suggest what he ought to say "he will just get mad."[58] When Dr. D. E. Buckingham told the newspapers that Mrs. Roosevelt had secured him his job as District veterinarian, she wrote him sharply, "You must realize that I never actually ask for anyone's appointment. I simply stated your qualifications as I would have done for anyone who had done anything for us. You have placed me in a very embarrassing position, by having made it appear that I had used my influence." And she advised the president of the District Commissioners

that in the future I will be very glad if my name is not used in connection with any recommendation which I make.

I write these letters merely to give any information which I have when a man's name is up for consideration, and I would not, under any condition, want to influence your decision or have you do anything which was not in accordance with your best judgment.[59]

In a story about Ickes' appointment of Ruth Bryan Rohde to attend an Inter-American Travel Congress, the *New York Times* reported that Mrs. Roosevelt had suggested the appointment. She quickly wrote the secretary:

I hope you do not think that I was the person who suggested Mrs. Rohde for any position. I simply wrote you because the President asked me to do so. There is such a concerted effort being made to make it appear that I dictate to F.D.R. that I don't want the people who should know the truth to have any misunderstanding about it. I wouldn't dream of doing more than passing along requests or suggestions that come to me.[60]

The issue of her influence with the president also arose in connection with her promptings of her husband during a press conference at Hyde Park. The president was accusing the anti-New Deal coalition in Congress of gambling with world peace and the economic well-being of the country, and in the informal atmosphere of Hyde Park Eleanor spoke up to remind him of some vivid phrases that he had used at breakfast to illustrate his point. Mrs. Roosevelt "has come into the open as the guiding spirit and co-phrasemaker of her husband's program," Arthur Krock of the *Times* wrote afterward.[61]

"Did you notice that Mrs. Roosevelt during a press conference prompted the President?" John C. O'Laughlin, publisher of the *Army and Navy Journal*, excitedly wrote his friend Herbert Hoover.

Are they hereafter to cooperate rather than each to work one side of the street? Is the idea to advance Mrs. Roosevelt for something or other, even the Presidency? A fantastic notion, but in Washington suspicion follows any Roosevelt act. It may be, too, that the pair thought it advisable to show complete harmony in view. If so, the President will go much farther to the left during the remainder of his term, for you are aware of the extreme radicalism of the First Lady. . . . In any event, the incident is interesting and is welcome by the Republicans, who now feel they can attack Mrs. Roosevelt as a politician and thus avoid criticism for assailing a woman.[62]

"I should have learned by this time to keep quiet when I happen to sit in at the President's conferences," Eleanor told another member of the staff of the *Times*,

for every time I have ever opened my mouth at one I have got into trouble. But it seemed to be such a shame that the phrase he had used, telling us the same things at the breakfast table, couldn't be repeated for the correspondents, because it just wasn't as good a story without those graphic expressions. So I tried to help him out—and that's all to that.[63]

As much as possible she sought to minimize and conceal from public view her intercessions with the president. In December, 1939, Walter White of the NAACP sent her a report on an investigation of two lynchings in Mississippi, in the hope of publishing the report with her sponsorship. She sent it to the president. Back came a memo: "You should not accept a place as a member of the group but I suggest that you ask the Attorney General to look into this whole case to smell out any interstate activity or effect in the crime." Eleanor sent the report to Attorney General Murphy, saying that the president had suggested he look into it, and Murphy assigned Assistant Attorney General O. John Rogge to the case. In writing to Walter White, however, she omitted any reference to the president. "I do not think it would be wise for me to give my name as a sponsor to the report you sent me, so I think this is one request I shall have to refuse. I am giving your letter to the Attorney General."

Louis Fischer, the writer and analyst of Soviet affairs, appealed to Eleanor to help get his wife and two sons out of the Soviet Union. At his request she agreed to speak to the president about it to find out if he would mention it to Soviet Ambassador Oumansky. The president had suggested that she invite Mrs. Oumansky for tea and talk to her about it, she reported to Fischer. The affair went well, and passports were issued to Fischer's family. When he later requested permission to describe the episode in a book he was writing and enclosed what he proposed to say, she wrote back:

I hate to spoil anything you have written, but I would rather you left out my letter and any reference to the President. I do not want more than a mention of the fact that you came to see me and I said I would do what I could. I do not want it said that I interfered.[64]

She sought to hide her influence and effectiveness, and she held no office in government. Yet at the end of her husband's second term, Raymond Clapper included her among "The Ten Most Powerful People in Washington," saying that she was "a force on public opinion, on the President and on the government . . . a cabinet minister without portfolio . . . the most influential woman of our times." Grace Tully called her "a one-woman staff for the President," and Jesse Jones thought of her as "Assistant President." Without office she had developed an immense following throughout the country. It was never tested in a vote, but a poll on the subject published by Dr. Gallup at the beginning of 1939 showed that 67 per cent of those queried approved of the way she had conducted herself as First Lady, with women endorsing her activities by an even larger ratio than men.[65]

The philosopher Alfred North Whitehead, close to death in Cambridge, realized what she had accomplished during her husband's first two terms in office. Writing on behalf of Mrs. Whitehead and himself, he said, "We cannot exaggerate our appreciation of the wonderful work which you are doing in transforming the bleak social agencies of the past by the personal exercise of kindness, interest and directive knowledge." She was never able to forget, she told S. J. Woolf, "that this country or any other country is in the final analysis a collection of human beings striving to be happy, and it is the human element which is the most important consideration."[66]

Why does she bother him with such trivial matters, the president's aides sometimes complained and oftener thought. Life might have been more tranquil for Franklin if she had not done so, but the texture of the Roosevelt years would have been different, a human touch would have been missing, the people and their government would have been less intimately involved with each other.

41. *Changes at Hyde Park*

———

ELEANOR ROOSEVELT HAD MANAGED as First Lady to remain herself, to be a person, not a personage, and to have the human being thus disclosed accepted by the American public. But to remain human she had to keep official duties from stifling her personal life. Sometimes she felt she was leading a Jekyll and Hyde existence—one moment the public personality, the next the private human being.

In 1937 Forbes Morgan, who had been married to Aunt Pussie, died. Eleanor's ties with him dated back to the year of her debut when as one of Pussie's suitors he had danced with her. The funeral services were in Washington, and as usual in family crises much of the responsibility fell upon Eleanor. She comforted "Boy," Forbes's son, went with him to meet members of the family who converged upon Washington, and the next day accompanied him on the sad journey to Tivoli where Forbes was laid to rest in the Hall family vault. Yet all during the two days she also had to attend to such official duties as the annual breakfast of the Congressional Club, to which she had hurried after meeting her Aunt Maude at the train, for, she explained,

these official duties, like the one yesterday and the one today, are scheduled so long in advance that it always seems to me unfair to break the engagement unless it is absolutely necessary.

But in some ways it is a rather curious thing to have to divide one's life into personal and official compartments and temporarily put the personal side into its little hidden compartment to be taken out again when one's official duties are at an end.[1]

There were people who spoke to the passionate side of her nature, to whom she was bound by the memories of shared joys and sorrows—members of her family, a few co-workers, a few of the waifs for whom she felt a special responsibility. They represented the "personal side" of her life. She wrote of her Aunt Maude:

There are comparatively few people in the world whom you are always sure of finding equally interested, equally sympathetic, and equally entertaining as when you last met. When your ties go back into your childhood, however, and you have always found that a given person comes up to your expectations, you pick up the threads of relationship just where you dropped them when last you were together, and you feel a security of understanding which you do not feel with many people.[2]

The president was immersed in public affairs, and her children were grown and gone. She had, moreover, always felt she had shared both her husband and her children with another woman, Franklin's mother. She needed to have people who were close to her, who in a sense were hers, to whom she was the one and only, and upon whom she could lavish help, attention, tenderness. Without such friends, she feared she would dry up and die. When such friends were in trouble she expected them to turn to her, and she felt rebuffed if they did not. When they came to Washington she insisted they stay at the White House, and when she was in New York City or whatever part of the country in which they lived, she planned, long in advance, the things they would do together. It gave her pleasure to bring them gifts, to take them to a new restaurant, to go to the theater with them. She corresponded with them faithfully, often writing longhand letters in the early hours of the morning. Their birthdays were listed in a little black loose-leaf book, their Christmas gifts in another, and in the bulging little engagement book that she kept in her purse (the pages for which were Lorena Hickok's annual Christmas present to her), the birthdays, Christmas parties, and wedding anniversaries that she unfailingly celebrated with them were the first entries. "As you know, Mrs. Roosevelt is always a year ahead of all the rest of us in her engagements," Tommy wrote Hick. "She asked me to drop you a note to tell you that she would like to have the pages for next year when you have time to do them."[3]

Eleanor's cousin Corinne Alsop was staying with Alice Longworth, she informed Eleanor, but she would like to come and have dinner or tea with Eleanor when Alice was otherwise engaged: "I know that in casually saying I want to see you I am treating you as 'Eleanor' and not quite as the Mistress of the White House and I am always finding myself shy in so doing." "For Heaven's sake," Eleanor remonstrated, "why shouldn't you treat me as Eleanor! I never think of myself as mistress of the White House with casual people, much less with my family." Corinne, like Cousin Susie and Henry Parish and Harry Hooker and Isabella Greenway, reached back to her youth. There were the friends made during the years she entered public life—Esther Lape and Elizabeth Read, Nancy Cook and Marion Dickerman, and Elinor Morgenthau; those like Lorena Hickok and Earl Miller, who dated back to the days at Albany; and a few like Mayris Chaney, a dancer, who had been introduced to her by Earl in the Washington years. She went to great lengths to get together with these people.[4]

In the 1936 campaign reporters were mystified when a petite, shapely blonde appeared on the presidential train during Roosevelt's tour through the Midwest. Who was she? they wanted to know, and gawked even more when the lady who they decided was someone's *femme fatale* rode in presidential parades in the same car with Mrs. Roosevelt. Finally a woman reporter was delegated to ask Eleanor who she was since no one else in the official party seemed able to tell them. She was, Eleanor willingly replied, Mayris Chaney, or "Tiny" as she called her, a dancer and a friend. But why on the campaign train? "Well," explained Marquis Childs in his newspaper column, "they had promised themselves a holiday together and when Mrs. Roosevelt discovered she would not be on the West Coast that fall she wired for her friend, Mayris, to tour with the Presidential party. It was as simple as that."[5]

When Tiny came to New York she stayed at the little hideaway apartment that Eleanor and Tommy maintained on East Eleventh Street in the Village, in a little house owned by Esther and Elizabeth. So did Eleanor's brother Hall. So did Earl. Eleanor no longer used the house on Sixty-fifth Street. When she and Franklin moved to Washington they had thought of selling it, but only if that also was Sara's wish. They dropped the plan when Sara wrote her son,

Yes, I should not care for being in New York and away from this house, which so exactly suits me and I have become fond of it. At the same time if we could get a good price, and if the money (half of the amount I get) would be a help to you, with your big family, I would willingly let it go and I should live in the country. Yet it would be a pity to sacrifice such fine property, for in time it will rise again in value.[6]

James and Betsy used the house briefly, as did Anna and her children after she divorced Curtis Dall, but Eleanor preferred her little apartment in the Village. "Dear Georgie," Tommy wrote the Negro maid, Miss Georgiana Turner, who worked for her and Eleanor in New York,

Mrs. Roosevelt will be in on Monday just in time to go to the theatre. Will you leave for her some crackers and milk, so that she and Mrs. Morgenthau can just have a bite before they go to the theatre. Then will you leave some sandwiches and some iced Sanka and some fruit so that they can have something to eat when they return from the theatre. Mrs. Morgenthau will spend the night, so you will have a bed ready for her, as well as for Mrs. Roosevelt.[7]

If Eleanor considered any place home, it was Hyde Park. "I am always given the reputation of being constantly on the move," she said to a group of women who were meeting in Washington, and added, her voice becoming a little high-pitched as it still did when she repeated something that seemed to her quite absurd,

in fact, one woman, I was told the other day, remarked that she did not see very much evidence that I ever stayed at home. As a matter of fact, I believe very strongly in deep roots in some piece of ground . . . some place that carried your memories and associations of many years. All of us need deep roots. We need to feel there is one place to which we can go back, where we shall always be able to work with people whom we know as our close friends and associates, where we feel that we have done something in the way of shaping a community, of counting in making the public opinion of that community.[8]

The Hudson Valley from Tivoli south to Hyde Park was that place for Eleanor, and Val-Kill particularly. For years the Stone Cottage, two miles east of the Big House—for which Franklin had given her, Nancy Cook, and Marion Dickerman lifetime use of the land (and where, as a measure of the intimacy of the three women, all the linen was marked EMN)—had been a refuge for her. There she found quietness when public life became too much, and devotion when, hurt by some new display of Franklin's casualness, she needed sensitive response and the feeling that she was really loved. Since the mid-twenties no one had been closer to Eleanor than Nan and Marion, especially Nan. But now her feelings began to change. She was constantly growing: "There is something rather exciting about starting a new thing and one's ideas run riot!" she wrote in 1937 when she was fifty-three. "If the day ever comes when some one talks to me about something and it does not at once start a dozen trains of thought, I shall feel that the real springs of life are slowing up and that age is truly upon me!" She told the Todhunter graduating class, "Don't dry up by inaction but go out and do new things. Learn new things and see new things with your own eyes."[9]

She lived by this rule, her friends less so. There was a small sign that the relationship between her and her friends had changed when in late 1937 Marion asked Eleanor's help in planning the expansion of Todhunter. Like Val-Kill, Todhunter was an enterprise in which the three women were partners, even though Eleanor had given up teaching when she went to Washington, except for a current-events class. She still came, however, for opening-day ceremonies and commencement, and still gave an annual party for the staff and had each graduating class at the White House for a week end. Although the school was an excellent one, it was Eleanor's association with it that made it unique. Eleanor agreed to help Marion with her new plans, even though Franklin cautioned her, "You realize, of course, that if a campaign is undertaken, you will have to go to several dozen pep talk dinners and that the campaign is really based on your effective leadership." She did most of the things that Marion asked of her, but she refused to be quoted in the fund-raising brochure as saying that she intended to make the school one of her chief interests after she left Washington; she hoped, in fact, that she would be able to go on with her column, her lectures, her radio work. "I am terribly sorry," she wrote the fund-raising firm, "but as I do not intend to make the school one of my chief interests, I feel it very much wiser to be absolutely honest. It will be one of my interests, but as I have no definite idea of what my other interests will be or where they will take me, I regret that I cannot change my statement." In the end, to Eleanor's relief, the expansion plans were abandoned because of the recession.[10]

But the shift in her interests might not have led to estrangement if Marion and Nancy had not reacted possessively. The break came when the three women decided to liquidate the Val-Kill Industries, which produced furniture, pewter, and woven materials. Eleanor wanted to take over the factory building, "The Shop" as it was called, and convert it into a house for herself and Tommy. According to Marion, they liquidated the factory because it had become too great a drain on Nancy: "The load that Nan carried nearly killed her," Marion was later quoted as saying. "I was carrying the school, but she carried the shop, the Democratic State Committee and was helping Eleanor with the homesteads."[11] Tommy's version was different: the furniture factory did not show a profit, and Eleanor was underwriting the losses; friends suggested that she get a business-minded person to manage the enterprise, and when Nancy objected they decided to dissolve the partnership.[12]

In return for clear title to the shop building, Eleanor proposed to relinquish her share in the Stone Cottage. It is not clear why Nan and Marion refused, except that they must have sensed that the new arrangements signified a change in Eleanor's feelings toward them and her withdrawal from a relationship that had been most significant in their lives. Franklin felt they had become too possessive; grateful as he was for the companionship they had given Eleanor—he had even agreed to their becoming members of the Cuff Links group—he was irritated, he told Agnes Leach, who was a good friend of all three women, by the way they went around saying "Eleanor this" and "Eleanor that," and he was outraged that after all Eleanor had done for them they should be making difficulties over the shop.[13]

That was the way matters stood when, in the summer of 1938, Marion went abroad. "While I was gone," she recalled three decades later, "something happened between Eleanor and Nancy. I don't know what. Nancy and Eleanor had a very tragic talk in which both said things they should not have said, but when I came back Nancy was crushed and Eleanor refused to see me. What took place I don't know."[14]

Eleanor did, however, spell out her version of what had happened in a letter to Marion on November 9, 1938, when she made a new attempt to gain clear title to the shop by turning over her share in the Todhunter School Fund to Nancy and Marion, and again, half a year later, when she finally insisted on withdrawing totally from Todhunter.

The talk I had with you last summer was a very preliminary one, but it was the result of a long period in which you may not have realized that you, Nan and I were having serious difficulties. After you left, I had a long and very illuminating talk with Nan which made me realize that you and Nan felt that you had spent your lives building me up. As I never at any time intended to put you in that position, and as I never had any personal ambitions, I was a little appalled to discover what was in Nan's mind, and of course must have been in yours. I know Nan well enough to know that you are a great influence and factor in her life.

In addition, on a number of occasions Nan has told me how extremely difficult my name made the school situation for you. You have told me that in spite of that, you wished me to continue my connection because we had begun together. However, in view of the fact that other factors have entered the situation which made me feel that we no longer had the same relationship that I thought we had in the past, there was no point in subjecting you to a situation which was detrimental. One real factor was that certain things came back to me through Franklin which made me realize many things which I had never realized before.

With a completely clear understanding, both financially and personally, I feel sure that we can have a very pleasant and agreeable relationship at Hyde Park. Any work I do in the future will of course be along entirely different lines which will not bring me into close contact with either of you in your work.

I shall always wish both you and Nan well in whatever you undertake, and I feel sure that we can all enjoy things at Hyde Park but not on the same basis that we have in the past.

I am looking forward very much to having you and Molly and the girls here on Friday. The arrangements which you suggested for Saturday have all been made, and the girls here invited for four o'clock.

She signed herself "affectionately." Marion replied that she had never used the expression "building up" nor even entertained the idea, and she knew nothing of what had come back to her from Franklin, with whom she had spoken for a few moments only after Eleanor had refused to talk with her for the second time. However, she accepted Eleanor's decision to sever her connection with the school and wished to consider a matter closed which had caused her much unhappiness and disillusionment. She, too, signed her letter "affectionately."

Eleanor's final transaction of giving up her share of the Todhunter School Fund, however, added to her disaffection from her friends. When Marion informed Franklin that she considered the fund a school trust and not the personal property of the three, Eleanor indignantly pointed out that they had all paid income taxes on their share of the fund which came out of the school profits; "If I were to die my executors would be obliged to get my share of that fund for my estate." If Marion did not consider this a fair way of compensating Nancy for her share in the shop building, Eleanor was prepared to agree to a cash payment. "I have, however, as great a desire to feel during my life I am living in a building which I own as you have to feel that this fund which you have earned shall be used for purposes which you decide on. Therefore, I will only live in the shop building if there is a tangible settlement of the cash values according to Nancy's accounts." And when Harry Hooker told her that she did not have to file a gift-tax return in connection with the transfer of the fund to Marion and Nancy, Eleanor stubbornly insisted she "would rather pay the gift tax, as I want to have it registered that I gave up something which I had possessed. It is not a school fund. It belonged to the three of us jointly."[15]

Eleanor brought all the financial papers to Elizabeth Read, who did her income-tax returns. Elizabeth was horrified by the injustice of the settlement, but she was unable to get Eleanor to change her mind. "Elizabeth, what you say is true—but I can never forget that these two girls are afraid of the future and I am not."[16]

For Eleanor, the chapter of Nancy Cook and Marion Dickerman was closed. She continued to include them in the Cuff Links dinners at the White House and invited them to the big entertainments at Hyde Park when the president was there, and she sent them a turkey at Thanksgiving and small gifts at Christmas, but she brushed off every attempt to revive the old relationship. The real state of her feelings was indicated by Tommy, who in writing a well-meaning gentleman said, "I doubt if it would be of much help to you to consult Miss Cook about anything concerning Mrs. Roosevelt."[17]

Eleanor thought of herself as a countrywoman, and at times even imagined that if she had been born under other circumstances she might have made "a fairly adequate farmer's wife, having the necessary health and energy." Those she had, but other rural talents she lacked. She was all thumbs; try as she would she was never able to achieve the results with furniture stains, flower arrangements, and vegetables that Nancy managed effortlessly. Fortunately, there were always friends eager to serve her, and while communications between the two houses at Val-Kill, which were only 150 feet apart and connected by a flagstone walk, were, after 1938, restricted to the amenities, the costs of landscaping and the flower beds continued to be shared and for a time were under Nancy's supervision.

But Eleanor wanted the cottage to be her own and had made that clear even before the break. Otto Berge, who built the furniture, should bring it to the house, but "I don't want anything moved into its place until I am there to direct it."[18] There was a good deal of pine paneling in the new cottage and she had the woodwork rubbed down to look the way the furniture did, but she was the judge of when a satisfactory stain had been achieved. The pool was in front of the Stone Cottage; she invited the contractor who had built it to come to Val-Kill with his family for a picnic "and incidentally show some of the rest of us what has to be done about the pool so if anything happens to the man in charge, there would be more than one individual who understood the works." She supervised the spring planting around her cottage herself, and the excitement of returning to the country a few weeks later to find all her plants and bushes growing so fast she hardly recognized them had a special savor. "I love contrasts in flowers as I do in people, the pale columbine is a good foil for the sturdier zinnia," and no garden was complete for her without "some old fashioned yellow rose bushes, a bed of lilies of the valley in some shady spot and sweet peas and pansies to grow more abundant the more you pluck them."[19]

She was happy at Val-Kill; it was her house in a way none had ever been before—a rambling, two-story stucco structure with some twenty rooms of all sizes and shapes, each with its own books and pictures that Eleanor took pleasure in selecting herself. Since the house in time accumulated wings, there were unexpected step-ups and step-downs, alcoves and recesses everywhere, and guests, if they wanted it, could have complete privacy. Eleanor's bedroom overlooked the pond in which the sunrise and sunset were reflected. She slept on a sleeping porch surrounded by trees; in the morning there was the chirping of the birds to awaken her and at night a croaking chorus of frogs. On her bedside table was her father's copy of the New Testament with his interlineations, the one that had accompanied him all around the world and that he and Anna had read together in the days of their courtship.

Tommy, who had become much more than Eleanor's secretary, had her own apartment in the cottage. When they had started to work together in the twenties at the New York Democratic State Committee, there had been one immediate bond between them: Eleanor had been no more experienced in dictating letters than Tommy had been in taking shorthand, and as a result they had gotten along famously. "Now Mrs. Roosevelt can dictate enough letters in one hour to keep me busy for two days," Tommy told friends in 1936. Working for Eleanor Roosevelt was her life, and she wanted no other. She had begun as a shy, awkward girl from the Bronx, the daughter of a locomotive engineer, and now was a poised woman of the world. She had a strong, determined chin and could even say "no" to "Mrs. R.," as she called her, in order to protect her. Once when Eleanor started to dictate a letter to an official asking him to do something on behalf of a petitioner, Tommy let her hands fall to her side: "You can't do that," she told Eleanor. "Of course I can," was the reply, to which Tommy's rebuttal was: "Don't you know he'll be back and ask to be invited to the White House as a return favor?" The letter was not written. During her White House years Tommy refused to go out socially. "If I lost my job tomorrow, those people wouldn't give me house room," she used to say. "And anyway you're always expected to pay for such favors—in some way."

Eleanor reciprocated Tommy's loyalty. Copy number 3 of *This Is My Story* went to her, and when Tommy became ill in 1938 and was taken to the hospital, Eleanor canceled all her appointments to be at her bedside.

Tommy's apartment in the Val-Kill cottage had two bedrooms and a screened porch where, on genial summer days, breakfast and lunch were served. A living room served as Tommy's office and a kitchen served as a bar, usually presided over by Henry Osthagen, a gruff-voiced employee of the Treasury Department who had been gassed in the war and who became Tommy's companion after she and her husband separated. Guests at the cottage usually assembled in Tommy's office-living room for drinks before going in to dinner, a ritual that Eleanor never allowed to become too protracted. It was a family joke that when mother announced dinner, there was no nonsense—"it was ready—now."

After dinner the guests went into the living room and sat around the fireplace. Conversation never flagged, with Eleanor, her fingers busy with some piece of knitting, setting the pace. She loved to read aloud, especially poetry, and often the much-used *Home Book of Verse* or Auntie Corinne's many books of poetry or, in the late thirties, "John Brown's Body" by Stephen Vincent Benét was brought out. She read well and without self-consciousness.

She managed an occasional week end at Val-Kill all through the winter but really lived there from Memorial Day until the end of September. The seasons in Dutchess County are very distinct, each with its own colors, shapes, and scents, and the changes and Eleanor's pleasure in them were faithfully chronicled in her letters and columns. In winter she walked the snow-deep trails in high walking boots, a captive of the peacefulness of the winter landscape, and in summer she rode through the same woods on her horse Dot. Occasionally she saw a deer silhouetted against the trees and in July "an old friend," a blue heron, flying out of the marsh. In July, too, the purple loosestrife, which grew in marshy ground, enveloped Val-Kill in a violet haze. The marshes were also a breeding ground for large wood-flies, which sometimes kept her from riding until the wind blew them away.

She swam daily in the pool, and her effort to go off the diving board head first was a demonstration of sheer grit: she bent over the edge slowly, her fingers reaching toward her toes, at last tilting into the pool with a great splash. She never mastered it; she never gave up trying. She was always on the lookout for games and sports with which to amuse her guests and keep herself in trim. One season it was archery, another it was skiing ("I tried coming down one hill and to everyone's amusement landed in a heap at the bottom").[20] But it was only deck tennis that she could enjoy herself rather than through her friends' pleasure.

Her guest rooms were usually occupied, and rare was the day without its special excitement, whether it was the child star Shirley Temple and her parents, for whose visit Eleanor collected as many grandchildren as she could, or NYA administrators, who came to discuss their problems with her and whose presentation, when Franklin drove over and the officials crowded around his open car, she skillfully steered so that they put their best foot forward, for she wanted them to get more funds.[21]

Much as she loved the peacefulness of Val-Kill and a rainy day alone there before an open fire, she loved people more. Whoever interested her was invited to spend the day and told to bring his bathing suit. Eleanor would be at the Poughkeepsie station to meet him, a summery figure in a linen skirt and cotton blouse, white shoes and white stockings, a white ribbon around her hair.

One summer day she received a letter from Frank Harting, writing on behalf of himself and two friends with whom he shared an apartment. They were three young businessmen, he wrote, and were "rabid Eleanor Roosevelt fans"; she headed the list of people they would like to meet. "I was very much amused and somewhat flattered by your letter," she wrote back. "I like young people very much as I have so many around me all the time, and I should like to know you three." She invited them to spend a day at Hyde Park. "Tell Earl," she instructed Tommy, "if he feels he should protect me he can plan to spend that Sunday here!"[22]

She enjoyed masculine company, whether it was Earl Miller, still a health magazine's dream of virile manhood, the fussy but thoughtful Frank Harting, or the tall, saturnine Adrian Dornbush, head of the WPA's Technical Services Laboratory, who came to her cottage to paint. Auntie Bye, too, had always been surrounded by a coterie of male votaries whom the family had called "Joe-Bobs." Bob Ferguson had been one of them before he married Isabella, as had Joseph Alsop before he courted and married Corinne.

Eleanor still mothered Earl. She made a special Christmas for him, got him fight tickets through Jim Farley, and helped him finance the house he built near Albany. As chief inspector of prison guards in New York State, he was frequently in the vicinity of Val-Kill and kept an eye on it for "the Lady," as he called her; a guest room was always there for him. Divorced in 1934, he presented to Eleanor a succession of ladies upon whom she showered gifts and kindnesses until they faded away. In 1941 he remarried. Eleanor wrote him faithfully, letters full of warmth and affection. Some of her friends were puzzled by her attachment to this "cop," but if Franklin could make Missy a part of his household, she could do the same with Earl.

She encouraged his romances as, indeed, she did her best to help true love along whenever it showed up among her friends. She had liked John Boettiger, a newspaperman who had covered Franklin for the *Chicago Tribune*, and when Anna, separated from Curtis Dall, fell in love with him, Eleanor thought it was wonderful and shielded the courtship from prying eyes until Anna and John were ready to disclose it. Ever afterward Eleanor reminded her daughter that she had known John before Anna did. It gave her pleasure to lend her new cottage to Martha Gellhorn and Ernest Hemingway as a hideaway before they were married, and she did the same for the author of this book and Trude Pratt. Her gift of empathy enabled her to enjoy vicariously the love affairs of her friends: for her "there was no love/save borrowed love."[23]

It was approximately two miles from the Big House on the Hudson to Val-Kill over a winding dirt road that went through woods and fields that belonged to Franklin, as did the wooded paths and hills behind Eleanor's cottage, for Franklin was a canny accumulator of land and could not resist buying a farm if it came on the market and was in the vicinity of the Roosevelt acres, which now numbered about two thousand.

When Franklin was at Hyde Park Eleanor moved to the Big House, although she still worked at Val-Kill with Tommy. The Big House still was dominated by Sara, who, though in her early eighties, kept a tight hold on the reins. At dinner Sara, as always, sat at one end of the table and Franklin at the other. She enjoyed the role of presiding dowager, and Eleanor was amused by Sara's calm assumption that it was to her and her son that the limelight belonged. When the Swedish crown princess visited Hyde Park, Eleanor was late because the royal party had come ahead of schedule, "but luckily," she reported, " my husband and my mother-in-law were the real hosts of the occasion so I managed to slip in unnoticed." Sara wanted to have the same precedence accorded her at the White House but Franklin said he could not overrule the protocol officers.[24]

There was a time when Sara's reproaches, complaints, and demands had upset Eleanor, but, as she wrote Maude, she was now so busy "I haven't time to worry about Mama and her feelings which is a help!"[25] She was considerate of her mother-in-law. It was still Eleanor who saw her off when she went abroad and was at quarantine to meet her on her return; but Eleanor lived her own life and when Franklin was not at the Big House she preferred her own cottage. For her part, Sara stayed aloof from Val-Kill, but Franklin did not. When he was at Hyde Park there was a steady flow of traffic between the Big House and the cottage. Eleanor had Franklin and his staff for steaks on her porch or, if he wanted to have a private luncheon at the Big House with some official, Eleanor had the rest of his household for a picnic, with James cooking the chops. On Labor Day the White House staff and newspaper people came for a picnic and baseball game. Usually, too, before the summer ended everyone journeyed to the Morgenthau farm at Fishkill for a "clambake," which, said Eleanor, Franklin enjoyed as much as any other early autumnal event in Dutchess County. She organized the newspapermen and women into a Virginia reel, with Franklin calling the numbers: "I feel very proud of my pupils," Eleanor noted in her column, "for I really started them . . . on the strenuous dance and they all seem to enjoy it and do it better each time I see them perform!" What the newspaper-men thought is not recorded.[26]

Eleanor sometimes wondered how they would organize their lives after Sara died and the years in the White House were over. She thought the day of the very large estates was drawing to an end. "Here on the Hudson River it seems to face one every day," she wrote a former Hudson River neighbor; "I ride over the Rogers place and wonder what is going to happen to it, and now the Vanderbilt place is in the same condition. Ogden Mills has given his to the state, but the state, after all, can't be expected to take everybody's land along the River." Republican Howland Spencer, whose estate, Krum Elbow, on the west bank of the Hudson faced the Roosevelts', disposed of his as a form of revenge against Franklin. In 1936 he had announced he was leaving the United States to settle on his 7,000 acres in the Bahamas as a protest against New Deal taxes. What do you think of "your friend" now, Franklin twitted his mother. "Dearest Son, I was rather upset this morning about the horrid paper you sent about Howland Spencer, & your dictated note calling him *my* friend. . . ." In 1938 Spencer declared that because of New Deal taxes he was unable to maintain Krum Elbow any longer and sold it to Father Divine, an eccentric self-appointed Negro preacher, for one of his "heavens." The country looked to Hyde Park. How would the president, with his strong streak of traditionalism and attachment for Hyde Park as it had been in his childhood, respond? It was Eleanor who commented through her column.

In Poughkeepsie I ran into some people who were much excited over the purchase by Father Divine of an estate across the river from my mother-in-law's home. I always feel sorry for anyone who has to sell a country place they have lived in for many years and enjoyed. One has so much more sentiment as a rule about one's country life. It must, however, be pleasant to feel that in the future this place will be "heaven" to some people, even if it cannot be to its former owner.[27]

Franklin wanted to keep Hyde Park not only the way it was in the thirties but the way it had been in his youth. The post offices that were built under his administration in Rhinebeck, Hyde Park, and Poughkeepsie were of gray field-stone, an architectural style that he called "early Dutch colonial" and that he insisted was indigenous to the Hudson Valley. He persuaded Mrs. VanAlen, the niece of Frederick Vanderbilt, to offer the magnificent Vanderbilt estate, three miles north of the Roosevelts', to the federal government; he then got the Historic Monuments Division to accept and maintain it not only as an example of the millionaire style of life at the turn of the century but for its trees, some of which were several hundred years old and not to be found elsewhere on the North American continent. And when he arranged to have his papers housed at Hyde Park in a fieldstone library building and for the Big House to go to the federal government, he spoke nostalgically of the "small boy" who "half a century ago" took especial delight in climbing trees, digging in woodchuck holes, and playing in creeks and fields that were not much different than they had been in the time of the Indians.

The Big House would always be his home but he, too, like Eleanor, wanted a place that would be built to his own specifications; he picked a hill-top behind Eleanor's cottage, where the sky seemed closer and over on the horizon the peaks of the Catskills could be glimpsed through the violet haze, to build "a little refuge to work in, where no one can come unless he invites them." Eleanor thought his plan to build a retreat on the Val-Kill side of his property "grand," and while he was cruising in Pacific waters on the U.S.S. *Houston* in the summer of 1938, her cables consisted chiefly of building progress reports: "Most of excavating for your house is finished"; "Walls of your house going up everything moving satisfactorily."[28]

Although she was less a traditionalist than her husband and was more adaptable to change, Eleanor shared his feeling about Hyde Park and was actively involved in the affairs of the village and of the Hyde Park Improvement Association. Franklin declined her invitation to take part in its meetings at her cottage, but he did make suggestions on what could be done to improve the village at the annual meetings of the Roosevelt Home Club which took place on the grounds of his farmer, Moses Smith.[29]

Eleanor always hated to see the summer end—"the tang of fall makes me very sad because it brings the winter and all of its excitement very close." She was perfectly sure "that some day when I have no longer any obligation to do anything in this world, I am going to be very happy enjoying rural quiet and watching nature carry on its drama of life from the sidelines."[30]

42. *Life with Mother and Father*

THERE IS A PICTURE of the Roosevelt family assembled at Hyde Park in September of 1934 for Sara's eightieth birthday—a large clan, including several great-grandchildren, gathered around the matriarch. It was a much photographed family, chiefly because it was the family that currently occupied the White House, but also because its members made a handsome group together.

"As I looked at my two daughters-in-law," Eleanor wrote about her fifty-third birthday party at the White House, "I could not help thinking how lucky we are! All the boys seem to have chosen, not only people that one can enjoy looking at, but the better you know them the more you like them. Best of all apparently we can all have good times together and I think it is a good thing for a family to be able to look back at happy times." On that occasion she and her brother Hall located a pianist, and while he played they all danced; later everyone gathered around the piano and sang, including Franklin, who amused them by singing some old college songs. It was long after midnight before Jimmy and Betsy and the Morgenthaus were permitted to go home, and then only by grace of a plea from Eleanor, who felt that parties should end "when everybody is still apparently having a good time," which meant 1:30 A.M. at the latest. But the two Franklins stayed up. "When I went in to see my husband this morning, he looked at me disgustedly and said: 'It was three o'clock before I went to sleep!' "[1]

The four boys and Anna were built like their parents—tall, long-limbed, and long-armed, with strong bone structures, and they were brimful of energy. One summer when Franklin Jr. visited Eleanor's Aunt Tissie at her shooting in Scotland, she walked the moors all day and played poker with him most of the night and never seemed weary. Why had she never told them about the Hall side of the family, Franklin Jr. asked his mother on his return; how could they help bursting with vitality since they got it from both sides of the family—the Halls as well as the Roosevelts? The Delanos did not lack for vitality either, Eleanor reminded her son. The children had their parents' zest for life, and "love of adventure came to them naturally."[2]

Family reunions were rambunctious affairs, full of "tribal affection" and equally uproarious argument and high jinks. Ike Hoover had written of the way Theodore Roosevelt's exuberant children had taken over the White House so that it became "one general playground for them and their associates . . . roller skating and bicycle riding all over the house . . . giving the pony a ride in the elevator. . . ." Eleanor and Franklin's children were older but equally high-spirited. Christopher Phillips recalled that at one Christmas party Franklin Jr. and John crept up behind the president's chair and tickled him. Roosevelt calmly reached his long arms behind him and pinioned them both. Muriel Martineau, over from London on a visit, thought the younger generation ill-mannered; the young girls staying at the White House were always late to dinner and kept the president waiting just because in New York it was fashionable to arrive a quarter to a half-hour late, and when the president came into the room many of the youngsters did not even get out of their chairs.[3]

But Franklin and Eleanor took youthful irreverence in their stride. Ickes described a dinner on the presidential train when they went to inspect the Grand Coulee dam site:

It resolved itself into a debate between the members of the Roosevelt family, with all of them frequently talking at one and the same time. Mrs. Roosevelt precipitated the discussion by raising some social question and her three sons at once began to wave their arms in the air and take issue with her. She expressed belief in a strict limitation of income, whether earned or not, and the boys insisted that every man ought to have a right to earn as much as he could. The President joined in at intervals, but he wasn't President of the United States on that occasion—he was merely the father of three sons who had opinions of their own. They interrupted him when they felt like it and all talked at him at the same time. It was really most amusing. At one stage when they were all going on at once, I raised my voice and observed to the President that I now understood how he was able to manage Congress. Senator Wheeler followed my remark with the observation that Congress was never as bad as that. That was about the sum and substance of outside contribution to the dinner talk that night, but it was all very interesting and very amusing.[4]

Eleanor and Franklin encouraged their children to have their own opinions and to express them without fear of embarrassing their parents. Yet Eleanor was slightly appalled when James, who was deeply involved in the politics of Massachusetts, a state with a large Catholic population, voiced his opposition to its ratification of the child-labor amendment. At the time newspaper publishers were insisting that the NRA Newspaper Code should permit employment of newsboys. "No civilization should be based on the labor of children," Eleanor said tersely. What about James' views, she was asked. She had written him in Boston asking for his reasons, she replied. "Of course, everybody is entitled to his own opinion," she added. "I am merely asking his. I would never dream of doing more. Jimmy must have reasons which seem sufficient to him. They wouldn't seem sufficient to me."[5]

She and the president were equally tolerant of Elliott in the late 1930s when, as a radio commentator over the Texas network of which he was an executive, he frequently voiced anti-New Deal views and as a politician allied himself with the anti-New Deal crowd which favored pledging the state's 48 votes to Garner in order to head off a third term. Elliott was a citizen of the United States and over twenty-one, and as such, Steve Early told the press, he was entitled to exercise his right of free speech. Although Eleanor and Franklin loyally defended Elliott's right to oppose his father's policies, a few months later Franklin, not without some satisfaction, filed in the family folder a news dispatch from Waco, Texas, reporting that supporters of a third term had drowned Elliott out with boos when he sought to introduce the keynoter, who favored pledging the state's delegation to Garner. And still later he filed another clipping, describing a thirty-minute ovation for the president that Elliott had precipitated at the Texas Democrats' state convention when he had defended New Deal spending and answered the charge of waste with the standard New Deal defense that hope had been kept alive.[6]

After his marriage to Anna, John Boettiger was offered and, with Franklin's encouragement and Eleanor's approval, accepted the publishership of the *Post-Intelligencer*, the Hearst paper in Seattle. "I shall miss them sadly but it does seem a grand opportunity and they will love it and so life is life, not always very pleasant," Eleanor wrote her husband, who was en route to Latin America on the U.S.S. *Indianapolis*. "I can hardly bear to have Anna & John go," she added a few days later, "but they are so happy that I wouldn't let them know for worlds but it is better than Europe for at least one can fly out if necessary."[7]

If Elliott and Ruth were associated with the anti-New Deal crowd in Texas, Anna and John were as staunch New Dealers as Eleanor herself, and this was an added bond between them. "Our voters reelected a complete New Deal delegation to Congress," John reported to his father-in-law in November, 1938. "So far as we are concerned in Washington [state], you can write your own ticket in 1940." The president did not comment on this last point when he replied to John; he was more concerned with his son-in-law's success as a publisher: "I am keen to hear all about the progress of the paper. Somebody told me that either you are in the black or about to get there. It goes to prove that a Hearst paper, minus Hearst's management, can be made to pay if it is run by a fellow like you." A few Seattle citizens were unhappy that, as a Hearst paper, the Boettigers published syndicated material critical of the president and First Lady; "they are not treating you and the President as they should as far as I can determine by the paper," one of them wrote Eleanor. "I assure you," she replied, "that they treat the President and myself with the highest respect and affection and the fact that they have one of Mr. Hearst's papers has nothing whatever to do with their attitude towards us personally."[8]

No sooner were Anna and John in their house in Seattle than Eleanor flew out, a "slow trip" because of low ceilings, to see them and to report to Franklin that their house was "lovely," that they were "making a real place for themselves," and that "Sis & Buzz are very well & happy. . . . Their teeth are being straightened so bars are rather in evidence."[9]

There were innumerable jokes, inside the family and out, about Eleanor's travels. "Dearest Babs," Franklin wrote her from the U.S.S. *Houston*, "The Lord only knows when this will catch up with my will o' the wisp wife, but at least I am proceeding according to schedule." Admiral Byrd set two places for supper at his South Pole hut just in case Mrs. Roosevelt should drop in; a child who heard the Robinson Crusoe story knew that the footprints in the sand were those of Mrs. Roosevelt; and the newswomen, in their 1936 stunt party, had Mrs. Roosevelt shooting to Mars in a rocket ship. The most famous story became a part of American presidential lore: the *New Yorker* cartoon in which two startled coal miners are looking up and saying, "Good gosh, here comes Mrs. Roosevelt." And when life did imitate art and Mrs. Roosevelt went down a coal mine in a miner's coveralls, Sara sent a barbed comment to her son, "I hope Eleanor is with you this morning. . . . I see she has emerged from the mine. . . . That is something to be thankful for." Sara never gave up trying. "So glad Eleanor is there with you dear," she wrote her son in Warm Springs, and sometimes she was even blunter: "I see Eleanor is back in Chicago, so perhaps you will have her at home tomorrow—I hope so."[10]

Yet much of Eleanor's traveling was done in order to keep in touch with the children. They were getting married (and divorced), settling down, having children, and setting up in business, and she was there to nurse them, to celebrate a birthday, to inspect a new grandchild, to counsel them, and to give them news of the rest of the family. She spent Christmas week, 1936, in Boston where Franklin Jr. was hospitalized for an operation on his sinuses, and stayed through New Year's Eve, sometimes in the company of, sometimes spelling, Ethel duPont, whom Franklin Jr. was to marry in June, 1937. Ten months later she was back in Boston to be with Johnny while he had four wisdom teeth removed, spending much of her time in the company of his fiancée, Anne Clark, a North Shore debutante. A few weeks later during Christmas of 1937 she canceled all engagements to fly out to be with Anna's family while Anna went into the hospital for an operation. And she made a special plane journey to Seattle to be with her daughter for the birth of her third child and to keep a promise to Buzz to be there for his ninth birthday, but she had to cancel the latter when the telephone rang at supper and she learned that Hall's son Danny had been killed in an airplane accident in Mexico. Dan Roosevelt had been a brilliant youngster, adventurous, with every promise of using the talents Hall had so tragically thrown away. "I am so deeply sorry for the boy's mother and my brother," Eleanor wrote an old friend, who had been one of the Morgan sisters of Staatsburgh. "Hall was so proud of Danny and was really very deeply affected. We can't put old heads on young shoulders and they seem always to confuse recklessness with courage." She left Seattle immediately to be with Hall and wrote him that "we must believe that there is a reason for all things in the universe, and turn to helping those, if we may, who are left behind, and will carry through life the scar of a great sorrow." She accompanied Hall to Dedham for the burial. "It meant a lot to us," Margaret Cutter, Hall's former wife, wrote her, "and I feel that you were the one person that kept Hall going. I was so terribly sad for him. Dan had been such a belated discovery and had proved such a perfect companion and was something for him to cling to."[11]

Eleanor was still the one the family turned to in moments of stress and tragedy. One wintry morning the telephone rang between 4:00 and 5:00 and she heard Franklin Jr.'s voice saying that he and Ethel had run into a car without lights parked on an icy road and were in the hospital. Would she come?

When she reached the hospital, she discovered that Franklin Jr. had a concussion and did not remember having called her and could not imagine how she came to be there; "his action was probably subconscious," she recalled in *This I Remember*, "a reassertion of the childhood habit of turning to one's mother automatically when one is in trouble."[12]

She was "well conditioned to coping with family crises," she wrote. She could not afford to go to pieces because the president could not be worried more than was absolutely necessary.

The wedding of a Roosevelt to a duPont, the family which had heavily subsidized the American Liberty League, was one of the story-book romances of the thirties. The day before the wedding Eleanor walked into her husband's oval study, but seeing a group of gentlemen engaged in what seemed to be a very serious conversation, began to back away, when Franklin motioned to her. "The question under discussion is, what do I do tomorrow afternoon? I don't think I had better stand in the line." She was not very helpful, she said, but remembering the way the guests had abandoned her and Franklin at their wedding to cluster around their Uncle Theodore, she murmured, "It doesn't really matter what you do, as long as you don't steal the show." The wedding was beautiful—that is, "the church part of it," Eleanor reported to a newspaperman to whom she wrote frequently to encourage him in his effort to cure himself of alcoholism; "Ethel was a most beautiful bride. There were so many people at the house for the reception, the bridal party never sat down for five hours and they were utterly exhausted." Eleanor herself had to abandon the receiving line at the duPont home in Greenville, Delaware, to make a broadcast in Washington. "I don't know whether to be happy or sad," she told reporters as she left, "but simply say prayers that fundamentally their lives may so develop that they may be useful lives and therefore happy ones." That was her attitude, too, a year later when John married. "So our last child is leaving us," she wrote Caroline Phillips in Italy. "He seems so very young, but he is determined to get married and I do love Anne Clark very much." To Anne she gave the last string of pearls from the five-string choke collar that Sara had given her on her wedding day. Had she also given any "motherly advice" to Anne and Johnny, a relentless press wanted to know. "I am not good at giving advice," she replied. "I believe in letting them work out their own plans."[13]

She was not inclined either to give advice or to make predictions as to how a marriage might turn out. The younger the couple was, the greater the hopes and dreams that were vested in the marriage relationship, yet when the fires of infatuation cooled who could be sure that the partnership would not fall apart, especially if because of immaturity neither husband nor wife understood that any human relationship to prosper must be carefully tended? "It would be better if people did not marry too young," she felt, "and if they waited until they had more experience. Unfortunately, most people in this world have to learn by experience." She partly blamed herself for the early marriages of James, Elliott, and Anna. The Governor's Mansion had not been a home, and they did not feel that the Sixty-fifth Street house was theirs, nor even Hyde

Park. That made them anxious to establish homes of their own and had added to their need to make money quickly.[14]

Elliott was the first to get a divorce. Anna was very close to him at the time, and at his bidding went to Chicago to talk things over with him. The family had heard rumors that he intended to get a divorce and marry Ruth Googins of Texas. "See if you can't keep him from rushing into it," Franklin asked his daughter. "He did not say he and Mother were opposed. He did not say 'don't do it' and when I called him from Chicago and told him Elliott was going to remarry right away, he was very annoyed, but his annoyance was at Elliott's doing it so quickly." Eleanor was more outspoken. She found it impossible to believe, she wrote her husband, that Elliott was considering remarriage, especially since he had no job. She flew to the West Coast to talk with him, but he was a restless young man, determined on his own course, and when he went ahead, despite his parents' pleas that he delay, they, of course, like most parents, loyally supported their headstrong child. Children should feel, Eleanor said, that they could always return to the home of their parents "with their joys or with their sorrows. We cannot live other people's lives and we cannot make their decisions for them." She had learned to accept "any change in her children's lives without making them feel guilty about it."[15]

She and Franklin had suffered so greatly from Sara's efforts to run their lives that they leaned over backward not to do the same with their children. They were unhappy when their children married too young and divorced too easily, but beyond being available to them for counsel and understanding when their private lives ran into difficulties, they resisted the impulse to interfere. Eleanor was more accessible than Franklin, for he, in addition to being tied down by his presidential duties, found it difficult to talk about intimate matters. Never once did either parent, although the children's divorces were a source of political embarrassment, advance political considerations as a reason for their not doing what they felt they had to do. The president said that "he thought a man in politics stood or fell by the results of his policies," Eleanor wrote; "that what their children did or did not do affected their lives, and that he did not consider that their lives should be tied to his political interests."[16]

Unlike Sara, Eleanor could not tell others what was right and what was wrong, since so often she was not sure herself. "Even if there were what the World calls sin," she replied to a woman who had written to criticize the Roosevelt children's divorces,

I think we should remember that the Christian religion is patterned on the life of Christ, and that Christ showed in many of his actions that he believed one should judge not so much by what people had done but by the motives and a complete knowledge of the situation. Few people ever have that about other human beings. That knowledge is given only to the Lord.[17]

She found it difficult to condemn divorce if behind the decision to do so there had been careful consideration and a genuine effort to make the marriage work. She thought the real culprit in most divorces was incompatibility:

"Incompatability of temper sounds like a trivial cause for divorce and yet I am not sure that it is not the most frequent cause. It is responsible for quarrels over money, and it drives husbands and wives away from each other to other interests and other people and brings about the most serious acts for which divorce is usually granted." For that reason she thought people should be able to separate legally without moral stigma:

Naturally, the people who, like the Catholics, believe that marriage is consummated in Heaven, are not going to agree on this point, but I think people can be made far more unhappy if they find they have developed different standards and different likes and dislikes, than they sometimes are by really very serious things. It does not seem to me necessary to brand everyone who gets a divorce with something as serious as adultery or desertion, when frequently it is a case of different development and different opportunities for development.[18]

Eleanor rejoiced in the marriage of Anna and John because she felt they had not gone into their second marriage in any lightness of spirit. Both had profited by the sufferings and mistakes of their first marriages and now were drawn together by shared values and interests and by temperaments that were attuned to each other.

She no longer felt that a marriage should be preserved for the sake of the children. She deplored divorce, she wrote, "but never for a minute would I advocate that people who no longer love each other should live together because it does not bring the right atmosphere into a home." It was very sad when a couple was unable to make a success of marriage, "but I feel it is equally unwise for people to bring up children in homes where love no longer exists." Such views did not sit well with the church.

I am afraid I cannot claim to be a very good churchwoman. In fact, when I was tendered the *Churchman's* Award this year for promoting goodwill among certain groups, I carefully explained that while my husband was a good churchman, I was not particularly orthodox. I have a religion but it does not depend especially upon any creed or church.[19]

There was another reason why she hesitated to judge her children critically: being the children of public figures, especially of a president, they were at all times in the pitiless spotlight of publicity, so that every misstep or case of bad judgment became the subject of headlines, the slightest scrape was blown out of all proportions, the most improbable tale given the widest currency. "It seems so futile," she wrote a woman in Jamesport, Missouri, "to answer such foolish statements. . . . However, I assure you that I have never seen any of my boys dance with a nude woman."[20]

"Incidentally, both our younger boys in college are having a very bad time as the sons of a man in public life," she wrote her Allenswood schoolmate, "Bennett." "It is not so easy . . . unless you never do anything or unless you have a Secret Service man with them all the time. Neither of these seems to go with the temperament of these two young things."[21]

The children resented the publicity. Franklin Jr. wanted to know why he should make headlines for actions which passed unnoticed when the Joneses or Smiths did them. His mother's reply that being the son of a president carried advantages as well as drawbacks, privileges as well as responsibilities never quite satisfied him. Franklin Jr., or "Brud" as he was called in the family, was a speed demon who held the unofficial Harvard-to-New-York record and was often stopped for speeding. "Will you speak seriously & firmly to F. Jr. & John about drinking & fast driving?" Eleanor begged her husband. "I really think it's important." Neither of the boys had any memory of their father having done so.[22]

"Father had great difficulty in talking about anything purely personal or private," Franklin Jr. recalled, "especially if it involved anything unpleasant. He left that to Mother." On one occasion, at Eleanor's insistence, Franklin finally agreed to speak sternly to "Brud" about his fast driving, but, Franklin Jr. recalled, his father "couldn't even bring himself to summon me to his little office on the porch of the Big House. It was Mother who had to say 'Your father wants to see you.' " When Franklin Jr. went in, his father hemmed and hawed and finally said, " 'Your Mother tells me I must ask you to give me your license until you have learned your lesson.' He put it all on Mother. That was a basic trait with him. He couldn't fire anyone. I'm the same way. I hate an unpleasant showdown with anyone."[23]

Bad as the publicity was, it was equally injurious when officials excused offenses for which a Smith or a Jones would have been penalized. On one occasion when Franklin Jr. was picked up for speeding, instead of fining him the judge took him home for dinner.* "Father was simply furious," Eleanor recalled. Her children, wrote Eleanor, were "five individualists who were given too many privileges on the one hand and too much criticism on the other."[24]

While Johnny was in Cannes in 1937 for the annual festival which ended in a "battle of flowers," he made international headlines when he was accused of having emptied a bottle of champagne in the mayor's plug hat. He denied the story, and William Bullitt, the U. S. ambassador to France, backed up his account. His parents believed the denial, and Eleanor was at the boat to meet him on his return:

If it had been one of my other boys I would have felt the incident was more than probable, for they have great exuberance of spirit. It just happens that John is extremely quiet, and, even if he had been under the influence of champagne, I doubt if he would have reacted in this manner.[25]

But these episodes of publicity were minor compared to the steady attack on the older children on the grounds that they were trading on their father's position in order to make money and win favors for their associates. The children felt that the reverse was true—that government officials bent over backward when Roosevelts were involved in order to avoid the suspicion of favoritism. This was Elliott's complaint to his mother when she visited him in Texas. "He is dreadfully upset," Eleanor wrote her husband,

* Franklin Jr. said his mother had sharpened the story to make her point. The judge fined him thirty dollars and *then* took him home for dinner.

FALDO
In Search of Perfection

FALDO
In Search of Perfection

Nick Faldo

With Bruce Critchley
Photographs by Dave Cannon

WEIDENFELD AND NICOLSON

Contents

Introduction
The Man Himself
8

The Open
Golf's Holy Grail
24

The Masters
Golf in the Garden of Eden
44

U.S. Tour
American Adventures
64

Team Faldo – Golf
The House That Lead Built
82

European Tour
Poor No More
94

World Golf
The Global Game
110

Team Faldo – Business
Success Management
126

The Ryder Cup
Us Against Them
138

Competition Record
159

Introduction

The Man Himself

• • • • • • • • • • • • • •

I have always been content with my own company and was able to amuse myself for hours when I was a child. The solitude of the practice ground and the hours spent there building a golf swing were a pleasure to me, whether in the early days after taking up the game, or later, when I took my swing to pieces with David Leadbetter and created another one.

I was an only child. I believe that was the single most important factor in the development of that part of my character that has led me to become a champion golfer. I was the apple of my parents' eye and received total encouragement in the pursuit of whatever interest – usually sporting – that grabbed me during my formative years.

I was always a big lad for my years, and as you grow up, size is often all you need to win, particularly in your age group. Being well coordinated as well, I won most sports I went in for and got a taste for winning. I was a good swimmer and before golf took over became a junior Hertfordshire county champion. But I suppose at some time or other I tried all the games that youngsters play, made the teams in team sports or did pretty well in individual ones.

Home was a council house in Knella Road, Welwyn Garden City. Dad worked on the financial side of ICI Plastics, and Mum was in the clothing business as a cutter and pattern designer. They were never all that well off and certainly never had much spare cash for expensive holidays or dinners out in nice restaurants. However, whenever I found a new pastime, whether it was bicycling, fishing, cricket or golf, they always managed to find the wherewithal to buy me a decent piece of equipment with which to pursue that particular interest.

More than some kids I know, once I took up an activity up, it kept me occupied for weeks, months, even years. Maybe I was aware that some sacrifice had been necessary to give me a fishing rod or cricket bat, so I had better make good use of it.

Early on I knew the office life was not for me.

I also had an innate curiosity as to how things work, and down the years comparisons have been drawn between the way I took a new bicycle to pieces and what I did with my golf swing. I can say that the only things I took to bits were the ones I was fairly confident I could put back together, and that went for both the bicycle and the golf swing.

Today I wish I had more time to tinker around with things. I used to love woodwork and metal work at school and would like to be able to do more of that now, but time and concern not to overstrain my arms, which are sensitive after so much practice in the 1980s, mean that hobby will have to wait.

That will also stop me building a children's tree-house in the garden, again something that I would dearly love to do. I suppose I will just have to be content with the design – and

With my parents in the early days.

supervision of construction! In the meantime I will just have to be happy with working on my clubs, which I do in my workshop at home.

Very early on I knew that the office life was not going to be for me. I had two rules: I was going to be my own boss, and I would somehow work outdoors. There was a time when I considered landscape gardening, and I suppose one day I will be — when I turn my attentions fully to being a golf-course designer.

Later I thought I might become a ranger in the Canadian forestry commission, but Dad, always well aware of the financial angle, said that it was a lot of hard work for not much pay. I was quite good at technical drawing and even considered a career in design, but that would have entailed too much time

indoors. Then along came golf and with it the end of any concern as to what I would do with my life.

Of all the interests I had in my youth, only fishing has survived into adulthood. Many of the old interests will, I am sure, re-emerge when Matthew is of an age to start wanting to take up sports himself, but until then the rod and a lonely stretch of river are a great antidote to all the stresses and strains that accompany tournament golf.

Once again, it was Dad who introduced me to fishing. In those days, we'd go out around Hertfordshire, to reservoirs and along river banks and fish with line and float for roach, perch and bream. Good old coarse fishing!

When we moved to the Wentworth area our local doctor, Mike Loxton,

The stylish early years.

11

turned out to be a bit of an expert, and he introduced me to the delights of trout fishing. Indeed, the first place he took me was the River Test in Hampshire; that's a bit like hitting your first golf shots at Augusta! Unlike the trout there, I was swiftly hooked.

Mike is a very good fisherman, be it trout or salmon. My preference is for trout, and with the Test nearby, it is easier for me to get at when I can find the odd day to sneak off. I find there is a very special buzz about trout fishing: the peace and quiet, the crystal-clear water, the knowledge that fish are there but have to be pursued with great stealth.

A lot of thought and care goes into catching trout. You have to know what they are eating, what they will take. Then you have to learn how to cast so the fly really lands on the water like the real thing. There is also the making of the flies themselves. Like golf, fishing is a multifaceted pastime, and all the more enthralling for it.

Fishing on the Avon before I discovered golf.

It wasn't long before I started thinking of buying my own stretch of river, but that is not as easy as it sounds, even if you have the cash. Good pieces of river don't come on the market very frequently, and I was very lucky to be able to join a small group of friends who had a nice stretch of the Test. It has been a bit like joining a rather exclusive fishing club.

If you are keen on fishing and can afford it, having a rod, as it is known, in a syndicate is important. Once people know you fish, invitations come from other devotees to have a go on their stretch, so it's nice to be able to reciprocate.

Golf has always been one of the great games for meeting pleasant and amusing people, but I have also made some good friends through shared days standing in a few feet of water while pursuing the elusive trout. Huey Lewis, the American rock star with his band The News, is both a keen golfer and trout fisherman. I met him at Kapalua in Hawaii one year and have since been to stay with him at his ranch in Montana, where he has a couple of miles of river to himself. He is not best pleased that golf as a subject is taboo, but we have had some great fishing.

Gareth Edwards, the great Welsh rugby player, is nowadays better

I find a lot of similarity between fishing and standing on the practice ground hitting shots.

Fishing with Huey Lewis in Montana. At least mine that got away was bigger.

known as a fishing guru and works for the Welsh River Authority. He is going to introduce me to sea-trout fishing sometime in the coming year, which he tells me takes place mostly at night. You get there around 11.00 pm and have a little drink to keep warm. The fishing really gets going about 2.00 am, and you fish all night. When I first got into fishing and heard tales of nights out in the rivers, I thought someone was having me on.

In return for introducing me to the Test, I took Mike Loxton to Sweden for a few days. We fished all day in a totally remote spot, working the banks of the lake until around tea time. Then we smoked some of the trout we'd caught over a wood fire, had them for tea, then fished some more. Sometimes there are moments of great perfection in life: that was one of them.

We'd get back around midnight,

have dinner and go to bed at 2.00 am – then do it all again the following day. I had never done anything like that, but it was great relaxation, so now I'm looking forward to the sea trout at night, this year or next.

I find a lot of similarity between fishing and standing on the practice ground hitting shots. You are always working to improve your technique, and neither is perfectible. There is also a lot in the stroke itself: there's a back-swing and a hit – though I suppose in fishing there's no follow through, at least not to the extent there is in golf. Above all, in both a slow back-swing and perfect timing is essential.

My other great interest outside golf and the family is helicopter-flying. A few years ago I started to find myself more and more often taking helicopters, either to get out of a tournament quickly to make a flight connection or to visit a number of course developments in a short space of time.

I remember thinking it would be a good idea if I took some lessons, if for no other reason that in the event of anything happening to the pilot, I could at least land the thing. Even in the bigger ones I usually find myself sitting 'up front' with the driver.

It was not something I could start in the middle of the season, so it had to wait until my big annual break around Christmas. At the turn of the year in 1991-2 I finally took myself along to Fairoaks Aerodrome at Chobham to have a go. I quickly found that it too was a great way of switching off from the torments and frustrations of tournament golf.

Suddenly finding yourself alone in the machine is very scary.

You cannot think of anything other than what you are doing; otherwise you make a nonsense of it — 'bend the skids', as the experts say. There is also a great sense of achievement as you take each step forward. Every lesson is different, and it too has a similarity with golf, in that some days it goes really well and on others you feel as if you have two left feet and are all thumbs.

There are lots of little milestones, all of which are important, and some will stay with me to the end of my days as moments of great satisfaction. The first day you get to hover without wobbling all over the place is wonderful. You only fly for 45 minutes each lesson and getting to that moment of being able to hold the machine some ten feet off the ground without the instructor laughing at your futile efforts while he sings 'A life on the ocean waves' took about four hours.

As has been apparent all my life, whenever I take something up I usually go flat out at it until mastering it. I basically learnt to fly in about a week. Every day I would drop the kids off at school and beetle over to Chobham for my lesson. After five days I could take off and land and hover those few feet off the ground.

But those first days had all been in a light five- to ten-mph breeze. On the Saturday, the wind was up to fifteen mph, and it was as if I had never had my hands on the controls before, I was all over the place. I tried really hard and was so completely exhausted by the effort and concentration that I had to hand it over before I put us all into the deck. That was a real blow to my confidence, but looking back, just as in golf, you have to have the bad moments to learn from and so move forward the next time.

I had to go away for a couple of weeks after that, but I thought about it a lot before I came back. Each evening I would sit for five minutes or so and mentally fly the helicopter: picking it off the ground, getting it to hover, flying it across the air field and landing it. I went through all the movements and checks each time, did everything just as though I was really there.

When I got back, I went straight to Fairoaks, got into the helicopter and did it, just as I had pictured each night while I was away. Again, the comparison with golf was uncanny: I was using the visualization trick we all use in golf, seeing the whole shot in my mind prior to hitting the ball.

My daughter Natalie receives some early training.

Not long afterwards I did my first solo flight. Not so much a flight really, just taking the chopper off, getting it to hover and then putting it down again. I nearly bottled out, thinking I might just leave it till the next time – but I made myself do it.

Suddenly finding yourself alone in the machine is very scary. The instructor stands a few feet in front of you as you go through the preliminaries and then lift off the ground. He watches while you hover there for a few seconds, then gives you the thumbs up and wanders off.

After about ten hours' tuition you are ready to attempt your own flight. They have a square round Fairoaks, and after taking off you go out there and fly the square, up to 700 feet, out over the trees and back down again.

The second time I did the circuit, I gave myself a nasty shock. I was up there going well, flying nicely, all the instruments working well, then suddenly at 700 feet I was in cloud for the first time, with or without an instructor. Did I panic! But I got myself under control, trusted the instruments and got down out of there.

I was in a real muck sweat for a few minutes after that.

The next time I went up, I was suddenly in traffic: the tower telling me there was an inbound aircraft from the south-east at 1000 feet. I thought to myself, 'Where the hell's south-east?' The trouble is, from the air, all the towns look the same. Even Woking and Guildford, with railways running through them, look similar.

I was at 700 feet, and you are supposed to have 500 feet clearance, so I quickly got back down to 500 feet and looked around for the other plane, but never saw it. It's amazing how quickly you start working out that 500 feet is only about a 5-iron, so it's a bit close in machines capable of going at the speed of a well-struck golf ball!

All in all I have now got more than thirty hours flying time under my belt and have completed the basic syllabus. Hopefully one winter I will have another two- to three-week course to complete the paperwork and get my licence. Thereafter, you only need about five hours a year to keep it, and I intend to do more than that.

I have no plans to buy my own helicopter. They are very expensive, and you would have to fly a lot more than I intend to make owning one worthwhile. Henry Cotton only ever gave me one piece of advice on the few occasions we met: 'There will be lots of incentive to surround yourself with expensive possessions. Don't. They cause worry and require much looking after. If you want anything, just rent it.' So I'll just hire them as and when I need them, and I will only ever be the auxiliary pilot. I would never fly regularly by myself.

Before the helicopter I got a reputation for driving fast cars. Once again the media blew that up out of all proportion. I did a high performance driving course more than ten years ago with an ex-Porsche racing driver, Mike Franey.

I have always loved Porsches. You can dawdle along in them, and they are as comfortable and easy to drive at 30 mph as they are at 130 mph. So many of the others are murder to go slow in; they keep stalling if you don't keep the revs up.

That session with Mike Franey was only a safety at speed exercise at an old air field, learning how to be thoroughly competent when going fast. The next time I went out with a professional was with Derek Bell a couple of years ago. The press speculated I was about to begin a career as a racing driver; at the very least I was no longer fully committed to golf!

It is a thrill to put a car right on the limit, but to go round and round a track quickly ceases to be much fun. Then there is the risk. At golf or fishing, if you lose concentration the ball is over the fence or the fish off the hook. Driving a car fast, you can do a bit more damage than that! With a family it just isn't worth it.

On that note: family, marriage and parenthood came at the time I was just beginning to see the light at the end of the golfing tunnel. Gill and I secretly married at a registry office on 3 January 1986 and had a service of blessing the following day. The registry office was to ensure privacy and the company of just a few good friends. The blessing was a bigger affair, and sure enough the press got wind and were there in force.

Natalie was born in September that year and mother and daughter were both at Muirfield when I won my first Open the following July — though I don't expect Natalie will be able to recall the occasion in later life. She was there in the Royal & Ancient caravan with me while I waited, with head in hands, not daring even to watch the television for Paul Azinger to finish and take five at the last to let me win. Indeed, it was a good distraction having to keep an eye on her, seeing she didn't get into any trouble during those endless final moments.

Matthew came along in 1989 and Georgia in the spring of 1993 — no prizes for guessing the inspiration of her name. Our main ambition for all our children is to bring them up as

British 3-man bob in 1993. Georgia and Green Ted are in the driver's seat.

normally as possible, bearing in mind all the hullabaloo that surrounds my life. When they witness the worse excesses, we try to treat it all as a game.

Like any father I like to take the kids to MacDonalds, but even there people come with napkins and old envelopes and ask for your autograph. 'Why are you signing that piece of paper for that man?' Matthew asks. I usually manage to make a bit of a joke about it.

Home for me as a kid in Welwyn was a two-up and two-down, and I was very happy there with my ladder shed and trees to play on. That was the norm. My kids are going to grow up in a bigger house and with more toys, but that for them will be the norm. Most important, though, will be that they respect the value of things, be they theirs or other people's. They will never be showered with cash and told to get on with life.

As a parent you want to give your kids opportunities, and ours will have a chance at most things they want to do. The last couple of years we have taken them skiing, and Matthew at four and a half years old was down those slopes like he'd been up a snow-covered mountain all his life. Natalie too. Both have intuition, and skiing will be second nature to all of them when they're grown up. Skiing will probably become a regular feature, as Christmas and January is my main holiday period. I spend

We try to make our home and our lives as normal as possible.

most of my working life in the sun, the children are often with me during their holidays, so crisp, clear sunny days in Switzerland are a novelty for all of us.

I don't ski; I'm too wary of breaking something or ripping some vital tendon. That would be my career gone, so it's just not worth it. Look what happened to Phil Michelson, broke both legs at the beginning of the 1994 season. Like golf, skiing is something to start young, and if I'd skied as a child I might still be doing it. All I can do with them is a bit of tobogganing, though I've ploughed all of us into the drifts on more than one occasion. Otherwise, its dressing up in the gear and following them with a camera for those two weeks. I get a great thrill watching them progressing so well so young, and clearly enjoying it.

I have been successful, so the children are going to have a great start in life, but both Gill and I intend that they enter adulthood with their feet firmly on the ground. No grandiose ideas about living in great luxury and never having to lift a hand. They'll have to earn their own pocket money.

Natalie looks as though she could turn out to be quite artistic, though her great love, as with many girls her age, is horses. She gets that from Gill, who rode a lot as a kid. Matthew looks to be well coordinated and could turn out to be a good sportsman. At the moment it wouldn't surprise me if he were taller than me, so maybe he will just become a second row forward!

Obviously I'd love him to be interested in golf so I could pass onto him everything I have learnt about the game; but there's no way I'm

The professor.

18

going to force him. He comes down to the practice ground with me now and then and whacks a ball about, but quite often he prefers to do something else, so the bug hasn't caught yet.

If he does become good, that will be great, but I know how difficult it is for sons to follow fathers who have established reputations. Look at the Jacklin and Nicklaus offspring: all the boys have had a go at the game, most professionally, but trying to learn a sport with the spotlight on you and Dad's shadow over you is hard indeed.

So we try to make our home and our lives as normal as possible. There must be lots of families where the father is away for two or three weeks at a time on a regular basis, and I'm probably around more than most Dads on the weeks I am not away. That said, the business side of my life — course design, working with my long-term sponsor on their products and charity work — seem to be taking ever more of the days when I am not at a tournament. I'll have to watch that.

GILL'S STORY

I suspect Nick is no different from most husbands in that domestic chores are not for him. Perhaps because he is away so much he really enjoys his children when he's at home. Being a small boy Matthew

Sculptor Jim Mathieson takes my measurements for Madam Tussaud's.

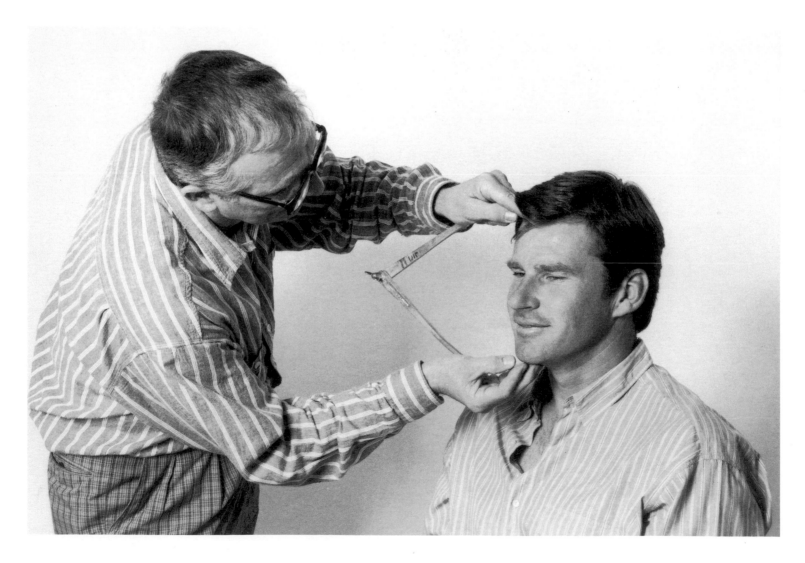

I told Elton to wear something inconspicuous – the other green jacket of 1990.

probably gets a little bit more attention, and he is the one who misses his Dad on the weeks he is away. 'How many more sleeps till Daddy comes home?' is the heartbreaking enquiry at bedtime every night. Nick is aware of this and tries to talk to all of us as often as possible when playing in tournaments. As a girl, Natalie seems much more self-sufficient, possibly a trait inherited from me.

Nick would very much like to have us travel with him more than we do, but with Natalie and now Matthew at school, that just isn't possible. In an ideal world, tournament golf would take place in term time and the rest periods would coincide with the children's holidays.

Nick is now very good at not bringing too much work home from the office. There was a time when he would brood for a long time after a bad round. He has now come to terms with golf not being perfectible, and his golf has benefited from it, not to mention lifting the clouds at home! Certainly since his last Open win he has become much more relaxed. That victory and the manner of it – having it sewn up, then nearly throwing it away, only to win it back again – and his emotional reaction to it, got a lot of warm reaction from many people we have since met.

That seemed to confirm to Nick finally that taking his swing apart and putting it back together again had not only been the right thing but was also perceived to be so. It was his fifth major and took him to another level of achievement. If he doesn't win another, he will still be pleased with what he has done, and all the effort will have been worthwhile.

That's not to say he's resting on his laurels, that he's no longer hungry to win and win the big ones. He still sets his goals every year – in fact, every week and every day – but if things don't go his way, he's much better at handling it. He still very much has the will to win, the drive, but he can take the disappointments better.

Part of the reason for Nick's success has been his ability to clear his mind of all unnecessary baggage and concentrate fully on the task in hand. Everything not directly connected to moving that little white ball around eighteen holes in the least number of shots, he leaves to others.

He relies totally on the people at IMG (Mark McCormack's client management company), and in particular John Simpson and Julie White, who deal with his business affairs. There are times when he gets deeply involved with corporate plans for Pringle or Mizuno, but day to day they have carte blanche to run his commercial life. I see myself filling much the same role on the domestic front – I head the home support team.

There was a time when I used to deal with a lot of the mail Nick gets at home, but when the children started to come something had to go, so now all correspondence gets dealt with by the office. Having worked for IMG myself – that's how we met – I am probably better equipped than most wives to talk on Nick's behalf with IMG without troubling him. I rather enjoy keeping my hand in, so to speak, but the kids and their well-being keep me more than fully occupied.

I am very protective of Nick's privacy and his time, all the more so since he won that 1992 Open Championship and the Johnnie Walker World Championship the following

Nick and Gill, with George.

December. Those wins seemed to spark an awareness wider than golf itself, rather like Seb Coe was a household name at the height of his powers, even to those that knew nothing about athletics.

Along with that increased fame has come even greater pressures to attend this or that function. Even on the weeks he is at home we have to be very selective about what we go to, otherwise we might never have any time on our own. Also, he finds purely social functions almost as stressful as coming up the last hole with a four to win. In fact he'd far rather cope with the pressure of getting that four than sit down to some five-course meal and make small talk. He's about a 24 handicap at that!

Along with the pleasure of having achieved as much as he has and the financial security that goes with it, Nick's success has opened doors that very few pass through. Golf is one of the pastimes of the rich and famous, and many is the giant of another walk of life that has been humbled by the game. That makes them as curious to meet you as you are to meet them, and it has been great fun to visit some really smart addresses.

The most surprising have been a couple of invitations to Number 10 and one to dine at the White House. George Bush is an enthusiastic golfer and has connections with the game in that an uncle, George Walker, was the one who presented the Walker Cup.

The occasion of our visit to the White House was the presentation of the Medal of Freedom to Margaret Thatcher. There was no reason for us to be there, but as we had been invited, we were certainly going to

make the effort. Nick came up from Florida, and I flew in from England.

At the dinner afterwards Nick found himself at the 'high table', near enough to Mr Bush to ask him about the Gulf War, which had just been won. He was most interesting, but all he really wanted to know was how to improve his putting.

The first Number 10 visit was also connected with George Bush, as he was visiting Mrs Thatcher at the time, and we were invited along as people he already knew! Then of course Dennis Thatcher is an avid golfer, and I suspect that had something to do with our second invitation there.

Those are just some of the many rewards that all Nick's endeavours have reaped, but I must honestly say that fame is very much a two-edged sword. Nick has already mentioned the incessant request for autographs, no matter where you are. Yes, it's flattering, but it very quickly becomes quite tedious.

All in all, though, I wouldn't change a day of it. Nick and I got together around the time he was going through his own personal hell of changing his swing. Those were dark days, but they have made the subsequent days in the sun all that more enjoyable. Genius in any form is never easy to live with, but the sharing in its success more than outweighs the sacrifices. I've enjoyed the ride. ◄

1
The Open
Golf's Holy Grail

• • • • • • • • • • • • •

The 1973 Open Championship was the very first time I watched golf live. My Dad and I went to Troon in a caravan, but the weather was terrible, wet and cold, and I remember having to wear pyjamas under my clothes all week to keep warm. The caravan wasn't all that warm either.

At the start I spent a lot of time just sitting on the practice ground, behind the players, watching them hit one perfect shot after another. I saw Tom Weiskopf early on. He was a very imposing figure, tall and with a wonderful swing.

One afternoon he was out there dressed in a sports coats and street shoes for the clubhouse, discussing different shafts with David Graham. Then he took his coat off and with no studs hit a stream of great shots — all with a 1-iron. I thought that was wonderful.

When the championship started I knew who I was going to follow: Weiskopf. In those days the galleries were allowed on the fairways to watch the second shots from behind. I used to watch him drive, then I would run ahead and catch his second shot, then sprint again up to the green. I think I saw him hit nearly every

Tom Weis-kopf, Open champion in 1973 at Troon, with Peter Oosterhuis.

shot that week — and of course he won.

We went to Lytham the next year, and again the practice ground was the main attraction for me. I was very impressed by Bruce Crampton, who had Nick de Paul caddying for him. You had to use your own practice balls then, and there was de Paul, with his big baseball glove, catching every single shot Crampton hit on the fly. Only when Crampton hit a driver did he let it bounce, and hardly

ever more than a pace to right or left.

Naturally I was aware by then of the Masters, having seen it on television a number of times, so I knew there were two big tournaments that were the most important in golf. Like any kid, when I was out there on my own at Welwyn, I used to imagine situations in which I had this putt for the Open or had to get down in two from the sand to win the Masters. Even then they were my goals, and of course they have remained so throughout my career.

Just two years later, at Royal Birkdale, I played in my first Open. At first I was a bit overawed to be alongside all those golfers whom I had watched so recently from behind the ropes. There was also the size of the crowds and all the marquees — it was massive. I am sure it is the same for any golfer who plays in a major championship for the first time. On top of which, The Open is by far the largest of all the majors, with more infrastructure than the other three put together. No European Tour event bears any comparison. Most American Tour events get big galleries, so their players have some experience of such an atmosphere, but in Europe in the mid-1970s, those watching could be counted in hundreds rather than thousands.

Only a couple of years after that I had my first real taste of contesting the closing stages. I finished just four shots behind Jack Nicklaus at St Andrews, the year he squeezed past New Zealander Simon Owen on the line. That was when I said to myself, 'I can win this one day.'

But it wasn't until 1983 that I really gave myself a chance. Before then it had been one bad round that kept me from being in contention to the end of the Championship. I realized at that level a bad round was something you just could not afford. At Royal Birkdale that year, I played really well to be up around the lead for all four days.

What I particularly remember was how comfortable I felt being at the centre of things. For the first time I felt I really

At the Open in 1983 I finally began to feel I belonged.

belonged to the Open. There was still all the hullabaloo, and I couldn't wait to get to the peace of the practice ground. Once there, I felt I was in my own private office, hitting shots and getting ready.

A few years later I might have won from that position, but at that stage I still had much to learn. I was leading as we played 13 on the last day, but Trevino holed a huge putt, and I three-putted. I did the same again at the next hole and dropped another at 16. In the end I finished eighth, five shots behind Tom Watson.

By 1987 my work with David Leadbetter was beginning to bear fruit. I came second in a minor event in Hattiesberg the same week as the Masters. All the big boys were obviously at Augusta but four rounds of 67 under tournament conditions was great for the confidence.

I didn't score all that well in the Scottish Open at Gleneagles the week before the Open at Muirfield, a few destructive shots undoing what was otherwise some good golf. I knew I was close to hitting the ball really well, and no one was taking much notice as I hadn't exactly threatened in Britain for the last few years.

A 68 and a 69 in the first two rounds of the Open put me close to the leaders at halfway. Then the Saturday was a horrid day: cold, wet and very windy. I struggled that afternoon, but the odd putt went in at the right moment and I came off the 18th green reasonably happy with my 71. I went off and tinkered with the grip on my putter. When I came back, I saw my 71 had taken me to the top of the leaderboard. I thought about it for a minute and realized that I was looking forward to the challenge, that I was ready for it.

Obviously the prospects of next day filled my mind, but that evening I could clearly envisage how things could unfold the following day. Gill and I knew there was no point in packing, that we'd have to stay the next night. I knew we'd be doing press conferences and then there'd be the

The one we all dream about: the putt to win the Open.

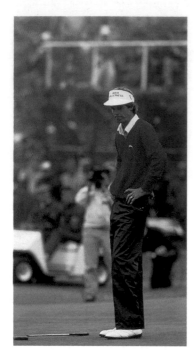

Azinger misses the last at Muirfield...

television crews at the hotel the morning after. Somehow I saw all this on the Saturday evening before.

By the following day I was in a true cocoon. I was in focus only as far as my footsteps in front of me, beyond that was just a blur. The contest was painfully close all the way. I was hitting the ball really well, but my putting was awful. I had chance after chance to build a winning lead, to get to the point where I could relax and enjoy it. The only putt I holed was from eight feet to save par at 11. I didn't set out to make eighteen pars, but it was a mucky day, cold and damp, and we'd started in a squall. Towards the end, the wind got up; at 16 I hit a 2-iron, the pin was only 186 yards away, but I still came up short — and I hit it well.

Playing 18 I knew it was close: you can feel it from the crowd, but I did not know who was doing what. When I set to the green I saw that Rodger Davis was four under, so I had to hole my five-footer to win. A tie and a play-off was not what I had foreseen the previous evening. I holed the putt and then sat in the Royal & Ancient van until the end.

There were televisions in there, but I couldn't bear to watch. Then I heard Peter Alliss say, 'the next fifteen seconds are going to change one of these young men's lives,' and

fortunately it was mine; Azinger missed his putt to tie.

Muirfield five years later was a totally different experience. I came into it as favourite, and in a sense I felt I was defending the title I won there the last time. I didn't mind favouritism because I was playing so well, almost as well as when I had won at St Andrews two years before. What I knew was important was to find the same attitude I had in 1987, to get comfortable with the occasion and be relaxed enough to produce winning golf on the day. There was still enormous pressure. When I started the last round with a four-shot lead, I was very aware I would be crucified by the media if I lost. I had to get rid of this feeling, so on a piece of paper I wrote: 'You are playing for yourself.'

...and the 1987 Open is mine.

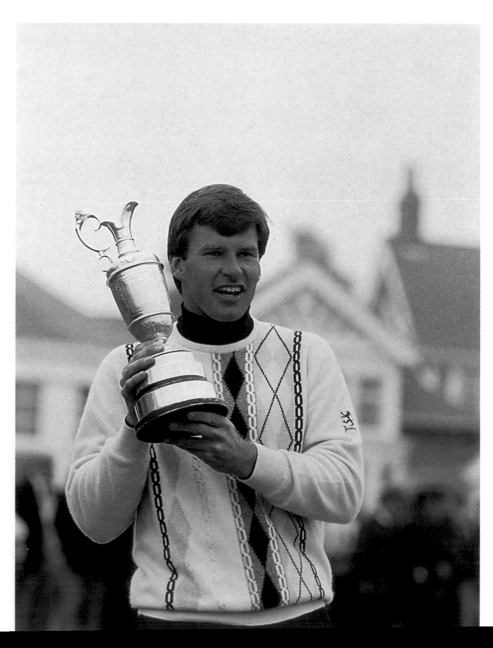

The 18th at Muirfield, 1992.

I played fine at the start of that final round, I had chances all through the front nine to wrap the tournament up there and then. I hit the ball better and better, but very much like 1987, I couldn't make a putt. I knew if I could just hole one, I would get into a comfort zone and have it all sewn up.

I was playing with Steve Pate, who wasn't paying that well, just hanging on, and it seemed no one else was coming at me. But then I started making mistakes. I missed the green left at 11, and the pin was over that side so there was no chance of getting down in two. Then I three-putted 13; it was only a 9-iron to that green, but I left it way short with the pin at the back.

I still felt fine, made a good swing at 14 into the wind, but the ball went sailing off into a bunker; I couldn't believe it. I wasn't nervous, but my concentration had gone; I was sure there was nothing wrong with the swing or tempo.

I nearly got away with a four at 14 but that was another shot gone. For the first time I looked at the scoreboard and could see that John Cook had come right back. I was now two behind. After driving out of bounds at the 9th, Cook had relaxed and started picking up shots where I was dropping them. From the turn he had picked up six shots on me in as many holes.

Walking to the 15th tee, I knew I was

John Cook at break-point at the 17th.

The scariest bunker shot at Muirfield. In 1992 I could have been there all day.

My third Open victory at Muirfield in 1992.

it back on the ground quickly. And that is exactly what I did at 15. There is always a bit of luck when a ball goes really close like that, but I had done my homework. The three there revived my confidence.

I was still going to need some help from John Cook, however. Don't ask me how, but I knew he would take five up to 18. This is no comment on him or his temperament, but 18 is a very hard hole at the best of times, and that day the wind was against and across from the right.

The pressure over those last few holes was colossal, more than anything I had ever experienced. I went from winning it to losing it and back again. I went right to the edge there and looked into the abyss, didn't like what I saw and thankfully went back the other way. Losing would have been very difficult to cope with.

I like to think I gained from that experience, that I was able to come back from behind and then emerge stronger as a result. One of things I am most proud of in my career is that I have hardly ever

facing the biggest crisis of my career. I had made some crucial mistakes earlier that summer and lost a number of tournaments I should have won, the French Championship in particular. I'd also wobbled when winning the Irish in June. Here I was again squandering a four-shot lead over the final nine holes. If I lost now, it would leave a bad mental scar. That was when I said to myself: 'I've just got to play the best four holes of my life.'

The second shot to 15 got me going. It was into the wind and 164 yards to the pin; just a three-quarter 5-iron, the type of shot I was playing perfectly just then. These little soft shots were something Lead and I had been working on, keeping the ball low, working it into the wind, hitting them right to left, left to right. The previous Sunday, and the wind had been howling at Muirfield, no one had gone out for fear of spoiling their swing. But I wanted to try a few shots in these conditions, so I went out for just four holes – 10, 11, 12, then back up 18. I played a lot of little middle irons; a 6-iron just 140 yards, keeping it low and getting

I needed a shoulder to lean on afterwards.

Muirfield 1992: the hardest of them all.

chucked in the towel. I have been very good at just battering away, even though I felt it was all going wrong. That Open at Muirfield in 1992 was my Championship: I was not going to give it away, and I was very pleased that I didn't.

St Andrews in 1990 was a different kind of situation. Right from the beginning I felt it would be a challenge between Greg Norman and me. Greg liked the course and had played a great round there in the final of the 1988 Dunhill Cup, so he was very comfortable with the course. I wasn't surprised when we were tied at twelve under after two rounds.

We had played the last two rounds together in the Australian Masters earlier in the year, and Greg had won that, but on a course that he liked, Huntingdale,

A great week of putting at St Andrews.

where he had won on five or six occasions. I liked the course, on the Melbourne sand belt, but have never played particularly well there.

I just felt the 1990 Open would be between me and Greg Norman.

Even so, that previous contest wasn't a factor; I was feeling very good. I knew every day I walked onto St Andrews that I would shoot between 66 and 68. I just

37

The end of a great day: on my way to a 67 in the third round.

didn't think I could do worse than that if the weather was good. It meant I could just go out and play, I didn't have to push too hard to make a score.

Everyone now puts the next day down as a significant day in Greg's career, a day that set him back a long way. I'm not sure about that, but I knew it was a contest between him and me and that however much we might say we were playing a medal round in a championship, this was a head-to-head situation. On the first hole, when we had similar putts and I went first, I knew I had to hole it. I did and he didn't, and I think that was important.

Greg is very competitive and flam-

For me the Open remains the greatest championship of all.

boyant. His style alone makes you more aware that you are playing him and not a quieter sort of guy. When he's around it just seems as if there is more going on, so to play with him you have to concentrate harder. There is certainly no gamesmanship about him, but while some other players simply knock it away, Greg's lights are flashing and it's more of a show.

I was interested to hear later that after the first couple of holes Greg changed his game-plan. He had been playing irons off every tee, going for position, but he suddenly started to go with his driver. He found one or two bunkers on the back nine, and again at 13 and those extra errors meant he finished the day too far behind to come back the following day.

The last day was difficult for me. Being five shots ahead meant I was bound to

I don't think Greg Norman enjoyed it as much as I did.

Almost home - the 18th tee at St Andrews, 1990. 5-shot lead – great!

play defensively. You want to play well, but you just can't take risks. I would have loved to hole some putts, just to make life easier, but nothing much happened. Again I didn't look at the scoreboard, but felt that they were closing in, I could sense it. In fact, it was Payne Stewart, and at one point he was within a couple of shots. It wasn't until I got a birdie at 15 that I looked at the leaderboard and saw I was safe: four ahead with four to play.

My first Open was enormously important to me, but to win at St Andrews is special. There is just so much history about the place and those last couple of holes finishing up in the town, so to speak. That Open was the only major where I could cruise in and look around me over those final holes. It was an experience I will long remember.

I also thought I was going to win in 1993, especially after a 63 in the second round. I was playing well, but the occasions when anyone can convert a two-shot lead – as I had at halfway – into an even greater one are rare. My third round of 70 was a bit disappointing, but the pin positions were very hard that day, and at the end I still held the lead, albeit in a tie with Corey Pavin.

On the final day Norman took over when Bernhard Langer and I both missed little putts at the 4th, and he never faltered from there on. In retrospect, my 67 in the last round of the Open would usually have been good enough, particularly if you start off in front, but Greg is the one person capable of the kind of golf he played that day. I didn't lose it, he won it.

For me the Open remains the greatest
championship of all. It is by far the most
representative of the majors, the Royal &
Ancient doing everything in their power
to scour the earth and ensure an even
balance of top players from around the
world. Also, links golf, while almost
unique to the British Isles, is perhaps the

*There was
much to
celebrate at
St Andrews
in 1990.*

most neutral ground on which to play a
championship. We may have grown up on
it, and any British player who has played a
year or two of top amateur golf is sure to
have played big medal events and the
Amateur Championship at the seaside,
but European Tour events hardly ever go
there, so now the wind and fast running
conditions are as foreign to us as the
Americans.

My Open Championships, and particularly the one at St Andrews, will
have pride of place when I review my
achievements, but those at Augusta will
not be far behind. ◀

*St Andrews:
to win at the
home of golf
is special.*

The Masters
Golf in the Garden of Eden

● ● ● ● ● ● ● ● ● ● ● ● ● ●

The Masters of 1971 was my very first contact with golf. I was thirteen years old and saw the last two days on television. With the Easter holidays just beginning, I told my parents that I wanted to have a go at the game, and off we went to Welwyn Garden City Golf Club.

Even though the game and the great players were completely unknown to me, Jack Nicklaus in 1971 made a clear impression on me. The commentators must have spoken of him in revered terms, and he drew my attention like a magnet, despite not winning that day. He shared the lead going into the last round, but nothing much went right for him, and he came third.

I was struck that weekend by the same things that hit everyone who experiences Augusta for the first time: the tall, dark pines, the green grass and the colourful golfers. What most impressed me, however, was the sound. Not the whooping of the crowds — though that is thrilling the first time — but the very sound of club on ball and the rush of air as the ball set off. I suppose the closeness and height of the trees exaggerate the sound, but I was very aware of that wonderful swoosh — the hit and the ball's launch are really all one noise.

When I took up the game, one of the things I was seeking was to recreate that unique sound. It was a long time — a year or so — before I hit one properly and heard it again. In any career there are certain important moments and events; that first really good strike was a vivid one for me.

When you first get to Augusta, having driven 150 miles due east from Atlanta, the town itself gives no hint of the jewel in its midst. You hardly even see the town as you turn off the highway into Washington Road before being assailed by classic American suburbia. Two-storey motels with flashing neon lights, restaurants and beauty parlours side by side, and churches mingling with shopping centres — surely the great Augusta National must be on the other side of town?

A mile or so down Washington Road, just past Silverstein's the Cleaners — all the clean laundary you can carry for $5 — is a wire fence with hedge behind. Past a couple of entrances into car parks with signs indicating 'The Tournament' appears the relatively understated turning into Magnolia Lane, with the old Plantation House instantly visible through the trees at the far end. If it weren't for the little plaque on the gate post that reads 'Augusta National Golf Club', it would be possible to pass it by.

On the other side of the gate is truly another world. The trees lining Magnolia Lane give the impression of a drive up to a French château, but the illusion is swiftly

At no other time or place is golf so right as at Augusta in the spring.

I hope I'll still be winning Majors at 46.

How can such beauty conceal such a beast?

dispersed by the presence of practice grounds on either side, as well as the distinct colonial style of the clubhouse itself.

The first thing that strikes you about Augusta is how small everything is. A moment's thought, and it is easy to realize that for a club with a mere 200 members anything bigger would be superfluous. But at Masters time it all seems rather crowded. What is extraordinary is that it can accommodate so many for that one week, while remaining the perfect members' club the rest of the year.

At no other time or place is golf so absolutely right as at Augusta in the spring. The U.S. Open, except when it is at Pebble Beach, could be anywhere, anytime U.S.A.; the U.S. P.G.A. should be anywhere *but* the U.S.A. in August, and even the Open Championship tests your commitment when you get a wet and windy one.

The majors have long been the sole peaks in the otherwise flat plane of the golf year. Recent years have produced not only a proliferation of tournaments, but the creation of some foothills: the Players Championship two weeks before the Masters and the Johnnie Walker World Championship in December are now more than just another stop along the year's golfing highway. Even so, there is still the seven-month gap between the last major of the previous year and the following year's Masters, and through that time the anticipation mounts.

I wasn't actually able to play in the Masters until 1979, because in those days there weren't as many slots available for Europeans as there are now. I got in then for finishing well up in Europe the previous year. But Augusta takes a bit of getting to know and it wasn't until 1984 that I made a decent show.

I was just two shots behind with a round to go and played with Ben Crenshaw, the eventual winner. I took 40 for the front nine and that was that. It was the first time I really got hammered by the media, coming as it did after I had blown the Open at Birkdale the previous

Ben Crenshaw at Augusta, 1984. That's when I first saw what good putting really was.

weather prevented the third round from being completed, and I was one of those still out. I had to stop with my ball in a horrid spot over the back of 13. The following morning I would have to bump the ball into that steep bank, skip it up onto the green and trickle it down to the pin across that step near the back left corner of the green.

They have practice facilities for everything at Augusta, and I found a spot not dissimilar on the practice ground. I must have had 50 or 60 goes at that very type of shot before going out the following morning. It was still a scary shot with the ground being so wet. I played it perfectly, however, judged the slope just right and got it down within six feet. I was thrilled. — then I missed the putt.

I was so disappointed that I three-putted the next hole and dropped another at 17. Par for the last six holes, what with the two par fives, is two under: I'd taken two over. I was now five behind, and with nothing to lose I changed putters and worked though the break on the putting green. I had picked up one of those black mallet-headed Wilson putters, the ones with three white stripes on the top. I taped over two of them, so I had just one line to set up with and off I went.

summer. That hurt, as did the disappointment of doing so badly, but even then I saw it as a learning experience. Apart from my poor play, my strongest memory of that day was standing at the edge of every green watching Crenshaw hole putt after putt on those unbelievable greens. I saw not only how to putt at Augusta — the sort of pace you had to strike the ball and the amount of borrow necessary to get it into the hole — but how Crenshaw coped with the pressures over those final few holes. So it wasn't all bad.

After that I was off into my wilderness years and didn't make much of a show again until 1989, the year I won my first title there. I had just played seven straight weeks in America without getting the sort of results I thought my play deserved. I was hitting the ball very well but not scoring. I remember deciding just to give it a go to see what would happen.

I played the first 27 holes really well; I was six under par and leading by three. Then I went straight backwards and after three rounds was one over. It was all so reminiscent of how things had been going that spring.

It was one of those years when bad

I was only on the front corner of the green at the first, and had this 25-yarder right across the slope. I would have been delighted just to get it close, but in it went. That sort of start is worth so much — I birdied two of the next three and felt I was back in with a fighting chance.

I had an awful putt, over the hog's back and down the other side.

I was still four, if not five, behind Scott Hoch at the turn. I got to 13 and hit a great wood shot on and birdied the hole. Then I hit it real close at the next, birdied 15 from over the back,

'Now come
and show me
how to putt
like that.' With
Ben Crenshaw
in 1984.

but the big breaks were at 16 and 17.

At 16 I was behind the pin. If the ball hadn't been one inch off the putting surface, it would have rolled back down past the hole. I was only fifteen feet away, but I had to borrow at least twelve feet left. There was no way of stopping it, but it went in.

It was the same thing at 17. The pin was in its usual last day place over on the right, and I dragged my approach fifteen yards left. I had an awful putt, over the hog's back and down the other side. Another huge borrow from the left, and frankly, I hit it much too hard. Afterwards an American friend said, 'If that putt had missed you'd have finished fourth, not second!'

It had started raining now, and as I was waiting to play my second up the last, water came through the umbrella and right onto my thumb, the one with the glove on — the worst place to get wet. Changing gloves would have only upset me further, so I hung on tight and the shot came off. It was such a good one, in fact, that I had quite a short putt for a three. I missed it and so tied with Hoch.

On the first extra hole, I was never going to do better than five. The tee shot was out right, and then I nearly hit a great second from 200 yards with a 4-iron but caught the edge of the bunker, and after all that rain, I was pleased to get it out somewhere close. In the end Hoch had a two-footer to win.

I stood at the side of the green and kept telling myself I was still going to win. I wasn't willing him to miss it, but it is important you continue to think positively. It was actually a very nasty putt, downhill and left to right, and he just hit it too hard. He was further away, and I remember wanting him to hole it

Afterwards there were press conferences and T.V. interviews.

3rd round, 11th hole, 1989 – just before my greatest win ever. It was getting dark, and Proj still wore dark glasses!

because that wasn't the way I wanted to win.

By now it was getting dark and raining hard. I hit a good drive but was still 210 yards from the hole with the wind blowing across from the right. With water on the left I aimed at the right edge of the green and saw the wind start to move the ball as it passed the trees by the 12 tee – perfect. It was just about the best 3-iron I ever hit.

Scott Hoch missed the green right and pitched to no better than eight feet, on that green and in that light a very difficult putt. I then had a chance to win, but it was so dark and misty that it was impossible to see the hole from where I was, 25 feet below it. It was so dark, in fact, Proj (caddy Andy Prodger) came over and said, 'It all looks a bit too misty to me, Guv, you'd better do this one on your own' – a great help. But I managed to hole it.

My abiding memories after that were of Sandy putting on the jacket in the cabin, and I think it must have been the one from the previous year, because the sleeves were so short. 'Never mind,' I said, 'it's the colour that counts.'

White Dogwood, 1989, 11th hole, where I won both my Masters titles.

Afterwards there were press conferences and T.V. interviews, and there was the members' dinner. You are allowed one guest, and with Gill at home after giving birth to Matthew just three weeks earlier, I took my manager John Simpson along.

Pearls of wisdom from the great man, Jack Nicklaus.

The turning point was probably at 12. It never looks too bad on television as the camera is right at the green and makes it look bigger than it really is. From the tee it appears to be a sliver of green. It's very difficult to get a visual image of the shot, and 'seeing' the shot you are going to play is very important to a golfer.

I found the bunker back left, and was plugged. From there it would be easy to leave it in or to knock it back over the green and into the creek. I played a great shot out, just cleared the lip of the bunker – but it still ran off the green on the other side. Holing the fifteen-foot putt back up the slope kept my round, not to mention my challenge, intact.

Walking off, I said to Nicklaus, 'Thank

And again, in 1990, before the play-off with Ray Floyd.

At the dinner you are the guest of the club's Chairman, who was Hord Hardin. John is always one for the quirky question and turned to Mr Hardin to ask whether he thought I should honour a commitment to play the following week in the Heritage or go home to my new family. After due consideration Mr Hardin replied, 'That's a good question, John, but I really think *Sandy* should stay and play.' Names have never been Mr Hardin's strong point.

At Augusta the following year my contest against Raymond Floyd was very similar, and not just because it again finished at the second extra hole. Once again I was several shots behind as we turned for home in the final round and had to press for everything to narrow the gap.

I was paired with Jack Nicklaus and had started off the last round three behind Floyd. On the first hole I started with a six: in the bunker off the tee, on in three and three putts. – great. Maybe that lapse helped me relax; I certainly knew I had to motor. Just as I had the previous year, I got a birdie at the 2nd, and then another at the 7th. Both are holes you are normally happy to get through with pars, and they kept me just about within range of Floyd.

The 8th hole on the par-3 course at Augusta: just as immaculate as the big one.

God we don't have to play that hole every week.' Jack responded, 'Hell, I've been playing it for the last 35 years.' To which I replied, 'That's older than me!' He didn't even smile. They were the first words we'd spoken all day, and don't forget, he was still trying to win the tournament.

I got my birdies at 13 and 15, the two par fives, then at 16 I had a putt on the opposite side to the year before. The night before I dreamt I made two at 16, and Fanny had had the same dream. It wasn't

I think I'll have the 11th hole at Augusta copied at my next home.

a difficult putt, perhaps the easiest you can get on that green, so neither of us was surprised when it went in. Two pars, and when Floyd three-putted 17, we were even. Once again, at the end of the final round, the leading golfer was defending his lead and getting caught.

I played 10, the first extra hole, just as I had the year before: drive off to the right and 3-iron into the bunker. Floyd got his drive down and round the corner and hit his approach right under the hole, no more than fifteen or eighteen feet away. It

Ben Hogan's Bridge.

was the sort of putt he'd fancy holing, but

I got my bunker shot out to four feet, and I think it shook him. He left his putt short.

The 11th tee is the only place on the course where there is what the Americans call a 'comfort station' — a loo, or at least one that is solely for the players. Raymond had to make a pit stop, so he was some way behind getting to our drives. I'd hit a good one, twenty yards past him, and whether he rushed because of having to catch up or was particularly confident after his good approach to 10, I don't know. But he'd no sooner got to his ball than he'd hit it and off into the water it went. That was the end of that.

As I was being driven back in the buggy, I remember thinking how nice it would be if Nicklaus were still around to give me the jacket. He'd been the only other player to win the Masters twice in a row. It would have been a great touch, and I'm sure if Nicklaus had

been asked he would have done it.

I sort of suggested it, but without anyone actually saying no, it didn't happen. Perhaps if they'd thought of it themselves they might have done it, but Mr Hardin did the presenting as usual. At least they had my jacket from the year before, so the size was right!

Throughout that early spell in America leading up to the Masters, thoughts about Augusta are always on your mind. I work on flighting the ball a little higher — the kind of shot, particularly with irons, you need there. Then I look to develop a draw for the tee shots, only the 1st and 18th there favouring a fade.

The 16th at Augusta. What a setting for unfolding drama.

The par-three course is a wonderful little course.

There's no point spending hours perfecting that little shot out of deep rough round greens: Augusta doesn't have any. Practising chipping into banks and bumps and finding practice greens with big slopes are the best way to prepare for Augusta's peculiarities.

If possible I like to get there the Sunday evening before the competition begins. Ideally, if I am playing well, I will do as little as possible to keep my swing ticking over. The hope is that the work of the previous five or six weeks will have brought my game together sufficiently so that all I need is little work-outs before and after playing. All the majors are difficult weeks, with lots of tension and hype surrounding them, so it is important to defuse all the external distractions.

There is a wonderful mystique and atmosphere about Augusta. Having played there for a number of years and being one of its winners, I find now there is a nice comfortable feel about the place. With its traditions it is very different from other clubs — where to go and what to do. Sometimes it is a bit like going back to school, feeling like you need to know which corridor to walk down so you don't bump into the headmaster. It has its own rules; what you can do for the other 51 weeks you cannot do there.

Every week on tour, for instance, whether here or in America, you can have your coach walk with you on practice rounds to watch you play and help you iron out the kinks. Not at Augusta. Apart from the players and their caddies, no one is allowed inside the ropes. No press, no photographers, no television even, so on balance, I am in favour of that.

It would be nice to have Lead there for

A great lay. At the 11th in 1990.

The 11th in 1990. They've come to take me away.

1990 at Augusta: Floyd made it easy for me in the end.

Sporting the green jacket in 1990, with Augusta's chairman, Hord Hardin.

Elated by a birdie on the third hole at the Masters in 1993.

the practice rounds, though, and I think the crowd would enjoy hearing what we were working on. I put the idea to Jackson Stevens, the current Chairman, and he listened and nodded, but I didn't get anywhere. I have never succeeded in getting Lead inside the ropes during practice.

I once went to Lead and told him I'd made a deal with the Chairman, but he'd have to dress as a caddie in white boiler-suit and vest. I got one of the white suits and the green hat with caddie written on it and had Lead put it on and took his picture. I didn't dare let him go outside — they can have a sense of humour failure at things like that!

Another reason for keeping the day work fairly light is that there are functions every night before the tourna-

Every time I learn or see something new. On the Wednesday is the competition over the par-three course. It is a wonderful little course, and with the crowd moving across from the big course there's tremendous atmosphere.

I like to be in one of the early groups to play the par three, otherwise there's a lot of hanging around; play can be slow there as well. There's no pressure to play in it, but it is fun and relaxing. You never want to win it because of the superstition that the winner has never gone on to win the main tournament.

The various prizes offered for special deeds both on the par three and in the main event are particularly nice. Closest to the hole or holes-in-one all get engraved crystal tumblers, as do eagles and albatrosses in the Masters

Before I won in 1989, I hadn't picked up any of the crystal and when I had a putt for a three at 13 in an early round, I was more conscious of 'this for that piece of glass' than its significance in the tournament. ◀

Join the club: Woosie's win in 1991.

ment starts. When I first went there, the only event was the club dinner for the international players on the Monday night. Now there is the champion's dinner on the Tuesday, and one year I won the American Player of the Year award, which meant going to the American Golf Writers dinner on the Wednesday.

Even though I know the course well, I still like to play three practice rounds.

3

U.S. Tour
American Adventures

● ● ● ● ● ● ● ● ● ● ● ● ● ●

*At the beginning of my career,
playing in America was essential because the European Tour
was so limited by comparison.
But with all the changes and
advancements made in Europe
the past dozen years, it is
sometimes difficult to remember
just how great the disparity
used to be.*

If you were in the top ten or fifteen players in Europe in 1980, you probably made a reasonable living, and the top half-dozen might actually have made enough to be putting something aside for a rainy day. The tournaments in Britain were mostly on quite good courses, but on the Continent golf was still a game for the elite few, and people who weren't too fussy about slick greens or well-raked bunkers.

While I have my doubts about our Tour starting in Europe as early in the year as it does now, no professional in any walk of life can wait until April to begin earning his or her living. Before sanctions there were enjoyable but lowly rewarded events in South Africa, and after that there was the Safari Tour through other parts of Africa. But thinking of those courses makes me realize I was being perhaps a bit harsh on the Continental ones. All this was in comparison to what was available in America. If you wished to make the most of your skills and believed sufficiently in yourself, America had to feature in your plans.

When I first went there in 1981 I did nor have my player's card, without which you couldn't play. People were still only talking about an all-exempt tour in which everyone had a ranking and you got into events based on where you were in the pecking order. The aim was to do away with the Monday qualifying events, which were administratively awkward and a nightmare to play in. When I started in America there were usually about 200 players looking for four or five slots in that week's tournament.

Being a Ryder Cup player, I was entitled to play in five events of my choosing. If I qualified one week, I was automatically exempted from the following week's tournament, without using up any more of my precious allocation.

I started playing tournament golf in the States early in 1981 in California, making the cut in the first seven events. At Los Angeles Open I finished seventh and by then had amassed enough points — or dollars, because that's how they measured it — to secure my card. I never had to go to any of the dreaded Monday events or, later, to the Qualifying School, which I can only imagine is like a week of Mondays!

America was a real eye-opener. To play week after week in glorious weather on courses that were in better condition than I believed possible and to experience the range of facilities provided for players — you felt if you couldn't play well there, you were never going to. It was during the first days on the American Tour that I learned what hard practice really meant. With superb ranges and an endless supply of balls, it was possible to hit shots as long as you wanted. Hour after hour to groove your swing was the culture there and one that appealed enormously to me.

There was indeed an endless supply of balls, but in those days, even in America, they weren't provided for free; it was $2 a bucket. Not having made much money then, I had to watch the pennies, or dimes. I remember getting my expenses into IMG pretty quick each week. In Europe we now take range balls, courtesy cars and Mizuno club-repair trucks very much for granted, but they have only come in the last five or six years, with the advent of the Tour sponsor, Volvo.

What is also easy to forget is that for much of my early career, indeed probably even as late 1987, I hardly ever had a matched set of clubs in my bag. Even on the odd occasions when they were all the same make, there was no way they could be described as matched by today's standards.

To get a new set of clubs in Europe meant taking a trip to the factory to be measured, then waiting three or four weeks for them to turn up. I don't ever remember having a set that was right even then. More often than not, there would be half a dozen clubs of the make I was contracted to play, but the 8, 9 and wedges, say, would be of another.

I had contracts to play with this or that club during that time, but the arrange-

Double-take on the swing.

66

1993 U.S.
Open, Baltus-
rol, New
Jersey.

ments were usually structured to allow me to mix and match. If the equipment did not meet my standards I could use others. Only with the arrival of Mizuno have we had sets of clubs available in Europe that I would truly call matched. They have set the standard, and other manufacturers have had to match them.

Again, America was different. The Wilson, Spalding or MacGegor reps were right there on tour, urging you to try this club or that, this shaft or that newfangled grip. If you found something you liked, they'd go away and make it up for you, and it would be there for you at the next stop. With that sort of service everyone tinkered around looking for the right mix of specifications to improve our games.

It was in the early days in America that I first began to question my swing. Until then I had been working at Welwyn Garden City with Ian Connolly, who had been my teacher from the beginning and who had done a brilliant job for me. America, though, was a whole new world; it opened up a new set of horizons. I was alongside the greatest players in the world, watching them go about their business in a totally different way. It was as though I had graduated to senior school, and an entirely new group of teachers.

A lot of people thought my efforts to alter my swing began in 1983 or 1984 with the arrival of David Leadbetter. Not so: I began experimenting a couple of years before that and had already made a number of changes myself before getting involved with Lead.

Jack Nicklaus dominated golf for more than two decades, and his successes had changed the way many top Americans thought and played. His very upright swing and steep descent into the ball had become the role model for most of the tall players. Jerry Pate, who had won the U.S. Open in 1976, was one, and when I first went there we talked often of the Nicklaus style, trying to incorporate the philosophy into our own games.

I never really could get it to work for

me; it was good some days, but then others I felt the bottom half of my body become detached from the top and a block to the right or a snap-hook was the result. I learnt then I would have to develop a method that was mine alone, not one borrowed from someone else.

I found the American Tour very much to my liking. In the early 1980s I would play twelve or thirteen weeks straight, particularly at the beginning of each year. I would probably have made my life there if I hadn't felt a responsibility to playing in Europe. With many of the courses on the Continent below standard and prize funds perhaps less than a third of what was on offer in America it would have been financial suicide to come back purely out of the goodness of our hearts, hence appearance money.

Every week there is an event worth more than a million dollars, and several with considerably more.

The pros and cons of that old chestnut have been aired often enough. My position remains that the presence of Seve, Sandy Lyle, Bernhard Langer, myself and latterly Ian Woosnam have enabled Ken Schofield to generate the prize funds we have today. Without appearance money the best players would always have gone to America and stayed there. Europe would have remained a golfing backwater, and quite probably we would never have had enough team spirit to win the Ryder Cup.

Detractors now say appearance money should cease, and in a sense it has. You no longer receive a fee for playing, but selected players are paid to appear on the Monday or Tuesday for special and often televised matches, such as shoot-outs or skins games.

In Europe it is still a case of supply and demand. There are now forty tourna-

ments, and sponsors and promoters would like you there every week, but that just isn't possible. Bearing in mind the shape of our Tour – the number of events and the few star players – the system we have really works quite well now.

In fact, trying to satisfy both tours contributed to my bad spell in the mid-1980s. In America I was trying to keep my card playing less than half the events there while attempting to play as much as possible in Europe. In 1983 I almost lost my U.S. Tour card: only by finishing second in the Walt Disney tournament after the Ryder Cup did I earn enough money. I won five times in Europe that year and had a great chance to win the Open, so it wasn't because I was playing badly.

Certainly a schedule of 34 or 35 events by the end of October and then off to Africa and Australia was a busy one. It was just too much, especially with the swing adjustments I was making. With hindsight, I should have cut back in 1984, let something go, even if it was my U.S. card; I would have come through that period of change much quicker if I had.

Two factors brought matters to a head. In 1986 Natalie was born, and a year later I won the Open. I couldn't face the upheaval that tournament play involved with a family, and the Open win meant I didn't have to. That was the point at which the European players started negotiations with Deane Beman of the U.S. Tour to get the number of tournaments we had to play down from fifteen to something more manageable.

We asked for a reduction to ten, but would have accepted twelve. Beman, however, wasn't having any of it. I suspect he was constantly having to deal with moans from the middle-ranking players about having 'non-Americans' – that was what we were called, never foreigners – on the Tour in the first place, so if he started showing us any favours he would get even more complaints.

In a sense they have been the losers. They have lost some of the best players as part of their tour, and we can now play there just about as much as we want: five regular Tour events, the three U.S. majors, the Tournaments Players Championship, plus the World Series and Tournament of Champions if you have won a qualifying event. That's about the ten we were looking for.

In my card-carrying Tour days life was not that easy for overseas players. To start with, there weren't as many as there are now, so you were a little band far from home. The top players were fine, especially when you became one of them. They could see the pluses of having the best from other parts of the world, both as competition and to enhance the reputation of their Tour.

All in all the pluses far outweighed the minuses. The weather, the crowds, the great consistency of the courses, not to mention all the ancilliary benefits of free cars for the week and telephone calls whenever and wherever you want.

Under Beman's stewardship the U.S. Tour has gone from strength to strength. With so many cities throughout the States all wanting tournaments and with local organizations keen to do their bit to make them a success, there is a tremendous grass roots energy that he has been able to harness.

Every week there is now an event worth more than one million dollars in prize money, and several with considerably more than that. It wasn't a casual decision to give all that up, and it is one I might well consider reversing in the future.

Recently I have made a leisurely start to the year, taking the only opportunity for a few weeks off at the beginning, with the golfing season now stretching from January to Christmas Eve. With a young family and increasing business commitments there is now a risk of golf becoming of secondary importance, something to be fitted in when time permits.

Some of my golf in the last year or so has not been as good as I would like, and I believe that can be laid at the door of competitive neglect. I have always told

my manager, John Simpson, that my golf comes first and other business activities must take a back seat to ensure I play to my fullest potential. The last thing I want is to look back on my playing career and feel it tapered off because I stopped giving it my fullest attention.

So it may well be that I will rejoin the American Tour for much of the early part of the year to take advantage of the great conditions and play a long stretch of tournaments up to and even through the Masters.

The schedule there is such that you do not have to travel more than a couple of hundred miles between events. Only trips from California or Arizona to Florida have to be done by plane. All the reasons that the United States was such an attractive option back in the early 1980s — great weather, tough courses in good condition and enthusiastic crowds —

U.S. P.G.A., 1988: I was watching Paul Azinger. Paul was watching me. And Jeff Sluman won!

still make playing there a pleasure.

Even when two tournaments are close together, as in Miami, there are large crowds each week, and they are the sole means of creating atmosphere. Playing week after week in front of large galleries is what give Americans the edge on most big occasions. It's another reason they do well on the last day of the Ryder Cup. Crowds in America tend to be much noisier than we are used to at, say, the Open Championship, but its cheerful noise is quite easy to get used to — or block out. And it can vary from one part of the States to another. An Open around New York, say at Baltusrol, will be far noisier than in California at Pebble Beach. But wherever you are, it is more noisy than anywhere else in the world. Indeed, if they were all suddenly to shut up as you were putting, it would be more off-putting than when they just natter on!

The swing through Florida ends with the Players Championship at Sawgrass, just two weeks before the Masters. It is as near a major championship as the U.S. Tour can put on, and was scheduled in late March to tap into all the top international players looking for competitive practice in America prior to the Masters.

The U.S. Open and P.G.A. are there to be won.

With most of the best players and the course a good test of golf, it takes some winning, particularly with one of the most demanding finishing holes in golf. As yet no one has gone on from victory in The Players Championship to take the Masters a fortnight later. In time it might get the same reputation as the par-three tournament on the eve of the Masters.

With the amount I have played in America over the years, I have felt these last few years that the spell in March prior to the Masters is enough to reacquaint myself with playing conditions over there. There is a view that I should play more

there before the U.S. Open and U.S. P.G.A., but that comes at an important time in the European calendar, what with our P.G.A. Championships and a number of the big Continental championships.

While I know Augusta well enough to need only the minimum of practice rounds, my ideal preparation for the other two American majors is to arrive the weekend before. This gives me every chance to see the course in all likely weather conditions and learn all there is to know about the course in question. If there are any fancy shots to be learnt, there is enough time to acquire the skill.

I am not totally out of touch with the peculiar conditions of American golf when in Europe. At home, I have a small putting green in the garden and have planted some Kentucky Blue grass and grown it to re-create conditions in America. There's not a week goes by in the season when I don't spend time practising on and around that green. After all, controlling the ball close to the hole from long grass is one of the hardest shots in golf, in America or anywhere else.

Usually I plan to play the event prior to each of these later majors to leave as much time for attunement as for acclimatizing myself. It doesn't always work out, as many of Europe's big events also take place around that time, and the gap between the Open Championship and the U.S. P.G.A. is awkwardly short.

I don't find it very easy to cope with time changes, so I just have to let it work through. I find it takes about five or six days to come completely right, and I am not averse to taking an afternoon nap to catch up. When I'm awake in the night, I sometimes use relaxation tapes to get me back to sleep, that or gentle music.

With the exception of my victories at Augusta, my American record is pretty thin. I only had my U.S. Tour card from 1981 to 1987, and during that time was either thinking about swing alterations or actually making them — a period that did not exactly coincide with my best golf.

I did have one success, at the Sea Pines

Heritage Classic at Harbour Town in South Carolina in 1984. It was the week after I had been in a good position to win the Masters but had lost to Ben Crenshaw through my bad playing and his putting.

I had been in America for fourteen straight weeks at that point and was ready to go home, especially after the disappointment of Augusta. I decided I would give it a real go that week, attack the course from the start and either win the tournament or fail to make the cut.

A bad spell of nine holes the previous week couldn't alter the fact that I must have been in good form just to be in contention, and as it turned out, I played exceptionally well. I had four rounds under 70, a fourteen-under-par total of 270 and victory by a shot. It was the first victory there by a British player since Tony Jacklin in 1972 and certainly removed some of the bad taste in the mouth left by Augusta.

By the time I had completed the major swing changes and started to win tournaments again, I had surrendered my U.S. card and chosen to use my few exemptions for a spring warm-up of several weeks in America, leading up to the Masters.

I suppose it is no coincidence that Europeans have not done as well in the latter two as in the Masters and our Open. To any non-American the Masters and the Open somehow have more standing than the two American championships. They seem more special, more individual, perhaps more truly international. The reverse is true if you are American, and if foreigners keep on winning the Masters, they might start to question its validity.

My best chance of winning the U.S. Open came in 1988 at the Country Club of Brookline. Tee to green, I played great: I only missed four fairways all week, but putted dreadfully. That particular course has always had the championship finish in a tie, including the time Francis Ouimet defeated Vardon and Ray to end British domination of golf, probably for ever.

It was another occasion when I had a

The crowd shares my excitement putting at the 1992 U.S. P.G.A. Championship.

The nearest I came to winning the U.S. Open was in 1988.

Championship makes it is awkward to do well, in particular if you have been in contention in the other two. It is another three weeks on and from the start of the U.S. Open, it is a long stretch to keep your game up to the mark. It is also too close to go off the boil and get back up again.

The P.G.A., the club pros body, run it and have to take it all over the States. The courses aren't set up as tightly as for the U.S. Open, but they sow special Bermuda-type grasses that the ball settles down in. At Shoal Creek in 1990 it was really severe: if you drove it in the rough you needed a wedge just to get it back on the fairway.

They've eased up a bit the last couple of years, and at Crooked Stick in 1991 and

premonition of what was going to happen. I was sure I was going to be involved in a play-off. Gill and I didn't pack, knowing we would to stay and play again on Monday. So I wasn't particularly surprised, or disappointed, when Curtis Strange got up and down at the 18th to force a play-off.

The following day, the difference was on the greens. He holed a few, and I got nothing. Maybe it would have been different if we'd finished the night before, as in other tournaments. On balance I prefer any tournament or championship to be sorted on the appointed day. Perhaps the Open Championship, with its few holes and then sudden death is the best solution.

I had another good chance in 1990 but left myself just a bit too much to do near the end. I thought I'd holed the putt on 18 that would get me in the play-off at Medinah. I still thought I had a chance until Hale Irwin holed one right across the last green to finish one ahead, to tie with Mike Donald.

That was the year I'd already won the Masters and went on to win the Open at St Andrews. It is difficult to understand the effect of people talking about doing the Grand Slam; it's certainly impossible to ignore. But you still go out and take every shot as it comes and keep the maybes at bay.

The timing of the U.S. P.G.A.

Hale Irwin to take a lap of honour at the 1990 U.S. Open. He still had the play-off to come.

U.S. Tour

*All that run-
ning – and at
his age!*

Things hotted
up at the 1993
U.S. P.G.A. in
Ohio.

Inverness this year they selected a couple
of excellent courses. Courses with a bit of
history, a bit of tradition would help the
P.G.A. – also an autumn date. But
changes in these days of tight schedules
and packed agendas are difficult to make.

1988 provided a good example of when
an unlikely player won. Jeff Sluman is
good, but he's not on everyone's lips
when the majors come around. I'd lost to
Strange at Brookline and was playing the
last day with Jeff Sluman at Oak Tree in
Oklahoma. Paul Azinger had seemed the
most likely threat, but Sluman was up
and away before either of us knew what
was happening.

I played perhaps my best in a U.S.
P.G.A. after playing well in the Open at
St Georges in 1993. After an indifferent
start to the year, I'd really begun to hit
the ball well in midsummer and hole a
few putts as well. I was feeling fresher
at the P.G.A. than usual. Inverness in
Toledo, Ohio, is an old and much respected course but not particularly long or difficult. The scoring was bound to be good,

1992 U.S.
P.G.A. at
Bellerive.

'You're aiming at the wrong flag, Faldo!' No wonder I didn't win at the 1993 U.S. P.G.A. at Inverness.

rain had softened the course more than was wanted. Along with the likes of Wadkins, Azinger and Norman I was picking up birdies here and there, staying in the thick of things. Then I took seven at a par four, the 13th, and those three shots were a lot to make up in soft conditions like that. I was going to have to catch up, they wouldn't come back.

The big difference between tour golf, on either side of the Atlantic, and the majors is the administration, on and off the course.

I finished the tournament fairly well and thought my eleven-under might be good enough for a play-off, but in the end both Azinger and Norman finished well. Coming so close after the Open, my abiding thought was that I had played really well in two major championships and won neither of them. I was 22 under par for the eight rounds and had nothing to show for it.

The one big difference between tour golf, either side of the Atlantic, and the majors is the administration, both on and off the course. The tours, with events week in week out, inevitably have achieved a consistency in the way they run the golf. The standard of refereeing is consistent, and they look to set courses up with similar green speeds, fairway widths and length of rough.

All the bodies that run the majors, Augusta for the Masters, the United States Golf Association for their Open, the Royal & Ancient for ours and the U.S. Professional Golfers Association (not the Tour) all run one big event for professionals, and they all go about it in a slightly different way. Augusta and the R & A are private clubs and run their championships with the enormous enthusiasm of knowledgeable memberships, but there the similarity ends. The Masters is a small, tight-

ly contained event where crowd numbers are strictly controlled and you get to play by invitation only. In recent years they have published the various categories under which invitations are issued. It is no longer the anxious wait each year to see if you are going to get one, but they still keep the odd special invite up their sleeve, particularly for overseas players.

The U.S.G.A. is different from the Royal & Ancient in that it is not a club but an elected body, the government of the game in the States voted into office by the clubs around the country. They too put great store by the traditions of the game.

You always know what the menu will be when you go to a U.S. Open; there will be narrow fairways, firm and fast greens and relatively rough close to the putting surfaces. It is a very stiff examination paper and one I would have expected to have a better record of in than the one I have. If I start to play more in America from 1995 onwards, then maybe my best performances are yet to come.

The U.S. P.G.A. are different again, the club professional body running their championships on courses in many ways similar to those chosen for the U.S. Open, but usually the questions asked are not so severe.

All in all, though, there is not a lot wrong with the way the upper reaches of the game are structured. The majors must have something special about them, otherwise they wouldn't be majors. A pity perhaps that three out of the four are played in America, but it won't stop me from trying to win them! ◄

In the rough at Bellerive, 1992.

U.S. Tour

Team Faldo – Golf
The House That Lead Built

It is in my nature to want to know exactly how things that are important to me work. The story of the new bicycle that I took to pieces and put back together is typical of my approach to life.

Not only do I want to know how things work, but if they are to be an integral part of my life, then it is most important they maximize their potential. For the past twenty years this has been my attitude to my golf swing, and the fascinating thing about golf is that it is infinitely perfectible. Put another way, it is a human activity impossible to perfect.

I started taking my swing to bits – questioning whether it was as good as it could and should be – when I went to the United States to play their tour in 1981. With the climate, perfect practice facilities and endless supply of balls, I was able to spend all my non-tournament days hitting shots. My lifelong fascination of finding out how, and how well, things worked, made it almost inevitable that I would want to examine the various parts of what was the most important working tool I possessed.

In those days there was a far greater practice ethic in America than I had ever come across in Europe. In addition, the U.S. Tour was a great deal more competitive than that in Europe. If you were going to succeed, indeed survive, you had to work really hard, because everybody else was. Life on tour really meant that. America is so large that there could only be a week, or at most two, when you could go home between tournaments. It really was a travelling circus, with golf the theme morning, noon and night. You played tournaments from Thursday to Sunday – provided you made the cut – flew or drove to the next event and practised Monday to Wednesday.

Most players would spend anything from five to fifteen weeks in succession on tour; when to play and when to rest depended very much how they were playing. In simple terms, if you were playing well, you kept going; if you had had a couple of bad weeks, it might be time to take a break. Even in America it was a case of grabbing

For me the swing change was fundamental.

the money while you could: you might not be around to collect tomorrow.

With the amazing advances in equipment technology nowadays the middle-aged can keep up with the young. Now it is more important to look after the mind, the nerve and the body – the only parts the likes of Mizuno or Bridgestone cannot replace.

Because there's so much golf to be played from one year's end to the other and such huge sums on offer each week, players are very aware of the need to conserve their mental and physical energies, and know they can afford to do so. They understand the dangers of burn-out, the risk of trying to play week in week out for years on end. Today there is plenty of evidence that careers really can be long and lucrative if you look after yourself. And if you are really careful, then there's that great honey pot, the Senior's Tour, in which you can do it all again, against the same opponents you have been challenging for the last twenty or thirty years.

New boys on tour will still play as many events as they can, but anyone who begins to make a success of it, wins a tournament or two, quickly starts to arrange his life around a schedule designed to extend his career into his thirties and forties. For those who have their eyes on the majors, that schedule will be structured to bring the player to a peak at the appropriate times of the year.

All that has changed in the last dozen years is that Europe has now truly caught the work ethic. With a full calendar from January to the end of October, there are plenty of players who spend weeks going from event to event, and when not playing a practice or tournament round, they will spend hour upon hour on the range. That's just how it was when I first went to America.

I have recalled the influence Jack Nicklaus had on the golf swings of his era, of how nearly every top-class golfer, at least all the tall ones, were very upright swingers of the club. Nicklaus at Augusta had been the inspiration for me taking the game up in the first place. With my height and the evidence of how the game was played at the highest level, it seemed inevitable I too would have an upright swing.

Make no mistake, it was a swing with which I had already achieved much by the time I went to America. I won three P.G.A. Championships in the four years after 1978, and in those days they were always played at Open Championship venues like Birkdale and St Georges. Those victories alone gave me some belief that the Open was a major that could well be within my grasp. There was also my first Ryder Cup match at Lytham in 1977, when I won all three of my matches.

But as with all golfers there are good days and bad days, and on the bad days I could play a whole round without ever feeling I was hitting the ball properly. With an upright swing and fair amount of lateral movement — that is a sway from right to left as the club goes through the ball — there were days when, quite simply, I got ahead of myself, the club-head came into the ball at too steep an angle, and I never hit it more than a glancing blow. The result was a shot that didn't go as far as a well-hit shot that tended to fly much higher and could go either right or left.

It has often been written that 5' 10" or thereabouts is the best height for a golfer. I am five inches more than that, and tall golfers have always had a problem fitting into a good golf swing. I am no exception.

What I needed to do was develop a swing that would enable me to flight the ball the correct height through the air the entire time. I later redefined my needs as being able to flight the ball high or low at will, depending on the wind and course conditions wherever I was competing.

This is where Mark O'Meara and his 'fanning' of the club head away from the ball came in. Mark joined the U.S. Tour the same year as I did, 1981. He was a more comfortable six feet tall, but wasn't getting very far with the upright swings so prevalent at the time. He was experimenting with opening the club-face as he took it away from the ball to achieve a lower plane

Mark O'Meara.

on the backswing. He was also working on bringing the club back to the ball on an even lower plane, so the shallower the angle of attack on the ball, the lower its flight.

This seemed the answer to me, so Mark and I worked together to develop this lower swing plane. Being three inches shorter, it was easier for him, and by 1984 he had mastered his changes to the point where he came second in the American order of merit — the official ranking system wherever tour golf is played — and has been a prolific money-winner ever since. He hasn't won that many tournaments, but has been a consistently fine player.

For me, however, it was a more fundamental change. Even though I was a few months younger, Mark had been through the American college system and was just starting out on his professional career. I had been a tournament professional since 1976, so my swing was more deeply ingrained. I am sure I had hit thousands more practice shots than Mark at that point in our lives. I began to work on the changes, making good progress at first and without interfering with my scoring ability. I was comfortably keeping my head above water in the States and still in the top five of the European order of merit each year. I won the T.P.C. at Hollingwell in 1982 and a number of events in 1983 — the French Open, the Martini, the Car Care, the Lawrence Batley and the Swiss Open — as well as making a good run at the Open.

My game in 1983 was more of a struggle in the United States, and only by finishing second in one of the last events of the year, the Walt Disney Classic, did I retain my card. The following spring I had my first real chance at the Masters but took 40 for the front nine when playing in the last pair with Ben Crenshaw, to finish well back. The win in the Heritage Classic the following week took care of my card over there for a couple of years, which, as it turned out, was just as well.

Rather than doubts about my swing and what I was doing to it, it was the failure to turn potential winning positions in two important majors – the Open of 1983 at Birkdale and the Masters the following spring – that worried me. In a sense, they reinforced my belief that I had to complete my changes, because the old method, or what was left of it, was not good enough to work on the big occasions.

I now redoubled my efforts to complete the transition and, not to put too fine a point on it, got into a tremendous muddle. During that year I spoke with both John Jacobs and Bob Torrance, as well as several of the teachers around the U.S. Tour, but no one seemed to be on my wavelength. Either they wanted me to work on their concepts, which in some way or other were at variance with what I thought was right, or thought I should go back to my old swing. Work with that, they said, and you will learn to handle the big occasions in due course. Even if they had been right, I don't believe you can get an old swing back after working hard on a new one, as all your muscle memory has changed. The old swing will no longer be there.

It was in the autumn of 1984 that I first met David Leadbetter. I was playing at Sun City, and he was there after moving to what was then Rhodesia when he was still a child. He grew up playing golf with, amongst others, Mark McNulty, Nick Price and Dennis Watson.

He turned professional at the same time they did and even played our tour in 1976 and 1977, but with little success. He later went to America and got into teaching with Phil Ritson, before setting up on his own at Greenleaf in Florida. He was soon working with McNulty, Price and Watson and their successes have, I am sure, much to do with their association with Lead. When I met him, Watson had just had the best year of his life in America, finishing fourth on the order of merit.

Lead impressed me as someone with his own ideas about the golf swing. He was the first person who said that if I got the early move in the golf swing right, it could correct six faults by itself. All the others had identified the faults but came up with corrections for each one. I agreed to think about what he had said and decide over the winter if I wanted to work with him.

Not much improved over the next few months. I missed the top 24 in the Masters by a shot, then failed to make much of a job defending my title at Hilton Head the following week. In some ways the miss at Augusta was the worst, as it meant I had failed to guarantee an invitation for the following year.

My next American tournament was Nicklaus's Memorial tournament at Muirfield Village. By then my golf was all over the place. I could look at a video and see all the faults but had no idea about how to put them right. I stood on the practice ground and felt like the mechanical man – with a short circuit! That's when I decided to meet with Lead again.

I was ready to put myself in his hands. I had reached the point where I knew I couldn't do it by myself, and of all the people I had talked to, Lead made the most sense. He didn't beat around the bush: it was a matter of breaking the whole swing down and starting over. With hindsight it obviously seems worth it, but there were many dark days along the way.

In retrospect, too, it would have been better not to start in mid-season. In those days, when a few of us were trying to keep a foothold on both the European and U.S. Tours, we were all fully committed during the summer months. Depending on how many events we had played in America before the Masters, we had to make sure we played our minimum quota of fifteen tournaments.

That inevitably meant a couple of returns to the United States at a time when Europe was staging its big events. May to September, and even October, were fully taken up just playing tournament golf – not the ideal time to embark on a major piece of reconstruction.

At the time, though, it seemed the only course of action and I felt reasonably confident after undertaking minor surgery and finding that I was still playing solid golf and learning new swing paths. But what Lead wanted to do was more drastic than anything I had done before.

My old swing was upright because I took the club away on the inside and then pushed it up over my head with a straight lift of the hands. Lead wanted me to rotate the arms to the right at the start of the backswing, making it wider, with the hands pushing the club on a more 'outside' path, resulting in a lower swing plane and a

flatter position at the top. It was very much the sort of position I had set out to find when working with Mark O'Meara, but it was a completely different method of getting there.

After some fairly intensive work with Lead at Muirfield Village, I was sure I knew what the correct swing felt like, and with hard work during the summer I could get it grooved in quite quickly. Without tournament play I think this would have been true, but there was still competitive golf to play. When I next saw Lead in September, my backswing was better, but I was still finding my old position at the top, so nothing had really improved.

That September was the first time I spent the best part of a week with Lead just hitting shots. It was to become a routine, and I have been back time and again for periods of several days. In later years it has become a fine-tuning exercise, but for a year and a half it was major surgery. No sooner had I mastered one part of the swing

Work, work, work. With David Leadbetter.

than the next bit had to be taken apart, analyzed and put back together again. First it was the backswing, retaining the new position at the top, then a different down-swing right through to the follow-through. It was a snail's pace, but at no time did I ever feel I wasn't making progress or that the whole thing was a terrible mistake.

The big difficulty was that I had to con-tinue playing tournament golf after a bad year in 1985, and now fully understanding how drastic the changes were, I had little confidence when it came to competitive playing. If 1985 was bad, 1986 was worse. But the reorganization of my swing took precedence over doing well in competition. Tournaments became a proving ground for the new swing as it developed, but some-how where I finished in those tournaments was secondary to how I hit the ball. I had no doubts that when the reconstruction was complete, I would get back to winning my fair share of tournaments. In the meantime, the roll of honour was on hold.

This I could live with, but it wasn't good news for my sponsors. Having won the order of merit with a run of victories in 1983, most of my contracts ran through to the end of 1985. With the form I was showing at the time, most of my sponsors dropped me like a hot potato. Very few people inside golf, let alone any on the out-side, understood what I was up to, and even fewer thought I was doing the right thing. I can appreciate that not many people thought I was a good investment.

Two companies stuck by me through those dark days: Pringle and Glynwed. The Pringle contract wasn't that large, nor were they a large company, but their faith in me was unflagging. With Glynwed the associa-tion was on a more personal basis, with the then Chairman, Sir Leslie Fletcher. I was still with them as I came out of the slump, but when he retired, the new broom decid-ed not to continue the sponsorship.

Perhaps the worst year of all was 1986. I slumped to 135th on the U.S. order of merit, and for the third year in a row I could not get into the top ten in Europe. The sponsors were deserting, and every

piece of media was taking me apart for destroying what they believed to have been a perfectly good golf game. But I still had faith in what I was doing and, more important, that Lead was the right man to do it with.

What gave me the encouragement that I was on the right track was that suddenly I could hit a shot or series of shots that were better than anything before. I'd hit a drive with real penetration or some iron shots that really went the way they should go. They were the stepping stones, the little boosts that kept me going.

Looking back, I see the reason it took as long as it did was that we were both learn-ing our differing trades at the same time. In a sense we were teaching each other. If another Nick Faldo went to him tomorrow, he could achieve what I did in about half the time. It was a case of trial and error for both of us.

In the spring of 1987 I went to Greenleaf again for another of what had become week-long sessions. I was approaching refinement time; there were no more ma-jor changes to be made. Lead thought dif-ferently.

Over the winter he had been studying the swings of many great players and had found that many of them brought the club back to the ball on a lower plane than the one they used for the backswing. Again, this coincided with what I had been tinker-ing with back in 1981 with Mark O'Meara. 'Shallowing the angle' he called it, and its real benefit was that it enabled me to fade the ball consistently for the first time.

Leaving Lead at the end of that week I went to Atlanta airport to pick up Gill and ran into some of the guys heading for Augusta. They turned left out of the air-port, I turned right for a little event in Hattiesburg. I hated that, but felt better about it when I posted four consecutive rounds of 67 and finished second.

The performance at Hattiesburg was another of those vital stepping stones that kept encouraging me. An even bigger one came about a month later when I won at Las Brisas in the Spanish Open, run by Seve

Ballesteros' promotions company, Amen Corner. He had ordered the course to be set up tough, so it was a true test of everyone's skills. I had to make four at the last, a drive and 5-iron, to win – and I did just that.

Greg Norman talks of his comeback win in the Canadian Open in 1992 as the most trying of his career, and I know exactly what he means. If you haven't won in a long time and have made significant changes, you don't really know if what you have done is right until you win again. When the chance comes, the pressures are enormous – it's like winning your first ever tournament, only more so.

When two months later I won the Open at Muirfield, all the anguish, all the hard work, was justified. I had finally proved to myself that I had been right all along to go back to the beginning and start again. I had now achieved more with the new version than I ever could have done with the old. Finally, the days of ever more dramatic changes were over.

Now came the consolidation and fine-tuning. In the last five or six years, Lead and I have established a pattern whereby we meet in Florida for the best part of a week at the beginning of each year to polish up the swing after the winter lay-off. We never just go back to where we were at the end of last season. A golf swing is an ever-changing, continually developing entity, like the human body itself. In many ways it ages as well, maybe gets a few wrinkles as time goes by, but hopefully gets more handsome too.

Lead is based at Lake Nona, a fine course de-

signed by Tom Fazio ten minutes from Orlando airport in Florida. In addition to excellent practicing facilities, it has nice rooms in the clubhouse and building plots being quietly and sensitively developed around the course. Lead and I meet there, usually in February, and spend the whole time on the practice ground, as well 0as working on and around the greens. When we were rebuilding in the mid-1980s, I thought nothing of hitting 1500 shots a day.

I work from early morning to 3.00 pm, go away and have a swim, rest up for an hour or two and then go back and do some

The fun only lasted so long.

Team Faldo at
the 1990 U.S.
Masters.

more around 6.00 pm. I used to love those evening sessions, the beautiful light, heat gone from the day. It used to be a confirmation of the day's work, rather like signing the post in the office.

Even if I wanted to, I couldn't work at that pace now. All those shots in the days of change and the more recent strength-building exercises have taken their toll. If I hit too many shots in a day, my hands and lower arms get sore. I still spend all day working with Lead, but now I restrict myself to little more than 300 shots in that time.

Ever since taking up golf, I have always loved spending an entire day with the game. As a kid my routine was no different. At Welwyn, I'd be up at the range by 8.15 am, and hit shots all morning until midday. Then I'd stop for lunch, chip and putt for an hour or so afterwards before going out to play maybe 27 holes, even 36 at times, and always finishing in the dark. I can still remember the evenings, coming up the last hole in almost total darkness.

Even if I didn't have to be careful, I would not hit as many shots now. The days of having to retrain the muscles to swing differently are past. Now we hit shots and analyze as we go along. We also have video cameras, so now I hit a few shots, note how they went and then review the pictures. With all this I sometimes cannot even get 300 shots away.

The sessions at the start of each year are now a mixture of repairing the ravages of a year's competitive toil and working in any refinements. Over the year errors can creep in to certain areas – areas where mistakes, should they occur under tournament pressures, are likely to originate.

For example, my hips have always been too 'active'; they tend to get involved in the swing too early and turn too much. Year after year this fault slips back in, regardless of what steps we take to eliminate it. Many, I am sure, have seen Fanny sitting on practice grounds behind me, hanging onto my legs. This is just one of the drills we use to try and keep the problem at bay.

In mentioning Fanny, I am referring to my caddy, Fanny Sunesson, who joined me at the beginning of 1990. She had previously learnt her trade working first for Jose Rivero and latterly with Howard Clark. During the previous year I had played a number of times with Howard and admired her professionalism. A brief talk with her and a request to Howard, and she came to work for me a couple of months before I won my second Masters.

On the refinement front, we concentrated in 1992 on acquiring greater skills with half-shots, not only learning to hit them consistently but how to move them right to left and vice versa. This paid huge dividends later in the year at the Open at Muirfield. It was a blustery week end and the little knocked-down half-shot was a great addition to the arsenal, never more so than when I had given away a two-shot lead to John Cook and was two behind with four to play. That great half 5 iron to eighteen inches at 15 was just one of those shots we had been working on.

Fanny herself is now a considerable expert.

Lead and I spend more time on the short game than we used to. He is particularly good around the green, with chips and little pitches. He has great imagination and has devised a number of shots to cope with specific situations. The first year I won at Augusta, Lead taught me a chip shot to play from just off the putting surface. The greens there have such sharp contours and are so fast that even though the grass is smooth enough to putt from off the green, a chip with a bit of backspin gives you more control. That little bit of backspin also stops the slope of the green affecting the run of the ball as early as it would do if struck with a putter. Lead got me to address the ball off my right toe and really lean forward so that my weight was over the ball, then pick the club straight up and give it a sharp descending blow. The ball would come out really low, and hop and skip up the green with a lot of

Playing a little football with Fanny during some time out at Gleneagles, 1990.

fizz. It was a shot played with a sand wedge, using the arms much like a pendulum – not much hands.

He has also been a lot of help with putting. I have a tendency to become too wooden, and my stroke loses its rhythm. He got me to practise putting with a 9-iron, gripping down the shaft and striking the ball at its equator, what we call blading the ball, a shot similar to one used by professionals when putting with their wedges from off the edges of greens if the ball is up against the collar of fringe grass. This exercise forces you to concentrate on striking the ball at a precise point with a precise point of the club. It also ensures that you follow through, and under tournament pressure it's the follow-through that tends to get choked off.

Lead and I meet regularly wherever I am playing. Your swing hardly stays the same from one day to the next and over a period of even a few weeks changes can creep in that shouldn't be there. If you play one week in the wind, that too can have a significant effect. So there is always plenty for us to do whenever we meet.

After working so long with Lead, I know nearly as much about my swing as he does and know what to look for. If something is awry, Fanny works the video and after just a few shots I can usually pick what is wrong and know how to put it right.

Fanny herself is now a considerable expert. Ever since she began working with me, she has attended all my weeks with Lead, and being a good golfer herself she has picked up much of what we discuss. At the start it was somewhat complicated for her to take in all the changes, and it took several visits before she came to terms with what we were up to. But she is a total professional and now has a pretty good grasp of the intricacies of the Faldo swing.

Once I was happy she understood what we were about, I encouraged her to speak up whenever she sees anything relevant. Between us, and with the use of the video on the practice ground, we can usually identify problems as we go, and nine times out of ten put them right. I now feel I have all the advice necessary, wherever I am and in whatever tournament, to be able to play golf to the best of my ability. ◄

Fanny's first Major carrying for me. The number 1 is always reserved for the defending champion.

European Tour
Poor No More

• • • • • • • • • • • • • •

The European Tour is now not that far short of its American counterpart, in stature, in strength of competition or in prize money. But it hasn't always been like that.

When I began my professional career, I always looked for the best places to play: where the most money was, where the competition was and, perhaps most important, where the best courses were. In the late 1970s and early 1980s that meant America from the beginning of the year to the Masters and even most of April. Then it was back to Europe for the summer, where there might not be a good tournament every week but where there was enough to keep busy. The autumn meant tournaments in South Africa and Australia.

The difference now is that Europe starts almost at the same time as America, in January, and there's a tournament every week. When the tours end in October, there is an ever-increasing scramble for the few dates in the weeks before Christmas. Instead of looking for tournaments you have to carefully pick through the year and make the best use of your time and energy.

Ten to fifteen years ago, I would play 35, maybe 38, weeks of the year. I certainly played nearly every week leading up to the Masters and perhaps the two or three immediately afterwards. That was when we were trying to keep our American cards, and that meant playing at least fifteen events over there, as well as giving the growing tour in Europe as much attention as possible.

My first event in Europe is usually in Spain around the end of April.

The European Tour is now up and running, and though I will still play here through the summer months, America could well see more of me during the early part of the year. I shall have to pace myself, as my hands and arms will no longer take as much work as they used to. Mind you, it is not the playing that puts them under strain but all the practice shots.

Planning my schedule at the beginning of each year is therefore very important, and I have a number of priorities: the first is to choose weeks to play that will ensure I get enough competition to stay in the best possible condition, both physically and mentally, for the majors. Four prime targets for the year is a good number, one could only wish that the last three of them weren't so close together.

In deciding on which weeks to play, of prime importance is the quality of the courses the events are being played on.

Ideally, I will play little stretches of two, possibly three weeks in a row, never more. By quality of courses I mean ones that test all the skills of the best players. The courses must be in good condition and be acknowledged classics in their own right or have been specifically designed with professional tournament play in mind.

One reason I believe we have not been competitive on the last days of recent Ryder Cups is that too many of our courses finish with holes that don't ask much of the golfer. Often three of the last five or

six holes will require just a wedge or nine iron to large greens with little protection from bunkers or other hazards.

In America, week after week, closing holes have some fiendish creeks or lakes that protect the approaches to the greens, and some even threaten wayward long shots as well. To win you not only have to hold off the opposition, you have to keep your nerve together and hit superb shots over frightening elements.

My first events in Europe, not counting the middle and Far East ones that have

Dubai in 1993. A great course in the desert.

The last putt at Hong Kong, 1990.

sprung up in recent years, have usually only been one on the Continent around the end of April, the Benson & Hedges, and then the Volvo P.G.A. Championship at Wentworth. Whether I do more than these depends on my early season form. If I have played well, maybe even won already, then I will play less than if things are not going well and I need the competitive practice.

After the U.S. Open, as with all majors now, I take a week off and then like to play the Irish and Scottish Opens the week before ours. These latter two are on good courses and ideal to keep the game in trim for the Open Championship.

August sees the U.S. P.G.A., and in a non-Ryder Cup year the prime objectives are then done with. How I have performed still dictates how much I play thereafter, but I still have in mind the end of season events, some of which come high in my list of priorities.

My objectives in Europe are clear: I always want to win the order of merit. It is often said that my only interest in tour events is to use them as practice for the majors. This is not true. I never enter an event without doing my best to win. What is true is that I may sometimes be working on refinements in my swing during the early part of an ordinary tournament week, but I will never do anything out on a round of golf

Volvo Masters 1989 in Valderrama, Spain, also site of the 1997 Ryder Cup.

to jeopardize how well I score that day.

I usually spend time on the range working on my drills and alterations, which creates a number of key thoughts that I take onto the course to see how they work under tournament conditions. By the week's end, they should be well enough integrated that I can concentrate on winning the tournament.

Tournaments can be won in a number of situations, but the increasing quality of play on the tour makes it more difficult to win from a lot of shots back. What is still true, though, is that those who go off like a shot out of a gun and are twelve or fifteen under for 36 holes inevitably become a bit defensive at the weekend and give those charging from behind the chance to catch up near the end.

The majors are different in that I hope to be comfortable with my game going into the week, not seeking any refinement to bring it together when the championship starts. I see the majors as real 72-

hole tournaments in which you have to go for the win right from the start. With all the best players present, you cannot afford to give them a start while you sort out your swing.

Although the approach may be different, I never tee up in a tournament without the intention to win. I was very conscious of my position as No. 1 in the Sony world rankings and was keen to keep it as long as possible. I used to keep an eye on those closest to me and sought week by week to do as well or better than them.

First of all, in 1991, Ian Woosnam was the one to watch, then came Fred Couples with his great winter of 1991–2, culminating with his Masters win that spring. A revitalized Greg Norman was the one who finally took that position away early in 1994. Someone was bound to take over one day, and few would argue with his form at that time. Just trying to stay on top, and indeed trying to get back there, has been enough to make sure I don't

Wentworth: my fourth win in the P.G.A. Championship.

The Irish Open, 1991.

treat tour events just as practice rounds for the majors.

It is certainly harder to win a major, but make no mistake, there is a lot of pressure involved in winning a tour event too. I had a bad run in 1992 and lost a couple of events I should have won. The worst was the French that year when I dropped shots over the last few holes. I'm as nervous as the next guy, but I have my rules for playing under pressure, certain disciplines to ensure a straight shot. I broke those rules in France and paid the price.

It would have been easy to become negative after that, but I saw it as a learning experience and tried to gain from it. I won a tournament every month for the next six months. I also wobbled a bit in winning the Irish Open, but what I learned in France helped me in Ireland. It also helped when I got into trouble over the closing holes at Muirfield in the Open in July.

I should also say that it's important to be nervous, it's part of being switched on for a tournament. Without it you will not be competitive. Perhaps nervous is the wrong word; getting a flow of adrenalin is probably more accurate, particularly when you are leading in a tournament and playing well. Nervous is what you get when you play badly and appear to be missing the cut.

I am also disciplined with my schedule because these days if you pull out of a tournament at the last minute, you upset a lot of people. If I say I am going to play in this or that event, promoters will build their publicity around it. Pull out and the media have a field day. So it is much easier to add tournaments to the schedule than to take them out.

I think what Ken Schofield has done with the tour over the last ten to fifteen years is fantastic. Quite simply, he has taken it from being a poor relation of the U.S. Tour to something that is almost its equivalent in every way. When I began, America was the only place to play if you

Shouldn't have been there in the first place.

Three in a row – a hat trick at the Irish Open in 1993.

There are great facilities now on the European Tour thanks to Volvo.

really wanted to make money at the game. The proof of Ken's success is that the likes of Seve, Langer and myself have been able to give up our U.S. cards and make a living at home.

Our successes in the Ryder Cup and in major championships have helped upgrade the status of the tour, and with it the money we play for each week. Of prime importance to me has been the attention the tour has paid to finding courses of the right calibre, and a lot of the fine-tuning is due to Volvo as tour sponsor. It has paid for the agronomy division as well as producing much better practising facilities – and not just better golf balls. I remember at Wilmslow in 1983, the practice ground was a field next door to the course, and there was clear evidence that the last occupants had been cows!

My only doubts have been whether the tour has grown too big, too long, starting in January with all the events in Spain and the neighbouring islands. It is asking a lot of one part of Europe to support the tour for so long, even though I fully support the concept of giving the up-and-comers every chance to make their mark while the seniors are tuning up in America for the Masters.

The foresight of looking to extend the tour into the early months of the year may well bear fruit if more tournaments start to appear in the Middle and Far East. Dubai and the Johnny Walker Classic are

very substantial events, and more like that can only be to the tour's advantage.

The argument for size is based on giving the maximum number of players the chance to compete in Tour events, and this is the best way to find the stars of the future. I believe anyone who is going to be that good will make it through anyway, so I would like to see smaller fields, make it tougher to get to compete at the highest level of tour golf.

A lot of people say, 'He's all right, he's made his money, he's bound to take that line.' But I'm as concerned as the next man about the ongoing success of the European Tour. I believe making it tougher to get onto the tour is one way to find winners among the next generation, not just players who survive in the lower reaches by paying their way from one tournament to the next.

Smaller fields would also make for better conditions, week in week out, for those who have made it. Our courses in our climate cannot handle fields of 156 players. If it rains the courses really go. With caddies, you've got over 300 people on every green, and for the later players that means bumpy greens and a lot of wear round the hole. The Tour officials can and have improved many aspects, but even they can't fix the weather.

This doesn't happen every time, of course, but you only have to look at events near the end of the season, with fields of 70 or 80, to see how much more quickly it moves. We have to be mindful of the entertainment value of our game both for spectators and television viewers, and slow play can be a bore.

All this, however, is only looking for refinements at the very top. The standard of play in Europe has continued to get better. I know, because I find myself having to play better to stay ahead. Ten years ago, if I led going into the last round, a 70 or 71 would have been good enough to win. Now you need to shoot 66 — that speaks for itself.

Everyone is practising much harder now than they used to. There was a time

Quiet please. The 1992 Scandinavian Masters at Malmö, Sweden.

The parting of the Red Sea.

of it. A couple of years back, I wrote to all the golf unions of Scotland, Ireland, England and Wales, and told them I was having a Master Class and asked them to send two guys. The Irish sent two, one of whom was Paul McGinley. He's done well since, as has Padraig Harrington, who was one of the few who did quite well in his Walker Cup matches.

The English Golf Union replied that the last thing they wanted to do was send anyone down to be mucked about by Faldo and Leadbetter — it had taken them forever to get rid of that stupid towel drill (when I wrap a towel around my upper torso and hold it there by keeping my arms close to my body through the swing). Scotland, though, weren't any better.

When I was at Wentworth practising for the P.G.A. Championship in 1993, a group of Scots lads came up and wanted a picture with me. One was a scratch player, and I asked if he was going for a place in the Open. He replied that the Scottish Union had told him not to waste his time as he had no chance of qualifying. But that's the only way to learn, you've got to have a go. You

when players could just bowl up, play the tournament, have a good time and still win. Those days are gone. You may still be able to make a living with that attitude, but that's all it will be. And when your playing days are over there won't be anything in the bank to cushion your retirement.

The way the Swedes have come from nowhere to being such a force today in the last ten years, for instance, has had something to do with this transformation. Some years before that they started their team system of coaching and playing, and today we see the results. Their system was based on correct coaching and lots of hard work. The only thing missing now is one individual who's got that little bit more to become a big winner, a force in the championships. I haven't seen that character yet — the Bjorn Borg of golf, if you like — but he will emerge. It will be that extra something in the heart.

I think we in Britain could learn much from what the Swedes have achieved. Attitudes are still wrong here, and by the time we get round to doing it right, I'll be retired. Of course it's got to start with the amateur game — look how poorly we did in the Walker Cup. But the amateur golf bodies don't seem to be doing anything to improve the system.

If someone were to take the system by the scruff of the neck, I'd love to be part

> **In one round on my own, I can learn all I need to know about a course.**

may surprise yourself and qualify, but succeed or not you will have learnt something, gained some experience.

But there has to be a change of attitude, a more professional approach among amateurs. The last Walker Cup side in America needed a professional coach who understood American conditions, like playing the heat. Diet is very important when it is hot, eat the wrong things, and you are bound to have a bad day afterwards. There are so many little things that can add up to the difference between success and failure. It may have been young, but it wasn't a bad team. It just didn't play anywhere near its potential.

As often as not, when I have time for a genuine practice round, I'll play it with some of the younger, newer guys on tour. Particularly on a course I know well, so I don't have to do a lot of homework to get to know it. If a Paul McGinley, a Peter Baker or a Roger Winchester ask to play sometime, I try to fix a game.

But I still like to play a practice round on my own, because I learn so much more. If you are playing with four other guys, there's bound to be a lot of chat, so it is easy to miss something vital. It may sound stand-offish, but what with shoot-outs and skins games, you sometimes go into a tournament without even having had a full practice round. I am certainly not complaining about how my career has panned out, but nowadays there are a lot of commitments that come with being a player they are promoting the tournament around.

In one round on my own, I can learn all I need to know about a course. In one's amateur days, you used to play two or three times before the event started, but we didn't know how to make full use of our time on the course, nor were we so confident about yardages and how far we hit the ball. As an amateur, you use your eyes and feel to judge distance much more than you do as a pro.

When I'm learning a course, especially one we are playing for the first time, I leave Fanny to do the yardages; I'm looking for where I want to be playing my shots into the green from. That can vary too, depending on where they put the pins each day. I pay closest attention, however, to the greens – charting the contours, working out where they are most likely to put the pins and the best places to aim for when the pin is in a certain position. I always want to leave myself an uphill putt.

I also take of notice of what happens if I miss a green, the sort of hazards at the sides and beyond greens. By the time I come off a course after a day of looking, I will be happy that there are no nasty surprises when I play the course in competition. I will understand how to play the course, how to play each hole.

Fortunately, all this care and preparation still translates into wins from time to time. Even if my main concern each year is the major championships, part of preparing for them is not only to pay competitive golf but to be in contention as often as possible. You can never have too much experience of coping with the pressures of finishing off a tournament. With the limited amount of play I allocate each year now, even if I were in contention every week with a chance to win it would still not be too often.

Winning the P.G.A. in only my second full year (1978) was a great start, but winning didn't become any sort of a habit till 1983. I won three of those P.G.A.s before anything else, two of them on links courses, Birkdale and St Georges. That may have been a throwback to my amateur days, when so much of the top competition is at the seaside.

I won the order of merit for the first time in 1983, not surprising as I won five times in Europe and was the first player to win £100,000 in a single season. Nowadays a top player would think he had a bad year if he didn't win double that amount. We did a study the other day at IMG to measure the increase in prize money between 1981 and 1991. It so happened that the same player came eightieth both times: in 1981 he won £4000 and ten years later £43,000, a good measure of the progress during those years of the European Tour.

Obviously the Spanish Open win in 1987 was crucial because it was the first proof to the home crowd that I wasn't a spent force.

> **There are enough players for me to know I will have to work hard to stay ahead.**

*The 1993
Spanish Open
in Madrid.*

The bigger the event, the more it means, so with the Volvo P.G.A. Championship being the tour's jewel in the crown, winning that counts for a lot. All in all, I have won it four times, though not since 1989. After that comes the Volvo Masters at Valderrama and winning there in its first year was important.

Certainly the rewards are more than sufficient to satisfy the most ambitious, though that shouldn't stop the best having a go in America, especially if they have major championship ambitions. It's not fair that three of the four top events each year should be played in the States, particularly now that the top players come from around the world. But that's the way it is, and likely to stay that way. Americans will remain the opposition to beat, at least in the Ryder Cup, so there is nothing like beating them there. ◀

6

World Golf
The Global Game

● ● ● ● ● ● ● ● ● ● ● ● ●

The last two months of the year, after the United States and European tours, provide the best opportunity for sponsors with big purses to entice the best players, from all parts of the world, to play in a number of limited field events.

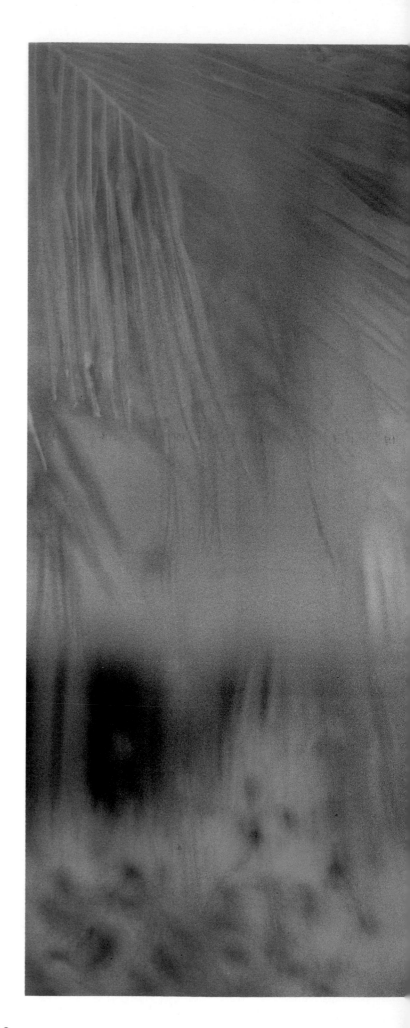

Clearly, the major championships are at the top of everyone's list of events they want to win. The Masters and the Open Championship probably have more world-wide recognition and status than the U.S. Open and P.G.A. Championships, but any one of the four will do nicely in a given year. But after those events one tends to look at one's own tour for meaningful competitions to win; in the U.S. it is likely to be the Players Championship in March or Tour Championship at the end of the year, while in Europe, the P.G.A. title and the Volvo Masters are their equivalent.

As individual titles go, one or two of the events that have become established at the end of the year, after the main tours have packed up for the year, certainly rank alongside the best of the tour events, and quite possibly ahead of them. In most cases the quality of the opposition, the presence of leading American Tour players in particular, will justify their position in the pecking order. But there is also a commercial side to the equation.

The significance of these events to an individual depends largely on how international that player is and where his sponsors are looking for and expecting exposure. My main sponsors – Mizuno, Bridgestone and Pringle, all globally recognized companies – are looking for me to win titles that have recognition worldwide rather than just in Europe. The best I can do for them in Europe is win the order of merit, which has more prestige than any one individual title. But tournaments like the World Match Play Championship and the Johnnie Walker World Championship in Jamaica are more widely seen around the world than, say, the Benson & Hedges or European Open, so are more important to those who back me.

One reason my golfing year seems to begin later each year is the proliferation of these year-end events. The Johnnie Walker World Championship, which I won in 1992, comes just before Christmas, a good time to keep my game in shape.

When you factor in the mental and physical demands of a Ryder Cup, you need a good break to recharge the batteries. The period from January to mid-February is now the only time to find a few weeks without an event of some significance. Even the Johnnie Walker Asian Classic is a bit early for me to

Digging it out from Down Under in 1990.

be ready for it, though I have managed to win it twice.

At the beginning of my playing career, when I used to hunt the globe for playing opportunities from one year's end to the next, there was little ordinary tour golf in Europe after the end of September. Even with an invitation to the World Match play, I would be off to the southern hemisphere before the end of October. Last year, a week before the Volvo Masters, I remember hearing the result of the Melbourne Cup on the radio and thinking that in the old days I had often been in Australia two weeks by the time the Melbourne Cup was run. Times change.

Hole number 5 at the Royal Melbourne.

The last couple of years I have, a bit reluctantly, taken Australia off my schedule. Even coming from places like Bangkok and Singapore, it is still a lot further to go, and as I have said, I am not one of those who can go charging through time zones without feeling the effect. Also, to make any sense of going there, I would have to couple a visit with my autumn trip to Japan, and that would mean being away from home for the best part of a month. The way I currently plan my life, that's too long.

This is a pity because the courses in Australia, particularly on the sand belt around Melbourne, are some of the best in the world. The soil is much the same as at Sunningdale and Wentworth, and the climate is immeasurably better. The great Alistair McKenzie built some of the early courses and was an enormous influence on the rest. In an area of a few square miles there are perhaps a dozen of exceptional quality. So I miss playing in Australia, but

I haven't done particularly well there in recent years. It may be because their big tournaments are either at the very end of the season and I am winding down, or so early the next year that I haven't really got going.

The best event down the years has been the Australian Masters, which often attracts a great field. The best I was able to do there was chase Greg Norman home in 1990; I was pleased to turn the tables in the Open at St Andrews later in the year.

I select my schedule for the autumn with as much care as for Europe and America earlier in the year. The same criteria of good courses and top-quality opposition apply, though the latter is guaranteed as only the best tend to get invited.

A typical year-end itinerary would read as follows: start off with the World Match Play, finish the European Tour off with the Volvo Masters, spend a week, perhaps two, in Japan, go to Sun City in early December and end up at the Johnnie Walker in Jamaica. This is not a particularly heavy schedule from a playing point of view, but it involves a lot of travel, which in itself is pretty wearing. I will have played more than enough golf earlier in the year and need relatively little practice to keep in tune for the World Championship just before Christmas.

Perhaps the most obvious omission from my schedule, particularly from a British point of view, is the Alfred Dunhill Cup. Even though it is at St Andrews, it sadly comes much to close after the Ryder Cup for me to be able to give it the effort and energy I would want. I think it wrong to accept an invitation to play representative golf when I am not able to give it 100 per cent of my ability

I take team commitments very seriously, and it was because I was part of a team in the Dunhill Cup in 1988 that I refused to play on one evening when England was playing Ireland. I was in the deciding match against Des Smyth and had to win the last hole to keep the game alive. As we came up the last hole, one of those Scottish mists came in, and even though I was no more than 40 yards from the green, it was completely lost in the mist. But the mist was only about fifteen feet off the ground so the students watching from the university building behind the 18th green could see me and the pin and thought I was causing an unnecessary fuss. They probably thought I was trying a bit of gamesmanship, and there was a lot of whistling and cat calling. But I simply couldn't see, and as darkness fell the final

At the end of the year it is nice to have a bit of variety.

A victory at the 1987 Dunhill Cup at St Andrews with Howard Clark and Gordon J. Brand.

moments had to be put off until the following morning. If I had been playing for myself, I might well have carried on, but I felt a responsibility to the team, so I stood my ground. As usual, I got a lot of media flack about it too.

For much the same reason I have only rarely played in the World Cup, the two-man team event that has stuttered along since it started life as the Canada Cup back in the 1950s. It is the prime example of the effect of poor players in a field leading to slow play. If you go to the World Cup, you know you will be in for six hours plus rounds, and that in itself is a disincentive.

It may seem strange that Sun City has been a regular feature in my autumn schedule. Quite simply, I enjoy playing there. For a long time, while it was politically impossible to play in South Africa, that was the one chance to visit a part of the world that I had much enjoyed in my earlier years. Now it just comes at a time when I need an event to keep my golf in trim for the World Championship in Jamaica.

On top of that, it meets my criteria of strong opposition and a challenging course. It is only a twelve-man field, but they are the pick of their respective tours, and the course demands every club in the bag.

Finally, it takes place at a time of year when it's nice to take the family somewhere warm. There's lots for the kids to do, and there are never a lot of people around to hassle you. The golf course, hotel and other facilities are all on one site, all of which makes it a very pleasant week in the sun, with a good prize to play for.

No such justification is necessary for the World Match Play Championship. It is now some 30 years old, and very few of the world's top players have not competed in it. The list of winners is a compendium of great players from Arnold Palmer and Jack Nicklaus to Greg Norman and Seve Ballesteros — including me along the way!

The fact that it is match play is a large

Lost in the mist somewhere in Scotland.

Victory at the 1989 Suntory World Match Play.

and by the weekend I'd get tired mentally, have a bad patch in mid-afternoon and lose matches I should have won.

I have now learnt to relax and pace myself during these games. Unless you have a runaway victory or are off form and get given a pounding, there will always be a lot of tooing and froing over 36 holes. I've learnt not to worry if I get three or four down, as there is plenty of time for the pendulum to swing back – and match play is a game of pendulums.

Sometimes there's more pressure in being two up rather than two down, particularly early on in these games. Almost inevitably the other player will get a good rhythm, have a few good holes and you soon realize how small such a lead is. But it is easy to get alarmed when you have been a few up, not done much wrong and are down. In the 1993 World Match Play I was three down to David Frost halfway through the morning round, but I kept working away, got down in a couple of chips and putts and went into lunch only one down. I am sure I felt more confident of winning in the afternoon than he did. That's just the psychology of these matches.

Wentworth is a good match-play course, it gets tougher towards the end: two or three down coming to final stretch and you still have a chance. The holes become narrower and it is easy to whip one in the trees at 13 or 15. Mind you, even though your opponent is in trouble, he can usually chip out, drop only one shot and you've still got to hit a 3-iron on the green and not take three putts. Then there are two par fives at the end – a pair of fours can win both.

One of my basic rules is to avoid all business during tournament golf.

part of its appeal. Week after week, we play 72-hole medal events, the staple diet of the major championships and tour golf. At the end of the year it is nice to have a bit of variety. All professionals will tell you they would rather play a match over 36 holes than eighteen, that is unless they believe the other player to be the better. One round is seen as the sprint distance. All sorts of golfers can have a golden patch and build a big lead that is impossible to recover in just eighteen holes. Over the full 36, I know I can weather the freak little storms and have time to come back and win.

The Epson Grand Prix at Chepstow was a prime example. One year I played Tony Johnstone in the first round and shot a 68. The trouble was that he went round in 64. If we had continued the game in the afternoon, I'd still have fancied my chances of catching him before the end.

It took me a few years to master the tactics of long matches. You always try to win every hole, but I used to fret if I got down early on. This took a lot out of me,

There's no doubt it is a tough event, both physically and mentally, coming as it does every other year quite soon after the

Ryder Cup. If I can, I like to pick up on my physical training for a week or two before, especially to get the legs in shape. 36 holes is double the normal distance we play, and it is usually cold and damp at that time of year, which makes it even more draining.

I didn't have any really good matches until I started to play well again in 1987. Before that, I had once been six up on Sandy Lyle in 1982 and lost 2/1 – shades of Tony Lema and Gary Player. That was in the days before I learnt to pace myself, to understand the intricacies of 36-hole matches.

When I first won the Open at Muirfield in 1987 I came to Wentworth pretty confident. I played Ian Woosnam in the semi-finals and was ten or eleven under par, but he beat me at the last. He has always been capable of some streaks of unbelievable golf, and that was his great

year when he first won a million pounds or thereabouts.

I caught him a couple of years later, though, in the final. The scoring that year was incredible: I was 42 under par for the 105 holes I played during the week. Even so, I was three down to Woosie with seven to play. He played the last seven holes in three under, but I had a couple of eagles, three birdies and caught him at the last.

The World Match Play usually comes a couple of weeks before the Volvo Masters, which officially marks the end of the European Tour. Started in 1988, the Volvo Masters has become established as a high note to finish the season very much on a par with the Tour Championship in the States.

Both are limited field events, only the leading players on tour during the year qualified to take part. Both also recognize the importance of a quality venue. Our

1989 World Match Play at Wentworth. Ian Woosnam was my partner in the Ryder Cup but was my opponent here.

Masters has always been played at Valderrama, as good a course as there is in Spain — or, indeed, Europe — and the reputation of course and event have grown together.

In recent years Deane Beman has taken his Tour Championship to some of the historically famous courses in America, such as Pinehurst in South Carolina and the Olympic Club in San Francisco. The combination of a quality field, good crowds and a highly respected course gives the Tour Championship all the ingredients to be a class event in every sense of the word. Along with the Players Championship at the end of March, it is as near to a major as Beman can create. These events come during the last week of

World Match Play Championship: Demolition Man.

October, after which I usually have a short break before setting off for Japan.

Japan is as near to a fully fledged business trip as I make during the year. Two of my biggest sponsors – Bridgestone and Mizuno – are based there, and the Japanese market is vital to two of my other sponsors, Pringle and Audemars Piguet.

One of my basic rules is to avoid all business, and indeed a lot of social, obligations during the weeks I am playing tournament golf. It is well known that when you are at the top anywhere in sport there are enormous demands on your time. The only way to cope is to find a way to handle them so that you can concentrate and do your job properly. Not mixing business with business, so to speak, is one of them. But on these fleeting visits to Japan, I break just about every rule in my book. Not only are there an endless rounds of business and social functions to attend, but my sponsors would be most put out if I did not play tournaments while I am there. I suppose I could have a couple of weeks of business meetings and then play a couple of tournaments, but that would break another of my golden rules: that of not spending more than two, at most three, weeks away from home and family.

I usually get to Tokyo on a Sunday to give myself as much time as possible to overcome jetlag and be in as good a condition as possible to play the tournament later in the week. Even the day I arrive there will be some function, a cocktail party or dinner, so there's no 24 hours grace before the gun goes.

The days before the tournament are very full. Monday might include a company outing, with a clinic in the morning and a few holes with each group of corporate clients. This all takes longer than back home, because there is a lot of translating going on. Before dinner there might be a couple of meetings with business groups to do with courses I am involved in designing. Although all the deals will be put together by my manager, John Simpson, they are still very keen that you be there to sign the contracts, with the attendant press conferences and photo calls. I visit the courses that are under construction, which is interesting, as when playing golf is no longer my main activity, I hope to become fully involved with course design and development – but those days are some way off.

As with a tournament weeks elsewhere

in the world, I try to get a practice round in each day before the start. This in itself is quite a performance, as it usually involves a long drive out to the course, perhaps not very far in distance, but the traffic is always heavy and any journey there seems to take at least an hour.

I am not a good person to play a practice round with when in Japan, as there are always twenty or thirty photographers following me right the way round, with all of them taking pictures of every shot I hit. Some even get into positions of extreme danger, being only a foot or two off where I am aiming the shot. They are particularly keen to do swing sequences, and I have to make a rule that I will only do them on the 18th tee, so they have to wait until then. And as you might imagine, getting off the 18th tee can sometimes take up to twenty minutes. All in all, it makes gathering information about the course very much a secondary exercise.

With all of these distractions it is not surprising that I have never won in Japan, though I have come second on a couple of occasions. Even were it not for the distractions, golf in Japan is different enough to be more difficult than most places to raid for a week or two and expect to win.

The greens are one big difference. Sown with a local grass, Korai, they resemble nothing so much as a tightly mown doormat. It has a strong grain – blades of grass that grow in a specific direction which can push the ball – which can sometimes go in two or three different directions en route to the hole. It requires a lot of local knowledge to putt well, the one commodity a visitor like me doesn't have.

The best Japanese players are as good as any in the world. Isao Aoki showed what can be achieved if sufficient time is devoted to playing in America or Europe. But he has really been the only one to concentrate his efforts abroad. The rest – the Ozaki brothers, Tommy Nakajima, Massy Kuramoto – only leave their own

tour fleetingly and never give themselves a real chance to show what they are capable of against the best international players.

The reason they seldom leave Japan, of course, is they make so much money in their country. They are treated like gods, and nothing they could achieve abroad would enhance their status. Their earnings are formidable, and I doubt even Greg Norman has a more exotic lifestyle than these fellows.

So why should they risk their glorious reputations in countries where the culture and the food are so different? If they go abroad and don't win, then there is great loss of face, and face is as important, perhaps even more so, than money and possessions. The major championships have by no means the same importance there as they do in States, Europe, Australia or South Africa, so they gain as much prestige by just being king of their own particular castles. I expect that would change if one of them won the Masters or the Open.

The big Japanese stars each have their own camps or groups of lesser professionals who are devoted to them. These usually younger players worship the Nakajimas, the Jumbo and Joe Ozakis; they dress like their particular hero, play the same clubs and balls, copy the great man's swing and try to emulate them in every way. You have to live within one 'camp' or other until you become one of the next generation of great players. In time they would then have their own band of camp followers.

Meanwhile, the functions continue, even during the tournament. The good thing is they start early by our standards, usually at 6.00 pm and finish at 8.00 pm. Your starting times are arranged so that you can be back in time to attend the event, and if it says 6.00 pm, they mean it: turning up a few minutes late is most impolite. They also finish bang on the dot, so there are no hidden late nights to contend with.

Wherever we go in the world, Fanny looks after the clubs. Now they mostly

have female caddies in Japan, but they are small and usually just control electric carts. To see a lady carrying a big bag seems wrong to them, and they are always trying to carry the bag for her when we arrive at the hotel or course. Sometimes it develops into quite a tug of war.

There was one occasion when I had been down to the Mizuno factory and actually had two sets of clubs in the bag. As usual, one of the porters rushed out to take the clubs out of the boot, thinking it would be no problem, after seeing Fanny carry the bag without much trouble. He wasn't very large and heaving the bag with its extra set up onto his shoulders, the sheer weight just swung him off his feet. Her stock went up right there and then!

Sadly for me Japan is really just the biggest corporate outing of the year. I would love to play better there. You always want people to see you at your best, particularly sponsors who are investing heavily in you. But the sheer demands in the short time make a peak performance unlikely, to say the least.

Which leaves only the Johnnie Walker

World Championship in Jamaica. Like a lot of new events, the sponsors and organizers haven't got everything completely right, but I think they have got a lot more right than wrong. It certainly is a tournament I want to win, so I try and raise my game for yet one more week of the year.

A field of that quality together means a lot of effort and expense has gone into it. I think that Johnnie Walker, with Jamaica and their Asian Classic, as well as their support of the Ryder Cup, have put a tremendous amount into golf. After all, we only have the large purses to play for because of the sponsors, and they just happen to be about the biggest and the best.

In some respects they have done the difficult bit by getting the tournament established and the players there. What is not yet right is the date and the venue. The week before Christmas really is too late for most of the top golfers to have much enthusiasm left for another big tournament. With the reputation gained in the short time it has been going, I

A busy week in Tokyo.

Sun, sand and golf: the 1992 Johnnie Walker Championship in Jamaica.

believe it now has the prestige to command a better date. Ideally it should come within a couple of weeks of the end of the European and U.S. tours, at the end of October.

The venue, Tryall, is a lovely place, but really just a resort course tricked up to make it tough for the players. With the wind, poor-quality greens and fairways and variable conditions from one hole to the next, the difficulties are down to flaws. The players now know the failings of Tryall and may start to go cold on it, feeling the course is not up to the status of the event.

The other major failing is the lack of spectators, and no one watching means little or no atmosphere. Whenever you have big galleries, as on the U.S. Tour, you feel you are at something worthwhile. That element you can never have in Jamaica, but were you to have 10,000 thousand people, the course is such that they couldn't see anyway. All this is, I'm sure, well known to those respon-

sible, and I suspect there will be some changes after 1994. I hope so, because I think they have an event that could really become established, like the World Match Play.

You can see why the end of term events need to be chosen carefully. It is the season when the carrots dangled are the largest, but take too many and you can have golfing indigestion around the time you should be tucking into the Christmas pud. ◄

Another tussle with Greg Norman.

The 14th: the start of a dramatic finish.

7
Team Faldo – Business
Success Management

• • • • • • • • • • • • • •

In my early days my business affairs amounted to trying to get the best deals. Later on, as I started winning tournaments and looked likely to be a good commercial property, my management company has dealt more with the considerable interest generated and selecting the best companies to go with.

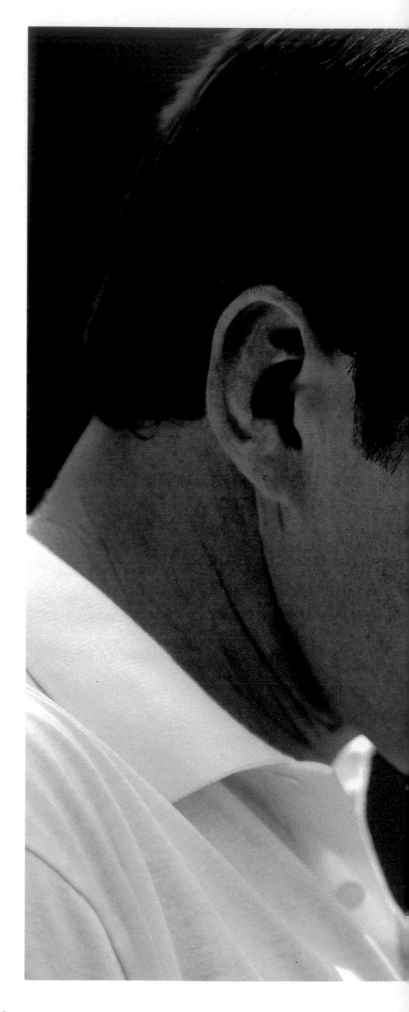

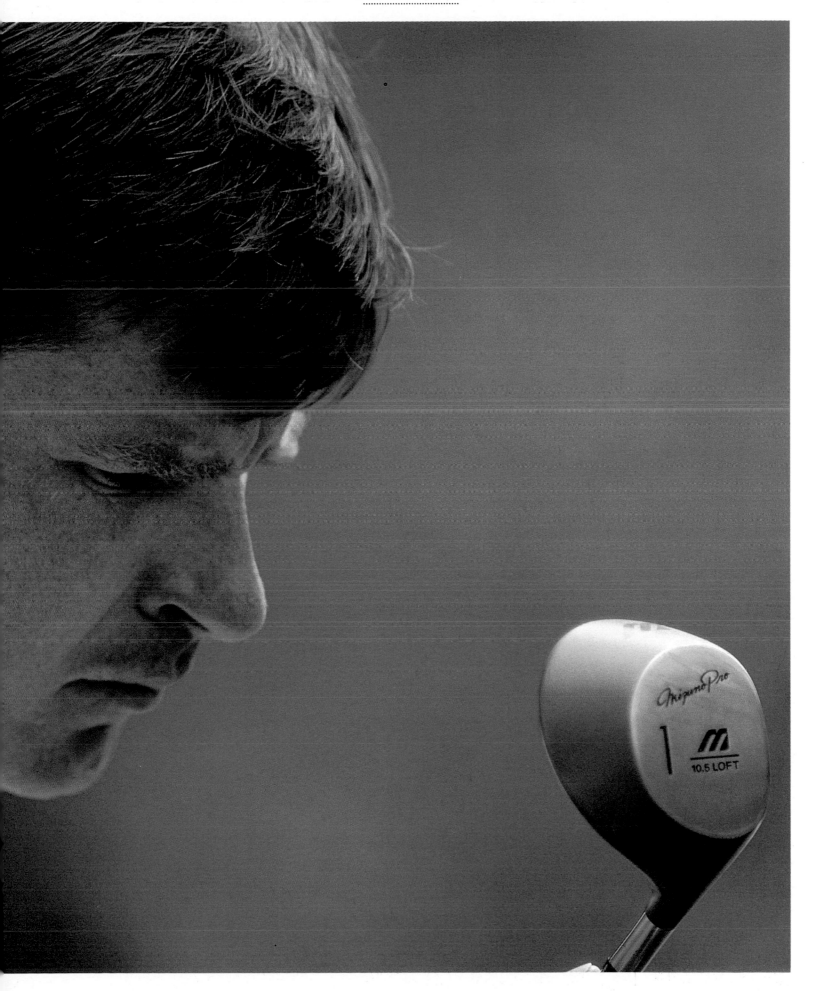

Mark McCormack's International Management Group have handled my affairs from the time I turned pro. IMG has always been very flexible with its clients, and I doubt whether any two business relationships are the same. They will do as much or as little for you as you want. I am happy for them to handle everything: all the deals, all the travel, hotels, cars and so on, and all my tax affairs. Now that we are getting into golf-course design, it is their in-house team that does the day-to-day work, and I give my input as and when required. This leaves me clear to concentrate on playing golf.

I turned professional when I was eighteen years old, and for a young lad from a fairly sheltered background the commercial end of sport seemed a bit of a jungle. At that time, in 1976, there were a number of individuals promoting themselves as being able to do a far better job than big conglomerates, such as IMG.

There was one chap, who must remain nameless, who came to me promising the earth, talking telephone numbers about what he could do for me and the money we would make playing round the world. Then, having made all this cash, a company called Norton Warburg would handle it and turn it into even more millions while I went on generating it all again on the golf course.

My Dad, with his accountancy background, checked up on the companies and said, 'You are either going to make a fortune with this decision, or lose the lot.' We went and saw this chap, who lived in a huge house with a Mercedes parked in front. While I was chatting to him, Dad goes into the local nursery and discovers that not only does he not own the house, he only rents the west wing and the Mercedes is on hire as well. He may have survived, but Norton Warburg went down with a bang a few years later, and a lot of high earners lost a fortune.

I was first introduced to Mark McCormack and his company by a South African called George Blumberg, with whom I used to stay when playing there

as an amateur. George was a sort of patriarch of golf there and was always getting good players to come down to play and looking after them when they came. He was a wonderful man, doing so much just out of a love of the game. His widow, Brenda, is still closely in touch with golf there and with IMG.

He was a close associate of McCormack, and I believe very helpful to him when he was looking to expand his activities outside America in the late 1960s. Mark and I had a game of golf in 1976, the only time we have ever played, and the one comment I remember him making was that he expected to make £100,000 a year out of me one day. Even with his percentage that meant I would be making four or five times that amount, huge sums in those days – not bad even today.

John Simpson has been responsible for me within IMG since 1978 – sixteen years, and just the length of time speaks for the kind of job he's done. I actually introduced him to IMG, having met him a couple of years before while playing at Royal St Georges.

I like to think we have grown together as a commercial partnership. As I have become more successful, his credence has risen within IMG, not just because I have done well, I hasten to add, but because he is also very good at his job. He now heads a team looking after the interests of all the European players on IMG's books, including Woosie, Langer and Lyle. For a time after we were married Gill liked to keep her hand in on the business side and took care of the correspondence that came my way, as well as liaising with IMG as we travelled around the world. The growing ages of the children has more or less brought a stop to all that, but she still has an eye for the business oppor-

I have been playing a role in design for my range of clothes.

tunity. I am sure IMG recognizes the benefit of having 'one of their own' in the camp.

Much of the day-to-day work – travel arrangements, correspondence sorting, and all the paraphernalia of the itinerant golfer – is now handled by Julie White who leads John's back-up staff. She very much puts the oil between the wheels of my life.

The likes of John really earn their corn in the early days with a player, before he has made any sort of a name for himself. They have to convince golf clubs or clothing manufacturers that they represent the next world beater who is worth the money they are asking to play their equipment or wear their clothes. When you do actually make it, the task is a bit easier, but they still have to know just how much you, the player, will be worth to the manufacturer by promoting their products to strike the best deal.

The first deal John did for me was with Robertsons Jam, and it doesn't take a genius to work out what I had stuck on my bag – that's right, a gollywog! We started with a company day for them, and there were a couple of gollywog balloons flying over the course. Today that would be deemed ethnically 'unsafe', as would John's comment when I arrived. 'Do you want the good news or the bad news?' he asked. 'The good is I have done the deal with Robertsons and you are to get £1500 (my, how times have changed!) for carrying their logo. The bad news is you are playing Calvin Pelle in the first round of the World Match Play next week!'

When I started winning a few tournaments, potential sponsors came knocking at the door, one of whom was Pringle. It was not the largest, but it made a good product and the management was anxious for my view on their golf products. In short, they were very nice people to be involved with.

More important, when I went through my slump in the mid-1980s, Pringle was one of the few companies to stick with me. That was at a time when many chose

With John Simpson and Julie White of IMG.

not to continue their contracts when they came up for renewal. I suppose Pringle still thought I looked good in their clothes even though I couldn't play!

After I won the Open in 1987, I could easily have gone elsewhere and got three times as much money, but they had stuck by me through thick and thin, and by then I had got to know and like the people there. Also, when I broached the idea of a Nick Faldo range of clothing, they were prepared to go along with it, despite being a considerable gamble for a company of their size.

Having said I like to leave all the administration of my life to others, I have found it interesting in recent years to get involved with the major companies I am linked with commercially and help them wherever possible. From the time of my first Open Championship win, I have been playing a role in design and marketing decisions for my range of clothing. That was how 'George', my geometric golfer logo, was born.

In the beginning, the golf market was the target area, and I was most insistent that we have a logo. I had travelled the world, and in places like France and Japan all golf clothing has a logo to identify each particular brand. Early on, it was only very up-market companies like Gucci

and Hermes that put distinctive labels on their goods, but by the late 1980s it had moved into sports clothing as well.

The things I'll do for a picture.

More recently, I feel I have been instrumental in encouraging Pringle to veer away from just the golf market and conceive of the range with the entire up-market leisure field in mind. Wives and girl-friends are now big purchasers of mens' sweaters both for themselves and for their menfolk. So we have put together a range that can be worn on any casual occasion, in the pub or on the golf course.

I meet with the company regularly to see each range a year in advance. While I do not have final say, they do listen, and over the years I am pleased to have been able to have had considerable input into the end product.

In line with aiming for a wider market than just golf, I have been encouraging them to go to more exciting venues for photoshoots, particularly ones without a golfing connection. This year's collection was shot in Sun City, and the background was anything but golf, but their golfing and Scottish heritage is difficult to shift. Two years ago we used the Johnnie Walker World Championships in Jamaica as a backdrop. A memo came from Graham Hayward, the Chief Executive of Pringle, to make it look as much like Scotland as possible!

As our range has grown, so has the company. In the recession Pringle has weathered the storm better than most. The Faldo line now makes up about a third of the company's turnover, and I am proud both of the product and the niche it has carved in the marketplace.

With my golf equipment, it is more complicated, as I can only use clubs and balls that I believe to be most suited to my game. At various times I have played with Wilson, Spalding and Macgregor clubs; now I use Mizuno. Usually the deals have been put in place before I have a set that I am completely happy with.

In 1986, after a couple of years out of the limelight and a previous club deal having gone by the board, Karsten

It takes a lot of people to make an instructional video. Valderrama, Spain, in 1994.

with a gear shift before moving onto automatic transmission.

The club that seemed right to me at that time was Mizuno. When they arrived in Europe in the mid-1980s, they had an approach to precision that was simply light years ahead of anything even in the States. In those days manufacturers would send you what they called a matched set of irons, and you could feel differences in weight and shaft flex. That was when I learnt how to take clubs to pieces and check on all the vital statistics so that when I went on to a course, I knew I truly had a matched set. Now I have a workshop in the back of the house, and I still check every club before I use it. It is nowhere near as necessary as it used to be, but having done so gives me that extra confidence that nothing has been left to chance.

Solheim's Ping company was looking to get me interested in playing with their clubs. A set was sent over in the summer of that year and I tried them out in the European Open at Sunningdale – and went round in 62. After the way I had been playing, John came down eager to make the deal, but I don't know what he must have thought when I said, 'I'm sorry, John, these just won't do, the ball goes too straight!'

I have always been a worker of the ball: I like to shape it left to right or right to left, never straight. The Pings are fine clubs, but I just couldn't manoeuvre the ball in the way I wanted. Pings are the frontrunners in perimeter weighted clubs, in which a much higher percentage of the weight is located at the heel and toe of the clubhead, giving a much wider 'sweet spot' than a traditional blade and are more forgiving to the handicap golfer. Their hooks and slices don't go as wide, but it was that very concept that made them unsuitable for me.

I would advise any youngster aspiring to be a great player to learn the game using blades rather than the 'game-improvement' type clubs. That is the only way to develop a quality of strike to see him through to the very top. Some of the top players now play with hollow-backed clubs, but they learnt their trade with the blade. It is a bit like learning to drive

The high standards set by Mizuno have dragged most top club manufacturers up in their wake, but for me they remain the market leaders. I was tinkering with their clubs in 1987, but it was 1991 before we cemented the deal. It is a bonus that they are the company that has sponsored the tour workshop and have trained the personnel that man it. They are the only people I trust to tinker with my clubs apart from myself.

Posing in Sun City for a Pringle shoot.

Barry Willett, a professional and club-maker, has been with Mizuno almost since the day they came to Europe. His problem in the beginning was that, as a Japanese company, they designed clubs for an average height that was two or three inches less than Westerners, which resulted in clubs with a flatter lie – a shallower angle between clubhead and shaft – than is normal for taller people, and short shafts.

Barry is the same height as I am, six feet three inches, and to start with he had trouble convincing them that for the European market, let alone America, they would have to alter some of the fundamentals. It was not until he stood one of their principal designers on a box, so that he was somewhere near Barry's height, that they understood the problem. They then sent their tallest club-maker, a relative giant of six feet one inch called Turbo, to be their senior man on the European Tour.

I base my schedule around trying to reach a peak for the majors.

Another change they had to make was on the leading edge of the clubhead. The turf in Japan is dryer than elsewhere in the world, and tougher. Hitting shots off their fairways is a bit like playing from a doormat, so the leading edge of their clubs tend to be razor sharp. Use them over here and that sharp edge would just dig into the ground. The rounded edge is designed to give the club a bit of bounce as it goes through our turf.

Bridgestone, despite its Western-sounding name, is also a Japanese company, and one that has for some time had more than 50 per cent of its domestic golf-ball market. I had for most of my competitive life played with Titleist, as have many professionals down the years.

Bridgestone were anxious to spread their sales to other golf-oriented countries, and part of that programme was to have a leading player play their ball. John Simpson had been talking to them for some time, and when he had the basis of a worthwhile deal, broached the subject with me. I had tried their product on one of my trips to Japan and have to say it no way matched up to my Titleist. I certainly wasn't the player to surrender a signifi-

cant playing advantage in return for huge sums to play an indifferent ball.

That didn't deter Bridgestone. They agreed to a deal, a significant part of which involved working closely with their research and development department. Early in 1990 they made me some balls, but they really weren't up to scratch. In discussions it emerged that one of the central problems was that the ball sounded wrong off the club, more of a thud than a click.

We had a session around the time of the 1991 U.S. Open, with a group of technicians who sat around listening to me hit shots, both with their ball and other

I love to fiddle with my clubs until I get them just right.

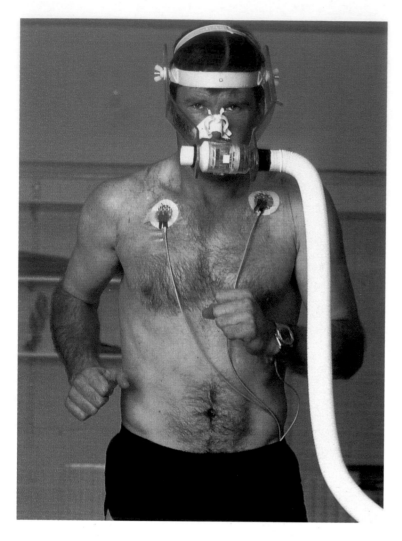

Working out on behalf of Bridgestone and the B.M.A.

is the best ball I have ever played. They have also developed a ball for playing in the wind, which I tried out the last time I went to Japan and found was extraordinary. In strong winds it flies lower for the same strike and travels just as far as an ordinary ball in calm conditions — all within the ball constraints laid down by the Royal & Ancient.

One of my other main contracts is with Audemars Piguet, though I feel there is not a lot I can add to their research and development department!

The policy with my portfolio of contracts has always been to have a small number of in-depth deals with blue-chip companies whose products I can get involved in with design and marketing strategies.

At the beginning of each year I sit down with John, and we agree when and where I am going to play during the year. I base my schedule around trying to reach a peak for the majors, while at the same time trying to play less when the kids are on holiday. Fortunately, the two aims coincide fairly well.

John and I work closely together on my schedule. The main criteria has always been to play the right number of events and to take the right amount of time with the family. In this way I feel I can prepare properly for the majors.

makes. They nodded sagely, said little and went away. Three months later they came back with a ball for me to try, and it was a revelation. They had completely redesigned the ball. It must have cost millions, but they said it was my comments about the sound that put them on the right track. They were prepared to go to any lengths to get it right: if I had suggested they move the factory, I think they might have done it.

The following summer we launched the ball, the Rextar, at the Open Championship at Muirfield. It will have done the launch and subsequent sales no harm that I went on to win the Championship.

I am now the test bed for all their technological advancements. They have gone on seeking further improvements and the ball I currently use, the Rextar Balata 40,

There have been too many golfers who have chased here and there for get-rich-quick events, to the detriment of their golf games. I have been fortunate enough to earn a sufficient amount just out of playing well to resist most of these. This enables me to pace my playing career to maximize the years I can compete at the highest level and to avoid the perils of burn-out.

In the early years this was easy. As a single guy keen to play as much as possi-

Golf-course design is an increasing part of my interest.

What a load of
. . .

ble, I played in everything I could. Europe still didn't have a full schedule, and sometimes John had to go looking for events for me to play in. Certainly any specials that came up were gratefully accepted. Some didn't turn out quite as planned.

In 1980 John sold me on the idea of a big charity event in Northern Ireland, which included an exhibition golf match. He did such a good selling job that I told him, 'If I go, you go' – so we both flew to Northern Ireland. The leading light was a Father O'Shea, and the match was to be between me and someone he referred to as 'Himself'. I didn't know then that was how most of Ireland referred to Christy O'Connor Senior, and for a while thought Father O'Shea really had some special connections.

As so often happens with golf in Ireland, thousands turned up to watch, and after the game there was an hour or two before the Gala Dinner. Christy and I

were being innundated with autograph-hunters, so to avoid the crush Father O'Shea invited us back to his house for 'a little something to refresh you after the day'.

Throughout the day we had been shadowed by a couple of security guards, and they came along as well, as did two members of the Ulster Constabulary who had been assigned to patrol the day's proceedings. No sooner were we in the good father's house than there came a knock at the door, and there stood a couple of Republican policemen, who often called on the priest, the border being just a mile or so away. Now there were four policemen, two from Eire and two from Northern Ireland.

Father O'Shea was clearly a well-known and much-loved local figure, trusted by both sides of that terrible dispute and who often visited political prisoners detained in the province. The last knock at the

At the first stroke, the time by Audemars Piguet is 11.42, exactly.

door turned out to be one of the worst villains recently released who wanted to thank the Father for his kindnesses while in jail. All their strife was forgotten in the presence of the great Christy O'Connor, and there cannot have been many occasions when all the political persuasions have had such a convivial drink together under one roof.

Golf-course design is an increasing interest. With the golf-course development boom of the 1980s there were many enquiries for me to become involved in a variety of projects, but it was not an area I was going to get into until I had my golf game where I wanted it and a few good titles under my belt.

I felt ready to devote some time to design projects by 1990, and the first course with which I have been involved, Chart Hills, was completed in 1993. At the moment I am progressing slowly, again because I don't want to get too committed while playing is still my main priority. I also want to learn the business fully before doing a lot of projects, as I would like eventually to become an authority on golf-course architecture.

That said, I have a number of schemes running in the Far East, as that is where the world economy is booming and many golf-related developments are taking place. I am able to visit them on my two yearly visits to Asia – in February for the Johnnie Walker Asian Classic and later for my business and tournament weeks in Japan.

In the long term I hope to work on projects in this country that will be aimed at the pay-and-play market but will have better and more facilities than what is currently available. As well as quality courses, there would be teaching centres based on the golf-academy concept with

How long I continue to play must remain a matter of conjecture.

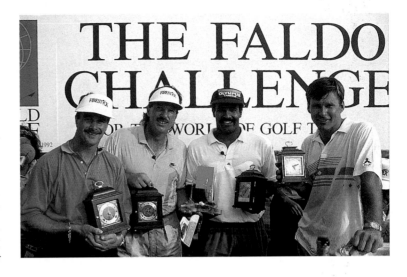

Not a great day – we lost! With Nigel Mansell, Ian Botham and Daley Thompson.

particular emphasis on opening the game up for juniors. I am well aware how risky investments in golf developments can be and fully intend to learn from the mistakes others have made.

How long I continue to play must remain a matter of conjecture, as I will go on as long as I can compete at the highest level and only as long as I enjoy playing competitively. I suspect that will depend on how long I am prepared to work as hard as I currently do. The lures of the Seniors Tour are too far away for me to have any ideas as to whether I will want to join that when the time comes. But it is rewarding to be in a sport that offers so many attractive opportunities for the time when you can no longer compete with the 'flat bellies', as Lee Trevino calls the young bloods of the principal tours around the world. ◀

The Ryder Cup
Us Against Them

• • • • • • • • • • • • • •

The Ryder Cup is, quite simply,
the most marvellous competition.
It is rather like the Olympics:
there is only one every two
years, against four
majors. You're on a team, even
though you are playing an
individual sport, and you know
the whole world is watching
and will see what you do,
whether you play well or badly.

Without a doubt the Ryder Cup is the most emotional, nerve-wracking week in golf. You are there because you have qualified to be there, have wanted to be there, and with no money at stake, it is somehow the ultimate test of your ability. There are simply no rewards for not winning; no few thousand pounds for being beaten in the first round, or having finalist in this or that world championship after your name. It is a week of agony and I love it.

It hasn't always been like that. When I first started playing it was still just Britain versus America, and although we might run them close once in a while, there never was much expectation of winning. In fact, not since Tony Jacklin was at his peak in 1969 had we even given them a good match. I suppose you went into the Ryder Cup hoping to play well, win your games but with no great thoughts about winning the match.

But every match has been memorable. My first was in 1977 at Royal Lytham & St Anne's and I was the new kid on the block. In those days there were only three matches, a foursomes, a four ball and a single on the last day. I was paired with Peter Oosterhuis, who was just about our best player, winning the order of merit four years in a row. It was a great start for me, but you knew you were one of the pairings that was expected to win a point or two.

For the foursomes, we were against Ray Floyd and Lou Graham. It was agreed that I would drive the odds, which meant I would hit the first tee shot and the first at Lytham is a short hole. On the practice ground I hit a lot of 4- and 5-irons, and when the moment came, I got it on the green.

So far so good, but Oosty was a bit off that day, and I found I was supporting him — it's been the reverse since then, when I was supposed to be the leader and had to be helped along. We were three down after ten holes, then Oosty got going and we won five of the next seven holes. I had my first point, and we won by 2/1.

The next day's fourballs was again against Floyd, who was teamed this time with Jack Nicklaus. I had just had some new graphite shafts put in my woods, and I was twenty yards past Nicklaus off every tee, and he was supposed to be the longest hitter there was.

With the arrival of so many new materials for clubs and golf balls that perform much better than they used to, length is less of an excitement factor these days — excluding John Daly. But back then there was great store set by who hit the ball the farthest. I can still remember walking up each fairway feeling Jack's eyes boring into the back of my neck for being so far past him.

I know I played the par fives better, and at the 11th, a huge hole back into the breeze, I was the only one on in two. That put us a couple ahead, and on we went to win 2/1 again.

The last day I drew Tom Watson, who was Open Champion at the time, having just won that fantastic contest against Nicklaus at Turnberry. After beating Nicklaus the previous day, some people thought the outcome was fixed. Neither of us played that well, but I just hung on to win at the last.

I had won all three games in my first Ryder Cup, beaten some of the best players in the world and still felt I was capable of playing better. I was aware it was quite a feather in my cap and a very big step in the building of my confidence.

I owed a lot to Peter Oosterhuis. In the 1970s he was living and playing in America and was one of the few players

I'm sure people felt if we couldn't win it at home, we didn't have a chance away.

on our side not overawed by 'them'. He too won his singles, and the four points between us were more than half the points won by the side.

*With my first
Ryder Cup
partner, Peter
Oosterhuis, at
Walton Heath
in 1981.*

The first time the Europeans took part in the Cup was 1979, but the appearance of Seve Ballesteros and Antonio Garrido in the team was far outweighed by the match being played on a totally typical American course. The Greenbrier is in West Virginia, and it was very hot and humid. The greens were faster than anything we had played on, and those well-documented collars of rough round each green were an examination we just weren't prepared for. Those were the days before a lot of us went and camped on the American circuit, so it took a lot of faith to believe we could win. I'm sure a lot of people felt if we couldn't win it at home, we didn't have a chance away.

Of the British, only Tony Jacklin had ever really made a success of playing there, and Peter Oosterhuis was never quite the player there he had been in Europe. But to this day he still has one of the best Ryder Cup records for players on either side.

After our good debut two years before, Oosty and I were paired up again, and this time we won two of our three games. I again got a point in the singles, though Lee Elder wasn't quite the scalp Tom Watson had been. Brian Barnes and Bernard Gallacher had a good match and overall we seemed to give them a better run than we had at Lytham a couple of years earlier.

With so much of the Ryder Cup played in pairs, the right chemistry is crucial.

With no disrespect to the Spanish, I think it took them a match or two to come to terms with the whole concept of the Ryder Cup. Representing a team and playing foursomes and fourball matches was foreign to them, and the whole history of the event was a bit of a closed book.

At Walton Heath in 1981 the Americans brought over just about the best team ever. Nicklaus and Watson at that time seemed to be carving up every major between them; Trevino was a superb match player, and Bill Rogers had won the Open at Sandwich. There was also Johnny Miller, who was capable of the most wonderful streaks of golf, and Ray F|oyd and Larry Nelson. Nelson had only just scraped into the side by winning the U.S. P.G.A., but prior to that his record in previous matches was nine wins from nine games – quite a last-minute addition.

We, of course, had shot ourselves in the foot by not having Seve Ballesteros playing. He had won the 1979 Open Championship and the 1980 Masters and felt he was entitled to appearance money in Europe for sacrificing the lucrative pastures of America to support his home tour. The authorities were trying to stamp out appearance money at that point and the result was stand-off. He hardly played an event in Europe, and being so at odds with everyone, he didn't get picked in the end. So we didn't actually go into the match as favourites.

John Jacobs was the captain, and he rightly tried to keep the Oosterhuis/Faldo partnership going, but without success. I didn't play very well, and Oosty was right off his game, so we were split and tried with different partners. All to no avail; neither of us got a point in either foursome or fourball. My one consolation was to beat Miller 2/1 in the singles.

Frankly, I don't think it would have mattered what we did against such a team. They would have beaten any side we ever put into the field and probably most of theirs as well. Indeed, it was extraordinary that the balance of power was to swing as quickly as it did, to the point where we nearly won the very next match.

By 1983 it had become obvious that Europe at last had some players who could expect to beat any American they came up against. Certainly half the side went over believing we could win, whether it was in America or at home. Those who believed, played well and won their matches, but some I feel were still in awe of the Americans and didn't play their best.

A disappointing loss in 1985.

Tony Jacklin was a big factor. His attributes and demands for everything to be first class are well known, but he was a captain very much of the generation of his players, and his record meant that no one questioned his right to be calling the shots. Above all, it was his enthusiasm that was infectious. At the end of each day it would be us calming him down. He would rave on about this shot or that, the way this match had turned our way or how we were so unlucky not to have won that, so that we would have to sit him in a corner with a large whisky and tell him to settle down.

He certainly got the whole team pulling for him, and that's one way of building great team spirit. If I had to sum up his best qualities for the job, I would say it was his ability to pull together a dozen players who apart from this one week every two years were fiercely independent competitive individuals. He turned us into a group of players who forgot about themselves and thought only of what the team might achieve.

He also had an instinct of who would play well together. His pairing of Ballesteros and Paul Way was an inspiration, giving Seve a paternal role in nursing a young first-timer that brought the best out of both. He saw that Bernhard Langer and I would get on and do a competent job and we won three points out of four.

With a sport as individual as golf, finding the right chemistry between two people is as important as their respective skills. Two players who get on well together, respect one another's strengths and play to them, and above all are comfortable out there for the three or four hours of the match, are going to do well.

With so much of the Ryder Cup played in pairs — sixteen of the 28 points come from foursomes or fourball — getting this chemistry right is crucial. In the nine matches I've played, I've had four partners with whom I've had a very good rapport. I had a great start with Peter Oosterhuis and in 1977 and 1979 lost only one game

together. In 1983 Langer and I got on well after losing our first match. That partnership might have flourished had I not been completely off the boil in 1985. Ian Woosnam and I did very well in 1987 and 1989, and I feel Colin Montgomerie and I will build on a more than competent performance last time.

Back to 1983. After two days and four series of matches it was square, and the Americans knew that there at last was a side that could beat them. I think that was the first time they ever really questioned whether they were the better team. For a time that final afternoon it looked very much like we would do it. You make a big effort to keep what's happening around you out of your mind, but even ignoring the scoreboards, you can't avoid the feeling of how it's going — and it was going all right.

The turning point must have been Seve not winning, having been three up with seven to play against Fuzzy Zoeller. Seve is such a mercurial player he might just have felt the job was done, particularly against a player who wasn't a 100 per cent fit. What we didn't know was how great a shot he had to play from a fairway bunker at the last to get a birdie and a half. But it was Seve who picked us up from the disappointment of losing so narrowly and said: 'This we must celebrate, this was a great victory for us. Now we know we can beat them and will do so next time.'

This was the point at which the Ryder Cup set off into the stratosphere and became the fascinating contest it has been ever since. It was the year when it turned into the most severe examination of a golfer's courage ever devised. Anyone who has played golf for a team knows the extra pressures it brings, but add to that the bright light of media attention and massive patriotic support and the pressure is multiplied a thousand times.

There was a lot of pressure before 1983, but it was more on the individual to perform well, as much for himself as for the team. With no great expectation of an overall victory, there wasn't the pressure there is today of having to get points on the board, to grasp every victory or half going, as it was sure to be vital come Sunday night.

At first it was great fun as we were breaking new ground. The last win had been in 1957 and only the halved match in 1969 had interrupted a string of American victories. That close-run affair the time before had given us an appetite for the match when we came to the Belfry for the first time in 1985.

Most of us turned up that year convinced we were going to win. Bernhard Langer had won the Masters in April and Sandy Lyle the Open in July. The Belfry was a course we all knew well — there was a tournament there every year — and even though they said it was American in style, it played like an inland British course with hard, bouncy fairways and slow greens. The main thing was that we arrived as a team and stayed that way. We got together regularly and discussed pairings, the way the course was playing and had all our meals together. That was important because there was so much hullabaloo now surrounding the match that you almost had to build an imaginary wall around the team to keep the pressure and the media hype at bay.

I think it probably shook the Americans when they arrived. Even the closely fought match in 1983 hadn't really woken the American public up to the excitement of the contest. They weren't prepared for the great buzz they found when they turned up two years later. It was noticeable that they

didn't behave like a team: they ate in twos and threes, then maybe disappeared to the movies. It was as though they still hadn't realized they were going to have to work really hard to keep the Cup.

In that way I don't think Trevino was a good captain. He is a great character and a fine player, but the psychological intricacies of captaincy weren't for him. I remember hearing he'd allowed arguments to develop about who would play with whom, and when and how the team should practice foursomes.

As for the match itself, we got a nasty shock the first morning. Seve and Manual Pinero won the top match, but the other three went comprehensively to the United States. Jacklin had quite understandably looked to put Bernhard Langer and me back in harness again. We had done so well two years before that he hoped we could rekindle the memories. It was not to be.

I was deep in my transitional period and while I was still sure I was going in the right direction, the various pieces of my new swing were still lying around on the workman's bench. I only played one game on the first two days and couldn't even beat dear old Hubie Green in the singles.

Fortunately it didn't matter. Ian Woosnam struck up a new partnership with Paul Way, Seve and Pinero went on winning most of their matches, and Craig Stadler missed a tiny putt on the 18th on the second morning, which really shook the Americans. It was probably the first time in the entire history of the matches that an American had so obviously buckled under pressure. Stadler has been vulnerable from short distances ever since.

The two Spanish pairings rushed off immediately after lunch and notched huge victories in the second series of foursomes.

Sam Torrance's winning moment at the Belfy in 1985.

Langer and Ken Brown got a point at the end, and suddenly we had a two-point lead going into the final day. Victory was in sight.

In the singles, Pinero was the inspiration. He asked for, and got, Lanny Wadkins and saw him off 3/1. Wadkins and Floyd had been put in at the top to try to get the two missing points back early on. The plan misfired as Paul Way beat Floyd as well.

Seve only halved his single again, this time against Tom Kite. But on this occasion he came back from three down to get something out of a match that had looked well lost. After that it was a fanfare ride home to the moment when Sam Torrance holed right across the 18th green to beat Andy North to win the match. Even though I had contributed nothing in the way of points, I still felt very much part of the team and revelled in the result along with everyone else.

With hindsight, 1985 at the Belfry and the following match at Muirfield Village two years later may well turn out to have been the high watermark of European fortunes. For the first time in Ryder Cup history Europe had not just one or two top class players but half a dozen – and the rest of the teams were great battlers.

The Americans on the other hand suddenly had no daunting personalities with which to intimidate the opposition. That was a first too. Perhaps advancing technology had enabled the likes of Nicklaus and Trevino to hang around longer than they might have done twenty years earlier, which in turn might have inhibited their own players from

1989 Ryder Cup: three Open champions on different missions. With Sandy Lyle and Tony Jacklin.

Seve and Olazabal did the same against Larry Nelson and Payne Stewart. Two all at lunch felt like a considerable victory.

That afternoon we did what no British or European team has done before: we won

Seve should hug him - he'd just knocked his first putt ten feet past. Ballesteros and Olazabal at Muirfield Village, 1987.

Woosie and I halving our foursome with Larry Mize and Hal Sutton in 1987.

developing fully into world beaters. Maybe the lush life on the U.S. Tour had finally sapped the American competitive spirit as many had predicted.

What is not in doubt is how well Europe played at Muirfield Village in 1987. Again we started poorly on the first morning and were down in all four foursomes matches by the turn. Fortunately Woosie and I got our game back under control and beat Wadkins and Mize on the last green, and all four matches — a whitewash. It was an unbelievable experience, greatly enhanced by the support of the small band of European fans. There were only some 2000 of them, but it seemed more like 20,000.

They were outnumbered five to one, but by sheer volume it seemed the other way round.

Woosie and I were playing Dan Pohl and Hal Sutton, who got quite cross and

The Dream Team in 1987

kept muttering, 'Is nobody supporting us?' I held Woosie back, so that when we walked onto the green second and waved to the crowd they just erupted.

That round and all the next day everyone played fantastic golf. Woosie and I, it seemed, just took turns getting in birdies, and it was much the same story in other matches. By the time the singles came around we had a huge five-point lead. It should have been plenty, but it nearly wasn't enough. Rather like going into the final round of a championship four or five shots ahead, it is very difficult to go further ahead. You inevitably become a bit defensive and the opposition, with nothing to lose, go for everything and narrow the gap.

All those who had played so well over the first two days suddenly ran out of inspiration. The final push to victory became a struggle against the tide. Sam Torrance and Howard Clark, who hadn't played since the first morning, were the only Europeans in the first seven matches to add to the overnight total. Howard beat Dan Pohl and Sam halved with Larry Mize. Of the rest, only Seve looked to be in control of his match with Curtis Strange.

Eamon Darcy had been a couple up on Ben Crenshaw, but came to the 17th one down. Crenshaw made a mess of 17 and then drove into the ditch at 18. Darcy frittered around too and had an awful downhill putt to win. If he had missed on that green, there was no way the ball would have stopped, and he would have been further away than before. He holed, and we heard Seve had beaten Strange 2/1 and that was that. Finally we had done something that no British or European team had done in the Ryder Cup before, we had won in America.

All wins are special in their way, and certainly I will take my victories in the majors, each and every one of them, to the grave. But for sheer euphoria, that win in America was the best. I suppose twelve people celebrating with wives and sweethearts, not to mention the fans, is likely to be a bit noisier than having a quiet celebratory supper with the missus.

The matches since then, particularly the two at the Belfry, have been that much harder. There is now a general presumption that we should win. Justifying favouritism has proved just as demanding mentally as playing David against America's Goliath.

Woosie and I continued our successful partnership in 1989, until running into Chip Beck and Paul Azinger in the second series of fourballs. We didn't play too badly, but they were thirteen under par for seventeen holes. I remember one shot by Azinger. We were on the front of the 15th green at the Belfry, the par five, in two. The approach is blocked by the bunkers that run out in front of the green from the left, and Azinger, who is a natural fader of the ball, needed to draw the ball about 30 yards in the air if he was to find the green. He not only did that, but put it by the pin to win with an eagle to our birdie. Sometimes a single shot can decide a match, and I think that was one of those occasions.

Another indifferent start in the foursomes had left us two points down at lunch on the first day, but we recovered to lead by two going into the singles. The pattern of all these close matches in recent times has been the same: we've managed to get our nose in front going into the last day, but only in 1985 have we actually won the singles.

As had been the case in 1987, it was those players who hadn't played very much during the first two days, or had not won many points, who managed to squeeze out the points to get us the half. One of the reasons has to be the different approach of two captains in selecting pairings and who plays when.

The Americans have always had a policy of trying to give every player a game on each day. With twelve players for only eight places in each series of games, they have even been prepared to break up successful partnerships to do it. Sometimes I feel that has worked against them over the first two days but has usually left them

Christy O'Conner Jnr's finest hour, beating Couples at the Belfry in 1989.

Top match in the singles at Kiawah Island at the 1991 Ryder Cup.

better prepared and fresher for the rigours of the singles. This goes back to the days when they used to win the matches comfortably and were more concerned that everyone felt they had played a real part in the match, because winning wasn't as big a concern as it is now.

Tony Jacklin, on the other hand, always went hell for leather to get points on the board and played his strong partnerships throughout. One might argue that this drains the top players, particularly as they have not done as well in the singles as they should. In 1989, Seve, Langer, Woosie and I all failed to win on the Sunday, so we were lucky in the end to halve the match.

It has been said that once the half had been achieved that Sunday – particularly after we had been down in virtually every match – the relief of retaining the trophy obscured the fact we still needed to win another point to win the match. Woosie and Faldo were still out there, and one of them was bound to get the job done, so we could get on with the celebrations.

I can only say the thought never crossed my mind. In spite of all the team hype of a Ryder Cup match, golf is still an individual game, and you go all out for your own personal satisfaction as much as for the team performance. Also, as professionals, you train yourself to keep the 'what ifs' at bay, concentrating fully on one shot at a time. That both Woosie and I hit the ball in the water at 18 had nothing to

Shooting out of the sand in at Kiawah Island.

do with relaxing because we had retained the cup or that there was an emotional let-down because no one was coming back to cheer us home. If anything, we ran out of steam after a long, hard week.

The 1991 match on Kiawah Island was one I would rather forget. It had not been a great year for me, my only victory being the Irish Open. Nor had I done much in the major championships, so I was certainly not brimful of confidence when I arrived. The Ryder Cup is not a time to go and find it. The Americans have an expression: 'If you don't bring it with you, you ain't going to find it when you get there.' That pretty well summed it up.

There was some doubt as to whether Woosie and I were going to play together, because Bernhard Gallacher had indicated earlier in the year that he wanted to split us up. With hindsight, that would have been the right thing to do. Woosie had won the Masters in April, as well as another tournament in the States, but his form had waned a bit, so neither of us was particularly cheerful about our prospects. Often, if one player is on form he can lift the other back to his best, but if both are down, you are not going to do very well. I think our gut feeling at the beginning of the week was that we shouldn't be playing together, which proved to be the case.

With what we had achieved in the two previous matches, a lot was riding on us to succeed. When we didn't, there didn't seem to be a plan B. Apart from Seve and Ole, no one was playing very well, and it wasn't until the second series of fourballs that a number of scratch pairings suddenly got us back into the match.

After the first day Woosie, Bernhard Langer and I all said we didn't think we were performing well enough. It was decided that I was the one who should play, but the question arose, with whom? The choice lay between David Gilford and Colin Montgomerie. I didn't know Monty that well, so I asked who was playing better. David was the reply; he was hitting everything straight down the middle.

In foursomes it is even more important for partners to get on well. David and I didn't know one another that well then, and the cauldron of the Ryder Cup wasn't really the time to start. We never really gelled, and if he missed a green, I didn't chip close enough to hole and vice versa. Everything that could go wrong, did.

The only good thing was that Bernhard and Woosie had their morning off and came back in the afternoon to win with Monty and Paul Broadhurst, respectively, as did Mark James and Steven Richardson. That got us back to all square with the singles to come.

I practiced very hard that second afternoon, for more than three hours with Lead. We then went up the opening holes and chipped and putted. At least I felt I had done as much as possible to get my game back, but when you are low, there is always the doubt it will work on the day.

That evening Bernie (Gallacher) told me I would be playing top, which was fine by me. When I drew Floyd, I thought, 'Great! He's not playing that well either.' He had won two of his games with Fred Couples, but mostly because Freddie was playing so well.

That night, though, I was the most nervous I have ever been. I had trouble getting off to sleep, and I was pacing round the room at 4.00 am with my heart going flat out. I thought I was going to have a heart attack. You get so much more nervous when you are not playing well, are not sure of yourself.

At least I knew what I had to do that morning. First out, you have to get the blue numbers on the board, holes up for your side. I made a great start and won the first three holes and went on from there. In the end I was four up with four to play, and even though Floyd dragged me up the last, I was still only one or two over par. Matches were being won later in the day with 78s and 80s.

For me, it became a matter of wait and see, of watching all the others struggle in the wind and on that extraordinary course. As in 1989, we never really looked like doing it and when Bernhard was three down with four to play, that appeared to be the end of it.

The rest will be forever etched on the minds of all who saw it, let alone played in it. But what really amazed me was how Bernhard bounced back and won a tournament the following week. That was real mental toughness.

There were a lot of problems that week. Bernie had the hardest job in the world following Jacklin as captain. He'd been Jacko's right-hand man in previous matches, but it is nothing like having the job yourself and having to make the decisions. Also the so-called strong players weren't playing well, and there was a higher percentage of first timers to be blooded. Everything worked much better at the Belfry two years down the track.

The result at the Belfry in 1993 was no better than at Kiawah, and indeed was known some time before the final putt was holed. But unlike Kiawah, it was a much stronger performance over the three days. At least that was the way it seemed, but that might be because I was playing much better myself.

In Colin Montgomerie I found another partner with whom I could build a sound golfing relationship. Maybe his amateur days has given him a sound understanding of partnership play and the importance of getting along. He certainly accepted that I needed to be in charge, though should he in the future find himself the strong man of the party, I am sure he will take the lead role without any problem. Most important of all, he is a great foursomes partner; he hits the ball straight and holes out well.

The partnership started really well. That first morning we saw off Floyd and Couples 4/3, then in the afternoon, with Paul Azinger joining Couples in place of Floyd, we had a superb fourball match. Both sides were round in a better ball of 63 and a half was a fair result.

The game couldn't be finished because we ran out of light. There had been a long delay for fog in the morning, and to be honest, it ceased to be playable by about the time we reached the 16th green.

Azinger and Couples had just birdied 16 to go one up, but I could see they were a lot less happy about continuing than we were. So I urged to play one more hole — a very different decision from the time I stopped in the fog at St Andrews in the Dunhill Cup, but the circumstances were different too. It was the right thing to do, as I got a birdie to square the match. By then it really was too dark to play.

The following morning it was pistols at dawn; all square with just the 18th to play. You go out and prepare as hard, if not harder, than before a normal competitive

They say that two heads are better than one. With Montgomerie in 1993.

round, including hitting a lot of drives. If there is a more frightening drive than the 18th at the Belfry in the Ryder Cup, it is hitting the same tee shot as your first of the day. In the end I had to hole a ten-footer for a four and a half. Nerve-wracking stuff!

I think the stress of having to go through that fifteen-minute exercise first thing on the Saturday morning took its toll later in the day. Monty and I played well enough to beat Wadkins and Pavin in the morning, but there seemed little inspiration left for the fourball in the afternoon.

On paper the combination of John Cook and Chip Beck looked less menacing than Azinger, Couples & Co., whom we had played before. We went one down after neither of us could get a par at the 8th, and every hole thereafter was halved. The putts suddenly stopped dropping, and however hard we tried, nothing worked. It was all most frustrating, particularly on an afternoon when Europe lost the initiative for the first time in the match.

We were never really able to get it back.

In the end, my match against Paul Azinger was of academic interest, but that didn't stop either of us going flat out to the wire. I have heard it said that had the match overall still been alive, then 'Faldo would have done it.' I'd like to think that would have been the case, but I don't think I could have played any better over the last few holes than I did. Just maybe, Azinger wouldn't have got a three at the last.

One final note about that hole in one at 14. All week I had been saying to Monty that I would hole a long shot. Against Couples and Azinger in the first fourball, the golf was so good, I kept saying 'Knock it in the hole' or 'I'm going to knock this one in.'

I really believed I was going to hole a full shot somewhere. So when I holed out at 14, I wasn't totally surprised. I had just made a mess of 13, and as I swept the leaves away from the tee, I said, 'Oh well, now's the time for that hole in one.' Honestly, ask Fanny. ◄

Mrs Montgomerie and Mrs Faldo: The style of the 1993 Ryder Cup.

A good pairing with Monty at the Belfry in 1993.

Competition Record

European Order of Merit Placings

1977	8th	£23,977
1978	3rd	£37,911
1979	21st	£14,910
1980	4th	£46,054
1981	2nd	£55,106
1982	4th	£68,252
1983	1st	£119,416
1984	12th	£46,958
1985	42nd	£18,959
1986	15th	£65,419
1987	3rd	£181,833
1988	2nd	£347,971
1989	4th	£261,552
1990	12th	£199,937
1991	10th	£245,892
1992	1st	£708,522
1993	2nd	£558,738

American Order of Merit Placings

1983	79th	$67,851
1984	38th	$167,000
1985	118th	$54,060
1986	135th	$52,965
1988	64th	$179,120
1989	31st	$327,981
(1990	37th	$345,262 – non Tour Member)

Team Member

Ryder Cup: 1977, 1979, 1981, 1983, 1985, 1987, 1989, 1991, 1993

Hennessy Cup: 1978, 1980, 1982, 1984 (captain)

Dunhill Cup: 1985, 1986, 1987, 1988, 1991, 1993

Tournament Victories

1977	Skol Lager Individual
1978	Colgate P.G.A. Championship
1979	ICL Tournament (SA)
1980	Sun Alliance P.G.A. Championship
1981	Sun Alliance P.G.A. Championship
1982	Haig Tournament Players Championship
1983	Paco Rabanne French Open
	Martini International
	Car Care Plan International
	Lawrence Batley
	Ebel Swiss Masters
1984	Heritage Classic (U.S.)
	Car Care Plan International
1987	Peugeot Spanish Open
	Open Championship
1988	French Open
	Volvo Masters
1989	U.S. Masters
	Volvo P.G.A. Championship
	Dunhill British Masters
	French Open
	Suntory World Match Play Championship
1990	U.S. Masters
	Open Championship
	Johnnie Walker Asian Classic
1991	Carrolls Irish Open
1992	Carrolls Irish Open
	Open Championship
	Scandinavian Masters
	European Open
	Toyota World Match Play Championship
	Johnnie Walker World Championship
1993	Johnnie Walker Classic
	Carrolls Irish Open
1994	Alfred Dunhill Open

First published in Great Britain in 1994 by
George Weidenfeld and Nicolson Ltd
The Orion Publishing Group
Orion House
5 Upper St Martin's Lane
London WC2H 9EA

Edited by Lucas Dietrich
Designed by Bradbury and Williams
Printed and bound in Italy

A cataloguing-in-publication record for this
book is available from the British Library.
ISBN 297 83278 6

THE
RHYTHMS
OF LIFE

THE
RHYTHMS
OF LIFE

Consultant Editors
Professor Edward S. Ayensu and
Dr Philip Whitfield

Crown Publishers, Inc., New York

Consultant editors : **Professor Edward S. Ayensu**
Director of the Department of
Biological Conservation
Smithsonian Institution, Washington DC

Dr Philip Whitfield Lecturer in Zoology
King's College, University of London

Text : **Dr Philip Whitfield**

Professor Paul Bohannan
Department of Anthropology
University of California, Santa Barbara

Dr John Brady Reader in Zoology
Imperial College of Science and Technology
University of London

Kendrick Frazier
Science journalist and
editor of *The Skeptical Inquirer*

Dr Martin Hetzel Consultant physician

Chris Morgan Writer and specialist in time,
science fiction and the future

Dr D.M. Stoddart Lecturer in Zoology
King's College, University of London

Dr Bryan Turner Lecturer in Zoology
King's College, University of London

Illustrations by : **Michael Woods**

Eugene Fleury
George Glaze
Tony Graham
Tom McArthur
Richard Orr
Jim Robbins

Editor: **Jinny Johnson**
Text editor: **Ruth Binney**
Art editor: **Mel Petersen**
Picture editor: **Zilda Tandy**
Assistant editors: **Rosanne Hooper**
                    Pip Morgan
Design assistant: **Linda Abraham**
Proof reader: **Gwen Rigby**
Production: **Hugh Stancliffe**

The Rhythms of Life was conceived, edited and designed by Marshall Editions
Limited, 71 Eccleston Square, London SW1V 1PJ

Inquiries should be addressed to Crown Publishers Inc.,
One Park Avenue, New York, New York 10016

Published simultaneously in Canada by General Publishing Company
Limited.

Library of Congress Cataloging in Publication Data
Ayensu, Edward S.
The Rhythms of Life
1. Biological rhythms. 2. Cycles I. Title
QH527.A93   754.1'882   81-9772
ISBN: 0-517-545233   AACR2

Printed and bound in The Netherlands by Smeets Offset B.V., Weert

© 1981 Marshall Editions Limited
First American edition 1982 by Crown Publishers Inc.

Contents

Introduction   6–7

Familiar rhythms   8–9
The vital rhythms   10–11
Rhythms of babyhood   12–13

Cosmic rhythms   14–15
The dawn of rhythms   16–17
Energy from the sun   18–19
The spinning Earth   20–21
The orbiting Earth   22–23
Winds and weather   24–25
Rhythms of the Ice Ages   26–27
Cycles of cold   28–29
The pull of the moon   30–31
Phases of the moon   32–33

Rhythms of the seasons   34–35
Temperate seasons   36–37
Seasons of the tropics   38–39
The changing hours of daylight   40–41
The growing season   42–43
A time to flower   44–45
A time to reap   46–47
Preparing for winter   48–49
The sleeping season   50–51

Rhythms within rhythms   52–53
The vocabulary of rhythms   54–55
Daily rhythms   56–57
Tidal rhythms   58–59
Yearly rhythms   60–61
The biological clocks   62–63

Rhythms of sex   64–65
Rhythms of conception   66–67
The annual display   68–69
The breeding season   70–71
Responses to weather   72–73
Rhythms of courtship   74–75
Rhythms of migration   76–77
The long-distance travellers   78–79
Spawning with the tides   80–81

Population cycles   82–83
Cycles of life   84–85
Alternating generations   86–87
Communities: the numbers game   88–89
The rise and fall of populations   90–91
Cycles of disease   92–93

Rhythms of growth   94–95
Cells: multiplication by division   96–97
Patterns of growth   98–99
The carbon cycle   100–101

Rhythms of energy   102–103
Fuelling body rhythms   104–105
Rhythms of breathing   106–107
The pulse of life   108–109
Rhythms of eating   110–111
A time for action   112–113
Cycles of sleep   114–115

Rhythms of motion   116–117
The art of flying   118–119
Hopping and jumping   120–121
The stepping sequence   122–123
On two legs   124–125
The wave makers   126–127
Rhythms through water   128–129

Rhythms of health and disease   130–131
The body clocks   132–133
'Owls', 'larks' and jet lag   134–135
Hormonal rhythms   136–137
Rhythms and asthma   138–139
Treatment and transplants   140–141

Rhythms of fate   142–143
Biorhythms   144–145
Waves of body and mind   146–147
Astrological cycles   148–149
Sunspot cycles   150–151

A sense of rhythm   152–153
Social rhythms   154–155
Contagious rhythms   156–157
Learning the beat   158–159
Music and movement   160–161
Rhythms of worship   162–163
Rhythms of work   164–165
The family beat   166–167
Communal rhythms   168–169

Rhythms of time   170–171
Concepts of time   172–173
The first clocks   174–175
Charting the years   176–177
Clocking the minutes   178–179
Ticking away the seconds   180–181
The race against time   182–183

Rhythm data   184–193
Index   194–198
Acknowledgements   199

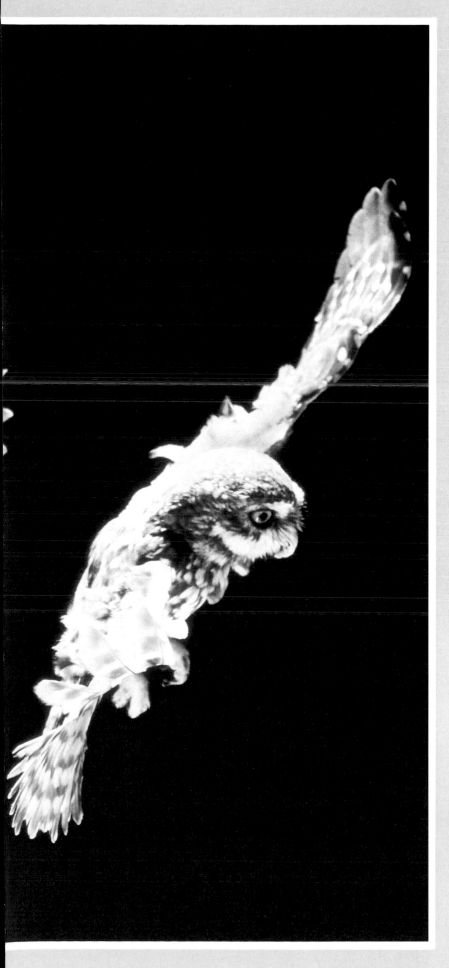

Introduction

While our ever-changing world appears more chaotic by the minute, the human mind yearns for the beauty of order and pattern. We turn up the hi-fi and the measured beats of music briefly smother the confusion. We stride out for a half hour's jogging, making paces to pre-empt the pacemaker. We re-form our family lives and links by seeking calm on an annual vacation.

What we probably fail to appreciate is that all these soothing influences are intrinsically rhythmic. Music has an obvious beat and rhythm, jogging is the rhythmic repetition of a cycle of movements and the calming beat of the ocean waves on the shore is a multi-dimensional rhythm in water.

Once you are aware of rhythms you find that they are everywhere, around you and also within. The earthly world the human race inhabits is orchestrated to create a rhythmical environment—albeit a complex one. Rhythms of day and night, the repetitive march of the seasons, the daily and monthly patterning of the ocean's tides and even the incredibly slow historical cycles of the earth's climate weave the rhythmical fabric of our surroundings.

Life takes on its own rhythms to match the rhythm of the environment. The sudden feel of your own heartbeat or awareness of your own breathing rhythm are just two everyday examples of the huge range of living rhythms. But the most staggering conclusion to emerge when these rhythms are analysed and examined in detail is that mankind, and nearly all the other creatures who share the planet, have an innate ability to measure time. With some of Superman's mystical powers, without reference to the hands of a clock, our bodies, and the bodies of animals and plants, beat in time with the environment. This is no magic trick, no special effect or sleight of hand or mind but the power that rules all life on earth.

If time is truly our planetary dictator, and rhythms the manifestations of that dictator's supremacy, then the study of rhythms becomes essential to the understanding of the way all life works. So the reason why this book was created—and why it should be read—becomes clear. Rhythms are the key to self knowledge and to knowledge of our surroundings. They put all life into a timely perspective.

Professor Edward S. Ayensu
Smithsonian Institution, Washington D.C.

Dr Philip Whitfield
King's College, University of London

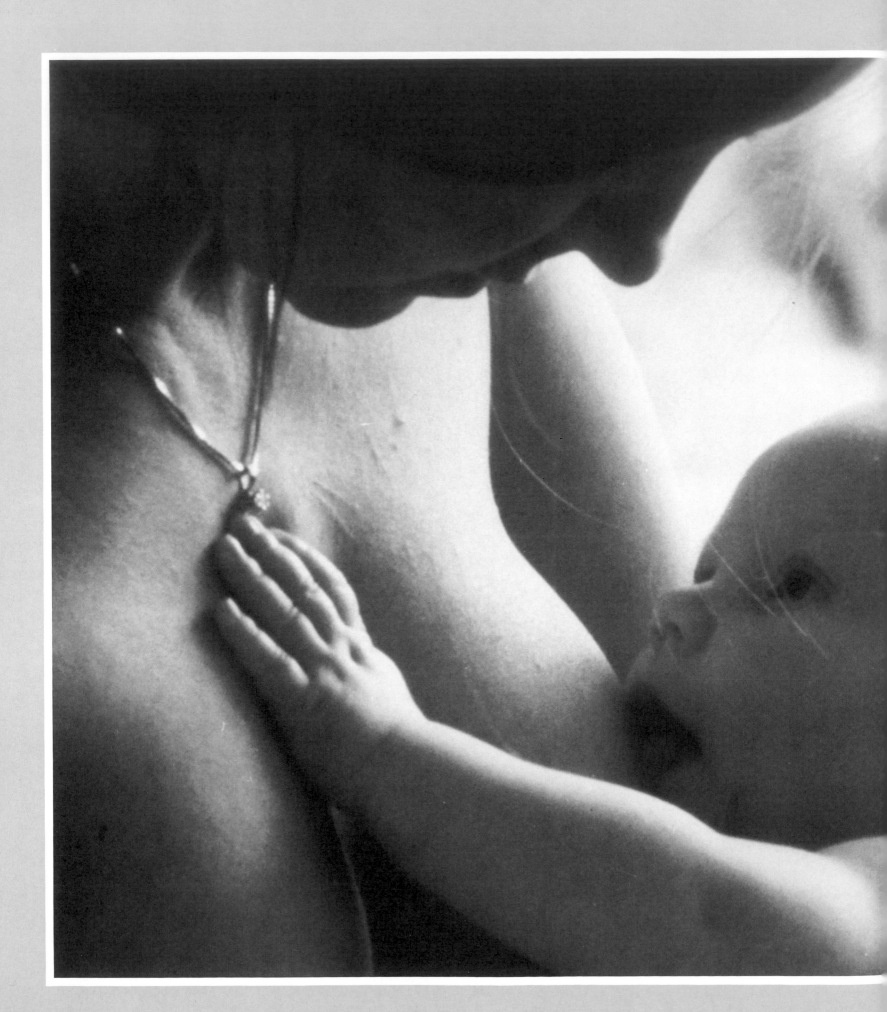

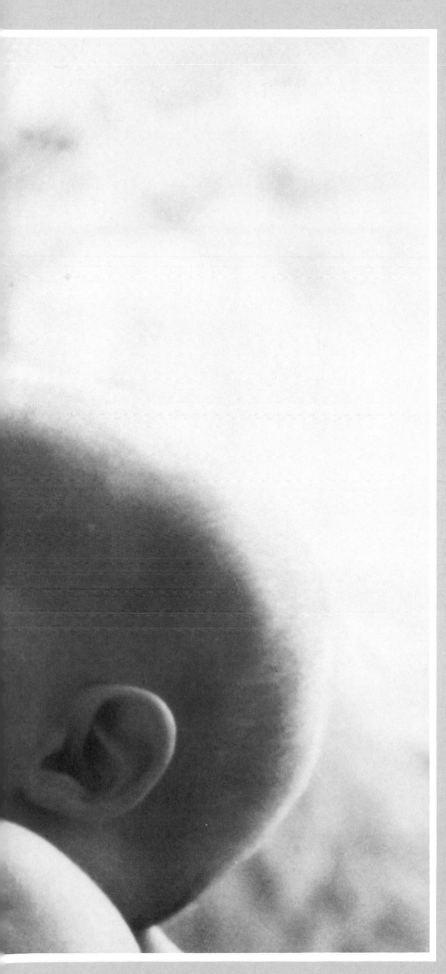

Familiar rhythms

In the ever-increasing complexity of human life we are surrounded by sights and sounds which are so commonplace that they pass unnoticed. The familiarity of everyday happenings can truly breed, if not contempt, then certainly a blunting of man's imagination. If our minds were not so hindered, then every sunrise, the birth of each new baby and the impact of every ocean wave on the shore would be recognized and greeted as the minor miracle that indeed it is. All these recurring miracles stem from one simple fact—life is rhythmic. This feature identifies the animals and plants of the planet Earth as effectively as a brand mark, but is so basic that even when it shapes our own lives we seldom honour it with a moment's careful attention.

Once the human mind has grasped the idea of rhythm, examples become obvious and all pervading. Our hearts beat rhythmically within us while our breathing follows a slower but equally repetitive pattern. We sleep, we wake. On a longer time-scale we can see that the lives of plants take the form of a yearly cycle. In a repeating and regular cycle a tree signals the seasons with its bare branches and inactive buds in winter, breaking buds in spring, a green profusion of growing leaves in summer and the fall of golden leaves in October and November.

A characteristic signature of every rhythm is its frequency, that is, the number of complete, even cycles that occur per second, minute, day, year, decade or even millenium. The frequency signature of a cycle provides a useful means of classifying biological rhythms and is a characteristic that can take on almost any value. So a baby's heartbeat might have a frequency of 100 beats a minute, a swallow's migratory rhythm a frequency of a single two-way journey per year. These two examples of frequency signatures reveal a startling diversity in the rapidity of life's rhythms—the baby's pulse is over 50 million times faster than the swallow's migratory rhythm. Such scales of difference make taxing demands on the imagination. At one end of the spectrum, for instance, insect wings vibrate at a frequency of hundreds of times per second, while at the other, it is possible that profound effects on animal evolution may have been brought about by rhythms in the earth's climate which have a frequency of one cycle every hundred thousand years or so.

Whatever their frequency, the cycles of life can be split into two distinct groups depending on whether or not the rhythms correspond to any external, rhythmical changes in the environment. So while the beat of the heart and the rhythm of breathing are not matched in frequency by any external rhythmical pattern, our cycle of sleep and wakefulness has a rhythm corresponding to the earth's external 24-hour rhythm of night and day. The breeding and migration of birds and the growth cycle of trees are examples of rhythms that occur in synchrony with the external cycle of the repeating seasons. Most scientists assume that by being 'tuned in' to the external rhythm of its surroundings an organism is gaining some benefit and, by inference, that the same plant or animal would be less efficient if it were operating out of step with its environment.

Man cannot isolate himself from the rhythmical imperatives of the world around him. He is part of the rhythms and the rhythms are part of him. Man has the same internal physiological rhythms as other animals, and similar daily and yearly rhythms, but he has created variations on the rhythmical theme which extend into every part of his life and society.

FAMILIAR RHYTHMS...*the vital rhythms*

Seen and unseen, rhythms and cycles exist both around and within us. To gain a general insight into the ubiquity and importance of biological rhythms and cycles, it is illuminating to indulge in some self-analysis and to consider carefully the animals we each know most intimately and intuitively—women and men, babies and children—the 'naked apes' as Desmond Morris has called us. It tickles human pride to itemize the ways in which man is unique among the earth's animals. Man has been described as the only animal with a true spoken language, the most enquiring of animals and the supreme toolmaker. It might not be an exaggeration to say that man is also the animal that demonstrates more facets of rhythmical phenomena in his life-span and life-style than any other. What makes man an exception is not the nature of his bodily rhythms, but the fact that he has taken rhythms, ritualized and formalized them, and made them an integral part of his existence. By means of technology he can also distort rhythms.

Before investigating some of these aspects of man's nature in depth, it is essential to clarify a difficult issue of terminology. The words rhythm and cycle have so far been used more or less interchangeably, but the similarities and differences between these two related terms must now be scrutinized more closely. Stated baldly, a rhythm is regularly repetitive in time—drumbeats, heartbeats and sunrises are all rhythmical phenomena. Defined in a similar fashion, cycles are chains of events that occur in a set order, and the order itself is repeated. ABCDABCD is a cycle of letters, while spring, summer, autumn, winter, spring, summer . . . is the cycle of the seasons. But what is the relationship between a rhythm and a cycle? Rhythms relate primarily to the timing of events, cycles to the order in which they occur. To this extent they are different, yet if cycles are completed at regular intervals in time they can be highly rhythmical, and it is in such contexts that rhythms and cycles become almost—but not precisely—synonymous.

To make the distinction between a rhythm and a cycle more concrete, think of an ordinary mechanical clock. When properly adjusted, the hour hand on such a clock behaves in a cyclical way; it points in turn to the numbers 1 to 12 over and over again in the same unvarying order. The same hand is also behaving rhythmically because it passes any particular number at regular 12-hour intervals. If the same clock were placed in the middle of a sandstorm, however, the sand would make the hand move irregularly—first fast, then slow and sometimes stopping as it circled round the clock face. In such circumstances the hand no longer moves rhythmically and passes the number one, for instance, at varying intervals of time which may be more or less than 12 hours. Although the rhythm is disturbed, the cycle of events is still preserved. The hand continues to move from one to two, two to three and so on and then repeats itself. So cycles may or may not be rhythmic, while rhythms are often generated by underlying mechanisms that are cyclical.

Against this background of theory we can begin to discern the principal rhythms and cycles of human life. Some of these are easily perceptible through our ordinary, unaided senses. Others require the most sophisticated and detailed analysis of the internal workings of the nerves, brain and glands before they become obvious. Yet others only become apparent when careful records of human behaviour and activity are made over the course of many days, months

The concept of the breath of life in Judeo-Christian religions and similar descriptions in other religions testify to the ancient spiritual significance of the breathing cycle. To pre-scientific societies breathing was the essential attribute of life—when breathing stopped so did all other vital processes. A single breathing cycle is made up of one breath in, followed by one breath out. At rest, while sleeping or during intense activity we breathe rhythmically quite unconsciously. Driving this rhythm is a portion of the brain stem that sends rhythmic sets of nerve impulses to the muscles of the chest wall and diaphragm.

Even in repose, with shallow breathing and a quiet, regular heartbeat, this woman is seething with other internal rhythms. She may seem static but many of her tissues are in a dynamic equilibrium of growth and decay—new cell growth and old cell removal balancing one another. Skin, finger nails, hair, cells in the lining of the intestines and the millions of cells in the bloodstream are continually renewed. All of these renewal processes are modulated by rhythms which usually have a 24-hour period. The body is buzzing with cellular activity which is organized in long, slow pulses, each lasting a day.

The daily beat of the body is apparent in many other disparate functions: there is a rhythm of urine flow which normally peaks between 10.30 am and 2.30 pm; a daily blood pressure variation; a rise and fall in body temperature and distinct changes in the hormone content of the blood.

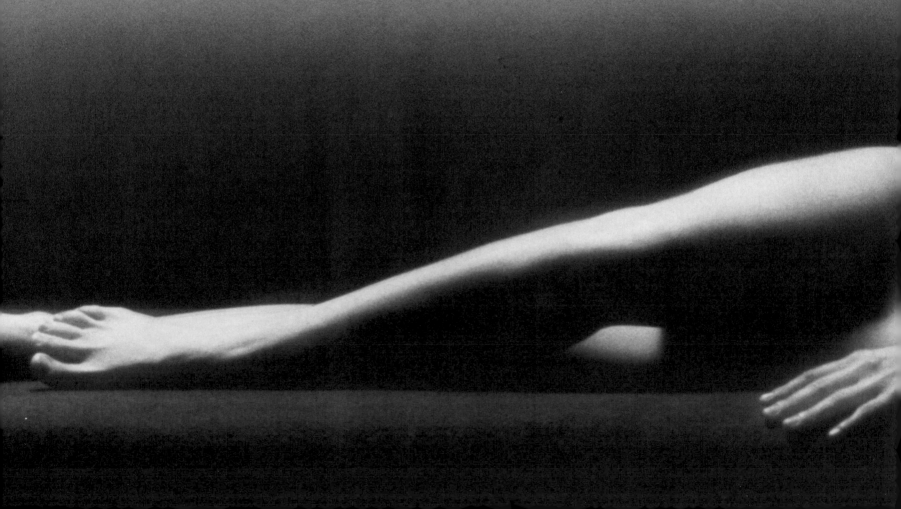

or even years and may even be a manifestation of the behaviour of whole human populations.

At the microscopic level the basic living units, the cells, from which the human body is constructed demonstrate cycles and rhythms which form the foundation of continued human existence. In order to work properly, many parts of the body need to renew themselves constantly, and to achieve this the cells multiply. Skin cells do so, and do so cyclically. Individual cells first double their genetic material which then splits into two identical halves. Then the cell itself divides so that each new daughter cell receives a complete set of genetic instructions. The whole process repeats itself in a cell cycle. Superimposed on this cell cycle is a larger scale rhythm in time because, in most tissues, more of the cells divide in the late evening and during the night than during the daylight hours.

Some body cells, such as those in the brain and nervous system, stop reproducing themselves once they have been formed. In specializing for their roles as the working components of a living computer, these cells seem to have forfeited their ability to divide and make replicas of themselves. Although nerve cells have given up their powers of division they still demonstrate their own high frequency rhythms. These are the rapid rhythmical changes in the surface electrical charges of nerve cells which create nerve impulses. Such impulses are the cell language by which nerves shuttle information around the body and the spikes of electrical activity, whose frequency is an information code, can occur at rates of hundreds per second.

Unlike cell divisions and nerve impulses, human breathing and heartbeat rates are directly perceptible. At rest our breathing and heartbeats are relatively constant rhythmical activities, the period or time gap between events being about five seconds in the case of breathing and about 0.85 seconds between heartbeats. These periods can be changed by a number of factors. Everyday experience tells us that exercise pushes up both rates—our hearts beat faster and we breathe more quickly and deeply. As with the pattern of cell division, there is also a daily rhythm of heart rate because, even when the body is resting, the heart generally beats faster during waking hours than it does during periods of sleep.

There are few physiological functions that man or his organs perform that do not conform to this general pattern of approximately 24-hour periodicity. Body temperature, urine flow, a huge diversity of hormone levels, the pattern of sleep and wakefulness and the timing of the beginning of labour are just some of the intricate body attributes that fluctuate with a daily rhythm. It is as if every organ in the body obeys the baton of an internal conductor who beats time very slowly, once every 24 hours. More remarkable still is the fact that many of these circadian or approximately daylength rhythms persist even when all external clues to the passage of time are removed.

Over periods longer than a day men and women continue to display rhythmical and cyclical behaviour. Most of these long-term rhythms seem to be generated by hormones, although when cycles have a yearly periodicity it is often difficult to disentangle the physiological from the psychological. A woman's menstrual cycle, however, falls neatly into the hormone-driven category. The menstrual cycle of a woman who is not pregnant, which ▷

A thousand years ago civilizations of Central and South America grasped one central fact about heart function. During their bloody, sacrificial rites they plucked out their victims' hearts and saw them still beat, though severed from the bodies. They knew that hearts have an intrinsic ability to beat. A heart is made up of cardiac muscle cells that, even in vertebrate embryos, have an innate facility for rhythmic contraction and elongation.

After puberty there is a rhythm in every non-pregnant woman's life so that, unlike most men, she can never be unaware of biological cycles. This so-called menstrual cycle is one of wonderfully orchestrated physiological and structural changes in the ovaries, the uterus and the vagina. The breakdown of the uterine lining and the consequent blood loss are the obvious parts of the cycle to its producer, but mid way between periods of bleeding is a key, often unperceived, event, an egg is released from one of the ovaries and, for a day or two, is available for fertilization.

Underlying the rhythmic changes of the menstrual cycle are complex cycles of hormone production. These hormones—estrogen and progesterone—have multiple effects so that the monthly changes coincide with cycles of mood, libido and other personality changes.

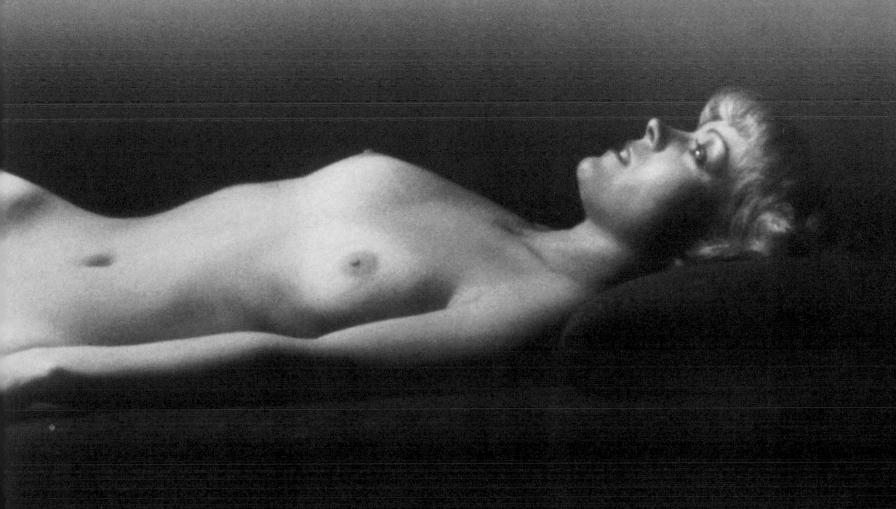

▷ normally averages between 28 and 29.5 days (it can vary between as few as 18 days and as many as 35), is often extremely regular, deviating only a day or so from its normal value over many years. Underlying the rhythm in time is a regular cycle of hormone-induced tissue changes in the ovaries, uterus and vaginal walls. A rhythmic cycle of mood and libido changes can often be linked with the hormone cycle and many female traits which are not immediately obvious, including sensitivity to painful skin stimuli, responsiveness to certain odours and the ability to distinguish changes in musical pitch, have all been shown to rise and fall in concert with the ups and downs of hormonal output during the menstrual cycle. We are rhythmic in more ways than we can know or understand.

While it is relatively easy to study many of the rhythms and cycles of particular cells, organs and systems of the body, it is impossible to comprehend the precisely coordinated, interlocking and interacting complex of human rhythms and cycles as a whole. It is not simply that each organ and activity has its own clocklike timekeeping ability, but there are obviously interdependent hierarchies of clocks within the body with unnervingly complicated patterns of dominance and subservience with respect to one another. We do not even know whether or not this hierarchy has an ultimate ruler—a single, central, all-determining time-giver.

In its changing activities and behaviour through time the human body is as intricate as an orchestra playing a symphony. Each organ, with its own internal rhythms, represents an instrument playing its own part in the symphony, but these rhythms only have a total significance in relation to the parts of all the other instruments. To discover more about the true nature of biological rhythms we must ask whether the full symphony of human activity is being played from the moment a baby is born. The answer to this crucial question seems to be 'no'. At birth a baby is playing only the rudiments of the final majestic opus and is performing on a few instruments alone. Through babyhood, childhood and puberty extra instruments—that is, extra organs and behaviour patterns—successively and accumulatively take up the overlapping rhythmical themes of the whole, so that it takes at least a decade of direct experience of day following night, the changing seasons and the succession of years before the human animal becomes fully attuned to the cyclically fluctuating world it inhabits.

The detailed story of our increasing understanding of the slow, stepwise development of human rhythms is a fascinating one. It shows how it has been possible for erroneous ideas about behaviour to arise, reveals how simple, but careful, observations can yield startlingly original results and demonstrates how even the youngest babies, with their simple responses to the world around them, already contain the embryo of adult rhythmicity. The aspect of a baby's development of circadian behaviour that is probably best understood is the cycle of sleeping and waking. This cycle is no more complicated than the alternating pattern in time of periods awake and periods spent sleeping. Most adults split each 24 hours into a reasonably regular array, with approximately 16 hours awake and eight hours asleep, each period of sleep or wakefulness starting at about the same time each day. And experiments on people with no access to watches or clocks, nor to external clues about time, such as the arrival

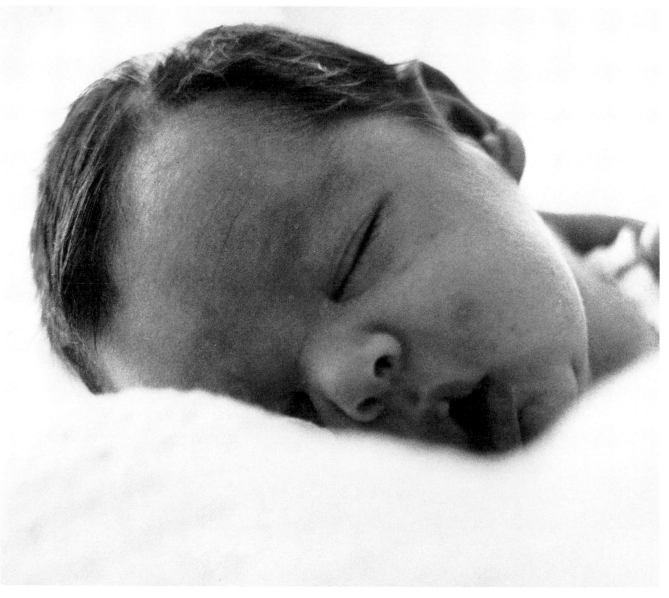

Coping with a baby's pattern of sleeping and waking is an aspect of parenthood that demands a considerable degree of compromise between adult and infant behaviour patterns. As the normal sleep rhythm develops, the growing child passes through a variable series of phases, from which the pattern of one period of sleep and one period of wakefulness in every 24 hours gradually emerges. Child-rearing gurus of the last two or three generations have argued as to how far this changing sleep pattern should be directly influenced by timed feeding regimes or left uninfluenced, as by the currently fashionable demand feeding method. Whichever stance is taken, a baby left to its own devices will not naturally wake at regular intervals during the first months of its life.

of dawn and the setting of the sun, show that such isolated human beings retain an internal personal ability to maintain a circadian rhythm of sleeping and waking. Expressed another way, man has an inbuilt or endogenous clock which commands that a period of sleep should begin once in about every 24 hours.

Parents the world over know that in their first weeks and months of life babies simply do not behave like this. Nights of disturbed parental sleep alone testify to the fact that a baby's pattern of sleeping and waking is very different from an adult one. A more detailed understanding of the pattern has, however, been hard to establish. In the first half of the century, for example, it was firmly believed that newborn babies, or neonates, needed to sleep almost continuously, that is for 22 hours out of every 24, and that during the first year of their lives that period gradually declined to more adult levels with the bulk of sleep taking place at night.

One piece of pioneering investigation, carried out in the United States in the 1950s by a pair of workers named Kleitman and Englemann, has done a great deal to change anecdote about infant sleep into hard data. Although their investigations were carried out on only 19 babies over the first six months of life, the central findings of Kleitman and Englemann's study are not only interesting but provide useful insights into specific aspects of child care, for example, whether babies should be fed every four hours by the clock or 'on demand'. The 19 babies were first monitored at three weeks and even at this early age were only sleeping for a total of approximately 15 hours out of 24, and there was already a slight excess of sleep in the nighttime hours. Between 8pm and 8am the babies slept for an average of $8\frac{1}{2}$ hours, while between 8am and 8pm they slept for only $6\frac{1}{2}$ hours. As the babies grew, this pattern gradually became accentuated and was accompanied by a gradual, but small-scale, decrease in the total amount of sleep. By six months the adult pattern was slowly emerging from the hint of the rhythm present at three weeks and the babies slept for an average of $13\frac{1}{2}$ hours in 24, but 10 of these were nighttime hours and only $3\frac{1}{2}$ were daytime sleeps.

In the developing child many of the high frequency physiological rhythms are obviously present before birth. Nerves produce rhythmic discharges and the heart is beating—albeit at a much higher rate than in adulthood—long before delivery. At the moment of birth, with the first breath, a true breathing rhythm is initiated with a marvellously articulated set of almost instantaneous changes in the heart, lungs and circulation.

Marked day-to-night or circadian rhythms arise in different body functions at characteristic periods of a baby's development. In the first days of life it is possible to show changes in the electrical resistance of a baby's skin between night and day. Body temperature fluctuations achieve a significant circadian pattern by two to three weeks, while similar changes in the rate of heartbeat and urine output arise between the fourth and twentieth weeks of life. Only with the onset of puberty and physical and sexual maturity in boys and girls, do the adult hormonal time patterns become established. With her first period, which in Western society occurs at an average age of 13, a girl is finally, and for the first time, demonstrating the full range of circadian and approximately month-long bodily rhythms and cycles.

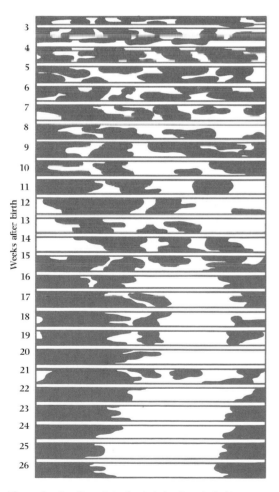

Age of child	Developing rhythmic functions
One week	Electrical skin resistance rhythm present
Two to three weeks	Body temperature rhythm begins to emerge
Four to twenty weeks	Sleep/wake rhythm nearly developed Body temperature rhythm present Heart rate rhythm present Excretion of urine, sodium, potassium and phosphate show daytime peaks
Five to nine months	All daily rhythms intensify and are present in nearly all observed functions
Sixteen to twenty-two months	Rhythm in excretion of creatine, creatinine and chloride develops

Significant day-night differences in bodily functions emerge through babyhood and childhood in a distinct and meaningful order. It is as though each process first operates in an unmodulated fashion and then, increasingly, comes under the influence and control of the body's inbuilt 'clock'. Once control is established there is a clear rhythm with a period of almost exactly 24 hours. Organs such as skin, which are well formed at birth, show a 24 hour rhythm in the first days of life. Others which do not fully mature until weeks or months after birth develop their rhythms correspondingly.

In his waking hours a baby gradually becomes aware of and attunes to the natural rhythms of his surroundings.

The understanding of rhythmic behaviour in babies was greatly increased by an experiment which monitored a child for the first six months of its life. In this simplified version of the data each horizontal bar represents the sleeping (dark area) and waking (light area) periods of one week and clearly shows the shifting pattern. After the first few chaotic weeks, a 25-hour rhythm emerges between weeks 5 and 25. This then switches to a 24-hour rhythm, with the bulk of sleep at night.

Cosmic rhythms

Imagine an alien creature, from a race infinitely more advanced than our own, whose life's task is to collect exotic organisms and then interpret their lifestyles. She sits in a control room in her far-off galaxy, activates her gravity-sink-space-warp device and scoops up a random collection of animals and plants from planet Earth, hundreds of light years distant.

She has gathered the organisms, but how can she possibly deduce anything about the world from which they came? In fact, woven into the structure, physiology and behaviour of those animals and plants is a remarkably precise inventory containing not only information about the conditions that exist on Earth, but also several vital facts about the nature of our solar system. This information is not fortuitous but is the physical manifestation of 3.5 billion years of organic evolution. The inexorable effect of the selective process at the heart of the evolutionary mechanism is to nudge the adaptiveness of reproducing organisms farther and farther into intimate concert with the conditions in which they must live. With almost infinite slowness—but without pause—animals and plants increase their fitness for life on Earth. Each minute addition to the appropriateness of their lives and physical organization makes them reflect the nature of their environment more clearly.

So the interstellar 'butterfly collector' could come to know much about our planetary home. The physical construction and temperature sensitivity of her specimens would provide vital clues. They would show first the approximate gravitational field, and hence the size of our planet, and second that most life on Earth must live in areas with a temperature range between -10 and $+40$ degrees centigrade (14 and 104 degrees F). The chemistry and lack of extreme anti-desiccation devices in the organisms would suggest a planet where water was plentiful. Simple experiments on the effect of various gas mixtures would reveal the type of atmosphere we possess.

Amazingly, these creatures, from trees to cockroaches, could provide information about the nature of our solar system because the intrinsic organization of almost every living thing on Earth—cockroaches included—conforms to a pattern of design dictated by the motions of the Earth and moon in space. Our intergalactic investigator would have to perform only the most cursory of temporal examinations on her collection to find that rhythmical phenomena of remarkably few particular frequencies constantly recurred in her sample.

Almost all the plants and animals would have circadian or daily rhythms with a beat of about 24 hours. The longer-lived life forms would all show some activity with a rhythmical period of about 350 days, that is, circannual rhythms. Any marine organisms in her sample would probably show both twice-daily and 14 or 28-day periodicities, corresponding to the time patterns of the tides. Any astute alien would thus conclude that planet X rotates about its axis once every 24 hours, completes its solar orbit in about 350 days and probably has a single satellite moon with an orbital period about X of 28 days, producing tidal surges in the planet's large water masses.

At the heart of this whimsical tale of science fiction is a sobering, unflippant fact. Each of us on Earth, each of the 10 million species that has evolved on and now swarms over its surface, carries the time signature of the planetary motion of our world indelibly stamped within it. We can now examine the physical basis of these signatures—the mechanisms that generate our rhythmical environment, an environment that has made us rhythmical creatures.

From man's first cave paintings, documented human history stretches back a few tens of thousands of years. Yet as an insight into the life-span of the Earth, this popular view of history is almost useless. To understand the astronomical influences that have shaped, and continue to shape the patterns of regular change in our environment, the concept of history must be expanded many orders of magnitude in time to encompass the life story of our solar system—the sun with its attendant flock of gravitationally tethered planets, asteroids, moons and comets.

To put our personal star the sun—and with it ourselves—into an ultimate context we must first determine our position in the universe. This is conceptually difficult because the map of the universe has no bottom left-hand corner. Instead, all positional descriptions have to be relative to other objects. There is no centre of the universe, no definitive grid reference. We are part of the rapidly expanding debris of the primordial 'big bang', the unimaginably violent single event that initiated our universe. Within very hazy limits this most pregnant of events, the true zero, can be set in history. It probably happened between 10 and 15 billion years ago, and the background radiation generated by that fireball still reverberates round the universe.

In the simplest models of the big bang, evenly distributed atoms of low mass spread ever outward from the explosion into space. But if the matter was, and remained smeared out in this way there would be no galaxies, no stars, no planets and no human beings. By some combination of causes which is as yet unknowable, the expanding universe gained large-scale structure so that matter became congregated into millions of spaced-out galaxies. Each galaxy is a tightly packed archipelago of stars, and each star is a huge concentration of matter. Between the galaxies are vast, almost empty gaps of intergalactic space.

Galaxies come in a huge range of types, but all are island universes on a scale that the imagination cannot grasp. They are so big that astronomers have to use a daunting vocabulary of units to describe them, of which the most dramatic is the light year, that is, the distance travelled by light at the rate of 186,000 miles (299,000 km) a second in a year—about 6,000 billion miles (9,600 billion km). In the night sky our own galaxy, or at least a small part of it, can be seen as the Milky Way. Viewed from outside it is a spiral galaxy with a flattened, lenslike shape and is quite large as spiral galaxies go. From edge to edge it stretches 100,000 light years and contains some 100 billion stars. One of these myriads is our sun, which is about 30,000 light years from the mysterious galactic core. This puts us firmly in our place, for it not only positions us but also emphasizes the insignificance of our whole solar system—in galactic terms we are in the outer suburbs.

In the context of the universe our solar system is comparatively young, having condensed out of a cloud of atoms by some process, which is as yet unknown, about five billion years ago. The precise nature of the origin of the sun and planets is a matter of intense scientific speculation but there is no doubt that the sun ended up with a most interesting assortment of planets—Mercury, Venus, Earth, Mars, Jupiter, Saturn, Uranus, Neptune and Pluto—each circling the sun in an elliptical orbit and each a world in its own right, but with fascinating differences.

Mercury, Earth, Venus and Mars, the four small inner planets, are all dense

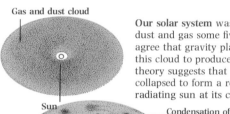

Our own Milky Way galaxy is like a multiple-armed spiral with a bulging centre. This has been deduced by examining the characteristics of far-distant galaxies and comparing them with our own. Since we are buried inside the Milky Way, along one of its arms, it is difficult to make direct observations of it. Optical and radio telescopes can discover the overall structure of typical configurations such as the whirlpool galaxy, *below*, which has a bright core and two prominent arms. The same instruments can provide information about the Milky Way from within. In a galaxy such as ours the stars are in spiral arms emanating from a dense centre, *left*. One arm of the Milky Way rotates about its centre every 200 million years.

Gas and dust cloud

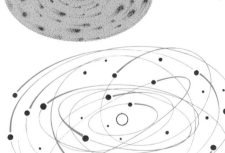

Sun

Condensation of gas and dust in disc

Our solar system was formed from a huge cloud of dust and gas some five billion years ago. All theories agree that gravity played a large part in condensing this cloud to produce the sun and the planets. One theory suggests that a spherical cloud of matter collapsed to form a rotating disc with a bright radiating sun at its centre, *left*.

Huge energy releases from this sun created a wide temperature range across the disc—hot near the sun, cold at the fringe. Such a range of heat may have led to the present planetary types— hot and rocky ones near the sun, cold gaseous ones farther away. The three lower diagrams, *left*, show many embryo planets in orbit; an intermediate stage of collisions which disturb their orbits; and the present state where the mature planets have settled down again into the plane of the disc.

Collisions cause randomization of orbits

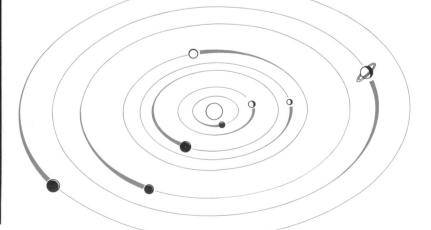

and rocky, with average densities between 4 and 5.5 times greater than water. The larger outer planets, excluding Pluto, are basically composed of gases. Their densities are much lower, being between 0.7 and 2.3 times that of water. To understand the conditions conducive to the existence of life, and the details of our global climatology, Earth is best compared with Venus and Mars. The initial surface temperature of Earth, dictated by the radiant energy reaching it from the sun 93 million miles (150 million km) away, was about 25 degrees centigrade (77 degrees F).

Carbon dioxide and water vapour, both gases arising largely from volcanoes, formed the original atmosphere. At the Earth's ambient temperature the carbon dioxide stayed as gas but most of the water condensed to form rivers, lakes and seas. Some of the carbon dioxide was removed from the atmosphere by being dissolved in the Earth's waters, while evaporation from the seas pushed water vapour into the atmosphere: clouds in the air and falling rain have been features of earthly weather for billions of years. The white clouds, however, are quite efficient at reflecting back into space some of the sun's short wavelength radiation, thus reducing the energy input into the planet below. As a result, the surface dropped to, and has remained at a mean value of about 15 degrees centigrade (59 degrees F).

To be provocatively simplistic, the presence of water, plus a physiologically mild temperature, led to the start of the evolution of life on Earth at least 3.5 billion years ago. Once cells evolved which, like those of modern green plants, could trap and use atmospheric carbon dioxide and release oxygen by the process of photosynthesis, the atmosphere altered dramatically. Oxygen was suddenly present in increasing quantities and today constitutes a fifth of the atmosphere's gases; a gigantic volume almost entirely biological in origin. The bulk of the atmosphere is now nitrogen, a gas which is only present in very tiny quantities in the gases emitted by volcanoes, but which has become accumulatively important because it is not appreciably consumed by any sort of biological activity.

Compared with Earth, Venus and Mars are worlds similar in size, rock composition and presumed early volcanic activity. So why is life absent on these planets? The answer seems to be simple: Venus is too near the sun, Mars, too distant. On Venus, only 67 million miles (107 million km) from the solar furnaces, the original surface temperature was about 87 degrees centigrade (189 degrees F). At this high temperature much of the water and all the carbon dioxide were in gaseous form. This thick gas shield produced an intense 'greenhouse effect', in which energy from the sun reached the planet's surface, but could not escape again because of the absorptive abilities of the gases. The resulting net energy gain has raised the Venusian surface temperature disastrously. It is now about 500 degrees centigrade (930 degrees F) with no possibility of life of an earthly type existing at all.

Mars is 142 million miles (225 million km) from the sun. Because of this remoteness its original surface was a chilling low of −30 degrees centigrade (−22 degrees F). At this temperature all the water vapour that reaches the atmosphere is immediately extracted again as ice. Even some of the carbon dioxide solidifies, resulting in a thin, denuded atmosphere in which no greenhouse effect of any significance can build up, so the temperature remains ▷

The Earth's atmosphere divides roughly into three zones of decreasing gas density—a dense troposphere, a thin stratosphere and a thinner upper atmosphere. Global weather occurs in the troposphere and is generated by the sun's radiation. Some radiation is reflected back into space by clouds, the atmosphere and by ice. The rest warms up the Earth, whose heat either fuels the weather machine or escapes into space. The poles receive less of this radiation and reflect more of it than the tropics, and this difference leads to the mass movements of air that are at the heart of the climate. The slice through the Earth, right, shows the extreme thinness of the atmosphere and the Earth's crust in relation to the size of the planet.

Spectacular images of Mars were taken as part of the NASA Viking expedition. The image, right, taken from 348,000 miles (560,000 km) away, shows three distinct volcanoes such as one would expect to find on a rocky planet. The image, below, taken from Viking Lander 1 shows the rocks and the drifts of dust on the Martian desert.

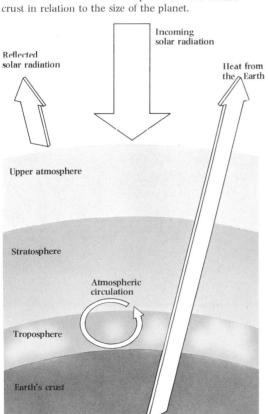

Reflected solar radiation

Incoming solar radiation

Heat from the Earth

Upper atmosphere

Stratosphere

Atmospheric circulation

Troposphere

Earth's crust

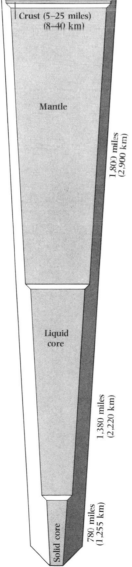

Atmosphere

Crust (5–25 miles) (8–40 km)

Mantle

1,800 miles (2,900 km)

Liquid core

1,380 miles (2,220 km)

Solid core

780 miles (1,255 km)

▷very low. The surface of Mars is a freezing desert, just as that of Venus is a superheated one. Again life is apparently out of the question, but if earthly life is a consequence of being on a rocky planet at the right distance from a star, then it is perfectly logical to argue that our galaxy contains many living planets apart from our own.

Once life evolved on Earth the sun's central significance assumed another degree of importance. As the greatest energy source in the solar system, the sun became the ultimate and only noteworthy provider of energy for all life processes; and it still fulfils this role today, making worship of the sun perhaps the most rational of all religions. The sun is an energy source of gigantic power, a vast ball composed of little more than hydrogen and helium, the two simplest elements in the universe. For five billion years the sun has been pumping out this energy and it will probably continue to do so for another five billion. But how can 10 billion years' worth of power come from two gases, which on Earth are relatively unreactive, unexciting inhabitants of chemistry laboratories? Unfortunately—terribly unfortunately—these gases are found in our world in other states. Perched atop every intercontinental ballistic missile is at least one potential, tiny uncontrolled sun. An exploding hydrogen bomb—a fusion device in the bland jargon of physics—illustrates the awesome power locked in the atomic structure of hydrogen, or indeed any other element.

Essentially the sun is a vast, balanced and controlled hydrogen bomb. The mass of the sun is so immense that, at its core, gravity ensures that matter is hot enough, and hydrogen nuclei packed tightly enough, for hydrogen fusion to occur. At earthly temperatures hydrogen normally exists as neutral atoms, each consisting of a nucleus made up of one positively charged particle, a proton, around which circles a negatively charged particle, an electron. But at the sun's heart, as a result of the high temperatures there, hydrogen exists not as neutral atoms but as protons, rocketing about in a matrix of electrons, forming a 'soup' or plasma of particles.

In all ordinary circumstances the positive charges of the protons would mean that, despite their motion, proton–proton collisions would be impossible because, like two magnetic North Poles, they would push each other apart. But at the temperatures of over 10 million degrees centigrade which prevail at the core of the sun, the protons move fast enough to collide occasionally, and with enough energy for them to fuse together. At the centre of the sun a complex chain of fusion reactions takes place in which hydrogen nuclei fuse to make a type of helium nucleus, denoted as helium–4 because it contains two protons and also two neutral particles, or neutrons. The first step in this reaction is the linking of two protons to form a deuteron (the nucleus of deuterium or heavy hydrogen). The last step is the collision of two helium–3 nuclei, each consisting of two protons and one neutron. This is the crucial reaction because the total mass of the products of the collision is slightly less than the total mass of the particles that bumped in nuclear contact.

A tiny discrepancy in the mass budget of helium might seem insignificant, but, in fact, it is this lost mass that keeps us alive. The reason is that the lost mass is converted directly into energy, and the rate of exchange of energy for mass is spectacular. For every single gram (0.03 oz) of helium–4 produced in this reaction, 175,000 kilowatt hours of energy are produced: roughly the

equivalent of a single-bar electric fire burning constantly for 20 years. So the lost mass is not an accounting error. It is the energy that keeps the sun hot, which produced the conditions suitable for the emergence of life on Earth, which ultimately still drives all biological activity, and which generates our climate.

Unlike the hydrogen bomb, the sun has a means of controlling the fusion reaction, and this control mechanism is inherent in its structure. Fusion only occurs deep in the centre of the sun's massive bulk where extraordinary conditions of high pressure and temperature prevail. At the very heart of our star the temperature is about 15,000,000 degrees centigrade, and the density of the plasma is about 160 grams per cubic centimetre of material—a density 12 times greater than that of lead. This hideously energetic core does not 'blow up' the sun because upon it is piled a layer of nonfusing hydrogen and helium some 300,000 miles (500,000 km) thick. The bottom 250,000 miles (400,000 km) of this stack is a zone of radiation transfer, where the matter is transparent enough for the heat generated at the core to shine through it. Most of the outer 60,000 miles (100,000 km) is a convection zone, where the gases are opaque enough to retard the outward spread of heat by radiation alone. As a result, large local temperature gradients are set up, and vast convection movements of hot gas transfer most of the heat.

The brilliant white-hot sphere we see as the sun is a thin layer of photosphere at the top of the convection zone. The temperature of the photosphere is comparatively low at about 6,000 degrees centigrade, so it consists of neutral gas atoms rather than ionized plasma. It is also in continuous turbulent motion because of the violent convection currents of gas jetting up from beneath. This convection sets up a surface pattern, or supergranulation, on the sun which is visible in telescopic photographs. In reality it is nothing much more than a gigantic version of the pattern of rising bubbles in a simmering pan of syrup; except that the bubbles are tens of thousands of miles wide.

Between the relatively cool, neutral photosphere and the corona—the vast outer atmosphere of the sun—is a thin chromosphere which acts as a transitional zone between the two. The enormous corona, which stretches out beyond the earthly orbit as solar wind, is paradoxically much hotter than the photosphere, reaching temperatures of around 2,500,000 degrees centigrade. Compared with the photosphere the corona emits a much dimmer light and this means that it can be seen clearly only when the dazzling photosphere is blocked out by the moon in an eclipse.

Both the corona and convective supergranulation patterns are constant features of the sun's structure and behaviour. Other features occur spasmodically, but often with an overall underlying rhythmic pattern, linked in some way to the sun's magnetic properties. Huge flares and prominences are projected from the sun's surface, and dark, cool blemishes or sunspots move across it then disappear. These sunspots can easily be seen to wax and wane in number with a considerable degree of regularity. The cycle has a periodicity of approximately 11 years and is linked to a 22-year cycle in which the magnetic poles of the sun reverse and subsequently regain their original polarity.

The behaviour of planet Earth, and of the organisms that inhabit it, are ▷

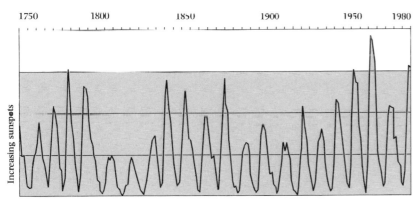

1750   1800   1850   1900   1950   1980

Increasing sunspots

Every 22 years the solar magnetic poles reverse twice, driving the 11-year rhythm of the sunspot cycle. The number of observable spots rises and falls during the cycle, directly indicating the amount of solar activity.

The sun is made up of four main layers:
Photosphere: the mottled surface is about 6,000°C, marked with sunspots.
Convection zone: 60,000 miles (100,000 km) thick, this is stirred by violent movements of hot matter.
Radiative zone: 250,000 miles (400,000 km) thick, up to 5 million°C, it increases in density toward the core. **Fusion core:** 12 times as dense as lead, 15 million°C it converts billions of tons of hydrogen into helium every second, creating solar energy.

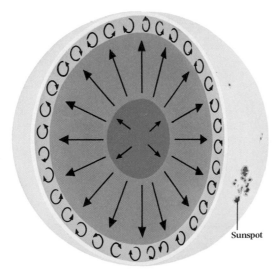

Sunspot

A vast prominence of luminous gas streams out from the sun into space, *left.* Each surface granule is really a bubbling cell of heat turbulence 620 miles (1,000 km) wide.

The internal, unobservable structure of the sun can be understood only by using complex calculations. Its heart is the fusion core (red); a radiative zone (orange) transmits energy to the convection zone (dark yellow) where the energy is expelled outward to shine from the photosphere (light yellow), whose light and heat is what we see and feel on planet Earth.

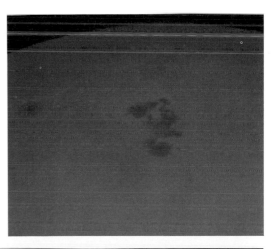

The discovery of sunspots spoiled man's idea of the sun as an unblemished sphere. They are relatively cool (4,000°C) areas of gas on the sun's surface. Usually they are 6,000 miles (10,000 km) across but can be 90,000 miles (150,000 km) wide. Appearing in pairs or clusters, they last a few weeks while moving with the sun as it rotates. Their strong magnetic field suggests that they are the visible effect of magnetic disturbances deep inside the sun.

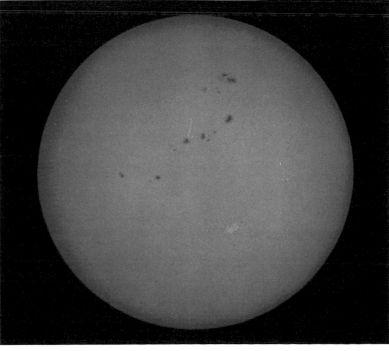

▷ intimately linked with the structure and working of the sun. The Earth is not an inert, unchanging rock ball, on which the story of the evolution of life is inscribed and played out by millions of species, but is in constant motion. Beneath the Earth's crust the great bulk of the planet's central mass is in a liquid or semi-liquid state. In this fluid, slow but massive convection currents, analogous to the immensely more powerful convection currents in the sun's substance, rise and fall.

Even the thin, solid crust that coats the outer surface of the Earth is more like a slow-moving sea of ice floes than a concrete platform. In a continual, slow jostling, which is clearly discernible only over millions of years, plates of the crust gradually creep past, over and under each other and then melt. The movements bring about the phenomenon of continental drift. They sometimes also cause earthquakes, in which the tensions set up by hundreds of years of relative plate motion are suddenly and violently released in rapid, spasmodic crustal movements—mere twitches on a global scale, but they can flatten cities. All the principal volcanic and seismic zones of the world, in which devastation is an awesome fact of life, are in the regions of the Earth where crustal plates make contact.

For all the living creatures on Earth, the most crucial pattern of planetary motion is the Earth's spin around its polar axis, the imaginary line linking the geographic North and South Poles. This spinning motion or, technically, rotation, generates day and night for any organism dwelling at a fixed point on the Earth's surface. The patterned division of time into a repeating cycle of dark and light periods is the strongest rhythmical environmental change to which

most earthly organisms are exposed. All the daily biological rhythms that life has evolved characteristically have a period of approximately 24 hours, and all such rhythms are a response to this dominant pattern of change.

The most obvious and dramatic differences between day and night is the discrepancy in light intensity. But the presence or absence of the energy-providing sun in the sky induces many other changes of great significance to living things. The most crucial pair are the ambient temperature and the relative humidity, that is, the degree to which the atmosphere is saturated with water vapour. Light, temperature and humidity are all enormously potent determinants of biological activity. The rapid changes in light intensity at dawn and dusk provide very clear-cut clues by which many organisms can monitor the procession of days. During the daylight hours, light itself is one of the forms in which the fusion power of the sun finally impinges on the Earth's life. The packets of light energy, or photons, from the sun, which strike green plants are used in the process of photosynthesis to create organic molecules.

Linked to the day-night cycle, temperature changes impose great constraints on all animals, plants and micro-organisms. All the biochemical processes that typify life are temperature dependent; they are speeded up by a temperature increase and slowed down as temperatures fall. Even a small, warm-blooded animal, such as any of the mammals or birds which can maintain a constant, high internal body temperature despite environmental temperature changes, must take note of the temperature alterations produced by night and day. The greater the temperature deviation up or down from the optimum, be it 37 degrees centigrade (98.6 degrees F) for man or 42 degrees

Solar radiation

Spin axis and geographic North Pole

Magnetic North Pole

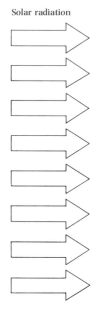
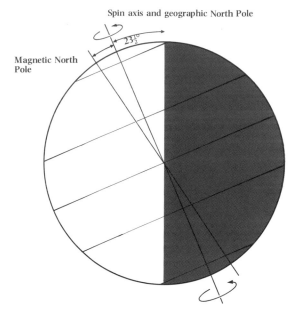

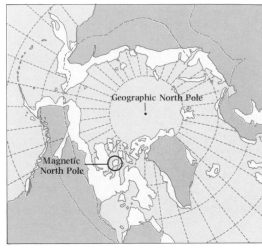

Today's positions of the geographic and magnetic North Poles are shown, *above*. All compasses point to the magnetic North Pole whose location is known to wander gradually through geological time.

Every 24 hours the Earth rotates about its spinning axis, so causing the rhythm of day and night. At midsummer in the northern hemisphere the spin axis tilts $23\frac{1}{2}°$ toward the direction of the sun's rays, *above*. This axis lies between the geographic north and south poles. The magnetic axis is at a small angle to, and rotates around, the spin axis. Satellites and spacecraft carry cameras which, in the past 20 years, have enabled man to photograph the whole Earth. This view, *left*, was taken during the Apollo 11 mission.

The rotation of the Earth is gradually slowing down: 400 million years ago the solar day was about 22 hours long; today it is 24 hours 4 minutes long. Evidence for this comes from parts of fossil corals from the middle Devonian era, *left*. The growth of these corals varied with tidal and daily cycles forming bands and ridges that corresponded to the lunar and daily periods respectively. The pattern of these bands suggests that the lunar month in the Devonian era had 30.8 days, rather than the present 29.5 days.

centigrade (107.6 degrees F) for a duck, the more work has to be done by the animal's metabolism to produce an internal temperature that is thermostatically stable.

Humidity variations are of especial importance to a wide range of invertebrates (animals without backbones) and wet-skinned, terrestrial vertebrates such as frogs, newts and toads. Because of the increased evaporation of water from the body surface at high temperatures and in dry air—typical daytime conditions—many such animals are necessarily nocturnal in their habits, and are active at night, when cooler conditions and wetter air mean that they can operate efficiently without excess water loss.

The physical changes wrought by the cyclical succession of days and nights produce an environment with a time pattern which animals and plants ignore at their peril. So dramatic are the alterations in character of a single habitat between day and night that all organisms have to make vital strategic choices about their life tactics in relation to these fluctuations. One of the central features of any animal's life-style is thus its pattern of activity throughout 24 hours. If an animal can be described as nocturnal, diurnal (active in the daytime) or crepuscular (active only at dawn or dusk), then this description encompasses some basic definitions of the animal's way of life.

To order their lives according to the spinning period of their mother planet, organisms have developed clocks whose hands can be reset by external clues. The most powerful of these is the circadian clock, tied irrevocably to the Earth's period of rotation. For all practical purposes, this period can be assumed to be 24 hours but, like all large-scale natural phenomena, it is subject to both long- and short-term variations. Measured against the reference point of a star, the Earth's rotational period is in fact a fraction over 23 hours 56 minutes, a value described as the sidereal day. The solar day—the time between one noon and the next for a fixed, earthbound observer—averages just under 24 hours 4 minutes, but varies throughout the year by an amount never more than 16 minutes either way. Superimposed on this predictable, large-scale variation is a wide range of very minor perturbations caused by redistributions of mass within the Earth's solids, fluids and atmospheric gases.

Perhaps the most intriguing of such changes are the very long-term ones. Analysis of ancient records leads to the inescapable conclusion that the Earth's spin is slowing down. Irrespective of short-term changes our days increase in length by approximately one millisecond (a thousandth of a second) every century. If this finding is projected back in time, then in the Devonian geological age 400 million years ago, a day would have lasted only 22 hours and each year 400 days. Such seemingly wild speculation is in fact substantiated by patterns in the growth rings visible in some fossils.

In most parts of the Earth, conditions change annually with the succession of the seasons. The primary source of much of the seasonal, year-to-year variations in earthly existence is the complex interaction between the precise orientation of the spinning axis of the Earth and the plane of the Earth's orbit around the sun. It is also believed that, over long time-spans, changes in the orientation of the spin axis may induce slow climatic changes which affect the whole Earth.

If the spinning axis of the Earth and the plane of the Earth's orbit of ▷

The spinning axis of the Earth is commonly thought to point directly at Polaris, the pole star. This is not quite true, for really the North Pole is directed to a point in the star field close to Polaris. Proof of the Earth's rotation is shown, *left*, in a continuous eight-hour photographic exposure taken through a fixed telescope. Each star has made a streak consisting of a third of a circle. The brightest arc near the centre shows the motion of Polaris. Over the next few thousand years the spin axis will be directed at a point even further away from Polaris. In about 21,000 years it will return, to point toward Polaris once again.

Three important variables of the environment show clear dramatic rhythms that correspond to the day and night cycle. Changes in light intensity, humidity and temperature through a 24-hour period at one point on the Earth's surface are shown, *right*. The measurements were taken at a place in the temperate mid-latitudes where the length of day was about 15 hours. Light intensity obviously leaps to a much higher value in the day than at night. As the temperature slowly rises the humidity falls and vice versa.

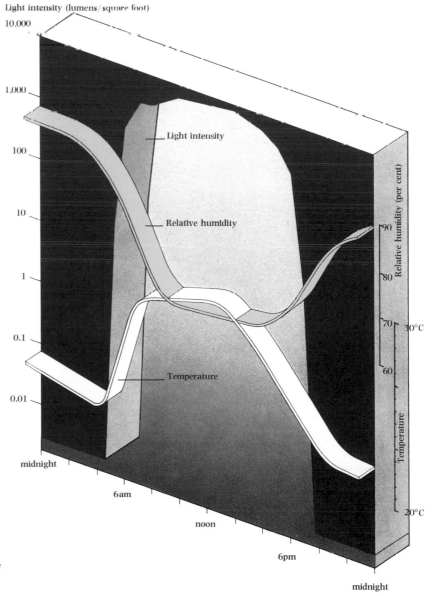

▷ revolution around the sun were orientated at right angles to one another, then the world would be an unrecognizable place. Everywhere on its surface, except for aberrant zones immediately around the North and South Poles, both days and nights would be unvaryingly 12 hours each throughout the year, and there would be no seasons as we know them. The vital role of the Earth's spinning axis in generating our seasons is difficult to grasp. If asked what makes summers hot and winters cold, most people, including those with some scientific training, would reply with a confused jumble of partially understood concepts. Perhaps the sun is farther away from the Earth in winter, perhaps the polar ice caps are involved in some way—or is it something to do with the height of the sun at noon?

The Earth's distance from the sun does alter with the seasons, although this has almost nothing to do with the differences between winter and summer, spring and autumn. But the answer to the question of seasonality has everything to do with the spin axis of the Earth, which is not at right angles to the planetary orbit, but inclined at about $23\frac{1}{2}$ degrees to it. And with gyroscopic stability, the axis points with great constancy—at least over many centuries—to one single point among the stars near the pole star, Polaris. This means that for half of each year the North Pole points obliquely at the sun, while for the other half the South Pole takes up this position.

The tilt of the Earth's axis of rotation divides the world into climatic zones, defined by the way in which the sun appears to move within them. At the top and bottom of the Earth are frigid zones, the outer boundary of each being $23\frac{1}{2}$ degrees of latitude from the Poles. In these areas there is constant night for at least one 24-hour day a year and, correspondingly, the sun is constantly in the sky for at least one other day. Here, within the context of cold, there are enormous extremes of temperature, and the maximum possible variation in day and night lengths. Round the centre of the Earth, bounded by the tropics of Cancer and Capricorn, each $23\frac{1}{2}$ degrees from the Equator, is the torrid or tropical zone. Here the sun is directly overhead at noon for at least one day a year, and throughout each 12 months daylengths alter very little from 12 hours. In all intermediate locations on Earth—the temperate regions—the sun never stays in the sky for 24 hours, nor is it ever directly overhead.

The interaction of the unchanging direction of tilt and the gravitationally driven orbit of the Earth produces the seasonally changing height of the sun in the sky at noon or, technically, its declination. At the summer solstice, 22 June, points $23\frac{1}{2}$ degrees of latitude north of the Equator experience a sun at the zenith, that is, overhead at noon. Anywhere in the northern hemisphere, this is the day on which the sun is at its highest in the sky and the daylight hours are longest. On 22 December, the winter solstice, the northern hemisphere experiences precisely the opposite set of conditions. The sun is at its lowest in the sky and the daylength is shortest. Within $23\frac{1}{2}$ degrees of the North Pole the winter solstice simply occurs in the middle of a long period of perpetual night. The southern hemisphere is the mirror image of the northern hemisphere in these respects, 22 June being the shortest and 22 December the longest day.

The $23\frac{1}{2}$ degree tilt of the Earth's axis of spin thus directly generates changing daylengths throughout the year and, during the same period, the alterations in height of the noonday sun. These fluctuations are both cyclical

The height of the sun at noon varies with the seasons. To an observer in the mid-latitudes of the northern hemisphere, *left*, the sun is always high or low in the southern sky. On 22 December the sun is directly above the Tropic of Capricorn: it is at its lowest point to the observer, whose shadow is long. On 22 June the sun is directly above the Tropic of Cancer: to the observer it is at its highest point and his shadow is short.

In winter the sun never climbs high in the sky, as this afternoon street scene in New York City shows. The Earth takes $365\frac{1}{4}$ days to orbit around the sun, *right*. The plane of this orbit is called the ecliptic, because only when Earth and moon are aligned in this plane can solar and lunar eclipses occur. The spin axis of the Earth is always tilted $23\frac{1}{2}°$ away from the perpendicular to the ecliptic. Because it tilts alternately toward and away from the sun the rhythm of the seasons is created. A tilt toward the sun means long days and more daily sunshine; a tilt away means short days and less sunshine. If the Earth were exactly perpendicular to the ecliptic the year would have only one season.

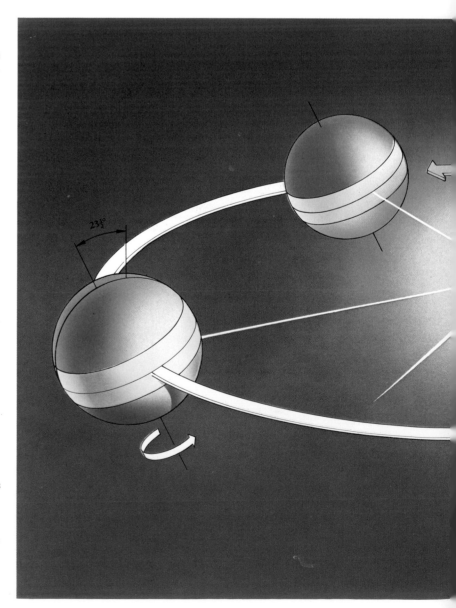

and rhythmic and, for the living creatures on Earth, provide a direct indication of the position of the Earth in its solar orbit. It is daylength, however, which communicates the march of the seasons most forcibly. On 22 December, at a position 60 degrees north, the sun is in the sky for close to eight hours. This means that the day must be 22 December. No other environmental clue such as temperature, rainfall, humidity or wind strength could give an organism that same information, although to receive it, the creature in question must have an accurate time sense in the form of some internal clock, against which external events can be measured.

As well as signalling the seasons, changing daylength and the altitude of the sun in the sky also generate the global pattern of climatic change that typify seasonality. All climate is sun-driven. Ultimately it amounts to no more than the heating effects of the sun and the movement of atmospheric gases—including water vapour—around the globe, although the movements are incredibly complex and the water vapour sometimes changes into tiny aerosol droplets (fog), large water drops (rain) or ice crystals (snow). Yet all the movements and heating are set into action and sustained by the interception of solar radiation by the Earth. Summer days are hot in the northern hemisphere because any point on the ground experiences longer days, and hence a longer period of heating, in each 24 hours. Also, the sun is at its highest so its radiation hits the ground at its least oblique angle, which means that there is a greater concentration of radiative energy on each unit area of the ground than at times when the rays are more oblique.

Despite the importance of the energy flux from the sun in determining the seasons, the distance of the Earth from the sun is not crucial in determining weather conditions. The Earth describes an elliptical orbit round the sun, but the sun does not lie at the centre of this orbit. Instead it is slightly displaced from it and is positioned at one of two foci. On average the Earth is some 93.5 million miles (149,589,000 km) from the sun, but the actual distance changes throughout the year in a cyclical way. And the Earth is not closest to the sun (in its perihelion position) in the middle of the northern hemisphere summer but in early January. At this time the Earth-sun distance is only 1.7 per cent shorter than the mean distance, so that any increase in the sun's heating power must be insignificant.

In the annual succession of the seasons, produced by the spin of the Earth around its tilted axis, animals and plants can use daylength to judge the time of year with considerable precision. Organisms need this information in order to organize their activities efficiently over long time-spans. So as well as dividing up their activities into appropriate patterns, with a periodicity of 24 hours to take account of night and day, they must also adjust their behaviour to be as successful as possible in the context of seasonal change.

Most of the seasonal changes in the environment are far more dramatic than the difference in length of day and night. Temperatures may vary by 50 degrees centigrade (122 degrees F) from one season to another, while rainfall can be completely absent in one season and more than an inch (2.5 cm) a day in the next. This sort of background change in the physical habitat generates secondary alterations in the environment during which both animals and plants respond to the climatic changes. Plants play a key role in determining ▷

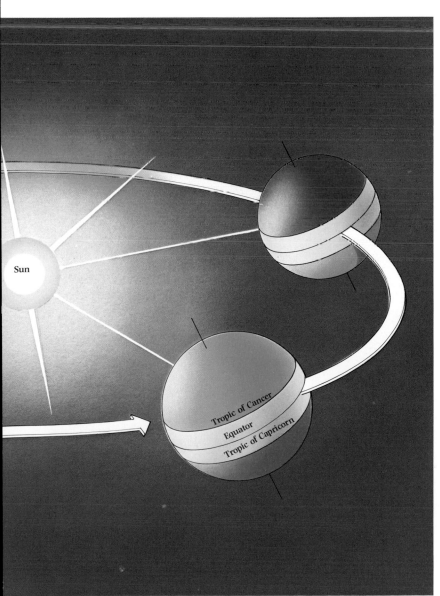

Spring

Summer

Autumn

Winter

Tropics

The length of day changes throughout the year in a pattern that is specific for any latitude north or south. For animals and plants this annual rhythm is the most predictable signal of the changing of the seasons. At the Equator the day is always 12 hours long. Everywhere else there is a seasonal variation: the same day of the same month will always be the same length in any year. The Earth's curvature, *below*, means that the density of solar radiation falling on it will be greater at the Equator than at higher latitudes.

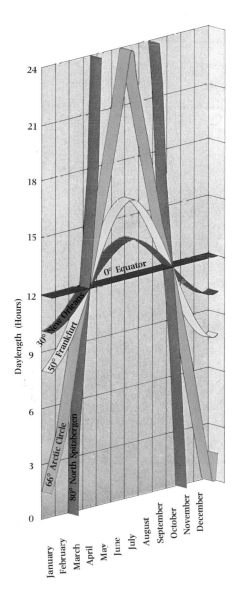

▷ the structure of animal communities, and the way in which animals respond to the seasons, because in most ecosystems (the ecological units into which any environment is divided) they are the primary producers of nutrients on which all other living creatures ultimately depend. So in many tropical dry savanna regions, the annual changes in the environment can be reduced to a cycle of hot dry seasons alternating with hot wet ones. In such a habitat some of the seasonal responses of the animals can be triggered by internal clock mechanisms, or by direct responses to changing humidity, but a great deal of the annual pattern in their lives is tied to the powerful and immediate response of the plants in the environment to the onset of the rains. Rapid initiation of grass growth in the newly wet soil not only transforms the landscape scenically but, overnight, produces a mass of new food resource for herbivores and, after a short time, for the carnivores that prey on those invertebrate and vertebrate herbivores. Insect, mammal and bird breeding seasons and migrations are inextricably tied to the vegetational changes wrought by the rain.

Around the world there are scores of different types of landscape, each with a characteristic vegetation and climate. Only a few of these zones possess no clear seasons. Such zones include the almost rainless desert areas near the Equator and, at the other extreme, some portions of the tropical rain forest which are perpetually hot and wet. Everywhere else in the world, the cyclical nature of the year is perceptible to micro-organisms, animals and plants as a simple or complex pattern of seasonal and climatic changes.

Of the many influences that shape the Earth's climate, some are almost as old as the Earth itself: for example, the effect on our atmospheric constitution of our precise distance from the sun. This distance, along with the gas-mix in the atmosphere, also plays a large part in determining the average temperature of the Earth's surface. Atmospheric conditions and mean global surface temperature are, in a sense, merely the most basic of ground rules in the game that global climate plays with the lives of all the organisms in our world. After over a century of accurate weather monitoring in many parts of the world, with weather ships dotted over the oceans, with the planet festooned with weather satellites and some of the world's largest computers at the disposal of meteorologists, we still have to admit that there are many detailed rules of the climate game that we do not yet understand.

The climate of our planet is often pictured as a huge machine—a heat engine whose working parts are the world's atmosphere, oceans, seas, lakes and rivers. For most of us the mental image of that engine would include wheels, cogs, pulleys and axles, all in concerted motion. Such an image is not inappropriate because, despite its enormous hierarchical complexity, the world's weather consists of an overlapping mass of cyclical phenomena.

The climatic heat engine of the Earth is driven by the sun. Radiated energy from the photosphere of our personal star continually reaches the Earth. This energy first interacts with the tenuous outer regions of the atmosphere, then with the denser lower layers of the Earth's gas shell, and finally strikes the Earth itself. Through the atmosphere, and on the Earth's surface, energy transfer takes place by radiation, conduction and convection. But because radiation is the dominant method of transfer, hardly any heating of the atmosphere has taken place by the time the incoming short wavelength energy from the sun

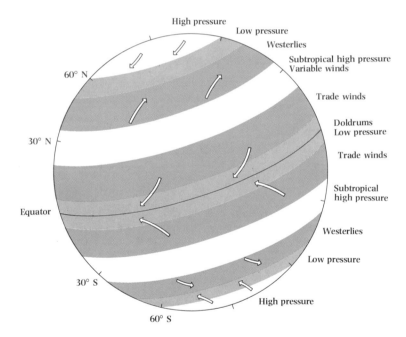

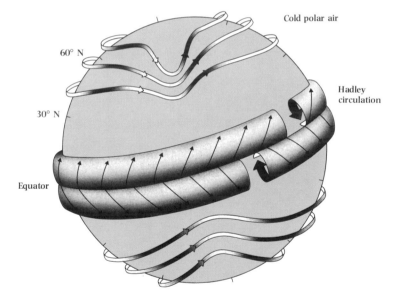

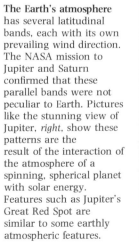

The Earth's atmosphere has several latitudinal bands, each with its own prevailing wind direction. The NASA mission to Jupiter and Saturn confirmed that these parallel bands were not peculiar to Earth. Pictures like the stunning view of Jupiter, *right*, show these patterns are the result of the interaction of the atmosphere of a spinning, spherical planet with solar energy. Features such as Jupiter's Great Red Spot are similar to some earthly atmospheric features.

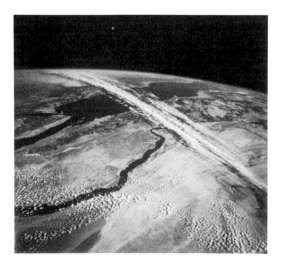

Hot equatorial air rises, moves north or south and returns close to the land to produce the trade winds. This Hadley circulation is one general feature that underlies local transient weather variations. It interacts with cold polar air, creating the strong westerly winds blowing around the world. In the northern hemisphere the interaction also creates a high speed wind called the jet stream. The streak of cirrus cloud, *right*, marks the course of a high altitude jet stream.

reaches the Earth's surface. The Earth itself—or at least its outer layers—absorbs the radiation that has passed through the atmospheric gases, is itself warmed up and re-radiates much of the heat energy as long wavelength heat radiation. Although the atmosphere is relatively transparent to the incoming short wave rays, its constituent gases, especially water vapour and carbon dioxide in the lower atmosphere, are much more efficient at absorbing the re-radiated long wavelength heat. This means that the lower zones of the atmosphere, up to altitudes far above the summit of Mount Everest, 29,030 feet (8,848 m) above sea level, are heated from below upward rather than directly from the sun, which explains why the top of Everest is covered with perpetual ice, while the foothills of the Himalayas have a semi-tropical climate.

The tilt of the Earth's spin axis induces different heating levels at different parts of its surface. In a tropical belt around the Earth, stretching nearly 40 degrees north and south of the Equator, the atmosphere/ocean systems are in heat surplus, that is, they absorb more solar heat than they radiate back into space. North and south of this belt the same systems are in deficit and radiate more than they receive. If this set of relationships persisted for any length of time, temperatures would progressively climb in the tropics from year to year while it became colder and colder in the rest of the world. In fact this does not occur. The heat budget is made to balance by massive circulatory movements of air which transfer heat from the central belt to the cooler regions north and south of it. The weather machine may be 7,900 miles (12,720 km) across and, round the Equator, spin at 1,000 miles (1,600 km) an hour, but while the sun continues to emit radiation energy, that machine will keep running.

The climate of the globe may seem to us to be perfectly stable but, like the ground beneath our feet, it has undergone dramatic and rhythmic perturbations in the course of history. So while the 'solid' Earth is, in reality, a thin, moving skin of solidified rock on a slowly seething furnace of hot molten rock, the climate of the globe too is in a state of change. Indeed, man's evolutionary history has unfolded in a period of the planet's history that has probably witnessed some of the most violent changes of climate and environment that have ever occurred in Earth's five billion year life-span. The last two million years of this evolutionary period is usually termed the Quaternary era or period. Conventionally it is split into the Holocene, encompassing the most recent 10,000 years, and the very much longer Pleistocene period which immediately preceded it. In terms of the total history of the Earth the span of the Quaternary is remarkably brief, taking up only one twenty-fifth of one per cent of the total time that has elapsed since the Earth was formed. But during this mere flicker of geological time, man came into existence, and the form and climate of the planet were spasmodically and recurrently altered.

These Pleistocene changes in global climate are commonly called the Ice or Glacial Age, although it is only one of three such eras. About 20,000 years ago the temperate world of the northern hemisphere we know today was almost unimaginably different. The difference was ice. If all the ice in the world today were concentrated in one place, it would form an amazing cube measuring 200 miles (320 km) along each of its edges. In the coldest period of the most recent Glacial Age, the Earth carried a mantle of ice with a mass that could have produced a cube three times as large. That alteration in ice mass has brought ▷

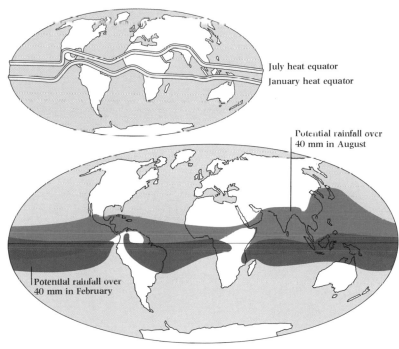

July heat equator
January heat equator

Potential rainfall over 40 mm in August

Potential rainfall over 40 mm in February

The patterns of winds and atmospheric circulation shown in the diagrams on page 24 are not constant throughout the year. The tilt of the Earth's spin axis forces these bands to shift up and down with a seasonal rhythm. The simple overall picture may be complicated locally by continents, mountains and oceans. The zone of the most direct solar heating shifts $23\frac{1}{2}°$ north to $23\frac{1}{2}°$ south and back again every year. This cycle of heating means the heat equator or the band of highest global temperatures itself moves cyclically. With a slight time delay after the summer and winter solstices, the heat equator, *above top*, reaches its northernmost and southernmost positions, respectively. Extreme solar heating over large oceans causes vast quantities of water to evaporate into the atmosphere and then precipitate as rain. So the zone of heavy and potentially constant rainfall generally coincides with the area of the heat equator. As a result, the band of heavy tropical rain, *above*, moves up and down the torrid zone, bringing the wet season.

The monsoon season in the Indian subcontinent and in Southeast Asia is one dramatic result of the seasonally shifting band of tropical rain. In winter huge evaporation occurs over the Indian Ocean and the west Pacific. In summer the water-laden air swings northward, dropping its cargo of rain on the land. For example, 95 per cent of Bombay's rain falls between June and September. Such rain is good for growing rice but can cause terrible flooding in low-lying areas.

▷ about, both directly and indirectly, incredible changes on the planet. Directly, much of the northern hemisphere was once buried under the ice. In the New World the ice sheets spread southwards to smother the eastern regions of Canada, much of the American Midwest and New England. More ice ground its way over Alaska, western Canada and the northwestern states of North America. On the other side of the Atlantic, from centres in Scandinavia and Scotland, the frigid juggernauts moved south to cover most of Britain and northern continental Europe. Smaller ice caps reached out from the Pyrenees and the Alps into the surrounding terrain. On a less extensive scale, ice caps grew in Argentina and Australasia, and tundra landscapes fringed all the ice sheets.

The indirect changes of the ice expansion were no less dramatic. With dropping temperatures and consequently changed habitats, animal and plant species were subjected to powerful new selection pressures. Some succumbed to extinction but others adjusted to the changing conditions by means of migrations or adaptations that made them more efficient in the new, cold world. The sheer weight of ice in some regions quite literally squashed the ground beneath it, sometimes producing rock deformations of many hundreds of feet.

The ice, locked up in solid form in the new ice sheets, had to come from somewhere and basically it came from the world's oceans. So great was the removal and conversion of water to ice, that worldwide ocean levels dropped as much as 350 feet (107 m). As this happened, extensive areas of the continental shelves around the world were exposed and became visible dry land. Continents expanded sideways and, as a result, some land masses which had previously been separate became continuous. Perhaps most dramatically, North America and Asia were linked by a land bridge in the area of the Bering Strait.

About 14,000 years ago the ice-spread reached its maximum extent. Net reconversion of ice into ocean water began, and the glaciers began to retreat as the levels of the oceans rose. About 7,000 years ago the ice cover of the Earth, its geographical climatic pattern and its vegetation systems were much as they are today. Thus, in broad terms, the Holocene period corresponds to this latter, most recent interval of raised global temperatures, shrunken ice sheets and high ocean levels.

This most recent spasm in the Earth's climate is the one that is best known, but it is reasonable—and also a wise precaution—to question its uniqueness. Has the world just passed through a completely unorthodox, single global twitch, or were these events just one of a succession of cyclical happenings? There seems little doubt that Glacial Ages themselves have an internal, periodic, rhythmic structure through time. It also appears very likely that the Pleistocene Ice Age was simply the last of three very widely spaced Ice Ages, which have gripped the Earth for relatively short periods during the last billion years or so of global history. Between these cold periods, most of the Earth's climatic history has been both warmer and wetter than it is during Ice Ages, and the ice sheets have been extremely restricted in extent or even non-existent.

The long-term climatic story of our planet is thus both cyclic and rhythmic. The Earth's weather pattern beats like a heart, but the beats are infinitely slow.

To be highly simplistic, the Earth's natural or typical climate is warm and wet, but superimposed upon this background has been a succession of colder, drier Ice Ages. The irregular alternations of the two climatic types constitute the cycles of the longest periodicity that are known about in the Earth's five billion years of development. Within the cold Ice Ages rhythmical patterns of climatic change are apparent, the planet cycling between relatively warm interglacial periods, such as the one we are experiencing now, and colder glacial periods in which the Earth's ice caps are much more extensive.

Our knowledge of the weather patterns that occurred thousands or even millions of years ago has not been acquired by chance. Rather it has only been made possible by a slow and painstaking accumulation and synthesis of many different types of evidence. To make informed speculations about climate during eras far back in geological history, an overlapping series of different techniques must be employed. With considerable precision and confidence we can back-track some 8,000 years in time. This is possible because of our ability to date organic material in the ground with radiocarbon (carbon–14) dating methods, cross-checked with tree-ring material of absolutely known age.

The radiocarbon technique measures the time that has elapsed since an organism died by measuring the proportion of different physical forms, or isotopes, of carbon, each having a slightly different atomic weight, in its preserved or fossilized remains. The technique is practical and accurate back to 50,000 years before the present day, but is particularly precise when calibrated against tree-ring material from bristlecone pine trees. These trees live above 9,000 feet (3,000 m) in mountains in the southwestern states of the United States of America. Some living trees are over 4,000 years old, which means that their seeds were germinating at the time when the first pyramids were being built. In the same area, dead wood with datable tree rings provides samples 8,000 years old. Using the radiocarbon technique it is possible to date fossil animals and plants over the past 50,000 years of the Quaternary era. And if the temperature requirements of these different types of organisms are known, it is possible to make detailed estimates about the climates in which they must have lived.

Another isotopic technique involves measuring the proportions of oxygen isotopes in ocean sediments laid down over the last million years of the Pleistocene period. This data provides a specific and subtle measure of the history of the global climate because, indirectly, it allows an assessment to be made of the volume of ice on Earth at any instant in the historical record. The scientific theory behind such a near-miraculous feat is as follows. When a volume of water freezes—leaving some water unfrozen—the oxygen isotope mixture in the ice and the residual water (both made of molecules consisting of one oxygen atom and two hydrogen atoms) is different. Compared with the original water the ice contains more light oxygen isotopes and the water fewer such isotopes. When the ice melts, the light isotope concentration in the water rises again.

During the expansion and contraction of ice sheets through a series of glacial and interglacial periods, these processes of freezing and thawing were going on not in a laboratory but throughout the world. Animals living in the oceans of the world were inhabiting an aqueous environment whose oxygen ▷

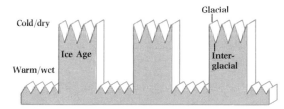

Each of the three Ice Ages of the last billion years had a rhythm of cold, dry glacials and warm, wet interglacials, *left*. We are probably now in an interglacial of the Pleistocene Ice Age.

Landscape changes generated by the expansion of ice and by glaciers and ice caps that persist in our interglacial world tell us about the last glacial period. The magnificent Bettmeralp glacier, *left*, in Switzerland shows the solid slow-moving river of ice, streaked with rocks, and dwarfing the town below. The gigantic isolated boulder, *below*, in California's Yosemite National Park, moved from a distant source by glacier power, is now a mute witness to former ice sheets.

Lakes in valley floors, U-shaped valley sides and parallel scratches on hard rock are signatures of a former glacier. The valley lake, *right*, is in the Black Cuillin mountains on the Isle of Skye off the coast of Scotland.

isotope concentration was changing in step with the climate, and their preserved bodies still carry the chemical evidence of those changes in water composition. In ocean sediment samples it is possible to map these fluctuations through time and to reconstruct the climatic changes. Each time the polar glaciers expanded, light isotopes of oxygen were effectively extracted from the world's oceans. When melting ice sheets retreated, the locked-up stores of light atoms of oxygen were returned to the oceans, thus restoring its isotopic constitution.

Using these and other techniques, it has been discovered that apparently most of the two million years of the Pleistocene era has consisted of large-scale shifts, from glacial to interglacial conditions and back again, with a basic period of about 100,000 years. This extreme instability of climate imposed profound constraints upon all the animals and plants on Earth. In every continent it is possible to see patterns of species production, species distribution and types of adaptation which are all the evolutionary results of the selection pressures imposed by a pulsating Ice Age.

The record in the rocks tells us that there were at least two previous Ice Ages before the one in which we are embedded, albeit in an interglacial period. The first of these occurred during the late Precambrian era, approximately 700 million years ago. Due to rock movements and erosion since then, it is impossible to deduce a distinct pattern of glacials and interglacials in this Ice Age, but glacial deposits of the correct antiquity are certainly widespread in southern Africa, Brazil and Australia.

The second Ice Age has been termed the Permocarboniferous Glacial Age. It

began just over 300 million years ago and lasted for more than 50 million years. In it continent-wide glaciation affected parts of South America, southern Africa, India and Australia. At that time these areas, and Antarctica, were fused together as a single, huge continent. Later, continental drift moved segments or plates of this continent apart to produce the separate southern hemisphere land masses we know today.

Continental drift has been proposed as a general explanation for the timing of the three main, extended periods of massive glaciation that the Earth has experienced. This theory suggests that wherever substantial continental land masses are shifted into zones near the poles, an increasing accumulation of ice occurs in those high latitudes. This build-up may possibly take place by means of a positive feedback mechanism, whereby, once initiated, the accumulations of ice reflect more solar energy directly back into space, so allowing further accumulation to occur. This hypothesis certainly seems to fit both of the last two Glacial Ages. In the Permocarboniferous, for example, Earth's continents were fused into a solitary supercontinent, Pangaea, centred on the Equator but stretching to the position of the South Pole. It is precisely those portions of Pangaea nearest the Pole that were glaciated. The present Glacial Age was probably precipitated by the shifting of North America and Eurasia towards the North Pole. In the northern hemisphere glaciers first started appearing about 10 million years ago.

Because it occurs too slowly, and does not have regular rhythmic components, the theory of continental drift cannot explain the decidedly regular 100,000-year rhythm of climate within the present Ice Age, as

Long-term cycles describe changes in the tilt and direction of the Earth's spin axis, and also in the shape of its orbit around the sun. These changes gradually alter the pattern of solar radiation falling on the Earth and profoundly influence the extent of the ice cover on the planet. Three cycles, with periods of about 21,000 years, 41,000 years and 100,000 years probably played a causal role in generating the observed pattern of glacial and interglacial periods within the Ice Ages. While these cycles account for the rhythm within an Ice Age, they do not, however, explain how an Ice Age is triggered in the first place.

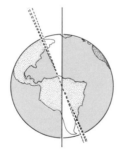

As the ocean waters froze during the last glacial of the Pleistocene Age, they expanded into huge glaciers. Spreading inexorably from the polar caps over great distances, the ice carved out the present northern landscape and altered the global climate patterns. The Arctic and Antarctic ice caps were much more extensive than they are today, and in the northern hemisphere what is now temperate land was then part of the polar region. The maps demonstrate the ice cover of the present day, *right*, and the extent of the Arctic ice sheet at the height of the last glacial of the Pleistocene Age, *below*, about 20,000 years ago.

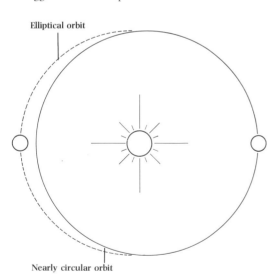

Elliptical orbit

Nearly circular orbit

The Earth nods up and down with respect to the sun. This is due to its spin axis tilting from 22 to $24\frac{1}{2}°$ and back to 22° every 41,000 years, *above*.

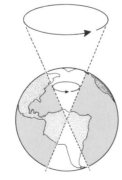

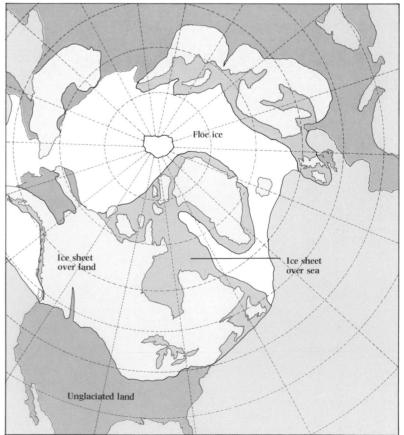

Floe ice

Ice sheet over land

Ice sheet over sea

Unglaciated land

The shape of the Earth's orbit changes every 90,000 to 100,000 years. The orbital path is basically elliptical with the sun at one focus of the ellipse. During one cycle the orbit oscillates between being more elliptical to being almost circular and back again, *above*. Together with the other two cycles, this produces complex changes in the amount of solar radiation reaching the ground at a particular latitude and at a particular season. These cycles and the changes they bring do not alter the total energy input from the sun. What they do alter is the way this energy is distributed over the Earth's surface. Global temperatures thus rise and fall enough to arrest or trigger glaciation.

The Earth is wobbling in space like a top spinning very slowly. Its spin axis describes a huge conical path against the stars every 21,000 years, *above*. The southern hemisphere has hotter summers than the north since the wobble is superimposed upon the nodding of the axis. In 10,000 years this situation will reverse.

demonstrated by isotopic oxygen and related studies. The best general theory so far propounded to explain the 100,000-year periodicity of climatic changes was first put forward by a Yugoslav mathematician Milutin Milankovitch, in 1920. In simple terms, Milankovitch suggested that three independent, rhythmic alterations in the Earth's celestial behaviour combine to produce temporal patterns in the amount of solar energy impinging on the Earth at different latitudes. The spin axis itself wobbles, with a complex dual periodicity of 23,000 and 19,000 years, in a movement known as precession. The tilt of the Earth's spin axis, relative to the orbit of the planet round the sun, can also vary cyclically between about 22 degrees and 24½ degrees, with a periodicity of some 41,000 years. Longest of all is a cycle, with a periodicity of between 90,000 and 100,000 years, in which the orbit of the Earth around the sun bounces between two configurations, one relatively elliptical, the other relatively circular. This is the eccentricity rhythm.

The eccentricity rhythm can obviously be tied to the dominant 100,000-year rhythm in the recent glacial/interglacial pattern. More startlingly, however, ocean sediment samples, analyzed by means of oxygen isotope estimations, also show minor periodicities of about 43,000, 24,000 and 19,000 years. These values are so close to the patterns predicted mathematically by Milankovitch, long before isotope studies were conceivable, that they represent a very powerful vindication of the basic truth of his theory.

It appears, then, that the Earth's cyclic and rhythmic climatic history is the consequence of a double interaction. First, the combined effects of planetary motion on the influx of radiant energy from the sun, and second, the combination of these mechanisms with the painfully slow creeping of the continental masses over the Earth's surface. Every smooth-sided glaciated valley, whether it be in Scotland, Scandinavia or Alaska, is the final, physical evidence of the effects of the different motions of the whole planet—motion through space and the motion of the Earth's crust.

Apart from the partisan fact that we happen to be living in it there is nothing unique about the present moment of planetary history. Milankovitch cycles do not stand still and the cyclical history of the Earth's climate, which is elegantly explicable in terms of the rhythms of planetary spin and orbital motion, must continue on into our future. What does this future hold? Can the evidence that has been gathered about previous Ice Ages, glacials and interglacials enable mankind to predict what the global climate will do over the next fifty, hundred, thousand or million years?

The usable evidence in this sort of speculation comes in three forms. First, we can use the mathematical predictability of the Milankovitch cycles which should, in theory, provide us with a broadly outlined picture of the major climatic changes due in the future. Second, we can attempt to extrapolate the detailed weather recordings of the past few centuries into the near future. Finally we must take account of the evidence suggesting that, in fact, man's presence in this planetary ecosystem is not climatically irrelevant because we are physically changing the atmosphere.

Taking these three categories of clues in turn, it seems that the basic cyclical patterns within the last million years suggest that we are only at the very beginning of an interglacial period. This evidence suggests that we are only just ▷

The temperature record of the last million years is based on oxygen isotope measurements taken from deep-sea sediment cores, *right*. The 100,000-year cycle of changes in the shape of the Earth's orbit could account for the seven or eight cold glacial peaks in the last 700,000 years.

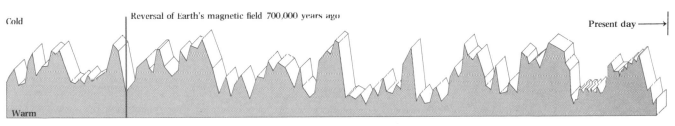

Cold

Reversal of Earth's magnetic field 700,000 years ago

Present day ⟶

Warm

Hooded crow

The hooded crow, *Corvus corone corvix*, has an unmistakable grey nape, back and chest.

Carrion crow

Carrion crows, *Corvus corone corone*, live in fairly open country and are all black. They form flocks, especially at roosting time, and nest in pairs on cliff ledges or in trees. Where they interbreed with the hooded crows, in narrow belts of land in Scotland and central Europe, the offspring all have darker feathers.

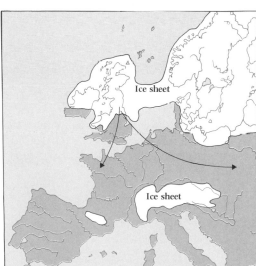

Ice sheet

Ice sheet

The ebb and flow of the ice sheets during the glacial and interglacial rhythm of the Pleistocene Ice Age has imposed profound evolutionary influences upon animals and plants. The ice changed their habitat so that they had to adapt, migrate or die. Carrion crows and hooded crows are both members of the same European crow species. The map, *right*, shows the distributions of these two subspecies which overlap only along a narrow zone of hybridization where they interbreed. An ancestral stock was possibly pushed south by the last glacial, see map *above*, and broken up into eastern and western populations. Over many years a segregation into two distinct forms has occurred.

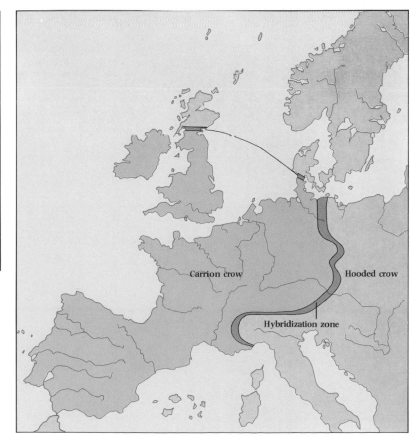

Carrion crow

Hooded crow

Hybridization zone

▷ entering many tens of thousands of years of relatively mild, moist weather. Looking at the past few hundred years of climate in the temperate mid-latitudes of the Earth we can distinguish many decades of unusually cold weather in the thirteen and fourteen hundreds and again in the seventeenth century. From around the year 1700 until the present day average temperatures seem to have been rising.

The possible influence that man may have on the future of his planet's climate is hard to judge, although it seems likely that his increasing utilization of forests might indeed have some impact. Since the beginning of the Industrial Revolution in the early nineteenth century the burning of coal, timber and then oil has led to an accumulative increase in atmospheric carbon dioxide levels. Tree destruction augments this change by reducing the extent to which carbon dioxide gas is removed from the air by the process of photosynthesis. It is impossible to make accurate estimates of this increasing carbon dioxide level but it is likely that today the natural equilibrium concentration of carbon dioxide in the atmosphere is 335 parts per million, compared with a figure of 270 parts per million in 1850, and is increasing by one or two parts per million each year.

These increments in carbon dioxide concentration, tiny though they are, could have profound effects on the Earth's weather. They could eventually increase the average temperature of the world a few degrees by means of an increasingly powerful greenhouse effect. Such a change could have dramatic consequences on the melting of the polar ice caps, sea levels, rainfall distribution and many other variables. Taken together, however, such changes tend to nudge the climate in the direction of typical interglacial weather so that man's activities over the foreseeable future are most likely to stabilize what is currently the Earth's natural state, namely that of interglacial mildness.

One of the cornerstones of the Milankovitch theory of variable planetary climate on the Earth is the effect of the precession of the Earth's spinning axis on solar energy input. The precessional movement of the Earth is exactly analogous to the rotating wobble that a spinning top develops as it begins to slow down. While the top is spinning fast, the orientation of its spin axis changes little, but as it slows down, so the rate of change of that orientation speeds up. In its precessional movement the spin axis of the Earth follows, in an approximate fashion, the surface of a cone whose tip-angle is 47 degrees, and it takes about 20,000 years for the orientation of the spin axis to describe a complete circle in the heavens.

The precession wobble of the Earth is essentially a gravitational effect, brought about by the influences of a small, close moon and a distant but massive sun on an Earth that is not a perfect sphere. Both the moon and the sun exert a complex gravitational pull on the Earth which has a bulge around the Equator—a sort of planetary paunch. Compared with the rest of the planet, this bulge experiences a slightly different pull from the moon and the sun and it is this that induces the precession wobble. Precession is an effect of lunar gravitation, not directly observable by any single ordinary person. Only over many generations is it possible to observe that geographical north points to slightly changing positions in the star field. At present the night sky in the northern hemisphere appears to revolve around a point near Polaris, the pole

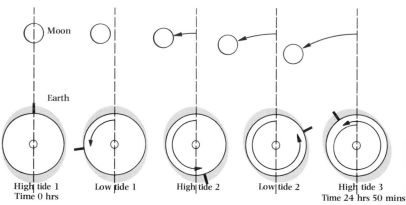

The moon's gravitational pull combines with centrifugal forces on the oceans to produce the daily rhythm of the tides. Gravitation is an attraction between the huge masses of Earth and moon. Centrifugal forces are due to these masses moving around a common centre of rotation. Together they produce a double water bulge on the Earth's surface. How the Earth's 24-hour rotation combines with the moon's motion to produce a tidal sequence is shown *above*. One spot on the earth, indicated by a vertical marker, moves through the water's bulges and troughs in a cycle lasting just longer than a day since the Earth rotates and the moon orbits in the same direction. If this were a seashore a biological zone would arise, each height on the shore experiencing different immersion times per cycle.

The seashore at Puerto Vallarta, Mexico, *right*, is a colourful example of an intertidal zone. Over just a few yards relatively large changes in light, temperature and moisture influence the organisms' way of life. A typical beach profile, *below*, shows the four main tidal levels and their associated zones where some plants live according to their metabolic and reproductive needs.

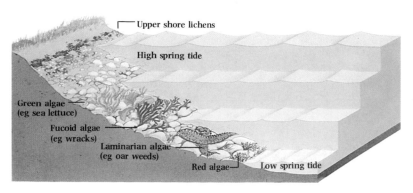

star, but because of the phenomenon of precession, this point is constantly—if slowly—on the move.

There is another effect of the moon's gravitational attraction that is simply and directly observable. Any child will tell you that at the seaside the tide goes in and out. It is common knowledge that in some way the tides—the cyclical advance and retreat of the ocean's fringe up and down the shoreline—are driven by the moon. But the gravitational dance of sun, moon and Earth that generates observed tidal patterns is, however, extremely complicated and, without recourse to rather abstruse mathematical formulations, only the major patterns and influences are comprehensible.

To begin at the beginning; all objects in the solar system attract one another gravitationally. Tidal systems are the particular result of one pattern of cyclically changing gravitational attraction on the waters of the Earth. In a more general sense, the passage of the moon over the Earth's surface in its approximately 28-day orbit raises tides other than oceanic ones. Atmospheric tides follow the circling moon and minute rock tides do the same. Ignoring the sun for a moment, and considering the moon poised over the Earth at a single instant in time, water particles on the side of the Earth closest to the moon will be attracted to it. If they are able to move these water particles will heap up to form a tidal bulge of deeper water beneath the moon's position, but that is not the only effect.

The moon does not really revolve around the planet Earth. The truth is that both the Earth and its solitary satellite revolve around a common centre of gravity placed on a line exactly joining their centres. The centrifugal acceleration that results from this movement varies with the distance from the common centre of gravity, and is, consequently, much larger on the portion of the Earth's surface directly opposite the moon's position than it is underneath the moon. The acceleration affects the Earth's waters in the same way as gravity. So, in effect, the moon's gravitational pull produces one bulge directly underneath it, while apparent centrifugal forces induce another on the opposite side of the Earth. If the Earth were a perfect sphere completely covered with water and only the moon affected that water, the tides would be produced by two symmetrically disposed bulges, through which any point on the rotating Earth would pass approximately twice every 24 hours.

That is the basic theoretical situation but, in reality, other factors complicate the real tidal phenomenon considerably. First, the sun cannot be ignored. It has a gravitational effect similar to that of the moon on the Earth's water, but the strength of its influence is only about half that of the moon's. When sun, moon and Earth are in a straight line the two tidal bulges are much larger than those produced by the moon alone. These are the spring tides which occur approximately every two weeks and which, inevitably, coincide with the appearance of a full or a new moon, because it is only at such times that the required linear configuration is achieved. Tides of this sort generate the highest high tide levels and also the lowest low tide levels. When, in contrast, sun, Earth, and moon are at right angles, the sun's gravitational influence will partially counteract that of the moon. The resulting less extreme, or neap, tides occur approximately one week after spring tides.

Real tides have other complex periodicities and irregularities. These result ▷

▷ from factors such as the friction between the ocean bottom and moving water masses, the physical blocking of water transfer by solid land masses, the resonance of water masses in relatively enclosed conditions and a number of other subtle physical effects. Taken together these perturbations make tidal prediction in the real world a highly sophisticated science. Specific predictions have to be made for every different geographical region of the Earth's ocean mass, simply because local conditions have an enormous influence on the basic tidal patterns. Some water masses, such as the Mediterranean, experience limited tidal effects while others, such as the coastlines on either side of the North Atlantic, demonstrate dramatically larger tidal changes. This particular difference is said to have caused the failure of one of Julius Caesar's attempts to invade England. Conditioned by the almost tideless Mediterranean, it appears that his captains underestimated the large tidal ranges along the English Channel coast, and this caused much of one invasion fleet to be wrecked on the shore.

The shoreline, the interface between two great ecosystem complexes, the sea and the land, is a life zone of staggering diversity. Even on a tideless planet the oceanic fringe of any land mass would be interestingly different from either the ocean or the land, in respect of the specialized organisms that lived there. All biological boundary regions have this property because, in them, a wide range of important physical parameters, such as light, temperature and the availability of water, undergo rapid change. On a tidal world such as planet Earth, the tides have the effect of spreading out the interface zone so that it extends over a considerable distance both horizontally and vertically. Tides also accentuate the way in which environmental factors fluctuate in the area of the shoreline.

The intertidal zone, that is, the region between the lowest tide marks and the highest, includes a complex community of animals and plants which often demonstrate very high productivity. The plants that live there, which are mostly algae (seaweeds) but include also lichens and a few flowering plants, have plentiful water, usually an unlimited supply of mineral salts from the sea, and sufficient light for the manufacture of foodstuffs by means of photosynthesis because, in this fringe zone, water levels are never very deep.

In all parts of the world the different nature of the intertidal zone depends on the physical form of the land abutting the sea, the exposure of the shoreline to strong wave action, the ambient climatic conditions and the physiological nature of the animal and plant life that inhabits it. Two extreme intertidal types would be a gently shelving mud or sandy shoreline, exposed only slightly to wave action, and a vertical cliff, facing the prevailing winds and pounded by waves with a long oceanic fetch. In between these two extremes are a wide range of intermediate types with moderate shore-profile gradients. But no matter how the intertidal band is stretched out, whether it is an almost flat expanse of mud several miles wide or a vertical cliff face, tide movements will provide extremely marked gradients of conditions for life throughout the zone.

The most basic of the gradients of the shoreline is that of immersion. At the base of the shoreline there will be a zone which is only exposed to the air during one or two low spring tides a year. At the top of the intertidal shore there will, likewise, be a band that is only covered by the sea on the same number of days.

The changing phases of the moon are the altering shapes an earthly observer sees of the sun-illuminated face of the moon. Probably the easiest of astronomical phenomena to observe, it must have been the earliest cosmic cycle to be recognized and revered by ancient man. Apart from sunspots, other easily detected features of the lunar disc are the only surface characteristics of any astronomical object that can be seen with the naked eye. Good unaided human vision can distinguish the broad dark plains called seas, the highland regions and a few of the largest craters. Through low-power telescopes and even binoculars much more detail can be seen, including the bright radiating rays that stretch out enormous distances from craters such as Tycho and Copernicus. These rays show the material ballistically thrown outward when the impact craters were formed by huge solid objects hitting the moon's surface. The lunar cycle, from crescent moon to full moon through to old moon, presents different opportunities to view the various surface features. Most detail is shown up when the moon is obliquely lit by the sun because then the topography casts large shadows. Thus the waxing or waning moon is the best time for lunar study.

Direction of solar illumination

New moon

Crescent moon

Old moon

Half moon third quarter

Half moon first quarter

Waning moon

Gibbous moon

Full moon

The moon is the only natural satellite of the Earth and has no mechanism for generating light of its own. It shines only by reflecting the light of the sun. From the moon the astronauts saw the Earth in precisely the same way—earthlight is also reflected sunlight. Apart from lunar eclipses, when the Earth comes exactly between the moon and the sun, half of the moon's nearly spherical surface is always illuminated by the sun: one half is always brightly lit, the other almost utter darkness. This is shown diagrammatically, *left*, in the inner ring of moon images. The appearance of the moon from the Earth varies, however, and the regular sequence of apparent changes of shape are termed phases. When the moon is between the Earth and the sun, its dark side is turned towards us and the moon cannot be seen. This is the new moon. When the Earth comes between the moon and the sun, the moon's face is turned toward us and we see a full moon. The intermediate phases of the moon, the crescent, the half moon, the gibbous, the waning, the last quarter and the old moon, are caused by a cycle of intermediate viewing conditions shown, *left*, in the outer ring of moon images. If the new moon is exactly between an observer and the sun a solar eclipse occurs.

In between there will be a more or less regular gradient with organisms being immersed for different proportions of their lives. This immersion gradient generates a wide range of secondary gradients in such features as temperature and desiccation. As a result of this superimposed series of gradients, all shorelines with marked tidal influences support a series of animal and plant communities, arranged in parallel from the top to the bottom of the intertidal area.

If you stand at any point on a graduated shoreline, it is possible to determine your position up or down the shore simply by identifying the animals and algae under your feet. Particular molluscs, worms and crustaceans inhabit—and are specifically adapted for—restricted zones of the shore. In the same way, the seaweed plant-cover of the intertidal zone consists of a series of specialized algal types, each operating most efficiently at a different degree of tidal immersion. On rocky temperate shores, for example, large brown laminarian kelps often dominate the low part of the shore, fucoid wracks, the centre zone and a mixture of green algae and rock-covering lichens, the upper shore.

For all these highly adapted organisms the cycle of high and low tides is the dominant environmental variable. This rhythm is more important in inducing adaptive behavioural patterns in the organism's life-style than any other physical cycle, including the changes that take place between day and night. So the animals of the intertidal zone organize their hunting and grazing, their meeting and reproduction according to tidal imperatives. The photosynthesis and reproduction of algae are likely, in a similar fashion, to be highly ordered by tidal sequences as well as day–night cycles.

The seashore may seem to be an unremarkable piece of seaside landscape, but it provides in microcosm an image of all rhythmic life processes. In a peculiarly direct way it is possible to perceive how an environmental rhythmic cycle—the pulsation of the tides—imposes both spatial patterning and behavioural patterning in time on all the creatures that are exposed to that elemental cycle. More than that, it is easy in this case to understand how the environmental rhythm is the direct consequence of a cosmic motion. All societies have realized that the moon governs the tides—no one with a boat and eyes lifted above the horizon could fail to grasp the inexorable linkage between the phases of the moon and the height of the tide.

The causal bonds between moon motion, tides and the behaviour of intertidal life are simply one set of ties, in a whole web of such connections, that link the motions of the solar system to the ebb and flow of life on our planetary home. The cyclical patterns can be so slow that we have no racial memory or human record of their passing. The glacial/interglacial pulsations, with their periodicities of many thousands of years, come into this category. The most rapid of the cycles, such as the twice-daily tides, occur at frequencies which demand that all but the most short-lived of organisms must perceive them and be influenced by them.

The astrologers of the past have been guilty of propounding some astonishing nonsense. Yet at the centre of their cosmic view they had grasped one jewel of truth, namely that all creatures on Earth, including man, have grown up reflecting in their daily lives the patterns and rhythms of the motions of the heavens.

The moon's pull is the main gravitational force on the Earth's oceans. Its nearness to Earth makes up for the moon's small size, and its pull is about twice that of the sun. The width of the broad arrows *left*, shows the relative size of the two forces. When the Earth, moon and sun are in a straight line, the combined pull of the sun and moon produce very high and low 'spring' tides. These occur about every two weeks, at the new and full moon. When the Earth, moon and sun form a right angle in space, *lower left*, in the days between the spring tides, the sun partly offsets the moon's pull. This results in the smaller high and low neap tides and occurs at a half moon. Such a rhythm, with its 14 and 28-day periods, is exemplified by the lunar month tide sequence, *below*, on the Atlantic seaboard of the United States near New York.

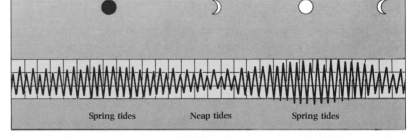

| Spring tides | Neap tides | Spring tides |

Rhythms of the seasons

When analyzing the attributes that have made *Homo sapiens* the most successful and widespread animal species on planet Earth, brain power is usually the skill that is emphasized first, followed, rather as an afterthought, by man's upright, two-legged stance. The blinkers of self-esteem stop us from seeing two other characteristics that must have been important to the evolutionary and social ascendancy of the human race—when considered alongside most of the other animals on earth we are comparatively huge and extremely long lived.

We human beings are not used to thinking of ourselves in such a comparative way, but more than 99.9 per cent of animal species are smaller and live shorter lives than we do. This combination of characteristics is in no way extraordinary because, for many years, biologists have recognized that there is a direct relationship between size and longevity or generation time. What is unusual is the additional degree of insight the acceptance of these two human attributes provides.

The large size of the human frame probably meant that during the early, crucial stages of man's evolution in the Pleistocene era, which began about two million years ago, there were few animals that he could not hunt and kill when operating in a cooperative group. Man's longevity opens some evolutionary doors but shuts others. He takes so long—a dozen years or more—to reach sexual maturity that his natural rate of increase can never approach that of fruit flies or white mice. But man's long life-span—three score years and ten according to biblical rule of thumb—allows for developmental possibilities and perceptions of the world forever barred to such 'boom and bust' reproducers.

The intellectual reward of human longevity is that it endows us with the long view. Emotionally and instinctively we never measure out our lives in minutes or seconds. The pattern of days is only the most immediate and fleeting aspect of our world view of time. Our natural milieu is the grand progress of seasons and years so that, if asked to describe the pattern of our lives, most of us naturally fall into a discussion of periods of this duration. For man, such a perception of time is a mental creation, but it is also rooted in fundamental biological processes which are only partly conceived in cerebral terms. Physiologically we respond to the changing seasons much as other large, long-lived organisms do.

If they are to survive to old age all large animals and plants must respond to the alterations in their habitats produced by the recurrent cyclical sequence of the seasons. Experience of these changing patterns by untold past generations has imposed constraining selection forces on the evolution of all organisms with a life-span of 12 months or more. Those strains or species of animals and plants which did not have appropriate behavioural responses to the onset of seasonal weather built into their genetic codes perished more often than those that did. Perennial insect-pollinated plants without the genetic instructions telling them to flower in the season when the appropriate insects were active, died out. They were simply fertilized less often, so their offspring came to represent less and less of the plant population.

Inexorable evolutionary forces shape responses to seasonal change, just as they act on structure or outward appearance. The result, seen in animals and plants throughout the world, is that in every latitude living things are precisely suited to the pattern of seasonal change characteristic of their own particular global location.

For most people living in Europe or North America talk of the seasons almost inevitably conjures up a fourfold sequence of periods that make up a year. Our languages give these four annual segments—spring, summer, autumn and winter—names that evoke a vivid mental picture of life in which the weather is only one element. This classical progression of the seasons, the sequence beloved of poets, is not a pattern that is equally valid all over the world.

The particular seasonal cycle experienced by an area of the globe is crucially dependent on its precise position. More specifically, latitude is the cycle's main determinant. Considered in the broadest terms, the apparently orthodox four-season year is a phenomenon typical of the mid-latitudes, the temperate regions of the earth sandwiched between the equatorial tropical zone and the frigid polar zones at the top and bottom of our planet. Where the quartet of seasons does occur, all four are characterized by particular patterns of the three most vital physical influences that mould the environment for all living creatures, including ourselves—temperature, light and water.

Temperature is important because it is the essential physical regulator of the rate at which the chemical processes that determine life can occur. This regulation is a direct consequence of the thermodynamic fact that most chemical and physical processes that need energy in order to take place are speeded up as temperatures increase, and slowed down as they decrease. This is, provided that the temperatures are not so extreme as to kill the organism or place it in a state of suspended animation.

In terms of energy, it is light from the sun that drives the biological ecosystems made up of animals and plants. Ultimately sunlight is the basic energy source for all net conversions of inorganic molecules into organic ones, such as proteins, fats, sugars and all the other complex substances of life. This conversion is achieved in plant cells containing the green pigment chlorophyll by means of the process of photosynthesis, which is driven by sunlight. Pared to its bare essentials, photosynthesis involves the combination of carbon dioxide from the atmosphere with water drawn up from the soil to make sugar molecules. As a result of this process, oxygen is released into the air. The products of plant photosynthesis provide the food for herbivorous animals, and these, in turn, are the food for carnivores, occupying higher and higher positions on the pyramid of predatory hierarchy. When a lion kills and consumes an eland it is, in terms of biological conversion, only one step away from eating grass. Sunlight also provides the necessary milieu for all seeing creatures. Without this light, vision, the most precise and specific of the senses, would not only be irrelevant but unimaginable.

Water constitutes a surprisingly large proportion of all living things. All living cells consist of at least 90 per cent water and all the chemical processes that go on in cells take place in aqueous solution. The amount of water available in an environment can often prove to be the overriding factor, enabling a biological activity to occur or prohibiting it.

Spring, summer, autumn and winter each have a consistent signature of light, temperature and water availability, but there is little doubt that in the temperate parts of the world, say between the latitudes of 30 and 70 degrees (from New Orleans to Murmansk in the northern hemisphere and from Durban to Alexander Island on the Antarctic fringe in the southern hemisphere),

Spring has always sparked off the annual farming cycle in temperate areas, as temperatures then rise above the crucial 43°F (6°C) necessary to initiate new plant growth. Seeds are sown, and the breeding season begins, setting in train the essential processes of life.

The Shepheard's Kalender

Summer begins in June, in the northern hemisphere. Medieval man observed the varying positions of the stars during the year, and linked the signs of the zodiac to the seasons. As illustrated in *The Shepheard's Kalender* he noted that the signs changed in mid-month.

Winter months, with freezing temperatures and long nights, are a feature of the cool temperate zones (between latitudes 30° and 70°). Melting snow may fall at 38°F (3°C), if the air is saturated and, as the air grows colder, the flakes become finer and settle.

Autumn, to medieval man, signified the harvesting of the year's basic food reserves. *The Shepheard's Kalender*, shows how life in the early 1500s revolved much more closely around the cycle of the seasons than do our technologically 'cushioned' lives today.

temperature is the key factor. In the mid-latitudes it is almost always temperature that modulates, for instance, the seasonal pattern of plant growth. In fact it is in relation to the absolute levels of temperature that the meaning of the word temperate, as applied to geographical zones, can be understood. In this context temperate certainly does not mean unchanging or moderate. Because of the tilted spinning axis of the Earth, the temperate regions experience temperatures intermediate between the consistently high values characteristic of the tropics and the much lower temperatures that prevail all the year round in the Arctic and Antarctic zones.

As well as producing a mean intermediate temperature level in mid-latitudes the tilt also, of course, produces a profoundly fluctuating one. When the tilt nods one hemisphere toward the sun, producing longer daylengths and less oblique rays of sunlight, then the temperature is high. When the same tilt angles the hemisphere away from the sun, generating shorter daylengths and more oblique sunlight, then the diametrically opposite seasonal period occurs and the temperature is low.

In the temperate zone seasonality is thus inextricably tied to a cyclical change of average temperature, from a summer high through the intermediate values of autumn to a winter low and then, via intermediate spring temperatures, to summer again. The two wide temperate bands around the earth between 30 and 70 degrees north and south contain a relatively distinct series of subzones, each with its own particular variants of the seasonal temperature cycle. These regions have been given a variety of names but those that are most immediately and directly understood are the warm temperate,

cool temperate and cold temperate regions.

These regions lie in sequence from Equator to pole, north and south of the Equator. Each region experiences its own cyclical seasonal pattern of temperature variation, but the range of temperature in each zone is different. This variable amplitude of temperature change is particularly vital to plant growth because almost all plant growth, including that of leaves, stems and flowers, stops at temperatures below 6 degrees centigrade (42.8 degrees F). Thus the proportion of days in a year on which the temperature is above this threshold constitutes, in a direct sense, the potential growing period for plants in that zone. The length of this growing period must inevitably be, in turn, a prime determinant of the amount of new plant material—an area's primary product—in any given year. The longer the growing period, the greater is the mass of new plant substance, and this productive effort constitutes the only net input of new organic material into communities of animals and plants.

Warm temperate areas are those in which the average temperature of the coldest month of the year does not drop below the magic, growth-enabling figure of 6 degrees centigrade (42.8 degrees F). In the northern half of the globe in the Old World, the warm temperate zone includes the whole of North Africa north of the Sahara, most of the Mediterranean region, and some of the Middle East, as well as Afghanistan and southern China. In the New World it takes in the sunny southern states of the USA. In the southern hemisphere, Chile, Argentina, South Africa and the south of Australia are largely in this zone, which stretches, broadly, from latitudes 30 to 40 degrees.

Next in the poleward sequence are the cool temperate geographical strips. ▷

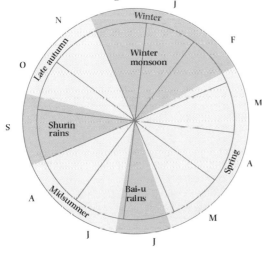

Japan, unlike other temperate countries, has six distinct seasons, three wet and three dry. The winter monsoon, the Bai-u rains in June and the late summer Shurin rains are each followed by a dry period.

The snowdrop, *Galanthus nivalis,* sometimes known in Britain as 'the fair maid of February', emerges through the melting snows of late winter. It heralds the transition into temperate spring, which brings longer days and fresh plant growth.

Temperatures fluctuate more dramatically inland than in coastal areas. In land-locked Winnipeg the annual temperatures range from −20°C to 20°C, while Vancouver, warmed by the heat stored in the oceans, rarely falls below 3°C.

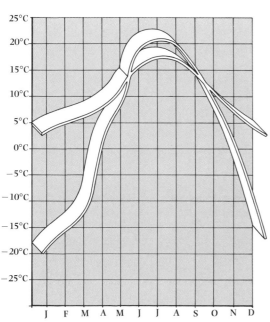

▷ These regions of the globe contain most of the rich and developed nations of the world, for in the northern hemisphere the cool temperate band includes most of the USA, the southern portion of Canada, most of Europe, southern Russia, northern China and Japan. There are hardly any cool temperate land masses in the southern hemisphere. It is a matter of some speculation whether the present coincidence of developed economic status and a particular climatic condition is fortuitous or causal. The cool temperate zone has at least one month in every year with a mean temperature below 6 degrees centigrade (42.8 degrees F) but not more than five such months. This frosty period is the true winter, which hardly exists in the warm temperate zone, and is characterized by a cessation of plant growth. It is in the cool temperate zone above all others that the four-season cycle is most characteristic.

Bordered on one side by a cool temperate zone and on the other by the treeless tundra of the polar regions is the cold temperate zone. Here it is normal to have temperatures below 6 degrees centigrade (42.8 degrees F) for at least six months out of every 12. The natural ecosystems in this zone have no deciduous trees of ordinary size, only miniature or creeping kinds, and plant life is dominated by vast tracts of coniferous, evergreen forests.

In the temperate parts of the world the dominant climatic theme is the cyclical seasonal variation in temperature. The tropical regions of the earth are, in contrast, typified by continous high temperatures but seasonal variations in rainfall. Everywhere between the Tropics of Cancer and Capricorn the sun is directly overhead on at least one day a year. Despite local variations, all this tropical zone is hot throughout the year, so that the sort of temperature-induced seasonal variation in plant growth, which is so vital in temperate regions, is of little importance near the Equator. Instead, where strong seasonal influences exist, they are centred around the availability of water, and the year is split into hot dry and hot wet seasons.

To synchronize the important activities of their lives, such as reproduction, both with each other and with the appropriate external climatic conditions, animals and plants that inhabit the temperate zones respond to the temperature changes or marked daylength alterations throughout the year. At first glance it might appear unlikely that animals living in the tropics in general, and those in regions on or near the Equator in particular, could behave in a seasonal fashion like their cousins in temperate zones. The reasons for this would be the absence of strong seasonal changes in either air temperature or daylength, implying an absence of clear-cut external clues, to which seasonal activity might be tied. In fact, even on the Equator itself, most animals still exhibit strong seasonality in their activities. This seasonality is present, despite the absence of any dramatic temperature variation to make an emphatic seasonal change in the appearance of the habitat.

In the tropics, the seasonal behaviour of animals can be the result of inbuilt annual activities or can be directly or indirectly tied to external seasonal clues, such as rainfall. In many of the tropical regions of the world there are broadly predictable changes in the amount of rainfall throughout the year, and there are also significant differences in this rainfall pattern. Nearest to the Equator there are many regions in which the seasonal variation in rainfall is low, but the absolute input of rain to the land masses is high. It is in these constantly wet

and hot zones that the true non-seasonal rain forest vegetation—the jungle—develops. These rain forests gradually merge into more seasonal forest belts where, for some periods of the year, drier conditions make a significant impact on plant success, restricting the amount of photosynthesis that occurs, and thus the amount of growth that can take place.

In many but not all of the zones within the tropics, the annual climatic cycle consists of two relatively wet and two relatively dry periods per year. It is these seasonal ups and downs in rainfall that trigger most of the clear-cut seasonal behaviour of tropical animals and plants. In any particular tropical location the total amount of rain that falls in the wet seasons depends on a number of factors, but of these distance from the sea and altitude above sea level are most important. As a rule, the wet seasons are wettest in sites closest to the sea because they receive air which has become water-laden as it has travelled landward over the ocean. Similarly, the higher an area is above sea level the fewer rainless months there are and the more rain there is in each rainy period. The reason for this is that water vapour condenses out into liquid raindrops more readily at the low temperatures of high altitudes. These variations within the tropics mean that the most dramatic transitions between wet and dry seasons occur in lowland zones, often those with savanna-type vegetation, in which the total annual rainfall is small. In such regions the seasonal changes are staggering, with the rains catapulting the landscape from arid, desiccated dormancy and inactivity to bursting plant growth and intense animal activity almost overnight.

The causes of the twice-yearly pattern of rains in the tropics can, like many other seasonal variations, be attributed to the Earth's tilted spinning axis. Because of the constant orientation of the Earth's axis, in the tropics, a zone of rainfall follows the apparent motion of the sun in a year—first northward, then southward then northward again. The rainfall belt is perhaps best described in relation to a specific location such as East Africa. Here the rain occurs in zones where water-laden air masses converge. Air rises in these zones, cools as it expands at lower pressure, and condenses into rain.

Of all these convergences, the one that is most important as far as East Africa is concerned is the intertropical convergence zone or equatorial trough. This zone is closely related to the heat equator of the globe and in it the massive tropical trade wind systems of the northern and southern halves of the world meet head on. If our planet were smooth and perfectly spherical like a billiard ball this convergence would create a girdle round the world that would follow the sun's apparent motion. On the earth's actual surface the mix of land masses and oceans means that the precise course marked out by the convergence zone is much more tortuous. None the less, it still sits astride Africa, and once each year moves up and down the central parts of that continent. The movement of the convergence zone alone can provide the essential clue to the puzzle of the double rainy period. At any spot in the tropics rain is likely to be associated with the twin passages of the convergence zone over that area—once as it moves north and once as it travels south again.

North of the Arctic Circle and south of its Antarctic equivalent, seasonality is tied to the third great ecological determinant—light. The polar year is divided, in different proportions at different latitudes, into periods of continuous ▷

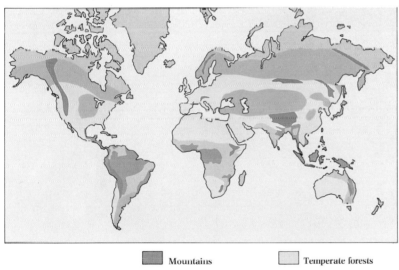

Desert · Savanna · Mountains · Snowlands · Taiga · Temperate forests · Tropical forests · Steppe

Tropical seasons are controlled by rain rather than temperature. At the Equator, the humid rain forests experience only slight variations in the intensity of rainfall. The huge belts of tropical grassland and savanna on either side, however, have extreme wet and dry seasons. Dry trade winds sweep across the area from June to October, and in January and February, bringing drought, *left*. Rainfall is minimal, existing moisture evaporates rapidly and the sun blazes. Animals huddle round the few remaining water holes and scour the scorched brown grassland for nourishment. In November and December, and from March to May, bands of low pressure bring the rains and transform the landscape almost overnight, *right*. Parched river beds become torrents, the dead, cracked earth melts under the moisture and becomes fertile again. Within days the strawlike tufts of burnt grass give way to fresh green vegetation. With this new abundance of good grazing, animals disperse and begin breeding, so giving their young the maximum chance to grow and thrive before the next dry season devastates the land.

The eight main vegetation types, which mirror precisely the world's climatic zones, weave irregular latitudinal patterns over the earth's surface. Jungle, steppe and desert are all created by weather systems.

These two views of the Tsavo National Park in southeastern Kenya reveal the extreme seasonal swings in the tropical savanna. The same landscape, brown and sun-parched in the dry season, *left*, is dramatically transformed by the first rains, *right*.

▷ daylight, continuous darkness and twilight periods. In the polar regions the truism that the sun is the ultimate source of all earthly life is dramatically illustrated as the sun appears and disappears for months on end. When darkness is the seasonal signature, animal and plant life plunges into the depths of dormancy. With the arrival of eternal day, frenetic activity ensues, so that organisms can rush through their essential reproductive processes, and collect and store enough food reserves to last them through the months of darkness.

Some of the most clear-cut and unambiguous clues that the weather machine can manufacture occur in various tropical regions of the world. The abrupt, almost instantaneous, transition of a landscape from arid, desiccated desert to a brilliant expanse of flowers, humming with insects, is not a signal that is easily ignored by other living creatures. But unambiguous though it is, such a stimulus cannot, by its very nature, be an accurate seasonal time check. Similarly, in the mid-latitude temperate zone of the world, the major climatic transitions of the seasons are roughly, but never exactly, at the same date each year. Autumn gales do, by definition, start in autumn, but in some years they are early, in others late—or they may be virtually non-existent. The last night frost of the year, a key event for any keen gardener with treasured tender specimens that need to be planted out, can never be pin-pointed in advance on the calendar, and may occur unexpectedly late when summer seems to be well on its way.

Meteorological signs can thus provide approximate signals about the time of year, but these messages can become garbled by the large part that chance plays in the pattern of weather at any specific spot on the earth's surface. The fact that weather signals, with a code of rain, temperature and winds, can give false information about seasonal time means that animals and plants can never place complete reliance upon such signals to order their own activities. But order their activities they must. Mates have to be found, breeding synchronized, nests built or flower buds made and opened at the correct time of year. Bad timing, a wrong extrapolation from freak warm weather in early spring, or a premature frost in late summer could make all the difference between disaster and a successful breeding season for an animal or abundant seed production for a plant.

Because of the inbuilt inaccuracy of forecasting by the weather, exact and consistent information about seasonal time is of life and death importance to living things. So how can organisms order their seasonal lives with apparently magical precision? Why do all the leaves of the trees in a beech wood spring out from their buds at very nearly the same time each year? And how do swallows, swifts and martins arrive back at their European nesting sites each breeding season with metronomic accuracy? In some ways it is surprising that the answer to these, and similar specific questions, was not arrived at until the 1920s and '30s. The answer is a single, technical word, photoperiodism. Dauntingly scientific it sounds, but all it means is changing daylength. Photoperiodism is nothing more esoteric or complicated than the fact that in temperate latitudes a day—that is, the number of sunlit hours—is longer in summer than it is in winter.

The transitions of daylength from, say, 16 hours in high summer to eight hours in midwinter, and the inverse change of the duration of nighttime, are

The number of daylight hours provides plants and animals with an accurate seasonal clock. As the tilted Earth orbits the sun each year, only the Equator experiences a constant 12-hour day. The higher the latitude, the more extreme the variations in daylength. At the poles, the days fluctuate between 24 hours of light in summer and none in winter.

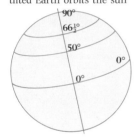

Latitude	Maximum daylength	No of days of max length	Minimum daylength	No of days of min length
90°	24	189	0	176
66½°	24	1	0	1
50°	16¼	7	7¾	6
0°	12	183	12	182

In temperate areas deciduous trees must produce well protected buds which will eventually replace the leaves that fall in autumn. The rudimentary leaves and stems held dormant inside the bud are ready to emerge the following spring when it opens. Changing daylengths induce the production, opening and falling of the leaves.

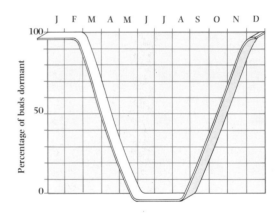

The annual activity of the colorado beetle, *Leptinotarsa decemlineata,* is ruled by the number of daylight hours. Only in the summer when there are more than 14 hours of light is this potato pest able to reproduce, grow and develop. When the days shorten in late summer and fall below this crucial level, the beetle becomes dormant.

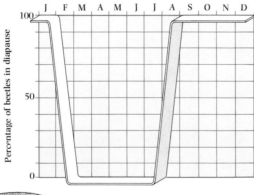

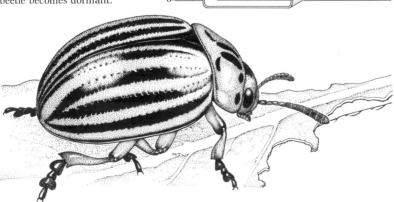

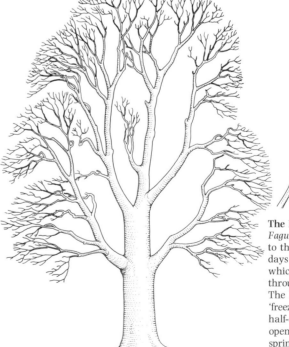

Dormant bud

The European beech, *Fagus sylvatica,* responds to the shortening autumn days by producing buds which remain dormant throughout the winter. The long dark nights 'freeze' the buds in their half-developed state, and open only when the spring days draw out to more than 12 hours.

not stepwise and abrupt. Daylength changes in a smooth, rhythmical cycle of alteration from a maximum at the summer solstice down to a minimum on the day of winter solstice, then back up to a summery maximum again. It needs chronometers and accurate record-taking to plot the smooth curve of change, but it takes no scientific sense to appreciate the reality. Everyone who lives in Europe, North America or Japan knows of long, balmy summer evenings and short, depressing winter days when the sun is low in the sky and the promise of spring far off.

Perhaps it was the very mundaneness of the phenomenon of the seasonal change in daylength that made zoologists, botanists and physiologists take so long to realize that this normal and all-pervading change in the environment is one of the most vital clues by which organisms impart temporal order to their lives. The fact that photoperiodism is normal and perceivable everywhere is central to an understanding of just why daylength is the external time signal by which living things run their seasonal lives efficiently. Unlike the weather, unlike wind speed or direction, unlike temperature, daylength is a message that simply cannot be jumbled or distorted. To change the signal you would have to stop the spinning, orbiting Earth in its celestial tracks. That the absolute length of a solar day on Earth has lengthened steadily over the billions of years of history of our planet is irrelevant. The changes are so small, amounting to perhaps a thousandth of a second a century, that every animal and plant has had more than enough evolutionary time in which to adjust to these minute alterations.

Except for a few underground, cave dwelling or deep-sea species, animals can see the enormous differences in light intensity between night and day. Day by day they can then integrate the total time-span of daylight (or night) and gather information about absolute daylength and whether it is becoming longer or shorter. The process might seem straightforward but, in reality, careful strategic safeguards and subtleties have to be built into the system. Gloomy overcast days must not be allowed to confuse the amount of daylight hours, and an accurate internal biological time sense is a necessity. With all this information computed, an animal located in a temperate climate can set its biological affairs in logical and efficient order. Most such animals are most active and reproduce during the warm months of late spring, summer and early autumn, timing their courtship and mating so that the young are born when conditions are most favourable for their survival. During the winter—if they do not avoid local climatic stresses by migrating to warmer areas—animals will usually reduce their activity so that they conserve as much body energy as possible, and will simply set about the business of survival on the minimum amount of food.

When firmly tied to external daylight, this overall pattern of change in the repertoire of an animal's activities offers other advantages that reach out farther than the individual life of a single animal. If all the members of a species use a common daylength as a trigger for the initiation of sexual development, the start of courtship and mating or nest building, then this will have the powerful and inevitable effect of synchronizing the breeding of all the animals in that species. In the mid-latitude climate of violently changing seasonal weather, tight synchronization of reproductive effort can be a necessity for the ▷

The male rock dove, *Columba livia*, like most birds, experiences a seasonal swelling and shrinking of its sexual organs. The lengthening spring days trigger hormonal changes which cause dramatic enlargement of the testes, equipping the bird for the breeding season. After breeding, their job done, the testes shrivel until the lengthening days of spring.

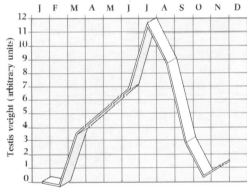

The lambing season coincides with the appearance of fresh spring grass, which will sustain the increasing sheep population. The sexual cycle begins in late summer when the shortening days induce ovary stimulation in the ewe and sperm production in the ram. Within four months the pair are ready to mate, and young are produced the next spring.

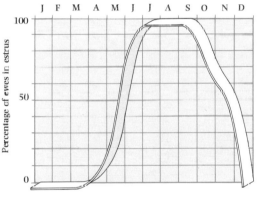

▷continuation of that species. It is never so common a practice, nor as vital to survival, in more climatically stable tropical ecosystems.

Like man, other animals use their eyes to acquire information about daylength and its photoperiodic change. But it is perhaps not quite so obvious that a plant—be it a garden weed or a giant redwood—can also monitor the changing period of nights and days throughout the year. In fact a plant's existence is, in every respect, infinitely more light-centred than that of an animal. The vital process of photosynthesis, in which organic matter is miraculously constructed out of gas and water, is powered by sunlight and all the rest of a plant's existence circles round this core of its activities. This being the case, it would be strange indeed if plants were not minutely aware of changing light levels in the world around them, and all green plants can not only perceive and react to light level changes but also have the capacity to measure time.

Plants are static. Compared with animals, which can change their position in small or majestically large ways, a leafy plant must stay in one spot and cope with whatever seasonal weather variations the local climate throws at it. In the winter an animal can move into a cave, nest or roosting place to reduce the amount of heat its body loses; in a desert noon it will disappear down a burrow or hide in the shade of a rock to achieve the reverse advantage and augment heat loss from its body. These are small-scale adaptive movements compared with those at the other end of the distance scale. These are migrations, mass movements of whole species, sometimes half way round the globe, to avoid, either wholly or partially, the vicissitudes of the climate. A plant in a mid-

latitudinal location never has these options, so in one extra but crucial respect, it must be sensitively aware of its time position within the march of the seasons. On each day of the year it must be performing efficiently in the prevailing conditions, but it must also be ready for the next inevitable phase of environmental change. Whatever happens the plant or its offspring will have to live through those seasonal changes, since it cannot move away.

The growing season of a plant is the section, or sometimes the sections, of a year in which the variables of the environment—light, water and temperature—are at appropriate levels to allow new plant cells to be produced, thus enabling the plant to grow. In most plants growth will begin when temperature levels are capable of sustaining metabolic activity and when there is enough water available for this active metabolism. The beginning of growth in different types of green plant may mean quite different sorts of change. The initiation of growth may be the germination of a seed, and the rapid development of the plant embryo lodged inside it into a seedling and then a whole plant. Or the beginning of growth may be the time at which buds open, so that the active cells (the primordia) of leaves and shoots, which were laid down in miniature in the preceeding season, are suddenly pumped up to their full functional size and burst out of their protective bud scales. Or growth may begin in less obvious areas, for example in underground bulbs, tubers and rhizomes. Once formed, the new, leafy portions of the plant above the ground will grow, and ultimately produce structures for reproduction—most usually flowers and fruits, but less showy structures in 'primitive' plants, such as seaweeds, mosses and ferns. This continues until external conditions fall short

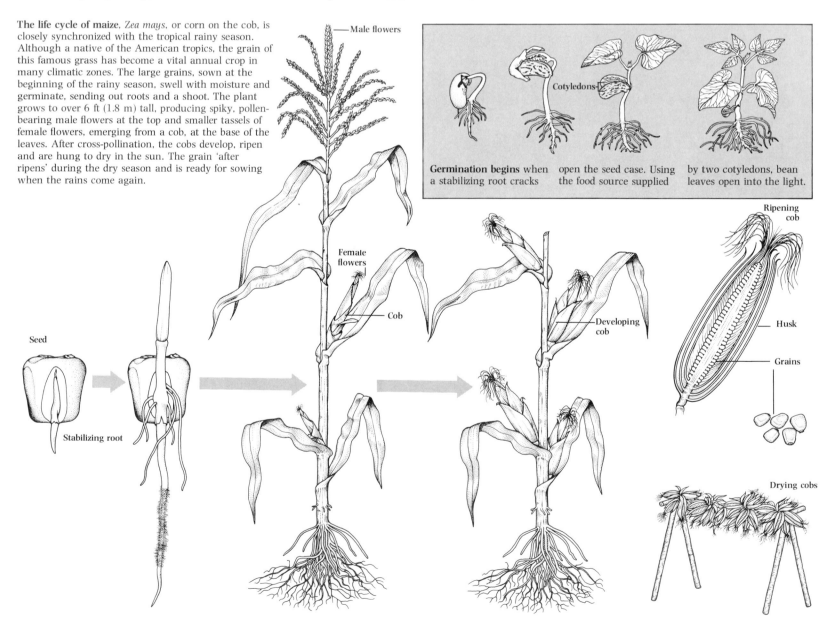

The life cycle of maize, *Zea mays*, or corn on the cob, is closely synchronized with the tropical rainy season. Although a native of the American tropics, the grain of this famous grass has become a vital annual crop in many climatic zones. The large grains, sown at the beginning of the rainy season, swell with moisture and germinate, sending out roots and a shoot. The plant grows to over 6 ft (1.8 m) tall, producing spiky, pollen-bearing male flowers at the top and smaller tassels of female flowers, emerging from a cob, at the base of the leaves. After cross-pollination, the cobs develop, ripen and are hung to dry in the sun. The grain 'after ripens' during the dry season and is ready for sowing when the rains come again.

Male flowers

Cotyledons

Germination begins when a stabilizing root cracks

open the seed case. Using the food source supplied

by two cotyledons, bean leaves open into the light.

Female flowers

Cob

Developing cob

Ripening cob

Husk

Grains

Seed

Stabilizing root

Drying cobs

of the necessary threshold levels in some way.

The unfavourable season for plant growth is not the same the world over. In the northern and southern temperate zones, conditions hostile to plant activity are usually related to cold. With the onset of winter, average temperatures drop too low for growth to occur. In the subtropical and tropical portions of the globe (except on mountain peaks), temperature is never, by itself, the limiting factor. Water is the growth factor whose absence makes a habitat inhospitable, and plants cease their activities near to the onset of the dry season. So plants have to be adaptable to cope with a cyclically varying pattern of seasonal climatic change most efficiently, although these adaptations vary between temperate and tropical regions. Whatever the specifics of such adaptation, one phase of each yearly cycle encourages plant growth and development, while the other prohibits it.

To solve this problem of seasonal change, plants have adopted utterly different life strategies. Annuals, which include nearly all weed species, are the plants that can grow quickly from a germinating seed at the beginning of the growing season, reach reproductive maturity rapidly and set seed, all within a matter of a few months at most. As resistant seeds they can last out the next danger period, be it one of drying heat or intense cold. Such plants are usually small in stature, have no woody tissues and can often squeeze in many seed-plant-flower-seed cycles during a single growing season.

Woody perennials, the world's shrubs, bushes and trees and many of its climbers, have a permanent structural framework of woody trunks and branches above ground which persists through many winters or dry seasons.

During these periods of inactivity, however, many tree species in the temperate zone, such as the deciduous oaks, beeches and maples, shed all their functional leaves. At the beginning of the next growing season dormant buds open to reveal new leaves that will be used for making food by photosynthesis during a single season. By the end of the growing season the tree or shrub will have produced a crop of seeds and also laid down a new set of buds for overwintering.

Non-woody herbaceous perennials, such as the grasses and a myriad other plants including irises, daffodils, snowdrops, anemones, primroses and tulips, persist through the harsh season by having a small amount of inactive foliage above ground or by means of below-ground storage organs, such as bulbs, corms, tubers or rhizomes. Spring initiates new growth in these plant parts—which incidentally act as organs of non-sexual reproduction—with the rapid production of new leaves, stems and flowers above ground.

Although the winters or the dry season are periods of hardship for plants, they have been utilized by those same plants as essential integrators of patterns of development. In cool and cold temperate regions, for example, seeds of plants of the rose family, Rosaceae, which includes apples, pears, apricots and peaches as well as roses themselves, need to experience severe cold before they can germinate. This process is a neat and convenient protective feature in the plant's life cycle. It ensures that seeds, produced early in the growing season, are not fooled by unseasonably mild weather into germinating just before winter sets in. In a similar way, some tropical and subtropical plants have seeds that need to go through a long dry season of conditioning before they are capable of germination.

▷

The crocus, *Crocus purpureus*, like many other temperate perennial plants survives the winter underground. Fuelled by food reserves stored in an underground corm, its cheerful flowers announce the end of winter. When the seeds have dispersed from the withered flowers in early summer, the leaves—their annual task complete—die down, leaving a new dormant corm above the old one. This then shrivels but lateral corms develop and break off to mature into separate plants the following spring. Meanwhile the seeds, which need the cold winter months to stimulate germination, grow into new plants, eventually producing their own corms and flowers. The crocus thus guarantees the rhythm of future generations by giving birth to two forms of offspring.

Stigma receives pollen

Male anthers produce pollen

Dispersal of seeds

New corm forming

Seedling produced from seed

Winter corm

The greenhouse is the gardener's way of beating nature's order. Controllable conditions allow him to grow otherwise impossible combinations of temperate and tropical plants. The natural variables of light, temperature, humidity and mineral nutrients can be automatically selected and controlled with the finest precision, enabling the horticulturalist to reconstruct a variety of conditions and habitats. While the normal rhythms of life persist outside, within the glasshouse a wide range of climates, seasons, soils and growing times are simulated convincingly enough for the plant to respond.

The seeds of flowering plants contain the embryos of new individuals and are the offspring of the plants that made them. Seeds are formed as a result of the complex process of pollination. During this process nuclei within a single male pollen grain fuse with nuclei within a female ovule of the flower. The ovule and pollen nuclei involved in this process of fertilization are made in a similar way to those of animal eggs and sperm and their fusion is analogous to the fertilization of an egg by a sperm.

There is nothing unusual about the fact that plants indulge in sexual reproduction. Plants use sex, and flowers are sexual organs. In the plant world flowers are the most sophisticated sort of sexual organs and are found in a staggering range of forms, with added layers of diversity generated by their scents and colours. Functionally, flowers can be divided into those adapted for pollination by means of physical agencies—most usually the wind but sometimes rain and very rarely water currents—and those that use animals as pollinators. Around the world, bees, wasps, ants, butterflies, moths, flies, beetles, slugs, birds, bats and even mice and marsupial possums are used by species of flowering plants as willing, if unwitting, partners in the pollination process. Urged on by some reward, which may be the gathering of pollen, guzzling nectar as food or even, in the case of some male wasps, the uncontainable urge to copulate with an orchid shaped and smelling like a mate, all these animals end up transferring pollen to new flowers, so achieving the cross-fertilization of the plants.

The male and female parts of the plant's reproductive equipment, respectively pollen-producing stamens and ovule-making ovaries, may both exist in one flower, although cross-fertilization with pollen from a different plant is usually necessary for seed to set. Male and female parts may be separate and located in different flowers on the same plant or even completely isolated from one another, in which case a plant species is divided into male and female plants. This explains why only the female plant of the holly tree, *Ilex*, can produce the showy red berries synonymous with Christmas and why only male trees of the North American shrub *Garrya* make the hanging display of eye-catching, pollen-producing catkins.

A flower is produced as a highly modified tip of a short branch, stem or twig. Indeed it is usually accepted that the petals of flowers and the sepals that surround them, which are usually green but may be brightly coloured and petal-like as in a tulip, are specialized forms of leaves, which gives the clue to the origin of the flower. In all flowering plants the growth of new stems and shoots occurs because of new cell production, concentrated into a small, but highly active, growth zone at the tip of the shoot. These points of seething plant activity are the meristems. At the end of a leafy shoot a meristem produces new cells that grow and elongate, then differentiate into particular cell types, including those that make up the tissues of new leaves.

The development of flower buds occurs when a hormone signal tells the meristems to begin making the cells of flower rather than those of a leafy shoot. It is in the control of the synthesis of such hormones—and also in more subtle ways—that photoperiodic stimuli come to exercise such a potent control over the timing of flowering. Many species of flowering plants can only begin to produce flowers, and thus begin their reproductive lives, when they experience

The flowering of most plants is triggered by a crucial number of daylight hours. The mature leaves perceive and interpret the photoperiodic changes and use the information to induce a wide range of physiological processes. Particular patterns of light and darkness stimulate internal chemical signals, which pass to the growing point of the plant and allow it to produce flowers instead of leafy shoots. While most plants cannot flower without receiving the relevant clues from the sun, some rely solely or partially upon other factors, such as temperature and humidity.

Apical meristem

Hormone signal

Long day plants such as spinach, Italian rye grass and henbane are so-called because they flower in the lengthening days of spring. Each plant has a critical photoperiod and only when the daylight lasts more than this crucial number of hours will the long day flowers appear.

Short day plants respond to the shortening days of late summer and autumn. The poinsettia, *Euphorbia pulcherrima*, for example, only flowers when there is less than 12.5 hours of daylight. Each plant produces its seed when its pollinators are active and conditions are most favourable for its development.

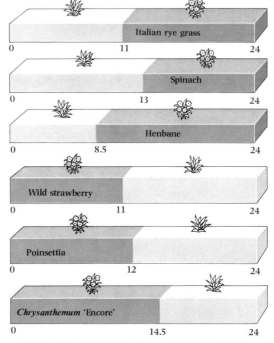

Italian rye grass
0   11   24

Spinach
0   13   24

Henbane
0   8.5   24

Wild strawberry
0   11   24

Poinsettia
0   12   24

Chrysanthemum 'Encore'
0   14.5   24

Since the annual changes in daylength vary according to latitude, the actual calendar date at which a plant reaches its critical photoperiod for flowering depends on where it is growing. A wild strawberry, for example, flowers when the days shorten to 11 hours. At 50° north of the Equator (Winnipeg, Canada; Land's End, England), this occurs in October, while were it to grow at 20° north (Mexico City) it would not flower until 21 December.

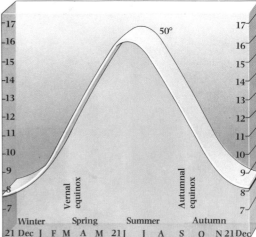

50°

Vernal equinox   Autumnal equinox

Winter   Spring   Summer   Autumn
21 Dec J F M A M 21 J J A S O N 21 Dec

particular lengths of daylight or, more commonly, darkness. It appears that it is the leaves that react to the length of days and nights by perceiving the changing patterns of light intensity created by the Earth's rotation round the sun. Acting almost like aerials, the leaves measure the photoperiod, and once the appropriate daylength occurs hormone signals are produced which switch on flower production. Because it is daylength and not the weather that is the crucial factor in the timing of flowering, gardeners can judge almost to the day when some of their specimens will bloom, and flower shows are often planned on this basis.

Some of the crucial early experiments that demonstrated the vital role of photoperiodicity in controlling the lives of long-lived organisms were carried out on plants. In 1920 two scientists named Garner and Allard, working in the US Department of Agriculture, first realized the crucial links between daylength and plant flowering. These workers were investigating a variety of the tobacco plant, *Nicotiana tabacum*, with the impressive name of 'Maryland Mammoth'. Irrespective of the date when the seeds which gave rise to the tobacco plants had been sown, the plants that grew from those seeds would only flower in the short days of winter. In experiments that have become models for much subsequent work in this field, Garner and Allard covered up some 'Maryland Mammoths' for part of each day during the long summer days. This simple and elegant manipulation was enough to fool the plants into believing that winter had arrived and they flowered out of season.

At a stroke, the experiment proved that, at least in these plants, flowering was controlled by daylength and that daylength was the master controlling factor, dominant over all other environmental clues. The plants rooted in their summer field were experiencing summer temperatures, but this signal was ignored because the photoperiod signal was telling a different story. In other experiments it proved possible to produce the reverse effect; in the winter it became feasible to prevent the tobacco plants from flowering by extending the apparent daylength with artificial lighting. These important studies from more than half a century ago created a conceptual revolution in botanical and agricultural thought. They also had immense practical and economic significance, because they showed with startling clarity how agriculturalists could manipulate the flowering period of some crop plants with relative ease.

Further studies have revealed that flowering plants can be conveniently divided into three categories on the basis of their response, in terms of flowering, to changing daylengths. 'Maryland Mammoth' tobacco plants are an example of short day plants, because short days and long nights induce such species and varieties to produce flowers while long days and short nights have an inhibitory effect on flowering. Chrysanthemums, dahlias, asters and golden rod are other good examples of short day plants. In contrast, long day plants will only flower when days are long and nights are short. When days are short their flowering is inhibited. Examples of such plants, which only flower in the lengthening days of late spring and early summer, include commercially important crops, such as clovers and beets. The final category comprises the 'daylength neutral' plants which appear to be able to flower whatever daylengths they are exposed to. Sunflowers, dandelions and tomatoes all respond in this fashion. ▷

Rainfall induced this Australian desert to bloom.

Once every 100 years the Chinese umbrella bamboo, *Thamnocalamus spathaceus*, flowers and dies. Other species of bamboo produce vegetation for 10, 20 or even 120 years, before all bursting into flower with an extraordinary display of species coordination. After flowering, the shoots die down, leaving roots and seeds to produce new plants. Sadly the giant panda has recently been a victim of the rare flowering of the umbrella bamboo, for its chief food source has died right down.

Flowering bamboo

▷ During the hunter-gatherer phase of man's evolutionary development, which must be considered to stretch back from about 10,000 years ago to man's origins among the large African apes between two and three million years ago, seeds and fruits must have been a highly significant component of his omnivorous diet. Why is it that these plant structures, which from the plant's viewpoint are protected embryonic offspring, are so important as foodstuffs? The answer is that they are usually packed with nutrients for the plant embryo to use when the seed begins to germinate. In the earliest phase of seed activation and germination, the tiny growing plantlet, first within the seed coats and then bursting out of them, is in a vulnerable position when it comes to food supplies. It is liable to begin its phase of explosive growth buried in the soil or under leaf litter, in other words in the pitch dark. While it is in this state it has water, but because it has no light photosynthesis cannot take place. Unlike its much larger, established parents, it cannot produce new nutrients for itself. Equally, until it has developed a functionally effective root system, it is unable to acquire mineral salts, vital to its biochemistry, from ground water.

To overcome these two early disadvantages, and to give the minute seedling a chance of becoming established, most seeds contain large stores of concentrated nutrients, including starches, fats and oils and rich protein mixtures, such as are found in peas, beans and other pulses and in nuts. Therefore, as long as it has a complement of biochemical catalysts or enzymes available within it, so that it can digest and mobilize these foods, plus some water, a seed is able to grow and develop with no sunlight and little, if any, access to mineral salts. During the first few days of life the seedling's nutritional organization slowly and progressively switches from dependence on these internal structures to nutritional independence. This final break from the food contained in the seed—which by this time is largely exhausted—comes with photosynthesis in the first seed leaves or cotyledons, and later in the first true leaves, which can fuel the plant's nutritional needs with the help of mineral salts and water drawn up by the newly formed roots.

Just as they attract animals to themselves to bring about the process of pollination, so plants also seduce creatures into activity as seed distributors by packaging small, tough, inconspicuous seeds in showy, colourful, juicy and sweet-tasting fruit flesh. As in pollination there is an evolutionarily generated plant-animal trade off. The animal is rewarded by fruit nutrients and vitamins for its role in dispersing the resistant, indigestible hard-coated seeds which are thrown aside, spat out or, if swallowed, pass through its gut undamaged. The seeds that travel the length of an animal's intestine before being deposited not only get a free ride to a new growing environment but are also deposited in their own patch of nitrogen-rich organic fertilizer—the animal's faeces. The efficacy of this partnership between animal and plant kingdoms is revealed in the rich crops of tomato plants that spring up every year in the sludge beds of sewage works.

About 10,000 years ago, in a number of sites around the world, societies of men and women took the first steps in the transition from being nomadic hunter-gatherers to forming settled agricultural groups. Instead of relying on their knowledge of the fruiting times of the natural plant forms in their habitats and, by their wanderings, making use of a wide range of plant food sources,

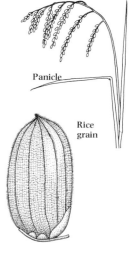

The rice harvest, at the beginning of the dry season, is perhaps the most significant event of the tropical year, as it feeds over half the world's population. In 1973, 320 million tons of rice were produced of which 15 million came from Thailand, *left*. The safe gathering of the crop is celebrated by many Asian rice growers as the beginning of the new year. Some perform a ritual symbolizing the successful union of two rice grains.

Panicle

Rice grain

Rice develops from a grain to a flowering panicle in about four months. Each panicle bears many tiny rice grains which mature 30 to 40 days after the flowers appear.

they began to plant their own crops. For each of the hundreds of plant species that has become domesticated by man and used for food, the story is roughly the same. A wild natural plant was originally gathered from its undisturbed setting and used as a source of nourishment. Then these completely unaltered plant types were grown together near human habitation. This was the crucial step, because once man started to select the seeds, suckers, tubers or bulbs that were to produce the next season's crop, an unconscious selection pressure was applied.

The human-induced selection pressure of selective breeding is immensely more powerful than the forces that operate in natural ecosystems and takes effect far more quickly. A woman living 10,000 years ago in an agricultural tribe, who, from a cluster of wild fruiting plants, took the seeds from only one plant with the biggest, juiciest fruits for sowing as the basis of the next year's crop, was changing the genetic structure of her domesticated stock. Modern geneticists and plant breeders have a much more sophisticated grasp of the processes underlying their activities and experiments, but the bulk of their work is conceptually the precise equivalent of that tribal woman's choice. So dramatic are the alterations brought about by just a few generations of domesticated breeding of plants—and animals too—that they were one of the key strands in Charles Darwin's web of interlinked evidence for evolutionary change.

The nutrition of modern man is completely dependent upon his ability to grow these radically altered, highly productive plant crops. Man's population is still increasing at an alarming rate, and the food requirements of the world's four billion people depend for their fulfilment on the evermore efficient husbandry of evermore productive crop plants. The phase of the agricultural process that conveys, above all others, the productivity of plant life and its significance to human societies is harvest. Harvesting is carried out when the cropable part of the domesticated plant has developed to a suitable and appropriate state for storage. Vital grain crops—wheat, rice, barley, oats and rye, which are all seeds of members of the grass family, Gramineae—we harvest when the seeds have dried out at the end of the growing season. Harvesting of soft fruit crops is timed to ensure the maximum survival time for the soft, edible part of the fruit, be it banana pulp, mango, strawberry or apple flesh.

In temperate climates one thinks instinctively of late summer and autumn as the time of harvest for, even though food crops are produced and mature all the year round, this is the time when the wheat is gathered in and most fruits plucked from their branches for winter storage. In tropical, subtropical and warm temperate climates harvest usually takes place at the end of the rainy growing season or at the beginning of a following dry season. The actual months depend, of course, upon exactly when the rainy and dry seasons occur. The sugar-cane harvest, upon which the economy of Cuba depends, takes place in the dry season from January to May, while groundnuts in the Kano region of Nigeria are lifted, and this lifting celebrated, after the rainy period in October and November. The completion of the harvest of any crop important to the survival of a community, even if the crop is poor, is usually a signal for a celebratory harvest festival. ▷

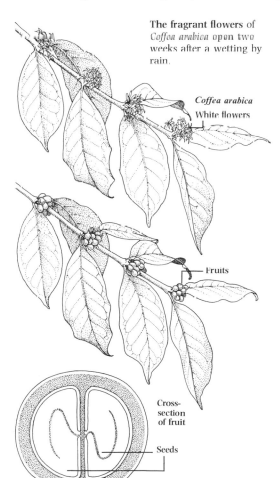

The fragrant flowers of *Coffea arabica* open two weeks after a wetting by rain.

Coffea arabica
White flowers

Fruits

Cross-section of fruit

Seeds

The evergreen coffee tree, *Coffea arabica*, which thrives in sub-tropical and tropical areas of Africa and America, produces 90 per cent of the world's coffee beans. The clumps of fruit, which develop 7 to 9 months after flowering, ripen over several weeks from a dull green to crimson, when they are ready for harvesting. Each fruit contains two seeds which are dried in the sun, and roasted to form coffee beans.

All wine-producing vines belong to a single species, *Vitis vinifera*, which prefers a temperate, Mediterranean climate. Left to itself, the vine grows rampant, sending out vigorous woody tendrils and poor fruit. In commercial vineyards the vine is regularly pruned, which channels the plant's energy into grape production. Most cultivated vines grow from grafted cuttings, and in the northern hemisphere sprout in April and May.

Tender vine shoots grow quickly into leaves and tendrils in mid-May.

Flowers appear in early June as soon as the days warm to 18°C (65°F).

Grapes form in June and begin to ripen in August for an October harvest.

▷ In Europe and North America the traditions and superstitions woven into the fabric of the harvest period provide some very powerful images. Many of these traditions, although now incorporated into notionally Christian ceremonies such as the autumnal harvest festival, undoubtedly stem from pre-Christian practices. In nutritional terms the grain harvest was often one of the most vital because, when properly dried, grass grain has excellent long-term storage properties. It is, perhaps, a mixture of unconscious racial memory of the importance of a fruitful harvest and the traditions that have been directly passed on down the generations that makes the image of the grain harvest so potent. Harvest time is linked in our minds with pictures of golden ripe corn rustling in the wind, of loaves plaited into sheaves, of corn dollies and of children bearing gifts of apples, pears and pumpkins.

It is easy to understand why spring and autumn, the transitional seasons of the temperate zone, in which the year's most dramatic changes take place, should have strong plant-related connotations. The most powerful images pass indelibly into the language; thus for North Americans, autumn is the fall and the fall is the annual, autumnal shedding of the leaves of deciduous trees. Leaf dropping is not, as might be imagined, the direct effect of the damaging environmental influences of the approaching winter. It is nothing to do with leaves being killed by declining temperatures or dropping nutrient levels in the soil. Leaf fall is a spectacular adaptation by plants, performed actively by the plants themselves, as a preparation for the damaging season which is soon—and predictably—to occur. This time-lag is crucial to an understanding of the whole process. The fact that the loss of leaves is a precautionary strategy means

that it cannot be triggered in time by the external environmental factors it is designed to avoid.

During the separation, or abscission, of leaf stalks (petioles) from tree branches, a layer of corky tissue is laid down between the end of the petiole and the branch. This abscission layer creates a seal to prevent the loss of vital sap from the branch and, once complete, allows the leaf to stay in position until only a breath of wind is needed to blow it off and carry it to the ground. The timing of abscission demands an elaborate chronological sense on the plant's part. At each moment it must know where it stands in the 12-month sequence of seasonal change and act at the appropriate time to drop its leaves before the onset of winter. As one might expect, the trick of perfect timing is accomplished by a photoperiodic response. Reacting to reducing daylength, rather than declining temperature, the temperate deciduous tree initiates the complex physiological process which, when complete, will leave it as a bare skeleton throughout the winter months. In the cool temperate subzone almost all the non-coniferous trees do shed their leaves before the onset of winter. The exceptions are so conspicuous by their unorthodoxy that they have often become endowed with supposedly magical powers. The laurel, holly and ivy are all excellent examples of broad-leafed evergreens with a firm place in folk culture and medicine.

The visual impact of the fall is not principally the result of leaf loss itself, impressive though that change may be. It is more the gloriously vivid shades of gold, red, orange and brown of the dying leaves that are unforgettable. Arguably, the eastern fringes of the world's major temperate continents have

Every year the Bactrian, or two-humped camel, grows an immensely thick winter coat, which allows it to travel for many days in freezing temperatures beyond the endurance of most large mammals. This makes it an invaluable beast of burden in its native Asian territory north of the Himalayas. The coat, which has a shaggy layer of long outer hairs and a lining of fine protective underwool, having protected the camel from the severe winter undergoes a dramatic moult in the spring. A fine film of summer hair replaces the woolly bulk, apparently reducing the animal to half its winter size, giving it a naked, shaven look and revealing the two fat-storing humps.

Seasonal changes in coat colour provide camouflage for many mammals living in the higher latitudes. The stoat, for example, adopts its white 'ermine' form during the winter, to hide from its prey in the snow.

Stoat   Ermine

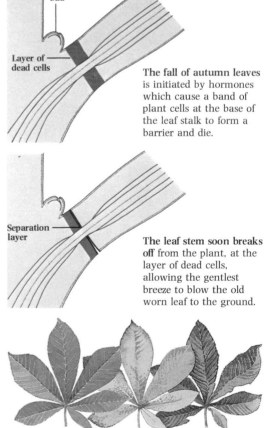

Axillary bud   Leaf stalk

Layer of dead cells

The fall of autumn leaves is initiated by hormones which cause a band of plant cells at the base of the leaf stalk to form a barrier and die.

Separation layer

The leaf stem soon breaks off from the plant, at the layer of dead cells, allowing the gentlest breeze to blow the old worn leaf to the ground.

The autumnal changes of colour in these horsechestnut leaves reflect the internal chemical changes which allow the tree to survive from year to year. During the winter when the soil is cold, it becomes more difficult for the plant roots to absorb water as quickly as the leaves transpire. So deciduous trees shed their leaves, having first stored the nutrients contained in them, and their functions slow down. Sugar, protein and the green-coloured chlorophyll are withdrawn, leaving carotenoid pigments, which produce the familiar autumn tints before the leaf falls.

the most splendid autumnal leaf displays. Certainly New England and the eastern edge of mainland China are noted for their abrupt and vibrant spectacles of fall. This is partly the result of meteorological factors which make the transition from summer to winter much more rapid in these regions. In the United Kingdom the autumn period is, in contrast, spread over several months often beginning in late August and persisting until as late as November or early December.

To understand why colour change is associated with leaf fall, it is essential to make a closer examination of the physiological processes that bring it about. In relation to the initiation of flowering, leaves are the aerials that detect changes in daylength. During the shortening days of autumn, leaves, which recognize this change, set in motion a series of alterations within themselves that bring about a form of voluntary euthanasia of the leaf.

The loss of all the leaves in their active, functioning state would represent an enormous loss of past investment on the part of the tree. It would mean the sacrifice of its 'stocks and shares'—great quantities of sugars, proteins and precious minerals such as magnesium, all of them garnered and constructed from raw materials at enormous energy cost. To avoid losses of this magnitude, the leaf cashes in its investments and is stripped of its removable nutrient assets before being relinquished for ever by the plant that built it. A wide range of nutrients is extracted and passed back into the framework of the tree. In particular, the principle complex molecule concerned with photosynthesis, namely the green pigment chlorophyll, is reabsorbed and removed from the leaves. It is this salvaging process that changes the leaf colour. Golds, reds and oranges are not pigments added to the leaf at fall time; they have been there all the time and are a variety of pigments related to carotene, the orange substance that gives carrots their colour. In summer the carotenoid pigments of most leaves are masked by a preponderance of green chlorophyll, and only when the chlorophyll is extracted, immediately before leaf fall, does the pattern of the other hues emerge.

Plants, especially trees, provide the most unmistakable and extensive colour changes that occur in living things on a seasonal basis, but animals also change their appearance with the seasons. Alterations of this sort may be brought about directly by changes in temperature or other external stimuli: lizards and amphibians become lighter in colour, for instance, as the temperature of their surroundings increases. This colour change is an adaptation which enables these cold-blooded creatures, which have no physiological machinery for controlling their body temperature from within, to reflect more heat when it is sunny and, conversely, to absorb more when the environment is cooler. Other animals change their colour or the nature of their outer covering to prepare themselves for a predictable, seasonal change and, as with leaf fall, this means that the changes must be triggered indirectly. Such changes are best seen in a range of adaptations employed by birds and mammals, which enable them to survive through the coming cold winter months.

The adaptations of birds and mammals may entail the swapping of dark plumage or fur for a white, camouflaging alternative for the snowy winter, and in the case of the ermine stoat, *Mustela erminea*, the white, dark-spotted winter fur has become highly prized by man and symbolic of aristocracy. The physical ▷

Apical bud bursting

Leaf stalk scar

The scars of the previous year's leaf fall can be seen on the budding horsechestnut twig, *above*. The old leaf's food and water-conducting vessels appear as 'nails' in the protective horseshoe-shaped cork seal.

This golden autumn in the Utah valley is typical of the spectacular fall in North America, where the transition from summer to winter is more rapid than in Europe. The endless revitalizing rhythm of the seasons is frozen in this view of millions of dying leaves.

▷ insurance premium for lasting out the winter may consist of a change in the thermal insulating properties of fur by an increase in the length or thickness of the hair. Changes of this sort, which pre-date the coming of the snow, are usually a mixture of inbuilt annual rhythms operating via hormonal changes and kept locked to real external seasonal time by photoperiodic clues. Only when daylength is short enough will the correct hormones be released to initiate the appropriate alterations in body structure. With the arrival of spring and increasing daylength, extra fur is moulted and colours change back to their summer shades.

Trees that are unable to escape the rigours of a snowy, cool temperate winter make use of leaf fall to protect themselves in the frigid months of the year. A very few vertebrate animals can make use of a protective method of coping with winter cold which is every bit as drastic as the defoliation of ashes, oaks, maples and the like. This method—hibernation—is used by only a small minority of warm-blooded vertebrate animals and all but one of these hibernators are mammals.

Some hedgehogs, woodchucks, ground squirrels, hamsters, bats and dormice hibernate, and the last of these examples provides a linguistic clue to the essential nature of the hibernation process. The dormouse is not, in strict zoological terms, a mouse at all. Its popular name comes from the French word *dormeuse*, meaning a sleeper. In the winter months, in the harsh conditions of the wild, hibernating animals change from the normal activity of warm-blooded creatures and enter a cold, sleep-like state. A single bird is known to undergo the same type of alteration, namely the North American 'poor-will'

nightjar, *Phalaeonoptilus nuttalli*. Many animals commonly supposed to hibernate, including bears, squirrels and badgers, do not, in fact, do so. Instead these animals enter a state of torpor.

What, then, is the difference between hibernation and torpor? Strictly, hibernation is the process confined to animals which can normally maintain a high and consistent body temperature close to 37.8 degrees centigrade (100 degrees F) against the ever-changing pattern of ambient temperature. Under some circumstances, however, the true hibernator can give up this controlled maintenance of body-warmth. Instead it behaves, at one level, like a cold-blooded reptile or amphibian by allowing its body temperature to fall to values close to those of its environment, which may be as low as freezing point, 0 degrees centigrade (32 degrees F).

For nearly all mammals and birds that do not hibernate body-cooling of this magnitude is rapidly lethal. In these typical forms a whole range of vital processes, such as the muscle contraction needed to maintain the heartbeat, collapses at temperatures well above freezing. In a hibernating animal, however, everything carries on working in the cold state. Breathing continues, but it is slow and shallow. The heart carries on beating and pushes chilled, thick blood around the body, but it beats much more slowly than at normal body temperatures. It is as if all the creature's life processes have dropped down into the lowest of low gears. The significance of the tremendous slowing of metabolism is an immense saving in energy expenditure.

Many scientists think that this technique of energy conservation in winter conditions is usually employed by mammals which first evolved in tropical and

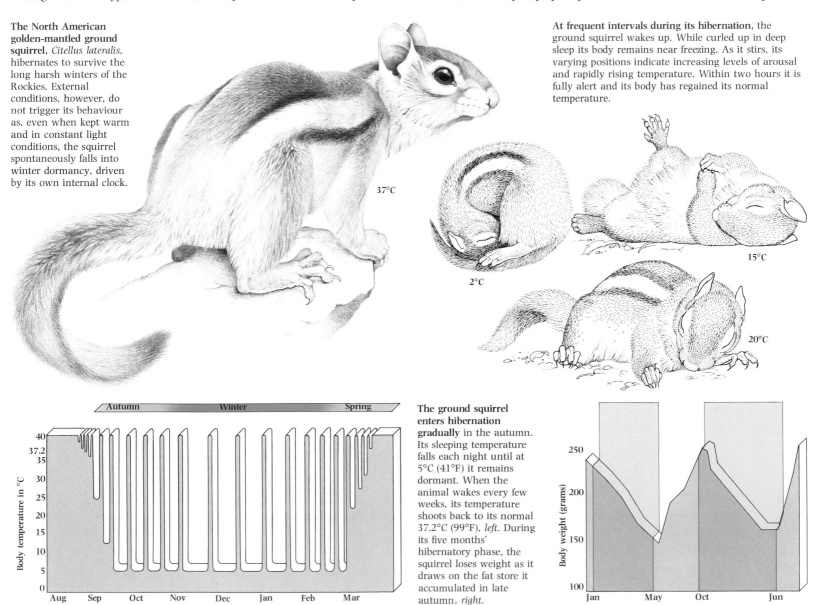

The North American golden-mantled ground squirrel, *Citellus lateralis*, hibernates to survive the long harsh winters of the Rockies. External conditions, however, do not trigger its behaviour as, even when kept warm and in constant light conditions, the squirrel spontaneously falls into winter dormancy, driven by its own internal clock.

37°C

At frequent intervals during its hibernation, the ground squirrel wakes up. While curled up in deep sleep its body remains near freezing. As it stirs, its varying positions indicate increasing levels of arousal and rapidly rising temperature. Within two hours it is fully alert and its body has regained its normal temperature.

2°C

15°C

20°C

The ground squirrel enters hibernation gradually in the autumn. Its sleeping temperature falls each night until at 5°C (41°F) it remains dormant. When the animal wakes every few weeks, its temperature shoots back to its normal 37.2°C (99°F), *left*. During its five months' hibernatory phase, the squirrel loses weight as it draws on the fat store it accumulated in late autumn, *right*.

subtropical climates, but which have later colonized cool temperate zones. The patterns of physiological adaptations acquired in the warmer initial habitats seem to have made adaptation to a life of high activity in cooling conditions difficult or impossible. Instead, the hibernator opts out of any active existence during the winter period. For animals, such as hedgehogs or bats, which feed predominantly on insect prey, winter is also a time when their essential food items are hard to come by, so hibernation gives them an added advantage in the survival game.

The two conditions of torpor and hibernation are similar but hibernation is, in all respects, more extreme. Hibernation involves lower body temperatures and greater metabolic slowing and lasts for much longer periods than typical torpor. In most respects these differences are those of degree rather than of type. Thus a torpid bear does have a reduced heart rate and breathing rate. Its metabolism is slowed and it may stop urinating for several months, but the torpid bear's body temperature is only a few degrees, at most, below that of an active summer bear and never approaches freezing point as that of a hibernating ground squirrel or dormouse does.

Within the entire animal kingdom there are a number of other changes and protective metabolic states which help the animals that employ them to survive in harsh conditions, occurring in a seasonably regular fashion. Many insects go into a switched-off state of suspended animation or diapause, often in response to daylength clues which signal that harsh environmental conditions are on their way. This is part of the answer to the question, 'Where do flies go in winter?' In the larvae of the Khapra beetle, *Trogoderma granarium*, a native of

India which infests stores of wheat, maize and other grains, diapause induced by low temperatures, desiccation or starvation, as well as changing daylength, may last as long as eight years. This long diapause has made these larvae a menace in the holds of grain-carrying cargo vessels because they are almost impossible to eradicate.

Some tropical vertebrates, living in habitats that cycle between intense dry heat and a flooded rainy season throughout a 12-month period, are able to protect themselves by entering a state of aestivation which is almost exactly the tropical equivalent of hibernation. During the dry season, when the availability of water drops to dangerously low levels, aestivating animals sit out the conditions in some protected location, using levels of metabolism that will only slowly consume nutrients stored within their bodies. The African lungfish, *Protopterus*, for example, burrows into the mud at the bottom of its swampy home in advance of the approaching dry season. When the dry season arrives in earnest, the swamps become completely dried up and the fish survive in mud cocoons beneath the baked mud surface. Months later, returning rains stimulate the fish back into activity, and they wriggle from their cocoons and escape from their burrows. Villagers in some parts of the Sudan use a novel method for discovering these tasty underground fish as the rainy season approaches. Village women walk over the hard, dried mud flats rattling their fingers loudly on gourds to make a sound like rain beating on the ground. Hearing the sound, the aestivating lungfish think the rains have arrived and start to emit grunting noises—at which moment they are promptly dug up and eaten.

Lack of insect food and an inadequate coat make hibernation a useful survival strategy for the hedgehog, *Erinaceus europaeus*. Sheltered in a hedgerow or under a pile of leaves, the hedgehog rolls into a tight prickly ball for the winter, relying on its thin spiky skin to deter predators and its store of fat to sustain it.

When milder weather returns in March, the hedgehog reinjects life into its sleepy body. Like other hibernators, it activates energy-rich deposits of brown fat to raise its temperature from near 0°C to 37°C (98.4°F). Within hours, enough energy is generated by the fat to return the body's physiological functions to normal.

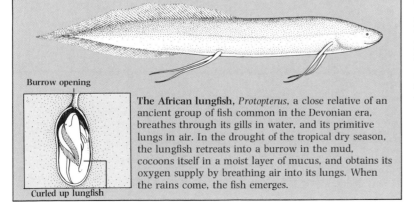

Burrow opening

Curled up lungfish

The African lungfish, *Protopterus*, a close relative of an ancient group of fish common in the Devonian era, breathes through its gills in water, and its primitive lungs in air. In the drought of the tropical dry season, the lungfish retreats into a burrow in the mud, cocoons itself in a moist layer of mucus, and obtains its oxygen supply by breathing air into its lungs. When the rains come, the fish emerges.

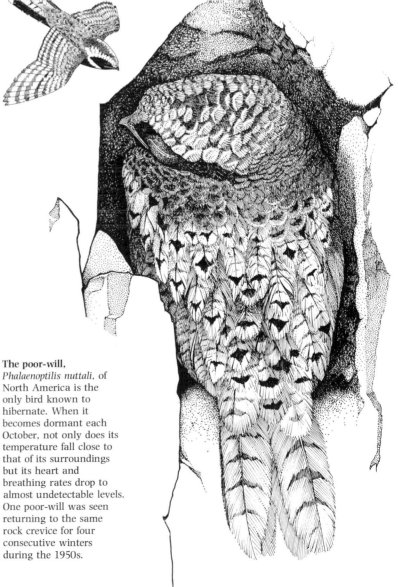

The poor-will, *Phalaenoptilis nuttali*, of North America is the only bird known to hibernate. When it becomes dormant each October, not only does its temperature fall close to that of its surroundings but its heart and breathing rates drop to almost undetectable levels. One poor-will was seen returning to the same rock crevice for four consecutive winters during the 1950s.

Rhythms within rhythms

Why is it that birds only sing in chorus at dawn? Why do crabs manage to hide under stones before low tide exposes them to the air? And why do cuckoos always arrive in the north in April? These and countless others, are examples of the way in which nature keeps abreast of the Earth's timetable of days, tides and seasons. The astronomical condition of living on a rotating planet which, together with its moon, circles around a star—the sun—places all of Earth's organisms in an environment whose time structure is composed of these three inescapable rhythms.

Night and day, high and low tide, summer and winter all involve spectacular differences in the amount of sunlight, dryness, temperature and many other environmental elements to which a creature is exposed. But few species are adapted to withstand the extremes that result from these rhythms. This problem is perhaps most obvious in tidal animals whose environment changes every six hours or so from being fully aquatic to being, in effect, terrestrial, but the rhythms of days and seasons can be equally dramatic. Animals are active either during the day or at night but usually not both, because to be both diurnal and nocturnal poses conflicting physiological demands—for example the ability to see well by night and also by day. While some creatures, such as cats and foxes, do have the ability to see and hunt well night and day, the structure of the eye of a nocturnal animal is actually different from that of the eye of a diurnal animal. Likewise for season: almost perversely it seems, snowdrops and crocuses come into flower in the depths of winter yet, by doing so, avoid direct competition from the quicker-growing but frost-sensitive annuals that smother them in summer.

These advantages of adjusting to nature's rhythms seem logical and reasonably easy to understand. But how and why did they arise, for surely primitive life had no need to be so sophisticated? The answer to this question may well lie in the composition of the Earth's early atmosphere. Four or five billion years ago, when life was struggling to assemble itself from the ingredients of the primeval soup, our planet was not protected from the sun's highly destructive ultra-violet radiation by an upper atmospheric screen of ozone as it is today. Thus the environment fluctuated violently between the searing radiation of the day and the freezing darkness of night, and it seems probable that primitive life would not have survived for long had it not developed some kind of timekeeping ability that restricted its more radiation-sensitive processes to the nighttime hours. That timekeeping ability ultimately became built into the genetic specification of early plants and animals, so that it not only had far-reaching implications for their lives but was passed on to the countless generations that followed.

All the many kinds of biological rhythms can be divided into two quite different and distinct categories. On the one hand there are all those biological functions which, especially in animals, just happen to work by oscillating—heartbeat, breathing, transmission of nerve impulses, and so on. These rhythms are not related to external time in any important sense, so that heartbeat and breathing, for example, vary mainly in relation to the demands of the body tissues for oxygen. Quite different are the rhythms by which animals and plants make the vital adjustments in their lives to the three basic periodicities of their environment—daily, lunar-tidal and annual. These three rhythms are specifically and exclusively concerned with environmental time and this chapter is devoted to them alone.

In an accurate but involuntary response to the daily, tidal, lunar and annual rhythms of the world around them, animals and plants have become adapted to their environment. These adaptations evolved so that organisms could order their lives according to the chronological arrangement of the world, and each species has its own characteristic relationship with the day, the tide or the year. From the opening of flowers to the mating behaviour of animals, all the members of a species must be active at roughly the same time if they are to breed and reproduce their kind successfully. Moreover, each individual of that species must have an inbuilt physiological timetable so that it can make suitable internal preparations in its body chemistry for the different activities which it performs around the clock.

This timetabling lies at the heart of all biological rhythms, whether daily, tidal, lunar or annual, and consists of two quite separate but closely interacting parts. One part is the organism's physiology, organized so that it cycles at approximately the right speed—once every 24 hours, or once each tide, or month, or year. The other part of the timetabling mechanism involves the environment and the responses the organism makes to the relevant cues, such as sunrise and sunset, which it receives from its surroundings about the passage of time. In this way the two parts interlock to keep the organism adjusted to local solar time, and they act together as if they comprised the mechanism of a clock—not a mechanical one, but a biological clock. We will come to the physiological reality and possible composition of such clocks later, but first it is necessary to be clear about some of the terms that are used to describe and to analyse them.

Both the rhythm of the organism and the rhythm of environmental change have some starting point—for example sunrise and waking up—and end up back at the same point 24 hours later, each having passed through one complete cycle of day and night, or activity and sleep. A rhythm is, thus, a continuous series of repeated cycles, each one very like the last. The result of this series of cycles is an oscillation, whether in the environment's light-dark cycle or in an animal's waking and sleeping behaviour. A pendulum does the same thing, repeatedly swinging through one full traverse and back again to complete each cycle of its oscillation, so providing a most useful and appropriate model rhythm with which to examine the terms that biologists have borrowed from physicists and engineers in order to study life's rhythms.

Imagine a pendulum set up with a pen fixed to it so that with each swing it traces an arc on to a piece of paper placed against it. If the paper is now moved downward at a steady speed, while the pendulum keeps swinging, the pen will trace a curving sinusoidal wave-form on to the paper. Turned on its side this wave will look like a smoothed-out version of the record of the 'sleep' movements of the leaf of the *Mimosa pudica* plant illustrated below, as it folds down its foliage at night and opens it up again during daylight. The up and down displacement of the line will show the amplitude of the pendulum's oscillation. The horizontal axis drawn along the paper represents time, and the distance between successive peaks of the trace is known as the period of the oscillation. The period of a rhythm is, thus, the time taken for the completion of one whole cycle, but here this is represented as distance along the paper—the actual distance depending on the speed at which the paper was moved.

The so-called 'sensitive' plant is a small species of the *Mimosa* genus that folds its leaves within a few seconds of being touched. The tiny leaflets close together against the leaf's midrib which then folds down at a joint in its stalk, *near left*. The plant also apparently 'goes to sleep' since at night the leaves fold in the same way, whereas by day they spread out in the sun. Few plants show the touch response but many show the daily rhythm of these sleep movements, especially those like *Mimosa pudica, far left*. which belong to the bean family (Leguminosae). This rhythm may be readily demonstrated using the apparatus, *above*. The leaf's midrib is joined by a thread to a light, pivoted arm at the other end of which is a small pen. The pen presses lightly on to a sheet of paper wrapped round a cylinder driven by clockwork to make one full revolution in a week. Thus, when the leaf rises during the day the pen moves down; when it folds down at night the pen moves up. The result is a roughly snake-shaped or sinusoidal record showing a rhythm with seven nighttime peaks and seven daytime troughs.

Another measure of the speed of a rhythm is its frequency, that is, the number of cycles it completes in a given time. Thus the frequency of a rhythm such as a human heartbeat is about 70 cycles a minute. This is, of course, a high frequency rhythm compared with the very low frequency of the environmental rhythms of day and night, moon and tides and the changing seasons: the frequency of the sleep-waking cycle is once every 24 hours, of leaf fall and renewal once a year. Mathematically frequency is the reciprocal of—or, colloquially, 'one over'—the period, so that as the period of a rhythm increases its frequency decreases and vice versa. And the pendulum shows this too. because the longer its arm, the longer its swing takes, so the greater its period and the lower its frequency.

Any particular point in a rhythm is a phase. It is essential to have some definable phase of a rhythm to know where the phase is in relation to the whole cycle and that of the rhythm itself. The period of the pendulum's rhythm, for example, can be identified by the positions of the peaks in its pen record. The peak is one convenient phase point to take but, equally, so is the trough or any other point in its oscillation. In theory, every cycle of a rhythm goes through an infinite number of phases, but in practice it is sensible to select easily identifiable ones. In the movement rhythm of the mimosa leaf, for example, any position of the leaves could be used as a reference phase, but it is easier to refer to the obvious phases of maximum daytime extension or maximum nighttime folding.

The phase of a rhythm is not only useful descriptively, but also brings out an important concept that ties the two parts of the biological clock mechanism

together—the physiological and the environmental. Mimosa has its leaves open by day and closed at night, and that is the phase-relationship between the plant's physiological rhythm (leaf position) and the rhythm of the environment (day/night). This phase-relationship stresses the significance of all such environmentally timed rhythms, whether they are daily, tidal, lunar or annual. There is a constant phase-setting of the organism's rhythm in relation to that of its environment. Thus nocturnal animals are active only at night, diurnal ones by day—the function of their biological timekeeping is to regulate this cycle of activity.

If the timing of the environmental cycle is changed, then the organism's cycle will be upset too, but it will, in due course, reacquire its old phase-relationship with the environment. In man the temporarily debilitating phenomenon of jet lag, after long-distance air travel across several time zones, sums up the problem admirably.

When you travel by jet aircraft from London to San Francisco your environment is changed so that it gets dark about eight hours later than you are used to. After a day or so, however, you adopt San Francisco time as your new temporal environment, although your underlying physiological rhythms may take several more days to catch up with your social schedule. In the laboratory it is easy to carry out equivalent experiments on animals or plants by changing their lighting schedule, and then seeing how they phase-shift to adapt themselves to the new conditions.

Except for organisms that live in tidal waters, and those such as bacteria that have a very short life-span, the most obvious expression of biological ▷

The main characteristics of any rhythm are illustrated on a record of the daily movement of the mimosa leaves, top right. The obvious oscillation is the daily repeated cycle of the up-down-up sequence of leaf movement. Each cycle is the same and lasts for 24 hours, which is the period of the rhythm. The rhythm's frequency is the number of cycles it completes in some chosen length of time, eg once in 24 hours. The amount by which the rhythm moves up and down is its amplitude, ie the maximum distance between the leaf's day and night positions. Any particular point in a rhythm is a phase: the phase of lowest leaf position is at midnight, for example, and of highest leaf position at noon. Each phase occurs only once per cycle and has a specific relationship with external solar time. This relationship can be changed experimentally by altering the cycle of light and dark. In this instance, below right, the first two days duplicate the external conditions of 12 hours light and 12 hours dark. The third dark period is extended by an extra eight hours and the plant's rhythm is temporarily suspended. When the lights are turned on again, the leaves resume their movement, but the phase of maximum leaf position has now shifted with respect to the record above it and hence to the real world.

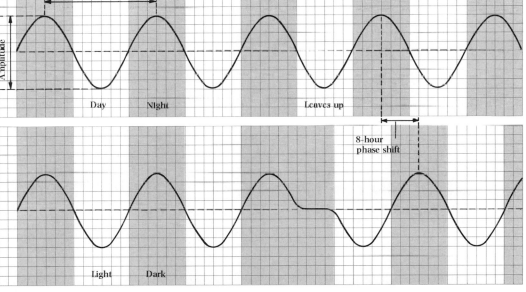

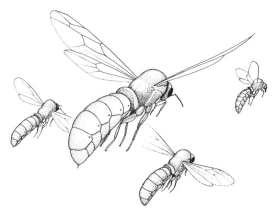

Varying rhythms allow different species to share out the environment's resources by using them at different times. The chart shows the flying times of five closely related male ant species of the genus *Dorylus* occupying the same habitat in the Ugandan jungle.

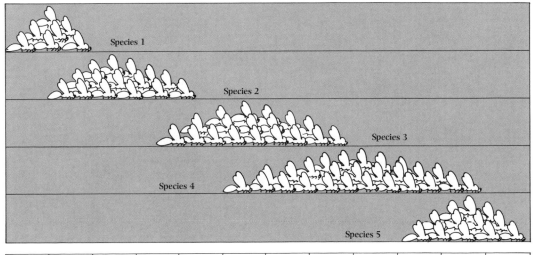

Sunset   Midnight   Sunrise

▷ timekeeping for virtually all organisms is their daily 24-hour rhythmicity. This property influences almost every aspect of their lives, making them hatch, grow, respire, feed, manufacture food products, move, mate and even die more at some times of day than at others. Even the simplest single-celled animals and plants have daily rhythms just as striking and almost as accurate as those of the mostly highly evolved mammals and the most complex flowering plants such as trees.

Because organisms tend to exploit their environment's resources at particular times they are firmly tied, in terms of both their behaviour and their physiology, to particular conditions of temperature, humidity and, most important of all, light. A simple answer to the question of why each different species has a particular phase-relationship with its environment could be that each responds to a particular phase of the daylight cycle—say dawn—and only becomes active because it is nudged by the environment to do so: just as a man can set his alarm clock to wake him up at the same time each morning. If this were so, then the logical implication would be that rhythms are nothing more than direct responses to environmental time cues and, therefore, no more inherently rhythmic than are the hands of a clock when deprived of a pendulum or hairspring to drive them.

There is, however, more to animal and plant rhythms than mere immediate responses to signals from their surroundings; organisms do seem to possess some form of internal timekeeping mechanism. While the animal or plant is in conditions of natural periods of daylight and darkness this inner mechanism may be impossible to detect. The solution is to bring the organism into the laboratory, subject it to experimental light schedules and then measure its activity.

First an organism must be chosen for experiment—say a golden hamster or a flying squirrel since both these mammals have clear activity rhythms. Next the creature must be placed in an artificial light cycle, set at a slightly different time from the natural day-night cycle outside the laboratory. When this is done one finds invariably that the animal takes a few days to settle down, while its rhythm gradually phase-shifts to meet the new timing of its environment, as it happens in a man who has just stepped off a transatlantic flight. The creature then adapts its normal phase-relationship to the light cycle. As all the other major environmental conditions, including temperature, humidity, noise and so on are kept constant throughout the experiment, two things are clear: one, that the rhythm does continue in a highly artificial situation with the only time cue present being that from the light cycle and, two, that the rhythm phase-shifts to a new setting if the timing of the light cycle is changed in any significant way.

This gradual phase-shifting over a few days strongly suggests that the animal may have an underlying internal rhythmicity. For if the activity rhythm were merely a direct response to the light cycle it would have changed immediately to the new setting, on the very first day of the experiment. Even so, the presence of the light cycle prevents us from knowing for sure that the animal's rhythm is not due, in large part, to the fact that the light rhythm is driving it.

The second part of the experiment must be to test what happens when the

The rhythms of locomotor activity of small mammals and large insects can be measured in the running-wheel apparatus, *below*. The wheel is joined to a pen-recorder so that each revolution completes an electrical circuit and makes a lateral 'blip' on an ink trace drawn on a piece of continuously moving paper. An animal, such as a flying squirrel or a cockroach, is placed in the wheel and left to run according to its own behavioural demands. The apparatus records the animal's activity as groups of 'blips' that signify bursts of running.

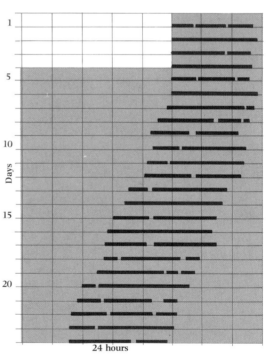

24 hours

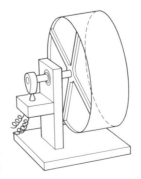

The North American flying squirrel, *Glaucomys volans*, is a nocturnal tree dwelling mammal. Folds of skin joining its front and hind legs enable it to glide from tree to tree.

Running wheel experiments ensure that the animal has ample food and water and is left undisturbed for several weeks in a strictly controlled environment. To analyze the record of its running activity, the paper is cut into lengths representing 24 hours, and each day is pasted up beneath the preceding one as shown *above*. The heavily inked parts of the trace correspond to the time when the animal was active. In this instance, a flying squirrel was used and for the first four days its activity coincided with night in the natural environment. From the end of the fourth night the squirrel was kept in constant darkness for the next 19 days so that it no longer had any 24-hour time cues from the light. Its rhythm nevertheless continued, slowly drifting with respect to external solar time. Still active for the same length of time, it began its activity about half an hour earlier each day. Its rhythm was thus free-running according to a $23\frac{1}{2}$-hour day, which is the squirrel's inherent circadian periodicity.

animal is deprived of all environmental time cues by placing it in constant and complete darkness. When this is done, two significant facts are revealed. First, the rhythm continues unabated, which means that its driving force certainly does not depend on a light cycle. Second, and even more interestingly, the rhythm does not continue at exactly 24 hours per cycle, but drifts relative to external, solar time as measured by the hands of the clock on the laboratory wall.

Had the rhythm of rest and activity continued in constant darkness with the same precise 24-hour period it showed in the 24-hour light cycle, it could conceivably have been due to the animal responding to unsuspected external time cues that were not controlled during the experiment—for instance, barometric pressure or magnetic field. But that did not happen. Instead, the rhythm ran at a frequency that differed slightly, but consistently, from 24 hours per cycle, whereas all the likely—and indeed unlikely—uncontrolled time cues from the environment run at the rate of exactly 24 hours because, like light and darkness, they arise from the effects of the earth's daily rotation about its axis.

This free-running drift of the 24-hour rhythm is strong evidence in favour of the proposition that the rhythm is internally controlled, that is, driven by a physiological 'clock' system from within the organism. The same drift is, in fact, characteristic of almost all the daily rhythms in plants and animals that have so far been studied. Moreover, the period of all such free-running rhythms in constant conditions rarely differs by more than an hour or two from 24, typically falling within the range of 22 to 28 hours per cycle. It is this narrow range of period that gives such rhythms their technical identifying description

of circadian, a word derived from the Latin words *circa* meaning about and *diem*, a day. Nearly all tidal, lunar and even annual rhythms that have so far been tested in constant conditions also free-run and are thus described as circatidal, circalunar (or circumlunar) and circannual.

Although circadian rhythms free-run in the laboratory it is obvious to even the most casual observer that they do not do so in nature. What happens, of course, is that each individual's rhythm is set so that it has a constant phase-relationship with the environment according to the day-night cycle. And this brings us full circle to the dual nature of biological rhythms: the rhythmicity of the environment is said to entrain the internal rhythm of the organism to an exact 24-hour periodicity.

It is just such a process of entrainment that goes into action when a plant or animal is subjected to a changed light cycle—as by a transatlantic flight or a laboratory experiment—and takes a few days of phase-shifting to get back into its normal phase-relationship with the new light cycle time. Circadian rhythms are normally entrained most strongly by the light intensity changes of the day-night cycle, particularly by dawn or dusk when light levels are changing fastest. But in the absence of a light cycle many organisms will entrain themselves to other 24-hour cues, for example to a temperature cycle, and for man, social time cues, such as the habit of working from nine to five and eating meals at regular times, may well be paramount in entraining his circadian rhythm.

While many plants and animals organize their activities around the cycle of day and night, the organisms of the seashore arrange their actions around the ▷

The morning glory, *Ipomoea*, takes its name from the fact that each pink flower, *above right*, opens in the morning and then withers away by early afternoon. Few flowers survive so briefly, although many species open only at fairly specific times of the day.

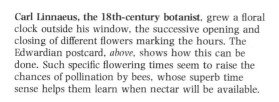

Carl Linnaeus, the 18th-century botanist, grew a floral clock outside his window, the successive opening and closing of different flowers marking the hours. The Edwardian postcard, *above*, shows how this can be done. Such specific flowering times seem to raise the chances of pollination by bees, whose superb time sense helps them learn when nectar will be available.

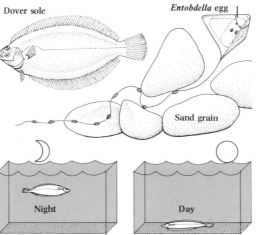

Dover sole

Sand grain

Entobdella egg

Night

Day

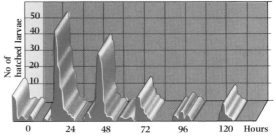

The common sole feeds and swims at night but rests by day in the top layer of sand on the sea bed. A skin parasite, *Entobdella soleae*, sheds its eggs into the same sand to which they become attached by a sticky thread, *left*. Larvae emerge at dawn, giving them 12 hours to find a new host. The daily hatching rhythm persists and free-runs in constant darkness, *above*.

▷ ebb and flow of the tides. Of all the habitats on Earth the one that exists between high and low tide levels is perhaps the most difficult and demanding. At high tide, although submerged and thus more or less typically marine, the creatures that live on the shore are subject to violent battering by the waves and a perpetual shifting of the sand, pebbles and rocks that form the substrata for all the habitat's plants and non-swimming animals. At low tide—a mere six hours later—the same site has become, to all intents and purposes, terrestrial, so that it is subject to rapid changes in salinity from rain, to freezing temperatures in winter, shadeless drying radiation in summer and, at all times, to merciless predation from sea birds. Small wonder, then, that the organisms which have evolved to exploit the riches of food in the intertidal zone, and which make the investigation of the beach at low tide such a pleasurable experience, have adopted sharp timekeeping, with the result that they can anticipate and avoid the worst of its radical, twice-daily changes in condition.

Just as the denizens of land, fresh water and open sea share out their habitat by using it at different hours of the day and night, so the intertidal habitat is divided up. But the division is not nearly as equal as the day versus night share-out. Nearly all intertidal animals are essentially aquatic and so breathe with gills, structures specifically designed to extract oxygen from water. It is, therefore, hard for these creatures to use the terrestrial low tide niche, and few species do so.

A rare exception to this intertidal rule is the fiddler crab, *Uca*, which comes out of its burrow to scavenge at low tide. More common are those species that are active within the advancing or receding tide front. Plants, of course, just

have to sit it out and wait; probably their only concession to the tidal cycle is to be rhythmic in the release of their reproductive spores, so that they shed these into the water only when they are submerged. Nearly all tidal plants are seaweeds (algae), and most live at the lower shore of the beach, so that they are uncovered for only brief spells at each low tide.

What we must now discover is whether these tidal rhythms are simply direct responses to the presence or absence of seawater. There are exceptions, such as barnacles, which will open up their shells at any time when they are under water, but, apart from these, all the other animals that have been tested in the laboratory show a typical free-running circatidal—that is, roughly 12-hour—rhythm when placed in constant conditions. They, therefore, drift in their timing relative to the tide times on the beach that was their home and from which they were collected, just as circadian rhythms drift relative to solar time.

The average duration of one tide cycle is 12.4 hours. This figure is rather close to half the 24-hour circadian period, so the activity rhythms of intertidal animals are very similar to the twice-daily activity patterns many terrestrial species adopt by being active at dawn and dusk, that is, crepuscular. Moreover, 24.8 hours, or two tide cycles, is well within the range of free-running circadian rhythms, so there is every reason to suppose that, even though they may have evolved independently, circatidal and circadian rhythms must operate along similar lines and by similar mechanisms. Certainly several animals, such as the common shore crab, *Carcinus maenas*, show a roughly 12-hour, free-running circatidal rhythm in the laboratory when they have been collected from a tidal

Tidal waters contain a rich array of plants and animals whose lives have to adjust to the twice-daily hazard of being alternately submerged and stranded by the high and low tides, *right*. Few animals can withstand being exposed for long at low tide and are thus rhythmic in their activities, burying themselves in the sand or under stones at roughly 12.4-hour intervals, as if in anticipation of the receding tide. The European shore crab, *Carcinus maenas*, shows a tidal rhythm of activity as it hides under stones at low tide, coming out to scavenge only when it is covered by water, *below right*.

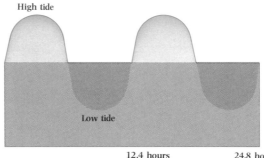

High tide

Low tide

12.4 hours   24.8 hours

The danger of being eaten by birds, such as this crab plover, is a major hazard facing animals at low tide.

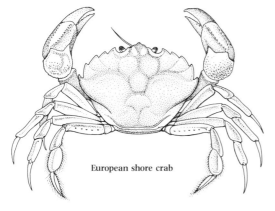

European shore crab

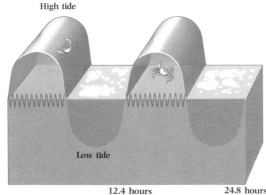

High tide

Low tide

12.4 hours   24.8 hours

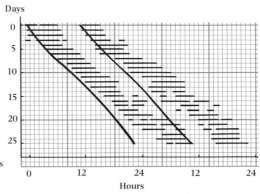

Days

0

5

10

15

20

25

0   12   24   12   24

Hours

A rare example of an animal that is active at low tide is the fiddler crab, *Uca* sp, which comes out of its burrow into the open air to look for food, *left*. Much research has been done on this crab in order to discover if its activity rhythm is triggered by the water or is governed by an internal ability to measure tidal time. The record, *above*, is the result of an experiment in which the crab was kept in constant conditions for 25 days. The twice-daily horizontal lines show the crab's activity; the sloping lines, the high tide times on its home beach. These drift by 50 minutes a day since the tidal 'day' is 24 hours 50 minutes long. That the crab's rhythm persists and also drifts faster than the tides shows that it is spontaneous and internally timed.

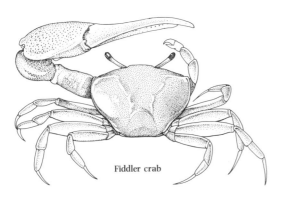

Fiddler crab

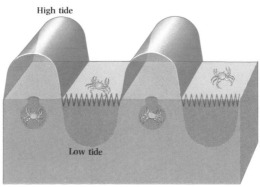

High tide

Low tide

12.4 hours   24.8 hours

shore, but a roughly 24-hour, circadian periodicity when they have been gathered from a tideless area such as a dock. This shows that the rhythm can become adapted to suit different conditions.

Apart from its shorter cycle time and the violence of its periodicity, the tidal habitat differs from all others by changing rhythmically with the phases of the moon. Twice in every lunar month of 28.5 days, when the moon and sun are in line—at the full and the new moon—the sun's gravitational pull on the sea augments that of the moon to cause tides considerably bigger than average. These are the spring tides, whose name often causes confusion because they are nothing to do with the seasons. The in between phase of smaller neap tides occurs when the sun's pull is at right angles to that of the moon.

The result of the moon's influence on the tides is that all coastal areas include three rather different habitats. There is a large central zone uncovered at every tide, a lower zone uncovered briefly twice a day only at maximum low-water spring tides and an upper zone that is covered briefly only at maximum high-water spring tides. The lower zone is almost always fully aquatic, the upper one almost always fully terrestrial, and there are animals that exploit both these features. A famous example is the grunion fish, *Leuresthes tenuis*, whose males and females swarm up Californian beaches to spawn, on the crest of high spring tides. There the fish bury their eggs, leaving them to develop in the warm sand until the next high spring tides wash them out to hatch in the open sea.

At the lower extreme of the tidal zone there is a highly unusual insect, a midge, *Clunio marinus*, whose larvae feed on the red algae growing at the most

seaward part of some European beaches. The adults live for only two hours, and must, therefore, emerge, mate and lay their eggs on the algae during a single low-water spring tide. Fascinatingly, when reared in the laboratory in a constant 24-hour light-dark cycle, the midges emerge from the culture in bursts at roughly 15-day intervals and thus demonstrate a clear, free-running semi-lunar rhythm.

Clunio is one of the few organisms in which a twice-monthly rhythm found in natural conditions has been shown to persist and free-run when transferred to the constant conditions of the laboratory. Another good example involves a plant, the large brown seaweed *Dictyota dichotoma*. In similar constant conditions this alga sheds its egg cells into the sea with a clear 17-day free-running rhythm. Both *Clunio* and *Dictyota*—and presumably most other inhabitants of the extreme tidal zones—thus possess the internal ability to measure out approximately 15-day intervals, presumably by means of a semi-lunar physiological clock mechanism.

There is one more aspect of lunar periodicity that affects at least some organisms, namely that of the full 29-day lunar month. Around coral reefs in the Pacific there is a particularly spectacular expression of this every year for just a few nights during the last quarter of each moon in October and November. During these nights, and only then, the surface of the sea swarms with an astronomical number of mating palolo worms of the species *Eunice viridis*. A more familiar example occurs in man—or rather in woman—as the menstrual cycle. Although in effect it free-runs, since it is not directly related to the timing of the real lunar cycle, this cycle can still be described as circalunar. ▷

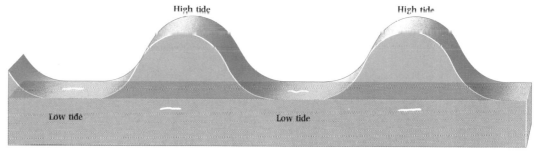

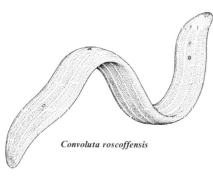

Convoluta roscoffensis

The small green marine worm, *Convoluta roscoffensis,* which lives just below the neap tide high-water mark in Brittany, is part animal and part plant. Its greenness comes from an alga that grows symbiotically in its tissues and from which it derives carbohydrate. This is made by photosynthesis, so the worm has to expose itself to sunlight. At high tide and at night it lies buried in the sand but at low tides during the day it crawls out into the light, *above*. Thus it possesses a combination of both a tidal and a circadian rhythm.

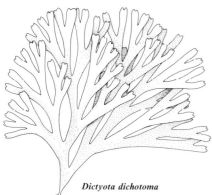

Dictyota dichotoma

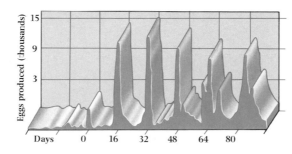

Every full and new moon the high tide is higher and the low tide is lower than usual. The 15-day rhythm of these spring tides causes the upper extreme of the tidal habitat to be covered for a few days and the lowest extreme to be uncovered. The brown alga, *Dictyota dichotoma*, lives in this lowest spring tide zone, where it discharges its eggs and sperm to fuse in the sea every 15 days during the smaller neap tides, presumably to avoid their being stranded by the low spring tide. In tideless conditions the rhythm of egg discharge persists, and free-runs every 17 days, *left*.

The aquatic larvae of the midge, *Clunio marinus,* feed on red algae growing in the low spring tide zones of many European shores. When the moon is full and new, the zone is exposed to the air for a few hours at each low tide. As waves break over them the larvae pupate, and when the tide is right out, quickly emerge as midges. The adults emerge, mate, lay eggs and die all within the few hours afforded by a single low spring tide. A larva that fails to pupate must wait two weeks before it has another chance. The timing of adult emergence with low spring tide is shown, *right*. In constant laboratory conditions the larvae persist in their rhythm, emerging as adults on one of four evenings at roughly 15-day intervals.

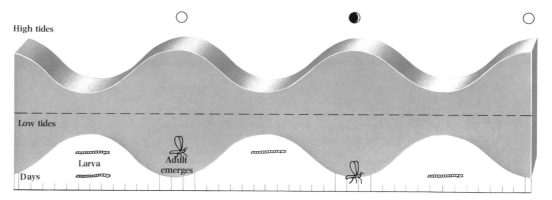

▷ There are several well-documented 29-day rhythms, clearly coupled to the moon's phases, to be found among invertebrate organisms, not only in marine species, where such behaviour might be expected from the cycle of the spring tides, but also in terrestrial species. For example, the emergence of some mayflies occurs in a peak just after the full moon. Most of these lunar rhythms are known only in their natural environment, but a few have been studied in the laboratory. A particularly good case is that of *Platynereis*, a European relative of the palolo, which swarms almost exclusively around the new moon in natural conditions, but shows a free-running circalunar rhythm when it is removed from its natural habitat and placed in an unchanging 24-hour light-dark cycle in the laboratory.

For the mayflies, palolo worm and *Platynereis* the function of this monthly swarming is presumably to bring the sexes together. But some tidal species show non-reproductive lunar rhythms, and it is difficult to see why they should have evolved this periodicity when the 15-day semi-lunar spring tide cycle must be much more important to their day-to-day survival. Nevertheless, all the cases so far investigated show free-running circalunar rhythms when they are placed in constant conditions, so they must all have evolved the internal ability to measure out a circalunar period, an ability indelibly inscribed in their genetic material.

Clearly none of these moon-caused rhythms, whether 12.4-hour, 15-day or 29-day, is free-running in nature. Just as with circadian rhythms they are kept to the correct, relevant environmental time—that is, they are entrained—by external time cues. In the few organisms that have been fully studied, semi-

lunar and circalunar rhythms are susceptible to entrainment by moonlight. Thus the rhythms of *Clunio*, *Dictyota* and *Platynereis*, for example, can be made to toe the environmental line by giving the organisms a few consecutive nights of artificial moonlight once a month in their otherwise unrelieved 24-hour cycles of light and dark. Experimentally this is done simply by replacing the total darkness of the relevant nights with dim light, controlled so that it is not confused with daylight.

For the twice-daily tidal rhythms, matters become a bit more complicated. The 24-hour day-night cycle that entrains circadian rhythms, although clearly discernible to most tidal species, is misleading because of its 0.8-hour (48-minute) difference from the 24.8-hour tidal 'day'. If tidal organisms used light cues to entrain their rhythms they would certainly get wholly out of phase with the tides in a few days. What these organisms use as tide-time cues are, therefore, the mechanical disturbance of the water as it rushes over them, or changes in temperature, salinity or pressure, or any combination of these reliable markers of the tidal cycle.

In the short term, the tidal environment creates the Earth's most demanding rhythm, but in the long term the changing year can be at least as exacting. Higher latitudes become totally uninhabitable in winter unless creatures stay hidden under sea ice, or go into a deep hibernation. And even in temperate latitudes, plants lie dormant and the food supply of many animals disappears. Anticipating this predictable annual crisis is, therefore, vital to survival for both plants and animals.

There are three ways in which one could imagine this adjustment being

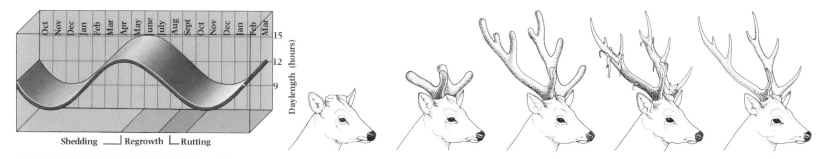

Shedding ⌐ Regrowth ⌐ Rutting

Most deer shed and regrow their antlers in an annual cycle. Like this American wapiti, *left*, they often add a branch or two over the years, so the complexity is a reflection of the stag's age. Generally antlers are shed in late winter or in early spring and then regrown in summer. Before the rutting season occurs in the autumn, the soft velvet under which the antlers develop must be lost. The annual antler cycle of the oriental sika deer is shown, *top left*, and the sequence of regrowth, *above*. If sika deer are kept in various lighting conditions, the antler cycle can be shown to be due to two factors. Mainly it is a response to the seasonal changes in daylength, which varies between 9 and 15 hours. It responds also to a weak, internal and roughly annual rhythm in the deer's physiology.

accomplished. First, organisms could merely switch into their winter dormancy or migratory phase when they first feel the pinch—say, from the first frost. Since frost, rain, drought and other such natural disasters arrive at the whim of the weather, however, they are unreliable markers for the change of season. The second possibility is that animals and plants use the totally reliable annual change of daylength as a predictor of seasons. This ability to measure out the number of hours of daylight is photoperiodism, and it is certainly used by many organisms, but to do so they must possess a sophisticated ability to measure daylength.

The third possibility would be for living things to have an internal annual clock—a circannual biological clock analagous with the circadian kind. Although this may sound improbable, such clocks do apparently exist in a wide variety of organisms. Circannual clocks were probably first noticed when European varieties of tree, normally exposed to changing daylength with the march of the seasons, were taken to the tropics by nineteenth-century colonists. There in an environment with virtually unchanging daylength, the trees continued to pursue their usual cycle of leaf opening, flowering and so on, although they tended to lose synchrony with the local year; they in fact free-ran in this natural laboratory.

More rigorously, although not very often because of the necessary experimental time involved, several animals and plants have now been shown to have free-running circannual rhythms in unchanging 24-hour light-dark cycles. The carpet beetle, *Anthrenus verbasci*, even shows a persistent circannual rhythm of adult emergence when kept for years in constant total darkness. In all these instances, the annual event that is actually timed in the free-running situation, such as mating, migration or moulting, can occur in the laboratory at any time of the year, and, therefore, quite out of phase with the real seasons outside. The experimental animals and plants are, therefore, not picking up uncontrolled cosmic cues, and must possess truly in-built circa-365-day clock systems within their bodies.

In natural surroundings, what is it that entrains these circannual rhythms to a precise year? The answer is not entirely clear, but is probably mainly a change in daylength. Certainly species such as deer and willow warblers show both circannual rhythmicity and responses to change in daylength. This sounds like a confusing mixture between photoperiodism, which is a direct response to daylength, and an organism's internal annual timing mechanism. Although quite different, the two phenomena do serve the same function in nature and go hand in hand. The circannual rhythm presumably makes the physiology of the animal, such as its production of sex hormones, change at roughly the right time of year so that it can correct its seasonal response when the appropriate daylength arrives.

All the observations and laboratory experiments performed on animals and plants leave us in absolutely no doubt that daily, tidal, lunar and annual rhythms are all controlled by underlying physiological timekeeping—that is, by physiological clocks. Such clocks clearly cannot be anything like man-made clocks, but any clock, whether biological or the product of human engineering, must, in principle, consist of the same five basic components. Number one constitutes the 'hands', the visible parts that indicate the clock's underlying ▷

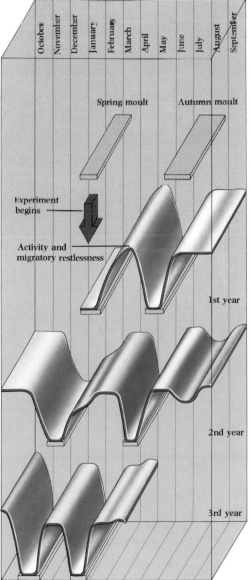

The willow warbler is a common European migrant, usually arriving in Britain in April. Like most other birds it moults twice a year: once in early spring before it migrates north, and once in late summer before it migrates south. When it moults its activity and migratory restlessness is reduced to a minimum. These moults are in part due to a response to seasonal changes in daylength. But if the warblers are kept for more than two years in a stable cycle of 12 hours light and 12 hours dark, they continue to moult roughly twice a year. The results of these experiments show that the interval between the spring moults and the interval between the autumn moults are both about 10 months. The birds must, therefore, have an internal and roughly annual clock to time the moults.

The European garden warbler has a circular migration route. In spring it migrates north across the Sahara and the eastern Mediterranean from its winter home in central Africa. In autumn it returns by flying over the Straits of Gibraltar, then southeast over the Sahara.

Northeast
(April–June)

Southwest
(Aug–Sept)

Southeast
(Oct–Dec)

Garden warblers know when to migrate and also the direction they must take. Built into the bird's behaviour is an ingenious annual schedule. Caged warblers in a migratory mood perform many repeated hops in the direction of their normal migratory flight path. These hops are easy to record, so for long periods the bird's attempts to migrate can be monitored. When the days are all kept the same length so the birds have no clue as to the time of year, their hops point in three directions, *above*, corresponding to their annual behaviour in the wild.

Autumn migration SW   Winter home range

Autumn migration SE

Spring migration N

▷ rhythm and show what time it is. Number two is a 'mainspring', the source of energy that drives the clock's mechanism. Three is an 'escapement' device, the basic regulating oscillator which, in mechanical clocks, governs the oscillation of the pendulum or combination of balance wheel and hairspring. Number four is the 'cogs', the couplings that link the escapement to the hands. Number five is an 'adjuster', the mechanism by which the clock can be corrected to tell local time.

In biological clocks, the 'hands' are all the visible, measurable rhythms, from running activity and leaf movement to migration and leaf fall. These observable rhythms are not an intrinsic part of the clock mechanism, but merely indicators of the state of the clock at any given moment. In theory the 'mainspring' should be the energy demands of the physiological mechanism, but these are so minute that they cannot be detected against the organism's general metabolism which uses comparatively huge amounts of energy. The 'escapement' of a biological clock is the key, unseen, driving oscillation, the essential timekeeping pacemaker.

The 'cogs' of the biological clock are those physiological coupling mechanisms such as hormones and nerves through which the 'escapement' drives the 'hands'. Although the environmental entraining time cue of the 'adjuster' mechanism is well known for many biological clocks—involving the perception of night and day by the eyes in circadian rhythms, for example—little or nothing is known about how this information is used within the body to reset the 'escapement' device.

For circadian rhythms, the two clock components about which most is

known are the 'escapement', or driving oscillator, and the coupling 'cogs'. Three plausible theories have been proposed for how the basic oscillator might work. The first theory places the clock mechanism in the cell's nucleus, the part of the cell in which hereditary information is contained in the chromosomes. These threadlike structures are composed of functional units, the genes, made up of the chemical deoxyribosenucleic acid (DNA) which acts as a coded series of instructions to control all life processes. The theory proposes that the circadian period is measured out by continuous reading of the genetic code along a very long loop of DNA in a chromosome. This idea has several attractive features and is supported by some experimental evidence, but it also has some flaws.

The second theory assumes that the clock has its roots in the organism's oscillating biochemistry. The problem is that it is theoretically difficult to construct a 24-hour clock from the known biochemical oscillations because these all have a high frequency with the time-span of each cycle measured in seconds or, at best, in minutes. The theory thus proposes that circadian rhythmicity is generated by an interaction of many of these high frequency chemical oscillations in such a manner that one inhibits another to create a net slow output. As yet, however, there is no concrete physiological evidence that this actually occurs.

The third theory of the biological escapement device envisages that the circadian oscillation occurs as a result of slow changes in the membranes within a cell. As a result of these changes, which affect the permeability of the membranes, ions, such as potassium, leak passively through a membrane from

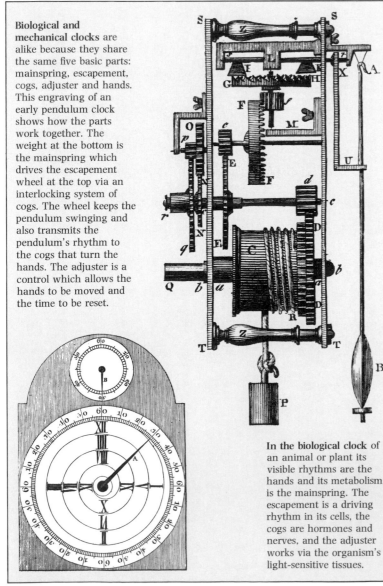

Biological and mechanical clocks are alike because they share the same five basic parts: mainspring, escapement, cogs, adjuster and hands. This engraving of an early pendulum clock shows how the parts work together. The weight at the bottom is the mainspring which drives the escapement wheel at the top via an interlocking system of cogs. The wheel keeps the pendulum swinging and also transmits the pendulum's rhythm to the cogs that turn the hands. The adjuster is a control which allows the hands to be moved and the time to be reset.

In the biological clock of an animal or plant its visible rhythms are the hands and its metabolism is the escapement. The escapement is a driving rhythm in its cells, the cogs are hormones and nerves, and the adjuster works via the organism's light-sensitive tissues.

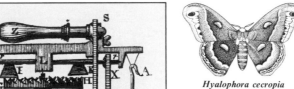

Hyalophora cecropia   *Antherea pernyi*

Tissue transplants are relatively easy to perform on these silkmoths because they are large and their body cavity is an open blood system without arteries or veins.

 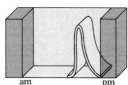

Moths of *Hyalophora* normally emerge from their pupal cases in the morning while those of *Antherea* emerge in the late afternoon.

am   pm   am   pm

 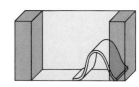

This circadian rhythm is lost if the brains are removed from the pupae; ultimately they still emerge normally, but at random times.

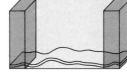 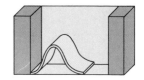

The normal daily rhythm of emergence can be restored if the removed brain is replaced in the abdomen of the brainless pupa.

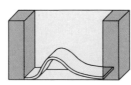 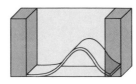

Rhythms are exchanged if the brain of one species is given to the other: *Hyalophora* then emerge in the late afternoon and *Antherea* in the morning.

An adult silkmoth emerges from its pupa at a particular time of day and, as the above series of experiments has shown, this is under physiological control. This emergence—the splitting and shrugging off of the cocoon—will occur at any time during the day if the brain is removed. But since the rhythm is restored when the brain is replaced in the pupa's abdomen, the brain is needed for a specifically timed emergence. A hormone must control this timing since the transplanted brain has no nervous connection with the abdomen but is only bathed in blood. This brain hormone switches on the circadian emergence rhythm.

The fact that the rhythm can be transferred from one moth species to the other when their brains are exchanged means the brain itself has a timing mechanism. Thus there is a clock in the pupa's brain that produces a hormone at a particular time of day and triggers the adult to emerge.

one part of a cell to another, and are then actively pumped back again in the reverse direction when a particular imbalance in their concentration is reached. There are good non-circadian models for this kind of thing in the membranes of nerves and other sorts of cell. Moreover, while most chemical treatments either have no effect on circadian clocks or put them permanently out of commission, chemicals such as alcohol and heavy water, which are known to alter the permeability of cell membranes, actually slow down or phase-shift circadian rhythms in both plants and animals. This implies that these substances are directly affecting the basic oscillators contained in the organism, so it looks as though the membrane clock does have a sound experimental basis.

Despite the attraction of a cell membrane 'escapement', it is still too early to dismiss the DNA theory completely. The reason is that one or two antibiotic drugs that selectively inhibit the manufacture of proteins in cells—a process that can only occur through the active participation of DNA—have also been shown to phase-shift circadian rhythms. The current view of the biological clock is, thus, that it may involve both slow changes in the permeability of cell membranes and also the nucleus, via its role in synthesizing membrane proteins.

So what of the 'cogs' that link the escapement device of the biological clock with its 'hands'? It is a basic assumption that circadian rhythmicity evolved in step with primitive life, and hence that it is an essential property of all cells. Certainly single-celled algae and protozoa, that is, the very simplest plants and animals, have circadian rhythms, and so do isolated cultured cells taken from higher plants and animals. But if each cell of the millions from which higher organisms are built contains a circadian clock mechanism, why do some specific operations on animals, such as removing the brain of a silkmoth, the pineal body from a bird or the suprachiasmatic nuclei from the hypothalamus of a rat, make these creatures arrhythmic? The answer is that these operations only stop overt *behavioural* rhythms. And that gives the lie to the whole circadian organization of these animals. There are clocks everywhere in the body but some cells, such as those in the silkmoth's brain, bird's pineal body and rat's suprachiasmatic nuclei, have acquired specialized timekeeping abilities and, as a result, act as driving clocks for other tissues throughout the creature's body.

The body of an animal or plant, thus, consists of a panoply of clocks at many levels of organization—in cell, tissue and organ—and in the whole organism they must all tick together. It seems that all these clocks are arranged in a hierarchical network, mutually entraining each other to some degree, but with the brain clocks that control behaviour being, in effect, the primary driving oscillators. In this hierarchy, all the other clocks are subservient to the brain clocks, but the clock in the adrenal gland seems to be higher on the organizational ladder than those in other hormone-releasing glands. Similarly, these hormonal clocks appear superior to those in individual cells. The brain clocks take on their dominant role because they control behaviour, but also because they are the only clocks directly connected to the eyes and, therefore, the only ones with a direct entraining influence from the powerful signal of daylight.

The pineal gland at the top of a bird's brain is probably the location of the clock controlling the bird's circadian rhythms. This 'third eye' is not used for seeing but is, nevertheless, sensitive to light. Its removal makes the bird's behaviour arrhythmic and its replacement restores the rhythms. If pineal glands are exchanged between two birds on different time schedules the recipient assumes the schedule of the donor. The pineal seems to be a circadian clock and also a rhythmic source of a behaviour-regulating hormone.

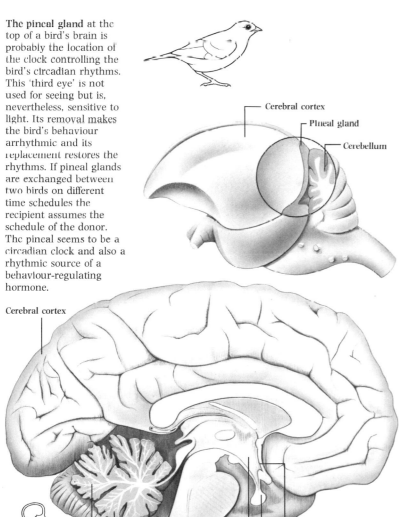

Cerebral cortex

Pineal gland

Cerebellum

Cerebral cortex

Suprachiasmatic nuclei

Cerebellum

Pituitary gland

Hypothalamus

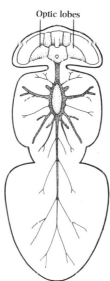

Optic lobes

The brain of an insect, such as a housefly, is the largest nerve centre in its body. Groups of brain cells seem to act as circadian clocks, which in some insects have been found in the optic lobes either side of the brain.

The daily activity rhythms of mammals and presumably, therefore, of man are driven by a clock in the hypothalamus—a key area of the mid-brain that controls body functions such as temperature, rate of metabolism, appetite and thirst. The actual clock cells are in two tiny groups called the suprachiasmatic nuclei. They are entrained and adjusted to external daylight by a specific nervous input from the eyes that has nothing to do with normal vision. Unlike the bird's pineal and the silkmoth brain, these cells exert their influence by a direct nervous route rather than via hormones.

Many biological functions of animals such as their behavioural activity show clear circadian rhythms. There are also rhythms in excretion, hormone production and in the metabolism of single cells. Normally these functions keep in time with each other and work in harmony. There is probably a hierarchy of clocks, perhaps as shown *below*. In a mammal, the hypothalamus is entrained by daylight via the eyes, and itself probably entrains the clocks of other organs, which in turn adjust the clocks of individual cells.

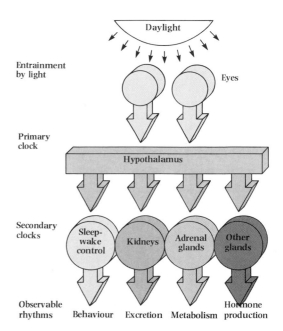

Daylight

Entrainment by light

Eyes

Primary clock

Hypothalamus

Secondary clocks

Sleep-wake control

Kidneys

Adrenal glands

Other glands

Observable rhythms

Behaviour

Excretion

Metabolism

Hormone production

Rhythms of sex

To ensure the continuance of their kind, animals must have a means of reproducing themselves. This process of reproduction does not, however, go on all the time and there are no species of animals capable of continuous reproduction. Some creatures are able to reproduce on many occasions during the year but others—the majority—are able to breed on only a few days in each 365. The reason why the annual rhythm of reproduction is so restricted is that it is essentially a process of development. A single egg cell is shed by the female which, after fertilization by one sperm from the male, eventually develops into a new, whole animal. Most invertebrate animals, the creatures without backbones, produce their eggs and sperm in batches and the processes of fertilization and egg development take place outside the body of the female, but in mammals, including humans, the egg is held inside the female's body. Following fertilization, a great deal of development occurs before birth so that reproduction requires a much longer involvement of the whole animal than, say, an act of movement, breathing or digestion.

Because of the inherent restrictions on continuous reproduction, there is a paramount need for the reproductive rhythms of males and females to be synchronized so that the male has ripe sperm ready just when the female has produced her eggs. If the rhythms of one sex are out of phase with those of the other then fertilization will be impossible and the species will not reproduce. The forces of evolution have seen to the attainment of synchrony, but simultaneous production of mature sex cells is not always enough. This is because many species—particularly among birds and mammals—must undergo a time consuming change in behaviour prior to mating. Without courtship, the mutual suspicion and aggression between the sexes may prevent mating from taking place. So courtship must precede mating and must itself be triggered by the body's changing chemistry as the process of sexual maturation progresses.

The actual cues that animals obey to time their breeding seasons are many and varied. Some creatures respond to the lengthening days of spring, others to the shortening days of autumn, yet others take their cue from the amount of rainfall or from the gradual change in temperature related to the seasons. But the timing of mating is always geared to the timing of birth or hatching, for if the young are to have a high chance of survival they must be born when the food and other resources they require are at their most abundant. This may mean that the adults have to make immense breeding migrations: some birds fly half way round the globe to breed and some whales cruise the length of an entire ocean.

Giving birth at the very best time for juvenile survival is the key to many of the fascinating aspects of reproductive rhythms of large, terrestrial animals. But in the sea, where there are few seasonal influences other than daylength, the chief problem is for the sexes to find one another, in order that fertilization can take place. Most marine animals mate in a rudimentary fashion: the females shed their eggs into the water all around them and the males do the same with their sperm. Therefore, considering the vastness of the oceans, it is absolutely imperative that eggs and sperm should be shed simultaneously if fertilization is to take place at all. It is the moon that is the all-important coordinator of these events because it exerts an influence on the sea through the tides, and those tides cause rhythmic changes in water pressure which synchronize and impart a rhythm to reproduction in marine animals.

The time of year during which an animal is fertile, and so ready and able to reproduce itself, is its breeding season. But although reproduction is an animal's most important function—the reason for its existence—many species have breeding seasons lasting only a few days. The exact timing of the annual rhythm of the breeding season depends upon a variety of environmental cues which change the animal from being sexually quiescent to being sexually active. Once the process of change has started, the sexual cycle begins its course.

In mammals, including humans, the cycle of sexual events is the estrous cycle of the female and is composed of two distinct phases, the follicular phase and the luteal phase. The follicular phase is the first of the two. During this part of the cycle developmental changes take place in the ovary of the female and some eggs ripen. The whole cycle is controlled by hormones, and the most vital are those that come from the front or anterior part of the pituitary gland, a small but influential organ situated at the base of the brain. The cycle starts when the anterior pituitary produces a hormone which acts specifically on the capsules, or follicles, in which the developing eggs are enclosed. This hormone, which is called the follicle stimulating hormone—or FSH for short—brings about an expansion of the follicles and an enlargement of the eggs within them. But FSH does more than just this, and its other actions sow the seeds of its own destruction. It causes the whole ovary to start secreting the female sex hormone, estrogen, which is soon sufficiently abundant to feed back to the anterior pituitary gland via the bloodstream and reduce the production of FSH.

The rise in the estrogen level and the fall in FSH marks the end of the

follicular phase of the estrous cycle. Next, under the influence of estrogen, and as a result of the absence of FSH, the anterior pituitary starts secreting a second hormone, luteinizing hormone (LH), which now acts on the ovarian follicle in a rather different way. The first effect of this hormone is to bring about the process of ovulation or egg release. Acting on the follicle walls it makes the follicle burst. The egg is shed into one of the Fallopian tubes that join the ovaries to the womb or uterus. The follicle, which nurtured the egg for so long, now has a new role to play. Under the influence of LH the follicle grows and fills up the space that was once occupied by the egg. The empty follicle, now yellowish in colour, is given the name of corpus luteum or yellow body.

This second phase of the estrous cycle, dominated by the emergence of the corpus luteum, is the luteal phase. The corpus luteum starts to secrete progesterone, the hormone necessary for maintaining pregnancy. If the egg or eggs from the female are fertilized just after their release from the ovary, then the corpus luteum left behind by each egg will continue to grow and pour out its life-supporting chemicals. But if the eggs are not fertilized, the corpus luteum gradually starts to shrink and its production of progesterone wanes. During all this time the output of estrogen has been declining, and when the corpus luteum is finally extinguished the production of progesterone stops. The cessation of progesterone production marks the end of one complete estrous cycle. Free from the restraints imposed upon it by estrogen and progesterone the anterior pituitary is now able to secrete another batch of FSH and so a new cycle begins.

Some species of mammal, such as the dog, are described as monestrous

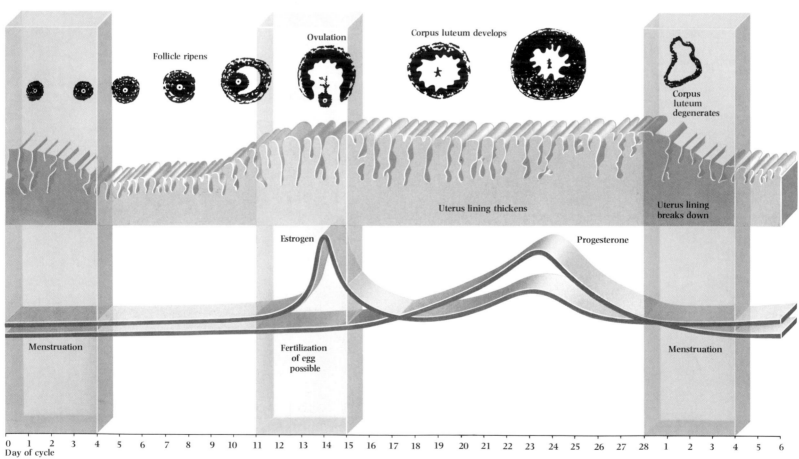

A **woman's menstrual cycle** is one of the most familiar human rhythms, with the same events taking place each month unless altered by pregnancy. An egg ripens in the ovary under the influence of follicle stimulating hormone (FSH), produced by the pituitary gland. Midway through the cycle ovulation occurs—an egg bursts from the ovary and travels down the Fallopian tube to the womb (uterus). The level of FSH drops and the level of luteinizing hormone (LH), also produced by the pituitary, rises. This hormone helps

the development of the yellow body (corpus luteum) in the ovary, which in turn produces progesterone. Under the influence of LH the egg, if fertilized, will implant itself in the uterus lining. If the egg is not fertilized the yellow body breaks down, the uterus sheds its lining and the progesterone level drops. Associated with menstruation is a temperature rhythm, *right*: the woman's body temperature rises with ovulation. This signal of fertility is used in the 'rhythm' method of contraception and is important in fertility therapy.

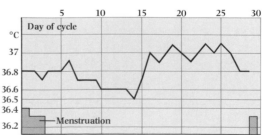

because they have just one estrous cycle during each breeding season. Others, such as the cow, mouse and rat, have several cycles in each breeding season and so are polyestrous. The smaller of the polyestrous species may be able to produce several litters of young during a single breeding season, a capacity for which mice are notorious.

Man, and a few species of ape, have no rigid breeding season. Instead, estrous cycles follow one another continuously throughout the year. The human cycle is known as the menstrual cycle, a name that comes from the Latin *mens*, meaning month, because it has a periodicity of approximately 28 days. Although the hormonal basis of the human menstrual cycle is identical with that of the estrous cycle, the two are different in one important respect. During the estrous cycle of mammals, apart from man and other menstruating species, there is a period of 'heat' during which mating normally occurs and this coincides with ovulation. In addition there are a number of behavioural changes, many of which are easily observed.

The hallmark of the human menstrual cycle is the periodic bleeding that normally occurs for between three and five days midway between ovulations. For a long time it was thought that menstruation was the equivalent of estral heat, and accompanied ovulation, but this is now known not to be so. In menstruating species, one of the effects of the hormone progesterone is to cause a thickening of the wall of the uterus in preparation for receiving and nourishing a fertilized egg should one become implanted in it. If fertilization does not occur, and the corpus luteum starts to degenerate, there is no support system of hormones left for the thick, blood-rich tissues. Sometimes slowly, and

sometimes with a rush, the uterine wall sloughs off its newly acquired thickness and prepares itself for the next cycle. Bleeding during the sexual cycle is not an exclusive attribute of man and some of his primate relations. A few species with estrous cycles bleed shortly before ovulation, but this bleeding is never as heavy, nor as long-lasting, as in menstruating species.

The rhythmic monthly changes in a woman's hormone levels are so great that they affect other parts of the human body, apart from the ovaries and uterus, in a regular fashion. Under the influence of progesterone a woman's breasts swell slightly, reaching their maximum size just before menstruation, and they may also become more sensitive to the touch and tingle slightly. The nose, too, suffers from the hormonal surges. During the time of ovulation— roughly 14 days after the start of menstruation—the sensitivity to musks and musklike odours increases tenfold or more, only to decrease sharply during the bleeding phase of the cycle. Progesterone also affects the tiny blood vessels in the nose, and many women suffer from nosebleeds and blocked noses during the latter part of their menstrual cycle. And because progesterone (produced now by the placenta) is secreted throughout pregnancy, some women suffer from mild nasal irritation at this time. The effect of the cyclic production of progesterone on the nervous system is not well understood, but it is well documented that many women suffer from premenstrual tension before their periods, a time during which they are abnormally anxious and tense. There are other strange effects: it has been found that toward the end of the cycle, women singers with the ability to pitch notes perfectly sometimes find their ability impaired. ▷

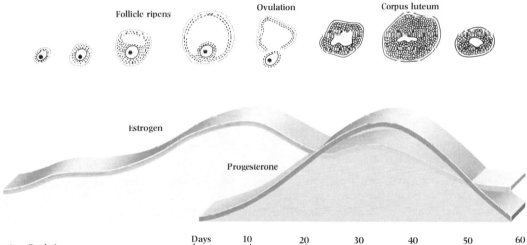

Follicle ripens · Ovulation · Corpus luteum

Estrogen

Progesterone

Most mammals are sexually receptive and fertile for a restricted number of short periods in each year and do not have a monthly cycle. During these periods of sexual activity an animal is 'on heat' and many behavioural changes accompany the physiological developments in the reproductive system. True estrus is marked by ovulation—the shedding of one or more eggs from the ovary—and is controlled by the same hormones as control the human menstrual cycle. In the few days immediately before estrus, external signs of fertility appear, such as changes in body coloration or the swelling of the vaginal area characteristic of some primates, and the production of a powerful body odour. After estrus the body is becoming prepared for pregnancy and this broody state of pseudopregnancy is typical of many species. If the animal is not pregnant the womb gradually shrinks back to its resting state to await the next breeding season.

→ Ovulation
▨ Estrus

Human females are sexually receptive throughout their cycle, although fertile for only a few days, *above*. This is a fundamental difference between man and other mammals. Some mammals have two or more estrous cycles during each mating season while others, such as dogs, experience just one. In general small mammals have many estrous cycles in quick succession. Larger animals, such as cattle and horses, have more widely spaced estrous cycles, though the actual duration of the 'heat' period may still be short. The opossum is a curious exception for although small it has long intervals between cycles.

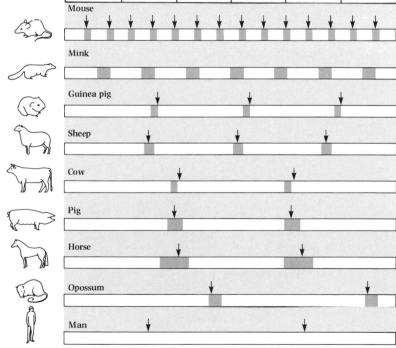

Ground squirrel

Rabbit

Mink

Days	10	20	30	40	50	60
Mouse						
Mink						
Guinea pig						
Sheep						
Cow						
Pig						
Horse						
Opossum						
Man						

The physical stimulus of copulation is needed by some animals to bring about ovulation. These 'induced ovulators' experience a regular estrous cycle but only release eggs when mating occurs, thereby running no risk of wasting eggs. The complete mechanism is not yet understood, but it seems that the stimulus of mating releases the hormone oxytocin from the pituitary gland, and triggers ovulation. Badgers, mink, rabbits, ground squirrels and many small rodents are all induced ovulators.

67

▷ In many species of mammals estrous cycles can be synchronized by certain odours or pheromones that emanate from both males and females. It has been suggested that human cycles are regulated by various odorous substances found in male urine and sweat, or even in the sweat of certain 'driver' women, but much more experimentation is required before the precise mechanism of this phenomenon is known—or is proven to be non existent.

Merely coming into estrus at a particular time is of little use if a potential mate is unaware that the time for mating has arrived. To overcome the problem of an overlooked estrus the females of most species have developed some means of signalling their readiness to mate. Since the signal is tied to the underlying sexual cycle it, too, makes itself apparent on a regular, cyclical basis. Animals use a wide variety of sensory cues to advertise their state. Deer and antelope, for example, make strutting movements which act as visual signals, while whales and dolphins sing complex songs. Very many mammals, including cats and dogs, produce specific sexual odours when they are ready to mate.

Among the most bizarre sexual advertisements in the whole animal kingdom are those of man's primate relatives. In many species, such as the chimpanzee, baboon, mangeby and macaque monkeys, the onset of estrus is heralded by a huge swelling of the vaginal lips. In some chimpanzees they not only swell up to huge spheres more than a foot (30 cm) across but also change colour, becoming deep pink or even crimson. The odour of the vaginal secretions is, however, able to influence the quality of the visual signal. At the end of her cycle, after conception has occured, the swelling of the female baboon is as large as before, but even so the male shows little sexual interest in

her. Clearly, then, the secretions bear a powerful olfactory (smell) message which cancels out the visual stimulus that was earlier of overriding importance.

In many of the more lowly primates, such as lemurs and tarsiers, the vaginal aperture is completely sealed off during the non-breeding season, so that mating is physically as well as physiologically impossible. As estrogens start to course through the bloodstream, the thin membrane which closes the orifice breaks down and the rim of the vagina starts to swell and flush with colour. At the peak of estrus the vagina is slightly everted, but quickly returns to normal at the end of the cycle. As if rear-end display were not enough, the gelada baboon, *Theropithecus gelada*, and a few other primates enhance its effectiveness with another form of display. During estrus the upper part of the female gelada's chest (her under or ventral surface), becomes slightly puffy and assumes a pink flush. Furthermore, a peripheral necklace of white promontories (tubercles) focuses attention on the pink skin within. Presumably the mimicking, ventral signal increases the chances that the message, carried primarily by the anal 'face', will get across to a willing, fertile male.

Clearly a message can only be understood—and acted upon—if the perceiver can read it. There is evidence that males of a number of animal species can only read the message telling them that a female is sexually prepared when they themselves are in breeding condition and ready to mate. Outside the breeding season both male and female sticklebacks, *Gasterosteus aculeatus*, look so much alike that it is hard to tell them apart. But as the male's testes develop, the hormone cycle induces a rich red flush to spread over his whole belly area.

When she is ready to mate, the female gelada baboon, *Theropithecus gelada*, signals her receptiveness by means of a thick, purplish-red swelling of her vagina and strong-smelling vaginal odours attractive to the male. Her chest also becomes pink and puffed up and surrounded by a 'necklace' of white promontories. These changes are brought about by a surge of the hormone estrogen which is essential to the release of an egg for fertilization

In the mating season, the belly of the male stickleback, *Gasterosteus*, turns bright red due to the influence of the hormone testosterone, made by his testes. This coloration deters other males from entering his breeding territory. The hormone also makes him extremely aggressive and he will attack any red object.

The female golden hamster, *Mesocricetus auratus*, sends out the message that she is ready to mate by marking her territory with strong-smelling vaginal secretions. Once an egg is released the number of markings drops rapidly.

▲ Days of estrus

When the male sets eyes on a silvery female he starts a courtship dance and she responds correctly, triggering off a chain reaction of events which ends in mating. A male in breeding condition will respond to anything coloured red, fearing a rival, but outside the breeding season, he is unaffected by red objects even when they are dangled close to him.

Other animals broadcast the news of their sexual readiness by applying special scents to various parts of their territories. Glands on the necks and chests of many species of primate are highly sensitive to sex hormones. As the sexual cycle progresses these glands pour out increasing quantities of odorous chemicals. This reaction is coupled with a cyclical variation in the frequency of scent-marking behaviour. Sometimes the scent is directed toward other individuals of the same sex—males of many big cats, for example, heavily mark an area that contains their females. With the golden hamster, *Mesocricetus auratus*, however, scent serves to attract the sexes to one another, for these animals are solitary creatures, coming together only for a brief period for mating. The female has a four-day estrous cycle but only during a receptive period of 20 hours will she allow a male to come close to her. To attract the male, the female indulges in frenetic scent-marking shortly before estrus. The odour of the vaginal secretions conveys a strongly attractive message, and the female spreads this widely about her home burrow, using a bobbing movement during which her vaginal orifice is dragged along the ground. The frequency of marking may be 30 times higher on the day before estrus than on the estral day itself.

Although humans do not have a breeding season, nor any obvious signal indicating ovulation, some research workers claim to have shown a rhythm in sexual activity. In Europe and North America most conceptions take place in spring and early summer, making January to March the favourite birthday months. In the southern hemisphere the same seasons are popular, even though the months are half a year apart. But there is no simple explanation to embrace the switch that occured in Puerto Rico between 1940 and 1960 from the typically northern pattern to the southern one. Other workers have tried to show that the frequency of intercourse is highest at a woman's mid-period point, and again shortly before menstruation, but there are great problems surrounding the collection of all such data.

In man, and in all other species in which the male inserts his penis into the female during copulation, the sex act itself is a rhythmic activity. The repeated physical thrusting of the human male induces waves of involuntary contractions in the smooth muscle of the vagina, which may assist in transporting the sperm high up into the uterus and on to the Fallopian tubes for fertilization to take place. These orgasmic waves which, contrary to popular belief, are not essential to conception, are approximately 0.8 seconds apart and closely follow the ejaculatory rhythm in the male during which the sperms and accompanying fluids are pumped out.

Since most species of animals are seasonal breeders, it is pertinent to ask what initiates the breeding season. The factors that trigger the beginning of breeding behaviour have long puzzled zoologists. In some northern species of birds and mammals the date of the start of the breeding season can be predicted with great accuracy, for example, the hare always mates in late March. In other ▷

A welcome summer resident of the northeastern oak forests of the USA is the scarlet tanager, *Piranga olivacea*. When males and females arrive after their winter in South America, both are the same drab, brownish-yellow colour, *right*, but as the days lengthen and the testes of the male develop, his drab plumage is moulted and replaced with resplendent scarlet cape and breast feathers, *below*. The pair build a nest of sticks and twigs high up in the trees and the brightly attired male defends his domain from pirates. He plays no part in incubating the eggs laid by the female but does help to fetch insect food for the hungry youngsters. After the breeding season the male sheds his bright plumage and returns to the nondescript coloring of his mate. As winter approaches the pair migrate south and return the following spring.

Non-breeding coloration

In an attempt to analyze human sexual behaviour in relation to the events of the menstrual cycle, 40 women recorded the timing of sexual intercourse and their periods over several years. The results, *right*, show a hint of maximum frequency of intercourse and orgasm around mid cycle, (at ovulation). Both fall to a minimum during menstruation.

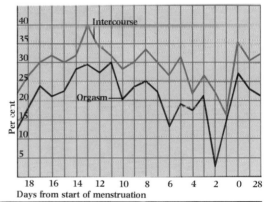

Copulation is prolonged in large predatory mammals such as the tiger, *Panthera tigris*, that do not risk being attacked during intercourse. Until she is in estrus, the female repeatedly pushes the male away. Then her powerful sex drive overcomes her fear and she allows him to approach and to mount. The first mating may last only a minute or two, but the pair will mate up to 20 times each day for the 3-week duration of the female's estrous period. In domestic cats it has been found that the friction of copulation stimulates the release of the egg from the ovary and the same is probably true of the tiger. Prolonged copulation also occurs in dogs and in some large herbivores.

▷ species the timing is more variable. Probably no single factor functions as the switch that turns on the breeding season. Instead it is more likely that the interaction of two or more environmental factors, such as daylength and temperature, start off a chain of physiological and behavioural events that leads to sexual union.

Many birds, including members of the duck family such as the shelduck, *Tadorna tadorna*, have a distribution range covering more than 15 degrees of latitude. Breeding starts earlier in the more southerly regions because here the daylength increases and the temperature rises considerably earlier than in the north. But to confuse the issue, there is some experimental evidence to suggest that there are no environmental switches at all, and that the initiation of the reproductive season is governed by some biological processes within the animal.

Studies have been performed on some male ducks in which the gradual, and cyclic, increase in the size of the testes, typical of the beginning of the breeding season, occurs in the total absence of light and of cues concerning temperature and other factors. The same cycles are seen whether the ducks are kept in total darkness or constant light, but it is apparent that the amplitude of these cycles is smaller than during normal seasonal changes, so that the testes do not become as big as they would under natural conditions. Also the periodicity of the changes is shorter, so that the breeding season does not last as long as usual. Other studies, in which sheep were kept in continuous light for three years, revealed that the time of the onset of breeding was no different from that of sheep kept in natural light conditions. Thus it has been speculated that some

animals have a built-in or endogenous sexual rhythm.

Such a rhythm has been postulated for birds that regularly migrate great distances and experience rapid changes of daylength and temperature. The short-tailed shearwater, *Puffinus tenuirostris*, which breeds in the Australian summer and spends the southern winter in the northern hemisphere in the Aleutian Islands before returning to the shores of Australia in September, maintains its normal breeding pattern in captivity, when exposed to a completely different range and pattern of light conditions from those it experiences in the wild.

Despite these complications, there is an abundance of evidence to show that, for many species of vertebrate animals, light is the trigger which initiates breeding. Some respond to a regular spring extension of daylength and are known as long day breeders because they breed when daylength is increasing, while others—the short day breeders—respond to the autumnal decrease in daylength. Small species with a short gestation period mate and give birth within a few weeks, and it is among these species, such as squirrels and other small rodents, small insectivores like shrews and hedgehogs, and small carnivores, such as cats, ferrets, raccoons, weasles and mongooses, that the breeding season is cued by an increase in daylength. By breeding in spring these species ensure that their young are produced in summer when food is most abundant and of the highest quality, and when environmental temperatures are higher, which gives offspring the best start in life and the best chance of surviving the winter when food is scarce.

Large species, with a gestation period of six months or more, cannot use

The key to successful breeding in the animal kingdom is to produce young at the time of year that will give them the best chance of survival. In the tropics breeding is often timed to coincide with the start of the wet season. In temperate latitudes, where winters are harsher, it is more advantageous for animals to give birth to young at the start of spring when food is plentiful. Large species with gestation periods of more than six months, such as goats, sheep and deer, must thus mate in autumn. These short day breeders mate when days are shortening.

The precise timing of the start of the breeding season depends on local climatic conditions. Species tend more often to breed in synchrony as they move to higher latitudes because the weather dictates that matings and births must be squeezed into a short period. The graph shows the number of species of birds producing eggs at the same time in various latitudes. The birds included the song thrush, *Turdus ericetorum*, the prothonotary warbler, *Protonaria citrea*, and the Californian white-crowned sparrow, *Zonotrichia leucophrys*.

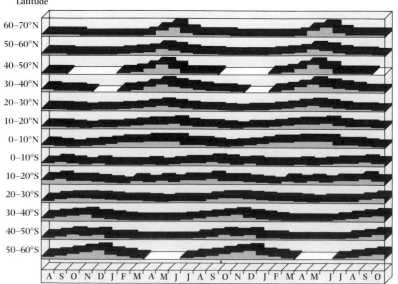

Small mammals, such as the cat, hare and ferret, have short gestation periods. They can thus mate towards the end of winter and give birth to their young in spring. These species are known as long day breeders because the cue that switches on the breeding cycle is an increase in daylight. It is not yet clear how the daylength cue actually triggers the hormonal mechanisms that allow breeding to begin, but the pineal body, in the brain, seems to be involved. Most rodents are long day breeders but in a mild autumn will produce young well into the winter.

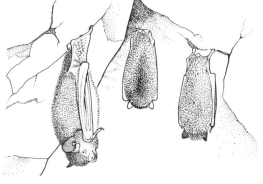

Bats spend the daylight hours inside dark caves and so cannot use daylength cues to trigger their breeding cycles. Despite this, bats such as *Miniopterus australis* always mate in September. It may be that the changing time of twilight, which marks the start of the bat's active period, is enough to begin the cycle, but the mechanism is still a mystery.

increasing daylength to start their surge of sexual activity. If they did, their young would be born in the autumn or early winter and would stand little chance of survival. So such animals are tuned to respond to decreasing daylength. Some short day breeders are sheep, goats and deer which all give birth in spring when food stocks are plentiful. Larger species, such as the horse, which have gestation periods of 10 months or more, respond to springtime cues of lengthening days, so timing the arrival of their young for the start of the following spring.

How do daylight cues actually influence the hormonal changes that are associated with the reproductive cycle? This is still a largely unanswered question, although significant progress toward understanding the mechanisms involved has been made. What is known is that no response in the gonads—the ovaries and testes—to daylength (photoperiod) occurs in animals which have no anterior pituitary gland. This is hardly surprising since it is the anterior pituitary that is responsible for the production of FSH early in the breeding cycle. What is surprising is that the eyes are not always essential to a gonadal response. In rats and ferrets, for instance, the eyes—and the optic nerves that link them to the brain—are necessary, whereas in ducks they are not. If a tiny glass fibre rod less than one twentieth of an inch (1 mm) in diameter is inserted into the brain of a male duck, and light is passed directly to the part of the brain adjacent to the pituitary gland, an increase in testis size takes place.

A largely mysterious and little-researched brain structure, the pineal body, has been implicated in the light-hormone pathway. In some lizards the pineal body actually pokes up through the skull, looking like a third eye on top of the head; in fact the pineal body is actually pigmented like a true eye and also has the ability to perceive light. Removal of the pineal body in male chameleons kept under natural light conditions results in enlargement of the testes. Thus, normally, the pineal seems to act in an inhibitory way, probably by secreting various substances into the blood which serve to regulate sexual development. In man and other mammals the pineal body does not seem to have a photoreceptive function because it is buried deep within the brain and light rays cannot reach it, nevertheless it appears to have some influence on sexual function. In one series of experiments the pineal bodies were removed from some female rats and the animals were then kept in complete darkness. It was found that these rats had larger ovaries than those not operated on and allowed normal access to light. Such experiments suggest that light, perceived either by the eyes or by the pineal body, acts on the pituitary gland and associated regions of the base of the brain, stimulating them to produce the various hormones that rule the sexual cycle.

The interrelationship between daylength and temperature in controlling the sexual cycle is clearly seen in a number of species. As far as the sex glands are concerned the breeding season consists of an enlargement phase and a shrinking phase. Like most small mammals, the American thirteen-lined ground squirrel, *Citellus tridecemlineatus*, starts to breed in spring. In midsummer the testes and ovaries start to shrink and by autumn are fully regressed. But if the squirrels are kept at a constant temperature of 4 degrees centigrade (39 degrees F), and under normal light, sex gland regression does not start until the end of autumn. This sort of link between sexuality and temperature does not ▷

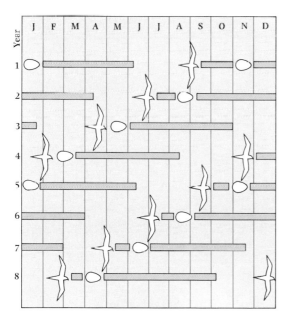

Most of the world's species of terns are migrators, covering incredible distances between their winter and summer quarters. Some tropical species do not migrate and one truly stay-at-home tern is the sooty tern, *Sterna fuscata*, which lives on the tropical Atlantic island of Ascension. The sooty tern breeds in a 9½-month cycle. Since the seasonal differences in daylength and average temperature are so slight it is not clear what triggers the breeding cycle, although it may be due to a cyclical variation in the abundance of fish food. Another explanation is that the sooty tern has an internal clock programmed to start the breeding cycle every 9½ months, allowing enough time for pairing, nest building, mating and moulting before the cycle restarts.

Flocks of sooty terns living on Ascension Island feed exclusively on fish. Each pair of terns lays its eggs in a crude nest on a crowded breeding ground where there is much squabbling, complaining and even open piracy. Despite this, enough chicks hatch each year to maintain the population.

▷ occur in all mammals, as studies on the European hamster, *Cricetus cricetus*, show. This creature normally hibernates in autumn, and before it does so its testes and ovaries are fully regressed. But if the hamsters are kept at 20 degrees centigrade (68 degrees F), so that they do not go into hibernation, their testes still regress in the usual way. So as for light, no simple rules about temperature apply to the regulation of mammalian breeding seasons.

Among the fish, cyclical temperature change is definitely an important cue for the sexual cycle. The environment enjoyed by fish has a relatively constant temperature, but this means that the smallest changes have significant repercussions on food supplies and, like mammals, fish also need to ensure that their young hatch out when food is available. In the male killifish, *Fundulus heteroclitus*, sperm formation, the process of spermatogenesis, starts when the water temperature reaches 10 degrees centigrade (50 degrees F), but is quite unaffected by daylength. Minnows, *Phoxinus phoxinus*, come into breeding condition as the water temperature rises, but full maturity depends upon the additional stimulus of long days. Interestingly, it has been shown that if minnows are kept under conditions of artificially short daylength, warm water inhibits sperm manufacture rather than stimulates it. Temperature also cues reproduction in certain lizards and amphibians, but again there is no universal rule governing this particular environmental influence.

A great many species of animals live either in the tropics, where light and temperature regimens undergo little annual variation, or in harsh environments where the likely food supplies for newborn young are unpredictable. Such species are seasonal breeders but even so they rely on certain environ-

mental triggers to set their sexual cycles in motion. Tropical animals rely on food availability, and the presence of certain compounds in fresh food seems to activate the cycle of sexual activity. In areas such as East Africa, where the year-round rainfall is relatively high, large mammals calve in every month of the year. This has been dramatically demonstrated in the case of the giraffe which has a gestation period of 15 months. In other parts of Africa, however, where rainfall is more seasonal, the timing of births corresponds more to the rainy season than to the dry season. Thus in the Kruger National Park in South Africa giraffes have two calving peaks corresponding to the periods of early summer and late summer rain.

Kangaroos are cued into breeding condition by daylength, and mate within a few days of becoming fully fertile. At ovulation, up to 20 eggs may be shed from the female and fertilized, but only one actually becomes implanted in the wall of the uterus and starts to develop. The others are held in a state of suspended animation, and may never be required. If there is adequate rainfall during the short gestation and throughout the first part of the youngster's pouch life, development will continue until the joey is weaned. The reserve eggs will then break down and disappear. If conditions of drought prevail, however, and the mother cannot find enough green vegetation sufficiently high in nutritive value to support both herself and her young, the embryo is expelled from the pouch before it has grown too large.

The cue that initiates this expulsion of the female kangaroo's burdensome embryo is the protein level of the forage; when it falls too low, the milk supply system is disturbed, resulting in the death of the young. Immediately this

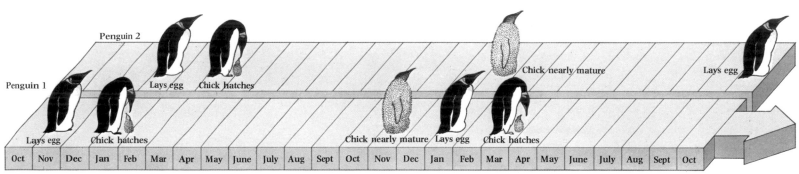

King penguins, *Aptenodytes patagonica,* must raise large chicks within one short Antarctic summer. They lay one egg at a time and can breed twice in every three years. In each season there are two peak periods of egg laying: one in November the other in January. Penguin (1) lays in November the first year and this chick is sufficiently independent for the parent to lay again in the January period of the next season. The third year, however, this second chick still needs its parent's attention and breeding is missed that year. Penguin (2) lays in January the first year. This chick is not fully grown the following season so the parent misses breeding that year but is free to lay early in the third year.

happens the corporea lutea in the ovary, which until this time have been suppressed, start secreting the hormone progesterone and one of the fertilized eggs from the reserve pool becomes implanted in the uterine wall. If the food supply does not improve this egg will go the way of its predecessor. This system of an environmental cue influencing the development of a new embryo is an excellent means of ensuring survival of a species in unpredictable surroundings, although it may seem wasteful, for in a year of intense drought many eggs will come to nothing.

Frogs and toads are other creatures whose reproduction is linked to water supplies. These animals need water in the form of a pool or puddle in which they can lay their eggs. Responding quickly to the sound and the feel of rain they actively seek out a mate and spawn before the water dries up. In some arid areas of the world tadpoles are dependent upon standing water for only a few days. A small African plains dwelling bird, the quelea, also needs rain before it will breed and in bad years no breeding will take place. Just the sound of rain falling on the parched earth is sufficient to induce gonad development, courtship and egg laying, although the precise mechanism by which the acoustic signals actually influence the hormonal balance is still a mystery.

The reproductive cycle of animals consists of more than just the physiological sexual cycle. Successful breeding embraces many behaviour patterns, including the courtship that precedes mating, and the eventual production and care of young. Perhaps one of the best-known behaviour patterns associated with breeding is the annual song cycle in birds. There are probably no birds whose song is absolutely constant throughout the year. In the northern

hemisphere, most small garden birds do not sing at all during the period from midsummer to late winter, although the red breasted European robin, *Erithacus rubecola*, is a tuneful exception to this rule. As the days begin to lengthen in February and March, the enlarging testes of the males of all the species produce increasing quantities of the male hormone testosterone, the same hormone that is made by the testes of mammals, including man. The birds' tendency to sing has been found to be closely correlated with the level of testosterone circulating in the blood.

As the mating season progresses—in April, May and June—and the testes approach their maximum size, the amount of song reaches its zenith. Experimentation has revealed that song production can be carefully controlled by artificially regulating daylength, and the songs of the birds can be kept at maximum level if the amount of light remains constant at its late spring or early summer level. This trick has long been known by bird fanciers who seek to lure migrating song birds to the ground. A caged member of the same species is kept at maximum singing level by means of controlled lighting, and is used as bait for its kin passing overhead.

Superimposed on the annual rhythm of bird song is a 24-hour daily rhythm. Most species sing less during the middle of the day than they do in the early morning or late afternoon. In hot, dry places the midday lull seems to be inextricably associated with heat and wind, but this cannot be the full story because the same phenomenon occurs in northern temperate areas. Certainly in arid regions any increase in humidity is usually associated with a renewed burst of song. Shortly after first light many male birds produce a burst of song, ▷

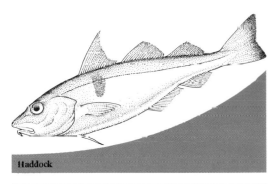

Haddock

The onset of breeding in fishes seems to be related to variations in water temperature, although the level of illumination may also play a part. Most fish species have a restricted range of temperatures within which they can breed. Giraffes, like man, are aseasonal breeders. Calves are born every month of the year with a slight increase coinciding with the onset of rains. Spadefoot toads, *Scaphiopus bombifrons*, inhabit the unpredictable environment of shallow pools which often dry up. During periods of drought the toads dig themselves into the mud and wait for rain. The arrival of the rain not only frees the toads but also triggers the development of the gonads and the production of spawn from which tadpoles emerge.

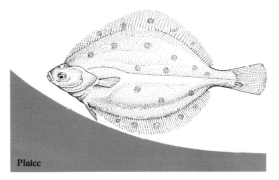

Plaice

▷ which lasts for about an hour. On wet, windy mornings it may be shortened or even absent, but on fine sunny mornings this dawn chorus can be dramatic. It seems to need just one particularly enthusiastic songster—often a blackbird—to start the entire choir into full voice. A few species of song birds sing only in the dawn chorus, but most sing later in the day as well, although the evening melodies are never as loud or as long as those of the early morning. Most ornithologists agree that the waves or bursts of song that punctuate the daily song period of any one bird are controlled by some innate factor, which is itself influenced by the level of production of testosterone.

There is certainly something spectacular about a great many animals all doing the same thing at the same time, and nowhere is mass activity more breathtakingly orchestrated than in the displays or leks of many game birds. Timing their activities for immediately after dawn, groups of male grouse and related species, such as prairie chickens, heath hens and blackcock, adopt the most ludicrous postures and swagger about in front of one another with a view to psychological intimidation. After many months of parading, the dominant cock emerging from this charade mates with the greatest number of females so that his traits of display are passed on to the next generation. The regularity of the lekking behaviour is remarkable, becoming earlier each day as daylength increases. Leks of a slightly different nature can be observed in certain species of bat, for example *Hypsignathus monstrosus*, the hammerhead bats of the Zaire Basin, which foregather in huge assemblies each evening just before twilight and sing loudly to one another.

Urban birds such as the starling, *Sturnus vulgaris*, perform the most intricate

aerial manoeuvres just as dusk is descending. Gathering in immense swarms of up to several thousand individuals, the entire mass rises into the air as one, wheeling and turning as if performing a carefully choreographed ballet. Just as suddenly as the aerial display starts it ends, with the dispersal of the flock. The function of these aggregations is not wholly understood, although it appears to be closely related to the prenuptial period and the assessment of the population size. It is not known how each individual actually responds to the assessment, although in certain years only a fraction of the adult population takes part in breeding. It may be that the stress of the display, or the activity it involves, tells more heavily on the weaker than on the stronger individuals in the flock and makes them less able to take, or to defend, a mate. What is particularly impressive, however, is the timing of these mass phenomena. Since they serve the important role of helping to prevent the population from becoming too large, they must occur at a clearly defined time of day. And the times of day at which light conditions are changing fastest—dawn and dusk—are clearly defined circadian landmarks.

The rhythmic movements of courtship often look like those of a ballet that has been professionally choreographed. In the crested grebe, *Podiceps cristatus*, for example, the male and female birds perform a sequence of courtship movements without which mating will not take place. As the male approaches the female he advertises his presence by raising the feathered, tuftlike crests on the top of his head and expanding his feathery ear flaps. As he gets nearer he adopts the 'cat' posture, hunching his neck and, at the same time, spreading out both wings to expose their white markings. The two birds then wag their

In the highlands of New Guinea young, unmarried tribesfolk take part in a type of mass 'courtship'. Couples traditionally rub their heads together and sing to one another before having sexual intercourse. Relationships forged in this ritual mating do not, in fact, lead to marriage. Instead, 'suitable' marriages are arranged by the families of young men and women. The rituals and rules of human courtship are different the world over and in the West are

undergoing rapid alteration related to more permissive attitudes and the changing role of women in society. In the animal world, matters are more rigid because courtship behaviour is largely governed by the levels of sex hormones in the blood. Closely related to courtship is aggressive behaviour between males with several rival males competing for the favours of one female. Paradoxically, behaviour such as fighting intimidates other males but may also attract a female.

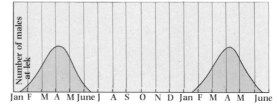

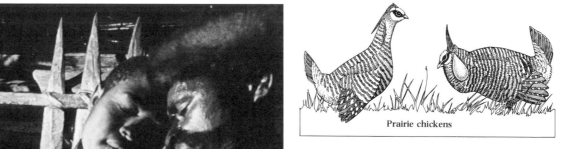

Prairie chickens

Before mating, males of many species of game birds, such as prairie chickens, *Tympanuchus cupidio*, strut about in front of one another for weeks or even months. Because it occurs in a traditional display place, or lek, this behaviour is described as lekking. When the few days for mating arrive, the highest ranking males will mate with the most females.

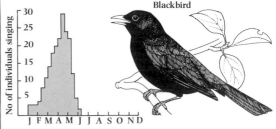

Like most garden songbirds, European blackbirds, *Turdus merula*, do not sing with the same intensity all year. From a slow start in January or February the number of individuals singing in early morning rises dramatically and reaches a peak in May. This peak corresponds with the nesting season. By July the number of birds singing has dropped and no song is heard from August to January.

heads at one another, pointing their bills rhythmically up and down.

After the head-wagging ceremony, the grebes may rise up out of the water and perform a 'penguin dance'. Both partners dive to the bottom of the pond, grab a piece of weed and rear out of the water face to face. Following this dance, or after head-wagging, one bird may retreat. It then faces its partner again and re-adopts the 'cat' display posture. The whole cycle of events is repeated several times before the pair go off to build their nest. Mating does not take place until the nest is finished and a platform of reeds has been built for the male to stand on. The male then drops his head to signal that he is ready to mate and the female stretches out her neck and flattens her crests to convey her readiness. A noisy copulation, with much wing-flapping by the male, is the culmination of the courtship ritual.

When it comes to courtship there are few animals that display a behaviour as rhythmic as that seen in fireflies. In many species of these nocturnally active beetles, which are members of the family Lampyridae, only the male is winged. The wingless female, who looks like a caterpillar and remains on the ground, is also commonly known as a glow-worm. Specialized light-producing or photogenic organs found on the undersurface of the abdomen in both sexes are used to help bring them together. The light from each male, which may be as strong as a fortieth of a candlepower, is flashed on and off rhythmically, with a frequency of about 5 seconds, each flash lasting about 0.2 seconds. The flashing, which is not like that of a lighthouse with a shutter temporarily obscuring the beam, but is the product of a controlled chemical reaction, continues as the flies rise and fall over the vegetation. Once a female on the ground flashes her light in reply, the male will fly down and copulate with her, but a male may flash his light rhythmically for many hours before he finds a mate and, because many males prefer to search together in a swarm, the twinkling effect is a delightful spectacle.

Although at first glance human courtship might appear to be devoid of any rhythmic or cyclic components, tribal peoples do still adhere to an ancient system of regular gatherings. The famous sun dances of the North American Indians, and the corroborees of the Australian Aborigines, although they have largely died out, were once gatherings of immense social significance, not least of which was to encourage courtship between members of different groups. They may also have allowed a population census to be made and this certainly happened in southwestern Asia during the era of the great nomadic caravanserais. Rather as the leks and massed swarms occur at the time of day at which they are most easily detected, early human social gatherings normally took place around the summer solstice, when the sun was at its highest in the sky. Regularly every year the tribes would gather to provide a formalized framework for intergroup trials of strength and stamina, as well as to encourage courtship dalliance. The reason these congregations took place in midsummer rather than in midwinter, which would have been equally distinctive, was because food was abundant in summer, so time could be spend on non-productive activities with equanimity.

Such social gatherings, tied to the calendar of the seasons, are a sort of social migration. Throughout the animal kingdom migration is a common phenomenon, although the reasons for its often vast scale of operation are sometimes ▷

Males compete for place on beach   Pregnant females come ashore   Females give birth   Males mate with females   Pregnant females return to sea

The breeding season of the southern elephant seal, *Mirounga leonina*, occurs on dry land. The first individuals ashore are the old bulls which squabble with one another over the division of the shore into territories. As the smaller females come on to land they are herded into harems by the bulls and many females are stolen by rival bulls. Within a few days any pregnant females give birth and spend much time suckling the young on rich, fatty milk. Meanwhile the bulls are busy inseminating the non-pregnant cows, all the time fighting off interested neighbours. About 10 days after giving birth the cows come into estrus again and they, too, are mated by the harem master. Soon afterwards they return to sea. The fertilized egg remains dormant for 3 to 4 months before development begins, and the new pups will be born after the adults have spent 11 months at sea.

▷obscure. Defined correctly, there are two components to a migration—an outward journey and a return journey. The irregular explosions of populations of Arctic and subarctic birds, such as waxwings, crossbills and sandgrouse, are one-way mass movements and certainly not predictable. In the truly migrant species the return and departure dates can be guaranteed as regular, rhythmic occurrences.

Breeding and feeding are, broadly speaking, the two reasons why animals adopt an annual migration pattern, but the two purposes may not be distinct. Subsidiary reasons for migration may include travel to a less hostile climate in which to give birth, so a species may undertake a migration to ensure that its young are born in an area in which the quantity or quality of food is optimal or the environment least damaging. Indeed there are few species that migrate for breeding or feeding only.

By definition, long distance migration must be a phenomenon restricted to those species that are highly mobile, the most dramatic examples being found among the birds, fishes and marine mammals and reptiles, and the large swift-footed land mammals. Small terrestrial mammals, reptiles and amphibians do not have the ability to move far but many, nevertheless, show a pattern of migratory movement. Thus the common toad, *Bufo bufo*, leaves the sanctuary of its home among vegetation every spring and searches for a pond—probably the one in which it was hatched—in which to spawn. After a few days, spent seeking for a mate and spawning, it returns to its former abode. In its own way this pattern of movement, in which the animal may travel only a few hundred yards, repeated year after year, is every bit as spectacular as the 17,000 mile

(27,000 km) breeding journey of the Arctic tern, or the 3,800 mile (6,000 km) trek of the caribou. Even rabbits, among the most sedentary of creatures, show a burst of activity annually at the start of the breeding season and build new sets of underground delivery rooms in which the mothers-to-be will incarcerate themselves to await the birth of their litters. Compared with the incredible breeding journeys of some species such activities differ only in scale—their purpose is the same.

A small number of species shows an annual pattern of migration that is associated only with feeding. This may be because of the seasonal pattern of rainfall, as it is with the annual east-west migration of herds of wildebeest, impala and zebra in Tanzania. Associated with these movements are migratory groups of hunting dogs, jackals and hyenas which prey upon the newborn and the weak. In these tropical areas breeding continues throughout the year with animals showing no preference for a special time or place. In North America huge herds of bison, *Bison bison*, once roamed the plains from northern Alberta to New Mexico, and from Oregon to Pennsylvania. They moved northward in spring and gave birth soon after the young, nutritious grass had started to sprout. In autumn the herds migrated southward again to avoid the harshness of the northern winter in which food was hard to find. Although the migration was primarily for feeding purposes, breeding regularly occurred at the start of the trek.

Depending for their survival upon the bison herds were the plains Indians, who regularly migrated northward and southward, following their quarry. Thus the Arapaho from central Colorado annually trekked a couple of

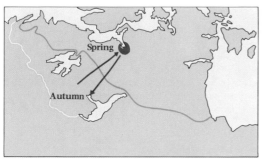

Migration means that an animal can have the best of both worlds—constant temperature conditions throughout the year and no shortage of food. Caribou, *Rangifer tarandus, below,* spend the winter in the forests of Alberta, Saskatchewan and Manitoba in Canada, *left,* and start their trek northward to the Barren Lands in spring. The deer head northward for almost 4,000 miles (6,400 km), lured by the prospect of lush lichens and spring grass during the Arctic summer. On the journey the calves are born and from their first day are initiated into a life of regular migration. Mating occurs in the summer pasture before the caribou begin their long march south.

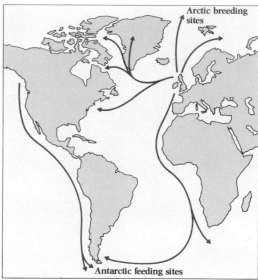

thousand miles through Wyoming, Montana and into Alberta in pursuit of bison. Humans, as we have seen, have no set breeding season, and births are recorded in every month of the year, so as far as the Arapaho people were concerned the annual migration was for feeding purposes alone.

The most astonishing breeding migrations are displayed by the birds that breed in the northern parts of the world in the summer months and spend the winter in southern latitudes. One such is the Arctic tern, *Sterna paradisea*, a marine bird which breeds in the summer as far north as Baffin Island and northwest Greenland, then flies off to Antarctica. By undertaking such vast migratory journeys from one polar region to the other, this bird is able to spend its whole life in more or less constant climatic conditions. During August, when its chicks are fully fledged and able to fend for themselves, the terns start to fly southward, following the northern coast of Labrador, and then off southeastward across the Atlantic.

Once they pick up the west coast of the Iberian peninsular, the migrating terns may be joined by others of their kind who have bred in northern Scotland and Scandinavia. As far south as the Azores the flocks tend to split up, one part following the west coast of Africa, the other the east coast of South America, until the Antarctic continent comes into sight. The return route is the same. The birds feed little on either their way south, or on their way back, although short resting periods do occur. A similar pattern of migration is seen in the European swallow, *Hirundo rustica*, which breeds in northern Europe and overwinters as far south as South Africa.

Why do these birds undertake such incredible journeys attended by dangers of every conceivable kind? There is no simple answer to this question, but the food resources at the breeding site certainly play a vital role in maintaining the migratory behaviour. Because the bulk of the earth's land mass lies in the northern hemisphere the amount of shallow seawater, in which the Arctic tern finds the whitebait on which it feeds, and the number of flying insects, upon which the swallow depends for sustenance, are far higher in the northern than in the southern half of the globe. The cost, in terms of both energy and life, of undertaking a huge migration, is more than offset by the riches of food to be found in the northern summer at journey's end.

For some terrestrial species the lure of such banquets is sometimes like a two-edged sword. The caribou of North America, *Rangifer tarandus*, which is identical with the European reindeer, spends its winters in the Canadian forests of Alberta, Saskatchewan and Manitoba. Caribou mate in late summer, just when they are preparing to leave the lichen-rich heaths of the northern Barren Lands, but the females do not feel the first birth pangs until some eight months later when they are migrating northward, again seeking nutritious lichens. But if the early spring weather is particularly inclement, the caribous' northward progress may be much slower than normal and the young may be born in a most inhospitable environment. Not only may the young perish in intense cold and blizzard conditions, but their mothers may also be unable to make sufficient milk to feed them during their first few shaky days of life. And like the hyenas following the wildebeest in Africa, there will be wolves eagerly awaiting their chance of an easy meal. Enough caribou survive, however, for there still to be large stocks of this courageous species.   ▷

Man is frequently a migrant species and his migrations are sometimes related to the movements of herds of large ungulates. In northern Europe the Lapps, *right*, have for countless generations followed the migration of vast herds of caribou (known in Europe as reindeer) as they seek out the rich plant growth of the high Arctic summer. Human reproduction is not linked to any phase of the migration—the association seems to have developed so that man can exploit his food resources more efficiently.

Among the most astounding of all the regular migrations undertaken by animals is the annual 17,000 mile (27,000 km) pilgrimage made by Arctic terns, *Sterna paradisea, left*, from their Arctic breeding sites to their Antarctic winter feeding sites. Flying over the open ocean as well as hugging continental coastlines, the birds use Atlantic winds to help them on their way. They stop infrequently, but spells of bad weather may force flocks to seek refuge for several days at a time. The tremendous effort of the journey is finally rewarded with a rich supply of whitebait.

▷ A number of truly outstanding breeding migrations involving fish, reptiles and mammals occur in the sea. The largest of all mammals, the whales, live mostly in the southern oceans where the continental shelf of Antarctica causes a vast upwelling of nutrients from the cool, deeper layers, which mix with the relatively warmer surface waters. Here microscopic plants and animals, which collectively compose the plankton, thrive as nowhere else on earth, and the whales cruise slowly through the dense plankton swarms, their mouths agape like the cutters of a combine as it passes through a field of wheat.

Although warm enough for well-insulated adult whales, the surface waters of the southern oceans are much too cold for newborn calves, which explains why many whales undertake breeding migrations towards the Equator, away from their feeding grounds. Thus the humpback whales, *Megaptera novae-angliae*, travel northward to the coastal regions of South America and southern Africa and there, in the warm and shallow waters, produce their calves. But while the diversity of planktonic organisms may be high in these regions, the sheer bulk of them is lacking. So once the calves are big enough to travel, the whales set off southward once again in search of the rich plankton pastures. During their migration the whales eat little, relying on their stored reserves of blubber to supply them with energy for movement and the nutrients to make milk for their calves. Humpbacks live in the north Atlantic as well as in the south, and the northern stock migrates to the warmer waters of the Caribbean shortly before giving birth. Since each stock travels toward the Equator in its own particular winter, the two communities do not meet at the breeding grounds.

Salmon, and a few related game fish, lay their eggs in fresh water, choosing fast-flowing rivulets with sandy or gravelly bottoms, high up among the headstreams of major rivers in Europe and North America. After hatching, the young fish spend the first two years or so of their lives in this relatively secure environment before embarking on a downstream adventure. With a remarkable physiological accommodation to the problems posed by passing from fresh to salt water, the young smolts head out into the Atlantic or Pacific oceans. There, at the edge of the continental shelf, they feed voraciously on the rich plankton whose pink colour is transmitted to the fishes' flesh. For one or two years they remain at sea then, as grilse, start the long haul back to their natal streams.

It is still not known how the grilse find their way back from 1,500 miles (2,400 km) out at sea to the coastline they left two years before, but once in the vicinity of the river mouth they can recall the odour of their home stream and, jumping huge waterfalls and negotiating tumultuous rapids, the adult salmon press on their way. They enter the rivers in August and September when in some early-running fish the gonads are not fully developed, but by October/November both males and females are fully mature.

Reaching the spawning grounds the fish court briefly and, as the female extrudes her eggs, the male sheds his sperm all over them. Huge stretches of the river may turn white because of the millions of sperm suspended in it. For the Pacific salmon—sockeye, chinook, coho, chum and humpback, all species of *Oncorhynchus*—spawning marks the end of their lives. The spent fish lie listlessly in the shallows, providing abundant food for foxes, wolves, brown

Because they encounter no physical barriers, water dwelling animals can migrate with comparative ease. Some migratory aquatic animals have to contend with physiological barriers, such as the change from fresh to salt water or vice versa, but migrant species have evolved means of overcoming these problems. Migration in the sea has the same function as migration on dry land, that is, it allows a species to breed in one place and to feed in another. How migration evolved is still a mystery, but it may be that the drifting apart of the continents in past eras was significant. Whatever the reason, the migrations of whales, eels, turtles and salmon are spectacular.

The world's two migratory populations of humpback whales, one in the northern hemisphere, the other in the southern, never compete for food at the breeding grounds because there is a six-month interval between the winters at the North and South Poles. The whales return to colder waters after calving.

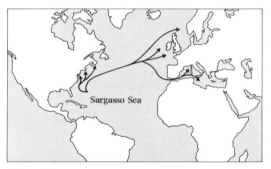
Sargasso Sea

Every eel or elver, *below,* found in European or North American waters, was born in the Sargasso Sea off the southeast coast of Florida, *left.* The 8,000 mile (12,800 km) journey to European waters takes up to three years. After several years the eels set out to retrace their journey and breed and die in the Sargasso.

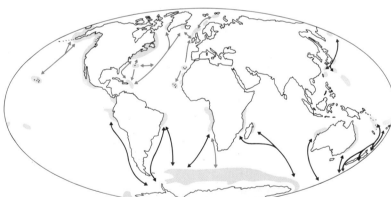

→ Migration routes of southern species

→ Migration routes of northern species

▭ Feeding and calving grounds

The nutrients in the currents of Antarctic waters support huge crops of krill, small shrimplike creatures on which the humpback whales feed. Despite this rich supply of food the whales migrate north in winter to the warm coastal waters of Africa, South America and Australia.

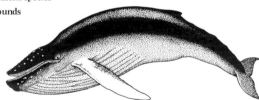

The humpback whale, *Megaptera novae-angliae,* lives in the freezing waters of the Arctic and Antarctic. Although nutrient-rich, these cold waters are no place for giving birth, so shortly before the winter the humpbacks migrate toward the Equator in search of warmer, shallower water. There the calves are born and the young suckled.

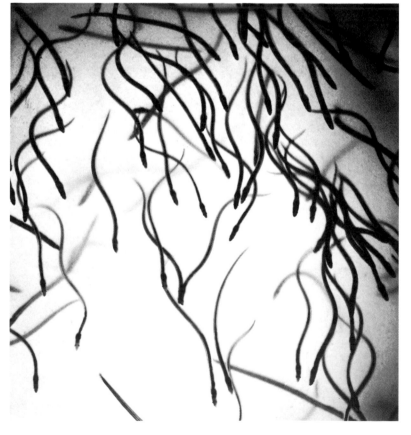

bears and bald headed eagles. But the spent Atlantic salmon, *Salmo salar*, has another chance. As thin, ragged-looking kelts they drift and float downstream, and while many perish from exhaustion on the way—for adult salmon do not feed from the moment they enter fresh water—a few manage to return to the oceanic feeding grounds. There, fortified with a rich plankton diet, they quickly rebuild their strength in readiness for the next spawning run. The timing of the run varies only slightly from year to year, so anglers can book salmon fishing holidays for the late summer with great confidence.

The annual breeding migrations of the European and American eels, *Anguilla anguilla* and *A. rostrata* respectively, are just as spectacular as those of the salmon. These fish are described as catadromous because they breed in the sea but feed in fresh water, in contrast to the anadromous salmon which behave in the opposite way. (Both types of creature have similar physiological problems to overcome when they pass from salt to fresh water and back again.) For almost three centuries zoologists have been actively trying to understand the biology of the eel, because sexually mature adults are never found in fresh water. Even Aristotle noticed this in the fourth century BC, declaring that eels arose from the 'entrails of the earth'. What appears to happen is that eels lay their eggs at great depth in the Sargasso Sea, some several hundred miles east of Florida. After hatching into tiny, flattened larvae, the baby eels begin their long swim toward fresh water.

For the American eels living in the eastern United States the journey takes only about a year, but the young European eels take three years to reach fresh water. By this time they are unmistakably small eels, or elvers, about 4 inches (10 cm) long. After some years in the rivers, the fully grown—but not sexually mature—eels set off again out into the ocean, heading for the Sargasso Sea. They swim at the great depth of 1,700 feet (500 m) or more, and on this journey their ovaries and testes develop. When they finally reach the Sargasso they spawn and die. No eel has ever been recorded as completing more than one spawning migration although American eels, because they have a far less strenuous journey than their transatlantic cousins, may spawn twice in a lifetime.

No account of breeding migrations could be complete without mention of the extraordinary travels of the green turtle, *Chelonia mydas*. Huge numbers of these large reptiles feed on rich growths of 'turtle grass' that fringe the eastern coast of Brazil. Green turtles breed on Ascension Island—a tiny outcrop of rock some 870 miles (1,400 km) distant in the south Atlantic ocean. Tagging studies have shown that young turtles hatched on Ascension return two years later to breed on the shore where they were born, but how they manage to find such a tiny target in such a vast ocean is a mystery. It is indeed a puzzle why turtles should bother to migrate at all for breeding, because perfectly adequate sites exist close to their feeding grounds. It has been argued that, before the process of continental drift separated the southern land masses of South America and Africa, Ascension Island was merely an offshore island, easily reached by the turtles in a day. Remaining faithful to their ancient breeding site as it moved eastward, the turtles were forced to make an ever more hazardous journey for breeding. That they succeed at all is a testament to their remarkable navigational ability. ▷

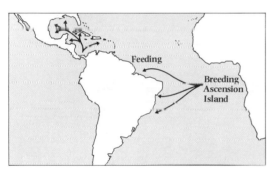

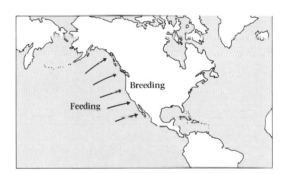

Salmon hatch in the headstreams of rivers and migrate out to sea, returning to fresh water to breed, *right*. After two or three years in fresh water, young Pacific salmon, *Oncorhynchus* spp, travel down the rivers and out to sea to enjoy the rich feeding grounds of the continental shelf. After two or three years young salmon feel the urge to breed and head back towards the land. On finding their natal stream they follow its branches until they reach the breeding shallows in which they were born. After spawning once, Pacific salmon die and provide an abundance of food for animals such as bears and bald eagles. The young hatch, develop and repeat the migration cycle.

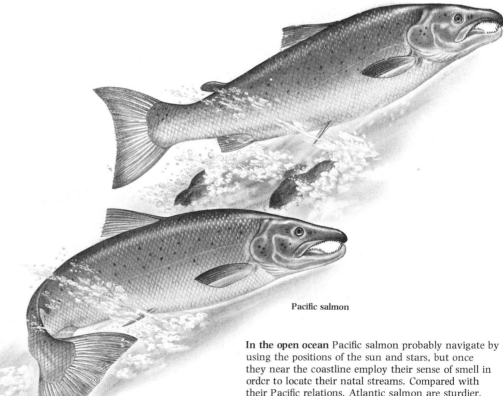

Pacific salmon

At breeding time, green turtles, *Chelonia mydas*, converge on Ascension Island 870 miles (1,400 km) from their feeding grounds off Brazil. The turtles may find their way by following the island's odour, which moves west in surface currents, and the turtles retain a memory of this odour in their brains. This memory is formed in the first days after hatching.

In the open ocean Pacific salmon probably navigate by using the positions of the sun and stars, but once they near the coastline employ their sense of smell in order to locate their natal streams. Compared with their Pacific relations, Atlantic salmon are sturdier, have a shorter journey, and can return to their breeding grounds to complete a second breeding cycle.

▷ The actual process of spawning, or egg laying, is also a rhythmical and carefully timed activity. An abundance of evidence indicates the rhythmic waxing and waning of the moon exerts a strong influence on spawning, either directly, through nighttime illumination levels, or indirectly, via its effect on the tides. There is a very good reason why the moon should be so influential: life in the sea is remarkably free from the pronounced seasonal effects to which terrestrial animals are exposed, and by which they synchronize their reproductive activities. And in a vast, homogeneous environment such as the sea it is absolutely crucial that the mechanism of reproduction be synchronized, so that the eggs of one individual stand a reasonable chance of being fertilized by the sperm of another.

Most marine invertebrates, such as molluscs, annelid worms, sea urchins, jellyfish and crustacea, simply cast their eggs and sperm in the waters in a haphazard fashion, so if all members of the population do this at the same time, the chances of fertilization are greatly increased. By far the most dramatic example of this is the South Pacific palolo worm, *Eunice viridis*. This worm, which is related to the common lugworm of temperate sandy shores, lives among coral reefs surrounding the Pacific islands of Samoa and Fiji. It breeds just once a year in a most curious manner. As the November spawning season approaches, the rear part of each worm becomes packed either with eggs, which impart a bluish hue, or sperm, which give a ruddy appearance. By day the worms remain curled up inside crevices in the reef, but at night they emerge to forage for microscopic invertebrates among the coral. During these forays they detect the level of lunar illumination. Then, around full moon, the rear

ends of the worms break free and wriggle to the water surface. There they burst open, and the sea turns white with the spilt sex cells or milt. The Samoans find baked palolo milt a great delicacy, so the November full moon signals an annual feast for them.

Careful experiments under controlled conditions show that it is the number of hours of lunar illumination that brings the worms to the peak of readiness— rather as the increasing daylength brings on sexual receptivity in mammals and birds, and triggers the dawn chorus—but the actual release of the sperm and egg bags is triggered by the pressure exerted by sea water in a particular phase of the tide.

A similar, though less dramatic effect is seen in several other types of worm. The Atlantic palolo, *Leodice fucata*, which lives among the coral rocks of the Tortugas islands off the coast of Florida, swarms every year within three days of the last quarter of the moon between 29 June and 28 July. A number of other species appear to relate their reproductive activity to the lunar rhythmicity, including many female 'fireworms' which flash luminescent lights to attract males during swarming.

Only one example is known of a sea urchin that responds to a lunar rhythm. The species *Diadema setosum* from the Red Sea spawns each full moon, requiring the intervening four weeks for the maturation of a new batch of eggs and sperm. Lunar periodicity of breeding is not known for any other species of sea urchins, even those that live in similar latitudes and habitats, but fishermen in the Mediterranean region still maintain that all sea urchins are best eaten at the time of the full moon.

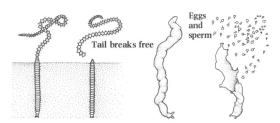

At spawning time the rear half of the palolo worm, *Eunice viridis*, thickens and becomes attracted to light. The worm's front half, *left*, stays in a crevice but the rear half breaks off, shedding eggs or sperm.

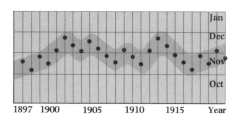

Palolo worms spawn around the November full moon, *left*. The end of each worm detects the waxing of the moon and when it reaches a maximum breaks off.

● Swarm

For many peoples of the South Pacific, including the Samoans, November full moon heralds a feast, because the palolo worms swarm at this time and can be caught in huge numbers. The South Sea islanders then bake the freshly caught morsels which are considered a delicacy. This fishery is one of the safest in the world, for no matter how many worms are caught the breeding stock is in no danger. The reason is that the parent worms, which released their bags of eggs and sperm, are safely ensconced in the dark crevices of rocks and coral reefs.

Through its action on the tides, the moon also influences reproduction in a few species of fish. In one, *Enchelyopus cimbrus*, from the east coast of Canada, the breeding season lasts several months, reaching its peak in July and August. The eggs are pelagic, that is, they float in open water toward the surface of the sea, and routine sampling of the surface waters shows a great abundance of eggs at the time of spring tides, when the moon is full. Between the spring tides of July and August the rate of egg production is almost nil. Even the neap tides—some 10 feet (3 m) lower than the east coast springs—are insufficient to trigger spawning. Since these fish live at a depth of 98 feet (30 m) or more, where temperature and illumination differences are likely to be insignificant, the actual cue that triggers off mating must be the rhythmic rise and fall of water pressure as the spring tide approaches.

Over on the west coast of North America, particularly in the San Pedro region of California, lives another fish with a remarkable sex life. This little fish, the grunion, *Leuresthes tenuis*, buries its clusters of eggs in the sand at the high water mark of the spring and neap tides. The moment the high water mark has been reached the grunion start to 'run'. They swim ashore in great numbers and can easily be observed mating and laying eggs in shallow scrapes which the female makes as the eggs pour out of her. The gentle lapping of the water covers the eggs with sand and within 60 seconds the adults have swum back out to sea. The eggs remain cool and damp, but are not exposed until the next spring tides. Then the erosion of their protective cover induces them to hatch, and the larval grunion head out to sea, starting their free life among the plankton. A much smaller run occurs at the neap tides, so there is a fortnightly cycle of

ripening eggs and sperm. It appears that the variation in water pressure associated with the tidal rhythm acts to control egg development, which continues unabated from March until June but peaks strongly in late April and May.

Synchronization of spawning with the phases of the moon may be far more widespread than has been thought up to now. It has been discovered, for example, that one species of mayfly, namely, *Povila adusta*, which inhabits the airspace over Lake Victoria and Lake Albert in East Africa, shows a lunar rhythm. The adult female mayflies lay their eggs in the water and these eggs hatch into water dwelling larvae. The emergence of swarms of adult flies from the eggs occurs about two days after the August full moon each year. The behaviour of the mayfly larvae also shows a circadian rhythm. During the day these larvae stay hidden and inactive in burrows made in the litter at the bottom of the lake, but at dusk they emerge and swim vigorously toward the water surface. Experiments in which the larvae are kept in conditions of continual darkness reveal that the rhythm is maintained, which suggests that it is inbuilt.

Future research into the rhythmic reproductive behaviour of animals may well reveal that most spawning species are affected by a combination of an annual reproductive season, the monthly periodicity of the moon and the tides, and the daily cycle of changing light intensity. The total purpose of all these rhythms is to bring the reproductive activities of a whole population into synchrony, perhaps during just a single hour, once each year. As with all reproduction, this behaviour ensures the continuance of the species.

The **Californian grunion**, *Leuresthes tenuis*, is a 6 in (15 cm) fish which spawns at night, either at full or crescent moon. Carried on to shore on a wave, the male and female intertwine and in a brief moment the female extrudes her eggs which are fertilized by the male and deposited about 2 in (5 cm) below the surface of the sand. The fish are carried out to sea and two weeks later, at the next spring high tide, the eggs hatch. More eggs may be laid every 15 days.

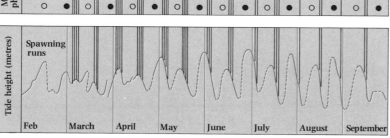

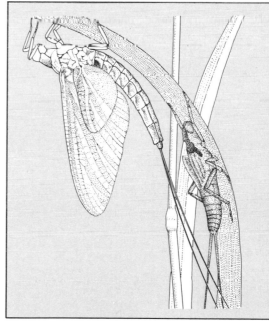

Lunar rhythms are usually confined to marine animals, but one exception is the mayfly, *Povilla adusta*, *left*, from Lake Victoria. Swarms of these hatch from aquatic larvae and are recorded about two days after the August full moon, *above*. The larvae are nocturnal in their behaviour, swimming to the surface at dusk, and this rhythm persists even if larvae are kept in total darkness.

Grunion spawn from March until September but the breeding season may end in late June. The runs may be controlled by changes in water pressure due to the rhythmic cycle of the tides, and by perception of the lunar phases. They can be predicted with great certainty since they always occur at the highest spring and neap tides. Because of this predictable availability, grunion fishing must be carefully regulated.

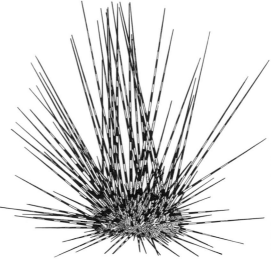

Only one sea urchin, namely, *Diadema setosum*, *left*, shows a lunar rhythm and in only one location. In the Suez region of the Mediterranean the urchins spawn at full moon, becoming ripe for further spawning at the next full moon. At Naples, Marseilles, Alexandria and on the Atlantic coast at Roscoff, there is no hint of moon-related spawning. Why this spawning should occur in such a limited way is as yet unexplained.

Population cycles

Every time a baby is born, utters its first yell and begins to breathe another human generation is complete. Both the mother and the father of this baby have brought their lives full circle and fulfilled, in reproductive terms, their *raison d'être* as part of the human race. Like man, all species of plants and animals that populate the earth have some sort of life cycle in which stages of development follow one another in an ordered sequence. The cyclical patterns have no beginning or end as long as the species persists, because an end to the cycle means extinction. For individuals the ring is broken if they do not or cannot reproduce themselves, or if they die of natural causes or are killed before they have a chance to procreate.

Often the word generation is used to mean the same thing as life cycle, but strictly a generation is the time that elapses between the birth of the parents and the birth of the offspring. The two are often synonymous but in some animals such as aphids, which infest plants, the life cycle contains several generations. Taking the egg produced in autumn and designed to last out the winter as the starting point in the aphid's life cycle, the next cycle will begin with the production of the next batch of overwintering eggs in the autumn of the next year. This annual life cycle is divided into many generations because the female aphids make many clones of female-only offspring with developing embryos of the next generation already forming inside them.

Annual breeding is commonplace in the living world. Man has extricated his reproduction from the web of the weather but for almost all other creatures the seasons have a profound effect upon their life cycles. Annual plants are a prime example, passing the winter as resistant seeds, then growing, flowering and setting fresh seed during the summer. Another big group of plants, the biennials, which includes many important root crops, such as parsnips, carrots, beetroot, swedes and sugar beet, takes two years to complete its life cycle. In their first year biennials grow from seed and lay down food stores in a swollen root or some other sort of storage organ. This food store carries the species through the winter so that it can grow rapidly in the following spring and produce flowers and seeds. Perennials—plants that live more than two years—have a persistent root system or storage structure, such as a bulb, corm or tuber, and make flowers and seeds every year.

Among the animals many soft-bodied invertebrates have annual life cycles but there may be one, two or three cycles squeezed into every 12 months. At the other end of the scale, the 17-year cicada, *Magicicada* spp, a native of North America, spends 17 years as a juvenile form or nymph, feeding underground on the sap of plant roots. Adults emerging from these nymphs in the same year spend a deafening summer of song, then mate, and the females lay their eggs. The young nymphs that hatch out burrow underground and 'disappear' for the next 17 years. This 17-year cycle is a local one so odd individuals which hatch out of phase with the majority have little chance of finding a mate.

In most populations patterns of change occur which encompass every developmental stage in a creature's life cycle. Animal and plant species usually have irregular populations which respond to changes in food or the climate, but some show definite cycles of change in which the number of individuals rises and falls. Four and ten-year cycles are common in some mammal and bird populations, while six to eight-year cycles occur in some moths, and two to four-year cycles are typical of several diseases, such as measles and rabies, which infect man and other animals.

The development of almost all plants and animals takes place as a cycle of events starting from a fertilized egg, progressing through various juvenile growth stages and ending with mature adults, which complete the cycle by producing eggs which are fertilized and give rise to the next generation. This is an organism's life cycle and, like all cyclical events, it goes through a sequence of stages before returning to its starting point. Exceptions to this basic cyclical pattern, which could begin anywhere but, purely for convenience, is taken as starting with the fertilized egg, are found throughout the animal and plant kingdoms. Many microscopic organisms, including bacteria, yeasts and a large proportion of single-celled animals (protozoa), reproduce simply by splitting into two in the process of fission, or by making buds which later break off the parent to become independent. The non-sexual life cycle is thus growth, fission and back to growth again. Occasionally these organisms have a 'sexual' stage inserted into the cycle. In this two different individuals of opposite 'sexes' or strains meet, fuse and give rise to a sort of egg, which may be useful by being resistant to specific environmental hazards.

Whether sexual or asexual, life cycles are by no means uniform and may differ in a number of distinct ways. One important variation is the length of time it takes for a life cycle to come full circle. For both animals and plants, the general rule is the bigger an organism, the longer its life cycle. So while it takes less than three weeks to increase the total cell-weight or biomass of a blowfly egg up to that of an adult, the microscopic egg of an elephant takes about 14 years to reach the 7,700 lb (3,500 kg) norm of an adult female capable of releasing fertile eggs. Most of the organisms that are a menace to man, be they

weeds, pests or diseases, are troublesome primarily because they are small and thus have a short generation time. In favourable environments brief lives allow for the rapid build up of the weed or pest, so large animals and plants can never be pests or weeds but mosquitoes and many grasses often can be.

The length of a life cycle has other important implications for the life-style of an organism. In a very short life cycle survival depends on quantity rather than quality of egg production, while for organisms with long life cycles the reverse is the case. Thus small creatures, such as insects with short life cycles, reach maturity quickly and release vast numbers of eggs, which are easily dispersed but just as easily destroyed or eaten by other animals. As a life cycle lengthens, so the time and energy invested in it by the advent of maturity is much greater, and there is, therefore, much more emphasis on covering the capital sum committed to the project by means of defence mechanisms, increased efficiency in obtaining food, and coping with competition. The eggs that are made tend to be few in number and well provided with food reserves to nourish the new individual in its first stages of growth and development. And the parents often expend considerable energy—as human parents will testify—in protecting and providing for the young of the next generation.

For some organisms habitat has a profound influence on their life cycle. Many plants and animals complete their life cycles in the same habitat. The young elephant, for example, has much the same structure and requirements as its parents, and if food or space became limited there would be direct competition between juveniles and mature adults for the available resources. In a forest this sort of competition is easy to observe. The mature trees are well

The life of the lung fluke, *Haematoloechus medioplexus,* cycles between three hosts, in water as well as on land. The adults of this common parasite live in the lungs of North American frogs, eg *Rana pipiens,* and toads, eg *Bufo americanus,* which frequent ponds and lakes. Eggs produced by the adult flukes are swept out of the lung by the action of its tiny hairs or cilia, and are subsequently swallowed, passing through the digestive system and out in the amphibian's faeces. The faeces, containing the first infective stage, are then eaten by an aquatic snail, which consumes organic

debris at the bottom of the pond. Enzymes in the snail's intestine stimulate the eggs to hatch, and the young parasites burrow through the gut wall and move into the snail's liver. Here they develop, multiply asexually and, in heavy infections, destroy the liver totally. After about three months the second infective stage, the cercariae, escape from the snail. These are able to swim, and live for only 30 hours during which time they must infect the next host, a young nymph of the dragonfly, *Sympterum.* Modified for respiration, the rectum of the nymph can pump water in and out via

the anus. Any nearby cercariae, drawn into the nymph's rectum by these respiratory currents, quickly burrow into the rectal tissue and form cysts around themselves. Frogs and toads eat either the nymphs or the freshly emerged adults which sit on leaves while their wings expand and their cuticles harden. The third infective stage emerges from the cyst in the amphibian's stomach, makes its way up the oesophagus and down into the lungs, so completing its cycle. The flukes mature in 37 days during the summer and remain in the frogs for up to 15 months.

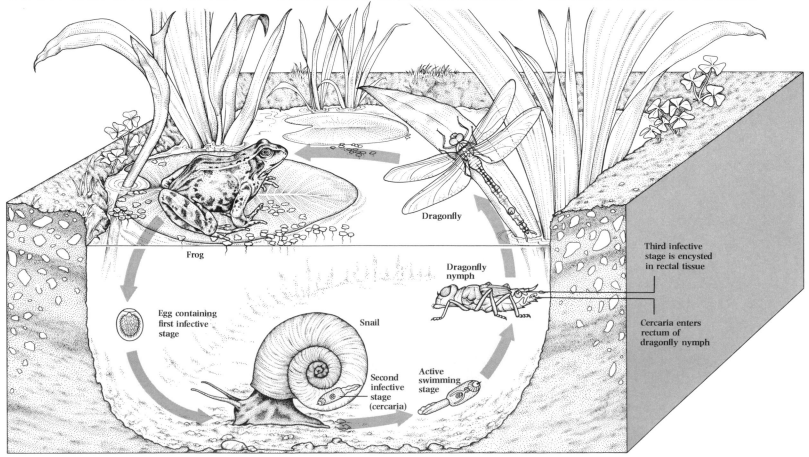

Frog

Dragonfly

Egg containing first infective stage

Snail

Dragonfly nymph

Second infective stage (cercaria)

Active swimming stage

Third infective stage is encysted in rectal tissue

Cercaria enters rectum of dragonfly nymph

spaced out with their canopies forming a continuous cover. This dense umbrella prevents sufficient light from reaching the forest floor and thus stops any tree seedlings from developing successfully. Clearings created by fallen or felled trees are, in contrast, a riot of young growth, and in time the vacant space in the canopy is filled by the most successful offspring.

To side-step the intense competition that may develop when the young and mature stages of a species both occupy the same habitat, many organisms make use of two different habitats during the course of their life cycle. Insects, for instance, which in terms of numbers of species are the most abundant of all organisms on earth, frequently double up on habitats, using one for the developing young and another for the mature adults. Most adult butterflies and moths exist primarily in the aerial habitat and feed on pollen, nectar and rotting fruits, but the herbivorous, land-locked larvae live for the most part on vegetation, chewing on leaves, stems and sometimes roots.

In fresh water, adult water beetles and water boatmen may share the available space and food with their offspring, but dragonflies, caddisflies and a host of other aquatic insects leave the water as adults to feed and live on land or in the air. Among the vertebrates those that make use of the land-water habitat duo are mostly amphibians, a group that represents the ancestors of the first backboned animals to leave the water for a life on land. Frogs, toads, salamanders and newts are all amphibians that use aquatic habitats for their juvenile tadpole stages, but exploit the land in a variety of ways as adults. These changes in habitat and feeding methods lead to dramatic alterations in shape and form—the contrast between caterpillar and butterfly, for example.

Competition between adults and their young is not the only reason for having a second home. In seasonal temperate environments, where the winter is distinct and cold, making use of two habitats may be a way of counteracting the effects of an adverse climate. In water the temperature fluctuates far less than it does on land, so an aquatic habitat has inbuilt buffers against rapid temperature change. Many insect larvae continue to grow and develop in fresh water during the winter, when the adults that gave rise to them have been killed off by the cold. Migration is another way of dealing with locally adverse conditions. Birds often use temperate food-rich regions of the world for raising their young, then move to a warmer zone to avoid the winter.

Parasites are animals or plants that live at the expense of—and often inside—other creatures which are known as their hosts. The life cycles of parasites differ widely in complexity and these differences are based on the theme of changing habitats. The body of the host is, by definition, the habitat of a parasite, but the host's own habitat may also influence the parasite. A few parasites complete their entire life cycle in a single host. For example, the pinworm, *Enterobius* sp, is a roundworm that commonly infests children, making its home in the lower section of the intestine and living on digested food. Repeated infection takes place when eggs are accidentally eaten as a result of lax hygiene. A similar situation is found in pigs who are prey to infestation by another roundworm by the name of *Ascaris*.

More commonly, parasites use two hosts so that the juvenile stages develop in one host, the mature egg-producing adults in another. The serious tropical disease bilharzia is caused by a parasitic flatworm *Schistosoma*. The adult ▷

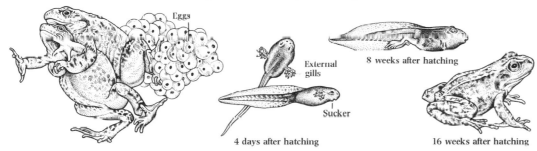

Eggs

External gills

8 weeks after hatching

Sucker

4 days after hatching

16 weeks after hatching

The larger an animal species, the longer is its life cycle. A full grown elephant weighs 3 to 4 tons and is at least 10 ft (3 m) high at the shoulder. The foetus spends nearly two years in the womb and only one offspring is produced at a time. Each baby has the same structure and food requirements as the adult, reaches sexual maturity in 13 to 17 years and lives for up to 70 years. The elephant's immense body requires a constant intake of food so it forages for most of the day. In some parts of Africa the elephant population is so large that vegetation has been seriously damaged.

In spring, frogs journey to the nearest pond to breed. A male grips a swollen female with his enlarged thumbs and is carried on her back for a few days. In the water, the female lays a cluster of between 3,000 and 6,000 eggs encased in a protective jelly. At the same time the male produces sperm which swim to the eggs and fertilize them. The eggs hatch into tadpoles, which are omnivorous and aquatic and look very different from the adult. The tadpole uses a sucker to hold on to vegetation and breathes through external gills. It slowly loses its gills, develops limbs and absorbs its tail. Four months after fertilization the tadpole has become a fully formed frog, is carnivorous and essentially terrestrial. Four years later it has become old enough to breed.

▷ worms live in the blood vessels of the human abdomen, including those of the gut and urinary bladder, while juvenile stages use snails as their hosts. In some parasites as many as three hosts are involved, with two separate hosts for the early and late juvenile stages and the third for the mature adult. But whatever a parasite's life-style, moving house from one host to the next is inevitably a hazardous business. Where these transfers take place in water the parasites often have active swimming stages, as can be seen, for example, in the fluke *Haematoloechus* which lives a sedentary life as an adult in the lungs of frogs and toads.

In terrestrial situations the risks are potentially much greater than they are in water because of the added problem of desiccation. The complex life cycle of the sheep liver fluke, *Dicrocoelium dendriticum*, illustrates one way of making the transfer from host to host in a wholly terrestrial situation. Eggs of *Dicrocoelium*, liberated in sheeps' faeces, are eaten by snails. Early juvenile stages develop which, in leaving the snails, irritate them so that they encase the parasites in balls of slime. The slime protects the parasites from fatal drying out and is also a highly attractive food for the second hosts, ants. After the ants have eaten the slime balls, the juvenile parasites escape and invade the ants' bodies. Following further development, some of the parasites move to the heads of the ants and begin to alter their behaviour in an odd way. The ants climb up grass stems and anchor themselves with their jaws. Stuck with lockjaw at the top of a blade of grass, an ant is likely to be eaten by grazing sheep and so the parasites in the ant are able to complete their life cycles by reaching their final host.

The number of offspring a creature produces and the way in which this is achieved vary widely. The elephant only has one offspring at a time. So too do tsetse flies of the genus *Glossina* and, 98 times out of 100, humans. In all these cases the survival rate of the offspring is high because the parents shepherd the young through its development until adulthood is achieved. In contrast, a frog produces several thousand eggs in each breeding season and the oyster is reputed to liberate several million eggs a year. In these cases survival depends on the way the numbers game is played—produce enough and a few are bound to surmount the rigours of the environment and the hazards of predation.

Safety in numbers is also the motto of social insects but these creatures have added insurance policies to protect their young. In such insects the fertile females, the queens, produce many offspring by laying huge numbers of eggs—up to several thousand a day in some termites—and these are well cared for by the infertile workers of the species so they have a high chance of survival. It is difficult to trace the life cycle of a social insect, such as a bee or termite, because, although the female may lay many millions of eggs in her lifetime, few will develop into new, virgin queens. The vast majority become workers and soldiers, which do not reproduce and so are reproductive 'dead ends'. In such instances it is more meaningful to think in terms of the life cycle of the colony as a whole, which is founded, grows large and eventually gives rise to potential queens, who leave to found new colonies of their own. Colonies tend to be large and long lived and create relatively few 'offspring' in the form of new self-contained colonies.

For most plants and animals, seeds or eggs are the primary means of producing offspring and increasing the number of individuals, but some species

A sex-change commonly occurs during the life cycle of the slipper limpet, *Crepidula fornicata*. Individuals live stacked upon each other, the youngest at the top and the oldest at the bottom. The young start as males, but later their male organs degenerate and they become temporarily sexless. If the stack contains no females the sexless limpet will become a female; if there are several females then it will revert to being male.

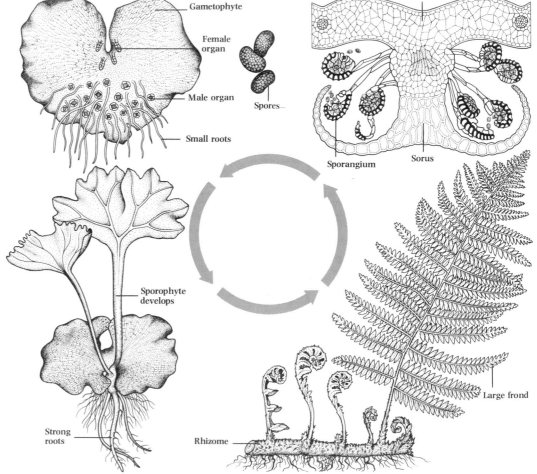

The life of a fern alternates between a sexual and an asexual phase. The large, leafy fern, familiar in woods and other moist habitats, is the culmination of its asexual generation. Starting as tight spirals growing from an underground rhizome, the young fronds unfold and expand into mature leaves, which possess small spore-containing structures or sori on their undersides. Within each sorus there are many stalked sporangia bearing clusters of asexual spores, which are liberated and dispersed when mature. On reaching a moist location they develop into small, flat, green, heart-shaped pads of tissue. These inconspicuous gametophytes are the short-lived sexual stages of the fern's life cycle. On the underside of this gametophyte are its male and female organs, and in moist conditions the male sperm swim to the female organs to fuse with the eggs. A fertilized egg develops into a young sporophyte, with simple leaves and a strong root system. The gametophyte then dies and the sporophyte grows into the large and characteristic fern, such as bracken, that often dominates the landscape.

use alternative methods of multiplication. Some species of parasitic wasp use a method which is a sort of cloning. In the body of its host—usually the caterpillar of another insect—the female wasp lays a single egg which then divides again and again to produce up to 3,000 identical wasp embryos. Although this system is rare, it can confer a distinct advantage if a female runs a serious risk of being damaged when she attempts to lay her eggs in the host.

The life cycles of many parasites contain phases in which the juveniles undergo a process of multiplication. Three of the parasites already mentioned, *Schistosoma*, *Haematoloechus* and *Dicrocoelium*, for example, all have multiplication stages, or sporocysts, in their intermediate snail hosts. This method of increasing the number of individuals in a population without sex is, in many ways, similar to the life cycle pattern with the rather confusing name of alternation of generations, which is seen in some plants and animals, notably insects. In such organisms the life cycle is divided into two parts with two offspring-producing stages or generations, one sexual, the other asexual. The confusion arises because the term generation is normally used synonymously with life cycle to encompass the time it takes for an offspring to grow up and produce new offspring. In alternation of generations a complete life cycle includes both sexual and non-sexual phases.

Reproduction by alternation of generations is well illustrated by the ferns. The familiar leafy fern frond is known as the sporophyte generation because it bears spore-producing organs on the underside of the frond. These spores are produced without sex. After they are liberated each of these spores is capable of developing into a small pad of tissue, the gametophyte generation, which bears

the male and female sex organs. Male cells or 'sperm' liberated from the male sex organs swim through drops of dew or rainwater deposited on the gametophyte to the female organs and fertilize the eggs they contain. The fertilized eggs then develop into new sporophytes, so completing the life cycle and also completing the alternation of generations between the sexually produced sporophyte and the asexually produced gametophyte.

Some of the most complex and highly variable life cycles of the living world are found among the aphids. The aphid life cycle is essentially annual and contains several 'generations', some sexual, some asexual. Different generations may be structurally and behaviourally distinct and induced by either genetic or environmental factors. Some generations lay eggs but most 'give birth' to live young. For even greater flexibility some aphid species switch hosts, either to prevent predators from congregating in regions of high aphid density, or to exploit more succulent new growth, or both. The sycamore aphid, *Drepanosiphum platanoides*, completes its life cycle on a single species, overwintering as an egg which hatches in spring as the sycamore leaves unfurl to produce the first of a series of female-only asexual generations. In autumn both males and females are produced and then mate and give rise to overwintering eggs. In contrast, the bird cherry/oat aphid, *Rhopalosiphum padi*, overwinters on bird cherry but switches to grasses and cereal crops in summer and has a wide variety of asexual generations.

Aphids, ants, humans and many other species live in groups or populations and occupy a particular situation or habitat. A population pulsates with change, often increasing or decreasing in size in naturally induced cycles. ▷

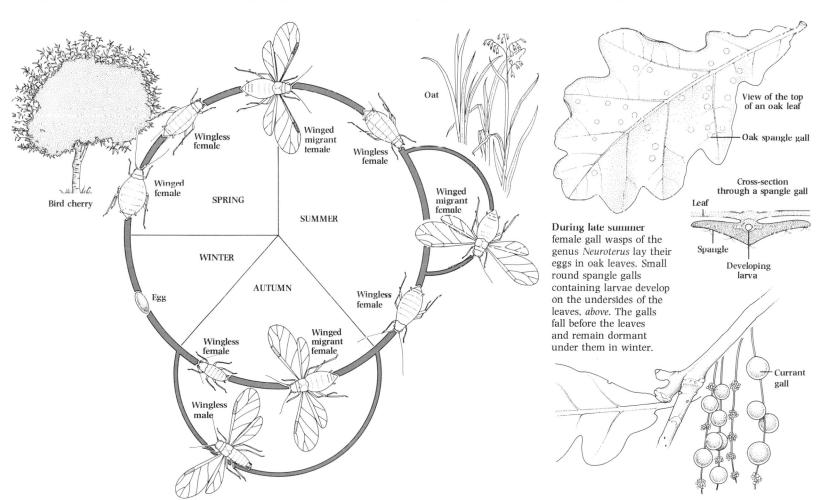

In its search for good quality plant sap the aphid, *Rhopalosiphum padi*, has developed a life cycle that not only alternates between sexual and asexual generations but also between the bird cherry tree and various grasses, such as the oat. The eggs overwinter in the bird cherry and in spring hatch into wingless females. These give birth to live wingless females

which produce live winged females that migrate to the oats in a nearby field. Overcrowding can cause one of the next generations to be winged, enabling them to move to a less populated area. In autumn, winged males and females are born and fly back to the bird cherry. The females give birth to live wingless females that mate with the males and lay eggs on the tree.

In the spring only female wasps emerge, flying up into the oak tree and laying unfertilized eggs in the buds. From these eggs larvae hatch and stimulate the oak to form round currant galls, *above*. Male and female wasps emerge from these galls in midsummer and mate. The females then lay their eggs on the undersides of the leaves and the life cycle begins again.

▷These changes in population size, which involve the processes of birth and death, emigration and immigration, occur regularly over long periods of time in any one locality.

In a perfect environment with unlimited resources, a population of almost any species of plant or animal will grow at its maximum or exponential rate. Imagine a population of bacteria, organisms consisting of a single cell, growing in a vast vat of nutrient-rich sludge. Every half-hour or so a bacterial cell will divide to give two cells. If we start with just one cell there will be two after 30 minutes, and four at the end of the first hour. After two hours the cell number rises to 16, and after three hours it is 64. At the end of the first 24 hours there will be approximately 2.8×10^{14} (280,000,000,000,000) cells. If this growth is plotted on a graph of numbers against time, the result is an exponential curve of increasing steepness and this shape is retained even if the time-scale of reproduction is altered.

In practice, however, environments are not perfect since they contain limited amounts of space, food, shelter and the other necessary requirements for the existence of a species. There is also a restriction on the volume of waste products they can accept and process. So while the population has a tendency to increase exponentially, as the population size increases the limitations of the environment's resources become increasingly apparent and exert an ever-more rigid restraint on unchecked exponential growth. Eventually a balance point is reached at which the growth and death rates of the population are equal, and this is the carrying capacity of the environment. The introduction of sheep to Tasmania in the early part of the nineteenth century is a good example

of such growth. To begin with the sheep multiplied exponentially, but then the rate of increase gradually slowed down, levelling out at a carrying capacity of 1.5 million sheep. Plotted out, this gives an S-shaped logistic growth-curve. Such a curve describes the population growth of many species in limited environments and occurs over and over again in both laboratory and natural situations.

If this pattern of growth is so widespread, we would expect the world's natural populations to remain constant. Some species do, in fact, maintain a steady rate of growth, but man's population is still enlarging exponentially while those of other species go through distinct cycles of expansion and contraction. Cyclical behaviour in population size has been extensively studied in certain Canadian populations of the lynx and the snowshoe hare, both of which have approximately ten-year cycles between peaks of population size. The cycling of lynx populations is easily explained. The lynx feeds primarily on the herbivorous snowshoe hare. When hares are abundant the lynx have plenty of food and can reproduce exponentially, or nearly so. When hares are scarce the lynx have difficulty in finding prey and so many die. Through its dependence on the hare for food, the population size of the lynx changes as the hare's population changes.

For other predators with pronounced population cycles similar explanations hold good. In the tundra regions, populations of the arctic fox show a four-year cycle linked to the population fluctuations of their principal prey, the lemming. Farther south on the forest margins, the marten and the red fox also have four-year population cycles synchronized to the changing size of the population of

A population of animals or plants will grow at its maximum rate if it lives in conditions where there is plenty of food and space and an absence of predators and disease. Humans are no exception to this, and in many countries the rate of population increase is near the maximum. In some developed countries there is a minimal increase, due to effective control measures. The global pattern of population, *below*, shows a continuing rise in numbers and also in the rate of increase. The world's population has doubled since 1940. In natural populations the environment effects its own controls and, unless man imposes his own restrictions on human populations, one or more of these natural controls will do it for him. There will be either a massive shortage of food or space, or some disease will spread. Technological advances, better agricultural practice, medical breakthroughs and a lack of regard for natural laws have buffered the human race from many natural population controls. When sheep were introduced into Tasmania they multiplied rapidly until they exceeded the population which Tasmania could carry. Their numbers then dropped from 2 to 1.5 million. Such an overshoot is common in natural populations and results from the time delay between the rate of population increase and the rate at which controls, such as lack of food, can come into effect. Improved farming has let numbers rise again.

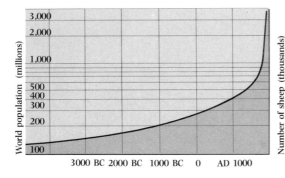

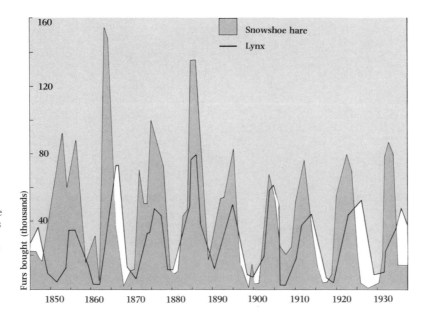

Populations of the lynx, *Felis canadensis*, and the snowshoe hare, *Lepus americanus*, reach a peak every 10 years. This regular cycle in their numbers is found in the records of furs bought from trappers by the Hudson's Bay Company in Canada. These show peak numbers of lynx are a year or two behind those of its prey, the hare. Lynx numbers rise if hares are abundant, but when most hares have been eaten, lynx numbers decline. The hare population cycle seems to be driven by climatic changes and the availability of plant food.

voles on which they feed. However, in parts of Canada the marten and the red fox feed on the snowshoe hare and so have ten rather than four-year population cycles. Similar explanations can be applied to the cyclical population changes in some predatory birds, such as snowy owls, which show cycles generated by changes in the populations of their prey.

Ample evidence exists to support the speculation that predator populations are controlled by the abundance of their prey, but what causes the cycling in the prey populations? A variety of answers has been put forward to explain the ten and four-year cycles in the herbivores. Some early analyses claimed to have found a link between the population cycles and sunspot cycles, but the fact that population cycles are not simultaneous across large tracts of land and show a huge site-to-site variability rules out any such global climatic influence. Another suggestion is that the predators have some force in driving the change. The idea is that the predator population grows in size as its food becomes more abundant, but that its demand for food eventually outstrips the rate at which the prey population is increasing, so that the prey population crashes because of over-exploitation by predators. The strongest argument against this idea is that the prey population's decline should be precipitous not gradual as, in fact, it is. Despite this objection, some insect populations seem to obey these rules of population growth and decline.

The influence of disease epidemics and changes in the physiology of individuals at high population densities have also been proposed to explain population cycles. Both do occur, but they, too, would produce more rapid reductions in population size than actually take place, so they may well be symptoms rather than the causes of change. A suggestion that fits the facts better is related to the abundance of the plant foods on which the hares, lemmings and voles feed. When population cycles are at their peak both the hares and small rodents behave as if they were searching for food. This is most noticeable among the lemmings which, at times of peak population, often embark on extensive, legendary migrations in search of new food resources. If food is scarce the juveniles are likely to be affected first so that the population decline begins with juvenile mortality, followed by the death of adults and a reduction in the numbers of offspring produced, so explaining a decline lasting several years.

The rise and fall of populations are part of a complex web of interactions that take place in an environment. Thus the population cycles of the hares and small rodents may regulate the cycles of their predators and also affect other species in the area. Several species of grouse, for example, show approximately ten-year cycles in Canada. The willow grouse has a ten-year population cycle in Canada but a four-year one in Norway, and these cycles are synchronized to the population cycles of the local hares or small rodents. Since the hares and grouse have different diets, depletion of one food source should have little effect on the other, but grouse are the favourite alternative prey for the Canadian predators of the snowshoe hare, such as the red fox and the goshawk, while in Norway the willow grouse stands in for the lemming as an alternative prey for arctic foxes and snowy owls. A decline in hare and small rodent populations, therefore, induces their predators to switch prey and so influences the population cycles of the grouse. ▷

Fighting breaks out when the density of a vole population increases, but aggressive individuals, while able to stay alive, cannot reproduce fast and are prone to disease. A reduced birth rate and an increased death rate cause the population to decline. This cycle of rise and fall in population size occurs approximately every four years. When the population density has fallen, less aggressive but faster breeding individuals make the population rise again.

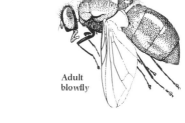

Adult blowfly

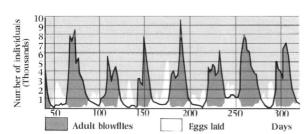

Number of individuals (Thousands)

Adult blowflies   Eggs laid   Days

The ecologist A.J. Nicholson grew colonies of the sheep blowfly, *Lucilia cuprina*, in a cage with a limited but renewed supply of food, and every day counted the numbers of flies and their eggs. Flies showed a regular cycle in their numbers, proving that they were being limited by the amount of food available for their larvae. At low densities there was ample food and many eggs were laid. At high densities few eggs were laid on the food because competing females obstructed one another. The two-week time delay between the laying of these differing egg numbers and the emergence of the adults governs the blowfly population cycle.

Vole

At the start of their breeding season male black grouse assemble at a certain place on the moors and make aggressive territorial displays to each other. A limited number of successful males is thus selected to mate with the females; the weaker ones are excluded and eventually killed by predators. As the population increases, these displays become more vigorous and more individuals are excluded from mating.

Black grouse

POPULATION CYCLES...*the rise and fall of populations*

▷ If population size is controlled by the effects of another species operating in the same environment then, according to the biotic school of thought, cycles develop because there is always a time-lag between the development of a regulator and its actual effect. This is like trying to control the temperature of an oven with a slow-acting thermostat. The oven temperature will rise and fall in a cyclical way. The faster the thermostat reacts, the smaller the fluctuations in temperature will be. Many of the early ideas of the biotic school were developed by entomologists studying the possibilities of controlling insect pests by using other insect species, and this concept of biological control is used today to deal with a wide range of pests around the world.

Opponents of this sort of argument have put forward the suggestion that animals regulate their own population sizes so that they do not overstep the carrying capacity of their habitat. Several mechanisms have been proposed to explain how this self-regulation is achieved. Some birds, mammals and even insects hold territories, patches of a habitat defended against intruders. Territory holders are at an advantage because having a territory may improve the chances of finding a mate or ensure space in the habitat in which a family can be successfully reared. Only a certain number of territories can be fitted into any one habitat and this automatically restricts the number of productive matings. Unsuccessful individuals who do not manage to raise a family will die out. In any habitat the amount of food will vary from year to year so that a territorial bird will have to evaluate the quality of a territory before deciding how big it should be. The poorer the conditions, the larger the territories will need to be and the fewer breeding pairs will be supported by the whole habitat.

In this situation population size is not, therefore, self-regulated but governed by the quality of the habitat, but the existence of territories does ensure that population levels do not outstrip the habitat's resources.

For many species the regular procession of the seasons creates a regular cycle of population size. Aphids, for example, build up their numbers throughout each summer before regular autumn and winter crashes. In less distinctly seasonal situations climate can also bring about marked changes in population size, but these are irregular. Small mammals and birds of the southern Sahara have populations that fluctuate in a non-rhythmical way in response to the erratic rainfall in the area, and in Australia grasshopper populations go up and down in a similar rain-induced way.

One striking climatic effect is seen on the western coast of South America. The cold, nutrient-rich Humboldt current sweeps up from the south and provides eminently suitable conditions for the development of large plankton and anchovy populations off the coast of Peru. Huge flocks of birds, tuna, whales and porpoises feed in these rich waters, and the Peruvian people harvest the anchovies for fish oil and meal and remove the bird droppings for fertilizer. At irregular intervals the wind patterns in the area change and warm, low-nutrient tropical waters displace the Humboldt stream, with catastrophic effects on the marine life, including the anchovies. As the anchovies die, all the other species that feed on them die too or leave the area. Population cycles of anchovies and pelicans are thus linked but show irregular patterns of change because of the vagaries of the climate. The notorious unpredictability of the weather means that regular patterns of population change are not linked to the

Catastrophe strikes the marine life and the fishing industry when 'El Niño'—the Christ child—comes to the waters off the coast of Peru. Occasionally, around Christmas time, unusually strong northeast trade winds bring warm nutrient-poor waters from the Equator to replace the cold nutrient-rich Humboldt current, flowing up from the Antarctic. This warm current causes a rapid rise in water temperature which kills the plankton and anchovies and, consequently, the larger animals that depend on them. Anchovies are the main catch for the Peruvian fishermen and also provide food for many of the birds, whose faeces form guano deposits which are used as fertilizer worldwide.

Brown pelican

Anchovies are the key to the pyramidal food chain that thrives in the cold waters of the Humboldt current. They feed on millions of tiny plankton and are themselves eaten by cormorants, pelicans, whales and porpoises. 'El Niño' kills the plankton and anchovies, and many of the animals dependent on them also die.

climate. Such patterns can only be the result of density-dependent processes—factors that exert an increasingly detrimental effect on the population as its numbers increase—and time-delays between cause and effect. The climate is density *independent*: the inflow of warm waters off Peru would kill the anchovies irrespective of how many there were.

By using computer simulations almost any pattern of population change can be mimicked and many modern ecologists believe that both climatic and biological influences are important in population dynamics, but that only biological, density-dependent factors can operate to generate cycles. The caterpillars of the larch budmoth, *Zeiraphera griseana*, feed on the needles of larch trees, and in parts of the European Alps have a regular seven-year population cycle. A detailed, long-term analysis of this species has revealed a complex interrelationship of mechanisms which together produce the population cycles.

Climate plays an important role in governing where these caterpillar cycles will occur, but does not influence the pattern of change itself. Unless they experience at least 120 days of cold weather, the overwintering eggs of the larch budmoth will not hatch. This delaying tactic or diapause, a quiescent period in an animal's life cycle common in many invertebrates, is usually broken by some specific external factor. The correct cold period is only found at specific Alpine altitudes. At high altitudes the climate is too cold for too long, so the eggs fail to develop, while at lower altitudes the eggs hatch too early, before the larch needles have burst from their buds. Conditions are best at between 5,000 and 6,000 feet (1,500 and 1,800 metres) and one of the most studied areas in this

range is the Upper Engadin Valley in Switzerland.

Within the larch budmoth populations there are two physiological strains—the 'strong' race and the 'weak' race—and much of the population cycle can be explained by the dominance of one race over the other. One of the key features in this story is that in the Upper Engadin the larch budmoth suffers from a unique virus disease. The virus lives latently in the 'weak' race, which is resistant, but the 'strong' race is highly susceptible to it. Parasitic wasps also play a role—they are more successful at laying their eggs in the 'weak' race than in the more active 'strong' race.

In several other cyclical species, including the western tent caterpillar, *Malacosoma* sp, and voles, separate races have been discovered which may exert an influence on population cycles. The 'strong' form of the moth is superior in almost all respects. Its eggs survive the winter better; its larvae grow more quickly, are bigger and more active; and the females of the 'strong' race lay more eggs. The success of a particular race, whether weak or strong, depends on the population density so that the regular oscillations in population size of the larch budmoth arise as a result of the changing fortunes of the 'weak' and the 'strong' races.

In the diseases that afflict man and other animals cyclical patterns can exist at two separate levels. The organisms that cause the disease may undergo cyclical population changes within their host, in much the same way as free-living species may rise and fall in numbers in a cyclical way in their own habitats. The prevalence of a disease among the individuals in the population that it attacks may also show cyclical patterns. These patterns are particularly ▷

Defoliation and extensive browning of larch trees occurs regularly in some parts of Switzerland, such as the Engadin Valley, *below*. Larvae of the larch budmoth, *Zeiraphera griseana*, feed on young larch needles, they cause most damage when their population reaches a maximum every seven to ten years.

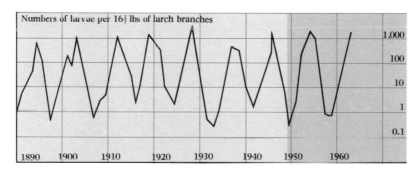

Numbers of larvae per 16½ lbs of larch branches

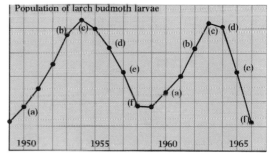

Population of larch budmoth larvae

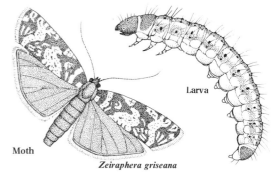

Moth

Larva

Zeiraphera griseana

A virus, parasitic wasps, competition between individuals, and a lack of tender larch needles all contribute to one complete cycle of the larch budmoth population, *above*. Two races make up its total numbers; a strong race, which is prone to the virus, dominates a weak race which carries the virus but is more often parasitized by the wasps. The population (*a*) grows as the strong race proliferates, and damage to the trees is noticeable. At high population densities (*b*) larvae compete for larch needles, and damage to the trees is most severe. Population growth slows (*c*) as female moths find it harder to discover fresh tender needles on which to lay their eggs, and the virus begins to spread. Population falls (*d*) as the virus kills the strong race, leaving the weak race to predominate. Population declines further (*e*) as many of the weak race are killed by the parasitic wasps. As population reaches its lowest density (*f*), the virus becomes latent in the weak race and so allows the strong race to proliferate once more.

▷ significant to the study of epidemics and may be useful to us all if they help scientists to plan preventive strategies for the future.

The life cycles of organisms that cause disease are often complex and they contain specific phases in which the organism is transmitted from one host to another. This may involve another species—a vector—or a new host may be infected directly. Transmission via a vector demands highly accurate synchronization between the behaviour of the virulent organisms and that of the vector species. In the tropics blood-sucking flies, such as mosquitoes, blackflies and tabanids, are frequently disease vectors, and throughout every 24-hour period they tend to have distinct feeding times. The disease-causing organisms these vectors transmit have behaviour patterns which ensure that forms of the organism suitable for transmission will be present in the blood vessels near the skin surface of an infected animal and will, therefore, be most likely to be taken up as the vector feeds. Loaiasis, for example, is an African disease, caused by the parasitic roundworm *Loa loa*, which is spread from human to human by several tabanid vectors which suck human blood during daylight hours. Transmission of *Loa loa* is, therefore, maximized because the greatest concentration of the infective stages in the superficial blood vessels occurs during the day in humans.

In other cases of diseases caused by roundworms, such as river blindness, or onchocerciasis, and elephantiasis, the infective stages also migrate to the superficial blood vessels to rendezvous with the biting vector. With malaria the situation is rather different. The single-celled protozoan *Plasmodium*, the cause of malaria, has a characteristic pattern of development in humans. Depending

on which species of *Plasmodium* is responsible for the disease, a periodic fever typically comes on every third or fourth day.

As part of its life cycle *Plasmodium* invades the red blood cells that are responsible for carrying oxygen round the body. When a parasite invades a red blood cell it divides four times to give 16 new infective stages or merozoites. The red blood cell then disintegrates, liberating the merozoites. Depending on the species it takes 48 or 72 hours for the 16 merozoites to be formed, and the fever is caused by the release of cell debris and waste products into the blood as the red cells disintegrate. What is particularly interesting is that the parasites are synchronized so that the merozoites are all released together. And the timing is so precise that the merozoites are liberated at a particular time of day, which explains why the tertian fever, typical of *Plasmodium vivax* infection, occurs every 48 hours in the early afternoon.

The fever period is not, however, the time at which the mosquitoes that transmit malaria bite and suck blood, nor are the merozoites infective to them. The timing is more subtle than this. Some of the merozoites are destined to become sexual cells, or gametocytes, designed to continue the infection in the mosquito. These gametocytes take between 30 and 36 hours to develop from the merozoites. Thus the very regular asexual cycle producing merozoites in the early afternoon ensures that the gametocytes will be at the correct stage of development some 30 to 36 hours later, that is, during the night of the following day. This fits perfectly with the nocturnal feeding habits of the mosquito vectors.

This system of disease transmission takes its time cues from the host. In most

The mosquito's need for human blood has caused millions of people to suffer from malaria. When it bites, it introduces into the wound asexual stages of the protozoan *Plasmodium*, present in the mosquito's salivary glands. These quickly make their way to the liver, where they multiply and live for many years, causing bouts of the disease. From the liver they enter the bloodstream periodically, invade the red blood cells and here develop and multiply. When mature they rupture the cell, and thousands of cells rupturing at the same time cause a fever. Most of the liberated spores invade other cells, so beginning the red blood cell cycle again. Others become male and female gametes, which will only develop and begin the sexual stage of the life cycle if they are sucked up in a mosquito's meal of blood.

Plasmodium develops in mosquito's stomach wall

Skin

Male and female gametes

Many *Plasmodium* cause red blood cells to rupture

Reinfection occurs

Red blood cell cycle

Red blood cell

Plasmodium divides

Brain

Spleen
Kidney

Colon

Liver

Liver cycle

Symptoms of malaria include kidney failure, enlargement of the spleen, disorders of the colon and, in fatal cases, brain damage.

The mosquito swallows the male and female gametes of *Plasmodium* and, when they enter its stomach, parasitic sexual reproduction occurs. The resulting parasites penetrate the stomach lining where they grow and eventually produce hundreds of cells which migrate to the salivary glands of the mosquito.

Once these cells are in human blood they can be transmitted by a mother to her foetus across the placenta causing abortions, stillbirths and infant mortality. Even in blood bank conditions *Plasmodium* cells remain viable for several weeks so that malaria can also be transmitted by transfusions.

Periodic fevers are the classic symptom of malaria but different *Plasmodium* species produce different patterns of fever. In all cases the fever occurs when the infected blood cells rupture and parasites, cell debris and waste products are released into the blood. *Plasmodium vivax* and *P. ovale* both take 48 hours to complete one blood cell cycle, and cause tertian fevers every third day. *P. malariae* takes 72 hours, causing quartan fevers every fourth day. The fevers begin in the middle of the day with a feeling of cold, and chattering teeth. The body temperature rises to 40°C (104°F) and headaches, vomiting and delirium may occur. After about three hours profuse sweating occurs, the temperature drops to normal and a feeling of well-being returns.

animals, including man, there are 24-hour cyclical changes in several physiological activities—temperature, blood acidity and hormone levels all fluctuate regularly during waking and sleeping. Night workers with malaria would, thus, experience the start of their fever just after midnight, that is, about half-way through their waking cycle. From experiments with malaria in animals it has been established that the *Plasmodium* organism makes use of slight temperature changes to synchronize its life cycle. If monkeys with malaria are cooled down under anaesthesia then their fever is delayed. *Loa loa* also employs temperature changes as cues for its timing, while *Wucheria bancrofti*, which causes elephantiasis, orders its activities according to changes in the oxygen levels of the lungs between day and night.

The cycles of human disease are frequently linked to the seasons but their periodicity may be greater than a year. Measles, for instance, has a two-year cycle, rabies a four-year one. It is unlikely that climate alone could produce such regular cyclical changes. More probably density-dependent factors, such as the proportion of susceptible people available, influence the populations of disease organisms, and so regulate their cycles. Season is important to several diseases. In temperate zones the crowded, intimate association of schoolchildren during winter and spring allows measles to spread easily among susceptible children. The virus is helped by the lowered resistance of children during the winter because of respiratory tract infections, and the typically warm, moist, enclosed classroom atmosphere is ideal for the transmission of airborne virus particles. Summer peaks occur in many diseases spread by accidental ingestion and via faeces. Salmonella food poisoning, cholera,

infective hepatitis and poliomyelitis are all such diseases. Summer peaks are also common in diseases spread by biting insects or ticks, whose populations are largest in the warmest months of the year.

Plague is a disease with both summer and winter peaks. The disease is spread by fleas which become increasingly active as the weather warms up. In late autumn small rodents, the natural reservoirs of the disease, tend to move into human houses to avoid the winter cold and this migration enhances the risk of cross-infection to man. Plague can be spread from man to man in air breathed out and there is a greatly improved chance of this causing infection in the enclosed atmosphere of winter accommodation.

In foxes, rabies shows a seasonal cycle linked to the fox life cycle. Male foxes are territorial creatures who aggressively defend their areas against intruders. Fox territories are established during the mating season which results in a considerable increase in the degree of contact between individuals. The prevalence of rabies in the fox population peaks in January or February, just after mating. Both rabies and foxes also show striking longer-term cycles of three, four or five years. Mathematical simulations have shown that these may result from a time-delayed density-dependent influence of rabies on foxes. Rabies reduces the fox population to such a low density that there are not enough individuals to spread the disease. This point of lowest density seems to be reached when the fox population drops below a single animal per square kilometre. The time-lag is determined by how long it takes the fox population to pick up and increase its numbers enough for the rabies virus to establish itself once more.

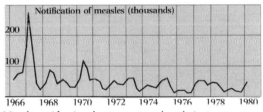

Measles epidemics show an annual cycle in temperate countries as the number of reported cases reaches a peak in spring. The incidence of the disease is markedly annual in North America but shows a two-year cycle in England and Wales, *above*. This biennial cycle persists even though vaccination, started in the late 1960s, has reduced the total number of cases.

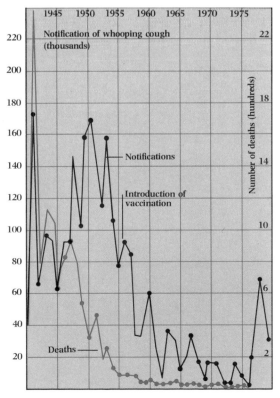

The incidence of **whooping cough** among children in England and Wales shows a distinct three to four-year cycle, *left*. This alarming disease is caused by a bacterium which is abundant in the sputum of infected children, and is spread by inhaling the drops expelled by the cough. Prior to 1950 the death rate was high, but it was reduced nearly to zero after vaccination was introduced in 1957. The total number of reported cases fell dramatically although the cycle of the disease persisted. Recent doubts about the safety of the vaccine have made many parents expose their children to the hazards of the disease rather than risk any side effects of the vaccine. As a result the incidence of whooping cough showed a sudden increase in late 1977 and 1978.

Rabies attacks the nervous system causing excessive salivation, a dread of water, paralysis, madness and eventual death. The red fox is the chief reservoir of rabies in Europe and a three to five-year cycle in the prevalence of rabid foxes has been found. In Africa the dog is the chief reservoir and in South America, the bat, although many animals can become infected. Virus particles are found in the saliva and one bite from a rabid animal is enough to spread the disease. The pitiful sight of a docile red fox whose hind legs lack coordination may inspire sympathy, but if approached it is liable to bite viciously. Change of temperament is an early symptom of the disease, normally docile animals becoming aggressive and vice versa. This is always followed by a phase when the animal bites readily and foams at the mouth.

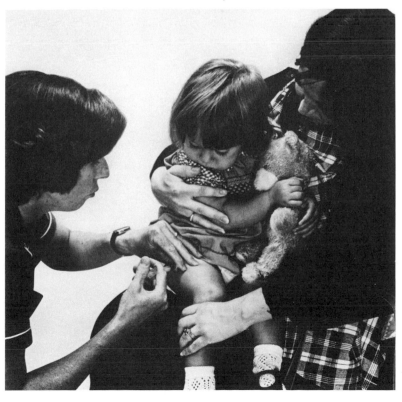

Rhythms of growth

No gardener, who completes the back-breaking task of clearing his vegetable patch only to find his precious plants overrun with weeds again in just a few weeks, could fail to believe that living things are capable of the most spectacular rates of growth. Or think of a human baby with a birthweight of 8 pounds (3.6 kg). Only nine months before, that baby was a living microdot weighing only a fraction of an ounce. Never again is human growth as fast as during these months in the womb. For other animals babyhood is also a time of staggering spurts of growth. Pups of the southern elephant seal, for example, who suckle on high-fat milk made by their mothers from stored blubber, put on weight at the rate of 20 pounds (9 kg) a day. Among plants, climbers are often the fastest growers, and a vigorous passion flower can add 20 feet (6 m) to its stature in a single growing season.

To increase in size, whether quickly or almost imperceptibly like a hardwood tree, living things do not simply blow themselves up like balloons, nor, like growing crystals, do they add on ready-made units to those already in existence. The secret of growth lies in the organization of the bodies of plants and animals into cells, units of life which are usually considerably less than 0.04 inches (0.1 mm) across. Whether an organism is constructed of just one cell or, like a human being, hundreds of millions of them, each cell has limited powers of expansion. For true growth to take place that cell must divide into two, and cells divide in a cyclical and often rhythmic way.

Unlike technological advance, which we accept with hardly a moment's thought, conceptual advances in science take years, if not centuries, to become accepted. Some of the slowness in coming to grips with new concepts arises because new hypotheses run counter to the superficial rules of common sense. If, for example, we cut a pat of butter in half we can go on cutting it into smaller and smaller pieces—but not for ever. The fact that butter is made of fat molecules which, when divided, turn into something else, is a conceptual leap that is in no way aided by common sense. The concept that living things are made up of cells has entered the common currency largely because it has become possible, with the help of sophisticated equipment, to look at and dissect them. Just as butter can only stay as butter if its molecules remain intact, so life can only continue if the integrity of its living boxes, its cells, is preserved. The complex molecules that make up those cells are not in themselves living but, to accomplish the process of growth, the cell has to ensure that all the essential molecules it contains, from its information store to its machinery for making new molecules, can be faithfully reproduced every time the cycle of cell division is completed.

The cycle of cell reproduction which underlies growth processes cannot continue unless, like all other living processes, it has a constant supply of energy. In the final analysis all this energy comes from our radiant provider, the sun, and is used by plants to make the energy-rich molecules which are either used directly by the plants themselves and by herbivorous animals, or indirectly by carnivores. The feeding chains of all the organisms on our planet interlock to form a vast energy cycle in which substances are constantly being trapped and used, processed and then pushed back into the atmosphere, from where they are trapped again and reused. Without this conservative cycle there would be no way in which the earth could support, in the long term, any form of life, least of all the voracious human race, seemingly intent on disrupting the cycle by wasting its energy-giving molecules.

Common sense, that most down to earth of human attributes, is bounded and constrained by the finite abilities of the body organs that help us to perceive the world around us. Our most detailed experience of the physical world is visual, and this vision is a prisoner of the wavelengths of light visible to us—unlike some creatures, such as the bees, we cannot receive and process light at the ultraviolet end of the spectrum. There is also a limit to the size of the objects we can see. Even with the finest optical microscopes we can see nothing smaller than the minimum wavelengths of the light our eye uses—about 0.00004 inches (0.0001 mm). The structure of our retina (the sensitive inner lining of the eye which receives light signals and converts them into nerve messages which are interpreted by the brain) means that only with great difficulty can we see objects less than 0.04 inches (0.1 mm) across with unaided eyes.

It is because of the constraints of our eyesight that emotionally we always regard the growth of living things as a continuous process. Over long time-spans we can see that a plant gets taller and adds new leaves to its collection, or that our children increase in stature, and everything our senses tell us about these natural changes adds up to a story of gradualism. The outward appearance of an elongating shoot is of a smooth, continuous extension, akin to toothpaste being squeezed from a tube.

The underlying process of growth is, however, quite different. Ultimately all sustained growth consists of the production of new living subunits, that is, cells. New cells can only be created by the process of cell division during which a parental cell, after carrying out extensive internal reorganization, divides itself into two. The pair of daughter cells resulting from this process of fission are,

after a time-lag which may vary from half an hour to many days, capable of repeating the fission process. By this essentially discontinuous and cyclical process cells reproduce themselves, new living material is formed and growth occurs. Down at the crucial level of organization, therefore, the growth activities of living things are not smooth expansions. Rather they consist of minute amounts of growth whose sum simply appears to be smooth. The situation perceived by the human eye is the averaged total of thousands or millions of individual cell divisions.

If it is to fit all the circumstances to which our language would apply the word growth, we must expand our detailed explanation of the cellular background to the phenomenon, although most normal examples fit in with the schema of typical cell growth in a straightforward fashion. Take, for instance, the growth of a human being. It is easy to concentrate on the growth processes that take place between birth and adulthood, such as the lengthening of the limbs and trunk, and forget that in some ways the most impressive and intense growth—at least in relative terms—occurs before the great event of birth itself. Each of us was conceived by the fusion of two single sex cells, or gametes, a sperm from our father and an ovum, or egg, from our mother, to form a single generative cell, the zygote, or fertilized egg. From this one individual, effectively invisible cell, a man or woman grew.

The extent of the total growth process is stupendous simply because one cell grows into billions of cells. All of this increase in size is generated by the cycle of cell division. Within each cell division cycle, however, another form of growth must occur. Before each parental cell divides, it must itself grow so that

The driving force of nearly all genuine growth is the multiplication of cells, the ultimate units of life. This mechanism can be explicitly revealed by cultivating colonies of bacteria in dishes of the nutrient jelly, agar. Individual bacteria are widely dispersed over the agar surface by making a dilute suspension of the cells in water then spreading this over the agar. The dishes are then incubated and each cell divides many times to become a colony, which is clearly visible, *left*, and whose specific appearance is helpful in identifying the bacteria that produced it.

Stained to show their chromosomes, cells from the root tip of an onion, *below*, are dividing. After the genetic material has been duplicated, daughter chromosomes move to opposite ends of the cell, *left*, before the chromosomes form two new nuclei, *right*.

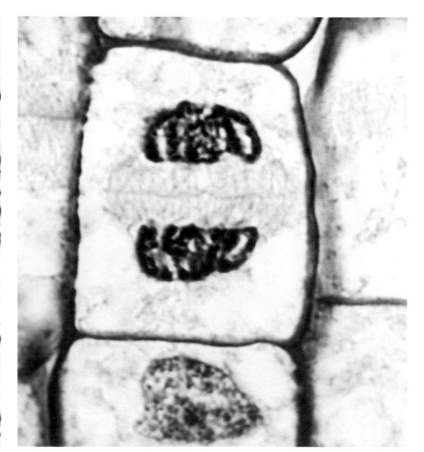

cell size increases. Without this form of expansionist policy each cell would halve in size every time it divides. Growth in cell size, or intracellular expansion, is the result of the production of brand-new complex organic molecules, principally proteins, within the cell, and nearly all dividing cells demonstrate this sort of increase in size.

In the case of one type of cell, specialized to carry out a particular job of work in a creature's life cycle, growth from within becomes enormously exaggerated and finally gives rise to single cells that are easy to see with the naked eye. These cells are eggs. There is no difficulty in seeing a boiled egg sitting in its cup waiting to be eaten at breakfast, and although a bird's egg is a complex structure in which the egg cell is surrounded by nutrients, various membranes and the shell, the ovum it contains is a truly gigantic cell.

The growth process that produces these gargantuan cells involves the laying down of both nutrient reserves, such as yolk, and information-containing molecules which, working together, will ensure that rapid cell divisions can take place after the egg has been fertilized by a sperm. These reserves mean that during the early embryological development of such creatures there is no significant increase in cell size. Instead, the original gigantic cell divides first into two, then four, then into eight cells, and so on until a rudimentary embryo is formed, which consists of hundreds of cells but has the same dimensions as the original fertilized egg.

In the vegetable world, seeds are, for flowering plants, the equivalent of fertilized animal eggs and they, too, are packed with nutrients for use in the first, crucial stages of development. Among plants there are some problems concerning the definition of growth. The first of these relates to the intriguing fact that a huge proportion of a tree is dead material. The living, cellular, section of a tree is very much smaller than the masses of material made up of cell skeletons. These skeletons are, in fact, cell walls composed of the tough plant carbohydrate cellulose, and it is cellulose, along with its chemical cousins, that makes up the skeletal bulk of a forest. The cellulose and other complex carbohydrates are laid down as secreted material outside the living cells of the plant. Thus a good deal of a tree's growth does not consist of living cells nor does its maintenance involve cell division.

The second growth 'oddity' of the plant kingdom involves cell expansions which do not depend on the standard method of the intracellular growth. When roots or shoots elongate, the new cells produced to sustain this growth undergo a marked expansion process which, although it puffs up the cell dimensions enormously, cannot strictly be thought of as growth. This cell elongation seems to be largely the result of changes which pump extra water into the cells, and these changes are caused by the process of osmosis. As the cell enlarges water is pulled into it as a result of alterations in the concentration of dissolved substances within.

Despite these two exceptions, the cyclical pattern of cell division underlies most biological growth activities. Cells grow internally then divide into two. One cell turns itself into two in a simple form of reproduction. The cyclical and repeating pattern of cellular growth, cellular division, then back to cellular growth is often rhythmical as well as cyclical, since the period of the cycle is reasonably constant in length, although its actual value varies from tissue to ▷

Like a cascade, cell numbers increase when a single cell divides. Cell division involves two separate cyclical processes. One is a cycle of cell enlargement and division, the other a doubling of the genetic material to ensure perfect replicas.

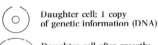

Daughter cell; 1 copy of genetic information (DNA)

Daughter cell after growth; 2 DNA copies present

Nucleus divides; 2 separate DNA copies present

Cell division producing 2 identical daughter cells

As a colony of bacteria grows from a single cell the formation of new DNA and new cells occur in two distinct cycles. If traced out through time, DNA formation appears to progress stepwise, *right*, because DNA is duplicated before the cell substance divides.

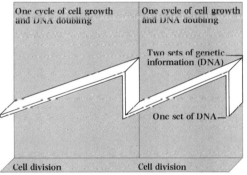

One cycle of cell growth and DNA doubling

One cycle of cell growth and DNA doubling

Two sets of genetic information (DNA)

One set of DNA

Cell division

Cell division

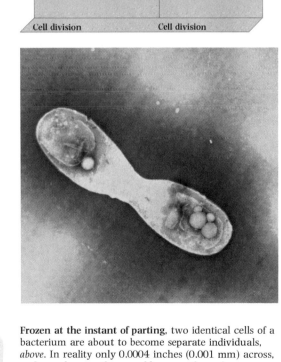

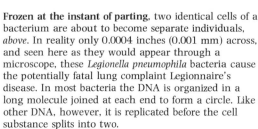

Frozen at the instant of parting, two identical cells of a bacterium are about to become separate individuals, *above*. In reality only 0.0004 inches (0.001 mm) across, and seen here as they would appear through a microscope, these *Legionella pneumophila* bacteria cause the potentially fatal lung complaint Legionnaire's disease. In most bacteria the DNA is organized in a long molecule joined at each end to form a circle. Like other DNA, however, it is replicated before the cell substance splits into two.

▷ tissue and species to species. Fundamental to the cycle is the splitting process. Within this partitioning of material there exists a cycle of change which is more important than the cell-halving process. It is a cycle without which the other processes could not occur and is the division of the material which, in every sense, forms the heart of the cell—the nucleus.

Within each cell of a living organism is a store of genetic information which is transmitted from generation to generation. This store is in the form of the chemical deoxyribosenucleic acid (DNA)—an awesome molecule housed largely in the nucleus—which contains, built into its atomic structure, codes for the construction of the key molecules of life. These molecules are: more DNA, its relative RNA (ribonucleic acid) and proteins, many of which, in the form of biochemical catalysts or enzymes, direct the life of a cell. The DNA information code, organized in the form of genes, is absolutely specific for any organism. Each and every cell in a particular organism bears exactly the same genetic code. If this were not so it would be impossible for the patterns of body shape and behaviour possessed by an organism, and essential to its survival and evolution, to be passed on to and used by future generations.

When a cell divides, the two daughter cells that are the offspring of the process must, therefore, contain an exact copy of the profoundly vital DNA. This biochemical imperative is obeyed in a complex and integrated series of changes which compose the cell cycle. In the cells of higher organisms, which contain separate nuclei within which the hereditary material is organized in long threadlike structures called chromosomes, the unvarying pattern of cyclical change obeys the following rules. The instant after it has been formed by

cell division, a daughter cell contains one complete copy of a unique genetic code sequence in the form of its cluster of chromosomes within the nucleus. Between that state and the daughter cell's next division three phases can be observed. First, there is an apparently quiescent or G_1 stage in which no DNA is produced. During this stage the enzymes needed for DNA copying are formed. Next comes the S, or synthesis, phase in which the exact new copy of the DNA sequences on the chromosomes is produced. The cell now has exactly twice the normal amount of DNA. In another apparently quiet period, the G_2 phase, synthesis of DNA stops while new proteins are made to provide the machinery needed for dividing the two sets of chromosomes by mitosis, the sort of cell division in which two identical daughter cells are created. Now the mechanics of mitosis take place and the cell splits into two, producing a new generation of daughter cells.

In single-celled, simple organisms, such as bacteria, the DNA sequence, although present, is not in the form of multiple chromosomes nor is it neatly packaged in a nucleus. In such life forms all the time between divisions is an S phase. Because DNA synthesis is going on continuously between one cell division and the next, there are no quiescent G stages. But for both higher and simple organisms the machinery of the living growth process is of paramount importance for survival. Except for a few privileged observers, who have seen the cells and chromosomes duplicate and divide by means of sophisticated optical equipment, no one has perceived the deeper processes of growth directly. Although they are carried on in such secrecy, these activities—and their observed results—are essential to understanding biological growth

A tortoise carries a date stamp indelibly marked on its hard shell, or carapace. This shell is divided into plates which give it a characteristic pattern, as shown in the Greek tortoise, *Testudo hermanni, below*. As the long-lived tortoise grows, its hard external skeleton must enlarge to provide space for its expanding body. Because the plates of the tortoise shell grow at different times of year, due to variations in external temperature and food supplies, annual banding patterns *right*, are elaborated in the growing plates.

Variations in colour and texture typify the bands of a tortoise shell, *left*. Until the rings are worn away, later in life, the animal's age can be estimated by counting the bands. For *T. hermanni* the method is reliable up to the age of about 20.

Life between the tides leaves its mark on the shells of many marine invertebrates such as the common cockle, *Cerastoderma edule, above*. The shell grows continuously during the cockle's life and has a complex pattern of bands reflecting annual growth, the tidal cycles and the cockle's inbuilt rhythms of daily life in a fluctuating environment.

The overlapping skin scales of a bony fish may show clear annual growth rings, *right*. These rings can be useful in analyzing the age composition of commercial fish stocks.

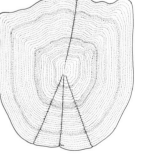

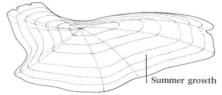

Summer growth

A fish carries its age marked in its ears as well as on its scales. The ear contains a stonelike structure, the otolith, which shows bands corresponding to a rhythmic growth pattern. In temperate species little if any growth takes place during the winter months, and this leads to variations in the rate at which new calcium-containing substance is laid down and, in turn, to the appearance of annual rings.

rhythms. If these rhythms are to be controlled, by the organism itself or by man, then strictures must be applied to the machinery of cell division from without or within.

The task of observing growth, and from these observations distinguishing rhythmical patterns of different frequency, can be difficult, simply because many organisms grow so slowly. For this reason continued experimental monitoring over extensive periods is necessary. In certain circumstances, however, animals and plants carry out their own record-taking for the human observer. These are the organisms that lay down hard skeletal materials internally or externally during part or all of their life-spans. The skeletons may be made of bones, scales, shells, wood or a number of other structures. The fact that such materials are progressively, and more or less continuously, constructed means, luckily for us, that the structures themselves may hold within their physical organization direct evidence of cyclical and rhythmical changes in the way in which they were produced.

At the level of an individual organism and its life-span, such rhythmical growth is conceptually similar to the age-long process of the deposition of sedimentary rocks at the bottom of the sea. In the case of such rocks the presence of different materials and fossils in the sequentially laid down sedimentary strata paints a frozen picture of a sequence of environmental and biological events that occured through those ages. In a similar way the shell of a marine snail might show a patterning that reveals a sequence of shell deposition and tells a clear story of changing shell growth rates tied, perhaps, to rhythms of both the years and the tides.

Among the most commonly recognized examples of such still pictures of rhythmically changing patterns of growth are the rings revealed when, in a forest in a temperate climate, a tree is cut down. Each double band of dark and then light wood, arranged in concentric circles outward from the heartwood to the bark, is a static, ossified image of a tree's annual increase in girth. Such banding patterns can be turned to aesthetic advantage in the beautiful effects of wood veneers, but in forestry, at a more practical scientific level, they are an aid to determining the age structure of a forest. A tree does not have to be felled and thus killed in order to count its annual rings, and so estimate its age. Boring from bark to core will produce a cylinder of wood containing the complete sequence of rings without sacrificing the tree.

Animal analogies of the tree-ring patterns are widespread in most types of invertebrates and in vertebrates which possess any sort of skeletal structures produced over long periods. Most often the practical use to which they are put is that of reasonably accurate ageing. Such knowledge can be of immense commercial significance. Around the world the stocks of many fish are, for instance, in danger of being overfished to the point of near extinction—as has happened in the recent past with the fishing of herring in the North Sea between the United Kingdom, Scandinavia and northern Europe. Only by understanding, in considerable detail, the age structure of a commercially harvested fish population is it possible to determine in advance what fishing strategy should be adopted to ensure a maximal, sustainable yield. Growth rings on fish scales provide sufficiently accurate information about their age to enable this sort of analysis to be undertaken. ▷

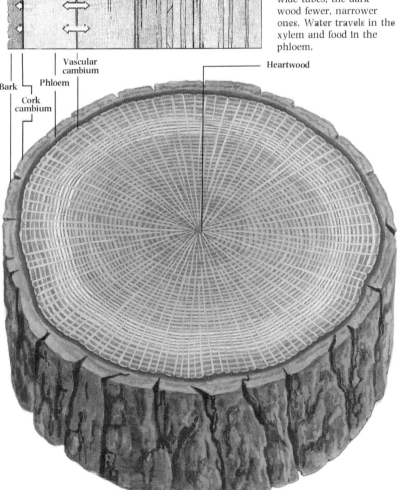

Wide xylem vessels
Narrow xylem vessels

A complete annual ring of a temperate tree contains two kinds of water-carrying tubes, or xylem vessels. The light wood contains many wide tubes, the dark wood fewer, narrower ones. Water travels in the xylem and food in the phloem.

Vascular cambium

Bark
Phloem
Cork cambium

Heartwood

Bristlecone pine
Pinus aristata

Analyzing growth rings on both dead and living trees can provide much information about past climatic conditions. The rings reflect climate because, for example, more large xylem vessels are made when water is most abundant. In a discrete area, specific conditions will produce identifiable and consistent variations in the rings. Long-lived trees, such as the California bristlecone pine, *left*, have survived for more than 4,600 years, making it possible to produce an overlapping chronology of ring patterns, *below*, extending far back into time.

The beautiful, complex cross-grain pattern of the wood of a tree trunk, *left*, reflects its cellular composition. Most of the wood consists of the tree's xylem vessels. At the centre of the trunk, in the heartwood, these vessels may be dead or obliterated by the deposition of substances within them. Xylem vessels are made by the division of cells in the vascular cambium, a cylindrical cell sheet around the trunk. The outer surface of this active layer splits off phloem vessels, which transport sugars and all other nutrients down from the leaves to every part of the tree. Outside this is another active layer, the cork cambium, whose cells divide to form the protective bark.

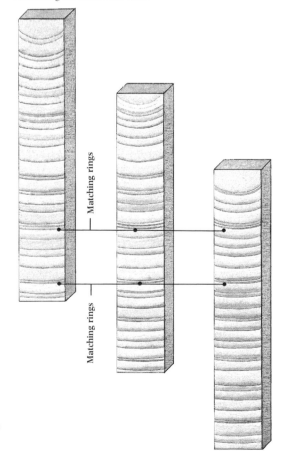

Matching rings

Matching rings

▷ The work of biologists in studying growth is closely linked with that of organic chemists. The chemicals around whose properties life itself was constructed are the organic or carbon-based molecules, and they come in a mind-boggling range of forms. Furthermore, the molecules are capable of indefinite expansion in all dimensions, so that their final diversity is effectively infinite. Organic molecules occur in the atmospheres and structures of the outer planets of the solar system, and by the use of spectrophotometry have even been identified in interstellar space. To date, however, planet Earth is the only location in the universe in which this plethora of carbon-centred molecules is known to be associated with life. Among this infinite chemical variation a single molecule stands supreme on earth as the most common—its name is cellulose and it is the structural building material of plant cell walls and, therefore, of wood and paper. There is little doubt that this most ordinary of substances occurs in quantities greater than those of any other organic substance, with the result that there are billions and billions of tons of it worldwide.

Cellulose, and ultimately all the other organic building blocks found in earthly ecosystems, are manufactured by plants in the chain of chemical reactions that compose the process of photosynthesis. Animals are essentially parasitic on the plant kingdom when it comes to obtaining their supply of complex organic molecules because, unlike plants, they cannot construct themselves and replace any deficient parts from a collection of non-organic starting reagents. The chemical magic of a plant is sun-powered alchemy. Radiant energy from the sun is, in the first analysis, the power source that drives the energy-requiring machinery of photosynthesis by which carbon dioxide is 'grabbed' from the atmosphere and fixed. In this fixation process the simple carbon dioxide gas, CO_2, made up of one atom of carbon and two of oxygen, is converted into the dramatically more complicated molecules of life, such as sugars. This increase in complexity can only be be paid for with an energy currency of which the sun is the final banker and it provides an extra dividend because oxygen gas is released into the atmosphere as a by-product of photosynthesis.

Not all parts of a plant can carry out photosynthesis. Only those cells that encounter significant intensities of sunlight will be in a position to carry out this process. Because of this fundamental restriction, roots, many woody stems and the central woody tissues of trees cannot do so, which means that their cells depend on the photosynthetic parts of the plant to provide them with the organic molecules they need for growth. All higher plants have a transport system of long, tubular cells or vessels, which together comprise the phloem tissue, by means of which this sort of nutrient translocation is achieved.

The cells that can carry out photosynthesis have an unmistakable brand mark. They are green. This colour, the indelible signature of the plant world, is formed by the pigment chlorophyll, a molecule that has changed the Earth from a dreary planet on which only yeastlike fermentation could take place in the absense of oxygen to the oxygen-rich globe we know today. It is the first in a highly ordered chain of molecules within green plant cells that effectively convert a photon, a package of light energy, into an energetic electron, and then trap some of the energy of several such electrons to drive vital chemical

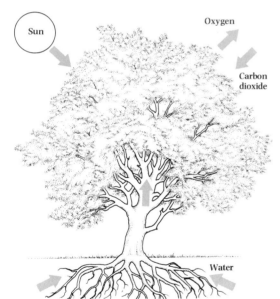

Green plants are the living links between the earth and the sun. The reason for this is that plants carry out the process of photosynthesis in which light energy from the sun is converted into chemical bonds in organic molecules. The chemical complexities of photosynthesis can be reduced to a single equation of change: under the influence of a light-generated energy source, carbon dioxide and a hydrogen-containing molecule combine to make organic molecules, such as sugars, which contain carbon, hydrogen and oxygen, plus water and the remnants of the hydrogen-donating molecule. For normal green plants the hydrogen donor is water (H_2O), so when the hydrogen is removed, oxygen is given off. As well as light, another essential mediator of photosynthesis is the green pigment chlorophyll, which gives most leaves their colour. The exceptions to these rules are some photosynthetic bacteria, which use hydrogen sulphide (H_2S) as their hydrogen source, and produce the element sulphur as a result of their sun-driven chemistry. Much is known about the electronic and chemical changes of photosynthesis. Not all the reactions need light, but the initial light reaction involves the interaction of a quantum of radiant energy from the sun with chlorophyll.

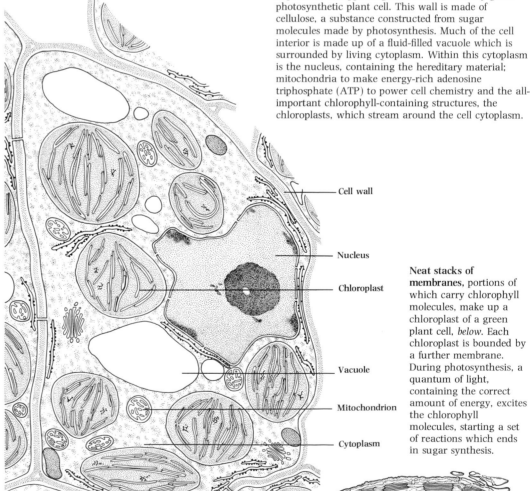

A protective, supporting wall surrounds every green photosynthetic plant cell. This wall is made of cellulose, a substance constructed from sugar molecules made by photosynthesis. Much of the cell interior is made up of a fluid-filled vacuole which is surrounded by living cytoplasm. Within this cytoplasm is the nucleus, containing the hereditary material; mitochondria to make energy-rich adenosine triphosphate (ATP) to power cell chemistry and the all-important chlorophyll-containing structures, the chloroplasts, which stream around the cell cytoplasm.

Cell wall

Nucleus

Chloroplast

Vacuole

Mitochondrion

Cytoplasm

Neat stacks of membranes, portions of which carry chlorophyll molecules, make up a chloroplast of a green plant cell, *below*. Each chloroplast is bounded by a further membrane. During photosynthesis, a quantum of light, containing the correct amount of energy, excites the chlorophyll molecules, starting a set of reactions which ends in sugar synthesis.

reactions, such as the fixation of atmospheric carbon dioxide gas and the manufacture of cellulose.

Green plant cells, such as those with which leaves are packed, reveal a Chinese puzzle of suntraps within suntraps. Leaves themselves are orientated so that they can intercept the sun's rays most efficiently. Within the leaves green chlorophyll-containing cells are dispersed so as to provide multiple opportunities for green cells to intercept light. Within each cell the chlorophyll and other chemical hardware of photosynthesis are packaged in stacks, and several stacks make up one chloroplast. Monomolecular layers of chlorophyll, bound to membranes in the chloroplasts, are the ultimate targets for the photons of light which left our personal star, travelling at 186,000 miles (297,600 km) per second, eight minutes or so before.

In two vital respects the mechanisms and implications of photosynthesis are cyclical in organization. First, the chemical complexities of carbon fixation itself involve a highly conservative self-replenishing cycle of molecular usage. Some of the key substances in the reaction are not consumed in the process of photosynthetic chemistry but are cyclically reconverted one into another. Second, jumping from the chemical to the more majestic, global scale, photosynthesis is at the heart of a planet-embracing cycle of carbon utilization with the apt name of the carbon cycle.

The carbon cycle of planet Earth involves two states of atomic carbon—organic compounds containing carbon and inorganic, carbon-containing molecules including carbon dioxide. In our world individual atoms of carbon shuttle between these two states. Carbon dioxide is fixed by the processes of photosynthesis and changed into organic compounds. These compounds are ultimately broken down during the process of respiration—either in the plant itself or in an animal that has eaten that plant—which turns the carbon in the respired molecules back into carbon dioxide again. Some forms of carbon, including deep carbonate rock strata and fossil fuels still undisturbed in the ground, are essentially unavailable to life processes in the short term. At another level non-organic carbon stocks in terrestrial and aquatic systems are partially separated from each other. In the air, carbon dioxide is found as a gas, while in the sea, a river or a lake it is present as dissolved carbon dioxide, carbonates or bicarbonates.

In total the absolute quantities of carbon being cycled by the life of our world are staggering. So, too, is the proportion of the available carbon cycled every year. The green plants of the world fix, very approximately, three and a half million billion ounces (a hundred million billion grams) of carbon every year, and pass about a third of it back into the atmosphere and the world's waters as carbon dioxide produced by plant respiration. The remaining two-thirds are eventually returned to the carbon dioxide pool, either as gas or in its dissolved state, as a result of the respiration of bacteria, fungi and animals, including ourselves, who either eat plant food or dine on herbivores who get their energy from plant-fixed organic material. Ignoring the seas and fresh water, it is likely that terrestrial communities or plants, animals and micro-organisms also process as much as 12 per cent of the total carbon dioxide in the atmosphere each year. Thus, on average, every atmospheric molecule of carbon dioxide must take part in the cyclical molecular dance of life every eight years.

All the key molecules from which earthly organisms are constructed are built around atoms of the element carbon. Linked in huge linear, branching or circular configurations, these carbon atoms provide a backbone for the attachment of other atoms. The central role of carbon means that the dynamic pathways, by which its atoms cycle between the living and inanimate components of our world, are vitally important. The most essential non-living forms of carbon are carbon dioxide gas in the atmosphere and dissolved carbon dioxide in the oceans. Together they form a carbon dioxide pool from which living things obtain carbon. These accessible reserves of carbon dioxide (CO_2) are trapped by terrestrial and aquatic plants and changed into sugar molecules by means of photosynthesis. The carbon dioxide is replaced as the plants themselves respire. In addition, animals eat plants and animals eat animals, and each action passes carbon down the chain. Respiration of herbivores and carnivores produces carbon dioxide, as does the decay of dead organisms or their carbon-containing excreta by micro-organisms.

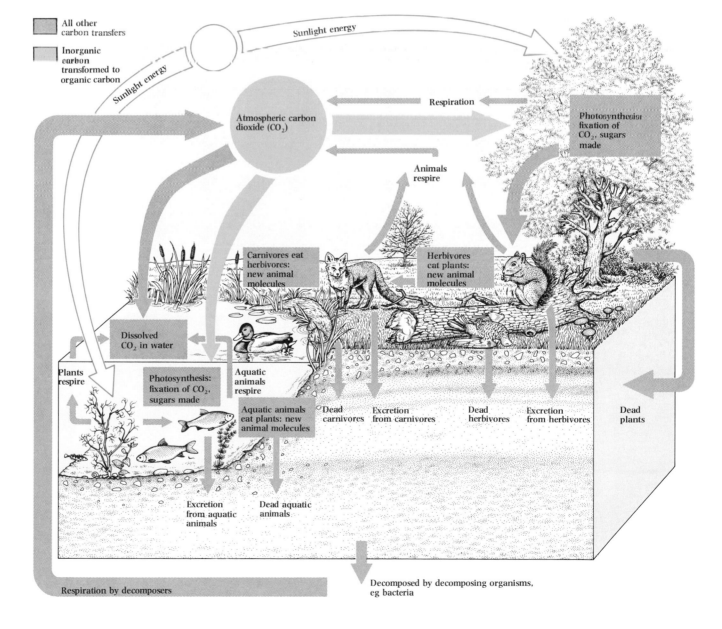

Rhythms of energy

All the activities that make life possible, and which together form the rhythms and cycles of the living world, require energy. The activity of animals is often dramatically obvious, like the sinuously muscular and rhythmic dash of a hunting cheetah in pursuit of an impala, or the laboured beating of the wings of an osprey as it rises from a lake with a trout twitching in its talons. Among plants, activities are usually less overt, none the less the activity patterns are there, from the rapid drooping of the leaves of a sensitive mimosa plant as they are touched by the tongue of a browsing goat, to the gradual blind extension of root tips through the soil in their quest for water or mineral salts.

Inside their bodies, although in a more subtle and covert fashion, animals and plants pulse with change. Food substances are absorbed; cells divide, grow and change their function; secretions are made, transported and even pushed out of the organism's body; nerves transmit electrical signals. At a microscopic level, and in a thousand ways a second, the internal organization of all living creatures teems with change.

All these varied patterns of activity are joined together by many different links, not least of which are the links forged by the connection of all life on planet Earth through a shared evolutionary past. At a fundamental level all the various life processes, from animal locomotion to molecular change inside cells, organs and tissues, need energy from some external source to make them happen. They involve work. They consist of events and phenomena which simply cannot occur without the application of energy.

If an animal is deprived of food for long enough, it will, in the end, not be able to move because it no longer contains any nutrients which can be burned with oxygen in the process of respiration to release the energy necessary for movement. Similarly, if a green plant is kept in the dark for long enough all its activities will grind to a halt because, for a plant, the only significant source of energy is the radiant energy of the sun. A plant can take up a collection of simple chemicals—carbon dioxide, water and mineral salts—and, with the sun's help, turn them into the myriad molecules of life by the process of photosynthesis. But animals must have their nutrients already made into complex organic molecules, such as proteins, sugars and fats, because they cannot build them from the inorganic molecules of the non-living world.

Activity, then, is multiple in form but always displays a basic link with energy supplied from outside. The fact that patterns of activity are so often cyclical or rhythmic in organization is the result of a series of constraints which operate on living things and the ecosystems in which they live, and which favour some processes rather than others. It is difficult to conceive of efficient locomotory systems, for instance, which do not have the cyclical features demonstrated by all running, swimming and flying.

The rhythmicity of locomotion arises because non-cyclical performances are intrinsically 'once only' affairs. A solid fuel rocket burns its fuel and produces movement. When the fuel is gone the movement stops until the rocket is refuelled. Animals and plants cannot function like this. Instead they power their movement by using small, repetitive event patterns that can be sustained indefinitely. Similarly, the constraints of the conservation of matter mean that many of the biochemical processes of life occur in a cyclical fashion. The biochemical cycles provide useful new molecules or energy, but they also generate some or many of their starting materials so that the system is both cyclical and potentially inexhaustible.

More than four billion years ago, when planet Earth was being formed, there was almost certainly no free oxygen gas in our atmosphere. When the first simple life forms began to develop on the earth's surface, probably between four and three billion years ago, the atmosphere was still devoid of this gas that is so crucial today. The absence of oxygen meant that all the first life forms had to make use of energy-obtaining strategies that had no need to 'burn' foods with oxygen. This meant that the cyclical movement of elements from the atmosphere to living things and back again was very different from the one that now exists.

The coming of green plants, and with them the process of photosynthesis, back in the Precambrian mists of prehistory more than 600 million years ago, induced a gigantic lurch in the organic evolution of life on earth. The first single-celled blue-green algae transformed the world. Because these organisms possessed the green pigment chlorophyll, they were able to take in the carbon dioxide already in the atmosphere and, using sunlight as an energy source and water as a donor of hydrogen atoms (water consists of oxygen and hydrogen), could make oxygen gas.

The oxygen gas that changed the world, which oxidized the minerals on the earth's surface and so potently altered the atmosphere and life that came to breathe it, was simply a waste product of plant activity. To begin with this oxygen was of little use to the plants themselves. The blue-green algae used their chlorophyll and the process of photosynthesis to produce organic molecules, such as sugar. However, the polluting waste from this piece of chemical conjuring turned out, inadvertently, to be the generator of a

biological breakthrough. It opened the door to a whole new cycle of molecular change and made possible a completely new way of producing energy for the activities of life.

If you take a tablet of pure glucose and heat it in the air at extremely high temperatures of several hundred degrees, it will eventually burn producing heat, carbon dioxide, water and nothing else. The matter in glucose is completely conserved by being burned with the oxygen in the air, but its atoms are changed from those of the glucose configuration—a ring of carbon atoms each bearing oxygen and hydrogen atoms—to a new configuration represented by the separate molecules of carbon dioxide and water. The heat energy produced by the process comes from the fracture of the chemical bonds that hold the glucose molecule together. But glucose does not give up its bond-energy easily. The great heating that was initially necessary to make the intrinsically stable glucose molecules burn was the energy input necessary to get the oxygen-adding—the oxidation or burning—process going.

The bodies of all animals, and those of plants and micro-organisms, all contain glucose, but it is inconceivable that they could obtain useful energy from this glucose by the burning process described. Such burning would be impossible for two reasons. First, animal, plant and microbial bodies are destroyed by the high temperatures required to make glucose burn spontaneously in oxygen. Second, the sort of energy provided by the uncontrolled burning of glucose, is in the wrong form.

All the forms of life which make use of oxygen—the aerobic organisms—employ a subtle manoeuvre to surmount these two problems. Instead of

Within each green leaf of any plant are many chlorophyll-rich cells which use solar energy for photosynthesis. In these cells carbon dioxide from the air and water drawn up by the roots are combined to produce sugar and oxygen. In the under part of the leaf, a spongy air-filled layer forms a passage for water vapour, which escapes through pores in the leaf underside as the plant transpires.

The opening and closing of each pore is controlled by water pressure in the surrounding 'guard cells'. During the day when the cells produce sugars more water is drawn into the guard cells making them swell and open. At night sugar is changed into starch, pressure falls and the pore closes.

Levels of light and transpiration follow the same rhythm, reaching a peak at noon. The leaf pores usually open to give off water and receive carbon dioxide, only when the sun provides energy for photosynthesis. Cacti, however, invert this rhythm to conserve water in desert conditions. At night the pores open to take in carbon dioxide. By day, pores closed, they photosynthesize using stored carbon dioxide.

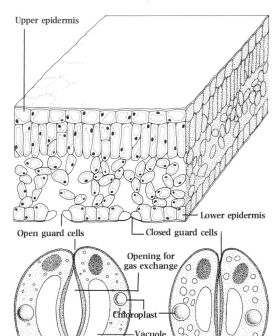

Upper epidermis

Lower epidermis

Open guard cells

Closed guard cells

Opening for gas exchange

Chloroplast

Vacuole

Starch grains

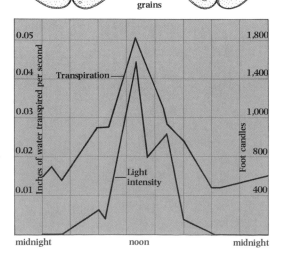

Inches of water transpired per second

Transpiration

Light intensity

Foot candles

midnight   noon   midnight

burning glucose directly to form carbon dioxide and water, the process takes place as a long sequence of tiny chemical steps, each controlled by specific enzymes. These enzymes, or biological catalysts, work in such a way that glucose can be broken down at physiologically harmless temperatures between 5 and 40 degrees centigrade (41 and 104 degrees F). The enzyme-regulated burning of glucose, which only ever takes place inside the cells of organisms, is thus known as internal respiration. In the same terms, external respiration comprises activities, such as the rhythmical movements of human breathing, which get oxygen into the body of an animal.

As well as taking place at non-lethal temperatures, internal respiration provides a usable form of energy for living things. It is an energy source of an unexpected kind—a complex organic molecule of adenosine triphosphate (ATP) containing three linked chemical groupings, all of which have phosphorus in them. ATP is the bank that issues the energy currency to cells, and it can drive almost any cell or body activity. During the process of internal respiration large amounts of ATP are made, and while it is being 'burned' with oxygen and broken down, one molecule of glucose is responsible for making 38 molecules of ATP.

Without the oxygen waste of the primeval blue-green algae, the energy-grabbing strategy of modern organisms and their countless predecessors would have been impossible. The concentration of oxygen in the atmosphere has slowly climbed since these early times until it now represents about 20 per cent of the gaseous envelope around our planet: a stupendous quantity of gas, all of it generated by living things. Once animals and plants had become biochemi-

cally adapted to the immense respiratory possibilities inherent in an oxygen-rich atmosphere, the next steps were those that had the effect of refining the process by which the atmospheric gases are transferred to the cells that need them. Plant cells need carbon dioxide and oxygen, while most animal cells need only oxygen.

Green plants, especially the larger, more complex, higher plants, such as ferns, conifers and the world's wealth of flowering plants, from herbaceous weeds to trees, have evolved a wide range of structures and cyclical processes designed to bring carbon dioxide and oxygen from the atmosphere to their internal cells for the essential processes of photosynthesis and internal respiration. Such plants also show rhythms in the way their water content is controlled. This control is critical because plants tend to lose water via pores, or stomata, in their leaves while they are in the process of trapping carbon dioxide for photosynthesis.

A wide range of animals, both aquatic and terrestrial, have developed respiratory structures to gather atmospheric oxygen for internal respiration. These structures work on the principle that the larger the surface area through which oxygen can diffuse, the more oxygen can be obtained. Gills are the surfaces favoured by water dwelling animals while land livers such as man use lungs. Animals of all kinds also show an elaborate and impressive variety of methods of ventilating these surfaces with oxygen-rich water or air during the process of external respiration.

The ventilating mechanisms used by animals to get oxygen to the tissues that need it for internal respiration are almost always cyclical in nature. ▷

Insects 'breathe' through valve-operated spiracles—tiny holes in the cuticle which open regularly to draw in oxygen from the air and to release carbon dioxide, and close to prevent water loss. An intricate system of air tubes which can subdivide into minute branches brings oxygen directly to the internal tissues by diffusion. The air flow is controlled by spiracles opening out of phase.

Tracheal channels   Air sac

Spiracle   Open spiracle   Closed spiracle

Many active insects increase the air flow by rhythmically pumping their abdomens. The locust, for example, contracts and relaxes its body in an up and down movement, which alternately squeezes and expands its air sacs, so replacing almost half the air in its body.

The honey-bee ventilates its body by pumping its air-filled abdomen in and out, accordion-style, in synchrony with the spiracle movements. Inspiration lasts 250 milliseconds during which the thoracic spiracles open for 25 milliseconds. These spiracles then close for one second before a one-second expiration phase when the abdominal spiracles open for 300 milliseconds.

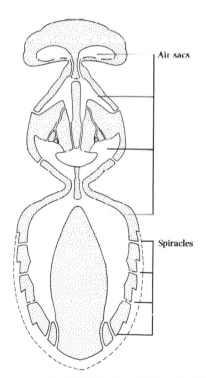

Air sacs

Spiracles

To avoid excessive water loss in dry, hot climates insects keep their spiracles shut for long periods, only opening them for brief bursts to allow carbon dioxide to escape. Before and after each burst, the spiracle valves flutter. The frequency of this cyclic respiration is largely controlled by ambient temperature and the insect's metabolic rate.

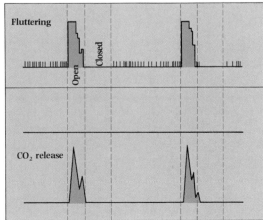

Fluttering   Closed

Open

CO_2 release

▷ Superficially there seems to be little intrinsic reason for using such methods of discontinuous pumping because it is perfectly possible to construct models of continuous-flow systems which would be just as efficient in providing good ventilation for lungs or gills. In fact a few 'greyhounds' of the fish world, bony fish such as mackerel and tunny, do create a continuous flow of water over their gills. These fish keep their mouths slightly open while they are swimming fast. Their swimming speed is so great that it maintains a steady water flow through the mouth and out over the gills, where oxygen is absorbed in exchange for carbon dioxide, which is the waste product of internal respiration. The water exits via the two opercula or flaps, on either side of the body, which cover the gill chambers in a bony fish. Mackerel need so much oxygen that they must swim continuously if the required quantities of water are to pass over their gills. In some species of shark it has been noticed that a mackerel-like continuous-flow strategy for external respiration operates when these predators are swimming, but active cyclical pumping of the water has to begin once swimming stops.

Since this continuous-flow tactic is workable, why is it that almost all other vertebrates, both aquatic and terrestrial, use discontinuous cyclical pumping, like that employed in a pump for inflating bicycle tyres or in any other man-made pumping machine? The answer probably lies in the nature of the equipment that animals have to work with. The basic material at an animal's disposal, for producing movement of either water or air, is muscle. Body muscles are intrinsically cyclical devices. They contract and, while they are contracting, can do work—this is phase one of the cycle. For anything more to

happen the muscle must then relax and elongate back to its resting length; this elongation makes up the second phase of the cycle. This two-phase cycle can be operated indefinitely, but its essentially cyclical nature means that any system of ventilation powered by animal muscles is likely to be cyclical and probably rhythmic. Given these limitations to the design, the range of successful products that has come off the evolutionary drawing-board is soberingly successful. Any commercial research and development team would be justifiably proud of the functional innovation displayed in the product range of respiratory equipment.

The smallest of all the creatures in the animal kingdom do not have to bother about active external respiration. Aquatic animals with a maximum body-length of up to about a quarter of an inch (6 mm) can obtain enough oxygen by diffusion, even at the centres of their tiny bodies. This process does not need an energy source because it is powered by the random motions of all molecules at temperatures above absolute zero. The process works in this way: a minute animal living in water containing dissolved oxygen has internal oxygen levels in its watery tissues that are almost equal to those of the surrounding water. If the creature now uses some internal oxygen in the process of burning glucose to make ATP, a new situation is produced in which the concentration of oxygen outside its body is higher than the concentration inside it. The random physical motions of oxygen molecules in the water automatically act to remedy this state of imbalance and oxygen flows into the animal.

The problem with diffusion, as far as animals are concerned, is that it is only

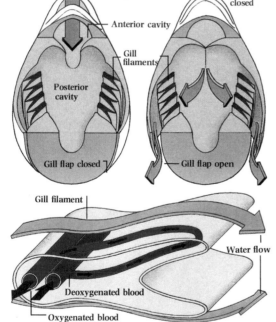

The muscles around the mouth and mouth cavity of bony fish operate to produce a muscular breathing pump that sends a continuous stream of water over the respiratory surface of the gills. The anterior and posterior cavities move slightly out of phase with each other, which ensures a continuous flow.

Mouth open

Mouth closed

Anterior cavity

Gill filaments

Posterior cavity

Gill flap closed

Gill flap open

Fish absorb as much as 80 per cent of the oxygen that reaches their gills. This is partly because blood to be oxygenated in the gill runs in the opposite direction to the water flow, allowing the maximum amount of oxygen to pass from the water into the blood.

Gill filament

Water flow

Deoxygenated blood

Oxygenated blood

Birds consume relatively more oxygen than many other creatures to fuel the exertions of flight. Air sacs, which act as reservoirs of air, help to increase the oxygen uptake by allowing a continuous one-way flow through the lung. This storage system prevents the mixing of oxygenated and deoxygenated air and means that the bird lung can operate highly efficiently.

Lung

Anterior sac

Lung

Posterior sac

Air sacs

Trachea

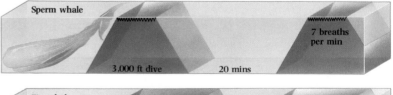
Sperm whale — 3,000 ft dive — 20 mins — 7 breaths per min

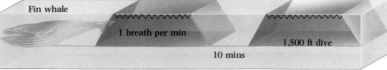
Fin whale — 1 breath per min — 1,500 ft dive — 10 mins

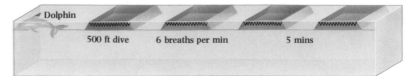
Dolphin — 500 ft dive — 6 breaths per min — 5 mins

effective over short distances, hence the upper size-limit on the animals that can depend on it as a mechanism for obtaining this metabolically vital gas. Unless they can play a physical trick and cut down the length of the transport path to the tissues so that diffusion can operate efficiently, all animals must supplement the diffusion mechanism by large-scale, usually muscle-powered, mass movements of air or water.

Fish are respiring aquatic animals, that is, they get their oxygen from water. This poses problems, not least because water is about 1,000 times more dense than air so much more muscle power has to be used to shift it about than is needed for moving air. In addition, any given volume of air will contain more oxygen, in absolute terms, than the same volume of water at the same temperature, so the respiratory dice are heavily stacked against water breathers. Fish are, in fact, highly efficient oxygen extractors. By means of a one-way flow system over the gills, powered by multistage muscle pumps in the mouth and gullet (pharynx), elegant gill design and subtle counter-current arrangements for transferring oxygen from the water to the blood within their gills, fish manage to remove oxygen from water more efficiently than man does from air. Some fish can extract 80 per cent of the oxygen in water while man removes only about 25 per cent of oxygen from the air he breathes.

For respiratory surfaces, the parts of animals that actually absorb oxygen (and at the same time get rid of carbon dioxide), design awards go to those which can pack the greatest area into the smallest volume. Absorption is a surface phenomenon—the more surface that can be crammed into a gill, the better it will work. The large surface areas inside the air-breathing lungs of

amphibia, reptiles and mammals are ventilated by tidal flows of air. Air is breathed in by muscle power into a highly subdivided respiratory sac, the lung, then the lung is partially emptied of air during expiration, like the tide rushing out. This in-out cycle is one reason why land dwelling vertebrates cannot attain the oxygen extraction results achieved by fish. The one-way flow arrangement of a fish's gills is intrinsically more efficient than our 'breathing bags' because the gills are constantly in oxygen-rich water, whereas the inner surfaces of our lungs are only in oxygen-rich air during one phase of the breathing cycle. As we breathe out the alveoli, the ultimate microscopic subdivisions of our lungs which ensure a big surface area for oxygen absorption, are exposed to a gas relatively low in oxygen.

For a cockroach, a pike, a sparrow or even an elephant, the ventilating rhythms of external respiration can only take oxygen as far as the respiratory surface. Oxygen travels across this surface by the process of diffusion and so is inside the animal, but it may still be a long way away from the tissues that urgently require oxygen for internal respiration and energy generation. Breathing rhythms can, for example, take air into a giraffe's lungs, and diffusion will pass oxygen across the giraffe's lung membranes, but neither ventilation nor diffusion can carry that oxygen the many feet that separate the giraffe's lungs from its brain.

All large many-celled animals must possess a transport system that can move oxygen—and at the same time nutrients, hormones and a thousand and one other substances—around the body. The problem is analagous to that of a central heating system. Having a boiler that burns fuel to produce usable heat is ▷

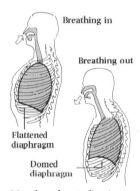

Man breathes to live in more ways than one, as demonstrated by Dizzy Gillespie, *right*. As air is sucked into the lungs, the rib cage is expanded, partly by a flattening of the diaphragm. Breathing out is a passive process. The rib cage sinks, air is squeezed out of the lungs and the diaphragm relaxes.

Whales and dolphins exhale a spectacular spout of compressed air through a blowhole when they surface for oxygen after a long dive. Their ability to store 40 per cent of their oxygen intake in their muscles, and to exchange 90 per cent of air in their lungs with each breath, allows these mammals to take less frequent though deeper breaths than man. Each species has its own breathing rhythm; the sperm whale breathes a mere 7 times per minute after a deep dive, *left*.

▷not, in itself, enough to warm a house. The boiler must be connected to a circulatory system of pipes to transfer heat from the boiler to every radiator in every room. The blood vessels of vertebrates, and the body spaces filled with the fluid haemolymph that exist in many invertebrates, represent the biological equivalent of the ducting of the heating system. These vessels take oxygen from the gills or lungs and transfer it around the body. The ultimate branches of this tubing system, the capillaries, ramify so extensively through the tissues that there are few cells in the body of a human being, or any other vertebrate, more than a fortieth of an inch (1 mm) away from these capillaries and the blood they contain.

Carrying the central heating analogy one stage further, blood is the working fluid of the body, equivalent to the water in the pipes and radiators. In fish, amphibians, reptiles, birds and mammals the blood in the circulatory system can carry oxygen in two distinct ways. In the simpler of these two forms of oxygen transport, the oxygen is dissolved in the watery background fluid or serum of the blood. Like seawater, rain, or the water in a lake or river, blood can dissolve a certain amount of gaseous oxygen. It is this oxygen, along with other gases, that emerges as bubbles when water is heated.

Merely dissolving oxygen in water is not a particularly efficient method of acquiring oxygen for active vertebrates that have high oxygen requirements. For this reason most vertebrates have specialized cells in their blood containing pigment molecules which combine with oxygen in the most avid fashion. The most common of these pigments is haemoglobin, a complex organic molecule consisting of a protein, globulin, linked to a ring-shaped cage of atoms

enclosing a single atom of iron, and it is the red colour of haemoglobin that gives blood its characteristic hue. In the oxygen transport system, haemoglobin is packed inside disc-shaped red blood cells.

The pigment haemoglobin is particularly useful because it has an amazing ability to combine with oxygen to make a new molecular arrangement, oxyhaemoglobin. The formation of oxyhaemoglobin happens most readily when haemoglobin is present in situations of high oxygen concentration, as it is in the lungs of a mammal or the gills of a fish. At the respiratory surfaces of gills and lungs, blood in vessels close to those surfaces picks up oxygen and immediately makes it into oxyhaemoglobin. In the tissues, where oxygen levels are lower, the oxygen contained in the oxyhaemoglobin becomes detached and can move into tissue cells to be used for energy production.

All blood circulatory systems, like all central heating systems, must have a pumping mechanism to maintain the flow around the system's closed network of ducts. In the blood system this pump is the heart and it is in its activity that some of the most clear-cut rhythmic aspects of bodily physiology are manifest. What can be more single-mindedly rhythmic and cyclical than a pulsating heart? The healthy human heart, from its elaboration in the early weeks of foetal life until its eventual failure at the end of a lifespan, is the ultimately efficient machine. It will contract ceaselessly, without pauses for maintenance or repair, for 70 years or more, which adds up to a quarter of a billion pulsations in a lifetime.

All hearts are built essentially to the same design. A portion of the blood vessel tubing is thickened by extra muscles in the walls. The space inside this

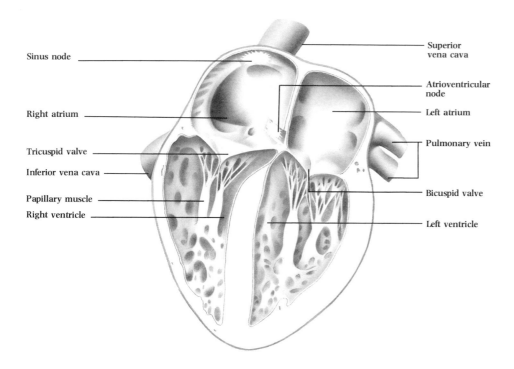

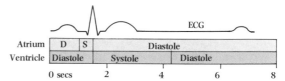

The heart's natural pacemaker, the sinus node is a small piece of muscle which initiates electrically induced rhythmic contractions, spreading first to the atria and a split second later to the ventricles. An ECG trace, *above*, measures the electrical charges triggering the contraction (systole) and relaxation (diastole), which produce the double heartbeat sounds as the valves close in rapid succession.

Heart rates of animals	Beats per minute at rest
Grey Whale	9
Elephant	25
Salmon	47
Cockroach	60
Housefly	60
Man	70
Seal	80
Sparrow	500
Shrew	600
Hummingbird	1200

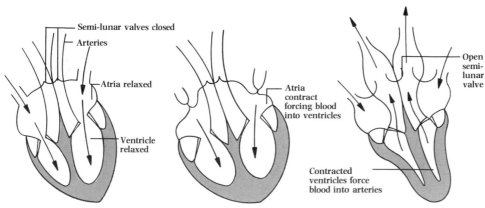

The continuous pumping of the heart ensures a constant oxygen supply to all parts of the body. Arteries carry oxygen-rich blood away from the heart, while veins bring blood back from the organs to the heart to be re-routed through the lungs. A separate circulatory loop feeds blood through the lungs for oxygenation before it returns to the rest of the body via the heart. Both sides of the heart beat in unison to ensure sufficient pressure is maintained. As the atria relax, blood flows from the lungs into the left atrium and from the rest of the body into the right atrium. Meanwhile, with a forceful contraction, the ventricles pump blood out into the arteries, then relax and refill with blood from the atria. A normal human heart beats 70 times a minute at rest, but increases to 200 after a release of adrenalin or heavy exercise.

muscular section of the ducting is functionally separated from the rest of the circulatory system by valves, flaps of tissue that allow flow in the appropriate direction, but restrict any backflow or make it impossible. As the muscular wall contracts, blood pooled within this region is forced out into the circulation via the open exit valve. Then the valve shuts, the wall relaxes and blood is drawn into the heart region through the entry valve, bringing the system back to its original condition, primed for another contraction or beat. During this two-phase sequence blood can only flow in one direction because of the presence of the valves—without them the system would produce no net circulation.

However, even in fish, the most primitive of the vertebrates that we commonly come across, the simplest of pumping mechanisms—the single-chambered heart—is not powerful enough to push the blood round the long circulatory path on its own. In a fish, blood from the heart travels in a single unbroken circuit from the heart, through the gills for oxygenation, and from there to all the other parts of the body before returning to the heart. On its journey the flow of blood is assisted by muscles in the walls of the vessels containing it and by other body muscles alongside them which, by contracting, help to squeeze the blood along. The fish heart has also a low pressure area, or atrium, that receives blood from the tissues, and a high pressure ventricle connected to the atrium that pushes blood round the body, via the gills.

In a mammal such as man a more sophisticated four-chamber pump is the rule. Here the lungs and the rest of the body each have a two-chamber pump of their own. The right side of the heart circulates blood through the lungs, so that it can pick up oxygen and dump its load of carbon dioxide waste, then passes this replenished blood to the left side of the heart from where it is delivered to the rest of the body. The blood coming back from the lungs rich in oxyhaemoglobin is bright cherry red; deoxygenated carbon dioxide-loaded blood returning from the body tissues is a dark purple-red colour. So blue blood is not the prerogative of kings nor of aristocrats—each of us is half blue blooded and half red blooded.

From the left side of the heart oxygenated blood travels outward through narrower and narrower arteries until it reaches the capillaries. Now the oxyhaemoglobin gives up its precious oxygen to tissue cells which use it to burn nutrients, such as glucose, in the controlled combustion of internal respiration which is governed by a series of biological catalysts. In fact, all cells which carry out this life-preserving process do so in specialized areas of their inner substance. These minute organelles, the mitochondria, each four hundred thousandths of an inch (0.001 mm) across, contain internal shelf-like partitions, the cristae, on which are packed in highly precise array the enzymes and other molecules needed, with the vital help of oxygen, to produce ATP. Like microscopic power houses, hundreds or even thousands of them to a cell, the mitochondria burn fragments of glucose to carbon dioxide and water in a self-replenishing chain of reactions named, after its elucidator, the Krebs cycle, which, at the level of molecular interactions, is a cyclical phenomenon.

The carbon dioxide released in the process of ATP formation now diffuses back into the blood in the capillaries. To complete the cycle, this deoxygenated blood flows back to the lungs to replenish its oxygen supply. This oxygen, the gas that respiratory and circulatory systems are designed to deal with, is the intangible, unseen agent that not only allows the mitochondria of an aerobic ▷

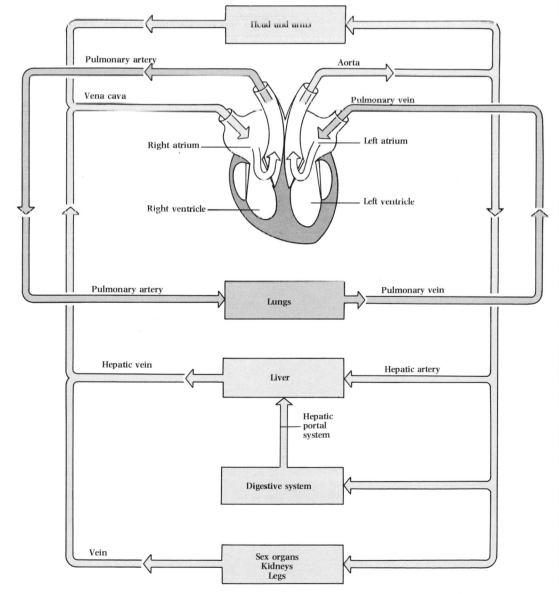

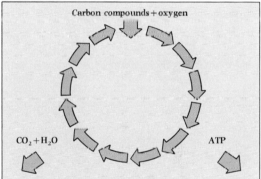

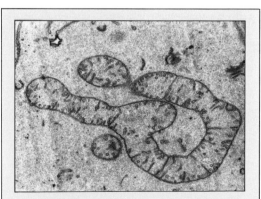

Energy is 'manufactured' within the body cells by minute membranous organelles called mitochondria, *above*. The carbon-containing breakdown products of glucose from other parts of the cell are passed into the mitochondria where a complex cycle of chemical processes, called the Krebs cycle, occurs. Air from the lungs oxidizes the carbon in these substances, producing carbon dioxide. At the same time water and molecules of ATP (adenosine triphosphate) are synthesized. The ATP molecules are an energy store that can be used to drive the energy-requiring processes of the body.

▷cell to produce ATP and so supply its energy needs but also enables a bonfire to burn and a car—or internal combustion—engine to run. But this is only half the story of energy generation. In animals the other half is ultimately food.

Why do we need to eat? The buying and growing of food, its preparation, the ritual of mealtimes, the inclusion of food imagery as a central part of our language are all such unexceptional and ordinary parts of our lives that we rarely stop to question the activity upon which they all centre. At the level of immediate motivation we eat because we feel hungry. Such an explanation can, however, be only the first step in unravelling the biological necessity for food consumption and merely leads us to another question. Why is it that we, and presumably other higher animals, have motivations or 'drives'—such as the internal trigger of hunger that pushes us into finding something to eat once the feeling of satiation created by our last meal has worn off—so firmly built into our patterns of behaviour?

Such patterns of internal behaviour control are necessary because we 'eat to live'—it is only the glutton who is chastised for 'living to eat'. Unlike plants, which can make all the sustenance they need, every animal, from the smallest microscopic creature to the mighty whale, must have food. The reason for this is, that in contrast to their green counterparts of the plant kingdom, even the most complex animals are absolutely incapable of constructing the complex molecules of life from simple inorganic ones.

The only means that an animal has of obtaining energy in the usable form of ATP is by the process of internal respiration in which sugars such as glucose, but also fats, are broken down. The metabolically incompetent animal must,

therefore, obtain its complex organic molecules ready-made. It may be difficult to think of lobster thermidor, ratatouille or a crusty loaf of bread with butter as fulfilling this chemically intimidating role, but that, apart from the pleasure of consumption, is all that any meal is for. The food we eat, thus, has two distinct but overlapping functions. First, it provides us with the organic building blocks originally constructed by plants from inorganic molecules with which we, as animals, can make new cells to replace those that have worn out, or can supplement existing structures to maintain the vast collection of cells we already possess. Second, food acts as fuel for the energy-releasing business of internal respiration to power all the energy-requiring processes and activities which our bodies carry out every minute of our lives.

The two functions of supplying raw materials for building and energy generation overlap because some of the substances that are good for burning as fuel also make excellent building bricks for constructing living cells. To take just two examples: the sugars that are the main starting point for energy production within cells are also essential components in the organization of DNA and RNA, the materials of the genetic code, which all life forms possess. Similarly, fatty acids, which form part of the fats, such as butter and margarine, in our diet can be burned as an energy source in place of sugars. Fats are also of vital importance structurally since they are employed as important raw materials in the construction of the membranes that surround all living cells.

A few of the foods that animals eat are already 'pre-processed' and arrive in the form of the small organic subunits that animals can utilize easily. Honey, for instance, which is made from plant nectars and pollens, contains both simple

Eskimos (the Inuet) are bound to a regular seasonal hunting pattern by the extreme variations in temperature and daylight. In Greenland, seal hunting for meat, oil and fuel begins in November when the sea forms a frozen sheet and seals can be caught coming up for air at their blowholes in the ice. In the summer many Eskimos decamp inland to hunt migratory birds and caribou, to fish river trout and gather autumn berries such as cranberries before returning to their coastal snow houses to prepare for the next sealing season.

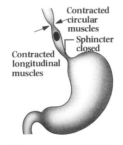
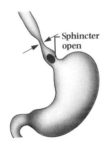

Contracted circular muscles
Sphincter closed
Contracted longitudinal muscles
Sphincter open

Eating involves a number of rhythmic processes which break food down into a digestible form. After each mouthful has been chewed into a manageable ball or bolus it passes into the oesophagus where a wave of muscular contractions pushes it towards the stomach. Circular muscles contract above the bolus forcing it downward and longitudinal muscles shorten the passage ahead, allowing the food to reach the stomach in 10 seconds. Contractions continue inside the stomach every 20 seconds while the food churns round.

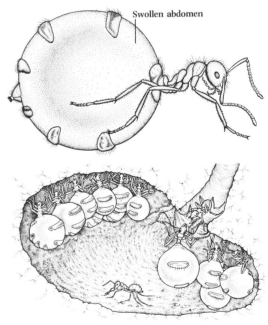

Swollen abdomen

The honeypot ants, *Myrmecocystus,* from the Colorado desert feed almost exclusively upon the sugary juices secreted by galls left on desert scrub oaks by gall wasps. Galls are only available for a few months of the year, so the ants have devised a storage system. They feed up several sterile female workers until they swell to eight times their normal size and leave them hanging from the ceiling of their burrow like a larder of honey sacs. In the dry season the females regurgitate food for the rest of the colony.

sugars and amino acids, the latter being the building blocks from which proteins can be constructed. These small organic substances can be directly absorbed across the gut wall of an animal by a mixture of diffusion—the same process by which oxygen travels into the bodies of minute organisms—and an energy-using system of active transport by which the nutrients are picked up by molecular ferries and given a ride from the space, or lumen, inside the intestinal tube into the bloodstream for transport to where they are needed.

Most of the food we eat is not, however, in such a readily available form. Rather it consists of complex mixtures of enormous molecules of fats, starches, proteins and nucleic acids such as DNA. These substances consist of huge molecules with molecular weights of more than 100,000 or even 1,000,000 compared with glucose with a molecular weight of only 180. These giant molecules cannot easily be absorbed in the state in which they are consumed. So first they have to be broken down into their constituent subunits—starches into simple sugars, fats into fatty acids and glycerol, proteins into amino acids and nucleic acids into building blocks named nucleotides.

It is the process of digestion which fragments these large molecules into their constituent parts. The mechanics of digestion begin when food is chopped up into small pieces by beaks, teeth and tongues; a task supplemented by the churning stomachs of mammals or grinding gizzards, filled with grit, in birds. The result of all these activities is a finely dispersed slurry of particles of the giant food molecules which is moved down the intestine by peristalsis, a kind of rhythmic pushing effected by muscular contraction. In its liquid form food is acted upon by digestive enzymes produced by the wall of the stomach and the intestine and by the neighbouring pancreas, which passes its secretions to the intestine through a tube. These enzymes do the job of chemical splitting so that the large molecules are converted into smaller ones which can be absorbed across the gut wall.

Just as the provision of oxygen for an organism is built around a number of rhythmic and cyclical processes, so feeding and food handling are often modulated in such a patterned way. Most of these patterns are imposed by, or firmly tied to, external environmental rhythms. So rats, for instance, even those kept in a laboratory with food and water instantly available for 24 hours a day, have a circadian rhythm of nocturnal feeding. During the hours of daylight the rats sleep, feed little, if at all, and produce almost no faeces. At dark they become active, start feeding and release faeces throughout the night until, near dawn, their activity subsides again. This complex pattern of cyclical change, of which feeding is an essential part, has nothing to do with the laboratory rats' food supply, but instead is a manifestation of their natural strategy of life which includes nighttime eating.

The circadian feeding rhythm of these laboratory rats is inextricably tied to the 24-hour cycle of day and night. The same rhythm can be used as a model for any animals that are decidedly nocturnal or diurnal—that is, daytime active—in their habits. Such patterning of general activity will almost always entail a parallel variation in feeding behaviour with nocturnal animals feeding, as one would expect, at night and diurnal ones during the day.

When displayed by predatory animals, such cycles usually imply that there is some restriction on available prey, or that the predator has become ▷

The short-tailed vole, *Microtus agrestis*, displays two different feeding rhythms. Within its longer 24-hour feeding rhythm, which reaches a peak just after sunset, the vole also feeds at 2–4 hour intervals as its stomach is so small.

Many game birds, including the ruffed grouse, *Bonasa umbellus*, of North America, select their diet seasonally according to both availability and preference. They enjoy the abundance of fruits and seeds in the summer months and substitute buds and twigs for them during the winter. The increase in insect consumption during the summer, however, reflects a physiological need, common to vegetarian birds, for protein before the breeding season. Males eat more during courtship; females double their food intake when egg-laying.

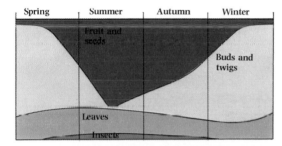

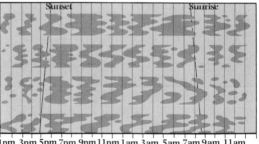

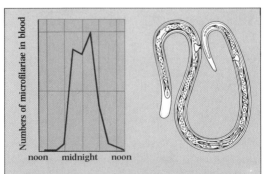

Three rhythms are involved in spreading the disease elephantiasis. Mosquitoes such as *Culex pipiens fatigans* pass larvae of the infecting worm *Wucheria bancrofti* into man's blood when they bite at night. During the day, the larval worms retreat into the victim's lungs, but return to the blood every night, ready to be sucked up by a mosquito, which will infect another man. If the host changes his pattern of sleep and waking, the worms adapt within a week.

▷ specialized to hunt only one or a few types of prey animals. So, for instance, a pied flycatcher, a bird that never flies at night, hunts solely during the hours of daylight for flying insects, and these it seeks and catches with the help of its keen sense of sight. In contrast a horseshoe bat, a totally nocturnal airborne mammal, catches night-flying insects, such as moths, on the wing. The bat is not hampered by the fact that there is no light and that it cannot use its eyes effectively because it uses a high precision system of ultrasonic radar to guide its movements. The bat emits pulses of high frequency sound through the strange horseshoe-shaped folds in its nose.

Other marked feeding patterns of animals have a seasonal or a yearly periodicity. Such rhythms may be tied, for instance, to the annual breeding activity of an animal, a period of migration or the seasonal availability of food. Animals such as birds, which collect food for their offspring confined to the nest, will often gather a quite different selection of food items for their young than they would to sustain themselves. Since this period, during which the young are being fed, normally occurs at a specific time of year, such changes of foraging or predatory behaviour add up, over a period of 12 months, to a reasonably regular annual cycle of food utilization.

Migrating animals commonly need to build up large reserves of fat before embarking on lengthy and arduous migrations during which the opportunities for feeding are likely to be few and far between, and also less successful than they are during the rest of the year. This requirement means that there is an intensive burst of feeding in the period immediately before the migratory journey. Fats are foods favoured by migrating animals, such as birds and butterflies, because, weight for weight, a food-store of fat burned with oxygen will give considerably more energy-providing ATP than the equivalent weight of any other nutrient, such as carbohydrates or proteins. For a flying migrant, payload considerations mean that the weight-to-energy ratio of the food (that is, fuel) it carries is of prime importance.

Naturally enough, feeding behaviour is only one facet of the many activity patterns exhibited by animals which demonstrate a regular rhythmic periodicity or a clearly cyclical organization in their lives. It is probably true to say that whatever energy-requiring activity one considers in the animal world, whether it is related to large locomotory movements, internal patterns of physiological activity, such as digestion or the rate of the heartbeat, or the performance of mental tasks, it is always possible to demonstrate that in some animals this behaviour exhibits rhythmical properties.

This generalization about animal activity can be shown to be valid for creatures as different in their size, habits and complexity as minute marine plankton and man himself. Marine plankton, made up of microscopic adult organisms and eggs and juvenile, larval stages of larger marine creatures, might easily be regarded as animals which could only be of interest to specialist zoologists with peculiar tastes. In fact the population sizes, distribution and migrations of plankton are of hard economic importance to every nation with a fishing fleet.

Zooplankton, the small planktonic animals in the sea, are absolutely crucial links in the complex web of food chains that exist in the seas of the world. Zooplankton feed on phytoplankton, microscopic free-floating marine plants

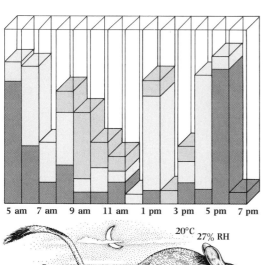

Birds time their daily activity according to their diet, size and predators. The activity of blackbirds, *left*, grows increasingly during the morning. Their feeding rhythm peaks at 5 pm. At dawn and dusk males sing to advertise and defend their territories.

Many desert rodents, including the jerboa, *left*, spend the day in burrows to avoid losing precious moisture in the intense heat. At night, when the fierce drying sun sets and cooler conditions return, the jerboa ventures out, returning to its humid burrow at dawn.

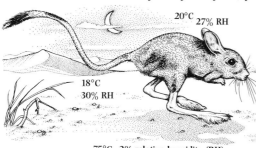

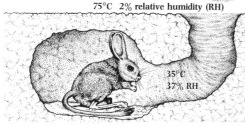

The night-active, red-backed salamander, *Plethodon cinereus, right,* normally follows a distinct pattern of movement. After a burst of activity at 10 am, it spends most of the day sleeping under stones and wood, until it re-emerges in the evening, and reaches a peak of activity at 9 pm. On nights with a full moon, however, this rhythm is subdued and the salamander remains quiet and still, shielding itself from the eyes of nocturnal predators.

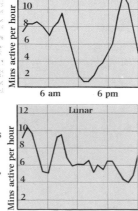

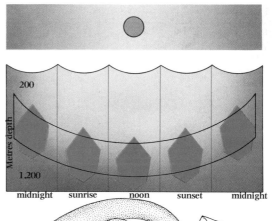

Many light-sensitive plankton species migrate into the ocean depths during the day and move back to the surface at night. Activated by light, temperature and salinity, the plankton swim to varying depths, determined by age, sex and water conditions. Many plankton-feeding fish follow their prey, so adopting the same rhythm.

which comprise the other half of the planktonic equation. Because they are green, the members of the phytoplankton are the primary producers, via the process of photosynthesis, of new organic material in the oceans. The fish that we eat feed on zooplankton or on smaller fish which have themselves grown fat on zooplankton. Much observation has been carried out by fisheries biologists of the daily activity patterns of these tiny, yet vital animals. Many of the zooplankton have been shown to carry out staggeringly extensive vertical migrations in the sea, moving downward during the day then returning to the surface each night in a regular circadian rhythm.

Although they may have the most powerful and versatile brains of any animal on earth, human beings are not excluded from the rhythmical imperatives of life. Much work has been done to examine the way that humans perform certain tasks and solve problems in an attempt to discover circadian, 24-hour rhythms in these abilities. The motivation for carrying out much of this research has been the possibility that work efficiency could be greatly improved if proper account were taken of intrinsic, through-the-day variations in the ability of all men and women—not just a selected few—to carry out specific types of task.

Most studies of this sort have concentrated on the normal, 'wakeful' or daytime phase of the sleep-wake cycle. A wide variety of scorable, or measurable, tasks have been devised by ingenious investigators and have been carried out by willing 'guinea pig' humans. For a remarkably wide range of problem-solving tasks, requiring either small or considerable muscle activity, a similar but distinct diurnal pattern of variation becomes obvious. And this

pattern holds true whether the subjects are tested on their ability to deal and sort playing cards, to draw on a piece of paper the image they see in a mirror or to perform multiplication sums. Within an hour or two of waking in the morning efficiency climbs relatively rapidly, reaching a peak sometime in the middle of the day, although these peaks are differently timed for different tasks. Thereafter, and often more gradually, efficiency declines again as nighttime approaches.

In a general way this pattern of change in performance corresponds to internal physiological rhythms of the human body, such as that of body temperature. When examined in detail, however, the two types of rhythm are rather different because, while efficiency rises rapidly and declines slowly throughout the day for moderately active adults, body temperature rises slowly throughout the day and in two phases. The first of these phases is fast and the second more gradual, but after the end of this second phase the decline in body temperature is rather rapid, so there is no simple and direct correlation between body temperature and levels of dexterity and skill.

The studies carried out on the ability of the human brain to solve problems, such as multiplication sums, were structured around a cycle of human existence that is normally thought of in terms of two phases—daytime wakefulness and nighttime sleep. The results concentrated on circadian patterns, that is, those with a periodicity of about 24 hours. In fact there is some evidence that underlying these relatively long-term cycles is a rhythm of change in human mental activity which has a far shorter period than 24 hours and which is present during both wakefulness and sleep.   ▷

Many animals have become nocturnal in response to negative pressure imposed by daylight. Frogs need humidity and are night-active to avoid dehydration. Mice come out at night to escape the many predators hunting by sight. Owls, however, have filled a niche with little competition from other predatory birds.

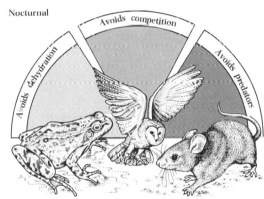
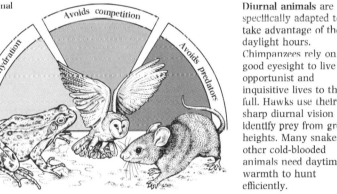

Nocturnal — Avoids competition — Avoids dehydration — Avoids predator

Diurnal animals are often specifically adapted to take advantage of the daylight hours. Chimpanzees rely on their good eyesight to live their opportunist and inquisitive lives to the full. Hawks use their sharp diurnal vision to identify prey from great heights. Many snakes and other cold-blooded animals need daytime warmth to hunt efficiently.

Diurnal — Good diurnal vision — Good vision — Needs warm temperatures

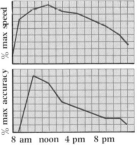

% max speed / % max accuracy

8 am   noon   4 pm   8 pm

Human efficiency levels, which fluctuate during the day, often follow the body temperature curve with one peak around midday and a low in the early hours of the morning. Mental performance is generally highest in the morning— multiplication is often most accurate at 10.30 am and most speedy at noon, *above.* Recalling digits also reaches a peak at noon, many important commercial decisions, *right,* may be influenced by the time of day.

▷ The first findings to suggest that these relatively rapid cyclical changes occur in the human body arose from important studies carried out in the 1950s. These studies showed that the sleep phase of the sleep-wakefulness cycle is not a blank, constant, unconscious nothingness. Indeed, in a prescientific way, the human dream experience showed long ago that this could not possibly be the case. Studies on human volunteers hooked up to electroencephalographs (machines which measure the electrical activity of the brain and produce traced recordings, or electroencephalograms (EEGs), of mental activity) as well as the results from a wide variety of other monitoring hardware, showed that sleep is divided into its own cyclical phases which alternate throughout the night in a way that is approximately rhythmic.

Sleep was, thus, found to have two phases which were remarkably different from one another in both behavioural and physiological ways. The first sort of sleep is rapid-eye-movement (REM) sleep because, as its name implies, during this phase rapid and transient eye movements occur beneath our closed lids. The second sort of sleep is non-rapid-eye-movement (NREM) sleep, and for its duration there are none of these paradoxical eye movements. So, rather surprisingly, a normal adult undergoes a complete cycle of REM then NREM sleep every 80 to 120 minutes, which means that, during an ordinary night's sleep of, say, eight or nine hours, we pass through at least four of these cycles.

Although the presence or absence of eye movements are the most obvious manifestations of the two phases of sleep, they are not the only differences between REM and NREM sleep. The pattern of electrical activity of the heart, as measured on an electrocardiogram (ECG), and the heart's rate of beating, the

breathing rate and the tone, or tautness, of the muscles all vary consistently between the two types of sleep. So it seems that something extremely basic alters within the body when we switch from one state of sleep to the other.

An intriguing and daring hypothesis has been put forward to account for the profound difference between these two states. This hypothesis suggests that the REM/NREM rhythm involves an alteration in the relative extent to which each of our two cerebral hemispheres controls our mental activities. The uppermost, newest, intelligent part of our brain, the cerebrum, is divided into distinct right and left halves, known from their shape as the two cerebral hemispheres, and between the two are some complicated criss-crossing nerve connections. There is little doubt that in most people the two halves of the cerebrum specialize in different mental tasks. In right-handed people (for handedness is part of this complex story of how the brain works) the right hemisphere is the expert on non-verbal, visual, spatial and artistic aspects of our perception of the world and has little to do with performing processes of logical analysis. The left half of the brain of a right-hander is the hemisphere concerned with written and spoken speech and features of our lives that are analytical and logical, such as mathematical ability.

The idea behind the new hypothesis of the phases of sleep is that during our sleeping hours the two halves of the brain take it in turns to run our mental processes. While the right hemisphere is in charge we pass through a phase of REM sleep, but when the nighttime autopilot sits on the left-hand side of the cerebral cockpit, we go through a period of NREM sleep. The eye movements themselves are an important clue to the veracity of this theory. The eyes are,

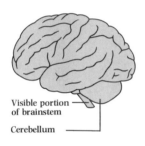

Evidence suggests that sleep may be induced by hormones which pass messages to an area of the brainstem, known as the reticular formation, which acts as the brain's switchboard and controls levels of arousal.

Visible portion of brainstem

Cerebellum

Rapid-eye-movement (REM) sleep, associated with one sort of dreaming, is typified by volleys of spiky brain waves. Breathing and pulse grow irregular, movement increases and body temperature rises.

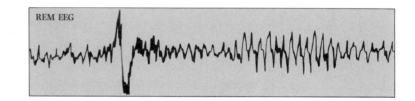

REM EEG

Human sleep is organized into four stages which can each be identified by the extent of electrical activity in the brain, *right*. One complete cycle lasts about 90 minutes and recurs 5 or 6 times each night, *far right*. Stage 1, the light sleep produces small undulations in the brain waves. As the brain reaches increasingly deep stages of sleep the EEG waves become larger and more random until the spindles disappear completely in Stage 4. The quality of sleep changes during the night, becoming lighter and more full of dreams towards morning, as body temperature rises and hormones thought to induce wakefulness become active. Poor sleepers tend to experience deep sleep spasmodically.

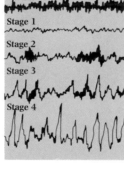

Awake

Stage 1

Stage 2

Stage 3

Stage 4

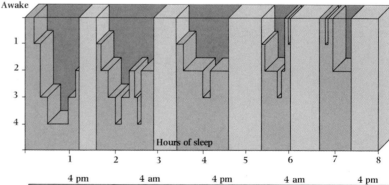

Awake

1

2

3

4

Hours of sleep

1   2   3   4   5   6   7   8

The length of a night's sleep and its internal rhythm varies with age. The most dramatic change is in the proportion of Stage 4 sleep which declines from 18 per cent of the night's sleep as a child, to 3 per cent in middle age, *right*. Stage 4 sleep is thought to fulfil a number of functions including the stimulation of the release of the growth hormone. Active, growing children thus have a far greater need for deep sleep. Tests have proved that children continually deprived of sleep do not grow fast and may become stunted.

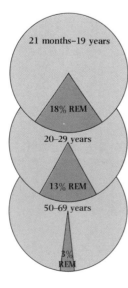

21 months–19 years

18% REM

20–29 years

13% REM

50–69 years

3% REM

Experiments on volunteers in deep caves show that our regular 24-hour sleep-waking cycle is largely coordinated by light cues. Without these external signals, the natural inclination is to allow the sleep pattern to lag slightly each day until it has drifted all the way round the clock. Most people have an innate cycle of about 25 hours which they entrain to the earth's 24-hour rhythm. Body temperature has an independent rhythm and during a period of free-running falls to a low at the onset not the end of sleep.

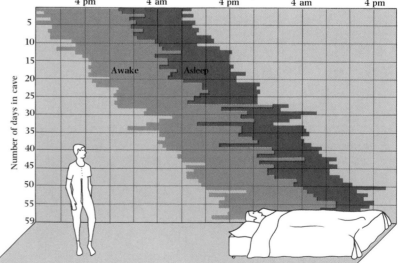

4 pm   4 am   4 pm   4 am   4 pm

5
10
15
20
25
30
35
40
45
50
55
59

Awake   Asleep

Number of days in cave

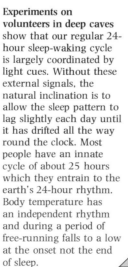

obviously, most active in the phase of sleep in which visual aspects are favoured, that is, right-sided REM sleep.

For the relationship between brain hemispheres and phases of sleep to be further substantiated, data was needed from people willing to act as subjects in sleep experiments which involved both monitoring and many disturbed nights. When these people were purposely woken up from continuous sleep in either the REM or the NREM phase (as judged by the evidence of EEG tracings), they reported different types of dream. On waking from REM sleep, volunteers described the types of dream associated with specific and clear visual images in which reality appears to be distorted—I dreamed that I was having dinner on top of the Statue of Liberty, for example.

In contrast, subjects surfacing from NREM sleep talked of a less easily remembered form of dream that does not readily fit into the common conception of what dreams are made of. These NREM dreams are less bizarre, less vivid, more thoughtful and rational than those of REM sleep. A dream in which a person is worried about passing an exam could be an example of a NREM dream. In other words, quite apart from the Freudian or other interpretations that might be placed on the content of our dreaming, it displays just the sort of dualism one would expect if our sleeping lives were controlled alternately by the left and right sides of our brains. All vertebrates are like us in having brains split into symmetrical halves about a line drawn from the nose to the top of the spine, and many mammals other than man have been shown to possess REM/NREM cycles of sleep. But what the functional significance of these cycles might be in, say, a cat or a mole is at present unclear.

One intriguing extension of the idea of the REM/NREM cycle has recently occurred to behavioural scientists, namely, that it is possible that the appropriate 100-minute mental rhythm is not confined to the sleeping phases of our lives. There appears to be some evidence that alternating dominance of the right and left sides of our brains also takes place during waking hours as well. Minutely detailed recording of human physiology during the day suggests that there are 90 to 110-minute rhythms in such human attributes as heart rate, the ability to maintain vigilance for a specific but unlikely event, and the fantasy content of our day dreams.

Following up these suggestions, Canadian workers have asked volunteers to carry out two types of task during their periods of wakefulness. The first of these tasks was highly orientated towards visual, non-verbal problem solving, while the second was specifically and closely linked to a written linguistic problem. Interestingly, these workers found significant 90 to 100-minute oscillations in the efficiency with which these two sorts of task are performed. Even more interesting is that while performance in one type of task improved, the other diminished. So it seems that there is a lot of sense in having a break from work when you feel that your performance is flagging, or leaving a problem aside and coming back to it an hour or two later; it could be that by then your brain is back in the correct phase to find the solution rapidly. Thus we are rhythmic in more ways than we know, for it is becoming increasingly clear that the two halves of our brains may rhythmically pass an important part of overall mental control to one another, like a tennis ball being hit back and forth across the net, throughout the hours of both wakefulness and sleep.

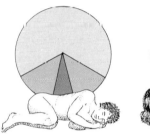

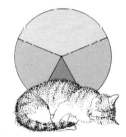

Awake
NREM
REM

The world's greatest sleeper appears to be the opossum which sleeps for 19 hours a day, of which 5.7 hours is spent in REM sleep. Turtles experience no REM and it comprises only 1 per cent of sleeping time in birds. Mammals such as moles cats, chimpanzees and man spend about 25 per cent of their sleep in REM while sheep show a mere 3 per cent. Humans, however, sleep for fewer hours than most animals.

Electroencephalograms (EEGs), *right*, monitor electrical frequencies in different areas of the brain. They are used to trace some of the internal rhythms of sleep. By identifying individual stages it has been possible to discern the effects of deprivation and thus the function of each phase of sleep. Severe lack of REM sleep can provoke emotional disturbance and even hallucinations, which suggests that it helps to maintain a psychological balance. Sleep loss, however, is normally made up the next night.

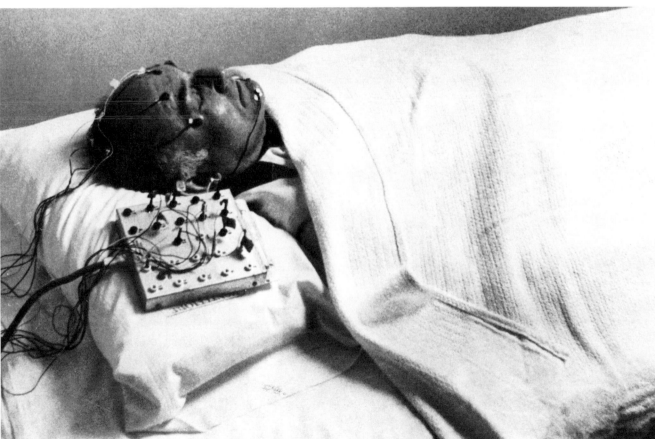

Rhythms of motion

Movement is an animal imperative. In sharp contrast to plants which have a settled existence, nearly all the animals on earth have the power to propel themselves through air, water or even the soil to collect food or find a mate. Because locomotion is a basic animal attribute it is not surprising that it exists in a huge range of patterns. Equally, since animals are dwarfed by the space in which they live, efficient locomotion demands the repeated performance of small cyclical acts, each of which moves the animal only a tiny distance. It is the repeated sameness of these acts that gives locomotion its essentially rhythmical character.

Of all the rhythms of life, those of animal locomotion are among the most obvious and overt. Movement rhythms occur quite fast—sometimes hundreds of times faster than the human eye can follow—and are usually both aesthetically and intrinsically pleasing. What can be more relaxing to the gaze than the unhurried wing-beat of the majestic swan or the regular jumping of a school of porpoises as it leads a ship to harbour? Some of the rhythms of locomotion are better understood than others and they can be explained in the language of physics, but they represent some of the most beautiful examples of functional adaptation in animals.

Over millions of years of evolution the rhythm of locomotion has been moulded according to the template provided by the physical development and needs of each species. The powers of evolution have also made locomotory rhythms extremely economical. Each separate propulsive cycle is as efficient as it can possibly be, and often one cycle leads into the next with some overlap so that the inertial force of the moving body is used to its fullest extent. In maximizing efficiency, counterbalances play a big part. Thus legs and wings, and often the tail or even the neck of an animal move in a particular way to help keep the creature balanced, or to pull it forward so that its centre of gravity falls within the base formed by its limbs. Some seemingly awkward rhythms, for example the swaying gait of the camel, are highly efficient in energy usage and admirably suited to the animal's body structure and its environment.

While some animals use the same pattern of locomotion irrespective of rapidity, others change their gait according to the speed at which they travel. Thus for man, running is little different from walking: the left foot still follows the right and the arms still swing to provide some balance, but a horse has a symmetry of movement when it is walking that is lost once it starts to gallop. Compared with many of his mammalian relatives man has rather an unspecialized means of locomotion and only puts up a mediocre performance. Yet man can run or walk tens of miles simply by getting into his stride and settling down to a steady rhythm. Top-class runners say that rhythm is all-important to success on the track and that any disruption, for instance by a stitch or cramp, can be disastrous.

Man may be able to run, but he certainly cannot fly. His flying machines, although they rely on the rhythmical and mechanical action of engines, do not mimic the flight patterns of birds and are, as a result, far less efficient. Similarly his boats are poor performers compared with their animal equivalents. In translating the rhythm in an engine to a rotating rhythm of an air or water screw, much energy is lost and the shapes of man's machines produce far too much drag. The more we understand about the design of machines, the more we marvel at nature which solved all the problems so elegantly many millions of years ago.

From the languid flapping of a stork to the angry buzz of a hornet, the rhythmic beating of wings gives animals the ability to fly through the air. Man has long marvelled at flight and, over the centuries, has made countless attempts to copy the birds he sees in the sky above him, but always without success. Strapping feathers to his arms, the birdman tries to fly by frantically beating his wings, but to no avail. Only after man discovered how to build successful aircraft did he begin to comprehend the mysteries of bird flight, and to understand how the rhythmic movement of wings allows a bird to climb heavenward with such apparent ease.

For any object—be it an aircraft, a bird or a paper dart—to travel through the air the force of gravity, which tends to pull the object to earth, must be counteracted by an opposite force of at least equal strength. This is lift, and the heavier the object the greater is the lift required to keep it airborne. But to hang motionless in the air is of little practical use to either animal or man and, furthermore, lift cannot normally be generated by a stationary organism or machine. So all fliers need the force of propulsion to drive them forward. The faster they wish to fly, the stronger that propulsive thrust must be. Like all fluids, air has a certain thickness and exerts a resistance on anything passing through it.

Of course air is much thinner than water or, say, molasses, but it is thick enough to stick to a wing and to try to stop it moving forward, so the propulsive force must be at least as great as this hampering force or drag. The three forces of lift, propulsion and drag underlie the physics of flight and every flying object, whether natural or man-made, must obey their rules.

Flying animals differ from man-made machines in that a single structure—the wing—provides them with both the lift and the propulsive force they need to become and to stay airborne. A bird's wing consists essentially of two parts, the inner part from 'elbow' to 'wrist' and the outer section from 'wrist' to 'fingertip'. It is the inner part of the wing that serves as an aerofoil to provide lift. In cross-section it looks like an aircraft wing with a blunt leading edge, a curved upper surface, concave lower surface and a thin trailing edge. As the wing is pushed along, the air striking the leading edge is deflected in two ways. Part of it shoots upward above the wing and part slips underneath it. The air that is deflected upward travels high above the wing and creates a slight suction above the wing's upper surface. To release the suction, the wing tends to be moved upward and this is what creates lift.

The mechanics of flight are complicated by the fact that air does not flow freely over the wing—instead it swirls around in small eddies. The efficiency of flight depends on the angle of attack between the wing and the direction in which the bird is flying. If this angle is too large the eddies become bigger and bigger. As long as the bird is flying fast enough the eddies are dissipated, but if it flies slowly the same eddies destroy the suction and make the lift force disappear in a sudden stall. To overcome this stalling effect at landing and take-off, birds push out a tiny tuft of feathers from the leading edge of the wing which helps to dissipate the eddies.

All the time it is flapping its wings in a repeated cycle of activities, a bird must have lift to counter the force of gravity. It is the outer part of the wing that provides propulsion and it does so in a rhythmical fashion. The two key factors in

Great black-backed gull

Stock dove

Hummingbird

Frequency of wing-beats is inversely proportional to the size of bird. The tiniest hummingbird performs a miraculous 100 beats per second, while a large gull languorously flaps twice per second. Crows and pigeons average 6 to 12 cycles per second.

Air travels farther over than under the curved leading edge of the wing. The resulting pocket of low pressure sucks the wing upward, lifting the bird.

Low pressure

High pressure

How hummingbirds beat their wings 100 times a second remains a mystery, as each cycle needs two muscle contractions, each lasting 10 milliseconds. These tiny birds hover motionless as the figure of eight pattern of their wings produces lift on both the up and down strokes.

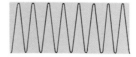

Doves are strong, versatile fliers, adapted to cope with a variety of environmental conditions. In normal flight they flap 12 to 14 times a second, but at high speeds their wing-beats become shallower and less frequent. Racing pigeons can sustain speeds of 100 miles (160 km) per hour.

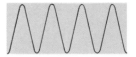

Slow, but powerful, crows cover long distances without rest, flapping their broad wings at a rate of 6 to 8 beats a second. To prevent stalling at low speeds, the crow spreads the tips of the primary feathers, allowing high pressure air to flow through the wing and smooth out turbulence above it.

The gull's flight muscles contract slowly, limiting the wings to two graceful flaps a second. This allows the gull to cruise nonchalantly over the ocean at about 34 miles (55 km) per hour. A huge wing area of over 155 in² (1,000 cm²) enables the gull to glide between periods of flapping flight.

propulsion are the mobile wrist joint, which allows the outermost or primary feathers of the wing to be turned outward so that they will beat almost backward, and the asymmetrical shape of the primary feathers themselves. As the wing is driven through a figure of eight, the wrist flexes back and forth, and in doing so provides maximum contact between the primaries and the air on the down beat, the minimum on the up beat. This is exactly how an oarsman feathers his oars: he rotates them at the same time as he speeds the blades forward for a new stroke. Just as the wing finishes its up stroke the pressure of air on the asymmetrical primaries makes them rotate and, as the next down stroke begins, they are beating backward; this is how propulsion is effected. The rhythm of the bird's wing-beat is synchronized with its rhythm of breathing.

Most birds fly with their bodies held almost horizontal, but one well-known exception to this rule is the tiny hummingbird as it hovers in front of a flower. Hummingbirds have mastered the rhythms of flight so effectively that the precision of their hovering defies the abilities of even the best helicopter pilot. The hummingbird can hold its body almost vertical so that the down and up strokes of its wings become, respectively, forward and backward strokes. The 'hand' part of the hummingbird's wing is relatively much longer than that of other birds. Because it is the 'wrist' that imparts flexibility, the hummingbird wing must be flexible over a greater part of its length than in most other birds. In hovering flight the wing-tips move through a symmetrical figure of eight in each cycle, with lift being provided by both the forward and backward sweeps. The propulsion created in the forward sweep is cancelled out by that created in

the backward sweep. The combination of forces generated over the whole cycle results in an effective upward force alone, but even a tiny change in the power supplied to one or other wing strokes is sufficient for the bird to move its position.

Every beat of the hummingbird's wing is effected by a contraction of the huge wing muscles—they may account for 40 per cent of the bird's body-weight—and the rapid repetition of the cycle, often as frequently as 80 times every second. The contraction of every muscle fibre is triggered off by a separate signal from a nerve, but how the nerve impulses and muscle contractions can work so fast is still a mystery. The frequency of the hummingbird's wing-beat, although remarkable in avian terms, is slow indeed when compared with some insects. The biting midge may beat its wings at the incredible rate of almost 1,000 times a second, but control of this rhythm is quite different from that of the hummingbird. It is impossible for nerve signals to be transmitted at this rate, so what the insect does is to switch its flight mechanism on to 'automatic pilot'.

Insects differ from vertebrate fliers, such as birds, in having skeletons outside their bodies, and their wings are merely extensions of that skeleton. The flexible cuticle of the insect skeleton can be bent by muscular action, with the energy generated by that distortion being dissipated via the wings. Furthermore, once the flight muscles have been switched on they produce their own impulses, so bypassing the higher nerve centres of the brain. The result is a rapid fibrillation that can rise to extraordinary frequencies. Despite its different mechanics, insect flight is aerodynamically essentially similar to bird flight and some insect ▷

Hooded crow

The pigeon's wing-tips trace a figure of eight in each flapping cycle. The wings, fully extended backward, are pulled forward and down by strong breast muscles (1). Half way down, pressure rotates the wing-tips (2) and as the wing swings forward propulsion is generated (3). For the recovery stroke, the wrist and elbow flex (4) and the shoulder rotates (5) to bring the wing up and back for the next downstroke (6).

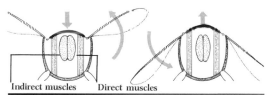

Indirect muscles   Direct muscles

The wings of tiny insects vibrate 1,000 times a second. Such frequencies are beyond nervous and muscular control and are powered by pulsations in the body of the insect. A contraction of the indirect flight muscles distorts the skeleton, forcing the wings down. The skeleton then clicks back into place, pushing the wings up. Once switched on, this mechanism runs by its own momentum, boosted by an occasional nervous impulse.

Dragonflies oscillate their two pairs of wings 25 times a second under the control of direct muscles attached to the wing-base —the system used by most large-bodied insects. Dragonflies perform sudden bursts of rapid wing-beats if chasing prey.

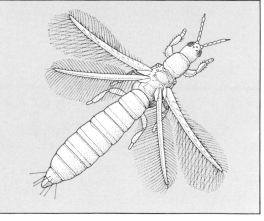

The tiny, delicate thrip is designed to drift rather than fly. Before launching into a zig-zagging flight, the thrip combs its finely feathered wings with its hind legs, which also provide the initial lift-off. Once airborne, the wings fan out and flutter rhythmically, just long enough for the wind to whisk the thrip high into the air for many miles.

▷ species have become specialized to ways of life requiring fast flight, slow flight and hovering. Honey-bees have evolved an extremely specialized launching technique. As they are unable to create lift for long on still days, they gather in small groups to fan their pairs of wings and build up a communal 'draught', strong enough to propel them into the air.

While many small animals make use of flight rhythms to get from place to place, comparatively few use jumping rhythms. Many small insects, such as fleas and springtails, jump to escape the attention of predators, but there is nothing cyclical or rhythmical about a single jump. Movement by rhythmical jumping or, more correctly, ricochetal locomotion, has been perfected by a number of mammals, most notably the kangaroos, and a few amphibians. But because jumping is only efficient when the body is long the common frog is about the smallest jumper, and even this creature has evolved certain anatomical adaptations to increase its body-length. There are no insects that use true richochetal locomotion and in man, for whom jumping rates low among his physical skills, the only sort of jumping that comes anywhere near it is the 'hop, step and jump', or triple jump, of athletic competition.

The least efficient sort of hopping is that employed by a frog. Each jump cycle has a clear beginning and end and does not lead naturally into the next. From a sitting position, with its head held up at an angle of about 45 degrees, a single backward kick of the hind legs launches the frog's body into the air. The front limbs are held pointing backward in a streamlined fashion, and at the peak of its jump the frog is aerodynamically quite stable. As it starts its descent the forelimbs are brought forward and extended, for they will be the first part of the

animal to make contact with the ground. The hind limbs come forward, too, so that once all four limbs are down, the frog can kick off on another cycle. An advantage of this type of hopping is that each jump can be made in a different direction from the previous one, so confusing a would-be predator.

Since all the power for the frog's jump comes from a single kick of its hind legs, it is essential for them to be in contact with the ground for as long as possible. The pelvic or hip girdle of the frog has become adapted to meet this requirement by an elongation of the bone on to which the thigh bones are attached. Furthermore, a strengthening strut, the urostyle, runs the length of the pelvic girdle and helps to translate the backward push into the considerable amount of kinetic energy necessary to propel the frog through the air. Just as the frog's pelvic girdle is adapted to jumping, so its shoulder or pectoral girdle is strengthened to absorb the shock of landing.

Compared with the ungainly hopping of a frog, the leaping of the kangaroo is a poetry of flowing grace. With seemingly effortless ease an adult red kangaroo in full flight can cover 14 feet (4.2 m) in a single jump, and can do so repeatedly for miles on end. Kangaroos only use true ricochetal locomotion when they are travelling at speeds above about 20 miles (32 km) an hour. When they are moving more slowly than this the short forelimbs are put on the ground while the massive hind limbs are slid outside them. The thick tail seems an unwelcome encumbrance during such slow movement, but when the kangaroo gets into its rhythmical stride, the tail comes into its own. At the start of a single jump cycle the tail is held out behind the body, then strong thigh muscles contract—just as in the frog—which tends to straighten the legs and

Long muscular legs unfold to launch the frog into the air at an angle of 45°. As the frog's toes spring off the ground, the body is already fully stretched, the extended backbone providing extra length. At the top of the jump, the frog draws up its hind limbs and brings the shock-absorbing forelimbs forward to cushion the impact of landing. It lands with a splat, readjusts the splayed hind legs for the next jump and the cycle begins again. Unlike the kangaroo, the frog can not use the momentum from the previous jump but treats each leap individually, the better to dart unpredictably away from a predator.

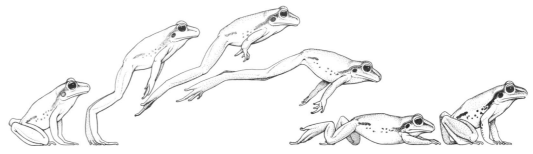

Small desert rodents find ricochetal jumping an essential adaptation to the desert environment, where scarcity of food makes speedy and long-distance travel necessary for survival. This two-legged hop not only enables the kangaroo rat and jerboa to bounce quickly across long stretches of sand but burns up much less energy than four-legged running. In these creatures a long tail acts as both a stabilizing counterbalance and a rudder. The tuft of fur at the tip provides directional control and a lash of the tail, mid-air, effects a change of direction. On landing, the jerboa's tail arches to make an air brake and prevents the animal toppling over. Larger species of jerboa can spring as high as 8 ft (2.4 m) and the legs of the tiniest species appear to vibrate, for their cycle of movement occurs at such high frequencies. The short forelegs, which are important for gathering food, are rarely used for running except at slow speeds.

The kangaroo rat hops on both legs simultaneously. Its toes spread for take-off, then gather and flex slightly as they swing forward for landing.

When jumping, the jerboa lands on one hind leg, then pushes forward taking one step before springing upward from the other hind leg.

lift the kangaroo forward and upward. As the kangaroo lands its body becomes more nearly horizontal. Because the tail assumes the same position relative to the body throughout the cycle, it is raised up, well clear of the ground. Acting as the perfect counterpoise, the tail now swings downward, so lifting the body up and forcing the centre of gravity rearward and the kangaroo is now ready for its next jump.

Speeds of up to 35 miles (55 km) per hour have been recorded for male kangaroos, while the female can achieve 40 miles (65 km) per hour for short bursts. When pursued and in danger a female kangaroo may jettison her young from the pouch to increase her speed. The pouch relaxes and the young drops, somersaulting along the ground for some way before ricocheting away at high speed. A kangaroo increases its speed by lengthening its stride rather than by hopping more frequently, so there is no marked change in rhythm with increasing speed as there is when a man changes from a jogging pace to a sprint. The duration of each hop thus remains constant over a wide range of speeds, although the time on the ground decreases and the time off the ground increases. The frequency of hops of each individual is determined by the length of the animal's leg.

In order to achieve the longest possible jump kangaroos, like frogs, have long legs and greatly elongated toes, but they do not have elongated pelvic girdles. Where kangaroos score over frogs is that they can use the elasticity of their leg muscles and tendons as springs which can be stretched and compressed. At the start of hopping, considerable energy is required to get the animal upward and off the ground. On landing, muscles which had contracted

to initiate the previous take-off are stretched, and the elastic recoil of these stretched muscles helps to provide some of the energy for the next cycle. So by contracting the muscles slightly before landing, their stretching releases some tension which, together with the stringy Achilles tendons and the pendulum-like motion of the tail, propels the kangaroo into the next cycle. Recent studies into the physiology of kangaroo locomotion have shown that this action of storing energy is highly efficient and requires far less energy for a given speed than would be required by a running species. To be able to travel so cheaply is a great asset to the kangaroo since it may have to go 20 miles just for a drink of water. This efficiency may also explain why the kangaroo survived in great numbers while its quadripedal counterparts, such as the marsupial lions, *Thylacole carniflex*, and the Tasmanian wolf, *Thylacinus cynocephalus*, became extinct when man and his dogs became hunters in Australasia.

It is interesting to note that among the other mammals that have taken up hopping many are desert dwelling species, living in a world of sparse food and even sparser water. The jerboa or desert rat shares many of the kangaroo's traits—long, strong hind legs with tough, elastic tendons and a long, counterbalancing tail. During its rhythmical hopping the jerboa's tail normally bobs up and down, but if the animal wants to change direction it need only lash its tail in the opposite direction to that in which it wishes to go, because a tuft of fur at the tail-tip acts like a rudder or sail to impart directional stability. The springhaas of southern Africa is about the size of a jackrabbit or European hare, and can hop tirelessly for immense distances of 5 miles (8 km) or more. As it does so, the heavy tail rises and falls, ever compensating for the rhythmic fore-and- ▷

Rhythmic grace and speed characterize the movement of the red kangaroo, *Megaleia rufa*. In one bound it can cover 27 ft (8.1 m), reach a height of 10 ft (30 m) and move at 40 miles (65 km) per hour. In the air, the heavy tail counter-balances the forward inclination of the body.

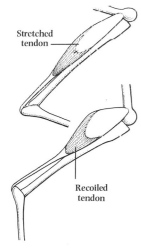

Stretched tendon

Recoiled tendon

At speeds over 11 miles (18 km) per hour, a kangaroo uses much less energy than a horse. The secret lies in the long Achilles tendon which runs from the calf muscle to the heel. On landing, the tendon tenses slightly, then stretches under the weight of the kangaroo. It then recoils by elastic contraction, providing the catapulting impulse for the next jump.

▷ aft movement of the centre of gravity. To stop the head from bobbing so much that it might cause damage to the brain, the neck is made inflexible by having bones (vertebrae) that are short and partially fused together.

Hopping is a very refined method of travel that almost certainly arose from the more usual four-legged or quadripedal running. But even running on four feet is restricted to comparatively few animals because most of the species that inhabit planet Earth have more than four legs, and some of them many more. Slow-moving invertebrates, such as millipedes and centipedes and even marine lugworms, have a large number of short limbs. To move forward, waves of locomotory activity pass forward from the rear to the front of the animal. Each limb is placed on the ground fractionally before the one in front, and also lifted from the ground fractionally before it. The result is a rippling type of leg movement, a metachronal rhythm.

A similar effect is seen in microscopic single-celled organisms such as *Paramecium* which live in stagnant water. These animals are covered with hairlike projections, or cilia. As the animal moves each cilium stiffens up and is beaten backward, to be followed by the neighbour in front of it, by the one before that, and so on. Like a whip being dragged up for another lash, the cilium then rises, again followed immediately and in succession by the neighbour in front of it. The ripple of movement of the cilia is like that of a field of corn blown by a gust of wind.

The golden rule of terrestrial locomotion is that if a creature has many legs and wants to travel fast, it must reduce the number of legs used in moving so that only a small number of limbs stays in contact with the ground. Insects have only six legs, and are capable of much higher land speeds than millipedes and centipedes. A cockroach, for example, can move more than a hundred times faster than a millipede, reaching a speed of 3 miles (4.8 km) per hour compared with the millipede's 0.02 miles (0.032 km) per hour. Typically, the rhythmic movement of an insect, such as a cockroach, is effected by an alteration of the triangular support, from the front and back legs on one side and the middle leg on the other, to the middle leg on the first side and the front and back on the other. The triangle formed in this action allows the legs previously used to recover and be ready for the next cycle. At high speeds the pattern changes, but it does not do so in a uniform fashion. Some species become quadripedal, simply ignoring the rear pair of legs, while others, such as the mantis, which are quadripedal at normal speeds, take to a six-legged gait. Spiders normally travel on all eight legs, which are well splayed out to prevent their tips from becoming entangled with one another, and in this way they can achieve a speed of 1.1 miles (1.76 km) per hour. Insects lying on their backs will continue to display rhythmic rather than random patterns of movement.

Like the wheels of a train all running on the same track, the limb-tips of millipedes must follow in the footsteps of their predecessors, because the limbs are all the same length. The variable limb-length of fast-moving invertebrates, such as insects, spiders and crabs, allows each limb to make contact with a different piece of ground from that of its neighbour. To get from place to place all the land-living vertebrates, the animals with backbones, have either four or two limbs. Compared with the many-legged invertebrates, and making due allowance for their size, the locomotory ability of these animals is far superior.

The sea gooseberry, like many other aquatic organisms, moves by waving its eight bands of tiny hairlike cilia in a rapid succession of ripples. Each cilium swings rigidly forward against the water a split second before the next, to produce a straight power stroke, and bends limply back like a whip for the recovery stroke to minimize the resistance to the water, *far right*. Each metachronal wave passes down the band a fraction of a second before the next. Viewed from above, the individual cilium of the sea gooseberry traces a clockwise circle, although in some other organisms, the cilia travel anti-clockwise.

The running millipede appears to travel on a gently moving wave which is caused by the action of the legs. In most species this wave passes forward over the body as each leg lifts, a split second before the leg in front. During the propulsive phase the legs spread to give a broad push-off and bunch together when swinging forward for the next stroke. Each pair of legs moves simultaneously and at any one time there will be as many legs on as off the ground, although each limb will be $\frac{1}{8}$ to $\frac{1}{12}$ of a step out of phase with the next. On average, 38 waves a minute pass along the body.

Long flexible legs allow the spider to scuttle along at a top speed of 1.1 miles (1.76 km) per hour. As the four pairs of legs are wide-spanning, each needs to be a slightly different length to prevent the spider tripping. Although the second and fourth legs are often synchronized, the spider's rather disorganized gait sometimes falls into a wavelike sequence. To speed up, the spider increases the frequency of each step, without altering its pattern of movement. A primitive device controls the spider's every stride: the legs can only be stretched by a sudden increase in hydraulic pressure of blood, although muscles bend them.

Beetles, cockroaches and all six-legged insects walk as if on a tripod and rhythmically alternate their three-legged triangle of support. The middle leg on one side is always synchronized with the two outer legs on the other side. To maintain the rhythm, the periods on and off the ground are equal and each limb is half a complete cycle out of phase with its opposite number, to prevent entanglement. This triangular gait makes the insect veer slightly from side to side with each step. An insect's speed is largely controlled by temperature: in hot surroundings, the muscles contract faster.

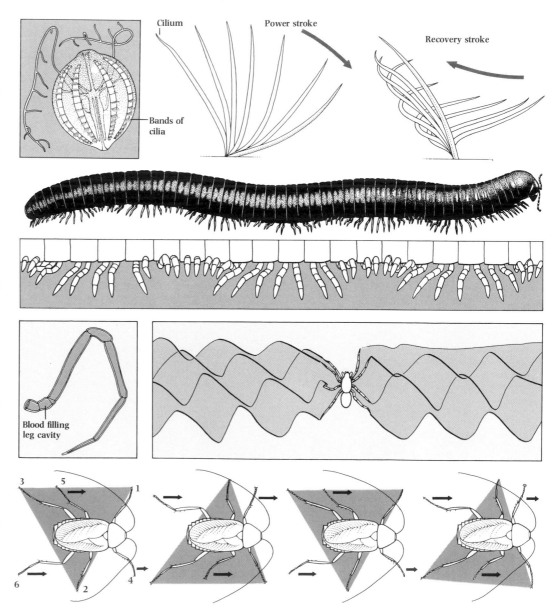

Cilium Power stroke

Recovery stroke

Bands of cilia

Blood filling leg cavity

The fundamental rhythm of movement for a terrestrial species, such as the horse, is essentially symmetrical—each leg is raised from the ground in turn and for the same amount of time. The pattern of hoof-fall is front left, back right, front right, back left. When viewed from above the horse's left side mirrors its right.

On increasing its speed from a walk to a trot, the horse has fewer hoofs in contact with the ground at any one time, so the pattern of the rhythm changes. Typically, the left hind and right front hoofs are in ground contact together, and are raised together, as the left front and right hind hoof are placed on the ground. But the symmetry of this gait is destroyed when the trot breaks into a gallop. Starting with the left hind foot striking the ground, the right hind, left front and right front follow in rapid succession, launching the horse upward and forward. All the feet are off the ground for perhaps four or five yards (3.6 to 4.5 m). This period of suspension, during which the horse is airborne, effectively increases the length of the stride, and with it the speed of movement.

The rhythmic pounding of a galloping horse's hoofs occurs more frequently than the rhythmic silent footfall of the cheetah because, during the suspension period, the feet of the horse are gathered up underneath its body. During the cheetah's suspension period its legs are stretched out to front and rear, and the animal's immensely flexible vertebral column curves up and down as the cheetah stretches for the longest stride. Rabbits and stoats are among the animals that employ a slightly different sort of rhythm, the half bound, in which both front feet touch the ground in unison, after which the rear feet are both put down together.

When humans ride terrestrial mammals, they have to flex and relax their legs in the stirrups in unison with the rise and fall of the animal's back and the constant shifting of the position of its centre of gravity. Yet even trained jockeys find difficulty in riding camels because, like giraffes, hyenas and a few other species with sloping backs, camels move both legs on one side forward, followed by both legs on the other side. A giraffe gallops in an ungainly fashion—its massive size precludes it from leaving the ground for more than the briefest moment—with the long neck swinging forward and backward twice in each stride, pulling the centre of gravity forward in concert with the forward movements of the legs. Because of its huge size, the maximum speed that a giraffe can achieve is little over 34 miles (55 km) per hour.

Using only two legs for walking and running—as man does—is a minority means of locomotion in the animal kingdom, but it is particularly fascinating because it is the human gait. Raising the body up from the ground and on to two legs means that the period of suspension during the running cycle may be more prolonged, so helping to achieve a high speed. However this is not the only critical factor, for fleetness of foot also depends on the flexibility of the spine, the length of stride and the power to weight ratio.

Among the lizards there is clear evidence that running on two legs and high speed are linked. Almost 40 species of lizards are quadripedal when moving slowly, but rear on to their hind legs, tuck in their forelimbs and run fast on two legs when danger threatens. The collared lizard, for instance, reaches speeds of 24 miles (38.6 km) an hour in this way. Unlike the legs of birds and mammals, which are positioned directly under the body, those of lizards project at right ▷

The horse's slow rhythmic walk follows a regular, symmetrical pattern of raising hind and forelegs on opposite sides. At normal speeds three legs are in contact with the ground at once. This rhythm is evident to the rider who bobs up and down twice in every cycle.

As a horse moves from a walk to a trot, the pattern and frequency of movement changes. Diagonally opposite legs move together, changing between swing and support phases, so that two legs are always on the ground. The head lifts to improve balance and stability.

For most of the galloping cycle, the horse is in mid-air. As it lands on one foot, the ligaments stretch to take the impact, *below,* before the other three feet follow asymmetrically, in rapid succession. A rider must move in unison with his horse to keep his seat.

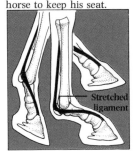

Stretched ligament

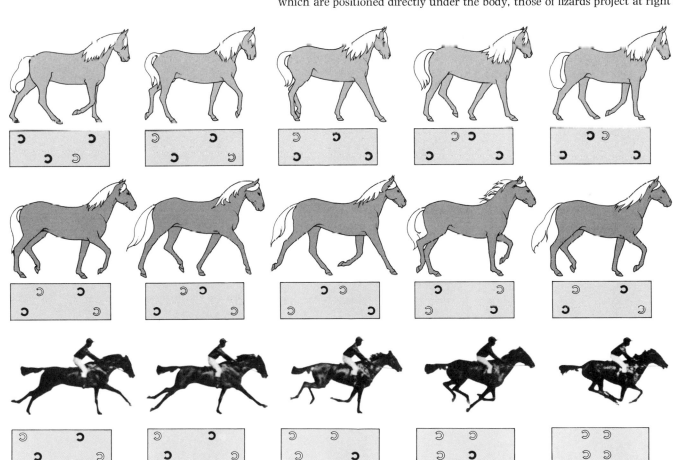

▷angles from the body and this gives them a rhythmical, rolling gait. During each cycle of limb movement the long axis of the body pitches up and down, being more steeply sloped during the early stages of the retraction of a hind limb and more nearly horizontal during the later stages. At the same time the body yaws from side to side—like a rowing boat riding out the wake of a ship. Both these characteristics of bipedal lizard locomotion result from the forward propulsive thrust being delivered by the foot some distance away from the centre of gravity. Bipedal lizards have long, heavy tails which bob up and down once during each cycle of movement of a hind limb and act as counterbalances. However, lizards are often found with damaged tails, so it seems that having a counterbalance is not vital to running on two legs. It is also interesting that the body-weight of these lizards is so widely distributed during running that some of them can travel several yards across water without risk of sinking and drowning.

Among the birds, ostriches, emus and cassowaries are all adapted for bipedal running, as was the moa of New Zealand which became extinct about 300 years ago. The ostrich is the fastest of all the running birds alive today and is reliably credited with speeds of 50 miles (80 km) an hour and more. In proportion to the size of its body, an ostrich's legs are extremely long, giving it a massive stride, and hingelike knees allow each foot to be raised far off the ground. Ostriches also have long necks which counterbalance the slight rolling motion produced by lifting first one, then the other leg. They appear to run effortlessly, almost as if they were on wheels. This is because several compensatory movements, built into the cycle of leg action, cut down

inefficient pitching and yawing to a minimum. Apart from the counterbalancing role of the long neck, the feet are long and pliable. As in a horse's foot there are strong elastic ligaments, which take the strain of landing and give some spring to the next stride, but while a horse breaks into an asymmetrical rhythm as it accelerates from a trot to a gallop, an ostrich merely increases the frequency of its symmetrical running cycle.

Walking upright on two legs, man is not nearly as well adapted for fast movement as an ostrich. Yet man can perform a great many other actions completely beyond the powers of the ostrich. It is the rhythm of man's walking that keeps him from falling on his face. As man walks, each stride starts when the calf muscles relax and the body sways forward under the influence of gravity. This sway moves the centre of gravity forward and outside the base provided by the feet. If nothing were done to correct this, the body would fall, so man moves one foot forward to widen his base and capture the moving centre of gravity. As he does so, the pelvis rotates and many muscles interplay to keep him on balance. Now the rear leg provides propulsion, using muscular energy which is transmitted first to the ball of the foot and then to the big toe, so terminating the 'stance' phase of the walking cycle. As the rear leg starts to move forward, so the 'swing' phase starts. Facilitated by the leg bending at hip, knee and ankle, the foot clears the ground and is straightened again immediately before footfall. The ankle stays bent, so the first contact with the ground is made by the heel. This action concludes the swing phase and starts a new stance phase, during which the point of contact between the foot and the ground moves inexorably from the heel to the tip of the big toe.

The ostrich, the world's fastest two-legged animal, can maintain and exceed speeds of 50 miles (80 km) per hour, over twice man's top speed. Adapted for speed, rather than variety as man is, the ostrich has powerful muscular legs, which are long in proportion to the body, and flex acutely at the knee to allow immense strides of over 12 ft (3.5 m). Strong elastic ligaments in the foot lend a spring to the ostrich's step and cushion the blow of landing. Evolution has reduced this pliable foot to two toes so strengthening and lightening it. To improve stability and counteract the swaying of the body, the slim neck swings back and forth and sideways. This 8 ft (2.4 m) tall bird may plunge its head in the sand, but it never takes flight.

	Maximum speed	Frequency of movement cycles
Millipede	0.02mph (0.03km/h)	38 per min
Giant tortoise	0.18mph (0.29km/h)	30 per min
Spider	1.1mph (1.76km/h)	10 per sec
Eel	2.2mph (3.52km/h)	1.7 per sec
Cockroach	3.13mph (5km/h)	20 per sec
Man	27mph (43km/h) for sprint.	6/7 per sec
Man	22mph (37km/h) for 100m (Olympic speed)	6 per sec
Cat	30mph (48km/h)	3.4 per sec
Giraffe	35mph (56km/h)	1 per sec
Greyhound	36mph (58km/h)	3 per sec
Jackrabbit	40mph (64km/h)	1.5 per sec
Horse	43mph (69km/h)	2.5 per sec
Red fox	45mph (72km/h)	2.6 per sec
Ostrich	50mph (80km/h)	2.5 per sec
Antelope	60mph (96km/h)	2.4 per sec
Cheetah	70mph (112km/h)	3.5 per sec

Throughout a stride, the human pelvis does not remain in quite the same plane, simply because the action of the rear leg in the stance phase drives it upward slightly—once for the action of the left leg and once for the right. Two people walking alongside one another, who wish to talk, find the rhythmical bobbing up and down irritating, which explains why they usually fall into step to synchronize their pelvic movements. The pelvis is not merely a passive partner in the walking cycle; it, too, undergoes rhythmic movements. During the stance phase, the contraction of the gluteus minimus and gluteus medius muscles underlying the buttocks tends to tilt the pelvis and stabilize it relative to the rear leg. At the same time it rotates slightly, so increasing the stride. This rotation, which is exaggerated in the mincing walk of theatre comedy, is not the same in both sexes. Because the proportions of the female pelvis are different from those of the male to allow for childbearing, a woman's hip cannot be thrown as far forward as a man's, so that for a given stride length a woman must rotate her pelvis through a greater angle. Fashion designers have exploited this by encouraging women to wear high heels, which further exaggerate the pelvic tilt and angle. However, styles of walking are much influenced by both individual anatomy and personality.

Accompanying the leg movements of human locomotion is a rhythmic pumping of the arms, which is much more pronounced in running than in walking. In walking, the right arm swings forward as the left leg starts its swing phase. As this leg enters its stance phase, the right arm travels back and the left swings forward, so that the four limbs move exactly the same as those of a walking horse. As the frequency of movement cycles increases, and man breaks into a run, the arm action becomes more prominent. This is partly to correct the yawing motion the rotating hips impart to the whole body, and partly to offset the imbalance produced by the body's being clear of the ground for part of each stride. Otherwise the rhythm of running is essentially the same as that of walking, although the heel is not placed so firmly on the ground at the end of each stride, and the body is bent forward so that the centre of gravity is pushed just that little bit farther from the base formed by the feet. For a fast sprint, these motions become more exaggerated: the body leans forward at a 25 degree angle, only the ball of the foot touches down, the knees are kicked higher and the arms pump aggressively through a wider angle and are held closer to the body for more efficient thrust.

The rhythmicity of human movement develops gradually. The hesitant movements and shaky coordination of young children improves as they grow and as the nervous system, which controls balance, timing and muscular control, becomes properly tuned.

Man's method of movement is well suited to a terrestrial existence, but is ill adapted for performance in water. Humans have to learn how to swim—but at least they can do it. The great apes, man's closest living animal relatives, simply do not possess the necessary motor skills for learning to swim, which means that apes can be kept safely in zoos behind a small water-filled moat. In the water man is very ungainly, for he must weld together the kicking of his legs and a sweeping, or rotation, of his arms to force his unstreamlined body through a medium some 800 times more dense than air.

Truly aquatic animals have a great degree of side to side or lateral flexibility ▷

Finding his rhythm becomes all-important to a top-class runner and this rhythm is largely dictated by the body's anatomical proportions. Swinging the arms in concert with the opposite leg helps to maintain rhythm and restores the balance, disrupted by lack of body support. As a human breaks into a run, the body leans forward to draw the centre of gravity forward, but then pulls upright again to maintain stability.

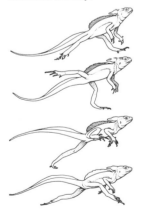

Some lizards are able to run on two legs. Their enlarged hind limbs are attached to the sides rather than the base of the body so they swing in wide circular arcs. The resulting sideways roll is partly corrected by the tail. The earnest-looking basilicus (left) can even sprint over water.

▷ (an attribute severely limited in man and extending only as far up as his hips) which provides them with extremely smooth and rhythmic activity of movement. All fish swim by making use of lateral undulations of their bodies. Those like eels, which are long and thin, rely on both wavelike undulations of their bodies and the lateral beating of a flattened tail fin to provide propulsion. Others, such as the trout, herring and tuna, adopt a combination of body undulation and fin action, while some highly specialized forms, which have abandoned fast swimming in favour of camouflage or some other device, use only fin action.

As an eel swims along, a wave of contractions of the muscles at the side of its body spreads backward down the fish, twisting the body first to the left and then to the right. In an adult eel there may be as many as three bends in the body at one time, but in younger, shorter individuals there may be only one or two. Each bend serves as a brake to stop the bent part of the body from slipping backward through the water as the part in front of it straightens up and forges forward. The forward propulsive force comes from the rhythmic lateral sweeping of the flattened tail, as well as from the forward thrusting of the body as the waves of undulations pass along it. If you watch an eel swimming just above the bottom of a muddy stream, you see a regular pattern of small whirls of water which seem almost to represent solid posts against which the undulations push.

Most fishes swim by flexing their tails rhythmically from side to side. This lateral flexure may be amplified by a rhythmic contraction of the body muscles which drive the base of the tail. As it moves from side to side, the tail fin bends because of the pressure of the water upon it, in rather the same way as the primary flight feathers on a bird's wing rotate as they move through the air. But water is much 'stickier' than air and so the lateral force of the tail fin is translated into a forward movement of the body to which it is attached. Directional stability is provided by other fins, which can be raised or lowered like brakes to keep the fish on the course it wishes to take. The speed of the fish depends on the dynamic shape of the body as well as the frequency and amplitude of the tail-beat.

Seahorses, boxfish and porcupine fish all have rigid skeletons that allow no lateral flexure of the tail base. Swimming is accomplished solely by the beating of a fin. This fin is not dragged from side to side, rather a ripple of waves runs down it from top to bottom. In the dorsal fin of the seahorse as many as seven waves may be in train at any one moment, with each wave lasting a tenth of a second. The many planes of pressure this series of waves produces means that the tiniest modifications allow for precise changes in position.

Seasnakes have a rhythmicity of action which closely parallels that of eels. Being air-breathing vertebrates, seasnakes often swim with their noses breaking the surface, and in calm water the bends in their bodies—the points of lateral thrust—can be seen as a tell-tale series of ripples which fan out at right angles from their point of origin. In swimming through water seasnakes are making the same movements as their terrestrial cousins do on dry land. In water, which has a much higher resistance to movement, a bend in the seasnake's body provides sufficient braking power to stop it from being pushed backward, but on dry land a simple bend is not enough. Most land snakes live in areas of dense vegetation and push against clumps of plants in order to achieve

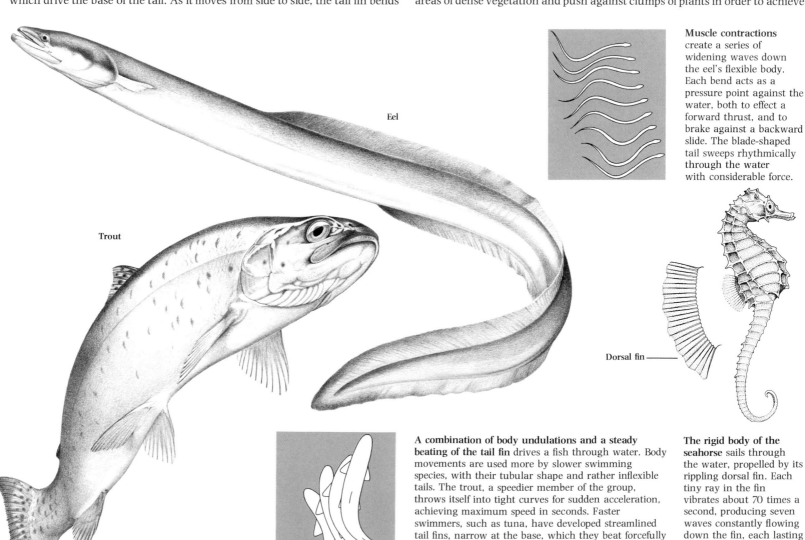

Eel

Trout

Dorsal fin

Muscle contractions create a series of widening waves down the eel's flexible body. Each bend acts as a pressure point against the water, both to effect a forward thrust, and to brake against a backward slide. The blade-shaped tail sweeps rhythmically through the water with considerable force.

A combination of body undulations and a steady beating of the tail fin drives a fish through water. Body movements are used more by slower swimming species, with their tubular shape and rather inflexible tails. The trout, a speedier member of the group, throws itself into tight curves for sudden acceleration, achieving maximum speed in seconds. Faster swimmers, such as tuna, have developed streamlined tail fins, narrow at the base, which they beat forcefully against the water, with a twist clockwise, when the fin moves left, and anti-clockwise, when it swings to the right. The frequency and span of the tail gradually increase with speed in these fast species, just as the undulations become more exaggerated in slower fish such as the herring.

The rigid body of the seahorse sails through the water, propelled by its rippling dorsal fin. Each tiny ray in the fin vibrates about 70 times a second, producing seven waves constantly flowing down the fin, each lasting $\frac{1}{10}$ second. Synchronized waves in the head and anal fins help increase the power and precision of these slow yet agile creatures.

forward thrust.

To exploit all the features of their environment as fully as possible, snakes can change their locomotory rhythms. If a snake enters a tunnel of any kind, such as might be found in a pile of boulders, it can switch from a simple undulatory rhythm to a concertina one. In this sort of movement a region at the front of the snake is thrown into two loops which press outward at their crests on to the wall of the tunnel. The rear of the snake is brought up by muscular contraction, then some new loops form at the rear. Thus held, the front relaxes, elongates and forms a new anchor.

Some snakes—notably vipers—are able to travel in a straight line, without the need for undulatory or concertina rhythms, although they do so only extremely slowly. These snakes have well-developed musculature and heavy scales on the underside of their bodies. At any one time there may be two waves of contraction passing down the body, but two short patches of the underneath, or ventral wall, of the body are firmly fixed to the ribs and act rather like athletes' starting blocks. Once the section of the snake in front of the patches is fully stretched, they relax and another two points immediately behind them take over.

Desert dwelling snakes, such as the rattlers, have to live in an environment often composed almost exclusively of sand. These snakes use the basic undulatory rhythm, but the whole body moves sideways. The snake only makes contact with the sand at two points, but because the whole body-weight bears down on just two points, enough static friction is developed to prevent these points from slipping. Against these effective anchors the body muscles

can exert a backward pressure, and so move the snake forward. This rhythmic 'sidewinding' leaves characteristic tracks in the sand, like parallel strokes inclined backward at an angle of about 30 degrees to the forward axis of the snake.

Because water is many times thicker than air, its extra resistance can be exploited in many ways and there are even more rhythms of locomotion associated with water than with air. Jet propulsion, for instance, is unknown in terrestrial animals but relatively common for aquatic species. Many types of clams and all octopuses use jet propulsion to escape their predators, but this is seldom rhythmical. Among the jellyfish and their relatives, however, rhythmic pulsing is well developed. Even the most sedentary of polyps send out tiny jellyfish barely visible to the naked eye to carry their reproductive cells into the upper layers of the water. Like their larger, more familiar, relatives, these jellyfish rhythmically pulsate their domes and so gain both height and sideways movement.

Although the musculature of jellyfish is primitive, each transparent mass that composes a jellyfish is supplied with a strong circular or coronal muscle running round the edge of its bell, and several radial muscles like the spokes of an umbrella, starting from the umbrella point and radiating out to the periphery. A single pulse starts with a slight shortening of the radial muscles as a result of impulses generated by nerve cells in the animal's sense organs, and is followed immediately by a strong contraction of the coronal muscles. This causes the dome to narrow and suck water in through an aperture of decreasing size, before a rapid contraction of the radial muscles thrusts the water out with ▷

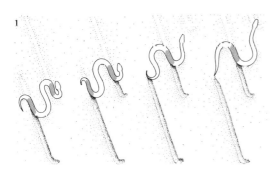

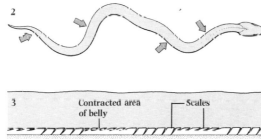

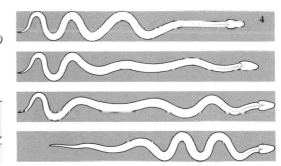

Snakes have adopted four different undulatory patterns, each using different push-off points, to suit a variety of habitats. The desert sidewinder leaves 'tramline' tracks in the sand (1). The more common

laterally bending snakes thrust sideways against plants and stones from alternate sides of the body (2). Rattlesnakes and vipers creep slowly forward in a straight line, using contracted areas of the belly for

'feet', as muscles haul the body forward inside the skin (3). When confined in a crevice a snake sends tight loops, concertina-style, down the body to press against the boulders, squeezing itself forward (4)

The sidewinders of North America have developed a highly efficient means of 'running' across the slippery desert sands. The snake is constantly poised on two anchoring push-off points with the rest of the body arched between. As the head reaches forward, the body follows and the snake lands on two new push-off points, resulting in a rapid sideways 'hobble'. The parallel tracks left in the sand by the contact points lie at a 45° angle to the forward direction of the snake.

▷considerable force. An adult individual of the common European jellyfish, *Aurelia*, blows out about 0.04 pints (22 ml) of water with each contraction. Slow, rhythmic pulsing of the bell can continue for long periods and carry the jellyfish many miles. As a general rule, the rate of muscle pulsation in jellyfish is higher in younger individuals, but it also increases in frequency with a rise in temperature of the sea water in which the animal lives.

Many aquatic species row themselves through the water. At its simplest this sort of action is similar to human rowing in boats with oars, but at its most elaborate becomes almost a sort of flight. Water beetles propel themselves by making beatlike movements of their middle and, sometimes, their hind legs. Starting with the 'oars' at the end of a stroke, the cycle of movement is as follows: the legs are rotated slightly to present a thinner profile and minimum surface area to the water. The legs are then drawn forward as far as they will go, rotated again so that the area of contact with the water is at a maximum, and then they are forced backward. Stiff bristles fringing the extremity of each leg now open up to provide an even greater area of contact with the water. At the end of the propulsive stroke the bristles fold down so that they do not hinder recovery.

A similar sort of rhythmical rowing is seen in the backswimmers and water boatmen, small bugs with elongated hind legs which pull rhythmically so drawing the creatures through the water. In water boatmen the body is flat and the back slightly concave. The creature's flat, paddlelike legs are employed to scull the animal over the water surface, while the long, slim middle legs are used for clinging to vegetation while the water boatman feeds. Once the animal releases its hold on these food materials it floats to the surface because its body

is lighter than water, and it will often shoot off through the water surface and take flight. Backswimmers are similar to water boatmen, living and swimming very close to the surface of the water. The big difference is that, as their name suggests, backswimmers swim on their convex, keeled backs. Backswimmers store bubbles of air under their wings in two channels formed by rows of hairs, and force themselves down into the water by rowing with their hind legs which, like those of water beetles, have hairy fringes for greater propulsion.

Whirligig beetles are also aptly named because they swim in circles on the water surface, although they move in straight lines when moving beneath the surface and when they dive. Both sorts of movement are made possible by rowing action of the four flat swimming legs (the other two foremost legs are much smaller), but in circular swimming the legs on one side of the body pull harder and more frequently than those on the other, rather in the same way that a novice rower with two oars fails to coordinate the actions of his two arms.

Turtles move through the water pulling rhythmically on their paired, bladelike forelimbs. These limbs are feathered during their recovery strokes and—like all oars, natural and man-made—are twisted at the start of the power stroke to present a broad, flat surface to the water. Although both the turtle's flippers beat together, the passage of the turtle through the water is not jerky because its streamlined shape allows its inertial mass to move fast enough between strokes to maintain its speed. Careful analysis of slow motion film of a turtle swimming reveals that the movement of the flippers shows some of

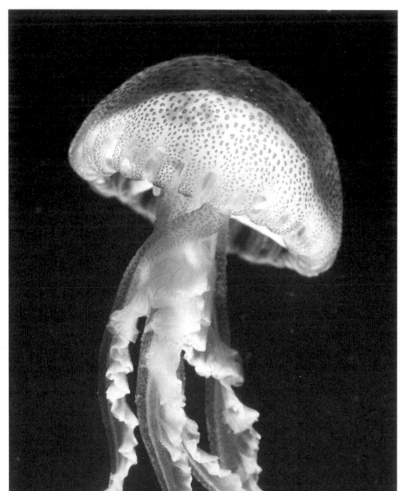

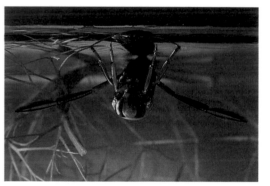

Rowing requires perfect synchrony for speed. A Cambridge boat crew, *below right*, mimics the techniques of the 'back-swimmer', *top*, presenting the broad side of the oar blades for the strong power stroke and the narrow side for the recovery, to minimize air resistance. Long oars produce a wide stroke in relation to the movement at the rowlock.

Gentle rhythmic pulsation propels the jellyfish through water. Spokelike muscles in the body dome contract, then a rapid contraction of a second set of muscles causes the dome to narrow and water to be sucked in. Further contraction of the spokelike muscles forces water out, driving the jellyfish upward.

the characteristics of birds' wings. On the down stroke the tip trails behind slightly, flicking backward, and producing forward propulsive thrust at the end of the power stroke and again at the start of the recovery stroke.

Even more like flying are the wing-beats of the rays, huge fish which can travel swiftly through the water with the grace and ease of a stork in the air. A large manta ray will beat its 'wings' once every three seconds—about one-third of the frequency of a stork's wing-beat. As the ray's huge wings beat downward, lift is produced exactly as in birds, with an area of low pressure being created above each wing, but it does not need to be as strong, since the relative weight of the ray in the dense water is low. A wave of ripples travels around the edge of the wing and serves to trim it to the particular manoeuvre being undertaken. During the recovery stroke the wing bends, allowing the springy wing-tip to travel back to its starting position without creating a downward force on the fish. Of all the rhythmic patterns of locomotion seen in aquatic animals, there can be few as aesthetically pleasing to the human eye as the graceful beating of the ray's wing.

Dolphins are streamlined, water dwelling mammals that have long fascinated man. Highly successful swimmers, dolphins can reach maximum speeds of about 25 miles (40 km) an hour. Most of the dolphin's normal swimming movement is brought about by the beating of its tail fin, powered by immensely strong body muscles. The tail fin, which is attached to the dolphin's body in a horizontal plane, beats up and down with a slight horizontal twist. Rhythmical swimming in the dolphin is made more efficient by adaptations of the animal's skin. When the dolphin suddenly increases or decreases its swimming speed, the skin of the lower half of the body wrinkles and these folds act to dissipate eddies of water round the body and so reduce drag. Fluid trapped within the wrinkles of skin is squeezed from high pressure areas of the body to low pressure areas, so that the water exerts a minimum of resistance on the dolphin. This pattern of skin wrinkles differs in males and females, but when individuals of either sex are moving at high speed, the waves move toward the rear of the body, each folding cycle lasting about two seconds.

As well as being excellent swimmers, dolphins and their close relatives make spectacular rhythmic jumping movements, which propel them out of the water. In such movement, the body muscles contract against the large vertical and horizontal extensions from the bones of the vertebral column, so that a wave of muscular contraction passes rapidly down the body. After the initial contraction, the rest of the jump cycle is essentially a passive process, until the next wave of contractions again forces the dolphin's body up above the surface of the ocean.

Sadly, man has exploited the low-drag, high-efficiency swimming abilities of dolphins and their close relations in two ways. For commercial purposes he has established dolphinariums in which animals are trained to perform before an audience. The body design of dolphins and porpoises has also attracted the attentions of military scientists. A number of experiments has been carried out in order to discover whether hull shapes or fluid-containing surface layers based on dolphin designs could be usefully applied to atomic submarines to improve their efficiency and reduce their drag as they surge powerfully through the world's oceans.

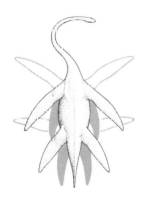

Plesiosaurs were agile paddlers of the prehistoric world. Although their 'oars' were rigid and could not be raised above shoulder level, they could flick them to make sharp turns and paddle backward. Such agility was useful when searching for fish which it would snap up by plunging its head into the water.

The loggerhead turtle, *Caretta caretta*, glides through the water by sculling both its elongated front flippers simultaneously. The smooth front edges of the flippers slice cleanly forward through the water before twisting to sweep the water back, and so propel the turtle forward. The flexible flipper-tip acts as a sensitive steering system. Some species have four flippers and may move diagonal pairs together.

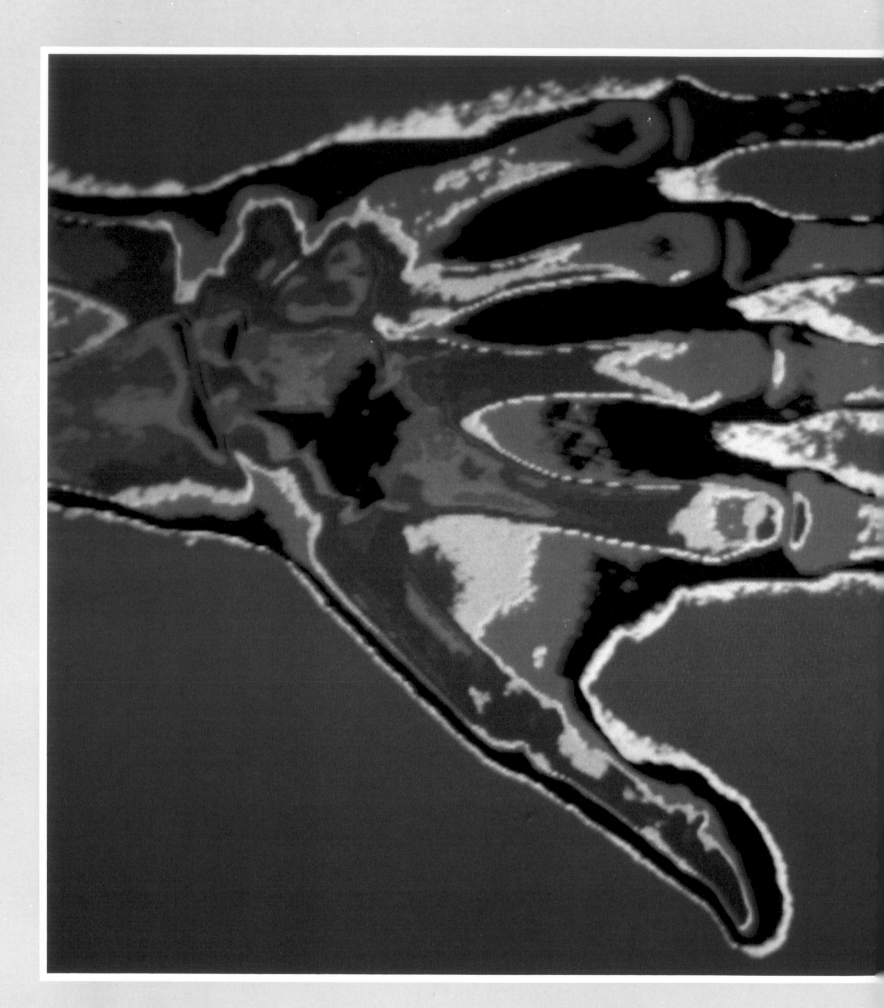

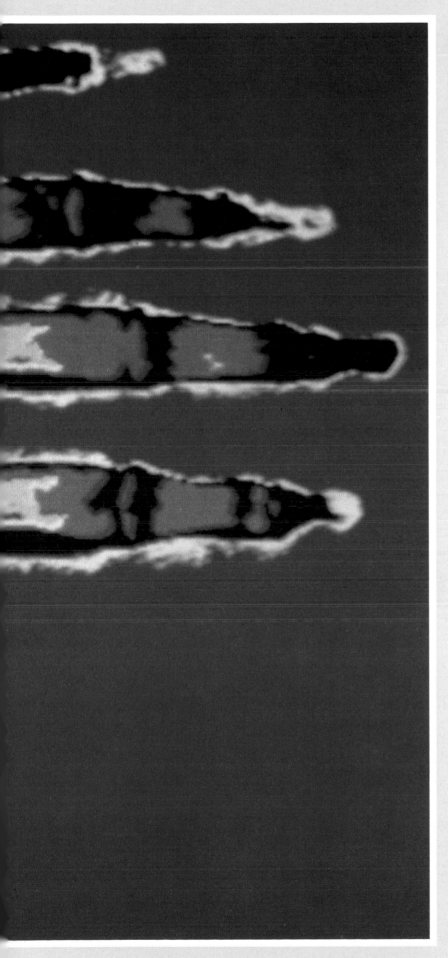

Rhythms of health and disease

By understanding something about our body rhythms we can all take steps to improve the way we do our jobs and make the decisions vital to our day-to-day well-being. Just judging whether you are at your best at crack of dawn or after dinner in the evening, and timing your work to fit in with this assessment, is a simple way to make a significant difference to the quality and quantity of your work. Knowledge of the rhythmic nature of human life is also beginning to have important implications in the diagnosis and treatment of disease. During every 24-hour period, for example, the body's internal chemistry changes, so making the symptoms of some illnesses show up more clearly at some times of day than others and, at the same time, altering the way in which the body will respond to treatment with drugs.

The human body is a remarkably rhythmic piece of machinery. Without any conscious control on our part, our hearts beat about 70 times a minute while we breathe in and out between 12 and 15 times. More subtle than these minute-by-minute rhythms are our daily or circadian rhythms, of which the most obvious by far is the rhythm of sleeping and waking. Other circadian rhythms involve biological functions which, at first sight, seem to be going on at a constant rate. The human pulse is a good example, for it does not stay at 70 beats a minute all the time. Over every 24 hours it shows a distinct variation, slowing down at night when the body is normally at rest and speeding up during the day. This rhythm continues even when the body is deprived of the natural daily change in illumination signalled by dusk and dawn, but not on a strictly 24-hour basis. Thus the heart rate rhythm of someone incarcerated in a pitch dark bunker or cave, and the rhythm of sleeping and waking, are found to have periods of between 25 and 27 hours, not 24 as you might expect, so that the body gradually gets out of phase with the time of day outside the cave, on the surface. The reason for this is that the biological clock, which drives the rhythm, normally synchronizes itself with the outside world but, when deprived of all time checks, free-runs and assumes its own slightly longer natural period.

Since the first orbital manned space flights of the 1960s scientists have taken great interest in the way in which human physiology changes under conditions of weightlessness and a day that is 90 minutes rather than 24 hours long. Indirect monitoring of the blood pressure of astronauts, for example, has shown that it follows a normal, approximately 24-hour rhythm in space, despite the drastically altered daylength.

In keeping the body healthy, and treating the diseases to which it succumbs, it is the approximately daily circadian rhythms that have so far proved most relevant, although the body does have medically significant monthly rhythms such as the female menstrual cycle. Many of the circadian rhythms which have been discovered show such a small variation between their highest and their lowest points that they can only be detected by meticulous and frequent measurements throughout each 24 hours, and may require the help of computers to reveal their underlying rhythmicity. But some rhythms in body functions have a larger variation and so are much easier to detect and study. Such rhythms include the pulse rate, blood pressure and body temperature, the production and release of hormones from some glands, the rate at which the kidneys produce urine and the brain's alertness. Knowing that the brain is least alert in the early hours of the morning, for example, gives the police a potential advantage over weary terrorists holding hostages.

The more we look for rhythms in our lives, the more we find. But despite an immense amount of study the true site and mechanism of the biological clock is still a mystery. Of all the many biological components from which the human machine is constructed, no one organ, tissue or group of cells can be singled out as the ultimate biological clock that drives all the body's 24-hour or circadian rhythms. Whether there is just a single clock or several, the human brain probably houses a master clock, which seems to synchronize itself with the outside world. This overall control ensures that our bodies are usually most active when we are awake and that internal body functions operate more slowly at night when we are asleep. The chief synchronizer of the master biological clock is probably light from the sun, which is received by our eyes, then transmitted to the brain by the optic nerves for interpretation. Other signals, such as the temperature of our surroundings, noise, and contact with our fellow human beings, which are received by other sense organs and sent to the brain for analysis, also act as synchronizers of human circadian rhythms.

For prehistoric man, who presumably had to hunt by day and hide from predators at night, a biological clock that stimulated him by day and encouraged him to hide and sleep when it was dark was a valuable aid to survival. Using artificial lighting, modern man has managed to change his environment so that, unlike his ancestors, he is no longer bound by the confines of the natural day; but the ordering of our activity in time is apparently so vital that the biological clock still persists. Experiments show that the clock is so strong that it is impossible to stop its natural rhythm for any length of time.

If the biological clock is in the human brain, it may control rhythms throughout the body directly via the nervous system, of which it is the ultimate coordinator, or indirectly by influencing the manufacture and release of hormones, chemical messengers which are carried in the blood to target organs where they exert their effects. A master clock in the brain may simply coordinate the timing of several subsidiary clocks in other parts of the body, or every individual body cell may have its own microscopic clock. It has been shown, for example, that animal hearts will retain their heart rate rhythm even when removed and kept alive in nutrient fluids—and even individual heart-muscle cells maintain a circadian rhythm, beating fast to correspond with daytime and moving slowly to correspond with nighttime.

The biological clock in the brain may regulate rhythms by operating through the unconscious or autonomic division of the nervous system. Without our knowing it, the autonomic nervous system sustains and controls all the essential functions that keep us alive. It keeps our hearts beating and the blood flowing round our arteries and veins. It makes the lungs pump air in and out and regulates the many aspects of the digestive process. It is also the autonomic nervous system that is operating when you get goosepimples from the cold or sweat because you are too hot.

The autonomic nervous system is itself divided into two parts whose actions tend to be contrary to one another, so that between them they keep the body 'on balance'. The two parts of the system act to control the flow of physiological traffic in the body rather like red and green traffic signals. When the 'green light' is showing, this means that all is well and the body can calmly get on with its work. The parasympathetic part of the autonomic nervous system is more

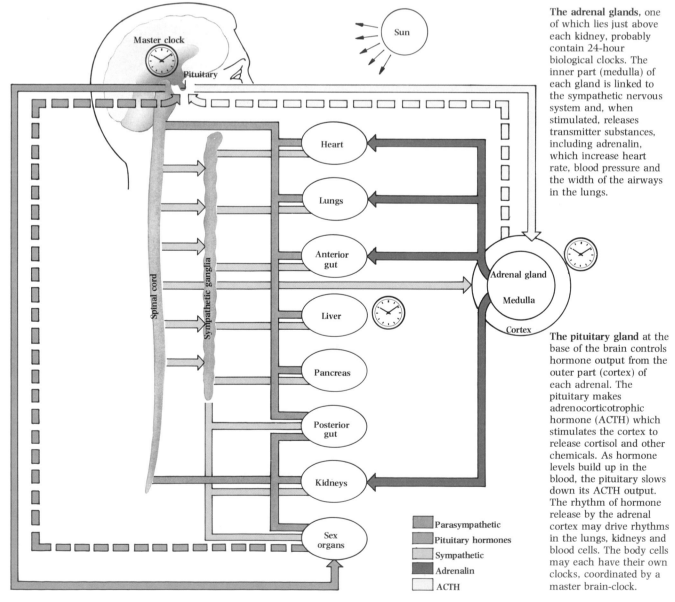

The machinery driving body rhythms includes both nerves and hormones. Information about the changes occurring in the course of the natural day is perceived by our sense organs and carried to the brain where it may act to synchronize a master clock. This clock drives rhythms in organs such as the heart and lungs. The system of control works through the unconscious or autonomic nervous system, either directly through nerves or indirectly via the release of chemicals. It also works through the controlling effect of the pituitary gland on hormone production. The autonomic nervous system is divided into two parts, the sympathetic and the parasympathetic. Nerves of the sympathetic system travel from the brain to the spinal cord and out between the bones of the spine to connect with relay stations, strips of nerve tissue (sympathetic ganglia), lying alongside the spine. Further links are made by different sets of nerves supplying individual organs. Most of the actions of the parasympathetic nerves are fulfilled by means of instructions carried in the vagus nerve supplying the lungs and abdomen.

The adrenal glands, one of which lies just above each kidney, probably contain 24-hour biological clocks. The inner part (medulla) of each gland is linked to the sympathetic nervous system and, when stimulated, releases transmitter substances, including adrenalin, which increase heart rate, blood pressure and the width of the airways in the lungs.

The pituitary gland at the base of the brain controls hormone output from the outer part (cortex) of each adrenal. The pituitary makes adrenocorticotrophic hormone (ACTH) which stimulates the cortex to release cortisol and other chemicals. As hormone levels build up in the blood, the pituitary slows down its ACTH output. The rhythm of hormone release by the adrenal cortex may drive rhythms in the lungs, kidneys and blood cells. The body cells may each have their own clocks, coordinated by a master brain-clock.

active at these times. It slows the heart rate and, at the same time, encourages the breakdown and absorption of food. The parasympathetic predominates during the night when the body is most relaxed.

Imagine you are asleep in bed and suddenly you are awakened by the knowledge that there is a stranger in your room. In an instant you are wide awake. Your heart is pounding, but you are ready to jump up and fight off the intruder or call for help. In such a situation it is the second part of the autonomic nervous system—the sympathetic section—that is working over-time. As a result of its stimulation of the body's internal organs, not only do heart rate and blood pressure increase but the hairs stand on end, just as they do on the neck of a frightened animal, and the pupils dilate. To help prepare the body for immediate action blood rushes to the muscles and is diverted away from those parts of the body, such as the intestines, whose working has temporarily become inessential. The feelings that your heart is in your mouth, that you are sick with terror, are rooted to the spot or want to run for your life are all brought about through the action of the sympathetic nervous system.

In the course of a normal day events are rarely as extreme as this, but the sympathetic and parasympathetic systems act as fine balancers. As you relax watching television the parasympathetic predominates—until something horrific comes on to the screen then the sympathetic has the upper hand again. It has been suggested that the circadian rhythms of the heart and lungs may be driven by the brain, the body's ultimate traffic controller, simply by varying the balance between these two parts of the autonomic system.

The job of preparing the body for action in times of stress is not the sole prerogative of the nerves that make up the sympathetic section of the autonomic nervous system. Hormones, too, are involved and these are released by the inner region (medulla) of the adrenal glands. These small glands are located over the kidneys and are supplied with nerve branches from the sympathetic system. It is the action of the adrenals that makes the body respond so instantly to danger that it can be fast asleep one minute and awake and ready for a fight the next. The secret ingredient that makes immediate action possible is the hormone adrenalin. As it pours out into the blood, adrenalin is carried to the internal organs and mimics the action of the sympathetic system, speeding up the heart, increasing the blood pressure, dilating the pupils and so on. Without this powerful adrenalin-motivated response the body would not be able to react quickly enough to save itself from danger—the midnight intruder would have burgled you or knocked you out before you were even properly awake. Adrenalin is not only involved in preserving the body from danger, but it also helps the body achieve the peak of performance. It is adrenalin that spurs on the marathon runner to reach the tape when he feels he cannot take another stride.

The body's output of adrenalin and other related hormones from the adrenal glands is not usually constant. In ordinary, everyday circumstances it, too, has a circadian rhythm and is lower during the night than during the day. Because of this rhythm, adrenalin and other adrenal hormones may act as a kind of local biological clock to control pulse rate and other body rhythms, either alone or by acting as relay stations from a master clock in the brain. Two circadian rhythms that seem to involve adrenalin can easily be shown. When your body ▷

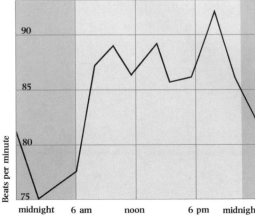

Detecting high blood pressure is important in the prevention of heart disease. Although there is a small rhythmical variation in blood pressure over 24 hours, most people are clearly normal or have high blood pressure. In borderline cases an evening reading may give an erroneous impression of high blood pressure.

The heart beats slowest at night and fastest in the afternoon, even if you lie in bed all day. The heart rate rhythm, *above*, may be controlled by a clock in the pacemaker, by the rhythms in the output of adrenalin and similar hormones from the adrenal gland, or by body temperature rhythms.

Taking the blood pressure gives a doctor valuable information about the state of the heart and arteries. As blood is pumped from the heart it presses on the elastic walls of the arteries. The resistance of the arteries to the flow of blood can be measured by finding out how high a column of mercury the pressure in the artery can support. To measure blood pressure, the brachial artery of the forearm is compressed by pumping air into a cuff. Pressure in the cuff is recorded by joining it to a mercury pressure gauge, or manometer. When the pressure in the cuff is gradually lowered, blood spurts through the artery as soon as the pressure in the cuff is the same as the maximum pressure the heartbeat can generate. This is the systolic blood pressure which produces a shock wave and a knocking sound that can be heard through a stethoscope. The knocking disappears when cuff-pressure falls far enough for the blood to flow continuously. The measurement at this moment, when the heart is resting between beats, is the diastolic pressure. The rhythm of blood pressure is most noticeable for the systolic measurement—the higher of the two.

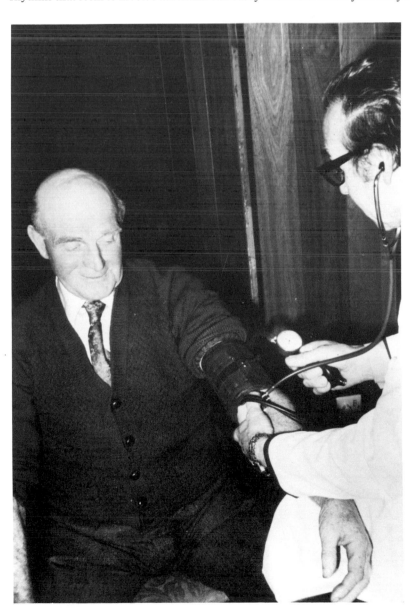

▷ is resting—that is, not being made to perform vigorous exercise—the heart beats slowly after you wake up in the morning and rises stepwise during the day. The total rise in pulse rate is often more than 10 beats a minute. In a similar way your blood pressure is lowest first thing in the morning and rises as the day goes on. Both rhythms are probably controlled, at least in part, by the adrenalin rhythm, which is at its lowest point in early morning, and both have some medical importance because changes in pulse rate and blood pressure may be early indicators of disease.

The outer parts of each adrenal gland secrete other hormones known as corticosteroids, which are made and used in artificial forms as cortisone and other steroid drugs. These corticosteroids are powerful chemicals and produce a huge range of vital effects in the body. They control the rate at which the body's metabolic reactions take place, help balance its mineral content, influence blood pressure and kidney action. To add to that, they have the ability to damp down the process of inflammation, which explains why the artificial versions are so valuable in treating rheumatoid arthritis, a disease in which the joints become inflamed, and why they help in preventing the rejection of organ transplants.

Control of corticosteroid output from the adrenals is not via the nervous system, as it is with adrenalin, but is governed by the pituitary gland, a pea-shaped projection on the underside of the brain. The cells of the pituitary have a remarkable inbuilt measuring machinery to 'test' the blood for the presence of one of the most important of the corticosteroid hormones, namely, cortisol. If the amount of cortisol in the blood is too low this triggers off the alarm bells in the pituitary. On 'hearing' these bells, the pituitary cells respond and set to work to make and send out a hormone to the adrenals so that cortisol output is stepped up. Laboratory measurements of cortisol levels in the blood throughout the day reveal that it has a marked circadian rhythm. This rhythm may be driven by the brain, which has a strong influence on the actions of the pituitary gland, or by a local clock situated in the adrenal gland itself.

The cortisol rhythm is so powerful that its effects overflow into other body systems. One of these is the blood system itself which contains two sorts of cells, the red cells, which carry oxygen round the body, and the white cells, which are involved in the body's natural defence against disease and play a part in allergic reactions. As the level of cortisol in the blood rises it makes the blood inhospitable to a type of white cell called an eosinophil, which is important in allergic reactions, and their numbers fall. So the circadian rhythm of eosinophil cell numbers is driven by the cortisol rhythm but is the mirror image of it. This is not altogether surprising because it has been shown that the rhythmical activity of the brain and of the heart, lungs and circulation are very closely related. What is more, most of the organs involved in these reactions are influenced by both the autonomic nervous system and the hormones released by the adrenal glands.

Many sorts of mental activity show circadian rhythms but the most obvious is the rhythm of sleep and wakefulness. Keeping the body awake depends on the activity of a system of nerve fibres joining the cerebral hemispheres of the brain and the brain stem, which contain centres which act as motors to drive breathing, the beat of the heart and the blood pressure. The rhythm of sleep and

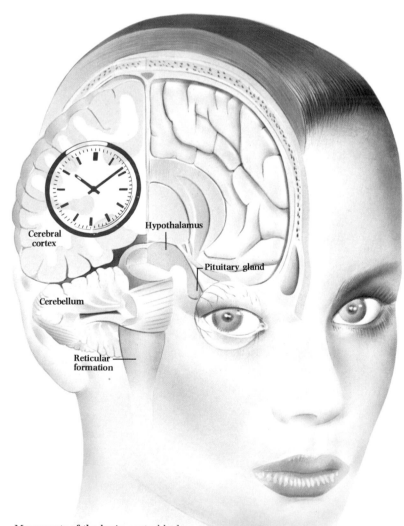

Many parts of the brain control body rhythms. The cerebral cortex helps to attune the biological clock to the environment. The hypothalamus controls temperature, with which many mental rhythms are linked. The pituitary controls hormonal rhythms, the reticular formation the rhythm of sleep and waking.

Cerebral cortex

Hypothalamus

Pituitary gland

Cerebellum

Reticular formation

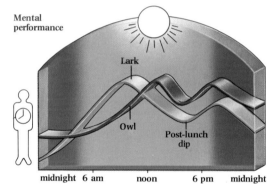

The ability to work well varies during the course of the day. 'Larks' do best in the morning but tire early in the evening. 'Owls' struggle to get going in the morning but liven up later. Both larks and owls experience a 'post-lunch dip', a sharp fall in performance around 1 pm, even if they do not eat.

Mental performance

Lark

Owl

Post-lunch dip

midnight 6 am noon 6 pm midnight

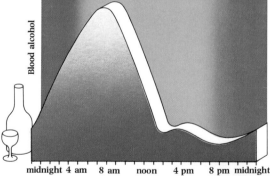

Measurements of the amount of alcohol in the blood, after regular, hourly intake of equal quantities, reveal a circadian rhythm in the rate at which alcohol disappears from the blood. Alcohol is metabolized most slowly from 2 to 7 am, when it depresses mental ability most. For least effect drink alcohol in the early evening.

Blood alcohol

midnight 4 am 8 am noon 4 pm 8 pm midnight

Rhythmic fluctuations in body temperature seem to be closely related to mental performance. The rhythm is easily shown by carefully taking the temperature inside the mouth at hourly intervals. This graph shows average results for a group of normal people over several days. Body temperature is lowest just before waking, rises to a peak around 9 pm, then falls rapidly. Values vary by 0.5°C (1°F) at most.

98.7
98.5
98.3
98.1
97.9
97.7
97.5

Body temperature °F

9 am 1 pm 5 pm 9 pm 1 am

wakefulness develops shortly after birth. To begin with, babies spend about eight hours awake out of every 24 but these hours are equally divided between day and night. By the time babies are two or three months old, the adult pattern is emerging, with most sleep taking place during the night. The adult rhythm depends on external stimuli to keep it synchronized with the outside world. Without such stimuli it free-runs and develops its own period of about 25 hours. Fortunately for modern man the rhythm of sleep and wakefulness adapts rapidly to new circumstances so that some of us can do shift work reasonably efficiently, although during the night we can never achieve the standards reached during the day. If, however, you are forced to stay awake without sleep the rhythm persists, which explains why people deprived of sleep find it hard to stay awake during the night, but in the morning find their fatigue is less marked although it returns more strongly the next night.

Mental performance rhythms are closely linked to the body temperature rhythm. Body temperature varies by about 0.5 degrees centigrade (1 degree F) over 24 hours, with lowest values in the early morning. This rhythm is not simply the result of increased heat production from chemical reactions, meals and exercise during the day, since it persists in people confined to permanent rest in bed and given meals equally spaced out over the 24 hours. Body temperature is controlled by a centre in the hypothalamus, the part of the brain that connects with the pituitary gland. The hypothalamus regulates sweating and the dilation and constriction of blood vessels in the skin, and, by stimulation of the pituitary gland, also influences the secretion by the thyroid gland of the hormone thyroxine, a chemical which speeds up the rate at which

cells consume oxygen, metabolize glucose and produce heat. Does this mean that the body's master clock is in or close to the hypothalamus? The answer is that we do not know, but a variation in the sensitivity of the temperature regulating centre may well be responsible for the temperature rhythm, so this rhythm could be a close guide to the time that is actually being shown by the 'hands' of the master clock.

As well as affecting our performance, circadian rhythms affect our moods. Most of us can classify ourselves either as 'larks', who wake early, work well during the morning but need to go to bed early, or 'owls', who find it hard to face the day but, once they get going, can work efficiently into the small hours. Some psychologists have gone further, claiming that larks are introverts, owls extroverts. These relationships—and the effect of the temperature rhythm— have been substantiated by a study on a group of sailors, who were classified by psychological testing and whose temperature rhythms were recorded. Introverts showed an earlier temperature rise in the morning but extrovert temperatures fell more slowly in the evening. Irrespective of psychological type, we all undergo a 'post-lunch dip'—a slight fall in mental efficiency around 1 pm. The cause of this phenomenon, which is seen in several other rhythms, is not known, but it is not due simply to eating lunch or to the effects of alcohol, since it persists even if you miss lunch and stay perfectly sober.

Rhythms of mood and body temperature, and the rhythm of sleep and wakefulness are all closely interrelated. Generally we are most anxious and depressed when we wake up in the morning, but become more cheerful as the day wears on. The sensation of fatigue, and performance in tests of mental ▷

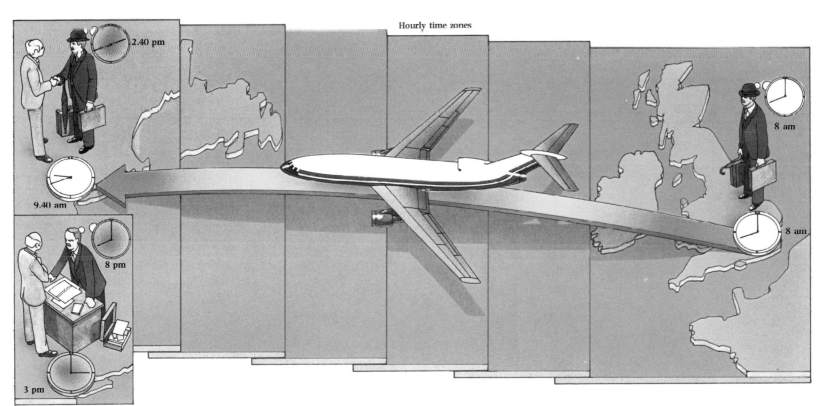

Hourly time zones

A British businessman leaves London for New York at 8 am, He travels 3,500 miles across five time zones in 6 hours 40 minutes and arrives at 9.40 am New York time, but his body clock registers 2 pm London time. Arriving at his American office at 1 pm he is in time for a working lunch and the serious business is done at 3 pm, when his American colleagues are at the end of their 'post-lunch dip' but he is at his mental peak. At 8 pm local time they go out to celebrate. The Englishman whose 'clock' is at 1 am finds that the wine goes to his head, but the Americans are at their peak for alcohol tolerance. It takes three days or more for all his body clocks to be reset to a new local time, *right*. On day 1, all the clocks tell London time, on day 2 they are all awry. By day 3 only the kidneys have not adapted completely.

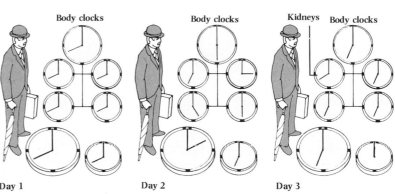

▷ agility, such as mental arithmetic, speed of dealing playing cards or reaction times in simulated motor vehicles, can be closely linked with the temperature rhythm, with the poorest responses occurring in the early morning when body temperature is lowest.

To help complete our knowledge of mental performance rhythms we can also consider the effects of alcohol. A group of enthusiastic volunteers has shown that alcohol is broken down and used more slowly, and thus has its maximum effect in clouding mental activity, between 2 and 7 am. The last drinks 'for the road' at the end of a late party can, therefore, be particularly dangerous as they will be metabolized more slowly.

Mental performance rhythms have many practical applications. It is useful to identify yourself as a lark or an owl and plan your day accordingly. If you are a lark, get up early and relax in the evening. If you are an owl, put in a hard stint of work around midnight. It is worth remembering the existence of the post-lunch dip, particularly if you are often involved in 'working' lunches. To gain maximum psychological advantage, tackle the important business before lunch, not after. Similarly, anyone involved in strenuous mental activity will probably benefit from a diversion for an hour or two after lunch.

The rhythm of sleep and wakefulness is vital to our lives. Because it exists, it is inevitable that night shift workers are less efficient than their counterparts on the day shift. The implications of the rhythm are particularly important for those involved in emergency services, for their own safety and that of those they treat. If at all possible, for example, surgeons should avoid performing operations at night as they cannot expect to perform as well as during the day.

This said, some people do adapt to night shift work better than others, and there does seem to be a 'learning' effect so that shift work gets easier the more you do it. To give the body time to adapt, it is sensible to go on night shift for a minimum of a week, because rapid changes of shift are most disruptive to the body clock.

Air travel does not allow time for the clock to adapt and jet lag is at least partly explained as fatigue experienced during the day as the clock remembers that it is bedtime back home. The addition of intercontinental ballistic missiles to the arsenals of the superpowers has given circadian rhythms a military significance. There are some areas of the USA and USSR which are 12 hours apart, although one could attack the other in a few minutes. The aggressor could, therefore, usefully time his offensive so that it occurs during the middle of the night for his enemy; for although his defences are manned around the clock, decision-making cannot be as good at night.

Circadian rhythms are significant to many sorts of disease but particularly to the diseases that affect the adrenal glands and to the problems of using cortisone and other steroid drugs to treat chronic diseases, such as rheumatoid arthritis, over a long period. The key to understanding the problems to which the adrenal glands are prone lies in the way the output of natural corticosteroid hormones is controlled. The mechanism of control is a feedback system which works like this: first the hypothalamus in the brain makes a chemical which travels to the neighbouring pituitary gland. This chemical tells the pituitary to make a hormone which acts as a kind of intermediary between the hypothalamus and the adrenal. The hormone, which has the rather daunting

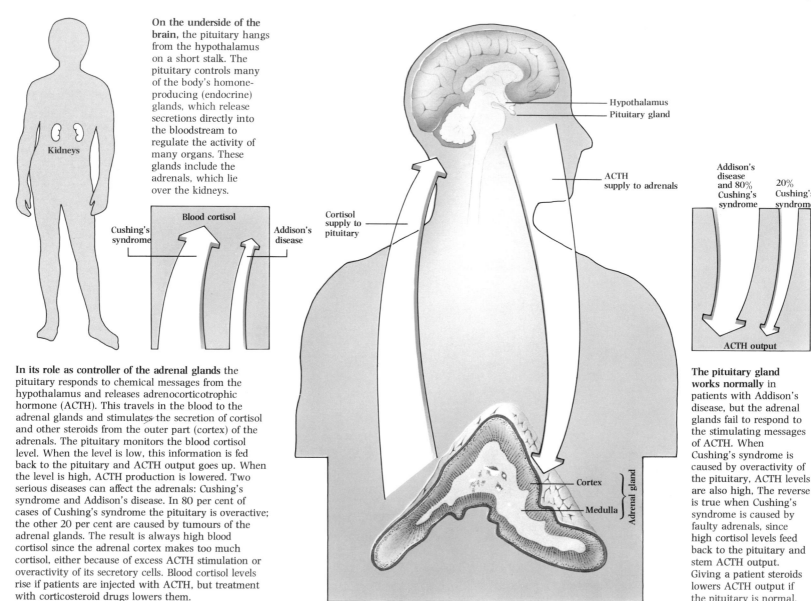

On the underside of the brain, the pituitary hangs from the hypothalamus on a short stalk. The pituitary controls many of the body's homone-producing (endocrine) glands, which release secretions directly into the bloodstream to regulate the activity of many organs. These glands include the adrenals, which lie over the kidneys.

Kidneys

Blood cortisol

Cushing's syndrome

Addison's disease

Hypothalamus
Pituitary gland

ACTH supply to adrenals

Cortisol supply to pituitary

Addison's disease and 80% Cushing's syndrome

20% Cushing's syndrome

ACTH output

Cortex
Medulla
Adrenal gland

In its role as controller of the adrenal glands the pituitary responds to chemical messages from the hypothalamus and releases adrenocorticotrophic hormone (ACTH). This travels in the blood to the adrenal glands and stimulates the secretion of cortisol and other steroids from the outer part (cortex) of the adrenals. The pituitary monitors the blood cortisol level. When the level is low, this information is fed back to the pituitary and ACTH output goes up. When the level is high, ACTH production is lowered. Two serious diseases can affect the adrenals: Cushing's syndrome and Addison's disease. In 80 per cent of cases of Cushing's syndrome the pituitary is overactive; the other 20 per cent are caused by tumours of the adrenal glands. The result is always high blood cortisol since the adrenal cortex makes too much cortisol, either because of excess ACTH stimulation or overactivity of its secretory cells. Blood cortisol levels rise if patients are injected with ACTH, but treatment with corticosteroid drugs lowers them.

The pituitary gland works normally in patients with Addison's disease, but the adrenal glands fail to respond to the stimulating messages of ACTH. When Cushing's syndrome is caused by overactivity of the pituitary, ACTH levels are also high. The reverse is true when Cushing's syndrome is caused by faulty adrenals, since high cortisol levels feed back to the pituitary and stem ACTH output. Giving a patient steroids lowers ACTH output if the pituitary is normal.

name adrenocorticotrophic hormone or ACTH for short, reaches the adrenal cortex through the bloodstream and orders it to begin making corticosteroids, including cortisol. All the time this is going on the amount of cortisol in the blood is monitored by the pituitary. If there is too much cortisol, ACTH production is turned down, but if there is not enough, then output is stepped up.

The circadian rhythm of cortisol production by the adrenal glands can be discovered by measuring the amount of cortisol in the blood at intervals over a complete 24-hour day, or by measuring the concentration of chemicals generated by the destruction of used hormones passed out of the body in the urine. The second of these lags slightly behind the first simply because of the time it takes for the kidneys to do their job of making and releasing urine. What these measurements show is that cortisol levels are lowest at midnight and in the early hours of the morning, after which they rise to a peak around 9 am.

The clock that drives this rhythm of cortisol production by the adrenals is probably in the glands themselves, since it has been shown that adrenal glands removed from hamsters and kept working in nutrient fluid continue to show rhythmic cortisol production. But the fact that the pituitary allows the rhythm to take place also implies that there must be a rhythm in the sensitivity of the pituitary to the presence of cortisol in the blood. As a result of this rhythm the message of maximum cortisol level at 9 am falls on deaf ears, yet at midnight the same cortisol level reaches a receptive audience and ACTH output falls considerably. This feedback mechanism can be tested by disrupting it with drugs; and in this way doctors can differentiate between faults in the pituitary and faults in the adrenals. If a tablet of one such drug is given to a healthy

person at 11 pm in the evening, it will provide the pituitary with exactly the same message and elicit the same response as a natural increase in the cortisol level. As a result ACTH output from the pituitary will go down and will, in turn, result in a lowering of cortisol output by the adrenals.

Understanding the cortisol rhythm is crucial to laboratory tests used to diagnose diseases of the adrenals, particularly Cushing's syndrome and Addison's disease. Cushing's syndrome, discovered by a Boston surgeon Harvey Cushing in 1932, results from excessive production of corticosteroids by the adrenals. In 20 per cent of cases it is caused by the presence of an adrenal tumour—a growth of abnormal cells which may be benign or malignant— while the remaining 80 per cent are due to tumours in the pituitary or to overactivity of the hypothalamus.

The signs and symptoms of Cushing's syndrome result from the presence of too much corticosteroid. Typically, the amount of fat under the skin increases, making the face become moon shaped, and a 'buffalo hump' of fat appears over the lower part of the neck and upper back. The trunk is obese, too, but the limb-muscles waste away, producing an appearance like a lemon on sticks. The skin is thin and bruises easily. Bones—particularly those of the spine—may weaken and fracture, and patients may become psychotic, or diabetic, or develop high blood pressure. To add insult to injury, men can become impotent and bald, while women grow excess body hair, lose their head hair and suffer from irregularities in their menstrual cycle.

From this horrific description you would think that such an unpleasant disease could easily be recognized, but in its early stages it can be hard to ▷

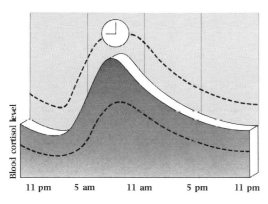

The normal daily cortisol output from the adrenals has a circadian rhythm. Peak output, at about 9 am, *left*, is more than twice as high as at midnight, but actual levels vary widely, as shown by the dotted lines. Because of the cortisol rhythm, cortisol levels must be measured at 9 am and midnight at least if disease is suspected.

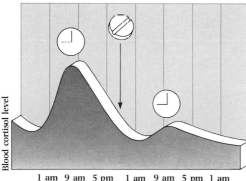

The integrity of the feedback loop between adrenals and pituitary can be tested with the steroid drug named dexamethasone. Given to a normal person at 11 pm the drug will lead to low cortisol levels at 9 am next day, *left*, showing that the pituitary has lowered its ACTH output and that the adrenals have made less cortisol.

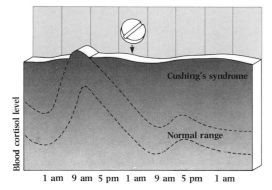

In Cushing's syndrome, cortisol levels are too high but the 9 am reading, *left*, may be within normal limits. Levels at midnight are, however, much higher than they should be. In borderline cases the drug dexamethasone is given to test the adrenals. If these glands are at fault this steroid will fail to suppress cortisol levels.

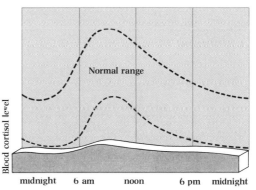

The cortisol rhythm is depressed in Addison's disease. Cortisol levels are low, but at midnight may be near normal in borderline cases. The rhythm is important to diagnosis, since a measurement at 9 am will reveal the low level. When the adrenals fail, the pituitary tries to stimulate them by making more ACTH.

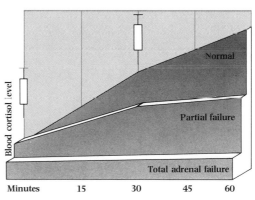

To confirm the diagnosis of Addison's disease, the hormone ACTH is injected and blood cortisol levels measured 30 and 60 minutes afterwards. Normal adrenal glands respond by making more cortisol than usual, but total adrenal failure produces no response. Partial adrenal failure or pituitary disease produces an intermediate response.

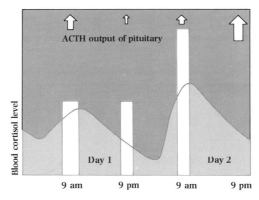

Prolonged treatment with steroids can reduce ACTH output and make the adrenals shrink. The drugs are usually given at 9 am and 9 pm (day 1). But at 9 pm the pituitary is most sensitive to steroids so ACTH output falls, switching off the adrenals and allowing them to degenerate. If all the steroids are given at 9 am (day 2) this effect is reduced.

▷diagnose. In such cases, measurement of cortisol levels is essential, but because of the circadian rhythm in cortisol output, a single high reading alone is not enough to make a diagnosis. At a minimum, measurements are needed at 9 am and at midnight. Only when both results are found to be above normal, and the rhythm abolished, is the diagnosis certain.

Addison's disease gets its name from the London physician Thomas Addison, who died in 1860, and is the reverse of Cushing's syndrome since it involves reduced corticosteroid production. Most cases are due to disease of the adrenal glands, but a few result from pituitary abnormalities. Patients with Addison's disease become very weak, lose weight and may have a craving for salt. They may vomit and become dehydrated. Their blood pressure falls and this can cut down the blood supply to the brain and make them feel faint. In the majority of cases, due to adrenal gland disease, the pituitary, in an attempt to correct the imbalance, becomes overactive and it also releases too much of another hormone which triggers over-production of the brown substance melanin—the pigment of a normal sun tan—in the skin, resulting in a darkening of the skin which is most marked in skin creases. Disruption of the normal 24-hour circadian rhythm of cortisol output is typical of Addison's disease and this fact is a valuable aid in diagnosis; in addition, cortisol levels remain consistently low throughout the 24 hours.

The adrenal rhythm is particularly relevant in the use of cortisone and other corticosteroid drugs in treating asthma, rheumatoid arthritis and other chronic diseases, and to the administration of similar drugs following transplant surgery. In all these conditions corticosteroids are used because they reduce

inflammation, or in the case of transplants, suppress the response which makes the body reject foreign tissue. Unfortunately, prolonged use of corticosteroids often brings about a host of problems, among them the abnormal fat distribution and collapse of the bones of the spine typical of Cushing's syndrome. The adrenal glands shrink and cannot respond to a stressful situation, such as a surgical operation, by producing more cortisol. This explains why steroid drugs can be dangerous if their doses are not kept to a minimum. Using the natural circadian rhythm, doctors can manipulate the drug dosage so it has the best effect. If all the day's steroid treatment is given in one dose at about 9 am, when the pituitary is least responsive to the drug, it will produce least interference with the feedback system. Theory and practice have certainly proved to coincide in the treatment of rheumatoid arthritis and it is hoped they will do so for other diseases.

In asthma there is a circadian rhythm so strong that even the sufferer is acutely aware of it. Even in the second and third centuries AD ancient physicians knew that asthma attacks are most common at night. In the seventeenth century it was thought that they were due to the body overheating at night, and only at the end of the last century did the discovery of an association between allergy and asthma offer a possible new explanation for these nocturnal attacks. Patients were believed to be reacting to feathers in their pillows or the house dust mite that lives in mattresses—agents to which asthma sufferers were less exposed during the day. It has also been suggested that the horizontal sleeping posture is the cause, but all these theories can be disproved by simple experiments. Nocturnal asthma occurs in patients without

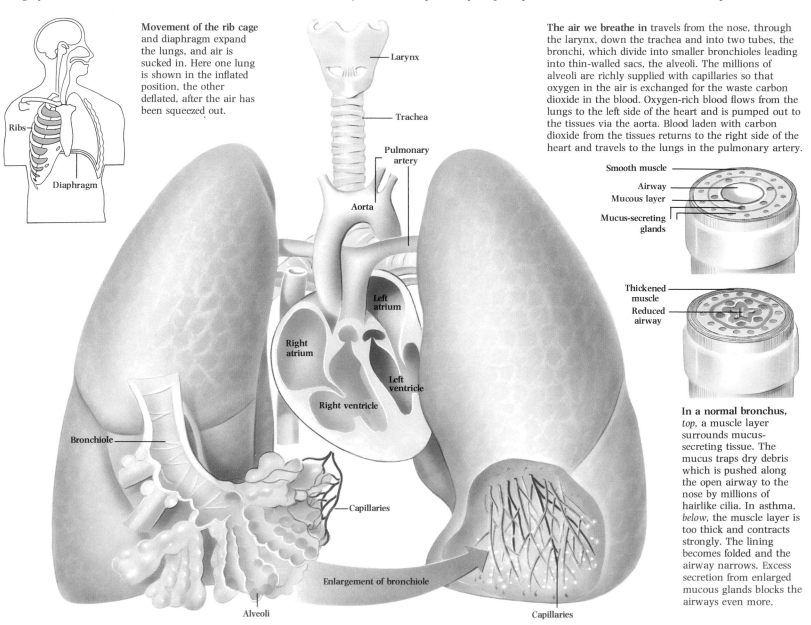

Movement of the rib cage and diaphragm expand the lungs, and air is sucked in. Here one lung is shown in the inflated position, the other deflated, after the air has been squeezed out.

Ribs

Diaphragm

Larynx

Trachea

Pulmonary artery

Aorta

Left atrium

Right atrium

Left ventricle

Right ventricle

Bronchiole

Capillaries

Enlargement of bronchiole

Alveoli

Capillaries

The air we breathe in travels from the nose, through the larynx, down the trachea and into two tubes, the bronchi, which divide into smaller bronchioles leading into thin-walled sacs, the alveoli. The millions of alveoli are richly supplied with capillaries so that oxygen in the air is exchanged for the waste carbon dioxide in the blood. Oxygen-rich blood flows from the lungs to the left side of the heart and is pumped out to the tissues via the aorta. Blood laden with carbon dioxide from the tissues returns to the right side of the heart and travels to the lungs in the pulmonary artery.

Smooth muscle
Airway
Mucous layer
Mucus-secreting glands

Thickened muscle
Reduced airway

In a normal bronchus, *top,* a muscle layer surrounds mucus-secreting tissue. The mucus traps dry debris which is pushed along the open airway to the nose by millions of hairlike cilia. In asthma, *below,* the muscle layer is too thick and contracts strongly. The lining becomes folded and the airway narrows. Excess secretion from enlarged mucous glands blocks the airways even more.

allergies and is not affected by posture, since it occurs just as often if patients spend the night sitting up in a chair.

The answer to the prevalence of asthma attacks at night lies in the true nature of the disease which has only recently been understood. In asthma the airways that lead air in and out of the lungs are abnormally sensitive. These tubes or bronchi are surrounded by coats of muscle which, when stimulated, contract too much, narrowing the airways almost to blocking point. In addition asthmatics produce excess amounts of mucus, a fluid which traps particles of dirt inhaled into the lungs so that they can be carried back up the airways in a constant stream which is regularly coughed up out of the lungs. In asthmatics this mucus is abnormally thick and sticky, so restricting the air flow even more. Even in people without asthma, a circadian rhythm occurs in the width of the bronchi. The tubes are at their widest between 4 and 6 pm, and at their narrowest on waking in the morning. The same rhythm is found in asthmatics, but its amplitude is much greater.

This circadian change in the width of the bronchi can be measured as the peak flow rhythm, the peak flow being the maximum rate of air flow a person can produce by blowing out as hard as he can. When the peak flow rate falls it means that the airways are narrowed, just as water comes out of taps more slowly if the pipes are furred. The mechanism driving the peak flow rhythm is still a mystery, but there are several likely explanations. The airways are dilated as a result of nerve messages from the sympathetic section of the autonomic nervous system—part of the set of reactions preparing the body to deal with stress—to help more air to get to the lungs. On the reverse side of the coin, the airways are constricted by nerve messages arriving via the parasympathetic nerves, and it may be that the rhythm results from the alternate activity of the two parts of the system, the balance being determined by a clock in the brain.

Another possibility is that the asthma rhythm results from the circadian rhythm in cortisol secretion by the adrenal glands. The reason behind this suggestion is that cortisone and similar drugs tend to widen the bronchi in asthmatics—an action described as bronchodilation—and help to cut down excess mucus production. It could be that the low nighttime level in natural cortisol output causes nocturnal asthma, but experiments suggest that this is not the case. The most plausible explanation is that, because adrenalin acts to widen the bronchi, the rhythm results from the rhythm in adrenalin production. The fall in adrenalin output during the night would allow the asthmatic airways to narrow and so bring on an attack.

The peak flow rhythm has become a useful tool for the treatment of asthma and many patients are learning to record their own peak flow rhythm at home. This enables asthma sufferers to recognize the early stages of an attack. If they notice severe falls in peak flow at night then this is a signal that their asthma has become unstable and that they need some treatment. The same practice is carried out in hospital if an asthmatic has to be admitted following a bad attack. Peak flow readings rise as the attack dies down, but large falls in peak flow at night are a sign that a relapse may be imminent. Thus the circadian rhythm provides a constant test of the sensitivity of the asthmatic airways—increased sensitivity means the risk of an attack and is heralded by severe nocturnal falls in peak flow rate. Sometimes asthma is difficult to diagnose because it only ▷

To **assess the width of their airways,** patients are asked to blow as hard as they can into an instrument which measures the maximum, or peak, flow of air out of the lungs, *left.* In asthma patients, regular measurements of peak flow reveal a circadian rhythm with lowest levels in the early morning and at night, *below,* which may be associated with asthma attacks. A similar pattern exists for people without asthma, but with much less variation between highest and lowest values. Nocturnal asthma seems to be an exaggeration of the normal circadian rhythm in the width of the airways.

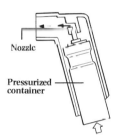

Routine treatment of asthma is with a drug released as a droplet spray from a pressurized aerosol, *left,* which is then inhaled, or with tablets. The drug works by imitating the effects of adrenalin and similar substances naturally produced by the inner, medulla region of the adrenal gland, which act to widen, or dilate, the airways of the lungs. Steroid drugs can also be useful in treating asthma because they dilate the airways, reduce excess mucus secretion and may also increase the sensitivity of the airways to other drugs.

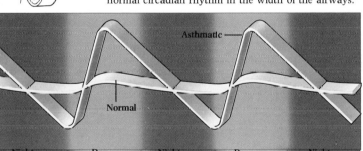

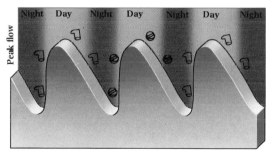

Effective treatment of asthma with drugs is difficult because of the practical problems of timing treatment to correspond with lowest levels in peak flow. Often patients wake up in the night with asthma attacks and need to take extra doses.

Shift work can be beneficial to an asthma sufferer. On the day shift peak flow is lowest at night, but when a worker goes on to the night shift his sleep-waking cycle is 12 hours out of phase with the normal pattern, *below.* This disrupts the clock that drives the peak flow rhythm and for a while the difference between the highest and lowest readings is drastically reduced, the minimum being when the asthmatic wakes at the start of the 'day'. The rhythm becomes synchronized with sleep and waking, but its amplitude does not reach a maximum until he returns to day working.

In hospital, asthma patients may be given drugs to dilate their airways continually via a drip into a vein in the arm. With constant administration, the nighttime falls in peak flow tend to be reduced, but they are not abolished.

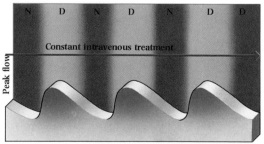

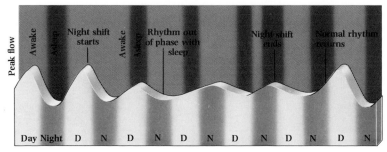

For an active asthmatic not in hospital, the best compromise between theory and practice is to take regular drug doses with an aerosol during the day and at night to take long-acting tablets which gradually release the drug into the blood. Nocturnal asthma attacks can thus be reduced.

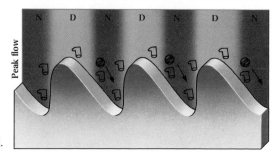

▷ causes symptoms at night and, because the lungs appear normal during the day, it may be mistaken for some types of heart disease, but a few days of recording the peak flow rhythm will usually clinch the diagnosis.

Like other circadian rhythms the peak flow rhythm responds to shift work. On changing to night shifts, the rhythm is disrupted for a day or two and its amplitude falls—a rare example of a beneficial effect of shift work. Patients with bad nocturnal asthma often find that their problem improves with a rapidly changing pattern of shift work, because the biological clock is disrupted and cannot stimulate the sensitive asthmatic airways. Because asthma is always worse during sleep and on first waking, if asthmatics go on to a night shift their asthma will become worse during the day.

The rhythm of asthma also affects its treatment. The drugs now given as tablets or pressurized aerosols for inhaling mimic the action of the sympathetic nervous system, to provide maximum stimulation of the asthmatic's defective receptors and relieve the spasm of the muscles surrounding the bronchi. Although effective, these drugs can be taken easily only during waking hours, not at night when they are needed most. To overcome this problem, slow-acting tablets taken at bedtime have proved helpful.

Interest is increasing in the potential importance of circadian rhythms in the treatment of other diseases as well, both by drugs and with the surgeon's knife. If they are to work, drugs must be taken into the body and transported to the parts of the body on which they are destined to have a useful effect. At the same time, some of the drug will travel to and be broken down (metabolized) by the liver. Usually this liver action diminishes the drug's effect, but the liver actually

converts some drugs into more potent forms. Drugs are eventually filtered by the kidneys into the urine, usually after the liver has metabolized them. All these processes may be susceptible to circadian rhythms, and may well be driven by individual clocks.

Most drugs are taken by swallowing, inhaling or injection, or are administered as suppositories. Because it is inconvenient to wake up to take them, treatment is usually at regular intervals during waking hours. In some cases, however, it is crucial for a doctor to consider whether this is the best thing. In diabetes, for example, insulin injections are used to replace deficient natural production by the pancreas. Diabetics have to mimic the natural rhythm of insulin output by anticipating the meals they will eat and controlling the quantity, quality and timing of their meals. Most find it best to take a big dose of insulin in the morning to cope with breakfast and lunch and a smaller evening dose to deal with dinner. Excessive insulin doses at night can be dangerous, for they may make the blood sugar level fall too low while the diabetic is asleep. Similarly patients with Addison's disease, who need to take corticosteroids, achieve the best results if they mimic the natural rhythm of the adrenal glands by taking most or all of their tablets at about 9 am.

Investigation of the liver and the kidneys reveals that both organs show circadian rhythms, so it is reasonable to expect a circadian rhythm in the way they deal with drugs. And if the rhythm is known, then drugs can be administered to maximum effect. Drugs broken down by the liver are best given at periods of low liver activity, but those that are converted to more active substances are most effective if administered when the liver is most active. In

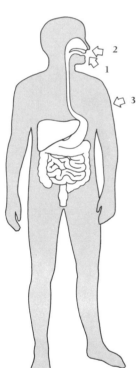

The most common method of drug administration is by mouth (1), but drugs taken in this way must be able to resist destruction by stomach acid and be easily absorbed through the intestine wall. The lungs have a rich blood supply, so some drugs can be inhaled (2). In emergencies, and for drugs destroyed in the stomach, an injection is made direct into the blood (3).

Several biological clocks may operate when the body deals with drugs. However they are given, all drugs are carried in the blood to the liver. Here, many drugs are broken down into inactive compounds or occasionally into more active ones, and liver cells show circadian rhythms in their activity. The end products of liver action are excreted by the kidneys which show circadian activity rhythms. The amount of a drug dose escaping the attention of the liver and kidneys is free to act on the end organ where it is needed; this organ may have a clock making it most sensitive to drugs at a certain time of day.

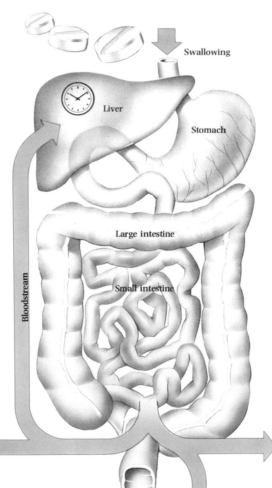

Swallowing

Liver

Stomach

Large intestine

Small intestine

Bloodstream

End organ

Kidney

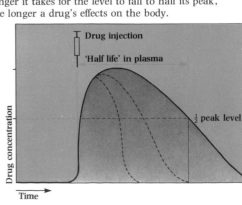

Elimination from bloodstream   Peak flow rate

'Half life'

The activity of a drug may show a circadian rhythm. Theophylline, taken by asthmatics to widen their airways and thus increase peak flow, is eliminated most quickly from the blood by the kidneys when given at night. This means that the drug's 'half life', the time it takes for the amount of a drug in the blood to reach half its highest level, is shortest at night when the drug is most needed by the patient to combat asthma attacks.

The breakdown of a drug by the body can be assessed by its stay in the blood. After injection, repeated blood samples are taken to measure the drug's concentration. This rises slowly as the drug leaves the stomach, then climbs to a peak. The level falls as the drug is broken down by the liver and/or excreted by the kidneys. The longer it takes for the level to fall to half its peak, the longer a drug's effects on the body.

Drug injection

'Half life' in plasma

½ peak level

Drug concentration

Time

the case of drugs that are got rid of by the kidneys without being metabolized, the timing of treatment should reflect the period of lowest excretion. The organs that react to the drugs may also show a circadian rhythm. The bronchi of the asthmatic are a prime example of this. Because the bronchi are least sensitive at night it is logical to give larger drug doses in the evening.

Studying the timing of drug action has generated results with great significance to the treatment of allergic diseases, such as hay fever and nettle rash, which is also known as hives or urticaria. In both of them substances, such as grass pollen and house dust (collectively known as allergens), to which patients are sensitive, react with antibodies. As a result of this link-up, the chemical histamine is released from most cells, making small blood vessels leak fluid to produce the red skin and the raised weals of nettle rash and the blocked or runny nose and streaming eyes of hay fever. The degree of a person's sensitivity to an allergen can be discovered by injecting a small quantity of it into his skin and measuring the size of the weal that results. If this is done at different times it is found that sensitivity is greatest at night and in the early morning.

Antihistamines are drugs that block the action of histamine, although they cannot stop its production. If antihistamines are given at various times of day, before skin tests with allergens are performed, a rhythm in the degree of protection that they give is evident. Antihistamines have their most prolonged action when taken at about 7 am. At 7 pm they do well at protection but not for as long. One serious side effect of antihistamines, particularly for drivers, is that they cause drowsiness but, applying the results of these experiments, smaller doses should be taken in the mornings, which reduces daytime drowsiness with little loss of protection.

Exciting prospects for the drug treatment of cancer are being based on body rhythms. Studies of artificially induced leukemia, a form of blood cancer, in mice show that there is a circadian rhythm in response to the drugs used to treat the disease. At about 6 pm these drugs destroy the rapidly dividing tumour cells most efficiently. Unfortunately the same drugs also destroy some normal cells, which limits their usefulness in treatment, and can make human patients and laboratory animals very ill. The tests on mice show, however, that the poisonous effects of the drugs on normal cells are greatest in the morning and so treatment at 6 pm is best all round. It is not yet known if similar rhythms exist in human cancer but, if they do, then careful timing could improve current treatments considerably.

Circadian rhythms could also hold the key to better results in transplant surgery. The greatest obstacle in this branch of medicine is rejection of the transplant, due to the activity of certain immune cells specialized to eliminate foreign materials from the body. These cells seem to operate in circadian fashion. The transplant is thus best carried out when the immune rhythm is at its low point, when the ability to start up the rejection reaction will be weakest. Corticosteroids and other drugs are used to suppress the immune reaction, often at the high price of troublesome and unpleasant side effects. Greater attention to the immune rhythm could make these drugs work better—in smaller doses and with fewer adverse reactions on the body—simply by giving them at the most appropriate time.

The time of day at which drugs are given may become important in treating cancer. Experiments on mice with leukaemia show that the cancer cells are most susceptible to drugs at about 6 pm. Conversely, this is the time when normal cells are least prone to being poisoned by drugs. If the same sort of rhythm occurs in man this may aid treatment.

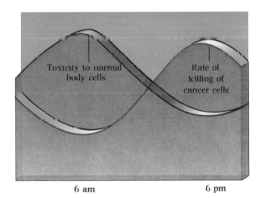

In human heart transplant surgery, *far right*, a small part of the recipient's old heart is left behind. This includes the pacemaker, a piece of tissue which controls the heart beat. The rhythms of donor and recipient pacemakers are slightly out of phase, showing that heart rate rhythm is probably driven by a clock in the pacemaker.

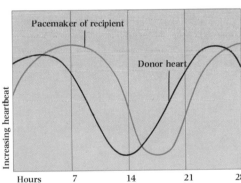

Time of transplantation may be crucial to the success of kidney transplants. A study on rats showed that the kidneys survived much longer if operations were performed at 8 pm. One explanation for this is that the operations coincided with the time at which the circadian rhythm in the immune response was minimal.

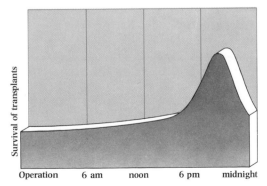

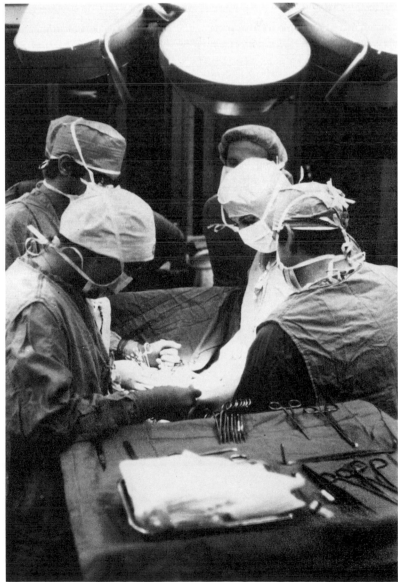

Rhythms of fate

Man is, at heart, a conservative creature. He may desire change in his life and environment but, when confronted with any drastic alteration, he panics. This inner terror is most real and most potent when change adopts the habit of disaster, leaving him with the feeling that his destiny is no longer in his own hands. It is man's sensation of inadequacy when confronted with the horrors of disease or drought, with earthquake and flood, with the death of those he loves, and with his own death, that has led him to try to explain—and if possible prevent—these happenings by summoning up the existence of forces that are not immediately obvious or measurable.

Many of the forces that man has come to believe in as the explanation and source of treatment for the unpleasant events of life are rhythmical or cyclical in nature, and all are controversial. Biorhythms, for example, are thought to operate cyclically within our bodies and brains to control our physical, emotional and intellectual performance, while the technique of biofeedback aims to give us power over the rhythmical activities of our brains by providing us with the machinery to record our innermost physiology. The medical art of acupuncture is based on the ancient belief that the energy that imbues us with life circulates round the body once every 24 hours. Both daily and yearly cycles are the essence of astrology, another of man's most ancient arts, and it is to the heavens that we look when we try to use the cycles of dark spots on the sun to explain the cyclical pattern of earthly weather.

Belief in these cycles and rhythms implies a large measure of faith because they cannot necessarily be measured scientifically. Such faith in rhythmic and cyclical forces is almost as old as man himself, since man has always been prey to death and destruction by natural disaster. The attitude we adopt today may be that nothing more precise could have been expected from prescientific man and that modern man should know better. We may view these forces with scepticism mingled, perhaps, with a sneaking feeling that there is a grain of truth in them somewhere, or we may take the view that the ancients were right after all, and that the trappings of modern life have blinded us to the potency of these rhythmical forces and that there are yet more to be discovered.

So who is correct? Are our lives determined by the cyclical movements of the heavens as interpreted by astrologers, or are we reacting to our inner biorhythms determined, like astrological influences, by our day of birth? Do natural disasters depend on the waxing and waning of sunspots? Can cancer be cured by acupuncture, which alters the cyclical flow of body energy, and can our rhythmical, electrical brain waves be controlled to rid us of anxiety and stress? The answer to most of these questions must be that we do not know. But because some of these rhythmical forces have been part of human belief for so many centuries, and because they are, for many, an ever-increasing part of modern medicine and psychology, they are well worth examining in depth.

In the study of rhythmical or cyclical events, but particularly those that seem to have a mystical component, statistical evidence is often employed to prove or disprove a theory. Every time we are told by the men and women of the media that there is a trend this way or that, we are reaping the results of statistical methods. The problem with such statistics is their precise interpretation. A sceptic would say that anything can be proved or disproved by statistics, so when we are trying to work out in our minds whether mysterious rhythmic and cyclical events are real, and are presented with statistical evidence, we must be as wary of the figures as of the phenomena.

To every owner of a human body, the machine that is the making of the man is the source and object of infinite speculation. But of all the phenomena displayed by the body, it is those that are rhythmical which prove to be among the most fascinating. We can all recognize with consummate ease the circadian, 24-hour cycle of sleeping and waking and could, if we wished, measure the rhythmic ups and downs of our body temperature or heart rate over any period of time, but it is impossible to convert our emotions into hard scientific data. Yet life does, indubitably, have its highs and lows, from the elation of success to the depths of failure; from the days when all seems right with our own personal world to those on which nothing goes well. Between these extremes are all those mediocre days, part good, part bad, on which there is little to record in the diary of events. So do these black, white and grey days fit into any sort of cyclical or rhythmic pattern and, if so, is it possible to predict them and to order our lives accordingly? Many people believe that the answer to this question is 'yes', and their faith has become known as the biorhythm theory.

Biorhythm theory began in the 1890s when a Viennese professor of psychology, Hermann Swoboda, noticed that the behaviour of his patients seemed to show a rhythmic pattern. This observation spurred him to make a meticulous study of his patients' case notes and from this study he arrived at the conclusion that behaviour fell into cycles with two distinct periods of 23 and 28 days. Putting his conclusions to practical effect, Swoboda devised a sort of slide rule from which patients could predict their 'critical' days. The 23 and 28-day cycles of behaviour were also 'discovered' quite independently by a German doctor, Wilhelm Fliess, at about the same time. Fliess was not a psychologist but

an ear, nose and throat specialist. Fliess based his study on examinations of the mucus-secreting cells that line the human nose, and his biorhythm theory depended on the periodicity of cell replacement. For Fliess, the significance of these cells was that they were supposedly male and female.

To the cycles of 23 and 28 days a German engineer, Alfred Teltscher, added another figure of 33 days, so the system of biorhythms now has three separate elements—a physical (P) cycle of 23 days, an emotional or sensitivity (S) cycle of 28 days and an intellectual (I) cycle of 33 days. These innate cycles begin, according to biorhythm theory, at the moment of birth and continue until death. The biorhythm hypothesis states that each cycle is divided into two equal phases and that a person's performance is best during the upper or positive half of the cycle and worst during the negative or lower half of the cycle. Our weakest, most vulnerable or 'critical' days are those on which a cycle crosses the zero line between positive and negative. If the theory is true then we should expect accidents and poor health on critical days in the physical cycle, depressions and bad personal relationships on critical days in the sensitivity cycle and poor judgment and learning on critical days in the intellectual cycle.

The total interpretation of these rhythms depends on the fact that they do not have the same periodicity. Because the cycles cross the zero line at different intervals there is only one day in about every six months on which all three cycles are critical together. This difference in periodicity would also explain, if the biorhythm theory is true, why we have so many ordinary days in our lives and so few extraordinary ones, because for most of the time the cycles are either moving away from or toward the zero line.

Physical

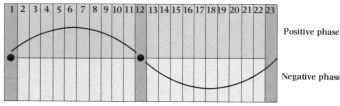

Positive phase

Negative phase

Emotional

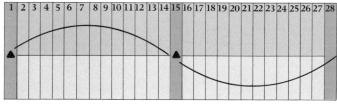

Intellectual

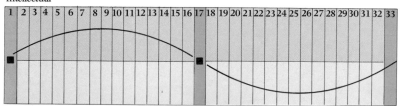

From the moment of birth and throughout life, three basic rhythms are believed to affect us. A 23-day physical rhythm supposedly governs our strength and endurance; a 28-day rhythm governs our sensitivity, moods and relationships; a 33-day intellectual rhythm controls our powers of judgement and thought. Each rhythm alternates regularly from a positive to a negative phase, becoming critical on the one day when it crosses over from one phase to another. A rhythm's phase on a particular day can inform us about ourselves. For example, when the physical rhythm is positive, strength and endurance are at a peak, so physical exertion can be attempted with confidence.

High positive days, low negative days and potentially dangerous critical days can all be predicted by using a biorhythm calculator, such as the Biomate, *left.* The serrated gear wheel at the bottom of the calculator turns the four dials, which show the date, and readings for each of the three biorhythms. To discover your biorhythms for a particular day in any calendar year, you must move the dial until the date of your birthday is aligned with the vertical axis line; the gear wheel is then disengaged. The settings for the biorhythm dials are found in the count list provided with the calculator, each biorhythm having a special setting according to how old you will be in that year. Each dial is turned, using a finger, until the right setting from the count list is lined up with the axis line. At this point the gear is re-engaged and the calculator will show your biorhythms for any day of the year. This biomate is set so that all three biorhythms are critical, which is a rare occurrence.

Racing along a highway near New Orleans, Jayne Mansfield, the film star, made a driving error, crashed into a truck in the opposite lane and died. Her biorhythms on that day, 29 June 1967, showed that she was physically critical a day after she had been emotionally critical, and a day before she was due to be intellectually critical. The fact that she died on the day when her biorhythms were so critical seems to support biorhythm theory. The record-breaking athlete, Sebastian Coe, won the final of the 1,500 metres at the Moscow Olympics on 1 August 1980. His biorhythms showed that he was emotionally critical, that he was physically low three days after being critical, and that he was intellectually low and approaching critical. According to the state of his biorhythms, Coe should not have won such a gruelling race, but the fact that he did win suggests that biorhythm theory is wrong. There are many similar examples that either support or contradict biorhythm theory.

The idea of a birthday-based biorhythm is one that has achieved considerable popularity, and it is now possible to buy a biorhythm calculator to work out your critical days so that you can order your life accordingly. The makers of one such calculator suggest, for example, that you should try to avoid driving whenever S and P criticals coincide and take particular care with business ventures on critical I and S days. Critical days in the P rhythm are those on which you are likely to be badly affected by drinking alcohol, while critical S days are bad for relationships. As you would expect, sporting performance peaks when the P rhythm is in its positive phase, but intellectual achievement is greatest when I is on the up. In business a combination of I and S in the positive phase augurs well for important deals, and the same duo helps give a gambler a lucky streak. People in creative jobs are advised to 'expect extraordinary ideas' on critical I days and to 'take notes for future use'.

All this sounds plausible indeed, and in Japan some companies even take steps to prevent workers from using machinery or driving trains on critical P days. But do biorhythms really exist? The statistical evidence is, at best, unconvincing, and much of it is based on samples too small to give significant results. In statistical studies of biorhythms it is found that the bigger the sample the less it conforms to the theory. In one test of 112,000 car drivers who had been involved in accidents—and for whom the biorhythms were worked out—there was no correlation between critical days on any of the three cycles and the dates on which the accidents occurred. According to one biorhythm protagonist, Arnold Palmer was in positive phase in all three rhythms when he won the British Open Golf Championship in 1962, and lost the American PGA

title two weeks later when low in all three. However, a detailed analysis of Palmer's achievements between 1955 and 1971 showed no significant correlation between his performance and his biorhythms.

In biological terms, one of the chief arguments against biorhythms is their incredible regularity. No known physiological rhythms are ever so well ordered and there is no evidence that biorhythms, when measured in subjects protected from all outside environmental influences, take up their own periodicity, or free-run. Another powerful objection to the biorhythm theory concerns the fact that all three cycles begin together on the day a person is born. On this day—which is undoubtedly stressful—all three cycles are set at 'critical' and, if this is so, you would expect many more babies to die at birth than in fact do so. And even after this, we all get through our triple criticals by some means. There is probably no truth in the biorhythm theory, but it might be an interesting exercise in self-analysis to try constructing your own chart, based on your physical, emotional and intellectual performance each day. Even if biorhythms do not work, belief in them may possibly serve the useful purpose of making us more self-aware and bringing us back to reality occasionally.

The improvement of mental and bodily well-being is also the aim of the technique of biofeedback which has a much more scientific background. There are countless processes continuously going on within our bodies of which we are normally totally unaware. The purpose of biofeedback is to make a person aware of these processes, many of which are rhythmic and cyclical, and to teach him to exercise conscious control over them.

The part of the body most intimately involved in biofeedback is the brain, the ▷

▷ final arbiter of all human actions, and it is the rhythms of the brain that were used in the first biofeedback experiments carried out by Dr Joe Kamiya in San Francisco in the 1960s. The human brain is a ferment of electrochemical activity, and the electrical pulses it generates are the physical clues to the work of its cells in sensory processing and the memorizing of information. The rhythms of the brain are recorded as electroencephalogram (EEG) traces, and produced by sticking a forest of electrodes to the scalp.

By means of EEG recordings it has been discovered that four distinct sorts of electrical rhythms take place in the brain. The first of these brain waves to be identified were the alpha rhythms, with a frequency of between 9 and 12 cycles per second, but sometimes between 8 and 13 cycles per second. The alpha rhythm is usually associated with a state of relaxed wakefulness. People undergoing a pronounced period of alpha activity describe their mental state as peaceful and sometimes mention a floating sensation. When your brain is producing alpha rhythms it is receptive, but you are not concentrating on any particular thought or activity.

Theta waves are about half the frequency of alpha waves, from 3.5 to 6.5 cycles per second, and rarely make up more than about 5 per cent of the total brain wave pattern. Theta waves are recorded most often when a person is drowsy or dreaming. Delta waves are even slower, with a frequency of 0.5 to 3 cycles a second, and are almost exclusively confined to the deepest stages of sleep. Nearly all the other electrical activity of the brain is classified as beta and its frequency ranges from 13 up to about 40 cycles a second. Beta is associated with alert behaviour and concentrated mental activity.

As so often in science, things are never clear and simple. Brain wave patterns are, in reality, a combination of the rhythmic and the irregular, and change so much from moment to moment that it is impossible to say with any certainty what a 'normal' brain wave pattern looks like. Despite this, the techniques of biofeedback can help a person to achieve a desired state of brain activity. The key to biofeedback, which has been applied with some success to the control of other body functions, such as blood pressure, muscle tension, skin temperature, sweating and heart rate, is to display to the subject monitored read-outs of the physiological function he wishes to control. Through a system of trial and error he then works at achieving the mental or physical state he is seeking, and can see the results of his efforts displayed before his eyes. The final accolade of biofeedback is awarded if he can achieve his goal without the machine. The technique has definitely shown encouraging results for people suffering from anxiety, who have few alpha brain waves.

Brain wave biofeedback has become a popular aid to meditation. Although it may not be true that experts of yoga and Zen have more slow alpha waves in their brain rhythms than the rest of us, mastering the art of relaxation is a worthwhile aim—with or without biofeedback—in the hurly burly of modern life. Mind control through transcendental meditation is claimed to increase the number of slow alpha and theta waves in the brain wave patterns. Research on the physiological effects of such meditation suggest that it does not result in an altered state of awareness, but in a mental state akin to sleep. This does not necessarily diminish its usefulness as an effective weapon against stress.

Like any machine, the human body is not perfect, and there can be no one

Yin

Yang

Yin and yang are the two opposing energies found in all things. They are both antagonistic and, at the same time, complementary. For example, the night is yin, the day is yang. The acupuncturist aims to restore the harmony between the yin and yang of the body.

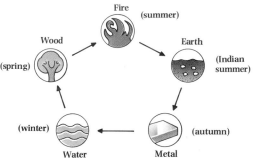

Fire (summer)

Wood

Earth (Indian summer)

(spring)

(winter)

(autumn)

Water

Metal

When a Zen Buddhist is meditating his body is relaxed, but his mind is alert. His brain is generating alpha, beta and theta rhythms and his skin shows a high electrical resistance. Without knowing it he is practising biofeedback, because he is learning about some function of his body or mind and controlling that function. Research into many forms of meditation has helped biofeedback therapists correlate the various states of awareness with the four principal brain rhythms: alpha, beta, theta and delta. As a result, people can now learn to relax their bodies and minds by finding out, with the aid of a therapist, how to develop their alpha and theta rhythms.

INCREASING YIN, WEAK YANG

3 am
1 am
5 am
Liver
Lungs
11 pm
Gall bladder
Colon
7 am
Triple warmer
Stomach
9 pm
9 am
Pericardium
Spleen
7 pm
Kidneys
Small Intestine
Heart
11 am
Bladder
5 pm
1 pm
3 pm

STRONG YANG, WEAK YIN

STRONG YIN, WEAK YANG

The five Chinese elements encompass all natural phenomena and together form the creative cycle of the seasons. Wood burns to create fire, which leaves behind the ashes of earth; from earth metals are mined, which become molten like water when heated; plants need water to grow and to make wood. These elements also qualify the 12 organs of the body through which the life energy, *chi*, courses every 24 hours. Starting at 3 am *chi* flows through the lungs and activates them. At 5 am it enters the colon and continues on its course, activating each organ in turn until it completes one cycle of this Chinese clock. Acupuncturists use this flow of *chi* in their diagnoses and treatments, and also the relationships of opposite organs on the clock: too much energy in the heart, for example, may upset the gall bladder and vice versa.

who can genuinely claim never to have had a day's illness in his life. The practice of medicine is thus as old as man himself and one of its most ancient branches is the Chinese art of acupuncture, which originated at least 5,000 years ago, but has only recently become popular in the West. All Oriental medicine is based on the twin towers of yin and yang. These are not tangible entities but tendencies in the movement of energy—yin is a tendency toward expansion, while yang is a tendency toward contraction. The theory is that all the rhythmical aspects of human physiology come about because of the constant flux that exists between these two extremes, pulling first one way, then the other. Thus yin and yang occur in a state of dynamic tension and interaction, but the end result is a state of perfect bodily harmony.

In the living world the forces of yin and yang, which underlie all aspects of Oriental life, are thought to operate by means of vibrating energy or *chi* which permeates all creatures. When a human body is healthy, the rhythm with which *chi* pulses is in harmony with the *chi* vibrations of the environment. Within the human body, life-giving *chi* energy circulates in specific systems, the *ching* or meridians. There are 12 regular meridians, each supplying particular body organs, and six 'extraordinary' meridians. Energy is thought to flow through these six emergency channels only when the normal 12 cannot handle the excess flow of energy generated by disease or disorder of any organ. Strategic points, located along all the meridians, and numbering about 1,000 in all, are the control valves that regulate energy flow and are the points for acupuncture treatment; anatomically the most important strands of the nervous system run along the meridians.

Acupuncture has a complex system of laws, but the one that stands out most clearly as a biological rhythm states that the *chi* circulates round the body once every 24 hours. Each of the 12 regular meridians—and hence their associated organs—is thought to have a two-hour period of maximum energy flow and a two-hour period of minimum flow. Using this knowledge, and their centuries of accumulated experience of when the disorders of any body system are likely to show the most acute symptoms, ancient Chinese medical practitioners drew up tables, still used today, of the most favourable times in each 24 hours for the treatment of disease by inserting needles into the appropriate point on a meridian to redistribute the excess energy.

Added to this clock is the knowledge of the opposite yin and yang properties of the various body organs. In acupuncture organs are treated in pairs, one member of each pair being a hollow, yang, organ such as the stomach, the other a dense, blood-filled yin organ such as the spleen. Thus if the kidney (yin) is stimulated the result is an improvement in the large intestine (yang). The treatment is best carried out in the evening because this is yin time and so coincides with the yin organ being stimulated. According to the acupuncture law of the five elements, the organs served by the 12 meridians are in six pairs and five of the pairs are equivalent to the elements wood, fire, earth, metal and water. The sixth pair are also 'fire' organs. Treatment is based on the interaction of the elements—for example, water (the kidney) quenches fire (the heart), so that if the kidney is sedated then the heart is stimulated.

No longer dismissed as 'quackery', but not heralded as a cure-all either, the practice, if not the theoretical background, of acupuncture is becoming ▷

The art of acupuncture is knowing where, in relation to which disease, to pierce the skin with needles. Each acupuncture point relates to a specific imbalance of yin and yang energies, which is diagnosed by the subtle assessment of the qualities of the pulse and the colour of the tongue and skin.

In acupuncture, the life energy that activates the 12 organs of the body is created by breathing and eating. It passes from one organ to the next along channels called meridians which, being neither arteries nor nerves, appear to have no place in the anatomy of the body. Each of the 12 main organs has one meridian associated with it, and each meridian is present on both the left and right sides of the body. Imbalances of yin and yang cause too much or too little energy to flow, thereby creating the symptoms specific to a disease. By carefully selecting the appropriate points, of which there are about 1,000, an acupuncturist can restore the harmony of the body's yin and yang.

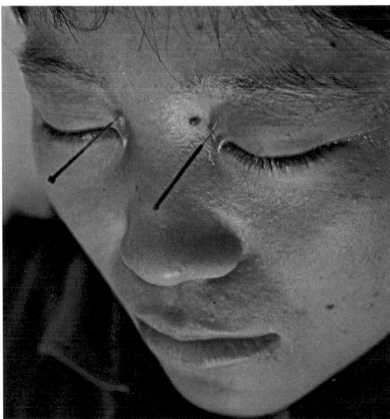

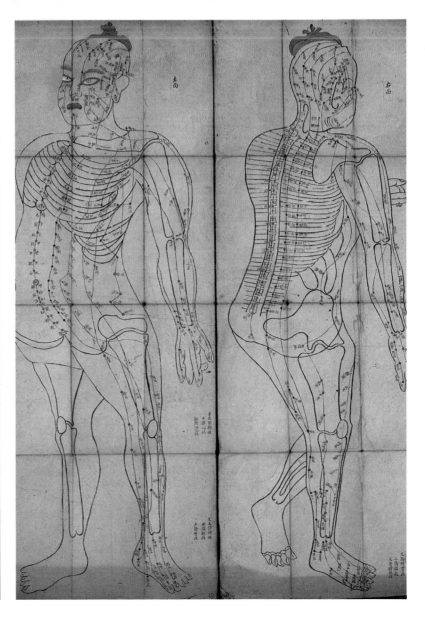

▷ accepted by many Western medical practitioners, particularly for the relief of chronic pain, for asthma and the treatment of stress-related disease. A few thin needles are inserted into points along particular meridians and either twisted or connected to electrical stimulators. The most recent research, carried out in both China and the West, suggests that acupuncture may work to relieve pain because it stimulates the pituitary gland at the base of the brain to release endorphins, natural morphinelike chemicals which numb pain.

Older even than acupuncture is the practice of astrology which, with astronomy, is one of the most ancient branches of science. There can be few of us who have never read our horoscope in the daily newspaper or do not know under which 'star sign' we were born; but what is the true basis of astrology and can it really foretell the future? Astrology has its basis in the cyclical movements that can be observed in the heavens. As for predicting tomorrow, any serious student would say that astrology is concerned more with defining trends than forecasting specific events, and that the horoscopes printed in newspapers and magazines are mere commercialization.

The deductions of astrology are based on the positions of the stars, sun, moon and planets in relation to the Earth. No astrologer would tell you that the Earth is the centre of the universe, this is just a convention that has persisted since ancient times. When studying the heavens the earliest astronomers and astrologers thought that the sky was a celestial sphere that revolved around the Earth. Taking the Earth as the centre of the sphere the sun seems to travel round it once each year along a regular path called the ecliptic. Following the same route as the sun, the moon and planets seem to trace a similar path in front of certain constellations, but stay within a zone extending 8 degrees on each side of the ecliptic containing the 12 constellations of the zodiac.

The full 360-degree circle of the zodiac is divided into 12 equal regions of 30 degrees. The dates for each sign are based on the position of the sun on 21 March, the spring equinox. In about 900 BC the sun appeared to enter the constellation Aries on that date, and this set the start of the zodiac circle. Astrology takes no account of the fact that the stars from which the signs were named have since taken up different positions relative to the Earth because of the 'wobble' or precession of the Earth's rotation about its axis.

Due to this precessional wobble, the Earth's spinning axis with respect to the stars shifts slightly. Astronomical calculations have arrived at a time-span of about 21,000 years for the Earth to return to exactly the same orientation in the heavens relative to any star, although astrologers take the figure to be 25,868 years. During this movement the Earth is thought by astrologers to pass through the influence of each sign of the zodiac in turn. Thus in the course of recorded history we have passed through the Age of Leo, which corresponds to the Stone Age around 9000 BC, and are now entering the Age of Aquarius which will last 2,160 years. Since Aquarius is associated with the dual concepts of science and humanity, astrologers predict that while man will become increasingly preoccupied with technological advancement, he will also strive towards gaining a victory for peace over conflict.

The apparent movements of the planets relative to the signs of the zodiac are among the cornerstones of astrology. For astrological purposes the sun and moon are included among the 'planets' and both are thought to be powerful

The sun and its retinue of planets are moving through space at a speed of 12.1 miles (19.4 km) per second toward the constellation of Hercules. As a result, the planets orbit the sun in spirals, the diameter of each spiral depending on the planet's distance from the sun Making a cross-section through this long body of the solar system is like stopping it in time and, like a horoscope, it tells the position of the planets at that one moment. The horoscope, *right*, is for the birth of the United States of America, when the Declaration of Independence was signed at Philadelphia at 3 am on 4 July 1776. Astrologers predict the fate of the United States and her people from the fact that Gemini was rising, and from the relationship of the planets to each other and to the signs they were in at that time.

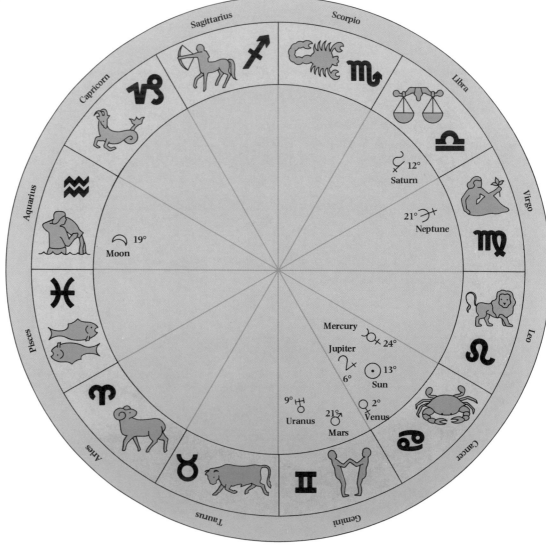

Horoscope of the USA
3 am 4 July 1776 at Philadelphia

influences, especially the sun. The farther a 'planet' is from the Earth, the more slowly it seems to move through the zodiac, so that while the sun takes a year to move in a complete circle relative to the Earth and the 12 zodiac signs, Pluto takes 248 years, and the moon only 28 days.

The most familiar of the cycles used by astrologers is the apparent yearly progression of the sun as it passes 'through' the dozen zodiac signs—in reality, of course, it is millions of miles in front of the constellations. It is from the position of the sun that you arrive at the fact that you were born, say, under the sign of Libra, because the sun is said to pass through Libra between 23 September and 22 October each year. To be born on the cusp means that your birthday is on the dividing line between two adjacent signs.

A person's horoscope, the prediction of his future and an analysis of his personality, is arrived at by more than just the position of the sun and can be thought of as a cross-section through the sun and its attendant planets as they spiral through space. In a true horoscope, therefore, the positions of the planets relative to the signs of the zodiac, and as viewed from Earth, are of great significance. The apparent angles of the planets, as they move in relation to one another and to the Earth, and calculated on the ecliptic, are the aspects. The aspects of the planetary groupings at the time of a person's birth are thought to be essential qualifiers of his 'vital energies', the forces that shape his whole life. When two planets are side by side, in conjunction, in a particular section of the zodiac, they have a combined influence. An angle of 60 degrees (a sextile) between planets, and its double, the 120 degree angle (a trine), are both considered to be beneficial influences, but angles of 90 degrees (a quarter) and

180 degrees (opposition) are disruptive.

As well as its yearly movement, the night sky seems to rotate around the Earth once every 24 hours. Like the yearly 'movement' of the sun, this diurnal rotation is divided into 12, the divisions being known as houses. Within each 24-hour period each planet appears to cross each of the 12 houses in turn. The houses are believed to have particular influences on an individual's life, from his personality and profession to his possessions and pastimes. In an individual horoscope the rising sign is also important. This is the sign of the zodiac on the eastern horizon at the moment a person is born.

There is no doubt that astrology is a fascinating subject, but also one about which it is difficult to be objective, because there always seems to be some part of an astrological assessment that 'fits' with reality. The statistical evidence seems to suggest that there is nothing in it—in one sample of 300 people there was, for example, no clear correlation between actual events and astrological predictions. In an attempt to bring astrology up to date, a new kind of astrology has been advanced. This cosmobiology dismisses traditional astrology but suggests that there is a statistical correlation between career choice or achievement and the positions of the planets. The French researcher Michel Gauquélin contends, for instance, that talented athletes are born when Mars is in the rising sign or in the mid-heaven—that is, has just passed its highest point in the sky. Others dispute their results and so the controversy rages on.

There is, however, no controversy about the fact that the cycles of the heavens are among the most impressive of all the cycles of nature, and it is hardly surprising that for thousands of years man has striven to associate these ▷

The annual revolution of the Earth around the sun is one of the main astrological rhythms, since a person's sun sign is decided by the date on which he was born. Because the Earth is orbiting around it, the sun appears to pass in front of each sign of the zodiac once every year. If a person is born between 20 February and 21 March the sun then is said to be 'in' Pisces as shown by the arrow, *below*, and the influence of the sun's vital force shapes the person's individuality in Piscean fashion. The planets also orbit the sun, but with different orbital periods, their influences changing as they pass from sign to sign. Jupiter, for example, orbits the sun every 11.8 years, spending nearly a year in each sign, so its influence is combined with the characteristics of the sign in which it happens to be.

Jupiter and Saturn were both in the middle of the sign of Taurus when John Lennon was born on 8 October 1940. This conjunction of the two planets occurs approximately every 20 years, since this is the average time of their two orbital periods. When they came together for their next conjunction, in the sign of Capricorn in 1960/61, Lennon was beginning to write, with Paul McCartney, the songs that were to make the Beatles famous. The following conjunction occurred in late 1980 and, just as Lennon was emerging once again into the public eye, he was murdered. The cycle of these successive conjunctions indicates a new start in a relationship and new social adjustments, both of which Lennon was embarking upon, but it is not the cause of the events that occurred.

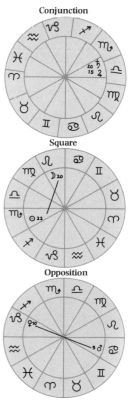

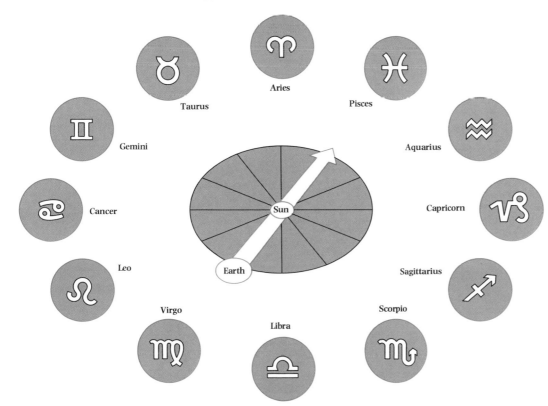

Aries

Taurus

Pisces

Gemini

Aquarius

Cancer

Capricorn

Leo

Sun

Sagittarius

Earth

Virgo

Scorpio

Libra

As planets orbit the sun at different speeds, they regularly make specific angles, or aspects, with the Earth and each other. Planetary aspects present at birth are shown on one's horoscope, and are part of the basis of astrologers' predictions. When planets are within 8° of one another in the sky, a conjunction occurs, *top right*. The planetary influences modify each other and signify the start of a new cycle. When planets form a right angle with Earth, the aspect is square, *middle right*, and the result may be disruptive, although determined people may derive energy from it. When planets form a straight line with Earth they are opposed, *right*, and although their influences complement one another, tension is usually created.

Conjunction

Square

Opposition

▷cycles with his own destiny. One of the astrological 'planets'—the sun—provides us with yet another natural cycle that seems to influence our lives. The ancient Chinese were probably the first people to notice that the dark spots visible on the sun seem to come and go. The first 'modern' astronomer to see these sunspots was Galileo, who carried out his work in the early seventeenth century, but the most thorough investigation made before the present century was by the German amateur astronomer Heinrich Schwabe in 1843. Since that time scientists and non-scientists alike have searched for a connection between the rhythmic appearance and disappearance of sunspots and cycles and the occurrence of events on earth such as earthquakes, droughts and floods.

Even before Schwabe's discovery that sunspots occur in 11-year cycles, the eminent English astronomer, William Herschel, had noticed that the numbers of spots varied, and in 1801 he suggested that the market price of wheat was closely correlated with sunspot numbers. Over the short-term period studied by Herschel this may have been true, but there was no correlation over a longer period. Since that time the quest for a relation between sunspot cycles and earthly events has been a curious one, and for every suggestion confirmed, several others have fallen by the wayside. The obvious reason for this is that two cyclical patterns may appear to be marching in step for a while, then move out of phase. The other is that human nature finds comfort in connections which explain events we cannot control.

Throughout the second half of the nineteenth century the fact that sunspots do come and go in a more-or-less regular 11-year cycle was common knowledge. Clear associations between sunspot cycles and magnetic storms on earth had been recorded and have since proved to be totally valid. The establishment of this connection led, however, to an explosion of supposed associations. In this burst of enthusiasm almost any cyclical occurrence could be used to play the sunspot game. Periodic epidemics of Asiatic cholera; mass uprisings around the world; the ups and downs of the world's financial markets; temperatures in tropical regions; wind direction in Argentina; the rabbit population of England; the levels of Lake Victoria; the depths of the Nile and the Thames; monsoons in India; soil temperatures in Scotland—all have been linked to the sunspot cycle at one time or another.

Some of these proposed links had a reasonable basis in fact, while others were totally arbitrary statistical associations with no rational back up. All of them were eventually disproved. Even today there is the occasional suggestion that stock market cycles have something to do with sunspot cycles, but these must be dismissed with the scorn they deserve. In the 1970s, a book was written suggesting that a complex chain of events involving sunspot cycles would lead to a massive series of earthquakes in 1982, when all the planets of the solar system will be within a 60 degree span on the same side of the sun. The combined gravitational effect, named the Jupiter effect, will, it was argued, come at a peak in the 11-year sunspot cycle and result in an especially high degree of solar activity. This will apparently alter the Earth's rotation and cause a devastating series of earthquakes in California. The idea rapidly captured the public imagination, but has since been retracted by its leading author.

Although earthquakes may not be influenced by events on the sun, there are some links between solar activity and earthly happenings that cannot be

dismissed so lightly. Sudden releases of magnetically pent-up energy, or solar flares, send out streams of high-energy particles, intensified X-rays, ultraviolet light and other forms of electromagnetic radiation. These charged particles race through space. Some collide with the earth's atmosphere and, through a series of complex reactions, create the beautiful and awesome spectacle of the aurora borealis or northern lights. The same emanations initiate geomagnetic storms that disrupt radio communications and cause power blackouts.

The frequency of these solar flares tends to ebb and flow roughly in phase with the 11-year sunspot cycle. The most intense and potentially dangerous flares—those that cause 'super' geomagnetic storms—occur mostly in the declining phase of the sunspot cycle, several years after sunspot numbers have reached their maximum. The sun reached a peak in the current sunspot cycle in late 1979 and early 1980 and will be in its declining phase in 1984. There is a real threat that intense solar flares will cause disruptive geomagnetic storms during this period.

As well as the sudden release of energy and particles in the form of solar flares, the sun continually issues forth a stream of charged particles, known as the solar wind. On earth, moderate magnetic storms seem to occur at 27-day intervals and this is roughly the same as the rotation period of the sun as viewed from earth. It has been discovered that openings in the magnetic field of the sun's outer atmosphere or corona, allow the escape of high speed solar wind particles. These coronal holes thus 'point' towards the earth once every 27 days, which explains the cycle. In addition, coronal holes tend to be more prominent during the declining phase of a sunspot cycle.

If events on the sun can cause magnetic storms on earth is there any truth in the rumour that sunspot cycles influence our weather and climate in a more general way? Since 1976, when it was conclusively shown that the sunspot cycle has not always been regular in the past, the search for the answer to this question has become more urgent. During the period 1645 to 1715, for example, practically no sunspots were observed and auroras and other earthly manifestations of strong solar activity were infrequent. This was, however, the time of the 'little Ice Age', so there may have been some connection. It is now known that over the past 7,000 years there have been many interruptions in the solar cycle, but it is not certain whether they have been responsible for the undoubted fluctuations in our climate.

After each 11-year sunspot cycle the magnetic field on the sun reverses, producing a 22-year magnetic cycle, which may prove to be more fundamental than the 11-year one. Certainly a striking and well-documented correlation exists between this 22-year cycle and widespread drought in the western United States. Studies on tree rings have successfully traced this correlation back to the seventeenth century.

Most investigators of the relationship between events on the sun and those on the earth view the connections with cautious optimism mixed with a liberal dose of necessary scepticism. But there is no arguing with the truth that the sun is a rhythmic body. The quest for a solar link-up has recently acquired a new respectability and sophistication, so the future may give us an entirely new perspective on our relationship with the sun's rhythms which will allow our climate to be more accurately predicted.

Sunspot numbers rise and fall every 11.1 years on average, and many attempts have been made to correlate events on earth with them. A Russian scientist, A.L Chizhevsky, studied many such cycles and found a corresponding cycle in the mass movements of people. In the year or two before peak sunspot numbers occur, people are excitable, nations are aroused to their greatest achievements, and revolutions, strikes and wars occur. Twentieth-century examples are the student riots and workers' demonstrations in Paris in 1968, *left*; the Russian Revolutions of 1905 and 1917; the British General Strike of 1926; the Spanish Civil War in 1936, and Iran's revolution in 1979.

Huge amounts of high-energy particles are released from the sun at times of peak sunspot numbers. With X-rays and ultraviolet light, these particles stream through space to interact with the earth's upper atmosphere, causing it to fluoresce. The night sky over the polar regions lights up in a display of bright colours—the aurora borealis of the northern hemisphere, the aurora australis of the southern hemisphere.

A sense of rhythm

Within an hour of birth babies flex their limbs and move their heads in approximate time to the rhythms of the human speech they hear around them. If a different language is used the actual movements of the babies alter slightly but the rhythm of their movements changes to match the language that is being spoken. This fascinating discovery was made in 1974. It is still not known when the sound of a child's native language becomes so firmly locked into his make-up that the switch from one rhythm to another is no longer automatic. What is certain is that human babies begin learning language—and with it culture—from the moment of birth on, and that they first do so through the rhythms of movement. Babies do not respond in this way to music of any kind, nor to random nor regular tappings.

As well as responding to cultural influences the human body also responds powerfully to the rhythms of the universe, to day and night and the march of the seasons. Most important of these cosmic rhythms are the 24-hour or circadian ones which set the pattern for day-to-day life. By the time a child is three months old circadian rhythms have become part of his physiological constitution, but the exact beat of these rhythms is determined by the cultural environment in which the child is reared. The result of this is that we all respond in roughly the same way to daily and seasonal change, but it is our cultural rhythms that give us an inner sense of feeling 'at home' in certain circumstances and ill at ease in others.

Just as surely as our bodies work according to rhythmic principles, so too do human societies. Cities are social clocks of great accuracy, with morning wakings, raucous noons, declining evenings punctuated by spurts of activity around midnight and, finally, sleep. These rhythms are repeated daily but vary in detail according to the day of the week or the season of the year.

The city is only one sort of cultural environment to which the body can adapt, and throughout our lives we constantly change according to our physical and cultural surroundings. But one of the ironic ambiguities of belonging to a culture is that we can consciously seek out synchronization with the rhythms around us and, at the same time, override some of our body rhythms dictated by the cosmos, such as the rhythm of sleeping and waking. The result is that we can understand when we are in synchrony with the rhythms of the universe and with the rhythms of our own bodies, and seek that kind of harmony, but we can also disregard that synchronization or deliberately put it out of our minds as we obey cultural mores or psychological demands.

The rhythms of the universe are not innately good or bad, it is cultural evaluations that label them—and cultural rhythms too. This means that in the end we all have to make these evaluations and take up a moral position with regard to ourselves, our neighbours and our environment. We can be like the yogi and search for 'oneness' with the universe. Or we can go to the opposite extreme and seek to control or exploit our natural and environmental rhythms (whatever the cost to the environment or the well-being of others). Some cultures, particularly those of the Western world, encourage us to overlook our natural rhythms as we search for some cultural ideal—or merely aim to be like everybody else. Because we have the power to disregard our body rhythms, and those of the world around us, we are masters of our own destiny. We can cooperate with or oppose those rhythms, or we can choose any number of intermediate strategies of life.

Culture penetrates every dimension of our lives. Even the most obvious characteristics which we share with our fellow members of the animal kingdom, such as our need to eat, reproduce or sleep, are in fact closely linked with the cultural requirements of the society in which we live. It is for this reason that actions which fall outside our particular social norms make us uncomfortable. One good reason for the discomfort we experience in foreign situations and environments is that we do not know exactly what is expected of us. Even more significant is the fact that our movements are not cued to the language, nor to the other rhythms around us. Speaking your own tongue after you have been abroad for a long time seems so delicious simply because your movements can again be ordered in the way you first learned them. We can all learn to speak other languages and adopt the mores of other cultures as if they were our own, but most people are most at ease in their 'native' surroundings.

In all cultures there are 'owls' and 'larks'—people who operate best either at night or in the morning. These habits and inclinations are cued to our body metabolism and so cross cultural boundaries, but different cultures make us respond to our basic rhythms in different ways. Most farming people, for example, begin work at dawn, or even before, and in such cultures owls are at a disadvantage. In an office operating flexible hours, on the other hand, the owls can work things to their benefit. Owls come into their own in any culture that adopts the use of artificial light because they can stay up later at night in a way that is not feasible for people reliant on the sun alone as a source of illumination.

The idea of a 'good night's sleep' is essentially a Western one and many

Westerners make themselves miserable because they cannot sleep at the particular time, and for the prescribed number of hours, that their culture—and their parents—tell them they should. The Tiv people of Nigeria, however, divide the night into three sleeps and expect to wake first around midnight, again at about 3 am and yet again just before dawn. For the Tiv, as for everyone else, personal biological rhythms are thus made to adjust to cultural rhythms. Many other people of the world sleep only when they are sleepy.

As with sleeping, our culture tells us when to eat, what we should eat and how our food should be prepared. Physiologically the human stomach contracts powerfully every 75 to 115 minutes both day and night, yet almost no human beings eat so often, and, at the other end of the scale, comparatively few adults eat only when they are hungry. The number of meals eaten in a day, and the timing of meals, conforms to many different patterns. In some European cultures four meals are prepared and eaten during the day—an Englishman once invited an American to tea and was taken aback by the response, 'I never eat between meals.' Most Americans eat three meals a day, most Asians eat two—one in the morning, the other in the evening. Some West African peoples produce one huge meal in the late afternoon then finish up the left-overs in the course of the next morning. Other societies allow, or even encourage people to have snacks whenever they feel hungry, yet others forbid it. An enormous amount of psychological motivation is needed to alter the rhythms of eating to which the body has become accustomed once cultural conditioning has done its work.

Both bodily and cultural rhythms work together to affect our moods. Most

people imagine they are in some sort of general command of their moods and do not notice small-scale mood changes, but when they keep meticulous diaries and records of the way they feel, it is sometimes possible to discern roughly rhythmical cycles of mood changes over many days. Scientists have not yet determined the major rhythms of these mood cycles, nor their causes, but certainly many people believe in them and some religions or pseudo-religions have tried to standardize them. The only known cycle which undoubtedly affects moods is the female menstrual cycle.

Many cultures allow their members to do things that have a considerable influence on the body's natural rhythms and many even dictate that such actions are carried out. Drugs, including alcohol, have a powerful effect on natural rhythms, including those of mood, and while some cultures forbid the use of all drugs to men and women of all ages, others encourage them, either overtly or unknowingly. Alcohol is a drug whose effects are both physiological and cultural. Cultural influences dictate how alcohol should make us feel—at a party, for example, we expect it to make us elated—but the alcohol itself affects our body rhythms such as our pattern of sleeping and dreaming. The use of these and other drugs—for example, the nicotine in cigarettes—is totally under cultural control. People of different ages or rank in society may be allowed quite disparate access to drugs, and the drug chosen may depend on one's age group. In Africa, for example, young men were traditionally allowed only a little beer—the bulk of the supply went to the old men and sometimes the old women of the society.

One of the most widespread and potent ways by which the basic body rhythms have been altered is through the use of the birth control pill. Whether or not a woman should take the pill is determined by medical and religious considerations. Some of the medical objections to it arise because doctors are wary about the damage that may be wrought by a long-term manipulation of the basic body rhythm of ovulation.

Natural body rhythms are also disrupted by stress. The stress of an illness or some other psychological pressure, the stress of unaccustomed physical effort or of social disaster may all bring about many changes. Even altering our daily routine is stressful, and travel to east or west puts more strain on the body systems than travel to north or south simply because it involves a disruption of our biological clocks. Furthermore, modern culture allows us to make these changes at great speed. In the days before air travel, when people crossed the Atlantic in liners and allowed their internal biological clocks to adjust day by day, there was no such thing as jet lag. So it may be that the more complex a culture becomes the more strain is imposed on human rhythms.

The internal rhythms of all animals, including man, are influenced or entrained by the rhythms of the environment, and without these external pacemakers a creature's internal rhythms will free-run and may become quite random. The way in which we receive the essential information about our surroundings is through our sense organs. Thus a flock of birds is made a flock by entrainment, each animal using delicate sensory mechanisms to pick up environmental cues, then adjusting its activities accordingly. Herding animals entrain their rhythms and so do people—even newborn babies take the rhythm of the adult speaking voice.   ▷

It has become culturally necessary in Western society to sleep only at night and for a prescribed number of hours, instead of falling asleep when we feel drowsy. Cat naps during the working day, *above*, are often frowned upon, but many societies condone 'siestas'.

Alcohol severely disrupts the body's natural rhythms. Hunger, sleep and temperature rhythms are thrown out of gear and the brain's normal perception of passing time is upset. Social and business drinking can become an integral part of the day's rhythm, but when alcohol becomes a problem, *right*, the timing of the next drink dictates the pattern for the whole day.

In all societies the day revolves around mealtimes, *left*, although the number of meals and their timing are usually influenced by class, occupation and religion. High tea in the north of England is often as early as 5 pm, while a restaurant dinner at midnight is normal in Latin cultures. The weekly pattern of Jewish Friday night dinners and the fasting month of Ramadan, however, are firmly rooted in religion.

▷ To observe the entrainment of human rhythms at first hand, stand on a busy street corner and watch the movement of traffic, each driver adjusting to the presence of others and each moving precisely attuned to his fellow road users. Although an accident may occur because of equipment failure, most road accidents arise when the rhythm is broken, either by miscueing, or by errors in perception or action by one or more drivers. Mile for travelled mile, the safest sort of driving is on freeways, motorways or *autobahns*, because these roads are controlled to cut down the number of variables. Speeds on freeways may be faster, but faults of rhythm, and hence accidents, are less likely. When they do happen, however, such accidents are likely to involve more cars.

Ballroom dancing is another good example of the way in which one human being can take the rhythm of another. To the accompaniment of music, which provides the basic beat—the fundamental external stimulus to which the body rhythms respond—the couple make their way around the floor, usually with the male partner in the 'lead' and the female partner 'following'. The skill of the dancers is directly related to the clarity with which the lead dancer can give signals and how skilful the following dancer is in responding to them. The more competent a dancer the more cues he can deal with, the ultimate being the intricate interrelated movements of ballet dancers.

Adopting the rhythm of another person is not limited to physical movements but can also be followed on an intellectual or emotional plane. A lecturer can, for example, sense whether the audience is following his argument, whether he is presenting his ideas too sketchily or too fully, whether those ideas are too difficult or too simple, and whether he is speaking too fast or too slowly. In the best lectures, as in the best theatrical performances, the lecturer or actor gets into conceptual synchrony with his audience. It is this that helps to create an inspired performance, and high points in the theatre always involve a rhythmic interchange which entrains the bodies and minds of the performers with those of their audience.

All human groups impose upon themselves a measure of social restraint but entrainment can work powerfully to break down the barriers of self control. Crowd phenomena, such as riots, arise when people take the rhythms of those around them, and are intricate examples of the way in which we can be entrained by the emotional rhythms of those around us and succumb to an emotional outpouring by means of rhythmic movements.

In our daily lives we can all notice examples of dysrhythmia, times when our fellows either fail to take our rhythms or do not set good rhythmic beats for us to follow. The pace of activity and the rhythms of the very young are, for instance, different from those of adults between the ages of puberty and senility. For a parent in a hurry, being patient while a child ties her shoelaces can almost qualify as sainthood and the natural tendency is, of course, to take over and do the job yourself. The child cannot, however, be expected to do up her laces quickly because she is inexpert in the complex pattern of movements and sequences the task involves. More than this, the basic rhythms she uses are quite different from those employed by an adult.

In a similar way, it is a common experience to stand behind an old lady in a queue who takes too long to find the exact coins she needs in the small purse lost somewhere in the depths of her shopping bag. As we get more and more

exasperated we fidget while she gets the contents of her bag together again before moving on. Old people boarding buses are often out of synchrony with the movements of other people and can disrupt our own performance, cause themselves embarrassment and even spark off a display of anger by the bus driver, the conductor or other passengers. Unconsciously we all adjust to take account of the different ages of the people around us, but once we reach a threshold of some sort—and this has not yet been seriously studied—we become aware that the other person is out of phase with our rhythms. This realization may be expressed as annoyance, pity or any sort of emotion in between.

Dysrhythmia may also be involved in illness. One of the reasons that hospitals are not better places to be is that, of necessity, the rhythms of the patients and the staff are set by different pacemakers. Illness of any sort upsets the human body rhythms and the patients are, almost by definition, dysrhythmic. The doctors march to their own busy schedules, while the nurses have the thankless—and unthanked—task of trying to adjust the rhythms of the patients to those of the doctors, and to the daily round of hospital activity. Moreover, nurses often have to work different shifts week by week, so their own body rhythms may be disrupted. Such disjointed, unconnected rhythms make it hard indeed for patients to realign their body rhythms. Once a patient leaves hospital he may find it equally hard to readjust his rhythms to those of the healthy people who now surround him.

In the field of mental health, one of the most promising aspects of research involves investigation of the ways in which diseases, such as autism, may display complex forms of dysrhythmia. Autistic children are either unable or unwilling to interact with other people as normal children do. They do not take cues from others and refuse to interact with their neighbours, often seeming as if such interaction is intensely painful. These children seem to be able to recognize no external pacemakers, which puts them out of phase with the rest of society, and the absence of such pacemakers also lets their various body rhythms free-run out of phase with one another. Such complicated dysrhythmia, arising from a lack of entrainment from external pacemakers, is also a symptom of schizophrenia. Psychiatrists and researchers into mental health are only just beginning a programme of research which promises to tell us much more about the way in which mental rhythms can be disrupted, and it is likely that by the end of the 1980s we will have a better understanding of the role of rhythms in individual and social health.

From the moment of birth onwards, external pacemakers help to create the rhythms to which human beings respond internally. At birth, babies have 50 to 60-minute cycles of rest and activity but, unlike adults, the rate at which their hearts beat does not vary between night and day. By the sixth week of life external factors—presumably both human and non-human—have set the rhythms for the child's bodily existence.

Physiologists claim that external factors, such as the patterns of family living, help to put the infant's rhythms into motion and these factors include the attitude of the parents towards feeding during the day and the night, the temperature and noise levels in and around the home and parental patterns of activity and rest. The synchronization of the child's rhythms with both the ▷

Group action is usually organized into a coordinated rhythm by one individual. This may be conscious as in an orchestra or choir where the conductor's role, *above*, is to set the pace and control the rhythm, or unconscious as in riots, *right*, when contagious emotion spreads to the masses from one or two leaders, causing an apparently spontaneous eruption. Similar though less involuntary cooperation is effected by the strict rhythms of a military band. Marching in step imposes discipline, and a sense of unity and purpose, upon a large body of men, who are encouraged by the synchronized movements to suppress their own individuality in favour of group identity. Two people walking along together tend to 'fall into step' and may even synchronize their breathing, to establish a rapport. In competitive sports, one individual sets the pace, which is taken up by the rest of the team or field and reflected in the crowd's movements. Even social and political trends follow the pattern mapped out by a leader.

▷ social and the natural world requires responses to such external pacemakers. The evidence is that without these entrainment forces the child's rhythms become increasingly random—only by entrainment can the infant organize his unordered rhythms to accord with those of his family and of the community of which he is a part.

The human infant is a helpless being who cannot survive unless tended by adults. Given his innate capacity for entrainment, the ministrations of adults provide the child with his first experience of coordination with human movement. So the mother's rhythms become an integral part of the child's experience of growing up and, along with other environmental rhythms, become built into the fabric of his internal physiology, making his 'mother rhythms' as natural as the rhythms established by light, temperature and gravity.

Rhythmic communications are closely associated with a baby's lifestyle in his first few months after leaving the womb. In many African societies, babies are carried on their mothers' backs. Tiv mothers in central Nigeria put their babies in slings. The baby's legs straddle the mother's back and the cloth sling is wrapped tightly round the child so that he can ride along as the mother goes to and fro from the fields or to market.

Among the !Kung Bushmen of southern Africa, a baby is carried in a sling at the mother's side. The baby looks out in the same direction as the mother and is approximately at her height from the ground so that the mother's actions are more or less duplicated in the child's body rhythms. In most Western societies, babies are not carried far by anybody, so they must learn interactional

synchrony in other ways; but taking their cues from African mothers, many Western mothers have adopted the practice of carrying their babies in slings. For a considerable part of the day, many eight or nine-month African babies are turned over to children of about ten. The ten-year-old carries the baby, tends to his needs, sees that he does not roam too far and is near his mother when he is hungry. Babies acquire a great deal of cultural information from older children in this way.

As they learn to creep, crawl and walk children take more and more of the rhythms of society into their own bodies. Although each of us has a characteristic gait, for example, there are cultural differences in the exact ways in which people walk: the way they pick up their feet, the precise order in which some of the muscular contractions are performed, the way in which the foot hits the ground, the manner in which the arms swing and how the shoulders are held. During the 1940s and 1950s, a characteristically English masculine walk depended on reducing the amount of movement in the hips. To prevent the hips from swinging as you walk it is necessary to lower your hip bones and shorten your stride. At the same period, a typically masculine walk for an American was associated with broad shoulders. To adopt this sort of gait you have to stand tall, raise your hips and push your breast bone up as high as possible. To add to this, the elbows are turned out slightly, the arms swung vigorously. The difference between these two styles of walking led the English to think that Americans walked like gorillas, while the Americans thought that the English minced. Both were trying to walk like 'real' men, but the resulting body rhythms communicated different messages.

When a baby spends the day strapped closely to his mother's back, side or breast, her natural rhythms become an integral part of the child's early experience. The soothing pulse of her heart, the gentle sway of her walk and the regular swinging of her body as she goes about her daily work, combined with the reassurance of close physical contact, become instilled into the baby's consciousness. The Malinke tribe from West Africa, *left*, who have a rich musical tradition, spend the first few months of life tucked snugly astride their mothers' stomachs. As in most cultures, exposure to music begins very young so that every child develops the taste for rhythm from the start. In some societies, particularly in Southeast Asia, children learn to dance almost as soon as they can walk, so that the rhythms of their own culture become 'second nature', and only when confronted with a different set of rhythms, do they become consciously aware of their own.

Encouraged by group skipping games, roller skating, dancing, basketball and other games, children soon learn that it is more fun and easier to move rhythmically. In later life they will use these rhythms not only in their leisure time but to move in harmony with their workmates. Children are not usually fully coordinated until the age of 12. Those who have difficulty moving rhythmically find visual stimuli more helpful than aural ones, as they can often improve their coordination through imitation.

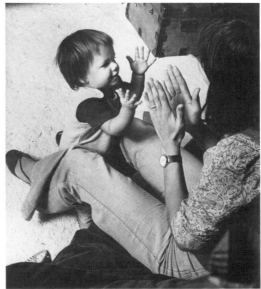

Clapping games are a popular and effective way of teaching children progressively complex rhythms, *left*. 'Pat-a-cake', for example, encourages a very young child to coordinate with other people and to pick up their rhythms. This ability to beat out a steady rhythm develops earlier than the ability to identify the rhythm in a piece of music. Children under eight cannot easily sustain long notes nor distinguish clearly between strong and weak notes. Individual rhythmic ability varies and continues to improve with practice well into adult life.

Culture and the rhythms of body movement are linked in other ways. Young children may learn the various methods of locomotion in a different order, so that crawling does not always precede walking, and some babies shuffle along on their bottoms before learning to walk. The cultural influence on such learning processes is well documented in Balinese babies, who first learn to squat, then to stand up from a squatting position. In contrast, most Western babies first pull themselves up into a standing position from their knees and only later—if at all—learn to sink into a squatting position. For Western people squatting, with the feet fully extended and the heels on the ground, is not usually employed as a way of resting the body and of sitting comfortably. The result is that most Westerners never learn how to get into a squatting position gracefully and rhythmically and, even if they do get there, find it extremely uncomfortable.

In some societies, children learn the rhythms of dance at an early age and babies may even be carried while their mothers dance. Even the smallest toddler can be seen 'bopping' to the beat of pop music, picking up the rhythm in a seemingly innate way. In a court session among the Tiv of Nigeria an energetic 14-month-old was even seen to pound on a drum, an activity normally reserved for adults only. The baby had a perfect right to be in court as long as he did not interrupt anything. On this occasion the judges paused, considered his dance rhythm, helped him to improve it, told him what a great boy he was and only then instructed his nurse to take him away so that the court could resume its deliberations.

As children grow up and are taught the technological skills of their society,

they use these skills in concert with the people around them. So they learn the rhythm of hoeing a field by hoeing in time with others, or pound grain in a mortar, lift heavy loads, or move goods along a production line in rhythms that set them in easy relationships with their workmates. By the time they are about 12 years old children are normally fully coordinated and can perform the full concerto of physical rhythms that they will use for the next 50 years or more. Our entire adult lives are rhythmical—whenever the rhythm is lost we become ill or maladjusted. Rhythms lie at the base of all normal social interactions and these cultural rhythms are learned early, usually by the time a child is four or five. Although adult rhythms have not yet emerged these basic social rhythms have, as much as our language, converted us into permanent members of our own particular culture.

The variations in the spectrum of body rhythms reflect the ways in which time can be organized, and we can sense these same differences in the nuances of poetry, dance and music. Poetry can be thought of as a reorganization of the rhythms of speech in such a way that both sound and meaning are heightened. Without changing the words of the language the poet orders the words he uses so that regular patterns emerge. The arrangement of words in poetry can thus become less complex than that of everyday speech, and to this special arrangement of words, which gives poetry its rhythm, is added the quality of reverberation which makes the poetry 'sing'.

Different languages lend themselves to distinct patterns of syllables and beats. The classic English iambic pentameter has five 'feet', each one made up of an unaccented syllable followed by an accented one. The French alexandrine ▷

▷ has six iambic feet arranged in such a way that a natural pause follows the third foot—it is almost impossible to write sensible alexandrines in English. Japanese, which lacks the stressed accent and depends on tone to do the same job, measures the number of syllables rather than the stresses. 'Free' verse may lack surface regularity, and also rhyme, but good free verse depends even more on meter and rhythm than rhyming verse.

The writer of good prose attends as closely to rhythm as the poet, but because prose does not have such an obvious pattern as poetry it does not have the same capacity to create a heightening of meaning. Both poetry and prose depend, however, on the rhythms of the spoken language, although the prose rhythm is more subtle and less restricted. One of the marks of poor prose is that it makes the tongue do unexpected things. A good lecture or political speech stands out because the rhythms of speech are controlled so that they flow nimbly and allow climaxes to be reached without noticeable effort on the part of the speaker.

The written word is frozen speech absorbed by the eye rather than the ear. People who do not read well 'translate' the words back into the 'proper' or spoken mode and may move their lips as they read. Even fast readers 'hear' a page of words at some level, despite the fact that they can read far faster than anyone can speak, and the eye can trip over dysrhythmias in the language as readily as the ear. The skill involved in writing prose that is easy to read comes less from vocabulary and sentence structure than from the mastery of prose rhythm, so that good writing is attuned to the rhythms of the human voice—just as the rhythmic movements of babies are.

Rhythm is only one element of music, but it is the element that ties music to the human body most directly: music 'soothes the savage breast' precisely because it provides us with a pacemaker to which we can entrain our rhythms. It can also be a moving emotional or intellectual experience. Whether music is peaceful or agitating depends in part on its relationship to body rhythms. Many people find that when music is playing they entrain any other activity they are involved in to its beat. Other musical components, such as scale, melody or timbre, do not travel as well across cultural boundaries as rhythm. Some Europeans cannot hear the intricate polyrhythms of African music so that it becomes just a blur, but the rhythm of foreign music is far more likely to be appreciated than its melody. The very way in which music is perceived differs from one culture to another and some languages do not have a word that translates the word 'music' found in all Indo-European tongues. Instead they have a plethora of words to indicate types of song and instrument.

The emotional effect of music is strongly linked with its relationship to body rhythms. The most natural rhythm is 80 to 90 beats a minute and any figure higher or lower than this sets up a state of inner tension. Many people react violently against both 'unnatural' and experimental rhythms when they first hear them. It was thus not merely the untraditional harmonies and un-conventional dancing that created the riotous reaction to the first night of Stravinsky's ballet, *The Rite of Spring*. The rhythms of the music, which most of us have learned to appreciate today, were strange and disturbing. The spontaneous reaction of the audience was not distaste but rage. A similar sort of reaction is felt by some older people to hard rock music. What distresses them—

apart from the volume—is the demanding pulsation of the beat. Subtle it is not, but coordinating it certainly can be, if one is not deafened in the process. However, some young people say that the purpose of the high decibels is to get the body membranes vibrating with the beat.

The choreography of the dance makes use of natural movements much as poetry employs natural language. These movements are, however, exaggerated and, most important of all, the pace is changed. Alteration of natural pace—usually a slowing down—and often the simplification of natural rhythms to a totally overt pattern, are the basic characteristic of all dancing everywhere. When we watch a prima ballerina we may admire the speed of her movements, but to see her gradually raise and unfold one leg in a *développé* can be a breath-taking experience. The wonder is not so much that she can do it, but that she can do it so slowly, and with such consummate grace and ease of movement.

African and Indonesian dances show us most clearly the nature of dance as a total experience. African dance, and music, concentrates on polyrhythms and the African orchestra is built around drums. A large drum with a fairly deep note is often the one that carries the basic beat while perhaps as many as a dozen smaller drums each have a different beat. The whole forms a pattern that is repeated after a given number of 'bars', but each drum comes in at a different place and often with a different rhythm. In most parts of Africa hand gongs or iron bells are added to the drums, while shawms (relatives of the oboe) and flutes may carry a tune.

African dancers make use of all the orchestra's rhythms. One part of the body—often the feet but equally often the trunk—maintains the basic beat, then the shoulders pick up part of the 'counterpoint', the arms and perhaps the knees another part. The head may move to the rhythm of the gongs or bells. Sometimes a number of people, often dancing in a ring around the orchestra, all perform the same steps and move in unison, creating an overwhelming impression of unity, but on other occasions the point of the dance may be the individual, creative use of rhythms intended to blend all the rhythms of the drums into a dramatic and pleasing whole. The best dancers are those whose bodies are filled with and express all the rhythms of the orchestra and who are graceful and agile. The result is both fast and subtle, but the audience must understand the process to appreciate the skill.

The *gamelan*, the orchestra of Bali and Java, is also built around percussion instruments, although flutes and stringed instruments may be added. The instruments of a Balinese *gamelan* are arranged in pairs with one member of the pair echoing the other. The basic pair of drums is called the male and the female (a similar division is also true in much of Africa), but they are slightly different in pitch and are beaten to create interlocking rhythms so that it sounds as if only one drum is playing. The two drummers control the tempo. The lead melodic instrument is the metallophone, which is like a xylophone but has metal bars rather than wooden ones. The first metallophone player is the melody maker and, especially if the male and female drums are silent, may influence the rhythm by becoming the pacemaker as well. The second metallophone is tuned a quarter tone from the first, but struck a fraction of a second after it. Thus every note has an answering call and this sets up a ▷

The tension caused by dancing to an accelerating rhythm can lead to a cathartic state of 'ecstasy'. The whirling dervishes in Turkey form a clockwise-moving ring, and as the music speeds up the dancers whirl wildly around in a trance. In this spiritually receptive state, these *sufi* seek total union with God.

The magic of the Fred Astaire and Ginger Rogers partnership was their perfect synchrony with each other and the music. They visualized the music's exaggerated rhythms in an exhilarating display of stylish coordination.

▷ reverberation—itself rhythmic in its vibrations—as well as complicating the rhythms set by the drums.

The cymbal players now come in to underline and shade the drums and metallophones, resulting in music that makes use of counterpoint of tone, melody and rhythm. The *gamelan* sits in a rough square and the rhythms echo across it from one side to the other and diagonally from corner to corner, so that the entire area reverberates. The whole is finally embroidered with smaller instruments playing fast, cascading 'flower parts' which provide the colour and make Balinese music so unmistakable to the ear.

Balinese music is arguably the most vibrant dance music in the world and young Balinese girls are among the most graceful dancers. The gestures of the dancers of Bali and Java, in which the shoulders shiver to the beat of the drums and the head and neck are moved in sinuous undulations, are carefully controlled, and each has a traditional meaning usually connected with religious myths and legends. The dancer is, therefore, not only unifying rhythm and motion but also the religion, history and literature of her people. Balinese dancers are taught by skilled instructors, usually themselves retired dancers. Student and teacher have a relationship of intense and close physical contact so that the student can sense and take the rhythm of the teacher in a type of entrainment process.

While the essence of a culture can thus be found in its music and dance, both are also tightly bound to the rituals of religion. Ted Shawn, the American dancer of the 1920s and '30s was an assiduous student of forms and styles of dancing throughout the world. His feeling on the matter was, 'I could not conceive of God being without rhythms, without grace, without intelligent expression, nor without possession of infinite forms of beauty through which to express His infinite Rhythmic Being.'

It is no accident, and certainly not a profane sentiment, that dance and religion have been intimately linked from man's earliest relationships with supernatural gods. Dance lies at the basis of religion because of its capacity to unleash our awareness of interlocking rhythms and to slow them down so that they are brought under conscious control. Music, always a dimension of dance, also lies at the root of religious experience. The cosmic rhythm is represented by the drums, the breath of the human spirit, by the woodwind, man's ability to be creative with his hands and mind, by the strings. The whole dance represents man's capacity to control his movements and express his own feelings.

Through its inextricable link with music, dance intermeshes the internal rhythms of the body with the immediate rhythms of the environment and ultimately with cosmic and celestial rhythms. The physical sensations that arise from controlling the coordination of one's own body are in themselves exhilarating, so that it is not surprising that in many eras and cultures dancing has been, and still remains, the primary means of communicating with the spirit world. Nor should it astound us that in some religions the gods who control the universe are thought of as dancers, or that one's own dancing body can be a receptacle for God himself to enter.

Yoga, a sort of static dancing, begins with breathing. As you prepare to assume the yoga positions you first become aware of the rhythm of breathing. Then you centre your mind and associate it with your body by consciously

At African curing ceremonies, the deep rhythm of a hand-beaten drum and the haunting sound of rhythmic chanting is believed to draw out evil spirits and cure illnesses.

In South Africa, Zulu mineworkers re-enact their ancestor's ritual war dance, *left*. Frenetic leaping and stamping dances used to build up the warriors' aggression to fever pitch, until they became thirsty for battle.

Muslims express their submission to God by bowing down in prayer five times a day. At dawn, noon, mid-afternoon, dusk and after dark, they remove their shoes and, facing towards Mecca, humbly pay homage to Allah.

slowing down, deepening your breathing and becoming quietly aware of your heartbeat. As concentration continues your heartbeat slows, your shoulders relax and so does the rest of your body, except for those muscles needed to hold the body in a particular yoga position. With an easy mind you can then use your brain to control your internal rhythms so that yoga becomes a spiritual and intellectual way of experiencing your intimate association with the rhythms of life.

Established Eastern religions, especially Buddhism, are highly sensitive to the impact of simplified, ordered rhythms on the state of body and mind. Many such religions use the mantra, or 'instrument of thought', as a sacred prayer or incantation to achieve a rhythmic 'self-centredness'. The mantra is personal— it is usually presented as a gift by a master—and is repeated in a single rhythm, over and over again. One of the aims of this monotonous, monorhythmic exercise is to disentangle the self from the disrupted rhythms of daily life. Using a mantra it is possible to capture an awareness of your own body rhythms, which are slightly different from those of anyone else.

In meditation the aim is for the body to be rested and the mind both rested and enlightened. In Eastern religion the mental state of meditation is thought to be essential if one is to re-establish contact with the rhythms of the universe, that is, with God. Western versions of meditation have lost their religious element, but make use of the same techniques to counter stress and to achieve peace of mind. The mental state of meditation has some similarities with the state of hypnosis. During meditation the electrical rhythms of the brain become more even, the heartbeat slows and the skin temperature drops, yet the

meditator is aware of the world around him. In hypnosis the same physical changes may occur, but the state of the mind is quite different from that of meditation because consciousness and memory are drastically altered.

A trance is quite opposite in its effects from meditation and can be accompanied by increased rapidity of body rhythms. The resulting feeling of ecstasy may take the form of a religious experience, and ecstasy is also associated, in religious history, with prophecy. The practice of prophecy during an ecstatic or hypnotic trance is still carried on in North and West Africa. Spirits, or *bori*, are said to enter or 'ride' human priests and allow them to prophesy or divine the cause of illness. At the insistence of Islamic officials, *bori* were banned in West Africa during the colonial era, but *bori* dancers kept appearing because their divinations were thought to be able to determine the cause of illness in a way that is beyond the scope of both modern and traditional medical techniques. These causes stem most often from ruptured social relationships, so that as well as being concerned with curing individual physical ills, *bori* seances, during which the spirits are summoned up, are said to heal social wounds.

Prophecy, music and dance all have their place in the Bible, the book that charts the history of the Jewish people and is the cornerstone of Christian faith. King David and the Israelites, for example, danced abandonedly before the Ark of God, and the Hebrew words originally used to describe the event can be translated as dancing, skipping, leaping and turning. Of all religious dancing, that of the 'devil dancers' of Sri Lanka is among the best documented and observed. In the area of Kandy, religious officials dance until they become ▷

163

▷ possessed by spirits, which the early Christians (missionaries) named devils. Once inside the dancers these spirits can be made to remove the illnesses from the beneficiaries of the performances, so that when the spirit leaves the priest, the disease also leaves the patient.

The religious practice of becoming entrained to the rhythms of the universe can be turned on its head so that, via religion, mankind can take upon his shoulders the task of being a pacemaker. As a result, many peoples of the world believe that if they do not perform certain specified rituals the seasons will not turn, crops will not ripen and the rains will fail to arrive. If our culture allows us we can, therefore, use our body rhythms to take on the responsibility for environmental rhythms. In some religions it is ritual and dance that are the pacemakers. The trouble with such dogmas is that there must always be an 'escape clause' to accommodate failure. Most usually the 'excuses' are that the practitioners did not keep taboos, were inaccurate in their ritual or were the unknowing targets of witches or evil spirits.

While rhythmic harmony is the essence of internal peace of mind, almost all human work is easier to do and produces more efficient results when performed in tune with a rhythmic pacemaker. Hunting and gathering people take their basic economic rhythms from the animals they hunt and the food they gather. The more hunters adapt to the rhythms of their prey, the better their results, because to be successful a hunter must observe his quarry and plan his actions accordingly. It is not surprising that game animals were worshipped by early hunters, because these men believed themselves to become the animal as they entrained their actions in order to kill it. Equally, survival of both the hunter

and the hunted are interdependent, because if an animal is overhunted it becomes extinct, and this adds to the religious significance of prey species.

The stock farmer or herdsman also entrains his rhythms to those of his animals, but over a longer period of time. African herdsmen are in constant contact with their beasts, and in their dancing imitate the movements and rhythms of their cattle. Like the herdsman, the peasant farmer synchronizes his daily, seasonal and annual rhythms to those of the living world, but adjusting to the rhythms of a plant is far more difficult than becoming entrained by an animal, because the psychological feedback of success may not arrive for a year or more. Nevertheless, such entrainment is vital to the subsistence farmer and even today is what gives a gardener his 'green fingers'.

With the coming of the industrial revolution, which began in Europe in the nineteenth century, man's rhythmic unity with his environment changed. Instead of entraining his rhythms to other living organisms, the worker had to adjust his body rhythms to machines, and his daily routine to the production line. The synchronization of factory workers with their machines meant that human rhythms had to be suppressed in the service of the machine. The human body was designed, over centuries of evolution, to detect and deal with environmental change. In the early days of life with the machine demands were totally different, and the constant repetition of identical movements at a fairly rapid rate became the imperative of work.

The machine that is the human body finds it difficult to maintain a single, repetitive motion in a monotonous rhythm. It is far better adapted for a variety of tasks in more complex rhythms. When a person entrains on a machine it is

the person who does all the adapting, so that work on an assembly line is both mechanical and monotonous. The lack of synchrony between human and mechanical rhythms was brilliantly caricatured by Charlie Chaplin in the film *Modern Times*: his muscles kept twitching long after he had finished work, while his body rhythms went completely crazy when the production line was speeded up. Chaplin thoroughly understood the rhythms of the body, and those of society, and used his knowledge to create a comic masterpiece.

The machine is the pacemaker to which the worker adapts but each machine has its own rhythm, making the array of industrial rhythms even more exhausting. In the office, the typewriter is a rhythm machine. The typist whose rhythm is even and secure not only types much faster but makes fewer mistakes than one whose rhythm is choppy. And the typing rhythm changes with content, which explains why copy typing, demanding little thought, is more rhythmic than composing copy straight on to the keys. Just as with reading, if you stumble over the rhythm, the words may well be written in the wrong order.

Hundreds of the machines we commonly use demand our rhythmic attention and entrainment. Sewing machines, food processors, agricultural machines—all demand careful integration of human rhythms with those of the machine and the result may be disastrous if we miss a beat. Of all man-made machines, the jack hammer or pneumatic drill is among the most rhythmic. You cannot control its rhythms, and must join in with them if the machine is to be of any use. The jack hammer shakes the human body into its own rhythm which can be felt for hours afterwards in the muscles of the arms and hands.

As well as the rhythms of machines, industrial society also imposes a diurnal nine-to-five rhythm on its workers, which is at odds with the diurnal rhythm of seasonal change. Most industrial rhythms do not alter with the seasons and the uncompromising clock has replaced the tempo dictated by the year. The weather outside the factory or office window makes little difference as we struggle to keep to a regular schedule, even if we are impeded by snowstorm or tropical hurricane. Whatever the weather, the production deadline will not wait. In many industries, work is organized in shifts which overlook the body's 24-hour circadian rhythms; although for 'owls', working an evening shift may be ideal and all but a few of us can eventually adjust to working a night shift, even if it takes several weeks to do so. For the purposes of production, however, one hour on the clock is no different from the next.

As more and more industrial processes become fully automated, and as more working men and women become involved in service industries rather than manufacturing, so the rhythm of work is changing. Compared with our fathers or grandfathers, we have more freedom to choose our times and hours of work and do not have to perform such demanding repetitions. Staggered working hours allow us to fit our working lives into the rest of our existence so that the pace of life is more comfortable. And today's innovators have begun to take human capacity into consideration when they design machines or machine systems. The work of the air traffic controller at a modern airport is an excellent example. Because one mistake can kill hundreds of people, the controller's rhythms must be correctly attuned to his equipment and his job must be planned with infinite care so that he works to maximum efficiency. ▷

Since the industrial revolution, man has had to submit his own rhythms to the overriding rhythms of machinery. On a production line each worker must adopt the pace set by the machine to maintain a smooth and effective flow. While it is less tiring to wield a scythe or an axe rhythmically, the unbroken monotony of factory rhythms can be exhausting. Music can delay fatigue and increase enthusiasm and thus the working speed of those performing mechanical tasks, but the inaccuracy that results from this distraction can prove dangerous and inefficient.

A SENSE OF RHYTHM...*the family beat*

Music is sometimes used to provide workers with a pacemaker. Sea shanties evolved to ease the task of sailors rigging a vessel, and for tribal and peasant peoples, singing together and working in rhythm to a song also seem to lighten the load by creating a sort of community rhythm. Even in modern offices and factories 'musak'—part tune, part gentle rhythmic beat—provides a background and increases output. Even without music, workers are usually rhythmically entrained. The rhythms of a good cook or the rhythms of cane cutters are a joy to the eye, and one of the most beautiful of all work rhythms is a crew of some 16 African fishermen handling a large canoe in the surf as they take each others' rhythms and constantly adapt to the ever-changing patterns of the sea.

Away from the rigours of work, men and women retreat to their homes and families. To provide themselves with living accommodation, people in different cultures build houses to all kinds of design. These houses, which may be large or small, rectangular or round, have a few large rooms or many small ones, are also home to a variety of family members—sometimes only a couple and their children, sometimes sets of siblings and all their children, sometimes all the members of several generations. All these kinds of households impose different rhythms upon the people who live in them. Every household has a daily round, which changes at weekends or on feast days, holy days or holidays, thus creating a weekly rhythm, while the cycle of the seasons may set the pace of yearly rhythms.

Division of labour among the many members of a household occurs worldwide. Careful coordination is essential to get all these jobs interlinked so that household life carries on smoothly. The rhythms of these tasks, and the tasks themselves, change from one culture to another, but the result is always a sort of domestic choreography which, when it works well and everybody fits comfortably together, can be both beautiful and rewarding.

Almost all the members of a household have schedules outside its four walls and leave it for work, to go to school, to participate in community activities, for sport or entertainment. Each member of the household must coordinate his or her personal schedule with the activities and schedules of others. The coordination of all this coming and going may take considerable skill, if tempers are not to become frayed and rhythms disrupted.

In traditional Western middle class families the husband or father is the only member of the family who 'works', which means that for five or more days a week he leaves the home. At that time, for some culturally decided period, he engages in another sort of activity, possibly alone but more probably with a small group of people who have no contact at all with the members of his family. His activities are directed toward goals quite different from those he aims for during his 'family time', but at the back of his mind he is aware that one of the purposes of his work is the economic support of his family. Increasingly in the West, wives, mothers and adult, unmarried children also leave the family home to work. The children go out to school or to a child minder, and so the basic rhythm of the household is created.

There are two points in this cycle at which the personal rhythms of the individuals involved must adapt, namely departure and re-entry. Like sliding your car into the pace and rhythm of the traffic on the freeway, human

rhythms must intermesh so that the activities of the household can continue on beat until all its members have returned. When a family reassembles a period of readjustment is both necessary and inevitable. However welcoming a home, or however much we have longed to be there, we may still experience a re-entry problem.

The best way of investigating the delicate intermeshing among family members is to examine families who have unusual rhythms. Oil workers on the pipeline and pumping stations in the snowy wastes of the northern shelf of Alaska are a perfect example. In this Arctic desert there are two people for every job—one is 'boss' and has a 51 per cent say in how the job is performed. The boss goes to the shelf and works for a week. With a 2½-hour overlap the boss and his alternate—and indeed the whole team—hand over their jobs before flying off home for a week.

During their week on the job, every person in the team has a single bunk room with a bath shared by one other person in the next room. Each room has two sets of lockable cupboards and drawers and is occupied for alternate weeks by members of the two different shifts. Work is arranged on the basis of a 12-hour day, but members of the management team are on call round the clock. At the end of the week everyone must re-enter their family world, and this is much more difficult after a week at work than just a day away from home. Ten minutes after his father walked into the house for his week 'at home' the eight-year-old son of one pipeline worker did something for which he needed a reprimand. The parents looked at each other but neither made a move. Then the mother said, 'Well, you're his father—are you going to let him get away

with that?' To which the father retorted, 'You want me to beat the child ten minutes after I get into the house?' The parents then talked over the problem, not just on that day but for the best part of the week. Since there were no cultural rules on which to base their behaviour they began to make their own rules and thus solved their own re-entry problem.

Fishermen, sailors and soldiers have to make a similar sort of adjustment at far longer intervals, as do men who choose to work in the all-male communities which have sprung up in the countries of the Middle East. A businessman who travels a lot may experience the same sort of problems as the Alaskan oil worker and even feel estranged from his wife and family until he readjusts his rhythms to those of his kin, rather than taking his cues from his workmates.

Every household also has a long-term rhythm. In Western society, newly married couples usually move into new households—if they do not they can severely disturb the normal family rhythm. When a child is born the rhythms of family life change, and this alteration will be largest if the mother gives up a job outside the home when the baby arrives. With the birth of subsequent children the rhythms change again, as they do when children start school and when they become adolescents. On each occasion the internal rhythms of the family have to adapt to the changing rhythms in the comings and goings of its members. When the children leave home the rhythms 'settle down' until the parents retire from full-time work. The final desolation of being a widow or widower is not only because of the loss of a loved one, but because the remaining member of the partnership is deprived of being in synchrony with another human rhythm.   ▷

All working people have to adapt to a different set of rhythms when they return home after a day's work. For coalminers, *left*, and others working anti-social hours and in unnatural conditions, the problems of adjustment are even greater. Food and drink may be the miner's first priority when he enters his front door, but the rest of his family may have conflicting physical and emotional demands. An acclimatizing period is essential for each individual before the household can regain its normal pattern. Family relationships may even begin to disintegrate if there is insufficient time for a harmonious rhythm to establish itself. But for many people, the best part of the day begins when the 're-entry' problems have been solved, and the familiar home routine takes over. This daily cycle of going to work and coming home again, with its inbuilt pressures, is itself a rhythm and when it is broken by retirement, unemployment, illness, or even weekends and holidays, there is a transitional period of re-orientation before a new set of rhythms can take over.

The intense elation and relief of returning home from war and reuniting with loved ones will inevitably be followed by a long period of readjustment. The soldier's long absence, coupled with his shattering experiences, which alienate him from those who have not shared them, make his integration into the family a long and difficult process. The household rhythms may no longer seem familiar or, like anyone returning home from an eye-opening trip, he may find them too familiar, too slow, too unchanging. Whether initially he rebels instinctively against the rhythms established by the rest of the family or tries consciously to fall in with them, it will take a while for both the 'returnee' and his family to regain some form of synchrony. During his time away, the children may have left home, creating a different pattern in the household to which he must adjust, or the family may have held firmly to the same reassuring daily cycle of activities, which they, in turn, may have to adapt to suit the different needs of the homecomer.

▷ In societies, such as those of many African and Asian peoples, in which households are large and are either polygamous or contain members of several generations, the family rhythm is less disrupted by arrivals and departures than it is in smaller units. Even in the West, comings and goings tend to disrupt rhythms more in small families. Paradoxically, in the big, easy-going family it seems much easier for everyone to intermesh their activities than it is in the small, tightly knit family unit.

The family is the basic unit of the community, but human relationships also involve the forging of bonds with other members of our species. And like the individuals of which they are composed, all human groups have their own rhythms. For a group to be welded into a unit, the rhythms of the single human components must blend easily with one another. The anthropologist Edward T. Hall, in his book *Beyond Culture*, notes that once he was sitting in an outdoor cafe on the Greek island of Mykonos when he saw a group of young people apparently listening to rock music on their portable transistor radio. As he observed them more closely, Hall concluded that the youngsters were not 'listening' to the music, rather they were using its rhythm as a 'sine wave' that would synchronize their movements with one another and, at the same time, increase group feeling and make the group-bond stronger.

A student of the same anthropologist once made a film of children in a playground. As he worked through the film he ran it at different speeds and examined it on a time-motion analyzer, a machine that makes it possible to run a film at any speed and stop at any frame. Gradually, he began to realize that a complex rhythm was taking place in that playground which had a 'tune' and a 'leader'. This leader was an extremely active child who moved long distances over the playground, interacting with each small group of children. Hall named that child the 'director or orchestrator of the playground rhythm'.

With the help of some musician friends the student then found a rock tune that fitted the complex rhythm of the children's play. The moment the music was put to the $4\frac{1}{2}$ minutes of the film sequence the rhythmic pattern was clear for all to see. What everyone asked was, 'How did you get the children to do all that in time to the music?' Some of the audience completely refused to believe that the music was added long after the film was made, and so was entrained to the 'music' that the playing children were making.

In a similar way, every traveller who goes from one city to another recognizes the changes he must make in the rhythms of his movements, if he is to fit in with the rhythm of the people in his new surroundings. The pace of some cities, such as New York, is fast and furious. London is a little slower, but still falls in the fast category. For a slow pace you must travel to a city such as Abidjan in West Africa. Some cities have mixed rhythms—Los Angeles, for example, is fast on the freeways but slow in the downtown areas. The rhythms within each city are many and complex. These rhythms change by the hour as people go about their daily routines, starting work, breaking for lunch and going home. Cities have high-energy areas that buzz with activity during daylight hours but are sleepy at night, while streets that seem dead during the day come alive when darkness falls. Even the rhythms of a neighbourhood change from street to street and block to block. Many of these fascinating city rhythms are as predictable as the daily and yearly activities of animals and

plants, but they remain largely unstudied.

At a much slower pace, long-term rhythms of activity and change make an indelible mark on the development, growth and decline of neighbourhoods. The linking of these developmental rhythms to the history of a particular city are purely incidental. Once an area has been built it seems to be typical of the very nature of its materials that it must become 'run down' before it can be rebuilt. Any idea of 'city maintenance' may even be incompatible with our present ideas of expansion and renewal because the rhythms do not blend with one another. On an even larger scale, countries and empires experience growth and decline through history and many democracies build a governmental rhythm into their constitution—thus the United States elects a new president every four years, France every seven years, while British governments can run for a five-year term before they must seek re-election.

All the rhythms of a community have their basis in the activities of the people that compose it, their goal, their jobs and the culturally determined way in which they go about the day-to-day business of living. The rhythms of the individuals that make up a city are an integral part of that city and the rhythms change with age. The alterations in the rhythms of any individual depend not only on his age but also on his health, the kind of work he does, the phase of family life he happens to be in, and on the many other environmental pacemakers to which his rhythms become entrained.

In concert with the changes in its inhabitants, the rhythms of the city also shift. If taken in tandem the rhythms of development, decay and renewal of a city, and the rhythms of ageing, health and work of the individuals in that city,

form a kind of infrastructure. It is the atmosphere of this infrastructure, determined by the rhythms of bricks and mortar and of living beings, that attracts you to one neighbourhood rather than another and so influences where you live, where you raise your family, where you play and, to a lesser extent, where you work.

The combination of cultural rhythms within one territory creates a number of habitats or niches within a city. The niche is the place in which any group, or an individual member of that group, finds security, enough to eat and sufficient services to satisfy at least a minimum of social needs. Survival of a population depends, at least in part, on the capacity—or luck—of its members to find a niche in which to prosper. The city is the sum of all the niches it provides, from Brooklyn to Greenwich Village in New York and from Soho to Hampstead in London.

It is the rhythms of our bodies, our culture and our cities that combine to make us what we are, just as we, in turn, make them. We may all think that our own methods of interaction and communication are universal, but that is far from the truth. One reason why we cannot understand why we are out of phase, and thus out of sympathy, with people from other cultures is that we overlook the differences in our basic rhythms, learned from our first experiences of language as babies and subconsciously adopted as normal. The rhythmic imperative is the essence of life, health and harmony, and the key to human well-being is the synchrony that can be achieved by keeping in step with the rhythms of our neighbours and also the rhythms inherent in the environment.

The market, which recurs every four or five days in many African societies, *far left*, divides time into a weekly rhythm. Not only a meeting place for social and business affairs, the market provides a regular focal point in the lives of every member of the community. In Western societies, weekends and holidays form similar focal points, drawing people out into the community, *left*, in contrast to the working week. Saints' days, religious festivals, school and summer holidays, pleasantly divide up the annual cycle.

Freeways and motorways not only reflect the increasing pace of modern society, but speed up the development of the world's big cities. 'Modernization' slowly regenerates declining neighbourhoods, new rhythms replace old, and growing areas rub shoulders with decaying ones. By its very nature, a city encompasses many diverse rhythms. Commercial, artistic, industrial, residential and municipal sectors each have their own pace, and come alive at different times of the day and the week. Diverse though less complex rhythms also exist side by side in rural communities.

Rhythms of time

From long before the beginnings of recorded history man has perceived that from day to day and year to year time moves with a cyclical rhythm. As civilization has developed, the desire to name and measure the natural cycles of time has grown, and as civilizations have become more complex so these accountings and measurements have become more exact—and ever more necessary. The natural days, months and years have been rigidly defined and reinforced by other measurements such as seconds, minutes, weeks, decades and centuries. Despite the fact that artificialities have been imposed upon it, the natural cyclical rhythm of time remains. As they continuously tick away, the cycles of time act as the lubricant that keeps modern society in motion. All our journeys, meetings, entertainments, plans and ceremonies are arranged and performed with reference to time.

Of all the natural cycles of time the most obvious one is that of day and night. Early man needed no special powers of intelligence to realize that he must gather food during the day and be sure of a safe, warm place to sleep at night. If he lived outside the tropics he could see that the relative lengths of day and night varied according to a regular pattern, but this mattered little until after civilization had become established.

To most primitive tribes the year was a relatively obvious cycle—not at first as any exact number of days, but in terms of the changing pattern of the weather and the relative abundance of both animal and vegetable foods. In temperate zones the regular procession of the seasons was unmistakable. The most accurate method of determining the length of the year, for the primitive and technologically aided observer alike, is to study the cycle of star patterns in the night sky. If, for example, you note the rising of a particular star above the horizon immediately before sunrise, exactly a year will pass before that star again rises immediately before the sun. It was this heliacal rising of Sirius or the Pleiades that enabled some early civilizations to calculate the length of a year to the nearest whole day.

Lunar months can be observed with no trouble, and for many tribes and civilizations have been the standard unit of timekeeping, each phase of the moon being used to name the parts of the month. Although the lunar cycle equates reasonably well to the menstrual cycle, and is a handy means of fixing the dates of feasts or religious services, it fits awkwardly with the solar year and is not allied to other natural cycles to the same extent as the day and the year.

From the natural cycles they perceived, early civilizations derived their various concepts of time. They learned to divide up the day into hours and to aggregate days into months and years. From the early Middle Ages men built increasingly sophisticated mechanical clocks so that today the accuracy of these timepieces exceeds that of the Earth's orbit around the sun. With greater precision in the measurement of the passing seconds time has become increasingly important, so that twentieth-century man is enormously dependent upon cycles of time.

In an attempt to rationalize the world we live in we have gradually become divorced from many of the natural seasonal and cosmic rhythms. Our festivals of Christmas and New Year, for example, are no longer linked to the shortest day but have artificially convenient dates. At the same time, split-second accuracy has gained an exaggerated importance. There seems to be so much to fit into our lives that they have become a race against time, with each passing second mourned as an irredeemable loss.

Assisted by a plethora of instruments and devices, modern man has developed a sophisticated way of telling the time. But the evolution of the concept of time, and the measurement of the passing minutes, have a long history that goes right back to man's beginnings. The least common concept of time used today is that of the Hopi Indians of Arizona. Unlike our compartmentalized or 'diary' time, the Hopi see time as an unquantifiable 'getting later'. For them, time is not a loss but a gain, so that each day is like a person who disappears and returns at sunrise in the same shape as yesterday but in a slightly older, more experienced form. In the timeless, Hopi view of the world, distinctions are not made between past, present and future but between momentary, continuing and repeated occurrences.

The ability of the Hopi to describe the universe without reference to either time or space is unusual, but it may well be far from primitive. It is much more likely that the time sense of the Australian Aborigines, who recognize the distant past as 'dreamtime' and treat everything else as a continuous present, is much nearer to man's earliest concept of time. Certain African and South American tribes believe in a concept of oscillating time. That time moves back and forth like a pendulum is an obvious, but simplistic, conclusion drawn from the observation of night and day, cold and heat, drought and flood, youth and age and so on.

From man's emergence up to the fourteenth century or later, the common people of most societies tended to view time as a cyclical progression of birth, maturity and death. Until this period men and women had no concept of the past or of the future stretching away from them, particularly as there was little change in their lives from year to year or from generation to generation. People would remember the recent past—the time of their own childhood or some important event—and would have hopes of a better future, but no more definite time sense than that. Thus there was little reason for such people to attempt to measure time for themselves.

Whatever the theory, it was chiefly for religious reasons that man began to count the passing days. For the men who directed the religious institutions of the common people there was good cause to divide up the days and to keep track of the years. Official religious views of the nature of time varied with the faith involved. According to most oriental faiths, and to the ancient Greeks, time was cyclical or, in the words of Aristotle, 'time itself is thought to be a circle'. This view was probably derived from observation of the cyclical rhythms of the patterns made by the stars in the sky, and of the seasons. In Greek mythology the idea of cyclical time is manifested as Oceanus which was, according to Homer, an 'immense stream' encircling the Earth which ebbed and flowed twice each day. Another chronological character of Greek mythology was the tail-eating serpent which encircled the universe and bore the cyclical zodiac on its back.

The idea of cyclical time is closely bound, in the Buddhist faith, with the idea of a continuous ever-rotating reincarnation. This concept of time is psychologically comfortable because it implies that there is no death of the body or of the universe. In ancient India time itself was supposed to progress in huge cycles, each lasting 1,080,000 years. Four of these cycles represented an even larger cycle of destruction and re-creation beginning with a Golden Age and

declining into dissolution before the next Golden Age 4,320,000 years later. The ancient Chinese also had a more positive circular model of time which included the cycle of years named after animals that persists today—the year of the rat, the year of the tiger and so on. In contrast to this concept of cyclical time, the Aztecs of South America believed in time as a constant linear progression. Linear time is also a tenet of the Christian faith, which charts a steady progression of mankind from the Fall in the Garden of Eden through to the final Day of Judgement. Linear time is traditionally symbolized as an 'ever-flowing stream'.

Most religions contain elements of both linear and cyclical views of time and the practicalities of measuring time began largely as a result of the inextricable link between time and religion. In many early cultures religious festivals were celebrated at times of equinox and solstice—or at some other specific time of year—and it was the responsibility of members of the priesthood to calculate exactly when these occurred. Priests were also responsible for marking off the years to record the length of a monarch's reign and the timing of certain important events, such as natural catastrophes, battles, eclipses and the like.

Religion was not always the impetus for measuring time. Sometimes the passing years were marked off just for the sake of keeping account. An outstanding example of this form of timekeeping is the Long Count of time kept by the Maya and the Aztecs. This was a running total of the number of days that had passed since a particular starting point. For the Maya this was the year 3113 BC, although the counting was begun some 2,000 years or so after that date. By counting in units of 20 the Maya were able to deal easily with numbers up in the millions, although it was probably only relatively few priests who really understood the system. The Long Count came to an end when the Spaniards destroyed the Mayan empire in the seventeenth century AD.

Although the day, month and year were natural divisions of time, the peoples of the earliest civilizations found it desirable to divide the day into hours and the month into weeks. The reason for having a week—a cyclical period of a few days—was both religious and commercial. It was widely agreed by the priests of many religions that one regular day in every so many should be kept free from the normal working routine and devoted to religious services and prayers. It also came to be a widespread practice, not tied to any one religion or culture, that on one particular day all people within walking distance would gather at an agreed central place to sell, buy and barter goods, an arrangement that was advantageous to both buyers and sellers. So the Sabbath and the market day came into being, and their periodicity gave rise to the week. This was not necessarily seven days in duration—although seven was well known as a magical number of great significance, probably related to the seven known planets. Weeks of as few as four days and as many as 10 have been known, but seven is a reasonable compromise used in Europe since Roman times and now universally accepted.

For thousands of years hours were a much more fluid concept than they are today. They have been used—at least in a primitive form—since before 2500 BC, but until the fourteenth century AD they were merely a convenient means of dividing up the varying period of daylight. Some peoples measured the span of daylight in six equal parts while others divided it into 12. At the latitude of ▷

The Taoists in ancient China believed that time consisted of recurrent cycles. The priest's satin robe, *far left*, symbolizes Taoist belief. The Pearl of Beginning created the cosmic rhythms of yin, the receptive, feminine force bringing matter to completion, and yang, the creative, masculine force acting with time and yin to initiate life and its cycles. Earthly yin, represented by the phoenix, and heavenly yang, symbolized as dragons and clouds, refer to the regular oscillations of night and day, negative and positive, feminine and masculine.

The Buddhists' search for a state of oneness with the universe and also for reincarnation through a cycle of lives is consonant with their view that time progresses in massive cycles or yugas of 1,080,000 years. These are grouped into larger recurring cycles of four yugas, which decline from Golden Age into dissolution. Buddha appears bottom centre in the Nepalese picture, *left*.

The death of Christ, depicted in Giotto's *Deposition, right,* initiated the concept of both eternal, linear time and our dating system.

▷ Britain the daylight 'day' can be as long as 16 hours in summer and as short as eight hours in winter, yet the day was still divided into 12 equal parts, irrespective of the season. These time divisions of varying length were traditionally known as hours but today are called 'temporary' hours.

Without reservation, we accept certain conventions concerning the way that time is divided up, for example, that the new day begins at midnight and the new year about 10 days after the winter solstice. In earlier societies, however, the conventions were different from those of today. The new day most frequently began at sunrise but, according to the practice still used by astronomers, it sometimes began at noon. In ancient Greece and Israel, and in Italy up to the Renaissance, sunset was taken as the start of a new day and practising Jews still adhere to this principle. Months have traditionally been counted from new moon to new moon or full moon to full moon, rather than in our more artificial system. Year end has been fixed at many different times in different societies and has been allied to the rutting of certain animals or to one of the equinoxes or solstices. Or the length of the year may bear no relation to the seasons and end simply after 12 lunar months have passed.

Early civilizations developed several ways of keeping track of the passing hours. Most of these were inaccurate by modern standards although some of them were quite ingenious. The earliest and most obvious method was to make use of the sun by measuring the changing length of the shadow it casts. The shadow clock was developed independently by the Chinese earlier than 2500 BC and by the Egyptians and Babylonians before 1000 BC. As with the counting of the days, the people who were responsible for this task seem to have been priests, who were probably anxious to fix the times and duration of religious services. By the end of the fourth century BC the Babylonians had developed a much more complex and efficient version of the shadow clock known as the hemicycle. In the hemicycle a hemispherical opening was cut into a clock of stone or wood and in the centre of the hemisphere was a pointer whose shadow travelled in an arc. The hours, indicated as a series of arcs, each with 12 parts, were engraved around the curved surface. These hours varied in length with the season and so were temporary hours. Sundials, which strictly tell the time by the angle, not the length of the shadow, were a common feature of the Roman world. Affluent families had one in the courtyard of their home and rich travellers carried portable models with them.

The Arabs made more advances in accuracy and used their sundials for astronomical purposes. Following an ordinance by Pope Gregory I in AD 600, most Christian churches had a simple scratch dial fixed to their walls. Up to the fourteenth century all sundials were inscribed in temporary hours, which meant that the hours spent in working, prayer and so on fluctuated with an annual rhythm dictated by the sun. It was only after mechanical clocks came into use during the fourteenth century that sundials were inscribed with equal hours. After 1300 their use persisted and their importance actually increased because, for at least three centuries, they were more accurate than their mechanical successors and were employed as a regular check on the time. Many different types of sundial were constructed, most of them extremely accurate—at least in a particular latitude—and some of them beautifully ornamented.

Even the earliest of civilizations recognized the need for an alternative to the shadow clock or sundial, namely, a method of timekeeping that would still work efficiently on a dull day and during the night. First conceived before 1400 BC, and employed throughout the Mediterranean lands and China, was the water clock or clepsydra. In principle the clock was designed to produce a gradually rising or falling water level which would show the time by revealing or concealing lines marked on its container. The idea was neatly symbolic of linear time as a flowing stream, but in practice it was virtually impossible to maintain a constant flow or drip of water. The reason for this was that the water evaporated or became frozen, and that changes in the viscosity of the water (which varies according to temperature) altered the rate of flow. Water clocks were thus notoriously inaccurate. They would have worked better if the markings had been in standard hours, but temporary hours were used to make them compatible with sundials. This meant that a series of different scales had to be inscribed, and that one needed to know the date in order to read off the correct time—or at least a rough approximation of it.

Some improvement in the clepsydra was made by the Greeks and Romans who managed to control the water outflow and thus increase its accuracy, but in order to avoid the problems of freezing, evaporation and changing flow rates the hourglass came into use, with sand representing the flow of time in place of water. The Greeks and Romans had clocks of this sort and, although they disappeared for a while during Europe's Dark Ages, they were reinvented during the eighth century AD. While temporary hours were the rule, different hourglasses were needed for summer and winter because of the different daylengths. Hourglasses were in regular and common use for many centuries and did not disappear as soon as mechanical clocks were introduced because they were cheaper, initially more accurate and, for several more centuries, superior under stormy conditions at sea.

Several other systems of non-mechanical timekeeping have been used over the centuries, including those that involve a constant rate of burning. Of these, candles with hour scales painted on the wax are the most familiar. Because the rate at which the candle burns depends upon the ambient draught, it was found to be much more satisfactory if the marked candle was enclosed in a lantern. In the Dark Ages, little glass was made, so such lanterns usually had a 'glass' face made of horn. In China more use was made of slow-burning ropes, incorporating tiny bells which would fall off and so strike each hour, and of powdered incense which was burned in shallow, mazelike containers. In sixteenth-century Japan, incense clocks were sometimes designed for 'smelling the time'. Small pieces of incense were burned one by one, each giving off a different smell and so indicating the time.

A later device, specifically designed for telling the time at night, was the aptly named nocturnal. This was an inscribed disc, normally made of brass, with scales and pointers attached to its hub. If one knew the date and the latitude the pointers could be set to the pole star and the Plough (the Great Bear) and the hour read off from the instrument's calibrations.

While it was relatively easy for man to devise the means of charting the rhythm of the days and hours reasonably accurately, designing a workable calendar was altogether a much more arduous task. Nature seems to abhor

Early man found the time of year written in the stars. The distinct rising and setting of the Pleiades, an open cluster with seven of its stars normally visible to the human eye, was often used to calculate planting and harvest times. In Southeast Asia, the Pleiades appear on the horizon around 1 June and at their zenith from the end of August and mid-September.

Water clocks, used by the ancient Chinese and Egyptians, were improved by the Romans who added a 24-hour dial. As water dripped constantly from the funnel into the flask, the float would rise, moving the clock hand slowly round the dial. Less accurate than shadow clocks, water clocks needed frequent adjustment.

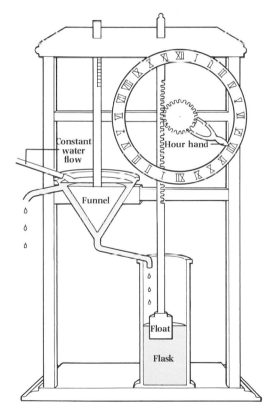

The nocturnal, *right,* was designed for telling the time at night from the positions of the pole star and the Plough. The inner plate is set for the date, the pole star is sighted through the hole and the long pointer aligned with the Plough. The angle between the pole star and the two stars in the Plough which always point towards it, gives the time to the nearest hour.

In AD 600 Pope Gregory I ordered a sundial to be put on every church. Since the Earth's orbit around the sun is not exactly circular, the speed of its rotation changes, and the $23\frac{1}{2}°$ tilt means that the height of the sun in the sky alters with the season. A solar day, therefore, varies during the year. A sundial can thus be up to 15 minutes behind or ahead of clock time at Greenwich.

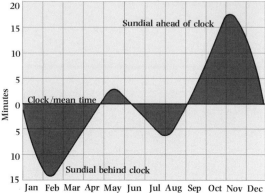

▷ round numbers. So while the rhythm of the Earth's orbit is almost constant, its period is an awkward one in terms of days (365.242) or of lunar months (12.368). For this reason considerable sophistication—particularly of astronomical observation—is required to design a calendar that will keep in step with the apparent motion of the sun over hundreds of thousands of years. All early civilizations tried and, to a greater or lesser extent, failed. Not until the sixteenth century was a system put into practice that was both workable and accurate.

It was probably the Egyptians who set up the earliest calendar, which was based on the heliacal rising of Sirius, the brightest star in the sky, and accepted the length of the year as 365 days. This calendar was used for the civil purposes of government and administration—the lunar calendar was still retained for the business of everyday life and agriculture. According to the civil calendar the year was divided into 12 unnamed months, each lasting 30 days, with the extra five days being tacked on all together at the end of the year,

The priests, whose job it was to mark off the days of the year, must soon have realized that their year was a little short compared with the solar year as the heliacal rising of Sirius would have been a day late at the end of every fourth year and another day later still with every successive four-year period. Yet no attempt was made to correct this error and it was allowed to build up over the centuries until, after 1,460 years (365 ×4), the heliacal rising of Sirius coincided once more with the beginning of the year. Even then the system was not changed. Because the Egyptians did not number their centuries or eras it is difficult to ascertain the starting date of the system. What is known is that their

new year coincided with the heliacal rising of Sirius in AD 139, so it must also have done so 1,460 years earlier in 1321 BC. The origin of the Egyptian calendar is thought to have been two cycles earlier still, in 4241 BC.

Among other ancient civilizations of the Mediterranean there was a great diversity of calendars. From about 2000 BC the Assyrians had a 360-day year of a dozen 30-day months, to which 15 days were added every third year. The Assyrians must have realized that they were getting out of step with the heliacal risings upon which their system was based, and it was altered in a number of ways before being merged with the Babylonian calendar soon after 1100 BC. The Babylonian calendar had evolved from being a lunar-based six-month year to a system of 12 lunar months. This made a total of only 354 days a year, so an extra month was inserted whenever dates seemed to be getting too much out of step. Later, in the fifth century BC, the Metonic cycle was imported from Greece. It was reasonably accurate but complex, employing both lunar and solar data and involving the addition of seven extra months into the calendar over a 19-year period.

Since the fourth century AD the Jewish calendar has also been based on the Metonic cycle of 19 years. In each cycle years 3, 6, 8, 11, 14, 17 and 19 all have 13 months. The extra month, inserted between months five and six, has 30 days. Because of religious festivals or fasts the year cannot begin on a Sunday, Wednesday or Friday so the length of the year is altered by one day if necessary, the addition or subtraction being made to the third month. The ancient Greek calendars, which existed from about 1200 BC, were peculiar to different city states and had various lengths and bases, but the 19-year Metonic cycle became

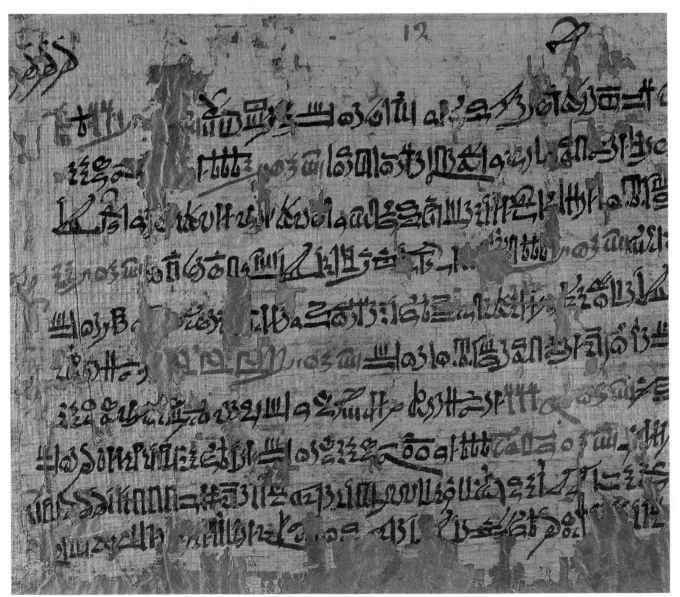

The ancient Egyptians originally used a lunar calendar with named days, which they synchronized with the rising of the star Sirius and the annual flooding of the Nile. They later devised a civil calendar with numbered days, based on the 365-day solar year. As the civil calendar did not take into account that the solar year was in fact $365\frac{1}{4}$ days long, the months were never truly synchronized with the seasons. Eventually an extra 30-day month was added to the civil calendar every 25 years to correct the error. The Egyptian calendar, *left* from 1230 BC marks the lucky named days in black and the unlucky ones in red.

The French Revolutionary calendar was introduced in 1793 to break away from the ecclesiastical Gregorian calendar. It consisted of twelve 30-day months, each with a name suitable for its season, and each divided into 10-day weeks.

generally accepted from the third century BC and many improvements were made to it.

Beyond the lands of the Mediterranean, other cultures attempted to devise calendars. In Central America the Mayan and Aztec civilizations had similar systems dating from around 3000 BC. Each recognized a 365-day solar year divided into 18 months, each lasting 20 days, plus five final 'evil' days; but despite this they regarded a 260-day cycle, which ran parallel to the solar year, to be of greater importance. These two cycles were meshed with great exactitude to produce a cycle of 52 years—the Calendar Round—having 18,980 days each with a different name. It is remarkable that the Mayan calendar is, in fact, more accurate than the one we use today as it loses only two days every 20,000 years compared with the loss on our calendar of three days every 10,000 years.

In Asia several different early calendar systems evolved independently. From the eleventh century BC, and possibly much earlier, the Chinese adopted a 60-day cycle of named days combined with a form of lunar calendar. At some time during the seventh century BC this was allied with a 12-year cycle. In order to keep the lunar cycles in step with the solar years, extra months were added on when necessary, but not in any planned way. The Hindus, Buddhists and Brahmans used lunar calendars—although with different month names—from as early as 1500 BC, adding days and months during each five-year period to keep in step with the solar year.

Circles and rows of standing stones, set up in northern Europe during the period 1500 to 500 BC, which had religious significance, were also used to identify the summer solstice. A number of other solar, lunar and stellar alignments have been claimed for these megaliths as the positions of the stone blocks can be used to measure the movements of the sun and moon and to chart the occurrence of eclipses. The best-known megaliths are at Stonehenge in southern England and Carnac in Brittany in northwest France.

Many of the early calendar systems have been replaced by the Gregorian calendar we use today. The Gregorian calendar is a direct descendant of the republican calendar of ancient Rome, which had 12 months, with names that mostly persist today, and a total of 355 days. Until 153 BC the year began on 1 March, but the change was then made to 1 January. Any extra days continued to be inserted into the 'last' month, February, although originally this was done after 23 February. In practice the republican calendar was interfered with for political ends so that by 46 BC it had fallen behind the seasons of the year by three months. The essential reform was carried out by Julius Caesar who, with the good advice of the astronomer Sosigenes, added 90 days to the year 46 BC and accepted a $365\frac{1}{4}$-day year. The accumulated quarters resulted in an extra day being added to February every fourth or leap year.

The resulting Julian calendar was so nearly correct that no discrepancies were noted for several centuries. The accumulated error was only one day in 128 years but nothing was done to correct it. In the 1470s, when the discrepancy totalled nine days, moves were made toward reform but the Pope's chosen astronomer was murdered and nothing was achieved. A century later Pope Gregory XIII appointed the German Jesuit mathematician Christopher Clavius to calculate the necessary changes. In October 1582 the calendar, now ▷

The Aztec calendar stone, from the Pyramid of the Sun in Mexico City, *left*, features symbols of all the previous epochs of the world, as well as a 260-day calendar. The Sun God is surrounded by symbols of the 20 day-names (reed, monkey etc), which were used with 13 day-numbers. The 260-day year ran parallel to the 365-day solar year, which was divided into 18 months of 20 days with 5 extra 'unlucky' days. The two serpents with touching fangs represent time.

Stonehenge, *above right, and right,* is a remarkably sophisticated 3,500-year-old megalithic calendar clock. From the remaining central stones and the pits of others, it has been possible to detect alignments pointing to sunrise and sunset at both winter and summer solstices, to the extreme positions of moonrise and moonset, and even to its eclipses. These positions have moved a few degrees since 1500 BC, but the readings were accurate at the time the stones were erected. The 30 Y and 29 Z holes which encircle the ring of stones may have been used by the pagan priesthood to count alternate months.

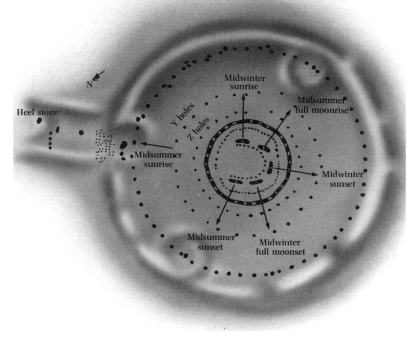

▷ known as the Gregorian calendar, was righted by advancing the date 10 days. At the same time a new rule was introduced to drop three leap days every 400 years, the change being made in century years unless they are divisible by four.

In 1582 it was only Roman Catholic countries which adopted this change. Protestant Europe persisted with the Julian calendar for almost another century. Britain only changed to the Gregorian calendar in 1752, and Russia only in 1917 after a Soviet government had replaced the rule of the Tsars, which means that the Soviet Union now celebrates the October revolution on November 7th. During the twentieth century the Gregorian calendar has been slightly amended so that the error will be reduced to only one day in 20,000 years—an excellent example of the way man has harmonized his timekeeping with the natural rhythm of planet Earth.

In parallel with the evolution of the calendar came a technological advance in clock design which allowed the passing hours and days to be recorded more accurately. The most significant advance came with the invention of the mechanical clocks, machines with integral power systems driven—at least for the first six centuries after their introduction—by falling weights or an uncoiling spring. The various timekeeping devices that operated by burning, or by the flow of water or sand, although they were often so complex that they struck a bell on the hour or triggered an alarm system telling the clock keeper to do so, were not truly mechanical.

No trial models or prototypes of the first mechanical clocks exist, nor are there any surviving descriptions of them. The earliest known public striking mechanical clock was built in 1335 and installed at the palace of the Visconti in Milan. Like most fourteenth-century clocks it had no face or hands but was placed in a tower and equipped with a bell to strike the hours. Several other clocks are known from before 1350—most are Italian and show considerable sophistication in their design. Commissioned and set in towers by noblemen, they struck the passing hours of day and night from one to 24, beginning at sunset. This was the period during which standard hours, unvarying throughout the year, came to replace temporary hours. Slowly the use of mechanical clocks spread across Europe. The earliest surviving example in England is the turret clock of Salisbury cathedral, installed in 1382, but it is not as complete as the one from Wells cathedral which dates from 1392 and is now displayed in the Science Museum in London.

Until the beginning of the sixteenth century all mechanical clocks were powered by falling weights. The principle of the mechanism is that as the weights fall they set in motion a system of gears to which a hand indicating the hour is attached. For the clock to run for any length of time the power in the weights must be used up slowly, not all at once. To achieve this one of the gears is first 'held' then released by means of an escapement device. In the first clocks this consists of a crossbar, carrying a weight on each side, which swings to and fro. Below the crossbar is an escape wheel with toothed notches attached to a vertical bar. Each time the crossbar swings, the vertical bar twists from side to side causing one tooth to be released and the next to slot in. The time of the swing of the escapement depends on the positioning and heaviness of the weights. Due to the inefficiencies of the escapement, these clocks frequently lost or gained as much as 15 minutes a day—a process exacerbated, no doubt, by

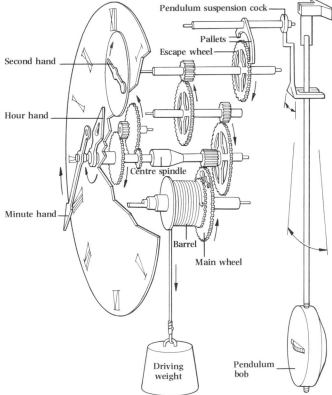

The ornate dial of the clock at Hampton Court Palace, which dates from 1540, indicates the hour, the day, the month, the number of days since the beginning of the year, the phases of the moon, the time of high water at London Bridge and the zodiacal signs. The original mechanism of the clock was replaced in 1835.

Falling weights were used as a driving force in clocks from the early 14th century, and towards the end of the 17th century the one-second pendulum was added as an accurate regulator. The pendulum's movement is transmitted through a pair of pallets which allow the escape wheel to rotate at the rate of one tooth per second. The power of the falling weights is thus only slowly consumed and the force of the escape wheel against the pallets keeps the pendulum swinging. The escape wheel is directly connected to the clock's second hand and, through a series of linking wheels, to the minute and hour hands. A slight loss or gain can be corrected by moving the pendulum bob up or down on the rod.

Pendulum suspension cock
Pallets
Escape wheel
Second hand
Hour hand
Centre spindle
Minute hand
Barrel
Main wheel
Driving weight
Pendulum bob

the fact that the mechanism was not cased, but open to dirt and the public. To set them right these clocks were checked against sundials.

Domestic clocks, with a face and a single hand to indicate the hours, were few and far between in the fourteenth century and were large, ugly and expensive. All these early clocks were made from wrought iron by a single workman who would complete one clock before starting the next. During the late fifteenth century there was a trend towards clocks with faces, but the first real improvement in clock design came with the use of a coiled metal spring to provide the motive power in place of falling weights. The development of these clocks is also shrouded in uncertainty, but the first working, spring-driven clock was probably made by Peter Henlein of Nuremburg in or around 1510. Spring-driven mechanisms were not only more accurate but allowed smaller timepieces to be built. And because spring-driven clocks were more likely to keep going if they were moved around, they led to the introduction, during the sixteenth century, of the first travelling clocks and watches.

The watches of the sixteenth century were certainly not pocket-sized, being typically 9 in (22.8 cm) in diameter by 5 in (12.7 cm) high. Known from their shape as drum clocks, they had a dial on the upper face and most were equipped with a hinged metal cover to protect the hour hand. Some were furnished with alarms, and almost all were beautifully finished, with an engraved case often embellished with gold or silver. Although little more accurate than their fourteenth-century predecessors, and only within the means of the rich, these watches represented a change in the order of things—man had begun to make the rhythm of his life fit in with an artificial division of night and day.

While previously only kings and princes had been able to afford them, during the sixteenth and seventeenth centuries there was a great demand for public and domestic clocks from the upper and middle classes of society. Gradually brass replaced wrought iron as the material used for clock making, making clocks lighter in weight and, because the metal was easier to work, more reliable. In Britain it took centuries for clock making to become an established craft. Most clocks were made by blacksmiths or locksmiths—often with mediocre results—but despite this a few handsome and reasonably accurate English clocks remain from the reign of Elizabeth I (1558–1603).

The most important single advance in the history of mechanical clocks was the introduction of the pendulum as a precise regulator of the escapement. The idea of the pendulum must be credited to Galileo, who was inspired in the late sixteenth century after watching a lamp swinging on a chain in Pisa cathedral, but the first clock to be regulated by a pendulum was designed by the Dutchman Christiaan Huygens in 1656. The first man to produce a pendulum with a beat of exactly one second was Dr Robert Hooke the English physicist, in about 1660.

The time of the pendulum's swing depends on its length and the one-second or Royal pendulum must be about 3 feet (90 cm) long and can be finely adjusted by means of a screw set in the bob. The significance of the one-second pendulum was that it enabled an enormous advance to take place in the accuracy of clocks. Minute hands were added to clock faces and the idea of dividing the minute into 60 seconds was readily accepted because it was possible, at last, to count off the seconds with great precision. Another of ▷

The oldest surviving clock in England *below* was installed in the tower of Salisbury cathedral in 1382. Although like other early European public clocks it had no dial, hands or case, it had a bell mechanism for striking the hours. It has been modernized over the centuries but much of the original wrought iron structure and verge escapement remain. This verge or crown wheel escapement mechanism, *right*, was the earliest means of regulating the speed of mechanical clocks. The crown wheel, which could be mounted vertically or horizontally, was prevented from using up all the force of the driving weights (not shown) by the foliot balance which swivelled from side to side, its pallets alternately releasing and blocking the teeth.

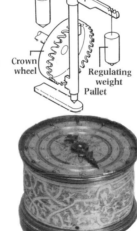

When spring-driven clocks were invented in the 1550s, a device was needed to produce a constant degree of power from the uncoiling spring. The most inspired method was the fusee, a tapered drum which housed the spring and allowed the force of the spring to be transmitted via a length of gut or cord. When fully wound, the cord winds first off the thin end of the drum, producing only a little power. As the day progresses, however, it begins to wind off the thick end, producing greater force to compensate for the reduced power of the uncoiling mainspring. Although the Italians were believed to have originated the fusee, the first man to insert this system into a clock was Jacob Zech of Prague in 1525.

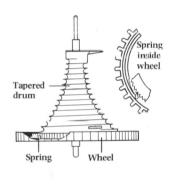

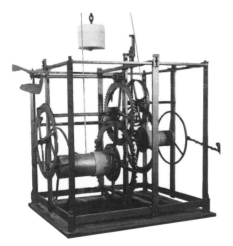

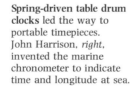

Spring-driven table drum clocks led the way to portable timepieces. John Harrison, *right*, invented the marine chronometer to indicate time and longitude at sea.

Our day begins at midnight, but until 1925 astronomers counted the days from noon. Until the last century, the nautical day ended at noon, *left*. So 6 am Monday civil time was also 6 am Monday in nautical time (but only 4 hours before Tuesday) yet it was 6 pm Sunday to astronomers.

Civil

SUNDAY		MONDAY		TUESDAY	
6 am	noon 6 pm	6 am noon	6 pm 6 am	noon	6 pm

Astronomical

SAT	SUNDAY		MONDAY		TUES
6 pm	6 am noon	6 pm	6 am noon	6 pm	6 am

Nautical

SUN	MONDAY		TUESDAY		WED
6 am noon	6 pm	6 am noon	6 pm 6 am	noon	6 pm

▷ Hooke's inventions, made at about the same time, was the recoil or anchor escapement which allowed a heavy pendulum to swing in a small arc.

These innovations changed the shape of clocks: the longer pendulum meant a taller clock and the English longcase or grandfather clock came into being. This period, the last quarter of the seventeenth century, was a time during which English clock and cabinet making were the best in Europe, and there are many grandfather clocks from the seventeenth and eighteenth centuries still keeping good time all over the world. Another effect of more accurate timekeeping, but one more difficult to quantify, was an increased awareness of small time intervals and the punctuality that they made possible.

Many refinements to clock mechanisms were made during the eighteenth century. Hooke's anchor escapement was replaced with the dead-beat escapement which made the swing of the pendulum more accurate by cutting out sway or vibration, and several solutions were found to the problem of a pendulum expanding—and thus moving more slowly, so causing the clock to lose time—in hot weather. If a steel pendulum is heated by 2 degrees centigrade (4 degrees F) it will lose one second a day. To compensate for this, metals were used whose expansion and contraction would cancel each other out.

The construction of ornamental clocks to act as decorations for the palaces and mansions of the rich was a lucrative business that required great imagination and reached its peak in France during the second half of the eighteenth century. Several French kings kept court clockmakers who produced many elaborate metal-cased clocks. Less tall than the English longcase clocks, these were designed to be placed on tables or mantlepieces.

Clocks have undoubtedly played a large part in influencing man's attitude to the rhythm of time but it is arguable that watches have been even more influential. The drum clocks of the sixteenth century were gradually improved in accuracy and reduced in size but watches did not become truly pocket-sized until the invention, around 1660, of the hairspring or balance spring, which was the essence of the seventeenth-century watch. The hairspring is a steel band or spring stressed by being bent or coiled which, when wound, acts as a store of energy. In early watches the spring was attached to the crossbar of a balance which, under the tension of the spring, swung first one way and then the other. The accuracy of the watch was controlled by a regulator which shortened or lengthened the spring and thus varied its tension.

As pocket watches became more popular, new types of escapement were developed specifically for them—the cylinder escapement in 1726 and the lever escapement in 1765. By this time most watches were almost as accurate as domestic clocks and by the end of the nineteenth century had become accessible to all. The wrist watch of today, if it is of the traditional type, has a balance in the form of a wheel with a heavy rim and a spring providing a restoring force. Electronic watches use another type of mechanism. A miniature high-density battery is used to power a minute tuning fork or a magnet and coil, and the vibrations produced are translated into digital signals that glow in gas-filled valves or activate liquid crystals.

The mass production of domestic clocks began in the nineteenth century and made such timepieces cheap enough to be standard items in every household. The factory manufacture of clocks started in America, but before

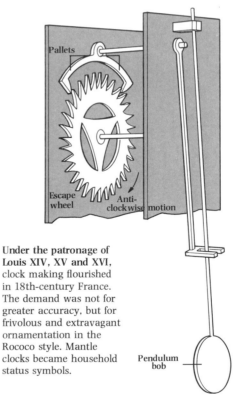

Under the patronage of Louis XIV, XV and XVI, clock making flourished in 18th-century France. The demand was not for greater accuracy, but for frivolous and extravagant ornamentation in the Rococo style. Mantle clocks became household status symbols.

The anchor or recoil escapement, *above*, invented in 1660 by Robert Hooke, was a great improvement on the verge escapement. The pallets are 'anchored' by a joining yoke, and alternately engage and release the escape wheel once per second to keep the pendulum swinging. The precision of this mechanism allowed seconds to be accurately counted. A second hand was therefore frequently incorporated in a smaller dial within the face of the clock, as in the early 18th-century English longcase clock, *right*. This escapement, however, tended to recoil against the pallets, so in 1715 a modified version—the dead-beat escapement—was developed by George Graham which corrected the defect by changing the shape of the pallet heads.

the end of the century cheap clocks were being made in quantity throughout Europe. Clocks were installed in every public building, in town squares and railway stations. Most men carried pocket watches and in the industrialized nations of the world people were becoming subservient to the rule of the clock.

The first electric clocks were designed and built in the 1840s, but it was another 50 years before electrical components were reliable enough for commercial production. In such an electric clock, a pendulum is kept in motion by regular electric impulses and, as a result, the hands move once a minute. This is the master clock and it can be used to drive many slave clocks, an invaluable system for factories and similar building complexes. As soon as a regular frequency of current was established—in 1918 in the USA and nine years later in Britain—it became possible to make synchronous clocks, powered by an alternating current of mains electricity. Such clocks are now in common use all over the world and should be accurate to within a few seconds over extended periods. Yet since this accuracy depends largely on the exactness of the voltage generated by power stations, these electric clocks do not really qualify as timepieces at all. They contain no timekeeping mechanism, only gears for reducing the frequency of current until it matches the required frequency of rotation for their hour, minute and second hands.

The twentieth century has witnessed a vast increase in the accuracy of timekeeping. The scientific clocks of today are far removed from even the most accurate wrist watches or domestic clocks, although there has been a significant spin-off from the laboratory to everyday life. In 1921 William H. Shortt invented the ultimate in mechanical clocks, the Shortt free pendulum

clock which varies by less than a few thousandths of a second a day. The clock consists of two separate clocks, one synchronizing the other. Every 30 seconds the swinging pendulum receives an impulse from a lever, which is released by an electric current transmitted from the secondary or slave clock. A synchronizing signal is then returned to the slave clock, so ensuring that the next impulse will follow exactly half a minute later.

More accurate clocks than the Shortt free pendulum have been based on an entirely different concept, that of the rhythm of natural vibrations. The quartz clock, for example, makes use of the oscillations given off by the mineral quartz crystal when alternating current is applied to it. These oscillations act in place of a pendulum to govern the motion of the clock. The principle is essentially the same as the mains electric clock, except that a much higher frequency of vibration or oscillation allows much greater accuracy—so much so, in fact, that a quartz crystal is more accurate than the rotation of the Earth around the sun. First developed in 1929, the quartz clock consists of a ring of quartz $2\frac{1}{2}$ inches (6.35 cm) across suspended on threads in an insulated chamber. Electrodes are attached to the ring and connected to a current to produce oscillations. The frequency of the oscillations is then reduced by a ratio of six million to one to make the ring rotate once every 60 seconds. This ring is then connected to a clock dial by means of mechanical gearing.

The atomic clock has evolved from the quartz clock and makes use of the natural oscillation frequency of atoms—usually those of the element caesium —as its pacemaker. The atomic clock is accurate to within one second over 30,000 years, a precision that the human mind finds hard to grasp. Thus in its ▷

Astronomical dials, showing the date, phase of the moon and time in different parts of the world, were popular features of grandfather clocks, *top.* Early watches were also ornate, often beautifully enamelled and gilded, *right,* with a metal lid to protect the hand. They became increasingly accurate and developed into 'fob' or pocket watches.

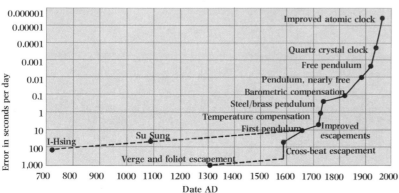

Accuracy of timekeeping improved only very gradually during the Middle Ages, and the earliest mechanical clocks were even less precise than sundials. Since the late 17th century accuracy has increased dramatically, particularly in the last 50 years, when modern atomic clocks losing less than a second every 30,000 years were developed.

Quartz crystal was first used in clocks in 1929 and was applied to electronic watches in the 1950s. In the watch, *above,* the crystal, supported inside a metal holder and sealed in a vacuum, has properties which cause it to vibrate at a steady frequency, when an alternating current is applied. The current is supplied by a long-lasting battery through an integrated circuit (a silicon chip). The frequency of the oscillation of the quartz crystal is converted into electronic impulses with a constant frequency determined by the size, shape and cut of the crystal—in this case 34,000 cycles per second. The impulses pass through another circuit which reduces the impulses to a frequency (eg 1 per second), which can be transmitted to the digital display, composed of tiny red dots.

▷ most rarified and artificial form, twentieth-century timekeeping takes its cue from the rhythm of the Earth's own building blocks.

With each year that passes, human society is becoming more and more time orientated. For most of us, there is a greater need than ever before to know the exact time of day, and to perform particular tasks at particular moments. Yet we possess no inborn sense of the passage of time. Our bodies maintain certain rhythms, which may be extremely accurate, but these rhythms cannot tell us precisely when a minute, an hour or a day has passed. As a result of this paradox, we all have our own subjective view of the rate at which time is passing and this, in turn, depends on our occupation, age and state of health. Also, we need continual prompting to tell us how quickly time really is ticking by. This means that watches and clocks are everywhere, that time-based systems have come to govern our lives and that references to time have become an important ingredient of our language.

Occasionally an individual can cultivate an accurate time sense. A soccer referee, for example, knows when 45 minutes have passed, while many professional broadcasters are skilled at judging the passage of time, from one minute to 30. But both referee and broadcaster have a clock or watch to back up, or correct, their estimate. Any of us can, if we wish, count off the passing seconds by muttering, 'one mississippi, two mississippi, three mississippi' and so on, but only when we are not otherwise occupied. It is much more usual for time to surprise us—sometimes going much faster than we think and sometimes much more slowly.

When we try to estimate the amount of time that has passed while we have been engaged in some activity or another, we are usually wrong, having been misled by our internal, subjective clock, of which the brain is a vital part. If the brain is dealing with new material, such as a movie or foreign surroundings, the amount of time spent is always overestimated—the more so if the movie is complex or if the trip abroad involves many varied activities. Conversely, the duration of those periods during which the brain receives little stimulus are underestimated. The best evidence of this is provided by volunteers who have spent periods of 100 days or more in deep caves. Cut off from all external stimuli, including the natural rhythm of day and night, such volunteers always estimate their spells of isolation to be shorter than they have been, sometimes by as much as 50 per cent.

The subjective perception of time varies with age so that the days seem to pass slowly for children, but rush past faster and faster with increasing age. The degree of mental stimulation in one's life is also involved in this phenomenon because for children everything is new, while old age brings few surprises. Another cause of this age-related difference in time sense is metabolic rate, that is, the rate at which the processes of body chemistry take place. Children have a slightly higher metabolic rate, and consequently a higher body temperature than adults, and for this reason can actually process more information than an adult in any given time, although they have a greater liability to boredom. The lower than average metabolic rate of the elderly, which gives them a lower body temperature, means that all their organic processes slow down and time seems to move correspondingly fast.

This relationship between body temperature and the subjective measure-

Ruled by schedules and high precision clocks, timetables and stop-watches, modern life has become a race against time. 'Time is money', 'time to get up' 'time for lunch', 'time's up' are constant reminders that we belong to a frenetic, time-ordered society which largely ignores natural human rhythms. It is one of the frustrating paradoxes of contemporary life that, having rushed to 'beat the clock' and arrive in time for a flight, train or bus, we must then queue and wait. Wrestling with time has increased efficiency but often at the cost of high blood pressure.

ment of time is equally valid when you are ill. When you have a fever your body temperature rises and time seems to pass slowly, but if you are subjected to extreme cold, time seems to go more quickly. There is even a mild but regular variation in our subjective clocks over the course of the day, which explains why time appears to go most slowly in the mornings.

The perception of time can be altered by the use of drugs. Stimulants, such as heroin, cannabis, LSD and other psychedelic drugs, and even the caffeine in coffee and tea, all speed up our subjective view of time and make us overestimate time intervals. Barbiturates, alcohol and other drugs that cause drowsiness are likely to have the opposite effect, so that considerable lengths of time can slip by unnoticed if you are under their influence. A state of trance, as produced by transcendental meditation and some forms of rhythmic dancing, also leads to underestimation of passing time and the same effect is produced by schizophrenia and some other mental disorders.

All around us are reminders of the extent to which we are obsessed with and governed by time. This is inevitable since a complex technological society with a high population density can only organize itself by conforming to timetables, schedules and timed appointments. Despite our criticism of public transport systems, most of them do run to time and, whether they are trains or aircraft, it is essential that they should do so, if fatal collisions are to be avoided. Our television and radio services work to exact schedules, while all entertainments, such as sporting events, films and plays, have pre-announced starting times and known durations.

The whole of industrial production is based on scheduled flows of manufacture and delivery. We are expected to be at our places of work between fixed hours and arrange to meet people at particular times. 'Time is money' is a catch phrase often used in business and for almost every moment of our waking lives there is some reference to time—it is coffee time, lunch time, tea time, going home time, bed time and so on. Alarm clocks wake us in the morning and breakfast is accompanied by radio or television shows which include frequent time-checks. Many of us jostle in a rush hour on the way to and from work and this may mean catching a bus or train at a particular time. When we do arrive at our work place, hopefully at the proper time, we may have to 'clock in' especially if we work 'flexitime' hours.

It seems to be an accepted part of the twentieth century ethos that 'faster is better'. World records are not only universally acclaimed but, for sports such as swimming and athletics, measured by split-second timing. Many companies have a department whose job it is to speed up all the others, while computers, and their software systems, are designed to process data more and more swiftly. All this adds up to an invitation to rush through life at breakneck pace, and results in a steady build-up of pressure on members of industrialized societies. To cope with this problem of 'future shock'—the disorientating effect of excess change in all areas of society—it is helpful to have the steady rhythm imposed by a time schedule, because it can act as a cushion by counterbalancing the effects of change in one or two areas of life. It may make it easier to move house or change jobs, for example, if you can maintain the rhythm of a particular journey to and from work, keep to the same mealtimes and watch the same television programmes in the evening.

The Hopi Indians have no word for past, present or future, but express time in terms of momentary, continuing or repeated events, and cannot conceive of things happing simultaneously. Their language suggests rather than defines the timing of an event. For example, 'a light flashed' to us states that the flash is already in the past, but the Hopi would simply say 'flash', to describe the duration of the flash. They also see time as varying with each observer, a view of time which does not lend itself to objective timekeeping.

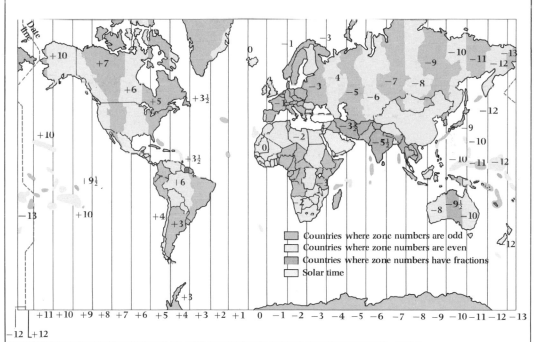

Noon (when the sun reaches its zenith) occurs at different times according to position on the earth's surface, hence the need for International Time Zones. High speed travel produces some bemusing effects—if a traveller crosses the International Date Line eastwards on his birthday, he will relive it, but if he crosses westward, he loses his birthday altogether.

Our perception of time changes considerably with age. Young children tend to overestimate short time-spans, but underestimate long ones, so that a week can seem as long as a year. A mature working man sees today as longer than the previous week because so much current information crowds his mind. Old people, on the other hand, look more to the past and feel time passes very fast. One explanation for this is that a slower metabolism and lower body temperature influence the consciousness of time.

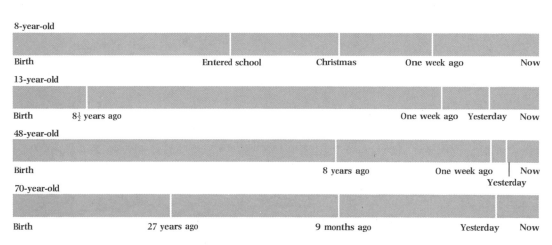

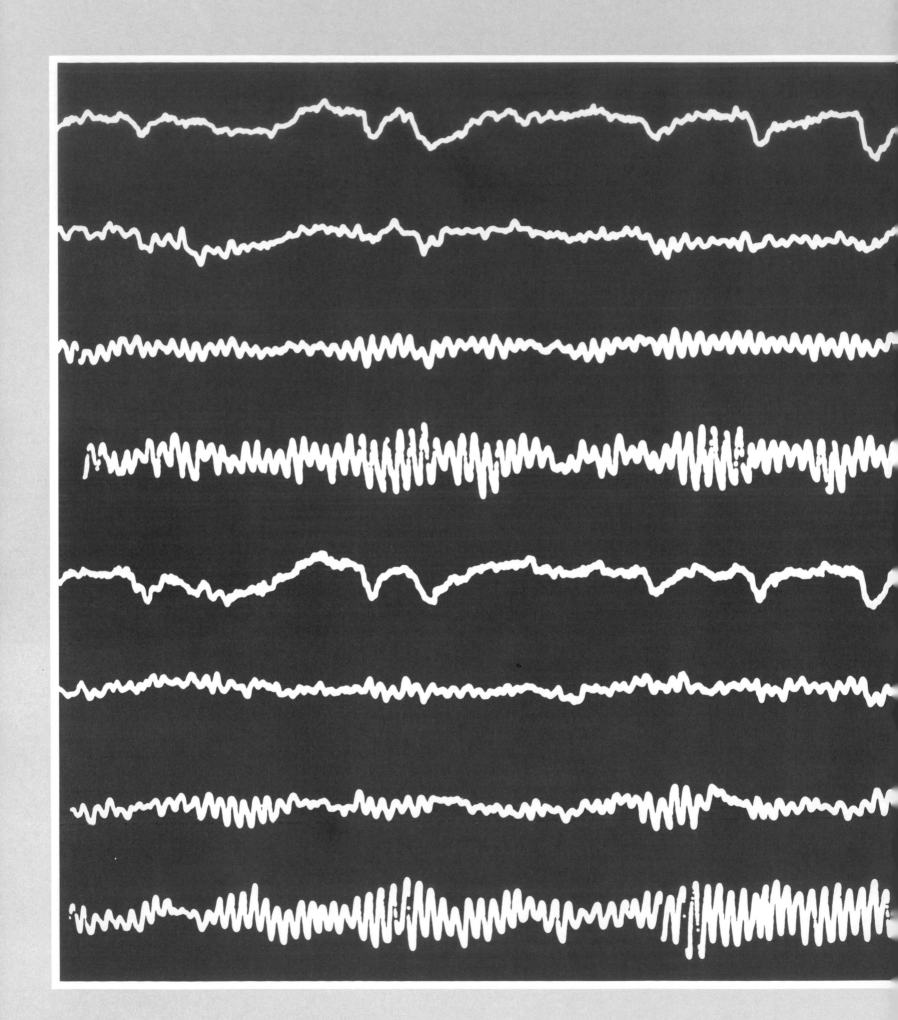

Rhythm data

Confronted with the awesome diversity of the universe and all it contains, the human intellect strives to recognize some sort of order. From the apparently ever-changing and complex physical and living worlds around him, man grasps at patterns. Of all these patterns the one that emerges most clearly and most often is the pattern of rhythm. As a result, rhythmic and cyclical phenomena are seen to be the central feature of a huge number of systems, processes and activities.

Over many thousands of years man has gathered the data that lends support to the idea of rhythms. This data concerns subjects as diverse as the revolution of galaxies and their stars and the rhythmical process of breathing. Although they might seem unconnected, these phenomena are inextricably linked because the celestial dance performed by the sun, moon and Earth has profound consequences for all earthly life. All life has evolved to respond to the complex, polyrhythmic beat of the physical world and the echoing counterpoint rhythms of biological clocks are to be found in almost all living things. In addition, all organisms demonstrate intrinsic activities and processes that are themselves rhythmic. From the growth of a tree to the flight of a bird, the processes of life are centred upon repetitive, rhythmical acts. And human life itself, constructed from a collection of biological and social components, reveals layer upon layer of rhythmical and cyclical patterns.

This final stage in the journey through the rhythms of life attempts to compress part of the enormous bank of data from which the preceding pages have drawn their inspiration. It is a catalogue of the types of events that most clearly demonstrate physical or living rhythms. Most of the lists extend or expand areas considered earlier, while a few embark on new areas of study. Most of the lists are entirely factual—they describe what certainly exists. A few others, such as the cycle of historical events, represent our desire to find patterns in everything, despite the fact that the evidence still remains insubstantial.

Planetary rhythms

The period of each planet's orbit round the sun is the length of its 'year'; the seasons on each planet are determined by the inclination of its Equator to the plane of its orbit; the length of the day on any planet is the time it takes to rotate about its axis. The distance of each planet from the sun determines its temperature and the composition of its atmosphere.
(*see pages 14–33*)

Planets	Period of orbit around the sun	Inclination of Equator to orbit	Period of rotation about axis	Distance from sun (miles)	Distance from sun (km)
Mercury	87.9 days	7°	58.5 days	36,000,000	57,920,000
Venus	224.7 days	3° 24′	243 days	67,200,000	108,100,000
Earth	365.2 days	23° 27′	24 hours 4 mins	92,957,200	149,600,000
Mars	687 days	23° 59′	24 hours 37 mins	141,600,000	228,000,000
Jupiter	11.8 years	3° 05′	9 hours 51 mins	484,300,000	779,100,000
Saturn	29.5 years	26° 44′	10 hours 14 mins	886,100,000	1,426,000,000
Uranus	83.8 years	97° 55′	10 hours 48 mins	1,783,000,000	2,870,000,000
Neptune	164.8 years	28° 48′	14 hours	2,793,000,000	4,493,000,000
Pluto	247.7 years	c.50°	6 days 9 hours	3,666,000,000	5,898,000,000

Comet cycles

Comets, like planets, orbit around the sun but, unlike them, have orbits that are often very large and eccentric. Comets are only visible when they come close to the Earth, and Halley's comet is the only bright comet to have an orbital period of less than a few centuries. Several other comets are listed here, although these are so faint that they cannot be seen with the unaided eye.

Comet	Orbital period (years)
Encke	3.3
Finlay	6.9
Tuttle	13.6
Crommelin	27.9
Halley	76.0
Grigg-Mellish	164.3

Meteor showers

Meteors are associated with comets and travel around the sun in swarms. When the Earth passes through a swarm, the meteors burn up in the Earth's atmosphere. They occur frequently throughout the year but, except for the Perseids, are not always consistently rich. Every 33 years the Leonids reach a peak of activity when as many as 100,000 shooting stars an hour can be seen.

Meteor showers	Dates
Quadrantids	1—4 January
Lyrids	19—22 April
Aquarids	1—13 May
Perseids	27 July—15 August
Orionids	15—25 October
Leonids	17 November
Andromedids	26 November—4 December
Geminids	9—13 December

Miscellaneous cosmic rhythms

Apart from the planets, comets and meteors, there are various other cosmic rhythms, a few of which are given here.
(*see pages 14–33*)

The period of the sun's revolution around the centre of the Milky Way	200 million years
Interval between one new moon and the next	29.53 days
Monthly revolution of moon around Earth	27.32 days
Daily revolution of moon around Earth	24 hours 50 mins
Interval between two perfectly straight alignments between Earth, moon and sun responsible for the solar eclipse cycle and for atmospheric tides produced by the moon	18.6 years
The meteorological drought cycle of the American Midwest: east of the Rocky Mountains, west of the Mississippi	18.6 years
Rotation of Earth's spin axis	21,000 years
Change in shape of Earth's orbit	c.100,000 years

Rainy seasons

Many tropical areas have a distinct annual season of heavy rainfall while the rest of the year is dry. Other areas, such as Lagos and parts of Ghana on the coast of the Gulf of Guinea, have two rainy seasons each year. Much of the life in these areas is shaped by the rhythm of the rainy season. The seasons given here are taken from the average monthly rainfall figures for the area concerned.
(*see pages 14–33 and 34–51*)

Africa

Conakry (Guinea)	June—October
Half Assini (Ghana)	March—July October—December
Kano (Nigeria)	May—September
Khartoum (Sudan)	July—September
Lagos (Nigeria)	April—July September—October
Mangoche (Malawi)	December—April
Wenchi (Ghana)	April—June September—October

Asia and Australasia

Bombay (India)	June—September
Broome (Australia)	December—April
Calcutta (India)	May—October
Colombo (Sri Lanka)	October—December March—May
Darwin (Australia)	November—April
Mandalay (Burma)	May—October

South and Central America, Caribbean and Hawaii

Havana (Cuba)	May—October
Honolulu (Hawaii)	November—March
Manaus (Brazil)	November—May
Mexico City (Mexico)	June—September
Port of Spain (Trinidad)	June—December

Breeding seasons

An animal's breeding season is timed so that the young are born at a time of year when they have the best chance of survival, that is, when there is plenty of food around and the climate allows them to complete the early stages of growth. The chart shows those times of year for various vertebrates, although the exact times vary with latitude. (*see pages 64–81*)

Animal	Scientific name	Breeding season
MAMMALS		
Armadillo	*Dasypus novemcinctus*	June—August
Bactrian camel	*Camelus bactrianus*	All year
Chimpanzee	*Pan troglodytes*	All year
Chipmunk	*Tamias striatus*	March—July
Common seal	*Phoca vitulina*	June—August (Atlantic) September (Pacific)
Common shrew	*Sorex araneus*	March—September
Fin whale	*Balaenoptera physalus*	November—March
Goat	*Capra hircus*	September—January
Hedgehog	*Erinaceus europaeus*	March—September
Lemur	*Lemur catta*	Late March—early July
Man	*Homo sapiens*	All year
Mandrill	*Papio sp*	All year
Mink	*Mustela vison*	March—April
Musk rat	*Ondatra zibethicus*	April—October
Platypus	*Ornithorhyncus anatinus*	July—October
Porpoise	*Phocoena phocoena*	July—August
Raccoon	*Procyon lotor*	January—June
Virginia opossum	*Didelphus marsupialis virginiana*	January—October
BIRDS (in NW Europe)		
Canada goose	*Branta canadensis*	March—April
Eider	*Somateria mollissima*	Late April—early September
Greylag goose	*Anser anser*	April—May
Mallard	*Anas platyrhyncos*	March—October
Mandarin	*Aix galericulata*	April—May
Mute swan	*Cygnus olor*	March
Shelduck	*Tadorna tadorna*	May—August
Teal	*Anas crecca*	Mid-April—July
Tufted duck	*Aythya fuligula*	Mid-May—early September
Wigeon	*Anas penelope*	June—August
REPTILES AND AMPHIBIANS		
American toad	*Bufo americanus*	February—July
Clawed toad	*Xenopus laevis*	All year
Eastern box turtle	*Terrapene carolina*	April—May
Mississippi alligator	*Alligator mississippiensis*	January—September
Moccasin snake	*Agkistrodon contortrix*	May
Prairie rattlesnake	*Crotalus viridis*	April—May
FISH		
Atlantic salmon	*Salmo salar*	September—February
European carp	*Cyprinus sp*	Spring—early summer
King salmon	*Oncorhynchus tschawytscha*	April—June
North Sea cod	*Gadus morhua*	February—April
Plaice	*Pleuronectes sp*	December—March
Sea lamprey	*Petromyzon marinus*	Spring
Yellow-fin tuna	*Thunnus albacares*	Spring—Summer

Estrous cycles and gestation periods

When a female mammal comes into 'heat' she is in estrus and capable of producing eggs for fertilization by a male. The estrous cycle is the sequence of biological events leading to egg production and fertilization. Many mammals have one or two estrous cycles a year, while the cycles of others such as our own species are continuous. (*see pages 64–81*)

Animal	Scientific name	Average estrous cycle (days)	Average gestation period (days)
Bactrian camel	*Camelus bactrianus*	15	400
Bushbaby	*Galago senegalensis*	32	115
Chimpanzee	*Pan troglodytes*	36	235
Cow	*Bos taurus*	21	284
Goat	*Capra hircus*	21	151
Golden hamster	*Mesocricetus auratus*	4	16
Gorilla	*Gorilla gorilla*	39	270
Guinea pig	*Cavia porcellus*	16	68
Horse	*Equus caballus*	22	336
Man	*Homo sapiens*	28.3	294
Mink	*Mustela vison*	8	53
Mouse	*Mus musculus*	4	25
Musk rat	*Ondatra zibethicus*	4	30
Pig	*Sus scrofa*	21	114
Platypus	*Ornithorhynchus anatinus*	60	12
Rabbit	*Oryctolagus cuniculus*	0	31
Rat	*Rattus norvegicus*	4	21
Red kangaroo	*Megaleia rufa*	35	33
Rhesus monkey	*Macaca mulatta*	28	170
Sheep	*Ovis sp*	16	148
Wallaroo	*Macropus robustus*	33	32

Bird migration times

Many birds that spend the winter in the tropics migrate north to breed in temperate regions during the summer. Birds that breed in the Arctic during the northern hemisphere's summer migrate south to temperate regions for the winter. The times of year are given when these birds are present in full force in the British Isles, California and Ottawa. (*see pages 64–81*)

Common name	Scientific name	Arrival	Departure
BRITISH ISLES			
Swallow	*Hirundo rustica*	Early April	Late October
Cuckoo	*Cuculus canorus*	Mid April	Early September
Nightingale	*Luscinia megarhyncha*	Mid April	Late August
Osprey (northward)	*Pandian haliaetus*	Late April	Early June
Quail	*Coturnix coturnix*	Mid May	Late September
Osprey (southward)	*Pandian haliaetus*	Late August	Mid October
Snow bunting	*Plectrophenax nivalis*	Early October	Late March
Little auk	*Plantus alle*	Early November	Mid February
CALIFORNIA			
Northern cliff swallow	*Petrochelidon albifrons*	Late February	Late October
Barn swallow	*Hirundo erythrogaster*	Early March	Early October
Northern black swift	*Nephoecetes niger*	Mid April	Mid September
Western tanager	*Piranga ludoviciana*	Early May	Late September
OTTAWA			
American woodcock	*Rubicolor minor*	Late March	Late October
Eastern kingbird	*Tyrannus tyrannus*	Early May	Late September
Ruby-throated hummingbird	*Archilochus colubris*	Early May	Mid October
Bobolink	*Dolichonyx oryzivorus*	Mid May	Mid September
Black-polled warbler	*Dendroica striata*	Mid May	Mid October

RHYTHM DATA

Flowering seasons

Many wild plants flower at the same time every year and their flowering often distinguishes the gradual changes of the temperate seasons. (*see pages 34–51*)

Garden flowers are the cultivated relatives of wild plants. Although selective breeding can produce plants that will flower at any time of the year, garden plants have specific times when they will flower. This chart is divided into annuals, which must be sown each year and perennials, which die down each winter and then grow again the following spring. (*see pages 34–51*)

Plant	Scientific name	Season
WILD FLOWERS:		
Bramble	*Rubus fruticosus*	May—September
Buckwheat	*Fagopyrum esculentum*	July—August
Butterbur	*Petastites hybridus*	March—May
Common sundew	*Drosera rotundifolia*	June—August
Deadly nightshade	*Atropa belladonna*	June—August
Dog's mercury	*Mercurialis perennis*	February—April
Fennel	*Foeniculum vulgare*	July—October
Gorse	*Ulex europaeus*	February—June
Heather	*Calluna vulgaris*	July—September
Hop	*Humulus lupulus*	July—August
Ivy	*Hedera helix*	September—November
Love-in-a-mist	*Nigella damascena*	June—July
Marsh mallow	*Althaea officinalis*	August—September
Marsh marigold	*Caltha palustris*	March—July
Mistletoe	*Viscum album*	February—April
Primrose	*Primula vulgaris*	December—May
Shepherd's purse	*Capsella bursa-pastoris*	January—December
Snowdrop	*Galanthus nivalis*	January—March
Sweet violet	*Viola odorata*	February—April
Touch-me-not balsam	*Impatiens noli-tangere*	July—September
TREES:		
Aspen	*Populus tremula*	March
Beech	*Fagus sylvatica*	March—April
Common maple	*Acer campestre*	May—June
Hazel	*Corylus avellana*	March—April
Ma-dake bamboo	*Phyllostachys bambusoides*	Every 120 years
Muli bamboo	*Melocanna sp*	Every 30 years
Rowan	*Sorbus aucuparia*	May—June
Sessile oak	*Quercus petraea*	April—May
Silver birch	*Betula pendula*	April—May
Small-leafed lime	*Tilia cordata*	July
Umbrella bamboo	*Thamnocalumnus spathaceus*	Every 90 years

Plant	Scientific name	Season
GARDEN FLOWERS:		
ANNUALS		
Bell flower	*Campanula medium*	July
Californian poppy	*Eschscholzia californica*	June—July
Hollyhock	*Althaea rosea*	June—July
Honesty	*Lunaria annua*	May—July
Lobelia	*Lobelia erinus*	June—October
Snapdragon	*Antirrhinum majus*	July—October
PERENNIALS		
Alyssum	*Alyssum saxatile*	April—June
Aster	*Aster novi-belgii*	September—October
Autumn crocus	*Crocus sativus*	October
Bougainvillea	*Bougainvillea spectabilis*	August—September
Columbine	*Aquilegia sp*	May—June
Cyclamen	*Cyclamen coum*	December—March
Bleeding heart	*Dicentra formosa*	April—June
Freesia	*Freesia sp*	March—April
Fritillary	*Fritillaria imperialis*	April
Gentian	*Gentiana asclepiadea*	August—September
Ginger lily	*Hedychium densiflorum*	May—June
Grape hyacinth	*Muscari armeniacum*	April—May
Hellebore	*Helleborus orientalis*	February—April
Lion's tail	*Leonitis leonurus*	October—December
Lotus	*Nelumbo nucifera*	July—September
Lupin	*Lupinus sp*	May—June
Mallow	*Malva moschata*	May—October
Mint	*Mentha spicata*	August
Oregano	*Origanum marjorana*	June
Primula	*Primula denticulata*	March—May
Sage	*Salvia officinalis*	May—June
Ice plant	*Sedum spectabile*	September—October
Lemon verbena	*Lippia citriodora*	August
Wisteria	*Wisteria sinensis*	May—June

Effects of daylength on flowering

All flowering plants can be divided into three categories: those that flower in autumn when the days are becoming shorter; those that flower in spring and early summer when the days are becoming longer; and those that do not depend on the length of day to flower. In the first two categories, the short day and long day plants, the plants will flower only when the length of the day has reached a certain critical value. (*see pages 34–51*)

SHORT DAY PLANTS	
Aster	*Aster novi-belgii*
Balsam	*Impatiens balsamina*
Chrysanthemum	*Chrysanthemum sp*
Coffee	*Coffea arabica*
Corn	*Zea mays*
Cosmos	*Cosmos sulphureus*
Lima bean	*Phaseolus lunatus*
Love-lies-bleeding	*Amaranthus caudatus*
Soy bean	*Glycine max 'Biloxi'*
Sweet potato	*Ipomoea batatus*

LONG DAY PLANTS	
Black-eyed Susan	*Rudbeckia speciosa*
Carnation	*Dianthus superbus*
Cloud grass	*Agrostis nebulosa*
Dill	*Anethum graveolens*
Gardener's garters	*Phalaris arundinacea*
Italian rye grass	*Lolium italicum*
Peppermint	*Mentha piperita*
Radish	*Raphanus sativus*
Scarlet pimpernel	*Anagallis arvensis*
Spinach	*Spinacia oleracea*

DAY NEUTRAL PLANTS	
Carrot	*Daucus carota*
Cayenne pepper	*Capsicum frutescens*
Cucumber	*Cucumis sativus*
Holly	*Ilex aquifolium*
Honesty	*Lunaria annua*
Marigold	*Calendula officinalis*
Onion	*Allium cepa*
Potato	*Solanum tuberosum*
Spanish clover	*Gomphrina globosa*
Tomato	*Lycopersicon esculentum*

Seasons to propagate cultivated plants

To multiply already existing stocks of cultivated plants certain methods and times of propagation are most successful. The most widely used method is given here, together with the optimum season to apply it. Many plants are not propagated by seed, since the seed may produce a new plant that differs from its parent. (*see pages 34–51*)

Plant	Scientific name	Propagation time and method
Alder	*Alnus* sp	Sow seeds in autumn
Beech	*Fagus* sp	Sow seeds in autumn
Cedar	*Cedrus* sp	Sow seeds in autumn
Chrysanthemum	*Chrysanthemum* sp	Take cuttings all year round
Dahlia	*Dahlia* sp	Make root division in spring
Elm	*Ulmus* sp	Sow seeds in spring
Eucalyptus	*Eucalyptus* sp	Sow seeds in spring
Fig	*Ficus carica*	Take cuttings in autumn
Fir	*Abies* sp	Sow seeds in autumn or spring
Juniper	*Juniperus* sp	Take cuttings in late summer
Magnolia	*Magnolia* sp	Sow seeds in autumn or spring
Maidenhair	*Ginkgo biloba*	Sow seeds in autumn or spring
Maple	*Acer* sp	Sow seeds in summer or autumn
Oak	*Quercus* sp	Sow seeds in autumn
Olive	*Olea europaea*	Take cuttings in winter or summer
Shagbark hickory	*Carya ovata*	Make bark graft in winter to spring
Strawberry	*Fragaria chiloensis*	Lay runners in summer
Vine	*Vitis* sp	Take cuttings in winter
Walnut	*Juglans* sp	Patch bud in spring to summer
Yew	*Taxus* sp	Take cuttings in autumn

Human circadian rhythms

The activity of many of our biological functions rises and falls every 24 hours. The timing of these ups and downs has important implications for our lives. Alcohol, for example, is more easily metabolized in the evening than in the morning. Colds are more easily caught at night when our immunity to infection is lowest. (*see pages 130–41*)

	Time of maximum	Time of minimum
Sleep	Night	Day
Activity	Day	Night
Heart rate	Day	Night
Immunity to disease and infection	Day	Night
Utilization of proteins	Morning	Evening
Blood cortisol level	Mid morning	Evening
Blood sugar level	Middle of the day	Night
Body temperature	Middle of the day	Middle of the night
Production of urine	Middle of the day	Night
Mental performance	Middle of the day	Middle of the night
Blood pressure	Late afternoon	Early morning
Blood amino acid level	Evening	Morning
Rate of alcohol metabolism	Evening	Morning
Blood clotting speed	Midnight	Midday
Cell division rate	Midnight	Midday
Growth hormone secretion in children	Midnight	Midday
Keenness of the senses	Middle of the night	Middle of the day

Linnaeus's flower clock

Various flowers open or close at particular times of the day, and Carl Linnaeus, an eighteenth-century botanist, was the first to arrange some of these into a flower clock. By simply glancing at the clock one could tell the time to within half an hour. (*see pages 52–63*)

Time	Flower	Scientific name	Activity
6 am	Spotted cat's ear	*Hypochoeris maculata*	Opens
7 am	African marigold	*Tagetes erecta*	Opens
8 am	Mouse-ear hawkweed	*Hieracium pilosella*	Opens
9 am	Prickly sowthistle	*Sonchus asper*	Closes
10 am	Common nipplewort	*Lapsana communis*	Closes
11 am	Star of Bethlehem	*Ornithogalum umbellatum*	Opens
12 noon	Passion flower	*Passiflora caerulea*	Opens
1 pm	Childing pink	*Dianthus* sp	Closes
2 pm	Scarlet pimpernel	*Anagallis arvensis*	Closes
3 pm	Hawkbit	*Leontodon hispidus*	Closes
4 pm	Bindweed	*Convolvulus arvensis*	Closes
5 pm	White water-lily	*Nymphaea alba*	Closes
6 pm	Evening primrose	*Oenothera erythrosepala*	Opens

Blood pressure rhythm in man

Blood pressure is measured in an artery in the arm and is a reflection of the heart's action. As the ventricles contract and pump blood around the body, the blood pressure rises. This is the systolic pressure. The pressure then falls to a resting level, when the atria pump blood into the ventricles. This is the diastolic pressure. (*see pages 102–15 and 130–41*)

Average blood pressure (mm mercury)	Systolic pressure	Diastolic pressure
Newborn	80	46
6 months/1 year	89	60
3 years	100	67
8 years	105	57
13 years	115	60
17 years male	121	74
female	116	72
20–24 years male	123	76
female	116	72
30–34 years male	126	79
female	120	75
45–49 years male	130	82
female	131	82
55–59 years male	138	84
female	139	84
70–74 years male	145	82
female	159	85

Hibernation

The metabolism of hibernating animals falls to a low level during the cold winter months. This slow metabolic rate is shown by the low rectal temperatures and low heart rates of some hibernating mammals and one bird, the American poor-will. (*see pages 34–51*)

Animal	External temp °C	External temp °F	Rectal temp °C	Rectal temp °F	Heart rate (beats/min)
Golden hamster	5	41	6	42.8	14
Hedgehog	−20	−4	3.7	38.7	6
Poor-will	4.8	40.6	4.8	40.6	18
13-lined ground squirrel	5	41	5.5	41.9	8
Woodchuck	−1	30.2	5	41	18

Human heart rates

The heart beats more slowly as people get older. As a general rule, the heart rates of women are slightly higher than those of men. The figures given here are for normal resting people. (*see pages 102–15 and 130–41*)

Age (years)	Heart rate (beats/min)	Age (years)	Heart rate (beats/min)
At birth	140	12 male	70
1 male	116	female	71
female	122	15 male	65
2 male	104	female	67
female	103	20 male	64
3 male	92	female	69
female	86	30 male	59
6 male	87	female	65
female	80	40–60 male	57
9 male	81	female	70
female	85	60–70 male	66
		female	71
		70 male	65
		female	73

Animal heart rates

As a general rule, the smaller an animal the faster is its resting heart rate. Voles, shrews and bats are all tiny mammals with dramatically fast heart rates. Every animal's heart rate increases rapidly when it is active or afraid. Reptiles and amphibians, which are cold-blooded, have heart rates that rise and fall with the external temperature. (*see pages 102–15*)

Animal	Scientific name	Heart rate (beats/min)
MAMMALS		
Bat	*Pipistrellus pipistrellus*	660
Bat (hibernating)	*Pipistrellus pipistrellus*	30
Adult camel	*Camelus bactrianus*	28
Newborn cat	*Felis domesticus*	168
Young cat	*Felis domesticus*	300
Adult cat	*Felis domesticus*	200
Newborn cow	*Bos taurus*	150
Adult cow	*Bos taurus*	50
Adult elephant	*Elephas indicus*	30
Adult giraffe	*Giraffa camelopardalis*	66
Adult goat	*Capra hircus*	81
Adult hare	*Lepus europaeus*	64
Hedgehog	*Erinaceus europaeus*	246
Adult hyena	*Hyaena* sp	55
Adult lion	*Felis leo*	40
Mouse	*Mus musculus*	376
Newborn pig	*Sus scrofa*	227
Shrew	*Sorex cinereus*	782
Vole	*Microtus arvalis*	522
White rat	*Rattus norvegicus*	305
BIRDS		
American robin	*Turdus migratorius*	570
Cassowary	*Casuarius casuarius*	70
Hooded crow	*Corvus cornis*	379
Mallard	*Anas platyrhynchos*	320
Mourning dove	*Zenaidura macroura*	135
Ostrich	*Struthio camelus*	65
Peregrine falcon	*Falco peregrinus*	347
Starling	*Sturnus vulgaris*	388
Turkey	*Meleagris gallopovo*	93
REPTILES AND AMPHIBIANS		
Crocodile	*Crocodylus* sp	30 (at 15°C)
		70 (at 23.5°C)
Leopard frog	*Rana pipiens*	7 (at 2°C)
		37 (at 22°C)

Heart rates of diving mammals

The slowing of the heart rate is an adaptation to diving and ensures a reduced rate of blood flow to all organs except the brain. Along with other adaptations, it allows these mammals to remain below the surface of the water for long periods. (*see pages 102–15*)

Animal	Scientific name	Normal Heart Rate (beats/min)	Heart Rate while diving (beats/min)
Beaver	*Castor canadensis*	140	10
Bottle-nosed dolphin	*Tursiops truncatus*	110	50
Dolphin	*Delphinapterus leucas*	150	15
Manatee	*Trichechus* sp	60	30
Seal	*Phoca vitulina*	100	10
Whale	*Beluga* sp	145	16

Human respiration rates

The respiration rate slows down as people grow older, but for adults averages about 12 breaths per minute. Heavy work, such as lifting large weights, nearly doubles the rate. For someone who is not in training, heavy exercise, such as running or climbing a steep hill, increases it to nearly one breath per second. (*see pages 102–15*)

	Breaths/min
Premature baby	34
Newborn baby	29
Adult male, 150 lbs (68 kg)	12
doing light work	17
doing heavy work	21
doing heavy exercise	up to 53
Adult female, 119 lbs (54 kg)	12
doing light work	19
doing heavy work	30

Animal respiration rates

The smaller an animal, the faster the rate at which it breathes air in and out. The respiration rate also increases with the amount of activity. It decreases during hibernation and when marine mammals dive. (*see pages 102–15*)

Animal	Scientific name	Respiration rate (breaths/min)
Beaver	*Castor canadensis*	16
Blue whale	*Balaenoptera musculus*	4
Chipmunk	*Tamias striatus*	65
Deer mouse	*Peromyscus leucopus*	135
Dog	*Canis familiaris*	18
Dolphin	*Tursiops truncatus*	2
Flying squirrel	*Glaucomys volans*	91
Giraffe	*Giraffa* sp	32
Goat	*Capra hircus*	19
Golden hamster	*Mesocricetus auratus*	74
Guinea pig	*Cavia porcellus*	90
Horse	*Equus caballus*	10
Jersey cow	*Bos taurus*	27
Marmot	*Marmota marmota*	8
Marmot (hibernating)	*Marmota marmota*	0.7
Mouse	*Mus musculus*	163
Rabbit	*Oryctolagus cuniculus*	37
Rat	*Rattus norvegicus*	86
Rhesus monkey	*Macaca rhesus*	33
Sheep	*Ovis aries*	20
Short-tailed shrew	*Blarina brevicauda*	186
Spiny ant-eater	*Tachyglossus aculeatus*	14
Australian lungfish (in water)	*Neoceratodus forsteri*	28
Canary	*Serinus canarius*	57
Cardinal	*Richmondena cardinalis*	45
House wren	*Troglodytes aëdon*	83
Mallard	*Anas platyrhynchos*	42
Ostrich (12°C, 53.6°F)	*Struthio camelus*	5
Ostrich (25°C, 77°F)	*Struthio camelus*	45
Sparrow	*Passer domesticus*	50

Wing-beat frequencies

As a general rule, the larger the surface area of a bird's wings, the slower its wing-beat frequency. This physical relationship holds good for flying animals as varied as birds, bats and insects. (*see pages 116–29*)

Animal	Scientific name	Beats/second
BIRDS		
Hummingbird, 0.07 oz (2 gms)	Family Trochilidae	50
Hummingbird, 0.12 oz (3.5 gms)	Family Trochilidae	32
Hummingbird, 0.21 oz (6 gms)	Family Trochilidae	24
Sparrow	*Passer domesticus*	14
Swift	*Apus apus*	10
Owl, 14 oz (400 gms)	Family Strigidae	4
Pigeon	*Columba livia*	4
Crow	*Corvus corone*	3.6
Buzzard	*Buteo buteo*	3
Gull, 35.3 oz (1,000 gms)	*Larus canus*	3
Heron	*Ardea cinerea*	2.5
Stork	*Ciconia ciconia*	2
Pelican	*Pelicanus sp*	1
INSECTS		
Biting midge	Family Ceratopogonidae	1,000
Honey bee (drone)	*Apis mellifica*	235
Cuckoo bee (queen)	*Psithyrus rupestris*	123
Common rose beetle	*Cetonia aurata*	101
Red-winged hadena	*Apamea laterita*	45
Cockroach	*Periplaneta americana*	35
Privet hawkmoth	*Sphinx ligustri*	30
Dragonfly	Order Odonata	25
Swallowtail butterfly	*Papilio machaon*	5.5
BATS		
Lesser horseshoe bat, 0.88 oz (25 gms)	*Rhinolophus hipposideros*	17
Mouse-eared bat, 0.74 oz (21 gms)	*Myotis myotis*	11.5
Spear-nosed bat, 3.17 oz (90 gms)	*Phyllostomus hastatus*	10

Cell division cycles

Many of the microscopic single-celled organisms that cause diseases and infections multiply very rapidly. Most of their reproduction is a simple division into two of each microbial cell. The time they take to complete this cell division cycle may be only a matter of minutes or hours at body temperature (37°C, 98.6°F). (*see pages 94–101*)

Organism	Action/environment	Cycle length	°C	°F
Amoeba proteus	Found in freshwater ponds	5 hours	27	80.6
Clostridium botulinum	Causes botulism	35 mins	37	98.6
Diplococcus pneumoniae	Causes pneumonia	24.5 mins	37	98.6
Entamoeba histolytica	Causes amoebic dysentery	5 hours	37	98.6
Escherichia coli	Found in human intestines	16.5 mins	37	98.6
Influenza A, PR-8 virus	Causes influenza	7 hours	37	98.6
Paramecium aurelia	Feeds on bacteria and yeast	5 hours	27	80.6
Rhizobium leguminosarum	Fixes nitrogen in root nodules of plants	130 mins	25	77
Salmonella typhimurium	Causes dysentery	29 mins	37	98.6
Staphylococcus aureus	Causes boils	27 mins	37	98.6
Trichomonas vaginalis	Found in woman's vagina	5.5 hours	37	98.6
Trypanosoma mega	Causes protozoan infection	19 hours	23	73.4

Human cell and tissue cycles

Many human body cells divide continually and different cell types divide at different rates. The cells of the stomach lining divide every two days. As a result of these cell cycles (C), whole tissues are renewed (T). the gums are renewed every 94 days on average. (*see pages 94–101*)

	Cycle length
Lining of the mouth	5 days (T)
Gums	94 days (T)
Oesophagus	6 days (T)
Stomach	2 days (C)
Duodenum	4 days (T)
Ileum (part of small intestine)	2 days (C)
Colon (part of large intestine)	30 hours (C)
Colon (part of large intestine)	4 days (T)
Rectum	13 hours (C)
Cells that make red blood cells	20 hours (C)
Red blood cells	120 days (T)
Skin	308 hours (C)
Skin with psoriasis (disease causing red scaly patches)	37.5 hours (C)
Skin	26 days (T)
Hair cycle (on arms, chest, ears, eyebrows, hands and legs)	$5\frac{1}{2}$ months (T)

Development of human alpha rhythms

The brain's electrical activity is measured with an electroencephalograph, which records the type of rhythm and the voltage that generates it. Recordings from children of different ages reveal that the alpha rhythm begins to emerge at 20 months and is developed by the age of four. (*see pages 102–15 and 142–51*)

Age	Voltage	Frequency of dominant rhythm
3 days	Low	Irregular
3 months	Low	$1\frac{1}{2}$–3 cycles per sec
5 months	Increasing	$1\frac{1}{4}$–4 cycles per sec
6 months	High	4 cycles per sec
11 months	Moderate	4–5 cycles per sec
20 months	High/moderate	High at 4 cycles per sec with moderate at 8 cycles per sec (alpha rhythm)
4 years	High	9 cycles per sec alpha rhythm
8 years	Moderate	9–10 cycles per sec alpha rhythm

Length of sleep cycles

Sleep is a cyclical phenomenon. Every 90 minutes we go through one complete four-stage sleep cycle, each stage having a typical brain rhythm. Before beginning the next cycle we go through a light dream-filled sleep characterized by rapid eye movements. (*see pages 102–15*)

	Total sleep (per 24 hours)	Cycle length (mins)	Percentage of REM sleep
Cat	14	26	28
Hamster	14	12	23
Man	8	90	23
Mole	8	10	25
Mouse	13	12	10
Opossum	19	23	29
Rabbit	7	42	11
Rat	13	9	20
Squirrel	14	13	25

Animal life spans

The life span of an animal is the period of its life cycle from birth to death. The figures quoted here are the maximum periods that have been authentically recorded, although the average life cycle periods are obviously much shorter. (*see page 82–93*)

Animal	Scientific name	Years
MAMMALS		
Man	*Homo sapiens*	115
Fin whale	*Balaenoptera physalus*	80
Asiatic elephant	*Elephas maximus*	70
Hippopotamus	*Hippopotamus amphibius*	51
Ant-eater	*Tachyglossus aculeatus*	$49\frac{1}{2}$
Horse	*Equus caballus*	46
Chimpanzee	*Pan troglodytes*	$44\frac{1}{2}$
Rhinoceros	*Rhinoceros unicornis*	40
Gorilla	*Gorilla gorilla*	$39\frac{1}{2}$
Bear	*Ursus arctos*	37
Seal	*Phoca vitulina*	34
Giraffe	*Giraffa camelopardalis*	$33\frac{1}{2}$
Cow	*Bos taurus*	30
Camel	*Camelus bactrianus*	$29\frac{1}{2}$
Wild cat	*Felis catus*	28
Pig	*Sus scrofa*	27
Deer	*Cervus elaphus*	$26\frac{1}{2}$
Tiger	*Panthera tigris*	26
Beaver	*Castor canadensis*	20
Dog	*Canis familiaris*	20
Sheep	*Ovis aries*	20
Goat	*Capra hircus*	18
Platypus	*Ornithorhynchus anatinus*	17
Bat	*Pipistrellus subflarus*	15
Squirrel	*Sciurus carolinensis*	15
Fox	*Vulpes vulpes*	14
Rabbit	*Oryctolagus cuniculus*	13
Mink	*Mustela vison*	10
Chipmunk	*Tamias striatus*	8
Guinea pig	*Cavia porcellus*	$7\frac{1}{2}$
Golden hamster	*Mesocricetus auratus*	4
Hedgehog	*Erinaceus europaeus*	4
Mouse	*Mus musculus*	$3\frac{1}{2}$
Rat	*Rattus norvegicus*	$3\frac{1}{2}$
Shrew	*Sorex palustris*	$1\frac{1}{2}$
BIRDS		
Raven	*Corvus corax*	69
Condor	*Gymnogyps californicus*	65
Ostrich	*Struthio camelus*	50
Chicken	*Gallus gallus*	30
Swift	*Apus apus*	21
Mallard	*Anas platyrhynchos*	$20\frac{1}{2}$
Starling	*Sturnus vulgaris*	16
REPTILES AND AMPHIBIANS		
Eastern box turtle	*Terrapene carolina*	85
Alligator	*Alligator mississippiensis*	56
Leopard frog	*Rana pipiens*	6
FISH		
Sturgeon	*Acipenser fulvescens*	152
Carp	*Cyprinus carpio*	47
Pike	*Esox lucius*	24
Salmon trout	*Salmo trutta*	18
Mackerel	*Scomber scombrus*	15
Salmon	*Salmo salar*	13
Electric eel	*Electrophorus electricus*	$11\frac{1}{2}$

Signs of the Zodiac

From the point of view of people on Earth, the sun appears to make an annual passage in front of the 12 constellations called the signs of the zodiac. The table lists the dates when the sun enters and leaves these signs. People's characters are believed to be shaped by the sign in which the sun happens to be at the time of their birth. (*see pages 142–51*)

Annual apparent passage of the sun through the 12 constellations (signs of the zodiac)	
Aries	22 March—20 April
Taurus	21 April—21 May
Gemini	22 May—22 June
Cancer	23 June—23 July
Leo	24 July—23 August
Virgo	24 August—23 September
Libra	24 September—23 October
Scorpio	24 October—22 November
Sagittarius	23 November—22 December
Capricorn	23 December—19 January
Aquarius	20 January—19 February
Pisces	20 February—21 March

Astrological ages

Astrologers believe that every 25,868 years the Earth completes a Great Year which is divided equally into 12 astrological ages. We are now nearing the end of the Piscean age and entering the age of Aquarius. The age of Pisces is symbolized by Jesus, whose disciples were fishers of men and who fed the multitude with loaves and fishes. The age of Aquarius is symbolized by humanity, communication, and the beginning of space travel. (*see pages 142–51*)

Astrological Ages: the 12 Great Months of the Great Year (Each Age is approximately 2,160 years)	
Age	**Approximate span**
Age of Leo	10000— 8000 BC
Age of Cancer	8000— 6000 BC
Age of Gemini	6000— 4000 BC
Age of Taurus	4000— 2000 BC
Age of Aries	2000— 0 BC
Age of Pisces	AD 0— 2000
Age of Aquarius	AD 2000— 4000
Age of Capricorn	AD 4000— 6000
Age of Sagittarius	AD 6000— 8000
Age of Scorpio	AD 8000—10000
Age of Libra	AD 10000—12000
Age of Virgo	AD 12000—14000
Age of Leo	AD 14000—16000

Astrological cycles of planetary conjunctions

Planets are in conjunction when they are within 8° of each other in the sky. The influences of the planets then combine and are astrologically significant. When the same planets return to the same positions they complete a cycle of conjunction. Astrologically, there is a cycle of relationship between the planets. The meaning of the relationship depends not only on the planets concerned, but also on the sign in which the conjunction occurs, and the position of the planets in a person's horoscope. (*see pages 142–51*)

Planets	Period of conjunction (years)
Pluto and Neptune	492
Uranus and Neptune	171
Saturn and Uranus	91
Saturn and Neptune	35
Saturn and Jupiter	20
Jupiter and Uranus	14
Jupiter and Neptune	13
Jupiter and Pluto	12

1 Pluto cycle	=	$1\frac{1}{2}$ cycles of Neptune
	=	3 cycles of Uranus
	=	$8\frac{1}{2}$ cycles of Saturn
	=	21 cycles of Jupiter
	=	132 cycles of Mars
	=	248 cycles of Earth
	=	400 cycles of Venus
	=	$1,033\frac{1}{3}$ cycles of Mercury

The astrological ages and life periods of man

Astrologers divide a person's life into seven ages and assign a planet to rule over each age. The character of each planet governs and shapes the age over which it rules. The three life periods of man approximately coincide with the Saturn cycle at the end of which—at the ages of 28, 56, 84—great changes may occur in a person's life. (*see pages 142–51*)

Age (years)	Planetary ruler	Characteristics
1— 4	Moon	Total dependence of infant on its mother
5—14	Mercury	Curiosity and education
14—22	Venus	Adolescence; sexual maturity; entrance to society
23—41	Sun	Peak time of virility, health and activity
42—56	Mars	Increase of sphere of influence; realization of ambitions
57—68	Jupiter	Reflection on earthly events; contemplation of spiritual reality
68—death	Saturn	Life-assessment and preparation for death
After death —before birth	Pluto	The after life

LIFE PERIODS Life period (years)	Characteristics
1—28	Establishment of the self; growth from birth to adulthood
28—56	Expansion of the self; cultivation of one's self in a chosen field; role as parent and spouse
56—84	Contraction of the self; goals are achieved or not achieved, rewards are reaped, debts paid; preparation of the soul for physical death

Yin and Yang

According to the Chinese principle of opposites, everything is composed of yin and yang which are both antagonistic and complementary. (*see pages 142 51*)

	Yang	Yin
In the natural world	Day	Night
	Clear day	Cloudy day
	Spring/summer	Autumn/winter
	East/south	West/north
	Upper	Lower
	Exterior	Interior
	Hot	Cold
	Fire	Water
	Light	Dark
	Sun	Moon
In the body	Surfaces of the body	Interior of the body
	Spine/back	Chest/abdomen
	Male	Female
	Clear or clean body fluid	Cloudy or dirty body fluid
	Energy	Blood
In disease	Acute/virulent	Chronic/non-active
	Powerful/flourishing	Weak/decaying
	Patients feels hot or hot to touch or has a high temperature	Patient feels cold or cold to touch or has below normal temperature
	Dry	Moist
	Advancing	Retiring
	Hasty	Lingering

Sunspot cycles and historical events

It has been controversially suggested that a cycle of historical events is synchronized with the sunspot cycle, and that nearly all major historical events have occurred in the three or four years leading up to and including the time of peak sunspot numbers. The dates of recent sunspot maxima are given with some of the major events of the time. (*see pages 142–51*)

1778	The American War of Independence (1775–83) led to the Declaration of Independence (1776) and to the defeat of the British.
1788–89	The American constitution was drafted (1787); the French Revolution succeeded (1789) and led to the rise of the middle classes.
1802–3	An Irish rebellion was suppressed (1799); parliamentary union of Great Britain and Ireland—the United Kingdom formed (1800).
1817	Duke of Wellington ended the Napoleonic era, defeating the French at Waterloo (1815) but Britain entered an economic depression.
1829–30	Irish Catholics were emancipated (1829); the first police force was established in London (1829); Greece became independent (1830).
1837	Trade unionism was born (1834); the People's Charter was drawn up by the Chartists (1836); Victoria became Queen of England (1837).
1849	Communist Manifesto produced by Marx and Engels (1848); French Republic proclaimed (1848); gold found in California (1848).
1860–61	Uprisings occurred in India (1857–8); Darwin published *Origin of Species* (1859); American Civil War broke out (1861).
1871	Westernization of Japan began (1868); education was made available to all British children (1870); Paris Commune was declared (1870).
1883–84	Germany, Austria and Italy signed Triple Alliance (1882); terrorism struck Britain and Russia (1880–2); Krakatoa erupted (1883).
1893	Uprisings by socialists and anarchists occurred in France, Spain and USA (1890–2); a great famine spread across Russia (1892).
1905–7	South Africa erupted with the Boer War (1899–1902); church and state separated in France (1905); Russian Revolution failed (1905).
1917	The Easter uprising occurred in Dublin (1916); Russian Revolution succeeded (1917); Palestine became national home for Jews (1917).
1926	The General Strike occurred in Britain (1926); Stalin assumed power in Russia (1926); women in Britain were enfranchised (1928).
1937	Hitler became dictator (1934); Spanish Civil War broke out (1936); Keynesian economics began (1936); Japan attacked China (1936).
1948	The United Nations was formed (1945); the state of Israel was proclaimed (1948); revolution succeeded in China (1946–9).
1957	Israel invaded Egypt which led to the Suez crisis (1956); Russia invaded Hungary (1956) and launched the first space satellite (1957).
1968–69	The Cultural Revolution occurred in China (1965–8); worldwide protests take place (1968); Irish troubles began (1968–9).
1979–80	Democracy began in Spain (1976); drought struck Britain (1976); revolution in Iran (1979); Russia invaded Afghanistan (1979).

Page numbers in bold type refer to subjects mentioned in captions to illustrations. The majority of these subjects also appears in the main text (eg Adrenalin, **133**).
Page numbers in ordinary type refer to entries in the main text only (eg Aborigines, 75, 172).
Page numbers in italic refer to subjects contained only in charts (eg *Aix galericulata, 187*).

A

Aborigines, 75, 172
Acer campestre, 188
Acipenser fulvescens, 192
Activity patterns, **12–13**, **52–63**, 103–15, **134–5**, **154–5**
Acupuncture, 143, **146**, 147–8
Adaptation, 35, 54
Addison, Thomas, 138
Addison's disease, **136–7**, 138, 140
Adenosine triphosphate (ATP), **100**, 105, 109, 110
Adrenalin, **133**
Adrenocorticotrophic hormone (ACTH), **132**, **133**, **137**
Aestivation, 51
Agkistrodon contortrix, 187
Aix galericulata, 187
Alcohol, 63
  effects of, **155**
  metabolism, **134**
  tolerance levels, **135**
Algae, 30, 32
  blue-green, 105
  fucoid, 30
  green, **30**
  laminarian, **30**
  red, **30**
Allard, H.A., 45
Allergies, 141
Alligator mississippiensis, 187, 192
Alpha rhythms, 146, *191*
Alternation of generations **86**, 87
Althaea officinalis, 188
  rosea, 188
Alyssum saxatile, 188
Anas crecca, 187
  penelope, 187
  platyrhyncos, 187, 190, 192

Anchovies, **90**
Anemone, 43
Anguilla anguilla, 79
  rostrata, 79
Anser anser, 187
Ant, **55**
  honeypot, **110**
Ant-eater, *190, 192*
Antelope, 68, *124*
Antherea pernyi, 62
Anthrenus verbasci, 61
Antihistamines, 141
Antirrhinum majus, 188
Aphid, 83, 87, 90
  oat, **87**
  sycamore, 87
Apollo 11 mission, **20**
Apple, 43
Apricot, 43
Aptenodytes patagonica, 72
Aquilegia sp, 188
Arapaho Indians, 76
Archilochus colubris, 187
Ardea cinerea, 191
Aristotle, 79, 172
Armadillo, *187*
Asia, 26
Aspen, *188*
Astaire, Fred, **161**
Aster, 45, *188*
Aster novi-belgii, 188
Asthma, 138–40
  treatment, **139**, 140
Astrology, 143, **148–9**, *192, 193*
  ages of, *192*
  cycles of planetary conjunctions, *192*
Atropa belladonna, 188
Auk, little, *187*
Aurelia, 128
Aurora australis, **151**
  borealis, **151**
Autism, 157
Autumn, 22, **23**, 35–51, **36**, **49**, **60**, **61**, **70**, **87**
Aythya fuligula, 187
Aztecs, 173, 177
  calendar stone, **177**
  Sun god, **177**

B

Baboon, gelada, **68**
Babyhood, biological rhythms in, **12**, **13**
  growth rates, 95
Babylonians, 174
  calendar, 176
Backswimmer, **128**
Bacteria, 84, 97, 101
Badger, **67**
Balaenoptera musculus, 190
  physalus, 187, 192
Bamboo, Chinese umbrella, **45**, *188*
Barley, 47

Bat, 51, **71**, *190, 191, 192*
  hammerhead, 74
  horseshoe, 112, *191*
Bear, *192*
Beaver, *190, 192*
Bee, 86, **105**
  flight, 120
Beech, European, **40**, *188*
Beet, 45
Beetle, **122**
  carpet, 61
  Colorado, **40**
  Khapra, 51
  water, 85, 128
  whirligig, 128
Bell flower, *188*
Beluga sp, 190
Bering Strait, 26
Beta rhythm, 146
Bettmeralp glacier, 27
Betula pendula, 188
Beyond Culture, E.T. Hall, 168
Bilharzia, 85
Biofeedback, 143, 145, **146**
Biological clock, 13, 53–63, 132–3, **140**
Biomate, **144**
Biorhythms, 143, 144–5
  calculations, **144**
Bird, activity, **112**
  bipedal running, 124
  breeding seasons, 24, 65–81, **72**
  feeding, **111**
  migration, 70, **71**, **76**, *77, 187*
  moulting, 49
  respiration, **106**
  song cycle, 73, **74**
  torpor, 50–1
  wing-beats, **118**, 119, *191*
Bison bison, 76
Blackbird, **74**, **112**
Blackcock, 74
Black Cuillin Mountains, **27**
Blackfly, 92
Blaring brevicauda, 190
Bleeding heart, *188*
Blood, 106–9
  circulation, 134
  hormone content, **10**
Blood pressure, 10, 11, **133**, *189*
  high, **133**
  of astronauts, 131
Blowfly, 84, **89**
Bobolink, *187*
Body rhythms, human, 9–13, 103–15, 131–41, 143–7, 153–9, *189*
Body temperature, 13, **50**, **51**, **66**, **113**, **134**, 135, *189*
Bonasa umbellus, 111

Bos taurus, 187, 190, 192
Bougainvillea spectabilis, 188
Boxfish, 126
Brain, **10**, 11, **62–3**, **113**, **134**, **135**
Brain waves, **114–15**, 146
Bramble, *188*
Branta canadensis, 187
Breathing, 9–13, **105–107**, **138–39**, *190*
Breeding seasons, 40–41, 65–81, **68**, **70**, **75**, **76**, **80**, **81**, *187*
Bronchi, **138**
Buckwheat, *188*
Buddhism, 163, **172**
Budmoth, larch, **91**
Bufo americanus, 84, 187
Bufo bufo, 76
Bulb, 43
Bushbaby, *187*
Buteo buteo, 191
Butterbur, *188*
Butterfly, 85, *191*
Buzzard, *191*

C

Caesar, Julius, 177
Calendar, 176–8
  Assyrian, 176
  Aztec, **177**
  Babylonian, 176
  Chinese, 177
  civil, 176
  early systems, 176–7
  Egyptian, **176**
  French Revolutionary, **176**
  Greek, 176
  Gregorian, **176**, 177, 178
  Jewish, 176
  Julian, 177–9
  lunar, **176**, 177
  Mayan, 177
Calendar Round, 177
Californian poppy, *188*
Calluna vulgaris, 188
Caltha palustris, 188
Camel, 123, *190, 192*
  Bactrian, 48, *187*
Camelus bactrianus, 187, 190, 192
Camouflage, animal, **48**, 49
Campanula medium, 188
Canary, *190*
Cancer, drug treatment of, **141**
Canis familiaris, 190, 192
Capra hircus, 187, 190, 192
Capsella bursa-pastoris, 188
Carbon cycle, 100–1, **101**

Carcinus maenas, 58
Cardinal, *190*
Caretta caretta, 129
Caribou, **76**, **77**, 110
Carnac, France, 177
Carnivores, 36, **101**
Carp, European, *187, 192*
Cassowary, 124, *190*
Castor canadensis, 190, 192
Casuarius casuarius, 190
Cat, big, **69**
  domestic, 69, **70**, **115**, *124, 190, 191*
  wild, *192*
Caterpillar, western tent, 91
Cavia porcellus, 187, 190, 192
Cell cycle, 11, 96–7, *191*
  division, 11, 95, **96**, **97**, 98, *191*
  plant, 100–1
Cellulose, **100**
Centipede, 122
Cerastoderma edule, 98
Cerebellum, **114**, **134**
Cerebral cortex, **134**
Chameleon, 71
Chaplin, Charlie, 165
Cheetah, *124*
Chelonia mydas, 79
Chicken, prairie, **74**
Chimpanzee, 68, **113**, **115**, *187, 192*
China, ancient, 174, **175**
Chipmunk, *187, 190, 192*
Chizhevsky, A.L., **151**
Chlorophyll, 49, 100, **104**
Cholera, 93
Chronometer, marine, **179**
Chrysanthemum, 45
Cicada, 83
Ciconia ciconia, 191
Circadian rhythms, 11–13, 15, 21, 56–7, **62**, **63**, 111, 113, 131–41, **137**, **139**, **140**, **141**, 153, *189*
  significance in disease, 136
Circannual rhythms, 15, 60–1
Citellus lateralis, 50
Citellus tridecemlineatus, 71
Clam, 127
Clavius, Christopher, 177
Clepsydra *see* Water clock
Climate, changes in, 23–30, **28**, 38–9
  effects on breeding, **70**
Climatic zones, 17, 22, 24, 36–40, **39**

Clock, 174–5, 178–81
  atomic, 181
  drum, **179**
  early, **174–5**
  electric, 181
  escapement, 178, **179**,
    180
  falling weights, **178**
  grandfather, **181**
  pendulum, **178**, 179
  quartz, **181**
  spring-driven, **179**
  water, 174, **175**
Clover, 45
Clunio marinus, **59**, 60
Cockle, **98**
Cockroach, 56, 122,
  122, *124*
Coe, Sebastian, **144**
Coffea arabica, **47**
Coffee tree, **47**
Columba livia, 41, *191*
Columbine, *188*
Comet cycles, *186*
Common maple, *188*
Community rhythms,
  168–9
Continental drift, 20, *20*
Convoluta roscoffensis, **59**
Copulation, animal, **67**,
  69
Corm, 43
Corpus luteum, 66, 67
Corticosteroids, 134,
  136–7
  as drugs, 138, 141
Cortisol, **132**, **133**, 134,
  136, **137**, 189
Cortisone, 134, 136
Corvus cornis, *190*
Corylus avellana, *188*
  corone corone, **29**, *191*
  corone corvix, **29**
Cosmic rhythms, 15–33,
  186
Coturnix coturnix, *187*
Courtship rituals, 65,
  73, **74–5**
Cow, **67**, *187*, *190*,
  192
Crab, European shore,
  58
  fiddler, **58**
Crepidula fornicata, **86**
Crepuscular animals, 21
Cricetus cricetus, 72
Crocodile, *190*
Crocodylus sp, *190*
Crocus, **43**
  autumn, *188*
Crocus purpureus, **43**
  sativus, *188*
Crommelin comet, *186*
Crop plants, **46**, **47**
Crossbill, 76
Crotalus viridis, *187*
Crow, **118**, *191*
  carrion, **29**
  hooded, **29**, **118**, *190*
Crustaceans, 33, 80

Cuba, 47
Cuckoo, *187*
Cuculus canorus, *187*
Culex pipiens fatigans, **111**
Cultural rhythms,
  153–69
Cushing, Harvey, 137
Cushing's syndrome,
  136, **137**
Cyclamen coum, *188*
Cygnus olor, *187*
Cyprinus sp, *187*, *192*

D

Daffodil, 43
Dahlia, 45
Dance rhythms, 156,
  158, 159, **161**
  African, 161
  Indonesian, 161
Dandelion, 45
Dasypus novemcinctus,
  187
Daylength, changes in,
  22–3, **23**, 38, 49, 51
  effects on plants, 44–5,
    48, *188*
Daylight, changes in,
  40–1
  cycles, 56
  effect on breeding, 71
  in polar regions, *40*
Day-night cycle, 20, 21,
  22–3, 55, 56
  and temperature
    changes, 20, **21**, 22
Deadly nightshade, *188*
Deer, **60**, **61**, **70**, **71**
  courtship display, 68
  sika, **60**
Delphinapterus leucas,
  190
Delta waves, 146
Dendroica striata, *187*
Deoxyribonucleic acid
  (DNA), 62, **96**, **97**, 98
Deposition, Giotto, 173
Dervishes, **161**
Desert, 24, **39**, **45**
'Devil dancers', Sri
  Lanka, 163
Devonian, **20**
Dexamethasone, **137**
Diadema setosum, 80, **81**
Dicentra formosa, *188*
Dicrocoelium dendriticum,
  86, 87
Dictyota dichotoma, **59**,
  60
Didelphus marsupialis
  virginiana, *187*
Digestion, 111
Disease, 83, 89, 91,
  92–3, 131–41
  treatment of, 140–1
Display, sexual, 68–9

Diurnal animals, 21, 53,
  113
DNA *see*
  Deoxyribosenucleic
  acid
Dog, 66, **67**, 68, **69**, *190*,
  192
  hunting, 76
Dog's mercury, *188*
Dolichonyx oryzivorus,
  187
Dolphin, 68, **106**, **107**
  bottle-nosed, *190*
  swimming pattern, 129
Dormouse, 50
Dorylus, 55
Dove, mourning, *190*
  rock, **41**
  stock, **118**
Dragonfly, **84**, 85, **119**
Drepanosiphum
  platanoides, 87
Drosera rotundifolia, *188*
Drug treatment, 140–1
  of cancer, **141**
Duck, 70, 71
  tufted, *187*
Dysrhythmia, 156, 157

E

Earth, 15, 17–25, *186*
  age of, 16
  atmosphere, **17**, **24**, 53
  crust, **17**
  curvature, **23**
  distance from sun, 22,
    23, 24
  evolution, 16
  heat radiation, 25
  humidity on, 20, **21**
  orbital plane, 21, **22**,
    28, **29**
  precessional wobble, 30
  revolution around sun,
    149
  rotation, 20, 21, 22
  spin axis, 20, **21**, **25**,
    28, 29, 37, 39
  temperature of, 17, 24
Earthquake, 20, 150
East Africa, rainfall belt,
  39
Eclipse, moon, 22, 32
  sun, 22, 32
Ecosystems, 24, 36, 38,
  100
Eel, **78**, 79, *124*, **126**
  electric, *192*
Efficiency levels, human,
  113
Egyptians, ancient, 174,
  175, 176
Eider, *187*
Electroencephalogram
  (EEG), 115
Elephant, 84, **85**, *190*
  Asiatic, *192*

Elephantiasis, 92, 93,
  111
Elephas indicus, *190*
  maximus, *192*
Emotional rhythms, 156
Emu, 124
Enchelyopus cimbrus, 81
Encke comet, *186*
Energy, **100–1**, **103–15**
  production of, 104–5,
    110
Englemann, T.G., 13
Enterobius sp, 85
Entobdella soleae, 57
Equator, 22, **22**, **23**, 24,
  25, 30, 37, 38, **39**, **40**
Equus caballus, *187*, *190*,
  192
Erinaceus europaeus, **51**,
  190, *192*
Erithacus rubecola, 73
Eschscholzia californica, *188*
Eskimos, **110**
Esox lucius, *192*
Estrogen, **11**, **66**
Estrous cycle, 66–9, **67**,
  69, *187*
Eunice viridis, **59**, **80**
Euphorbia pulcherrima,
  44

F

Fagopyrium esculentum,
  188
Fagus sylvatica, **40**, *188*
Falcon, peregrine, *190*
Falco peregrinus, *190*
Family rhythms, 166–7
Feeding, **110–2**
Felis catus, *192*
  domesticus, *190*
  leo, *190*
Felix canadensis, 88
Fennel, *188*
Fern, 86, 87
Ferret, **70**, 71
Fertilization, 65
Finlay comet, *186*
Firefly, 75
Fish, bony, **98**, **106**
  growth rings, **98**
  respiration, **106**, 107
  sexual cycle, 72, **73**
  spawning, 80–1
  swimming, **126**
Flea, 120
Fliess, Wilhelm, 144
Flight, 118–20
  bird, **118**, **119**
  insect, **119**, 120
Flowering seasons,
  44–5, *188*
Fluke, lung, **84**, 86
  sheep liver, 86
Fly, tsetse, 86
Flycatcher, pied, 112
Foeniculum vulgare, *188*

Follicle stimulating
  hormone (FSH), **66**, 71
Food chains, 95, 112
Forest, rain, **39**
  temperate, **39**
  tropical, **39**
Fox, arctic, 88
  rabies cycle, **93**
  red, 88, 89, **93**
Freesia, *188*
Fritillaria imperialis, *188*
Frog, 21, 73, **85**, *113*,
  120, *190*, *192*
  leopard, *190*, *192*
Fundulus heteroclitus, 72

G

Galago senegalensis, *187*
Galanthus nivalis, **37**,
  188
Galileo, 150, **179**
Gamelan, Balinese, 161,
  162
Garner, W.W., 45
Garrya, 44
Gasterosteus aculeatus, **88**
Gauquélin, M., 149
Gentian, *188*
Gentiana asclepiadea, *188*
Gestation period, 70,
  187
Ginger lily, *188*
Giraffa camelopardalis,
  190, *192*
Giraffe, 72, **73**, 123, *124*,
  190, *192*
Glaciers, effects of,
  26–8, **27**, **28**
Glaucomys volans, 56,
  190
Glossina, 86
Goat, **70**, 71, *187*, *190*, *192*
Golden rod, 45
Goose, Canada, *187*
  greylag, *187*
Gorilla gorilla, *187*, *192*
Gorse, *188*
Goshawk, 89
Graham, George, **180**
Grain crops, **46**, 47
Gramineae, 47
Grape, **47**
Grebe, crested, **74–5**
Greece, ancient, 174
  calendar, 176
Gregory I, Pope, 174,
  175
Gregory XIII, Pope, 177
Greyhound, *124*
Grigg-Mellish comet, *186*
Groundnut, 47
Group patterns, human,
  168–9
Grouse, 74
  black, **89**
  ruffed, **111**
  willow, 89

Growth, **95–101**
Grunion, **81**
Guinea pig, **6**, *187*, *190*, *192*
Gull, *191*
  great black-backed, **118**

H

Hadley circulation, **24**
Haematoloechus medioplexus, **84**, 86, 87
Halley's comet, *186*
Hampton Court Clock, **178**
Hamster, 50
  European, 72
  golden, **68**, 69, *187*, *190*, *192*
Hare, **70**, *190*
  snowshoe, **88**, 89
Harrison, John, **179**
Harvesting, 47, 48
Hawk, **113**
Hay fever, 141
Hazel, *188*
Heart, **108–9**
Heartbeat, 9, 53, 134, **158**
  in infancy, 9, *189*
  rates of, 9, **11**, 55, 108, **109**, 131, **133**, *189*, *190*
Heart disease, **133**
Heath hen, 74
Heather, *188*
Hedera helix, *188*
Hedgehog, 50, **51**, 70, *187*, *190*, *192*
Hedychium densiflorum, *188*
Hellebore, *188*
Helleborus orientalis, *188*
Henbane, **44**
Henlein, Peter, 179
Hepatitis, 93
Herbivore, 36, **101**
Heron, *191*
Herring, 99, **126**
Herschel, William, 150
Hibernation, **50–1**, *189*
Himalaya mountains, 25
Hippopotamus amphibius, *192*
Hirundo rustica, 77, *187*
Hives *see* Nettlerash
Hollyhock, *188*
Holly tree, 44
Holocene, 25, 26
Honesty, *188*
Honey-bee, **57**, **105**
  flight, 120
Hooke, Dr Robert, 179, **180**
Hop, *188*
Hopi Indians, 172, **183**

Hormones, 133, 134
  levels of, 11
  output, **132–3**
  production cycles, 11, 66–7, 131
  sex, **66–7**, 69, **132**
Horse, **67**, *187*, *190*, *192*
  locomotion, 123, **123**, **124**
Horsechestnut, **48–9**
Hourglass, 175
Housefly, **63**
Humboldt current, **90**
Hummingbird, **118**, 119, *191*
  ruby-throated, *187*
Humulus lupulus, *188*
Huygens, Christiaan, 179
Hyaena sp, *190*
Hyalophora cecropia, **62**
Hydrogen, 18, 104
Hyena, 76, 123, *190*
Hypothalamus, **63**, **134**, 135, **136**, 137
Hypsignathus monstrosus, 74

I

Ice Ages, 25–9, **26**, **27**, **28**, **29**
Ice caps, **28**
Ice plant, *188*
Ilex, 44
Impala, 76
Impatiens noli-tangere, *188*
India, **25**
Indian Ocean, **25**
Industrial rhythms, **165**
Insects, breeding seasons, 24, 75
  diapause, 51
  social, 86
  ventilating mechanisms, **10**
  wing vibration, 9, **119**, 120
International Date Line, **183**
International Time Zones, **183**
Ipomoea, **57**
Iris, 43
Israel, ancient 174
Italy, 174
Ivy, *188*

J

Jackal, 76
Jellyfish, 80, 127, **128**
  European, 128
Jerboa, **112**, 120, 121
Jet lag, **135**, 136, 155

Jet propulsion, in aquatic creatures, 127
Jumping, **120–1**
Jupiter, 16, *186*

K

Kangaroo, 72, 120, **121**
  red, **121**, *187*
Kelp, laminarian, 33
Killifish, 72
Kingbird, eastern, *187*
Kleitman, N., 13

L

Lambing season, **41**
Lamprey, *187*
Lampyridae, 75
Larus canus, *191*
Legionella pneumophila, **97**
Legionnaire's disease, **97**
Lek, **74**
Lemming, 88
Lemon verbena, *188*
Lemur, 68, *187*
Lemur catta, *187*
Lennon, John, 149
Leodice fucata, 80
Leonitis leonurus, *188*
Leptinotarsa decemlineata, **40**
Lepus americanus, **88**
Lepus europaeus, *190*
Leukemia, studies of, 141
Leuresthes tenuis, **81**
Lichen, 30, 32, 33
Life span, 83–7, *192*
Lime, small-leafed, *188*
Limpet, slipper, **86**
Linnaeus, Carl, **57**, *189*
  flower clock, **57**, *189*
Lion, *190*
  marsupial, 121
Lion's tail, *188*
Lippia citriodora, *188*
Lizard, 124, **125**
  basilicus, **125**
  collared, 123, **124**
Loa loa, 92, 93
Loaiasis, 92
Lobelia, *188*
Lobelia erinus, *188*
Locomotion, 117–29
  amphibian, **120**
  bird, **118–9**, **124**
  fish, **126**, **127**
  frog, **120**
  insect, **119–20**, **122**, **128**
  invertebrate, **122**, **128**
  lizard, **125**
  mammalian, **120–1**, **123**
  snake, **127**
  turtle, **129**

Locust, **105**
Lotus, *188*
Love-in-a-mist, *188*
Lucilia cuprina, **89**
Lugworm, marine, 122
Lunaria annua, *188*
Lunar rhythms, 60
  effects on spawning, 80–1
Lung, **138**, 139
Lungfish, **51**, *190*
Lupin, *188*
Luscinia megarhyncha, *187*
Luteinizing hormone (LH), **66**
Lynx, 88, **89**

M

Macaca mulatta, *187*
  rhesus, *190*
Macaque monkey, 68
Mackerel, *192*
Macropus robustus, *187*
Magicicada spp, 83
Maize, **42**
Malacosoma sp, 91
Malaria, **92**
Mala moschata, *188*
Malinke tribe, West Africa, **158**
Mallard, *187*, *190*, *192*
Mallow, **188**
Mammals, activity, 112–13
  breeding seasons, 24, 66–72
  camouflage, **48**
  hibernation, **50–1**
  locomotion, **120–25**
  respiration, **107**
  sleep, 114–5
Man, beliefs, **143–51**, **162–3**, **172–3**
  biological cycles, 9–13, **131–41**
  discovery of agriculture, 46
  eating, **110**
  evolution, 35, 46
  health, **131–41**, **146–7**, **154–5**
  life cycle, 83
  life-span, 35, *192*
  locomotion 117, 123, **124–5**
  mental performance, **113**, **134–5**
  reproduction, **66**, 67, 69, 75, *187*
  respiration, **107**, *190*
  sexual behaviour, **69**, 75
  sleep, **115–6**
Manatee, *190*
Mandarin, *187*

Mandrill, *187*
Mangebey, 68
Mansfield, Jayne, **144**
Mantis, 122
Marmot, *190*
Marmota marmota, *190*
Mars, 16, **17**, 18, *186*
Marsh mallow, *188*
Marsh marigold, *188*
Marten, 88
Mayan timekeeping, 173, 177
Mayfly, 60, **81**
Meal patterns, 154, **155**
Measles, 83, **93**
Meditation, **146**, 163
Medulla, **136**
Megaleia rufa, **121**, *187*
Megaptera novaeangliae, **78**
Meleagris gallopovo, *190*
Melocanna sp, *188*
Menstrual cycle, 11–12, 59, **66**, 67, **69**, 155
Mentha spicata, *188*
Mercurialis perennis, *188*
Mercury, 16, **17**, *186*
Mesocricetus auratus, **68**, 69, *187*, *190*, *192*
Meteor showers, *186*
Metonic cycle, 176
Microtus agrestis, **111**
  arvalis, *190*
Midge, 59, 119, *191*
Migration, 75–9, 85, **112**
  bird, 9, 24, 76, **77**, *187*
  fish, **78**, **79**
  human, 77
  mammalian, 76, **77**, **78**
  turtle, **79**
  see also Birds
Milankovitch, Milutin, 29
  theory of variable planetary climate, 29–30
Milky Way, **16**
Millipede, **122**, **124**
Mimosa pudica, **54**, **55**
Miniopterus australis, 70
Mink, **67**, *187*
Minnow, 72
Mint, *188*
Mirounga leonina, **75**
Mistletoe, *188*
Moa, 124
Modern Times (film), 165
Mole, **115**
Mollusc, 33, 80
Mongoose, 70
Monkey, rhesus, *187*, *190*
Monsoon season, **25**, *186*
Moon, craters, 32
  eclipses, 32
  gravitational pull, 30–31, 32, **33**
  influence on sexual cycles, 65

Moon (*cont.*)
  phases of, **32–3**
  see also Lunar cycles,
    Tides
Morning glory, **57**
Mosquito, **92, 111**
Moth, 85
Mouse, **67, 113**, *187,*
  190, 191, 192
  estrous cycle, **67**
Muscari armeniacum, 188
Music, 160–2
  Balinese, 161, 162
  emotional effects of,
    160
Musk rat, *187*
Mus musculus, 187, 190,
  192
Mustela erminea, 48, 49
  vison, 187
Myotis myotis, 191
Myrmecocystus, 110

N

Nelumbo nucifera, 188
Neoceratodus forsteri, 190
Neolithic revolution,
  46–7
Nephoecetes niger, 187
Neptune, 16, *186*
Nerve impulses, 53
Nervous system,
  autonomic, 11, 132–3,
  132
Nettlerash, 141
Neuroterus, 87
Newt, 21, 85
Nicholson, A.J., 89
Nicotiana tabacum, 45
Nigella damascena, 188
Nightingale, *187*
Nocturnal animals, 21, **113**
Nocturnal (timepiece),
  175, **175**
North American
  Indians, 75

O

Oak, sessile, *188*
Oat, 47, **87**
Octopus, 127
Onchocerciasis, 92
Oncorhynchus spp, 78, 79
Ondatra zibethicus, 187
Opossum, **67, 115**, *191*
  Virginia, *187*
Oregano, *188*
Orgasm, **69**
Origanum marjorana, 188
Ornithorhyncus anatinus,
  187, 192
Oryctolagus cuniculus,
  187, 190, 192
Osprey, *187*

Ostrich, **124**, *190, 192*
Ovis sp, 187, 190
Ovulation, **66, 67,** 69
Owl, **113**, *191*
  snowy, 89
Oxygen, 17, 27, 28, 29,
  100, 101, 104–5, **106,**
  107, 108, **109, 138**

P

Palmer, Arnold, 145
Pandian haliaetus, 187
Pangaea, 28
Panthera tigris, 69
Pan troglodytes, 187, 192
Papio sp, 187
Paramecium, 122
Parasite, **84,** 85–6, 87,
  89, 91, 92, 111
Passer domesticus, 190,
  191
Peach, 43
Pear, 43
Pelican, *191*
  brown, 90
Penguin, 72
  King, **72**
Performance levels,
  human, **113, 134,**
  135, 136
Permocarboniferous, 28
Peromyscus leucopus, 190
Petastites hybridus, 188
Petrochelidon albifrons,
  187
Petromyzon marinus, 187
Phalaeonoptilus nuttalli,
  50, **51**
Pheromone, 68
Phoca vitulina, 187, 190,
  192
Phocoena phocoena, 187
Photoperiodism, 40–1,
  44, 45, 70, *188*
Photosphere, 19, 24
Photosynthesis, 17, 20,
  36, 42, 46, 49, **59,**
  100, 101, 104, 105
Phoxinus phoxinus, 72
Phyllostachys
  bambusoides, 188
Phyllostomus hastatus,
  191
Pig, **67,** *187, 190, 192*
Pigeon, **118, 119,** *191*
Pike, *192*
Pine, bristlecone, 27, **99**
Pineal, **63,** 71
Pinworm, 85
Pipistrellus pipistrellus,
  190
  subflarus, 192
Piranga ludoviciana, 187
  olivacea, 69
Pituitary gland, **132,**
  133, 134, 135, **136,**
  137

Plague, 93
Plaice, **73,** *187*
Planets, 15, **16,** 17, 18,
  149, *186, 192, 193*
Plankton, 112–3
Plants, alternation of
  generations, **86,** 87
  carbon cycles, 100–101
  cells, **96–7, 100,** 104
  cultivated, **42, 43, 46,**
    47, *189*
  daily cycles, **54,** 56–7
  flowering, 37, **43, 44–5,**
    83, *188*
  germination, **42**
  leaf-fall **48–9**
  seasonal growth cycle,
    9, **23,** 35, **36–49,** 83
  seed distribution, **46**
  transpiration, **104**
  see also Photosynthesis
Plantus alle, 187
Plasmodium malariae, 92
  ovale, 92
  vivax, 92
Platynereis, 60
Platypus, *187, 192*
Pleiades, **175**
Pleistocene, 25, 26, **27,**
  28, 29, 35
Plesiosaur, **129**
Plethodon cinereus, 112
Pleuronectes sp, 187
Plover, crab, **58**
Pluto, 16, 17, *186*
Podiceps cristatus, 74–5
Poinsettia, **44**
Polaris, **21, 22,** 30, **175**
Polar years, 39–40
Polar zones, 36, 37, **40**
Poles, geographic, **20,**
  21, 22
  magnetic, **19,** 20
Pole star *see* Polaris
Poliomyelitis, 93
Pollination, **44,** 46
Polyp, 127
Poor-will nightjar, 50,
  51, *189*
Populations, 83–93
Populus tremula, 188
Porcupine fish, 126
Porpoise, *187*
Povilla adusta, **81**
Precambrian, 28
Premenstrual tension, 67
Primrose, 43, *188*
Primula vulgaris, 188
  denticulata, 188
Procyon lotor, 187
Progesterone, **11, 66,** 67
Protonaria citrea, **70**
Protopterus, **51**
Protozoa, **84, 92**
Psychedelic drugs, 183
Puffinus tenuirostris, 70
Pulse rate, **11,** 108, **109,**
  131, **133, 134,** *147*
Pyramid of the Sun,
  Mexico City, **177**

Q

Quail, *187*
Quaternary, 25, 27
Quelea, 73
Quercus petraea, 188

R

Rabbit, 66, **67,** 76, 123,
  124, *187, 190, 191, 192*
Rabies, 83, **93**
Raccoon, 70, *187*
Radiocarbon dating, 27
Rainfall, 23, 24, **25, 37,**
  38, 39, 45, 51, *186*
  effects on breeding, **73**
  see also Monsoon
Rain forest, 39
Ramadan, **155**
Rana pipiens, 84, 190,
  192
Rangifer tarandus, 76, 77
Rat, **67,** 71, 111, *187,*
  190, 191, 192
  kangaroo, **120**
  white, *190*
Rattlesnake, **127,** *187*
Rattus norvegicus, 187,
  190, 192
Ray, manta, 129
Religious rituals, 162–3
  African, **162**
  Islamic, **162**
Reproduction, 64–81,
  83–93
  in amphibians 73
  in birds, **69, 70, 71**
  in fish, 73, 76–81
  in mammals, 65, **66,**
    67, 68, 70, 71, **73**
  see also Breeding
    seasons, Migration
Respiration, 10, 103–9,
  105–7, 114–5, **138–9,**
  190
Rheumatoid arthritis,
  136, 138
Rhinoceros unicornis, 192
Rhinolophus hipposideros,
  191
Rhizome, 43
Rhopalosiphum padi, **87**
Ribonucleic acid (RNA),
  98
Rice, **46,** 47
Richmondena cardinalis,
  190
River blindness, 92
RNA *see* Ribonucleic
  acid
Robin, American, *190*
  European, **73**
Rogers, Ginger, **161**
Root crops, 83
Rosaceae, 43

Roundworm, 92
Rowan, *188*
Rubicolor minor, 187
Rubus fruticosus, 188
Running, **122–3, 124–5,**
  144
Rye, 47
Rye grass, **44**

S

Sage, *188*
Salamander, 85
  red-backed, **112**
Salisbury cathedral,
  turret clock, 178, **179**
Salmon, **78, 79,** *187,*
  192
Salmonella, 93
Salmo salar, 79, 187, 192
  trutta, 192
Salvia officinalis, 188
Sandgrouse, 76
Saturn, 16, *186*
Savanna, 24, **38, 39**
Scaphiopus bombifrons,
  73
Schistosoma, 85, 87
Schwabe, Heinrich, 150
Scomber scombrus, 192
Sea gooseberry, **122**
Seahorse, **126–7**
Seal, *187, 192*
  elephant, **75,** 95
Seashore, 30, **31,** 57,
  58–9
Seasnake, 126
Sea urchin, 80, **81**
Seaweed, 30, **59**
Sedum spectabile, 188
Serinus canarius, 190
Sexual cycles *see*
  Breeding seasons
Sexual display, **68–9**
Shadow clock *see*
  Sundial
Shearwater, 70
Sheep, **67, 70,** 71, *187*
Shelduck, 70, *187*
Shepheard's Kalender,
  The, 36
Shepherd's purse, *188*
Shift work, 136, **139,**
  166–7
Shortt, William H., 181
Shrew, 70, *187, 190,*
  192
Sidereal day, 21, 176
Sidewinder, **127**
Silkmoth, **62**
Silver birch, *188*
Sirius, **176**
Sleep, animal, 114, **115**
  human, 9, 11, **12,** 13,
    55, 113, **114–5, 134,**
    135, 136, **139, 155,** *191*
Snake, **113, 127**
  moccasin, *187*

Snapdragon, *188*
Snowdrop, 37, 43, *188*
Social rhythms, 12–13, 113, 134–5, 144–5, 154–69, 171–83
Solar day, 21, 171–7, 179
see also Circadian rhythms
Solar flare, **151**
Solar system, 15–33
Solar year, 171, 176–7, **183**
Sole, 57
Somateria mollissima, 187
Sorbus acuparia, 188
Sorex araneaus, 187
cinereus, 190, 192
palustris, 192
Sosigenes, 177
Sparrow, *190, 191*
Californian white-crowned, 70
Spawning, 76, 78, **80–1**
Speech rhythms, 159, 160
Spider, **122**, *124*
Spinach, **44**
Springhaas, 121–2
Springtail, 120
Squirrel, 70, *191, 192*
flying **56**, *190*
ground, 50, **66, 67**, 71
Starling, 74, *190, 192*
Stars, 16, **21**, 22, 30, **175**, 176
Sterna fuscata, **71**
paradisaea, **77**
Steroid drugs, 134, 136, **137**
Stickleback, **68, 69**
Stoat, 123
ermine, **48, 49**
Stonehenge, **177**
Stork, *191*
Stratosphere, **16**, 17
Stress, 115, 134–5, 136–7, 155
Struthio camelus, 190, 192
Sturgeon, *192*
Sturnus vulgaris, 74, *190, 192*
Sufi, **161**
Sugar cane, 47
Summer solstice, 22, **25**, **44**, 176, **177**
Sun, 16, 18, **19**, **22**
energy from, **16**, 18–19, **20**, 21, 23, 24–5, **28, 100, 101**, 103, **104**
Sundial, 174, **175**
Sunflower, 45
Sun sign, **148–9**
Sunspots, **18, 19**, 150–1, *193*
Sus scrofa, 187, 190, 192

Swallow, barn, *187*
European, 77, *187*
Northern cliff, *187*
Swan, mute, *187*
Sweet violet, *188*
Swift, *191, 192*
Northern black, *187*
Swimming, **126–7**
see also Fish
Swoboda, Hermann, 144
Sympterum, **84**

T

Tabanid, 92
Tachyglossus aculeatus, 190, 192
Tadorna tadorna, 70, *187*
Tadpole, 73, **85**
Tamias striatus, 187, 190, 192
Tanager, scarlet, **69**
Western, *187*
Taoists, **173**
Tarsier, 68
Tasmania, introduction of sheep, **88**
Teal, *187*
Teltscher, Alfred, 144
Temperate regions, **20**, 21–5, **36–51**, 72–3
Temperature, environmental **20, 21**, **29**, 36, **37**, 38–51, 72–3, 112–3, 180
Termite, 86
Tern, Arctic, 76, **77**
sooty, **71**
Terrapene carolina, 187
Testosterone, 73
Testudo hermanni, **98**
Thamnocalamus spathaceus, 45, 188
Theropithecus gelada, 68
Theta waves, 146
Thrip, **119**
Thrush, 70
Thunnus albacares, 187
Thylacinus cynocephalus, 121
Thylacole carniflex, 121
Thyroid gland, **136**
Tides, 30, 31, 32, **33**, 55, 58–9, **80–1**
neap, 31, **33, 59**, 60, 65
spring, 31, **33, 59**
Tiger, **69**
Tilia cordata, 188
Time, 171–83
cyclical, 172–3
nautical, **179**
perception, 182, **183**
Timekeeping, **178–81**
ancient practices, 174, 175
Tiv people, Nigeria, 154, 158, 159

Toad, 21, 73, 85
American, *187*
clawed, *187*
common, 76
spadefoot, **73**
Tobacco plant, 45
Tomato, 45
Tortoise, **98**
giant, *124*
Touch-me-not balsam, *188*
Trade winds, **24**
Trance, 163
Transplant surgery, 138, **141**
Trees, 9
deciduous, **40**, 43, **48**, 50
disease, **91**
growth rings, 99
leaf-fall, **48**, 50
ring-dating, 27, **99**
Trichechus sp, *190*
Troglodytes aëdon, 190
Trogoderma granarium, 51
Tropical rain forest, 24, 38, **39**
Tropic of Cancer, **22**, 38
Tropic of Capricorn, 22, 38
Troposphere, 16, **17**
Trout, **126**
salmon, *192*
Tsavo National Park, **38, 39**
Tuber, 43
Tulip, 43
Tuna, **126**
yellow-fin, *187*
Turdus ericetorum, 70
merula, **74**
migratorius, 190
Turkey, *190*
Tursiops truncatus, 190
Turtle, **78, 115**, 128
Eastern box, *187*
green, **79**
loggerhead, **129**
Tuttle comet, *186*
Tympanuchus cupido, **74**
Tyrannus tyrannus, 187

U

Uca sp, **58**
Ulex europaeus, 188
Uranus, 16, *186*
Urine flow, **10, 11, 13**, *189*
Ursus arctos, 192
Urticaria *see* Nettlerash
Utah Valley, **49**

V

Vancouver, **37**
Venus, 16, 17, *186*

Vine, **47**
Viola odorata, 188
Visconti, Palace of the, 178
Viscum album, 188
Vitis vinifera, **47**
Vole, 89, *190*
short-tailed, 111

W

Walking, **123**, 124–5
Wallaroo, *187*
Wapiti, **60**
Warbler, black-polled, *187*
European garden, **61**
prothonotary, **70**
willow, **61**
Wasp, **87**
Watch, 180, **181**
Water boatman, 85, **128**
Water clock, 174, **175**
Waxwing, 76
Weasel, 70
Weather, 24–7, 30, **39**, 40, 151
effects on reproductive cycles, 70, 72, 73
Whale, 68, **78, 107**, *190*
blue, *190*
fin, **106**, *187, 192*
humpback, **78**
sperm, **106**
Whooping cough, **93**
Wigeon, *187*
Wildebeest, 76
Wind, **24, 25**
solar, 151
trade, **39**
Winter solstice, 22, **25**, **44**, 174
Wisteria sinensis, 188
Wolf, Tasmanian, 121
Woodchuck, 50
Woodcock, American, *187*
Working rhythms, 113, **134–5, 144–5, 164**, **165**
Worm, 33, 80
palolo, 59, 60, **80**
Wren, house, *190*
Wucheria bancrofti, 93, **111**

X

Xenopus laevis, 187

Y

Yeasts, 84
Yin and yang, **146, 147**, **173**, *193*

Yoga, 146, 162–3
Yosemite National Park, 27

Z

Zea mays, **42**
Zebra, 76
Zech, Jacob, **179**
Zeiraphera griseana, 90, **91**
Zenaidura macroura, 190
Zen Buddhism, **146**
Zodiac, signs of **148**, 149, *192*
Zonotrichia leucophrys, **70**

ACKNOWLEDGEMENTS

The authors contributed text as follows:

Dr Philip Whitfield	8–13, 14–33, 34–51, 94–101, 102–115, 185
Dr John Brady	52–63
Dr D.M. Stoddart	64–81, 116–129
Dr Bryan Turner	82–93
Dr Martin Hetzel	130–141
Kendrick Frazier	142–151
Paul Bohannan	152–169
Chris Morgan	170–183

The Publishers received invaluable help during the preparation of **The Rhythms of Life** from:
Mary Corcoran, picture researcher; Libby Wilson, editorial assistant; Ann Kramer, who compiled the index; Robert De Filipps of the Office of Biological Conservation, Smithsonian Institution; Barbara Anderson; Candy Lee; Nigel O'Gorman

Typesetting by Servis Filmsetting Limited, Manchester
Origination by Adroit Photo Litho Limited, Birmingham

Throughout this book a billion = 1,000,000,000

The Publishers wish to thank the photographers and agencies listed below for their help in providing material for this book. The following abbreviations have been used: *t top; tr top right; tl top left; c centre; l left; r right; br bottom right; bl bottom left; b bottom.*
Cover:
1 Babout/Rapho; 2/3 Tony Stone Associates; 4/5 Courtesy of National Film Archive/Stills Library; 6/7 Stephen Dalton/Bruce Coleman (owls), A. Wetzel/ZEFA (moon), Spectrum Colour Library (cloud); 8/9 Camera Press; 10/11 John Garrett; 12 John Bigg; 13 Lorna Minton; 14/15 Bill Brooks/Masterfile; 16 Space Frontiers Ltd; 17 *t* Space Frontiers Ltd; 17 *b* Jet Propulsion Laboratory; 18/19 Space Frontiers Ltd; 20 *l* Space Frontiers Ltd; 20 *r* Dr C.T. Scrutton, University of Newcastle upon Tyne/*New Scientist*; 20/21 Lick Observatory Photograph; 22 Michael Boys/Susan Griggs Agency; 24 Space Frontiers Ltd; 25 Santosh Basak/Frank Spooner Pictures; 26 Aerofilms Ltd; 27 *l* Oxford Scientific Films; 27 *r* John Cleare; 30/31 Horst Munzig/Susan Griggs Agency; 32/33 Lick Observatory Photographs; 34/35 Denis Waugh; 36 Ann Ronan Picture Library; 37 Adam Woolfitt/Susan Griggs Agency; 38 Heather Angel; 39 P.H. & S.L. Ward/Natural Science Photos; 41 Ardea London; 45 The Photographic Library of Australia; 46 Mireille Vautier; 47 H.W. Silvester/Rapho; 48 Roland & Sabrina Michaud/John Hillelson Agency; 49 Dr J.A.L. Cooke/Oxford Scientific Films; 52/53 David Thompson/Oxford Scientific Films; 56 Stouffer Productions/Bruce Coleman; 57 Wayne Lankinen/Bruce Coleman; 60 Charlie Ott/Bruce Coleman; 62 The Mansell Collection; 64/65 R. Kruschel/Okapia; 68 Varin-Visage/Jacana; 69 Leonard Lee Rue III/Bruce Coleman; 71 Valerie Taylor/Ardea London; 72 Francisco Erize/Bruce Coleman; 73 *l* Carol Hughes/Bruce Coleman; 73 *r* Joe McDonald/Oxford Scientific Films; 74 P. Jones-Griffiths/John Hillelson Agency; 75 Massart/Jacana; 76 *l* P. Bading/ZEFA; 76 *r* David & Katie Urry/Ardea London; 77 Bryan & Cherry Alexander; 78 Jane Burton/Bruce Coleman; 80 Ted Spiegel/John Hillelson Agency; 82/83 Tadanori Saito/Rex Features; 85 Alan Root/Bruce Coleman; 86 Nigel O'Gorman; 90 Marion Morrison; 91 Swiss National Tourist Office; 93 Mike Abrahams/Network; 94/95 David Thompson/Oxford Scientific Films; 96 Carolina Biological Supply Co/Oxford Scientific Films; 97 E.H. Cook/Science Photo Library; 98 Zig Leszczynski/Oxford Scientific Films; 102/103 Adam Woolfitt/Susan Griggs Agency; 104 F.G. Bass/Natural Science Photos; 106 Ken Balcomb/Bruce Coleman; 107 David Redfern; 109 Oxford Scientific Films; 110 Tibor Hirsch/Susan Griggs Agency; 111 Wayne Lankinen/Bruce Coleman; 113 Spectrum Colour Library; 114 Edward Hausner/NYT Pictures/John Hillelson Agency; 116/117 Pete Turner/The Image Bank; 119 Stephen Dalton/NHPA; 120 Stephen Dalton/Oxford Scientific Films; 121 Jean-Paul Ferrero/Ardea London; 123 The Royal Photographic Society; 124 *l* Philippe Varin/Jacana; 124 *r* Root/Okapia; 125 Leo Mason; 127 David Hughes/Bruce Coleman; 128 *l* Dr Giuseppe Mazza; 128 *tr* Heather Angel; 128 *br* Colorsport; 129 Dr Giuseppe Mazza; 130/131 Howard Sochurek/John Hillelson Agency; 133 John Watney; 141 L.L.T. Rhodes/Daily Telegraph Colour Library; 142/143 Michael Friedel/Woodfin Camp & Associates/Susan Griggs Agency; 144 *r* Kobal Collection; 145 Sporting Pictures (UK) Ltd; 146 Alan Hutchison Library; 147 *l* Bruno Barbey/John Hillelson Agency; 147 *r* Roland & Sabrina Michaud/John Hillelson Agency; 150 Bruno Barbey/John Hillelson Agency; 151 Spectrum Colour Library; 152/153 Anthony Crickmay; 154 Phelps/Rapho; 155 *l* Marc Tulane/Rapho; 150 *r* Sergio Larrain/John Hillelson Agency; 156 Patrick Thurston; 157 *l* Clive Barda; 157 *r* Abbas/Frank Spooner Pictures; 158 *l* John Bulmer; 158 *r* Richard & Sally Greenhill; 159 Mike Abrahams/Network; 160/161 Peter Carmichael/Aspect Picture Library; 161 Kobal Collection; 162 *l* Tony Carr/Colorific!; 162 *r* Rabout/Rapho; 163 Marc Riboud/John Hillelson Agency; 164/165 Tadanori Saito/*The Sunday Times*, London; 166 John Sturrock/Report, London; 167 Associated Press; 168 *l* Juliet Highet/Alan Hutchison Library; 168 *r* Spectrum Colour Library; 169 George Hall/Susan Griggs Agency; 170/171 The Mansell Collection; 172 *l* Victoria & Albert Museum; 172 *r* Michael Holford Library/Musée Guimet, Paris; 173 Scala/Vision International; 174 Octopus/California Institute of Technology & Carnegie Institution of Washington; 175 *l* Ann Ronan Picture Library; 175 *r* Angelo Hornak; 176 Michael Holford/Courtesy of the Trustees of the British Museum; 177 *tl* Werner Forman Archive/National Museum of Anthropology, Mexico; 177 *bl* Giraudon; 177 *r* Aerofilms Ltd; 178 The Mansell Collection; 179 *l* *Salisbury Times & Journal* Co Ltd; 179 *c* Victoria & Albert Museum; 179 *r* Ann Ronan Picture Library; 180 Victoria & Albert Museum; 181 *l* Victoria & Albert Museum; 181 *c* Victoria & Albert Museum; 181 *r* Paul Brierley; 182 Alain Keler/Sygma/John Hillelson Agency; 183 Peter Newark's Western Americana; 184/185 Science Photo Library